INNER LIVES
AND
SOCIAL WORLDS

INNER LIVES

—— AND ——

SOCIAL WORLDS

READINGS IN SOCIAL PSYCHOLOGY

EDITED BY

James A. Holstein
Jaber F. Gubrium

New York   Oxford
OXFORD UNIVERSITY PRESS
2003

Oxford University Press

Oxford   New York
Auckland   Bangkok   Buenos Aires   Cape Town   Chennai
Dar es Salaam   Delhi   Hong Kong   Istanbul   Karachi   Kolkata
Kuala Lumpur   Madrid   Melbourne   Mexico City   Mumbai   Nairobi
São Paulo   Singapore   Taipei   Tokyo   Toronto

and an associated company in Berlin

Published by Oxford University Press, Inc.
198 Madison Avenue, New York, New York 10016
http://www.oup-usa.org

Oxford is a registered trademark of Oxford University Press

ISBN 0-19-514727-8

Printing number: 9   8   7   6   5   4   3   2   1

Printed in the United States of America
on acid-free paper

CONTENTS

PREFACE

Psychology and sociology each describe how thoughts, feelings, and actions are influenced by others. The individual and society are crucial to each discipline. *Psychological* social psychology typically focuses on how the individual—a configuration of temperaments, perceptions, cognitions, and attitudes—responds to social stimuli. In contrast, a well-established form of *sociological* social psychology traditionally concentrates on how external social forces—such as socioeconomic status, cultural norms, and social roles—influence individual behavior.

The differences between the two disciplines have clearly shaped how social psychology is presented to students. Social psychology courses taught in psychology departments are usually quite different from those taught in sociology departments. Nevertheless, both disciplines continue to highlight the contrast between the individual and society—between inner, psychic regions on the one hand, and outer, social worlds on the other. Reifying this difference leads to the division of experience into private and public realms, as if these were somehow independent of one another.

Inner Lives and Social Worlds provides a distinctly sociological perspective on social psychology without separating the social from the psychological. This perspective centers on the actual *practice* of everyday life, rather than on the inter-relationship of distinct individual and social spheres. The focus on social interaction blurs the contrast between public and private realms. The leading idea is that our domains of inner experience derive from social encounters and, at the same time, our social worlds are built up from the interactions of purposeful agents in concrete social settings. Inner lives and social worlds are thoroughly intertwined in practice. The individual and the group—self and society, to use more sociological terms—are two sides of the same coin. If one wishes to understand the psychological "inside," one needs to turn to the social "outside," and vice versa. Social interaction connects these insides and outsides. It's the ordinary working glue that holds them together.

Although *Inner Lives and Social Worlds* features a sociological perspective, it doesn't discount important and familiar psychological constructs. It simply views them from a social standpoint. The book takes such stalwart psychological concepts as the self, personality, perception, motives, emotions, and attitudes very seriously, but it addresses these concepts in interactional terms. By the same token, the book does not take the fundamental constructs of sociology for granted. It also treats social structures such as gender, race, culture, and institutions as products of social interaction. The unifying theme is the interplay of inner lives and social worlds as they are produced in the practice of everyday life.

The reading selections in this book address a wide variety of topics that have long interested social psychologists and students of everyday life. Some would certainly be considered classics. Other readings provide new and innovative commentary on social life and experience. The essays that introduce each part of the book thematize the readings. Short introductions also set the stage for each section and provide an orientation to the reading selections that follow.

The book is divided into four parts. Part 1—Points of Departure—offers a general introduction to the book's perspective. Part 2—Social Interaction—shows how interaction is the source of both inner lives and social worlds. Part 3—Inner Lives—and Part 4—Social Worlds—deal with how the seemingly separated inner and outer realms of everyday life grow out of common sources in social interaction. Throughout the book, we discuss and illustrate how the social and the psychological continually relate to one another. As the cover art from expressionist painter Paul Klee suggests, the faces of our lives resonate with many others, all of which bear on the demeanor of experience.

As editors, we have tried to present the reading selections in as near to their originally published form as possible. Although we have pieced together some of the classic readings from different sources, most of the selections are from a single, original text. Whenever possible, we have tried to preserve the integrity of the authors' original presentation and arguments by publishing selections in their entirety.

We have had a great deal of help in developing the themes and selecting the readings for *Inner Lives and Social Worlds*. We are grateful to the many friends and colleagues who have generously suggested readings and offered ideas and direction for how to organize the presentation. Dozens of people made recommendations, advising us about their favorite readings; the following list acknowledges our deep gratitude for the important role they played in assembling this book. Our thanks to (in alphabetical order) Patti Adler, Peter Adler, Malin Åkerstrom, Pertti Alasuutari, David Altheide, Leon Anderson, Sylvia Ansay, Jun Ayukawa, Diane Bartel, Carl Bertoia, Amy Best, Joel Best, Kathleen Blee, Robert Bogdan, Craig Boylstein, Kendal Broad, Spencer Cahill, Kathy Charmaz, Susan Chase, David Cheal, Jeff Chin, Candace Clark, Adele Clarke, Mark Cohan, Roberta Coles, Peter Collier, Martha Copp, Stephen Cornell, Jeff Coulter, Sara Crawley, Arlene Kaplan Daniels, Norman Denzin, Marjorie Devault, Robert Dingwall, Jim Dowd, Donna Eder, Carolyn Ellis, Bob Emerson, Chris Faircloth, Joe Feagin, Jessica Fields, Gary Alan Fine, Lara Foley, Andy Fontana, Kathy Fox, Steve Franzoi, Josh Gamson, Carol Gardner, James Gilsanen, Scott Grills, Bill Gronfein, Tim Halkowski, Douglas Hartman, Sharlene Hesse-Biber, Richard Hilbert, Arlie Hochschild, Daphne Holden, Joe Hopper, Ruth Horowitz, Scott Hunt, Peter Ibarra, Val Jenness, John Johnson, Rick Jones, Kathy Kalab, David Karp, Jack Katz, Stephen Katz, Sharon Kaufman, Robin Kelley, Michael Kimmel, John Kitsuse, Sherryl Kleinman, Joe Kotarba, Lyn Lofland, Doni Loseke, Kathe Lowney, Mike Lynch, David Maines, Peter Manning, Amir Marvasti, Douglas Mason-Schrock, Doug Maynard, Linda McDowell, Jay Meehan, Gale Miller, Leslie Miller, David Morgan, Susan Murray, Nancy Naples, Kirin Narayan, Christina Nippert-Eng, Virginia Olesen, Anssi Perakyla, Mel Pollner, Anne Rawls, Laurel Richardson, Catherine Riessman, Carol Ronai, Paul Rosenblatt, Dana Rosenfeld, Clint Sanders, Kurt Sandstrom, Joseph Schneider, Michael Schwalbe, Diane Scully, Connie Shehan, David Silverman, David Snow, Jack Spencer, Liz Stanley, Bob Stebbins, Pattie Thomas, Carol Thompson, Barrie Thorne, Lisa Tillman-Healy, David Unruh, Hernan Vera, Carol Warren, Susan Watkins, Darin Weinberg, Janet Wirth-Cauchon, Michelle Wolkomir, and Bob Young.

We also thank the people at Oxford University Press for doing their usual exemplary and professional job of producing this book: Jeffrey Broesche for his work at the start, Peter La-Bella for finishing up, and Christine D'Antonio, Sean Mahoney, Scott Burns, and Wendy Almeleh for their fine work of assembling the volume and presenting it to our colleagues and their students.

PART 1

POINTS OF
DEPARTURE

Inner lives and social worlds are well-known features of the social psychological landscape. Even though we can't actually see them, we believe that inner lives contain important aspects of experience. They are the personal, interior spaces that we figure are really us. We also recognize that we live in social worlds. These are the outer regions of experience, external territory that we share with others.

We commonly refer to inner lives and social worlds as if they were totally separate domains. We view one as private, the other as public. Inner lives are composed of selves, feelings, thoughts, and motives. We believe that these and myriad other personal characteristics make up who we are inside. In contrast, social worlds are "out there." They are populated by other people and made up of social forms, such as the family, community, and culture. We experience our lives in relation to these social worlds. They influence what we think, feel, and do. But as much as social worlds may affect—even shape—who we are, we don't think of them as the same as what we are inside. These outer worlds seem distinctly different from what we are within.

It's a strong contrast: inner lives and social worlds. Black and white, no shades of gray. We certainly speak of experience in such clear-cut terms. Thoughts are "in our heads." Emotions are "in our hearts." We talk as if our minds, attitudes, preferences, and prejudices inhabit our inner reaches. We say that they are "personal" characteristics. At the same time, we refer to society as if it were an entity unto itself. It's a domain we treat as independent of us, seeming to impose itself on us from the outside. We say that society acts upon us, "making us" do things. Likewise, the economy "constrains" our life chances. Religion "dictates" morality. Our words commonly locate these social forces outside of us, in society. The disciplines of psychology and sociology provide sophisticated vocabularies that formalize the distinction.

But is experience so clearly partitioned in practice? Is it neatly divided into inner and outer realms? Sometimes what seems plainly evident turns out to be more complicated. As much as inner lives and social worlds appear to be separate domains, the two intersect in the give-and-take of everyday life. In practice, it's not clear where one ends and the other begins. This can make us uncomfortable at times. If we are uncertain of who we are and confused about how to act, we sort it out at the intersection of inner lives and social worlds.

Consider, for example, the unsettling circumstances in which Sara Wilder recently found herself. Sara was about to graduate from college, and she and her boyfriend, Alex Ross, had finally decided to get married. They'd been seeing each other since their freshman year and, as graduation approached, they figured it was a good time to tell their parents about their plans. Both sets of parents were delighted at the news, but, as parents often do, they also expressed reservations about how the couple would manage on their own: "Where will you live? How will you support your selves? How are you going to pay off your college loans?"

Sara and Alex expected questions like these. Parents have a right to be a little concerned. But it did catch Sara off guard when Alex's mother, Jane, from out of the blue, invited her to lunch. "We'll be in town a couple of days before graduation, and I think it would be a wonderful idea for us to meet and talk—just the two of us—to get to know each other better."

Sara had met Alex's mother on several occasions, and she really liked her. More than that, she admired her. Jane Ross was a modern-day success story. From everything Alex had said about his mother, Ms. Ross was Soccer Mom and CEO all rolled into one: married 29 years to Alex's father, two children both graduated from college, and the founder and director of a flourishing marketing and public relations firm. Capable, courageous, ambitious, successful. Quite an imposing mother-in-law-to-be!

As much as she admired Ms. Ross, Sara was anxious. She really wanted Ms. Ross to like her. Sara didn't lack for confidence herself; she was no slouch. She had always been well liked. She'd made the Dean's List almost every semester and was graduating with honors. She had several good job interviews lined up, so work wasn't going to be a problem. She'd taken enough business courses to make her way in a corporate environment, even if she was an English major.

But how would she act around her future mother-in-law? Wasn't it natural to try to impress such a new and important figure in her life? Then why did she feel apprehensive? What was the problem?

As levelheaded as Sara appeared to be and as well prepared for life after college as she was, there was another side to her. One of her dreams—which she'd confided to Alex, but not to many others—was to be a songwriter, maybe even play keyboards and sing with a rock 'n' roll band. She'd taken years of piano lessons and fooled around playing with some friends in high school. She even joined a couple of bands during summers. Her notebooks were filled with bits and pieces of melodies and lyrics that constantly ran through her head.

Still, every fall, Sara dutifully put her music down and got serious about her schoolwork. It paid off in a nice grade point average, but she couldn't get the music out of her system. She told her parents that she was majoring in English because it was excellent preparation for law school. That was true. But deep down, Sara knew it wasn't the whole story. She loved literature and poetry; expressing the depths of experience was important to her. The business courses were, in part, a concession to her parents. After all, her parents were footing some of the bill, and they were just being sensible by insisting that Sara get something practical out of college. But Sara was only mildly interested. All those job interviews? All Sara really wanted right now was a day job that would pay the bills while she found out if she actually could be a musician. She needed to find out if that was what she really wanted. Alex was all for it, but what about his parents?

We've all experienced some of Sara's anxiety. Some of it came from the conflict she was feeling about the impression she would make on Ms. Ross. "I've always been responsible," Sara thought to herself. "I could do very well as a businesswoman, but what would she think about her son marrying a musician, a songwriter, or maybe a flake?" Sara was a bit confused because the social world she was about to enter was making her real self more uncertain than it had ever been.

Sara didn't want to get off on the wrong foot with her new family, so she decided that, for the time being, she would simply be the person she thought Ms. Ross expected—even if it wasn't obvious who Sara really was to herself. She didn't need to bring up the music stuff, did she? She'd just let Ms. Ross see her more practical side. That wasn't being a phony, was it? She was actually practical most of the time. She really was responsible and mature. She fully intended to get a respectable job and contribute her full share to support the household. She just wasn't prepared to tell Ms. Ross that she wanted a day job that would allow her to find out if she was the next Sheryl Crow. That would sound impulsive, maybe a little immature. The last thing she wanted was to make a bad impression.

Sara was guarded about which aspects of her inner life she would reveal to Ms. Ross. She wanted to create a positive impression, carefully crafted out of those parts of her self that she knew were "respectable." The facets of the self that Sara presented—her thoughts, motives, and achievements—would all appeal to Ms. Ross's superwoman sensibilities. "Maybe it isn't completely me," Sara told herself, "but I'll just have to live with that for now."

Their lunch turned out to be quite pleasant, even if it was a bit nerve-racking. The conversation was lively. Sara was bright and personable. Ms. Ross gently quizzed her about her prospects and plans. What was she looking for in her first job? Was this going to be a stepping-stone to a serious career? Did Sara know where she wanted to be in five years? And what about a family?

Sara was cagey, revealing only those aspects of herself that she felt were safe. She figured that she'd respond just like Jane Ross might have done if she were in her shoes. "I want to get a solid job, where I can learn everything I can as I work my way up." "Money isn't the most important thing, but it does matter." "We're not sure yet where a family fits into all of this." Not bad. Modest, yet ambitious. Serious without being pretentious. Professional, with domestic undertones. This was Sara, even if it wasn't *all* of Sara.

Then Jane Ross threw Sara a curve. "English major, huh? It's tough putting that to use in a career." "True," Sara replied, searching Jane's expression for any sign of what she made of it. "It took me a long time to decide on a major. The English department here is one of the best. Law schools love English majors. I figured I could take some business courses on the side. I almost have a minor in marketing." Sara was uncomfortable. Everything she said was true, yet there was so much more to it. She couldn't exactly let on that, deep down, she was several "me's."

"That's interesting," replied Ms. Ross. "You know, there are times when I kick myself for jumping into business so quickly. There's so much I missed, so much that I wish I had tried out. I was so committed to getting started and being a success, being a successful *woman,* that I didn't allow myself any choices. I could have been an art major, but I got on the fast track and had no idea what I might be missing. It was only when I decided to start my own business, that I stepped back to look at who I really was. What did I really want to be? You know why I started a PR firm? It's my creative outlet. It's my job to express things in new and exciting ways. I paint word pictures. I even like producing marketing slogans and those little jingles we use to plant an idea in people's heads."

Suddenly, Sara's outlook changed. She could feel a new inner life starting to take shape that very moment. "You know, I couldn't agree with you more," Sara almost blurted. "I think we should all try to find out our true calling and not let opportunities pass us by." Wow! This was really something. Ms. Ross really wasn't *all* business after all. Sara thought, "I bet she would understand how important music is to me. She'd really like that side of me."

With this, Sara started to see and present herself in rather different terms. The social world formed in talking with Ms. Ross significantly altered who Sara figured she could be. She actually began to think of herself as a new person. And there, right in front of her, was a model of the kind of person she might actually be. Maybe art, music, and business could come together in a way that satisfied Sara *and* others like her parents and the Rosses.

The social world "out there" now seemed to hold a new set of options for who Sara could be. Sara became increasingly aware of this possibility as she fit Jane Ross into her own social world and fit herself into Jane's. Anticipating Ms. Ross's concerns and proclivities, Sara tried to sort out who she—Sara—really was. But she couldn't do so solely on her own terms. She saw herself as others saw her, too. This was the only way she could get the full picture of who she really was. It soon became to clear to Sara that her real self was not something separate and distinct from what others figured her to be. She was part of the social world, and it was part of her inner life.

Sara's story highlights three important points about inner lives and social worlds, two of which are already familiar. The familiar ones deal with how we orient to inner lives and social worlds *in theory.* One point is that we approach experience *as if* our inner lives are our own. We assume that they belong to us and not to others. They aren't "out there"; they are "in here." To be sure, we feel like our inner lives reflect and respond to our social worlds, but fundamentally, they are who we are inside. The second familiar point parallels the first. We approach social worlds *as if* they were "out there," not "in here" within ourselves. We may gear our inner lives to social worlds, but we act as if they were separate domains of experience.

A third point refers to the relationship between inner lives and social worlds *in practice.* This point may be puzzling and a bit ironic, but it's a major theme of this book. As we can see from Sara's situation, inner lives and social worlds are intimately connected in the practice of everyday life. They are two sides of the same coin. This may seem strange, given that we typically think of the two as separate. But in practice, things are not always as simple or straightforward as they seem to be in theory. Actual experience is not this clear-cut, as Sara's interaction with Ms. Ross revealed.

Sara discovered that her true self was pretty complex. It became apparent that what she thought of as herself was actually assembled from the social world that confronted her. With Alex at the heart of one social world, Sara felt comfortable being a musician-waiting-to-be-discovered. When Ms. Ross entered the picture, so did Sara's more businesslike self, alongside her musical self. Ms. Ross brought Sara into a social world that, in a matter of minutes, seemed to reshape who Sara could be. In the process, Sara felt herself becoming a different person, one who was constructed in a way she'd only glimpsed before.

The actual connection between inner lives and social worlds is not always apparent. If we look and listen closely, however, we can see and hear it working itself out in the give-and-take of everyday interaction. The connection becomes visible in practice, even while we act as if inner lives and social worlds are separate and distinct in theory. Sara's social world actually began to change when she realized that she was going to have to interact with Ms. Ross as a daughter-in-law. The mere anticipation of this relationship transformed the social landscape "out there" for Sara. During the ensuing lunchtime conversation, Sara progressively assembled a self that initially didn't seem to fit together. But when Ms. Ross revealed her passion for art and her regrets about her own education, she turned Sara's social world upside down. The interaction altered Sara's picture of Ms. Ross's social world, as well as her sense of Ms. Ross's inner life. Jane Ross's inner life—who Sara figured Ms. Ross was "inside"—became a new part of Sara's social world. This, in turn, helped reshape Sara's inner life.

It's noteworthy that such a simple exchange of information deeply affected how Sara defined both the social world and her place in it. It was as if Ms. Ross told Sara to think about the world differently when she revealed that she had once wanted to be an art major. What we initially took to be distinct—inner lives and social worlds—were suddenly linked in the ordinary exchange of a lunchtime conversation.

Social interaction made all the difference in the world, so to speak. It's the key linkage between inner lives and social worlds. Talk and interaction work to build up what we understand about ourselves and others. In turn, interaction produces the social worlds that we inhabit. As the book proceeds, we will elaborate on this connection. The relationship between inner lives and social worlds is complex, so describing them can be tricky. It's hard to tell where one stops and the other takes over, so it's difficult to describe inner lives without talking about social worlds, and vice versa. Far from being separate domains of experience, we will show that they are intricately woven together in the course of everyday life.

AN INTERACTIONAL PERSPECTIVE

Social interaction is the key to this book's approach to social psychology. As the source of inner lives and social worlds, it's where it all happens, so to speak. The book's essays and reading selections offer a social psychology of everyday life that emphasizes how people interacting with one another assemble both their inner lives and their social worlds. The basic premise is that everyday reality as we know it is socially constructed. As people interact, what they say and do creates a working sense of what is real for them. They establish, negotiate, and modify who and what they are in the course of the give-and-take of daily living, constructing and reconstructing their social worlds in the process.

Of course, this doesn't mean that there's no substance to reality, that it's a mere figment of imagination. It doesn't imply that reality can be conjured up out of thin air. Rather, people communicate what things mean to them as they interact with one another. What something means—what that something actually is to them—depends upon how they come to know it in the context of actually dealing with others. Recall that Sara formulated a new sense of the reality of Jane Ross's social world through interacting with her. This interaction, in turn, altered Sara's social world and Sara's self. The personal and professional implications of combining art and business became apparent as Ms. Ross and Sara chatted about their lived experiences. The realities of their lives didn't appear out of nowhere.

When we turn to inner lives in Part 3, we will focus on interior matters, such as selves, minds, emotions, and motives. As we noted earlier, we typically think of these matters as personal and private. But our interactional perspective will show how seemingly internal characteristics are given their shape and character in the course of everyday life. Similarly, when we turn to social worlds in Part 4, we will show how these, too, are built up through interchanges with others. Social worlds comprise the shared panorama of experience. They are reality as we take it to be *together*—at least for the time being. A social world is way of seeing and experiencing the reality we share with others. But as far-reaching and inclusive as social worlds can be, they aren't just out there either, as we commonly assume. They are sorted and assembled through the tangle of social relations. The book will also illustrate how various social worlds, with their distinctive features, come together interactionally.

Social Situations

As we explore the interactional construction of everyday reality, we need to be aware of factors that influence the process. High on the list of conditions that shape interaction are the social situations in which inner lives and social worlds are constructed. When and where reality is constructed are tremendously important for what reality looks like.

Returning to Sara's story, for example, it's important to note the situation in which Sara's inner life and social world were constructed. Sara went to great lengths to show her responsible side as she chatted with her future mother-in-law. The social context was definitely important to how Sara saw and presented herself. Imagine how she might have come off if she were dealing with someone else. It would make quite a difference, for instance, if she were meeting a friend of Alex who was interested in starting a rock band. Sara's social world would also have been different if she were having lunch with Alex's cousin, who was merely passing through on his way to a Tibetan monastery.

Situations like this prompt a variety of questions about the interactional process. Who is involved? What is the mutual history of the people who are interacting? What is likely to happen in their future together? Where does the interaction take place? Put more generally, how does the situated context of everyday interaction influence the practice of reality construction?

Years ago, social psychologist W. I. Thomas urged colleagues to take account of the when's and where's of people's lives in order to understand their actual thoughts, feelings, and motivations. Thomas coined the famous phrase "definition of the situation" to capture the situated character of inner lives and social worlds. He used the term to underscore how much social context effects what people figure they are, what they say, and what they do. In *The Child in America* (1928/1956: 572), Thomas wrote, "If [people] define situations as real, they are real in their consequences." This was his way of saying that the inner lives and social worlds that people construct are real *for them* in their circumstances, no matter what we, as outsiders, may think about it. We emphasize "for them" because it signifies that reality is in the eye of the beholder, so to speak. This is what everyday reality refers to—the real according to its adherents. Equally important, it suggests that realities are socially situated. Social context, Thomas tells us, is real and consequential for the people who experience it, when and where it occurs. Alter the context, and you are likely to alter people's everyday realities.

Take a teenage boy named Seth, for example, who has been in and out of trouble at school and has had a couple of minor brushes with the law. He's consistently late to class and has even cut school a few times. Recently, Seth was sent home from school for wearing a T-shirt with an obscenity printed on it. And then there were the incidents with the law. Once the police brought Seth home for being on the street after curfew. On another occasion, Seth and his buddies were caught "toilet-papering" his geometry teacher's house. Seth's mother had to pick him up at the police station after that one.

Thomas would tell us that whether or not we view the boy as a delinquent depends on how one defines the situation. Around the house, where he is one of four brothers being raised by a single mother, Seth may be considered willful or spirited. His mother and brothers view him as "just a kid who gets excited about stuff." At the police station, however, Seth is viewed as a troublemaker. Police officers see him as a "problem kid" with a growing "rap sheet" of increasingly significant offenses. When Seth was remanded for psychological counseling, staff members looked at his family life and decided it was dysfunctional. He was being raised by a single parent, after all. For many, this is the first sign of trouble. In this context, Seth was viewed as psychologically damaged, certainly not just spirited or a problem kid. The byword was "emotionally disturbed." Interestingly enough, Seth's friends put a positive spin on his personality, constructing Seth and the world they shared with him in glowing terms. You never hear them use phrases, such as "emotionally disturbed" or "dysfunctional." These aren't part of the normal working vocabulary of teenage boys "on the street." To his friends, Seth is just "one of the guys." He's absolutely "normal," even "cool." In each case, what Seth's "really" is depends on how others define the situation.

Clearly, the reality of everyday life is not uniform or stable. Definitions contrast dramatically. Yet each may be perfectly viable, given the situation in which the defining takes place. Complicating matters, definitions of situations seldom remain constant. A psychological counselor may define Seth's behavior as "obviously" pathological when discussing Seth at a staff meeting. But she may talk about him quite differently over dinner with friends or family. There, Seth may simply be "screwed up," a phrase the counselor wouldn't dream of using seriously with colleagues. At work, a counselor's professional responsibilities demand technical terminology, made up of psychological symptoms, syndromes, and the like. The professional context prompts her to apply a specialized way of seeing and describing inner lives. In contrast, the informal context at home is a different discursive environment, with its own vocabulary of troubles.

If that's not complicated enough, one person's definition of the situation can be affected by another's, as we saw in Sara's interaction with Ms. Ross. Seth, for example, has his own definitions of the situations in which he participates. He isn't simply a definitional puppet in his relations with others. He influences the interaction he has with his family, the police, his friends, his teachers, and his counselor. If he develops a reputation as a "bad" kid, he may respond in a number of ways. He may angrily reject the definition and be hostile to those who believe in it. This behavior may turn him into a social outcast of sorts, which would confirm the very definition that started things along this road in the first place. In the manner of a self-fulfilling prophecy, Seth may actually become the bad kid that these others think he is. "They think I'm a loser, no matter what I do. Well, I'll show them." Going along, Seth could eventually come to define himself as these others have defined him. Alternatively, he may persistently offer a more positive view of himself. In time, this view could serve to convince others that he is "basically a good kid underneath it all."

Whichever of these possibilities develops depends both on Seth's input into the matter and on the situated contingencies of social interaction. Teachers and administrators may view Seth and his friends as troublemakers at school, but this isn't a universal or comprehensive definition. This vision of who and what the boys really are, and the kinds of social worlds they inhabit, is built up in the offices and classrooms of the school. But after school, just outside on the basketball court with a bunch of other teenagers, a different set of situated contingencies kicks in. Seth and his friends are defined in a strikingly different way. Their inner lives and social worlds unfold in different terms, in what they and others say and do, in how they are treated, and in how they respond to it. Make a game winning shot, and you're a hero. Dribble the ball off your foot, and you're a jerk. Heroes and jerks are far from being troublemakers or bad kids. The reality of the moment is very much a product of the situation at hand.

Pioneering social psychologist William James (1892/1961: 46) had such situations in mind when he wrote that people "have as many selves [and inner lives] as there are individuals who recognize [them] and carry an image of [them] in their minds." James shared the notion that inner lives and social worlds are not fixed in experience. He extended this notion by suggesting that these inner lives and social worlds are produced through talk and interaction with a wide variety of individuals. Teachers in school construct Seth and his friends differently than do players on the basketball court. Get other people involved, and the boys would likely be defined in still other ways.

Sociologist Erving Goffman (1959) tried to capture the same idea using the language of the theater. He saw society as a series of dramatic performances. Whereas James noted that we have as many selves as there are people we interact with, Goffman viewed the situated construction of inner lives and social worlds as analogous to the roles that actors play on stage. From Goffman's perspective, there are as many selves—as many inner lives—as there are everyday dramas that call for their presentation. Each drama conjures up a distinct social world, with its particular set of inner lives in tow.

According to Goffman, everyday interactions are not extemporaneous, but are more or less scripted. We construct what we say and do in relation to social expectations. We play roles in real life, just as actors do on stage. Among our friends, we may be "cool guys" or "basketball stars," but we take up other roles in school, at home, and in myriad other social contexts. We may give better or worse performances, but each performance presents a recognizable version of who we are and the social world we engage. As we will show in the reading selections from his work, Goffman provides a powerful framework for understanding these contingencies of social situations.

Many of the essays and readings that follow emphasize the importance of social situations. While they are significant influences on how people formulate the meaning of experience, we remind readers that situations don't *determine* inner lives and social worlds. They provide resources and reasons for action, but they don't prescribe what we see, say, and do. Moreover, the definitions and meanings of social situations are themselves socially constructed. They don't stand above and beyond the interactional reality construction process, dictating what is locally real. They are part of the process itself. We will return to this issue when we discuss the *reflexivity* of social interaction in Part 2.

Time and Experience

An interactional approach to the construction of inner lives and social worlds addresses time as well as social context. Time relates to the construction of experience in both the long and the short run. Different historical periods, for example, present different ways of constructing reality in the long run. Centuries ago, we couldn't conceive of an inner world of "ids," "egos," and "superegos" like some people do today. There literally were no "libidos," "defense mechanisms," or "Oedipal complexes" to speak of. Sigmund Freud developed this way of thinking and talking about inner life less than a hundred years ago. Prior to Freud, our inner lives were constructed in different terms.

Time also bears on who and what we are in the short run. For example, repeatedly feeling stressed at the start of the day may lead a working mother to suspect that something is wrong with her. To be anxious before anything has happened may suggest that something is amiss in her inner life. Having the same feelings after a long, hard day at the office, a teacher conference, a soccer game, supper at Chuck E. Cheese's, and a bout with algebra homework may lead her to quite different conclusions. Her inner life isn't the problem. Her social world is. Although the stress this woman feels may be the same, the time it is experienced can be used to put it in an entirely different light.

Whether we view time in the long run or the short run, it doesn't just flow with experience. The meaning of things and actions aren't the simple by-products of the passage of time. Rather, in practice, individuals *actively* use the concept of time to assign meaning to their actions. This requires a new way of thinking about time. Once again, theory doesn't necessarily square with practice. Typically, we think of time as a continuum along which events occur in an irreversible progression from the past through the present to the future. We see our lives as embedded in time. Talk and interaction are suspended in it. Given this view, there is a sense of inevitability about what time means and what happens as time passes.

We often assume that lives develop along the continuum of time in a deterministic way. That is, we presume that our pasts are more or less set in stone. We may have lapses of memory, but the past itself remains the same. We also assume that our present flows from the past. Similarly, our futures follow a trajectory established by what's gone before. In this view, inner life flows with time, as do the sum and substance of the social worlds that surround it.

This is a passive view of time and experience. Time and its effects are simply *there*. Returning to Seth, for example, we can see a variety of ways in which this understanding of time affects how we apprehend his inner life and social world. Let's say we learn that Seth had a difficult childhood. His family life was chaotic, he had unsavory friends, and he was far from being a model student. Given a passive orientation to time, we may conclude that these past experiences played a significant role in his current troubles. Seth's early social world provides a basis for understanding the inner life he developed in his formative years, which, in turn, affects what he is now. We'd say that his present is rooted in his past.

Looking ahead, we'd likely figure that the past and present provide grounds for predicting what Seth's future will be. Seth may think this way himself. He started down the path to no good, he may observe, and he's likely to continue down that road. We wouldn't be surprised to hear others offer dire forecasts for his future: "That kid's headed for all kinds of trouble. I wouldn't be surprised if he ended up in jail." There's an almost inevitable pathway of experience implied here, based on the assumption that Seth's inner life and social worlds are entities that flow with time. One thing leads to another, as it were. We can see what lies ahead in terms of what came before.

Seen this way, the past, the present, and the future are continuous. They are all made of the same cloth. Each follows its predecessor, and each predicts its successor. Of course, some periods may be more or less important to us than others, but, essentially, time marches on. And, of course, so do inner lives and social worlds. Each moment that passes, we believe, tells us about what we have been, what we are at present, and what we can expect to become. In this passive view of time and experience, we take it for granted that time will flow in the expected direction. In due course, so will everyone's sense of his or her inner life and social world.

In contrast, if we take the more active view that reality, including time, is interactionally constructed, a different sense of time results. The meaning of time and its passage aren't given. Time doesn't simply surround and shape experience. Instead, individuals actively use the concept of time in various situations to build up a sense of what its passage means for their inner lives and social worlds. In this view, time becomes a resource for constructing meanings in everyday life. People aren't locked into particular versions of the past, present, and future. The word *versions* suggests that the meaning of time in relation to experience is not set in stone. Its meaning is established and modified in interaction, just like all other meanings. The connections between different events and points in experience are not fixed simply because one precedes or follows another. Rather, in practice, individuals actively pick and choose how they will relate the passage of time to the meanings of events. That is, they use particular understandings of time to form definitions of situations and the people who participate in them.

To illustrate, recall how Seth's presumed difficult childhood and chaotic family life were used to interpret his present behavior and circumstances. But that was only one version of time and experience. The sense of Seth's past as difficult and chaotic starts from the assumption that he is presently a troubled youth. But if we view Seth's present more positively—say the version shared by his family members at home or the version held by Seth's friends—Seth's past can take on a different meaning. The language of dysfunction and chaos isn't really appropriate for describing the social setting that Seth came from if Seth appears to be more or less normal *now*. The terms aren't readily congruent with a more positive picture of Seth in the present. Consequently, Seth's past is likely to be constructed in more optimistic terms. His family life may be understood more as "typical of the times" than as dysfunctional, for example. Once his past is established as "unremarkable," Seth's present can be affirmed to be "normal" as well.

Note how an active orientation to time can reverse the place of the past and present in the construction of Seth's inner life and social world. This alternate interpretation of who Seth is and why he's turned out that way begins, oddly enough, with the present, not with the past. The present is used as a resource to construct Seth's past. Because Seth is currently seen as "normal," his past can't be viewed as a source of "trouble." The past, therefore, is not fixed in time. Rather, it is actively constructed to fit with a different version of the present. With a different understanding of the present firmly in mind, we then look back at the past and formulate its meaning accordingly.

APPLYING THE PERSPECTIVE

An interactional perspective on the construction of reality establishes some common concerns for social psychology. In one way or another, the authors of the reading selections in this book all share these concerns.

A Focus on Everyday Life

One common concern is a focus on everyday life. Each of the authors urges us to consider inner lives and social worlds as they unfold in actual experience. Everyday life includes all the ordinary times and places where we see, do, and say things to each other. We don't need special occasions or scientific laboratories to show us how we experience ourselves and our worlds. For example, if researchers want to understand how boys and girls construct the meaning of gender, they should study them in the places where they live out their lives experiencing gender: on playgrounds, in school cafeterias, in backyards, or down the block where they meet after school. Researchers who want to understand what the aging process means should go to places where aging is an ongoing concern. These places may include obvious ones, such as senior centers and nursing homes, but we also can learn a great deal about what it means to age in unexpected places. For instance, one can learn what growing "old" means for the exotic dancers who make a living in nightclubs by showing off their bodies. When young bodies are a premium, every passing day can have foreboding consequences related to looking young or old, even for women in their teens and 20s. Age isn't simply a concern for the elderly.

Because social research usually is associated with science, the idea of doing research has always connoted something over and above simply listening to and observing people in ordinary situations. In a sense, this would be too simple. To be scientific, we are told, we need standardized research methods and technology. These methods tend to take researchers a distance from everyday life. The pursuit of science has traditionally turned social psychologists away from directly listening to people, observing their behavior on its own terms, or interacting with them at the times and in the actual places they conduct their lives. More psychologically inclined researches have frequently conducted experiments. Many like to work in laboratories. The aim is to carefully control the variables that may affect subjects, then take note of which of these variables seem most influential. Unfortunately, such laboratory settings are often far removed from real-life situations. Experimenters are aware of this problem and have done their best to simulate real life within the laboratory. Usually, they only partially succeed. While they want laboratory life to be as much like real life as possible, they don't want to give up the control they can exert in the process.

More sociologically inclined researchers often prefer survey interviewing. They, too, study inner lives and social worlds under controlled conditions. Structured interview questions and mechanical interviewing techniques provide fairly uniform ways of delving into people's experience. The scientific aim is to elicit uncontaminated information from respondents' stores of information. Standardization is the key. Interviewers ask respondents identical questions in the same way. They limit respondents' options for answering questions by presenting a fixed set of response choices. Of course, researchers are aware of the problem of "putting words into people's mouths" during interviews that wouldn't necessarily be there in real life. As a result, they take care to formulate questions and responses that are based on real-life sensibilities, but these questions and responses are still guided by a primary concern for standardization.

While the work that appears in this book is also scientific, it is inspired by a keener appreciation for the rich texture of everyday living. The authors' sensibilities tell them to "go to the people," wherever and whenever they may be. For them, talk, interaction, and its varied situations are their laboratories. They study places where people actually conduct their lives. The result is a different kind of science—the science of everyday life.

A Concern for Meaning Making

The importance of a science of everyday life rests on a concern for meaning making. Two reading selections provide us with points of departure for understanding this concept. One is by William Foote Whyte, the author of a classic study, *Street Corner Society* (1943), a portrayal of street life in an impoverished Italian American community in the late 1930s. From the start, Whyte tells us to be alert for the everyday meaning-making processes that appear around every turn.

Whyte calls the neighborhood he studied "Cornerville" because so much of its activity takes place on street corners. In poor neighborhoods, street life is a central part of daily living. Significant things go on in surprisingly public circumstances. The public and the private often blend, making street scenes as intimate and important as households and workplaces. Whyte tells us that hanging out on the corner is not meaningless or a symptom of social disorganization. It isn't the result of having nothing better to do, as it may appear to outsiders whose lives are anchored in a more formal allocation of time and space. Rather, hanging out is an integral part of being a member of Cornerville society. Cornerville's street scenes are important locations for formulating selves and designating identities, the cornerstones, so to speak, of residents' inner lives and social worlds.

Whyte teaches us that social worlds exist in surprising places and take many forms. Such places may be unseemly or unimportant to outsiders. Whyte warns us about jumping to such conclusions. We can find meanings-in-the-making virtually anywhere, he warns. A fascinating social world may be under our very noses, but we could miss it because we aren't accustomed to what we see. Worse yet, we may ignore it for alleged scientific purposes. Looking for the familiar, we may easily overlook something surprisingly different. To really see Cornerville's social world, Whyte cautions, we must be willing to look for meaning where we least expect to find it.

> There is a pattern to Cornerville life. The middle-class person looks upon the slum district as a formidable mass of confusion, a social chaos. The insider finds in Cornerville a highly organized and integrated social system. (P. xvi)

If Whyte advises us not to jump to conclusions, the selection from Erving Goffman's work alerts us to how we should be prepared to observe. Whereas Whyte urges us to shed familiar lenses, "go to the people," and "enter their worlds," Goffman cautions us that social worlds and inner lives are not simply there for the looking and the listening. We need to be especially sensitive to the activity that makes them meaningful—meaning *making*.

Like Whyte, Goffman (1961) urges researchers to get up close to observe what goes on in everyday life. As he explains in relation to his study of a psychiatric hospital,

> My immediate objective in doing fieldwork at St. Elizabeth's [psychiatric hospital] was to try to learn about the world of the hospital inmate, as this world is subjectively experienced by him. . . . It was then and still is my belief that any group of persons—prisoners, primitives, pilots, or patients—develop a life of their own that becomes meaningful, reasonable, and normal once you get close to it, and that a good way to learn about any of these worlds is to submit oneself in the company of the members to the daily round of petty contingencies to which they are subject. (Pp. ix–x).

But Goffman is more concerned than Whyte with the strategic or active side of meaning making. Meaning making is strategic because people are aware of the impressions that they "give off" to others, as Goffman puts it. Goffman cautions us not to take meanings and their social worlds for granted because they are always in process. He turns our attention to the activity involved in literally "putting on" or performing social worlds. He urges us to look closely at the effort that people put into constructing everyday realities. The social construction of meaning is *work,* after all. While Whyte emphasizes the meanings of inner lives and social worlds as they exist on their own terms, Goffman stresses the processes by which social worlds and their inner lives are presented, performed, and sustained as everyday realities.

FINAL REMINDERS

In looking ahead to the reading selections, we remind readers of two important features of an interactional perspective. Keep them in mind as you read about the construction of inner lives and social worlds.

The Priority of Social Interaction

First and foremost, remember that inner lives and social worlds are constructed through social interaction. As we put it earlier, interaction is where it's at. It's the working foundation of everyday reality.

Since, in practice, inner lives and social worlds both grow out of talk and interaction, inner lives and social worlds stand on equal footing as aspects of experience. Neither can be considered prior to, or more essential than, the other. The perspective presented in this book doesn't accentuate inner lives by starting out to consider how they relate to interaction within various social worlds. Such a view easily leads to treating inner lives as if they were responsible for interaction, not the other way around. Nor does the perspective begin with social worlds and take inner lives to be by-products of interaction within those worlds. This view can lead to social determinism, in which society is viewed as molding who and what we are as persons.

Instead, the perspective presented here is oriented to inner lives and social worlds as being equally constructed within talk and interaction. Who we are inside and what we share with others are both assembled in the practice of everyday life. A good rule of thumb for avoiding the pitfalls of putting either inner lives or social worlds ahead of the other is always to place social interaction first.

Continual Connection

Our second reminder is that inner lives and social worlds are always connected. Many of the authors are even reluctant to distinguish them. We have hesitated to define them too precisely ourselves. To do so would make them seem like separate and distinct things, which would isolate them from each other. Instead, we have tried to point to their continual connection in practice. Even though the book has separate parts devoted to inner lives and to social worlds, we discuss both in each part. Throughout, we show how inner lives and social worlds constantly inform one another. We can't easily deal with questions related to inner life without knowing something about the social world taken to surround it. By the same token, knowing social worlds generally entails knowledge of the inner lives of those involved. Whenever you consider one, you inevitably consider the other.

There's a good rule of thumb that can prevent the separation and reification of inner lives and social worlds: always look for the working linkage between them. And look for that linkage in social interaction. The themes and messages conveyed in the readings will make much better sense if readers keep both in mind.

REFERENCES

Goffman, Erving. 1959. *The Presentation of Self in Everyday Life.* New York: Doubleday.

Goffman, Erving. 1961. *Asylums.* New York: Anchor Books.

James William. [1892] 1961. *Psychology: The Briefer Course.* New York: Harper & Row.

Thomas, W. I. [1928] 1956. *The Child in America.* New York: Alfred A. Knopf.

Whyte, William Foote. 1943. *Street Corner Society.* Chicago: University of Chicago Press.

PART 2

SOCIAL INTERACTION

Talk and interaction are the keys to inner lives and social worlds. Where would we be without them? How would we know what's going on with people around us? Would we have any sense of others' worlds, or of our own, for that matter? Could we even know ourselves if we didn't know what others saw in us? As important as these questions are, we seldom stop to think about them. We go about our lives with hardly a thought to how social interaction assembles and nourishes who we are and the worlds we share with others.

But social interaction is the process from which individuals and society are made. What is inner life other than the sense of what each of us is, gleaned from our relations with others? What is society other than people interacting with other people, working out how to live together in some meaningful way? Interpersonal routines and patterns of interaction make our inner lives and social worlds understandable and predictable—at least enough so that we get from day to day without much trouble.

INTERACTION AND MEANING

As we interact with one another, we establish what we mean by what we say and do. It's this meaningful component that makes human interaction distinctive. We just don't drift along or mill about like schools of fish or flocks of sheep. Our social transactions aren't automatic or mechanical, although through habit they may sometimes appear to be. In contrast to sheep, fish, and other animals, we take each other meaningfully into account in social interaction. It's not so much what people visibly do to, or with, each other that's significant. It's the meaning of what they say and do that matters. This is how people are different socially from fish and sheep.

We differ from other animals in that we don't respond to each other instinctively, as a matter of uncontrollable reflex. Certainly, we do things without really thinking. But we're not Pavlov's dogs, salivating uncontrollably at the sound of a dinner bell. Sometimes we're like children clamoring at the sight of McDonald's golden arches, but this isn't a knee-jerk reaction to the physical environment. Dogs and children can be "conditioned" to anticipate a meal, for instance, but there's a big difference between the unmediated connection between stimulus and response that sets a dog to drooling, on the one hand, and the elaborate constellation of meanings that ignites a McDonald's feeding frenzy, on the other. Happy Meals. Play structures. Big Macs. Skinny french fries. It's not just stomachs and salivary glands that spring to life. It's all the meaningful associations with McDonald's that spark imaginations and anticipations as much as appetites. It's more than hunger that drives children to Mickey D's.

Meaning is central to how we respond to things and each other. It makes everyday life a varied and complex environment. Consequently, social realities are always a bit "messy." They are fluid and changeable because they are continually constructed and reconstructed. They're never final and clear-cut. They are always filled with, and surrounded by, meaning. Our responses to them are never automatic because meanings are involved.

Take the situation that confronted 12-year-old twin brothers, Zach and Josh, who were in trouble at school. The guidance counselor, Sally Jeffers, telephoned the boys' mother, Mrs. Skinner, for an after-school conference in her office. According to their teacher, the boys were acting out in class, disrupting lessons and causing a general uproar. The crux of the problem was their inappropriate language. "There's no other way to put this," said Jeffers, "Your kids have foul mouths, and it's got to stop. The teacher's at her wits' end. Their cursing and swearing is completely unacceptable."

Wanting to be helpful, Ms. Jeffers discussed possible remedies with Mrs. Skinner. She provided literature on difficult children, including a brochure on behavior modification. The gist of the pamphlet was that one could shape and reform a child's behavior through the use of positive and negative reinforcements. Reward desired behaviors and punish those that you want to extinguish. Be firm and consistent and, in no time, the child will behave in the desired way. This was "scientific," far more sophisticated than washing the children's mouths out with soap.

"I guess I've just gotten used to this," thought Mrs. Skinner to herself. "But it's got to stop, and right now! Beginning tomorrow morning," she vowed to herself, "I'll tolerate no foul language. Positive and negative reinforcement. I'll snuff this out. Extinguish it, like the brochure says." *Conditioning* the boys, she figured, would do the trick.

As usual, the next morning the boys bolted into the kitchen, demanding breakfast. "What would you like to eat?" their mother asked.

"I'll have some f——kin' oatmeal!" blurted Zach impatiently.

"Here we go, again," thought Mrs. Skinner. Grabbing the newspaper that was rolled up on the breakfast table, she swatted Zach a crisp shot across the back of his head. Zach was stunned.

"I said, what do you want to eat?" Mrs. Skinner repeated.

"What the hell?" puzzled Zach. "Are you out of that f——kin' oatmeal?"

Whack! Another smack with the newspaper, this time on the seat of Zach's pants. And with a good deal more gusto and authority.

"Now, one more time, what do you want for breakfast?"

"Geeze," replied Zach, cowering. "I'll take whatever ya got."

"That's much better," replied Mom, as she served up a bowl of Frootie Tooties.

"And now, what's *your* pleasure?" asked Mom, turning to Josh, who'd been watching from across the room. "What can I get you for breakfast?"

Sitting down cautiously at the table, Josh pondered for a moment. "Well, I really don't give a damn, as long as it's not that f——kin' oatmeal."

This is an old story, a joke often told by behavioral psychologists. But its point is noteworthy. In the human social world, connections aren't automatic. Swats of any kind don't stand in one-to-one relationship with anything in particular. While Mrs. Skinner figured that a swat was punishment enough to extinguish her sons' swearing, the boys assigned an entirely different meaning to their breakfast table interactions. The little drama makes it clear that the way we define objects, actions, and situations is crucial to how we respond to them.

When we interact, we deal in meanings, not automatic associations. Meanings both enter into, and arise within, social interaction. They're at the heart of everyday life. We inform one another about who and what we are, what we are doing, and how we regard others in the process. Of course, meaning may not always be communicated perfectly. Clearly, Mrs. Skinner failed to make her point with the boys, even though she had a definite plan in mind. Still, she was communicating meaning. It just wasn't the meaning she intended.

MEANING AND COMMUNICATION

We communicate with one another as we interact, using all manner of signs, symbols, and gestures. It's how we construct and transmit meaning. Communication may be verbal or nonverbal, written, or conveyed otherwise. Talk is perhaps the most common way of communicating meaning.

Words and other forms of communication don't straightforwardly stand for particular things. Objects and words don't simply correlate with one another; there's no set relation among words, things, and meanings. Rather, the meaningful realities of a word can vary. Consider the word "state," for example. The word has a particular meaning in the context of governmental or legal jurisdiction, as in the State of California. It means something distinctly different in the context of "a state of confusion," where it signifies a mental or emotional condition or disposition. And, of course, there are "secretary of state," "state of mind," "lying in state," "state of equilibrium," and "state your piece!" Examples of words with multiple meaning are easy to find: "leather belt," "seat belt," "Bible Belt," "belt a home run," "belt down a shot of whiskey," "belt out a song," "cast a ballot," "the cast of a Broadway musical," "plaster cast," "cast a glance," and so forth.

Swiss linguist Ferdinand de Saussure (1959) tells us that the meaning of a word doesn't lie in the word itself. It stems from the connections that are made with other words. These connections establish meaningful contexts for words. No context, no meaning. The term "state," for example, means one thing when it's used to designate "state-as-a-territorial designation," and quite another to signify "state-as-a-psychological disposition." One meaning derives from the word's connection with geographic territory, while the other meaning comes from its connection with mental status. The word may mean any number of other things, depending on its context. Indeed, think of what may happen if you simply asked a friend what "state" means without linking the term to something else so as to communicate its meaning. Your friend would almost surely answer your question with another question: "What do you mean, 'state'?"

For the most part, we take the communication of meaning for granted. We seldom reflect on how talk and interaction function in our everyday lives. We just do them. But even the most mundane, seemingly trivial interactions can help build the meaning of things. Imagine how hard it would be to make sense of things if you couldn't hear the talk surrounding them. Let's say that late one night, you decide to watch television. You turn on the TV, but the cable is out of order. You get the picture, but not the sound. You're not sleepy and don't want to go to bed. You've got nothing better to do, so you sit down and begin to watch an old movie. People interact with one another, inaudibly talking, gesturing, laughing, and scowling. You watch for a couple of minutes, and it's not too interesting. There's not a lot of action to capture your attention. Things are going on, but you're not sure just what. All in all, it's pretty boring. Boring, that is, until you start trying to make sense of it.

Trying to make sense of it means that you put *words* to it! What are the people saying? What could they possibly mean? You imagine the conversations, what individuals are communicating, even if you can't hear them. In other words, you imagine the talk in the interaction. You create fragments of plots, filling in the dialogue, then wait to see if subsequent actions fit with the story you're assembling. In this way, you furnish the meanings that the missing dialogue typically supplies for you. It's only then that the action starts to make sense. But this is a sense you've assigned to the action in the connections you're making between the words you supply and the things on the screen. It's like a game, filling in the words and story for the missing sound track. But, interestingly enough, it's very much like the meaning making we do in everyday life.

Back to the TV show. After a commercial, as the movie resumes, a written message silently announces "Our Late Night Feature: *Monkey Business.*" Now here's something to work with! The title *Monkey Business* gives you a clue of its own for making sense of what you're seeing. The title isn't much—just two words—but it now provides an additional set of meanings for how you now may understand what's going on. Is this a documentary about monkeys in the tropics? Nope, no rainforest scenes here. Is it about simian entrepreneurs? Nah, no baboons in business suits.

Maybe you shouldn't take the title literally. Remember how we often find humor in the double meanings of words. "Monkey business" sometimes refers to silly, mischievous, or deceitful acts. Language in context, remember? Maybe it's a comedy. Perhaps it's an old Marx Brothers flick. Or that classic with Cary Grant and Marilyn Monroe. No, neither of those. Unfortunately, like other things, it's hard to find humor without the words that convey it.

Then, miraculously, the sound is back. You begin to hear the movie's dialogue. "We've got to stop this shipment of Mandrills from Guinea." "Maybe we should pay the ransom. Right now it's our only option." "If we don't, they'll spread the dreaded Ebola virus all across North America." "But where do we get that kind of money?" In a matter of seconds, the conversation provides information that fills the screen with meaning. Instantly, you start making sense of what had previously been meaningless, except, of course, for the meanings that you assigned to the action on the previously silent screen. Definitions of formerly puzzling situations become "obvious." Of course, now they mean something different from what they did before.

Sitting back and thinking about it, you notice that language works back and forth among events, context, and meaning. Meaning isn't especially stable, but appears to unfold and change, in the process of making sense of things. Without knowing that "monkeys" are central to the plot of the movie, you may not know what is being shipped from Guinea. Mandrills, after all, are not as familiar as house cats to the average viewer. Knowing the "shipment" is from Africa helps solidify the meaning of Mandrill. Knowing that African mammals are involved helps pinpoint the meaning of "the dreaded Ebola virus." And so on.

Language and meaning continually elaborate and inform one another. Each helps make sense of the other. In their connection, they construct the context of things, what the things in question mean. Nothing simply stands for itself. Nothing is meaningful outside the context in which it is encountered. Context provides the connections with other words that construct meaning. Without communication, the world is a strange and barren place, like a movie without a sound track—virtually meaningless. Unless we take action and supply the sound and dialogue, there's simply nothing to tell us what's going on.

INTERACTION AND INNER LIFE

Communication and meaning provide the basis for inner life as well. Even the meaning of our most private thoughts and feelings emerges from talk and interaction. We learn about ourselves—what we experience, what we call that experience, what we think and feel about that experience—through the ways that others respond to and communicate with us. Even the deepest sensations, such as so-called altered states of mind, are social matters. Let's see how that's possible.

The inner feelings that smoking marijuana induces seem to be pleasurable for many people, but not for everybody. Not everyone "gets high," especially not the first time or two that he or she tries it. Some feel that it doesn't do a thing for them. Others find it outright obnoxious, no more appealing than inhaling exhaust fumes from a bus. Sociologist Howard Becker (1973) was interested in how such differences come about. Perhaps, Becker reasoned, there's something in the experience, besides the drug itself, that makes marijuana appealing. After all, marijuana doesn't have the same powerful chemical effects as other psychoactive drugs. It isn't addictive. Users can stop without undergoing withdrawal symptoms or uncontrollable cravings. Its effects aren't necessarily captivating and controlling. So how do users get high?

Becker maintained that getting high has a great deal to do with social interaction. For one thing, one has to learn how to define what one is feeling while smoking. A user has to be taught what to feel. Even after one learns the proper smoking technique, he or she may not get high. Sure, the sensations caused by marijuana may be present, but a first-time user may not know how to recognize them as pleasurable. It's not until the sensations are viewed as part of being high that the user actually experiences a high. That's something cultivated through interaction with others, according to Becker. Other users have to enlighten the neophyte about how it feels—what it means—to get high.

Listen to how one marijuana user whom Becker interviewed described the process:

I didn't get high the first time. . . . I don't think I held it in long enough. I probably let it out, you know, you're a little afraid. The second time I wasn't sure, and he [smoking companion] told me, like I asked him for some symptoms or something, how would I know, you know. . . . So he told me to sit on a stool. I sat on—I think I sat on a bar stool—and he said, "Let your feet hang," and then when I got down my feet were real cold, you know.

And I started feeling it, you know. That was the first time. And then about a week after that, some time pretty close to it, I really got it on. That was the first time I got on a big laughing kick, you know. Then I really knew I was on. (Pp. 49–50)

Another novice told how he discovered that he was high for the first time:

They were just laughing the hell out of me because like I was eating so much. I just skoffed [ate] so much food and they were just laughing at me, you know. Sometimes I'd be looking at them, you know, wondering why they were laughing, you know, not knowing what I was doing. . . . Like, you know, like I'd ask, "What's happening?" and all of a sudden I feel weird, you know. "Man, you're on you know. You're on pot. . . ." I said, "No, am I?" Like I don't know what's happening. (P. 50)

Others identified different ways of knowing that they were high. They were all immersed in social interaction. Here's another example:

I heard little remarks that were made by other people. Somebody said, "My legs are rubbery," and I can't remember all the remarks that were made because I was very attentively listening for all these cues for what I was supposed to feel like. (P. 50)

One novice user, a musician, pointed directly to others in explaining how important they are in recognizing a high, as well as explaining why he was enjoying himself!

. . . I mean, like that first time it was more or less of a mild drunk. I was happy, I guess, you know what I mean. But I really didn't know I was high, you know what I mean. It was only after the second time I got high that I realized I was high the first time. Then I knew that something different was happening.

. . . How did I know? If what happened to me that night would have happened to you, you would've known, believe me. We played the first tune for almost two hours—one tune! Imagine, man! We got on the stand and played this one tune, we started at nine o'clock. When we got finished I looked at my watch, it's quarter to eleven. Almost two hours on one tune. And it didn't seem like anything.

I mean, you know, it does that to you. It's like you have much more time or something. Anyway, when I saw that, man, it was too much. I knew I must really be high or something if anything like that could happen. See, and then they [his fellow musicians] explained to me that that's what it did to you, you had a different sense of time and everything. So I realized that that's what it was. I knew then. Like the first time, I probably felt that way, you know, but I didn't know what's happening. (P. 51)

This musician felt high, but he didn't actually know it until his buddies clued him in. Only after the fact did he realize that he had been high on the previous occasion, too. It's as if the present were reinterpreting the past. Now that he knew what it was like, he also knew that he liked it. Being high was as much a by-product of interacting with other marijuana users as it was a drug-induced experience.

Getting high clearly isn't just a function of marijuana use. Users depend on the social situation, talk, and interaction to provide suggestions, concrete referents, and even instructions for what to feel. Since the sensations produced by marijuana aren't automatically or necessarily pleasant, getting high is a socially acquired taste. After all, is being fuzzy, dizzy, thirsty, or tingly necessarily a good feeling? Is misjudging time and distance undeniably a pleasant experience? If these sensations aren't experienced positively, then getting high isn't going to be appealing.

I felt I was insane you know. Everything people done to me just wigged me. I couldn't hold a conversation, and my mind would be wandering, and I was always thinking, oh, I don't know, weird things, like hearing music different. . . . I get the feeling that I can't talk to anyone. I'll goof completely. (P. 53)

The larger point here is that any experience, no matter how personal or private, is socially constructed. Even feelings like physical pain (Zborowski 1952), anger, joy, and fear (Schachter and Singer 1962) are defined by way of interaction and the resulting meanings that we take from and share with others.

INTERACTION AND SOCIAL WORLDS

Social worlds are also interactionally constructed. The statuses we acquire, the positions we occupy, and the situations in which we participate all result from what we say and do with one another. As we just showed, the world of the marijuana user doesn't simply appear out of thin air to someone who smokes marijuana. It's socially generated.

Establishing definitions of situations and the working identities of the people in them is important interactional work. Situations don't appear to us as objectively meaningful, as if, like clothing, they came labeled for brand recognition. Nor can we automatically match available definitions with our observations. We always engage in interpretation in order to understand what things mean. This, too, involves talk and interaction.

Let's examine how the definition of a situation as an act of "vandalism" and the construction of the identity "juvenile delinquent" are put in place in relation to circumstances in which what's going on isn't completely evident. One day at school, Jason Howard, a 14-year-old high school freshman, was summoned to the principal's office. This was quite unsettling for Jason because things like this never happened to him. He just didn't get into trouble. But trouble was on the horizon, as the principal, Dr. Warren, beckoned Jason into his office. There, to Jason's surprise, sat his neighborhood friend, Mike Ryan, sullenly awaiting his unknown fate. The boys barely acknowledged one another as they sat facing the principal.

"Gentlemen," Dr. Warren proceeded, "Officer Klein would like to have a word with you." Only then did Jason realize that the man seated next to Dr. Warren's desk was a police detective. "I'm going to leave you to have a little chat," the principal concluded as he left the room.

"You boys know why I'm here?"

The boys shook their heads silently, indicating they knew nothing.

"You know each other?"

"Yeah, we hang out now and then," offered Mike coolly. "Sometimes we work on a little homework." Jason nodded in agreement.

It was true. Mike and Jason had been classmates off and on for five years. They'd been in many "talented and gifted" and accelerated learning programs together in elementary and intermediate school. While they now traveled in different circles, they still spent time together now and then, doing nothing special. They'd both tried out for the high school basketball team and enjoyed playing together, until Mike got cut from the team. They were definitely friends, if not the best of buddies.

"Listen, I bet I know what happened here," sympathized Officer Klein. "You're hanging out, nothing to do. You wander over to the construction site. You see the bulldozer. One thing leads to another. Who's got the nerve to get behind the wheel? Who's gonna take the dare? And once you get started, why not just take down the outhouse? Is that about right? Some kind of stupid prank?"

The boys remained silent. Not a hint of recognition. Jason knew nothing of such an escapade.

"Come on, it's no big deal. You know you're gonna have to pay for the outhouse, but it's just, you know, kid stuff. Screwin' around. We're gonna have to tell your parents, and the rest is up to them."

Stone silence. "Tell my parents?" thought Jason. "He's got nothing to tell them. I don't know what this guy's talking about." Officer Klein waited.

"OK. If that's the way you want it. You wanna be smart guys? We *are* gonna get to the bottom of this, whether you cooperate or not. You [indicating Mike], take a seat outside. I'll get to you later."

Sitting down behind the desk across from Jason, Officer Klein turned up the heat. "I don't know why you're holding out, boy. We know you were there. We know that it was you. We've got the evidence."

"I'm sorry, sir, but I don't know what you're talking about."

"You think this is all hot air? You think I'm just making this up?" Klein shot back. "You think I'm stupid?"

"No, sir. I just don't know what you're talking about."

"You been hanging out at that construction site at the end of Plum Street?"

"No, sir."

"You mean to tell me you don't know anything about how that outhouse got tipped over?"

"No, sir, I don't."

"You got an identification bracelet?" Klein paused. "You lose an ID bracelet recently?"

"I never had an identification bracelet, sir."

"Never? Never lost one down at that construction site?"

Dr. Warren had slipped back into the room, and now Officer Klein rose from behind the desk. He tossed something across the room to Jason. It was a "dog tag," the kind worn by members of the military. It read: "Jason Howard, 980 Plum Street, Concord, California." "What's that, smart guy?"

"It's a dog tag, sir. You said 'ID bracelet.' This was mine, but I probably lost it in about the third grade."

"How's it going here?" Dr. Warren interjected. He could sense that things were at an impasse. "Is Mr. Howard giving you the straight story? He's not usually in this kind of trouble."

"Well, we seem to have a bit of a discrepancy," allowed Officer Klein.

"You know," continued Dr. Warren, "Jason's got a point. That's not an ID bracelet. And it's rusty enough to be pretty old. Tell me, Jason, you get pretty good grades, right? Honor roll? Play on the basketball team? Take an extra class during A period [before school]? It's not like you to be involved in this sort of thing." Jason just nodded.

Officer Klein began to waver. "So you don't know anything about this stuff? [To Dr. Warren] You sure he's tellin' the truth. Well . . . you seem like a decent kid. I don't want to find out that you've been up to something. . . . Let's see what your friend has to say?"

With that, Jason was escorted to a chair outside the door, and Mike took his place in the hot seat. Jason could overhear the proceedings as Klein conducted his interrogation. Mike was just as adamant as Jason that he knew nothing about the outhouse incident. Eventually, though, he grew impatient with the relentless accusations. "This is bulls——it," he exclaimed defiantly when Officer Klein stated unequivocally that he had him "dead to rights."

"Listen Officer Krupke [referring to the character from *Westside Story*], you don't have a thing on me," Mike taunted Klein. "It's just like you cops. You can't tell an outhouse from an a——hole." Klein bristled.

Jason could hear Dr. Warren and Officer Klein conferring. This wasn't the first time Mike had been in trouble, the two noted. Klein said Mike had several referrals to juvenile court, and Warren acknowledged that Mike was no stranger to the principal's office. Parents divorced. Living with a single mother. Mike even looked like trouble waiting to happen. He was well over six feet; he'd been a head taller than his classmates all his life. (Jason, by contrast, was a mere five feet eight.) Mike had probably been shaving since he was 10. And he had a foul mouth, a bad attitude besides.

This was a matter for further investigation, the two men concluded. "We seem to have a budding juvenile delinquent on our hands, a real smart guy. It looks like we're gonna have to take this punk down to lock-up," Officer Klein concluded. "We'll sift through the details of this crime and see what shakes out. Would you [Warren] call his mother and arrange for her to meet us down at the station?" On the way out of the office, Dr. Warren dismissed Jason, quickly writing him a pass to get back into class. Officer Klein had one parting shot. "Keep away from this guy [Mike]. He's a badass, nothing but trouble."

An amazing amount of interactional, interpretive work was involved in coming to this conclusion. At the start, the situation was defined as "kid stuff," a "stupid prank." Eventually, however, it became a full-blown "crime." From a couple of guys "just hanging out" and "one thing leads to another," Mike and Jason were transformed into a "punk" and a "decent kid," respectively. Their social worlds were implicated in the process. How did this happen, when the facts of the case remained essentially unchanged?

As the interaction unfolded, Officer Klein offered his initial take on the matter—his definition of the situation. What had transpired, he posited, was a simple teenage prank. Two kids, hanging out together, with time to kill and temptation at hand. The boys' steadfast refusal to buy into this account called his interpretation into question. Maybe these weren't just "boys bein' boys" after all. Maybe they were "smart guys," even "badasses," delinquents not pranksters. The possibility that this was a prank faded as Klein came to see the boys in a different light.

Officer Klein slipped into this frame of mind as he began to interrogate, then accuse, Jason. The situation was looking more and more like a crime to him. And as this interpretation took shape, Klein began to figure Jason was "holding out," not admitting to being on the construction site. Viewing Jason in this way made it reasonable, in turn, to look for evidence to confirm the identity "smart guy." The ID bracelet immediately became convincing proof of Jason's complicity. It was proof that Jason had been on the scene, and now he was lying to cover up. Even the denial of the crime could be seen as fitting the typical image of the smart guy—a delinquent with a penchant for covering his tracks.

Dr. Warren, however, defined the situation differently when he revealed that this sort of trouble was really out of character for Jason. This cast matters in a new light. Jason's impeccable schoolboy credentials made it seem plausible that the damning evidence represented by the ID bracelet was just what Jason said it was: a long-lost dog tag and nothing more. Jason wasn't being dishonest or a smart guy. He was just being truthful and accurate. If Jason was basically a "decent kid," he wasn't likely to have committed a criminal act.

All this happened by way of social interaction. The definition of the situation didn't automatically jump out from the facts of the crime scene. Nor did it flow directly from either boy's character. In fact, more than one definition came into play. As information emerged in the interaction, different schemas began to make their own kind of sense. Observed features of the now-apparent past, as well as aspects of the immediate interaction—for example, Jason's respectful demeanor—added pieces to the reformulated puzzle. As Officer Klein began to rearrange the pieces, the definition of Jason as a decent kid became increasingly plausible. Again, the present was making sense of the past.

Another definition kicked in when Officer Klein turned to Mike. Initially, Mike was a strong candidate for being a smart guy. The ensuing conversation did nothing to dissuade Klein from this opinion. While less evidence pointed to Mike than to Jason, Officer Klein remained steadfast. Why the difference? First, there was no alternate character sketch—no credible competing identity—to challenge the one that Klein was constructing for Mike. Indeed, everything that transpired during their conversation bolstered the smart-guy image. For his part, Mike was openly defiant, unlike Jason, who was respectful, if politely insistent in his denials. Mike was antagonistic. He was profane. He was, from all appearances, a genuine "badass." His wisecracks about cops, outhouses, and a——holes left no doubt on that score.

Dr. Warren added substance to this identity. By mentioning Mike's school troubles and his family situation, Warren supplied new pieces to the puzzle, drawing a familiar, if not always accurate, social world into the picture. They fit perfectly with the popular image of a bona fide juvenile delinquent. What Dr. Warren *didn't* say also sustained the image. Omitting the fact that Mike was among the brightest kids at the school left the badass identity intact. Several teachers counted Mike among their favorite students because of his intelligence, wit, and intellectual curiosity, but their views weren't introduced into the discussion. Such information might have challenged Officer Klein's emerging interpretation or opened the possibility for an alternate scenario.

In the end, the emerging definition of the situation, the social worlds that were marshaled as confirming evidence, and the identities that unfolded in the principal's office were artfully constructed. The nature of an alleged act (a "crime" or a "prank"), the identities and moral character of the two boys (a "decent kid" versus a "smart guy"), and the social background that was used to shed light on the situation (a single-parent household in Mike's case) were assembled interactionally. They were produced within ongoing talk and interaction.

FINAL REMINDERS

The leading theme of the book—that inner lives and social worlds are constructed through social interaction—is apparent in the reading selections that follow. We remind you to think about the everyday relationships among language, meaning, and communication as you go through the readings. Keep the following features of interaction in mind.

Meaning Making

First, remember that social interaction is meaning-making activity. When we interact, we construct the realities of our everyday lives. This takes time and effort. We don't deal automatically with one another, as if experience had meaning separate from our conduct. Rather, we put together what our everyday social worlds look like. We assemble the identities of the inhabitants of those social worlds. And, in the process, we make those inner lives and social worlds meaningful. In a word, interaction is the active meaning-making *work* of reality construction.

Also bear in mind that meaning making is practical social activity. Participants don't just behave. They make connections between words and things, between words and other words. In the process, they make meaning. Without communication, things appear meaningless, as they did in the *Monkey Business* example. It is through communicative practice—through everyday talk and interaction—that we define situations and assemble the meaningful realities of our inner lives and social worlds.

Reflexivity

Second, social interaction both makes meaning and, in turn, draws upon and is shaped by the meanings it produces. It is "reflexive," as sociologist Harold Garfinkel (1967) put it. Reflexivity is a tricky concept, even if we see its traces everywhere. In the sense that we use it here, reflexivity means self-producing and self-sustaining. The artist and master illusionist M. C. Escher's famous picture *Drawing Hands* nicely illustrates the concept. The picture is composed of a right hand holding a pencil, drawing a left hand. The left hand in the picture is also holding a pencil. It, in turn, is drawing the right hand that ostensibly drew the left hand. *Reflexivity.* The first hand draws the second hand, which, in turn, has drawn the first hand. The first hand both produces and is produced by the second hand.

It's the same with social interaction. Interaction produces the meaningful situations of everyday life. These situations, in turn, provide the basis for interaction itself. In the situation involving Mike and Jason, we saw how Officer Klein, Dr. Warren, Jason, and Mike reflexively assembled both the actions and actors in question. There was an interpretive give-and-take as information was introduced, interpreted, reinterpreted, and fit into the emerging picture. The resulting definition, in turn, became the basis for treating Jason as the "good kid" and Mike as the "badass." Parts of the puzzle made up the whole picture, while the whole picture provided a place for each part to fit.

REFERENCES

Becker, Howard. 1973. "Becoming a Marijuana User." *American Journal of Sociology* 59:235–242.

Garfinkel, Harold. 1967. *Studies in Ethnomethodology.* Englewood Cliffs, NJ: Prentice Hall.

Saussure, Ferdinand de. 1959. *Course in General Linguistics.* New York: Philosophical Library.

Schachter, Stanley and Jerome E. Singer. 1962. "Cognitive, Social, and Physiological Determinants of Emotional State." *Psychological Bulletin* 69:379–399.

Zborowski, Mark. 1952. "Cultural Components in Responses to Pain." *Journal of Social Issues* 8:16–30.

INTERACTION IN EVERYDAY LIFE

Needless to say, scientists like to be scientific. Just as physicians are attracted to clinics and medicine and lawyers are drawn to the courtroom and the law, scientists practice their trade in laboratories. Their special skills and problems call for distinctive *wares* and workplaces. Centrifuges, spectrometers, test tubes, and microscopes are part of the hardware that signifies what it means to be scientific.

Social scientists are no different. They also have their wares. Sample surveys, standardized interviews, mathematical models, psychological tests, and behavioral experiments are just a few of the procedures they use to obtain information about human experience. The places where many social scientists ply their trades may actually be formal laboratories and other highly controlled research settings. Surveys, for example, take place in locations designated by the researcher. Interviewing is governed by a strict set of rules also set up by the researcher. The respondent's role is simply to answer questions, nothing more. As in formal laboratories, strict measures are taken to show that social researchers are being scientific.

Wares differ from *trappings*. Scientific wares are required to do scientific work. Trappings, in contrast, are paraphernalia used for the sake of appearance. Trappings are like window dressing. They serve to convince people that what is going on is, indeed, what it appears to be. Scientifically speaking, trappings are things we could do without.

Social scientists are aware of the distinction between wares and trappings. They study people, not things, and people may resist or misunderstand the application of scientific procedures to their experience. Too many trappings can make research subjects uncomfortable. They make situations unnatural. This can hamper research. A highly structured, formal interview, for example, may cause respondents to be silent or respond glibly. Respondents are less likely to answer questions in the complex and sensitive ways that they typically do in everyday circumstances. Coming on too strong as a scientist may simply turn people off. Excessive trappings may actually cause them to mislead researchers.

Minimizing research trappings allows for a more natural view. Getting to know people and their worlds by involving oneself in the places they live and work can be a highly effective way of seeing social reality as it is actually practiced. Unobtrusive research procedures may not give a research project the appearance of science, but they often produce more valid results.

Researchers who are interested in naturally occurring interaction try to minimize the disruptive influence of their research procedures. They avoid wares, such as laboratory simulation and standardized interviewing, because these wares distort everyday life. The talk and interaction that unfolds in places such as street corners, shopping malls, playgrounds, and households doesn't easily accommodate scientific wares, let alone trappings. The natural flow and complex meanings of everyday life may actually resist science, since scientific wares are designed for much more formally controlled circumstances.

The social scientists whose work appears in this section conduct their research in the ordinary contexts of daily life. The absence of formal scientific control allows the researcher to see how people assign meaning to their conduct and activities on their own terms. These social scientists feel that this is the only way to gain access to the lives and worlds of the people they hope to understand. For these researchers, everyday life is its own laboratory.

ABOUT THE READINGS

A brief excerpt from the introduction to **William Foote Whyte's** classic study *Street Corner Society* (1943), entitled "**Cornerville and Its People,**" opens this section on interaction in everyday life. Whyte describes everyday life in the late 1930s on the street corners of an impoverished neighborhood he calls "Cornerville." It's an Italian immigrant slum located in "Eastern City." Whyte is especially concerned with how easy it is for "respectable people" to get the wrong picture of Cornerville. To the outsider, it's tempting to see Cornerville as a lifeless collection of depressing statistics about a neighborhood in decline. Those who limit themselves to this kind of information miss the vibrant, well-organized features of everyday life that give Cornerville its social character.

Whyte urges us to leave these stereotypic perceptions and images behind. Instead, he insists that we look for ourselves. Whyte argues that wherever everyday life appears, it's organized on its own terms. This may be a far cry from the kind of orderliness that "respectable people" are familiar with, but it's orderly just the same. Listen to how people talk. Watch as they interact. Only then will you be able to see the exquisite patterns of social life. This is sage advice coming from a trailblazing social researcher. Whyte was being quite daring by suggesting that social researchers need to stay clear of scientific wares and trappings to discover the actual ways people live their lives.

In "**The Sociology of Everyday Life,**" **Jack D. Douglas** also directs us to study everyday life. He provides rules of thumb for understanding it on its own terms. At every turn, Whyte's voice seems to echo in the background. First, Douglas suggests that we steer away from "scientific manipulation," which, he argues, can easily get in the way of seeing how people watch people as they actually interact. Second, he encourages us to drop our scientific pretenses and, instead, adopt the standpoint of members of these situations. If these rules appear to be simple, they are profoundly different from the way social scientists and "respectable people" with preconceived notions often proceed.

Hugh Mehan and **Houston Wood** show us what we may see if we follow Whyte's and Douglas' advice. They outline "**Five Features of Reality**" that characterize the organization of everyday life, wherever it occurs. First, everyday life is "reflexive," whether it takes place in Cornerville, among the Azande tribe of Africa, or in the boardroom of an American corporation. Talk and interaction construct understandings of inner life and social worlds. These understandings, in turn, provide the basis and substance for further talk and interaction. Second, in everyday life, people construct *coherent* bodies of knowledge about themselves and their worlds. They continually straighten things out when knowledge seems incompatible or fill in the gaps when it's missing. A third feature is that the reality of everyday life is always interactional. Reality construction is part of the ongoing work of social interaction. Fourth, because it is always under construction, reality is not set in stone. It is as fragile and fluid as the work that holds it together. And, finally, reality is not a single, homogeneous entity. Rather, it's comprised of the many social worlds and associated inner lives that ebb and flow in our ongoing experience in society. We live and participate in multiple realities.

1 | CORNERVILLE AND ITS PEOPLE
William Foote Whyte

In the heart of "Eastern City" there is a slum district known as Cornerville, which is inhabited almost exclusively by Italian immigrants and their children. To the rest of the city it is a mysterious, dangerous, and depressing area. Cornerville is only a few minutes' walk from fashionable High Street, but the High Street inhabitant who takes that walk passes from the familiar to the unknown.

For years Cornerville has been known as a problem area, and, while we were at war with Italy, outsiders became increasingly concerned with that problem. They feared that the Italian slum dweller might be more devoted to fascism and Italy than to democracy and the United States. They have long felt that Cornerville was at odds with the rest of the community. They think of it as the home of racketeers and corrupt politicians, of poverty and crime, of subversive beliefs and activities.

Respectable people have access to a limited body of information upon Cornerville. They may learn that it is one of the most congested areas in the United States. It is one of the chief points of interest in any tour organized to show upper-class people the bad housing conditions in which lower-class people live. Through sight-seeing or statistics one may discover that bathtubs are rare, that children overrun the narrow and neglected streets, that the juvenile delinquency rate is high, that crime is prevalent among adults, and that a large proportion of the population was on home relief or W.P.A. during the depression.

In this view, Cornerville people appear as social work clients, as defendants in criminal cases, or as undifferentiated members of "the masses." There is one thing wrong with such a picture: no human beings are in it. Those who are concerned with Cornerville seek through a general survey to answer questions that require the most intimate knowledge of local life. The only way to gain such knowledge is to live in Cornerville and participate in the activities of its people. One who does that finds that the district reveals itself to him in an entirely different light. The buildings, streets, and alleys that formerly represented dilapidation and physical congestion recede to form a familiar background for the actors upon the Cornerville scene.

One may enter Cornerville already equipped with newspaper information upon some of its racketeers and politicians, but the newspaper presents a very specialized picture. If a racketeer commits murder, that is news. If he proceeds quietly with the daily routines of his business, that is not news. If the politician is indicted for accepting graft, that is news. If he goes about doing the usual personal favors for his constituents, that is not news. The newspaper concentrates upon the crisis—the spectacular event. In a crisis the "big shot" becomes public property. He is removed from the society in which he functions and is judged by standards different from those of his own group. This may be the most effective way to prosecute the lawbreaker. It is not a good way to understand him. For that purpose, the individual must be put back into his social setting and observed in his daily activities. In order to understand the spectacular event, it is necessary to see it in relation to the everyday pattern of life—for there is a pattern to Cornerville life. The middle-class person looks upon the slum district as a formidable mass of confusion, a social chaos. The insider finds in Cornerville a highly organized and integrated social system.

2 | THE SOCIOLOGY OF EVERYDAY LIFE
Jack D. Douglas

The sociology of everyday life is a sociological orientation concerned with the experiencing, observing, understanding, describing, analyzing, and communicating about people interacting in concrete situations. There are three important points in this definition.

First, the sociologist of everyday life studies social interactions by observing and experiencing them in natural situations, that is, in situations that occur independently of scientific manipulation. These are situations common to everyday life. The focus leads to the name, the sociology of everyday life. Other names referring to this sociological orientation are "microsociology," "interactionism," and "naturalistic sociology." Natural situations are the opposite of experimentally controlled situations. This does not mean that the sociologists of everyday life never use experimental controls to study human beings. On the contrary, the social scientist of everyday life sometimes makes use of a previously established understanding of everyday life to manipulate variables in a study. These studies are called "natural experiments." (See the discussion of natural experiments in Douglas, 1976.) All such scientific controls, however, are derived from earlier experience and observation of natural situations. We must first learn what human beings feel, perceive, think, and do in natural situations before we can determine how to conduct observations with controls that will not distort or bias the realities we observe.

Second, the sociology of everyday life begins with the experience and observation of people *interacting in concrete, face-to-face situations. Concrete situations*[1] are those in which the members of society actually are engaged in face-to-face interaction with other members of society—feeling, perceiving, thinking, and doing things. Sociologists of everyday life begin by experiencing and observing what is happening naturally, rather than by hypothesizing about what *might* happen or by questioning the members of society

about what they think happens or did happen or will happen. Introspection and questioning are sometimes used by the sociologists of everyday life after they know from experience and observation what in fact does happen naturally. The sociologists of everyday life do not record what people say on an abstract level (such as their responses to an opinion poll or questionnaire survey), because abstract responses are often quite different from what people really feel, perceive, think and do in concrete situations.

Third, all analysis of everyday life, of concrete interactions in concrete situations, begins with an analysis of the *members' meanings.* Members' meanings are often called "common-sense meanings" or "everyday-life meanings" by sociologists of this school. "Meaning" is used to refer to the feelings, perceptions, emotions, moods, thoughts, ideas, beliefs, values, and morals of the members of society. In short, "meaning" refers to the internal experience of the members that is most relevant to a particular social interaction. Sociologists of everyday life do not begin by imposing their own meanings on their observations. They do not say "I think premarital intercourse is immoral because. ...." They are concerned with finding what the members perceive, think, and feel. For example, do those being studied feel premarital intercourse is immoral? Sociologists of everyday life, then, first try to understand and analyze social situations *from the standpoint of the members.* Later analyses generally go beyond members' meanings, but they try to retain those meanings in as undistorted a way as possible. (This is what sociologists of everyday life often call "being true to the natural phenomena.")

THE PARTIAL SITUATEDNESS OF LIFE

All life is partially interdependent with the concrete situations or environments in which it exists. This truth is well recognized in everyday life and is expressed by numerous common-sense expressions, such as "It depends on the situation," "It all depends," "That depends on the circumstances," and so on.

All of this may sound simple enough and almost obvious today. But it was anything but obvious to most social scientists before the 1960s. Sociology and psychology in the nineteenth and early twentieth centuries was primarily built on methods that imposed controlled situations of observation on the human beings studied and that arrived at theories that include no direct consideration of the partial situatedness of concrete actions. In order to understand the importance, problems, and nature of the sociologies of everyday life, we must first understand how these earlier theories came about and what their basic ideas were.

Probably the most important mistake the early social scientists made as a result of their imitating the natural scientists was their adoption of the experimental method and the hypothetical model with which to formulate their theories. (For detailed treatments of this see, for example, Douglas, 1967 and 1971.) We now know from our own experience, as well as from experience in the numerous fields of behavioral biology, that the experimental method and the hypothetical model were the wrong approaches for a new science of human beings. The reasons are simple. The experimental method assumes, first, that one can make controlled observations of phenomena without the method itself changing the phenomena observed. And, second, the experimental method assumes that all of the important natural phenomena can be precisely reproduced under the controlled conditions of an experiment, so the scientist can see in the controlled situation all of the phenomena of fundamental importance. Both assumptions are quite untrue when applied to higher forms of life, especially to social animals—and especially untrue when applied to human beings. All higher forms of life, especially the higher social animals, are highly reactive to social observations; above all to any observation by strangers. Most animals will not allow people to get near enough to them to observe their natural behavior in any detail. Indeed, most early observations of animal life were of flight behavior only, which is important but hardly representative of the whole repertoire of animal behavior. Human be-

ings also are extremely sensitive about being observed by other people. The distinction between private areas (not observable by strangers) and public areas (observable by strangers) varies in intensity from one group or individual to another, but it is always there and always important. In our society the distinction is basic. As Sartre noted, the difference between being unobservable (completely private), and the *possibility* of being observed by any human being, is a vast difference for human beings. We all know how carefully people "put their best foot forward" when they are observed.

The failure to see the interdependency of life with its concrete situations led to the assumption that the observational reactivity of human beings is insignificant. Once scholars assumed that rigorous experimental methods should be used to study human beings, then they began to observe people in labs, to use "objective" tests or questionnaires to study their intelligence or their love lives, and even to study their physiological responses with computers. Of course, many scientists using experimental methods for observing people recognized that people change according to the situation they are in. Not all social scientists used the methods of the Skinnerians or others who studied human beings by putting pigeons or rats into mazes and boxes. Those who studied human beings in labs often tried to hide the experimenter's presence by using one-way mirrors. Over time, subjects studied in this way probably became less reactive to the observations of scientists, as long as the "subjects" were engaging in public forms of behavior. But that does not mean that their "subjects" were not affected by the methods of observation, nor does it mean that they were ever able to study anything but the most unconflictful forms of public behavior.

The failure of sociologists to see the fundamental interdependency of human beings and their situations also derived from the abstractionist fallacy of the structural sociologies. If one assumes the situation does not affect what people feel, think, or do, then one does not bother to observe concrete situations and instead looks for the causes of human behavior only in non-situational factors. The sociologies of the nineteenth and early twentieth centuries found those non-situational factors in the abstract shared values of social groups. The structuralists (also called structural-functionalists because they were concerned with the functions social structures supposedly served) produced a great deal of literature arguing that the abstract and publicly expressed values of a society determine the basic patterns of actions in the society.

One well-known work of the structuralists was Seymour Martin Lipset's *First New Nation* (1963). The basic argument of this book is that the major patterns of American society over the past two centuries have been determined by the conflict between a commitment to equality and a commitment to achievement, both of which are abstract values. The evidence for such a position is obvious enough. When asked in public-opinion questionnaires whether they believe in the values of equality and achievement almost all Americans will say yes. They will also express agreement on a large number of other abstract values such as love and honesty. It seems likely that even more agreement would be found on abstract values like "individual freedom," which, after all was the "slogan" of Americans in the nineteenth century and remains so for many millions. Almost all the members of all the industrial societies of the Western world express roughly the same abstract values in response to public opinion polls. This led Talcott Parsons (1951) and others to argue that Western societies can be described in terms of their position on general value dimensions. Parsons' structural analysis was far more abstract than Lipset's and thus even more removed from concrete situations.

Anyone assuming that the concrete actions of Americans are determined by abstractly shared values would expect to find almost universally similar human behavior. Such an analyst might expect to find everyone doing the same things. For example, the structuralist might expect all Americans to act in such a way as to produce total equality and total freedom. There are, however, intense social conflicts over specific or concrete interpretations of the values of equality or freedom. For example, today government officials and many judges insist that equality of education can be achieved through "busing," but approximately 80 percent of the people disagree, some violently. Again, libertarians insist that "individual freedom" means that individuals should be able to make their

own decisions on economic matters, public nudity, drugs, or prostitution. What one person defines in a concrete situation as "equality," another sees as "government tyranny"; what one defines concretely as "freedom," another defines as "licentiousness" or "social disorder."

The pervasiveness of such conflicts led Lipset and other structuralists to argue that the abstractly shared values conflict with each other. They argued that abstract value conflicts produce conflicts over meanings and actions. But what determines which particular values will come into conflict in any given situation? What determines who will invoke what values in what order, to what degree? Above all, what determines which value will win out or which interpretation of what values will win out? Suppose, for example, that American history is determined by a conflict between an abstract value of equality and an abstract value of achievement. What determines why some people will line up on the side of "universal equality," while the other 80 percent line up on the side of "achievement"? Even more to the point, what determines which side will win in such a conflict? How, for example, would one predict that a society committed above all to freedom and due process of law would be one in which the minority of 20 percent would win out over the majority of 80 percent?

Thus, the recognition of a vast gap between the social theory of the structuralists and the everyday world around us led more and more sociologists to question the meanings imputed by the structuralists to the members of society. Were these meanings the ones the members of society were using in their everyday lives to determine what they did? Durkheim and other structural sociologists, for example, had given an abstract definition to suicide, that of a "death resulting from the act of an individual against himself which he knew would have the consequence of producing death." Durkheim argued against using a definition that involved any idea of intention, because he thought intention was too problematic or uncertain for a social scientist to be able to determine reliably. Durkheim also assumed that his abstract definition of suicide was the same as the concrete meanings of suicide imputed in concrete cases by coroners, medical examiners, and others who had gathered the official statistics on suicide that Durkheim used in his study. It was easy to show that the truth was the exact opposite. "Intention to kill oneself" is the most common idea involved in the everyday use of the word suicide; the officials who constructed the statistics used by Durkheim were using the term in that way. (The officials rarely even knew what the legal definition might be, but it also generally involved some idea of intention. See Douglas, 1967, 1971). If it was so simple to find that, why did not a brilliant man like Durkheim find it? The reason was simple: he did not look at human beings in everyday life. He *assumed* that concrete situations do not affect the meanings and actions of human beings. Durkheim assumed that the concrete meanings and actions are determined by the abstract meanings. In the long run, however, concrete situations are of fundamental importance and determine abstract meanings.

THE PARTIALLY PROBLEMATIC NATURE OF LIFE

Everyone knows that life is partially problematic, that is, unpredictable. We cannot always predict whether we shall go to work in the morning or whether we shall eat dinner at home at the usual time. More importantly, we all know, or recognize as soon as we think about it, that we cannot predict *exactly* what will happen in any given concrete situation. If we could predict with complete accuracy the exact details of what will happen in concrete situations, then we would say that life worked like "clock work," because clocks work as automatically as anything. Yet we know that clocks do break down and do run fast or slow. "Clock work" is about as unproblematic as anything ever gets in natural situations, yet clock work remains partially problematic. Needless to say, we all know that the important things and situations in our lives, such as love and marriage, are far more problematic than that. The question "What is love?" has perplexed human beings of all ages, and the question "Am I in love?" perplexes most people most of the time. The situatedness of life and its problematic nature are actually two different ways of looking at the same thing. If natural situations and our actions in them were totally predictable, totally unproblematic,

then we could program our lives to avoid situations and actions in situations we do not like. But, of course, life is not totally predictable; life is always partially problematic. Our own feelings, thinking, and actions are problematic because we cannot totally predict what situations will arise. We therefore must always remain open to changing situations. We must adapt partially to concrete situations as they arise or emerge, independently of our earlier feelings, perceptions, thoughts, or anticipation of situations and actions.

Life is situated because it is problematic, and it is problematic because it is situated. Or, life is both partially situated and partially problematic because, for whatever unknown reason, behavior that can change according to the situation at hand is the most adaptive (genetically successful).

The only known human beings who act totally "out of situation," that is, who act always in the same programmed way, are the Don Quixotes. Don Quixotes always find evil windmills to attack in the same way. And what happens when Don Quixotes always perceive the same things in the world, always interpret them the same way, always act in the same ways—always feel, think, and act independently of the concrete situations they face? They meet disaster very quickly. Those who do not take into consideration the partially problematic nature of reality and adapt their feelings, thinking, and actions to concrete natural situations are "absolutists." Absolutists who merely talk absolutely, which is, after all, quite common, may succeed quite well. Those who act absolutely quickly meet disaster. That, presumably, is why all of our studies of human beings in everyday life reveal them to be almost always unabsolutist—or absolutist talkers and unabsolutist actors! People who are truly absolutist are normally already labeled mental patients and are said to be "acting out of situation"—that is, without regard to the situation or to the problems it poses.

THE PARTIALLY TRANS-SITUATED AND PARTIALLY ORDERED NATURE OF LIFE

We have emphasized that life is only partially situated and problematic. There has been a tendency for some sociologists of everyday life to react against the extreme of structuralism, in which life is seen as totally unsituated and unproblematic, by going to the opposite extreme of seeing life as totally situated and totally problematic.

Life is a matter of degree. Some things are highly problematic and situated, while others are highly unproblematic and unsituated (or trans-situated). Consider, for example, those forms of behavior which are almost completely programmed in the human being. These are the simplest forms of reflexes, such as the prehensile reflex by which our feet tend to grasp something that exerts a moderate and general stimulus. It is an almost completely unproblematic and unsituated form of behavior, an automatic behavior. Because it is almost always adaptive to human beings to grasp the ground surface and, thus, to balance themselves on their feet, we have evolved a reflex that leads the feet to grasp the surface on which we are walking. Yet even that behavior is not totally programmed. If the stimulus is "sharp," then another and opposite reflex will supersede it (that of suddenly collapsing and retracting the foot). Some reflex actions, therefore, are dependent upon the stimulus of a situation. Of course people can choose to walk on very sharp objects that injure the feet, to override an instinctive reflex. Situations do occur in which it would be more adaptive to accept injury to the feet than to avoid it. Thus, all higher animals are able to abstract themselves from concrete situations, that is, to partially transcend the concrete situations they face in order to achieve some future situation: we can partially abstract ourselves from our injured feet perhaps to achieve greater safety. But, of course, when we do so we almost always do it with very cautious concern for the concrete situation in order to minimize the injury and maximize the chances of getting through safely without permanent maiming.

It is easy in everyday life to observe ourselves going through all degrees of problematicness and situatedness in feeling, thinking, and acting. Sometimes we are very uncertain about whether we are in love. Other times we feel certain. Sometimes we are highly flexible and open to new ideas about a situation. Other times we insist on acting in only one way because "it is a matter of principle." People must constantly adapt to situations requiring varying degrees of problematic decision making. Principles, absolute in theory, have a

way of bending in concrete situations. We may feel "certain for ever," but new situations sometimes remind us of our old uncertainties or stimulate new ones. The sociologist of everyday life must be concerned with *how* problematic and *how* situated individual and social life are, not with one extreme or the other, since these extremes are almost nonexistent.

THE SOCIAL CONSTRUCTION OF MEANINGS AND PATHS OF ACTION

Because meanings and actions are partially problematic, individuals must construct (or create) concrete meanings and actions for the concrete situations that emerge in their everyday lives. The more problematic the meanings and actions, the more creative or constructive the work they must do. Some meanings and paths of action in some situations are almost totally shared and routinized. For example, members of our society almost always put on clothes that hide their sex organs before appearing in any public setting. This is one of the most shared and routinized patterns of action in our society. Nevertheless, there are people who deviate from this norm. Individuals do in fact have choices to make about whether they appear nude or clothed. Small children exercise this choice rather freely, causing parents to do a great deal of constructive work to convince children to wear clothes. Moreover, a great amount of constructive work goes into clothing and dressing, including that which "reveals by first hiding and then emphasizing" the clothed sex organs. (For discussions of the social meanings of nudity and clothing, see König, 1973; and Douglas and Rasmussen, with Flanagan, 1977).

Other meanings and paths of action are extremely problematic. Most sexual matters are quite problematic for the members of Western societies, but of course the degree varies greatly with individuals and from one group to another. Some of the rules might be very clear for some people, but feelings have a distinct tendency to go in different directions from the rules, causing many people to make highly creative interpretations of the rules and not infrequently to create deviant paths of action for themselves.

Most of the meanings we impute and most of our actions are made up more or less of the problematic.

Most of the words we use in conversations have shared meanings within our particular social group for any concrete situation we face. But some words and many statements made by people are experienced by others as problematic, forcing others to consciously set about constructing the meanings for them. We do this by asking questions ("What do you mean by that?"), by giving answers, by qualifying and explaining, by interpreting, by inferring, and guessing.

Most of our everyday lives are lived in roughly the same way we cook something. That is, there are certain basic rules of cooking (use heat or microwaves to cook) that are almost universally shared and largely unproblematic. There are certain other shared meanings—pepper is hot, for example—and shared paths of action related to these which are not very problematic—such as always go easy on the pepper. There are also general sets of meanings and rules and paths of action that can be put together in relatively unproblematic ways to make up *recipes for living* in most of the concrete situations that emerge in our lives. Like any cooking recipes, these everyday life recipes give us certain pat or largely unproblematic *stocks of knowledge* (see Schutz, 1962, and Altheide, 1977) and rules. But they do not eliminate the problems involved in living, especially those involved in living well. We still must be very careful to put knowledge together in the right way, always taking note of the special properties of the concrete situation we face. (On hot days the bread dough will rise more easily than on cold days, so. . . . But just how hot is today? And will the humidity or breeze make a difference?) As anyone who has ever cooked knows, cooking remains a rather problematic thing for everyone, and even the best cook can spoil the simplest dish by burning it, oversalting it, undercooking it, or doing many other things that have problematic, unintended consequences. Even the most careful

and wise construction cannot eliminate all problems or missteps that bring disaster. Life's concrete situations are partially constructed in accord with our recipes for living, but they always remain partially open, uncertain, problematic, and situated. Moreover, the rapid pace of change and conflict in Western societies today have made life far more problematic. Many more individual constructions of meanings must be made to avoid disasters.

NOTE

1. Other terms frequently used to refer to concrete situations and interactions are "face-to-face situations," "immediate situations," "mundane interaction," "practical interaction," and "micro-interaction."

REFERENCES

Altheide, David. *Creating Reality.* Beverly Hills, Calif.: Sage Publications, 1977.

Douglas, Jack D. *The Social Meanings of Suicide.* Princeton, N.J.: Princeton University Press, 1967.

Douglas, Jack D. *American Social Order.* New York: The Free Press, 1971.

Douglas, Jack D. *Investigative Social Research.* Beverly Hills, Calif.: Sage Publications, 1976.

Douglas, Jack D., and Paul K. Rasmussen, with Carol Ann Flanagan. *The Nude Beach.* Beverly Hills, Calif.: Sage Publications, 1977.

Eibl-Eibesfeldt, Irenaus, and Wolfgang Wickler. "Ethology," *International Encyclopaedia of the Social Sciences.* vol. 5. New York: Crowell Collier, 1968.

König, Rene. *A la Mode.* New York: The Seabury Press, 1973.

Lipset, Seymour Martin. *The First New Nation.* New York: Basic, 1963.

Parsons, Talcott. *The Social System.* New York: The Free Press, 1951.

Schutz, Alfred. *Collected Papers.* The Hague: Martinus Nijhoff, 1962.

3 | FIVE FEATURES OF REALITY
Hugh Mehan and Houston Wood

REALITY AS A REFLEXIVE ACTIVITY

When the Azande of Africa are faced with important decisions, decisions about where to build their houses, or whom to marry, or whether the sick will live, for example, they consult an oracle. They prepare for these consultations by following a strictly prescribed ritual. First a substance is gathered from the bark of a certain type of tree. Then this substance is prepared in a special way during a seancelike ceremony. The Azande then pose the question in a form that permits a simple yes or no answer, and feed the substance to a small chicken. The Azande decide beforehand whether the death of the chicken will signal an affirmative or negative response, and so they always receive an unequivocal answer to their questions.

For monumental decisions, the Azande add a second step. They feed the substance to a second chicken, asking the same question but reversing the import of the chicken's death. If in the first consultation sparing the chicken's life meant the oracle had said yes, in the second reading the oracle must now kill the chicken to once more reply in the affirmative and be consistent with its first response.

Our Western scientific knowledge tells us that the tree bark used by the Azande contains a poisonous substance that kills some chickens. The Azande have no knowledge of the tree's poisonous qualities. They do not believe the tree plays a part in the oracular ceremony. The ritual that comes between the gathering of the bark and the administration of the substance to a fowl transforms the tree into an oracle. The bark is but a vessel for the oracle to enter. As the ritual is completed the oracle takes possession of the substance. The fact that it was once a part of a tree is irrelevant. Chickens then live or die, not because of the properties of the tree, but because the oracle "hears like a person and settles cases like a king" (Evans-Pritchard, 1937:321).

The Westerner sees insuperable difficulties in maintaining such beliefs when the oracle contradicts itself. Knowing the oracle's bark is "really" poison, we wonder what happens when, for example, the first and second administration of the oracle produces first a positive and then a negative answer. Or, suppose someone else consults the oracle about the same question, and contradictory answers occur? What if the oracle is contradicted by later events? The house site approved by the oracle, for example, may promptly be flooded; or the wife the oracle selected may die or be a shrew. How is it possible for the Azande to continue to believe in oracles in the face of so many evident contradictions to his faith?

What I have called contradictions are not contradictions for the Azande. They are only contradictions because these events are being viewed from the reality of Western science. Westerners look at oracular practices to determine if in fact there is an oracle. The Azande *know* that an oracle exists. That is their beginning premise. All that subsequently happens they experience from that beginning assumption.

The Azande belief in oracles is much like the mathematician's belief in certain axioms. Gasking (1955:432) has described such unquestioned and unquestionable axioms as *incorrigible propositions:*

> An incorrigible proposition is one which you would never admit to be false whatever happens: it therefore does not tell you what happens. . . . The truth of an incorrigible proposition . . . is compatible with any and every conceivable state of affairs. (For example: whatever is your experience on counting, it is still true that 7 + 5 = 12.)

The incorrigible faith in the oracle is "compatible with any and every conceivable state of affairs." It is not so much a faith about a fact in the world as a faith in the facticity of the world itself. It is the same as the faith

---

many of us have that 7 + 5 always equals 12. (cf Polanyi, 1958: 190–193; 257–261).

Just as Gasking suggests we explain away empirical experiences that deny this mathematical truth, the Azande too have available to them what Evans-Pritchard (1937:330) calls "secondary elaborations of belief." They explain the failure of the oracle by retaining the unquestioned absolute reality of oracles. When events occurred that revealed the inadequacy of the mystical faith in oracles, Evans-Pritchard tried to make the Azande understand these failures as he did. They only laughed, or met his arguments:

> sometimes by point-blank assertions, sometimes by one of the evasive secondary elaborations of belief . . . sometimes by polite pity, but always by an entanglement of linguistic obstacles, for one cannot well express in its language objections not formulated by a culture (Ibid.:319).

Evans-Pritchard (Ibid.:319–320) goes on to write:

> Let the reader consider any argument that would utterly demolish all Zande claims for the power of the oracle. If it were translated into Zande modes of thought it would serve to support their entire structure of belief. For their mystical notions are eminently coherent, being interrelated by a network of logical ties, and are so ordered that they never too crudely contradict sensory experience, but, instead, experience seems to justify them. *The Zande is immersed in a sea of mystical notions, and if he speaks about his poison oracle he must speak in a mystical idiom.* (italics mine.)

Seeming contradictions are explained away by saying such things as a taboo must have been breached, or that sorcerers, witches, ghosts, or gods must have intervened. These "mystical" notions reaffirm the reality of a world in which oracles are a basic feature. Failures do not challenge the oracle. They are elaborated in such a way that they provide evidence for the constant success of oracles. Beginning with the incorrigible belief in oracles, all events *reflexively* become evidence for that belief.[1]

The mathematician, as Gasking suggests, uses a similar process:

> But it does lay it down, so to speak, that if on counting 7 + 5 you do get 11, you are to describe what has happened in some such way as this: Either "I have made a mistake in my counting" or "Someone has played a practical joke and abstracted one of the objects when I was not looking" or "Two of the objects have coalesced" or "One of the objects has disappeared," etc. (Gasking, 1955; quoted in Pollner, 1987:56).

Consider the analogous case of a Western scientist using chloroform to asphyxiate butterflies. The incorrigible idiom called chemistry tells the scientist, among other things, that substances have certain constant properties. Chloroform of a certain volume and mix is capable of killing butterflies. One evening the scientist administers the chloroform as usual, and is dismayed to see the animal continue to flutter about.

Here is a contradiction of the scientist's reality, just as oracle use sometimes produces contradictions. Like the Azande, scientists have many secondary elaborations of belief they can bring to bear on such occurrences, short of rejecting the Western causal belief. Instead of rejecting chemistry they can explain the poison's failure by such things as "faulty manufacturing," "mislabeling," "sabotage," or "practical joke." Whatever the conclusion, it would continue to reaffirm the causal premise of science. This reaffirmation reflexively supports the reality that produced the poison's unexpected failure in the first place.

The use of contradictions to reaffirm incorrigible propositions can be observed in other branches of science. In the Ptolemaic system of astronomy, the sun was seen as a planet of the earth. When astronomers looked at the sun, they saw it as an orb circling the earth. When the Copernican system arose as an alternative to this view, it offered little new empirical data. Instead, it described the old "facts" in a different way. A shift of vision was required for people to see the sun as a star, not a planet of the earth.

Seeing the sun as a star and seeing it as a planet circling the earth are merely alternatives. There is no a priori warrant for believing that either empirical determination is necessarily superior to the other.

How is a choice between equally compelling empirical determinations made? The convert to the Copernican system could have said: "I used to see a planet, but now I see a star" (cf. Kuhn, 1970:115). But to talk that way is to allow the belief that an object can be both a star and a planet at the same time.

Such a belief is not allowed in Western science. So, instead, the Copernican concludes that the sun was a star all along. By so concluding, the astronomer exhibits an incorrigible proposition of Western thought, the *object constancy assumption*.[2] This is the belief that objects remain the same over time, across viewings from different positions and people. When presented with seemingly contradictory empirical determinations, the convert to Copernicanism does not consider that the sun changed through time. Instead he says: "I once took the sun to be a planet, but I was mistaken." The "discovery" of the sun as a star does not challenge the object constancy belief any more than an oracular "failure" challenges the ultimate reality of Azande belief.

The reaffirmation of incorrigible propositions is not limited to mystical and scientific ways of knowing. This reflexive work operates in commonsense reasoning as well. Each time you search for an object you knew was "right there" the same reflexive process is operating. Say, for example, you find a missing pen in a place you know you searched before. Although the evidence indicates that the pen was first absent and then present, that conclusion is not reached. To do so would challenge the incorrigibility of the object constancy belief. Instead, secondary elaborations—"I must have overlooked it," "I must not have looked there"—are invoked to retain the integrity of the object constancy proposition.

Without an object constancy assumption, there would be no problems about alternative determinations. But, with this assumption as an incorrigible proposition, the person faced with alternative seeings must choose one and only one as real. In choosing one, the other is automatically revealed as false. The falsehood of the rejected alternative may be explained in various ways. It may be due to a defective sensory apparatus, or a cognitive bias, or idiosyncratic psychological dynamics. We explain the inconstancy of the experienced object by saying that inconstancy is a product of the experiencing, not a feature of the object itself.[3]

Once an alternative seeing is explained away, the accepted explanation provides evidence for the object constancy assumption that made the explanation necessary in the first place. By demanding that we dismiss one of two equally valid empirical determinations, the object constancy assumption leads to a body of work that validates that assumption. The work then justifies itself afterward, in the world it has created. This self-preservative reflexive process is common to oracular, scientific, and commonsense reasoning.

So far I have approached the reflexive feature of realities as if it were a form of reasoning. But reflexivity is not only a facet of reasoning. It is a recurrent fact of everyday social life. For example, *talk itself is reflexive* (cf. Garfinkel, 1967; Cicourel, 1973). An utterance not only delivers some particular information, it also creates a world in which information itself can appear.

Zimmerman (1973:25) provides a means for understanding the reflexivity of talk at the level of a single word. He presents three identical shapes:

The first and third differ from the second: they each contain single words. These words interact with the box in which they appear so as to change the nature of that box. In so doing, they reflexively illumine themselves. For example, the word "projection," appearing in some other setting, would not mean what it does here. For me it means that I am to see the back panel and the word "projection" as illustrative of a projection. The word "projection" does not merely appear in the scene reporting on that scene. It creates the scene in which it appears as a reasonable object.

Similarly, the word "indentation" not only takes its meaning from the context in which it appears, it reflexively creates that very context. It creates a reality in which it may stand as a part of that reality.

These examples only hint at the reflexivity of talk. [Escher's "Drawing Hands" provides another visual intimation of reflexivity.] Actual conversations are more complex than single words. The social context in which talk occurs, while analogous to one of these static boxes, is enormously ambiguous and potentially infinitely referential. Nonetheless, conversation operates like the printed "projection" and "indentation." An analysis of greetings can be used to show how talk partially constitutes the context and, then comes to be seen as independent of it.[4]

To say "hello" both creates and sustains a world in which persons acknowledge that (1) they sometimes can see one another; (2) a world in which it is possible for persons to signal to each other, and (3) expect to be signaled back to, by (4) some others but not all of them. This is a partial and only illustrative list of some of the things a greeting accomplishes. Without the superstitious use of greetings, no world in which greetings are possible "objects" would arise. A greeting creates "room" for itself. But once such verbal behaviors are regularly done, a world is built up that can take their use for granted (cf. Sacks, Schegloff, and Jefferson, 1974).

When we say "hello" and the other replies with the expected counter greeting, the reflexive work of our initial utterance is masked. If the other scowls and walks on, then we are reminded that we were attempting to create a scene of greetings and that we failed. Rather than treat this as evidence that greetings are not "real," however, the rejected greeter ordinarily turns it into an occasion for affirming the reality of greetings. He formulates "secondary elaborations" of belief about greetings. He says, "He didn't hear me," "She is not feeling well," "It doesn't matter anyway."

Reflexivity provides grounds for absolute faith in the validity of knowledge. The Azande takes the truth of the oracle for granted, the scientist assumes the facticity of science, the layman accepts the tenets of common sense. The incorrigible propositions of a reality serve as criteria to judge other ways of knowing. Using his absolute faith in the oracle, the Azande dismisses Evans-Pritchard's Western science contradictions. Evans-Pritchard, steeped in the efficacy of science, dismissed the oracle as superstitious. An absolute faith in the incorrigibility of one's own knowledge enables believers to repel contrary evidence. This suggests that all people are equally superstitious.

REALITY AS A COHERENT BODY OF KNOWLEDGE

The phenomenon of reflexivity is a feature of every reality. It interacts with the coherence, interactional, fragility, and permeability features I describe in the rest of this chapter. These five features are incorrigible propositions of the reality of ethnomethodology. They appear as facts of the external world due to the ethnomethodologist's unquestioned assumption that they constitute the world. In other words, these features themselves exhibit reflexivity.

This reflexive loop constitutes the interior structure of ethnomethodology. This will become clearer as I describe the second feature of realities, their exhibition of a coherent body of knowledge. To illustrate this feature I will extrapolate from the work of Zimmerman and Wieder (n.d.), who investigated the life of a number of self-named "freaks," frequent drug users within America's counterculture. Both freaks and their academic ethnographers (e.g., Reich, 1970; Roszack, 1969) describe freaks as radical opponents of the straight culture from which they sprang. As Zimmerman and Wieder (n.d.: 103) write:

> From the standpoint of the "straight" members of society, freaks are deliberately irrational. . . . they disavow an interest in efficiency, making long-range plans, and concerns about costs of property (etc.) which are valued by the straight members of American society and are understood by them as indicators of rationality.

On first appearance, here is a reality that seems anarchical. Nonetheless, Zimmerman and Wieder (Ibid: 102–103) found that:

> when it comes to those activities most highly valued by freaks, such as taking drugs, making love, and other "cheap thrills," there is an elaborately developed body of lore. Freaks and others use that knowledge of taking drugs, making love, etc., reasonably, deliberately, planfully, projecting various consequences, predicting outcomes, conceiving of the possibilities of action in more or less clear and distinct ways, and choosing between two or more means of reaching the same end.

The most vivid illustration that freaks use a coherent body of knowledge comes from Zimmerman's and Wieder's discoveries about the place of drugs in the everyday freak life. At first glance such drug use appears irrational. Yet, among freaks, taking drugs "is something as ordinary and unremarkable as their parents regard taking or offering a cup of coffee" (Ibid:57). Freak behavior is not a function of the freaks' ignorance of chemical and medical "facts" about drugs. The freaks studied knew chemical and medical facts well. They organized these facts into a different, yet coherent corpus of knowledge.

One of the team's research assistants, Peter Suchek, was able to systematize the freaks' knowledge of drugs into a taxonomic schemata (Table 1).

What the freak calls "dope," the chemist calls "psychotropic drugs." Within the family of dope, freaks distinguish "mind-expanding" and "body" dope. Freaks further subdivide each of these species. In addition, freaks share a common body of knowledge informing them of the practicalities surrounding the use of each type of dope. All knowledge of dope use is grounded in the incorrigible proposition that dope is to be used. One must, of course, know how to use it.

Zimmerman and Wieder (Ibid.: 118) found the following knowledge about "psychedelic mind-expanding dope" to be common among freaks:

The folk pharmacology of psychedelic drugs may be characterized as a method whereby drug users ratio-

Table 1 The Folk Pharmacology for Dope (after Zimmerman and Wieder, n.d.: 107)

Types of Dope	Subcategories
Mind expanding dope	(Untitled)
	"grass" (marijuana)
	"hash" (hashish)
	"LSD" or "acid" (lysergic acid)
	Psychedelics
	Mescaline
	synthetic
	organic
	natural, peyote
	Psilocybin
	synthetic
	organic
	natural, mushrooms
	"DMT"
	miscellaneous (e.g., Angel's Dust)
Body dope	"speed" (amphetamines)
	"downers" (barbiturates)
	"tranks" (tranquilizers)
	"coke" (cocaine)
	"shit" (heroin)

nally assess choices among kinds of drugs, choices among instances of the same kind of drug, the choice to ingest or not, the time of the act of ingestion relative to the state of one's physiology and relative to the state of one's psyche, the timing relative to social and practical demands, the appropriateness of the setting for having a psychedelic experience, the size of the dose, and the effectiveness and risk of mixing drugs.

Freaks share similar knowledge for the rest of the taxonomy. Being a freak means living within the auspices of such knowledge and using it according to a plan, as the chemist uses his. Both the freaks' and the scientists' realities are concerned with "the facts." Though the facts differ, each reality reflexively proves its facts as absolute.

Consider how the freak assembles the knowledge he uses. He is not loath to borrow from the discoveries of science. But before accepting what the scientist says, he first tests scientific "facts" against the auspices of his own incorrigible propositions. He does not use the scientists' findings to determine the danger of the drug, but rather to indicate the particular dosage, setting, et cetera, under which a drug is to be taken.

Scientific drug researchers frequently attend to the experiences of freaks in a comparable way. They incorporate the facts that freaks report about dope into their coherent idiom. The two then are like independent teams of investigators working on the same phenomenon with different purposes. They are like artists and botanists who share a common interest in the vegetable kingdom, but who employ different incorrigibles.

The freak's knowledge, like all knowledge, is sustained through reflexive interactional work. For example, the knowledge contained in the drug taxonomy (Table 1) sometimes "fails," that is, it produces not a "high" but a "bummer." The incorrigible propositions of freak pharmacology are not then questioned. Instead, these propositions are invoked to explain the bummer's occurrence. "For example," Zimmerman and Wieder (Ibid.: 118) write:

a "bad trip" may be explained in such terms as the following: it was a bad time and place to drop; my head wasn't ready for it; or it was bad acid or mescaline, meaning that it was cut with something impure or that it was some other drug altogether.

The reflexive use of the freak taxonomy recalls my previous discussion of the Azande. When the oracle seemed to contradict itself, the contradiction became but one more occasion for proving the oracular way of knowing. The reality of oracles is appealed to in explaining the failure of the oracle, just as the reality of freak pharmacology is used to explain a bad trip. It would be as futile for a chemist to explain the bad trip scientifically to a freak as it was for Evans-Pritchard to try to convince the Azande that failures of the oracle demonstrated their unreality.

The coherence of knowledge is a reflexive consequence of the researcher's attention. Zimmerman and Wieder, in the best social science tradition, employed many methods to construct the freak's taxonomy. Freaks were interviewed by sociology graduate students and by their peers. These interviewers provided accounts of their own drug experiences as well. Additional freaks not acquainted with the purposes of the research were paid to keep personal diaries of their day-to-day experiences. Zimmerman and Wieder used a portion of this massive data to construct the freak taxonomy, then tested its validity against further portions of the data.

Such systematizations are always the researcher's construction (Wallace, 1972). To claim that any reality, including the researcher's own, exhibits a coherent body of knowledge is but to claim that coherence can be found *upon analysis.* The coherence located in a reality is found there by the ethnomethodologist's interactional work. The coherence feature, like all features of realities, operates as an incorrigible proposition, reflexively sustained.

Consider the analogous work of linguists (e.g., Chomsky, 1965). Within language-using communities, linguists discover the "rules of grammar." Although the linguist empirically establishes these grammatical rules, speaker-hearers of that language cannot list them. Rules can be located in their talk, upon analysis, but language users cannot describe them.

Similarly, freaks could not supply the taxonomy Zimmerman and Wieder claim they "really" know. It was found upon analysis. It is an imposition of the researcher's logic upon the freak's logic.

Castaneda's (1968, 1971) attempts to explain the reality of Yaqui sorcery further illustrates the reflexity of analysis. In his initial report, *The Teachings of Don Juan,* Castaneda (1968) begins with a detailed ethnography of his experiences of his encounter with a Yaqui sorcerer, Don Juan. In this reality it is common for time to stop, for men to turn into animals and animals into men, for animals and men to converse with one another, and for great distances to be covered while the body remains still.

In the final section of his report, Castaneda systematizes his experiences with the sorcerer. He presents a coherent body of knowledge undergirding Don Juan's teachings. Thus Castaneda, like Zimmerman and Wieder, organizes a "nonordinary" reality into a coherent system of knowledge.

In a second book Castaneda describes Don Juan's reaction to his systematization of a peyote session, a "mitote." Castaneda told Don Juan he had discovered that mitotes are a "result of a subtle and complex system of cueing." He writes (1971:37–38):

> It took me close to two hours to read and explain to Don Juan the scheme I had constructed. I ended by begging him to tell me in his own words what were the exact procedures for reaching agreement.
>
> When I had finished he frowned. I thought he must have found my explanation challenging; he appeared to be involved in deep deliberation. After a reasonable silence I asked him what he thought about my idea.
>
> My question made him suddenly turn his frown into a smile and then into roaring laughter. I tried to laugh too and asked nervously what was so funny.
>
> "You're deranged!" he exclaimed. "Why should anyone be bothered with cueing at such an important time as a mitote? Do you think one ever fools around with Mescalito?"
>
> I thought for a moment that he was being evasive; he was not really answering my question.
>
> "Why should anyone cue?" Don Juan asked stubbornly. "You have been in mitotes. You should know that no one told you how to feel, or what to do; no one except Mescalito himself."
>
> I insisted that such an explanation was not possible and begged him again to tell me how the agreement was reached.
>
> "I know why you have come," Don Juan said in a

mysterious tone. "I can't help you in your endeavor because there is no system of cueing."

"But how can all those persons agree about Mescalito's presence?"

"They agree because they *see*," Don Juan said dramatically, and then added casually, "Why don't you attend another mitote and see for yourself?"

Don Juan finds Castaneda's account ridiculous. This rejection is not evidence that Castaneda's attempt at systematization is incorrect. It indicates that the investigator reflexively organizes the realities he investigates. All realities may *upon analysis* exhibit a coherent system of knowledge, but knowledge of this coherence is not necessarily part of the awareness of its members.

Features emerging "upon analysis" is a particular instance of reflexivity. These features exist only within the reflexive work of those researchers who make them exist. This does not deny their reality. There is no need to pursue the chimera of a presuppositionless inquiry. Because all realities are ultimately superstitious, the reflexive location of reflexivity is not a problem within ethnomethodological studies. Rather, it provides them with their most intriguing phenomenon.

My discussion of these first two features of realities also shows that any one feature is separate from the other only upon analysis. In my description of reflexivity, I was forced to assume the existence of a coherent body of knowledge. Similarly, in the present discussion I could not speak about the existence of coherent systems of knowledge without introducing the caveat of "upon analysis," an implicit reference to reflexivity. This situation will continue as I discuss the remaining three features. Though I attempt to keep them separate from one another, I will only be partially successful, since the five are inextricably intertwined. Nevertheless, I will continue to talk of them as five separate features, not as one. I acknowledge that this talk is more heuristic than literal—it provides a ladder with five steps that may be climbed and then thrown away (cf. Wittgenstein, 1921).

REALITY AS INTERACTIONAL ACTIVITY

Realities are also dependent upon ceaseless social interactional work. Wood's study of a mental hospital il-

lustrates the reality of this reality work. He discovered that psychiatric attendants shared a body of knowledge. Wood's (1968:36) analysis of the attendants' interaction with the patients uncovered labels like: "baby," "child," "epileptic," "mean old man," "alcoholic," "lost soul," "good patient," "depressive," "sociopath," and "nigger." Though borrowed from psychiatry, these terms constitute a corpus of knowledge which reflects the attendants' own practical nursing concerns. These terms can be arranged in a systematic taxonomy (see Table 2). Each is shown to differ from the others according to four parameters of nursing problems.

Wood's study explored how the attendants used this taxonomy to construct meanings for the mental patients' behavior. One explanation of label use is called a "matching procedure." The matching model of labeling patient behavior is essentially a psychological theory. It treats behavior as a private, internal state, not influenced by social dimensions. The matching model assumes the patients' behavior has obvious features. Trained personnel monitor and automatically apply the appropriate label to patients' behavior.

Wood presents five case histories that show that labels are not applied by a simple matching process. They are molded in the day-to-day interaction of the attendants with one another and with the patients. The labeling of patients is a social activity, not a psychological one.

Wood (Ibid.: 51–91) describes the labeling history of patient Jimmy Lee Jackson. Over the course of his three-month hospitalization, Jackson held the same official psychiatric label, that of "psychoneurotic reaction, depressive type." However, the ward attendants saw Jackson within the web of their own practical circumstances. For them, at one time he was a "nigger," at another a "depressive," and at yet another a "sociopath." These seeings reflected a deep change in the meaning Jackson had for the attendants. When he was seen as a "nigger," for example, it meant that the attendants considered he was "lazy, and . . . without morals or scruples and . . . that the patient is cunning and will attempt to ingratiate himself with the attendants in order to get attention and 'use' them for his own ends" (Ibid.: 52). When Jackson became a depressive type, all these negative at-

Table 2 The Meaning of the Labels (Wood, 1968:45)

Psychiatric Attendant Label	NURSING TROUBLE				
	Work	Cleanliness	Supervisory	Miscellaneous	Frequency × 60
mean old man	yes	yes	yes	yes	2
baby	yes	yes	yes	—	20
child	yes	yes	—	yes	4
nigger	yes	—	yes	yes	1
epileptic	—	yes	—	yes	4
sociopath	yes	—	—	yes	3
depressive	—	—	—	yes	2
alcoholic	—	—	yes	—	8
lost soul	yes	—	—	—	12
good patient	—	—	—	—	6

tributes were withdrawn. The change in attribution, Wood shows, cannot be explained by a matching procedure. The attendants' social interactional work produced the change, independent of Jackson's behavior. This suggests that realities are fundamentally interactional activities.

One evening Jackson was suffering from a toothache. Unable to secure medical attention, he ran his arm through a window pane in one of the ward's locked doors. He suffered a severe laceration of his forearm which required stitches. When the attendants who were on duty during this episode returned to work the following afternoon, they discovered that the preceding morning shift had decided that Jackson had attempted suicide. Jackson was no longer presented to them as a nigger. The morning shift found that persons who had not even witnessed the event had given it a meaning they themselves had never considered. Nevertheless, the evening shift accepted the validity of this label change.

The label change indexed a far larger change. Jackson's past history on the ward was reinterpreted. He now was accorded different treatment by attendants on all shifts. He was listened to sympathetically, given whatever he requested, and no longer exhorted to do more ward work. All the attendants came to believe that he had always been a depressive and that they had always seen him as such.

A few weeks later Jackson became yet another person, a "sociopath." The attendants no longer ac-

cepted that he was capable of a suicide attempt. The new label was once again applied retrospectively. Not only was Jackson believed to be incapable of committing suicide now, he was thought to have always been incapable of it. The attendants agreed that the window-breaking incident had been a "fake" or "con,"—just the sort of thing a sociopath would do. Attendants who had praised Jackson as a hard worker when he was labeled a depressive now pointed to this same work as proof he was a "conniver." Requests for attention and medicine that had been promptly fulfilled for the depressive Jackson were now ignored for the sociopath Jackson, or used as occasions to attack him verbally.

Yet, as Wood describes Jackson, he remained constant despite these changes in attendant behavior. He did the same amount of work and sought the same amount of attention and medicine whether he was labeled a nigger or a depressive or a sociopath. What Jackson was at any time was determined by the reality work of the attendants.

In the final pages of his study, Wood (Ibid.: 137–138) further illustrates the power of interactional work to create an external world:

The evening that he [Jackson] cut his arm, I, like the PAs [psychiatric attendants], was overcome by the blood and did not reflect on its "larger" meaning concerning his proper label. The next day, when I heard all of the morning shift PAs refer to his action as a suicide attempt, I too labeled Jackson a "depressive" and the cut arm as a suicide attempt. When the label changed in future weeks I was working as a PA on the ward up to 12 hours a day. It was only two months later when I had left the ward, as I reviewed my notes and my memory, that I recognized the "peculiar" label changes that had occurred. While I was on the ward, it had not seemed strange to think that cutting an arm in a window was a serious attempt to kill oneself. Only as an "outsider" did I come to think that Jackson had "really" stayed the same through his three label changes.

As Wood says, Jackson could never have a meaning apart from *some* social context. Meanings unfold only within an unending sequence of practical actions.[5]

The *matching* theory of label use assumes a correspondence theory of signs (cf. Garfinkel, 1952:91ff.; Wieder, 1970). This theory of signs has three analytically separate elements: ideas that exist in the head, signs that appear in symbolic representations, and objects and events that appear in the world. Meaning is the relation among these elements. Signs can stand on behalf of the ideas in the head or refer to objects in the world. This theory of signs implies that signs stand in a point-by-point relation to thoughts in one's mind or objects in the world. Meanings are stable across time and space. They are not dependent upon the concrete participants or upon the specific scenes in which they appear.

Wood's study indicates that labels are not applied in accordance with correspondence principles. Instead, labels are *indexical expressions.* Meanings are situationally determined. They are dependent upon the concrete context in which they appear. The participants' interactional activity structured the indexical meaning of the labels used on the ward. The relationship of the participants to the object, the setting in which events occur, and the circumstances surrounding a definition, determine the meaning of labels and of objects.

The interactional feature indicates that realities do not possess symbols, like so many tools in a box. A reality and its signs are "mutually determinative" (Wieder, 1973:216). Alone, neither expresses sense. Intertwining through the course of indexical interaction, they form a life.

THE FRAGILITY OF REALITIES

Every reality depends upon (1) ceaseless reflexive use of (2) a body of knowledge in (3) interaction. Every reality is also fragile. Suppression of the activities that the first three features describe disrupts the reality. Every reality is equally capable of dissolution. The presence of this fragility feature of realities has been demonstrated by studies called "incongruity procedures" or "breaching experiments."

In one of the simplest of these, Garfinkel used 67 students as "experimenters." These students engaged a total of 253 "subjects" in a game of tick-tack-toe. When the figure necessary for the game was drawn, the experimenters requested the subject to make the first move. After the subject made his mark, the experimenter took his turn. Rather than simply marking another cell, the experimenter erased the subject's mark and moved it to another cell. Continuing as if this were expected behavior, the experimenter then placed his own mark in one of the now empty cells. The experimenters reported that their action produced extreme bewilderment and confusion in the subjects. The reality of the game, which before the experimenter's move seemed stable and external, suddenly fell apart. For a moment the subjects exhibited an "amnesia for social structure" (Garfinkel, 1963:189).

This fragility feature is even more evident in everyday life, where the rules are not explicit. People interact without listing the rules of conduct. Continued reference is made to this knowledge nonetheless. This referencing is not ordinarily available as long as the reality work continues normally. When the reality is disrupted, the interactional activity structuring the reality becomes visible. This is what occurred in the tick-tack-toe game. A usually unnoticed feature of the game is a "rule" prohibiting erasing an opponent's mark. When this unspoken "rule" is broken, it makes its first public appearance. If we were aware of the fragility of our realities, they would not seem real.

Thus Garfinkel (Ibid: 198) found that when the "incongruity-inducing procedures" developed in games:

> were applied in "real life" situations, it was unnerving to find the seemingly endless variety of events

that lent themselves to the production of really nasty surprises. These events ranged from . . . standing very, very close to a person while otherwise maintaining an innocuous conversation, to others . . . like saying "hello" at the termination of a conversation. . . . Both procedures elicited anxiety, indignation, strong feelings on the part of the experimenter and subject alike of humiliation and regret, demands by the subjects for explanations, and so on.

Another of the procedures Garfinkel developed was to send student experimenters into stores and restaurants where they were told to "mistake" customers for salespersons and waiters. The following is a sample of what the experimenters reported about the results of these procedures.

One experimenter went to have lunch at a restaurant near a university. Her host directed her toward a likely subject. She began by saying to him:

(E): I should like a table on the west side, a quiet spot, if you please. And what is on the menu?

(S): [Turned toward E but looked past and in the direction of the foyer.] Eh, ah, madam, I'm sure. [Looked past E again, looked at a pocket watch, replaced it, and looked toward the dining room.]

(E): Surely luncheon hours are not over. What do you recommend I order today?

(S): I don't know. You see, I'm waiting . . .

(E): [Interrupted with] Please don't keep me standing here while you wait. Kindly show me to a table.

(S): But Madam—[started to edge away from door, and back into the lounge in a slightly curving direction around E].

(E): My good man—[at this S's face flushed, his eyes rounded and opened wide.]

(S): But—you—I—oh dear! [He seemed to wilt.]

(E): [Took S's arm in hand and propelled him toward the dining room door slightly ahead of herself.]

(S): [Walked slowly but stopped just within the room, turned around and for the first time looked directly and very appraisingly at E, took out the watch, looked at it, held it to his ear, replaced it, and muttered, "Oh dear."]

(E): It will take only a minute for you to show me to a table and take my order. Then you can return to wait

for your customers. After all, I am a guest and a customer, too.

(S): [Stiffened slightly, walked jerkily toward the nearest empty table, held a chair for E to be seated, bowed slightly, muttered "My pleasure," hurried toward the door, stopped, turned, looked back at E with a blank facial expression.]

At this point, E's host walked up to S, greeted him, shook hands, and propelled him toward E's table. S stopped a few steps from the table, looked directly at, then through E, and started to walk back toward the door. Host told him E was a young lady whom he had invited to join them at lunch. (He then introduced her to S, who was one of the big names in the physics world, a pillar of the institution.) S seated himself reluctantly and perched rigidly on his chair, obviously uncomfortable. E smiled, made light and polite inquiries about his work, mentioned various functions he had attended and at which he had been honored, and then complacently remarked that it was a shame E had not met him personally. If she had, he said, she would not have mistaken him for the maître d'. The host chattered about his long-time friendship with E, while S fidgeted and looked again at his pocket watch, wiped his forehead with a table napkin, and looked at E but avoided meeting her eyes. When the host mentioned that E was studying sociology at UCLA, S suddenly burst into loud laughter, realized that everyone in the room was looking in the direction of our table, abruptly became quiet, and said to E, "You mistook me for the maître d', didn't you?"

(E): Deliberately, sir.

(S): Why deliberately?

(E): You have just been used as the unsuspecting subject in an experiment.

(S): Diabolic. But clever, I must say [to our host] I haven't been so shaken since —— denounced my theory of —— in 19—. And the wild thoughts that ran through my mind! Call the receptionist from the lobby, go to the men's room, turn this woman to the first person who comes along. Damn these early diners, there's nobody coming in at this time. Time is standing still, or my watch has stopped. I will talk to —— about this, make sure it doesn't happen to "somebody." Damn a persistent woman. I'm not her "good man." I'm Dr. —— and not to be pushed around. This can't be happening. If I do take her to that damned table she wants, I can get away from her, and I'll just take it easy until I can. I remember —— (hereditary psychopath, wife of one of the "family" of the institution), maybe if I do what *this* one wants she will not make any more trouble than this. I wonder if she is "off." She certainly looks normal. Wonder how you can really tell? (Garfinkel, 1963:224–226).

The breaching experiments were subsequently refined, such that:

the person [subject] could not turn the situation into a play, a joke, an experiment, a deception, and the like . . . ; that he have insufficient time to work through a redefinition of his real circumstances; and that he be deprived of consensual support for an alternative definition of social reality (Garfinkel, 1964; in 1967:58).

This meant that subjects were not allowed to reflexively turn the disruption into a revalidation of their realities. The incorrigible propositions of their social knowledge were not adequate for the present circumstances. They were removed from the supporting interactional activity that they possessed before the breach occurred.

These refinements had the positive consequence of increasing the bewilderment of the subjects, who became more and more like desocialized schizophrenics, persons completely devoid of any social reality. These refinements produced a negative consequence. They were immoral. Once subjects had experienced the fragility, they could not continue taking the stability of realities for granted. No amount of "cooling out" could restore the subject's faith.

THE PERMEABILITY OF REALITIES

Because the reflexive use of social knowledge is fragile and interaction dependent, one reality may be altered, and another may be assumed. Cases where a person passes from one reality to another, dramatically different, reality vividly display this permeability feature.

Tobias Schneebaum, a painter who lives periodically in New York, provides an example of a radical shift in realities in his book, *Keep the River on Your Right* (1969). Schneebaum entered the jungles of Peru in 1955 in pursuit of his art. During the trip the book describes, he gradually lost interest in painterly studies. He found himself drawn deeper and deeper into the jungle. Unlike a professional anthropologist, he carried no plans to write about his travels. In fact, the slim volume from which I draw the following discussion was not written until 13 years after his return.

He happened upon the Akaramas, a stone age tribe that had never seen a white man. They accepted him quickly, gave him a new name, "Habe," meaning "ignorant one," and began teaching him to be as they were.

Schneebaum learned to sleep in "bundles" with the other men, piled on top of one another for warmth and comfort. He learned to hunt and fish with stone age tools. He learned the Akaramas' language and their ritual of telling stories of their hunts and hikes, the telling taking longer than the doing. He learned to go without clothing, and to touch casually the genitals of his companions in play.

When one of the men in Schneebaum's compartment is dying of dysentery, crying out at his excretions of blood and pain, the "others laugh and he laughs too" (Ibid.: 109). As this man lies among them whimpering and crying in their sleeping pile at night, Schneebaum writes (Ibid.: 129): "Not Michii or Baaldore or Ihuene or Reindude seemed to have him on their minds. It was as if he were not there among us or as if he had already gone to some other forest." When he dies, he is immediately forgotten. Such is the normal perception of death within the Akarama reality. As Schneebaum (Ibid.: 109) describes another incident: "There were two pregnant women whom I noticed one day with flatter bellies and no babies on their backs, but there was no sign of grief, no service . . ."

Gradually, Schneebaum absorbed even these ways and a new sense of time. At one point he left the Akaramas to visit the mission from which he had embarked. He was startled to find that seven months had passed, not the three or four he had supposed. As he was more and more permeated by the stone age reality, he began to feel that his "own world, whatever, wherever it was, no longer was anywhere in existence" (Ibid.: 69). As the sense of his old reality disappears, he says, "My fears were not so much for the future . . . but for my knowledge. I was removing my own reflection" (Ibid.: 64–65).

One day, a day like many others, he rises to begin a hunting expedition with his sleeping companions. This day, however, they go much farther than ever before. They paint themselves in a new way and repeat new chants. Finally they reach a strange village. In they swoop, Schneebaum too, shouting their sacred words and killing all the men they can catch, disemboweling and beheading them on the spot. They burn all the huts, kidnap the women and children. They then hike to their own village, without pause, through an entire night. At home, a new dance is begun. The meat of the men they have murdered and brought back with them is cooked. As a new movement of the dance begins, this meat is gleefully eaten. Exhausted at last, they stumble together on the ground. Then the last of the meat is put to ceremonious use:

> we sat or lay around the fires, eating, moaning the tones of the chant, swaying forward and back, moving from the hip, forward and back. Calm and silence settled over us, all men. Four got up, one picked a heart from the embers, and they walked into the forest. Small groups of others arose, selected a piece of meat, and disappeared in other directions. We three were alone until Ihuene, Baaldore, and Reindude were in front of us, Reindude cupping in his hand the heart from the being we had carried from so far away, the heart of he who had lived in the hut we had entered to kill. We stretched out flat upon the gound, lined up, our shoulders touching. Michii looked up at the moon and showed it to the heart. He bit into it as if it were an apple, taking a large bite, almost half the heart, and chewed down several times, spit into a hand, separated the meat into six sections and placed some into the mouths of each of us. We chewed and swallowed. He did the same with the other half of the heart. He turned Darinimbiak onto his stomach, lifted his hips so that he crouched on all fours. Darinimbiak growled, Mayaarii-ha! Michii growled, Mayaarii-ha!, bent down to lay himself upon Darinimbiak's back and entered him (Ibid.: 106–107).

Mass murder, destruction of an entire village, theft of all valuable goods, cannibalism, the ritual eating of the heart before publicly displayed homosexual acts—these are some of the acts Schneebaum participated in. He could not have done them his first day in the jun-

gle. But after his gradual adoption of the Akarama reality, they had become natural. It would have been as immoral for him to refuse to join his brothers in the raid and its victory celebration as it would be immoral for him to commit these same acts within a Western community. His reality had changed. The moral facts were different.

Schneebaum's experience suggests that even radically different realities can be penetrated.[6] We would not have this account, however, if the stone age reality had completely obliterated Schneebaum's Western reality. He would still be with the tribe. The more he permeated the Akaramas' reality, the more suspect his old reality became. The more he fell under the spell of the absolutism of his new reality, the more fragile his old reality became. Like the cannibals, Schneebaum says: "My days are days no longer. Time had no thoughts to trouble me, and everything is like nothing and nothing is like everything. For if a day passes, it registers nowhere, and it might be a week, it might be a month. There is no difference" (Ibid.: 174).

As the vision of his old reality receded, Schneebaum experienced its fragility. He knew he must leave soon, or there would be no reality to return to. He describes his departure:

> A time alone, only a few weeks ago, with the jungle alive and vibrant around me, and Michii and Baaldore gone with all the other men to hunt, I saw within myself too many seeds that would grow a fungus around my brain, encasing it with mold that could penetrate and smooth the convolutions and there I would remain, not he who had travelled and arrived, not the me who had crossed the mountains in a search, but another me living only in ease and pleasure, no longer able to scrawl out words on paper or think beyond a moment. And days later, I took myself up from our hut, and I walked on again alone without a word to any of my friends and family, but left when all again were gone and I walked through my jungle . . . (Ibid.: 182).

The Akarama would not miss him. They would not even notice his absence. For them, there were no separate beings. Schneebaum felt their reality obliterating "the me who had crossed the mountains in a search." Schneebaum was attached to this "me," and so he left.

In the previous section, I listed three conditions

necessary for successful breaches: There can be no place to escape. There can be no time to escape. There can be no one to provide counter evidence. The same conditions are required to move between realities. That is, as Castaneda's (1968, 1971, 1972) work suggests, in order to permeate realities, one must first have the old reality breached. Castaneda has named this necessity the establishment "of a certainty of a minimal possibility," that another reality actually exists (personal communication). Successful breaches must establish that another reality is available for entry. Thus, as Don Juan attempted to make Castaneda a man of knowledge, he first spent years trying to crack Castaneda's absolute faith in the reality of Western rationalism.

Castaneda's work suggests many relations between the fragility and permeability features. It is not my purpose to explore the relations of the five features in this book. But I want to emphasize that such relations can be supposed to exist.

I relied on the "exotic" case of a person passing from a Western to a stone age reality to display the permeability feature of realities. However, any two subsequent interactional encounters could have been used for this purpose. All such passages are of equal theoretic import. Passages between a movie and freeway driving, between a person's reality before and after psychotherapy, between a "straight" adquiring membership in the reality of drug freaks, or before and after becoming a competent religious healer, are all the same. The differences are "merely" methodological, not theoretical. Studying each passage, I would concentrate on how the reflexive, knowledge, interactional, and fragility features effect the shift.

ON THE CONCEPT OF REALITY

Many ethnomethodologists rely on Schutz's concept of reality (e.g., 1962, 1964, 1966). My use of "reality" contrasts with Schutz's view. For Schutz (e.g., 1962:208ff.), the reality of everyday life is the *one* paramount reality. Schutz says that this paramount reality consists of a number of presuppositions or assumptions, which include the assumption of a tacit, taken for granted world; an assumed practical interest in that world; and an assumption that the world is intersubjective (e.g., 1962:23). Schutz argues that other realities exist, but that they derive from the paramount reality. For example, he discusses the realities of "scientific theorizing" and of "fantasy." These realities appear when some of the basic assumptions of the paramount reality are temporarily suspended. The paramount reality of everyday life has an elastic quality for Schutz. After excursions into other realities, we snap back into the everyday.

My view of realities is different. I do not wish to call one or another reality paramount. It is my contention that every reality is equally real. No single reality contains more of the truth than any other. From the perspective of Western everyday life, Western everyday life will appear paramount, just as Schutz maintains. But from the perspective of scientific theorizing or dreaming, or meditating, each of these realities will appear just as paramount. Because every reality exhibits the absolutist tendency I mentioned earlier, there is no way to look from the window of one reality at others without seeing yourself. Schutz seems to be a victim of this absolutist prejudice. As a Western man living his life in the Western daily experience, he assumed that this life was the touch-stone of all realities.

My concept of reality, then, has more in common with Wittgenstein (1953) than with Schutz. Wittgenstein (e.g., 1953:61, 179) recognizes that human life exhibits an empirical multitude of activities. He calls these activities language games. Language games are forever being invented and modified and discarded. The fluidity of language activities do not permit rigorous description. Analysts can discover that at any time a number of language games are associated with one another. This association, too, is not amenable to rigorous description. Instead, language games exhibit "family resemblances." One can recognize certain games going together. But one could no more articulate *the* criteria for this resemblance than one could predict the physical characteristics of some unseen member of a familiar extended family. Wittgenstein (Ibid.: 119, 123) calls a collection of language games bound together by a family resemblance, a *form of life*.[7] Forms of life resemble what I call "realities." Realities are far more aswarm than Schutz's terms "finite" and "province" suggest. Forms of life are always forms of life forming.[8] Realities are always realities becoming.

NOTES

1. See Pollner's (1975, 1987) discussions of the reflexive reasoning of the Azande, and Polanyi's (1958:287–294) examination of the same materials. In the Apostolic Church of John Marangue, illness is not bodily malfunction, it is sin. Sin is curable not by medicine, but by confessional healing. When evangelists' attempts to heal church members were not accompanied by recovery, Jules-Rosette (1973:167) reports that church members did not lose their faith in the confessional process. They looked to other "causes" of the "failure." They said things like: Other persons must have been implicated in the sin, and untrue confession must have been given. Once again, contradictions that could potentially challenge a basic faith do not, as the basic faith itself is not questioned.

2. See Gurwitsch (1966) for a more technical discussion of the object constancy assumption. Later in this chapter, I show that the object constancy assumption is not a belief that exists in the head. A body of interactional work is required to achieve a constant world.

3. The pen–not pen and planet-star examples are adapted from Pollner (1975). Much of this discussion of reflexivity derives from Pollner's thinking on these matters.

4. Riel (1972) illustrates how talk reflexively constitutes the context it then seems to independently reference. Trying to make a certain point, she reports turning away from an inadequate sentence she had written to explore notes and texts again. Forty-five minutes later she wrote the now-perfect sentence, only to discover it was exactly the same sentence she had rejected before.

5. Cicourel (1968) examines the interactional work that accomplishes external objects in greater detail. He shows that juvenile delinquents and crime rates are constituted by the social activities of law enforcement personnel.

6. For an account of a reality shift in the other direction, from the stone age to industrial Western society, see Kroeber's *Ishi in Two Worlds* (1961). Again the transition was never total, but this was a result of a political decision on the part of the author's husband. As Ishi's official keeper, he wished to keep him primitive for his own and anthropology's benefit.

7. Blum (1970) has previously explored the importance of Wittgenstein's notion of "form of life" for social science.

8. This phrase, like much of this chapter, has been adapted from the unpublished lectures of Pollner. For Pollner's published writings see Zimmerman and Pollner, 1970; and Pollner, 1975, 1987.

REFERENCES

Blum, Alan. 1970. Theorizing. In Jack D. Douglas (ed.), *Understanding Everyday Life*. Chicago: Aldine Publishing Company.

Castaneda, Carlos. 1968. *The Teachings of Don Juan*. Berkeley: University of California Press.

———. 1971. *A Separate Reality*. New York: Simon & Schuster.

———. 1972. *A Journey to Iztlan*. New York: Simon & Schuster.

Chomsky, Noam. 1965. *Aspects of the Theory of Syntax*. Cambridge: The M.I.T. Press.

Cicourel, Aaron V. 1968. *The Social Organization of Juvenile Justice*. New York: John Wiley & Sons.

———. 1973. *Cognitive Sociology*. London: Macmillan & Co.

Evans-Pritchard, E. E. 1937. *Witchcraft, Oracles and Magic Among the Azande*. London: Oxford University Press.

Garfinkel, Harold. 1952. Perception of the Other. Unpublished Ph.D. dissertation. Harvard University.

———. 1963. A Conception of and Experiments with "Trust" as a Condition of Concerted Stable Actions. In O. J. Harvey (ed.), *Motivation and Social Interaction*. New York: The Ronald Press Company.

———. 1964. Studies of the Routine Grounds of Everyday Activities. *Social Problems* 11:225–250 (Chapter 2 in Garfinkel, 1967.)

———. 1967. *Studies in Ethnomethodology*. New York: Prentice-Hall.

Gasking, Douglas. 1955. Mathematics and the World. In Anthony Flew (ed.), *Logic and Language*. Garden City, N.Y.: Doubleday & Company; Anchor Books.

Gurwitsch, Aron. 1966 *Studies in Phenomenology and Psychology*. Evanston, Ill.: Northwestern University Press.

Jules-Rosette, Bennetta. 1973. Ritual Context and Social Action. Unpublished Ph.D. dissertation. Harvard University.

Kroeber, Theodora. 1961. *Ishi in Two Worlds*. Berekley: University of California Press.

Kuhn, Thomas S. 1970. *The Structure of Scientific Revolutions*. Chicago: University of Chicago Press.

Polanyi, Michael. 1958. *Personal Knowledge*. Chicago: University of Chicago Press.

Pollner, Melvin. 1975. "The Very Coinage of Your Brain": The Anatomy of Reality Disjunctures. *Philosophy of the Social Sciences*. 5:411–30.

———. 1987. *Mundane Reason*. Cambridge, England: Cambridge University Press.

Reich, Charles A. 1970. *The Greening of America*. New York: Random House.

Riel, Margaret M. 1972. The Interpretive Process. Unpublished paper presented to a seminar led by Paul Filmer, University of California, San Diego.

Roszak, Theodore. 1969. *The Making of a Counter Culture*. Garden City, N.Y.: Doubleday & Company.

Sacks, Harvey, Emmanuel Schegloff, and Gail Jefferson. 1974.

A Simplest Systematics for the Analysis of Turn Taking in Conversation. *Language.* 50:696–735.

Schneebaum, Tobias. 1969. *Keep the River on Your Right.* New York: Grove Press, Inc.

Schutz, Alfred. 1962. *Collected Papers I: The Problem of Social Reality.* The Hague: Martinus Nijhoff.

———. 1964. *Collected Papers II: Studies in Social Theory.* The Hague: Martinus Nijhoff.

———. 1966. *Collected Papers III: Studies in Phenomenological Philosophy.* The Hague: Martinus Nijhoff.

Wallace, H. Thomas. 1972. Culture and Social Being. Unpublished M.A. thesis. University of California, Santa Barbara.

Wieder, D. Lawrence. 1970. Meaning by Rule. In Jack D. Douglas (ed.), *Understanding Everyday Life.* Chicago: Aldine Publishing Company.

———. 1973. *Language and Social Reality.* The Hague: Mouton.

Wittgenstein, Ludwig. 1961 [1921] *Tractatus Logico-Philosophicus.* London: Basil Blackwell, & Mott.

———. 1953. *Philosophical Investigations.* London: Basil Blackwell & Mott.

Wood, Houston. 1968. The Labelling Process on a Mental Hospital Ward. Unpublished M.A. thesis. University of California, Santa Barbara.

Zimmerman, Don H. 1973. Preface to Wieder, 1973.

Zimmerman, Don H., and Melvin Pollner. 1970. The Everyday World as a Phenomenon. In Jack D. Douglas (ed.), *Understanding Everyday Life.* Chicago: Aldine Publishing Company.

Zimmerman, Don H., and D. Lawrence Wieder. n.d. *The Social Bases for Illegal Behavior in the Student Community: First Year Report.* San Francisco and Santa Barbara: Scientific Analysis Corporation.

FURTHER READING

Berger, Peter and Thomas Luckmann. 1966. *The Social Construction of Reality.* New York: Doubleday.
- Aspects of the social construction of inner lives and social worlds from the perspective of social phenomenology.

Douglas, Jack D. (ed.). 1970. *Understanding Everyday Life.* Chicago: Aldine.
- Essays focused on the everyday world as a phenomenon, how the appearance of everyday reality is interactionally produced and sustained.

Garfinkel, Harold. 1967. *Studies in Ethnomethodology.* Englewood Cliffs, NJ: Prentice Hall.
- Essays by the founder of ethnomethodology on the practical procedures that construct our everyday sense of reality.

Karp, David A. and William C. Yoels. 1993. *Sociology in Everyday Life* (2d ed.). Itasca, IL: Peacock.
- A symbolic interactionist perspective on everyday life.

Sarbin, Theodore R. and John I. Kitsuse (eds.). 1994. *Constructing the Social.* London: Sage.
- Studies of everyday constructions of inner lives and social worlds, including the social construction of life histories, genius, anxiety, sexual dysfunction, and family.

———— SECTION 2 ————

LANGUAGE AND COMMUNICATION

People view social interaction in many ways. At one end of the spectrum, it's seen in economic terms. Social exchange is like monetary exchange. One person gives an item of value to another, who, in turn, reciprocates with another valued item. The exchange is fair or balanced if the items traded are of equal or similar value. Some social exchanges are actually monetary, such as paying a fair price for an automobile. Other exchanges deal in gestures without material value. We extend thanks or condolences in measures figured to be appropriate in the marketplace of sentiments, for example. Interaction doesn't always deal with goods, but it's always centered on the exchange of values of some kind.

At the other end of the spectrum, people view social interaction as an exchange of meanings. Here, the emphasis is not on distinct values and equitable exchanges. Instead, the focus is on how participants communicate and share meaning through social encounters. In the economic model, values or meanings are predetermined, or, at the least, they are calculated in exact terms in the course of interaction. Viewing interaction as an exchange of meanings, however, directs us to the processes by which meanings are social constructed. In this view, meaning (or the interpretation of what is exchanged) isn't predetermined or otherwise precisely designated. It's reflexively constructed as interaction unfolds.

This perspective on interaction pays special attention to language and communication. Meaning can't be discerned from people's behavior alone. It can't be calculated apart from the communication process. The result is that meaning is usually plural, rather than singular. A gesture may have different meanings, depending on how it's interpreted by others. We must listen to how others respond to actually know a gesture's practical meaning for them. A clenched fist, for example, may be seen as either a threat or as a sign of solidarity. It may even be a gesture of momentary pain. We can't tell which meaning is at work unless we know how persons who receive the gesture respond to it. What's more, there's no guarantee that a gesture will be understood the same way on different occasions. A clenched fist, for example, may initially be interpreted as a threat. If the situation changes and the persons involved come to an understanding, however, the same gesture may later mean that the parties stand together.

Language and communication aren't merely neutral channels for getting meanings across. They aren't just transport vehicles that convey set meanings through interaction, as if interaction were an unobstructed pipeline to understanding. Instead, language and communication actively shape the course of interaction as it progresses. Categories and metaphors, for example, provide understandings of what experience is like. A metaphor borrows meaning from one situation to characterize a second situation. In doing so, however, it does more than merely describe the second situation. It constitutes its meaning, giving it a substance that is otherwise lacking. Calling someone a "bulldog" constructs a different reality than calling him a "pussy cat," for example. In practice, language and communication not only convey messages but actually enter into the work of constructing the meaning of everyday life.

ABOUT THE READINGS

In **"Meaning and Social Interaction," George Herbert Mead** stresses that language plays a major role in constructing meaning. For Mead, language is not a passive vehicle for communicating meaning. In practice, it actively produces and assembles meaning in the course of social interaction. As Mead notes, "Language does not simply symbolize a situation or object that is already there in advance; it makes possible the existence or the appearance of that situation or object." Meaning is not just "there" ahead of communication. It comes into being as an outcome of talk and interaction. Language and communication are parts of what Mead calls the "social process." It's the give-and-take between people interacting with one another.

Herbert Blumer was Mead's student at the University of Chicago in the 1920s. One of Blumer's most important contributions was to extend Mead's ideas about language and communication. In **"Society as Symbolic Interaction,"** Blumer argues forcefully that society *is* a communicative process. It doesn't exist over and above everyday life. In Blumer's view, society shouldn't be seen as an object surrounding social interaction, bearing down on it from the outside. Nor is society something we internalize, only to have it direct our actions from within. Rather, society is made up of meaningful social exchanges. Sometimes, however, we reflexively respond to society *as if* it were separate and distinct from us. We do so because we fail to see how our everyday talk and interaction continuously produce social worlds and inner lives.

George Lakoff and **Mark Johnson** elaborate on the constructive character of communication in their essay **"Metaphors We Live By."** If metaphors are something "we live by," then they are more than just poetic devices for embellishing existing meaning. They are a powerful devices for meaning making. As Lakoff and Johnson put it, everyday life "is fundamentally metaphorical in nature." Here, again, we see an active view of language, one that casts metaphors as the building blocks of meaning.

Jonathan Potter and **Margaret Wetherell's** discussion of the place of **"Categories in Discourse"** lays the groundwork for analyzing how individuals use the ordinary categories of language to make things meaningful. The authors show how categories, such as "mother" and "father" or "violent" and "peaceful," organize our understanding of people and events. Without the application of categories, experience is meaningless. We respond to the meaning of things, not things in their own right. Categories supply meaning to things. Potter and Wetherell show us how to analyze the meaning-making process using "categorization analysis," which draws heavily from sociologist Harvey Sacks's visionary work on "membership categorization devices." The authors illustrate how categorization analysis can be used to understand aspects of inner lives and social worlds as wide ranging as racial slurs and the meaning of community.

4 | MEANING AND SOCIAL INTERACTION
George Herbert Mead

Symbolization constitutes objects not constituted before, objects which would not exist except for the context of social relationships wherein symbolization occurs. Language does not simply symbolize a situation or object which is already there in advance; it makes possible the existence or the appearance of that situation or object, for it is a part of the mechanism whereby that situation or object is created. The social process relates the responses of one individual to the gestures of another, as the meanings of the latter, and is thus responsible for the rise and existence of new objects in the social situation, objects dependent upon or constituted by these meanings. Meaning is thus not to be conceived, fundamentally, as a state of consciousness, or as a set of organized relations existing or subsisting mentally outside the field of experience into which they enter; on the contrary, it should be conceived objectively, as having its existence entirely within this field itself. The response of one organism to the gesture of another in any given social act is the meaning of that gesture, and also is in a sense responsible for the appearance or coming into being of the new object—or new content of an old object—to which that gesture refers through the outcome of the given social act in which it is an early phase. For, to repeat, objects are in a genuine sense constituted within the social process of experience, by the communication and mutual adjustment of behavior among the individual organisms which are involved in that process and which carry it on. Just as in fencing the parry is an interpretation of the thrust, so, in the social act, the adjustive response of one organism to the gesture of another is the interpretation of that gesture by that organism—it is the meaning of that gesture.

At the level of self-consciousness such a gesture becomes a symbol, a significant symbol. But the interpretation of gestures is not, basically, a process going on in a mind as such, or one necessarily involving a mind; it is an external, overt, physical, or physiological process going on in the actual field of social experience. Meaning can be described, accounted for, or stated in terms of symbols or language at its highest and most complex stage of development (the stage it reaches in human experience), but language simply lifts out of the social process a situation which is logically or implicitly there already. The language symbol is simply a significant or conscious gesture.

Two main points are being made here: (1) that the social process, through the communication which it makes possible-among the individuals implicated in it, is responsible for the appearance of a whole set of new objects in nature, which exist in relation to it (objects, namely, of "common sense"); and (2) that the gesture of one organism and the adjustive response of another organism to that gesture within any given social act bring out the relationship that exists between the gesture as the beginning of the given act and the completion or resultant of the given act, to which the gesture refers. These are the two basic and complementary logical aspects of the social process.

The result of any given social act is definitely separated from the gesture indicating it by the response of another organism to that gesture, a response which points to the result of that act as indicated by that gesture. This situation is all there—is completely given—on the non-mental, non-conscious level, before the analysis of it on the mental or conscious level. Dewey says that meaning arises through communication.[1] It is to the content to which the social process gives rise that this statement refers; not to bare ideas or printed words as such, but to the social process which has been so largely responsible for the objects constituting the daily environment in which we live: a process in which communication plays the main part. That process can give rise to these new objects in nature only in so far as it makes possible communication among the individual organisms involved in it. And the sense in which it is responsible for their existence—indeed for the existence of the whole world of common-sense objects—is the sense in which it determines, conditions, and makes possible their abstraction from the total structure of events, as identities which are relevant for everyday social behavior; and in that sense, or as having that meaning, they are existent only relative to that behavior. In the same way, at a later, more advanced stage of its development, communication is responsible for the existence of the whole realm of scientific objects as well as identities abstracted from the total structure of events by virtue of their relevance for scientific purposes.

The logical structure of meaning, we have seen, is to be found in the threefold relationship of gesture to adjustive response and to the resultant of the given social act. Response on the part of the second organism to the gesture of the first is the interpretation—and brings out the meaning—of that gesture, as indicating the resultant of the social act which it initiates, and in which both organisms are thus involved. This threefold or triadic relation between gesture, adjustive response, and resultant of the social act which the gesture initiates is the basis of meaning; for the existence of meaning depends upon the fact that the adjustive response of the second organism is directed toward the resultant of the given social act as initiated and indicated by the gesture of the first organism. The basis of meaning is thus objectively there in social conduct, or in nature in its relation to such conduct. Meaning is a content of an object which is dependent upon the relation of an organism or group of organisms to it. It is not essentially or primarily a psychical content (a content of mind or consciousness), for it need not be conscious at all, and is not in fact until significant symbols are evolved in the process of human social experience. Only when it becomes identified with such symbols does meaning become conscious. The meaning of a gesture on the part of one organism is the adjustive response of another organism to it, as indicating the resultant of the social act it initiates, the adjustive response of the second organism being itself directed toward or related to the completion of that act. In other words, meaning involves a reference of the gesture of one organism to the resultant of the social act it indicates or initiates, as adjustively responded to in this reference by another organism; and the adjustive response of the other organism is the meaning of the gesture.

Gestures may be either conscious (significant) or unconscious (non-significant). The conversation of gestures is not significant below the human level, because it is not conscious, that is, not *self*-conscious (though it is conscious in the sense of involving feelings or sensations). An animal as opposed to a human form, in indicating something to, or bringing out a meaning for, another form, is not at the same time indicating or bringing out the same thing or meaning to or for himself; for he has no mind, no thought, and hence there is no meaning here in the significant or self-conscious sense. A gesture is not significant when the response of another organism to it does not indicate to the organism making it what the other organism is responding to.

Much subtlety has been wasted on the problem of the meaning of meaning. It is not necessary, in attempting to solve this problem, to have recourse to psychical states, for the nature of meaning, as we have seen, is found to be implicit in the structure of the social act, implicit in the relations among its three basic individual components: namely, in the triadic relation of a gesture of one individual, a response to that gesture by a second individual, and completion of the given social act initiated by the gesture of the first individual. And the fact that the nature of meaning is thus found to be implicit in the structure of the social act provides additional emphasis upon the necessity, in social psychology, of starting off with the initial assumption of an ongoing social process of experience and behavior in which any given group of human individuals is involved, and upon which the existence and development of their minds, selves, and self-consciousness depend.

NOTE

1. [See *Experience and Nature,* chap. v.]

5 | SOCIETY AS SYMBOLIC INTERACTION
Herbert Blumer

A view of human society as symbolic interaction has been followed more than it has been formulated. Partial, usually fragmentary, statements of it are to be found in the writings of a number of eminent scholars, some inside the field of sociology and some outside. Among the former we may note such scholars as Charles Horton Cooley, W. I. Thomas, Robert E. Parks, E. W. Burgess, Florian Znaniecki, Ellsworth Faris, and James Mickel Williams. Among those outside the discipline we may note William James, John Dewey, and George Herbert Mead. None of these scholars, in my judgment, has presented a systematic statement of the nature of human group life from the standpoint of symbolic interaction. Mead stands out among all of them in laying bare the fundamental premises of the approach, yet he did little to develop its methodological implications for sociological study. Students who seek to depict the position of symbolic interaction may easily give different pictures of it. What I have to present should be regarded as my personal version. My aim is to present the basic premises of the point of view and to develop their methodological consequences for the study of human group life.

The term "symbolic interaction" refers, of course, to the peculiar and distinctive character of interaction as it takes place between human beings. The peculiarity consists in the fact that human beings interpret or "define" each other's actions instead of merely reacting to each other's actions. Their "response" is not made directly to the actions of one another but instead is based on the meaning which they attach to such actions. Thus, human interaction is mediated by the use of symbols, by interpretation, or by ascertaining the meaning of one another's actions. This mediation is equivalent to inserting a process of interpretation between stimulus and response in the case of human behavior.

The simple recognition that human beings interpret each other's actions as the means of acting toward one another has permeated the thought and writings of many scholars of human conduct and of human group life. Yet few of them have endeavored to analyze what such interpretation implies about the nature of the human being or about the nature of human association. They are usually content with a mere recognition that "interpretation" should be caught by the student, or with a simple realization that symbols, such as cultural norms or values, must be introduced into their analyses. Only G. H. Mead, in my judgment, has sought to think through what the act of interpretation implies for an understanding of the human being, human action, and human association. The essentials of his analysis are so penetrating and profound and so important for an understanding of human group life that I wish to spell them out, even though briefly.

The key feature in Mead's analysis is that the human being has a self. This idea should not be cast aside as esoteric or glossed over as something that is obvious and hence not worthy of attention. In declaring that the human being has a self, Mead had in mind chiefly that the human being can be the object of his own actions. He can act toward himself as he might act toward others. Each of us is familiar with actions of this sort in which the human being gets angry with himself, rebuffs himself, takes pride in himself, argues with himself, tries to bolster his own courage, tells himself that he should "do this" or not "do that," sets goals for himself, makes compromises with himself, and plans what he is going to do. That the human being acts toward himself in these and countless other ways is a matter of easy empirical observation. To recognize that the human being can act toward himself is no mystical conjuration.

Mead regards this ability of the human being to act toward himself as the central mechanism with which the human being faces and deals with his world. This mechanism enables the human being to make indications to himself of things in his surroundings and thus to guide his actions by what he notes. Anything of which a human being is conscious is something which he is indicating to himself—the ticking of a clock, a knock at the door, the appearance of a friend, the remark made by a companion, a recognition that he has a task to perform, or the realization that he has a cold. Conversely, anything of which he is not conscious is, *ipso facto,* something which he is not indicating to himself. The conscious life of the human being, from the time that he awakens until he falls asleep, is a continual flow of self-indications—notations of the things with which he deals and takes into account. We are given, then, a picture of the human being as an organism which confronts its world with a mechanism for making indications to itself. This is the mechanism that is involved in interpreting the actions of others. To interpret the actions of another is to point out to oneself that the action has this or that meaning or character.

Now, according to Mead, the significance of making indications to oneself is of paramount importance. The importance lies along two lines. First, to indicate something is to extricate it from its setting, to hold it apart, to give it a meaning or, in Mead's language, to make it into an object. An object—that is to say, anything that an individual indicates to himself—is different from a stimulus; instead of having an intrinsic character which acts on the individual and which can be identified apart from the individual, its character or meaning is conferred on it by the individual. The object is a product of the individual's disposition to act instead of being an antecedent stimulus which evokes the act. Instead of the individual being surrounded by an environment of pre-existing objects which play upon him and call forth his behavior, the proper picture is that he constructs his objects on the basis of his on-going activity. In any of his countless acts—whether minor, like dressing himself, or major, like organizing himself for a professional career—the individual is designating different objects to himself, giving them meaning, judging their suitability to his action, and making decisions on the basis of the judgment. This is what is meant by interpretation or acting on the basis of symbols.

The second important implication of the fact that the human being makes indications to himself is that his action is constructed or built up instead of being a mere release. Whatever the action in which he is engaged, the human individual proceeds by pointing out to himself the divergent things which have to be taken into account in the course of his action. He has to note what he wants to do and how he is to do it; he has to point out to himself the various conditions which may be instrumental to his action and those which may obstruct his action; he has to take account of the demands, the expectations, the prohibitions, and the threats as they may arise in the situation in which he is acting. His action is built up step by step through a process of such self-indication. The human individual pieces together and guides his action by taking account of different things and interpreting their significance for his prospective action. There is no instance of conscious action of which this is not true.

The process of constructing action through making indications to oneself cannot be swallowed up in any of the conventional psychological categories. This process is distinct from and different from what is spoken of as the "ego"—just as it is different from any other conception which conceives of the self in terms of composition or organization. Self-indication is a moving communicative process in which the individual notes things, assesses them, gives them a meaning,

and decides to act on the basis of the meaning. The human being stands over against the world, or against "alters," with such a process and not with a mere ego. Further, the process of self-indication cannot be subsumed under the forces, whether from the outside or inside, which are presumed to play upon the individual to produce his behavior. Environmental pressures, external stimuli, organic drives, wishes, attitudes, feelings, ideas, and their like do not cover or explain the process of self-indication. The process of self-indication stands over against them in that the individual points out to himself and interprets the appearance or expression of such things, noting a given social demand that is made on him, recognizing a command, observing that he is hungry, realizing that he wishes to buy something, aware that he has a given feeling, conscious that he dislikes eating with someone he despises, or aware that he is thinking of doing some given thing. By virtue of indicating such things to himself, he places himself over against them and is able to act back against them, accepting them, rejecting them, or transforming them in accordance with how he defines or interprets them. His behavior, accordingly, is not a result of such things as environmental pressures, stimuli, motives, attitudes, and ideas but arises instead from how he interprets and handles these things in the action which he is constructing. The process of self-indication by means of which human action is formed cannot be accounted for by factors which precede the act. The process of self-indication exists in its own right and must be accepted and studied as such. It is through this process that the human being constructs his conscious action.

Now Mead recognizes that the formation of action by the individual through a process of self-indication always takes place in a social context. Since this matter is so vital to an understanding of symbolic interaction it needs to be explained carefully. Fundamentally, group action takes the form of a fitting together of individual lines of action. Each individual aligns his action to the action of others by ascertaining what they are doing or what they intend to do—that is, by getting the meaning of their acts. For Mead, this is done by the individual "taking the role" of others—either the role of a specific person or the role of a group (Mead's "generalized other"). In taking such roles the individual seeks to ascertain the intention or direction of the acts of others. He forms and aligns his own action on the basis of such interpretation of the acts of others. This is the fundamental way in which group action takes place in human society.

The foregoing are the essential features, as I see them, in Mead's analysis of the bases of symbolic interaction. They presuppose the following: that human society is made up of individuals who have selves (that is, make indications to themselves); that individual action is a construction and not a release, being built up by the individual through noting and interpreting features of the situations in which he acts; that group or collective action consists of the aligning of individual actions, brought about by the individuals' interpreting or taking into account each other's actions. Since my purpose is to present and not to defend the position of symbolic interaction I shall not endeavor in this essay to advance support for the three premises which I have just indicated. I wish merely to say that the three premises can be easily verified empirically. I know of no instance of human group action to which the three premises do not apply. The reader is challenged to find or think of a single instance which they do not fit.

I wish now to point out that sociological views of human society are, in general, markedly at variance with the premises which I have indicated as underlying symbolic interaction. Indeed, the predominant number of such views, especially those in vogue at the present time, do not see or treat human society as symbolic interaction. Wedded, as they tend to be, to some form of sociological determinism, they adopt images of human society, of individuals in it, and of group action which do not square with the premises of symbolic interaction. I wish to say a few words about the major lines of variance.

Sociological thought rarely recognizes or treats human societies as composed of individuals who have selves. Instead, they assume human beings to be merely organisms with some kind of organization, responding to forces which play upon them. Generally, although not exclusively, these forces are lodged in the make-up of the society, as in the case of "social system," "social structure," "culture," "status position," "social role," "custom," "institution," "collective rep-

resentation," "social situation," "social norm," and "values." The assumption is that the behavior of people as members *of a society* is an expression of the play on them of these kinds of factors or forces. This, of course, is the logical position which is necessarily taken when the scholar explains their behavior or phases of their behavior in terms of one or another of such social factors. The individuals who compose a human society are treated as the media through which such factors operate, and the social action of such individuals is regarded as an expression of such factors. This approach or point of view denies, or at least ignores, that human beings have selves—that they act by making indications to themselves. Incidentally, the "self" is not brought into the picture by introducing such items as organic drives, motives, attitudes, feelings, internalized social factors, or psychological components. Such psychological factors have the same status as the social factors mentioned: they are regarded as factors which play on the individual to produce his action. They do not constitute the process of self-indication. The process of self-indication stands over against them, just as it stands over against the social factors which play on the human being. Practically all sociological conceptions of human society fail to recognize that the individuals who compose it have selves in the sense spoken of.

Correspondingly, such sociological conceptions do not regard the social actions of individuals in human society as being constructed by them through a process of interpretation. Instead, action is treated as a product of factors which play on and through individuals. The social behavior of people is not seen as built up by them through an interpretation of objects, situations, or the actions of others. If a place is given to "interpretation," the interpretation is regarded as merely an expression of other factors (such as motives) which precede the act, and accordingly disappears as a factor in its own right. Hence, the social action of people is treated as an outward flow or expression of forces playing on them rather than as acts which are built up by people through their interpretation of the situations in which they are placed.

These remarks suggest another significant line of difference between general sociological views and the position of symbolic interaction. These two sets of views differ in where they lodge social action. Under the perspective of symbolic interaction, social action is lodged in acting individuals who fit their respective lines of action to one another through a process of interpretation; group action is the collective action of such individuals. As opposed to this view, sociological conceptions generally lodge social action in the action of society or in some unit of society. Examples of this are legion. Let me cite a few. Some conceptions, in treating societies or human groups as "social systems," regard group action as an expression of a system, either in a state of balance or seeking to achieve balance. Or group action is conceived as an expression of the "functions" of a society or of a group. Or group action is regarded as the outward expression of elements lodged in society or the group, such as cultural demands, societal purposes, social values, or institutional stresses. These typical conceptions ignore or blot out a view of group life or of group action as consisting of the collective or concerted actions of individuals seeking to meet their life situations. If recognized at all, the efforts of people to develop collective acts to meet their situations are subsumed under the play of underlying or transcending forces which are lodged in society or its parts. The individuals composing the society or the group become "carriers," or media for the expression of such forces; and the interpretative behavior by means of which people form their actions is merely a coerced link in the play of such forces.

The indication of the foregoing lines of variance should help to put the position of symbolic interaction in better perspective. In the remaining discussion I wish to sketch somewhat more fully how human society appears in terms of symbolic interaction and to point out some methodological implications.

Human society is to be seen as consisting of acting people, and the life of the society is to be seen as consisting of their actions. The acting units may be separate individuals, collectivities whose members are acting together on a common quest, or organizations acting on behalf of a constituency. Respective examples are individual purchasers in a market, a play group or missionary band, and a business corporation or a national professional association. There is no empirically observable activity in a human society that does not spring from some acting unit. This banal statement needs to be stressed in light of the common practice of sociologists of reducing human society to social units that do not act—for example, social classes in modern society. Obviously, there are ways of viewing human society other than in terms of the acting units that compose it. I merely wish to point out that in respect to concrete or empirical activity human society must necessarily be seen in terms of the acting units that form it. I would add that any scheme of human society claiming to be a realistic analysis has to respect and be congruent with the empirical recognition that a human society consists of acting units.

Corresponding respect must be shown to the conditions under which such units act. One primary condition is that action takes place in and with regard to a situation. Whatever be the acting unit—an individual, a family, a school, a church, a business firm, a labor union, a legislature, and so on—any particular action is formed in the light of the situation in which it takes place. This leads to the recognition of a second major condition, namely, that the action is formed or constructed by interpreting the situation. The acting unit necessarily has to identify the things which it has to take into account—tasks, opportunities, obstacles, means, demands, discomforts, dangers, and the like; it has to assess them in some fashion and it has to make decisions on the basis of the assessment. Such interpretative behavior may take place in the individual guiding his own action, in a collectivity of individuals acting in concert, or in "agents" acting on behalf of a group or organization. Group life consists of acting units developing acts to meet the situations in which they are placed.

Usually, most of the situations encountered by people in a given society are defined or "structured" by them in the same way. Through previous interaction they develop and acquire common understandings or definitions of how to act in this or that situation. These common definitions enable people to act alike. The common repetitive behavior of people in such situations should not mislead the student into believing that no process of interpretation is in play; on the contrary, even though fixed, the actions of the participating people are constructed by them through a process of interpretation. Since ready-made and commonly accepted definitions are at hand, little strain is placed on people in guiding and organizing their acts. However, many other situations may not be defined in a single way by the participating people. In this event, their lines of action do not fit together readily and collective action is blocked. Interpretations have to be developed and effective accommodation of the participants to one another has to be worked out. In the case of such "undefined" situations, it is necessary to trace and study the emerging process of definition which is brought into play.

Insofar as sociologists or students of human society are concerned with the behavior of acting units, the position of symbolic interaction requires the student to catch the process of interpretation through which they construct their actions. This process is not to be caught merely by turning to conditions which are antecedent to the process. Such antecedent conditions are helpful in understanding the process insofar as they enter into it, but as mentioned previously they do not constitute the process. Nor can one catch the process merely by inferring its nature from the overt action which is its product. To catch the process, the student must take the role of the acting unit whose behavior he is studying. Since the interpretation is being made by the acting unit in terms of objects designated and appraised, meanings acquired, and decisions made, the process has to be seen from the standpoint of the acting unit. It is the recognition of this fact that makes the research work of such scholars as R. E. Park and W. I. Thomas so notable. To try to catch the interpretative process by remaining aloof as a so-called "objective" observer and refusing to take the role of the acting unit is to risk the worst kind of subjectivism—the objective observer is likely to fill in the process of interpretation with his own surmises in place of catching the process as it occurs in the experience of the acting unit which uses it.

By and large, of course, sociologists do not study human society in terms of its acting units. Instead, they are disposed to view human society in terms of structure or organization and to treat social action as an expression of such structure or organization. Thus, reliance is placed on such structural categories as social system, culture, norms, values, social stratification, status positions, social roles and institutional or-

ganization. These are used both to analyze human society and to account for social action within it. Other major interests of sociological scholars center around this focal theme of organization. One line of interest is to view organization in terms of the functions it is supposed to perform. Another line of interest is to study societal organization as a system seeking equilibrium; here the scholar endeavors to detect mechanisms which are indigenous to the system. Another line of interest is to identify forces which play upon organization to bring about changes in it; here the scholar endeavors, especially through comparative study, to isolate a relation between causative factors and structural results. These various lines of sociological perspective and interest, which are so strongly entrenched today, leap over the acting units of a society and bypass the interpretative process by which such acting units build up their actions.

These respective concerns with organization on one hand and with acting units on the other hand set the essential difference between conventional views of human society and the view of it implied in symbolic interaction. The latter view recognizes the presence of organization to human society and respects its importance. However, it sees and treats organization differently. The difference is along two major lines. First, from the standpoint of symbolic interaction the organization of a human society is the framework inside of which social action takes place and is not the determinant of that action. Second, such organization and changes in it are the product of the activity of acting units and not of "forces" which leave such acting units out of account. Each of these two major lines of difference should be explained briefly in order to obtain a better understanding of how human society appears in terms of symbolic interaction.

From the standpoint of symbolic interaction, social organization is a framework inside of which acting units develop their actions. Structural features, such as "culture," "social systems," "social stratification," or "social roles," set conditions for their action but do not determine their action. People—that is, acting units—do not act toward culture, social structure or the like; they act toward situations. Social organization enters into action only to the extent to which it shapes situations in which people act, and to the extent to which it supplies fixed sets of symbols which people use in interpreting their situations. These two forms of influence of social organization are important. In the case of settled and stabilized societies, such as isolated primitive tribes and peasant communities, the influence is certain to be profound. In the case of human societies, particularly modern societies, in which streams of new situations arise and old situations become unstable, the influence of organization decreases. One should bear in mind that the most important element confronting an acting unit in situations is the actions of other acting units. In modern society, with its increasing criss-crossing of lines of action, it is common for situations to arise in which the actions of participants are not previously regularized and standardized. To this extent, existing social organization does not shape the situations. Correspondingly, the symbols or tools of interpretation used by acting units in such situations may vary and shift considerably. For these reasons, social action may go beyond, or depart from, existing organization in any of its structural dimensions. The organization of a human society is not to be identified with the process of interpretation used by its acting units; even though it affects that process, it does not embrace or cover the process.

Perhaps the most outstanding consequence of viewing human society as organization is to overlook the part played by acting units in social change. The conventional procedure of sociologists is (a) to identify human society (or some part of it) in terms of an established or organized form, (b) to identify some factor or condition of change playing upon the human society or the given part of it, and (c) to identify the new form assumed by the society following upon the play of the factor of change. Such observations permit the student to couch propositions to the effect that a given factor of change playing upon a given organized form results in a given new organized form. Examples ranging from crude to refined statements are legion, such as that an economic depression increases solidarity in the families of workingmen or that industrialization replaces extended families by nuclear families. My concern here is not with the validity of such propositions but with the methodological position which they presuppose. Essentially, such propositions either ignore the role of the interpretative behavior of acting units in the given instance of change, or else regard the interpretative behavior as coerced by the factor of change. I wish to point out that any line of social change, since it involves change in human action, is necessarily mediated by interpretation on the part of the people caught up in the change—the change appears in the form of new situations in which people have to construct new forms of action. Also, in line with what has been said previously, interpretations of new situations are not predetermined by conditions antecedent to the situations but depend on what is taken into account and assessed in the actual situations in which behavior is formed. Variations in interpretation may readily occur as different acting units cut out different objects in the situation, or give different weight to the objects which they note, or piece objects together in different patterns. In formulating propositions of social change, it would be wise to recognize that any given line of such change is mediated by acting units interpreting the situations with which they are confronted.

Students of human society will have to face the question of whether their preoccupation with categories of structure and organization can be squared with the interpretative process by means of which human beings, individually and collectively, act in human society. It is the discrepancy between the two which plagues such students in their efforts to attain scientific propositions of the sort achieved in the physical and biological sciences. It is this discrepancy, further, which is chiefly responsible for their difficulty in fitting hypothetical propositions to new arrays of empirical data. Efforts are made, of course, to overcome these shortcomings by devising new structural categories, by formulating new structural hypotheses, by developing more refined techniques of research, and even by formulating new methodological schemes of a structural character. These efforts continue to ignore or to explain away the interpretative process by which people act, individually and collectively, in society. The question remains whether human society or social action can be successfully analyzed by schemes which refuse to recognize human beings as they are, namely, as persons constructing individual and collective action through an interpretation of the situations which confront them.

6 | METAPHORS WE LIVE BY

George Lakoff and Mark Johnson

Metaphor is for most people a device of the poetic imagination and the rhetorical flourish—a matter of extraordinary rather than ordinary language. Moreover, metaphor is typically viewed as characteristic of language alone, a matter of words rather than thought or action. For this reason, most people think they can get along perfectly well without metaphor. We have found, on the contrary, that metaphor is pervasive in everyday life, not just in language but in thought and action. Our ordinary conceptual system, in terms of which we both think and act, is fundamentally metaphorical in nature.

The concepts that govern our thought are not just matters of the intellect. They also govern our everyday functioning, down to the most mundane details. Our concepts structure what we perceive, how we get around in the world, and how we relate to other people. Our conceptual system thus plays a central role in defining our everyday realities. If we are right in suggesting that our conceptual system is largely metaphorical, then the way we think, what we experience, and what we do every day is very much a matter of metaphor.

But our conceptual system is not something we are normally aware of. In most of the little things we do every day, we simply think and act more or less automatically along certain lines. Just what these lines are is by no means obvious. One way to find out is by looking at language. Since communication is based on the same conceptual system that we use in thinking and acting, language is an important source of evidence for what that system is like.

Primarily on the basis of linguistic evidence, we have found that most of our ordinary conceptual system is metaphorical in nature. And we have found a way to begin to identify in detail just what the metaphors are that structure how we perceive, how we think, and what we do.

To give some idea of what it could mean for a concept to be metaphorical and for such a concept to structure an everyday activity, let us start with the concept ARGUMENT and the conceptual metaphor ARGUMENT IS WAR. This metaphor is reflected in our everyday language by a wide variety of expressions:

ARGUMENT IS WAR

Your claims are *indefensible.*
He *attacked every weak point* in my argument.
His criticisms were *right on target.*
I *demolished* his argument.
I've never *won* an argument with him.
You disagree? Okay, *shoot!*
If you use that *strategy,* he'll *wipe you out.*
He *shot down* all of my arguments.

It is important to see that we don't just *talk* about arguments in terms of war. We can actually win or lose arguments. We see the person we are arguing with as an opponent. We attack his positions and we defend our own. We gain and lose ground. We plan and use strategies. If we find a position indefensible, we can abandon it and take a new line of attack. Many of the things we *do* in arguing are partially structured by the concept of war. Though there is no physical battle, there is a verbal battle, and the structure of an argument—attack, defense, counterattack, etc.—reflects this. It is in this sense that the ARGUMENT IS WAR metaphor is one that we live by in this culture; it structures the actions we perform in arguing.

Try to imagine a culture where arguments are not viewed in terms of war, where no one wins or loses, where there is no sense of attacking or defending, gaining or losing ground. Imagine a culture where an argument is viewed as a dance, the participants are seen as performers, and the goal is to perform in a

---

balanced and aesthetically pleasing way. In such a culture, people would view arguments differently, experience them differently, carry them out differently, and talk about them differently. But *we* would probably not view them as arguing at all: they would simply be doing something different. It would seem strange even to call what they were doing "arguing." Perhaps the most neutral way of describing this difference between their culture and ours would be to say that we have a discourse form structured in terms of battle and they have one structured in terms of dance.

This is an example of what it means for a metaphorical concept, namely, ARGUMENT IS WAR, to structure (at least in part) what we do and how we understand what we are doing when we argue. *The essence of metaphor is understanding and experiencing one kind of thing in terms of another.* It is not that arguments are a subspecies of war. Arguments and wars are different kinds of things—verbal discourse and armed conflict—and the actions performed are different kinds of actions. But ARGUMENT is partially structured, understood, performed, and talked about in terms of WAR. The concept is metaphorically structured, the activity is metaphorically

structured, and, consequently, the language is metaphorically structured.

Moreover, this is the *ordinary* way of having an argument and talking about one. The normal way for us to talk about attacking a position is to use the words "attack a position." Our conventional ways of talking about arguments presuppose a metaphor we are hardly ever conscious of. The metaphor is not merely in the words we use—it is in our very concept of an argument. The language of argument is not poetic, fanciful, or rhetorical; it is literal. We talk about arguments that way because we conceive of them that way—and we act according to the way we conceive of things.

The most important claim we have made so far is that metaphor is not just a matter of language, that is, of mere words. We shall argue that, on the contrary, human *thought processes* are largely metaphorical. This is what we mean when we say that the human conceptual system is metaphorically structured and defined. Metaphors as linguistic expressions are possible precisely because there are metaphors in a person's conceptual system. Therefore, whenever in this book we speak of metaphors, such as ARGUMENT IS WAR, it should be understood that *metaphor* means *metaphorical concept.*

7 | CATEGORIES IN DISCOURSE
Jonathan Potter and Margaret Wetherell

Categorization is an important and pervasive part of people's discourse. In the course of conversation everyone populates their lives with friends, doctors, Americans, extraverts, immigrants and a thesauras of other categories of people. Pick up any newspaper and many of the stories will concern people who are described, evaluated and understood not in terms of any unique features of their biography but through their category membership: "model reveals star's secret life," "wife found murdered."

Categorization is no less fundamental to the social scientist. Much of social psychology is concerned with the attributes of social groups—males, political extremists, working-class adolescents—and experimental or survey findings from representative samples of these people are recurrently extrapolated to other group members. That is, people are taken to be members of relatively enduring social categories, and *in virtue of their category membership* inferences are made from the attributes of individuals to the attributes of the rest of the category. Social categories are, in one way or another, the principal building blocks in many areas of social research.

As well as being a resource for both lay and scientific explanations of behaviour, social categories have increasingly become a topic of research in themselves. Social psychologists have focused on the *cognitive processes* underlying categorization and its *consequences*. What is the cognitive mechanism involved in categorization? How do people break up the social world into distinct groupings? And, given that a category has been applied, what effect will this have on people's perception or understanding? In this tradition, categorization is seen as a natural phenomenon rather like breathing; people automatically transform the polluting detritus of their over-complex physical and social reality into a simplified and readily assimilable form.

In contrast to this approach, workers in the more linguistically orientated traditions of ethnomethodology and discourse analysis have been interested in how categories are constituted in everyday discourse and the various functions they satisfy. Instead of seeing categorization as a natural phenomenon—something which just happens, automatically—it is regarded as a complex and subtle *social accomplishment*. This emphasizes the action orientation of categorizations in discourse. It asks how categories are flexibly articulated in the course of certain sorts of talk and writing to accomplish particular goals, such as blamings or justifications.

In this chapter we will overview the social psychological and discourse approaches in turn. We will stress in particular the implications of the discourse analyses for social psychological work on categorization, and suggest certain lessons for social research more generally.

SOCIAL PSYCHOLOGY AND SOCIAL CATEGORIES

Imagine looking at a television screen in an area of extremely poor reception. An image is there, but it is very difficult to decipher in the sea of dots. Someone familiar with the programme then points out that this is a talk show with two personalities in a studio set.

You can now 'see' the image more clearly. Two vague shapes coalesce into people while the fuzziness around becomes the studio. The shapes have become both more integral and more distinct. The categories (people/studio set) clarify and simplify; certain regions are seen as more similar than before and certain contrasts are heightened. The traditional social psychological approach assumes that processes of *social* categorization are ultimately derived from perceptual mechanisms of this kind.

Categories and the Physical World

A number of experiments have demonstrated effects of this type with nonsocial objects. In one classic study, for example, Tajfel and Wilkes (1963) showed people sets of lines with different labels on them and asked for an estimate of their length. All the lines differed, some were long and some short. The crucial finding was that if all the shorter lines were labelled A, and the longer ones B, the difference in length between the lines was exaggerated. At the same time there was a tendency for the lines carrying the same label to be seen as more similar. That is, if the lines could be viewed as members of *separate* categories— A and B—*differences* were accentuated and if they could be viewed as members of the *same* category *similarities* were accentuated.

It is claimed that this kind of categorization process is adaptive; it clarifies and systematizes the physical environment. With less confusing noise, and less complexity to handle, the argument runs, the person is better prepared for action (Tajfel, 1981, 1982; Tajfel and Forgas, 1981). These kinds of categorization processes have thus been more or less explicitly glossed in evolutionary terms. The image of the hunter on the savanna, simplifying and systematizing tasty zebras from the irrelevant grass and worrying leopards is difficult to resist. However, what happens when we make categorizations in the social arena?

Categories and the Social World

One common answer to this question is: nothing changes. The effect of perceiving *people* in terms of categories is exactly the same as perceiving *objects* in this way. And indeed a body of research has demonstrated the same kind of effects. Wilder (1978), for example, showed some experimental participants a videotape of four people, one of whom was offering his opinions on various topics. In one version of the video the people were presented as a group (they sat at the same table and wore identifying tags), while in another version they were merely shown as unrelated individuals (other differences were, of course, held constant). The task of the participants was to judge how similar the opinions of the others were to the speaker. In line with the experimental hypothesis, Wilder found that seeing people as a group led to judgements of greater similarity between their views.

In another experiment, Allen and Wilder (1979) randomly split a number of boys into two groups and asked them about the opinions and preferences of the boys in their own and the other group. As expected, the boys perceived the opinions and preferences of members of their own group as similar to their own views but different to those of the other group. Moreover, the preferences and beliefs of the boys in the other group were seem as similar to one another. So, as in the Tajfel and Wilkes experiment on the length of lines, the opinions of people categorized together in Wilder's video, and the views of the boys in the same group were seen as more like each other. Similarly, the differences in perceived opinions between the two categories of boys were exaggerated and accentuated.

What has really excited social psychologists about this kind of research is the possibility of understanding and explaining racial stereotyping and hence discrimination. Could it be a natural consequence, as it were, of the way we have evolved to organize the world into categories? Could prejudice be the unfortunate outcome of the biases which emerge when the differences between categories are exaggerated and the differences within them downplayed?

A number of researchers (Hamilton, 1979; Taylor, 1981) have argued exactly that. As Wilder pithily writes, "categorization, per se, propels the individual down the road to bias" (1986: 293). This is a depressing conclusion, and one that we will argue against later, for it suggests that bias and stereotyping are not social and psychological aberrations, induced perhaps by faulty child-rearing or distorting ideo-

logical processes, but an inevitable product of the way our cognitive system is organized, to respond to categories.

Categories and Prototypes

Up to now we have described research on the perceptual *consequences* of categorization. However, there is another strand of work which is much more directly concerned with the mechanisms underlying this process: with how people "think" in terms of categories, how, they assign a particular person to a specific category, for example. Social psychologists have again plundered the theoretical storehouse of cognitive psychology to deal with this problem.

The suggestion offered by Cantor and Mischel (1977, 1979) is that categories are cognitively organized around prototypes; a prototype being a typical or paradigm example. The theory of prototypes has, of course, been developed mainly in cognitive psychology by Eleanor Rosch and her associates (Rosch et al., 1976). Thus, moving out of the social arena for a moment, if we think of birds, the prototypical bird is something like a blackbird or sparrow. This is a classic and familiar example of the category "bird" which shares most of its main features (has wings, flies, goes tweet and so on). At the same time we are aware that there are other birds such as ostriches and penguins which are very different from the prototype and may be treated as borderline cases; indeed, there may well be disagreement about whether they should be treated as full members of the category at all.

Using this notion, Cantor and Mischel offer a more precise statement of how members are assigned to categories. They suggest that the process is one of matching the potential member to the relevant prototype. Each person carries around a large set of preformed, mentally encoded prototypes; if the potential member shares enough features with one of these it will be included in the category. Thus, if we want to decide whether someone we meet should be categorized as an extravert we compare them to our model instance of extravert (loud voice, goes to lots of parties etc.). If they display enough of these features they will be so categorized.

It is important to note here that Cantor and Mischel

are not proposing this process is like following a mechanical algorithm. It may well be that *no* one feature is essential for inclusion. They stress that social categories are not homogeneous entities where each member shares a specified set of features and no others; rather they are "fuzzy sets" in which members have many things in common but also many differences.

A further feature of the theory of prototypes is the claim that categories will come in hierarchical clusters. To use Cantor and Mischel's example, we will not have one, unitary prototype of a "cultured person"; rather this will be split up into lower level categories (e.g. "patron of the arts") which can be subdivided even further ("donator to art museum" and so on—see Figure 1). Consistent prototypes will be drawn upon only at this more basic level of categorization; and hence it is here that stereotyping of category members will be most evident (Brewer et al., 1981).

PROBLEMS WITH TRADITIONAL CATEGORIZATION RESEARCH

There is now a large and theoretically sophisticated body of research on the topic of categorization and its role in fostering stereotyping and intergroup discrimination (see Tajfel, 1981; Wilder, 1986, for reviews from different perspectives). Despite providing some important insights and findings it is prone to certain

difficulties. We suggest these are a consequence of problematic base assumptions about the phenomenon of categorization and the failure to examine categorization as a social practice involving certain sorts of language use. Later in the chapter we will go on to examine some research which develops this alternative perspective. To begin with, though, let us enumerate these problem assumptions.

1. *Inevitability of biased categorization.* Social psychological research has come to view stereotyping as a consequence of purportedly basic and adaptive cognitive processes. People's very perception is seen to be based on categorizations which simplify, and thus result in distorted stereotypes.

2. *Categories have a fixed structure.* The theory of prototypes suggests that categories are fuzzy sets organized around prototypical instances. Categorical perception is dependent on a process of matching stimuli to prototypes, which are further organized in hierarchical structures.

3. *Categories are preformed and enduring.* People are viewed as carrying around a mentally encoded set of preformed and enduring prototypes of category members. These will be stable and will determine perception and understanding.

All these assumptions flow from the basic social cognition approach which attempts to explain social

Figure 1 The Organization of Sub-Prototypes. *Source:* Cantor and Mischel, 1979.

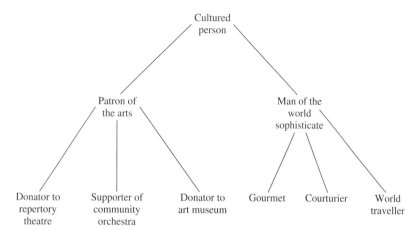

phenomena within the framework of cognitive psychology. It is cognitive processes and structures which
are seen as the causal determinants here. The social
phenomenon of stereotyping is caused by the way our
cognitive systems operate on information, reducing
and distorting in the light of the organized structures
of prototypes.

If we take a discourse-orientated approach to categorization each of these assumptions becomes rather
less convincing. We can contrast the cognitive perspective with the image of the person using their discourse to perform different kinds of acts which we
have been developing throughout this book. From this
perspective we predict that instead of being a "victim"
of mechanical categorization processes people will
both draw flexibly on preformed categories and construct the sense of categories as they talk.

Categorization and Particularization

In an important critique, Michael Billig (1985) had
radically questioned the first of the assumptions identified above. He has argued against the idea that perception should be the primary metaphor for prejudiced
judgement and that simplifying categorizations are
necessarily adaptive.

He starts with a basic but telling point. The perceptual model leads us to overlook the fact that people
are constantly prejudiced against groups whose members they have never met and hence we ignore the social convention component in prejudice. Furthermore,
the stress on perception seems to make the expression
of prejudice *in talk* a secondary or epiphenomenon.
Given that many people spend considerable time pro-
pounding racist views in casual conversation about
groups they may have rarely or never seen, this relegation seems entirely pointless. Like discourse analysts (see also van Dijk, 1985, and Reeves, 1983), Billig suggests that to understand prejudice more fully
we need to bring talk or rhetoric back to centre stage,
displacing perception.

In contrast to the claim that categorization is a natural and adaptive process, Billig suggests that both
categorization and the *opposite* process of particularization (splitting categories in parts, or distinguishing
specific instances from categories) are necessary for
dealing with the world. The distorted emphasis on the

process of categorization alone has led to what Billig
describes as a "bureaucratic model of thought":

> much of thinking is seen as a process of locking
> the unfamiliar into safe, familiar categories . . . the
> image of the person to emerge from this approach
> resembles that of a bureaucrat sensibly ordering
> the messy stimulus world. . . . Just as a bureaucrat
> might defend office procedures, so these theorists
> [Hamilton, 1979; Snyder, 1981; Rothbart, 1981] talk
> of organization, order, management, efficiency, etc.
> (1985: 87–8)

What is lacking in discussion of social cognition is the
ability to transcend the limits of familiar categories, to
develop new procedures, and to reach out, through
particularization, to the unique features of individual
cases. These abilities are equally "natural" to social
life as those of grouping, classifying and categorizing.

Finally, Billig suggests that if we think about the
reality of racist and stereotyped categorizations we
can see the importance of both rigidity *and* flexibility
in prejudiced judgement. For example, if a white
British person is going to rigidly maintain that, say,
West Indians are "lazy and unmotivated" they will
probably need to also constructively and flexibly manipulate their discourse to deal with any information
threatening this generalization. Perhaps they will need
to generate all sorts of subcategories of West Indians
to neutralize potentially problematic examples of
hard-working and motivated West Indian behaviour.
That is, they may well rely on the very techniques of
making exceptions and particularizing undervalued by
the categorization approach to maintain their biased,
prejudiced response. Billig proposes that instead of
trying to understand prejudice in terms of the operation of the single process of categorization we should
move to looking at how both categorization and particularization are managed wherever talk is manifested. Let us now go on to examine the research traditions which have followed this procedure.

PROTOTYPES AND VARIABILITY

Discourse analysts use the detailed examination of
variability in accounts as a basic research strategy.
Different versions and forms of talk are the analyzable
trace of the way language is used to bring about differ-

ent ends. Varying accounts can be thought of as the residue of the social practices through which people organize their lives; practices ranging, as we have seen, from persuading others of the correctness of a large-scale scientific theory through to accounting for the refusal of a party invitation; from justifying racial inequality in a society to choosing a turn of phrase which starts to close down a telephone conversation.

At the same time, the embarrassing presence of radical and pervasive variability calls into question those theoretical perspectives—whether they focus on attitudes, rules, the self—which were meant to reveal an illuminating consistency in social life. To be of heuristic value, theories of this kind should be able to explain actual patterns of social behaviour, and allow us to predict patterns in the future. Failure in this central task is fatal.

Cantor and Mischel's theory of the operation of prototypes in the perception of category membership has similar general goals to the theories we criticized in earlier chapters. As we indicted, their model of prototypes suggests that people come to identify category members, and indeed grasp the meaning of categories via typical or paradigm examples which all properly socialized members of the group share. The category is "anchored" to the prototype. If people's perception and understanding are determined by their prototypes in this way we should expect to find considerable consistency between descriptions of category members given by people from within the same subculture.

Prototypes of Maoris

We have looked at this issue of prototype variability in a study conducted with Ruth McFadyen (Wetherell et al., 1986) on middle-class, white, New Zealanders' discourse about Maoris, the indigenous people colonized by the British. In the course of semi-structured interviews, descriptions of Maoris came up repeatedly, in topics such as positive discrimination, land rights, and the South African rugby tour of 1981. If white New Zealanders do use stable prototypes of the category Maori there ought to be a high degree of consistency in the depiction of Maoris across different topics.

The problem for the theory of prototypes is that this consistency was not there, although the New Zealand situation resembles many other "race relations" situations in Britain, America, Canada etc. and categorization theory is supposed to be particularly relevant to prejudice and stereotyping issues. Indeed, we did not need to look very far to find examples of highly variable discourse about this category of people. For example, we chose four interview transcripts at random and noted all adjectives the participants applied to Maoris. The entire list is reproduced in Figure 2. Out of a total of sixty-two adjectives, only three were the same: using the term "friendly." Of course, if we repeat this exercise with more transcripts we find some increase in overlapping terms—but we also find a concomitant increase in unique terms. It is clear that the variability is at least as striking as any consistency.

A common technique social psychologists have introduced to deal with variability of this kind is the use of some form of gross categorization. That is, the adoption of a categorization scheme which is broad and ambiguous enough to eliminate variability, or at least to cut it down. This kind of scheme could, for example, classify together apparently similar adjectives such as "dirty" and "scruffy." The problem here, however, is that consistency becomes an achievement of the researcher rather than a feature of the discourse. For example, participants themselves may, on occasion, see important differences between the sense of "dirty" and "scruffy"; "dirty" may be used to denote the distasteful and uncivilized, while "scruffy" may refer to a laid back, streetwise demeanor which could be essentially positive. These significant nuances would be lost if researchers simply aggregated terms. Classifications of this kind should not come from the researcher's commonsense semantics, but from a detailed analysis of participants' own use of discourse.

Even gross categorization of this kind would be unable to handle much of the variation found in this material. It is not easy to find sensible classifications which encompass contradictory adjectives such as "they're proud" and "they've lost their pride and dignity"; "lazy race" and "such hard-working people"; "lack of greed" and "quite selfish and greedy" (see Figure 3). For just about every statement made about Maoris an opposing or contradictory statement was also offered somewhere in the material.

Figure 2 Four Speakers' Descriptions of Maoris

SPEAKER ONE
Independent
Responsibility in family gone
Mature
Worldly
Lost their culture
Stirring
Like to congregate
Lovely ethnic feeling for each other
Like driving
Like playing with machinery
Tend to go for jobs which are manual
Make good soldiers
Haven't got stickability
What you've got is theirs
They steal

SPEAKER TWO
Passive
Not interested in language revival
Don't take advantage of education
Dirty
Scruffy
Evil-looking
Hot-heads
Isn't a leader

SPEAKER THREE
Proud
Wonderful
Don't want to share their culture
Busy reestablishing themselves
Trendy
No motivation
Takes care of her children

Friendly relaxed manner
Music lovely
Use same sort of expression
Friendly

SPEAKER FOUR
Feel disadvantaged
Slow
Feel they have no self-esteem
Need to take a positive view of their life
Must look at selves and decide strengths and weaknesses
Feeling money will put disadvantages right
Feelings inside all wrong
Simply need not get together
Get cracking
All work together
Behaving in unacceptable way
Wider family is important to them
Balance good feelings: body, spirit, soul
Not observing own standards of hygiene
Not observing own cultural beliefs
Great difficulty opening up their hearts, telling how they feel
Demanding
Expecting
Need a bit more insight
Need more exercise and self control
Marvellous
Very good
Courteous
Smile
Welcome
Friendly
Happy

Figure 3 Inconsistencies Between Respondents' Descriptions of Maoris

Lazy race	Such hard-working people
They're proud	Lost their pride and dignity
Proud of all their background	Humble
Want to split this society	Passive
They really know how to put a story across, to get the message across, are orators	They come across as clueless they don't know how to express their views
Great respect of older folks	Very good at taking advantage of their old
Less materialistic and more diverting in their culture	Quite selfish and greedy
Relaxed friendly manner	Ill at ease

Can Prototype Theory Be Sustained?

One way of responding to findings of this kind might be to suggest that different participants were drawing upon different prototypes. Variable accounts, then, would merely be a consequence of people's variable individual prototypes. However, the difficulty here is that variation was pervasive and extreme even within the talk of the same participants. One respondent, for instance, described Maoris as having "an innate understanding of their land" and claimed shortly after that "their land is just a bit of dirt to them."

Another type of response to this inconsistency might be to argue that it is a consequence of the different *levels* of categorization operating (Brewer et al., 1981). In this view, contradictions are produced by people moving between different subprototypes of Maoris—Maori children, Maori parents, Maori leaders etc. Thus inconsistency only appears if the researcher assumes participants are working with the broad super-ordinate: Maori.

The first thing to note about this view is the danger of making the theory so flexible and post hoc that it can predict virtually anything. We reach the point where a prototype is posited to explain every single variation in accounts of Maoris, and the theory becomes empirically empty. However, even if we remain with the limited splitting into subtypes indicated above, the problem of variability returns to haunt the theory. When our data were analysed in terms of the sorts of subtypes where prototype theorists might expect consistency we again found variability. In our respondents' discourse Maori parents, for example, are both "very fond of their children" and they "aren't interested in their kids"; Maori leaders are "often too radical" and "you don't see them agitating."

Of course it might well be possible for a prototype theorist to do some judicious splitting into subsubcategories, and to further emphasize individual differences, and thereby provide some sort of account of these data. But this is going to get very clumsy indeed. Our claim is that discourse analysts are able to provide a much more workable explanation of the variations which occur in participant's discourse. By highlighting the functions of talk we can explain why a category of people should be described in one way on one occasion and in a different way on another. Rather than demonstrate this in detail with the above data (see Wetherell) et al., 1986, for examples) we will turn to ethnomethodologically inspired work on social categories, which was the first look at social categorization from this general perspective.

MOTIVES AND MEMBERSHIP CATEGORIES

Given that ethnomethodology's central concern is with the way people make sense of their world—their ordinary reasoning—and given that ethnomethodologists take a strongly functional view of talk, it is not surprising that they took an early interest in people's social categorizations. For these researchers, this was an area of discourse fundamentally involved in the way ordinary people make sense of social structure and provide coherence to their social worlds. At the same time, the ethnomethodological concern with the active *accomplishment* of social phenomena and interaction sensitized them to the possibility that categories might be more than simplifying perceptual sunglasses but deliberate constructions fitted for many tasks.

Harold Garfinkel himself took this approach in a detailed and fascinating case study of "Agnes," a would-be transsexual (Garfinkel, 1967). Garfinkel adopted the view that membership of the gender categories "male" and "female" is not merely a factual matter of biology but, in social psychological terms, negotiated *achievement*. The study documents the complex and subtle procedures Agnes had to learn so that she/he could successfully bring herself/himself off as a woman.

Harvey Sacks took the study of categories in another direction. He was particularly concerned with the kinds of inferences people make when category terms are used and, as a consequence of this, the ends categories work towards. In a paper edited from a lecture given in 1965 (Sacks, 1979) we can see just how radically his view of categories differed from the standard social psychological formulation.

Hotrodders and Teenage Drivers

Sacks starts with the question of why American kids generate so many new typologies of cars. Why, he asks, are the existing terms not good enough? Sacks notes how different category terms are enmeshed in, and can be used to exemplify, different world views. For a contemporary example we only have to think of "gay" and "faggot" as competing descriptive terms for "homosexuals" (Watson and Weinberg, 1982). The example Sacks uses are the competing descriptions, "teenage driver" and "hotrodder" (remember, this is 1965). The former term is used by adults and reflects an adult view of teenagers who drive cars. The latter term, however, reflects an alternative, non-adult, world view; a world which revolves around customizing cars and racing them in the street, much to the displeasure of the police.

Sacks illustrates the way these competing descriptions are managed using a piece of recorded dialogue. To understand this exchange we need to know that a Pontiac Bonneville is the sort of souped-up car driven by a "hotrodder," while a Pontiac station wagon is an everyday, straight from Detroit, motor car, the sort that might be driven by a "teenager." The categories of cars are linked to the categories of people. (The transcription is slighly simplified and edited from the original.)

1. *Ken:* In that Bonneville of mine, I could take that thing out, an' if I've gotta <u>tie</u>, and a sweater on, an' I look clean ninety nine percent of the time a guy could pull up to me, the <u>same</u> car, same colour, same year the whole bit, roar up on his pipes, and he's inna dirty grubby tee shirt, an' the guy [policeman] will pick the guy up in the dirty grubby <u>tee</u> shirt before he'll pick <u>me</u> up.
   (2.0)
   ( ):   hheh
   Ken: J'st just for   uh
   Al: (But) not many people get picked up in a Pontiac station wagon.
                                                    (Sacks, 1979: 7)

Ken is claiming that he can go out, smartly dressed, in what we learn from Al's interruption is his, in fact, non-customized Pontiac, get into drag races and then—because of his clothes and car—not get picked up by the police. Sacks suggests that Ken is seen to be trying to have his cake and eat it. He is claiming to be a hotrodder; while at the same time remaining loyal to the safe adult version of the world. Hence Al's sarcastic deflation: why would the police pick someone up in a Pontiac like that? One reason for generating typologies of cars, then, is to mark alternative social categories. That is, the selection from the category of cars "Bonneville"/"Pontiac" displays membership of the category "hotrodder" versus "teenager." Al has picked Ken up on, in effect, an illegitimate claim to be a member of the category "hotrodder." What we are seeing here, according to Sacks, is the policing of a category and, ultimately, the preservation of an alternative version of the social world (see also Cuff and Hustler, 1982).

Membership Categorization and Ordinary Reasoning

In his later work, Sacks (1972, 1974) went on to pay detailed attention to people's use of categories in their ordinary reasoning. On this topic, his best-known contribution concerned membership categories and categorization devices. Although this began with some of the most mundane features of our category discourse, its aim was to use these to illuminate the details and subtleties of complex social acts, such as blamings and mitigations.

A membership category is simply a commonsense equivalence class for the identification of people in talk, e.g. "teenagers," "Maoris." A membership categorization device groups together membership categories. Thus "family" is a membership categorization device (MCD) which groups together "brother," "mother," "baby" and so on while the MCD "gender" groups together the categories "male" and "female."

It might seem that this is a rather clumsy way of referring to the fact, noted earlier in our discussion of prototypes, that categories may be ordered into hierarchies. However, the use of the term "device" reflects the ethnomethodological emphasis on the *constructive* nature of talk; the collection of a set of categories together and the creation of an MCD are active accomplishments. Categories are not nested in a clear-cut, natural way like Russian dolls, for example, one inside another, but are grouped into collections by the use of potentially complex and contradictory sets of interpretative procedures. We shall return to these differences between ethnomethodological and social cognition approaches to categorization later.

Sacks suggests that there are certain basic practices which people draw on in their everyday discourse concerning categories. For example, there is a maxim of "consistency" which states that if one category from a MCD has been used it may well be appropriate to use another from that MCD. For the hearer of the discourse this means that if two categorizations which could be from the same MCD (but are not necessarily so) are used, they will be heard as coming from the same MCD. For example, the categorization "sister" could appear in the MCD "family" and the MCD "feminists." How it will be interpreted will depend in part on, for instance, whether the category "father" or the category "activist" has already appeared in the discourse.

Sacks further points out that certain categories have what he calls "duplicative organization." What he means by this is that the category is not merely a boundary to an independent set of individuals; rather, the individuals may also be seen having some kind of interpersonal organization. We can contrast categories such as "family" and "gang" which are duplicatively organized and those such as "redheads" or "Scots" which may not be. The former may have "in-group loyalty" and "stick together"—the latter may not have these features (Watson, 1978). It is important to note that interpersonal features such as in-group loyalty are occasioned rather than necessary. That is, they are available to be established in the course of a particular account rather than intrinsically linked to the categories.

The overall point is that people draw upon knowledge of the organization of categories as a resource for producing economical and intelligible conversation. As well as relying on this kind of knowledge, Sacks notes that people also draw on conventional knowledge about the *activities* of members of categories. For example, one of the things we conventionally expect members of the category "baby" to do is cry. Crying can thus be seen as an activity bound to the category "baby." Likewise, giving medical help and writing prescriptions are category-bound activities belonging to doctors. In fact, as Watson (1978) and Jayyusi (1984) have noted, it is not just activities which are conventionally bound to categories; a whole cluster of features may be expected of categories: the traits and preferences of the incumbents, where they live, what they look like, what they wear and so on.

The fact that membership categories can be conventionally tied to, or associated with, specific activities and other features, provides people with a powerful resource for making sense of their social worlds. In particular, it allows them to make inferences, or discursive connections to the category membership of the actors. And, conversely, given that they know only a person's category membership, they can make a good guess as to the kinds of things that person is likely to be doing. If someone is writing out a prescription we

expect them to be a doctor; if there is crying we may look around for the baby. Put another way, if we hear a doctor crying or see a baby writing a prescription we will expect an account of the special circumstances which led to this aberrant behaviour.

Now of course, these features of categorization have also been identified by social psychologists. Tajfel (1981), for instance, talks about inductive category errors where people mistakenly work from some features of an individual, ignoring other features, in order to categorize them. Nevertheless a very different perspective underlies the similar points made by ethnomethodologists and social psychologists. This difference will become more and more obvious as we proceed to research examples.

The basic ethnomethodological insights have provided some powerful tools for revealing some of the details of social phenomena such as blamings, accusations, and mitigations (Drew, 1978; Jayyusi, 1984; Lee, 1984; Watson, 1978, 1983; Watson and Weinberg, 1982; Wowk, 1984). To illustrate how they can be used, we will take examples from studies by Rod Watson and Maria Wowk on the role of categorizations when blame is being allocated in a murder investigation.

Race, Gender and Blame

One of the attractions of studying murder confessions and police interrogations of suspects is that they bring issues of culpability and motive to the forefront of discourse. In general, suspects know that certain sorts of motivations may be seen as more culpable than others, and that a range of circumstances may make them appear less blameworthy and more understandable. Thus when suspects construct descriptions of their crimes they do "motive work" (Mills, 1940). That is, they construct a version of the crime and what led them to commit it in such a way that the act is mitigated or even justified (Scott and Lyman, 1968). In British and American legal systems punishment is not an automatic consequence of the sheer behaviour of killing someone; circumstances, beliefs and motives are all taken into account and punishment varied accordingly.

In this context, categorization is a resource which suspects frequently draw on to help produce the most appropriate motive account. Take the extract below, for example. Watson notes that there are at least three plausible motivations for the murder of a black female by the black male who is doing the speaking: financial, sexual and racial; and he suggests that this passage of talk works to preserve the racial motive and disclaim the financial one.

2. Then he turned off the ignition then the one in the back he said "alright who doing whoring around out here?" Then [the victim] said well if you want money, I don't have money so the [accomplice] in the back said we don't want your money [ ] and then he said "we disgusted him every time one of his *black sisters* goes to bed with *white men* and was going to put a stop to it." He asked [the victim] again why she went to bed with the *white men* and she told him she had three kids and he said [she] was a God damn liar and punched her in the face and about the body a couple of times. (Watson, 1983: 50, emphasis added)

In this part of the interview the suspect deploys two membership categorizations: "black sister" and "white men." In terms of Sacks' consistency rule, we can clearly see the predicates "black" and "white" as from the MCD "race"; however, it is not easy to view "sister" and "men" as from a single MCD. Watson suggests that this complex of categorizations, which both follows and flouts the consistency rule, is carefully constructed to produce a particular effect.

The category "sister" is derived from the MCD "family" which, as we noted above, is generally understood as duplicatively organized; it groups together categories of people who are then seen to have a variety of interpersonal bonds. The (black) suspect's categorization of the victim as a black sister thus stresses his co-incumbency of the category "black" and trades on the affiliative, team-like properties of that co-incumbency. Watson's point is that the categorizations pull together the suspect and victim while contrasting the victim with those she purportedly goes to bed with ("white men" note, not "white brothers"). This construction provides the motive. The impassioned murder of someone who has dragged her whole family—even if it is only a family in metaphorical terms—into the mire of disrepute is so much more understandable

than the cold-blooded murder of a young woman where the only motive is the theft of a small quantity of money.

While in Watson's example the motive work is done more or less directly by the use of explicit categorizations, the categorization in the murder confession analysed by Maria Wowk must be inferred. The confession contains what Watson and Weinberg (1982) have described as a "category puzzle", a set of behaviours is described and the listener has the task of making sense of them. The problem they are faced with is: what kind of category member would act in this way? Here are some extracts from the confession.

3. *Suspect.* I got to the intersection (.2) of Brookland and Slade (1.0) when this girl walked up to me (.6) and propositioned me
(1.0)
Policeman. what did she exactly say to you Lewis?
Suspect. you look like a tough guy (1.2) y'look like the member of a gang (1.2) I told her I'm not a member of a gang (.) I'm an independent (.7) and she propositioned me again
[ ]
Policeman. what did she ask actually say to you
[ ]
Suspect. she asked me if I would like to get laid
[later in confession]
Suspect. urh (1.4) the girl got (.8) might say kind of (.2) pricky (1.0) and er::
[ ]
she propositioned me again (.6) and then she called me a prick hh (.) a no good sonofabitch (.) hhh and she threw what was left at (.2) the remainder (.) of the bottle of beer at me
[ ]
at that (1.2) I threw al (.) a right handed punch (.2) from the waist towards her shoulder . . . [goes on to describe killing] (Wowk, 1984: 80–1)

As we noted above, one powerful resource used in everyday reasoning is the idea of the category-boundedness of activity. People conventionally make inferences from categories to the activities of incumbents and, conversely, from activities to the category membership of actors. In this extract we are presented with both a category— "a girl"—and activities—propositioning the suspect, calling him a "prick" and a "no good sonofabitch," throwing beer at him etc. The puzzle for the listeners is to provide a categorization which can account for these activities in a way that "girl" fails to do.

Wowk suggests that, given the described activities, the conventional puzzle solution will be to further specify the category membership of the girl as a "tramp," "slut" or even "hooker," all categories which have strongly derogatory implications. These provide a negative moral assessment in the way "girl" does not. Yet, as they are not offered explicitly by the suspect, he can make a negative moral assessment of the victim available, while maintaining a position which allows him to deny that he views the victim as a slut. Nevertheless, reapportioning some of the blame in this way is exactly the upshot of the suspect's account.

In both of these analyses, then, we see a very different picture of the way categories operate from the one offered by social cognition researchers such as Wilder and Cantor. Rather than viewing the process of categorization as a defect in perception—albeit an adaptive one—these researchers have demonstrated how categorizations can be carefully inserted into discourse as part of the joint activities of blaming (the victims) and mitigation, and thus how categories can be read.

CATEGORIES, CONTENT AND COMMUNITY

One of the features of the traditional social psychological approach to categorization is its tendency to treat categories as if they were distorting enclosures anchored to unitary consistent prototypes. Their damaging social consequences are said to arise from effects such as the over-inclusion of people into the category, and the possibly stereotyped nature of the prototype (Pettigrew et al., 1958; Tajfel, 1969).

The studies examined in the last section reveal a rather different set of categorization phenomena. They display categorizations used not so much for their "boundary work," grouping and separating individu-

als, but for the category-based inferences made available. Watson demonstrated in Extract Two how the suspect's use of "white men" and "black sister" was not simply an exercise in inclusive grouping (although it inevitably achieved this) but the groundwork for an imputation of motive. Although, on the face of it, the idea of categories carrying a cluster of category-based attributes is similar to the notion of categories anchored to a prototype with a limited set of features, there is a crucial difference between these two models.

For the social cognition researcher the prototype determines perception through the operation of a feature matching process; if the stimulus shares the prerequisite number of features with the prototype it will be included in the category. For those who study the operation of categories in discourse, however, the cluster of category-based attributes is not viewed as a kind of mental picture influencing perception but as a potentially inconsistent cluster of expectations and associations drawn on in an *occasioned* manner. The point is that these expectations are selectively managed, in the context of passages of talk and writing, to present certain effects (Drew, 1978; Jayyusi, 1984). Thus some features may be made focal, others ignored, and yet others reconstructed. An understanding of the effectiveness of categorizations will thus depend on both elucidating the relevant cluster of attributes and the detail of their deployment in discourse. We will illustrate how this can be done by looking at a detailed study of how the categorization "community" was used in accounts of a "riot" (Potter and Reicher, 1987; see also Halliday and Potter, 1987; Reicher and Potter, 1985).

Uses of "Community"

In the spring of 1980 an event occurred in Bristol which came to be known as the "St. Paul's riot." Fighting took place between police and youths on the streets of the St. Paul's area of Bristol over a period of some hours. Several police vehicles and properties were destroyed, a number of police and civilians were injured—although none seriously—and the event dominated the next day's national news coverage and resulted in an emergency debate in Parliament. This seemed an ideal opportunity to look at the way social categories are used in the representation of conflict.

The study worked with an archive of documents: copies of reports and editorials from the local and national press, transcripts of television news and current affairs programmes, records of parliamentary proceedings, official reports and transcripts of interviews with people who were actively involved in the events.

Since much of the time the discourse of conflict was addressed to defining the nature of the protagonists, it was an especially rich context in which to study people's use of categorizations, and in particular their use of the categorization "community."

The analysis was initiated by selecting out from the archive all instances of the term "community" and its synonyms, and went on to identify the different predicates used with the term, along with the varying ways it was adopted to refer to the protagonists in the events. It was immediately apparent that certain sorts of predicates were repeatedly used, in particular predicates describing a certain cohesive style of social relation-ship: "closeness," "integration" and "friendliness," and those associated with certain metaphors: spatial ("close-knit"), organism ("growth") and agency (a community "acts")—see Figure 4. Without exception, where the term "community" was used with a strongly evaluative force it was positive: "community" was seen as a good thing.

Despite the broad agreement in the attribute cluster connected with the category "community," considerable variability was evident in the application of the term. In some accounts, for example, the "community" had been "disrupted" or even "finished" by the "riot"; in others the "riot" was merely a sign of the cohesiveness of the "community." In some accounts the police were depicted as part of the "community"; in others the disturbance was a conflict between the "community" and the police. Variability on this scale has now become a very familiar phenomenon. Yet it represents an enormous headache for any realist approach to participants' discourse, and particularly for those researchers bent on reconstructing exactly what went on, between whom, in the disturbance. It is for this reason that research generally uses procedures which render variability invisible. But, if we look to the action orientation of the accounts, differences become much more understandable.

One major difference in the data occurred between a broad group of accounts which depicted the events in St. Paul's as a "community relations" problem and another group of accounts which treated them as a direct conflict between the "community" and the police. Contrast the following passages which illustrate these two versions. The first is a statement by the then Home Secretary, William Whitelaw, made in the parliamentary debate which followed the disturbance; the second is from the beginning of a report in the newspaper *Socialist Challenge*.

4. *Whitelaw.* As to what the Right Honourable Gentleman says about the community relations work of the police, it does so happen that a police officer in this particular area of Bristol, as I understand, has been very active indeed in the area of Community Council. He has been one of the most highly respected members of that council who have done a great deal of the sort of work that the Right Honourable Gentleman has in mind.

5. ON WEDNESDAY 2nd April, the mainly black population of St. Paul's, a Bristol inner-city district, responded to police harassment by mounting a counter attack. The police are the most visible instrument of state repression of the black minority in Britain today. Almost exactly a year after the police riot in Southall, the black community of St.

Figure 4 Predicates and Metaphors Used with "Community"

Sample Predicates	Metaphors (where relevant)
Friendly	
Warm	
Happy	
Harmonious	
Close-knit	Spatial
Integrated	
Tight	
Grows	Organic
Evolves	
Matures	
Acts	Agency
Knows	
Feels	

Paul's fought back against police brutality and won.

Extract Four was typical of one kind of interpretation of the disturbance. Whitelaw was responding to a question about "community policing." He formulated his reply in the rather broader terms of the "community relations work of the police" and claimed that this work already existed, citing an active member of the "Community Council." The effect is to include problems of policing under the topic of "community relations"—which he had earlier characterized as good—and to support this characterization with strongly positive, but at the same time very vague, allusions to the work of a "community police officer."

Throughout the parliamentary debate the "riot" was described in this manner as a problem of "community relations" and the police were depicted as part of the "community"; thus preparing the way for a response to the events which follows from the cluster of features bound to the category "community." If a "*community*" had been disturbed the problem will be one of fractured interpersonal relationships and trust. Thus the proposed response is directed at these points. It includes further representation of police on community bodies as in Extract Four, the development of personal relationships and trust between police and locals, and a construal of the conflict in "human terms." In general, the use of "community" in this way leads inexorably to the introduction of "community policing": the perfect solution to "community relations problems."

Extract Five is very different. Instead of formulating the event as a riot triggered by ailing "community relations" it is depicted as an open conflict, with the two sides explicitly characterized as the "black community" and the police. Furthermore, a clear-cut and straightforward causal story of the conflict is offered: the "black community" was responding to "harassment" and "brutality," so the conflict is a *natural* part of an ongoing *intergroup* struggle.

In accounts of this kind, the cluster of category-bound attributes and the positive force of "community" contribute three consequences. First, the police are implicitly blamed; for "communities" are not reasonable targets for police attack (unlike, say, "thugs" or "crazed rioters"—see Trew, 1979). Second, actions against the police are legitimated. As "communities" have the category-bound attribute of harmonious personal relationships, if they become involved in violence it will most likely be seen as externally caused and justifiable. Third, any potential dismissal of people fighting with police as marginal or pathological is undermined; depicting them as "the community" they are made central and indeed representative of the area. Versions of this kind lead to a distinct, alternative set of solutions. Instead of "community policing" being the answer the curbing of a repressive and racist police force is proposed.

CATEGORIES AND THE CONSTRUCTION OF DISCOURSE

Earlier in the chapter we identified three kinds of assumptions which are perenially made in traditional social psychological work on categories and which become questionable when a discourse-oriented perspective is adopted. These were that categories are preformed and enduring, they have a fixed structure and inevitably lead to biased perception. Having explored some of the research on categories in discourse we are now in a position to see the problems with these assumptions more clearly.

The idea that categories are enduring, preformed entities is hard to maintain in the light of widespread variation in the content of category accounts (as well as papers cited above, see Gilbert and Mulkay, 1984: ch. 5; Yearley, 1984). This variation and the active reconstruction of categories cannot be easily reconciled with the popular cognitive models in this area, especially Eleanor Rosch's theory of prototypes, but is perfectly compatible with discourse theory which sees variation as thrown up in the wake of action.

Likewise, the concept of categories structured as fuzzy sets anchored to prototypes and organized in hierarchies differs markedly from the notion of structure revealed in discourse analyses. As we saw in the previous section, the relatively static exemplar or prototype is replaced with the idea of a cluster of potentially inconsistent features and expectations. It would be wrong to think of these expectations as constituting a clear-cut, prestructured, enduring list. Nor should our talk of the "function" of category accounts be taken to mean that categorizations *in themselves* notably lead to certain consequences. The relevance and detailed nature of the expectations associated with a category is worked up in passages of discourse. This is not to say that prior expectations and understanding are not important; rather that these are drawn on as a resource from which the detailed sense and implication of the category account is manufactured.

The suggestion that categories have a fundamental role in biasing perception is replaced, in the discourse analytic work, with the idea of categories being actively constructed and drawn on for many *different* actions: bias and tolerance effects included. It may well be that categorizations are often associated with phenomena such as over-inclusion and simplification; however, research on categories in discourse has shown that categorization is very far from the mechanical cognitive process implied by traditional work. Many different studies have shown that categories are selected and formulated in such a way that their specific features help accomplish certain goals. This accomplishment does not depend merely on the homogenizing properties of categorization, their ability to group a set of stimuli, but on features specific to the category. For example, we saw how accounts could use descriptions of actions bound to the category "tramp" in the course of a blaming, or features bound to the category "community" to provide certain actions with legitimacy.

One of the benefits of the discourse approach to categorization is that it has directed attention away from the cognitive processes assumed to be operating under people's skulls and on towards the detail of how categories are actually used. The study of categories unfolds into the general study of the organization of discourse and its consequences (Billig, 1985, 1987). It is not surprising that categories are so important, because they are the nouns from which we construct versions of the collectivities in which we live. In a sense, they are the building blocks of our many versions of the social world; however, once we look closely at the blocks we see that they themselves are not solid and defined, but have to be moulded in discourse for use in different accounts.

APPENDIX: TRANSCRIPTION NOTATION

The form of notation used throughout this chapter was developed by Gail Jefferson. A more complete description is found in Atkinson and Heritage (1984).

Extended square brackets mark overlap between utterances, e.g.:

A: Right ⌈ so you
B: ⌊ I'm not sure

An equals sign at the end of a speaker's utterance and at the start of the next utterance indicates the absence of a discernable gap, e.g.:

A: Anyway Brian =
B: = Okay, okay

Numbers in brackets indicate pauses timed to the nearest tenth of a second. A full stop in brackets indicates a pause which is noticeable but too short to measure, e.g.:

A: I went (3.6) a lot further (.) than I intended

One or more colons indicate an extension of the preceding vowel sound, e.g.:

A: Yea::h, I see::

Underlining indicates that words are uttered with added emphasis; words in capitals are uttered louder than the surrounding talk, e.g.:

A: It's not right, not right AT ALL

A full stop before a word or sound indicates an audible intake of breath, e.g.:

A: I think .hh I need more

Round brackets indicate that material in the brackets is either inaudible or there is doubt about its accuracy, e.g.:

A: I (couldn't tell you) that

Square brackets indicate that some transcript has been deliberately omitted. Material in square brackets is clarificatory information, e.g.:

A: Brian [the speaker's brother] said [ ] it's okay

REFERENCES

Allen, V. L. and D. A. Wilder (1979) "Group Categorization and Attribution of Belief Similarity," *Small Group Behaviour,* 10:73–80.

Atkinson J. M. and J. C. Heritage (eds.) (1984) *Structures of Social Action: Studies in Conversation Analysis.* Cambridge: Cambridge University Press.

Billig, M. (1985) "Prejudice, Categorization and Particularization: From a Perceptual to a Rhetorical Approach," *European Journal of Social Psychology,* 15:79–103.

Billig, M. (1987) *Arguing and Thinking: A Rhetorical Approach to Social Psychology.* Cambridge: Cambridge University Press.

Brewer, M. B., V. Dull and L. Lui (1981) "Perception of the Elderly: Stereotypes as Prototypes," *Journal of Personality and Social Psychology,* 41:656–70.

Cantor, N. and W. Mischel (1977) "Traits as Prototypes: Effects on Recognition Memory," In L. Berkowitz (ed.), *Advances in Experimental Social Psychology* Vol. 9. London: Academic Press.

Cantor, N. and W. Mischel (1979) "Prototypes in Person Perception," in L. Berkowitz (ed.), *Advances in Experimental Social Psychology* Vol. 12. London: Academic Press.

Cuff, E. C. and D. E. Hustler (1982) "Stories and Story-Time in an Infant Classroom: Some Features of Language in Social Interaction," *Semiotica,* 42:119–45.

van Dijk, T. A. (ed.) (1985) *Handbook of Discourse Analysis* Vols 1–4. London: Academic Press.

Drew, P. (1978) "Accusations: The Occasioned Use of 'Religious Geography' in Describing Events," *Sociology,* 12:1–22.

Garfinkel, H. (1967) *Studies in Ethnomethodology.* Englewood Cliffs: Prentice Hall.

Gilbert, G. N. and M. Mulkay (1984) *Opening Pandora's Box: A Sociological Analysis of Scientists' Discourse.* Cambridge: Cambridge University Press.

Halliday, Q. and J. Potter (1987) "Community Leaders in Discourse: Lay Environmental Psychology in Accounts of a 'Riot,'" mimeo, University of St Andrews.

Hamilton, D. L. (1979) "A Cognitive-Attributional Analysis of Stereotyping," in L. Berkowitz (ed.), *Advances in Experimental Social Psychology* Vol. 12. New York: Academic Press.

Jayyusi, L. (1984) *Categorization and the Moral Order.* London: Routledge and Kegan Paul.

Lee, J. (1984) "Innocent Victims and Evil-Doers," *Women's Studies International Forum,* 7:69–73.

Mills, C. W. (1940) "Situated Actions and Vocabularies of Motive," *American Sociological Review,* 5:904–13.

Pettigrew, T. F., G. W. Allport and E. V. Barnett (1958) "Binocular Resolution and Perception of Race in South Africa," *British Journal of Psychology,* 49:265–78.

Potter, J. and S. Reicher (1987) "Discourses of Community and Conflict: The Organization of Social Categories in Accounts of a 'Riot'" *British Journal of Social Psychology,* 26.

Reeves, W. (1983) *British Racial Discourse: A Study of British Political Discourse about Race and Race-Related Matters.* Cambridge: Cambridge University Press.

Reicher, S. and J. Potter (1985) "Psychological Theory as Intergroup Perspective: A Comparative Analysis of 'Scientific' and 'Lay' Accounts of Crowd Events," *Human Relations,* 38:167–89.

Rosch, E., C. B. Mervis, W. D. Gray, D. M. Johnson and P. Boyes-Braem (1976) "Basic Objects and Natural Categories," *Cognitive Psychology,* 8:382–439.

Rothbart, M. (1981) "Memory Processes and Social Beliefs," in D. L. Hamilton (ed.), *Cognitive Processes in Stereotyping and Intergroup Behaviour.* Hillsdale, N.J.: Erlbaum.

Sacks, H. (1972) "An Initial Investigation of the Usability of Conversational Data for Doing Sociology." in D. Sudnow (ed.), *Studies in Social Interaction.* New York: Free Press.

Sacks, H. (1974) "On the Analyzability of Stories by Children," in R. Turner (ed.), *Ethnomethodology.* Harmondsworth: Penguin.

Sacks, H. (1979) "Hotrodder: A Revolutionary Category," in G. Psathas (ed.), *Everyday Language: Studies in Ethnomethodology.* New York: Irvington.

Scott, M. B. and S. Lyman (1968) "Accounts," *American Sociological Review,* 33:46–62.

Snyder, M. (1981) "On the Self-Perpetuating Nature of Social Stereotypes," in D. L. Hamilton (ed.), *Cognitive Processes in Stereotyping and Intergroup Behaviour.* Hillsdale, N.J.: Erlbaum.

Tajfel, H. (1969) "Cognitive Aspects of Prejudice," *Journal of Biosocial Sciences,* 1, Supplement Mon. No. 1, *Biosocial Aspects of Race,* 173–91.

Tajfel, H. (1981) "Social Stereotypes and Social Groups," in J. Turner and H. Giles (eds), *Intergroup Behaviour.* Oxford: Blackwell.

Tajfel, H. (1982) *Human Groups and Social Categories.* Cambridge: Cambridge University Press.

Tajfel, H. and J. Forgas (1981) "Social Categorization: Cognitions, Values and Groups," in J. Forgas (ed.), *Social Cognition.* London: Academic Press.

Tajfel, H. and A. Wilkes (1963) "Classification and Quantitative Judgement," *British Journal of Psychology,* 54:101–14.

Taylor, S. E. (1981) "A Categorization Approach to Stereotyping," in D. L. Hamilton (ed.), *Cognitive Processes in Stereotyping and Intergroup Behaviour.* Hillsdale, N.J.: Erlbaum.

Trew, T. (1979) "Theory and Ideology at Work," in R. Fowler, B. Hodge, G. Kress and T. Trew (eds), *Language and Control.* London: Routledge and Kegan Paul.

Watson, R. (1978) "Categorization, Authorization and Blame-Negotiation in Conversation," *Sociology* 12:105–13.

Watson, R. (1983) "The Presentation of Victim and Motive in Discourse: The Case of Police Interrogations and Interviews," *Victimology,* 8:31–52.

Watson, R. and T. Weinberg (1982) "Interviews and the Interactional Construction of Accounts of Homosexual Identity," *Social Analysis,* 11:56–78.

Wetherell, M. S., R. McFadyen, J. Potter and B. Rothwell (1986) "Categories in Discourse," mimeo, University of St. Andrews.

Wilder, D. (1978) "Perceiving Persons as a Group: Effects on

Attributions of Causality and Beliefs," *Social Psychology*, 1:13–23.

Wilder, D. A. (1986) "Social Categorization: Implications for Creation and Reduction of Intergroup Bias," in L. Berkowitz (ed.), *Advances in Experimental Social Psychology* Vol. 19; New York: Academic Press.

Wowk, M. T. (1984) "Blame Allocation, Sex and Gender in a Murder Interrogation," *Women's Studies International Forum*, 7:75–82.

Yearley, S. (1984) 'Proofs and Reputations: Sir James Hall and the Use of Classification Devices in Scientific Argument', *Earth Sciences History*, 3:25–43.

FURTHER READING

Cahill, Spencer. 1986. "Language Practices and Self-Definition: The Case of Gender Identity Acquisition." *Sociological Quarterly* 27:295–311.

- Illustrates the importance of categorization for the formation of gender identity.

Cassirer, Ernst. 1944. *An Essay on Man.* New Haven, CT: Yale University Press.

- A popular philosophical essay on the significance of symbols and communication for understanding the shape of the social world.

Filmer, Paul, Michael Phillipson, David Silverman, and David Walsh. 1973. *New Directions in Sociological Theory.* Cambridge, MA: MIT Press.

- Addresses the so-called linguistic turn in the study of social life.

Whorf, Benjamin Lee. 1956. *Language, Thought, and Reality.* Cambridge, MA: MIT Press.

- Classic essays on the relation among language, communication, and social reality.

Zerubavel, Eviatar. 1994. *The Fine Line: Making Distinctions in Everyday Life.* New York: Free Press.

- How perspectives and social categories organize the meanings of objects and events.

─────── SECTION 3 ───────

THE WORK OF SOCIAL INTERACTION

Social interaction is so ordinary we take it for granted. We meet others, talk things over, and go on with our lives with hardly a thought to the interaction involved. It's almost automatic. At the same time, the outcomes of the simplest conversation or the most fleeting of chance encounters can be truly disturbing. We say to ourselves "I wish I hadn't said that" or "Where did I go wrong?" admitting that interaction does make a difference. Even the most trivial comment can shape the meaning of things. Saying or doing something can change the reality we share with others. A chance encounter can alter our inner lives.

When Sigmund Freud wrote about "slips of the tongue," he wasn't being cute. These weren't just amusing stories from his clinical practice. Rather, he was suggesting that the most trifling interactions can reveal realities otherwise unknown to us. Consider what happens when someone says "excuse my lust," instead of the intended "excuse my dust." According to Freud, such a slip of the tongue speaks volumes about one's underlying feelings and intentions. Freud was famous for connecting features of ordinary interaction to what he called the "unconscious." It was his habit to point out the unrecognized reality-defining work that's accomplished in "inadvertently" saying things like "excuse my lust." This, of course, contrasts significantly with the reality-defining work accomplished by saying "excuse my dust." For Freud, a mere slip of the tongue could reveal identities and relationships that exist far beyond our awareness.

We needn't conjure up the unconscious to realize that there's more work to social interaction than we may think. Some people plan endlessly to "come off" as, say, smart or sophisticated. Some work nonstop to look like they're busy, in order to avoid additional responsibilities or to seek favorable employee evaluations. Regardless of the payoff, we work hard to communicate our identities, our intentions, and the things that are significant to us. Or at least we work at giving those impressions. This work is evident in the practice of everyday life. It's not hidden in the recesses of the unconscious.

In practice, we concertedly work to shape our selves and identities—who we are to ourselves and others. Others work at our identities, too. It begins when we're born. Parents, for example, outline our futures the very moment they begin to define our genders. These definitions are precarious, since the meaning of gender is not what it used to be. The possibilities for being boys and girls are virtually endless, yet people still have to work to establish gendered identities. Adulthood is not only a matter of getting older. It's a product of the definitional work that establishes "grown-up" identities. In adulthood, we work at seeming to be faithful in marriage, truthful in the courtroom, and vivacious at Saturday night cocktail parties. We hope that others, in turn, define us as good spouses, honest witnesses, and lively "party animals."

Clearly, we don't construct our inner lives and social worlds on our own. No person is an island. Sometimes we deal with competitors in defining who and what we are. Other times, we often collaborate in teams to sustain the apparent reality of an occasion. The work of everyday social interaction is anything but individual or automatic. If we slack off on our reality-constructing jobs, the results are likely to show in how situations are redefined.

ABOUT THE READINGS

W. I. Thomas made significant early contributions to the study of social interaction. The reading selections from his work—entitled **"The Definition of the Situation"**—are taken from two of his books, *The Unadjusted Girl* (1923) and *The Child in America* (1928). One of Thomas's projects was to understand the way individuals and groups constructed their lives. He coined the famous phrase, the "definition of the situation," to depict the process. For Thomas, reality construction was highly consequential work. "If men define situations as real," he argued, "they are real in their consequences."

Later, **Erving Goffman** pointed to the deeply social character of definitions of situations. The reading selection **"Teamwork"** is taken from his popular book, *The Presentation of Self in Everyday Life* (1959). Goffman deeply appreciates the continuing effort individuals exert to sustain their realities. In this chapter, however, he takes the social process a step further. He illustrates how "performance teams" can be involved in staging definitions of the situation. Goffman instructs us about the coordinated efforts people make to define shared identities and social situations. He's especially concerned with how individuals work together, as teams, to manage and sustain particular appearances. The lesson is that inner lives and social worlds are only as stable as the work that goes into constructing them.

Echoing both Thomas and Goffman, **Joan P. Emerson** takes us to a somewhat unusual social situation to study interactional work. In **"Behavior in Private Places: Sustaining Definitions of Reality in Gynecological Examinations,"** Emerson shows us how much the definition of the gynecological examination depends on the reality-constructing efforts of those who are involved. Because the examination is so intimate, its definition teeters on the brink of the sexual. The event could be defined as purely professional and impersonal. But without the related definitional work, it can easily become personal, with decided sexual overtones. It's never automatic which situation it will be. This study is an important test case because the definition of this situation is so precarious. When its interactional work is carried out successfully, a medical situation emerges. Should this work fail, the situation risks the embarrassment and professional shame that can easily come when sexual definitions prevail.

The definitional process involves the entire situation: the physical environment of the examination room; the patient's attire; and the words, gestures, and demeanor of the doctor, attending nurse, and the patient herself. Definitional work includes speaking in innocuous ways, avoiding explicit references to the genitals, maintaining disinterested eye contact, and "draping" the patient so as to distance the bodily site of the examination from the selves of the participants. Instructions to the patient can make all the difference in the world. To benignly direct the patient to "let your knees fall apart," instead of blurting "spread your legs," is significant interactional work in this situation. The cooperation of all participants, as a team, "brings off" the medical reality of the situation, according to Emerson. Reading her article, we realize that there's more to sustaining the reality of gynecological examinations than medical competence alone provides.

8 | THE DEFINITION OF THE SITUATION
W. I. Thomas

Preliminary to any self-determined act of behavior there is always a stage of examination and deliberation which we may call *the definition of the situation.* And actually not only concrete acts are dependent on the definition of the situation, but gradually a whole life-policy and the personality of the individual himself follow from a series of such definitions.

But the child is always born into a group of people among whom all the general types of situation which may arise have already been defined and corresponding rules of conduct developed, and where he has not the slightest chance of making his definitions and following his wishes without interference. Men have always lived together in groups. Whether mankind has a true herd instinct or whether groups are held together because this has worked out to advantage is of no importance. Certainly the wishes in general are such that they can be satisfied only in a society. But we have only to refer to the criminal code to appreciate the variety of ways in which the wishes of the individual may conflict with the wishes of society. And the criminal code takes no account of the many unsanctioned expressions of the wishes which society attempts to regulate by persuasion and gossip.

There is therefore always a rivalry between the spontaneous definitions of the situation made by the member of an organized society and the definitions which his society has provided for him. The individual tends to a hedonistic selection of activity, pleasure first; and society to a utilitarian selection, safety first. Society wishes its member to be laborious, dependable, regular, sober, orderly, self-sacrificing; while the individual wishes less of this and more of new experience. And organized society seeks also to regulate the conflict and competition inevitable between its members in the pursuit of their wishes. The desire to have wealth, for example, or any other socially sanctioned wish, may not be accomplished at the expense of another member of the society,—by murder, theft, lying, swindling, blackmail, etc.

It is in this connection that a moral code arises, which is a set of rules or behavior norms, regulating the expression of the wishes, and which is built up by successive definitions of the situation. In practice the abuse arises first and the rule is made to prevent its recurrence. Morality is thus the generally accepted definition of the situation, whether expressed in public opinion and the unwritten law, in a formal legal code, or in religious commandments and prohibitions.

The family is the smallest social unit and the primary defining agency. As soon as the child has free motion and begins to pull, tear, pry, meddle, and prowl, the parents begin to define the situation through speech and other signs and pressures: "Be quiet," "Sit up straight," "Blow your nose," "Wash your face," "Mind your mother," "Be kind to sister," etc. This is the real significance of Wordsworth's phrase, "Shades of the prison house begin to close upon the growing child." His wishes and activities begin to be inhibited, and gradually, by definitions within the family, by playmates, in the school; in the Sunday school, in the community, through reading, by formal instruction, by in-

formal signs of approval and disapproval, the growing member learns the code of his society.

In addition to the family we have the community as a defining agency. At present the community is so weak and vague that it gives us no idea of the former power of the local group in regulating behavior. Originally the community was practically the whole world of its members. It was composed of families related by blood and marriage and was not so large that all the members could not come together; it was a face-to-face group. I asked a Polish peasant what was the extent of an "okolica" or neighborhood—how far it reached. "It reaches," he said, "as far as the report of a man reaches—as far as a man is talked about." And it was in communities of this kind that the moral code which we now recognize as valid originated. The customs of the community are "folkways," and both state and church have in their more formal codes mainly recognized and incorporated these folkways.

. . . If men define situations as real, they are real in their consequences.

The total situation will always contain more and less subjective factors, and the behavior reaction can be studied only in connection with the whole context, i.e., the situation as it exists in verifiable, objective terms, and as it has seemed to exist in terms of the interested persons. Thus, the behavior records of the child clinics are contributing important data by including the child's account of the difficult situation, the often conflicting definitions of this situation given by parents, teachers, etc., and the recording of such facts as can be verified about the situation by disinterested investigators.

In the field of psychiatry the context becomes particularly significant, and it is desirable to have here a multiplication of records showing how situations are appreciated and motivate behavior, but the records should be made not without regard to the factual elements in the situation. To the degree that the psychiatric cases are approached from the standpoint of the total situation it will appear that the problems of behavior taken all together assume an aspect of totality. The unfortunate separation of the "abnormal" from the "normal" in behavior studies will disappear, and the abnormal, pathological and criminal behavior reactions will appear not as "disease" but as socially (and individually) undesirable behavior reactions in given situations, and from this standpoint they will lend themselves more readily to study from the behavioristic standpoint. . . .

With the progress of our studies of the various behavior-forming situations we may hope to approach the still more obscure problem of mass behavior—the participation of whole populations in common sentiments and actions. This is represented by fashions of dress, mob action, war hysteria, the gang spirit, mafia, omertà, fascism, popularity of this or that cigarette or tooth paste, the quick fame and quick infamy of political personalities, etc. We are unable to define this total situation satisfactorily, but it involves the interaction of language and gesture and gossip and print and symbols and slogans and propaganda and imitation, and seems, more than anything else, the process eventuating in the formation of the distinctive character of communities, nationalities and races. The process itself may be described as a series of definitions of situations whereby behavior norms are established.

In the same connection (while we do not advocate anthropological and historical studies as remunerative behavioristic studies in themselves and are of the opinion that the past contains no models on which we may build in the present) it would be useful to extend our studies of this situational character to the large cultural areas, to the contemporaneous races and nationalities, in order to understand the formation of behavior patterns comparatively, in their most general and particular expressions, and appreciate the capacity of human nature to work under various and widely contrasted habit systems. Furthermore, behavior studies within these wide limits may be expected to reveal comparatively and in the most general way the situations within which particular maladjustments (delinquency, crime, the psychoneuroses) tend to appear, and the situations and habit systems unfavorable to their appearance, or, more positively, the situations within which the activities are integrated about particular interests, leading to pursuits, roles and careers.

9 | TEAMWORK
Erving Goffman

In thinking about a performance it is easy to assume that the content of the presentation is merely an expressive extension of the character of the performer and to see the function of the performance in these personal terms. This is a limited view and can obscure important differences in the function of the performance for the interaction as a whole.

First, it often happens that the performance serves mainly to express the characteristics of the task that is performed and not the characteristics of the performer. Thus one finds that service personnel, whether in profession, bureaucracy, business, or craft, enliven their manner with movements which express proficiency and integrity, but, whatever this manner conveys about them, often its major purpose is to establish a favorable definition of their service or product. Further, we often find that the personal front of the performer is employed not so much because it allows him to present himself as he would like to appear but because his appearance and manner can do something for a scene of wider scope. It is in this light that we can understand how the sifting and sorting of urban life brings girls with good grooming and correct accent into the job of receptionist, where they can present a front for an organization as well as for themselves.

But most important of all, we commonly find that

the definition of the situation projected by a particular participant is an integral part of a projection that is fostered and sustained by the intimate co-operation of more than one participant. For example, in a medical hospital the two staff internists may require the intern, as part of his training, to run through a patient's chart, giving an opinion about each recorded item. He may not appreciate that his show of relative ignorance comes in part from the staff studying up on the chart the night before; he is quite unlikely to appreciate that this impression is doubly ensured by the local team's tacit agreement allotting the work-up of half the chart to one staff person, the other half to the second staff person.[1] This teamwork ensures a good staff showing—providing, of course, that the right internist is able to take over the catechism at the right time.

Furthermore, it is often the case that each member of such a troupe or cast of players may be required to appear in a different light if the team's over-all effect is to be satisfactory. Thus if a household is to stage a formal dinner, someone in uniform or livery will be required as part of the working team. The individual who plays this part must direct at himself the social definition of a menial. At the same time the individual taking the part of hostess must direct at herself, and foster by her appearance and manner, the social definition of someone upon whom it is natural for menials to wait. This was strikingly demonstrated in the island tourist hotel studied by the writer (hereafter called "Shetland Hotel"). There an over-all impression of middle-class service was achieved by the management, who allocated to themselves the roles of middle-class host and hostess and to their employees that of domestics—although in terms of the local class structure the girls who acted as maids were of slightly higher status than the hotel owners who employed them. When hotel guests were absent, little nonsense about a maid-mistress status difference was allowed by the maids. Another example may be taken from middle-class family life. In our society, when husband and wife appear before new friends for an evening of sociability, the wife may demonstrate more respectful subordination to the will and opinion of her husband than she may bother to show when alone with him or when with old friends. When she assumes a respectful role, he can assume a dominant one; and when each

member of the marriage team plays its special role, the conjugal unit, as a unit, can sustain the impression that new audiences expect of it. Race etiquette in the South provides another example. Charles Johnson's suggestion is that when few other whites are in the region, a Negro may call his white fellow worker by his first name, but when other whites approach it is understood that mistering will be reintroduced.[2] Business etiquette provides a similar example:

> When outsiders are present, the touch of businesslike formality is even more important. You may call your secretary "Mary" and your partner "Joe" all day, but when a stranger comes into your office you should refer to your associates as you would expect the stranger to address them: Miss or Mr. You may have a running joke with the switchboard operator, but you let it ride when you are placing a call in an outsider's hearing.[3]
>
> She [your secretary] wants to be called Miss or Mrs. in front of strangers; at least, she won't be flattered if your "Mary" provokes everyone else into addressing her with familiarity.[4]

I will use the term "performance team" or, in short, "team" to refer to any set of individuals who co-operate in staging a single routine.

Until now in this report we have taken the individual's performance as the basic point of reference and have been concerning ourselves with two levels of fact—the individual and his performance on one hand and the full set of participants and the interaction as a whole on the other. For the study of certain kinds and aspects of interaction, this perspective would seem sufficient; anything that did not fit this framework could be handled as a resolvable complication of it. Thus co-operation between two performers each of whom was ostensibly involved in presenting his own special performance could be analyzed as a type of collusion or "understanding" without altering the basic frame of reference. However in the case-study of particular social establishments, the co-operative activity of some of the participants seems too important to be handled merely as a variation on a previous theme. Whether the members of a team stage similar individual performances or stage dissimilar performances which fit together into a whole, an emergent team impression arises which can conveniently be treated as a fact in its own right, as a third level of fact located between the individual performance on one hand and the total interaction of participants on the other. It may even be said that if our special interest is the study of impression management, of the contingencies which arise in fostering an impression, and of the techniques for meeting these contingencies, then the team and the team-performance may well be the best units to take as the fundamental point of reference.[5] Given this point of reference, it is possible to assimilate such situations as two-person interaction into the framework by describing these situations as two-team interaction in which each team contains only one member. (Logically speaking, one could even say that an audience which was duly impressed by a particular social setting in which no other persons were present would be an audience witnessing a team-performance in which the team was one of no members.)

The concept of team allows us to think of performances that are given by one or more than one performer; it also covers another case. Earlier it was suggested that a performer may be taken in by his own act, convinced at the moment that the impression of reality which he fosters is the one and only reality. In such cases the performer comes to be his own audience; he comes to be performer and observer of the same show. Presumably he intracepts or incorporates the standards he attempts to maintain in the presence of others so that his conscience requires him to act in a socially proper way. It will have been necessary for the individual in his performing capacity to conceal from himself in his audience capacity the discreditable facts that he has had to learn about the performance; in everyday terms, there will be things he knows, or has known, that he will not be able to tell himself. This intricate maneuver of self-delusion constantly occurs; psychoanalysts have provided us with beautiful field data of this kind, under the headings of repression and dissociation.[6] Perhaps here we have a source of what has been called "self-distantiation," namely, that process by which a person comes to feel estranged from himself.[7]

When a performer guides his private activity in accordance with incorporated moral standards, he may associate these standards with a reference group of some kind, thus creating a non-present audience for his activity. This possibility leads us to consider a further one. The individual may privately maintain standards of behavior which he does not personally believe in, maintaining these standards because of a lively belief that an unseen audience is present who will punish deviations from these standards. In other words, an individual may be his own audience or may imagine an audience to be present. (In all of this we see the analytical difference between the concept of a team and that of an individual performer.) This should make us go on to see that a team itself may stage a performance for an audience that is not present in the flesh to witness the show. Thus, in some mental hospitals in America, unclaimed deceased patients may be given a relatively elaborate funeral on the hospital grounds. No doubt this helps to ensure the maintenance of minimal civilized standards in a setting where back-ward conditions and the general unconcern of society can threaten these standards. In any case, on occasions when kinfolk do not appear, the hospital minister, the hospital funeral director, and one or two other functionaries may play out all the funeral roles themselves and, with the dead patient now laid out, perform a demonstration of civilized regard for the dead before no one present.

It is apparent that individuals who are members of the same team will find themselves, by virtue of this fact, in an important relationship to one another. Two basic components of this relationship may be cited.

First, it would seem that while a team-performance is in progress, any member of the team has the power to give the show away or to disrupt it by inappropriate conduct. Each teammate is forced to rely on the good conduct and behavior of his fellows, and they, in turn, are forced to rely on him. There is then, perforce, a bond of reciprocal dependence linking teammates to one another. When members of a team have different formal statuses and rank in a social establishment, as is often the case, then we can see that the mutual dependence created by membership in the team is likely to cut across structural or social cleavages in the establishment and thus provide a source of cohesion for the establishment. Where staff and line statuses tend to divide an organization, performance teams may tend to integrate the divisions.

Secondly, it is apparent that if members of a team must co-operate to maintain a given definition of the situation before their audience, they will hardly be in a position to maintain that particular impression before one another. Accomplices in the maintenance of a particular appearance of things, they are forced to define one another as persons "in the know," as persons before whom a particular front cannot be maintained. Teammates, then, in proportion to the frequency with which they act as a team and the number of matters that fall within impressional protectiveness, tend to be bound by rights of what might be called "familiarity." Among teammates, the privilege of familiarity—which may constitute a kind of intimacy without warmth—need not be something of an organic kind, slowly developing with the passage of time spent together, but rather a formal relationship that is automatically extended and received as soon as the individual takes a place on the team.

In suggesting that teammates tend to be related to one another by bonds of reciprocal dependence and reciprocal familiarity, we must not confuse the type of group so formed with other types, such as an informal group or clique. A teammate is someone whose dramaturgical co-operation one is dependent upon in fostering a given definition of the situation; if such a person comes to be beyond the pale of informal sanctions and insists on giving the show away or forcing it to take a particular turn, he is none the less part of the team. In fact, it is just because he is part of the team that he can cause this kind of trouble. Thus the isolate in the factory who becomes a rate-buster is none the less part of the team, even if his productive activity embarrasses the impression the other workers are attempting to foster as to what constitutes a hard day's work. As an object of friendship he may be studiously ignored, but as a threat to the team's definition of the situation, he cannot be overlooked. Similarly, a girl at a party who is flagrantly accessible may be shunned by the other girls who are present, but in certain matters she is part of their team and cannot fail to threaten the definition they are collectively maintaining that girls are difficult sexual prizes. Thus while teammates are often persons who agree informally to guide their efforts in a certain way as a means of self-protection and by doing so constitute an informal group, this in-

formal agreement is not a criterion for defining the concept of team.

The members of an informal clique, using this term in the sense of a small number of persons who join together for informal amusements, may also constitute a team, for it is likely that they will have to co-operate in tactfully concealing their exclusiveness from some non-members while advertising it snobbishly to others. There is, however, a meaningful contrast between the concepts team and clique. In large social establishments, individuals within a given status level are thrown together by virtue of the fact that they must co-operate in maintaining a definition of the situation toward those above and below them. Thus a set of individuals who might be dissimilar in important respects, and hence desirous of maintaining social distance from one another, find they are in a relation of enforced familiarity characteristic of teammates engaged in staging a show. Often it seems that small cliques form not to further the interests of those with whom the individual stages a show but rather to protect him from an unwanted identification with them. Cliques, then, often function to protect the individual not from persons of other ranks but from persons of his own rank. Thus, while all the members of one's clique may be of the same status level, it may be crucial that not all persons of one's status level be allowed into the clique.[8]

A final comment must be added on what a team is not. Individuals may be bound together formally or informally into an action group in order to further like or collective ends by any means available to them. In so far as they co-operate in maintaining a given impression, using this device as a means of achieving their ends, they constitute what has here been called a team. But it should be made quite clear that there are many means by which an action group can achieve ends other than by dramaturgical cooperation. Other means to ends, such as force or bargaining power, may be increased or decreased by strategic manipulation of impressions, but the exercise of force or bargaining power gives to a set of individuals a source of group formation unconnected with the fact that on certain occasions the group thus formed is likely to act, dramaturgically speaking, as a team. (Similarly, an individual who is in a position of power or leadership may increase or decrease his strength by the degree to which his appearance and manner are appropriate and convincing, but it is not claimed that the dramaturgical qualities of his action necessarily or even commonly constitute the fundamental basis of his position.)

If we are to employ the concept of team as a fundamental point of reference, it will be convenient to retrace earlier steps and redefine our framework of terms in order to adjust for the use of team, rather than individual performer, as the basic unit.

It has been suggested that the object of a performer is to sustain a particular definition of the situation, this representing, as it were, his claim as to what reality is. As a one-man team, with no teammates to inform of his decision, he can quickly decide which of the available stands on a matter to take and then wholeheartedly act as if his choice were the only one he could possibly have taken. And his choice of position may be nicely adjusted to his own particular situation and interests.

When we turn from a one-man team to a larger one, the character of the reality that is espoused by the team changes. Instead of a rich definition of the situation, reality may become reduced to a thin party line, for one may expect the line to be unequally congenial to the members of the team. We may expect ironic remarks by which a teammate jokingly rejects the line while seriously accepting it. On the other hand, there will be the new factor of loyalty to one's team and one's teammates to provide support for the team's line.

It seems to be generally felt that public disagreement among the members of the team not only incapacitates them for united action but also embarrasses the reality sponsored by the team. To protect this impression of reality, members of the team may be required to postpone taking public stands until the position of the team has been settled; and once the team's stand has been taken, all members may be obliged to follow it. (The question of the amount of "Soviet self-criticism" that is allowed, and from whom it is allowed, before the team's position is announced, is not here at issue.) An illustration may be taken from the civil service:

> At such committees [Cabinet Committee meetings] civil servants share in the discussions and express their views freely, subject to one qualification: they will not directly oppose their own Minister. The possibility of such open disagreement very rarely arises, and ought never to arise: in nine cases out of ten, the Minister and the civil servant who attends the committee with him have agreed beforehand what line is to be taken, and in the tenth the civil servant who disagrees with his Minister's view on a particular point will stay away from the meeting where it is to be discussed.[9]

Another illustration may be cited from a recent study of the power structure of a small city:

> If one has been engaged in community work on any scale at all, he is impressed over and over with what might be termed the "principle of unanimity." When policy is finally formulated by the leaders in the community, there is an immediate demand on their part for strict conformity of opinion. Decisions are not usually arrived at hurriedly. There is ample time, particularly among the top leaders, for discussion of most projects before a state of action is set. This is true for community projects. When the time for discussion is past and the line is set, then unanimity is called for. Pressures are put upon dissenters, and the project is under way.[10]

Open disagreement in front of the audience creates, as we say, a false note. It may be suggested that literal false notes are avoided for quite the same reasons that figurative false notes are avoided; in both cases it is a matter of sustaining a definition of the situation. This may be illustrated from a brief book on the work problems of the professional concert-artist accompanist:

> The nearest that the singer and pianist can get to an ideal performance is to do exactly what the composer wants, yet sometimes the singer will require his partner to do something which is in flat contradiction to the composer's markings. He will want an accent where there should be none, he will make a *firmata* where it is not needed, he will make a *rallentando* when it should be *a tempo:* he will be *forte* when he should be *piano:* he may sentimentalize when the mood should be *nobilmente.*
>
> The list is by no means exhausted. The singer will swear with his hand on his heart and tears in his eyes that he does and always aims to do exactly what the composer has written. It is very awkward. If he sings it one way and the pianist plays it another way the re-

sult is chaotic. Discussion may be of no avail. But what is an accompanist to do?

At the performance he must *be with the singer,* but afterwards let him erase the memory of it from his mind . . .[11]

However, unanimity is often not the sole requirement of the team's projection. There seems to be a general feeling that the most real and solid things in life are ones whose description individuals independently agree upon. We tend to feel that if two participants in an event decide to be as honest as they can in recounting it, then the stands they take will be acceptably similar even though they do not consult one another prior to their presentation. Intention to tell the truth presumably makes such prior consultation unnecessary. And we also tend to feel that if the two individuals wish to tell a lie or to slant the version of the event which they offer, then not only will it be necessary for them to consult with one another in order, as we say, "to get their story straight," but it will also be necessary to conceal the fact that an opportunity for such prior consultation was available to them. In other words, in staging a definition of the situation, it may be necessary for the several members of the team to be unanimous in the positions they take and secretive about the fact that these positions were not independently arrived at. (Incidentally, if the members of the team are also engaged in maintaining a show of self-respect before one another, it may be necessary for the members of the team to learn what the line is to be, and take it, without admitting to themselves and to one another the extent to which their position is not independently arrived at, but such problems carry us somewhat beyond the team-performance as the basic point of reference.)

It should be noted that just as a teammate ought to wait for the official word before taking his stand, so the official word ought to be made available to him so that he can play his part on the team and feel a part of it. For example, in commenting on how some Chinese merchants set the price of their goods according to the appearance of the customer, one writer goes on to say:

One particular result of this study of a customer is seen in the fact that if a person enters a store in China, and, after examining several articles, asks the price of any one of them, unless it is positively

known that he has spoken to but one clerk, no answer will be made by him to whom the question is put until every other clerk has been asked if he has named a price for the article in question to the gentleman. If, as very rarely happens, this important precaution is neglected, the sum named by different clerks will almost invariably be unlike, thus showing that they fail to agree in their estimates of the customer.[12]

To withhold from a teammate information about the stand his team is taking is in fact to withhold his character from him, for without knowing what stand he will be taking he may not be able to assert a self to the audience. Thus, if a surgeon is to operate on a patient referred to him by another doctor, common courtesy may oblige the surgeon to tell the referring doctor when the operation will be and, if the referring doctor does not appear at the operation, to telephone him the result of the operation. By thus being "filled in," the referring doctor can, more effectively than otherwise, present himself to the patient's kinfolk as someone who is participating in the medical action.[13]

I would like to add a further general fact about maintaining the line during a performance. When a member of the team makes a mistake in the presence of the audience, the other team members often must suppress their immediate desire to punish and instruct the offender until, that is, the audience is no longer present. After all, immediate corrective sanctioning would often only disturb the interaction further and, as previously suggested, make the audience privy to a view that ought to be reserved for teammates. Thus, in authoritarian organizations, where a team of superordinates maintains a show of being right every time and of possessing a united front, there is often a strict rule that one superordinate must not show hostility or disrespect toward any other superordinate while in the presence of a member of the subordinate team. Army officers show consensus when before enlisted men, parents when before children,[14] managers when before workers, nurses when before patients,[15] and the like. Of course, when the subordinates are absent, open, violent criticism may and does occur. For example, in a recent study of the teaching profession, it was found that teachers felt that if they are to sustain an impression of professional competence and institutional authority, they must make sure that when angry parents come to the school with complaints, the principal will support the position of his staff, at least until the parents have left.[16] Similarly, teachers feel strongly that their fellow teachers ought not to disagree with or contradict them in front of students. "Just let another teacher raise her eyebrow funny, just so they [the children] know, and they don't miss a thing, and their respect for you goes right away."[17] Similarly, we learn that the medical profession has a strict code of etiquette whereby a consultant in the presence of the patient and his doctor is careful never to say anything which would embarrass the impression of competence that the patient's doctor is attempting to maintain. As Hughes suggests, "The [professional] *etiquette* is a body of ritual which grows up informally to preserve, before the clients, the common front of the profession."[18] And, of course, this kind of solidarity in the presence of subordinates also occurs when performers are in the presence of superordinates. For example, in a recent study of the police we learn that a patrolling team of two policemen, who witness each other's illegal and semi-illegal acts and who are in an excellent position to discredit each other's show of legality before the judge, possess heroic solidarity and will stick by each other's story no matter what atrocity it covers up or how little chance there is of anyone believing it.[19]

It is apparent that if performers are concerned with maintaining a line they will select as teammates those who can be trusted to perform properly. Thus children of the house are often excluded from performances given for guests of a domestic establishment because often children cannot be trusted to "behave" themselves, i.e., to refrain from acting in a way inconsistent with the impression that is being fostered.[20] Similarly, those who are known to become intoxicated when drink is available and who become verbose or "difficult" when this occurs constitute a performance risk, as do those who are sober but foolishly indiscreet, and those who refuse to "enter into the spirit" of the occasion and help sustain the impression that guests tacitly unite in maintaining to the host.

I have suggested that in many interaction settings some of the participants co-operate together as a team or are in a position where they are dependent upon this co-operation in order to maintain a particular definition of the situation. Now when we study concrete social establishments we often find that there will be a significant sense in which all the remaining participants, in their several performances of response to the team-show put on before them, will themselves constitute a team. Since each team will be playing through its routine for the other, one may speak of dramatic interaction, not dramatic action, and we can see this interaction not as a medley of as many voices as there are participants but rather as a kind of dialogue and interplay between two teams. I do not know of any general reason why interaction in natural settings usually takes the form of two-team interplay, or is resolvable into this form, instead of involving a larger number, but empirically this seems to be the case. Thus, in large social establishments, where several different status grades prevail, we find that for the duration of any particular interaction, participants of many different statuses are typically expected to align themselves temporarily into two team groupings. For example, a lieutenant at an Army post will find himself aligned with all the officers and opposed to all enlisted men in one situation; at other times he will find himself aligned with junior officers, presenting with them a show for the benefit of senior officers present. There are, of course, aspects of certain interactions for which a two-team model is apparently not suitable. Important elements, for example, of arbitration hearings seem to fit a three-team model, and aspects of some competitive and "social" situations suggest a multi-team model. It should also be made clear that whatever the number of teams, there will be a sense in which the interaction can be analyzed in terms of the co-operative effort of all participants to maintain a working consensus.

If we treat an interaction as a dialogue between two teams, it will sometimes be convenient to call one team the performers and to call the other team the audience or the observers, neglecting momentarily that the audience, too, will be presenting a team-performance. In some cases, as when two one-person teams interact in a public institution or in the home of a mutual friend, it may be an arbitrary choice as to which team to call the performer and which to call the audience. In many important social situations, however, the social setting in which the interaction occurs is assembled and managed by one of the teams only, and contributes in a more intimate way to the show this team puts on than to the show put on in response by the other team. A customer in a shop, a client in an office, a group of guests in the home of their hosts—these persons put on a performance and maintain a front, but the setting in which they do this is outside of their immediate control, being an integral part of the presentation made by those into whose presence they have come. In such cases, it will often be convenient to call the team which controls the setting the performing team, and to call the other team the audience. So, too, it will sometimes be convenient to label as performer the team which contributes the more activity to the interaction, or plays the more dramatically prominent part in it, or sets the pace and direction which both teams will follow in their interactive dialogue.

The obvious point must be stated that if the team is to sustain the impression that it is fostering, then there must be some assurance that no individual will be allowed to join both team and audience. Thus, for example, if the proprietor of a small ladies' ready-to-wear is to put a dress on sale and tell his customer that it is marked down because of soilage, or end of the season, or last of a line, etc., and conceal from her that it is really marked down because it won't sell, or is a bad color or style, and if he is to impress her by talking about a buying office in New York which he does not have or an adjustment manager who is really a salesgirl, then he must make sure that if he finds it necessary to hire an extra girl for part-time work on Saturday he does not hire one from the neighborhood who has been a customer and who will soon be one again.[21]

It is often felt that control of the setting is an advantage during interaction. In a narrow sense, this control allows a team to introduce strategic devices for determining the information the audience is able to acquire. Thus, if doctors are to prevent cancer patients from learning the identity of their disease, it will be useful to be able to scatter the cancer patients throughout the hospital so that they will not be able to learn from the identity of their ward the identity of their disorder. (The hospital staff, incidentally, may be forced to spend more time walking corridors and moving equipment because of this staging strategy than would

otherwise be necessary.) Similarly, the master barber who regulates the flow of appointments by means of a scheduling book open to his public is in a position to protect his coffee break by filling a properly timed appointment with a dummy code name. A prospective customer can then see for himself that it will not be possible for him to have an appointment at that time. Another interesting use of setting and props is reported in an article on American sororities, where a description is given of how the sorority sisters, who give a tea for prospective members, are able to sort out good prospects from bad without giving the impression that guests of the house are being treated differentially:

> "Even with recommends, it's hard to remember 967 girls by just meeting them for a few minutes in a receiving line," admitted Carol. "So we've worked out this gimmick to separate the good ones from the dull characters. We have three trays for the rushees' calling cards—one for golden girls, one for look-agains, one for pots.
>
> "The active who is talking with the rushee at the party is supposed to escort her subtly to the appropriate tray when she's ready to leave her card," Carol continued. "The rushees never figure out what we're doing!"[22]

Another illustration may be cited from the arts of hotel management. If any member of a hotel staff is suspicious of the intentions or character of a guest couple, a secret signal can be given to the bellboy to "throw the latch."

> This is simply a device which makes it easier for employees to keep an eye on suspected parties.
>
> After rooming the couple, the bellman, in closing the door behind him, pushes a tiny button on the inside of the knob handle. This turns a little tumbler inside the lock and makes a black stripe show against the circular center of the latch on the outside. It's inconspicuous enough so as not to be noticed by the guest, but maids, patrols, waiters and bellmen are all trained to watch for them . . . and to report any loud conversations or unusual occurrences which take place behind them.[23]

More broadly, control of the setting may give the controlling team a sense of security. As one student suggests concerning the pharmacist-doctor relation:

The store is another factor. The doctor often comes to the pharmacist's store for medicine, for bits of information, for conversation. In these conversations the man behind the counter has approximately the same advantage that a standing speaker has over a sitting audience.[24]

One thing that contributes to this feeling of the independence of the pharmacist's medical practice is his store. The store is, in a sense, a part of the pharmacist. Just as Neptune is pictured as rising from the sea, while at the same time being the sea; so in the pharmaceutical ethos there is a vision of a dignified pharmacist towering above shelves and counters of bottles and equipment, while at the same time being part of their essence.[25]

A nice literary illustration of the effects of being robbed of control over one's setting is given by Franz Kafka, in *The Trial*, where K.'s meeting with the authorities in his own boardinghouse is described:

> When he was fully dressed he had to walk, with Willem treading on his heels, through the next room, which was now empty, into the adjoining one, whose double doors were flung open. This room, as K. knew quite well, had recently been taken by a Fraulein Bürstner, a typist, who went very early to work, came home late, and with whom he had exchanged little more than few words in passing. Now the night-table beside her bed had been pushed into the middle of the floor to serve as desk, and the inspector was sitting behind it. He had crossed his legs, and one arm was resting on the back of the chair.
>
> ... "Joseph K.?" asked the inspector, perhaps merely to draw K.'s distracted glance upon himself. K. nodded. "You are presumably very surprised at the events of this morning?" asked the inspector, with both hands rearranging the few things that lay on the night-table, a candle and a matchbox, a book and a pincushion, as if they were objects which he required for his interrogation. "Certainly," said K., and he was filled with pleasure at having encountered a sensible man at last, with whom he could discuss the matter. "Certainly, I am surprised, but I am by no means very surprised." "Not very surprised?" asked the inspector, setting the candle in the middle of the table and then grouping the other things around it. "Perhaps you misunderstand me," K. hastened to add. "I mean"—here K. stopped and looked round him for a chair. "I suppose I may sit down?" he asked. "It's not usual," answered the inspector.[26]

A price must, of course, be paid for the privilege of giving a performance on one's home ground; one has the opportunity of conveying information about oneself through scenic means but no opportunity of concealing the kinds of facts that are conveyed by scenery. It is to be expected then that a potential performer may have to avoid his own stage and its controls in order to prevent an unflattering performance, and that this can involve more than the postponement of a social party because the new furniture has not yet arrived. Thus, of a slum area in London we learn that:

> ... mothers in this area, more than mothers elsewhere, prefer their children to be born in hospital. The main reason for this preference seems to be the expense of an at-home birth since proper equipment must be bought, towels for instance, and bathing basins, so that everything measures up to the standards required by the midwife. It also means the presence in the home of a strange woman, which in turn means a special cleaning out.[27]

When one examines a team-performance, one often finds that someone is given the right to direct and control the progress of the dramatic action. The equerry in court establishments is an example. Sometimes the individual who dominates the show in this way and is, in a sense, the director of it, plays an actual part in the performance he directs. This is illustrated for us by a novelist's view of the ministerial functions at a wedding ceremony:

> The minister left the door ajar, so that they [Robert, the groom, and Lionel, the best-man] might hear their cue and enter without delay. They stood at the door like eavesdroppers. Lionel touched his pocket, felt the round outline of the ring, then put his hand on Robert's elbow. As the cue word approached, Lionel opened the door and, on cue, propelled Robert forward.
>
> The ceremony moved without a hitch under the firm and experienced hand of the minister, who came down hard on the cues and used his eyebrows to menace the performers. The guests did not notice that Robert had a hard time getting the ring on the bride's finger; they did, however, notice that the bride's father cried overmuch and the mother not at all. But these were small things soon forgotten.[28]

In general, the members of the team will differ in the

ways and the degree to which they are allowed to direct the performance. It may be noted, incidentally, that the structural similarities of apparently diverse routines are nicely reflected in the like-mindedness that arises in directors everywhere. Whether it is a funeral, a wedding, a bridge party, a one-day sale, a hanging, or a picnic, the director may tend to see the performance in terms of whether or not it went "smoothly," "effectively," and "without a hitch," and whether or not all possible disruptive contingencies were prepared for in advance.

In many performances two important functions must be fulfilled, and if the team has a director he will often be given the special duty of fulfilling these functions.

First, the director may be given the special duty of bringing back into line any member of the team whose performance becomes unsuitable. Soothing and sanctioning are the corrective processes ordinarily involved. The role of the baseball umpire in sustaining a particular kind of reality for the fans may be taken as an illustration.

> All umpires insist that players keep themselves under control, and refrain from gestures that reflect contempt for their decisions.[29]
>
> I certainly had blown off my share of steam as a player, and I knew there had to be a safety valve for release of the terrific tension. As an umpire I could sympathize with the players. But as an umpire I had to decide how far I could let a player go without delaying the game and without permitting him to insult, assault, or ridicule me and belittle the game. Handling trouble and men on the field was as important as calling them right—and more difficult.
>
> It is easy for any umpire to thumb a man out of the game. It is often a much more difficult job to keep him in the game—to understand and anticipate his complaint so that a nasty rhubarb cannot develop.[30]
>
> I do not tolerate clowning on the field, and neither will any other umpire. Comedians belong on the stage or on television, not in baseball. A travesty or burlesque of the game can only cheapen it, and also hold the umpire up to scorn for allowing such a sketch to take place. That's why you will see the funnymen and wise guys chased as soon as they begin their routine.[31]

Often, of course, the director will not so much have to

smother improper affect as he will have to stimulate a show of proper affective involvement; "sparking the show" is the phrase sometimes employed for this task in Rotarian circles.

Secondly, the director may be given the special duty of allocating the parts in the performance and the personal front that is employed in each part, for each establishment may be seen as a place with a number of characters to dispose of to prospective performers and as an assemblage of sign-equipment or ceremonial paraphernalia to be allocated.

It is apparent that if the director corrects for improper appearances and allocates major and minor prerogatives, then other members of the team (who are likely to be concerned with the show they can put on for one another as well as with the show they can collectively stage for the audience) will have an attitude toward the director that they do not have toward their other teammates. Further, if the audience appreciates that the performance has a director, they are likely to hold him more responsible than other performers for the success of the performance. The director is likely to respond to this responsibility by making dramaturgical demands on the performance that they might not make upon themselves. This may add to the estrangement they may already feel from him. A director, hence, starting as a member of the team, may find himself slowly edged into a marginal role between audience and performers, half in and half out of both camps, a kind of go-between without the protection that go-betweens usually have. The factory foreman has been a recently discussed example.[32]

When we study a routine which requires a team of several performers for its presentation, we sometimes find that one member of the team is made the star, lead, or center of attention. We may see an extreme example of this in traditional court life, where a room full of court attendants will be arranged in the manner of a living tableau, so that the eye, starting from any point in the room will be led to the royal center of attention. The royal star of the performance may also be dressed more spectacularly and seated higher than anyone else present. An even more spectacular centering of attention may be found in the dance arrangements of large musical comedies, in which forty or fifty dancers are made to prostrate themselves around the heroine.

The extravagance of the performances found at royal appearances should not blind us to the utility of the concept of a court: courts in fact are commonly found outside of palaces, one instance being the commissaries of Hollywood production studios. While it seems abstractly true that individuals are convivially endogamous, tending to restrict informal ties to those of their own social status, still, when a social class is examined closely, one may find it to be made up of separated social sets, each set containing one and only one complement of differently placed performers. And frequently the set will form around one dominant figure who is constantly maintained as the center of attention in the center of the stage. Evelyn Waugh suggests this theme in a discussion of the British upper class:

> Look back twenty-five years to the time when there was still a fairly firm aristocratic structure and the country was still divided into spheres of influence among hereditary magnates. My memory is that the grandees avoided one another unless they were closely related. They met on state occasions and on the racecourse. They did not frequent one another's houses. You might find almost anyone in a ducal castle—convalescent, penurious cousins, advisory experts, sycophants, gigolos and plain blackmailers. The one thing you could be sure of not finding was a concourse of other dukes. English society, it seemed to me, was a complex of tribes, each with its chief and elders and witch-doctors and braves, each with its own dialect and deity, each strongly xenophobic.[33]

The informal social life conducted by the staffs of our universities and other intellectual bureaucracies seems to break up in something of the same way: the cliques and factions which form the smaller parties of administrative politics form the courts of convivial life, and it is here that local heroes can safely sustain the eminence of their wit, their competence and their profundity.

In general, then, one finds that those who help present a team-performance differ in the degree of dramatic dominance given each of them and that one team-routine differs from another in the extent to which differentials in dominance are given its members.

The conceptions of dramatic and directive dominance, as contrasting types of power in a performance, can be applied, *mutatis mutandis,* to an interaction as a whole, where it will be possible to point out which of the two teams has more of which of the two types of power and which performers, taking the participants of both teams all together, lead in these two regards.

Frequently, of course, the performer or team which has one kind of dominance will have the other, but this is by no means always the case. For example, during the showing of the body at a funeral home, usually the social setting and all participants, including both the bereaved team and the establishment's team, will be arranged so as to express their feelings for the deceased and their ties to him; he will be the center of the show and the dramatically dominant participant in it. However, since the bereaved are inexperienced and grief-laden, and since the star of the show must stay in character as someone who is in a deep sleep, the undertaker himself will direct the show, although he may all the while be self-effacing in the presence of the corpse or be in another room of the establishment getting ready for another showing.

It should be made clear that dramatic and directive dominance are dramaturgical terms and that performers who enjoy such dominance may not have other types of power and authority. It is common knowledge that performers who have positions of visible leadership are often merely figureheads, selected as a compromise, or as a way of neutralizing a potentially threatening position, or as a way of strategically concealing the power behind the front and hence the power behind the power behind the front. So also, whenever inexperienced or temporary incumbents are given formal authority over experienced subordinates, we often find that the formally empowered person is bribed with a part that has dramatic dominance while the subordinates tend to direct the show.[34] Thus it has often been said about the British infantry in World War I that experienced working-class sergeants managed the delicate task of covertly teaching their new lieutenants to take a dramatically expressive role at the head of the platoon and to die quickly in a prominent dramatic position, as befits public-school men. The sergeants themselves took their modest place at the rear of the platoon and tended to live to train still other lieutenants.

Dramatic and directive dominance have been mentioned as two dimensions along which each place on a team can vary. By changing the point of reference a little, we can discern a third mode of variation.

In general, those who participate in the activity that occurs in a social establishment become members of a team when they co-operate together to present their activity in a particular light. However, in taking on the role of a performer, the individual need not cease to devote some of his effort to non-dramaturgical concerns, that is, to the activity itself of which the performance offers an acceptable dramatization. We may expect, then, that the individuals who perform on a particular team will differ among themselves in the way they apportion their time between mere activity and mere performance. At one extreme there will be individuals who rarely appear before the audience and are little concerned with appearances. At the other extreme are what are sometimes called "purely ceremonial roles," whose performers will be concerned with the appearance that they make, and concerned with little else. For example, both the president and the research director of a national union may spend time in the main office of the union headquarters, appearing suitably dressed and suitably spoken in order to give the union a front of respectability. However one may find that the president also engages in making many important decisions whereas the research director may have little to do except be present in body as part of the president's retinue. Union officials conceive of such purely ceremonial roles as part of "window dressing."[35] The same division of labor can be found in domestic establishments, where something more general than task-qualities must be exhibited. The familiar theme of conspicuous consumption describes how husbands in modern society have the job of acquiring socio-economic status, and wives the job of displaying this acquisition. During somewhat earlier times, the footman provided an even more clear instance of this specialization:

> But the chief value of the footman lay in one of these [domestic] services directly. It was the efficiency with which he advertised the extent of his master's wealth. All domestics served that end, since their presence in an establishment demonstrated their master's ability to pay and maintain them in return for little or no productive work. But all were not equally effective in this respect. Those whose uncommon

skills and specialized training commanded a high remuneration reflected more credit upon their employers than those who were paid at lower rates; those whose duties brought them obtrusively into view more effectively suggested their master's wealth than those whose work kept them constantly out of sight. Livery servants, from the coachman down to the footboy, were among the most effective of the lot. Their routines endowed them with the highest visibility. Moreover, the livery itself emphasized their remoteness from productive labor. Their effectiveness achieved its maximum in the footman, for his routine exposed him to view more consistently than did that of any of the others. He was, in consequence, one of the most vital parts of his master's display.[36]

It may be remarked that an individual with a purely ceremonial role need not have a dramatically dominant one.

A team, then, may be defined as a set of individuals whose intimate co-operation is required if a given projected definition of the situation is to be maintained. A team is a grouping, but it is a grouping not in relation to a social structure or social organization but rather in relation to an interaction or series of interactions in which the relevant definition of the situation is maintained.

We have seen, and will see further, that if a performance is to be effective it will be likely that the extent and character of the co-operation that makes this possible will be concealed and kept secret. A team, then, has something of the character of a secret society. The audience may appreciate, of course, that all the members of the team are held together by a bond no member of the audience shares. Thus, for example, when customers enter a service establishment, they clearly appreciate that all employees are different from customers by virtue of this official role. However, the individuals who are on the staff of an establishment are not members of a team by virtue of staff status, but only by virtue of the co-operation which they maintain in order to sustain a given definition of the situation. No effort may be made in many cases to conceal who is on the staff; but they form a secret society, a team, in so far as a secret is kept as to how they are co-operating together to maintain a particular definition of the situation. Teams may be created by individuals to aid the group they are members of, but in aiding themselves and their group in this dramaturgical way, they are acting as a team, not a group. Thus a team, as used herein, is the kind of secret society whose members may be known by non-members to constitute a society, even an exclusive one, but the society these individuals are known to constitute is not the one they constitute by virtue of acting as a team.

Since we all participate on teams we must all carry within ourselves something of the sweet guilt of conspirators. And since each team is engaged in maintaining the stability of some definitions of the situation, concealing or playing down certain facts in order to do this, we can expect the performer to live out his conspiratorial career in some furtiveness.

NOTES

1. Writer's unpublished study of a medical service.

2. Charles S. Johnson, *Patterns of Negro Segregation* (New York: Harper Bros., 1943), pp. 137–38.

3. *Esquire Etiquette* (Philadelphia: Lippincott, 1953), p. 6.

4. Ibid., p. 15.

5. The use of the team (as opposed to the performer) as the fundamental unit I take from John von Neumann and Oskar Morgenstern, *The Theory of Games and Economic Behavior* (2nd ed.; Princeton: Princeton University Press, 1947), especially p. 53, where bridge is analyzed as a game between two players, each of whom in some respects has two separate individuals to do the playing.

6. Individualistic modes of thought tend to treat processes such as self-deception and insincerity as characterological weaknesses generated within the deep recesses of the individual personality. It might be better to start from outside the individual and work inward than to start inside the individual and work out. We may say that the starting point for all that is to come later consists of the individual performer maintaining a definition of the situation before an audience. The individual automatically becomes insincere when he adheres to the obligation of maintaining a working consensus and participates in different routines or performs a given part before different audiences. Self-deception can be seen as something that results when two different roles, performer and audience, come to be compressed into the same individual.

7. See Karl Mannheim, *Essays on the Sociology of Culture* (London: Routledge & Kegan Paul, 1956), p. 209.

8. There are, of course, many bases of clique formation. Edward Gross, *Informal Relations and the Social Organization of Work in an Industrial Office* (unpublished Ph.D. dissertation, Department of Sociology, University of Chicago, 1949), suggests that cliques may cross ordinary age and ethnic lines in or-

der to bring together individuals whose work activity is not seen as a competitive reflection upon one another.

9. H. E. Dale, *The Higher Civil Services of Great Britain* (Oxford: Oxford University Press, 1941), p. 141.

10. Floyd Hunter, *Community Power Structure* (Chapel Hill: University of North Carolina Press, 1953), p. 181. See also p. 118 and p. 212.

11. Gerald Moore, *The Unashamed Accompanist* (New York: Macmillan, 1944), p. 60.

12. Chester Holcombe, *The Real Chinaman* (New York: Dodd, Mead, 1895), p. 293.

13. David Solomon, "Career Contingencies of Chicago Physicians" (unpublished Ph.D. dissertation, Department of Sociology, University of Chicago, 1952), p. 75.

14. An interesting dramaturgical difficulty in the family is that sex and lineal solidarity, which crosscut conjugal solidarity, make it difficult for husband and wife to "back each other up" in a show of authority before children or a show of either distance or familiarity with extended kin. As previously suggested, such crosscutting lines of affiliation prevent the widening of structural cleavages.

15. Harold Taxel, "Authority Structure in a Mental Hospital Ward" (unpublished MA., thesis, Department of Sociology, University of Chicago, 1953), pp. 53–54.

16. Howard S. Becker, "The Teacher in the Authority System of the Public School," *Journal of Educational Sociology,* XXVII, p. 134.

17. Ibid., from an interview, p. 139.

18. E. C. Hughes, "Institutions," *New Outline of the Principles of Sociology,* ed. Alfred M. Lee (New York: Barnes and Noble, 1946), p. 273.

19. William Westley, "The Police" (unpublished Ph.D. dissertation, Department of Sociology, University of Chicago, 1952), pp. 187–96.

20. In so far as children are defined as "non-persons" they have some license to commit gauche acts without requiring the audience to take the expressive implications of these acts too seriously. However, whether treated as non-persons or not, children are in a position to disclose crucial secrets.

21. These illustrations are taken from George Rosenbaum, "An Analysis of Personalization in Neighborhood Apparel Retailing" (unpublished M.A. thesis, Department of Sociology, University of Chicago, 1953), pp. 86–87.

22. Joan Beck, "What's Wrong with Sorority Rushing?" *Chicago Tribune Magazine,* January 10, 1954, pp. 20–21.

23. Dev Collans, with Stewart Sterling, *I Was a House Detective* (New York: Dutton, 1954), p. 56. Ellipsis dots the authors'.

24. Anthony Weinlein, "Pharmacy as a Profession in Wisconsin" (unpublished M.A. thesis, Department of Sociology, University of Chicago, 1943), p. 105.

25. Ibid., pp. 105–6.

26. Franz Kafka, *The Trial* (New York: Knopf, 1948), pp. 14–15.

27. B. M. Spinley, *The Deprived and the Privileged* (London: Routledge and Kegan Paul, 1953), p. 45.

28. Warren Miller, *The Sleep of Reason* (Boston: Little, Brown and Company, 1958), p. 254.

29. Babe Pinelli, as told to Joe King, *Mr. Ump* (Philadelphia: Westminster Press, 1953), p. 141.

30. Ibid., p. 131.

31. Ibid., p. 139.

32. See, for example, Donald E. Wray, "Marginal Men of Industry: The Foreman," *American Journal of Sociology,* LIV, pp. 298–301, and Fritz Roethlisberger, "The Foreman: Master and Victim of Double Talk," *Harvard Business Review,* XXIII, pp. 285–94. The role of go-between is considered later.

33. Evelyn Waugh, "An Open Letter," in Nancy Mitford, editor, *Noblesse Oblige* (London: Hamish Hamilton, 1956), p. 78.

34. See David Riesman, in collaboration with Reuel Denny and Nathan Glazer, *The Lonely Crowd* (New Haven: Yale University Press, 1950), "The Avocational Counselors," pp. 363–67.

35. See Harold L. Wilensky, "The Staff 'Expert': A Study of the Intelligence Function in American Trade Unions" (unpublished Ph.D. dissertation, Department of Sociology, University of Chicago, 1953), chap. iv. In addition to his thesis material, I am indebted to Mr. Wilensky for many suggestions.

36. J. J. Hecht, *The Domestic Servant Class in Eighteenth-Century England* (London: Routledge, Kegan Paul, 1956), pp. 53–54.

BEHAVIOR IN PRIVATE PLACES
Sustaining Definitions of Reality in Gynecological Examinations

10

Joan P. Emerson

INTRODUCTION

In *The Social Construction of Reality,* Berger and Luckmann discuss how people construct social order and yet construe the reality of everyday life to exist independently of themselves.[1] Berger and Luckmann's work succeeds in synthesizing some existing answers with new insights. Many sociologists have pointed to the importance of social consensus in what people believe; if everyone else seems to believe in something, a person tends to accept the common belief without question. Other sociologists have discussed the concept of legitimacy, an acknowledgment that what exists has the right to exist, and delineated various lines of argument which can be taken to justify a state of affairs. Berger and Luckmann emphasize three additional processes that provide persons with evidence that things have an objective existence apart from themselves. Perhaps most important is the experience that reality seems to be out there before we arrive on the

scene. This notion is fostered by the nature of language, which contains an all-inclusive scheme of categories, is shared by a community, and must be learned laboriously by each new member. Further, definitions of reality are continuously validated by apparently trivial features of the social scene, such as details of the setting, persons' appearance and demeanor, and "inconsequential" talk. Finally, each part of a systematic world view serves as evidence for all the other parts, so that reality is solidified by a process of intervalidation of supposedly independent events.

Because Berger and Luckmann's contribution is theoretical, their units of analysis are abstract processes. But they take those processes to be grounded in social encounters. Thus, Berger and Luckmann's theory provides a framework for making sense of social interaction. In this paper observations of a concrete situation will be interpreted to show how reality is embodied in routines and reaffirmed in social interaction.

Situations differ in how much effort it takes to sustain the current definition of the situation. Some situations are relatively stable; others are precarious.[2] Stability depends on the likelihood of three types of disconforming events. Intrusions on the scene may threaten definitions of reality, as when people smell smoke in a theater or when a third person joins a couple and calls one member by a name the second member does not recognize. Participants may deliberately decline to validate the current reality, like Quakers who refused to take off their hats to the king. Sometimes participants are unable to produce the gestures which would validate the current reality. Perhaps a person is ignorant of the relevant vocabulary of gestures. Or a person, understanding how he should behave, may have limited social skills so that he cannot carry off the performance he would like to. For those who insist on "sincerity," a performance becomes especially taxing if they lack conviction about the trueness of the reality they are attempting to project.

A reality can hardly seem self-evident if a person is simultaneously aware of a counter-reality. Berger and Luckmann write as though definitions of reality were internally congruent. However, the ordinary reality may contain not only a dominant definition, but in addition counterthemes opposing or qualifying the dominant definition. Thus, several contradictory definitions must be sustained at the same time. Because each element tends to challenge the other elements, such composite definitions of reality are inherently precarious even if the probability of disconfirming events is low.

A situation where the definition of reality is relatively precarious has advantages for the analysis proposed here, for processes of sustaining reality should be more obvious where that reality is problematic. The situation chosen, the gynecological examination,[3] is precarious for both reasons discussed above. First, it is an excellent example of multiple contradictory definitions of reality, as described in the next section. Second, while intrusive and deliberate threats are not important, there is a substantial threat from participants' incapacity to perform.

Dramaturgical abilities are taxed in gynecological examinations because the less convincing reality internalized by secondary socialization is unusually discrepant with rival perspectives taken for granted in primary socialization.[4] Gynecological examinations

share similar problems of reality-maintenance with any medical procedure, but the issues are more prominent because the site of the medical task is a woman's genitals. Because touching usually connotes personal intimacy, persons may have to work at accepting the physician's privileged access to the patient's genitals.[5] Participants are not entirely convinced that modesty is out of place. Since a woman's genitals are commonly accessible only in a sexual context, sexual connotations come readily to mind. Although most people realize that sexual responses are inappropriate, they may be unable to dismiss the sexual reaction privately and it may interfere with the conviction with which they undertake their impersonal performance. The structure of a gynecological examination highlights the very features which the participants are supposed to disattend. So the more attentive the participants are to the social situation, the more the unmentionable is forced on their attention.

The next section will characterize the complex composition of the definition of reality routinely sustained in gynecological examinations. Then some of the routine arrangements and interactional maneuvers which embody and express this definition will be described. A later section will discuss threats to the definition which arise in the course of the encounter. Measures that serve to neutralize the threats and reaffirm the definition will be analyzed. The concluding section will turn to the theoretical issues of precariousness, multiple contradictory definitions of reality, and implicit communication.

THE MEDICAL DEFINITION AND ITS COUNTERTHEMES

Sometimes people are in each other's presence in what they take to be a "gynecological examination." What happens in a gynecological examination is part of the common stock of knowledge. Most people know that a gynecological examination is when a doctor examines a woman's genitals in a medical setting. Women who have undergone this experience know that the examination takes place in a special examining room where the patient lies with her buttocks down to the edge of the table and her feet in stirrups, that usually a nurse is present as a chaperone, that the actual examining lasts only a few minutes, and so forth. Besides knowing what equipment to provide for the doctor, the nurse has in mind a typology of responses patients have to this situation, and a typology of doctors' styles of performance. The doctor has technical knowledge about the examining procedures, what observations may be taken to indicate ways of getting patients to relax, and so on.

Immersed in the medical world where the scene constitutes a routine, the staff assume the responsibility for a credible performance. The staff take part in gynecological examinations many times a day, while the patient is a fleeting visitor. More deeply convinced of the reality themselves, the staff are willing to convince skeptical patients. The physician guides the patient through the precarious scene in a contained manner: taking the initiative, controlling the encounter, keeping the patient in line, defining the situation by his reaction, and giving cues that "this is done" and "other people go through this all the time."

Not only must people continue to believe that "this is a gynecological examination," but also that "this is a gynecological examination going right." The major definition to be sustained for this purpose is "this is a medical situation" (not a party, sexual assault, psychological experiment, or anything else). If it is a medical situation, then it follows that "no one is embarrassed"[6] and "no one is thinking in sexual terms."[7] Anyone who indicates the contrary must be swayed by some nonmedical definition.

The medical definition calls for a matter-of-fact stance. One of the most striking observations about a gynecological examination is the marked implication underlying the staff's demeanor toward the patient: "Of course, you take this as matter-of-factly as we do." The staff implicitly contend: "In the medical world the pelvic area is like any other part of the body; its private and sexual connotations are left behind when you enter the hospital." The staff want it understood that their gazes take in only medically pertinent facts, so they are not concerned with an aesthetic inspection of a patient's body. Their nonchalant pose attempts to put a gynecological examination in the same light as an internal examination of the ear.

Another implication of the medical definition is that the patient is a technical object to the staff. It is as if the staff work on an assembly line for repairing bodies; similar body parts continually roll by and the staff have a particular job to do on them. The staff are concerned with the typical features of the body part and its pathology rather than with the unique features used to define a person's identity. The staff disattend the connection between a part of the body and some intangible self that is supposed to inhabit the body.

The scene is credible precisely because the staff act as if they have every right to do what they are doing. Any hint of doubt from the staff would compromise the medical definition. Since the patient's nonchalance merely serves to validate the staff's right, it may be dispensed with or without the same threat. Furthermore, the staff claim to be merely agents of the medical system, which is intent on providing good health care to patients. This medical system imposes procedures and standards which the staff are merely following in this particular instance. That is, what the staff do derives from external coercion—"We have to do it this way"—rather than from personal choices which they would be free to revise in order to accommodate the patient.

The medical definition grants the staff the right to carry out their task. If not for the medical definition the staff's routine activities could be defined as unconscionable assaults on the dignity of individuals. The topics of talk, particularly inquiries about bodily functioning, sexual experience, and death of relatives might be taken as offenses against propriety. As for exposure and manipulation of the patient's body, it would be a shocking and degrading invasion of privacy were the patient not defined as a technical object. The infliction of pain would be mere cruelty. The medical definition justifies the request that a presumably competent adult give up most of his autonomy to persons often subordinate in age, sex, and social class. The patient needs the medical definition to minimize the threat to his dignity; the staff need it in order to inveigle the patient into cooperating.

Yet definitions that appear to contradict the medical definition are routinely expressed in the course of gynecological examinations. Some gestures acknowledge the pelvic area as special; other gestures acknowledge the patient as a person. These counterdefinitions are as essential to the encounter as the medical definition. We have already discussed how an actor's lack of conviction may interfere with his performance. Implicit acknowledgments of the special meaning of the pelvic area help those players hampered by lack of conviction to perform adequately. If a player's sense of "how things really are" is implicitly acknowledged, he often finds it easier to adhere outwardly to a contrary definition.

A physician may gain a patient's cooperation by acknowledging her as a person. The physician wants the patient to acknowledge the medical definition, cooperate with the procedures of the examination, and acknowledge his professional competence. The physician is in a position to bargain with the patient in order to obtain this cooperation. He can offer her attention and acknowledgment as a person. At times he does so.

Although defining a person as a technical object is necessary in order for medical activities to proceed, it constitutes an indignity in itself. This indignity can be canceled or at least qualified by simultaneously acknowledging the patient as a person.

The medical world contains special activities and special perspectives. Yet the inhabitants of the medical world travel back and forth to the general community where modesty, death, and other medically relevant matters are regarded quite differently. It is not so easy to dismiss general community meanings for the time one finds oneself in a medical setting. The counterthemes that the pelvic area is special and that patients are persons provide an opportunity to show deference to general community meanings at the same time that one is disregarding them.

Sustaining the reality of a gynecological examination does not mean sustaining the medical definition, then. What is to be sustained is a shifting balance between medical definition and counterthemes.[8] Too much emphasis on the medical definition alone would undermine the reality, as would a flamboyant manifestation of the counter-themes apart from the medical definition. The next three sections will suggest how this balance is achieved.

SUSTAINING THE REALITY

The appropriate balance between medical definition and counterthemes has to be created anew at every

moment. However, some routinized procedures and demeanor are available to participants in gynecological examinations. Persons recognize that if certain limits are exceeded, the situation would be irremediably shattered. Some arrangements have been found useful because they simultaneously express medical definition and countertheme. Routine ways of meeting the task requirements and also dealing with "normal trouble" are available. This section will describe how themes and counterthemes are embodied in routinized procedures and demeanor.

The pervasiveness of the medical definition is expressed by indicators that the scene is enacted under medical auspices.[9] The action is located in "medical space" (hospital or doctor's office). Features of the setting such as divisions of space, decor, and equipment are constant reminders that it is indeed "medical space." Even background details such as the loudspeaker calling, "Dr. Morris. Dr. Armand Morris" serve as evidence for medical reality (suppose the loudspeaker were to announce instead, "Five minutes until post time"). The staff wear medical uniforms, don medical gloves, use medical instruments. The exclusion of lay persons, particularly visitors of the patient who may be accustomed to the patient's nudity at home, helps to preclude confusion between the contact of medicine and the contact of intimacy.[10]

Some routine practices simultaneously acknowledge the medical definition and qualify it by making special provision for the pelvic area. For instance, rituals of respect express dignity for the patient. The patient's body is draped so as to expose only that part which is to receive the technical attention of the doctor. The presence of a nurse acting as "chaperone" cancels any residual suggestiveness of male and female alone in a room.[11]

Medical talk stands for and continually expresses allegiance to the medical definition. Yet certain features of medical talk acknowledge a nonmedical delicacy. Despite the fact that persons present on a gynecological ward must attend to many topics connected with the pelvic area and various bodily functions, these topics are generally not discussed. Strict conventions dictate what unmentionables are to be acknowledged under what circumstances. However, persons are exceptionally free to refer to the genitals and related matters on the obstetrics-gynecology service. If technical matters in regard to the pelvic area come up, they are to be discussed nonchalantly.

The special language found in staff-patient contacts contributes to depersonalization and desexualization of the encounter. Scientific-sounding medical terms facilitate such communication. Substituting dictionary terms for everyday words adds formality. The definite article replaces the pronoun adjective in reference to body parts, so that for example, the doctor refers to "the vagina" and never "your vagina." Instructions to the patient in the course of the examination are couched in language which bypasses sexual imagery; the vulgar connotation of "spread your legs" is generally metamorphosed into the innocuous "let your knees fall apart."

While among themselves the staff generally use explicit technical terms, explicit terminology is often avoided in staff-patient contacts.[12] The reference to the pelvic area may be merely understood, as when a patient says: "I feel so uncomfortable there right now" or "They didn't go near to this area, so why did they have to shave it?" In speaking with patients the staff frequently uses euphemisms. A doctor asks: "When did you first notice difficulty down below?" and a nurse inquires: "Did you wash between your legs?" Persons characteristically refer to pelvic examinations euphemistically in staff-patient encounters. "The doctors want to take a peek at you," a nurse tells a patient. Or "Dr. Ryan wants to see you in the examining room."

In one pelvic examination there was a striking contrast between the language of staff and patient. The patient was graphic; she used action words connoting physical contact to refer to the examination procedure: feeling, poking, touching, and punching. Yet she never located this action in regard to her body, always omitting to state where the physical contact occurred. The staff used impersonal medical language and euphemisms: "I'm going to examine you"; "I'm just cleaning out some blood clots"; "He's just trying to fix you up a bit."

Sometimes the staff introduce explicit terminology to clarify a patient's remark. A patient tells the doctor, "It's bleeding now" and the doctor answers, "You? From the vagina?" Such a response indicates the ap-

propriate vocabulary, the degree of freedom permitted in technically oriented conversation, and the proper detachment. Yet the common avoidance of explicit terminology in staff-patient contacts suggests that despite all the precautions to assure that the medical definition prevails, many patients remain somewhat embarrassed by the whole subject. To avoid provoking this embarrassment, euphemisms and understood references are used when possible.

Highly specific requirements for everybody's behavior during a gynecological examination curtail the leeway for the introduction of discordant notes. Routine technical procedures organize the event from beginning to end, indicating what action each person should take at each moment. Verbal exchanges are also constrained by the technical task, in that the doctor uses routine phrases of direction and reassurance to the patient. There is little margin for ad-libbing during a gynecological examination.

The specifications for demeanor are elaborate. Foremost is that both staff and patient should be nonchalant about what is happening. According to the staff, the exemplary patient should be "in play": showing she is attentive to the situation by her bodily tautness, facial expression, direction of glance, tone of voice, tempo of speech and bodily movements, timing and appropriateness of responses. The patient's voice should be controlled, mildly pleasant, self-confident, and impersonal. Her facial expression should be attentive and neutral, leaning toward the mildly pleasant and friendly side, as if she were talking to the doctor in his office, fully dressed and seated in a chair. The patient is to have an attentive glance upward, at the ceiling or at other persons in the room, eyes open, not dreamy or "away," but ready at a second's notice to revert to the doctor's face for a specific verbal exchange. Except for such a verbal exchange, however, the patient is supposed to avoid looking into the doctor's eyes during the actual examination because direct eye contact between the two at this time is provocative. Her role calls for passivity and self-effacement. The patient should show willingness to relinquish control to the doctor. She should refrain from speaking at length and from making inquiries which would require the doctor to reply at length. So as not to point up her undignified position, she should not project her personality profusely. The self must be eclipsed in or-der to sustain the definition that the doctor is working on a technical object and not a person.

The physician's demeanor is highly stylized. He intersperses his examination with remarks to the patient in a soothing tone of voice: "Now relax as much as you can"; "I'll be as gentle as I can"; "Is that tender right there?" Most of the phrases with which he encourages the patient to relax are routine even though his delivery may suggest a unique relationship. He demonstrates that he is the detached professional and the patient demonstrates that it never enters her mind that he could be anything except detached. Since intimacy can be introduced into instrumental phys-ical contact by a "loving" demeanor (lingering, ca-ressing motions and contact beyond what the task re-quires), a doctor must take special pains to ensure that his demeanor remains a brisk, no-nonsense show of efficiency.[13]

Once I witnessed a gynecological examination of a forty-year-old woman who played the charming and scatterbrained Southern belle. The attending physician stood near the patient's head and carried on a flippant conversation with her while a resident and medical student actually performed the examination. The pa-tient completely ignored the examination, except for brief answers to the examining doctor's inquiries. Un-der these somewhat trying circumstances she attempt-ed to carry off a gay, attractive pose and the attending physician cooperated with her by making a series of bantering remarks.

Most physicians are not so lucky as to have a col-league conversing in cocktail-hour style with the pa-tient while they are probing her vagina. Ordinarily the physician must play both parts at once, treating the pa-tient as an object with his hands while simultaneously acknowledging her as a person with his voice. In this incident, where two physicians simultaneously deal with the patient in two distinct ways, the dual ap-proach to the patient usually maintained by the exam-ining physician becomes more obvious.[14]

The doctor needs to communicate with the patient as a person for technical reasons. Should he want to know when the patient feels pain in the course of ex-amination or information about other medical matters, he must address her as a person. Also the doctor may want to instruct the patient on how to facilitate the ex-amination. The most reiterated instruction refers to re-laxation. Most patients are not sufficiently relaxed when the doctor is ready to begin. He then reverts to a primitive level of communication and treats the pa-tient almost like a young child. He speaks in a soft, soothing voice, probably calling the patient by her first name, and it is not so much the words as his man-ner which is significant. This caressing voice is rou-tinely used by hospital staff members to patients in critical situations, as when the patient is overtly fright-ened or disoriented. By using it here the doctor height-ens his interpersonal relation with the patient, trying to reassure her as a person in order to get her to relax.

Moreover even during a gynecological examina-tion, failing to acknowledge another as a person is an insult. It is insulting to be entirely instrumental about instrumental contacts. Some acknowledgment of the intimate connotations of touching must occur. There-fore, a measure of "loving" demeanor is subtly inject-ed. A doctor cannot employ the full gamut of loving insinuations that a lover might infuse into instrumen-tal touching. So he indirectly implies a hint of intima-cy which is intended to counter the insult and make the procedure acceptable to the woman. The doctor conveys this loving demeanor not by lingering or su-perfluous contact, but by radiating concern in his gen-eral manner, offering extra assistance, and occasional-ly by sacrificing the task requirements to "gentleness."

In short, the doctor must convey an optimal com-bination of impersonality and hints of intimacy that si-multaneously avoid the insult of sexual familiarity and the insult of unacknowledged identity. The doctor must manage this even though the behavior emanating from each definition is contradictory. If the doctor can achieve this feat, it will contribute to keeping the pa-tient in line. In the next section, we will see how the patient may threaten this precarious balance.

PRECARIOUSNESS IN GYNECOLOGICAL EXAMINATIONS

Threats to the reality of a gynecological examination may occur if the balance of opposing definitions is not maintained as described above. Reality in gynecologi-cal examinations is challenged mainly by patients.

Occasionally a medical student, who might be considerably more of a novice than an experienced patient, seemed uncomfortable in the scene.[15] Experienced staff members were rarely observed to undermine the reality.

Certain threatening events which could occur in any staff-patient encounter bring an added dimension of precariousness to a gynecological examination because the medical aegis screens so much more audacity at that time. In general, staff expect patients to remain poised and in play like a friendly office receptionist; any show of emotion except in a controlled fashion is objectionable. Patients should not focus on identities of themselves or the staff outside those relevant to the medical exchange. Intractable patients may complain about the pain, discomfort, and indignities of submitting to medical treatment and care. Patients may go so far as to show they are reluctant to comply with the staff. Even if they are complying, they may indirectly challenge the expert status of the staff, as by "asking too many questions."

Failure to maintain a poised performance is a possible threat in any social situation. Subtle failures of tone are common, as when a performer seems to lack assurance. Performers may fumble for their lines: hesitate, begin a line again, or correct themselves. A show of embarrassment, such as blushing, has special relevance in gynecological examinations. On rare occasions when a person shows signs of sexual response, he or she really has something to blush about. A more subtle threat is an indication that the actor is putting an effort into the task of maintaining nonchalant demeanor; if it requires such an effort, perhaps it is not a "natural" response.

Such effort may be indicated, for example, in regard to the direction of glance. Most situations have a common visual focus of attention, but in a gynecological examination the logical focus, the patient's internal organs, is not accessible; and none of the alternatives, such as staring at the patient's face, locking glances with others, or looking out the window are feasible. The unavailability of an acceptable place to rest the eyes is more evident when the presence of several medical students creates a "crowd" atmosphere in the small cubicle. The lack of a visual focus of attention and the necessity to shift the eyes from

object to object requires the participants to remain vaguely aware of their directions of glance. Normally the resting place of the eyes is a background matter automatically managed without conscious attention. Attentiveness to this background detail is a constant reminder of how awkward the situation is.

Certain lapses in patients' demeanor are so common as hardly to be threatening. When patients express pain it can be overlooked if the patient is giving other signs of trying to behave well, because it can be taken that the patient is temporarily overwhelmed by a physiological state. The demonstrated presence of pain recalls the illness framework and counters sexual connotations. Crying can be accredited to pain and dismissed in a similar way. Withdrawing attention from the scene, so that one is not ready with an immediate comeback when called upon, is also relatively innocuous because it is close to the required passive but in play demeanor.

Some threats derive from the patient's ignorance of how to strike an acceptable balance between medical and nonmedical definitions, despite her willingness to do so. In two areas in particular, patients stumble over the subtleties of what is expected: physical decorum (proprieties of sights, sounds, and smells of the body) and modesty. While the staff is largely concerned with behavioral decorum and not about lapses in physical decorum, patients are more concerned about the latter, whether due to their medical condition or the procedure. Patients sometimes even let behavioral decorum lapse in order to express their concern about unappealing conditions of their bodies, particularly discharges and odors. This concern is a vestige of a nonmedical definition of the situation, for an attractive body is relevant only in a personal situation and not in a medical one.

Some patients fail to know when to display their private parts unashamedly to others and when to conceal them like anyone else. A patient may make an "inappropriate" show of modesty, thus not granting the staff the right to view what medical personnel have the right to view and others do not. But if patients act as though they literally accept the medical definition this also constitutes a threat. If a patient insists on acting as if the exposure of her breasts, buttocks, and pelvic area are no different from exposure of her arm or leg, she is "immodest." The medical definition is supposed to be in force only as necessary to facilitate specific medical tasks. If a patient becomes nonchalant enough to allow herself to remain uncovered for much longer than is technically necessary she becomes a threat. This also holds for verbal remarks about personal matters. Patients who misinterpret the license by exceeding its limits unwittingly challenge the definition of reality.[16]

Neutralizing Threatening Events

Most gynecological examinations proceed smoothly and the definition of reality is sustained without conscious attention.[17] Sometimes subtle threats to the definition arise, and occasionally staff and patient struggle covertly over the definition throughout the encounters.[18] The staff take more preventive measures where they anticipate the most trouble: young, unmarried girls; persons known to be temporarily upset; and persons with reputations as uncooperative. In such cases the doctor may explain the technical details of the procedure more carefully and offer direct reassurance. Perhaps he will take extra time to establish personal rapport, as by medically related inquiries ("How are you feeling?" "Do you have as much pain today?"), personal inquiries ("Where do you live?"), addressing the patient by her first name, expressing direct sympathy, praising the patient for her behavior in this difficult situation, speaking in a caressing voice, and affectionate gestures. Doctors also attempt to reinforce rapport as a response to threatening events.

The foremost technique in neutralizing threatening events is to sustain a nonchalant demeanor even if the patient is blushing with embarrassment, blanching from fear, or moaning in pain. The patient's inappropriate gestures may be ignored as the staff convey, "We're waiting until you are ready to play along." Working to bring the scene off, the staff may claim that this is routine, or happens to patients in general; invoke the "for your own good" clause; counterclaim that something is less important than the patient indicates; assert that the unpleasant medical procedure is almost over; and contend that the staff do not like to cause pain or trouble to patients (as by saying, "I'm sorry" when they appear to be causing pain). The staff

may verbally contradict a patient, give an evasive answer to a question, or try to distract the patient. By giving a technical explanation or rephrasing in the appropriate hospital language something the patient has referred to in a nonmedical way, the staff member reinstates the medical definition.

Redefinition is another tactic available to the staff. Signs of embarrassment and sexual arousal in patients may be redefined as "fear of pain." Sometimes sexual arousal will be labeled "ticklishness." After one examination the doctor thanked the patient, presumably for her cooperation, thus typifying the patient's behavior as cooperative and so omitting a series of uncooperative acts which he had previously acknowledged.

Humor may be used to discount the line the patient is taking. At the same time, humor provides a safety valve for all parties whereby the sexual connotations and general concern about gynecological examinations may be expressed by indirection. Without taking the responsibility that a serious form of the message would entail, the participants may communicate with each other about the events at hand. They may discount the derogatory implications of what would be an invasion of privacy in another setting by dismissing the procedure with a laugh. If a person can joke on a topic, he demonstrates to others that he possesses a laudatory degree of detachment.

For example, in one encounter a patient vehemently protests, "Oh, Dr. Raleigh, what are you doing?" Dr. Raleigh, exaggerating his southern accent, answers, "Nothin'." His levity conveys: "However much you may dislike this, we have to go on with it for your own good. Since you know that perfectly well, your protest could not be calling for a serious answer." Dr. Raleigh also plays the seducer claiming innocence, thus obliquely referring to the sexual connotations of where his hand is at the moment. In another incident Dr. Ryan is attempting to remove some gauze which has been placed in the vagina to stop the bleeding. He flippantly announces that the remaining piece of gauze has disappeared inside the patient. After a thorough search Dr. Ryan holds up a piece of gauze on the instrument triumphantly: "Well, here it is. Do you want to take it home and put it in your scrapbook?" By this remark Dr. Ryan ridicules the degree of involvement in one's own medical condition which would induce a patient to save this kind of memento. Later in the same examination Dr. Ryan announces he will do a rectal examination and the (elderly) patient protests, "Oh, honey, don't bother." Dr. Ryan assures her jokingly, "It's no bother, really." The indirect message of all three jokes is that one should take gynecological procedures casually. Yet simultaneously an undercurrent of each joke acknowledges a perspective contrary to the medical definition.

While in most encounters the nurse remains quietly in the background, she comes forward to deal actively with the patient if the definition of reality is threatened. In fact, one of the main functions of her presence is to provide a team member for the doctor in those occasional instances where the patient threatens to get out of line. Team members can create a more convincing reality than one person alone. Doctor and nurse may collude against an uncooperative patient, as by giving each other significant looks. If things reach the point of staff collusion, however, it may mean that only by excluding the patient can the definition of reality be reaffirmed. A more drastic form of solidifying the definition by excluding recalcitrant participants is to cast the patient into the role of an "emotionally disturbed person." Whatever an "emotionally disturbed person" may think or do does not count against the reality the rest of us acknowledge.

Perhaps the major safeguard of reality is that challenge is channeled outside the examination. Comments about the unpleasantness of the procedure and unaesthetic features of the patient's body occur mainly between women, two patients or a nurse and a patient. Such comments are most frequent while the patient gets ready for the examination and waits for the doctor or after the doctor leaves. The patient may establish a momentary "fellow-woman aura" as she quietly voices her distaste for the procedure to the nurse. "What we women have to go through" the patient may say. Or, "I wish all gynecologists were women." Why? "They understand because they've been through it themselves." The patient's confiding manner implies: "I have no right to say this, or even feel it, and yet I do." This phenomenon suggests that patients actually have strong negative reactions to gynecological examinations which belie their acquiescence in the actual situation. Yet patients' doubts are expressed in an in-

nocuous way which does not undermine the definition of reality when it is most needed.

To construct the scene convincingly, participants constantly monitor their own behavior and that of others. The tremendous work of producing the scene is contained in subtle maneuvers in regard to details which may appear inconsequential to the layman. Since awareness may interfere with a convincing performance, the participants may have an investment in being as unself-conscious as possible. But the sociologist is free to recognize the significance of "inconsequential details" in constructing reality.

CONCLUSION

In a gynecological examination the reality sustained is not the medical definition alone, but a dissonance of themes and counter-themes. What is done to acknowledge one theme undermines the others. No theme can be taken for granted because its opposite is always in mind. That is why the reality of a gynecological examination can never be routinized, but always remains precarious.

The gynecological examination should not be dismissed as an anomaly. The phenomenon is revealed more clearly in this case because it is an extreme example. But the gynecological examination merely exaggerates the internally contradictory nature of definitions of reality found in most situations. Many situations where the dominant definition is occupational or technical have a secondary theme of sociality which must be implicitly acknowledged (as in buttering up the secretary, small talk with sales clerks, or the undertaker's show of concern for the bereaved family). In "business entertaining" and conventions of professional associations a composite definition of work and pleasure is sustained. Under many circumstances a composite definition of action as both deviant and unproblematic prevails. For example, while Donald Ball stresses the claim of respectability in his description of an abortion clinic, his material illustrates the interplay of the dominant theme of respectability and a countertheme wherein the illicitness of the situation is acknowledged.[19] Internally inconsistent definitions also are sustained in many settings on who persons are and what their relation is to each other.

Sustaining a sense of the solidness of a reality composed of multiple contradictory definitions takes unremitting effort. The required balance among the various definitions fluctuates from moment to moment. The appropriate balance depends on what the participants are trying to do at that moment. As soon as one matter is dealt with, something else comes into focus, calling for a different balance. Sometimes even before one issue is completed, another may impose itself as taking priority. Further, each balance contains the seeds of its own demise, in that a temporary emphasis on one theme may disturb the long-run balance unless subsequent emphasis on the countertheme negates it. Because the most effective balance depends on many unpredictable factors, it is difficult to routinize the balance into formulas that prescribe a specific balance for given conditions. Routinization is also impractical because the particular forms by which the themes are expressed are opportunistic. That is, persons seize opportunities for expression according to what would be a suitable move at each unique moment of an encounter. Therefore, a person constantly must attend to how to express the balance of themes via the currently available means.

Multiple contradictory realities are expressed on various levels of explicitness and implicitness. Sustaining a sense of solidity of reality depends on the right balance of explicit and implicit expressions of each theme through a series of points in time. The most effective gestures express a multitude of themes on different levels. The advantages of multiple themes in the same gesture are simultaneous qualification of one theme by another, hedging (the gesture lacks one definite meaning), and economy of gestures.

Rational choices of explicit and implicit levels would take the following into account. The explicit level carries the most weight, unless countered by deliberate effort. Things made explicit are hard to dismiss or discount compared to what is left implicit. In fact, if the solidification of explication is judged to be nonreversible, use of the explicit level may not be worth the risk. On the other hand, when participants sense that the implicit level is greatly in use, their whole edifice of belief may become shaken. "I sense that a lot is going on underneath" makes a person wonder about the reality he is accepting. There must

be a lot he does not know, some of which might be evidence which would undermine what he currently accepts.

The invalidation of one theme by the concurrent expression of its countertheme must be avoided by various maneuvers. The guiding principle is that participants must prevent a definition that a contradiction exists between theme and countertheme from emerging. Certain measures routinely contribute to this purpose. Persons must try to hedge on both theme and countertheme by expressing them tentatively rather than definitely and simultaneously alluding to and discounting each theme. Theme and countertheme should not be presented simultaneously or contiguously on the explicit level unless it is possible to discount their contradictory features. Finally, each actor must work to keep the implicit level out of awareness for the other participants.

The technique of constructing reality depends on good judgment about when to make things explicit and when to leave them implicit, how to use the implicit level to reinforce and qualify the explicit level, distributing themes among explicit and implicit levels at any one moment, and seizing opportunities to embody messages. To pursue further these tentative suggestions on how important explicit and implicit levels are for sustaining reality, implicit levels of communication must be explored more systematically.

NOTES

Arlene K. Daniels has applied her talent for editing and organizing to several drafts of this paper. Robert M. Emerson, Roger Pritchard, and Thomas J. Scheff have also commented on the material. The investigation was supported in part by a predoctoral fellowship from the National Institute of Mental Health (Fellowship Number MPM-18,239) and by Behavioral Sciences Training Grant MH-8104 from the National Institute of Mental Health, as well as General Research Support Grant I-SOI-FR-05441 from the National Institutes of Health, U.S. Department of Health, Education, and Welfare, to the School of Public Health, University of California, Berkeley.

1. P. Berger & T. Luckmann (1966), *The social construction of reality,* Garden City, NY: Doubleday.

2. The precarious nature of social interaction is discussed throughout the work of Erving Goffman.

3. The data in this article are based on observations of approximately 75 gynecological examinations conducted by male

physicians on an obstetrics-gynecology ward and some observations from a medical ward for comparison. For a full account of this study, see J. P. Emerson (1963), "Social functions of humor in a hospital setting," unpublished doctoral dissertation, University of California at Berkeley. For a sociological discussion of a similar setting, see W. P. Rosengren & S. DeVault (1963), "The sociology of time and space in an obstetrical hospital," in E. Freidson (Ed.), *The hospital in modern society* (pp. 266–292), New York: Free Press of Glencoe.

4. "It takes severe biographical shocks to disintegrate the massive reality internalized in early childhood; much less to destroy the realities internalized later. Beyond this, it is relatively easy to set aside the reality of the secondary internalizations." Berger & Luckmann (1966), p. 142.

5. As stated by Lief and Fox: "The amounts and occasions of bodily contact are carefully regulated in all societies, and very much so in ours. Thus, the kind of access to the body of the patient that a physician in our society has is a uniquely privileged one. Even in the course of a so-called routine physical examination, the physician is permitted to handle the patient's body in ways otherwise permitted only to special intimates, and in the case of procedures such as rectal and vaginal examinations in ways normally not even permitted to a sexual partner." H. I. Lief & R. C. Fox (1963), "Training for 'detached concern' in medical students," in H. I. Lief et al. (Eds.), *The psychological basis of medical practice,* New York: Harper & Row, p. 32. As Edward Hall remarks, North Americans have an inarticulated convention that discourages touching except in moments of intimacy. E. T. Hall (1959), *The silent language,* Garden City, NY: Doubleday, p. 149.

6. For comments on embarrassment in the doctor-patient relation, see M. Balint (1957), *The doctor, his patient, and the illness,* New York: International Universities Press, p. 57.

7. Physicians are aware of the possibility that their routine technical behavior may be interpreted as sexual by the patient. The following quotation states a view held by some physicians: "It is not unusual for a suspicious hysterical woman with fantasies of being seduced to misinterpret an ordinary movement in the physical examination as an amorous advance." E. Weiss & O. S. English (1949), *Psychosomatic medicine,* Philadelphia: W. B. Saunders; quoted in M. Hollender (1958), *The psychology of medical practice,* Philadelphia: W. B. Saunders, p. 22. An extreme case suggests that pelvic examinations are not without their hazards for physicians, particularly during training: "A third-year student who had prided himself on his excellent adjustment to the stresses of medical school developed acute anxiety when about to perform, for the first time, a pelvic examination on a gynecological patient. Prominent in his fantasies were memories of a punishing father who would unquestionably forbid any such explicitly sexual behavior." S. Bojar (1961), "Psychiatric problems of medical students," in G. B. Glaine, Jr., et al. (Eds.), *Emotional problems of the student,* Garden City, NY: Doubleday, p. 248.

8. Many other claims and assumptions are being negotiated or sustained in addition to this basic definition of the situation. Efforts in regard to some of these other claims and assumptions have important consequences for the fate of the basic definition. That is, in the actual situation any one gesture usually has relevance for a number of realities, so that the fates of the various realities are intertwined with each other. For example, each participant is putting forth a version of himself which he wants validated. A doctor's jockeying about claims about competence may reinforce the medical definition and so may a patient's interest in appearing poised. But a patient's ambition to "understand what is really happening" may lead to undermining of the medical definition. Understanding that sustaining the basic definition of the situation is intertwined with numerous other projects, however, we will proceed to focus on that reality alone.

9. Compare Donald Ball's account of how the medical definition is conveyed in an abortion clinic, where it serves to counter the definition of the situation as deviant. D. W. Ball (1967, Winter), "An abortion clinic ethnography," *Social Problems, 14,* 293–301.

10. Glaser and Strauss discuss the hospital prohibition against examinations and exposure of the body in the presence of intimates of the patient. B. Glaser & A. Strauss (1965), *Awareness of dying,* Chicago: Aldine, p. 162.

11. Sudnow reports that at the county hospital he studied, male physicians routinely did pelvic examinations without nurses being present, except in the emergency ward. D. Sudnow (1967), *Passing on: The social organization of dying,* Englewood Cliffs, NJ: Prentice-Hall, p. 78.

12. The following quotation suggests that euphemisms and understood references may be used because the staff often has the choice of using "lewd words" or not being understood. "Our popular vocabulary for describing sexual behavior has been compounded of about equal parts of euphemism and obscenity, and popular attitude and sentiment have followed the same duality. Among both his male and female subjects, the interviewers found many who knew only the lewd words for features of their own anatomy and physiology." N. N. Foote (1955), "Sex as play," in J. Himelhock & S. F. Fava, *Sexual behavior in American society,* New York: Norton, p. 239.

13. The doctor's demeanor typically varies with his experience. In his early contacts with patients the young medical student may use an extreme degree of impersonality generated by his own discomfort in his role. By the time he has become accustomed to doctor-patient encounters, the fourth-year student and intern may use a newcomer's gentleness, treating the scene almost as an intimate situation by relying on elements of the "loving" demeanor previously learned in nonprofessional situations. By the time he is a resident and focusing primarily on the technical details of the medical task, the physician may be substituting a competent impersonality, although he never reverts to the extreme impersonality of the very beginning. The senior doctor, having mastered not only the technical details but an attitude of detached concern as well, reintroduces a mild gentleness, without the involved intimacy of the intern.

14. The management of closeness and detachment in professional-client relations is discussed in C. Kadushin (1962, March), "Social distance between client and professional," *American Journal of Sociology, 67,* 517–531. Wilensky and Lebeaux discuss how intimacy with strangers in the social worker-client relation is handled by accenting the technical aspects of the situation, limiting the relationship to the task at hand, and observing the norms of emotional neutrality, impartiality, and altruistic service. H. L. Wilensky & C. N. Lebeaux (1958), *Industrial society and social welfare,* New York: Russell Sage Foundation, pp. 299–303.

15. For a discussion of the socialization of medical students toward a generally detached attitude, see Lief & Fox (1963), pp. 12–35. See also M. J. Daniels (1960, November), "Affect and its control in the medical intern," *American Journal of Sociology, 66,* 259–267.

16. The following incident illustrates how a patient may exceed the limits. Mrs. Lane, a young married woman, was considered by the physicians a "seductive patient," although her technique was subtle and her behavior never improper. After examining Mrs. Lane, an intern privately called my attention to a point in the examination when he was pressing on the patient's ovaries and she remarked to the nurse: "I have this pain in intercourse until my insides are about to come out." The intern told me that Mrs. Lane said that to the nurse, but she wanted him to hear. He didn't want to know that, he said; it wasn't necessary for her to say that. The intern evidently felt that Mrs. Lane's remark had exceeded the bounds of decorum. A specific medical necessity makes the imparting of private information acceptable, the doctor's reaction suggests, and not merely the definition of the situation as medical.

17. There is reason to think that those patients who would have most difficulty in maintaining their poise generally avoid the situation altogether. Evidence that some uncool women avoid pelvic examinations is found in respondents' remarks quoted by Rainwater: "I have thought of going to a clinic for a diaphragm, but I'm real backward about doing that. I don't even go to the doctor to be examined when I'm pregnant. I never go until about a month before I have the baby." "I tell you frankly, I'd like a diaphragm but I'm just too embarrassed to go get one." L. Rainwater (1960), *And the poor get children,* Chicago: Quadrangle, pp. 10, 31.

18. An example of such a struggle is analyzed in J. P. Emerson (1970), "Nothing unusual is happening," in T. Shibutani (Ed.), *Human nature and collective behavior. Papers in honor of Herbert Blumer,* Englewood Cliffs, NJ: Prentice-Hall.

19. Donald Ball (1967).

FURTHER READING

Drew, Paul and John Heritage (eds.). 1988. *Talk at Work.* Cambridge, England: Cambridge University Press.
- Essays on how everyday conversation constructs social context in a variety of institutional settings.

Hughes, Everett. [1962] 1984. "Going Concerns." Pp. 52–64 in *The Sociological Eye: Selected Papers,* edited by David Riessman and Howard S. Becker. New Brunswick, NJ: Transaction Books.
- Features social institutions as patterned interactional work.

Silverman, David. 1998. *Harvey Sacks: Social Science and Conversation Analysis.* New York: Oxford University Press.
- Extensive discussion of the work of the founder of conversation analysis.

Sudnow, David (ed.). 1972. *Studies in Social Interaction.* New York: Free Press.
- Leading scholars in the area present various studies of the work of social interaction.

Willis, Paul. 1990. *Common Culture.* Boulder, CO: Westview Press.
- Presents the symbolic creativity entailed in producing the ordinary culture of everyday life.

PART 3

INNER
LIVES

Our inner lives stand for who we really are. At least that's the way we typically think and talk about ourselves. Who we are "inside" is the essence of our individuality, our uniqueness. We consider our inner lives to be separate from other people and our varied social worlds. As social as modern life has become, we still cling to the idea that what we are within is somehow special. It's known to us—and only to us—in a way that's inaccessible to others. Even though others' actions and opinions do matter in what we think and feel about ourselves, we consider our inner lives to be private. They're ours alone.

As linguists George Lakoff and Mark Johnson (1980) told us in Part 2, the "metaphors we live by" help sustain this belief. A metaphor is a figure of speech in which a word or phrase typically associated with one thing is applied to another. For example, "a mind like a sieve" is a familiar metaphor that conveys a particular image of inner life. It implies that the container of our inner thoughts and memories is "leaky." It's full of holes, like a sieve. Thoughts seep right out. The metaphor helps us understand what it means to "lose one's mind," for instance, as we sometimes say about a person who suffers from senile dementia. But it also paints a picture of forgetfulness that can happen to anyone.

We use all sorts of metaphors to convey inner states. Students, for example, often "cram" for exams until their minds virtually "burst" with knowledge. They know the material inside-out. When a student can't recall an answer for an exam question, we may say "his mind went blank." Another student may write a confusing essay, noting all the key terms from the course, but missing the main points altogether. We may say this student "can't see the forest for the trees." In the first instance, we're comparing the mind to a slate or a computer screen, both of which, of course, can be inadvertently erased or "go blank." In the second instance, we're comparing the mind to a thick woods. The forest isn't visible in its entirety, however, because the surrounding thicket obscures the student's vision. Metaphors such as these convey complex or obscure meanings through easily understood images.

We use myriad terms like "inside" and "outside," and "deep down" to communicate the contours of experience. Our everyday vocabularies readily distinguish the public from the private, the individual from the social. Parents and teachers ask children to think for themselves and not to blindly follow others. It's important to have a "mind of one's own." The media tell us that a "mind is a terrible thing to waste." This phrase suggests that mind comes in quantities that are valuable. Children would do well to preserve and cultivate what they have. Indeed, we often judge them on the basis of whether they seem to realize the importance of their special inner domains—their selves, minds, feelings, and intelligence.

The belief in the distinctiveness of inner life applies to adolescence, too. In fact, it seems to lurk around every corner. Adolescence is a time of transition from the dependence of childhood to the independence of maturity. As we raise children, we figure they will eventually "grow up." In part, this means that kids will ultimately develop "minds of their own." But the teenage years bring a wave of new crises. A strong need to conform with others—the dreaded "peer group pressure"—seems to undermine the independence valued in adulthood. Many adults will tell you that teenagers don't seem to have minds of their own. This is especially true, we hear, when teenagers "hang" in groups. Then, they compulsively "go with the flow," doing what others do while forfeiting their own identities. This behavior is exasperating, from an adult point of view, because we constantly nag teenagers to develop distinctive inner selves.

Adulthood is also marked by the belief that we have inner lives separate from other realms of experience. Today, more than ever, adults are expected to be autonomous and independent—in their thoughts, feelings, and actions. For example, when a wife asks her husband what he thinks about a particular social or political issue, she expects to hear her husband's inner thoughts and opinions, not someone else's. These are parts of who he *really* is. She wants to know where he truly stands on, say, women's reproductive rights or welfare reform. She doesn't want to hear the echoes of his father's partisan rantings, nor the innocuous equivocations that her husband's boss might demand. She expects the real "him" to speak up. Anything less would mean that her husband wasn't "his own man."

Today, we are constantly plied with questions about how we think and feel inside, especially deep down. Indeed, we are likely to believe that feelings more than thoughts actually mark the core of our inner lives. Our deep emotions are increasingly treated as the best indicators of our most authentic selves. Thoughts and actions, in this context, are merely veneer. As a matter of everyday belief, we figure we must plumb the depths of inner life to find out who we truly are (Gubrium and Holstein 2000).

INNER LIFE IN PRACTICE

As much as we believe in distinct inner lives, actually getting in touch with them is another matter. They exist in theory, but these sequestered, private realms are far from obvious in the *practice* of everyday life. Being "inner," a person's private side is, by definition, hidden from public display. Others have no direct access to it. What we commonly take to be the manifestations of others' inner lives are apparent only in what others say and do. These are outward signs that may or may not reflect what others really believe or actually feel. We can read these signs, but we can't see their concrete referents. Similarly, others can glean who we are only from what we do and what we say. These outward signs may or may not reveal the "real" me presumed to be deep inside each of us.

When we refer to "practice," we mean the entire range of actions we undertake as we conduct our everyday lives. It includes all the interpretive activities by which we come to know the world we inhabit. In practice, what I see and hear when I watch and listen to you is not your inner life at all. I only see signs of it. I observe your bodily movements, your demeanor, your clothing, what you say, and how you say it. These are just a few of the visible features of who and what you ostensibly are within. I have no immediate access to those inner realms that we refer to as "minds," "thoughts," and "feelings."

Whatever access I have is indirect. What I know about you "deep inside" also comes by way of external sources, such as emotional outbursts and facial expressions. The precise problem for understanding the private realms of everyday life is that we need to use things that are *not* private to figure out what the private is. We have no other option. We have no recourse but to use external, accessible features of experience to construct what we believe lies within. In practice, everything we do to figure out another's inner life is done publicly. Everything we convey about ourselves is equally public.

Consider how the body is used to figure inner constitution. Body size and form, we presume, tell us something, say, about a person's mettle. The connection is implicit, but familiar to us all. Years ago, for example, advertisements in magazines, newspapers, and comic books touted the Charles Atlas body-building program as a way to develop staunch character and fortitude. These advertisements featured the body as a significant path to inner reaches of mind and virtue. A familiar illustration showed "bullies" on the beach, kicking sand in the face of a puny young man. The poor guy didn't have the gumption to stand up for himself. He just accepted the humiliation. The message was clear: a puny body harbors a timid heart and weak resolve. The advertisement's pitch was equally clear. Build your body with the Charles Atlas program and not only will your appearance improve, but your moral valor will burgeon. Driving home the theme, the last frame of the advertisement shows the formerly puny young man now dramatically transformed. Handsome and muscular, he's no longer a pushover. Now popular with the girls, he's the one who's kicking sand in other guys' faces.

Even today, we hear traces of the same message. "Sound body, sound mind" is a hallmark of the self-improvement industry. Clothing, too, is taken as an important outer sign of inner life. We hear about "power" suits and ties. We believe that what's visible outside announces what's present inside. We turn to assertiveness training, public speaking courses, and cosmetic "makeovers" to improve our demeanor, communication skills, and appearance. But we also see them as ways of developing positive messages about our inner selves. Virtually any external facet of an individual can be taken as a marker of his or her inner life.

Despite the proliferation of external signs, inner life remains elusive. It's virtually invisible. The everyday location of "inner" is problematic in its own right. Philosopher Gilbert Ryle (1949) once commented on the problem when he critically assessed the commonplace expression "in my head." His argument was that although we often use that part of our body to convey what is on or in our minds, we don't actually mean it literally. That is, we don't really capture a catchy tune or trace the steps we'll take in solving a puzzle within the actual cranium that sits above our shoulders. As Ryle noted,

> No one thinks that when a tune is running in my head, a surgeon could unearth a little orchestra buried inside my skull or that a doctor by applying a stethoscope to my cranium could hear a muffled tone, in the way in which I hear the muffled whistling of my neighbor when I put my ear to the wall between our rooms. (Pp. 35–36)

Ryle went on to explain that whereas we use such expressions to locate the mind, we do so metaphorically. We understand that we are experiencing a catchy tune or solving a puzzle only *as if* they were inside our heads. Of course, in the long run, "as if" has a way of becoming "actually" for all practical purposes. Out of habit, we simply take it that inner life exists within the head, especially its more cognitive facets, such as our minds, thoughts, and motives. As Ryle might have put it, the "logical geography" of mind doesn't extend below the neck. We don't figure that other locations—say, the feet—could properly house such eminent facets of our inner lives.

While we commonly use the head to locate inner life—especially the mind—it's important to note that the mind is not the same thing as the brain. The brain and other organs of the head and the body are anatomical structures. Ryle's surgeon could certainly "unearth" each of them. Inner life, in sharp contrast, is a domain we can't tangibly discover. Instead, we speak of, and act in relation to, it *as if* it were located inside us. Inner life has textual and practical status in our experience, not actual anatomical presence. In other words, we act as if our interior regions were the locations of our thoughts, feelings, motives, and other aspects of who we view ourselves to be as persons.

We should also note that the duration of inner life is different from that of anatomical structures, such as the brain or the heart. Unlike a bodily organ, an aspect of inner life can be imagined well before a person is born and live on well after he or she dies. Parents, for example, start constructing the inner life of an unborn child—especially the kind of self an unborn child will have—well before birth. Everyday comments, such as "She's going to be the smartest girl in school" and "He's going to be a real tiger," construct inner qualities before the child even arrives.

Inner life doesn't die with the body, either. Although the body may be dead and gone, a person's thoughts, beliefs, mind, and soul may live on for years—in others' recollections. Many cultures have taken this sort of "after life" seriously, developing communal ways of sustaining the disembodied. Our own society often relegates the construction and management of such matters to historians or religious institutions. In its own way, each preserves the inner lives of those who have physically departed.

The private facets that we call "feelings" or "emotions"—the affective side of inner life—fare similarly in practice. Emotions are as invisible as minds. We don't actually see emotions. We only observe their outward manifestations or expressions. A smile suggests a positive inner state, a frown something less benign. Like the outward evidence of mind, we can sometimes misjudge what is or isn't behind a smile or a frown. A smile may hide a great deal of anger. A frown may be a contrived tactic for gaining sympathy. The only way to know "for sure" is to check these signs against other outward manifestations of related inner states. But here's the rub again: we never have direct access to feelings. We can't check outward signs against what's really going on "in there." We can only compare outward signs against other outward signs.

Of course, the locations for the different facets of inner lives are not capricious or arbitrary.

They derive from long cultural traditions. Cognitive aspects of inner life, for example, are usually signified with references to the head. We convey what's in or on our minds by pointing to our skulls, for instance. Or we signify mental confusion or "craziness" by tracing quick circles in the air near our temples. Signs for the more affective regions of our inner lives are more diverse. The head, for instance, is hardly ever used. Indeed, romanticist inclinations tend to draw a sharp distinction between matters of the head and emotional matters. The heart is the most prominent and familiar location for the passions, especially love, and, of course, heartache and sorrow. Other emotions, such as anger and guilt, are not so uniformly located, but can nonetheless be signified by the body.

An important question remains concerning the experience of inner life in practice. It's evident that we have only indirect access to others' inner lives and must therefore attend to public signifying practices to know them. But must we do the same with our own inner lives? Do we have only indirect access to our own inner lives? The belief in a distinct inner life would suggest that our own inner realms would be there, waiting to be experienced firsthand. After all, we do appear to have direct access to our own thoughts and feelings. But how do we know, in practice, what's in our minds and hearts? Do we actually experience our own thoughts and emotions directly? Do we know in some immediate fashion what we think and feel?

Our interactional perspective would suggest that access to one's own thoughts and feelings is as indirect as it is with others' inner lives. While we commonly believe that we can "know our own mind" or be "at one" with ourselves, practice suggests otherwise. To start, consider the questions we regularly ask ourselves in our inner conversations. George Herbert Mead (1934) referred to these conversations as "mind" itself. For him, internal conversations were communicatively much like the social exchanges we have with others. And these conversations reveal *to ourselves* who we are, what we think, and how we feel, just as external conversations may reveal those things to others. In talking to ourselves, we answer questions like "Am I really that kind of person?" "Do I really think that way?" "What's actually on my mind?" "What do I genuinely feel about myself?" "What are my true motives?" "Am I actually as smart as I think I am?" Daily experiences of all kinds raise these questions "in our minds" about all aspects of our inner lives, from our thoughts and motives to our feelings and sense of competence.

The fact that we regularly raise these questions about ourselves, even in our most private moments, suggests that we, too, address our inner lives indirectly. We converse with ourselves just as we do with others and as others do with us. We find out about ourselves through these conversations. We may even conclude that we can't really know ourselves directly, so we turn to others for answers about who and what we are. Indeed, it isn't all that unusual for others to tell us that they know us better than we do ourselves. And we often agree that it's true! Indeed, many of us pay good money to others—who claim to be experts on inner life—to help us gain access to our most private thoughts and deepest feelings. Psychotherapy is precisely this kind of business.

At this point, the practical duality of inner life poses a bit of a quandary. We take inner life to be *inside,* but all evidence of it comes from *outside.* Mead and others recognized this duality as a key feature of social interaction—even of the inner conversation we call "mind." In Mead's view, mind is not something we exclusively possess. Emotions aren't something that we privately feel. Rather, both are products of talk and interaction with others, as well as our conversations with ourselves. Our relations with ourselves, Mead argued, are communicatively identical with our relations with others. They are practical and indirect. We have no immediate access to ourselves. We must learn about ourselves just as we learn about others. We must pose the kinds of questions to ourselves that were presented in the preceding paragraph. And we must respond to them in order to know ourselves.

Selves, minds, thoughts, feelings, and motives come to us by way of the communicative work we do to understand who and what we are. Even on our own, we don't experience these things directly just because they are ostensibly within us. We can address them only from afar, so to speak. We must answer our own questions before we can get a sense of what we are experiencing within. Even our own inner lives must be approached this way. In effect, we step outside ourselves to ask who and what we are. We then step back inside to *be* these things.

Philosopher Ludwig Wittgenstein (1953) had a slightly different take on this issue. He discussed inner lives in terms of what he called the "private language" problem. Wittgenstein asked several important questions. Do we have an inner realm that we can call our own? Do we address ourselves differently than we address others? Is inner life distinct from the many socially shared ways we have of addressing ourselves? Wittgenstein drew upon the concept of "language games" to answer these questions. We experience privacy and inner domains, Wittgenstein argued, because we are in the habit of dividing up and talking about experience *in those terms*. That is, we take part in the language game of "inner lives." We readily engage in this language game—with ourselves and others—and, in the process, turn a belief into a reality. The language game of "inner life" gives us a way of experiencing each other and ourselves as having private, inner regions that are separate and distinct from social worlds. The "social worlds" language game operates in the same way, but constructs realms of experiences we share with others. In either case, the way we use language *in practice*—in the course of interaction—shapes the experiential realities of our inner lives and social worlds.

Constructing Inner Life

This concern for language use brings us right back to square one: inner lives and social worlds are inextricably linked through social interaction. Even the deepest reaches of privacy—our most intimate thoughts and feelings—are formed in the terms of the language we share. In this sense, the personal is always social. Inner lives are fashioned from the vocabulary and metaphors that are culturally available to us. Talk and interaction reveal our inner regions to us and to each other.

Questions that bring inner lives to our attention are immensely significant in this process. Inquiries of ourselves as well as of others—such as who and what we are, what we feel, and why we take particular actions—are a first step toward constructing our private, inner lives. Such questions pique our interest in a *presumed* world within. This realm wouldn't be an object of interest if the questions weren't posed in the first place. We begin to look for the things that we wonder about, so to speak.

But where do the answers to these questions come from? Once again, it is important to look at the actual practice of social life, rather than take everyday realities for granted. It would be easy to say that we merely look at or inside people to see who and what they are. But that's too simple. In practice, we can look as intently as we please, but we can never actually see thoughts, motives, or emotions. We have figures of speech that suggest this possibility—"I can read your mind," for example—but they are merely that: figures of speech. In practice, the mind and its reading are conjured up out of speech—talk and interaction. They aren't "just there."

This means we need to take a different approach to understanding how we answer questions about who and what we are. One strategy is to begin by asking about the kinds of ideas, frameworks, metaphors, and vocabularies people use to construct experience. These questions point us to the *possible* ways that inner life could be conceptualized. If we start down this path, we quickly learn that the belief in thoughts and emotions has been around for a long time, but people have not always constructed them in the same way. Social historian Michel Foucault (1977) provided a fascinating illustration.

Foucault was curious about the massive social transformations taking place in France at the end of the 18th century. One interesting development was a distinct change from a widespread sense that individuals had little or no private inner lives of their own to a new belief that each person has an interior space that he or she commands. Foucault opens his book *Discipline and Punish* by depicting a horrific execution scene, drawing from newspaper accounts of the day. His description shocks us with the dreadful torture of a man named Damiens, who was condemned to death for attempting to assassinate King Louis XV. We cringe as Damiens's body is flayed, burned, drawn, and quartered, all in public view.

> On 2 March 1757 Damiens the regicide was condemned "to make the *amende honorable* before the main door of the Church of Paris," where he was to be "taken and conveyed in a cart wearing nothing but a shirt, holding a torch of burning wax weighing two points," then, "in the said care, to the Place de Grève, where, on a scaffold that will be erected there, the flesh will be torn from his breasts, arms, thighs, and calves with red-hot pincers, his right hand, holding the knife with which he committed the said parricide, burnt with sulphur, and, on those places where the flesh will be torn away, poured molten lead, boiling oil, burning resin, wax and sulphur melted together and then his body drawn and quartered by four horses and his limbs and body consumed by fire, reduced to ashes and his ashes thrown to the winds. (P. 3)

Foucault asks why criminals were subjected to such horrible bodily torture. His answer grows from his observation that, at the time, people held different beliefs about who and what individuals were *as subjects.* By subjects, we mean the supposed agents who are responsible for their actions. At the time, Damiens—like everyone else—was conceived literally as an appendage of the king's being. His body and soul were inseparable extensions of the crown. Damiens's assassination attempt was therefore like an infection that besieged the king. It had to be attacked in turn, as a red hot iron rod may be used to cauterize a festering wound.

For Foucault, the spectacle of the execution was not a scene whose central character was an independent subject with a mind and sentiments of his own. Although there was no question that Damiens could think and feel, these were not figured to be his *own* thoughts and feelings. If they were, observers might have considered the spectacle to be cruel and inhuman. Only now, given our current sense of inner lives being owned and experienced by individuals on their own, can we feel deeply sorry for what Damiens "must have gone through" or how "he must have felt." To do so requires a belief in a sympathetic inner self.

But in the 18th century, people believed that Damiens's life in total—body and soul—was not his own, at least not in the sense that we believe today. It was not a significant object for people to worry about. Damiens was not so much an individual with a mind and feelings of his own as he was an offending accessory to the crown that had to be excised. He was considered to be something like a cancer on the sovereign. At the time, it was simply inconceivable to view him as an object of sympathy or compassion. No one could think that Damiens's own wits and habits might be reformed to bring him back into the fold.

A mere 80 years later, according to Foucault, torture as a public spectacle had gradually disappeared in France. He notes that the "gloomy festival of punishment" was dying out. It was replaced by a humanizing regimen, informed by the belief in an independent, thinking subject with a "mind of his own." People now believed that criminality in such a subject is correctable. Persons were viewed as having inner lives that were under their own control. They were separate and distinct from the crown or the state. This is a new kind of subject, not a mere appendage of the king. The individual can, in effect, reason on his or her own and, as such, is open to rehabilitation.

Today, when things go wrong, the "new" individualized subject can be reshaped or reformed, rather than brutally excised from the public realm. Foucault, however, is careful to note that inner life is still public in practice. The new interior subjectivity still draws the sense of who and what it is from the outside. While the new individualized self is apparently autonomous, it nonetheless formulates and manages itself in terms shared with others. Individuals exercise control over themselves by addressing themselves in terms they take from their social world. They formulate who and what they are from the start in those very terms. Once again, we see the unceasing linkage between inner lives and social worlds, drawn through talk and interaction. Foucauldian scholar Nikolas Rose (1990) makes the point directly in relation to the contemporary scene:

> Our intimate lives, our feelings, desires and aspirations, seem quintessentially personal. Living at a time when we are surrounded by messages of public troubles that appear overwhelming—war, family, injustice, poverty, disease, terrorism—our mental states, subjective experiences and intimate relationships offer themselves as perhaps the only place where we can locate our real private selves. There is, no doubt, much comfort to be afforded by such a belief. But it is profoundly misleading.
>
> Our personalities, subjectivities, and "relationships" are not private matters, if this implies that they are not the objects of power. On the contrary, they're intensively governed. Perhaps they always have been. Social conventions, community scrutiny, legal norms, familial obligations and religious injunctions have exercised an intense power over the human soul in past times and other cultures. . . . Thoughts, feelings, and actions may appear as the very fabric and constitution of the intimate self, but they are socially organized and managed in minute particulars. (P. 1)

Recently, we've seen the proliferation of "new and improved" ways to construct minds, thoughts, and feelings. Self-help and self-improvement books, videos, and TV shows endlessly tell us how to reform what we are, inside and out. The psychological-sciences now offer countless ways of constructing and reconstructing inner life. They supply virtual blueprints for our inner regions. Indeed, we may refer to the past 100 years or so as "the psychological era" of the human subject. It was only in the 20th century that we wholeheartedly came to believe in the inner, private subject—the subject we now take ourselves to be.

Perhaps the most influential design for inner life is the model Sigmund Freud devised early in the 20th century. Whereas Freud is considered the father of psychoanalysis, he was far more than just a pioneering "shrink." His ideas about how inner life is organized literally revolutionized the way Westerners think about their personal selves and experiences. Today, it's hard to talk about anything that goes on "inside our heads" without retracing Freud's road map of our interior regions.

Freud viewed inner life as more than just a space where one reasoned. It was not simply a private region where individuals organized their thoughts and sentiments in response to the world around them. Instead, it comprised an intricate network of sophisticated psychic structures. Borrowing from literature, mythology, philosophy, and existing psychological theories of mental life, Freud divided inner life into three now-famous components: the *id,* the *ego,* and the *superego.* According to Freud, the id was the original, unformed and unconscious psychological energy we all are born with. It comprised the socially untamed, biologically based desires that flood our lives at the start. It's focus is entirely on food; tactile stimulation; comfort; and, yes, sex. In Freud's original German text, the id was simply called "it" (*es*). "It" is a splendid name because the id isn't concerned at all with social niceties or what things mean. It's an undisciplined cauldron of desire and potential until it enters into communicative relations with others. Only then is it structured into something meaningful.

For better or worse, the term eventually became objectified into *the* id (the it). It came to be viewed as *the* unformed material foundation of Freud's model of psychological structure and process. As the id encounters a world of others, its rampant desires are soon thwarted, however. Others tend to get in the way of unvarnished self-indulgence. As the id is increasingly immersed in social encounters, a new process and structure emerges. Freud called this process and structure "ego," which in German is simply "I" (*ich*). Ego represents the conscious awareness of self and others. By hook or by crook, the ego reasons its way through life. It doesn't unabashedly pursue its desires. Instead, it tries to get what it wants, but it also considers the consequences of its actions. Where the id is purely impulsive, the ego is calculating. It, too, has been objectified, into *the* ego (the I), giving it further standing and substance as a structure of inner life.

Finally, Freud identified a third psychic structure, ostensibly the most social of the three. Indeed, it's conceived as an internal mirror of society, one that reflects the ideal member of the community. Freud called this structure "superego," which in German is literally "above me" (*über ich*). It, too, has eventually been objectified into *the* superego.

In developing this terminology, Freud did more than merely name a tripartite organization for inner life. He and his followers gave these structures objective status. That is, these parts of the psyche became reified objects, not just labels for abstract processes. To refer to id (it), ego (I), and superego (ideal I) is one thing. To preface each with "the" is quite another. The addition of this simple linguistic convention for referencing a thing—the "the"—literally solidified this psychic terrain. Following Freud's original inspiration, inner life could be structured into objectified regions. In this imagery, different psychic provinces stood apart and distinct from each other. They might even metaphorically resemble competing, if not warring, factions of mental life. We can all remember cartoons, for example, with little devils and angels inside a character's head, arguing over the course of action to be pursued. "Do it! It will be great," urges the devil, the crass embodiment of pure id. "Don't do it! It's just not right," counters the angel, speaking as the heavenly superego. As trivial as this example seems, it clearly demonstrates how concretely we can envision our psychic processes.

Freud conceived of the id, ego, and superego as parts of a system. They were separate domains of inner life, but each also influenced the others. None was completely independent, in Freud's view. Over time, this Freudian terminology and the images it presents have become familiar to us. Indeed, most of us talk about our egos or our unconscious minds from time to time, even if we've never read a word of Freud's. That's Freud's great significance. Nearly all members of contemporary Western societies construct inner lives at least partially in Freudian terms.

The familiar, of course, is enticing. Because Freud's psychic model is so commonplace, we readily assume that inner life is organized precisely in these terms. We just take it for granted.

When we casually talk about ourselves as having "damaged egos" or say someone has a "overdeveloped superego," we are constructing in practice the very structures Freud theorized. We act toward ourselves and others as if these structures of the mind actually exist, even if we can't directly see them.

Today, we couch many of our experiences in psychological, if not Freudian, terms. We seek help for "personal problems" in these very terms. Scholarship and science remind us of Freud's model, even if the details have changed over the years. Talk shows and radio psychologists constantly reaffirm that we have inner regions carved into conscious and unconscious realms, divided into distinct psychic entities. Conscience, libido, reason, personality, sex drive. We commonsensically believe these to be components of inner lives. They may not be precisely Freudian. They may sometimes stray from the cranium. But we talk about them so frequently—and so naturally—that we come to regard the inner life that they produce *as if* it truly exists apart from our constructions of it. A vocabulary that was originally devised as a means of imagining and describing inner life has become a way to actually address ourselves and others as psychological beings.

Of course, Freud doesn't own the franchise on inner lives. For example, inner life is increasingly constructed in the language of computer systems. We now use the vocabulary of hardwiring, high-speed processors, hard drives, system crashes, and the like to construct and communicate who and what we are (Kearns 1987; Sternberg 1990). This is especially true with respect to thought and intelligence. Character is constructed from the vocabulary of professional football. Teenage romantic passion takes the form of "'N Sync" harmonies. Our private reaches increasingly take their shape from the images and metaphors of popular culture.

Even personal morality is constructed in popular terms. As C. Wright Mills (1940) suggests later in this book, motives are subject to fashion. The reasons we offer for why we've acted in particular ways draw on customarily accepted accounts. To say "the devil made me do it" is not as socially acceptable as it once might have been. We aren't likely to seriously account for actions in those terms in this day and age. But we do frequently hear that things are done "for family reasons." We hear it so frequently, in fact, that it's becoming a modern-day exculpatory cliché, an all-purpose excuse. The point is not whether the motive is true or simply a pretext or lame justification. Rather, it's that motives and values—no matter what they are—are supplied externally, though talk and interaction, even if we believe that they are located internally.

FINAL REMINDERS

We conclude this essay by reiterating that inner life is *socially* constructed from available metaphors and recognized ways of speaking. It's like all other domains of experience in this regard. In everyday life, we talk about inner life *as if* we could actually observe it, even though it is never directly available to us. It's always hidden, yet we construct it through highly visible interactional practices. This is a fascinating paradox: inner life has external sources.

As you read the selections in this part of the book, bear "in mind" that no surgeon could open our heads to find the ids, egos, and superegos of Freud's grand vision. Nor could a surgeon find high-speed processors, search engines, or fiber optic connections. Motives, emotions, and the like would be similarly elusive. The language of inner life—with its familiar and enticing terms—is merely a way of addressing ourselves and others *as if* this were what inner life is like. This brings us back, full circle, to where we started. There is an unceasing linkage between inner lives and our social worlds, a linkage forged in social interaction.

REFERENCES

Foucault, Michel. 1977. *Discipline and Punish.* New York: Vintage.

Gubrium, Jaber F. and James A. Holstein. 2000. "The Self in a World of Going Concerns." *Symbolic Interaction* 23:95–115.

Kearns, Michael S. 1987. *Metaphors of Mind in Fiction and Psychology.* Lexington: University Press of Kentucky.

Lakoff, George and Mark Johnson. 1980. *Metaphors We Live By.* Chicago: University of Chicago Press.

Mead, George Herbert. 1934. *Mind, Self, and Society.* Chicago: University of Chicago Press.

Mills, C. Wright. 1990. Situated Actions and Vocabularies of Motive. *American Sociological Review* 5:904–13.

Rose, Nikolas. 1990. *Governing the Soul: The Shaping of the Private Self.* London: Routledge.

Ryle, Gilbert. 1949. *The Concept of Mind.* Chicago: University of Chicago Press.

Sternberg, Robert J. 1990. *Metaphors of Mind: Concepts of the Nature of Intelligence.* Cambridge, England: Cambridge University Press.

Wittgenstein, Ludwig. 1953. *Philosophical Investigations.* New York: Macmillan.

SELVES AND IDENTITIES

As personal as they seem, our selves and identities are extremely social. They are hallmarks of our inner lives, yet they take shape in relation to others. We establish who and what we are through social interaction. In some respects, selves and identities are two sides of the same coin. Selves are the subjects we take ourselves to be; identities are the shared labels we give to these selves. We come to know our selves in terms of the categories that are socially available to us. Gender, race, age, "good," bad," "smart," "clueless," and other identities are all formulated and conferred socially.

Managing everyday social relations involves organizing and presenting our selves and relating to possible identities. Think about the sorts of complications that arise on special occasions, such as the first day of classes of a fall semester. It can be a bit jarring when the self we present by way of a tank top and baggy shorts encounters everyone else dressed in jeans and T-shirts. Of course it's not the end of the world, socially speaking. We all live through these moments. Still, we do say something about ourselves by virtue of how we look. We make claims to particular kinds of identity images and send messages about who we are inside by the way we craft our appearance outside. Who can forget how important these impressions were in our younger days? Making the wrong fashion statement in junior high might have led to mortifying embarrassment or torrents of tears.

Usually, we have plenty of identities to chose from. There are countless categories of who and what we could possibly be. Going back to junior high, the options for self-definition were almost endless. The social menu included "cool," "nerd," "brain," "jock," "Goth," "freak," and "airhead," among many others. It's much the same in the workplace later in life. The categories change, but the process of self-construction is the same. "Rate buster," "executive material," "Dilbert," and other labels replace the school-yard terms, but who we are inside still derives from the raft of identities that come our way. Over the life course, identities associated with race, gender, sexuality, and ethnicity cross our lives, too. The media, of course, play a big role. Movies, television, and talk shows offer up colorful and exaggerated identities to which we often aspire.

Time and place also have their ways of influencing selves and identities. A matter of hours can alter the way we view ourselves. The "nerdy" kid who is the laughing stock of afternoon soccer practice can be the "star" of the chess club that night. The loving and patient mother who has time for her daughters' every whim goes to work to become a demanding and shrewish boss known as the "dragon lady." Day in and day out, as we move from situation to situation, we reorganize who and what we are to ourselves and others

Sudden and untimely overlaps between situations can sometimes throw our selves into a tizzy. We all worry a little bit about what people from one sphere of our lives may think if they see us in another sphere. Our selves and identities are at stake. That's why both an honor student and her philosophy professor may cringe at the prospect of running into one another at a Hooters restaurant—where she's a waitress and he's a patron. The claims of self and identity made on campus are severely at odds with those presented "after hours." These complications involving our inner lives are part of the routine business of everyday life. They make our selves and identities anything but constant. And they show how these are far from private realms.

ABOUT THE READINGS

For centuries, the self was the object of philosophical reflection and theological contemplation. In the late 19th and early 20th centuries, however, William James, Charles Horton Cooley, George Herbert Mead, and others, who called themselves "pragmatists," redefined the self as much more ordinary and practical. They viewed it as a social image, reflected by others. From the most outrageous to the most conventional, everyone has a self that guides behavior. With this realization, the pragmatists democratized the self, setting the stage for viewing it as a ubiquitous feature of experience.

The pragmatists didn't create a special jargon for describing this ordinary self. It didn't need extraordinary terms of reference. In **"The Me and the I,"** notice how **William James** refers to the self in plain terms. For him, "the I" serves as the standpoint from which we and others address ourselves. To this he adds "the Me," that which we learn about ourselves through interaction with others. Together, the I and the Me constitute the self. For James, this was an "empirical self" in that it came into being with experience. This empirical self was as real and as obvious as its roots in everyday interaction. Being a product of social interaction, the self in practice was many selves. According to James, we have as many selves as there are others who view us in particular ways.

Referring directly to James, **"The Looking-Glass Self"** by **Charles Horton Cooley** extends the discussion of the I and the Me. Cooley tells us that the relation between the two facets of self is similar to the way we respond to ourselves when looking into a mirror. Our selves, Cooley explains, are as evident as the steps we take in responding to our images. We first imagine who or what we are from someone else's point of view. We then figure what the other person thinks of us. Finally, we respond to those thoughts with "some sort of self-feeling." This process of self-construction is interactional, even if we are interacting only with ourselves. The process has come to be know as "the looking-glass self."

"The Self," by **George Herbert Mead** also emphasizes the social contours of the self. Mead is especially concerned with the key feature of the self's communicative character: the self can be an object to itself and thus can speak to itself. Mead underscores the importance of everyday talk and interaction even more than does James or Cooley. He also traces the self to early life experiences, especially to children's play. According to Mead, in childhood games, we virtually practice society by taking the various social roles that make up the games.

Decades later, **Erving Goffman** borrowed from the language of the theater to elaborate our understanding of the self. In **"The Presentation of Self,"** he shows how profoundly social the self is in the presence of others. He richly illustrates how we manage to "come off" as authentic through our public performances. What we "give off," in other words, *is* the self, for all practical purposes. Everyday life is like the theater in that we act in ways that present who and what we are. What you see is what you get, so to speak. The self is a matter of public performance. Multiple performances produce multiple selves. For Goffman, there are as many selves as there are situations for who we are to others.

In **"Salvaging the Self,"** **David A. Snow** and **Leon Anderson** show how poignant the work of maintaining the self can be. The authors consider the plight of the homeless, looking closely at the selves of persons who are "down on their luck." The chapter illustrates not only how others assign degraded identities to the homeless, but how the homeless, in turn, attempt to rescue themselves from these identities.

Finally, **Kathleen S. Lowney** and **James A. Holstein** turn to the self-constructive role that entertainment media play in **"Victims, Villains, and Talk Show Selves."** This chapter visits the construction site of some public selves—daytime talk shows, such as the *Jerry Springer Show.* We see how familiar, if despicable, identities provide the grist for the "freak shows" that now populate the airwaves. As we encounter these identities, we once more see how social categories construct the personas we come to be.

11 | THE ME AND THE I
William James

THE ME AND THE I

Whatever I may be thinking of, I am always at the same time more or less aware of *myself,* of my *personal existence.* At the same time it is *I* who am aware; so that the total self of me, being as it were duplex, partly known and partly knower, partly object and partly subject, must have two aspects discriminated in it, of which for shortness we may call one the *Me* and the other the *I.* I call these "discriminated aspects," and not separate things, because the identity of *I* with *me,* even in the very act of their discrimination, is perhaps the most ineradicable dictum of common-sense, and must not be undermined by our terminology here at the outset, whatever we may come to think of its validity at our inquiry's end.

THE EMPIRICAL SELF OR ME

Between what a man calls *me* and what he simply calls *mine* the line is difficult to draw. We feel and act about certain things that are ours very much as we feel and act about ourselves. Our fame, our children, the work of our hands, may be as dear to us as our bodies are, and arouse the same feelings and the same acts of reprisal if attacked. And our bodies themselves are they simply ours, or are they *us?* Certainly men have been ready to disown their very bodies and to regard them as mere vestures, or even as prisons of clay from which they should some day be glad to escape.

We see then that we are dealing with a fluctuating material; the same object being sometimes treated as a part of me, at other times as simply mine, and then again as if I had nothing to do with it at all. *In its widest possible sense,* however, *a man's Me is the sum total of all that he* CAN *call his,* not only his body and his psychic powers, but his clothes and his house, his wife and children, his ancestors and friends, his reputation and works, his lands and horses, and yacht and bank-account. All these things give him the same emotions. If they wax and prosper, he feels triumphant; is they dwindle and die away and die away, he feels cast down—not necessarily in the same degree for each thing, but in much the same way for all.

THE SOCIAL ME

A man's social me is the recognition which he gets from his mates. We are not only gregarious animals, liking to be in sight of our fellows, but we have an in-

From *Psychology: The Briefer Course* by William James. [1892] 1961 by Harper and Co.

nate propensity to get ourselves noticed, and noticed favorably, by our kind. No more fiendish punishment could be devised, were such a thing physically possible, than that one should be turned loose in society and remain absolutely unnoticed by all the members thereof. If no one turned round when we entered, answered when we spoke, or minded what we did, but if every person we met "cut us dead," and acted as if we were non-existing things, a kind of rage and impotent despair would ere long well up in us, from which the cruelest bodily tortures would be a relief; for these would make us feel that, however bad might be our plight, we had not sunk to such a depth as to be unworthy of attention at all.

Properly speaking, *a man has as many social selves as there are individuals who recognize him* and carry an image of him in their mind. To wound any one of these his images is to wound him. But as the individuals who carry the images fall naturally into classes, we may practically say that he has as many different social selves as there are distinct *groups* of persons about whose opinion he cares. He generally shows a different side of himself to each of these different groups. Many a youth who is demure enough before his parents and teachers, swears and swaggers like a pirate among his "tough" young friends. We do not show ourselves to our children as to our club-companions, to our customers as to the laborers we employ, to our own masters and employers as to our intimate friends. From this there results what practically is a division of the man into several selves; and this may be a discordant splitting, as where one is afraid to let one set of his acquaintances know him as he is elsewhere; or it may be a perfectly harmonious division of labor, as where one tender to his children is stern to the soldiers or prisoners under his command.

The most peculiar social self which one is apt to have is in the mind of the person one is in love with. The good or bad fortunes of this self cause the most intense elation and dejection—unreasonable enough as measured by every other standard than that of the organic feeling of the individual. To his own consciousness he *is* not, so long as this particular social self fails to get recognition, and when it is recognized his contentment passes all bounds.

A man's *fame,* good or bad, and his *honor* or dishonor, are names for one of his social selves. The particular social self of a man called his honor is usually the result of one of those splittings of which we have spoken. It is his image in the eyes of his own "set," which exalts or condemns him as he conforms or not to certain requirements that may not be made of one in another walk of life. Thus a layman may abandon a city infected with cholera; but a priest or a doctor would think such an act incompatible with his honor. A soldier's honor requires him to fight or to die under circumstances where another man can apologize or run away with no stain upon his social self. A judge, a statesman, are in like manner debarred by the honor of their cloth from entering into pecuniary relations perfectly honorable to persons in private life. Nothing is commoner than to hear people discriminate between their different selves of this sort: "As a man I pity you, but as an official I must show you no mercy"; "As a politician I regard him as an ally, but as a moralist I loathe him"; etc., etc. What may be called "club-opinion" is one of the very strongest forces in life. The thief must not steal from other thieves; the gambler must pay his gambling-debts, though he pay no other debts in the world. The code of honor of fashionable society has throughout history been full of permissions as well as of vetoes, the only reason for following either of which is that so we best serve one of our social selves. You must not lie in general, but you may lie as much as you please if asked about your relations with a lady; you must accept a challenge from an equal, but if challenged by an inferior you may laugh him to scorn: these are examples of what is meant.

12 | THE LOOKING-GLASS SELF
Charles Horton Cooley

It is well to say at the outset that by the word "self" in this discussion is meant simply that which is designated in common speech by the pronouns of the first person singular, "I," "me," "my," "mine," and "myself." "Self" and "ego" are used by metaphysicians and moralists in many other senses, more or less remote from the "I" of daily speech and thought, and with these I wish to have as little to do as possible. What is here discussed is what psychologists call the empirical self, the self that can be apprehended or verified by ordinary observation. I qualify it by the word social not as implying the existence of a self that is not social—for I think that the "I" of common language always has more or less distinct reference to other people as well as the speaker—but because I wish to emphasize and dwell upon the social aspect of it.

The distinctive thing in the idea for which the pronouns of the first person are names is apparently a characteristic kind of feeling which may be called the my-feeling or sense of appropriation. Almost any sort of ideas may be associated with this feeling, and so come to be named "I" or "mine," but the feeling, and that alone it would seem, is the determining factor in the matter. As Professor James says in his admirable discussion of the self, the words "me" and "self" designate "all the things which have the power to produce in a stream of consciousness excitement of a certain peculiar sort."

Since "I" is known to our experience primarily as a feeling, or as a feeling-ingredient in our ideas, it cannot be described or defined without suggesting that feeling. We are sometimes likely to fall into a formal and empty way of talking regarding questions of emotion, by attempting to define that which is in its nature primary and indefinable. A formal definition of self-feeling, or indeed of any sort of feeling, must be as hollow as a formal definition of the taste of salt, or the color red; we can expect to know what it is only by experiencing it. There can be no final test of the self

except the way we feel; it is that toward which we have the "my" attitude. But as this feeling is quite as familiar to us and as easy to recall as the taste of salt or the color red, there should be no difficulty in understanding what is meant by it. One need only imagine some attack on his "me," say ridicule of his dress or an attempt to take away his property or his child, or his good name by slander, and self-feeling immediately appears. Indeed, he need only pronounce, with strong emphasis, one of the self-words, like "I" or "my," and self-feeling will be recalled by association.

As many people have the impression that the verifiable self, the object that we name with "I," is usually the material body, it may be well to say that this impression is an illusion, easily dispelled by any one who will undertake a simple examination of facts. It is true that when we philosophize a little about "I" and look around for a tangible object to which to attach it, we soon fix upon the material body as the most available *locus;* but when we use the word naïvely, as in ordinary speech, it is not very common to think of the body in connection with it; not nearly so common as it is to think of other things. There is no difficulty in testing this statement, since the word "I" is one of the commonest in conversation and literature, so that nothing is more practicable than to study its meaning at any length that may be desired. One need only listen to ordinary speech until the word has occurred, say, a hundred times, noting its connections, or observe its use in a similar number of cases by the characters in a novel. Ordinarily it will be found that in not more than ten cases in a hundred does "I" have reference to the body of the person speaking. It refers chiefly to opinions, purposes, desires, claims, and the like, concerning matters that involve no thought of the body. *I* think or feel so and so; *I* wish or intend so and so; *I* want this or that; are typical uses, the self-feeling being associated with the view, purpose, or object mentioned. It should also be remembered that "my" and "mine" are

From *Human Nature and the Social Order* by Charles Horton Cooley. [1902] 1964 by Schocken Books.

as much the names of the self as "I," and these, of course, commonly refer to miscellaneous possessions.

The social self is simply any idea, or system of ideas, drawn from the communicative life, that the mind cherishes as its own. Self-feeling has its chief scope *within* the general life, not outside of it; the special endeavor or tendency of which it is the emotional aspect finds its principal field of exercise in a world of personal forces, reflected in the mind by a world of personal impressions.

That the "I" of common speech has a meaning which includes some sort of reference to other persons is involved in the very fact that the word and the ideas it stands for are phenomena of language and the communicative life. It is doubtful whether it is possible to use language at all without thinking more or less distinctly of some one else, and certainly the things to which we give names and which have a large place in reflective thought are almost always those which are impressed upon us by our contact with other people. Where there is no communication there can be no nomenclature and no developed thought. What we call "me," "mine," or "myself" is, then, not something separate from the general life, but the most interesting part of it, a part whose interest arises from the very fact that it is both general and individual. That is, we care for it just because it is that phase of the mind that is living and striving in the common life, trying to impress itself upon the minds of others. "I" is a militant social tendency, working to hold and enlarge its place in the general current of tendencies. So far as it can it waxes, as all life does. To think of it as apart from society is a palpable absurdity of which no one could be guilty who really *saw* it as a fact of life.

The reference to other persons involved in the sense of self may be distinct and particular, as when a boy is ashamed to have his mother catch him at something she has forbidden, or it may be vague and general, as when one is ashamed to do something which only his conscience, expressing his sense of social responsibility, detects and disapproves; but it is always there. There is no sense of "I," as in pride or shame, without its correlative sense of you, or he, or they. Even the miser gloating over his hidden gold can feel the "mine" only as he is aware of the world of men over whom he has secret power; and the case is very

similar with all kinds of hid treasure. Many painters, sculptors, and writers have loved to withhold their work from the world, fondling it in seclusion until they were quite done with it; but the delight in this, as in all secrets, depends upon a sense of the value of what is concealed.

In a very large and interesting class of cases the social reference takes the form of a somewhat definite imagination of how one's self—that is any idea he appropriates—appears in a particular mind, and the kind of self-feeling one has is determined by the attitude toward this attributed to that other mind. A social self of this sort might be called the reflected or looking-glass self:

> *"Each to each a looking-glass*
> *Reflects the other that doth pass."*

As we see our face, figure, and dress in the glass, and are interested in them because they are ours, and pleased or otherwise with them according as they do or do not answer to what we should like them to be; so in imagination we perceive in another's mind some thought of our appearance, manners, aims, deeds, character, friends, and so on, and are variously affected by it.

A self-idea of this sort seems to have three principal elements: the imagination of our appearance to the other person; the imagination of his judgment of that appearance, and some sort of self-feeling, such as pride or mortification. The comparison with a looking-glass hardly suggests the second element, the imagined judgment, which is quite essential. The thing that moves us to pride or shame is not the mere mechanical reflection of ourselves, but an imputed sentiment, the imagined effect of this reflection upon another's mind. This is evident from the fact that the character and weight of that other, in whose mind we see ourselves, makes all the difference with our feeling. We are ashamed to seem evasive in the presence of a straightforward man, cowardly in the presence of a brave one, gross in the eyes of a refined one, and so on. We always imagine, and in imagining share, the judgments of the other mind. A man will boast to one person of an action—say some sharp transaction in trade—which he would be ashamed to own to another.

13 | THE SELF
George Herbert Mead

The self has a character which is different from that of the physiological organism proper. The self is something which has a development; it is not initially there, at birth, but arises in the process of social experience and activity, that is, develops in the given individual as a result of his relations to that process as a whole and to other individuals within that process.

The self has the characteristic that it is an object to itself, and that characteristic distinguishes it from other objects and from the body. It is perfectly true that the eye can see the foot, but it does not see the body as a whole. We cannot see our backs; we can feel certain portions of them, if we are agile, but we cannot get an experience of our whole body. There are, of course, experiences which are somewhat vague and difficult of location, but the bodily experiences are for us organized about a self. The foot and hand belong to the self. We can see our feet, especially if we look at them from the wrong end of an opera glass, as strange things which we have difficulty in recognizing as our own. The parts of the body are quite distinguishable from the self. We can lose parts of the body without any serious invasion of the self. The mere ability to experience different parts of the body is not different from the experience of a table. The table presents a different feel from what the hand does when one hand feels another, but it is an experience of something with which we come definitely into contact. The body does not experience itself as a whole, in the sense in which the self in some way enters into the experience of the self.

It is the characteristic of the self as an object to itself that I want to bring out. This characteristic is represented in the word "self," which is a reflexive, and indicates that which can be both subject and object. This type of object is essentially different from other objects, and in the past it has been distinguished as conscious, a term which indicates an experience with, an experience of, one's self. It was assumed that consciousness in some way carried this capacity of being an object to itself. In giving a behavioristic statement of consciousness we have to look for some sort of experience in which the physical organism can become an object to itself.

When one is running to get away from someone who is chasing him, he is entirely occupied in this action, and his experience may be swallowed up in the objects about him, so that he has, at the time being, no consciousness of self at all. We must be, of course, very completely occupied to have that take place, but we can, I think, recognize that sort of a possible experience in which the self does not enter. We can, perhaps, get some light on that situation through those experiences in which in very intense action there appear in the experience of the individual, back of this intense action, memories and anticipations. Tolstoi as an officer in the war gives an account of having pictures of his past experience in the midst of his most intense action. There are also the pictures that flash into a person's mind when he is drowning. In such instances there is a contrast between an experience that is absolutely wound up in outside activity in which the self as an object does not enter, and an activity of memory and imagination in which the self is the principal object. The self is then entirely distinguishable from an organism that is surrounded by things and acts with reference to things, including parts of its own body. These latter may be objects like other objects, but they are just objects out there in the field, and they do not involve a self that is an object to the organism. This is, I think, frequently overlooked. It is that fact which makes our anthropomorphic reconstructions of animal life so fallacious. How can an individual get outside himself (experientially) in such a way as to become an object to himself? This is the essential psychological problem of selfhood or of self-consciousness; and its solution is to be found by referring to the process of social conduct or activity in which the given person or individual is implicated. The apparatus of reason would not be complete unless it swept itself into its own analysis of the field of experience; or unless the individual brought himself into the same experiential field as that of the other individual selves in relation to whom he acts in any given social situation.

The individual experiences himself as such, not directly, but only indirectly, from the particular standpoints of other individual members of the same social group, or from the generalized standpoint of the social group as a whole to which he belongs. For he enters his own experience as a self or individual, not directly or immediately, not by becoming a subject to himself, but only in so far as he first becomes an object to himself just as other individuals are objects to him or in his experience; and he becomes an object to himself only by taking the attitudes of other individuals toward himself within a social environment or context of experience and behavior in which both he and they are involved.

The importance of what we term "communication" lies in the fact that it provides a form of behavior in which the organism or the individual may become an object to himself. It is that sort of communication which we have been discussing—not communication in the sense of the cluck of the hen to the chickens, or the bark of a wolf to the pack, or the lowing of a cow, but communication in the sense of significant symbols, communication which is directed not only to others but also to the individual himself. So far as that type of communication is a part of behavior it at least introduces a self. Of course, one may hear without listening; one may see things that he does not realize; do things that he is not really aware of. But it is where one does respond to that which he addresses to another and where that response of his own becomes a part of his conduct, where he not only hears himself but responds to himself, talks and replies to himself as truly as the other person replies to him, that we have behavior in which the individuals become objects to themselves.

Such a self is not, I would say, primarily the physiological organism. The physiological organism is es-

sential to it, but we are at least able to think of a self without it. Persons who believe in immortality, or believe in ghosts, or in the possibility of the self leaving the body, assume a self which is quite distinguishable from the body. How successfully they can hold these conceptions is an open question, but we do, as a fact, separate the self and the organism. It is fair to say that the beginning of the self as an object, so far as we can see, is to be found in the experiences of people that lead to the conception of a "double." Primitive people assume that there is a double, located presumably in the diaphragm, that leaves the body temporarily in sleep and completely in death. It can be enticed out of the body of one's enemy and perhaps killed. It is represented in infancy by the imaginary playmates which children set up, and through which they come to control their experiences in their play.

The self, as that which can be an object to itself, is essentially a social structure, and it arises in social experience. After a self has arisen, it in a certain sense provides for itself its social experiences, and so we can conceive of an absolutely solitary self. But it is impossible to conceive of a self arising outside of social experience. When it has arisen we can think of a person in solitary confinement for the rest of his life, but who still has himself as a companion, and is able to think and to converse with himself as he had communicated with others. That process to which I have just referred, of responding to one's self as another responds to it, taking part in one's own conversation with others, being aware of what one is saying and using that awareness of what one is saying to determine what one is going to say thereafter—that is a process with which we are all familiar. We are continually following up our own address to other persons by an understanding of what we are saying, and using that understanding in the direction of our continued speech. We are finding out what we are going to say, what we are going to do, by saying and doing, and in the process we are continually controlling the process itself. In the conversation of gestures what we say calls out a certain response in another and that in turn changes our own action, so that we shift from what we started to do because of the reply the other makes. The conversation of gestures is the beginning of communication. The individual comes to carry on a conversation of gestures with himself. He says something, and that calls out a certain reply in himself which makes him change what he was going to say. One starts to say something, we will presume an unpleasant something, but when he starts to say it he realizes it is cruel. The effect on himself of what he is saying checks him; there is here a conversation of gestures between the individual and himself. We mean by significant speech that the action is one that affects the individual himself, and that the effect upon the individual himself is part of the intelligent carrying-out of the conversation with others. Now we, so to speak, amputate that social phase and dispense with it for the time being, so that one is talking to one's self as one would talk to another person.

This process of abstraction cannot be carried on indefinitely. One inevitably seeks an audience, has to pour himself out to somebody. In reflective intelligence one thinks to act, and to act solely so that this action remains a part of a social process. Thinking becomes preparatory to social action. The very process of thinking is, of course, simply an inner conversation that goes on, but it is a conversation of gestures which in its completion implies the expression of that which one thinks to an audience. One separates the significance of what he is saying to others from the actual speech and gets it ready before saying it. He thinks it out, and perhaps writes it in the form of a book; but it is still a part of social intercourse in which one is addressing other persons and at the same time addressing one's self, and in which one controls the address to other persons by the response made to one's own gesture. That the person should be responding to himself is necessary to the self, and it is this sort of social conduct which provides behavior within which that self appears. I know of no other form of behavior than the linguistic in which the individual is an object to himself, and, so far as I can see, the individual is not a self in the reflexive sense unless he is an object to himself. It is this fact that gives a critical importance to communication, since this is a type of behavior in which the individual does so respond to himself.

We realize in everyday conduct and experience that an individual does not mean a great deal of what he is doing and saying. We frequently say that such an individual is not himself. We come away from an in-

terview with a realization that we have left out important things, that there are parts of the self that did not get into what was said. What determines the amount of the self that gets into communication is the social experience itself. Of course, a good deal of the self does not need to get expression. We carry on a whole series of different relationships to different people. We are one thing to one man and another thing to another. There are parts of the self which exist only for the self in relationship to itself. We divide ourselves up in all sorts of different selves with reference to our acquaintances. We discuss politics with one and religion with another. There are all sorts of different selves answering to all sorts of different social reactions. It is the social process itself that is responsible for the appearance of the self; it is not then as a self apart from this type of experience.

A multiple personality is in a certain sense normal, as I have just pointed out. There is usually an organization of the whole self with reference to the community to which we belong, and the situation in which we find ourselves. What the society is, whether we are living with people of the present, people of our own imaginations, people of the past, varies, of course, with different individuals. Normally, within the sort of community as a whole to which we belong, there is a unified self, but that may be broken up. To a person who is somewhat unstable nervously and in whom there is a line of cleavage, certain activities become impossible, and that set of activities may separate and evolve another self. Two separate "me's" and "I's," two different selves, result, and that is the condition under which there is a tendency to break up the personality. There is an account of a professor of education who disappeared, was lost to the community, and later turned up in a logging camp in the West. He freed himself of his occupation and turned to the woods where he felt, if you like, more at home. The pathological side of it was the forgetting, the leaving out of the rest of the self. This result involved getting rid of certain bodily memories which would identify the individual to himself. We often recognize the lines of cleavage that run through us. We would be glad to forget certain things, get rid of things the self is bound up with in past experiences. What we have here is a situation in which there can be different selves, and it is dependent upon the set of social reactions that is involved as to which self we are going to be. If we can forget everything involved in one set of activities, obviously we relinquish that part of the self. Take a person who is unstable, get him occupied by speech, and at the same time get his eye on something you are writing so that he is carrying on two separate lines of communication, and if you go about it in the right way you can get those two currents going so that they do not run into each other. You can get two entirely different sets of activities going on. You can bring about in that way the dissociation of a person's self. It is a process of setting up two sorts of communication which separate the behavior of the individual. For one individual it is this thing said and heard, and for the other individual there exists only that which he sees written. You must, of course, keep one experience out of the field of the other. Dissociations are apt to take place when an event leads to emotional upheavals. That which is separated goes on in its own way.

The unity and structure of the complete self reflects the unity and structure of the social process as a whole; and each of the elementary selves of which it is composed reflects the unity and structure of one of the various aspects of that process in which the individual is implicated. In other words, the various elementary selves which constitute, or are organized into, a complete self are the various aspects of the structure of that complete self answering to the various aspects of the structure of the social process as a whole; the structure of the complete self is thus a reflection of the complete social process. The organization and unification of a social group is identical with the organization and unification of any one of the selves arising within the social process in which that group is engaged, or which it is carrying on.

The problem now presents itself as to how, in detail, a self arises. We have to note something of the background of its genesis. First of all there is the conversation of gestures between animals involving some sort of co-operative activity. There the beginning of the act of one is a stimulus to the other to respond in a certain way, while the beginning of this response becomes again a stimulus to the first to adjust his action to the oncoming response. Such is the preparation for the completed act, and ultimately it leads up to the conduct which is the outcome of this preparation. The conversation of gestures, however, does not carry with it the reference of the individual, the animal, the organism, to itself. It is not acting in a fashion which calls for a response from the form itself, although it is conduct with reference to the conduct of others. We have seen, however, that there are certain gestures that do affect the organism as they affect other organisms and may, therefore, arouse in the organism responses of the same character as aroused in the other. Here, then, we have a situation in which the individual may at least arouse responses in himself and reply to these responses, the condition being that the social stimuli have an effect on the individual which is like that which they have on the other. That, for example, is what is implied in language; otherwise language as significant symbol would disappear, since the individual would not get the meaning of that which he says.

Another set of background factors in the genesis of the self is represented in the activities of play and the game. We find in children something that answers to this double, namely, the invisible, imaginary companions which a good many children produce in their own experience. They organize in this way the responses which they call out in other persons and call out also in themselves. Of course, this playing with an imaginary companion is only a peculiarly interesting phase of ordinary play. Play in this sense, especially the stage which precedes the organized games, is a play at something. A child plays at being a mother, at being a teacher, at being a policeman; that is, it is taking different rôles, as we say. We have something that suggests this in what we call the play of animals: a cat will play with her kittens, and dogs play with each other. Two dogs playing with each other will attack and defend, in a process which if carried through would amount to an actual fight. There is a combination of responses which checks the depth of the bite. But we do not have in such a situation the dogs taking a definite rôle in the sense that a child deliberately takes the rôle of another. This tendency on the part of the children is what we are working with in the kindergarten where the rôles which the children assume are made the basis for training. When a child does assume a rôle he has in himself the stimuli which call out that particular response or group of responses.

He may, of course, run away when he is chased, as the dog does, or he may turn around and strike back just as the dog does in his play. But that is not the same as playing at something. Children get together to "play Indian." This means that the child has a certain set of stimuli which call out in itself the responses that they would call out in others, and which answer to an Indian. In the play period the child utilizes his own responses to these stimuli which he makes use of in building a self. The response which he has a tendency to make to these stimuli organizes them. He plays that he is, for instance, offering himself something, and he buys it; he gives a letter to himself and takes it away; he addresses himself as a parent, as a teacher; he arrests himself as a policeman. He has a set of stimuli which call out in himself the sort of responses they call out in others. He takes this group of responses and organizes them into a certain whole. Such is the simplest form of being another to one's self. It involves a temporal situation. The child says something in one character and responds in another character, and then his responding in another character is a stimulus to himself in the first character, and so the conversation goes on. A certain organized structure arises in him and in his other which replies to it, and these carry on the conversation of gestures between themselves.

If we contrast play with the situation in an organized game, we note the essential difference that the child who plays in a game must be ready to take the attitude of everyone else involved in that game, and that these different rôles must have a definite relationship to each other. Taking a very simple game such as hide-and-seek, everyone with the exception of the one who is hiding is a person who is hunting. A child does not require more than the person who is hunted and the one who is hunting. If a child is playing in the first sense he just goes on playing, but there is no basic organization gained. In that early stage he passes from one rôle to another just as a whim takes him. But in a game where a number of individuals are involved, then the child taking one rôle must be ready to take the rôle of everyone else. If he gets in a ball nine he must have the responses of each position involved in his own position. He must know what everyone else is going to do in order to carry out his own play. He has to take all of these rôles. They do not all have to be present in consciousness at the same time, but at some moments he has to have three or four individuals present in his own attitude, such as the one who is going to throw the ball, the one who is going to catch it, and so on. These responses must be, in some degree, present in his own make-up. In the game, then, there is a set of responses of such others so organized that the attitude of one calls out the appropriate attitudes of the other.

This organization is put in the form of the rules of the game. Children take a great interest in rules. They make rules on the spot in order to help themselves out of difficulties. Part of the enjoyment of the game is to get these rules. Now, the rules are the set of responses which a particular attitude calls out. You can demand a certain response in others if you take a certain attitude. These responses are all in yourself as well. There you get an organized set of such responses as that to which I have referred, which is something more elaborate than the rôles found in play. Here there is just a set of responses that follow on each other indefinitely. At such a stage we speak of a child as not yet having a fully developed self. The child responds in a fairly intelligent fashion to the immediate stimuli that come to him, but they are not organized. He does not organize his life as we would like to have him do, namely, as a whole. There is just a set of responses of the type of play. The child reacts to a certain stimulus, and the reaction is in himself that is called out in others, but he is not a whole self. In his game he has to have an organization of these rôles; otherwise he cannot play the game. The game represents the passage in the life of the child from taking the rôle of others in play to the organized part that is essential to self-consciousness in the full sense of the term.

The fundamental difference between the game and play is that in the latter the child must have the attitude of all the others involved in that game. The attitudes of the other players which the participant assumes organize into a sort of unit, and it is that organization which controls the response of the individual. The illustration used was of a person playing baseball. Each one of his own acts is determined by his assumption of the action of the others who are playing the game. What he does is controlled by his being everyone else on that team, at least in so far as those attitudes affect his own particular response. We get then an "other" which is an organization of the attitudes of those involved in the same process.

The organized community or social group which gives to the individual his unity of self may be called "the generalized other." The attitude of the generalized other is the attitude of the whole community. Thus, for example, in the case of such a social group as a ball team, the team is the generalized other in so far as it enters—as an organized process or social activity—into the experience of any one of the individual members of it.

14 | THE PRESENTATION OF SELF
Erving Goffman

When an individual enters the presence of others, they commonly seek to acquire information about him or to bring into play information about him already possessed. They will be interested in his general socio-economic status, his conception of self, his attitude toward them, his competence, his trustworthiness, etc. Although some of this information seems to be sought almost as an end in itself, there are usually quite practical reasons for acquiring it. Information about the individual helps to define the situation, enabling others to know in advance what he will expect of them and what they may expect of him. Informed in these ways, the others will know how best to act in order to call forth a desired response from him.

For those present, many sources of information become accessible and many carriers (or "sign-vehicles") become available for conveying this information. If unacquainted with the individual, observers can glean clues from his conduct and appearance which allow them to apply their previous experience with individuals roughly similar to the one before them or, more important, to apply untested stereotypes to him. They can also assume from past experience that only individuals of a particular kind are likely to be found in a given social setting. They can rely on what the individual says about himself or on documentary evidence he provides as to who and what he is. If they know, or know of, the individual by virtue of experience prior to the interaction, they can rely on assumptions as to the persistence and generality of psychological traits as a means of predicting his present and future behavior.

However, during the period in which the individual is in the immediate presence of the others, few events may occur which directly provide the others with the conclusive information they will need if they are to direct wisely their own activity. Many crucial facts lie beyond the time and place of interaction or lie concealed within it. For example, the "true" or "real" attitudes, beliefs, and emotions of the individual can be ascertained only indirectly, through his avowals or through what appears to be involuntary expressive behavior. Similarly, if the individual offers the others a product or service, they will often find that during the interaction there will be no time and place immediately available for eating the pudding that the proof can be found in. They will be forced to accept some events as conventional or natural signs of something not directly available to the senses. In Ichheiser's terms,[1] the individual will have to act so that he intentionally or unintentionally *expresses* himself, and the others will in turn have to be *impressed* in some way by him.

The expressiveness of the individual (and therefore his capacity to give impressions) appears to involve two radically different kinds of sign activity, the expression that he *gives,* and the expression that he *gives off*. The first involves verbal symbols or their substitutes which he uses admittedly and solely to convey the information that he and the others are known to attach to these symbols. This is communication in the traditional and narrow sense. The second involves a wide range of action that others can treat as symptomatic of the actor, the expectation being that the action was performed for reasons other than the information conveyed in this way. As we shall have to see, this distinction has an only initial validity. The individual does of course intentionally convey misinformation by means of both of these types of communication, the first involving deceit, the second feigning.

Taking communication in both its narrow and broad sense, one finds that when the individual is in the immediate presence of others, his activity will have a promissory character. The others are likely to find that they must accept the individual on faith, offering him a just return while he is present before them in exchange for something whose true value will not be established until after he has left their presence. (Of course, the others also live by inference in their dealings with the physical world, but it is only in the world of social interaction that the objects about which they make inferences will purposely facilitate and hinder this inferential process.) The security that they justifiably feel in making inferences about the individual will vary, of course, depending on such factors as the amount of information they already possess about him, but no amount of such past evidence can entirely obviate the necessity of acting on the basis of inferences. As William I. Thomas suggested:

> It is also highly important for us to realize that we do not as a matter of fact lead our lives, make our decisions, and reach our goals in everyday life either statistically or scientifically. We live by inference. I am, let us say, your guest. You do not know, you cannot determine scientifically, that I will not steal your money or your spoons. But inferentially I will not, and inferentially you have me as a guest.[2]

Let us now turn from the others to the point of view of the individual who presents himself before them. He may wish them to think highly of him, or to think that he thinks highly of them, or to perceive how in fact he feels toward them, or to obtain no clear-cut impression; he may wish to ensure sufficient harmony so that the interaction can be sustained, or to defraud, get rid of, confuse, mislead, antagonize, or insult them. Regardless of the particular objective which the individual has in mind and of his motive for having this objective, it will be in his interests to control the conduct of the others, especially their responsive treatment of him.[3] This control is achieved largely by influencing the definition of the situation which the others come to formulate, and he can influence this definition by expressing himself in such a way as to give them the kind of impression that will lead them to act voluntarily in accordance with his own plan. Thus, when an individual appears in the presence of others, there will usually be some reason for him to mobilize his activity so that it will convey an impression to others which it is in his interests to convey. Since a girl's dormitory mates will glean evidence of her popularity from the calls she receives on the phone, we can suspect that some girls will arrange for calls to be made, and Willard Waller's finding can be anticipated:

> It has been reported by many observers that a girl who is called to the telephone in the dormitories will often allow herself to be called several times, in order to give all the other girls ample opportunity to hear her paged.[4]

Of the two kinds of communication—expressions given and expressions given off—this report will be primarily concerned with the latter, with the more theatrical and contextual kind, the non-verbal, presumably unintentional kind, whether this communication be purposely engineered or not. As an example of what we must try to examine, I would like to cite at length a novelistic incident in which Preedy, a vacationing Englishman, makes his first appearance on the beach of his summer hotel in Spain:

> But in any case he took care to avoid catching anyone's eye. First of all, he had to make it clear to those potential companions of his holiday that they were of no concern to him whatsoever. He stared through them, round them, over them—eyes lost in space. The beach might have been empty. If by chance a ball was thrown his way, he looked surprised; then let a smile of amusement lighten his face (Kindly Preedy), looked round dazed to see that there *were* people on the beach, tossed it back with a smile to

himself and not a smile *at* the people, and then re-sumed carelessly his nonchalant survey of space.

But it was time to institute a little parade, the pa-rade of the Ideal Preedy. By devious handlings he gave any who wanted to look a chance to see the title of his book—a Spanish translation of Homer, classic thus, but not daring, cosmopolitan too—and then gathered together his beach-wrap and bag into a neat sand-resistant pile (Methodical and Sensible Preedy), rose slowly to stretch at ease his huge frame (Big-Cat Preedy), and tossed aside his sandals (Carefree Preedy, after all).

The marriage of Preedy and the sea! There were alternative rituals. The first involved the stroll that turns into a run and a dive straight into the water, thereafter smoothing into a strong splashless crawl towards the horizon. But of course not really to the horizon. Quite suddenly he would turn on to his back and thrash great white splashes with his legs, some-how thus showing that he could have swum further had he wanted to, and then would stand up a quarter out of water for all to see who it was.

The alternative course was simpler, it avoided the cold-water shock and it avoided the risk of appearing too high-spirited. The point was to appear to be so used to the sea, the Mediterranean, and this particular beach, that one might as well be in the sea as out of it. It involved a slow stroll down and into the edge of the water—not even noticing his toes were wet, land and water all the same to *him!*—with his eyes up at the sky gravely surveying portents, invisible to oth-ers, of the weather (Local Fisherman Preedy).[5]

The novelist means us to see that Preedy is improper-ly concerned with the extensive impressions he feels his sheer bodily action is giving off to those around him. We can malign Preedy further by assuming that he has acted merely in order to give a particular im-pression, that this is a false impression, and that the others present receive either no impression at all, or, worse still, the impression that Preedy is affectedly trying to cause them to receive this particular impres-sion. But the important point for us here is that the kind of impression Preedy thinks he is making is in fact the kind of impression that others correctly and incorrectly glean from someone in their midst.

I have said that when an individual appears before others his actions will influence the definition of the situation which they come to have. Sometimes the in-dividual will act in a thoroughly calculating manner, expressing himself in a given way solely in order to give the kind of impression to others that is likely to evoke from them a specific response he is concerned to obtain. Sometimes the individual will be calculat-ing in his activity but be relatively unaware that this is the case. Sometimes he will intentionally and con-sciously express himself in a particular way, but chiefly because the tradition of his group or social sta-tus require this kind of expression and not because of any particular response (other than vague acceptance or approval) that is likely to be evoked from those im-pressed by the expression. Sometimes the traditions of an individual's role will lead him to give a well-designed impression of a particular kind and yet he may be neither consciously nor unconsciously dis-posed to create such an impression. The others, in their turn, may be suitably impressed by the individ-ual's efforts to convey something, or may misunder-stand the situation and come to conclusions that are warranted neither by the individual's intent nor by the facts. In any case, in so far as the others act *as if* the in-dividual had conveyed a particular impression, we may take a functional or pragmatic view and say that the individual has "effectively" projected a given def-inition of the situation and "effectively" fostered the understanding that a given state of affairs obtains.

There is one aspect of the others' response that bears special comment here. Knowing that the indi-vidual is likely to present himself in a light that is fa-vorable to him, the others may divide what they wit-ness into two parts; a part that is relatively easy for the individual to manipulate at will, being chiefly his ver-bal assertions, and a part in regard to which he seems to have little concern or control, being chiefly derived from the expressions he gives off. The others may then use what are considered to be the ungovernable aspects of his expressive behavior as a check upon the validity of what is conveyed by the governable as-pects. In this a fundamental asymmetry is demonstrat-ed in the communication process, the individual pre-sumably being aware of only one stream of his communication, the witnesses of this stream and one other. For example, in Shetland Isle one crofter's wife, in serving native dishes to a visitor from the mainland of Britain, would listen with a polite smile to his polite claims of liking what he was eating; at the same time she would take note of the rapidity with which the visitor lifted his fork or spoon to his mouth, the eagerness with which he passed food into his mouth, and the gusto expressed in chewing the food, using these signs as a check on the stated feelings of the eater. The same woman, in order to discover what one acquaintance (A) "actually" thought of another acquaintance (B), would wait until B was in the presence of A but engaged in conversation with still another person (C). She would then covertly examine the facial expressions of A as he regarded B in conversation with C. Not being in conversation with B, and not being directly observed by him, A would sometimes relax usual constraints and tactful deceptions, and freely express what he was "actually" feeling about B. This Shetlander, in short, would observe the unobserved observer.

Now given the fact that others are likely to check up on the more controllable aspects of behavior by means of the less controllable, one can expect that sometimes the individual will try to exploit this very possibility, guiding the impression he makes through behavior felt to be reliably informing.[6] For example, in gaining admission to a tight social circle, the participant observer may not only wear an accepting look while listening to an informant, but may also be careful to wear the same look when observing the informant talking to others; observers of the observer will then not as easily discover where he actually stands. A specific illustration may be cited from Shetland Isle. When a neighbor dropped in to have a cup of tea, he would ordinarily wear at least a hint of an expectant warm smile as he passed through the door into the cottage. Since lack of physical obstructions outside the cottage and lack of light within it usually made it possible to observe the visitor unobserved as he approached the house, islanders sometimes took pleasure in watching the visitor drop whatever expression he was manifesting and replace it with a sociable one just before reaching the door. However, some visitors, in appreciating that this examination was occurring, would blindly adopt a social face a long distance from the house, thus ensuring the projection of a constant image.

This kind of control upon the part of the individual reinstates the symmetry of the communication process, and sets the stage for a kind of information game—a potentially infinite cycle of concealment, discovery, false revelation, and rediscovery. It should be added that since the others are likely to be relatively unsuspicious of the presumably unguided aspect of the individual's conduct, he can gain much by controlling it. The others of course may sense that the individual is manipulating the presumably spontaneous aspects of his behavior, and seek in this very act of manipulation some shading of conduct that the individual has not managed to control. This again provides a check upon the individual's behavior, this time his presumably uncalculated behavior, thus reestablishing the asymmetry of the communication process. Here I would like only to add the suggestion that the arts of piercing an individual's effort at calculated unintentionality seem better developed than our capacity to manipulate our own behavior, so that regardless of how many steps have occurred in the information game, the witness is likely to have the advantage over the actor, and the initial asymmetry of the communication process is likely to be retained.

When we allow that the individual projects a definition of the situation when he appears before others, we must also see that the others, however passive their role may seem to be, will themselves effectively project a definition of the situation by virtue of their response to the individual and by virtue of any lines of action they initiate to him. Ordinarily the definitions of the situation projected by the several different participants are sufficiently attuned to one another so that open contradiction will not occur. I do not mean that there will be the kind of consensus that arises when each individual present candidly expresses what he really feels and honestly agrees with the expressed feelings of the others present. This kind of harmony is an optimistic ideal and in any case not necessary for the smooth working of society. Rather, each participant is expected to suppress his immediate heartfelt feelings, conveying a view of the situation which he feels the others will be able to find at least temporarily acceptable. The maintenance of this surface of agreement, this veneer of consensus, is facilitated by each participant concealing his own wants behind statements which assert values to which everyone present feels obliged to give lip service. Further, there is usually a kind of division of definitional labor. Each participant is allowed to establish the tentative official ruling regarding matters which are vital to him but not immediately important to others, e.g., the rationalizations and justifications by which he accounts for his past activity. In exchange for this courtesy he remains silent or non-committal on matters important to others but not immediately important to him. We have then a kind of interactional *modus vivendi*. Together the participants contribute to a single over-all definition of the situation which involves not so much a real agreement as to what exists but rather a real agreement as to whose claims concerning what issues will be temporarily honored. Real agreement will also exist concerning the desirability of avoiding an open conflict of definitions of the situation.[7] I will refer to this level of agreement as a "working consensus." It is to be understood that the working consensus established in one interaction setting will be quite different in content from the working consensus established in a different type of setting. Thus, between two friends at lunch, a reciprocal show of affection, respect, and concern for the other is maintained. In service occupations, on the other hand, the specialist often maintains an image of disinterested involvement in the problem of the client, while the client responds with a show of respect for the competence and integrity of the specialist. Regardless of such differences in content, however, the general form of these working arrangements is the same.

In noting the tendency for a participant to accept the definitional claims made by the others present, we can appreciate the crucial importance of the information that the individual *initially* possesses or acquires concerning his fellow participants, for it is on the basis of this initial information that the individual starts to define the situation and starts to build up lines of responsive action. The individual's initial projection commits him to what he is proposing to be and requires him to drop all pretenses of being other things. As the interaction among the participants progresses, additions and modifications in this initial informational state will of course occur, but it is essential that these later developments be related without contradiction to, and even built up from, the initial positions taken by the several participants. It would seem that

an individual can more easily make a choice as to what line of treatment to demand from and extend to the others present at the beginning of an encounter than he can alter the line of treatment that is being pursued once the interaction is underway.

In everyday life, of course, there is a clear understanding that first impressions are important. Thus, the work adjustment of those in service occupations will often hinge upon a capacity to seize and hold the initiative in the service relation, a capacity that will require subtle aggressiveness on the part of the server when he is of lower socio-economic status than his client. W. F. Whyte suggests the waitress as an example:

> The first point that stands out is that the waitress who bears up under pressure does not simply respond to her customers. She acts with some skill to control their behavior. The first question to ask when we look at the customer relationship is, "Does the waitress get the jump on the customer, or does the customer get the jump on the waitress?" The skilled waitress realizes the crucial nature of this question. . . .
>
> The skilled waitress tackles the customer with confidence and without hesitation. For example, she may find that a new customer has seated himself before she could clear off the dirty dishes and change the cloth. He is now leaning on the table studying the menu. She greets him, says, "May I change the cover, please?" and, without waiting for an answer, takes his menu away from him so that he moves back from the table, and she goes about her work. The relationship is handled politely but firmly, and there is never any question as to who is in charge.[8]

When the interaction that is initiated by "first impressions" is itself merely the initial interaction in an extended series of interactions involving the same participants, we speak of "getting off on the right foot" and feel that it is crucial that we do so. Thus, one learns that some teachers take the following view:

> You can't ever let them get the upper hand on you or you're through. So I start out tough. The first day I get a new class in, I let them know who's boss . . . You've got to start off tough, then you can ease up as you go along. If you start out easy-going, when you try to get tough, they'll just look at you and laugh.[9]

Similarly, attendants in mental institutions may feel that if the new patient is sharply put in his place the first day on the ward and made to see who is boss, much future difficulty will be prevented.[10]

Given the fact that the individual effectively projects a definition of the situation when he enters the presence of others, we can assume that events may occur within the interaction which contradict, discredit, or otherwise throw doubt upon this projection. When these disruptive events occur, the interaction itself may come to a confused and embarrassed halt. Some of the assumptions upon which the responses of the participants had been predicated become untenable, and the participants find themselves lodged in an interaction for which the situation has been wrongly defined and is now no longer defined. At such moments the individual whose presentation has been discredited may feel ashamed while the others present may feel hostile, and all the participants may come to feel ill at ease, nonplussed, out of countenance, embarrassed, experiencing the kind of anomy that is generated when the minute social system of face-to-face interaction breaks down.

BELIEF IN THE PART ONE IS PLAYING

When an individual plays a part he implicitly requests his observers to take seriously the impression that is fostered before them. They are asked to believe that the character they see actually possesses the attributes he appears to possess, that the task he performs will have the consequences that are implicitly claimed for it, and that, in general, matters are what they appear to be. In line with this, there is the popular view that the individual offers his performance and puts on his show "for the benefit of other people." It will be convenient to begin a consideration of performances by turning the question around and looking at the individual's own belief in the impression of reality that he attempts to engender in those among whom he finds himself.

At one extreme, one finds that the performer can be fully taken in by his own act; he can be sincerely convinced that the impression of reality which he stages is the real reality. When his audience is also convinced in this way about the show he puts on—and this seems to be the typical case—then for the moment at least, only the sociologist or the socially disgruntled

will have any doubts about the "realness" of what is presented.

At the other extreme, we find that the performer may not be taken in at all by his own routine. This possibility is understandable, since no one is in quite as good an observational position to see through the act as the person who puts it on. Coupled with this, the performer may be moved to guide the conviction of his audience only as a means to other ends, having no ultimate concern in the conception that they have of him or of the situation. When the individual has no belief in his own act and no ultimate concern with the beliefs of his audience, we may call him cynical, reserving the term "sincere" for individuals who believe in the impression fostered by their own performance. It should be understood that the cynic, with all his professional disinvolvement, may obtain unprofessional pleasures from his masquerade, experiencing a kind of gleeful spiritual aggression from the fact that he can toy at will with something his audience must take seriously.[11]

It is not assumed, of course, that all cynical performers are interested in deluding their audiences for purposes of what is called "self-interest" or private gain. A cynical individual may delude his audience for what he considers to be their own good, or for the good of the community, etc. For illustrations of this we need not appeal to sadly enlightened showmen such as Marcus Aurelius or Hsun Tzŭ. We know that in service occupations practitioners who may otherwise be sincere are sometimes forced to delude their customers because their customers show such a heartfelt demand for it. Doctors who are led into giving placebos, filling station attendants who resignedly check and recheck tire pressures for anxious women motorists, shoe clerks who sell a shoe that fits but tell the customer it is the size she wants to hear—these are cynical performers whose audiences will not allow them to be sincere. Similarly, it seems that sympathetic patients in mental wards will sometimes feign bizarre symptoms so that student nurses will not be subjected to a disappointingly sane performance.[12] So also, when inferiors extend their most lavish reception for visiting superiors, the selfish desire to win favor may not be the chief motive; the inferior may be tactfully attempting to put the superior at ease by simulating the kind of world the superior is thought to take for granted.

I have suggested two extremes: an individual may be taken in by his own act or be cynical about it. These extremes are something a little more than just the ends of a continuum. Each provides the individual with a position which has its own particular securities and defenses, so there will be a tendency for those who have traveled close to one of these poles to complete the voyage. Starting with lack of inward belief in one's role, the individual may follow the natural movement described by Park:

It is probably no mere historical accident, that the word person, in its first meaning, is a mask. It is rather a recognition of the fact that everyone is always and everywhere, more or less consciously, playing a role . . . It is in these roles that we know each other; it is in these roles that we know ourselves.[13]

In a sense, and in so far as this mask represents the conception we have formed of ourselves—the role we are striving to live up to—this mask is our truer self, the self we would like to be. In the end, our conception of our role becomes second nature and an integral part of our personality. We come into the world as individuals, achieve character, and become persons.[14]

This may be illustrated from the community life of Shetland.[15] For the last four or five years the island's tourist hotel has been owned and operated by a married couple of crofter origins. From the beginning, the owners were forced to set aside their own conceptions as to how life ought to be led, displaying in the hotel a full round of middle-class services and amenities. Lately, however, it appears that the managers have become less cynical about the performance that they stage; they themselves are becoming middle class and more and more enamored of the selves their clients impute to them.

Another illustration may be found in the raw recruit who initially follows army etiquette in order to avoid physical punishment and eventually comes to follow the rules so that his organization will not be shamed and his officers and fellow soldiers will respect him.

As suggested, the cycle of disbelief-to-belief can

be followed in the other direction, starting with conviction or insecure aspiration and ending in cynicism. Professions which the public holds in religious awe often allow their recruits to follow the cycle in this direction, and often recruits follow it in this direction not because of a slow realization that they are deluding their audience—for by ordinary social standards the claims they make may be quite valid—but because they can use this cynicism as a means of insulating their inner selves from contact with the audience. And we may even expect to find typical careers of faith, with the individual starting out with one kind of involvement in the performance he is required to give, then moving back and forth several times between sincerity and cynicism before completing all the phases and turning-points of self-belief for a person of his station. Thus, students of medical schools suggest that idealistically oriented beginners in medical school typically lay aside their holy aspirations for a period of time. During the first two years the students find that their interest in medicine must be dropped that they may give all their time to the task of learning how to get through examinations. During the next two years they are too busy learning about diseases to show much concern for the persons who are diseased. It is only after their medical schooling has ended that their original ideals about medical service may be reasserted.[16]

While we can expect to find natural movement back and forth between cynicism and sincerity, still we must not rule out the kind of transitional point that can be sustained on the strength of a little self-illusion. We find that the individual may attempt to induce the audience to judge him and the situation in a particular way, and he may seek this judgment as an ultimate end in itself, and yet he may not completely believe that he deserves the valuation of self which he asks for or that the impression of reality which he fosters is valid. Another mixture of cynicism and belief is suggested in Kroeber's discussion of shamanism:

Next, there is the old question of deception. Probably most shamans or medicine men, the world over, help along with sleight-of-hand in curing and especially in exhibitions of power. This sleight-of-hand is sometimes deliberate; in many cases awareness is perhaps not deeper than the foreconscious. The attitude, whether there has been repression or not, seems to be as toward a pious fraud. Field ethnographers seem quite generally convinced that even shamans who know that they add fraud nevertheless also believe in their powers, and especially in those of other shamans: they consult them when they themselves or their children are ill.[17]

STAGING AND THE SELF

The general notion that we make a presentation of ourselves to others is hardly novel; what ought to be stressed in conclusion is that the very structure of the self can be seen in terms of how we arrange for such performances in our Anglo-American society.

In this report, the individual was divided by implication into two basic parts: he was viewed as a *performer,* a harried fabricator of impressions involved in the all-too-human task of staging a performance; he was viewed as a *character,* a figure, typically a fine one, whose spirit, strength, and other sterling qualities the performance was designed to evoke. The attributes of a performer and the attributes of a character are of a different order, quite basically so, yet both sets have their meaning in terms of the show that must go on.

First, character. In our society the character one performs and one's self are somewhat equated, and this self-as-character is usually seen as something housed within the body of its possessor, especially the upper parts thereof, being a nodule, somehow, in the psychobiology of personality. I suggest that this view is an implied part of what we are all trying to present, but provides, just because of this, a bad analysis of the presentation. In this report the performed self was seen as some kind of image, usually creditable, which the individual on stage and in character effectively attempts to induce others to hold in regard to him. While this image is entertained *concerning* the individual, so that a self is imputed to him, this self itself does not derive from its possessor, but from the whole scene of his action, being generated by that attribute of local events which renders them interpretable by witnesses. A correctly staged and performed scene leads the audience to impute a self to a performed character, but this imputation—this self—is a *product* of a scene that comes off, and is not a *cause* of it. The self, then, as a performed character, is not an organic thing that has a

specific location, whose fundamental fate is to be born, to mature, and to die; it is a dramatic effect arising diffusely from a scene that is presented, and the characteristic issue, the crucial concern, is whether it will be credited or discredited.

In analyzing the self then we are drawn from its possessor, from the person who will profit or lose most by it, for he and his body merely provide the peg on which something of collaborative manufacture will be hung for a time. And the means for producing and maintaining selves do not reside inside the peg; in fact these means are often bolted down in social establishments. There will be a back region with its tools for shaping the body, and a front region with its fixed props. There will be a team of persons whose activity on stage in conjunction with available props will constitute the scene from which the performed character's self will emerge, and another team, the audience, whose interpretive activity will be necessary for this emergence. The self is a product of all of these arrangements, and in all of its parts bears the marks of this genesis.

The whole machinery of self-production is cumbersome, of course, and sometimes breaks down, exposing its separate components: back region control; team collusion; audience tact; and so forth. But, well oiled, impressions will flow from it fast enough to put us in the grips of one of our types of reality—the performance will come off and the firm self accorded each performed character will appear to emanate intrinsically from its performer.

Let us turn now from the individual as character performed to the individual as performer. He has a capacity to learn, this being exercised in the task of training for a part. He is given to having fantasies and dreams, some that pleasurably unfold a triumphant performance, others full of anxiety and dread that nervously deal with vital discreditings in a public front region. He often manifests a gregarious desire for teammates and audiences, a tactful considerateness for their concerns; and he has a capacity for deeply felt shame, leading him to minimize the chances he takes of exposure.

These attributes of the individual *qua* performer are not merely a depicted effect of particular performances; they are psychobiological in nature, and yet they seem to arise out of intimate interaction with the contingencies of staging performances.

And now a final comment. In developing the conceptual framework employed in this report, some language of the stage was used. I spoke of performers and audiences; of routines and parts; of performances coming off or falling flat; of cues, stage settings and backstage; of dramaturgical needs, dramaturgical skills, and dramaturgical strategies. Now it should be admitted that this attempt to press a mere analogy so far was in part a rhetoric and a maneuver.

The claim that all the world's a stage is sufficiently commonplace for readers to be familiar with its limitations and tolerant of its presentation, knowing that at any time they will easily be able to demonstrate to themselves that it is not to be taken too seriously. An action staged in a theater is a relatively contrived illusion and an admitted one; unlike ordinary life, nothing real or actual can happen to the performed characters—although at another level of course something real and actual can happen to the reputation of performers *qua* professionals whose everyday job is to put on theatrical performances.

And so here the language and mask of the stage will be dropped. Scaffolds, after all, are to build other things with, and should be erected with an eye to taking them down. This report is not concerned with aspects of theater that creep into everyday life. It is concerned with the structure of social encounters—the structure of those entities in social life that come into being whenever persons enter one another's immediate physical presence. The key factor in this structure is the maintenance of a single definition of the situation, this definition having to be expressed, and this expression sustained in the face of a multitude of potential disruptions.

A character staged in a theater is not in some ways real, nor does it have the same kind of real consequences as does the thoroughly contrived character performed by a confidence man; but the *successful* staging of either of these types of false figures involves use of *real* techniques—the same techniques by which everyday persons sustain their real social situations. Those who conduct face to face interaction on a theater's stage must meet the key requirement of real situations; they must expressively sustain a definition of the situation: but this they do in circumstances that have facilitated their developing an apt terminology for the interactional tasks that all of us share.

NOTES

1. Gustav Ichheiser, "Misunderstandings in Human Relations," Supplement to *The American Journal of Sociology,* LV (September, 1949), pp. 6–7.

2. Quoted in E. H. Volkart, editor, *Social Behavior and Personality,* Contributions of W. I. Thomas to Theory and Social Research (New York: Social Science Research Council, 1951), p. 5.

3. Here I owe much to an unpublished paper by Tom Burns of the University of Edinburgh. He presents the argument that in all interaction a basic underlying theme is the desire of each participant to guide and control the responses made by the others present. A similar argument has been advanced by Jay Haley in a recent unpublished paper, but in regard to a special kind of control, that having to do with defining the nature of the relationship of those involved in the interaction.

4. Willard Waller, "The Rating and Dating Complex," *American Sociological Review,* II, p. 730.

5. William Sansom, *A Contest of Ladies* (London: Hogarth, 1956), pp. 230–32.

6. The widely read and rather sound writings of Stephen Potter are concerned in part with signs that can be engineered to give a shrewd observer the apparently incidental cues he needs to discover concealed virtues the gamesman does not in fact possess.

7. An interaction can be purposely set up as a time and place for voicing differences in opinion, but in such cases participants must be careful to agree not to disagree on the proper tone of voice, vocabulary, and degree of seriousness in which all arguments are to be phrased, and upon the mutual respect which disagreeing participants must carefully continue to express toward one another. This debaters' or academic definition of the situation may also be invoked suddenly and judiciously as a way of translating a serious conflict of views into one that can be handled within a framework acceptable to all present.

8. W. F. Whyte, "When Workers and Customers Meet," Chap. VII, *Industry and Society,* ed. W. F. Whyte (New York: McGraw-Hill, 1946), pp. 132–33.

9. Teacher interview quoted by Howard S. Becker, "Social Class Variations in the Teacher-Pupil Relationship," *Journal of Educational Sociology,* XXV, p. 459.

10. Harold Taxel, "Authority Structure in a Mental Hospital Ward" (unpublished Master's thesis, Department of Sociology, University of Chicago, 1953).

11. Perhaps the real crime of the confidence man is not that he takes money from his victims but that he robs all of us of the belief that middle-class manners and appearance can be sus-

tained only by middle-class people. A disabused professional can be cynically hostile to the service relation his clients expect him to extend to them; the confidence man is in a position to hold the whole "legit" world in this contempt.

12. See Taxel, op. cit., p. 4. Harry Stack Sullivan has suggested that the tact of institutionalized performers can operate in the other direction, resulting in a kind of *noblesse-oblige* sanity. See his "Socio-Psychiatric Research," *American Journal of Psychiatry,* X, pp. 987–88.

"A study of 'social recoveries' in one of our large mental hospitals some years ago taught me that patients were often released from care because they had learned not to manifest symptoms to the environing persons; in other words, had integrated enough of the personal environment to realize the prejudice opposed to their delusions. It seemed almost as if they grew wise enough to be tolerant of the imbecility surrounding them, having finally discovered that it was stupidity and not malice. They could then secure satisfaction from contact with others, while discharging a part of their cravings by psychotic means."

13. Robert Ezra Park, *Race and Culture* (Glencoe, Ill.: The Free Press, 1950), p. 249.

14. Ibid., p. 250.

15. Shetland Isle study.

16. H. S. Becker and Blanche Greer, "The Fate of Idealism in Medical School," *American Sociological Review, 23,* pp. 50–56.

17. A. L. Kroeber, *The Nature of Culture* (Chicago: University of Chicago Press, 1952), p. 311.

15 | SALVAGING THE SELF
David A. Snow and Leon Anderson

To be homeless in America is not only to have fallen to the bottom of the status system; it is also to be confronted with gnawing doubts about self-worth and the meaning of existence. Such vexing concerns are not just the psychic fallout of having descended onto the streets, but are also stoked by encounters with the domiciled that constantly remind the homeless of where they stand in relation to others.

One such encounter occurred early in the course of our fieldwork. . . . The homeless were congregating in front of the Sally (the Salvation Army) for dinner. A school bus approached that was packed with Anglo junior high school students being bused from an east-side barrio school to their upper-middle- and upper-class homes in the city's northwest neighborhoods. As the bus rolled by, a fusillade of coins came flying out the windows, as the students made obscene gestures and shouted, "Get a job." Some of the homeless gestured back, some scrambled for the scattered coins—mostly pennies, others angrily threw the coins at the bus, and a few seemed oblivious to the encounter. For the passing junior high schoolers, the exchange was harmless fun, a way to work off the restless energy built up in school; but for the homeless it was a stark reminder of their stigmatized status and of the extent to which they are the objects of negative attention.

Initially, we did not give much thought to this encounter. We were more interested in other issues and were neither fully aware of the frequency of such occurrences nor appreciative of their psychological consequences. We quickly came to learn, however, that this was hardly an isolated incident. The buses passed by the Sally every weekday afternoon during the school year; other domiciled citizens occasionally found pleasure in driving by and similarly hurling insults at the homeless and pennies at their feet; and, as we have seen, the hippie tramps and other homeless in the university area were derisively called "Drag worms," the police often harassed the homeless, and a number of neighborhoods took turns vilifying and derogating them.

Not all encounters with the domiciled are so stridently and intentionally demeaning, of course, but they are no less piercingly stigmatizing. One Saturday morning, for instance, as we walked with Willie Hastings and Ron Whitaker along a downtown street, a woman with a station wagon full of children drove by. As they passed, several of the children pointed at us and shouted, "Hey, Mama, look at the street people!" Ron responded angrily:

> "Mama, look at the street people!" You know, it pisses me off the way fucking thieves steal shit and they can still hold their heads high 'cause they got money. Sure, they have to go to prison sometimes, but when they're out, nobody looks down on them. But I wouldn't steal from nobody, and look how those kids stare at us!

The pain of being objects of curiosity and negative attention are experienced fairly regularly by the homeless, but they suffer just as frequently from what has been called "attention deprivation." In *The Pursuit of Attention,* Charles Derber commented that "members of the subordinate classes are regarded as less worthy of attention in relations with members of dominant classes and so are subjected to subtle yet systematic face-to-face deprivation."[1] For no one is Derber's observation more true than for the homeless, who are routinely ignored or avoided by the domiciled. As previously noted, pedestrians frequently avert their eyes when passing the homeless on the sidewalk, and they often hasten their pace and increase the distance between themselves and the homeless when they sense they may be targeted by a panhandler. Pedestrians sometimes go so far as to cross the street in order to avoid anticipated interaction with the homeless. Because of the fear and anxiety presumably engendered in the domiciled by actual or threatened contact with the homeless, efforts are often made at the community level, as we saw earlier, to regulate and segregate the homeless both spatially and institutionally. Although these avoidance rituals and segregative measures are not as overtly demeaning as the more active and immediate kinds of negative attention the homeless receive, they can be equally stigmatizing, for they also cast the homeless as objects of contamination. This, too, constitutes an assault upon the self, albeit a more subtle and perhaps more insidious one.

Occurring alongside the negative attention and attention deprivation the homeless experience are an array of gestures and acts that are frequently altruistic and clearly indicative of goodwill. People do on occasion give to panhandlers and beggars out of sincere concern rather than merely to get them off their backs. Domiciled citizens sometimes even provide assistance without being asked. One evening, for instance, we found Pat Manchester sitting on a bench near the university eating pizza. "Man, I was just sitting here," he told us, "and this dude walked up and gave me half a pizza and two dollar bills." Several of the students who worked at restaurants in the university area occasionally brought leftovers to Rhyming Mike and other hippie tramps. Other community members occasionally took street people to their home for a shower, dinner, and a good night's sleep. Even Jorge Herrera, who was nearly incoherent, appeared never to wash or bathe, and was covered with rashes and open sores, was the recipient of such assistance. Twice during our field research he appeared on the streets after a brief absence in clean clothes, shaved, and with a new haircut. When we asked about the changes in his appearance, he told us that someone had taken him home, cleaned him up, and let him spend the night. These kinds of unorganized, sporadic gestures of goodwill clearly facilitate the survival of some of the homeless, but the numbers they touch in comparison to those in need are minuscule. Nor do they occur in sufficient quantity or consistently enough to neutralize the stigmatizing and demeaning consequences of not only being on the streets but being objects of negative attention or little attention at all.

In addition to those who make sporadic gestures of goodwill, thousands of domiciled citizens devote occasional time and energy to serving the homeless in an organized fashion in churches, soup kitchens, and shelters. Angels House kitchen was staffed in part by such volunteers, and their support was essential to the operation of the kitchen. Yet the relationship between these well-meaning volunteers and the homeless is highly structured and sanitized. The volunteers typically prepare sandwiches and other foods in a separate area from the homeless or encounter them only across the divide of a serving counter that underscores the distance between the servers and the served. Thus, however sincere and helpful the efforts of domiciled volunteers, the structure of their encounters with the homeless often underscores the immense status differences and thereby reminds the homeless again of where they stand in relation to others.

Gestures of goodwill toward the homeless and the kinds of attention they receive are not constant over time. Instead, they tend to follow an annual cycle, with sympathetic interest increasing with the first cold snap in the fall and reaching its zenith during the Christmas holiday season. This pattern is clearly seen in Figure 1. Based on a frequency count of newspaper stories on the homeless across the country, the figure reveals a dramatic increase in the number of stories as the Thanksgiving/Christmas holiday season approaches. Moreover, once Christmas passes, coverage declines precipitously.[2] This same pattern was seen in Austin in the activities both of the media and of many community residents. At times this expression of holiday concern reached almost comical dimensions. One Thanksgiving Day, for instance, the homeless were inundated with food. In the morning several domiciled citizens came to the Labor Corner to hand out sandwiches, and a few gave away whole turkeys, assuming they would be devoured on the spot. The Assembly of God Church served a large meal around noon, and the Salvation Army served its traditional Thanksgiving meal in midafternoon. At one point in the early afternoon the Sally officials appeared to be worried that

Figure 1 Newspaper Stories on Homelessness by Month in *New York Times Index,* 1975–1989.

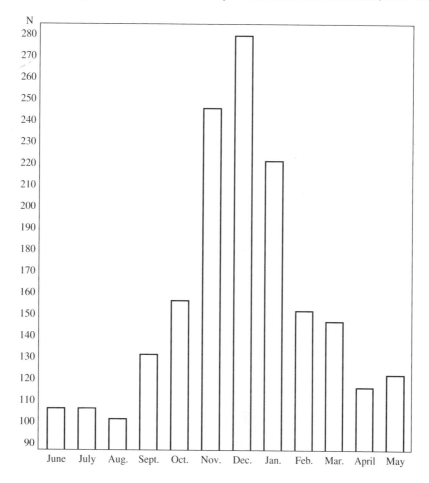

only a few people would show up for the meal. Newspaper and television reporters lingered around the Sally much of the afternoon, taking pictures and interviewing both officials and street people for stories that
would be aired that evening or would appear in the
morning newspaper.

After Christmas, charitable interest in the homeless declined dramatically. The public span of sympathy seemed to have run its course. Thus, except for a
two- to three-month period, the homeless tend to be
recipients only of negative attention, ignored altogether, or dealt with in a segregated and sanitized fashion
that underscores their stigmatized status.[3]

The task the homeless face of salvaging the self is
not easy, especially since wherever they turn they are
reminded that they are at the very bottom of the status
system. As Sonny McCallister lamented shortly after
he became homeless, "The hardest thing's been getting used to the way people look down on street people. It's real hard to feel good about yourself when almost everyone you see is looking down on you." Tom
Fisk, who had been on the streets longer, agreed. But
he said that he had become more calloused over time:

> I used to let it bother me when people stared at me
> while I was trying to sleep on the roof of my car or
> change clothes out of my trunk, but I don't let it get
> to me anymore. I mean, they don't know who I am,
> so what gives them the right to judge me? I know I'm
> okay.

But there was equivocation and uncertainty in his
voice. Moreover, even if he no longer felt the stares
and comments of others, he still had to make sense of
the distance between himself and them.

How, then, do the homeless deal with the negative
attention they receive or the indifference they encounter as they struggle to survive materially? How
do they salvage their selves? And to what extent do
the webs of meaning they spin and the personal identities they construct vary with patterns of adaptation?
We address these questions in the remainder of the
chapter by considering two kinds of meaning: existential and identity-oriented. The former term refers to
the kinds of accounts the homeless invoke in order to
make sense of their plight; the latter refers to the kinds
of meaning they attach to self in interactions with
others.

MAKING SENSE OF THE PLIGHT OF HOMELESSNESS

The plight of human beings brought face-to-face with
the meaning of their existence by suffocating social
structures, unanticipated turns of events, dehumaniz-
ing living conditions, or the specter of death has been
a long and persistent theme in both literature and philosophy. Underlying this strand of writing, generally
discussed under the rubric of existentialism, are two
consistent themes: that the quest for meaning, while
an ongoing challenge in everyday life, is particularly
pressing for those individuals whose routines and expectations have been disrupted; and that the burden of
finding meaning in such disruptive moments rests on
the shoulders of the individual.[4] From this perspective, meaning is not an essence that inheres in a particular object or situation, but a construction or imputation; and the primary architects of such constructions
are human actors. The burden of infusing problematic
situations with meaning is heavier for some actors
than for others, however. Certainly this is true of
the homeless, with their pariah-like status, limited
resources, and the often demeaning treatment they
receive.

How do the homeless carve out a sense of meaning in the seemingly insane and meaningless situation
in which they find themselves? Are they able to make
sense of their plight in a fashion that helps to salvage
the self?

Some are able to do so and others are not. Many of
the homeless invoke causal accounts of their situation
that infuse it with meaning and rescue the self; others
abandon both concerns by drifting into the world of
alcoholism or into an alternative reality that is in this
world but not of it and that is often treated as symptomatic of insanity by those not privy to it. Of the
two lines of response, the first is clearly the most
pronounced.

Invoking Causal Accounts

By causal accounts we refer to the reasons people give
to render understandable their behavior or the situations in which they find themselves. Such accounts are
essentially commonsense attributions that are invoked
in order to explain some problematic action or situa-

tion. Whether such accounts seem reasonable to an observer is irrelevant; what is at issue is their meaningfulness to the actor.

These explanatory accounts are seldom new constructions. Rather, they are likely to be variants of folk understandings or aphorisms that are invoked from time to time by many citizens and thus constitute part of a larger cultural vocabulary. This view of causal accounts accords with the contention that culture can best be thought of as a repertoire or " 'tool kit' of symbols, stories, rituals, and world views which people use in varying configurations to solve different kinds of problems."[5] These stories, symbols, or accounts are not pulled out of that cultural tool kit at random, however. Instead, the appropriation and articulation process is driven by some pressing problem or imperative. In the case of the homeless, that predicament is the existential need to infuse their situation with a sense of meaning that helps to salvage the self. In the service of that imperative, three folk adages or accounts surfaced rather widely and frequently among the homeless in Austin in their conversations with us and each other. One says, "I'm down on my luck." Another reminds us, "What goes around, comes around." And the third says, "I've paid my dues."

"I'm down on my luck"   The term *luck,* which most citizens invoke from time to time to account for unanticipated happenings in their lives, is generally reserved for events that influence the individual's life but are thought to be beyond his or her control.[6] To assert that "I'm down on my luck," then, is to attribute my plight to misfortune, to chance. For the homeless, such an attribution not only helps to make sense of their situation, but it does so in a manner that is psychologically functional in two ways: it exempts the homeless from responsibility for their plight, and it leaves open the possibility of a better future.

Exemption from personal responsibility was a consistent theme in the causal accounts we overheard. As Willie Hastings asserted aggressively in discussing with Ron Whitaker and us the negative attention heaped on all of us just a few minutes earlier by the children in the passing car:

> Shit, it ain't my fault I'm on the streets. I didn't choose to become homeless. I just had a lot of bad luck. And that ain't my fault. Hell, who knows? Those kids and their old lady might get unlucky and wake up on the streets someday. It can happen to anyone, you know!

Ron chipped in:

> Yeah, a lot of people think we're lazy, that we don't give a shit, that this is what we want. But that sure in hell ain't so—at least not for me. It wasn't my fault I lost my job in Denver. If I'd been working down the street, maybe I'd still be there. I was just at the wrong place at the wrong time. Like Willie said, some people just ain't got no luck!

Sonny McCallister, Tom Fisk, Tony Jones, Tanner Sutton, and Hoyt Page would all have agreed, in large part because their recently dislocated or straddler status makes them take street life less for granted than the outsiders do and therefore prompts them to try to explain their situation. But why invoke luck? Why not fix the blame for their plight on more direct, tangible factors, such as family discord, low wages, or being laid off? Not only are such biographic and structural factors clearly operative in their lives, but reference to them can also exempt people from personal responsibility for their plight. After all, it was not Tony Jones's fault that he lost his job as a security guard at a Chicago steel mill when the plant cut back. Yet, although he referred to this event as the one that triggered his descent onto the streets, he still maintained that he was primarily the victim of "bad luck" rather than less mysterious structural forces that clearly intruded into his life. Apparently, he felt that had he chanced to work at a different job or in a different factory, his fate would have been different.

The same logic is evident in Hoyt's efforts to make sense of his situation. His biography is strewn with a host of factors not of his own doing, such as having been orphaned and not having received proper attention for a learning disorder, which could have been woven into a responsibility-free account for being homeless. Yet, he too often said that he was simply "down on my luck."

This tendency to cling to the luck factor in lieu of structural or biographic accounts of homelessness does not stem from ignorance about these other factors or from false consciousness regarding their causal influence. The homeless often name structural and biographic factors when discussing the reasons for their homelessness. But the bad-luck account more readily allows for the possibility of a better day down the road. The victim of bad luck can become the recipient of good luck. "Luck changes," as we were frequently reminded. So, too, do structural trends and biographic experiences, but perhaps not so readily or positively from the standpoint of the homeless. Luck is also more fickle and mysterious, and its effects are supposedly distributed more randomly across the social order than are the effects of most structural trends. For good reason, then, some of the homeless cling to the luck factor.

Yet, the lives of most homeless are devoid of much good fortune, as is clear from the biographies of virtually all of our key informants. Why, then, do some of the homeless talk as if good luck is about to come their way? The answer resides in two other frequently invoked causal accounts that are intertwined with the luck factor: "What goes around, comes around," and "I've paid my dues."

"What goes around, comes around" Insofar as there is a moral code affecting interpersonal relations on the streets, it is manifested in the phrase, "What goes around, comes around." But the relevance of this phrase is not confined solely to the interpersonal domain. It is also brought into service with respect to the issue of meaning in general and the luck factor in particular.

Regarding the former, the contention that "what goes around, comes around" suggests a cyclical rather than linear conception of the process by which events unfold. This circularity implies, among other things, a transposition of opposites at some point in the life course. Biblical examples of such transpositions abound, as in the New Testament declarations that "The last shall be first and the first last" and "The meek shall inherit the earth." Although few homeless harbor realistic thoughts of such dramatic transpositions, many do assume that things will get better because "what goes around, comes around."

This logic also holds for luck. Thus, if a person has been down on his or her luck, it follows that the person's luck is subject to change. Hoyt, among others, talked as though he believed this proposition.

"Look," he told us one evening over dinner and a few beers at a local steak house:

> I've been down on my luck for so damn long, it's got to change. . . . Like I said before, I believe what goes around, comes around, so I'm due a run of good luck, don't you think?

We nodded in agreement, but not without wondering how strongly Hoyt and others actually believed in the presumed link between luck and the cyclical principle of "what goes around, comes around." Whatever the answer, there is certainly good reason for harboring such a belief, for it introduces a ray of hope into a dismal situation and thereby infuses it with meaning of the kind that helps keep the self afloat.

"I've paid my dues" This linkage is buttressed further by the third frequently articulated causal account: "I've paid my dues." To invoke this saying is to assert, as Marilyn Fisch often did in her more sober moments, that "I deserve better" after "what I've been through" or "what I've done." The phrase implies that if there are preconditions for a run of good luck, then those conditions have been met. Thus, Gypsy Bill told us one afternoon that he felt his luck was about to change as he was fantasizing about coming into some money. "You may think I'm crazy," he said, "but it's this feeling I've got. Besides, I deserve it 'cause I've paid my dues." A street acquaintance of Gypsy's, a man who fancied himself as "a great blues harmonica player," broke in:

> Yeah, man, I know what you mean. I was playing the blues on Bleeker Street once when Jeff Beck comes by and tells me I'm the best blues harmonica player he's ever heard. "Where do you live?" he asks me. And I tell him, "Here on this sidewalk, and I sleep in the subways." And he asks me, "What do you want from me?" And I tell him, "Nothing, man. A handshake." And he reaches into his pocket and pulls out a hundred-dollar bill and gives it to me 'cause I had it coming! I know the blues, man. I live them. I sleep on the fucking street, paying my dues. That's why no one plays the blues like me!

He then pointed to the knapsack on his back and asked if we knew what was in it. We shook our heads, and he said, "My jeans, man. I fucking pissed in 'em last night, I was so drunk. That's what I'm saying: I know the blues, man! I've paid my dues."

So a streak of good luck, however fleeting, or anticipation of such a streak, albeit a more sustained one, is rationalized in terms of the hardships endured. The more a person has suffered, the greater the dues that have been paid and the more, therefore, a run of good luck is deserved. Perhaps this is why some of those with the longest stretches of time on the streets, namely, outsiders, were heard to assert more often than others that "I've paid my dues." As Shotgun explained in one of his moments of sobriety, "I been on the streets for about fifteen years. . . . I've rode the boxcars and slept out in the wintertime. That's how you pay your dues." Yet, many outsiders do not often invoke this phrase. The reason, we suspect, is that they have been down on their luck for so long that their current fate seems impervious to change and they have therefore resigned themselves to life on the streets. Those who assert that they've paid their dues, however, invoke the phrase in service of the luck factor and the corollary principle of what goes around, comes around. And for good reason. Together, these accounts both exempt the homeless from responsibility for their plight and hold the door ajar for a change in luck.

Avenues of Escape: Alcohol and Alternative Realities

Not all homeless attend to the existential business of making sense of their situation by invoking conventional folk understandings. Some individuals may have been on the streets too long or have endured too many hardships, experienced too many frustrations, and suffered too many insults to the self to bother any longer with the accounting process. Instead, they gradually drift down alternative avenues for dealing with the oppressive realities of street life and the resultant brutalization of the self. These avenues, while stigmatized by the larger culture, are often consonant with the subculture of street life itself. One such avenue is alcoholism; the other involves the creation or adoption of alternative realities frequently associated with mental illness.

The suggestion that some of the homeless drift into alcoholism and mental illness as a consequence of the hopeless and demeaning situation in which they find themselves runs counter to the tendency to treat these conditions as precipitants of homelessness or at least as disabilities that increase vulnerability to becoming homeless.[7] That this presumed causal connection holds for some of the homeless is no doubt true, but it is also true that alcoholism and mental illness sometimes function as means of coping psychologically with the traumas of street life. Clearly, they do not guarantee literal escape from the streets, but they can serve as insulation from further psychic assaults and thereby create illusions of personal autonomy and well-being. How often this process occurs is unclear, but that it is not an infrequent occurrence we are certain.

Evidence of this tendency for substance use to escalate with increasing time on the streets also comes from our key informants. Hoyt is an avowed alcoholic, but he reminded us a number of times that he did not come to the streets as a chronic alcoholic. Instead, his "drinking problem," as he referred to it, developed over the course of eleven years on and off the streets. He began with drugs, primarily marijuana and speed, but gradually came to use alcohol more heavily because it was cheaper and "didn't get you into as much trouble with the law." During the past several years, he has used alcohol almost exclusively and has recently come to the realization that he has "a serious drinking problem" that must be attended to if he is to get off the streets permanently. Marilyn's experience with alcohol is similar. As she explained one morning over coffee:

> I didn't have much of a drinking problem before I landed on the streets. But I found it all so depressing. And everybody else was drinking and asking me to drink. So I said, "Why not?" I mean, what did I have to lose? Everything was so depressing. Drinking sure couldn't make it any worse!

Her claim of gradually increasing levels of drinking was substantiated by our frequent contacts with her for over two years. When we first met her Marilyn, like many of the homeless, was a spree or binge drinker, but as time passed the period between the sprees became shorter and her drinking became more chronic, all of which was manifested in her increasingly emaciated, weathered, and scarred physical appearance.[8] The experiences of Shotgun, Gypsy, Nona George, and JJ and Indio, as well as other outsiders we met, are all quite similar: increasing use of alcohol with the passage of time, resulting eventually in apparent physiological and psychological dependence.

Why this drift toward alcohol? Reasonable explanations are not hard to come by. One is subcultural. Drinking is, after all, one of the more salient features of street life, and, as Marilyn found, there is often normative pressure to join in either by sharing what one has or by drinking a portion of what has been offered. Boredom is another explanatory factor. Idleness is also a salient characteristic of street life, as the one thing many homeless have to fritter away is unscheduled time. But the explanatory factor that was most often cited by the homeless we came to know is psychological. In a word, it is escape—not so much from boredom as from the travails and miseries of street life, or from the past, or perhaps from both. Hoyt often noted how his reach for the bottle was driven by the need to escape the moment, to get away from the wretchedness and humiliation of his current experience. Shelters, he told us, activated this urge more than anything else:

> You're in there, with lotsa people you don't know. They look like shit and smell like it, too. And they remind you of where you are and who you are. It ain't pleasant. So you begin to crave a drink.

Hoyt was also aware that the drive to drink was sometimes prompted by the need to escape thoughts of the past. He told us once of a former street friend in Dallas who initially drank to obliterate the pain he experienced whenever he thought about the daughter he had lost through divorce:

> He did what a lot of us do when you think about something like that or about where you are now. You think about it and you get pissed off about it and you get drunk and forget about it. At least for a while, and then you start all over. It's just a cycle, a vicious cycle.

Hoyt, JJ, Indio, Nona, Marilyn, Gypsy, and others were all caught in this vicious cycle. Most were not ignorant about what they were doing, but they knew that they were ensnarled in a "catch-22" of sorts. On the one hand, there was awareness of both the physiological and the psychological hazards of chronic drinking; on the other hand, alcohol was often seen as the only

avenue for escaping the traumas of the past or present and the meaningless of it all. "At times," as Hoyt once put it, "it seems like the only way out."

Viewed in this light, drinking clearly functions for some of the homeless as adaptive behavior that provides a psychological antidote to the pains of existence. For the chronic drinkers, to be sure, it is an adaptive behavior that has gotten out of control. But it did not begin that way for all of them. Much of the drinking behavior on the streets, including that which has gone awry, thus constitutes a variant of behaviors Erving Goffman has called "secondary adjustments," ways in which individuals who find themselves trapped in demeaning social contexts attempt to stand "apart from the role and the self" implied. They are "undertakings that provide something for the individual to lose himself in, temporarily blotting out all sense of the environment which, and in which, he must abide."[9]

Like much of the drinking that occurs on the streets, some of the behaviors and verbalizations customarily read as symptomatic of mental illness can be construed as forms of adaptive behavior. Undoubtedly, some of the homeless who might be diagnosed as mentally ill were that way prior to their descent onto the streets, but others evince symptoms of such illness as a result of the trauma of living on the streets. The symptoms we refer to are not those of depression and demoralization, which are understandably widespread on the streets,[10] but more "bizarre" patterns of thought and behavior that are less prevalent but more conspicuous.[11] These include auditory and visual hallucinations, that is, hearing or seeing things to which others are not privy; conspiratorial delusions, such as the belief that others are talking about you or are out to get you; grandiose delusions, like the belief that you have extraordinary powers, insights, or contacts; and the public verbalization of these hallucinations and delusions as well as audible conversations with others not present. Such beliefs and behaviors suggest an alternative inner reality that is neither publicly shared nor fully accessible to others and is therefore "out of this world." Although such alternative realities frequently invite both folk labels of "nuts" and "crazy" and clinical labels of schizophrenia and paranoia, they may often be quite functional for some individuals who find themselves in a demeaning and inhumane context in which they are the frequent objects of negative attention or attention deprivation. After all, if you are rarely the recipient of any positive attention or are ignored altogether, creating and retreating into a private reality that grants you privileged insights and special status may be more adaptive than it appears at first glance.

Certainly this appeared to be the case with Tanner Sutton, the badly burned and disfigured Sally street employee who was preoccupied with the occult and higher forms of consciousness and who claimed to be a "spiritually gifted person" with "special mystical powers" that enabled him "to read people," live in "many different dimensions of space," and "look into the future when humans will be transformed into another life form." Taken at face value, such claims appear to be outlandish and perhaps even symptomatic of psychosis. Even some of Tanner's street associates regarded him as "far out," as we saw earlier. Yet Tanner was able to function quite resourcefully on the streets, as was evidenced by his ability to discharge his duties at the Sally. Moreover, however weird or bizarre Tanner's claims, to evaluate him in terms of their veracity misses the point. Tanner's biography and the context in which he found himself make the issue one not of verisimilitude but of psychological functionality. For Tanner, as for others who appear to have lodged their self in some alternative reality, that reality provides a psychological alternative to the material world in which they find themselves, thus insulating them from further psychic assaults emanating from that world and providing an alternative source of self-regard.

Such secondary adjustments, albeit psychological ones, are not fashioned in a highly conscious and intentional manner. Instead, they are drifted into unwittingly over a period of time in much the same way some of the homeless drift into chronic alcohol use. Evidence of this drifting process was clear in the life histories of both Tanner and Lance McCay. Lance's case is particularly revealing: he was admittedly and visibly mentally ill at the time we met him, but his behavior became increasingly bizarre over the two-year period we maintained contact with him. More often

than not, such changes seemed to be triggered by an abbreviated visit home, after which he could be seen ranting and raving about his parents, incessantly talking to himself and engaging in more delusional thinking. It seemed clear to us that such outbursts were in large part defensive reactions to feelings of abandonment and exclusion that were magnified by the attention deprivation he experienced on the streets. Not only did we rarely see him conversing with others who were physically present, but other people made a point of avoiding him. In response, Lance retreated into his inner world. That world consisted of conspiratorial thoughts and behaviors, as when he wrote to his mother that he was considering moving to Billings, Montana, where "people won't be prejudiced against me because they won't even know me," as well as grandiose delusions, such as his claim to be "a writer like Hemingway."

Such statements and claims may appear to be strikingly outlandish at first glance, but their strangeness dissipates when they are put in context.[12] For example, it seems less odd that Lance's talk and behavior were peppered with examples of paranoia and delusional thinking when it is remembered that he was frequently rejected and excluded. Moreover, these two sets of observations were linked together in a kind of interactive, self-fulfilling dynamic: the longer Lance was on the streets and the more he experienced rejection and exclusion, the more pronounced his conspiratorial and delusional thinking became and the more bizarre he appeared.[13]

The point is that the bizarre patterns of thought and behavior exhibited by Tanner and Lance, among others, and commonly taken as symptomatic of mental illness can be understood, in part, in terms of their psychological survival value. This is not to suggest that individuals like Lance are not mentally ill in a clinical sense. But to frame their mental functioning and the realities they identify with solely in that fashion is to gloss the extent to which these alternative realities can function as adaptive shields against the painful realities of street life and thereby render superfluous the need to account for that existence in terms of conventional folk understandings. Like alcohol, then, bizarre, alternative realities can provide psychological escape from a brutalizing world out of which physical escape seems unlikely.

CONSTRUCTING IDENTITY-ORIENTED MEANING

However the homeless deal with the issue of existential meaning, whether by stringing together causal accounts borrowed from conventional cultural vocabularies or by seeking refuge in alcohol, drugs, or alternative realities, they are still confronted with establishing who they are in the course of interaction with others, for interaction between two or more individuals minimally requires that they be situated or placed as social objects.[14] In other words, situationally specific identities must be established. Such identities can be established in two ways: they can be attributed or imputed by others, or they can be claimed or asserted by the actor. The former can be thought of as social or role identities in that they are imputations based primarily on information gleaned from the appearance or behavior of others and from the time and location of their action, as when children in a passing car look out the window and yell, "Hey, Mama, look at the street people!" or when junior high school students yell out the windows of their school bus to the homeless lining up for dinner in front of the Sally, "Get a job, you bums!" In each case, the homeless in question have been situated as social objects and thus assigned social identities.[15]

When individuals claim or assert an identity, by contrast, they attribute meaning to themselves. Such self-attributions can be thought of as personal identities rather than social identities, in that they are self-designations brought into play or avowed during the course of actual or anticipated interaction with others.[16] Personal identities may be consistent with imputed social identities, as when Shotgun claims to be "a tramp," or inconsistent, as when Tony Jones yells back to the passing junior high schoolers, "Fuck you, I ain't no lazy bum!" The presented personal identities of individuals who are frequent objects of negative attention or attention deprivation, as are the homeless, can be especially revealing, because they offer a glimpse of how those people deal interactionally with their pariah-like status and the demeaning social identities into which they are frequently cast. Personal identities thus provide further insight into the ways the homeless attempt to salvage the self.

What, then, are the personal identities that the homeless construct and negotiate when in interaction with others? Are they merely a reflection of the highly stereotypic and stigmatized identities attributed to them, or do they reflect a more positive sense of self or at least an attempt to carve out and sustain a less demeaning self-conception?

The construction of personal identity typically involves a number of complementary activities: (a) procurement and arrangement of physical settings and props; (b) cosmetic face work or the arrangement of personal appearance; (c) selective association with other individuals and groups; and (d) verbal construction and assertion of personal identity. Although some of the homeless engage in conscious manipulation of props and appearance—for example, Pushcart, with his fully loaded shopping cart, and Shotgun, who fancies himself a con artist—most do not resort to such measures. Instead, the primary means by which the homeless announce their personal identities is verbal. They engage, in other words, in a good bit of identity talk. This is understandable, since the homeless seldom have the financial or social resources to pursue the other identity construction activities. Additionally, since the structure of their daily routines ensures that they spend a great deal of time waiting here and there, they have ample opportunity to converse with each other.

Sprinkled throughout these conversations with each other, as well as those with agency personnel and, occasionally, with the domiciled, are numerous examples of identity talk. Inspection of the instances of the identity talk to which we were privy yielded three generic patterns: (1) distancing; (2) embracement; and (3) fictive storytelling.[17] Each pattern was found to contain several subtypes that tend to vary in use according to whether the speaker is recently dislocated, a straddler, or an outsider. We elaborate in turn each of the generic patterns, their varieties, and how they vary in use among the different types of homeless.

Distancing

When individuals have to enact roles, associate with others, or utilize institutions that imply social identities inconsistent with their actual or desired self-conceptions, they often attempt to distance themselves from those roles, associations, or institutions.[18] A substantial proportion of the identity talk we recorded was consciously focused on distancing from other homeless individuals, from street and occupational roles, and from the caretaker agencies servicing the homeless. Nearly a third of the identity statements were of this variety.

Associational Distancing Since a claim to a particular self is partly contingent on the imputed social identities of the person's associates, one way people can substantiate that claim when their associates are negatively evaluated is to distance themselves from those associates.[19] This distancing technique manifested itself in two ways among the homeless: disassociation from the homeless as a general social category, and disassociation from specific groupings of homeless individuals.

Categoric associational distancing was particularly evident among the recently dislocated. Illustrative is Tony Jones's comment in response to our initial query about life on the streets:

> I'm not like the other guys who hang out down at the Sally. If you want to know about street people, I can tell you about them; but you can't really learn about street people from studying me, because I'm different.

Such categorical distancing also occurred among those individuals who saw themselves as on the verge of getting off the street. After securing two jobs in the hope of raising enough money to rent an apartment, Ron Whitaker indicated, for example, that he was different from other street people. "They've gotten used to living on the streets and they're satisfied with it, but not me!" he told us. "Next to my salvation, getting off the streets is the most important thing in my life." This variety of categorical distancing was particularly pronounced among homeless individuals who had taken jobs at the Sally and thus had one foot off the streets.

These individuals were frequently criticized by other homeless for their condescending attitude. As Marilyn put it, "As soon as these guys get inside, they're better than the rest of us. They've been out on the streets for years, and as soon as they're inside, they forget it."

Among the outsiders, who had been on the streets for some time and who appeared firmly rooted in that life-style, there were few examples of categorical distancing. Instead, these individuals frequently distinguished themselves from other groups of homeless. This form of associational distancing was most conspicuous among those, such as the hippie tramps and redneck bums, who were not regular social-service or shelter users and who saw themselves as especially independent and resourceful. These individuals not only wasted little time in pointing out that they were "not like those Sally users," but were also given to derogating the more institutionally dependent. Indeed, although they are among the furthest removed from a middle-class life-style, they sound at times much like middle-class citizens berating welfare recipients. As Marilyn explained, "A lot of these people staying at the Sally, they're reruns. Every day they're wanting something. People get tired of giving. All you hear is gimme, gimme. And we transients are getting sick of it."

Role Distancing Role distancing, the second form of distancing employed by the homeless, involves a self-conscious attempt to foster the impression of a lack of commitment or attachment to a particular role in order to deny the self implied.[20] Thus, when individuals find themselves cast into roles in which the social identities implied are inconsistent with desired or actual self-conceptions, role distancing is likely to occur. Since the homeless routinely find themselves being cast into or enacting low-status, negatively evaluated roles, it should not be surprising that many of them attempt to disassociate themselves from those roles.

As did associational distancing, role distancing manifested itself in two ways: distancing from the general role of street person, and distancing from specific occupational roles. The former, which is also a type of categorical distancing, was particularly evident among the recently dislocated. It was not uncommon for these individuals to state explicitly that they should "not be mistaken as a typical street person." Role distancing of the less categoric and more situationally specific type was most evident among those who performed day labor, such as painters' helpers, hod carriers, warehouse and van unloaders, and those in unskilled service occupations such as dishwashing and janitorial work. As we saw earlier, the majority of the homeless we encountered would avail themselves of such job opportunities, but they seldom did so enthusiastically, since the jobs offered low status and low wages. This was especially true of the straddlers and some of the outsiders, who frequently reminded others of their disdain for such jobs and of the belief that they deserved better, as exemplified by the remarks of a drunk young man who had worked the previous day as a painter's helper: "I made $36.00 off the Labor Corner, but it was just nigger work. I'm twenty-four years old, man. I deserve better than that."

Similar distancing laments were frequently voiced over the disparity between job demands and wages. We were conversing with a small gathering of homeless men on a Sunday afternoon, for example, when one of them revealed that earlier in the day he had turned down a job to carry shingles up a ladder for $4.00 an hour because he found it demeaning to "do that hard a work for that low a pay." Since day-labor jobs seldom last for more than six hours, perhaps not much is lost monetarily in foregoing such jobs in comparison to what can be gained in pride. But even when the ratio of dollars to pride appears to make rejection costly, as in the case of permanent jobs, dissatisfaction with the low status of menial jobs may prod some homeless individuals to engage in the ultimate form of role distancing by quitting currently held jobs. As Ron Whitaker recounted the day after he quit in the middle of his shift as a dishwasher at a local restaurant:

My boss told me, "You can't walk out on me." And I told her, "Fuck you, just watch me. I'm gonna walk out of here right now." And I did. "You can't walk out on me," she said. I said, "Fuck you, I'm gone."

The foregoing illustrations suggest that the social identities lodged in available work roles are frequently inconsistent with the desired or idealized self-

conceptions of some of the homeless. Consequently, "bitching about," "turning down," and even "blowing off" such work may function as a means of social-identity disavowal, on the one hand, and personal-identity assertion on the other. Such techniques provide a way of saying, "Hey, I have some pride. I'm in control. I'm my own person." This is especially the case among those individuals for whom such work is no longer just a stopgap measure but an apparently permanent feature of their lives.

Institutional Distancing   An equally prevalent distancing technique involved the derogation of the caretaker agencies that attended to the needs of the homeless. The agency that was the most frequent object of these harangues was the Sally. Many of the homeless who used it described it as a greedy corporation run by inhumane personnel more interested in lining their own pockets than in serving the needy. Willie Hastings claimed, for example, that "the major is money-hungry and feeds people the cheapest way he can. He never talks to people except to gripe at them." He then added that the "Sally is supposed to be a Christian organization, but it doesn't have a Christian spirit. It looks down on people. . . . The Salvation Army is a national business that is more worried about making money than helping people." Ron Whitaker concurred, noting on another occasion that the "Sally here doesn't nearly do as much as it could for people. The people who work there take bags of groceries and put them in their cars. People donate to the Sally, and then the workers there cream off the best."[21] Another straddler told us after he had spent several nights at the winter shelter, "If you spend a week here, you'll see how come people lose hope. You're treated just like an animal."

Because the Salvation Army is the only local facility that provides free shelter, breakfast, and dinner, attention is understandably focused on it. But that the Sally would be frequently derogated by the people whose survival it facilitates may appear puzzling at first glance, especially given its highly accommodative orientation. The answer lies in part in the organization and dissemination of its services. Clients are processed in an impersonal, highly structured assembly line-like fashion. The result is a leveling of individual differences and a decline in personal autonomy. Bitching and complaining about such settings create psychic distance from the self implied and secure a modicum of personal autonomy.[22] This variety of distancing, though observable among all of the homeless, was most prevalent among the straddlers and outsiders. Since these individuals have used street agencies over a longer period of time, their self-concepts are more deeply implicated in them, thus necessitating distancing from those institutions and the self implied. Criticizing the Sally, then, provides some users with a means of dealing with the implications of their dependency on it. It is, in short, a way of presenting and sustaining a somewhat contrary personal identity.

Thus far we have elaborated how some of the homeless distance themselves from other homeless individuals, from general and specific roles, and from the institutions that deal with them. Such distancing behavior and talk represent attempts to salvage a measure of self-worth. In the process, of course, the homeless are asserting more favorable personal identities. Not all homeless individuals engage in similar distancing behavior and talk, however. As is indicated in Table 1, which summarizes the foregoing observations, categorical distancing tends to be concentrated among the recently dislocated. Among those who are

Table 1 Types of Distancing, by Type of Homeless*

Types of Homeless	Categoric Distancing[a] (N: 16)	Specific Distancing[b] (N: 23)	Institutional Distancing[c] (N: 23)
Recently dislocated	68.8%	—	8.7%
Straddlers	12.4%	60.9%	43.5%
Outsiders	—	34.8%	47.8%
Mentally ill	18.7%	4.3%	—

*$\chi^2 = 41.88$, df = 6, P < .001.

[a]Comments or statements coded as categoric distancing include those indicating dissociation or distancing from such general street-role identities as transient, bum, tramp, or drifter, or from other street people in general.

[b]Comments or statements coded as specific distancing include those indicating dissociation from specific groupings of homeless individuals or from specific survival or occupational roles.

[c]Comments or statements coded as institutional distancing include those indicating dissociation from or disdain for street institutions, such as the Salvation Army or soup kitchens.

more firmly entrenched in street life, distancing tends to be confined to distinguishing themselves from specific groups of homeless, such as novices and the institutionally dependent, from specific occupational roles, or from the institutions with which they have occasional contact.

Embracement

Embracement connotes a person's verbal and expressive confirmation of acceptance of and attachment to the social identity associated with a general or specific role, a set of social relationships, or a particular ideology.[23] So defined, embracement implies that social identity is congruent with personal identity. Thus, embracement involves the avoval of implied social identities rather than their disavowal, as in the case of distancing. Thirty-four percent of the identity statements were of this variety.

Role Embracement   The most conspicuous kind of embracement encountered was categoric role embracement, which typically manifested itself by the avoval and acceptance of street-role identities such as tramp and bum. Occasionally we would encounter an individual who would immediately announce that he or she was a tramp or a bum. A case in point is provided by our initial encounter with Shotgun, when he proudly told us that he was "the tramp who was on the front page of yesterday's newspaper." In that and subsequent conversations his talk was peppered with references to himself as a tramp. He said, for example, that he had appeared on a television show in St. Louis as a tramp and that he "tramped" his way across the country, and he revealed several "cons" that "tramps use to survive on the road."

Shotgun and others like him identified themselves as traditional "brethren of the road" tramps. A number of other individuals identified themselves as "hippie tramps." When confronted by a passing group of young punk-rockers, for instance, Gimpy Dan and several other hippie tramps voiced agreement with the remark one made that "these kids will change but we'll stay the same." As if to buttress this claim, they went on to talk about "Rainbow," the previously mentioned annual gathering of old hippies which functions in part as a kind of identity-reaffirmation ritual. For these street people, there was little doubt about who they were; they not only saw themselves as hippie tramps, but they embraced that identity both verbally and expressively.

This sort of embracement also surfaced on occasion with skid row—like bums, as was evidenced by Gypsy Bill's repeated references to himself as a bum. As a corollary of such categoric role embracement, most individuals who identified themselves as tramps or bums adopted nicknames congruent with these roles, such as Shotgun, Boxcar Billie, Gypsy Bill, and Pushcart. Such street names thus symbolize a break with their domiciled past and suggest, as well, a fairly thoroughgoing embracement of life on the streets.

Role-specific embracement was also encountered occasionally, as when Gypsy would refer to himself as an "expert dumpster diver." Many street people occasionally engage in this survival activity, but relatively few pridefully identify with it. Other role-specific survival activities embraced included panhandling, small-time drug-dealing, and performing, such as playing a musical instrument or singing on a street corner for money. "Rhyming Mike," as we have seen, made his money by composing short poems for spare change from passersby, and routinely referred to himself as a street poet. For some homeless individuals, then, the street roles and routines they enact function as sources of positive identity and self-worth.

Associational Embracement   A second variety of embracement entails reference to oneself as a friend or as an individual who takes his or her social relationships seriously.[24] Gypsy provides a case in point. On one occasion he told us that he had several friends who either refused or quit jobs at the Sally because they "weren't allowed to associate with other guys on the streets who were their friends." Such a policy struck him as immoral. "They expect you to forget who your friends are and where you came from when you go to work there," he told us angrily. "They asked me to work there once and I told them, 'No way.' I'm a bum and I know who my friends are." Self-identification as a person who willingly shares limited resources, such as cigarettes and alcohol, also occurred frequently, particularly among self-avowed tramps and bums.

Associational embracement was also sometimes expressed in claims of protecting buddies. JJ and Indio repeatedly said they "looked out for each other." When Indio was telling about having been assaulted and robbed while walking through an alley, JJ said, almost apologetically, "It wouldn't have happened if I was with you. I wouldn't have let them get away with that." Similar claims were made to one of us, as when two straddlers said one evening after an ambiguous encounter with a clique of half a dozen other street people, "If it wasn't for us, they'd have had your ass."

Although protective behaviors that entailed risk were seldom observed, protective claims, and particularly promises, were heard frequently. Whatever the relationship between such claims and action, they not only illustrate adherence to the moral code of "what goes around, comes around," but they also express the claimant's desire to be identified as a trustworthy friend.

Ideological Embracement   The third variety of embracement entails adherence to an ideology or an alternative reality and the avowal of a personal identity that is cognitively congruent with that ideology. Banjo, for example, routinely identifies himself as a Christian. He painted on his banjo case "Wealth Means Nothing Without God," and his talk is sprinkled with references to his Christian beliefs. He can often be found giving testimony about "the power and grace of Jesus" to other homeless around the Sally, and he witnesses regularly at the Central Assembly of God Church. Moreover, he frequently points out that his religious beliefs transcend his situation on the streets. As he told us once, "It would have to be a bigger purpose than just money to get me off the streets, like a religious mission."

A source of identity as powerful as religion, but less common, is the occult and related alternative realities. Since traditional occupational roles are not readily available to the homeless as a basis for identity, and since few street people have the material resources that can be used for construction of positive personal identities, it is little wonder that some of them find in alternative realities a locus for a positive identity. As we noted earlier, Tanner Sutton identifies himself as a "spirit guide" who can see into the future, prophesying, for instance, that "humans will be transformed into another life form."

Like mainstream religious traditions and occult realities, conversionist, restorative ideologies such as that associated with Alcoholics Anonymous provide an identity for some homeless people who are willing to accept AA's doctrines and adhere to its program. Interestingly, AA's successes seldom remain on the streets. Consequently, those street people who have previously associated with AA seldom use it as a basis for identity assertion. Nonetheless, it does constitute a potentially salient identity peg.

We have seen how the personal identities of the homeless may be derived from embracement of the social identities associated with certain stereotypic street roles, such as the tramp and the bum; with role-specific survival activities, such as dumpster-diving; with certain social relationships, such as friend and protector; or with certain religious and occult ideologies or alternative realities. We have also noted that the use of embracement tends to vary across the different types of homeless. This can be seen more clearly in Table 2, which shows that categoric embracement in particular and embracement talk in general occur most frequently among outsiders and rarely among the recently dislocated.

Fictive Storytelling

A third form of identity talk engaged in by the homeless is fictive storytelling about past, present, or future experiences and accomplishments. We characterize as fictive stories that range from minor exaggerations of experience to full-fledged fabrications. We observed two types of fictive storytelling: embellishment of the past and present, and fantasizing about the future.[25] Slightly more than a third of the identity statements we recorded fell into one of these two categories.

Embellishment By *embellishment* we refer to the exaggeration of past *or* present experiences with fanciful and fictitious particulars so as to assert a positive personal identity. Embellishment involves enlargement of the truth, an overstatement of what transpired or is unfolding. Embellished stories, then, are only partly fictional.

Examples of embellishment for identity construction abound among the homeless. Although a wide array of events and experiences, ranging from the accomplishments of offspring to sexual and drinking exploits and predatory activities, were embellished, such storytelling was most commonly associated with past and current occupational and financial themes. The typical story of financial embellishment entailed

Table 2 Types of Embracement, by Type of Homeless*

Types of Homeless	Categoric Embracement[a] (N: 16)	Specific Embracement[b] (N: 23)	Ideological Embracement[c] (N: 23)
Recently dislocated	—	10.0%	7.7%
Straddlers	5.1%	35.0%	46.1%
Outsiders	87.2%	45.0%	30.8%
Mentally ill	7.7%	10.0%	15.4%

*$\chi^2 = 21.11$, df = 6, P < .05.

[a]Comments or statements coded as categoric embracement include those indicating acceptance of or attachment to street people as a social category or to such general street-role identities as bum, tramp, drifter, or transient.

[b]Comments or statements coded as specific embracement include those indicating identification with a situationally specific survival role, such as dumpster diver or street performer, or with a specific social-relational role, such as friend, lover, or protector, or with an occupational role.

[c]Comments or statements coded as ideological embracement include those indicating acceptance of a set of beliefs or ideas, such as those associated with a particular religion.

an exaggerated claim regarding past or current wages. A case in point is provided by a forty-year-old homeless man who spent much of his time hanging around a bar boasting about having been offered a job as a Harley-Davidson mechanic for $18.50 per hour, although at the same time he constantly begged for cigarettes and spare change for beer.

Equally illustrative of such embellishment was an encounter we overheard between Marilyn, who was passing out discarded burritos, and a homeless man in his early twenties. After this fellow had taken several burritos, he chided Marilyn for being "drunk." She yelled back angrily, "I'm a sheetrock taper and I make 14 bucks an hour. What the fuck do you make?" In addition to putting the young man in his place, Marilyn thus announced to him and to others overhearing the encounter her desired identity as a person who earns a good wage and must therefore be treated respectfully. Subsequent interaction with her revealed that she worked only sporadically, and then most often for not much more than minimum wage. There was, then, a considerable gap between claims and reality.

Disjunctures between identity assertions and reality appear to be quite common and were readily discernible on occasion, as in the case of a forty-five-year-old straddler from Pittsburgh who had been on the streets for a year and who was given to substantial embellishment of his former military experiences. On several occasions he was overheard telling about "patrolling the Alaskan/Russian border in Alaskan Siberia" and his encounters with Russian guards who traded him vodka for coffee. Since there is no border between Alaska and Siberia, it is obvious that this tale is outlandish. Nonetheless, such tales, however embellished, can be construed as attempts to communicate specifics about the person and the person's sense of self. Additionally, they focus a ray of positive attention on the storyteller and thereby enable him or her to garner momentarily a valued resource that is typically in short supply on the streets.

Fantasizing   The second type of fictive storytelling among the homeless is verbal fantasizing, which involves the articulation of fabrications about the speaker's future. Such fabrications place the narrator in pos-

itively framed situations that seem far removed from, if at all connected to, his or her past and present. These fabrications are almost always benign, usually have a Walter Mitty/pipe dream quality to them, and vary from fanciful reveries involving little self-deception to fantastic stories in which the narrator appears to be taken in by his or her constructions.[26]

Regardless of the degree of self-deception, the verbal fantasies we heard were generally organized around one or more of four themes: self-employment, money, material possessions, and women.[27] Fanciful constructions concerning self-employment usually involved business schemes. On several occasions, for example, Tony Jones told us and others about his plans to set up a little shop near the university to sell leather hats and silver work imported from New York. In an even more expansive vein, two straddlers who had befriended each other seemed to be scheming constantly about how they were going to start one lucrative business after another. Once we overheard them talking about "going into business" for themselves, "either roofing houses or rebuilding classic cars and selling them." A few days later, they were observed trying to find a third party to bankroll one of these business ventures, and they even asked us if we "could come up with some cash."

An equally prominent source of fanciful identity construction is the fantasy of becoming rich. Some of the homeless just daydreamed about what they would do if they had a million dollars. Pat Manchester, for instance, assured us that if he "won a million dollars in a lottery," he was mature enough that he "wouldn't blow it." Others made bold claims about future riches without offering any details. And still others confidently spun fairly detailed stories about being extravagant familial providers in the future, as Tom Fisk did when he returned to town after a futile effort to establish himself in a city closer to his girlfriend. Despite his continuing financial setbacks, he assured us, "I'm going to get my fiancée a new pet monkey, even if it costs a thousand dollars. And I'm going to get her two parrots too, just to show her how much I love her."

Fanciful identity assertions were also constructed around material possessions and sexual encounters with women. These two identity pegs were clearly illustrated one evening among several homeless men along the city's major nightlife strip. During the course of making numerous overtures to passing women, two of the fellows jointly fantasized about how they would attract these women in the future. "Man, these chicks are going to be all over us when we come back into town with our new suits and Corvettes," one exclaimed. The other added, "We'll have to get some cocaine too. Cocaine will get you women every time." This episode and fantasy occurred early in the second month of our fieldwork, and we quickly came to learn that such fantasizing was fairly commonplace and that it was typically occasioned by "woman-watching," which exemplifies one of the ways in which homeless men are both deprived of attention and respond to that deprivation.

One place homeless men would often watch women was along a jogging trail in one of the city's parks adjacent to the river. Here on warm afternoons they would drink beer and call out to women who jogged or walked along the trail or came to the park to sun themselves. Most of the women moved nervously by, ignoring the overtures of the men. But some responded with a smile, a wave, or even a quick "Hi!" Starved for female attention, the homeless men are quick to fantasize, attributing great significance to the slightest response. One Saturday afternoon, for example, as we were sitting by the jogging trail drinking beer with Pat Manchester and Ron Whitaker, we noticed several groups of young women who had laid out blankets on the grassy strip that borders the trail. Pat and Ron were especially interested in the women who were wearing shorts and halter tops. Pat called out for them to take their tops off. It was not clear that they heard him, but he insisted, "They really want it. I can tell they do." He suggested we go over with him to "see what we can get," but he was unwilling to go by himself. Instead, he constructed a fantasy in which the young women were very interested in him. Occasionally the women glanced toward us with apprehension, and Pat always acted as though it was a sign of interest. "If I go over there and they want to wrap me up in that blanket and fuck me," he said, "man, I'm going for it." Nonetheless, he continued to sit and fantasize, unwilling to acknowledge openly the obdurate reality staring him in the face.[28]

Although respectable work, financial wealth, material possessions, and women are intimately interconnected in actuality, only one or two of the themes were typically highlighted in the stories we heard. Occasionally, however, we encountered a particularly accomplished story-teller who wove together all four themes in a grand scenario. Such was the case with the straddler from Pittsburgh who told the following tale over a meal of bean stew and stale bread at the Sally, and repeated it after lights-outs as he lay on the concrete floor of the winter warehouse: "Tomorrow morning I'm going to get my money and say, 'Fuck this shit.' I'm going to catch a plane to Pittsburgh and tomorrow night I'll take a hot bath, have a dinner of linguine and red wine in my own restaurant, and have a woman hanging on my arm." When encountered on the street the next evening, he attempted to explain his continued presence on the streets by saying, "I've been informed that all my money is tied up in a legal battle back in Pittsburgh," an apparently fanciful amplification of the original fabrication.[29]

Although both embellished and fanciful fictive storytelling surfaced rather frequently in the conversations we overheard, they were not uniformly widespread or randomly distributed among the homeless. As is indicated in Table 3, embellishment occurred among all the homeless but was most pronounced among the straddlers and outsiders. Fantasizing, on the other hand, occurred most frequently among those

Table 3 Types of Fictive Storytelling, by Type of Homeless*

Types of Homeless	Embellishment[a] (N: 39)	Fantasizing[b] (N: 31)
Recently dislocated	2.6%	45.2%
Straddlers	42.1%	32.2%
Outsiders	50.0%	9.7%
Mentally ill	5.3%	12.9%

*$\chi^2 = 24.35$, df = 3, P < .001.

[a]Comments or statements were coded as embellishment if they entailed the elaboration and exaggeration of past and present experiences with fictitious particulars. See note 25 for criteria used for determining the fictive character of comments and stories.

[b]Comments or statements were coded as fantasizing if they entailed future-oriented fabrications that placed the narrator in positively or strangely framed situations. See note 25 for criteria used for determining the fictive character of comments and stories.

who still had one foot anchored in the world they came from and who could still envision a future, and it occurred least often among those individuals who appeared acclimated to street life and who tended to embrace one or more street identities. For these individuals, especially those who have been on the streets for some time, the future is apparently too remote to provide a solid anchor for identity-oriented fictions that are of this world. It is not surprising, then, that it is also these individuals who exhibit the greatest tendency to drift into alternative realities, as did a thirty-three-year-old black female who claimed to be "the Interracial Princess," a status allegedly bestowed on her by "a famous astrologer from New York."

We have elaborated three generic patterns of talk through which the homeless construct and avow personal identities. We have seen that each pattern of this identity talk—distancing, embracement, and fictive storytelling—contains several varieties, and that their frequency of use varies among the types of homeless. Categoric role and associational distancing and the construction of fanciful identities occur most frequently among the recently dislocated, for example; whereas categoric embracement and embellishment tend to manifest themselves most frequently among the outsiders. Overall, then, many of the homeless are active agents in the construction and negotiation of identities as they interact with others. They do not, in other words, passively accept the social identities their appearance sometimes exudes or into which they are cast. This is not to suggest that the homeless do not sometimes view themselves in terms of the more negative, stereotypical identities frequently imputed to them. One afternoon, for example, we encountered Gypsy stretched out on a mattress in the back of his old car. Drunk and downhearted, he muttered glumly:

> I've just about given up on life. I can't get any work and all my friends do is keep me drunk. Crazy, just crazy—that's all I am. Don't have any desire to do anything for myself. This car is all I've got, and even it won't work. It's not even worth trying. I'm nothing but an asshole and a bum anymore.

But on other occasions, as we have seen, Gypsy was not only more cheerful but even managed to cull shreds of self-respect and dignity from his pariah-like existence. Moreover, we found that self-deprecating lamentations like Gypsy's were relatively rare compared to the avowal of positive personal identities. This should not be particularly surprising, since every human needs to be an object of value and since the homeless have little to supply that sense of value other than their own identity-construction efforts.

SUMMARY

All animals are confronted with the challenge of material subsistence, but only humans are saddled with the vexing question of its meaning. We must not only sustain ourselves physically to survive, but we are also impelled to make sense of our mode of subsistence, to place it in some meaningful context, to develop an account of our situation that does not destroy our sense of self-worth. Otherwise, the will to persist falters and interest in tomorrow wanes. The biblical prophets understood this well when they told us that "man does not live by bread alone." The homeless appear to understand this existential dilemma, too, at least experientially; for while they struggle to subsist materially, they confront the meaning of their predicament and its implications for the self. These concerns weigh particularly heavily on the recently dislocated, but they gnaw at the other homeless as well—sometimes when they drift off at night, sometimes when they are jarred from sleep by their own dreams or the cries of others, and often throughout the day when their encounters with other homeless and with the domiciled remind them in myriad subtle and not-so-subtle ways of their descent into the lowest reaches of the social system and of their resultant stigmatized status.

In this chapter we have explored the ways the homeless deal with their plight, both existentially and interactionally, by attempting to construct and maintain a sense of meaning and self-worth that helps them stay afloat. Not all of the homeless succeed, of course. The selves of some have been so brutalized that they are abandoned in favor of alcohol, drugs, or out-of-this-world fantasies. And many would probably not score high on a questionnaire evaluating self-esteem.[30] But the issue for us has not been how well the homeless fare in comparison to others on measures of self-esteem, but that they do, in fact, attempt to salvage the self, and that this struggle is an ongoing feature of the experience of living on the streets.

The homeless we studied are not the only individuals who have fallen or been pushed through the cracks of society who nevertheless try to carve a modicum of meaning and personal significance out of what must seem to those perched higher in the social order as an anomic void. Other examples of such salvaging work have been found in mental hospitals, concentration camps, and among black street-corner men.[31] In these and presumably in other such cases of marginality, the attempt to carve out and maintain a sense of meaning and self-worth seems especially critical for survival because it is the one thread that enables those situated at the bottom to salvage their humanity. It follows, then, that it is not out of disinterest that some people find it difficult to salvage their respective selves, but that it results instead from the scarcity of material and social resources at their disposal. That many of the homeless are indeed able to make some culturally meaningful sense of their situation and secure a measure of self-worth testifies to their psychological resourcefulness and resolve, and to the resilience of the human spirit.

Considering these observations, it is puzzling why most research on the homeless has focused almost solely on their demographics and disabilities, to the exclusion of their inner lives. Perhaps it is because many social scientists have long assumed that the issues of meaning and self-worth are irrelevant, or at least of secondary importance, in the face of pressing physiological survival needs. This assumption is firmly rooted in Abraham Maslow's well-known hierarchy of needs, which holds that the satisfaction of physiological and safety needs is a necessary condition for the emergence and gratification of higher-level needs such as the need for self-esteem or for a positive personal identity.[32] This thesis has become almost a cliché in spite of the fact that relevant research is scanty and ambiguous at best. Our finding that concern with both existential and identity-oriented meaning can be readily gleaned from the talk of homeless street people, clearly some of the most destitute in terms of physiological and safety needs, provides an empirical counter-point to this popular assumption. Moreover, our observations suggest that the salience of such cognitive concerns is not necessarily contingent on the prior satisfaction of physiological survival requisites. Instead, such needs appear to coexist, even at the most rudimentary levels of human existence. The homeless we came to know clearly evidence such concerns.

NOTES

1. Derber (1979: 42).

2. If expression of concern for and interest in the homeless were associated primarily with cold weather, then media coverage should be greatest during January and February, the coldest months of the year across the country. Instead, public sympathy for the down and out, and perhaps for others as well, is ritualized most conspicuously during the Thanksgiving/Christmas holiday season. As a *Los Angeles Times* editorial noted on Christmas Day, 1988: "The charity of the holiday season is traditional—and welcome. The problem is that so much is seasonal. . . . Come January, when most people go back to their normal routines, the hunger and homelessness recognized in the holiday season will remain. It would be nice if most of the spirit of giving remained too."

3. That sympathy for the homeless would be compressed into a two- to three-month period is hardly surprising theoretically. In his essay on "the visibility of evil," Coser (1969) notes that the degree to which individuals identify sympathetically with victims of catastrophe or injustice varies considerably across time. He argues that "we share at all times the capacity for not seeing what we do not wish to see" (1969: 104), in part because we have only so much emotional energy and yet we live in a world filled with inhumanity and injustice. In order to protect ourselves both emotionally and morally, we are thus inclined toward denial or what Myrdal (1944) referred to as the "convenience of ignorance." The implication is that there is no necessary or direct correspondence between the magnitude and empirical visibility of injustice or evil in a society and the degree to which it enters the perceptual and emotional field of the more fortunate.

4. For discussion of these and related themes from a sociological standpoint, see Douglas and Johnson (1977) and Fontana (1980).

5. Swidler (1986: 273).

6. For conceptualization and general discussion of luck, see Gunther (1977) and Morrow (1981).

7. This vulnerability thesis is clearly articulated in the parallel works on today's homeless by Rossi (1989: 143–79) and Wright (1989: 95–114), and it is suggested by a host of other writings focusing on symptoms of mental illness on the streets and particularly on the link between deinstitutionalization and homelessness.

8. In a review of research on the drinking patterns of homeless men through the 1960s, Bahr suggests that this pattern

of spree or periodic drinking was fairly common, occurring among one-third to one-fourth of the drinkers. But, as Bahr cautioned, "[I]t is probable that many of them are merely heavy drinkers whose consumption is periodic because of financial or other factors" (Bahr, 1973: 103).

9. Goffman coined the term to capture the ways that inmates of mental asylums take leave without actually leaving the facility and thereby get "around the organization's assumptions as to what [they] should do and get and hence what [they] should be" (1961a: 189). We think the concept provides analytic leverage when applied to other contexts as well. For a thorough discussion and empirical grounding of the concept in relation to asylums, see Goffman (1961a: 188–320). Material quoted in the text comes from pages 189 and 309.

10. Research on the mental health of the homeless of the 1980s has found that they suffer from considerably higher rates of depression and demoralization than the domiciled, including the domiciled poor (see Rossi, 1989: 147–52; LaGory et al., 1990). Rossi found, for example, that 47 percent of the sample of homeless he interviewed in Chicago were classified as high on the depression scale he used. Such findings do not strike us as surprising. Indeed, not only would we expect to find considerable depression on the streets considering the trials and exigencies of street life, but we suspect such depression might be interpreted as a fairly normal response to a strikingly abnormal situation.

11. For discussion of some mental disorders as "bizarre behaviors," see Eaton (1986: 1–41).

12. Much diagnostic and epidemiological research on mental illness has proceeded as if symptoms of psychosis could be understood out of context. But some students of mental illness have argued instead that symptomatic behaviors are inherently neither normal nor abnormal but have meaning only in relation to the social setting in which they are embedded. See, for example, Coleman (1967), Eaton and Weil (1953), Edgerton (1969), Goffman (1971), and Laing and Esterson (1970).

13. This dynamic is consistent with Lemert's (1962: 19) observations regarding paranoia. He argues that "while the paranoid person reacts differently to his social environment, it is also true that 'others' react differently to him and . . . that these differential reactions are reciprocals of one another, being interwoven and concatenated at each and all phases of a process of exclusion." Thus, he concludes, "delusions and associated behavior must be understood in a context of exclusion."

14. This is one of the cardinal principles of social interaction. See Stone (1962), Turner (1968), and McCall and Simmons (1978).

15. This conceptualization of social identity is consistent with both Goffman (1963: 2–3) and McCall and Simmons (1978: 62), as well as with Turner's (1978: 6) "appearance principle," which holds that "people tend to conceive another person [and thus impute social identities] on the basis of the role behavior they observe unless there are cues that alert them to the possibility of a discrepancy between person and role."

16. This conceptualization differs from Goffman's (1963: 57) and McCall and Simmons's (1978: 62–63) in that they define personal identity in terms of unique, biograpic facts and items that function as pegs upon which social identities can be hung. It is our contention that biographic facts and experiences, like social roles, influence but do not fully determine the construction and assertion of what we call personal identities. In other words, rather than taking for granted the relationship between biography and personal identity, we see it as problematic and variable.

17. These identity statements were not elicited by asking the homeless how they see themselves or other such direct questions. Instead, they arose as the homeless interacted with one another as well as others. The statements were secured primarily by the two relatively unobtrusive forms of listening discussed earlier: eavesdropping and nondirective, conversational listening. All told, we heard 186 statements that we read as bearing directly on the issue of identity. Although these statements came from only 40 percent of our field informants, this subsample was comparable to the larger sample in terms of age, gender, and ethnicity. More important for our purposes, each of the different types of homeless is represented by the identity statements we secured. Consequently, we are reasonably confident that the identity talk we overheard is representative of the homeless living in or passing through Austin.

18. For discussions of such distancing in various contexts, see Goffman (1961b), Levitin (1964), Stebbins (1975), and Sayles (1984).

19. As Anderson (1976: 214) observed, based on his research among domiciled black street-corner men, claims to a particular identity depend in part "on one's ability to manage his image by drawing distinctions between himself and others he does not want to be associated with."

20. See Goffman (1961b) for the initial conceptualization.

21. It was in fact true that some Salvation Army employees loaded bags of groceries into their cars before leaving for the day, but the reason was not, as is implied in this statement, so that they could take them home for personal use. Rather, they were transporting the groceries to needy families in the community.

22. Wiseman (1970: 187–88, 194–98) similarly noted the "harsh sentiments" of skid-row alcoholics toward their seeming benefactors. Similar patterns of bitching and griping have been observed in relation to more all-encompassing institutions, such as prisons and mental hospitals. In commenting on such verbal insubordination, Goffman (1961a: 319) pushes an interpretation that dovetails with ours: "This recalcitrance is not an incidental mechanism of defense but rather an essential constituent of the self" that allows the individual "to keep some distance, some elbow room, between himself and that with which others assume he should be identified."

23. This conception of embracement is derived from Goffman's (1961b: 106–7) treatment of role embracement, but with two differences. First, we conceive of embracement as a gener-

ic process through which attachment to and involvement in a particular entity or activity are expressed, with role embracement constituting only one of many forms of embracement. And, second, we think embracement need not entail disappearance into the activity at hand and corresponding inattention to the flow of other proximate activities. Such engagement should be viewed as a variable feature of embracement, not as a defining characteristic.

24. Anderson (1976) found that the identity work of the black street-corner men he studied was composed mainly of associational distancing and embracement. Evidence of both this and role embracement is also reported by Rooney (1973) in his study of skid-row men in the 1960s. He found that those who were on skid row for longer than a year were much more likely to identify themselves as skid-row members, and that this tendency was even more pronounced among those with friends on skid row. Thus, such embracement appears to be more pronounced the longer the time on the streets and the greater the number of street associates.

25. Given the categorization of this line of talk as "fictive," it is important to make explicit the criteria used to determine whether a particular narration was indeed fictive. We talked with and listened to each of the seventy individuals within our identity subsample, seeing nearly all of them in a range of situations at different times, with an average of 4.5 encounters per individual. We were thus able to monitor many of these individuals across time and space. Any story we identified as fictive contained one or more of three kinds of narrative contradictions: (1) those among multiple stories told by the same individual, as when a street person claims to be thirty-six years old on one occasion and forty-six on another; (2) those between stories and observed behaviors in various situations, as when someone claims to be working regularly but is seen panhandling or intoxicated during the day; and (3) those between current situations and future projections and claims, as when a disheveled, penniless street person claims to have a managerial job awaiting him at a local business. In each of these situations, credulity is strained because of objective discrepancies or because of the vast gap between current and projected realities.

26. Fanciful identities are constructed by other people as well, but it is our sense that with movement up the class structure they tend to be privatized and temporally or spatially ritualized, rather than publicly articulated, ongoing features of everyday life, as was the case with many of the homeless we studied and the black street-corner men observed by Liebow (1967) and Anderson (1976). Regarding the latter, Liebow (1967: 213) noted that the construction of fictive identities allows them to "be men once again providing they do not look too closely at one another's credentials." Although many of the personal identities they construct, such as "going for brothers," are different in content from those constructed by the homeless, they are functionally similar.

27. That these four factors function as springboards for fanciful identities constructed by homeless men is hardly surprising, considering that success as an adult male in America is defined in large part in terms of job, money, possessions, and women. This thematic connection also suggests that although the life-style of homeless males stands outside the normative order, their dreams and fantasies are nonetheless very much of that order. It could hardly be any other way, of course, since dreams and fantasies are, in large part, culturally embedded.

28. The unsolicited sexual overtures of homeless males understandably make most women uncomfortable. One stereotypic image of the homeless man is that of a potential sex offender, and some of the tactics the men use to gain attention, such as Pat's calling to the young women to undress, overstep public propriety (although the talk and actions certainly are no more lewd than much locker-room humor and singles-bar activities). A large measure of the perceived threat in such interactions may well be a transformation of class offense into sexual terms. In any case, women generally try to avoid encouraging homeless men. Usually the homeless accept this refusal of social involvement, but sometimes, especially when the refusal seems particularly direct, they respond angrily to the loss of face it entails. This can lead to a quick escalation of aggressive interaction, such as that which we witnessed one afternoon in the downtown area when we were hanging out with Ron. He was watching young women walking down the sidewalk after work. As they passed, Ron called out, "Hey, honey, lookin' good!" Most of them responded either by ignoring him or by giving a small grin and accelerating their pace. When one young woman instead scowled and lifted her head in disdain, Ron took off after her, calling out angrily, "Rich bitch! Rich goddamn bitch!" as she hurried up the street.

29. It is important to note that this amplification was elicited by one of us rather than by another homeless individual. As we indicated in the last chapter, we rarely overheard the homeless call into question each other's stories and asserted identities. Whatever the reasons for not challenging publicly another's identity claims, the outcome is a mutually deferential stance that increases the prospect of embellishment and storytelling, thus making the homeless unwitting co-conspirators in the spinning and maintenance of outlandish personal identities.

30. The issue of self-esteem or worth has not been explored in research on today's homeless, but Bahr and Caplow's survey of skid-row men of the 1960s did reveal that they "were much more likely than the non–skid row respondents to admit negative self-conceptions" (1973: 287).

31. See, for example, Goffman's study of asylums (1961a), Liebow's (1967) and Anderson's (1976) ethnographies of black street-corner men, and the observations of Bettelheim (1943), Frankl (1963), and Dimsdale (1980) on the psychological coping strategies of concentration-camp inmates.

32. Maslow (1962).

REFERENCES

Anderson, Elijah. 1976. *A Place on the Corner.* Chicago: University of Chicago Press.

Bahr, Howard M. 1973. *Skid Row: An Introduction to Disaffiliation.* New York: Oxford University Press.

Bahr, Howard M., and Theodore Caplow. 1973. *Old Men Drunk and Sober.* New York: New York University Press.

Bettelheim, Bruno. 1943. "Individual and Mass Behavior in Extreme Situations." *Journal of Abnormal Social Psychology* 38:417–452.

Coleman, Jules V. 1967. "Social Factors Influencing the Development and Containment of Psychiatric Symptoms." Pp. 158–168 in Thomas J. Scheff, ed., *Mental Illness and Social Processes.* New York: Harper and Row.

Coser, Lewis A. 1969. "The Visibility of Evil." *Journal of Social Issues* 25:101–109.

Derber, Charles. 1979. *The Pursuit of Attention: Power and Individualism in Everyday Life.* New York: Oxford University Press.

Dimsdale, Joel E. 1980. "The Coping Behavior of Nazi Concentration Camp Survivors." Pp. 163–74 in Joel E. Dimsdale, ed., *Survivors, Victims and Perpetrators: Essays on the Nazi Holocaust.* Washington: Hemisphere.

Douglas, Jack D., and John M. Johnson, eds. 1977. *Existential Sociology.* New York: Cambridge University Press.

Eaton, Joseph W., and Robert J. Weil. 1953. "The Mental Health of the Hutterites." *Scientific American* 189:31–37.

Eaton, William W. 1986. *The Sociology of Mental Disorders.* Second edition. New York: Praeger.

Edgerton, Robert B. 1969. "On the Recognition of Mental Illness." Pp. 49–72 in Stanley C. Plog and Robert B. Edgerton, eds., *Changing Perspectives on Mental Illness.* New York: Holt, Rinehart and Winston.

Fontana, Andrea. 1980. "Toward a Complex Universe: Existential Sociology." Pp. 155–181 in Jack D. Douglas, Patricia A. Adler, Peter Adler, Andrea Fontana, C. Robert Freeman, and Joseph A. Kotarba, eds., *Introduction to the Sociologies of Everyday Life.* Boston: Allyn and Bacon.

Frankl, Viktor. 1963. *Man's Search for Meaning.* New York: Washington Square Press.

Goffman, Erving. 1961a. *Asylums.* Garden City, N.Y.: Anchor.

———. 1961b. "Role Distance." Pp. 85–152 in *Encounters: Two Studies in the Sociology of Interaction.* Indianapolis: Bobbs-Merrill.

———. 1963. *Stigma: Notes on the Management of Spoiled Identity.* Englewood Cliffs, N.J.: Prentice-Hall.

———. 1971. "The Insanity of Place." Pp. 335–390 in Erving Goffman, *Relations in Public.* New York: Harper and Row.

Gunther, Max. 1977. *The Luck Factor.* New York: Macmillan.

LaGory, Mark, Ferris J. Ritchey, and Jeffrey Mullis. 1990. "Depression Among the Homeless." *Journal of Health and Social Behavior* 31:87–101.

Laing, R. D., and A. Esterson. 1970. *Sanity, Madness and the Family.* Second edition. Baltimore: Penguin Books.

Lemert, Edwin M. 1962. "Paranoia and the Dynamics of Exclusion." *Sociometry* 25:2–20.

Levitin, T. E. 1964. "Role Performances and Role Distance in a Low Status Occupation: The Puller." *Sociological Quarterly* 5:251–60.

Liebow, Elliot. 1967. *Tally's Corner: A Study of Negro Streetcorner Men.* Boston: Little, Brown.

Los Angeles Times. 1988. "If Only the Spirit of Giving Could Continue." December 25.

McCall, George J., and J. L. Simmons. 1969. *Issues in Participant Observation: A Text and Reader.* Reading, Mass.: Addison-Wesley.

Maslow, Abraham H. 1962. *Toward a Psychology of Being.* New York: Van Nostrand.

Morrow, Lance. 1981. "The Importance of Being Lucky." *Time,* April 27:79–80.

Myrdal, Gunnar. 1944. *An American Dilemma: The Negro Problem and Modern Democracy.* New York: Harper and Row.

Rooney, James F. 1973. "Friendship and Reference Group Orientation Among Skid Row Men." Ph.D. dissertation, University of Pennsylvania.

Rossi, Peter. 1989. *Down and Out in America: The Origins of Homelessness.* Chicago: University of Chicago Press.

Sayles, Marnie L. 1984. "Role Distancing: Differentiating the Role of the Elderly from the Person." *Qualitative Sociology* 7:236–252.

Stebbins, Robert A. 1975. "Role Distance, Role Distance Behavior and Jazz Musicians." Pp. 133–141 in D. Brissett and C. Edgely, eds., *Life as Theater: A Dramaturgical Sourcebook.* Chicago: Aldine.

Stone, Gregory P. 1962. "Appearance and the Self." Pp. 86–118 in Arnold M. Rose, ed., *Human Behavior and Social Processes.* Boston: Houghton Mifflin.

Swidler, Ann. 1986. "Culture in Action: Symbols and Strategies." *American Sociological Review* 51:273–286.

Turner, Ralph H. 1968. "The Self-Conception in Social Interaction." Pp. 93–106 in C. Gordon and K. J. Gergen, eds., *The Self in Social Interaction.* New York: John Wiley and Sons.

———. 1978. "The Role and the Person." *American Journal of Sociology* 84:1–23.

Wiseman, Jacqueline. 1970. *Stations of the Lost: The Treatment of Skid Row Alcoholics.* Chicago: University of Chicago Press.

Wright, James D. 1989. *Address Unknown: The Homeless in America.* New York: Aldine de Gruyter.

16 | VICTIMS, VILLAINS, AND TALK SHOW SELVES
Kathleen S. Lowney and James A. Holstein

Just when you think it can't get any worse, switch channels and you'll find the latest episode of "I'm African American and I Hate Black People!" or "Dad Wants to Be a Woman!" Perhaps you'll channel surf across "Back Off, Boys! I'm a Lesbian and You'll Never Have Me." Jerry, Ricki, Sally, and Jenny. Misfits, perverts, lowlifes. Flailing, biting, scratching. Fear, conflict, pain, exploitation. Cultural and psychic casualties. Drivel. Trash.

Some say that daytime television talk shows have become the traveling circus—the carnival sideshow—of the late 20th century (see Gamson 1998; Lowney 1999; Twitchell 1992). But, reviled as they may be (see Abt and Seesholtz 1994; Heaton and Wilson 1995), talk shows are an exploding (and explosive) entertainment genre that offers viewers an important "window on the world"—or at least some very outrageous corners of that world.

Talk shows, like all TV programming, rely upon a reliable stock-in-trade to garner viewers and support high ratings. Indeed, the production conventions of *The Oprah Winfrey Show* or *The Jerry Springer Show* are becoming as familiar to viewers as those of the nightly news or *The Tonight Show*. While myriad production techniques contribute to their success—their "personality" hosts, topical subject matter, "colorful" or "intriguing" guests, just to name a few—a staple of the daytime talk show is the interpersonal carnival that serves up the selves of "outrageous" guest subjects for public scrutiny, inquisition, approbation, and/or condemnation. As Everett Hughes (1984) might have put it, the on-camera pageant of captivating, scandalous, even contemptible, characters is a principal "going concern" of the TV talk show. More and more, the spectacle of human torment, degradation, and depravity has become the driving impulse behind talk show programming.

This chapter examines the ways in which TV talk shows—especially the new, more confrontational shows that dominate programming at the turn of the century—convene and assemble troubled identities for their guests in order to produce the contentious scenarios their audiences crave. Of course the individuals who populate talk shows bring with them their own biographical particulars, their own lived experiences. Guests are diligently selected for the personal attributes, attitudes, and actions that make them popular with viewers (Gamson 1998; Lowney 1999). Nevertheless, production conventions, combined with the interactional manipulation of identities—"good, bad, and ugly" personas, so to speak—produce selves to fill all three rings of the postmodern talk show circus.

Constructing talk show selves, as we shall see, is deliberate and artful. Hosts and producers adroitly manage guests so as to present shocking characters and sensational stories. While these selves are virtual works of art, they are by no means "originals." Whereas each guest is presented as a unique package of traits and troubles, taken together, talk show participants represent a rather limited range of standard—even classic—cultural images. Show after show formulaically—almost ritualistically—conjures up types of persons who are effectively guaranteed to arouse viewers passions.

If talk shows draw upon familiar archetypes as identity templates for their guests, the general personas of "victims" and "villains" are the most commonly invoked. They repeatedly employ familiar self-construction formats to provide uniquely embodied, yet recognizable, "stock" characters that generate the emotion and excitement upon which their audiences thrive. While individual selves are deftly constructed, with considerable situational nuance, these are also ritualized *re*-productions of sympathetic and despised cultural icons. As we compare numerous episodes of different talk shows, it's evident that the selves produced are both formulaic and inventively crafted at the same time.

THEMATIC CONVENTIONS

Talk show programming has transmuted, if not evolved, since its popular explosion in the 1980s. Initially daytime versions of nighttime "variety" shows with well-known guests who both performed and chatted with hosts, talk shows also began exploring controversial social and moral issues. This development required shows to produce the characters—with extravagant selves and memorable identities—necessary to titillate, provoke, and entertain, if not appall, curious audiences.

During the 1980s and early 1990s, talk shows were typically organized around three major conventions, each of which still exists today, although in changing measure (see Lowney 1999). First, there is the *informational* convention. These shows usually involve topics relating to health, medicine, psychiatry/psychology, science, or social policy and politics. In this convention, shows teach audience members about how to cope with medical, personal, or social problems in order to improve their lives. Their titles signal the informational themes: "Shortened Hospital Stays Are Dangerous to Newborns," "Obsessive-Compulsive Behavior in Children and Adults," and "Memory Loss and Other Mental Deficiencies."

The second traditional convention is pure *entertainment,* involving popular culture or "show business" themes. Such shows are also easy to identify: "Celebrity News: Star Predictions for the Coming Year," "Oprah and Viewers in Hollywood," and "Inside the Life of a Celebrity." Some of these shows include well-known Hollywood insiders or movie critics, whose expertise provides clues about what is going to be popular, and why. Other shows feature entertainment "personalities" themselves, promoting their latest books or movies while viewers peer into the "private" selves of these "public" figures.

A third convention is *salvational.* These shows attempt to rescue people from destructive, sick, or "deviant" lifestyles, habits, or relationships. In many respects, shows of this ilk resemble the carnival-revival of centuries past (Snow 1983). They provide both entertainment and titillation, offering some of the spontaneity, rowdiness, and even chaos of the carnival, while also serving up the almost sacred rhetoric of re-

vivalism's "conversion" testimonials. These shows typically revolve around guests who have fallen prey to their own weaknesses or foibles, or have been ensnared by others with pernicious intent. The guests typically have their psychic or social afflictions graphically exposed, but, eventually, they are set on the road to recovery or redemption (see Lowney 1994, 1999). *Salvation* shows thus require subjects who are first degraded, but who can subsequently be resurrected. Identity construction, while often far from subtle, is nonetheless artful in that it must conjure up spoiled selves that retain the potential for change or deliverance.

Through the 1980s into the mid-1990s, the salvational convention dominated talk show programming. In 1996, for example, approximately 70 percent of all "mainstream" shows aimed at salvation in one way or another (Lowney 1999). But by the late 1990s, a close relative of the salvation theme has come to dominate many of TV's daytime talk shows. While many themes were adumbrated, if not fully exploited, in salvational programming, the appearance of shows like *The Ricki Lake Show, The Jerry Springer Show,* and *The Jenny Jones Show* transformed the carnival-revival into a "real-life" hybrid of the circus side show and "Big Time Wrestling"—with clear vestiges of the spectacle and carnage of ancient Romans throwing Christians to the lions in the Coliseum. In place of crowds yelling "kill, kill, kill," *Jerry Springer* viewers chant "Jer-ry, Jer-ry, Jer-ry" (see Gamson 1998, p. 8).

This new convention is broadly based on *confrontation.* It is conflict TV, plain and simple, built on virtual showdowns between persons, beliefs, and lifestyles. By comparison, shows from the other conventions seem tame, short on energy and excitement. Even ostensibly "responsible" mainstream hosts have dipped deeper into this new convention (for example, Sally Jessy Raphael), while other traditional stalwarts like Phil Donahue have retired from the scene. More and more, talk shows present guests with something merely outrageous and provocative to say, and who are likely to say it loudly—even if it has little intrinsic informational or entertainment value. These are characters hell-bent on conflict, whose appeal lies in their "shock value." As Joshua Gamson (1998, p. 75) tells us, these new talk shows "need heat, and the easiest thing to do is to find people to espouse readily recognizable conflict packages."

The subjects required for *confrontation* shows have to be "up front" and "out there." Guests are expected to interact passionately with one another, to trade insults and condemnations. If they actually assault one another, so much the better. Interpersonal conflict, relational strife, social rebellion, and other antisocial attitudes and behaviors are acted out broadly, coarsely, and violently; physical encounters are the pièce de résistance. Onstage "street fights" and "school yard brawls" have now been added to the parade of relational "freaks" comprising the talk show *circus maximus*. There's no holding back in the presentation of these selves, no place for self-consciousness or reserve.

While physical confrontation is now almost formulaic on *The Jerry Springer Show* (with guests sometimes assaulting one another even before words are exchanged), it's not a necessary ingredient for all shows of this genre. Bizarre personas, cultural misfits, guests who flagrantly and outrageously confront, deny, and flaunt societal norms or mores, or interpersonal renegades who profess not the slightest regard for social conventions, manners, or niceties can propel a show without physical confrontations—although this is becoming increasingly rare. Even if guests don't actually brawl with one another, a character spewing "I don't give a rat's ass about what anybody thinks or feels" is bound to disgust and offend most viewers, and arouse *some* emotion in virtually everyone. Confrontation—physical or not—emanates from the audacious, even bodacious, selves that clash with conformity and convention, if not with one another.

The titles of confrontation shows trumpet the convention: "Outrageous Confessions," "You're Gay. How Dare You Raise a Child," "Listen Family, I'm Gay. It's Not a Phase. Get Over It," "Girly to Burly: Women Who Become Men," "You're Not the Man I Married," "Teen Boys Tell Their Moms, 'I Want to Be a Woman,'" "Family Secrets: Straight Women, Gay Husbands," "My Boyfriend Turned Out to Be a Girl." What could be more quintessentially confrontational than "Watch Me! Today I'm Going to Break Up My Ex and His New Chick"? (See Gamson pp. 254–59.)

Close cousins, salvation and confrontation themes are not totally distinct from one another. Rather they exist on a continuum from those emphasizing redemption to those merely promoting violent spectacle. Even Jerry Springer, who hosts shows where physical aggression is clearly the raison d'être (indeed, shows where violent combat is so predictable that it has lost its element of surprise), delivers a brief "sermonette" at the close of each show, admonishing viewers to repudiate the "bad examples" he has just aired.

This chapter concentrates on talk shows drawn from the confrontation and salvation conventions. Based on the examination of dozens of transcripts of talk shows from the past decade, we analyze how the shows draw upon troubled social identities to construct the selves that such shows require. First, we consider the production devices, then the formulas, that are used to produce the talk show personas that will captivate—even outrage—viewers. We discuss some of the ritualistic institutional practices and schemes that produce the selves upon which such shows rely. Then, we turn to some of the nuances of interactional identity work that constitute talk show selves.

IDENTITY-PROMOTING DEVICES

Talk shows are relatively brief, typically an hour long. To ensure that the desired characters emerge within that hour, which may be divided among several guests, talk shows must expeditiously promote conspicuous, intrepid, loathsome, or sympathetic identities for their central participants. They need brazen on-screen personas to fulfill the dramatic or spectacular promise of their conventions, and they need them fast in order to set the frenzied pace audiences have come to expect. Booking the "right" guests, of course, is crucial. Talk show producers go to great lengths to line up the sorts of characters their shows demand (see Gamson 1998; Lowney 1999). But simply recruiting captivating guests and opening up controversial discussions doesn't guarantee the desired effect. Merely introducing teenage prostitutes, transvestites, or satanists doesn't make "good" talk show TV.

Addressing this problem, talk shows employ a broad spectrum of identity-promoting devices to cultivate the characters that populate their stages. Depending upon the preferred outcome, the raw material—the biographical particulars—of the recruited guest must be framed, managed, and profiled so as to achieve the shows' implicit salvational or confrontational goals. Clearly, the sympathetic, even pathetic "loser" is a prime candidate to be "saved" on *Geraldo,* and the more outrageous and combative the character, the better for Jerry Springer and company. But even the less flamboyant *Phil Donahue Show,* for example, routinely attempted to portray "outcast" guests—those with stigmatizing features or stigmatized lifestyles—as being "just like you or me," at least to some extent. Phil would regularly present ordinary-appearing, rational-sounding guests who would reveal their "secret" deviance with reserve and dignity (Gamson 1998). The objective was to "normalize" the "abnormal," to literally redeem the guest in the eyes of the audience. This is a far cry from how Ricki Lake or Jenny Jones today might shape the persona of a guest from one of these very same groups whom they hope to thoroughly glamorize or demonize.

Achieving the desired personas requires skillfully deployed implements of self-design, including techniques such as *framing* and *staging.* Talk shows use these standard production devices to ensure that guests become the on-air personalities that programming conventions demand.

Framing

Talk shows depend heavily upon affective framing to establish the desired appreciation of guests and their situations. The outrageous personality, the social pariah, and the casualty of interpersonal or cultural turmoil all depend upon a certain emotional "shock value" to achieve maximum viewer appeal. Aiming for emotional arousal, talk shows unveil persons to be pitied, blamed, mocked, or saved from "monsters" or appalling social circumstances that inspire viewer disgust, aversion, and contempt. The task is often to make sure one guest is viewed as sympathetic, while another is seen as despicable, worthy only of disdain.

A variety of framing devices are central to this interpretive process. Titles and opening statements or introductions, for example, announce to the audience the types of persons that are about to appear. They serve as prefaces (see Holstein and Gubrium 2000) or schemes of interpretation (Schutz 1970) that pave the way for subsequent narratives of self and experience. Visual and audio production devices (for example, graphics, montages, camera angles) augment and accent aspects of the persons and circumstances to underscore salient plot lines and identity features. Geraldo Rivera, for instance, often modulates his voice when introducing a topic in the salvational convention, beginning his opening introductions in a loud voice and slowly lowering it, until he is barely whispering as he describes the pitiful plight of an unfortunate victim. He sounds almost confessional by the time he suggests the gravity of the issues he is about to explore.

Verbal framing often personalizes the issues at stake in order to make it absolutely clear how the audience is to feel about the guests. Manifestly, the host introduces topics and guests, but, in doing so, he or she also cues the audience into the "actual" selves behind, or deep inside, the persons, in the process instructing viewers as to how they should relate emotionally to these characters. Consider the following introductory segment from *Geraldo* (11/17/97):

> You've seen the images of the young ladies of the night. They're out there in their impossibly sexy or provocative outfits, their very, very short skirts, their—their spiked heels. You know that they're hookers. You know that they're very, very young. You wonder at times what brought those ladies to that place in their life, why they're working the streets. Why are they putting themselves at such tremendous risks? Why, at that tender age, are they doing, perhaps, the most dangerous profession they could possibly be following? Take a look, ladies and gentlemen, at the young ladies on our panel today. They are all, each of them, teenagers. They are also moms. They are all also prostitutes. Some of them began at the age of just 13 years old. They are teens turning tricks, they tell us, for their toddlers. On a good night, Stephanie—hi, Stephanie . . . brings home a grand, $1000. . . . She says she does it for her two-year-old son. His father—the kid's father is in jail. The father of the baby used to be Stephanie's pimp. Now she has a new boyfriend. She . . . also is

expecting her second child. And you're just a baby, really, Stephanie. Are you really doing it for your—for your kids, or are you doing it because you choose it as your calling? . . . How'd this guy get you into it?

Clearly, the subjects of this show could reasonably be seen as despicable characters: sluts, whores, incorrigible children, and indiscreet parents. But Geraldo adroitly crafts from contrasting depictions both what these teenagers could (wrongly) be taken to be, and what they "actually" are. Portrayed as "young ladies," "teenagers," and "moms" of a "tender age," Geraldo casts them as immature, innocent victims of circumstance and exploitative and uncaring adults. While their actions are suspect, their motivations, Geraldo implicitly assures us, are honorable (that is, they are "turning tricks," but doing it to support their kids), undermining the moral condemnation usually reserved for members of their "profession." The selves behind or underneath the appearances are virtuous, even if they have fallen prey to circumstance.

As Geraldo personalizes his introduction, he speaks directly to the girls, but his monologue simultaneously teaches viewers how to understand the identities of these guests, casting them in a sympathetic light, preparing the audience to accept them as victims of difficult lives. The introductory framing is a virtual discourse of guilelessness and sympathy-worthiness. While Geraldo temporarily withholds explicit judgment, he skillfully adumbrates the pain, grief, abuse, and bad choices that will soon be splashed across the screen. Again, it's not what the girls have done, but who they "actually" are, that Geraldo seeks to portray.

Typically, the opening gambit of a talk show segment designates how the characters should be interpreted, at least initially. While subsequent presentations of alternate selves or "startling revelations" may alter audience opinions, the initial framing provides a predisposition—a paradigm for understanding (Kuhn 1962)—for how viewers should interpret and react to the "facts" and characters of these little dramas.

Staging

While talk shows foster the appearance of being unrehearsed, on-screen actions are typically staged to achieve the desired outcomes. This doesn't mean the shows are literally scripted or "fake," but it does involve manipulating what the audience will see and how, concretely, it will be presented. In a sense, identity staging involves the "material mediation" of self-disclosure (see Holstein and Gubrium 2000). This means that unfolding self-presentations (Goffman 1959) may entail the use of strategic physical "props" as well as concerted "teamwork" to pull off the desired effects.

Some staging is merely practical (see Abt and Mustazza 1997; Gamson 1998). For instance, shows have rules about what is considered appropriate on-air attire. Guests (and, for that matter, even audience members) are frequently told what to wear. Audience members are instructed to remove (if possible) all clothes that suggest seasons or holidays, since shows are often rerun. Guests and audience members are also told not to wear beige or white, for these colors "fade out" too much against background sets.

On many occasions, however, clothing and other aspects of superficial appearance become integral to establishing the guests' identities. It's not just about the "look" of the guest, but also about constructing the character behind the appearance—the innocence, evil, or helplessness of those concerned. When Nazi youth are featured, they appear as tattooed "skinheads." "Big hair" and profuse makeup are de rigueur in establishing some outlandish feminine identities, while leather and chains underscores other "deviant" personas, both masculine and feminine. Viewers are implicitly told that embedded in these material trappings are the selves whose features are being conveyed.

While material staging may seem "matter of fact," it can also be the dramatic centerpiece of a talk show segment. For example, in an episode of the *Sally Jessy Raphael Show* (2/14/96), two teenage girls talk with Sally about their mothers, whom they claim are the town "sluts." They accuse the mothers of acting and dressing like "hookers," calling them, among other things, "spandex queens." According to the girls, their mothers go braless, wear "short shorts," "wear things that you can see their butts . . . navels . . . cleavage . . . breasts." One of the girls, Tammy, is upset because her mother, Linda, "will go to the grocery store, and she will wear a tight black dress, two sizes too small, mini—and when she bends over, she has no underwear." Tammy is concerned that many people think that she behaves just like her mother, something Tammy vehemently denies.

Later, Sally greets the mothers, but they don't simply appear on camera. Instead, they sashay on stage, as if on a fashion show "runway," "spandex queens" literally on parade. As advertised by their daughters, they are revealingly clad, looking much like the "sluts and hookers" the daughters described. While the daughters' dialogue framed the mothers from the girls' point of view—predisposing viewers to see the bad side of the mothers—the mothers' full-blown material presence provides a thoroughly visceral understanding of the girls' disgust with their mothers' appearance and a deep appreciation for the mothers as the culprits of this scenario. Their physical, material comportment assures us that they *are* the despicable selves their daughters have portrayed them to be. While Sally goes on to try to "save" these women from their wanton ways, their sheer corporeal appearance etches their contemptible identities into viewers' hearts, minds, and *eyes*. They *are* women who disrespect themselves and their families by putting it all "out on the street."

In many such instances—where salvation and "makeovers" are the ultimate design—ignoble guests enter dramatically from offstage, allowing the audience ample opportunity to scrutinize their offending selves. This is quite different from the typical presentation of "innocent" accusers, who typically are onstage from the beginning, sitting demurely as they recount their stories. "Miscreants," in contrast, quite literally march in review in front of the audience, like circus performers, fashion models, or sideshow freaks. Material staging draws moral boundaries between and around the audience, the "good" guests, the hosts, and those with troubled selves. On the sets of the more "chaotic" shows like *The Jerry Springer Show,* the hovering presence of "bouncers" posing as stagehands provides further material evidence of the types of characters that are likely to appear. Production conventions and devices thus ensure that identity types are visibly embodied by "in-the-flesh" guests.

CONSTRUCTING VICTIMS AND VILLAINS

If staging and framing are standard self-construction tools, then character archetypes are the "blueprints" for talk show selves. To varying degrees, both salvation and confrontation shows thrive on clashes between "good" and "evil" to produce either the basis for redemption or fuel for conflict. One of the primary means of setting up (and setting off) emotional shock waves is to cast guests in the starkly personal terms of virtue versus depravity. Passion often boils over when the contrast personifies veritable *victims* and *villains*. While the means of developing these character types may vary, the desired outcome is the clear authorization of one party as the innocent "prey," "dupe," or "casualty" of the heinous victimizer. Indeed, establishing a victim typically requires the simultaneous manufacture of the villain (Holstein and Miller 1990). Accordingly, talk shows conscientiously develop obvious victims and villains, or victimizers, as the case may be. By ritualistically reproducing these identity icons, the shows supply ready-made conflict packages rife with confrontation.

Producing Victims

One way of envisioning "victimization" is to think of it as the process whereby someone is interpretively constituted as a person unjustly harmed or damaged by forces beyond his or her control (Holstein and Miller 1990). This involves dividing the world into oppositional categories: good and bad, hero and scoundrel, innocent and guilty, victim and villain. The categories provide good reasons to despise, punish, or rehabilitate the perpetrator and sympathize with and heal the victim. The categories help us appropriately formulate our emotions.

Clearly, victimization generates much of talk shows' emotional energy. Unjust pain and suffering propel their narrative themes and emotional momentum. Their discursive and affective environments center on the harm that one party gratuitously inflicts upon another. Indeed, victims are typically talk shows' central characters, "co-starring," of course, with their victimizers. They are often introduced first and allowed to tell their stories relatively uninterrupted. This predisposes viewers to their point of view, and promotes an initial sympathy for the character. (Villains, however, may also appear first for a similar reason—to develop instant and initial antipathy. See Lowney 1999.)

Talk shows serve up many forms of victimization, from criminal exploitation, physical harm, and sexual assault, to emotional betrayal and infidelity. The point is to establish at least one (temporarily) sympathy-worthy self, whether it is to set him or her up for salvation, to establish the victimizer as worthy of punishment or rehabilitation, or to simply generate conflict and audience antagonism toward the guests onstage. By cultivating stereotypic images of their guests, talks shows almost ritualistically reproduce emotionally charged, culturally familiar characters.

Sometimes there's no question about who is being portrayed as the victim and who is cast as the villain. This can be achieved by simply allowing a sympathy-worthy guest to tell his or her story in extended, graphic detail. On one episode of *The Montel Williams Show* (11/27/95), for example, the topic for the day was "box-cutter assaults." In order to establish the hideous nature of this new "trend" in crime, and to indelibly imprint upon the audience just how serious the injuries were, Montel sympathetically invited Peaches, a 17-year-old female, to recount her horrifying experience.

Her narrative is several minutes long, a virtually uninterrupted tale of how Peaches's best friend, Aires, had suddenly and inexplicably attacked Peaches with a box cutter during lunch hour at school. The story is graphically dramatic. The audience shares Peaches's horror and confusion when a typical school day results in a trip to the hospital and scars for life—both physical and emotional—as Peaches is literally shredded with a box cutting knife. The shock and gore are revolting; blood flows narratively as Peaches stands by helplessly, not even trying to defend herself.

Over the course of her account, Peaches did far more than describe the action, however. Just as importantly, her self-presentation established that she was a "victim" on different levels. As she tells the story, she narrates her own essential innocence as well as the horrible transmutation of character that somehow motivates Aires's assault. Viewers learn that the girls were "really close," "best friends" who shared the intimacies of adolescence. Peaches makes it clear that both girls cared for and trusted one another deeply. Right to the end, Peaches is baffled by Aires's attack. Simultaneously, she outlines a dark transformation in Aires, one that Peaches could only sense, but could not explain. In its entirety, Peaches's account is, figuratively (but almost literally), the story of an innocent lamb being led to slaughter.

Presented this way, it's "obvious" that Peaches is the victim of an unprovoked assault; her narrative leaves no doubt about who is the casualty and who is the cause. The moral certainty conveyed in the presentation guarantees sympathy for Peaches and animosity toward her victimizer. The deep pathos attending the incident results as much from the identities that are presented as from the attack itself. This helps fulfill the institutional expectation—even demand—that the show produce victims clearly worthy of viewers' sympathy and villains who will raise viewers' ire.

Frequently, talk show hosts are active in interactionally promoting the "victimization" of their guests. In the previous example, Montel merely provided the space and incitement for Peaches to tell her tale, but in the following instance, we see Sally Jessy Raphael actively working during the on-screen interview (see Holstein and Gubrium 1995) to ensure that her guest was thoroughly identified as the victim. There was considerable challenge to this, since the topic at hand was "I'm Ready to Divorce My Children" (2/15/96), an act that only an ostensibly "heartless" mother might consider. In this case, Penny was attempting to rid herself of her 12- and 13-year-old daughters. This, of course, contradicts our cultural predisposition to adore children and to mandate parental responsibility to off-spring. The challenge confronts Sally as she sets out to "victimize" Penny—that is, to interpretively make a victim out of her.

SALLY: Please meet Penny. Penny is in bad shape, aren't you Penny? Penny says that she has two daughters, 12-year-old Ashlee and 13-year-old Amanda, and they are the demons from hell. She says that the 12-year-old started sleeping with boys when she was 11 and since then she has slept with four boys. We are assuming not using protection of any kind.

PENNY: No, none.

SALLY: She says that her 13-year-old has a violent temper. Will throw food and ashtrays at you?

PENNY: Yes.

SALLY: At your head.

PENNY: Yes, anything she can get her hands on at the time.

SALLY: Now, Penny says that it is impossible to control the 12- and 13-year-olds. Tell me what each one is doing. What's—why so violent?

PENNY: Ashlee—

SALLY: I mean they are 12 and 13.

PENNY: Right. Ashlee is the 12-year-old, she's having sex, she's drinking, she's smoking. She chases men, not boys. Because she says she's "hot."

SALLY: She's hot? And she's 12.

PENNY: And she's 12.

SALLY: Someone told me that she steals more than any of the other girls that we've ever met.:

PENNY: She is a good thief. . . . She steals pocketbooks, nighties. . . . Yes, she can sit and talk to you, look you straight in the face and at the same time have her hand in your purse taking all your money. . . . She's—she's taken money from my friends. She's not allowed to go to a neighbor's house now, because she did steal from her, steal her money. She's taken—

SALLY: Penny, what's—what's the problem here? I mean, what—do you have any ideas—

PENNY: I've tried everything. I tried to be the best mother I can. I worked until two years ago when I got sick. I took care of them, I gave them anything and everything. She has no reason to steal. She has no reason to, you know, everything that she has asked for, I've tried to provide for them and everything that they need.

SALLY: How does this make you feel? Having these kids. I mean, why come to see me?

PENNY: Well, I was mad. I've been mad for a long, long time. But now it hurts, because I feel like I am doing wrong. And I've tried everything. I've taken them to counseling. I've kept her on house arrest. I body search her every time we go somewhere, tried to embarrass her. I've embarrassed her in front of her friends. I've busted her behind, it does no good. She doesn't care.

SALLY: People in town think you are a bad mother?

PENNY: Yes, my—I had her in the store one day, and she calls me a bitch and a whore and a slut and told me that because I wouldn't buy her what she wanted, you know, she'd get it: "I'll get it." . . .

SALLY: Okay, you're Amanda. Amanda, let's start with you. You have heard how upset your mother is about your behavior. Do you care about your mother's feelings?

AMANDA: No, I don't.

Here, at least part of Sally's objective is to present Penny as the victim of disrespectful daughters. Prefacing the segment with "Penny is in bad shape," she allows Penny to tell her side of the story before the "demons from hell" (the daughters) are introduced. Along the way, Sally prompts elaborations with calculated, pointed questions at key junctures. She asks about the girls' violent tempers, elicits a graphic response, then probes for elaboration. Several times, she inquires into other grave transgressions, prompting Penny to embellish her account. Sally also anticipates questions that skeptical viewers might harbor about Penny's competence as a mother, and Penny's strategies for dealing with the girls. In doing so, Sally affords Penny the opportunity to defend herself against unstated accusations and to show the wide range of remedies she has tried. This helps create a sympathetic vision of Penny as a mother who has tried to do right by her "out-of-control" children. Ultimately, Sally ventures "inside" Penny's emotions, asking her how she feels about the situation. This, of course, reveals the extent to which Penny's inner self is an emotional casualty of this domestic turmoil, further warranting her desire to "divorce" herself from her kids.

Building victims' sympathy worthiness is key to talk show construction of selves. It's artful identity work, but it's done using familiar cultural resources. In addition, it may involve the creation of a compassionate emotional climate as much as presenting the "facts" of a guest's circumstance. This is the objective in the following example, where Sally Jessy Raphael gently but diligently produces an atmosphere that is conducive to understanding deep "betrayal" on a show titled "We Just Said 'I Do,' Now We're Through" (3/23/99).

Sally introduces this segment by reminding viewers that Tamica, a young African American woman, had appeared on the show several weeks ago, revealing at the time that she had been unfaithful to her husband, Duane, on the fourth night of their marriage. At that time, Tamica and Duane agreed to reconcile, to try to make the marriage work. It's now four weeks later and Duane, also an African American, has telephoned Sally to report on recent developments. Sally invites him to appear on the show once more.

SALLY: Okay, last week you called us. What's wrong?

DUANE: Well, Tamica is back to her same ways again.

SALLY: What's she doing?

DUANE: She's staying out. She's not coming home. I believe she's cheating on me again.

SALLY: Why are you so desperate to save this marriage?

DUANE: Because a marriage is something that you take pride in, something that you treasure. Not something you throw away just like that. I mean, I love my wife and I made a vow to her to be with her, no matter what . . .

SALLY: How do you live like this, not being sure?

DUANE: I don't sleep at night. I take long walks at night. I think about it. I ask myself is it the right thing to do. . . . Or am I just being a fool?

At this juncture, Tamica makes her entrance from backstage, greets Duane, and sits down in the chair next to him. Her demeanor is cordial, if slightly cool.

SALLY: [To Tamica] So, what's the "*qué pasa*"?

TAMICA: I am not cheating on Duane. I'm not. He is only telling you one side of the story. . . . He goes out, he don't tell me where he goes. He's not affectionate to me. He calls me names because I've gained weight. . . . I thought I loved him.

SALLY: [Breaking in] Do you love him?

TAMICA: I care about him because he's the father of my child, but I do not love him. . . . I want to be with Darrell [the ex-boyfriend with whom she had previously cheated]. I'm sorry. . . .

SALLY: Tamica, you are being very honest. I appreciate your honesty. Are you in love with anyone else?

TAMICA: I care about Darrell. I really do. . . . Yes, I am in love with him [Darrell]. [At this point an ex-

tended, heated argument breaks out between Duane and Tamica concerning what it takes to be married.]

SALLY: Duane, are you in love with her?

DUANE: Very much. Because she's my wife. . . . Yes I am.

[Sally responds very sympathetically at length.]

TAMICA: He [Darrell] is a good man. I'm not doggin' Duane, but I deserve a good man and I don't think that I have that from him. And I want to tell you, that I'm here to tell you, I really want to get a divorce.

At this point, the video cuts abruptly to a shot of the audience, where a young African American woman rises to comment. "Hi Duane," she coos. "You are one good lookin' brother. I just want to say that I'm available, baby." And on that note, the segment ends.

Sally's interviewing technique is clearly instrumental in establishing Duane's sympathy worthiness, in making him out to be the victim in this case. She elicits his side of the story, then draws him into a verbal commitment to the sanctity of marriage in principle, and to his marriage to Tamica, specifically. While treating Tamica gently, too, Sally undermines Tamica's moral position from the start. She listens to some of Tamica's depiction of marital discord, but is clearly not interested in its elaboration. Indeed, she even avoids pursuing the issue of weight gain, which is well known to be one of Sally's favorites. At the first opportunity, Sally interrupts Tamica to bring the issue of Tamica's love and commitment to the fore. Playing off her earlier discussion with Duane, Sally gets Tamica to deny that she loves Duane, then immediately provokes Tamica to declare her love for Darrell.

The conversational production and juxtaposition of Duane's and Tamica's stances on love and marriage are clear byproducts of Sally's introduction and questioning. The lead-in divulges Tamica's "fourth-day indiscretion" and Duane is allowed to establish his willingness to stick with the marriage, despite the hurt he has suffered. When Tamica appears, Duane "obviously" comes off as the victim, an artifact of both what Sally has incited, and what she has chosen to ignore. Despite her denials of further sexual betrayal, Tamica is coaxed into admitting that her heart belongs to another, and, finally, to wanting a divorce—even though she is the one who is the marital transgressor. Finally, as if to underline Duane's sympathy worthiness, the show's editors attach the audience member's reaction, which literally embraces Duane as the object of solace and affection. It's clear that Sally and her producers have used cultural models of relational fidelity and betrayal to craft the victim and victimizer, respectively, creating both the conflict necessary to sustain viewer interest, and an emotionally satisfying resolution. Duane's upstanding character is rewarded by an audience member's advances, while Tamica is left sitting alone.

Producing Villains

Constructing victims allows the host, the audience, and perhaps even the victims themselves, to understand in an emotional, visceral way how sullied they have become, how conflict may have damaged them, and how they deserve sympathy, if not salvation. Following this thematic path, the construction of the "victim's" self almost always implicates a "victimizer." Interpretively speaking, one needs the other. Consequently, as talk shows set about designating victims, they simultaneously produce the villains that are necessary to sustain the salvational or confrontation themes of the shows. We can return to the *Sally Jessy Raphael Show* about "divorcing children" to illustrate aspects of this process.

In the segment we previously discussed, not only does Sally help construct the motivation for the audience to compassionately embrace Penny, but she subsequently helps "expose" just how bad the children really are. In order to justify Penny's desire for a "divorce," the daughters must come off as thoroughly odious. If Penny is to be a sympathy-worthy victim, her daughters need to be totally vile, completely unsympathetic. Sally is aggressively complicit in producing this outcome.

After completing her generally sympathetic interview with Penny, Sally brings the daughters, 12-year-old Ashlee and 13-year-old Amanda, onstage. They are instantly rude to Sally, to audience members, and of course, to their mother. Rather than offering the "kid gloves" treatment typically afforded children (Lowney 1999), Sally pointedly interrogates the girls, following up on Penny's accusations, underscoring Penny's indictments. She asks the girls if they steal and if they call their mother obscene names. The

daughters belligerently answer yes. Sally then inquires about the allegations of sexual promiscuity. Merely questioning a 13-year-old about having unprotected sexual intercourse is symbolically degrading; eliciting a defiant answer ("Everybody has got to die sometime") solidly confirms the daughters' depravity. For a salvation episode, Sally needs to establish the segment's principal characters in order to designate who will be "saved," who will be rehabilitated. In this instance she not only depicts Penny as the sympathy-worthy victim, but simultaneously constructs the daughters as reprehensible children, the true villains of the scenario.

Confrontation shows also need their victims and villains, most obviously to spark the onstage combat that has become their stock-in-trade. Jerry Springer is masterful at "springing" a surprise revelation on an ostensibly unsuspecting guest in order to set off a combustible confrontation. And he can turn up the emotional heat of audience indignation if it can be made clear just who the "real" villain is. Consider, for example, how Jerry engineers the delivery of a relational "bomb-shell" in the following segment (3/15/99), where he invites a tall, attractive African American "woman" to the stage. "Diamond" has a secret to tell Ed, her boyfriend of several months. With Diamond alone onstage, Jerry begins:

JERRY: What is your secret you want to reveal?

DIAMOND: I'm really a man!

[Audience gasps, then commences to chant "Jer-ry, Jer-ry, Jer-ry."]

JERRY: And you're going to reveal this to your boyfriend? He doesn't know you're a guy?

DIAMOND: Well look at me Jerry. [Diamond is very attractive, if atypically tall for a woman. Initially she appears totally feminine.]

JERRY: How long have you been going with him?

DIAMOND: Three months.

JERRY: For three months. So, you've been going out with him for three months and, uh, have you kissed him?

DIAMOND: . . . We've kissed. We've, like, had oral sex.

[Audience gasps, boos, and chants "Jer-ry, Jer-ry."]

JERRY: Okay. Do you love him?

DIAMOND: I care for him. . . . I've met his family. We did stuff together on the holidays. [She continues, providing details of a family get-together.]

JERRY: The holidays . . . and it never came up over the turkey that maybe you should tell him?

DIAMOND: No, no . . .

JERRY: All right, well let's see what he says.

Jerry now invites Ed to join Diamond onstage. Ed is an attractive, masculine-looking African American male. He walks confidently up to Diamond, kisses her affectionately, then takes a seat in the chair next to her. Jerry, standing in the audience, reiterates some of the history of their relationship, then turns to direct a question to Ed:

JERRY: How long have you been together?

ED: Three months.

JERRY: And the relationship is good?

ED: Yeah, fine. [Ed elaborates on the nature of the relationship.]

JERRY: [To Diamond] Now you have something you want to tell him.

DIAMOND: [Pause] Well, I'm really not a woman. I'm a man.

At this point, Ed rises from his seat, anger spreading across his face. He charges Diamond, they struggle hand-to-hand. Ed shoves Diamond to the floor. As stagehands intervene and the scuffle continues, Diamond distances herself from Ed, then taunts him:

DIAMOND: You forget that under all this makeup and nails, I'm still a man.

ED: You coulda told me that.

DIAMOND: You didn't ask me!

Ed goes after Diamond again, more scuffling ensues, and they are separated. All the while the audience chants "Jer-ry, Jer-ry, Jer-ry." The dialogue is now virtually unintelligible with every other word a "bleeped out" obscenity. The two exchange what are plainly sexual insults regarding penis size. The crowd cheers. The guests end up vehemently calling each other "Faggot!" Throughout the exchange, Ed is indignant, Diamond defiant. Finally, Jerry gains control of the conversation, and addresses Diamond:

Look, you are what you are, and God bless you, but you have to know that you're playing with people's lives and their feelings and their hearts when you deceive them. [The segment ends as the show goes to commercial.]

Diamond is clearly the villain in this confrontation, but Jerry's stage management primes the audience's reception. While the disclosure of being a man might, in itself, provide sufficient shock to set off the desired confrontation, Jerry also gets Diamond to admit that 1) she has known Ed for quite some time, 2) they have been sexually intimate, 3) she cares for Ed, and 4) she has participated in family gatherings generally reserved for trusted intimates. In light of all this, her "secret" is even more deceitful, more treacherous. Jerry then gets Ed to confirm some of Diamond's description, and sets the stage for betrayal, humiliation, and confrontation by having Ed publicly confirm that he feels that the relationship is going well—"Yeah, fine." Ed, of course, is set up as the dupe extraordinaire. Jerry has seen to that. But, not fully satisfied, Jerry, by way of conclusion, sanctimoniously reaffirms where the fault lies in this whole mess, reminding Diamond that she is, in fact, responsible for the deception. While seemingly gratuitous, Jerry's comment underscores the identities that were at stake and the self-destruction that has occurred.

Victim Contests

While conflict between victims and villains provides both grounds for salvation and fuel for confrontation, talk shows turn up the emotional heat by actively involving the host and audience in on-screen identity contests. One recurring format designed for this purpose explicitly creates a victim contest in which observers act as de facto arbiters in deciding who is the victim and who is the victimizer or villain. Sometimes the host seizes this responsibility, simply (but authoritatively and sanctimoniously) pronouncing that one guest is the "bad guy" while another has been wronged. Whether the audience agrees or disagrees, the strong opinion raises the emotional pitch and often instigates even more conflict and confrontation.

Other programming formats build character judgment explicitly into the planned action. Some shows, for example, establish the pretense that the host or audience will "impartially" or "objectively" mediate disputes between guests. For instance, a *Sally Jessy Raphael Show* (2/15/96) titled "Prove That You're Not Cheating" featured three couples in which the female partner suspected the male of infidelity. But rather than stage confrontations in the typical "accusation and rejoinder" fashion, Sally arranged for the men to take polygraph tests to ascertain the truth of the matter. What could be more objective and evenhanded?

Of course, Sally doesn't sit idly by and let the process unfold on its own. Rather, she's solicitous and supportive as the women tell their stories, often reassuring them that contrary to what the men were saying, they (the women) "were not crazy" for being suspicious. Repeatedly referring to the men as "cheaters," Sally demands that the men be truthful to their partners and skeptically—sometimes sarcastically—parries with the men as they tell their stories. Fueling these domestic controversies with her own suspicions, Sally fans audience members' passions, building a confrontational tension that is intensified by the knowledge that *somebody* is going to be revealed as being either "crazy" or a liar. In effect, Sally uses cultural typologies to clarify the identities at stake and to set up the episode's emotional climax. The test results are withheld until the final eight minutes of the show, and they all reveal the men to be the cheating cads that their partners, Sally, and the audience "always" believed them to be.

While the polygraph is a popular tool for deciding victim contests on some talk shows, the on-screen paternity test is even more exciting, since the suspense entailed adds to a contest's dramatic realization. Another growing favorite embroils the audience in elections over victimhood. Jenny Jones regularly allows viewers to vote for who is right and wrong, good or bad, guilty or innocent. As she put it at the beginning of one show (4/15/99), "I'll be judge Jenny and you can be my jury."

This episode, titled "I Want My Stuff Back," is a classic confrontation show in that the explicit aim is to create and adjudicate discord and, in the process, to decide who is the villain and who is the victim. Family members or close friends comprise the guest pairings. In each segment, one party claims that the other has inappropriately or unfairly expropriated his or her

property and won't give it back. One side tells a story, then the other responds. For example, a pair of female former roommates wrangle over possession of household items after they've moved into separate apartments. One claims that the other has kept her stereo, TV, VCR, and some clothes for over a year and won't let her take them back. In another segment, a daughter insists that her parents won't let her claim her rightful personal possessions—a new TV, kitchenware, and the like—after the parents "threw [her] out of the house." The parents counter with tales of the daughter borrowing money to buy the stuff, signing loan agreements with them, then failing to repay any of the money.

The format of this show resembles many of the mock courtroom shows so popular on daytime TV (for example, *People's Court, Judge Judy*), but without the legal trappings. Jenny attempts some mediation but, in the end, she allows the audience to decide who should get to keep "the stuff" in each case. Audience members are outfitted with prepared signs that they hold up to indicate their votes. Each segment concludes with the vote and comments from the audience as to why the vote was justified. The sorts of disputes adjudicated in this fashion range from property claims and legal rights to highly personal opinions (for example, "You May Be Proud of What You've Got, But a Model You Are Not!").

The significant feature of such shows in relation to guests' identities is that self-construction becomes a formally institutionalized part of the programming format. It's neither accidental nor incidental; the express objective of such shows is to endorse locally embodied identities. Such shows quite deliberately constitute the selves they need to entertain; indeed, the self-construction process becomes part of the entertainment itself.

CONFOUNDING THE DISTINCTION

Whereas salvational shows may require victims to be saved and confrontational shows thrive on the clash of good and evil, both have considerable latitude with respect to how characters might be developed to suit their needs. While victims and villains are integral components, they need not be diametrically opposed to achieve the desired effect. Indeed, on some shows it appears that as long as a plethora of character flaws and aberrant behavior emerges, it doesn't matter much who is at fault or who reaps the most harm. Many shows of this type literally commingle victimhood and villainy in the same characters, denying any pure distinction, but building confrontational and salvational possibilities along the way. Consider the following excerpt, again from *The Jerry Springer Show* (3/15/99).

The second segment of this show involves a couple—Heather and Rick—who had been together for seven years. Heather is introduced first—a young, attractive, white female, dressed casually and provocatively, braless with bare midriff. She enters confidently, even defiantly, resembling Rocky Balboa dancing into a boxing ring. Jerry's introduction indicates that Heather doesn't consider Rick to be her partner any longer. He's now her "ex," Heather claims, and he will not leave Heather and her new boyfriend alone. The implication is that Rick is somehow stalking or harassing them.

The audience initially gasps and groans in sympathy as Heather urges them on, claiming that Rick demands that she choose between him and her family, a choice she alleges Rick originally forced upon her when Heather was only 15 years old. She chose Rick, and he then moved Heather to some far-off places where she felt isolated from all other aspects of her former life. Heather then recounts a recent incident when Rick told Heather that if she (Heather) didn't "have sex with another woman" (apparently Rick wanted to watch), he would abandon Heather. Despite her bravado, Heather is obviously staking claim to being the victim of Rick's domestic domination, if not his sexual perversion.

Now Jerry invites Rick on stage, and Rick appears with a bouquet of flowers. He is a young, slightly built white male, not very imposing in stature or demeanor. The image is not one of the domestic dictator that Heather implied; instead, Rick projects the figure of a sincere, gentle suitor—an almost classic romantic archetype. As he approaches Heather with the flowers, they exchange words:

HEATHER: Don't come by me. [She curses him vehemently at length, berating him about his "girlfriend,"

and complaining that Rick is harassing Heather and her new boyfriend, Billy.]

RICK: I'm not up here to fight with you. I'm up here to tell you that I love you. . . .

HEATHER: Are you gonna tell your girlfriend that you love me?

RICK: Yeah, I'm gonna tell her. I love *you*. . . . I know that I want a relationship, that I want my family back. You got my kids. [This is the first mention of children as part of the relationship.]

HEATHER: [Goes on to say that Rick is no father to the kids and that they now call her new boyfriend "Daddy."] . . . I'm not going to let you see the kids as long as you have a girlfriend.

RICK: . . . You should not keep those kids from their father. . . . I won't have them calling no other guy Daddy.

At this point, Heather launches an extended complaint about how Rick has mistreated her over the years. She recounts an incident when she was eight months pregnant and Rick took the money that she had been saving for a baby crib and used it to play poker. Rick denies this. On another occasion when one of the children was sick, Heather claims, she had to call Rick five times to get him to take the child to the hospital.

When Jerry finally takes command of the conversation, he turns to Rick: "Rick, you say you want to be back with her but you have a girlfriend." "Yeah," Rick replies, "I got a girlfriend." At this point Jerry invites Michele, Rick's girlfriend, onstage, and she immediately assaults Heather. They scuffle and are separated by stagehands, invectives and obscenities flying freely. The audience chants "Jer-ry, Jer-ry." Rick stands by helplessly, shaking his head, finally taking a seat between the two women, who continue to curse each other. Michele is trying to tell Jerry that Rick has made repeated attempts to see the kids, each time to be thwarted by Heather, but soon the two women are fighting again. As stagehands separate them, Michele sternly challenges Heather: "Come on, bitch, come and get it."

Jerry now summons Heather's new boyfriend, Billy. No sooner is he onstage than Rick charges at him and a brawl ensues. The crowd cheers and chants "Jerry." The onstage dialogue now consists almost entirely of "bleeped-out" obscenities. The women continue to scream at one another. Eventually, we hear Michele ask Heather how she supports the kids, to which Heather replies that she has a job.

MICHELE: What kind of a job, bitch?

HEATHER: I'm a dancer.

MICHELE: So, you spread your legs for everyone.

Amid the confusion and confrontation, the segment ends as the show goes to commercial.

During this interaction, Heather and Rick repeatedly swapped "victim" and "villain" identities. The initial trajectory of the segment cast Heather as the victim of Rick's domineering ways, but Rick's meek presence, attempts at reconciliation, and professions of love and devotion to Heather and their children turn the tables on Heather. Now she's the "bad" one who curtly rejects the father of her children. Introducing Michele and Billy provides the confrontational icing on this dysfunctional family cake. Their presence physically embodies the complications to what started out as a seemingly simple story of domestic tyranny.

The ethos of the confrontation show calls for conflicting personas, but sets no demands on moral purity or self-constructional consistency. Assuredly, villains and victims are fuel for incendiary interpersonal relations, but roles and identities needn't be firmly affixed. Indeed, there appears to be a perverse appeal to situations in which sin and virtue shift back and forth in the give-and-take of accusations and condemnations. Enduring moral certainty takes a back seat to immediate, flagrant transgression. Salvation only requires that someone, at some juncture, be amenable to rehabilitation or redemption. Confrontation demands someone to "dish it out" and someone to "take it," but there's no fundamental need to establish a permanent hierarchy of sympathy or blame. Pure conflict, not its explanation or resolution, is the objective; confounding the victim and villain identities may heighten, not undermine, the explosiveness of the outrageous interpersonal showdowns that talk shows cultivate.

Talk show hosts eagerly play upon the thirst for confrontation. Whereas we saw earlier how Sally Jessy Raphael, on occasion, works hard to clearly establish victims and villains, on other occasions, hosts simply promote conflict, letting the identity chips fall where they may. There's an almost perverse delight in exposing one party, then the other, as the cad of the moment. On one episode of *The Jerry Springer Show* (4/12/99), for instance, the theme of "Scandalous Confessions" would seemingly capitalize on one partner admitting something scandalous, while the other suffered its indignity. It's a surefire recipe in the villain/victim paradigm. Jerry, however, has some tricks up his sleeve.

After the initial revelation is played out at the start of each segment, open conflict predictably erupts. Through the cursing and fighting, the transgressor and the victim clearly emerge. Then Jerry introduces a new twist. Addressing the momentarily prevailing "victim," he coyly asks, "And now what surprise do you have to tell [your partner]?" In each instance, the second revelation is more startling and egregious than the first.

In one segment, for example, Eric makes his scandalous confession, telling his steady girlfriend, Kiki, that he has been sleeping with her sister, Shannon. After a few moments of Eric's futile explanations and Kiki's indignant outrage, Kiki spits back that she (Kiki) has been sleeping with Eric's sister, who now rushes onstage and into Kiki's arms. Homosexuality trumps infidelity as the confrontational grounds shift and the mantles of victim and villain transmute before our very eyes. Partners scuffle with partners, siblings pummel siblings. The women grope each other shamelessly in an open display of sexual passion while their brother/lover looks on.

The original designations of victim and villain are lost in the confusion. To be sure, transgressors and human casualties abound, but the distinction between their embodiments blurs as different individuals occupy the roles. Victim and villain personas remain crucial, but a prevalent moral agnosticism makes it unnecessary to affix them permanently. As elements of sheer confrontation, their inconstancy provides renewable resources for outrage, a seemingly inexhaustible supply of surprises, and targets of indignation.

"TAKE CARE OF YOURSELF"

Perhaps there's no good reason to watch daytime TV talk shows. But millions still do. Part of the reason may lie in the identity formulas we see enacted day after day, so predictably that we know, before we actually see the particulars, that two guests on *The Jerry Springer Show* are going to end up fighting. The selves that talk shows construct for their guests provide outrageous entertainment, to be sure, but they also serve as constant exemplars that may very well serve a self-identifying function.

Jerry Springer and his ilk offer characters who captivate our interests, in part, simply by displaying unforgivable transgressions, despicable selves, and brute passions. Viewers' responses are largely visceral, unthinking reactions to the graphic and energetic staging of acts and persons so contemptible, so atrocious, that they nearly defy belief—even among viewers whose everyday lives desensitize them to the rude, crude, violent, and bizarre. We watch for the same reasons freak shows and automobile accidents attract attention; we're inexplicably drawn to the hideous, to the outlandish selves talk shows construct for our viewing pleasure. The victim/villain contrast adds to our intrigue.

At the same time, these selves provide viewers with points of reference against which viewers must assuredly compare favorably. The extremes of relational insensitivity, defiance of social convention, and disdain for civility probably outpace even our most unseemly behaviors, on even our worst days. They're negative identity exemplars of a sort, living embodiments of *what we are not*. As Emile Durkheim (1964) told us long ago, we need the visible presence of the "pathological" to assure us of what is "normal." Talk shows may help us sense the boundaries of the acceptable; by negative example, they show us the normative contours of self and society (Erikson 1964).

At least that's what Jerry Springer might want us to think. Indeed, his shows routinely point this out to us, as they did on the "Scandalous Confessions" episode we discussed earlier. The final segment of the show involved two sisters who learned on the show that they had both been sleeping with the same man. The revelation was accompanied with the chaos, physical attacks, recriminations, and vulgar denunciations that typify Jerry's shows. But even though he'd betrayed both women, the sisters were still fighting over the man. In the show's final segment, Jerry usually allows audience members to take the microphone and ask questions of the guests—although the questions often turn into vile indictments. In this particular instance, a young woman of approximately the same age as the female guests took the microphone. Addressing the two combative women, and referring to the insults and recriminations that they had previously exchanged, the audience member asked a question and made her point:

> You said he [the man sleeping with the two sisters] had a little (pause) a little weenie. Well tell me, why was you up there fightin' with your sister over a guy with a little weenie? You never catch me doin' somethin' like that.

The point is clear. Talk shows demonstrate things that we should never do; they construct selves that we should never be. "You never catch me doin' somethin' like that." Durkheim couldn't have said it better himself. But, of course, Jerry tries.

In the epilogue to the show, he serves up his daily sermonette. All the guests are now onstage, over a dozen in all. They're packed in, disheveled from the combat, a veritable sideshow of the morally depraved. Ripped clothing dangles from necks and shoulders. Hairpieces are missing. Two men stand naked from the waist up, their shirts completely destroyed, their bodies scratched and bleeding. Jerry is poised alongside this motley crew, on the set, not in the audience. He turns to the guests, thanks them for appearing on the show, then continues:

> I hope you are able, if not to repair your relationships, at least, ah, your family relationships. I hope you're able to work that out. Good luck to you. [Turning to face the camera.] You know, in case you're wondering, this is not how most people live. Most of us don't sleep with our boyfriend's or girlfriend's sister. We don't grab the lover of a cousin. We don't screw our best friend's mate. Most of us aren't like that. I don't know, the moral fiber seems nonexistent here, and the only thing more lacking than good sense is respect. There's no respect for family, for bed-mates, for even the most basic customs and traditions of society. It's little more than "I'll sleep with who I want, when I want, the hell with all of you." I know how often we have heard on these shows, "Hey it just happened," or "We'd been drinking." Well, that, of course, is no excuse. Look, a

good rule of thumb to remember here is that, as you are heading for the bedroom or the backseat of the car, if (pause) the face you're with is one you've seen around the Thanksgiving dinner table, or other family functions, then just say no. 'Til next time, take care of yourself and each other.

The message is clear. Jerry has used these characters to teach us all a valuable lesson in social relations. He constructs these selves so we may learn from them. But mark his words well, talk show guests. Guard your selves, because Jerry will surely appropriate them to his own purposes. Take care of your selves, or Jerry will take care of them for you.

REFERENCES

Abt, Vicki, and Leonard Mustazza. 1997. *Coming After Oprah: Cultural Fallout in the Age of the TV Talk Show.* Bowling Green, Ohio: Bowling Green State University.

Abt, Vicki, and Mel Seesholtz. 1994. "The Shameless World of Phil, Sally, and Oprah: Television Talk Shows and the Deconstructing of Society." *Journal of Popular Culture.* 28:171–91.

Durkheim, Emile. 1964. *The Rules of Sociological Method.* New York: Free Press.

Erikson, Kai. 1964. "Notes on the Sociology of Deviance." In *The Other Side,* ed. Howard S. Becker, 9–21. New York: Free Press.

Gamson, Joshua. 1998. *Freaks Talk Back.* Chicago: University of Chicago Press.

Goffman, Erving. 1959. *The Presentation of Self in Everyday Life.* New York: Anchor.

Heaton, Jeanne Albronda, and Nona Leigh Wilson. 1995. *Tuning in Trouble: Talk TV's Destructive Impact on Mental Health.* San Francisco: Jossey-Bass.

Holstein, James A., and Jaber F. Gubrium. 1995. *The Active Interview.* Thousand Oaks, Calif.: Sage.

———. 2000. *The Self We Live By: Narrative Identity in a Postmodern World.* New York: Oxford University Press.

Holstein, James A., and Gale Miller. 1990. "Rethinking Victimization: An Interactional Approach to Victimology." *Symbolic Interaction* 13:103–22.

Hughes, Everett C. 1984. *The Sociological Eye.* New Brunswick, N.J.: Transaction Books.

Kuhn, Thomas. 1962. *The Structure of Scientific Revolution.* Chicago: University of Chicago Press.

Lowney, Kathleen S. 1994. "Speak of the Devil: Talk Shows and the Social Construction of Satanism." In *Perspectives on Social Problems,* vol. 6, ed. James A. Holstein and Gale Miller, 99–128. Greenwich, Conn.: JAI Press.

———. 1999. *Baring Our Souls: TV Talk Shows and the Religion of Recovery.* Hawthorne, N.Y.: Aldine de Gruyter.

Schutz, Alfred. 1970. *On Phenomenology and Social Relations.* Chicago: University of Chicago Press.

Snow, Robert P. 1983. *Creating Media Culture.* Beverly Hills: Sage.

Twitchell, J. B. 1992. *Carnival Culture: The Trashing of Taste in America.* New York: Columbia University Press.

FURTHER READING

Adler, Patricia A. and Peter Adler. 1989. "The Gloried Self: The Aggrandizement and the Constriction of Self." *Social Psychology Quarterly* 52:299–310.
- A study of changes in the selves of college athletes that result from their entry into a world of celebrity.

Goffman, Erving. 1959. *The Presentation of Self in Everyday Life.* New York: Doubleday.
- A classic presentation of selves as shared performances.

Holstein, James A. and Jaber F. Gubrium. 2000. *The Self We Live By: Narrative Identity in a Postmodern World.* New York: Oxford University Press.
- Discusses the birth of the ordinary self and its development into an institutional phenomenon.

Gubrium, Jaber F. and James A. Holstein (eds.). 2001. *Institutional Selves: Troubled Identities in a Postmodern World.* New York: Oxford University Press.
- Ethnographic studies of institutional self-constructions.

Schwalbe, Michael L. and Douglas Mason-Schrock. 1996. "Identity Work as Group Process." *Advances in Group Processes* 13:113–147.
- Examines the process by which groups create shared identities.

MIND

Mind is the object we construct to carry out the rational, cognitive work of our lives. As we've noted, not even a brain surgeon can find the mind, even though we would all swear it occupies the head. Rather, our interactional, constructive activities give us each a mind. We place these minds in our heads and act *as if* that is where thoughts, beliefs, wishes, and the like originate and brew. By the same token, our interactional, constructive activities can strip us of our minds, so to speak, as when we insist that "I'm losing my mind."

As a distinctive enclave of inner life, the mind has unique characteristics of its own. If feelings occupy the emotional corners of our interior, mind is the locus of reason. In practice, the mind and the emotions are commonly constructed in opposition to each other. We regularly refer to what we think as opposed to how we feel. We've all said things, such as "I really feel great about being asked to apply for the job, but I don't think there's a chance in hell they'll hire me" or "I think the President will get reelected, but really don't feel strongly about it." And there's the cliché, "My heart tells me one thing, but my head tells me another." The important point is that when inner life is constructed, it's often partitioned into specialized realms.

Mind links up with the social world differently than other aspects of inner life. For example, while today it may seem old-fashioned, mind and feelings have traditionally been gendered in stereotypical ways. The life of the mind was, and in some circles still is, considered a hallmark of male experience. The realm of feelings is female territory. The operating communicative styles of the mind and the emotions are also distinguished along gendered lines. Mind echoes speech, written texts, logic, and mathematics. Feelings hint of bodily gestures, expressiveness, the senses, and the arts. If prose is the language of the mind, poetry speaks from the heart.

Mind, then, is something we "do" as much as it is something we construct as part of inner life. Here, again, the *as if* clause enters the picture. The traditional opposition between thoughts and feelings divides the world of experience between reason and rationality on one side and sentiment and emotion on the other. It orients us to ourselves and others as if experience is actually divided against itself. We commonly think and speak of matters of the mind versus matters of the heart. Rightly or wrongly, we often approach others as if their lives were guided more by one department of inner life than the other.

For example, we tend to describe men's activities and occupations in the language of reasoning and logic. We are more likely to characterize women's actions and jobs with images and symbols of emotional experience. In turn, we come to see the gender differences in terms of these constructions. We treat them *as if* they were actual features of inner life, not products of our own depictions of inner life. When we look within, to the deepest reaches of our beings, we see each other in terms of the categories we have used to construct one another as males and females. Gendered identities are social to the core. In practice, mind—like all aspects of inner life—is as much a social activity as it is a private structure.

ABOUT THE READINGS

In **"The Locus of Mind," George Herbert Mead** begins the readings in this section by boldly stating that the mind is not located inside the individual. Mead doesn't mean that we don't experience mind as if it were within. Nor does he suggest that we don't orient to others in this way. Rather, Mead focuses on the everyday *practice* of our concern with our own and others' minds. He maintains that we experience being "minded" in the course of our various encounters with others.

According to Mead, language makes mind possible. At the same time, he reminds us that mind isn't just words. Mind is built up in the concrete interaction within which language is embedded. It's *mind in practice*. When Mead states that "out of language emerges the field of mind," he is emphasizing the unceasing relationship between the social and individual aspect of our everyday experiences. "It is by means of reflexiveness—the turning-back of the experience of the individual upon himself—that the whole social process is thus brought into the experience of the individuals involved in it," Mead writes. This statement underscores how mind is constructed in terms that we share with others.

The other reading selections in this section apply this perspective to everyday experiences of mind. **"The Social Preservation of Mind: The Alzheimer's Disease Experience"** considers our ordinary relations with persons who have Alzheimer's disease (AD) or senile dementia. Following in Mead's footsteps, **Jaber F. Gubrium** argues that even when medical opinion suggests that a mind is seriously compromised or even gone, we can sometimes continue to interact with the afflicted person as if his or her mind were intact. Gubrium maintains that since medical opinion in this area is based on the status of the brain, not the mind, concrete medical facts can't readily explain how we interact with the demented. His observations of support groups for adult caregivers of AD sufferers show that AD minds are persistently constructed by those who still care about them—even when the brain begins to fail. Caregivers virtually "preserve" the minds of their loved ones when they speak and act as if those minds are still active. They even offer personally and socially convincing evidence to that effect. The moral of Gubrium's story is that when the mind is viewed as a precious thing, we can go to great lengths to construct and sustain it.

The final reading selection by **Clinton R. Sanders** turns us to the world of companion dogs. In **"Understanding Dogs: Caretakers' Attributions of Mindedness in Canine-Human Relationships,"** Sanders doesn't take for granted that dogs don't have minds. Instead, he explores the many familiar ways that we act as if they do. Sanders shows us the complex ways in which owners construct the inner lives of their pets through their interactions with them. What emerges from this practice are highly minded animals, ones with their own beliefs, desires, motives, and concerns for their owners and themselves. The reflexive relation between minds and social worlds that Mead noted is clearly evident in Sanders's chapter. Not only do owners construct their dogs' minds as they interact with them, but the owners, in turn, respond to their own constructions. They offer opinions and express feelings in response to what they believe their dogs "have in mind" and aim to do. The process is clearly reminiscent of Cooley's "looking-glass self."

17 | THE LOCUS OF MIND
George Herbert Mead

The locus of mind is not in the individual. Mental processes are fragments of the complex conduct of the individual in and on his environment. . . . Mentality on our approach simply comes in when the organism is able to point out meanings to others and to himself. This is the point at which mind appears, or if you like, emerges. What we need to recognize is that we are dealing with the relationship of the organism to the environment selected by its own sensitivity. The psychologist is interested in the mechanism which the human species has evolved to get control over these relationships. The relationships have been there before the indications are made, but the organism has not in its own conduct controlled that relationship. It originally has no mechanism by means of which it can control it. The human animal, however, has worked out a mechanism of language communication by means of which it can get this control. Now, it is evident that much of that mechanism does not lie in the central nervous system but in the relation of things to the organism. The ability to pick these meanings out and to indicate them to others and to the organism is an ability which gives peculiar power to the human individual. The control has been made possible by language. It is that mechanism of control over meaning in this sense which has, I say, constituted what we term "mind." The mental processes do not, however, lie in words any more than the intelligence of the organism lies in the elements of the central nervous system. Both are part of a process that is going on between organism and environment. The symbols serve their part in this process, and it is that which makes communication so important. Out of language emerges the field of mind.

It is absurd to look at the mind simply from the standpoint of the individual human organism; for, although it has its focus there, it is essentially a social phenomenon; even its biological functions are prima-rily social. The subjective experience of the individual must be brought into relation with the natural, sociobiological activities of the brain in order to render an acceptable account of mind possible at all; and this can be done only when the social nature of mind is recognized. The meagerness of individual experience in isolation from the processes of social experience—in isolation from its social environment—should, moreover, be apparent. We must regard mind, then, as arising and developing within the social process, within the empirical matrix of social interactions. We must, that is, get an inner individual experience from the standpoint of social acts which include the experiences of separate individuals in a social context wherein those individuals interact. The processes of experience which the human brain makes possible are made possible only for a group of interacting individuals—only for individual organisms which are members of a society, not for the individual organism in isolation from other individual organisms.

Mind arises in the social process only when that process as a whole enters into, or is present in, the experience of any one of the given individuals involved in that process. When this occurs the individual becomes self-conscious and has a mind; he becomes aware of his relations to that process as a whole, and to the other individuals participating in it with him; he becomes aware of that process as modified by the reactions and interactions of the individuals—including himself—who are carrying it on. The evolutionary appearance of mind or intelligence takes place when the whole social process of experience and behavior is brought within the experience of any one of the separate individuals implicated therein and when the individual's adjustment to the process is modified and refined by the awareness or consciousness which he thus has of it. It is by means of reflexiveness—the turning-

---

back of the experience of the individual upon him-self—that the whole social process is thus brought into the experience of the individuals involved in it; it is by such means, which enable the individual to take the attitude of the other toward himself, that the indi-

vidual is able consciously to adjust himself to that process, and to modify the resultant of that process in any given social act in terms of his adjustment to it. Reflexiveness, then, is the essential condition, within the social process, for the development of mind.

THE SOCIAL PRESERVATION OF MIND
18 | The Alzheimer's Disease Experience
Jaber F. Gubrium

In his critique of Watson and behaviorism, George Herbert Mead (1934) presented an alternative view of mind. It was Mead's contention that mind, self, or in-telligence—he often used these interchangeably (see Mead, 1934:50, 134, 186, 191, 192)—was a discur-sive process. Thinking was likened to internal conver-sation (p. 47). Mead took care to point out that, while individuals came to have selves or minds, the latter were not emergent products of nascent structures pres-ent at birth, but, rather, were outcomes of the "social side of human experience" (p. 1). Quoting from Mead:

> Mind arises in the social process only when that process as a whole enters into, or is present in, the experience of any one of the given individuals in-volved in the process. When this occurs the individ-ual becomes self-conscious and has a mind . . . (p. 134)

Although Mead's theory of mind has not been without explanatory controversy (see Blumer, 1973, 1977, 1980; Huber, 1973a,b; Lewis, 1976, 1977, 1979; McPhail and Rexroat, 1979, 1980), mind's "logical geography" (cf. Ryle, 1949:chaps. 1–2) re-mains individualistic both in symbolic interactionism and in the most recent social behaviorism. While it is generally agreed that self or mind is not an inherent individual possession, it is nonetheless thought to be a state of being located in and about the individual per-son whose physical presence, with experience, comes

to embody it. As Mead (1934: 50) argued against Wundt: "The body is not a self, as such; it becomes a self only when it has developed a mind within the con-text of social experience." Being self-conscious and socially formed, the individual mind is, in turn, trans-formed through social interaction.

A variety of commonplace experiences suggests a need to refine Mead's view. In his many dogfight illus-trations, Mead asserts that we take it for granted that, while dogs may engage in vivid "conversations of gestures," the gestures are not "significant." The ges-tures are not products of, nor do they concretize, ca-nine selves. As Mead (1934: 43) says: "We do not as-sume that the dog says to himself, 'If the animal comes from this direction he is going to spring at my throat and I will turn in such a way.'" The conduct of dogs is understood to be mindless, the outcome of their mutual conditioning. Yet what are we to make of the common experiences where the assumption is relaxed or even reversed? At times, people do take it for granted that dogs, let alone any quick or inanimate object, significantly reference themselves, have minds, and behave accordingly (cf. Casteneda, 1968, 1971, 1972; Wieder, 1980). In light of such definitions and experiences, is not an a priori assumption to the contrary unduly restrictive? More inclusive would be a radically social version of Thomas' (1923) notion of "the definition of the situation" (cf. McHugh, 1968).

While some might judge the interpretation of canine conduct and the consideration of what fuels dogfights as marginal to the symbolic depth of human experience, or the ordinary attribution of mindedness to animals as incidental to the ultimate realities and individual location of selves, there is striking evidence of such conduct in the realm of human affairs. As a case in point, the Alzheimer's disease (senile dementia) experiences of patients, caregivers, and concerned others show that it is not routinely assumed that the demented are mindless but, rather, the assumption, in its own right, is a recurring issue of treatment and caregiving. The patient-oriented actions of the concerned cannot be adequately understood in terms of an internal conversational view of self-location, notwithstanding its social sensitivity. Only the treatment of mind as a social preserve, as an "internal" entity assigned and sustained both by, and for, whomever assumes it to exist, can account for what is taken to be the minded conduct of the mindless, the belief and attitude that the demented have minds when it may be less evident than in the conduct of dogs.

This article presents data toward a more fully social appreciation of Mead's seminal understanding of mind. Following a medical description of the disease and the study from which the data are drawn, four features of the social preservation of mind are examined: (1) the idea of the hidden mind and the problem of its realization, (2) the question of who is mind's agent, (3) discernment and articulation rules, and (4) the organization of mental demise. In conclusion, suggestions are offered for a dialogical view.

THE DISEASE

Called "the disease of the century" (Alzheimer's Disease and Related Disorders Association, 1982), Alzheimer's or senile dementia is now considered to be the single most devastating illness of old age (Reisberg, 1983: xvii). Long after its discovery in 1906 (Alzheimer, 1907, 1911), it was believed to affect those aged thirty to fifty and thus also referred to as a presenile dementia. Recent neuropathological research (Terry, 1978a) indicates that the distinction between presenile or Alzheimer's dementia and its senile form is probably arbitrary, implying that the behavioral and organic markers of both forms of debility are actually one disease.

Alzheimer's is a devastating disease. There is a progressive decline in mental functioning in which victims experience confusion, forgetfulness, depression, disorientation, and agitation. The inability to plan and organize actions leaves one unable to complete the simplest tasks of daily living. While in the early stages, a patient can lead a moderately independent life, severe dementia virtually disables its victim such that one, for example no longer recognizes the once-familiar faces of a spouse or child and is rendered incapable of managing routine activities like eating, voiding, and grooming (see Reisberg, 1981).

However severe the cognitive decline, the victim may be remarkably physically fit. It is said that the only physical markers of Alzheimer's disease may be the senile plaques, neurofibrillary tangles, and ancillary bodies found in the victim's brain, observable upon autopsy. While bioptic examination of the living brain is possible, it is not without considerable risk and rarely done. As such, the diagnosis of Alzheimer's disease remains clinical, based on cognitive evaluation by means of mental status inquiries, family histories, and physical examinations to rule out confounding or concurrent illnesses (Katzman, 1981, 1982; Katzman and Karasu, 1975).

At present, there is no prevention or cure for Alzheimer's disease. While a variety of experimental drugs holds some promise for the treatment of milder symptoms, there is still no effective medical means of reducing severe senile dementia. Medical treatment remains managerial, commonly psychopharmacological intervention. Primarily a custodial problem, the Alzheimer's disease patient becomes the virtual ward of those upon whom he/she is dependent—frequently family members.

The cognitive and pathological status of the disease is even more ominous when its connection with the aging process is taken into account. Although there are repeated reminders, both in the medical and popular literature, that Alzheimer's disease is not normal aging (e.g., Alzheimer's Disease and Related Disorders Association, 1982), there is good evidence that the distinction between the disease and the aging process may be quantitative, not a difference in kind

(Tomlinson, Blessed, and Roth, 1968, 1970; Terry, 1978b; Johnson, 1985). As a result, it is not clear whether the inexorably progressive symptoms of the disease are endemic to it or are the characteristics of becoming very aged, prematurely or in due course.

The combination of conditions has meant that Alzheimer's disease virtually has "two victims"—the person afflicted and the caregiver. Its so-called living death devolves into a caregiving problem, not a medical one. Founded in 1979, the Alzheimer's Disease and Related Disorders Association (ADRDA), a nationwide network of local chapters and support groups, aims to encourage medical research to eventually find a prevention or cure but, more immediately, to aid, educate, and counsel family members, concerned others, and the public-at-large in dealing with and caring for victims. At the same time, the ADRDA serves as a forum for the mutual support and enlightenment of caregivers.

Both in theory and practice, from medical opinion to custodial concern, the Alzheimer's disease experience is considered to be an interpersonal one, as the "two victims" theme suggests, never the sole problem or burden of the victim proper. The experience virtually exists in the nexus of the "disease that dims bright minds," a now-familiar phrase, and the burden of care. In and about the daily disease affairs of those who coexist there is the abiding everyday problem of mind, the enduring concern over what is left of the patient's self and, if anything, how to decipher it.

THE STUDY

Consideration of the social organization of mind emerged in conjunction with general reflections on field data and the analysis of disease literature from a larger study of the descriptive structure of senility (Gubrium, 1986). Participant observation was conducted in a variety of sites. A small day hospital for the care of Alzheimer's disease patients was studied over a four-month period. Informal activities were observed, as were scheduled events such as therapeutic recreation, reality orientation, activities of daily living, field trips, utilization reviews, staff conferences, and a support group for the patients' primary caregivers. Fieldwork also was conducted in the ADRDA

chapters of two cities, focusing on their caregiver support groups. Few of the support groups permitted patient participation. Some specialized exclusively in the concerns of adult children; others were limited to victims' spouses. Local chapter meetings also were attended; their function tended to be more administrative and educational than expressly supportive.

In addition, diverse documents and texts were analyzed for related themes. The mind of the Alzheimer's patient, in theory and in practice, is the frequent topic of both prose and poetry in the disease literature. The presentations and transcribed discussions of medical conferences (e.g., Eisdorfer and Friedel, 1977; Katzman, Terry, and Bick, 1978; Katzman, 1983) show evidence for formal concern for issues raised casually by caregivers: "How does the victim lose a mind?" "How can the mental status of the Alzheimer's patient be assessed when the patient is characteristically incommunicable?" An exploding body of professional and semiprofessional literature addresses the questions, too, presenting the results of controlled studies as well as advice for practical application. With the growth of public concern over the disease and the emergence of an Alzheimer's disease movement centered in the ADRDA, a number of how-to books for caregivers has appeared (see Heston and White, 1983; Mace and Rabins, 1981; Powell and Courtice, 1983). In their own fashion, the books offer a range of practical solutions—rules—for the discernment and preservation of mind. Mind also is thematised in the prose and frequently appearing poems of the disease's folk literature, especially the newsletters of the many local chapters of the ADRDA. It is the poetry, more than any form of written text, that, even in its simplicity and sentimentality, brings the reader or listener to the very heart of mind.

A HIDDEN MIND

A persistent question for all concerned is "What significance is assigned to the patient's gestures and expressions?" For most caregivers, it is evident that the patient, to paraphrase a widely used slogan, at one time had a bright mind now dimmed by the disease. The victim was once intelligible, fully in command of wit and wisdom. As another slogan puts it, the disease seems to steal that mind away. Yet, while the victim's outward gestures and expressions may hardly provide a clue to an underlying humanity, the question remains whether the disease has stolen it all or only the capacity to express it, leaving an unmanifested, hidden mind.

A focal theme of newsletters and support groups, the issue of the hidden mind bridges two native senses of mind, one individualistic but more structured than Mead's, the other structured but more fully social. Newsletters and support group proceedings show that there is a clear sense that it is individual persons who possess minds. While the social origin of mind is rarely discussed, its social sustenance frequently is. Caregivers and concerned others commonly deliberate over, share information, and offer each other practical advice about how to maintain whatever remains of the Alzheimer's victim's mental life.

In one sense, mind is more structured than Mead's conception in that it is taken to be less an internal communicative process than an objective "thing," an entity owned by the person that, once secured, can be expressed. This is evident in varied common references to "the state of mind," whether a patient has fully "lost his/her mind, when he/she will be completely "out of his/her mind," "what his/her mind is really like," "how to get into a victim's mind," among many similar expressions. In the Alzheimer's experience, such statements are more than casual metaphors; they are taken to be concrete references.

In contrast to this usage is a sense of mind more fully social than Mead's. While mind as entity is, in a manner of speaking, what all concerned are up against, it is at the same time a thing that is existentially tied to all. Because it is hidden—if not completely stolen—by the disease, others are charged with its realization. A common sentiment, it is said to be "up to us" to look and listen carefully for what the Alzheimer's victim is really trying to communicate. A familiar claim, only those who truly love the person, who may hate the disease, can make the difference between the continued realization of the victim's person as opposed to his/her loss to the "mere shell" of a former self. The contrast with Mead is a mind that persists in and through social assignment, the external (public) preservation of self.

The following exchange, drawn from the proceedings of one of the support groups observed, illustrates both senses of mind. The group is comprised mainly of the elderly spouses of Alzheimer's patients. Attention is centered on the mental status of a particular patient. The patient's spouse (call her Rita), asks what to think about her husband's very demented condition of late.

> I just don't know what to think or feel. It's like he's not even there anymore, and it distresses me something awful. He doesn't know me. He thinks I'm a strange woman in the house. He shouts and tries to slap me away from him. It's not like him at all. Most of the time he makes sounds but they sound more like an animal than a person. Do you think he has a mind left? I wish I could just get in there into his head and see what's going on. Sometimes I get so upset that I just pound on him and yell at him to come out to me. Am I being stupid? I feel that if I don't do something quick to get at him that he'll be taken from me altogether.

Immediately responding to Rita, another participant, Sara, explains:

> We all have gone through it. I know the feeling . . . , like, you just know in your heart of hearts that he's in there and that if *you* let go, that's it. So you keep on trying and trying and trying. You've got to keep the faith, that it's him and just work at him, 'cause if you don't . . . well, I'm afraid we've lost them. That's Alzheimer's. It's up to the ones who care because they [the victims] can't do for themselves.

In the exchange, mind is both individual and social. It is an entity possessed by the victim; yet the possession is also a gift allocated faithfully toward its subsequent realization. It is evident that, in practice, Rita, Sara, and their coparticipants, are literally "doing" mind in order to realize it (see Garfinkel, 1961; Mehan and Wood, 1975). Applying Mead's conversational metaphor, we can interpret their activity as a radically social turn on individual mental life. The status of the victim's internal conversation is, simultaneously, an articulation and practical realization of whomever enters into it. As Sara's response implies, it is those concerned who preserve mind, as ably as they can.

Following Sara's response, several participants

question the wisdom of maintaining faith in the face of decreasing evidence that the victim still has a mind. With this, participants directly confront the understanding so central to Mead's view: the status of mind's internal conversation. Participants deliberate over the warrants of their faith. One of them, Jack, asks Sara whether she wouldn't feel foolish to realize that all her faith in, and effort to communicate with, her husband were for naught because, as he claims of his own spouse, "she's like the living dead." He adds:

> That's why I'm looking for a nursing home for her. I loved her dearly but she's just not Mary anymore. No matter how hard I try, I can't get myself to believe that she's there anymore. I know how that can keep you going, but there comes a point where all the evidence points the other way. Even at those times (which is not very often) when she's momentarily lucid, I just know that's not her speaking to me but some kneejerk reaction. You just can't let that sort of thing get your hopes up because then you won't be able to make the kind of decision that's best for everyone all around. You know what I mean?

Sara interjects:

> Well, I know what you've gone through, and I admire your courage, Jack. But you can't be too sure. How do you *really* know that what Mary says at times is not one of those few times she's been able to really reach out to you? You don't *really* know for sure, do you? You don't really know if those little plaques and tangles are in there, do you? I hate to make it hard on you, Jack, but I face the same thing day in and day out with Richard [her husband]. Can I ever finally close him out of my life and say, "Well, it's done. It's over. He's gone"? How do I know that the poor man isn't hidden somewhere, behind all that confusion, trying to reach out and say, "I love you, Sara"? [she weeps].

In this touching scene, we find that even the attempt to empirically confirm or disprove the supposition of mind can't penetrate its existence or the possibility that it has been altered. Mind's existence seems to be experientially tied, in the final analysis, to the faith of those concerned and to the social preservation of the assignment, to minding. The working sense of mind found in the Alzheimer's disease experience is, at once, individual, social, and discursive. It radicalizes Mead's vision of social individuality. Rather than

presenting mind as secured individual property, the Alzheimer's disease experience repeatedly raises the question of how to define it as such. Although essentially hidden, when mind is faithfully assigned, it is an entity, a structure, articulated as much by those concerned as by those for whom there is concern. All are equally mind's agents, in common ownership of those who seek it. Unassigned, mind is no longer in hiding and thereby experientially nonexistent, its apparent expressions meaningless.

THE QUESTION OF AGENCY

As a thing located somewhere behind gesture and expression, mind never presents itself directly to those who take it into account. Hidden as it is, mind must be spoken for. As the Alzheimer's disease experience plainly shows, persons may not be able to speak their own minds. It should be noted, though, that the Alzheimer's disease experience is not unique in this regard, only more visible and urgent in the presentation of what is otherwise a universal problematic. Daily life is full of the pursuit of others' insights into individual minds as well as claims to know individual mind's better than those who ostensibly possess them. As the professionalization of mental concern indicates, agency has even been commodified, a purchasable service available to those desiring expert access to their minds.

Speakers for the victim's mind are a motley set. They may be a formal group, as is the health-care team who reviews a patient's conduct to keep it in tow. In the day hospital observed, the team consisted of a physician, psychiatrist, nurses, a recreation therapist, and a social worker. In varied ways and degrees, each team member spoke for the patient as a means of arriving at a shared sense of his/her mental status for diagnostic, prescriptive, and therapeutic purposes. In the Alzheimer's disease experience, of course, the caregiver is a key spokesman, his/her assertions warranted by intimate daily contact. At times, the patient may also serve as agent for this own mind; at other times, his/her very vocal, insistent, or seemingly intelligible testimony on his/her own behalf may be discounted because of his/her disease (see Gubrium, 1980). There is no guarantee, in practice, who will serve or be accepted as mental agent, only that mind emerges by way of agency.

Before mind is spoken for, the issue of who speaks credibly must be resolved. For example, in ascertaining the victim's mental status, the victim may be taken to speak competently for himself, even at the end stages of the disease when he might otherwise be considered vegetative. As the earlier extracts showed, the concept of "lucid moments" raised the possibility that there were occasions when the virtually fully demented were to be taken as temporary agents for minds still functioning behind the disease. As such, the disease is a communicative malfunction, the lucid moment serving to convey aspects of a mind otherwise hidden. The issue of agency may become lodged in deliberations over the lucidity of such moments, over the question of whether what was said and heard was, in fact, lucid (a clear and distinct expression of the victim's mind) or the mere appearance of lucidity (perhaps a so-called parroting). The discernment of lucidity may itself turn on the assessment of discernment credentials, as one or another party to a deliberation claims to know best in such matters because of experience, education, or insight, among a host of interpretive warrants. Indeed, the figure and ground of warrants and discernments continually shift in the flow of mental discourse.

Mind experientially persists to the extent that some agent preserves it, be the agent the one whose mind is at stake or some other. While in theory, mind is referenced as a thing, it is articulated and realized by a type of existential labor. Agents are themselves practicing features of mind, even though mind, in its own right, is taken to be a separate and essentially hidden entity. As a support group participant explained:

> Look, you and I know that if we don't make a real, loving effort to listen, to really hear, what they're [Alzheimer's patients] trying to say to us, that you might as well call it quits. I know that Dad hasn't said a word for years, but when I touch his hand or put my arms around him—God bless him—he knows. He really knows! You can't tell me he's gone. As far as I'm concerned, Dad's as much with us as he always was. The damned disease has just made it impossible for him to communicate with us. It's an effort and someone's got to believe in them. You just

can't ever forget that it's a life and you can't give up on it.

Now, of course, not all of those gathered in this or in other support groups feel as this devoted daughter did. Some cease to be the victim's agent because they consider it foolish to do so, not because it is foolish to care but, rather, foolish to continue caring for something they no longer believe exists. Those continuing to maintain what is called the illusion of the patient's lucidity, who try to preserve the semblance of the victim's former self, are said to be "denying," the irrational sustenance of mind. In contrast, for others, the ultimate question of mind's existence experientially overshadows whatever evidence is brought to bear in the matter. For them, denial is mere rhetoric, someone's way of being diagnostic. When all is said and done, the question remains, as Sara put it earlier, "How do I know that . . . behind all that confusion, [he's not] trying to reach out and say: 'I love you, Sara.'?"

Given the liberal tenor of Mead's philosophy, he understandably tended to limit agency to the individual, embodied articulators of mind, as if to say, when self-consciousness occurs, an individual can speak his/her own mind. Diverse, casual evidence and the Alzheimer's disease data suggest the need for a broader interpretation, cast as discursive and practical individualization. Accordingly, mind is anyone's responsibility, everyone being a potential agent, the person conceivably self-conscious despite himself/herself.

ARTICULATING MIND

Hidden as it is, mind requires articulation. In Mead's view, it is the individual person, in possession of self-consciousness and sensitive to others, who expresses himself/herself, to others and to himself/herself. The Alzheimer's disease experience poignantly confronts those concerned with the everyday issue of articulation. While there are any number of agents for the victim's mind, how do they go about their work? Consider here the social organization of preservation; in the next section, we turn to closure or mental demise.

A difficult task confronts the caregivers and concerned others who seek the Alzheimer's victim's mind: to read outward signs of mind bereft of common meaning. The disease is said to destroy the victim's capacity to communicate by gesture or expression. Left with little or no memory, muddled speech, erratic movement, or other unintelligible activity, in diverse combinations, the usual route to mind is virtually nonexistent.

In the face of this, rules of thumb are offered to facilitate articulation, some based on professional practice, others being "tips" for hearing what the patient is trying to say drawn from individual caregiving experiences. Articulation rules are regular features of the disease literature, especially nursing and social work writings, the advice books for caregivers, and the many ADRDA chapter newsletters.

The foremost rule is that those concerned must be *prepared* to articulate what the patient is trying to communicate. Before the actual interpretation process begins, agents must sharpen their perception so that whatever clues there are to the patient's inner intentions can be captured, obscure and fleeting as they may be. Called "active listening" by some (e.g., Philadelphia ADRDA *Newsletter,* January 1983) and a "special kind of listening" by others (e.g., Bonjean, 1979), preparation is said to require *objectivity*. An active listener attempts to hear without being judgmental, which would confound what the patient means. As explained in the Philadelphia ADRDA *Newsletter* (and reprinted in other chapter newsletters):

> This method [active listening] conveys nonjudgmental interest and a sincere willingness to understand the other person. The result is a clarification of the situation for both the person speaking and the "active" listener, and—in many cases—the person with the problem is able to come up with more insight about his/her problem through the conversation. (p. 3)

The rule not only prepares the listener to perceive the patient's intentions but, through the active listener's effort, both the listener's and the patient's insight into the latter's mind is achieved. As such, active or special listening is preparatory to the common realization of intention.

The preparatory rule has a selection provision. While the active listener should be objective, he/she should not listen to everything the patient conveys, for much of what is said and done is meaningless, arbitrary, or unintended. As a result, one listens for what

the patient is *truly* saying, not literal expressions. As Bonjean (1979:8) advises: "Sometimes, listening means attempting to hear what is felt rather than what is reported, what is meant rather than what is actually said." And as pointed out in the Philadelphia *Newsletter:* "In active listening, one listens not only to the literal meaning of the words spoken but also to the emotional content underlying the words" (p. 3).

The active listener fine-tunes for affective messages. This resolves the challenge of communicating with the incommunicable. As defined by the rule, in the final analysis the route to mind is by way of feelings. From physicians to caregivers, those concerned repeatedly reminded each other that, while the Alzheimer's victim may be cognitively deficient, it does not mean he/she doesn't have feelings, the very heart of mind. Needless to say, this puts a considerable interpretive burden on listeners.

Other rules link details of the patient's conduct with particular meanings. Some of the most explicit are described in a widely quoted article by Bartol (1979) titled "Nonverbal Communication in Patients with Alzheimer's Disease." Explicit rules are suggested in the following passages.

> Pacing the halls, restless behavior, and inability to sleep tell us clearly that the patient is anxious, [the patient asking us] "What is wrong with me? Can't you see I am getting worse? How much worse will I get?"
>
> Withdrawn behavior and signs of nervousness tell us that the patient may be afraid [the patient saying to us] "I am frightened of what is happening to me! Help me!"

Not all interpretive rules are as straightforward. Many emerge from deliberations over the particular meaning of unintelligible gestures or expressions. From professional staffings to support group proceedings and casual conversation, the concerned inform each other of how to interpret the patient's conduct, warranting their claims on grounds as varied as training, expertise, and intimacy of contact. Whether formal or casual, the application of interpretive rules is organized in usage. Rules themselves are interpreted, transformed, and applied as the need arises, working guides for making sense of individual expressions, discovered, interpreted, and applied case by case.

Just as words are believed to stem from mind, feelings are taken to have a source. But what thing do feelings express? The answer lies in the affective analog of hidden mind: the referential heart.

Time and again, in speech and text, those concerned distinguish between the feelings and words the patient conveys, as do rules for active listening. Words and feelings are located, respectively, in references to matters of mind and heart. For some, heart is the mind that has all but failed, the spirit of intention, the heart of mind. As frequently noted, "His mind might no longer be active, but he's still got a heart and feelings."

The heart of mind has the same discursive properties as mind itself. It is a thing, hidden, inferentially describable. Where there can be mental anguish, so, too, there is heartache. Where there is sincerity, there also are heartfelt intentions. Even mind's past—remembrances—has its counterpart in heart's memories. Originally appearing in the Kansas City ADRDA *Newsletter* and reprinted in the August 1984 issue of the Des Moines ADRDA *Newsletter,* extracts from a poem titled "Heart's Memories," said to be written by an Alzheimer's disease victim, share the heart of mind's past:

> *I remember you with my heart*
> *My mind won't say your name*
> *I can't recall where I knew you*
> *Who you were*
> *Or who I was.*
> . . .
> *But I do know you*
> *I know I knew you*
> *And I do love you*
> *I know how you make me feel*
> *I remember the feelings we had together*
> *My heart remembers*
> *It cries out in loneliness for you*
> *For the feeling you give me now.*
> . . .
> *Please, please don't forget me*
> *and please don't stay away*
> *Because of the way my mind acts*
> *I can still love you*
> *I can still feel you*

> *I can remember you with my heart*
> *And a heart memory is maybe*
> *The most important memory of all.*

While the folk poetry of the disease experience would be judged crude by some, its place in the conduct of the concerned cannot be judged on literary grounds. The folk poetry not only reveals how the ultimate structure of mind is envisioned by those concerned, it is also a way of voicing, by means of words, what words cannot convey. Ironic as that may be, it is taken to articulate the heart of mind, a thing indescribable in its own right.

A commonplace dilemma, caregivers and concerned others frequently complain that they "just can't put into words" the feelings they and/or their patients are experiencing or desire to communicate. It is not a problem of "really knowing deep down," but one of articulation. More than any other vehicle, it is the growing poetry of the disease that succinctly serves that purpose. For example, in one support group session, several participants were struggling to describe to each other the inner feelings of their respective patients. For some time, one caregiver in particular tried unsuccessfully to do so. She claimed to know very well what was in her demented husband's heart, what the disease progressively and insidiously had hidden from her, but had difficulty articulating what she knew. Many agreed that it was hard for them, too. At one point, though, as she once again attempted to describe her husband's heart, she fetched a poem from her purse and read it aloud. On the face of it, its words were no different than the words she had earlier used ineffectively to convey the feelings. Yet, when she had read the poem, her message was received with clear understanding, various members of the group acknowledging that "it said it all." What that was, of course, cannot be described. The point of the poetic message was that, despite its words, it was taken to be clear communication: emotive discourse. The poem was what the poem did; thereby, poetry-in-use became a social relationship—common understanding, community.

THE DEMISE OF MIND

For some participants, the function of support groups is to teach one to realize, as a veteran put it, "that there comes a point where to keep thinking that they're still sensible and lucid underneath it all is ridiculous and blind." The attitude is not necessarily uncaring but realistic, for, just as those who claim to find definitive evidence of mind and heart in the conduct of their patients, others become equally convinced of their absence. As a daughter explained:

> When all is said and done, for all the finagling they do trying to figure out Mother's strange speech and erratic ways, Mother's just not there anymore. You might just as well be talking to a wall. It's a plain fact as clear as day. All that listening and all the clues in the world are not going to tell you that that brain's still working up there. Everyone should realize that sooner or later. If you ask me, it's more in *their* [caregivers'] minds than in the patient's.

The comment brings us face to face with the social nature of mind and minding. It informs us that, as entities, heart and mind are objects-for-us. The sentiment is that minding should in due course cease, for it eventually represents no conscious thing, nothing. Continued, unrestrained minding itself becomes an affliction—pathological denial—further victimizing the "other patient" of the disease, the victim's caregiver.

In a study of the social organization of death in two hospitals, Sudnow (1967) described dying as a social state of affairs. He reported on the physical preservations and closures linked with interpretations of the social worth of the dying. The Alzheimer's disease experience shows that closure is not only social but, for some, programmatic, processed by rules as formal as those serving articulation. The interpersonal relations of the patient and the caregiver are sometimes said to have a natural history. In veteran and professional judgment, it is only natural for, say, the wife of a recently diagnosed spouse to eagerly search for a cure or some other means of sustaining his "once bright mind." Indeed, the search and hope might last for years, well into the most debilitating stages of the disease. For some, the search virtually outlives the victim, as the former caregiver retrospectively attempts to regain the semblance of what the patient "really must have [meant or] felt even though he couldn't even remember his own name, where he'd been, or where he was going." Yet, as those who claim to know from experience or from being expert in such matters,

there comes a point when it's only natural to begin closing off one's affairs with the hopelessly demented.

The professional rationalization of intervention is crystallized around a developmental-stage view of the closure process. Discussions and advice columns in ADRDA chapter newsletters and the human service literature of the disease show that Kübler-Ross' (1969) well-known formula of the five stages of dying has been adapted to Alzheimer's disease counterparts. A familiar concern is where the caregiver or a support group "is at." *Is at* refers to some point in the natural history of concern. For example, in regard to a particular caregiver, it may be said that he/she is at the stage of denial or in the acceptance phase, respectively, meaning that he/she refuses to close off his affairs with the person behind the disease or comes to accept the need for closure with what is now only the shell of a former self. Support groups also are said to progress naturally through stages of concern. A group comprised of novice caregivers is likely to dwell on articulation, particularly the cure that will again reveal the minds of those who were once so bright. A group of experienced participants is more likely to have confronted, discussed, and perhaps come to terms with mental demise. Indeed, support groups are described as more or less mature depending on whether they are, as a geriatrician put it, "still preoccupied with cure or are getting their own lives in order."

While in theory the natural history view is a linear vision of closure, even veteran caregivers and mature support groups, on occasion, confront that persistent question: "How do I know . . . behind all that . . . , [he's not] trying to reach out . . . ?" Sometimes, the question rushes ahead of its own deliberation, the fact of it having raised it in the first place taken to be callous and uncaring, the assumption made that, "of course," the victim still has feelings, if not the ability to rationally express them. In the circumstance, closure may be transformed into urgent preservation, with former hard evidence of total mental demise, of so-called brain failure, becoming previously unrecognized clues of the living person behind the disease. There are support groups sessions where ongoing shifts in the discourses of articulation and closure serve to construct, deconstruct, and reconstruct the victim's mind. As such, mind experientially dies and is reborn time and again, in and through formal and informal concern, an ongoing achievement.

CONCLUSION

Consider two principles of Mead's theory of mind in light of the Alzheimer's disease experience. One is the principle of minded individuality; the other is the principle of social formation. As set forth in Mead's eponymous book, *Mind, Self and Society,* the first refers to Mead's treatment of mind as individual property, as an owned internal conversation. The second principle discerns mind as a social achievement, formed and transformed in and through experience, in relation to others. Mead could be interpreted as seeing the principles as in continual dialog, neither one in that regard being a first principle but, rather, simultaneously operative, as Blumerians would prefer (see Blumer 1969). In this sense, the Alzheimer's disease experience suggests that mind is pervasively dialogical, an individual product of its own discourse.

At times, though, Mead's statements reveal a distinct inequity in the application of the principles. Certain usages suggest that, once enlivened, the individual mind takes on more than an empirically independent existence. Mead speaks of the occurrence of self-consciousness and, then, the presence of mind. But the treatment is such that, while social in development, mind is occasionally described *theoretically* as referencing a self-conscious entity, embodied in the individual, foreclosing the further analysis of the dialogical status of that now separate and distinct internal conversation.

This sense of mind's logical geography constrains the data of the Alzheimer's disease experience, where mind is a poignantly problematic category, the common responsibility and property of those concerned. The concerned may settle their affairs with the heart of mind, concluding that there is indeed a self-conscious, feeling entity hidden somewhere behind the disease, or they may not. In either case, it is continually subject to their brand of epistemological scrutiny. They have the work of assigning and reassigning internality to portions of the common dialog of mind, whose participants include all conversant from victims to caregivers and concerned others (cf. Todorov, 1984).

The practical dialog that now constructs, deconstructs, and then reconstructs mind is not an epistemological dilemma for its participants. They work at its components, they are not numbed by its overall challenge. Thus we sometimes find caregivers raising the question "How can we *really* know?" together with the understanding that knowing is essentially tied to the faith of those concerned. Yet, at other times, they set that aside to deal with the object of their concern, as if to temporarily stop the dialogical whirlwind in order to see through to its major point of reference, to mind.

The Alzheimer's disease experience suggests that Mead's principles be detached from their bourgeois individualism and appreciated as concrete dialogical themes. With that, mind becomes a more fully social entity, one born with attention to self-consciousness unfettered by a conclusive self-possession. Not far removed from Mead's internal conversation metaphor, minding is open dialog centered on its essentially unarticulated, but phenomenally describable source: mind.

REFERENCES

Alzheimer, A. 1907. "Über eine eigenartige Erkrankung der Hirnrinde," *Allgemeine Zeitschrift für Psychiatrie* 64:146–148.
———. 1911. "Über eigenartige Krankheitsfälle des Späteren Alters." *Zeitschrift für Gesamte Neurologle und Psychiatrie* 4:356–385.
Alzheimer's Disease and Related Disorders Association (ADRDA). 1982. *A Disease of the Century: The Case for the Alzheimer's Disease and Related Disorders Association and its Fight Against Alzheimer's and Related Diseases.* Chicago: A DR DA.
Bartol, M.A. 1979. "Nonverbal Communication in Patients with Alzheimer's Disease." *Journal of Gerontological Nursing* 5:21–31.
Blumer, H. 1969. *Symbolic Interactionalism: Perspective and Method.* Englewood Cliffs, N.J.: Prentice Hall.
———. 1973. "A Note on Symbolic Interactionism." *American Sociological Review* 38:797–798.
———. 1977. "Comment on Lewis's 'The Classic Pragmatists as Forerunners to Symbolic Interactionism'." *Sociological Quarterly* 18:285–289.
———. 1980. "Social Behaviorism and Symbolic Interactionism." *American Sociological Review* 45:404–419.
Bonjean, M.J. 1979. *Making Visits Count.* Madison/Milwaukee: University of Wisconsin System.

Casteneda, C. 1968. *The Teaching of Don Juan.* Berkeley, Calif.: University of California Press.

———. 1971. *A Separate Reality.* New York: Simon & Schuster.

———. 1972. *A Journey to Ixtlan.* New York: Simon & Schuster.

Eisdorfer, C. and R.O. Friedel (eds.) 1977. *Cognitive and Emotional Disturbance in the Elderly.* Chicago: Year Book Medical Publishers.

Garfinkel, H. 1961. *Studies in Ethnomethodology.* Englewood Cliffs, N.J.: Prentice-Hall.

Gubrium, J.F. 1980. "Patient Exclusion in Geriatric Staffings." *Sociological Quarterly* 21:335–348.

———. 1986. *Oldtimers and Alzheimer's: The Descriptive Organization of Senility.* Greenwich, CT: JAI Press.

Heston, L.L. and J.A. White. 1983. *Dementia: A Practical Guide to Alzheimer's Disease and Related Illnesses.* New York: W.H. Freeman.

Huber, J. 1973a. "Symbolic Interaction as a Pragmatic Perspective: The Bias of Emergent Theory." *American Sociological Review* 38:274–284.

———. 1973b. "Reply to Blumer: But Who Will Scrutinize the Scrutinizers?" *American Sociological Review* 39:798–800.

Johnson, H.A. (ed.). 1985. *Relations Between Normal Aging and Disease.* New York: Raven Press.

Katzman, R. 1981. "Early Detection of Senile Dementia." *Hospital Practice* 16:61–76.

———. 1982. "The Complex Problem of Diagnosis." *Generations* 7:8–10.

Katzman, R. (ed.). 1983. *Branbury Report 15: Biological Aspects of Alzheimer's Disease.* Cold Spring Harbor, N.Y.: Cold Spring Harbor Laboratory.

Katzman, R. and T.B. Karasu. 1975 "Differential Diagnosis of Dementia." Pp. 103–134 in W. Fields (ed.) *Neurological and Sensory Disorders in the Elderly.* New York: Grune and Stratton.

Katzman, R., R.D. Terry, and K.L. Bick (eds.). 1978. *Alzheimer's Disease: Senile Dementia and Related Disorders.* New York: Raven Press.

Kübler-Ross, E. 1969. *On Death and Dying.* New York: Macmillan.

Lewis, J.D. 1976 "The Classic American Pragmatists as Forerunners to Symbolic Interactionism." *Sociological Quarterly* 17:347–359.

———. 1977. "Reply to Blumer." *Sociological Quarterly* 18:291–292.

———. 1979. "A Social Behaviorist Interpretation of the Median 'I'." *American Journal of Sociology* 85:261–287.

Mace, N.L. and P.V. Rabins. 1981. *The 36-Hour Day.* Baltimore: Johns Hopkins University Press.

McHugh, P. 1968. *Defining the Situation.* Indianapolis: Bobbs-Merrill.

McPhail, C. and C. Rexroat. 1979. "Mead vs. Blumer: the Divergent Methodological Perspectives of Social Behaviorism and Symbolic Interactionism." *American Sociological Review* 44:449–467.

———. 1980 "Ex cathedra Blumer or ex libris Mead?" *American Sociological Review* 45:420–430.

Mead, G.H. 1934. *Mind, Self & Society.* Chicago: University of Chicago Press.

Mehan, H. and H. Wood. 1975. *The Reality of Ethnomethodology.* New York: Wiley Interscience.

Philadelphia ADRDA Newsletter. 1983. "Summary of January Meeting on Active Listening." Philadelphia ADRDA Newsletter (January): 2–3.

Powell, L.S. and K. Courtice. 1983. *Alzheimer's Disease: A Guide For Families.* Reading, Mass.: Addison-Wesley.

Reisberg, B. 1981. *Brain Failure.* New York: Free Press.

———. 1983. "Preface." Pp. xvii–xix in B. Reisberg (ed.), *Alzheimer's Disease: The Standard Reference.* New York: Free Press.

Ryle, G. 1949. *The Concept of Mind.* Chicago: University of Chicago Press.

Sudnow, D. 1967. *Passing On.* Englewood Cliffs, N.J.: Prentice-Hall.

Terry, R.D. 1978a. "Aging, Senile Dementia, and Alzheimer's Disease." Pp. 11–14 in R. Katzman, R. D. Terry, and K.L. Bick (eds.) *Alzheimer's Disease: Senile Dementia and Related Disorders.* New York: Raven Press.

———. 1978b. "Physical Changes in the Aging Brain." Pp. 205–220 in J.A. Behnke, C.E. Finch, and G.B. Moment (eds.) *The Biology of Aging.* New York: Plenum.

Thomas, W.I. 1923. *The Unadjusted Girl.* Boston: Little Brown.

Todorov, T. 1984. *Mikhail Bakhtin: The Dialogical Principle.* Minneapolis: University of Minnesota Press.

Tomlinson, B.E., G. Blessed, and M. Roth. 1968. "Observations on the Brains of Non-Demented Old People." *Journal of Neurological Sciences* 7:331–356.

———. 1970. "Observations on the Brains of Demented Old People." *Journal of Neurological Sciences* 11:205–242.

Wieder, D. L. 1980. "Behavioristic Operationalism and the Life World: Chimpanzees and Chimpanzee Researchers in Face-to-Face Interaction." *Sociological Inquiry* 50:75–103.

UNDERSTANDING DOGS

19 | Caretakers' Attributions of Mindedness in Canine-Human Relationships

Clinton R. Sanders

Words are the source of misunderstanding.
—*Antoine de Saint Exupery (from* The Little Prince)

Few associations are as intense and emotionally involving as those we have with companion animals. Despite the frequency and importance of relationships between humans and animals, analyses of interspecies interaction are noticeably rare in the social scientific literature (for exceptions, see Arluke 1988; Bryant 1991; Crist and Lynch 1990; Helmer 1991; Hickrod and Schmitt 1982; Mechling 1989; Nash 1989; Sanders 1990; Robins, Sanders, and Cahill 1991; Wieder 1980).

To a major degree, this lack of attention to animal-human exchanges is due to the conventional sociological belief that "authentic" interaction is premised on the abilities of social actors to employ conventional linguistic symbols. Language enables interactants to construct and share a mutually defined reality and provides the vehicle for the internal conversation that constitutes mind.

Because they are presumed to lack the ability to understand and use shared linguistic symbols, animals are, in the conventional sociological view, excluded from all but the most simple social exchanges. Mead ([1934] 1964) presented nonhuman animals as ongoingly involved in communicative acts involving the use of natural signs. He conceived of animal exchanges as immediately situated and involved in direct references to physically present objects or intentions. The only connection between the sign/gestures presented by animals and the subsequent behaviors of their cointeractants was due, according to Mead, to instinct or conditioning.

In establishing this phonocentric view, Mead effectively excluded the routine encounters of people with their nonhuman companions from all but the most cursory of examinations. Because animals are not full-fledged social actors from the Meadian point of view, their encounters with humans are one-way exchanges, lacking the intersubjectivity at the heart of true social interaction. People interact with animals as objects. From the conventional perspective, dog owners[1] babbling endearments to their canine companions are simply taking the role of the animals and projecting humanlike attributes onto them (see Pollner and McDonald-Wickler 1985). Interpreting the behavior of dogs as authentic social responsiveness is the same form of anthropomorphic projection in which people engage when they "interact" with a computer (Turkle 1984), automobile, or other inanimate object (Cohen 1989).

In contrast, caretakers of companion animals and others who live in everyday situations entailing frequent and intimate interaction with nonhuman animals and who have practical interests in making ongoing sense of their behavior consistently see animals as subjective actors and define interactions with them as being "authentic" and reciprocal social exchanges (see Crist and Lynch 1990; Griffin 1984; Hearne 1987; Shapiro 1990; Ristau 1990). People grant this (at least, limited) mindedness to animals even when the situation in which they encounter the animal-other is formally constrained by a reductionist ideology demanding that they be seen and dealt with as scientific objects. Arluke's (1988, 1990) studies of animal care technicians in medical research facilities and Wieder's (1980) work with chimpanzee researchers, for example, amply illustrate the persuasiveness of everyday encounters in prompting people to regard nonhuman animals as minded coactors.

This discussion focuses on dog owners' definitions of the companion animals with whom they have ongoing relationships. Based on routine, intimate interac-

Clinton R. Sanders, *Journal of Contemporary Ethnography* 22: 205–226, copyright © 1993 by Clinton R. Sanders. Reprinted by permission of Sage Publications, Inc.

tions with their dogs, caretakers come to regard their animals as unique individuals who are minded, empathetic, reciprocating, and well aware of basic rules and roles that govern the relationship. Caretakers come to see their dogs as consciously behaving so as to achieve defined goals in the course of routine social exchanges with people and other canines. The dogs are regarded, in short, as possessing at least a rudimentary ability to "take the role of the other." This interpretation of the dogs' actions and reactions as "expressions of competence" (Goode 1992)—as thoughtfully constructed and reciprocating—requires owners, in turn, to take the role of the animal other in order to establish the "natural rituals" (Collins 1989) that constitute their ongoing relationship.

Following a brief presentation of the various sources of data on which this discussion is grounded, I expand on the key elements outlined above. Drawing parallels to the sociological work on interactions between able-bodied people and ostensibly less competent human others (e.g., Bogdan and Taylor 1989; Goode 1992; Gubrium 1986), I first describe how owners construct perspectives on their dogs as minded actors and what they see to be the nature of their subjective experience. Next, I present the owners' definitions of their animals as possessors of unique, historically grounded personalities. I then focus on the central emotional component of the canine-human relationship. Owners typically view their canine companions as having an emotional life and as being ongoingly aware of and appropriately responsive to the emotional experience of their human companions. The substantive discussion closes with a description of how caretakers incorporate their dogs into the social networks and key routines that encompass and comprise their intimate lives. The article's conclusion points to areas of further research and focuses on how investigations of animal-human relationships can expand sociological perspectives on such central issues as mind, identity construction, and interpersonal intimacy.

THE RESEARCH

The data on which this discussion is based are drawn from three sources. First, I call on material included in an "autoethnography" constructed as I systematically

observed and recorded personal experiences with my own dogs (three Newfoundland females) over a 4-year period. As the term implies, autoethnography is a combination of autobiography and ethnography. As such, it rejects the traditional ethnologic convention of positioning the researcher as an objective outsider describing and interpreting observed events. Instead, autoethnography emphasizes the value of information drawn from the systematic examination of personal experiences, emotions, and interpretations (see Denzin 1989; Ellis 1991; Hayano 1979; Shapiro 1990).[2]

The second body of data was amassed during 9 months of participant observation in a large veterinary clinic located in the Northeast. The field data of central importance to this article consist of detailed observations of owners and their dogs as they waited for a veterinarian to come into the examination room, the conversations that owners had with me during this time, and the exchanges that occurred between clients and veterinarians in the course of the service encounter. Unless asked directly who I was, I did not identify myself as a sociologist to the clients. In general, clients assumed that I was a veterinary student or a technician employed by the clinic. As a participant in the setting, I routinely made myself generally useful, holding animals for various procedures, fetching equipment and supplies, helping clean examination rooms, offering nonmedical advice, and in a variety of other ways assisting with the business of the clinic.

Finally, information is drawn from relevant portions of a series of in-depth, semistructured interviews conducted with 24 dog owners initially contacted when they presented themselves at the veterinary hospital or who agreed to be interviewed following their involvement in an 8-week-long puppy-training class sponsored by the clinic. These interviews averaged between 60 and 90 minutes in length and were tape-recorded with the interviewee's permission. All interviews were conducted in the interviewee's homes, and in all cases the owner's dog was present during the encounter, thereby allowing me to observe exchanges between the informant and his or her animal in their most familiar interactional setting.

I do not maintain that this description of owners' orientations toward and interactions with their dogs encompasses all such exchanges. It is certainly the case that owners construct a variety of identities for their dogs—from object through make-believe person to surrogate child—and consequently treat them in a variety of ways. I do contend, however, that the interactants and canine-human exchanges presented here are fairly typical of the people, dogs, and relationships one finds in the average American household.

The informants were drawn from and observations were made in a veterinary practice that provided services for a largely middle-class clientele. A recent national survey commissioned by the Veterinary Medical Association (1988) reveals that approximately 38% of American households include an average of 1.5 dogs and that close to 78% of dog owners visit a veterinarian an average of about 2.5 times a year. People with canine companions encountered in a veterinary clinic, therefore, can reasonably be seen as fairly typical dog owners. Certainly, one would expect to encounter rather different orientations and relationships (probably more on the functional/object end of the continuum; see e.g., Jordon 1975) were research done with lower-class owners and/or those who never seek veterinary services.[3]

ASSIGNING THE DOG A HUMANLIKE IDENTITY

The designation of another as "human" is an eminently social activity. The exclusion of certain people from this category has been a fairly common sociohistorical phenomenon. "Primitives," African Americans, and members of various other human groups routinely have been, and continue to be, denied the status of human (see Spiegel 1988), and studies of interactions in total institutions (e.g., Bogdan et al. 1974; Goffman 1961; Goode 1992; Vail 1966) are filled with descriptions of the "dehumanization" of inmates by staff members, principally on the grounds that the inmates do not possess the requisite level of mind.

In their study of the interactions of nondisabled people with severely disabled family members, Bogdan and Taylor (1989) discussed the ways in which the social meaning of humanness is created and the criteria used by "normals" to assign a human identity to severely disabled intimates.[4] This definitional activity entails attending to four basic factors. First, the

nondisabled *attribute thinking* to disabled others. The latter are seen as minded—able to reason, understand, and remember. The caretakers regard the disabled individuals as partners in the inter-subjective play of social interaction, interpret their gestures, sounds, postures, and expressions as indicators of intelligence, and are adept at taking the role of the disabled others.

Second, the nondisabled see the others as *individuals.* They regard the disabled persons as having distinct personalities, identifiable likes and dislikes, authentic feelings, and unique personal histories.

Third, the disabled persons are seen as *reciprocating,* as giving as much to the relationship as they receive from it. For nondisabled associates, the others are true companions who help to expand their lives by providing companionship, acting as objects of caring, and opening up situations in which they can encounter new people (see Messent 1983; Robins, Sanders, and Cahill 1991).

Finally, Bogdan and Taylor (1989) described how disabled persons are humanized by being *incorporated into a social place.* Through defining the disabled persons as integral members of the family and involving them in ongoing domestic rituals and routines, the nondisabled actively situate the others into the intimate relational network.

The owners I interviewed and encountered in the veterinary hospital engaged in a process of identity construction very similar to that described by Bogdan and Taylor. They routinely used their day-to-day experience with their dogs to define their animals as minded social actors and as having, at least, a "person-like" status.[5] Caretakers typically saw their dogs as reciprocating partners in an honest, nondemanding, and rewarding social relationship.

The skeptical reader of what follows may well discount caretakers' identity construction of their dogs as "mere" anthropomorphic projections. Even if this were the case, we should not disregard people's definitions of the other as the central element in understanding how human-animal relationships—or relationships between "normals" and alingual others more generally—are organized (see Pollner and McDonald-Wickler 1985).

Evaluating the subjective experience of others is always a tricky procedure (Schutz 1970; Goffman

1959). Most basically, the chaining of interactions is a practical endeavor; estimations of coactors' perspectives are assumed, altered, or discarded with regard to what works. Intimate familiarity with others—animal or human—is an effective teacher.

As I write these words, for example, one of my dogs comes to my study and stares at me. She then walks back down the hall to the door opening onto the porch and rings the bell she uses to signal her desire to go outside. Because I am not immediately responsive, she returns to my study, pokes me with her nose, and returns to the door. Grumbling about the intrusion, I get up, open the door, and she goes out to lie down in her usual spot.

I maintain, and the dog owners presented below would maintain, that the most reasonable interpretation of this mundane sequence of events is to see it as an authentic social exchange. My dog has encountered a problem, realized on the basis of remembered past events that my actions hold the potential for solving her problem, purposefully behaved in a manner that effectively communicated her "request," and, in so doing, shaped my behavior to her defined ends.

Seeing this simple encounter as involving communication of a definition of the situation, mutual taking the role of the other, and projection of a short-term future event does not, however, require that we *literally* see dogs as people. Defining companion animals as "people in disguise" (Clark 1984, 24) is as degrading to them as is the view that they are mere behaviorist automatons. My informants, in describing their dogs' humanlike qualities and actions, did not regard them as literally human. Nor did they facilely place them in a "keyed frame" as "pretend" people (Hickrod and Schmitt 1982). The point they were making, and the focus of this discussion, is that their animal companions were far more than objects; they were minded, creative, empathetic, and responsive. The animal-human relationships they shared were authentically social.

The Dog as Minded Actor

The owners with whom I spoke had little doubt of their dogs' cognitive abilities, and all could recount examples of what they defined as minded behavior. Dogs' thought processes were generally seen as fairly

basic ("He's not exactly a Rhodes scholar"), and, to a certain extent, thoughtful intelligence was seen as varying from animal individual to individual and from breed to breed. Because they were dogs and not humans, the companion animals were typically described as engaging in thought processes that were "wordless" (Terrace 1987). Thought was characterized as being nonlinear, composed of mental images, and driven largely by emotion (see Gallistel 1992). When asked if she thought that her malamute cross could think, an interviewee replied,

> Yes I do. I don't think [dogs'] heads are empty. I think their thinking process is different from ours. I think they think on emotions. If the environment is happy and stable, they are going to act more stable—pay more attention to what you are doing. They are going to be more alert. If everything is chaotic, they would not be thinking externally but be more concerned with themselves internally—protecting themselves and not paying attention to my cues. I would call that thinking, but it is not what you would call linear thinking. . . . They are making decisions based on emotional cues.

No matter what the mode of mental representation defined by caretakers, most agreed that the issues *thought about* were rather basic. The dog's mind was focused predominantly or immediate events and matters of central concern to his or her ongoing physical and emotional experience:

> I think that [my dogs] are here just to get approval. [They are here for] feeding or to get petted or get their ears rubbed. I think they think enough not to get yelled at, not to get into trouble. That's the way dogs are. I don't think they can reason like people.

On the other hand, some owners did see their animals as going beyond these basic physiological and emotional concerns. One typical type of example offered by informants focused on their dogs' play activities and the adjustments they made while being trained. The dog's purposive modification of behavior was seen as indicating a basic ability to reason. For example, one owner described the actions of his hunting dog in the course of learning to retrieve objects from the water:

> This is the smartest dog I have ever had. We are having him trained professionally, and we were with the

trainer with my dog and some of the other dogs he was training. He said, "Look here. I'll show you how smart your dog is." He threw the retrieving dummy out into the middle of this long pond there. My dog jumped in and swam to the thing, grabbed it in his mouth, and took a right turn. He swam to the land and walked back to us with the dummy in his mouth—all proud. He was the only one smart enough to walk back. The other dogs all swam out, retrieved the thing, and swam all the way back.

While watching my own dogs play, I was struck by the adjustments they made—behavioral alterations that, were they made by hairless bipeds, clearly would be seen as demonstrating thought. Soon after the introduction of a new puppy into my household, I made the following entry in my autoethnographic notes following a walk in the woods:

Today Isis [my 3 year old Newfoundland] appeared to come to a realization about how she had been attempting to play "chase" and this prompted her to alter the play process somewhat—essentially altering the assumption of roles. On each of the walks so far, Isis has attempted to initiate chase by acting as the chaser. She runs off at a rapid pace, turns back, runs toward Raven [the puppy], bowls her over, runs past, etc. This doesn't work because of the size and strength difference. Raven just cowers, runs to one of us for protection, cries out. So, this time when Raven made a run at her at one point in the walk, Isis ran off a little ways until Raven followed. Isis then ran further and soon Raven was in hot pursuit. Isis led her on a merry chase over fallen trees, through thickets, into gullies. It was particularly interesting to watch because Isis was adjusting the game on the basis of her knowledge of Raven's, as yet, limited abilities. She would run just fast enough so that Raven wouldn't get more than a few feet behind and would occasionally slow down enough that Raven could grab hold of some hair on her side or legs. Isis would also toy with the other player by jumping over larger falls or into gullies with deep, vertical sides—obstacles she knew were beyond Raven's limited abilities.

Owners frequently offered stories in which their dogs acted in ways that were thoughtfully intended to shape the owners' definitions of the situation and to manipulate their subsequent behavior to desirable ends. A number of informants told of dog behavior such as the following:

We have a beanpot that we keep filled with dog cookies. Every time the dogs go out and "do their business" they get a cookie. They have interpreted this as "all we have to do is cross the threshold and come back and we get a cookie." So it will be raining and they won't want to go out and they will just put one foot outside the door and then go over to where the cookies are kept: "Well, technically we went out."

Though rarely successful, this sort of behavior indicated for the owners an attempt by the dog to deceptively manipulate their definition of the situation (dog went out) so as to shape their behavior (give cookie). Caretakers also provided descriptions of situations in which they observed their dogs engaging in deceptive actions while playing with other dogs. For example, a veterinarian offered the following story when we were discussing the issue or whether or not dogs think:

I believe that dogs think. My dogs play a game called "bone." One of them will get the rawhide bone and take it over to the other one and try to get him to try and get it. Or one will try to get the bone if the other one has it. One day I was watching and the youngest one was trying to get the bone without much luck. So he goes over to the window and begins to bark like someone is coming up the driveway. The other dog drops the bone and runs over to the window and the puppy goes and gets the bone. There wasn't anyone in the driveway—it was just a trick. Maybe it was just coincidence but . . .[6]

The Dog as an Individual

Although many caretakers did see certain personality characteristics as breed related, they regularly spoke of their own dogs as unique individuals. Few informants had any trouble responding at some length to my routine request that they describe what their dog "was like." Owners currently living with multiple dogs or those who had had serial experience with dogs often made comparisons in presenting their animals' unique personal attributes. For example, an interviewee with two springer spaniels responded to my question about his dogs' personalities as follows:

It's interesting. A good way to look at this is to compare her with my other dog. I look at my older springer and she is always begging for attention. Sometimes I misinterpret that as wanting something to eat. I'll just be studying and she is happy just to sit there and have her head in my lap while I scratch her behind the ears. On the other hand, Ricky really likes attention and she seeks it. But if you're not willing to give it to her, she'll go find something else to entertain herself. She's bold, she's aggressive. At the same time she is affectionate—willing to take what you will give her.

Owners also were adept at describing their dogs' unique personal tastes. Informants typically took considerable pleasure in talking about individual likes and dislikes in food, activities playthings, and people. For example, when asked by the veterinarian whether her dog liked to chew rocks (he had noticed that the dog's teeth were quite worn), a woman described her female Doberman's special passion:

> She just loves big rocks—the bigger the better. When she finds a new one she is so happy she howls. She'll lie and chew them all day. She puts them in her water bucket, and sometimes it takes two hands to get them out.

Owners also attributed individuality to their dogs by embedding them in a readily recountable narrative history. Interviewees took great pleasure in telling stories about their dogs' exploits and how they were acquired. In somewhat more abstract terms than those used by my informants, Shapiro (1990) presented the individuality of his own dog, stressing its embeddedness in their shared historical experience:

> History informs the experience of a particular animal whether or not it can tell that history. Events in the life of an animal shape and even constitute him or her. . . . [My dog] is an individual in that he is not constituted through and I do not live toward him as a species-specific behavioral repertoire or developmental sequence. More positively, he is an individual in that he is both subject to and subject of "true historical particulars". . . . I can not replace him, nor, ethically, can I "sacrifice" him for he is a unique individual being. (p. 189)

The Dog as Emotional and Reciprocating

As mentioned above, owners typically understood their dogs as having subjective experiences in which some form of reasoning was linked with emotion. The most common theme that emerged from the encounters in the clinic and interviews with owners was that dogs are eminently emotional beings. Dogs were, for example, described as experiencing loneliness, joy, sadness, embarrassment, and anger. Interviewees often focused on this last emotional experience—anger—because it was linked to incidents in which dogs responded in ways which owners saw as indicating vindictiveness. For example, one owner described her Shar Pei puppy's displeasure at being abandoned and his playfully vengeful response to her absence:

> It's funny. Usually after I have been at work all Friday I don't go out unless I am sure that somebody is going to watch him. But one time I left him alone and when I got home HE WAS ANGRY. He just let me know. [How did he let you know?] He'd follow me around and he would look up at me and he would just bark. It was like he was yelling at me. And I would say, "What is it with you?" and when I would stop talking he would look at me and bark—like "You left me. How could you do that?" You could read it in his face. When he was younger and I would go to work and leave him during the day, he would find some way to let me know that he wasn't pleased—like he would shred all his newspapers. Every day was something new. He would move his crate, or he would flip his water dish, or something like that.

In the course of my research, I routinely asked owners whether they thought that their dogs had a "conscience." Although there was some considerable difference of opinion among informants about how effective their animals' consciences were in constraining unwanted behavior, all saw their dogs as possessing a basic sense of the rules imposed by the human members of the household. In turn, they all could offer descriptions of incidents where their animals violated the rules and subsequently responded in ways that indicated the subjective experience of guilt. Typical guilt responses entailed clearly readable body language—bowed head, tucked tail, ears down, sidelong glances. For example:

> Some major problems existed with Diz when he was younger and learning the house rules—what's proper and what's not proper. [Do you think Diz has a conscience?] He knows what he should and shouldn't do. If he gets into something. . . . He came up the stairs with a big old flower in his mouth, this silk flower, and his ears go forward. That's his look, "Am I doing something I'm not supposed to be doing?"

He'll get something in his mouth and he'll put his head down and his ears go down and his little tail is kind of wagging. It is a body language that says to me, "Am I supposed to be doing this?"

Because caretakers saw their dogs as experiencing a subjective world in which emotion played a central role, they frequently understood their relationships with the animals as revolving around emotional issues. The chief pleasure they derived from the animal-human relationship was the joy of relating to another being who consistently demonstrated love—a feeling for the other that was honestly felt and displayed and not contingent on the personal attributes or even the actions of the human other. One indication of the intensely positive quality of their relationship with their animals were the owners' perceptions that their dogs were attuned to their own emotions and responded in ways that were appropriate and indicated empathy. A man and his teenage daughter, for example, spoke of their dog's ability to read their emotions and his attempts to comfort them when they felt sad:

DAUGHTER: He's just fun. He keeps us lighthearted. And he certainly senses our moods. If you're sad and crying he will come snuggle next to you.

FATHER: He just seems to sense it somehow, you can be in a different room and be down. Recently when Mary was in her room he just seemed to know where to go. . . . He sensed that somewhere in this house—his doghouse—there was something that was not quite right. He sought Mary out and was just there. One day I was sitting on the front porch kind of blue about some things and he just snuggled in there—totally noninvasive, just "If you want to pet me, pet me. I'm here if you need me."

Owners saw their intimate relationship with their dogs as premised on intersubjectivity and shared emotion. However, caretakers defined the animal-human relationship as unique because it was free from the criticism and contingent feelings that typified relationships with human intimates. This prompted owners to feel intense emotional ties to their dogs. The centrality of emotional connectedness is obvious in this story offered by a client in the veterinary clinic as she responded to my request for her to tell me about how she acquired her dog:

A lady down the street had a litter. I went in and im-

mediately he came right over to me. It was love at first sight—he chose me. I remember it was really snowing that night and we couldn't get to the grocery store. My mother made him chicken soup. To this day he goes wild when he smells chicken soup. Every time I make it he gets half. Sometimes this annoys my roommate—"Hey, I wanted some of that." But he is more important. He's not a dog to me. He's my best friend. He loves me and I love him. When I come home from work he's happy to see me and I am happy to see him. I try to spend quality time with him every day. . . . He gives me love. He can't live without me and I can't live without him. It's so hard to see him getting old. I just don't know what I would do without him.

Affording the Dog a Social Place

Because their dogs were regarded by owners as displaying these essentially humanlike attributes, they actively included their animals in the routine exchanges and the special ritual practices of the household. The dogs typically were considered as being authentic family members.[7] Shared family routines commonly centered around feeding and food preparation, playing with or exercising the dog, and some more idiosyncratic routines that evolved in the course of the shared relationship. One interviewee, for example, referred to her own childhood experiences while describing the daily breakfast routine she shared with her newly acquired puppies:

I love these dogs. They are people dogs. We do have a set course of activities during the course of the day. We seem to meld very nicely with one another. Anywhere from 5:30 on, the dogs will start to bark which means to me that it is time to get up—the activities of the day have begun. I come downstairs and they are on the back porch waiting to come in for breakfast. I bring them in the house and I talk to them. We talk about what we are going to do today and what do you want for breakfast? Of course, they have no choice—they get the same thing every meal. But it is very important for me to talk to them, and I'm sure they know what I am saying because they will go into the pantry and get a biscuit. So I go in and get the bag of Purina®, and I show it to them and say, "This is what we're having for breakfast." They'll sit down and look, and I will go the refrigerator and get the . . . yogurt out, and I will put a spoonful in each dish, and I will always be sure that I leave a little on the spoon so the kids can lick it. I do that because it reminds me of when I was a kid, and whenever my mother made frosting she would leave a little on the spoon. That was always the highlight of frosting a cake—licking the spoon. Then I take the dishes out and they eat. I go get my coffee and read the paper and talk to them. They will walk around and poop. They will play for a while. The day has begun.

Informants regularly spoke of key ritual activities they shared with their animals. Most, for example, celebrated their dogs' birthdays. Cakes were baked, presents were bought, parties were organized, favorite foods were prepared, and other special steps were taken by owners to ritually commemorate their animals' births. The other typical ritual in which the dogs were included was that surrounding Christmas or other religious holidays. A young woman, for example, described her puppy's first Christmas:

> He just loved Christmas. Somehow he figured out which were his presents under the tree and he happily opened them all himself. He had his own ornaments on the tree—I got some that were unbreakable and put them on the bottom branches. He would take one carefully in his mouth and come running into the other room with it all proud to show it off. He loved the tree. He thought we had brought it in from the outside just for him.

At the same time that owners presented their dogs as thinking, emotional, creative, role-taking individuals they realized that conventional social definitions tended to situate dogs outside the bounds of humanness. Companion canines are customarily regarded as objects, toys, or creatures whose ostensibly human characteristics are "actually" the result of anthropomorphic projection on the part of overinvolved owners. However, intimate experience and the practical recognition that treating their animals as minded and competent coactors *worked* as an effective context in which to understand and accomplish ongoing collective action convinced owners that rigidly placing dogs outside the social category of "person" was unwarranted. The recognition that their views of their dogs violated conventional boundaries between humans and "others" and could potentially be seen as stigmatizing was apparent in the discomfort often expressed by my interviewees when I asked them if they regarded their dogs as "people." For example:

> In a sense they are [people]. They have feelings. There is a mutual caring for one another and although they may hurt one another it is done in a playful manner. Yeah, they are people, but I hesitate to say that to too many individuals because they would think I am nuts. Because I don't think many people think of animals as being people. The majority of people think of animals as pets and they are to be kept at a distance. It is very important to me to have these "kids" portrayed as part of my family. Because they are part of my family. I do treat them as people. I care about them and I would never deliberately hurt them. It is very important for me to convey to them that I do care very much for them. I'm sure they understand that.

CONCLUSION

This discussion has focused on the categories of evidence used by dog owners to include their animals inside the ostensibly rigid but actually rather flexible boundaries that divide minded humans from mindless others. The picture that emerges is of the person experiencing his or her companion dog as an authentic, reciprocating, and empathetic social actor. Canine companions are effectively involved with their caretakers in routine social exchanges premised on the mutual ability of the interactants to take the role of the other, effectively define the physical and social situation, and adjust their behavior in line with these essential determinations. In much the same way as the ablebodied construct identities of intimate human others who have severely limited abilities, caretakers use the evidence at hand to define their dogs as possessing minds, emotional lives, unique personalities, and readily identifiable tastes. These humanlike characteristics qualify dogs to be incorporated into the rituals and routines that symbolize and constitute owners' daily lives and intimate social networks.

This discussion of people and their dogs has touched on only one small segment of human interactions with nonhuman animals. Sociological attention could be directed at a wide variety of related issues and situations—for example, people's interactions with species other than canines; occupational and recreational settings incorporating animals; class, ethnic, and racial variations in human-animal interactions; and intensely interdependent relationships, such as those between people and guide dogs or other assistance animals.

Within the larger context of how animal "humanness" is constructed as a practical accomplishment, this discussion has presented mind as similarly constituted. Much like those who intimately and regularly interact with Alzheimer's patients (Gubrium 1986), the owners on whom I focused regarded their dogs as possessing minds revealed in the knowledge drawn from intimate experience. The import of this view is that it moves away from the Meadian orientation toward mind as an individual internal conversation/object. Instead, mind is reconceived as more fully social, enduring in its social classification by those who are most connected to and knowledgeable of the alingual other. Like Gubrium's (1986) Alzheimer's patient caregivers, dog owners actively engage in "doing mind": They act as agents who identify and give voice to the subjective experience of their animals. Dog caretakers also make claims for the minds of their animals because they, like the intimates of the severely retarded and those with Alzheimer's disease, can "listen with their hearts." Owners foster and value the emotional connections that bind them to their dogs. To a major degree, the intimate relationship and interaction that the owner shares with his or her animal is, as Gubrium put it, an "emotive discourse" (p. 47).

The generative context within which this emotionally focused construction of animal mind takes place involves the accretion of mutual experience of what Collins (1989) referred to as "natural rituals." Caretakers and their dogs ongoingly share activities, moods, and routines. Coordination of these natural rituals requires human and animal participants to assume the perspective of the other and, certainly in the eyes of the owners and ostensibly on the part of the dogs, results in a mutual recognition of being "together."

Most broadly then, this discussion has been about how identities are constructed. Sociogenic identities (Goode 1992) are created and projected in immediate interactional contexts. Perspectives on the other and evaluations of his/her/its capabilities are affected centrally by preexisting expectations and ideologies.

Those who routinely interact with alingual companions draw from their ongoing experience information about the other, effectively disconfirming folk beliefs, occupational ideologies, or academic doctrines that present the inability to talk as rendering one mindless and incompetent. Investigations of people's relationships with companion animals, like those focused on affiliations with speechless humans, emphasize the undue emphasis traditionally placed on language as the foundation of intimate interaction, mind and thoughtful behavior, and the generation of social identities.

This, then, is part of the promise of the investigation of people's relationships with companion animals—expansion of sociological perspectives on mind and modes of mental representation ("iconographic mind"), illumination of procedures whereby minded identities are socially generated and the interactional contexts which constrain these procedures, extension of analyses of "the other," and the opportunity to further develop our views of intimate relationships and the emotional elements which are central to these essential social bonds. Seen in this light, systematic attention to animal-human relationships offers symbolic interactionists a challenging and rewarding prospect.

NOTES

AUTHOR'S NOTE: An earlier version of this discussion was presented at the International Conference on Science and the Human-Animal Relationship, Amsterdam, March 1992. I am indebted to Patti Adler, Peter Adler, Arnold Arluke, Emma, Ann Goetting, Isis, Eleanor Lyon, Raven, Gaye Tuchman, Françoise Wemelsfelder, and two anonymous reviewers for their assistance.

1. Despite the significant power difference symbolized by the terms "owner" and "caretaker," I use these designations interchangeably throughout the article.

2. The focus of this discussion on people's relationships with dogs flows, in part from my own lifelong experience with dogs, my respect for them as a species, and the ready access afforded by my currently living intimately with them. Further, dogs are the nonhuman animals with which humans have the longest history of intimate association (Budiansky 1992; Porter 1989) and for whom people have the most intense attraction (Endenburg 1991). The dog's highly social nature accounts, in part, for this lengthy and emotional relationship with people and also means that human interaction with dogs lends itself ideally to sociological analysis.

3. My informants were not, as one anonymous reviewer skeptically put it, "wacky" and lonely people who are over-involved with their pets, dress them in silly outfits, etc. At the veterinary clinic in which I participated, clients with this sort of overinvolved orientation were identified as such, were commonly referred to as "animal nuts," and were frequently the focus of gentle derision. None of the data on which this discussion is based are drawn from observations of or conversations with this readily identifiable category of client.

4. One reviewer of an earlier version of this article expressed some concern with the apparent implication that dogs are "like" severely disabled human beings. Some discussions (e.g., Regan 1983) emphasize that infants, the mentally retarded, and others with limited or nonexistent verbal and social capacities are regarded as human and afforded a consequently appropriate moral place, whereas animals are typically denied similar considerations (see Frey 1980). I do not intend to imply necessarily that because dog owners consistently define their animal companions as minded and humanlike that, therefore, dogs and their interests are morally equivalent to those of humans. This discussion is about the social construction of the companion animal's identity in the context of intimate relationships. While not irrelevant to the issue of animal rights, this description focuses on a sociological phenomenon. The rights of companion animals and the attendant responsibilities of humans are matters of philosophical and legal debate beyond the scope of this article.

5. Of the owners interviewed by Cain (1985), 72% said that their dog usually or always had "people status" (see also Veevers 1985).

6. For interesting discussions of play interactions between dogs and people, see Mitchell and Thompson (1990, 1991) and Mechling (1989).

7. The most common categories used by caretakers to situate their relationships with their dogs was to regard them as either family members or close friends. General studies of pet owners show that this is extremely common. Somewhere between 70% (Beck and Katcher 1983) and 99% (Voith 1983) of pet caretakers define their animals as members of the family and from 30% (Nieburg and Fischer 1982) to 83% (Bryant 1982) consider the pet a "special" or "close" friend.

REFERENCES

Arluke, A. 1988. Sacrificial symbolism in animal experimentation: Object or pet? *Anthrozoos* 2:98–117.
———. 1990. Moral evaluation in medical research. *Advances in Medical Sociology* 1:189–204.
Beck, A., and A. Katcher. 1983. *Between pets and people.* New York: Putnam.
Bogdan, R., and S. Taylor. 1989. Relationships with severely disabled people: The social construction of humanness. *Social Problems* 36:135–48.
Bogdan, R., S. Taylor, B. deGrandpre, and S. Haynes. 1974. Let them eat programs: Attendants' perspectives and programming on wards in state schools. *Journal of Health and Social Behavior* 15:142–51.
Bryant, B. K. 1982. Sibling relationships in middle childhood. In *Sibling relationships: Their nature and significance across the lifespan,* edited by M. E. Lamb and B. Sutton-Smith, 87–122. Hillsdale, NJ: Lawrence Erlbaum.
Bryant, C. 1991. Deviant leisure and clandestine lifestyle: Cockfighting as a socially disvalued sport. *World Leisure and Recreation* 33:17–21.
Budiansky, S. 1992. *The covenant of the wild: Why animals chose domestication.* New York: Morrow.
Cain, A. 1985. Pets as family members. In *Pets and the family,* edited by M. Sussman, 5–10. New York: Haworth.
Clark, S. 1984. *The nature of the beast.* New York: Oxford University Press.
Cohen, J. 1989. About steaks liking to be eaten: The conflicting views of symbolic interactionists and Talcott Parsons concerning the nature of relations between persons and nonhuman objects. *Symbolic Interaction* 12:191–214.
Collins, R. 1989. Toward a neo-Meadian theory of mind. *Symbolic Interaction* 12:1–32.
Crist, E., and M. Lynch. 1990. The analyzability of human-animal interaction: The case of dog training: Paper presented at the annual meeting of the International Sociological Association, Madrid, Spain.
Denzin, N. 1989. *Interpretive interactionism.* Newbury Park, CA: Sage.
Ellis, C. 1991. Sociological introspection and emotional experience. *Symbolic Interaction* 14:23–50.
Endenburg, N. 1991. *Animals as companions.* Amsterdam: Thesis.
Frey, R. G. 1980. *Interests and rights: The case against animals.* Oxford: Clarendon.
Gallistel, C. R., ed. 1992. *Animal cognition.* Cambridge: MIT Press.
Goffman, E. 1959. *The presentation of self in everyday life.* Garden City, NY: Doubleday.
———. 1961. *Asylums.* Garden City, NY: Doubleday.
Goode, D. 1992. Who is Bobby? Ideology and method in the discovery of a Down syndrome person's competence. In *Interpreting disability: A qualitative reader,* edited by P. Ferguson, D. Ferguson, and S. Taylor, 197–213. New York: Teachers College Press.
Griffin, D. 1984. *Animal thinking.* Cambridge, MA: Oxford University Press.
Gubrium, J. 1986. The social preservation of mind: The Alzheimer's disease experience. *Symbolic Interaction* 9:37–51.
Hayano, D. 1979. Auto-ethnography: Paradigms, problems, and prospects. *Human Organization* 38:99–104.
Hearne, V. 1987. *Adam's task.* New York: Alfred A. Knopf.
Helmer, J. 1991. The horse in backstretch culture. *Qualitative Sociology* 14:175–95.

Hickrod, L. J. H., and R. L. Schmitt. 1982. A naturalistic study of interaction and frame: The pet as "family member." *Urban Life* 11:55–77.

Jordon, J. 1975. An ambivalent relationship: Dog and human in the folk culture of the rural south. *Appalachian Journal* 2:68–77.

Mead, G. H. [1934] 1964. *George Herbert Mead on social psychology.* Edited by Anselm Strauss. Chicago: University of Chicago Press.

Mechling, Jay. 1989. "Banana cannon" and other folk traditions between human and nonhuman animals. *Western Folklore* 48:312–23.

Messent, P. 1983. Social facilitation of contact with other people by pet dogs. In *New perspectives on our lives with companion animals,* edited by A. Katcher and A. Beck, 37–46. Philadelphia: University of Pennsylvania Press.

Mitchell, R., and N. Thompson. 1990. The effects of familiarity on dog-human play. *Anthrozoos* 4:24–43.

———. 1991. Projects, routines, and enticements in dog-human play. In Perspectives in ethology: Human understanding and animal awareness, edited by P.P.G. Bateson and P. Klopfer, 189–216. New York: Plenum.

Nash, J. 1989. What's in a face? The social character of the English bulldog. *Qualitative Sociology* 12:357–70.

Nieburg, H., and A. Fischer. 1982. *Pet loss.* New York: Harper & Row.

Pollner, M., and L. McDonald-Wickler. 1985. The social construction of unreality: A case of a family's attribution of competence to a severely retarded child. *Family Process* 24:241–54.

Porter, V. 1989. *Faithful companions: The alliance of man and dog.* London: Methuen.

Regan, T. 1983. *The case for animal rights.* Berkeley: University of California Press.

Ristau, C., ed. 1990. *Cognitive ethology: The minds of other animals.* Hillsdale, NJ: Lawrence Erlbaum.

Robins, D., C. Sanders, and S. Cahill. 1991. Dogs and their people: Pet-facilitated interaction in a public setting. *Journal of Contemporary Ethnography* 20:3–25.

Sanders, C. R. 1990. Excusing tactics: Social responses to the public misbehavior of companion animals. *Anthrozoos* 4:82–90.

Schutz, A. 1970. *On phenomenology and social relations.* Chicago: University of Chicago Press.

Shapiro, K. 1990. Understanding dogs through kinesthetic empathy, social construction, and history. *Anthrozoos* 3:184–95.

Spiegel, M. 1988. *The dreaded comparison: Human and animal slavery.* Philadelphia: New Society.

Terrace, H. 1987. Thoughts without words. In *Mindwaves: Thoughts on intelligence, identity and consciousness,* edited by C. Blakemore and S. Greenfield, 123–37. New York: Blackwell.

Turkle, S. 1984. *The second self.* New York: Simon & Schuster.

Vail, D. 1966. *Dehumanization and the institutional career.* Springfield, IL: Charles C Thomas.

Veevers, J. 1985. The social meaning of pets: Alternative roles for companion animals. In *Pets and the family,* edited by M. Sussman, 11–30. New York: Haworth.

Veterinary Medical Association. 1988. *The veterinary services market for companion animals.* Overland Park, KS: Charles, Charles Research Group.

Voith, V. 1983. Animal behavior problems: An overview. In *New perspectives on our lives with companion animals,* edited by A. Katcher and A. Beck, 181–86. Philadelphia: University of Pennsylvania Press.

Wieder, D. L. 1980. Behavioristic operationalism and the lifeworld: Chimpanzees and chimpanzee researchers in face-to-face interaction. *Sociological Inquiry* 50:75–103.

FURTHER READING

Bogdan, Robert and Steven J. Taylor. 1989. "Relationships with Severely Disabled People: The Social Construction of Humanness." *Social Problems* 36: 135–148.

- A study of the way mental competence is socially sustained for the disabled.

Coulter, Jeff. 1979. *The Social Construction of Mind.* Totowa, NJ: Rowman & Littlefield.

- A discussion of how the mind is socially constructed.

Coulter, Jeff. 1993. "Materialist Conceptions of Mind: A Reappraisal." *Social Research* 60: 117–142.

- A critical discussion of the materialist concept of mind.

Fox, Kathryn J. 1999. "Changing Violent Minds: Discursive Correction and Resistance in the Cognitive Treatment of Violent Offenders in Prison." *Social Problems* 36: 135–148.

- A field study of a violence-reduction program for prison inmates.

Harré, Rom and Grant Gillett. 1994. "Thoughts." Pp. 37–49 in *The Discursive Mind.* London: Sage.

- Presents the concept of thought as a way of internalizing language.

Ryle, Gilbert. 1949. *The Concept of Mind.* New York: Barnes & Noble.

- A pioneering discussion of mind as a social construct.

—————— SECTION 3 ——————

EMOTIONS

Emotions seem to be the quintessential elements of inner life. Indeed, we often hear that emotions convey our deepest truths. The mind deals in reason, but its communications may easily be twisted and altered through reasoning's calculating schemes and machinations. Feelings, we believe, simply express what they are; they are the most authentic manifestations of our inner being. We believe that we can manipulate our thoughts, but emotions are beyond control. They arise spontaneously, as in "moments of madness" or "crimes of passion." Our minds may deceive or misrepresent our hearts and emotions, but feelings, we believe, still represent the most genuine aspects of our inner lives.

If our feelings appear to come from inside, they aren't always attached to the same bodily location. We may say, for example, that anger comes in the form of a "hothead." We picture someone doing a "slow burn," with head and face so "steamed" that they may explode. We feel love in our hearts and rejection in the hollow pits of our stomachs. Hate resides in our "guts," "gnawing" at one's insides. We believe the body reveals inner feelings by way of facial expressions, posture, subtle gestures, and the like. If we notice a friend's failure to smile, her downcast expression, or lack of eye contact, we're likely to assume that she's despondent, if not depressed. We expect "body language" to speak out for emotions inside us.

As we noted earlier, emotions are often constructed in opposition to mind. Thought and reason, being features of mind, are said to be the products of a "cool head." Emotions are more passionate. There's nothing cool about rage, lust, fervor, or desire. At the same time, emotions convey meanings unfathomable to rationality. They communicate the heart and soul in ways that the mind can't comprehend. While the mind speaks, feelings are often incommunicable. One can feel "too sad for words," for example.

While it's clear that we construct our feelings as inner phenomena, we've said little about the everyday practice of emotional experience. We've left a lot of important questions unanswered. For instance, what meanings do we assign to our own feelings? How do we know that what we feel "in our guts" is hate, for example, not unrecognized love? When do we perceive facial expressions as depression, rather than boredom? How do we know that we feel "blue?" How do others interpret our expressions?

These questions lead us back to social worlds and social interaction. Social psychologists Stanley Schachter and Jerome Singer (1962) (see Further Reading) devised an experiment to answer some of these questions. In an elaborately designed deception, experimenters injected experimental subjects with adrenaline under the guise of giving them a benign vitamin supplement. In doing so, they induced a state of physical arousal for which the subjects had no immediate explanation. One might say that they felt a "raw emotion" but didn't know what it meant. As the experiment continued, the subjects began to attach various emotional labels to their states of arousal. These labels were suggested by the subjects' immediate social environments. If others with whom they interacted seemed happy, the subjects reported that they felt happy. If others were anxious or angry, the subjects "became" angry or anxious, too. The experiment was a fascinating study in the social construction of emotions.

This study also points out that emotions are also socially organized. The social environment serves up answers to everyday questions of what we feel inside. At parties, for example, we are expected to feel happy. The "feeling rules" of the occasion suggest that we construe our inner feelings as "pleasure" and take others' outward appearances as signs of enjoyment. Other circumstances present contrasting rules. Funerals, for example, encourage weeping. These situated differences suggest that the bodily sensations we experience as interior emotions are defined by our social worlds.

ABOUT THE READINGS

In an earlier reading selection, Erving Goffman stressed the importance of everyday performances for conveying the meaning of inner life. Goffman believed that we have no choice but to use the expressions that individuals "give off" to figure who and what they are. This would seem to apply to all aspects of inner life, including emotions. Goffman typically focused on strategic interaction within social encounters, but paid less attention to the emotional aspects of experience.

Arlie Russell Hochschild combines these concerns in **"Emotion Work."** Hochschild begins by noting that we "act" or manage our everyday performances in two ways—outwardly and inwardly. Following Goffman, she notes that we use body language to openly communicate our emotions to others. But Hochschild is especially concerned with how we manage our performances inwardly, an area that Goffman ignored. Here, she turns to the writings of Russian theatrical director Constantin Stanislavski for inspiration. In contrast to mere impression management, Stanislavski conceptualized inner or "deep acting," the processes by which we convince ourselves and others that the roles we play are our actual identities. The idea is that the identities we incorporate into our actions on stage become the selves we are. Being a good actor, in Stanislavski's view, was a matter of learning how to feel that one actually *is* the role one is playing. He called this "method acting."

Hochschild applies the notion of "deep acting" to social interaction. According to Hochschild, in everyday life we use a variety of methods to convince ourselves of how we feel on different occasions. If we don't experience a particular emotion in a situation that demands a particular feeling, we may be surprised, even shocked. We believe that our emotions should coincide with the emotional norms of the occasion. Feeling otherwise suggests that something is wrong with us. This leads to an important point: an occasion's emotional expectations or "feeling rules" have a significant impact on how we feel about *ourselves,* no matter what we are conveying to others. Social worlds and their emotional norms thus have implications for the deepest, most private reaches of the emotional self.

Hochschild notes that institutions are increasingly involved in emotion management. They seem to be displacing our own emotional control. Businesses, prisons, schools, and churches, among other institutions, present us with feeling rules. We all cooperate in this process, Hochschild maintains, because we willingly follow their rules. We act and feel the way we are expected to act and feel. We take jobs that require us to display all the "right" emotions. We even seek therapeutic help when we don't feel the way we're told to feel. Hochschild is especially concerned with the commercialization of deep feelings. In the organization she studied—Delta Airlines—flight attendants were asked to shape their selves and emotions to please airline customers. Hochschild worries that doing so amounts to selling our deepest experiences to others. Her chapter leaves little doubt that our inner lives are profoundly influenced by our social worlds.

"The Development of Feeling Norms Underlying Romantic Love Among Adolescent Females" visits the love lives of teenage girls. Authors **Robin W. Simon, Donna Eder,** and **Cathy Evans** focus on the feelings rules that go along with girls' romantic experiences. From in-depth interviews and participant observation in a midwestern middle school, the authors describe the feeling norms that the girls develop. The girls readily speak of these rules as they come to understand the meaning of love and romance. But it's also evident that the rules don't strictly govern their feelings. Rather, these girls take them into account, but sometimes resist them, as they come to grips with their own experiences. The authors provide us with a view of how emotions can be social without being entirely socially determined.

20 | EMOTION WORK
Arlie Russell Hochschild

MANAGING FEELING

He who always wears the mask of a friendly man must at last gain a power over friendliness of disposition, without which the expression itself of friendliness is not to be gained—and finally friendliness of disposition gains the ascendancy over him—he is benevolent.

—*Nietzsche*

"Sincerity" is detrimental to one's job, until the rules of salesmanship and business become a "genuine" aspect of oneself.

—*C. Wright Mills*

We all do a certain amount of acting. But we may act in two ways. In the first way, we try to change how we outwardly appear. As it is for the people observed by Erving Goffman, the action is in the body language, the put-on sneer, the posed shrug, the controlled sigh. This is surface acting.[1] The other way is deep acting. Here, display is a natural result of working on feeling; the actor does not try to *seem* happy or sad but rather

expresses spontaneously, as the Russian director Constantin Stanislavski urged, a real feeling that has been self-induced. Stanislavski offers this illustration from his own experience:

At a party one evening, in the house of friends, we were doing various stunts and they decided, for a joke, to operate on me. Tables were carried in, one for operating, the other supposedly containing surgical instruments. Sheets were draped around; bandages, basins, various vessels were brought.

The "surgeons" put on white coats and I was dressed in a hospital gown. They laid me on the operating table and bandaged my eyes. What disturbed me was the extremely solicitous manner of the doctors. They treated me as if I were in a desperate condition and did everything with utmost seriousness. Suddenly the thought flashed through my mind, "What if they really should cut me open?!"

Now and then a large basin made a booming noise like the toll of a funeral bell.

"Let us begin!" someone whispered.

Someone took a firm hold on my right wrist. I felt a dull pain and then three sharp stabs. I couldn't help trembling. Something that was harsh and smarted was rubbed on my wrist. Then it was bandaged, people rustled around handing things to the surgeon.

Finally, after a long pause, they began to speak out loud, they laughed, congratulated me. My eyes were unbandaged and on my left arm lay a new-born baby made out of my right hand, all swaddled in gauze. On the back of my hand they had painted a silly, infantile face.[2]

The "patient" above is not pretending to be frightened at his "operation." He is not trying to fool others. He is really scared. Through deep acting he has managed to scare himself. Feelings do not erupt spontaneously or automatically in either deep acting or surface acting. In both cases the actor has learned to intervene—either in creating the inner shape of a feeling or in shaping the outward appearance of one.

In surface acting, the expression on my face or the posture of my body feels "put on." It is not "part of me." In deep acting, my conscious mental work—the effort to imagine a tall surgeon looming over me, for example—keeps the feeling that I conjure up from being part of "myself." Thus in either method, an actor may separate what it takes to act from the idea of a central self.

But whether the separation between "me" and my face or between "me" and my feeling counts as estrangement depends on something else—the outer context. In the world of the theater, it is an honorable art to make maximum use of the resources of memory and feeling in stage performance. In private life, the same resources can be used to advantage, though to a lesser extent. But when we enter the world of profit-and-loss statements, when the psychological costs of emotional labor are not acknowledged by the company, it is then that we look at these otherwise helpful separations of "me" from my face and my feeling as potentially estranging.

Surface Acting

To show through surface acting the feelings of a Hamlet or an Ophelia, the actor operates countless muscles that make up an outward gesture. The body, not the soul, is the main tool of the trade. The actor's body evokes passion in the *audience's* soul, but the actor is only *acting* as if he had feeling. Stanislavski, the orig-

inator of a different type of acting—called Method acting—illustrates surface acting in the course of disparaging it:

> [The actor portrayed] an important general [who] accidentally found himself alone at home with nothing to do. Out of boredom he lined up all the chairs in the place so that they looked like soldiers on parade. Then he made neat piles of everything on all the tables. Next he thought of something rather spicy; after that he looked aghast over a pile of business correspondence. He signed several letters without reading them, yawned, stretched himself, and then began his silly activities all over again.
>
> All the while [the actor] was giving the text of the soliloquy with extraordinary clarity; about the nobility of highly placed persons and the dense ignorance of everyone else. He did it in a cold, impersonal way, indicating the outer form of the scene without any attempt to put life or depth into it. In some places he rendered the text with technical crispness, in others he underscored his pose, gesture, play, or emphasized some special detail of his characterization. Meantime he was watching his public out of the corner of his eye to see whether what he was doing carried across.[3]

This is surface acting—the art of an eyebrow raised here, an upper lip tightened there. The actor does not really experience the world from an imperial viewpoint, but he works at seeming to. What is on the actor's mind? Not the chairs that he has commanded to line up at attention, but the audience, which is the nearest mirror to his own surface.

Stanislavski described the limitations of surface acting as follows:

> This type of art (of the Coquelin school) is less profound than beautiful. It is more immediately effective than truly powerful; [its] form is more interesting than its content. It acts more on your sense of sound and sight than on your soul. Consequently it is more likely to delight than to move you. You can receive great impressions through this art. But they will neither warm your soul nor penetrate deeply into it. Their effect is sharp but not lasting. Your astonishment rather than your faith is aroused. Only what can be accomplished through surprising theatrical beauty or picturesque pathos lies within the bounds of this art. But delicate and deep human feelings are not subject to such technique. They call for natural emo-

tions at the very moment in which they appear before you in the flesh. They call for the direct cooperation of nature itself.[4]

Deep Acting

There are two ways of doing deep acting. One is by directly exhorting feeling, the other by making indirect use of a trained imagination.[5] Only the second is true Method acting. But in either case, Stanislavski argued, the acting of passions grows out of living in them.

People sometimes talk as much about their *efforts* to feel (even if these efforts fail) as they do about having feelings.[6] When I asked students simply to describe an event in which they experienced a deep emotion, the responses were sprinkled with such phrases as "I psyched myself up, I squashed my anger down, I tried hard not to feel disappointed, I forced myself to have a good time, I mustered up some gratitude, I put a damper on my love for her, I snapped myself out of the depression."* In the flow of experience, there were occasional common but curious shades of will—will to evoke, will to suppress, and will to somehow allow a feeling, as in "I finally let myself feel sad about it."[7]

Sometimes there was only a social custom in mind—as when a person wished to feel sad at a funeral. But other times there was a desperate inner desire to avoid pain. Herbert Gold describes a man's effort to prevent himself from feeling love for a wife he no longer has:

> He fought against love, he fought against grief, he fought against anger. They were all linked. He reminded himself when touched, moved, overwhelmed by the sights and smell of her, or a sight and smell which recalled her, or passing their old house or eating their foods, or walking on their streets; don't do this, don't feel. First he succeeded in removing her from the struggle. . . . He lost his love. He lost his anger. She became a limited idea, like a newspaper death notice. He did not lose her entirely, but chipped away at it; don't, don't, don't, he would remind himself in the middle of the night; don't feel; and then dream what he could.[8]

These are almost like orders to a contrary horse (whoa, giddyup, steady now), attempts to exhort feeling as if feeling can listen when it is talked to.† And sometimes it does. But such coaching only addresses the capacity to duck a signal, to turn away from what evokes feeling.[9] It does not move to the home of the imagery, to that which gives power to a sight, a sound, or a smell. It does not involve the deeper work of retraining the imagination.

Ultimately, direct prods to feeling are not based on a deep look into how feeling works, and for this reason Stanislavski advised his actors against them: "On the stage there cannot be, under any circumstances, action which is directed immediately at the arousing of a feeling for its own sake. . . . Never seek to be jealous, or to make love, or to suffer for its own sake. All such feelings are the result of something that has gone before. Of the thing that goes before you should think as you can. As for the result, it will produce itself."[10]

Stanislavski's alternative to the direct prodding of feeling is Method acting. Not simply the body, or immediately accessible feeling, but the entire world of fantasy, of subconscious and semiconscious memory, is conceived as a precious resource.‡

If he were in the hands of Stanislavski, the man

---

* In each instance the individual indicates awareness of acting on a feeling. A passive stance toward feeling was reflected in other examples: "I found myself filled with pride," "My stomach did a trapeze act all by itself."

† It also presupposes an *aspiration* to feel. The man who fought against love wanted to feel the same about his former wife as he thought she felt about him; if he was a limited idea to her, he wanted her to be that for him. A courtly lover in twelfth-century France or a fourteen-year-old American female rock fan might have been more disposed to aspire to one-sided love, to want it that way. Deep acting comes with its social stories about what we aspire to feel.

‡ In *An Actor Prepares,* Stanislavski points out an apparent contradiction: "We are supposed to create under inspiration; only our subconscious gives us inspiration; yet we apparently can use this subconscious only through our consciousness, which kills it" (1965, p. 13). The solution to this problem is the indirect method. The subconscious is induced. As Stanislavski notes: "The aim of the actor's preparation is to cross the threshold of the subconscious. . . . Beforehand we have 'true-seeming feeling,' afterwards 'sincerity of emotion.' On this side of it, we have the simplicity of a limited fantasy; beyond, the simplicity of the larger imagination, [where] the creative process differs each time it is repeated" (p. 267).

who wanted to fight off love for his former wife would approach his task differently. First, he would use "emotion memory": he would remember all the times he had felt furious at his wife's thoughtlessness or cruelty. He would focus on one most exasperating instance of this, reevoking all the circumstances. Perhaps she had forgotten his birthday, had made no effort to remember, and failed to feel badly about it afterwards. Then he would use the "if" supposition and say to himself: "How would I feel about her if this is what she really was like?" He would not prompt himself not to feel love; rather he would keep alive the cruel episode of the forgotten birthday and sustain the "if." He would not, then, fall naturally out of love. He would actively conduct himself out of love through deep acting.

The professional actor simply carries this process further for an artistic purpose. His goal should be to accumulate a rich deposit of "emotion memories"—memories that recall feelings. Thus, Stanislavski explains, the actor must relearn how to remember:

> Two travelers were marooned on some rocks by high tide. After their rescue they narrated their impressions. One remembered every little thing he did; how, why, and where he went, where he climbed up and where he climbed down; where he jumped up or jumped down. The other man had no recollection of the place at all. He remembered only the emotions he felt. In succession came delight, apprehension, fear, hope, doubt, and finally panic.[11]

To store a wealth of emotion memories, the actor must remember experiences emotively. But to remember experiences emotively, he or she must first experience them in that way too, perhaps with an eye to using the feelings later.* So the conceiving of emotion memory as a noun, as something one *has,* brings with

it a conceiving of memory and of spontaneous experience itself as also having the qualities of a usable, nounlike thing. Feeling—whether at the time, or as it is recalled, or as it is later evoked in acting—is an object. It may be a valuable object in a worthy pursuit, but it is an object nonetheless.

Some feelings are more valuable objects than others, for they are more richly associated with other memorable events; a terrifying train ride may recall a childhood fall or a nightmare. Stanislavski recalled, for example, seeing an old beggar killed by a trolley car but said that the memory of this event was less valuable to him as an actor than another one:

> It was long ago—I came upon an Italian, leaning over a dead monkey on the sidewalk. He was weeping and trying to push a bit of orange rind into the animal's mouth. It would seem that this scene had affected my feelings more than the death of the beggar. It was buried more deeply into my memory. I think that if I had to stage the street accident I would search for emotional material for my part in my memory of the scene of the Italian with the dead monkey rather than in the tragedy itself.[12]

But emotion memory is not enough. The memory, like any image drawn to mind, must *seem real now.* The actor must *believe* that an imagined happening *really is happening now.* To do this, the actor makes up an "as if," a supposition. He actively suspends the usual reality testing, as a child does at play, and allows a make-believe situation to seem real. Often the actor can manage only a precarious belief in *all* of an illusion, and so he breaks it up into sturdier small details, which taken one by one are easier to believe: "*if* I were in a terrible storm" is chopped up into "*if* my eyebrows were wet and *if* my shoes were soaked." The big *if* is broken into many little ones.[13]

The furnishings of the physical stage—a straight horse-hair chair, a pointer leaning against the wall—are used to support the actor's *if.* Their purpose is not to influence the audience, as in surface acting, but to help convince the person doing deep acting that the *if* events are really happening.

---

* The mind acts as a magnet to reusable feeling. Stanislavski advises actors: "Imagine that you have received some insult in public, perhaps a slap in the face, that makes your cheek burn whenever you think of it. The inner shock was so great that it blotted out all the details of this harsh incident. But some insignificant thing will instantly revive the memory of the insult, and the emotion will recur with redoubled violence. Your cheek will grow red or you will turn pale and your heart will pound. If you possess such sharp and easily aroused emotional material, you will find it easy to transfer it to the stage and play a scene analogous to the experience

you had in real life which left such a shocking impression on you. To do this you will not need any technique. It will play itself because nature will help you" (1965, p. 176).

Everyday Deep Acting

In our daily lives, offstage as it were, we also develop feeling for the parts we play; and along with the workaday props of the kitchen table or office restroom mirror we also use deep acting, emotion memory, and the sense of "as if this were true" in the course of trying to feel what we sense we ought to feel or want to feel. Usually we give this little thought, and we don't name the momentary acts involved. Only when our feeling does not fit the situation, and when we sense this as a problem, do we turn our attention to the inward, imagined mirror, and ask whether we are or should be acting.

Consider, for example, the reaction of this young man to the unexpected news that a close friend had suffered a mental breakdown:

> I was shocked, yet for some reason I didn't think my emotions accurately reflected the bad news. My roommate appeared much more shaken than I did. *I thought that I should be more upset by the news than I was.* Thinking about this conflict I realized that one reason for my emotional state might have been the spatial distance separating me from my friend, who was in the hospital hundreds of miles away. I then tried to focus on his state . . . and began to picture my friend as I thought he then existed.

Sensing himself to be less affected than he should be, he tried to visualize his friend—perhaps in gray pajamas, being led by impassive attendants to the electric-shock room. After bringing such a vivid picture to mind, he might have gone on to recall smaller private breakdowns in his own life and thereby evoked feelings of sorrow and empathy. Without at all thinking of this as acting, in complete privacy, without audience or stage, the young man can pay, in the currency of deep acting, his emotional respects to a friend.

Sometimes we try to stir up a feeling we wish we had, and at other times we try to block or weaken a feeling we wish we did not have. Consider this young woman's report of her attempt to keep feelings of love in check.

> Last summer I was going with a guy often, and I began to feel very strongly about him. I knew, though, that he had broken up with a girl a year ago because she had gotten too serious about him, so I was afraid to show any emotion. I also was afraid of being hurt,

so I attempted to change my feelings. *I talked myself into not caring about him* . . . but I must admit it didn't work for long. To sustain this feeling I had to *invent bad things about him and concentrate on them* or continue to tell myself he didn't care. It was a hardening of emotions, I'd say. It took a lot of work and was unpleasant because I had to concentrate on anything I could find that was irritating about him.

In this struggle she hit upon some techniques of deep acting. "To invent bad things about him and concentrate on them" is to make up a world she could honestly respond to. She could tell herself, "If he is self-absorbed, then he is unlovable, and *if* he is unlovable, which at the moment I believe, then I don't love him." Like Stanislavski during his make-believe "operation," she wavers between belief and doubt, but she nevertheless reaches for the inner token of feeling that it is her part to offer. She wavers between belief and doubt in her beloved's "flaws." But her temporary effort to prevent herself from falling in love may serve the grander purpose of waiting for him to reciprocate. So in a way, her act of momentary restraint, as she might see it, was an offering to the future of their love.

We also set a personal stage with personal props, not so much for its effect on our audience as for the help it gives us in believing in what we imagine. Serving almost as stage props, often, are fellow members of the cast—friends or acquaintances who prod our feelings in a desired direction. Thus, a young woman who was trying not to love a man used her supporting cast of friends like a Greek chorus: "I could only say horrible things about him. My friends thought he was horrible because of this and reinforced my feelings of dislike for him."

Sometimes the stage setting can be a dismayingly powerful determinant of feeling. Consider this young woman's description of her ambivalent feelings about a priest forty years her senior: "I started trying to make myself like him and fit the whole situation. When I was with him I did like him, but then I'd go home and write in my journal how much I couldn't stand him. I kept changing my feelings." What she felt while facing the priest amid the props of a living room and two cups of afternoon tea collapsed when she left that setting. At home with her diary, she felt free of her obligation to please her suitor by trying to like him. There, she felt another obligation—to be honest to her diary. What changed between the tea party and the diary session was her sense of which feeling was real. Her sense of realness seemed to shift disconcertingly with the stage setting, as if her feeling of liking the priest gained or lost its status as "real" depending on its context.

Sometimes the realness of a feeling wavers more through time. Once a love story is subject to doubt, the story is rewritten; falling in love comes to seem like the work of convincing each other that this had been true love. A nineteen-year-old Catholic college student recalled:

> Since we both were somewhat in need of a close man-woman relationship and since we were thrown together so often (we lived next door to each other and it was summertime), I think that we convinced ourselves that we loved each other. I had to try to convince myself that I loved him in order to justify or somehow make "right" sleeping with him, which I never really wanted to do. We ended up living together supposedly because we "loved" each other. But I would say instead that we did it for other reasons which neither of us wanted to admit. What pretending that I loved him meant to me was having a secret nervous breakdown.

This double pretending—pretending to him and pretending to herself that she loved him—created two barriers to reflection and spontaneous feeling. First, she tried to feel herself in love—intimate, deeply enhanced, and exquisitely vulnerable—in the face of contrary evidence. Second, she tried not to feel irritation, boredom, and a desire to leave. By this effort to orchestrate feeling—to keep some feelings above consciousness and some below, and to counter inner resistances on a daily basis—she tried to suppress reality testing. She both nurtured an illusion about her lover and doubted the truth of it. It was the strain of this effort that led to her "secret nervous breakdown."

In the theater, the illusion that the actor creates is recognized beforehand as an illusion by actor and audience alike. But in real life we more often participate in the illusion. We take it into ourselves, where it struggles against the sense we ordinarily make of things. In life, illusions are subtle, changeable, and hard to define with certainty, and they matter far more to our sanity.

The other side of the matter is to live with a dropped illusion and yet want to sustain it. Once an illusion is clearly defined as an illusion, it becomes a lie. The work of sustaining it then becomes redefined as lying to oneself so that one becomes self-stigmatized as a liar. This dilemma was described by a desperate wife and mother of two:

> I am desperately trying to change my feelings of being trapped [in marriage] into feelings of wanting to remain with my husband voluntarily. Sometimes I think I'm succeeding—sometimes I know I haven't. *It means I have to lie to myself and know I am lying.* It means I don't like myself very much. It also makes me wonder whether or not I'm a bit of a masochist. I feel responsible for the children's future and for my husband's, and there's the old self-sacrificer syndrome. I know what I'm doing. I just don't know how long I can hold out.

On stage, the actress doing Method acting tries to delude herself; the more voluntary, the more richly detailed the lie, the better. No one thinks she actually *is* Ophelia or even pretending to be. She is borrowing Ophelia's reality or something from her own personal life that resembles it. She is trying to delude herself and create an illusion for the audience, who accept it as a gift. In everyday life there is also illusion, but how to define it is chronically unclear; the matter needs constant attention, continual questioning and testing. In acting, the illusion starts out as an illusion. In everyday life, that definition is always a possibility and never quite a certainty. On stage, the illusion leaves as it came, with the curtain. Off stage, the curtains close, too, but not at our bidding, not when we expect, and often to our dismay. On stage, illusion is a virtue. But in real life, the lie to oneself is a sign of human weakness, of bad faith. It is far more unsettling to discover that we have fooled ourselves than to discover that we have been fooling others.

This is because for the professional actor the illusion takes on meaning only in relation to a professional role whereas in real life the illusion takes on meaning with reference to living persons. When in private life we recognize an illusion we have held, we form a different relation to what we have thought of as our self. We come to distrust our sense of what is true, as we know it through feeling. And if our feelings have lied to us, they cannot be part of our good, trustworthy, "true" self. To put it another way, we may recognize that we distort reality, that we deny or suppress truths, but we rely on an observing ego to comment on these unconscious processes in us and to try to find out what is going on despite them.

At the same time, everyday life clearly requires us to do deep acting. We must dwell on what it is that we want to feel and on what we must do to induce the feeling. Consider, for example, this young man's efforts to counter an apathy he dreaded:

> I was a star halfback in high school. [But in my senior year] before games I didn't feel the surge of adrenalin—in a word, I wasn't "psyched-up." This was due to emotional difficulties I was experiencing at the time, and still experience. Also, I had been an A student but my grades were dropping. Because in the past I had been a fanatical, emotional, intense player—a "hitter," recognized by coaches as a hard worker and a player with "desire"—this was very upsetting. I did everything I could to get myself "up." I tried to be outwardly rah-rah, I tried to get myself scared of my opponents—anything to get the adrenalin flowing. I tried to look nervous and intense before games, so at least the coaches wouldn't catch on . . . when actually I was mostly bored, or in any event, not "up." Before one game I remember wishing I was in the stands watching my cousin play for his school.

This young man felt a slipping sense of realness; he was clear that he felt "basically" bored, not "really" up. What also seemed real to him was the sense that he should feel driven to win and that he wanted to feel that way. What also felt real to him in hindsight was his effort to seem to the coaches like a "hitter" (surface acting) and his effort to make himself fearful of his opponents (deep acting).

As we look back at the past, we may alternate between two understandings of "what really happened." According to one, our feeling was genuine and spontaneous. According to the other, it seemed genuine and spontaneous, but in fact it was covertly managed. In doubt about which understanding will ultimately make sense, we are led to ask about our present feelings: "Am I acting now? How do I know?" One basic appeal of the theater is that the stage decides that question for us: we know for sure who is acting.

In sum, what distinguishes theater from life is not illusion, which both have, need, and use. What distinguishes them is the honor accorded to illusion, the ease in knowing when an illusion *is* an illusion, and the consequences of its use in making feeling. In the theater, the illusion dies when the curtain falls, as the audience knew it would. In private life, its consequences are unpredictable and possibly fateful: a love is killed, a suitor rejected, another hospital bed filled.

Institutional Emotion Management

The professional actress has a modest say over how the stage is assembled, the props selected, and the other characters positioned, as well as a say over her own presence in the play. This is also true in private life. In both cases the person is the *locus* of the acting process.

But something more operates when institutions are involved, for within institutions various elements of acting are taken away from the individual and replaced by institutional mechanisms. The locus of acting, of emotion management, moves up to the level of the institution. Many people and objects, arranged according to institutional rule and custom, together accomplish the act. Companies, prisons, schools, churches—institutions of virtually any sort—assume some of the functions of a director and alter the relation of actor to director. Officials in institutions believe they have done things right when they have established illusions that foster the desired feelings in workers, when they have placed parameters around a worker's emotion memories, a worker's use of the *as if*. It is not that workers are allowed to see and think as they like and required only to show feeling (surface acting) in institutionally approved ways. The matter would be simpler and less alarming if it stopped there. But it doesn't. Some institutions have become very sophisticated in the techniques of deep acting; they suggest how to imagine and thus how to feel.

As a farmer puts blinders on his workhorse to guide its vision forward, institutions manage how we feel.* One of the ways in which they do this is to pre-arrange what is available to the worker's view. A teaching hospital, for example, designs the stage for medical students facing their first autopsy. Seeing the eye of a dead person might call to mind a loved one or oneself; to see this organ coldly violated by a knife might lead a student to faint, or flee in horror, or quit medicine then and there. But this seldom happens. In their study of medical training, Lief and Fox report:

> The immaculate, brightly lit appearance of the operating room, and the serious professional behavior required, justify and facilitate a clinical and impersonal attitude toward death. Certain parts of the body are kept covered, particularly the face and genitalia, and the hands, which are so strongly connected with human, personal qualities, are never dissected. Once the vital organs have been taken out, the body is removed from the room, bringing the autopsy down to tissues, which are more easily depersonalized. The deft touch, skill, and professional attitude of the prosector makes the procedure neater and more bloodless than might otherwise be the case, and this increases intellectual interest and makes it possible to approach the whole thing scientifically rather than emotionally. Students appear to avoid talking about the autopsy, and when they do talk about it, the discussion is impersonal and stylized. Finally, whereas in laboratory dissection humor appears to be a widespread and effective emotional control device, it is absent in the autopsy room, perhaps because the death has been too recent and [humor] would appear too insensitive.[14]

Covering the corpse's face and genitalia, avoiding the hands, later removing the body, moving fast, using white uniforms, and talking in uniformed talk—these

are customs designed to manage the human feeling that threatens order.†

Institutions arrange their front stages. They guide the way we see and what we are likely to feel spontaneously. Consider the inevitable institutional halls, especially those near the areas where people wait. Often in medical, academic, and corporate settings we find on the walls a row of photographs or oil paintings of persons in whom we should have full confidence. Consider Allen Wheelis's description of a waiting-room picture of a psychiatrist:

> With the crossed legs you claim repose, tranquility. . . . Everything is under control. With the straight shoulders you say dignity, *status*. No matter what comes up, this guy has nothing to fear, is calmly certain of his worth and of his ability. With the head turned sharply to the left you indicate that someone is claiming his attention. No doubt hundreds of people would like this guy's attention. He was engrossed in his book, but now he's being interrupted. And what was he reading? *Playboy? Penthouse?* The funny papers? Oh, no; he's into something heavy. We can't see the title, but we know it's plenty important. . . . Usually it's Osler's *Principles and Practice of Medicine.* And the finger marking his place? Why, he's been at it so intently, so diligently, he's already halfway through. And the other hand, lying so lightly, so gracefully, on the book. That shows intelligence, experience, mastery. He's not scratching his head trying to figure out what the hell the author is getting at. . . . Anytime you knock on this guy's door, you'll find him just like that, dressed to the nines, tie up tight in his buttoned-down collar, freshly pressed jacket, deeply immersed in one of these heavy tomes.[15]

The professional's own office, of course, should

---

* We commonly assume that institutions are called in when individual controls fail: those who cannot control their emotions are sent to mental hospitals, homes for disturbed children, or prisons. But in looking at the matter this way, we may ignore the fact that individual failures of control often signal a prior institutional failure to shape feeling. We might ask instead what sort of church, school, or family influence was unavailable to the parents of institutionalized patients, who presumably tried to make their children into adequate emotion managers.

---

† Scientific writing, like scientific talk, has a function similar to that of covering the face and genitalia. It is an extension of institutional control over feeling. The overuse of passive verb forms, the avoidance of "I," the preference for Latinate nouns, and for the abstract over the concrete, are customs that distance the reader from the topic and limit emotionality. In order to seem scientific, writers obey conventions that inhibit emotional involvement. There is a purpose in such "poor" writing.

be done up in a pleasant but impersonal decor, not too messy and colorful but not too cold and bare; it should reflect just the amount of professional warmth the doctor or lawyer or banker himself ought to show. Home is carefully distinguished from office, personal flair from professional expertise. This stage setting is intended to inspire our confidence that the service is, after all, worth paying a lot for.

Airlines seem to model "stage sets" on the living rooms seen on daytime television serials; the Muzak tunes, the TV and movie screens, and the smiling flight attendants serving drinks are all calculated to "make you feel at home." Even fellow passengers are considered part of the stage. At Delta Airlines, for example, flight attendants in training are advised that they can prevent the boarding of certain types of passengers—a passenger with "severe facial scars," for example. The instructor elaborated: "You know, the other passengers might be reminded of an airplane crash they had read about." The bearer of a "severe facial scar," then, is not deemed a good prop. His or her effect on the emotion memory of other money-paying passengers might be all wrong.*

Sometimes props are less important than influential directors. Institutions authorize stage directors to coach the hired cast in deep acting. Buttressed with the authority of a high office or a specialized degree, the director may make suggestions that are often interpreted at lower levels as orders.

The director's role may be simple and direct, as in the case of a group of college students training to be clinicians in a camp for emotionally disturbed children, studied by Albert Cohen. These students, who composed the junior staff, did not know at first how they were supposed to feel or think about the wild behavior of the disturbed children. But in the director's chair sat the senior counselors, advising them on how to see the children: "They were expected to see the children as victims of uncontrollable impulses somehow related to their harsh and depriving backgrounds,

and in need of enormous doses of kindliness and indulgence in order to break down their images of the adult world as hateful and hostile."[16]

They were also taught how to *feel* properly toward them: "The clinician must never respond in anger or with intent to punish, although he might sometimes have to restrain or even isolate children in order to prevent them from hurting themselves or one another. Above all, the staff were expected to be warm and loving and always to be governed by a 'clinical attitude.'"[17] To be warm and loving toward a child who kicks, screams, and insults you—a child whose problem is unlovability—requires emotion work. The art of it is passed down from senior to junior counselor, as in other settings it passes from judge to law clerk, professor to graduate student, boss to rising subordinate.

The professional worker will implicitly frown on certain uses of emotion memory. The senior counselor of disturbed children will not allow herself to think, "Tommy reminds me of the terrible brat I had to babysit when I was thirteen, and if he's like that I'll end up hating him." Instead, she will reconceive Tommy in another way: "Tommy is really like the other kid I used to babysit when I was fourteen. He was difficult but I got to like him, so I expect I'll get to like Tommy despite the way he pushes me away suspiciously."

A proper way to *experience* the child, not simply a proper way to seem to feel, was understood by everyone as part of the job. And Cohen reports that the young caretakers did admirably: "To an extraordinary degree they fulfilled these expectations, including, I am convinced, the expectation that they *feel* sympathy and tenderness and love toward their charges, despite their animal-like behavior. The speed with which these college students learned to behave in this way cannot be easily explained in terms of gradual learning through a slow process of 'internalization.'"[18]

In more circuitous ways, too, the formal rules that prop up an institution set limits to the emotional possibilities of all concerned. Consider, for example, the rules that guard access to information. Any institution with a bit of hierarchy in it must suppress democracy to some extent and thus must find ways to suppress envy and resentment at the bottom. Often this is done by enforcing a hierarchy of secrets. The customary

---

* I heard the rationale for this company regulation discussed in class on February 19, 1980. (It was also stated in the training manual.) Whether it has ever been enforced, and with what result, I don't know.

rule of secrecy about pay is a case in point: those at the bottom are almost never allowed to know how much money those at the top get each month, nor, to the fullest extent, what privileges they enjoy. Also kept secret are deliberations that determine when and to what level an individual is likely to rise or fall within the organization. As one University of California administrative memorandum explained: "Letters concerning the disposition of tenure review cases will be kept confidential, in order that those involved not hold grudges or otherwise harbor resentment toward those unfavorably disposed in their case." In this situation, where the top depends upon being protected from the middle and the bottom—from "those involved" as the memo put it—leaks can cause panic.[19]

Finally, drugs of various sorts can be used to stimulate or depress mood, and companies are not above engineering their use. Just as the plow displaced manual labor, in some reported instances drug use seems to be displacing emotional labor. The labor that it takes to withstand stress and boredom on the job can be performed, some workers have found, by Darvon and Valium. Workers at the American Telephone and Telegraph Company, for example, found that nurses in its medical department gave out Valium, Darvon, codeine, and other drugs free and without prescription. There are a number of ways, some of them company-sponsored, to "have a nice day" on the job, as part of the job.[20]

An Instrumental Stance Toward Feeling

The stage actor makes the finding and expressing of feeling his main professional task. In Stanislavski's analogy, he seeks it with the dedication of a prospector for precious metal. He comes to see feeling as the object of painstaking internal mining, and when he finds it, he processes it like gold. In the context of the theater, this use of feeling is considered exciting and honorable. But what happens when deep and surface acting become part of a day's work, part of what we sell to an employer in return for a day's wage? What happens when our feelings are processed like raw ore?

In the Recurrent Training class for experienced flight attendants at Delta Airlines, I observed borrowings from all types of acting. These can be seen in the ways students answered when the instructor asked how they tried to stop feeling angry and resentful at passengers:

> If I pretend I'm feeling really up, sometimes I actually get into it. The passenger responds to me as though I were friendly, and then more of me responds back [surface acting].
>
> Sometimes I purposely take some deep breaths. I try to relax my neck muscles [deep acting with the body].
>
> I may just talk to myself: "Watch it. Don't let him get to you. Don't let him get to you. Don't let him get to you." And I'll talk to my partner and she'll say the same thing to me. After a while, the anger goes away [deep acting, self-prompting].
>
> I try to remember that if he's drinking too much, he's probably scared of flying. I think to myself, "he's like a little child." Really, that's what he is. And when I see him that way, I don't get mad that he's yelling at me. He's like a child yelling at me then. [deep acting, Method acting].

Surface and deep acting in a commercial setting, unlike acting in a dramatic, private, or therapeutic context, make one's face and one's feelings take on the properties of a resource. But it is not a resource to be used for the purposes of art, as in drama, or for the purposes of self-discovery, as in therapy, or for the pursuit of fulfillment, as in everyday life. It is a resource to be used to make money. Outside of Stanislavski's parlor, out there in the American marketplace, the actor may wake up to find himself actually operated upon.

FEELING RULES

> A restless vitality wells up as we approach thirty.
>
> —*Gail Sheehy*

> Measuring experience against a normative model set up by doctors, people will be as troubled by departures from the norm as they are troubled by [Gail Sheehy's] "predictable crises" themselves, against which medical norms are intended to provide reassurance.
>
> —*Christopher Lasch*

Since feeling is a form of pre-action, a script or a moral stance toward it is one of culture's most powerful tools for directing action.[21] How do we sense these scripts or, as I shall call them, feeling rules? In this chapter we discuss the various ways in which all of us identify a feeling rule and the ways in which we discover that we are out of phase with it—ways which include noting the duration, strength, time, and placement of a feeling. We explore the areas of love, hate, grief, and jealousy, to which these private rules apply.

The purpose of this effort is to expose the outlines of a private emotion system. This system involves emotion work (deep acting). Feeling rules are what guide emotion work by establishing the sense of entitlement or obligation that governs emotional exchanges. This emotion system works privately, often free of observation. It is a vital aspect of deep private bonds and also affords a way of talking about them. It is a way of describing how—as parents and children, wives and husbands, friends and lovers—we intervene in feelings in order to shape them.

What are feeling rules? How do we know they exist? How do they bear on deep acting? We may address these questions by focusing on the pinch between "what I do feel" and "what I should feel," for at this spot we get our best view of emotional convention. The following snapshots of people caught in moments of emotional deviance, moments in which they stand naked of convention, are not exactly candid shots since people pose even in their confessions. But they are clear pictures of how people see their own actions in relation to emotional convention. And just as we may infer from conscious emotion work the possibility of unconscious forms of it, so we may infer the possibility of unconscious feeling rules, harder to get at but just as probably there.[22]

How do we recognize a feeling rule? We do so by inspecting how we assess our feelings, how other people assess our emotional display, and by sanctions issuing from ourselves and from them.[23] Different social groups probably have special ways in which they recognize feeling rules and give rule reminders, and the rules themselves probably vary from group to group.[24] On the whole, I would guess that women, Protestants, and middle-class people cultivate the habit of suppressing their own feelings more than men, Catholics, and lower-class people do. Our culture invites women, more than men, to focus on feeling rather than action; it invites Protestants into an in-

ner dialogue with God, without benefit of church, sacrament, or confession as an intermediary structure; and it invites those in middle-class occupations to manage feeling in service jobs. To the extent that it does these things, the very ways in which we acknowledge feeling rules reflect where we stand on the social landscape. Indeed, the amount of interest people have in feeling rules and emotion work may tend to follow these social lines.

How do we recognize a rule reminder? We can experience it as a private mumbling to ourselves, the voice of a watchful chorus standing to the side of the main stage on which we act and feel.* We also receive rule reminders from others who ask us to *account* for what we feel.[25] A friend might ask, "Why do you feel depressed? You've just won the prize you've always wanted." Such friends are generally silent when we feel as they expect us to, when events visibly explain our feeling. A call for account implies that emotional conventions are not in order and must be brought up to consciousness for repair—or, at least in the case of weak conventions, for a checkup. A wink or ironic tone of voice may change the spirit of a rule reminder. Such gestures add a meta-statement: "That's the feeling rule, all right, but we're disregarding it, aren't we?" We are reminded of the rule by being asked to disregard it.

We also know feeling rules by the way others react to what they think we are feeling. These external reactions or "claims"—both as they are intended and as they are interpreted—vary in directness or strength. Some claims are both direct and strong: "You should be ashamed of yourself." "You have no right to feel so jealous when we agreed to an open marriage." "You ought to be grateful considering all I've done for you." Other claims may be presented in the guise of questions, as in "Aren't you just thrilled about Evelyn's news?" Such a question may actually be meant and understood as a claim, a statement of what another ex-

---

* We may also believe *that* there shouldn't be a feeling rule in a given instance. One father, for example, reported: "When Jeffrey was little, and squalled interminably one morning—I felt like throwing him on the floor. I was horrified at my rage. But I told myself, it's all right to feel the rage. It's just bad to act on it."

pects. Such questions as "Hey, isn't this fantastic music?" or "Isn't this an incredible party?" remind us of what the world expects of the heart. Rule reminders also appear disguised as statements about what we supposedly *do* feel, as in "You're just as pleased as punch, I know you are."

Sanctions common on the social scene—cajoling, chiding, teasing, scolding, shunning—often come into play as forms of ridicule or encouragement that lightly correct feeling and adjust it to convention. Mainly it is the gentle, benign gesture that puts a feeling into line. For instance, one woman recalled: "When I got the news that my father had died, I found that I couldn't cry over my loss. Everyone of course expected me to cry, and words such as '*It's okay to let go*' made me cry just by their suggesiveness."[26]

Through the idea of "inappropriate affect," psychiatrists have had a lot to say about feeling rules. For them, "inappropriate affect" means the absence of *expected* affect, and from it they infer that a patient is reacting to an event in an unexpected way. When a patient has "an idiosyncratic conceptualization of the event," the psychiatrist will inspect the patient's other experiences, especially childhood ones, in order to find something that might account for the feeling.[27]

What is taken for granted all along is that there are rules or norms according to which feelings may be judged appropriate to accompanying events.[28] Like the rest of us, psychiatrists use cultural measures of appropriateness. We, like them, seek reasons for feelings that stand out as strange.

But the psychiatrist and the sociologist take different viewpoints on feelings that do not fit the conventions designed for them. We can get at this difference by comparing how a psychiatrist and a sociologist might analyze the following report by a recent bride:

> My marriage ceremony was chaos, unreal, completely different than I imagined it would be. Unfortunately, we rehearsed at eight o'clock the morning of the wedding. I had imagined that everyone would know what to do, but they didn't. That made me nervous. My sister didn't help me get dressed or flatter me, and no one in the dressing room helped until I asked. I was depressed. I wanted to be so happy on our wedding day. I never ever dreamed how anyone could cry at their wedding. That's the happiest day of one's

life. I couldn't believe that some of my best friends couldn't make it to my wedding. So I started out to the church with all these little things I always thought would not happen at my wedding going through my mind. I broke down—I cried going to the wedding. I thought, "Be happy for the friends, the relatives, the presents." But I finally said in my mind, "Hey, people aren't getting married, *you* are." From down the long aisle we looked at each other's eyes. His love for me changed my whole being from that point. When we joined arms I was relieved. The tension was gone. From then on, it was beautiful. It was indescribable.

A psychiatrist might respond to this roughly as follows: "On the face of it, the young woman seems anxious. In her anxiety, the rules seem overcathected (unduly important to her). The cause of her anxiety may lie in her ambivalence about marriage, which might be related to childhood impressions of her own parents' marriage or perhaps to the sexual aspects of it. I would need to know more to say for sure."

A sociologist would look at the wedding from quite another point of view. To begin with, he or she would consider the ceremony as a ritual event of significance to the assembled witnesses as well as to the bride and groom; attention would be paid to where various relatives and friends sat and how involved each person seemed to be. But the sociologist could also be concerned with what happened in the realm lying between feelings and the external events of the ritual—the realm of feeling rules and emotion management. In preparing for and participating in the wedding ritual, the bride assumes the right and obligation to experience a certain skew of vision and a certain elation. Rights and obligations also apply to her outward display of joy and radiance.* Drawing on her

---

* This raises the issue of display and display rules. It raises the issue of the "falseness," as distinct from the "wrongness," of a feeling. Wrongness refers to a discrepancy between "what I *do* feel and think" and "what I *should* feel and think." Falseness refers to a discrepancy between "what I *do* feel and think" and "what I *appear* to feel and think." For example, the bride may say "I'm so happy" with such a forced smile that she seems false to others. One of the display rules at weddings is that the bride should seem natural and unforced.

understanding of the general rules for how brides should see and feel and seem, the bride makes herself up. She acts like a bride. When everything goes well, she experiences a unity between the event (the wedding), the appropriate way to think about it (to take it seriously), and the proper way to feel about it (happy, elated, enhanced). When that happens, the ritual works.

But for the bride considered here, the ritual almost fails. As she sees it, she should feel beautiful but in fact she doesn't. She should feel happy but in fact she feels depressed and upset. The "ought" of the feeling struggles with the "is." Her notion of a bride's-way-of-seeing a wedding and a bride's-way-of-feeling about it is for a time unhinged from the factual role of bride and detached from the occasion of the wedding. What she imagined or hoped might be her experience of the wedding ("the happiest day of one's life") made her privately miserable.

Almost any emotional convention makes room for lapses and departures. Thus while the bride may aspire to feel central, beautiful, and happy at the supreme moment of marching down the aisle, she can usually also tolerate temporary anxiety or ambivalence and feel fine about that. In fact, some anxiety is prescribed, for it shows how seriously she takes marriage.

Sensing a gap between the ideal feeling and the actual feeling she tolerated, the bride prompts herself to "be happy."* Precariously and for the moment, but without falseness, this seems to work; her emotion work leads into emotion. She probably thought little about how *appropriate* her feelings were at the time or about how her private feeling rules matched some publicly shared code. She simply disliked what she felt. She wanted to feel differently, as a private and individual matter. If she admitted to having feeling rules, she would probably say that she made them up

herself; after all, it was *her* wedding. Yet in one sense, it was not her wedding. The throwing of rice is a medieval fertility rite, the wearing of white a Victorian addition, and the very idea of a father but not a mother giving away a daughter but not a son derives from Saxon times, when a father would sell his daughter for her labor. (Only after the Crusades, when women exceeded men in number, did the father come to "give her away.") It was her wedding in the sense that it was *her* borrowings from culture, as well as her borrowings from public notions about what she should inwardly experience on such a day.[29]

To get the emotion-management perspective clear, we have ignored two other principles that organize social life. The first of these, considered primarily by psychiatrists, is pain avoidance. The bride may try to struggle out of her depression not because it is proper to be happy but because she wants to avoid the unspeakable ache of being depressed. The second principle, which Erving Goffman and other sociologists take as primary, is advantage seeking in the social arena. The bride may try to be happy in order to win the affection of her in-laws, to attract the envy of her unwed girl friends, or to provoke jealousy in a former suitor. As principles, avoiding pain and seeking advantage explain patterns of emotion management, but it is important to note that both operate within a context of feeling rules.

The virtue of the focus on feeling rules lies in the questions it opens up. How, for example, does a change in feeling rules change the way brides experience weddings? In a society in which there is a rising divorce rate and a growing sense of contingency about the idea of marital commitment, the bride may get inadvertent reminders from her friends to take a rather nonchalant attitude toward the ceremony and to behave more as she would at an informal party. If she has any feelings about the religious solemnity of the occasion, she may be asked to keep them to herself; and, indeed, if she is to indicate that she shares the feeling rules of her modern friends, she will have to try to express a certain degree of shame about experiencing her marriage in a more old-fashioned way. Even while pain avoidance and advantage seeking stick as fixed principles of emotional life, feeling rules can change.

---

* What can be *expected* (at this stage, on this occasion) and what is *wished for* in experience deserve a certain analytic separation. But in the American middle class, there may be an "optimism norm" so that what we realistically expect and what we think is ideal are closer together than they are in other classes and other cultures.

Misfitting Feelings

A feeling itself, and not simply the way it is displayed on face and body, can be experienced as misfitting a situation in a surprising number of ways. We can suggest a few of them by considering how one might feel at a funeral.

A funeral, like a wedding, symbolizes a passage in relationships and offers the individual a role that is limited in time. The role of mourner, like that of bride, exists before and lives on after the rite. But rules about how to feel during the rite are linked to an understanding of the rite itself and of the bond it commemorates.

A funeral is ideally suited to inducing spontaneous sadness and grief. This is because the ritual usually reminds the bereaved of the finality of death while at the same time offering a sense of safety and comfort in this realization.[30] In response, the bereaved generally senses that this is the right time and right place to feel grief and not much else. Yet in a wondrous variety of ways it is possible for a griever to misgrieve.

One way is not to feel sad, as at the funeral recalled by this woman, now thirty-one:

> When I was around nine or ten, my fourteen-month-old sister died. I had one other sibling—a sister who was three years older. I remember feeling important telling people my baby sister had died; I enjoyed the attention. At the funeral our immediate family was sitting in a special side room separated from the other guests by a transparent curtain. At the point when the rabbi drew the curtain open, the whole family simultaneously blew their noses. I thought that was quite funny and started laughing, which I masked into crying. When my piano teacher [who came to our house to give me lessons] asked why the mirror was covered (a Jewish custom), I nonchalantly told her that my little sister had died, at which point she became hysterical and ran to express her grief to my mother. Of course I was aware that I was supposed to be sad and grieving . . . but my parents were so aggrieved and preoccupied that I was just brought along [to the funeral] and not dealt with individually. My status of youngest child was back, along with more attention from my parents, and my little sister hadn't developed a great personality yet, so there wasn't much to miss. Though I understand the dynamics of the situation in retrospect, I still feel a little guilty, like there's something wrong with me and I'm exposing myself for not having felt bad. Actually at this point I honestly feel it would be lovely to have a younger sister.

This child felt happy at being more important both because she was close to an event that affected many people and because she had one less rival for her parents' attention. In this case, her shame about feeling happy at her baby sister's death attached itself to these childhood feelings only when she later reinterpreted the event through adult eyes. In other cases, of course, time does not elapse between having the feeling and appreciating the unwritten convention that it does not fit.

We can offend against a feeling rule when we grieve *too much* or *too little,* when we overmanage or undermanage grief. As a nineteen-year-old woman recalled: "A few months ago when my grandfather died, I was very upset and sad. My sadness was mostly for mother and my grandmother, but it was also for myself. I kept feeling I shouldn't be this upset because I wasn't that close to my grandpa and I didn't love him that much." In assessing her feelings, this young woman seemed to choose between two rules, one that would apply if she had loved her grandfather very much and another that would fit if she hadn't loved him "that much."

Even if we very much love someone who has died or is about to die, how much of what kind of stoicism is appropriate for a given situation? This can be a problem, as two sociologists found in the case of parents anticipating the death of their children, who were hospitalized with leukemia and tumors:

> The parents were frequently described by the medical staff as being strong, though occasionally this behavior was interpreted as reflecting "coldness" or lack of sincere concern. The parents were also often aware of this paucity of emotional feeling, frequently explaining it on the grounds that they "could not break down" in the presence of the children or their physicians. However, the parents would occasionally verbalize their confusion and even guilt over not feeling worse.[31]

Ordinarily we expect the bereaved to be shocked and surprised at death; we are not supposed to expect death, at least not too confidently. Yet many deaths—from cancer, stroke, or other terminal illness—occur gradually and come finally as no surprise. Not to feel shock and surprise may show that even before a person dies physically, he or she can die socially. In these cases, kin and friends often offer each other permission to feel relief, accepting the fact that they may have mourned a genuine loss "too early."

Another way to feel unfittingly about death is to resent the labor and sacrifice the dead person has caused relatives. It is not fitting to hold a grudge beyond the grave. One forty-eight-year-old woman recalled:

> The death of my father brought a mixture of grief and relief. Taking care of him and my mother required that I move them out of their own home, rent an apartment, and start housekeeping for them while my own family, my husband and three teenagers, were home. This was my first long separation from my husband and children. My nerves were raw; my dad seemed never to sleep except in the daytime, while my only time for sleeping was at night. *I didn't give much thought about what I should feel, but I felt bad,* and guilty to be relieved and sorry at the same time. I handled my feelings by simply asking my dead father for forgiveness and by accepting the fact that I was weak.

In the overwhelming majority of cases, it is women who give care to aged parents, and it is probably more their burden to feel resentment about the sacrifices they have made and therefore to feel ambivalent about the deaths of their parents.

Another way in which feelings can seem to misfit a situation is in their timing. Indeed, many moments of "misfeeling" express the difference between a personal and a cultural clock. Sometimes a problem in timing can lead others to draw undesirable inferences. As a middle-aged woman recalled:

> When my husband died I thought I should feel a great sense of loss and grief. Instead I found a sense of freedom at being able to do as I pleased and to make decisions about my life without having to consult him or face anger or hurt feelings if I went against him. I felt really guilty about this and dealt with it by putting aside all emotions connected with my husband, acting as if he existed only in some dim memory. In fact, I could remember very little of the

eleven years we spent together. I couldn't tell anyone how I felt, but I proceeded to make a new life for myself, with new friends, activities, and experiences. *My old friends, of course, could not understand this and interpreted it as evidence that I had not loved him.*

More than a year later, after moving to a new location and becoming involved in a serious relationship to which I was willing to commit myself, I was at last able to come to terms with my feelings and memories about my husband. Then I felt the grief I was unable to feel before and was able to share my children's grief.

It sometimes takes the right context, one that reduces the press of inhibitions, for grief to emerge. If that context does not present itself quickly, family and friends may decide that grief has emerged too late. Sometimes the bereaved are taken by "anniversary reactions," periods of grief and depression occasioned by the anniversary of a loved one's death. To those who know nothing about anniversary reactions, a sudden spell of depression can seem inexplicable and frightening. Those acquainted with the syndrome, however, can provisionally expect its results and can define the grief as being, in a way, "on time" after all. What is early and what is late is as profoundly a social affair as what is too much and what is too little.

There is a *public* aspect to the proprieties of timing, and sometimes social scientists can themselves establish the proprieties. For example, Dr. Robert Weiss, with colleagues at the Laboratory of Community Psychiatry, developed a "seminar for the bereaved." He has written:

> We were hesitant about scheduling a party for the bereaved because we thought that many of them defined themselves as still within that period of mourning when gaiety is prohibited. But we . . . discovered to our surprise that participants brought to [the party] an excitement; there was a good deal of eager planning for it; some of the women came to it in formal dresses. On looking back, one might guess that they had interpreted the party as establishing their right to reenter the social world, but we could never have guessed that this is what the party would mean.[32]

In addition to problems of timing, there are problems of placing. Being in the right place to grieve involves being in the presence of an audience ready to receive your expressions. It can make a big difference whether one is surrounded by grieving aunts and uncles or by curious sixth graders:

> I was in the sixth grade at the time my grandfather died. I remember being called to the office of the school where my mother was on the phone from New York (I was in California). She told me what had happened and all I said was, "Oh." I went back to class and a friend asked me what happened and I said, "Nothing." I remember wanting very much just to cry and tell everyone what had happened. But a boy doesn't cry in the sixth grade for fear of being called a sissy. So I just went along as if nothing had happened while deep down inside I was very sad and full of tears.

Males especially may have to wait for ceremonial permission to feel and express. Even within the ceremonial setting, even when men do cry, they may feel more constrained not to sob openly.[33] In that sense men may need ceremonies more than women, who in any case, may cry without losing respect according to the standards imposed on men.

In each instance above, from the mourner's viewpoint, the same event, a funeral, is misexperienced. In each case, the event seems to prescribe a "proper" range of inner feelings and corresponding outer display. Ideals in grieving vary depending on the type of funeral ceremony and the cultural understanding of grief on which it draws. Thus in many ways normal ambivalences can be privately reshaped to fit social rules we are scarcely aware of.[34] The ways in which people think they have grieved poorly suggest what a remarkable achievement it is to grieve well—without violating the astonishingly exact standards we draw from culture to impose on feeling.

Misinterpreted Relations and Inappropriate Feeling

A bride and a mourner live out roles that are specific to an occasion. Yet the achievements of the heart are all the more remarkable within roles that last longer and go deeper. Parents and children, husbands and wives, lovers and best friends expect to have more freedom from feeling rules and less need for emotion work; in reality, however, the subterranean work of placing an acceptable inner face on ambivalence is ac-

tually all the more crucial for them. In fact, the deeper the bond, the more emotion work, and the more unconscious we are of it. In the most personal bonds, then, emotion work is likely to be the strongest. At the other extreme, it is a wonder that we find emotion work at all—and not simple pretending—in the bill collector and the flight attendant. But we do, and because their contacts do not cut so deep, their emotion work rises more readily to the surface of consciousness where it can be seen and talked about. We may look at it where it is easiest to see in order to infer where, in the cement of the most personal bonds, it is strongest.

The family is often considered a "relief zone" away from the pressures of work, a place where one is free to be oneself. It may indeed be a refuge from the emotion work required on the job, but it quietly imposes emotional obligations of its own. Of these, perhaps the feeling obligations of parent for child are the clearest. Here, if nowhere else, we say love is "natural." Culture may govern its expression, psychology may explain its unfolding, but we take parental feeling itself to be "natural." It needs no normative shield, no feeling rules, we think, because nature does the work of a convention for us. In fact, however, we do seem to need conventions here—not because parental love is unnatural but because it is so important to security and sometimes so difficult to sustain.

The relation of parent to child differs from other close relations in three basic ways. First, the bond usually endures. Especially during the child's tender years, we feel that a parent should not emotionally "divorce" a child. Second, the bond is tight because in the beginning a child depends upon it for virtually everything. Third, the bond is usually embedded in a wider network of kin and friends. Any bond like the one between parent and child is subject to ambivalence and the rules that contain it. The child loves and hates the parent, and the parent loves and hates the child. But cultural rules in each case prescribe acceptable mixes of feeling. These rules come to consciousness as moral injunctions—we "should" or "shouldn't" feel this, we "have a right" or "don't have the right" to feel that.

There are tests of parental love. A parent may habitually lie or rage against a child without explanation.

And when the child cannot muster the love or sympathy that a father, for example, thinks himself owed, anger may emerge unprotected by the shield of entitlement to it:

> Two years ago my father quit his job and in the process admitted himself into Langley Porter Psychiatric Hospital for treatment of what was then diagnosed as manic-depressive psychosis. After being released, he admitted to the family many cruel and deceiving things he had been doing behind our backs for the past ten years. At the time I remember thinking that I should show him my love now more than ever before, that I should forgive this pitiful man who had lost the respect of his wife, his co-workers, his friends, his children, and most of all himself. But all I could feel was anger at his deception, anger at his once "funny" behavioral quirks that now suddenly came into sharp focus. I fought the obligation to love because I needed to hate. I had to resolve my own feelings before I could worry about his.

This son really wanted to forgive his father and to respond to his father's desperate need for self-respect; he also felt obliged to feel forgiving. Yet because he himself felt deceived and angry at being deceived, he could not feel as he wanted to and thought he ought to. He could not see his father's activities as "quirks"; he could not sustain that *as if* and feel the love he would experience if they were just quirks. Instead, these activities felt like deceptions. And given the serious reality of the deception, the boy felt angry. He did not revise what he sensed he owed his father—loyalty and love. He did not reconceive of his former love for his father as overpayment. He did not conceive of his father as being in emotional debt. Rather, the rule stayed in place and he "fought the obligation to love" because he needed to hate. He did not change the feeling rule. He acted on a strong need to violate it.

Such events differently interpreted often create problems between parents and children. In the following example, what the mother might have seen as a trying episode for a single parent, deserving of sympathy and understanding, was to the daughter simply inexcusable selfishness. As the daughter, a twenty-year-old college student, wrote:

> I was alone in the house with my mother, who had been very unhappy and was making all of our lives

miserable. Part of it stemmed from her hating the house in which we lived, and on this particular night the hate was very profound. She was in her room— crying, yelling, and banging things around very audibly and making angry references to my father, my sister, and, to a lesser extent, myself. I know I was the one person who was not involved in her hate—*I felt I was supposed to feel sorry for her, comfort her,* call someone who might be able to help. However, what I felt was intense anger at her; if she hated our family, I wanted to be included in that hate and I wanted her to quit making our lives miserable whether she was capable of controlling her emotions or not. I didn't know what to do, I cried to myself and wanted to run from the situation entirely. I just didn't want to have anything to do with it.

Like the deceiving father, the distraught mother poses a test to love; she makes the rule that one should love a parent seem temporarily intolerable. Is the father crazy, forgivable, and lovable, or is he deceiving, unforgivable, and unlovable? Is the mother unable to control herself, in need of help, and basically well-meaning, or is she cruelly manipulative, using emotional blackmail to win an ally in a family war? What should a child feel? The choice in each case was hard not only because the child was violently torn between two reactions but because of a "should" that bolstered one reaction and not the other. As the daughter said, "I felt I was supposed to feel sorry for her, comfort her."

An incapacity to control rage, or to tell the truth, or to fulfill sexual agreements, or to hold a job are all human flaws which, up to a point, we may try to ignore or forgive but which we are also free to criticize. Being mentally retarded, on the other hand, is a problem that is no one's fault, but it can lead to the same sort of emotional predicament: "My younger and only sister is severely mentally retarded. Though she is nearly normal physically, she has no intellect. I often think that I should feel love for her, but I don't. There is nothing there for me to love—the fact that she is my sister is not enough. I feel guilty about my feelings, but I'm content that at least I can be honest with myself." This sibling feels guilty about not feeling love for a sister "with no intellect." He confronts a "should" that he must reject in order to feel honest.

Like the bond between parent and child, the bond between wife and husband may be strained in the battle between sanction and feeling. Freud, in his essay "Modern Sexual Morality and Modern Nervousness," describes the problem well:

> Let us take for instance the case observed so frequently of a woman who does not love her husband because owing to the conditions of her union and to her matrimonial experience she has absolutely no reason for loving him; *she would like to love him, however,* because that is in accord with what she has been brought up to consider as the ideal of married life. She will accordingly suppress all the instincts that would reveal the truth and counteract her ideal endeavor. She will take special care to act like a loving, tender, and thoughtful wife [my emphasis].[35]

"Like to love him" is one of those threads in the weave that differ by culture. A fourteen-year-old Indian girl in an arranged marriage to a wealthy sixty-year-old man may be required to serve him (and may even feel obliged to try to love him), but she may be internally freer to dislike him; she is not responsible for having chosen him. The "love ethic" in a free market exchange, on the other hand, places more exacting standards of experience on marriage. If the actual feelings between the spouses fall short of the ideal, it is not the institution of marriage but one's own poor choice of a partner that is to blame.[36]

Between husband and wife or between lovers, sexual jealousy and love are usually presumed to go together. But the sociologist Kingsley Davis has suggested that sexual jealousy is not natural between mates and that it is often the proprietary claims that husband and wife make upon each other that cause adultery to evoke jealousy.[37]

Following this logic, some couples strive to rid themselves of the agreement to be monogamous and therefore of the right to jealousy. Making love to someone outside the marriage is defined not as adultery but as "sharing your love." Since monogamy has been a common way of expressing emotional commitment, other ways of expressing that commitment are given more importance. But if these other ways fail, at least one partner may feel rejected. Consider the situation reported by this young woman:

> About four years ago when I was living down South, I was involved with a group of people, friends. We used to spend most evenings after work or school together. We used to do a lot of drugs, acid, coke, or just smoke dope, and we had this philosophy that we were very communal and did our best to share everything—clothes, money, food, and so on. I was involved with this one man, and I thought I was "in love" with him. He in turn had told me that I was very important to him. Anyway, another woman who had been a very good friend of mine at one time started having a sexual relationship with this man, supposedly without my knowledge. I knew, though, and had a lot of mixed feelings about it. I thought, intellectually, that I had no claim to the man, that no one should ever try to own another person. I also believed that it was none of my business, that their relationship together really had nothing to do with my friendship with either of them. I also believed in sharing. *But I was horribly hurt, lonely, and depressed,* and I couldn't shake the depression. And on top of those feelings, I felt guilt for having those possessively jealous feelings. And so I would continue going out with these people every night and try to suppress my feelings. My ego was shattered. I got to the point that I couldn't even laugh around them. So finally I confronted my friends and left for the summer and traveled with a new friend. I realized later what a heavy situation it was, and it took me a long time to get myself together and feel whole again.

The clash between the feeling she could muster under the countercultural feeling rule and the feeling of hurt and jealousy she experienced seemed like a private nightmare. Yet the origin of this sort of conflict and pain is also profoundly social, for it is through social institutions that a basic view of sexual access is elaborated and a moral code promoted. That is why institutions or subcultures that develop a total system of punishments for jealous behavior, and rewards for unjealous behavior, may go some distance toward eliminating jealousy. As two sociologists comment about a communal experiment:

> At Twin Oaks in Virginia, sexual freedom is the community norm and jealousy is a common problem. Cat Kincade, . . . one of the founders, describes jealousy management at Twin Oaks: "The biggest bulwark against jealousy is our heavy community disapproval of it . . . nobody gets group reinforcement for feeling or expressing jealousy. A surprising amount of it is wiped out by that fact alone . . . Most of us here do not approve of our bad feelings when we have them.

Just as a person with a Puritan conscience can often control his erotic impulses by reference to what he believes, so a person with a communitarian conscience can control his repressive impulses by reminding himself what his principles are.[38]

Had the young woman's friends and neighbors taken more care to reinforce her communitarian view and more closely supported her emotion work, it is conceivable that her story would have ended differently.

A social role—such as that of bride, wife, or mother—is partly a way of describing what feelings people think are owed and are owing. A role establishes a baseline for what feelings seem appropriate to a certain series of events. When roles change, so do rules for how to feel and interpret events. A rising divorce rate, a rising remarriage rate, a declining birthrate, a rising number of working women, and a greater legitimation of homosexuality are the outer signs of changing roles. What, when she works outside the home, *is* a wife? What, when others care for children, *is* a parent? And what, then, *is* a child? What, when marriages easily dissolve, *is* a lover and what *is* a friend? According to which standard, among all those that are culturally available, do we assess how appropriate our feelings are to a situation? If periods of rapid change induce status anxiety, they also lead to anxiety about what, after all, the feeling rules are.*

In times of uncertainty, the expert rises to prominence. Authorities on how a situation ought to be viewed are also authorities on how we should feel. The need for guidance felt by those who must cross shifting social sands only adds importance to a more fundamental principle: in the matter of what to feel, the social bottom usually looks for guidance to the social top. Authority carries with it a certain mandate over feeling rules. A parent may show a child how much fear to feel about the new bull terrier on the block. An English literature professor may suggest to

students how strongly they should feel about Rilke's first Duino Elegy. A supervisor may comment on a cheer worn thin in a secretary's "Here's your correspondence, sir." It is mainly the authorities who are the keepers of feeling rules.[39] And so when an authority like Gail Sheehy tells us that "a restless vitality wells up as we approach thirty," it can, as Christopher Lasch points out, become part of the experience of turning thirty to address the "restless vitality" norm. Similarly, it can become part of the experience of greeting a passenger, or collecting a bill, to address official ideas about what we should feel as we do it.

NOTES

EPIGRAPHS: F. W. Nietzsche (1874), cited in Gellhorn (1964); C. Wright Mills, *White Collar,* p. 183.

Gail Sheehy, *Passages: Predictable Crises of Adult Life,* p. 138; Christopher Lasch, *New York Review of Books,* September 30, 1976.

1. As suggested by Goffman's description of "Preedy" on the beach, in *The Presentation of Self in Everyday Life* (1959), surface acting is alive and well in Goffman's work. But the second method of acting, deep acting, is less apparent in his illustrations, and the theoretical statement about it is correspondingly weak. Goffman posits a self capable of surface acting, but not one capable of deep acting.

2. Stanislavski (1965), p. 268.

3. Ibid., p. 196.

4. Ibid., p. 22.

5. There is actually another distinguishable way of doing deep acting—by actively altering the body so as to change conscious feeling. This surface-to-center approach differs from surface acting. Surface acting uses the body to *show* feeling. This type of deep acting uses the body to *inspire* feeling. In relaxing a grimace or unclenching a fist, we may actually make ourselves feel less angry (ibid., p. 93). This insight is sometimes used in bio-feedback therapy (see Brown 1974, p. 50).

6. The direct method of cognitive emotion work is known not by the result (see Peto 1968) but by the effort made to achieve the result. The result of any given act is hard enough to discern. But if we were to identify emotion work by its results, we would be in a peculiar bind. We might say that a "cooled-down anger" is the result of an effort to reduce anger. But then we would have to assume that we have some basis for knowing what the anger "would have been like" had the individual not been managing his anger. We are on theoretically safer ground if we define emotion management as a set of acts *addressed* to feeling. (On the nature of an act of will, as separate from its effect, see Jean Piaget in Campbell 1976, p. 87.)

7. By definition, each method of emotion work is active,

---

* Indeed, we are most likely to sense a feeling rule as a feeling rule, and deep acting *as* deep acting, not when we are strongly attached to a culture or a role but when we are moving from one culture or one role to another. It is when we are *between* jobs, between marriages, or between cultures that we are prone to feel at odds with past feeling rules.

but just how active, varies. At the active end of the continuum we contort reality and grip our bodily processes as though gripping the steering wheel of a car. At the passive extreme we may simply perform an act upon an act—as in deliberately relaxing already existing controls or issuing permission to "let" ourselves feel sad. (For a discussion of active versus passive concentration in autogenic training, see Wolfgang Luthe, quoted in Pelletier 1977, p. 237.) In addition we may "ride over" a feeling (such as a nagging sense of depression) in the attempt to feel cheerful. When we meet an inward resistance, we "put on" the cheer. When we meet no inward resistance, we amplify a feeling: we "put it out."

8. Gold (1979), p. 129.

9. Stanislavski (1965), p. 38. Indeed, an extra effort is required *not to focus* on the intent, the effort of trying to feel. The point, rather, is to focus on seeing the situation. Koriat et al. (1972) illustrated this second approach in a laboratory experiment in which university students were shown films of simulated wood-chopping accidents. In one film a man lacerates the tips of his fingers; in another, a woodworker cuts off his middle finger; in a third, a worker dies after a plank of wood is thrust through his midsection by a circular saw. Subjects were instructed to detach themselves when first viewing the films and then, on another viewing, to involve themselves. To deintensify the effect of the films, the viewers tried to remind themselves that they were just films and often focused on technical aspects of production to reinforce this sense of unreality. Others tried to think of the workers in the films as being responsible for their own injuries through negligence. Such detachment techniques may be common in cases when people victimize others (see Latane and Darby 1970). To intensify the films' effect, the viewers reported trying to imagine that the accidents were happening to them, or to someone they knew, or were similar to experiences they had had or had witnessed; some tried to think about and exaggerate the consequences of accidents. Koriat et al. conceive of these deintensifying or intensifying devices as aspects of appraisal that precede a "coping response." Such devices may also be seen as mental acts that adjust the "if supposition" and draw on the "emotional memory" described in Stanislavski (1965).

10. Stanislavski (1965), p. 57.

11. Ibid., p. 163.

12. Ibid., p. 127.

13. Stanislavski once admonished his actors: "You do not get hold of this exercise because . . . you are anxious to believe all of the terrible things I put into the plot. But do not try to do it all at once; proceed bit by bit, helping yourselves along by small truths. If every little auxiliary act is executed truthfully, then the whole action will unfold rightly" (Ibid., p. 126).

14. Lief and Fox (1963) quoted in Lazarus (1975), p. 55.

15. Wheelis (1980), p. 7.

16. Cohen, (1966), p. 105.

17. Ibid.

18. Ibid.

19. The very way most institutions conduct the dirty work of firing, demotion, and punishment also assures that any *personal* blame aimed at those who fire, demote, and punish is not legitimized. It becomes illegitimate to interpret an "impersonal act" of firing as a personal act, as in "You did that to me, you bastard!" See Wolff (1950), pp. 345–378.

20. See Robert Howard, "Drugged, Bugged, and Coming Unplugged," *Mother Jones,* August 1981.

21. Feeling rules are not the only channel through which social factors enter feeling. Without giving it quite this name, many social scientists have discussed feeling rules. Among the earlier classics, Émile Durkheim offers a general statement, in *The Elementary Forms of the Religious Life:* "An individual . . . if he is strongly attached to the society of which he is a member, feels that he is *morally held to participating* in *its sorrows and joys;* not to be interested in them would be equivalent to breaking the bonds uniting him to the group; it would be renouncing all desire for it and contradicting himself" (1965, p. 446). Following Durkheim, Mary Douglas uses this concept in her *Natural Symbols* (1973, see p. 63), as does Charles Blondel (1952) when he refers to "collective imperatives." Freud, too, touches upon feeling rules, although his interest is in how they form part of intrapsychic patterns as part of the superego. On the creative margins of the Freudian tradition, R. D. Laing illuminates the idea of feeling rules in his important essay "The Politics of the Family" (1971), as does David Riesman in his exquisitely sensitive explanations of faces in *The Lonely Crowd* (1953; see also 1952). Richard Sennett makes a particular application of feeling rules to anger (1973, p. 134), and Talcott Parsons offers a general discussion of "affectivity" (Parsons et al. 1953, p. 60; also Parsons 1951, pp. 384–385).

22. Some people doubtless reflect on feeling less than others. In any given instance, when an individual has no sense of "feeling inappropriately," one of three conditions applies: (1) the rules for his or her situated feeling are internalized but unavailable to consciousness; (2) he or she is not disobeying the rules and therefore is not aware of them; (3) the rules are in fact weak or nonexistent.

23. People assess their feelings as if they were applying standards to feeling. These acts of assessment are secondary reactions to feeling. From secondary reactions to feeling we may postulate the existence of rules. The concept of a feeling rule makes sense of stable patterns into which many acts of assessment fit. An assessment, then, can be taken as an "application" of a more general rule. Using fragments of data on assessment, we may begin to piece together parts of a more general set of rules that guide deep acting, a set that is socially variable and historically changing. A feeling rule shares some properties with other rules of etiquette that govern acts one can see. As with rules of etiquette, we do not presume a given set of feeling rules to be universal or objectively valid according to any moral criteria. They are, instead, culturally relative traffic rules. But they govern the inner realm. They are the etiquette of preaction or "deep etiquette."

As with rules of etiquette, we often disobey but guiltily. At the minimum, we acknowledge a rule. For example: "I'm reading *National Lampoon* and come across the comic section by Rodriguez called 'Hire the Handicapped.' This pokes fun at people with handicaps and I find it hilarious, one of the funniest series of comics I've ever seen. I feel that this is not something to laugh about, that I *should* feel sympathy and not laugh. I *continue to laugh anyway because it's really funny*. Tragedy is often funny in the proper perspective." Feeling rules, like rules of behavior, delineate zones. Within a given zone we sense permission to be free of worry, guilt, or shame. Each zoning ordinance describes a boundary—a floor and a ceiling with room for motion and play between the two. The reader above was comfortable about his temporary delight in the *Lampoon* comic; but if his mirth had been more intense or more enduring, had a certain boundary been reached, he might have experienced signs of the boundary—worry, guilt, or shame. "What's wrong with me that I find this so hilarious? Am I a sadist? Do I identify with the lame too little? Or too much?"

The act of assessing feeling may occur nearly simultaneously with the feeling. For example, we may feel angry and know we have no right to feel angry at nearly the same time. We may *focus* more fully on self-disapproval after the fact, but we *sense* it peripherally *while* the anger is rising.

24. The importance accorded to feeling rules may vary from culture to culture. The emotion-management perspective itself raises questions about its own cross-cultural limits. In addition, there are probably cross-cultural variations in the formation of different types of tension in the leeway that exists between what we *do* feel and what we *expect* to feel, between what we *expect* to feel and what we *want* to feel, between what we *think we should* feel and what we *expect* to feel.

25. See Lyman and Scott (1970). Some authors, like George Herbert Mead (1934), focus on internal dialogues and thus on private rule reminders. Others, like Erving Goffman, focus on external dialogues. Socially and morally, Goffman's people tend to come alive only in social interactions, and Mead's only in private soliloquies.

26. If the permission granted (as in "go ahead and cry") is not properly received, an encounter may not go "as it should." By not being in the sort of psychological shape that requires permission, there is some risk of offense. The comforter may not feel offended that her comfort is not working, but she may feel some slight *right* to feel offended. The more accountable for her feelings the individual can be held to be (the more she resists her sick role), the more this is true.

27. See Beck (1971), p. 495. As Schafer notes: "Anna Freud . . . pointed out that in child analytic work, where the free association method cannot be used, the analyst can use the absence of the expected affect as an indicator of specific unconscious conflicts. On many occasions the analyst of adults also interprets just this absence of predictable emotion" (1976, p. 335).

28. R. D. Laing takes us a step forward theoretically by questioning the background assumptions concerning appropriate affect. By raising examples of patients in "crazy-making" situations to which "crazy" responses seem reasonable ones, Laing focuses our attention on the situation and the *doctor's* expectations. In the same vein, C. Wright Mills notes: "There are few attempts to explain deviations from the norms in terms of the norms themselves, and no rigorous facing of the implications of the fact that social transformations would involve shifts in them" (1963, p. 43).

29. There may be, then, an element of consent to her experience. Commenting on primitive religious groups, Émile Durkheim said something similar: "When the Christian, during the ceremonies of commemorating the Passion, and the Jew, on the anniversary of the fall of Jerusalem, fast and mortify themselves, it is not in giving way to a sadness which they feel spontaneously. Under these circumstances, the internal state of the believer is out of all proportion to the severe abstinences to which they submit themselves. *If he is sad, it is primarily because he consents to being sad*. And he consents to it in order to affirm his faith" (1965, p. 446). Now, a Christian's consent to be sad is an individually authored consent. But that authorship is influenced by the church, by religious beliefs (about rewards and punishments among other things), and by the community. The young bride's feeling rules are privately authored in the same sense that the Christian's are. And her acts of management are likely to fit a public code about weddings that is shared by others of her sex, age, religion, ethnicity, occupation, social class, and geographic locale.

30. The dual aspect of the funeral is suggested in Mandelbaum's study of the Kotas, a people who live in South India: "There is no inclination to enlarge the intensity or scope of the mourner's grief. The bereaved are given a formal opportunity for complete self-immersion in grief, but there is also an effort to curtail their sorrow, to distract them by pleasing figures of the dance" (1959, p. 191). Mandelbaum also notes that since the Kotas have become more influenced by the practices of high-caste Hindu villagers, they have become more uncertain about the propriety of dancing at a funeral. (On grief, see Lindemann 1944; Glick et al., 1974; Lewis 1961; Lofland 1982.)

31. Friedman et al. (1963), p. 617.

32. Weiss (1975), p. 25.

33. This may not be confined to Anglo-Saxon culture. Mandelbaum notes about the Kotas of India: "On the first morning of the Dry Funeral a band of musicians . . . plays a lament. . . . Bereaved women stop in their tracks. A rush of sorrow suffuses them; they sit down where they are, cover their heads with their shoulder cloths, and wail and sob through much of that day and the next. Men of the bereaved household have much to do in preparation for the ceremony and do not drop everything to mourn aloud as do the bereaved women" (1959, p. 193; also see Gorer 1977).

34. Psychoanalytic theory now typically deals with unconscious feelings that are too guilt-invoking to bear and are therefore repressed. For example, one may unconsciously think, in

the case of death, "I'm glad it wasn't me." Horowitz (1970) discusses the cognitive patterns characteristic of various personality types facing the trauma of an accidental death.

35. Freud's interest in what she "has been brought up to consider as the ideal" is expressed in his next sentence: "Neurotic troubles will soon follow upon that attempt at self-repression; a neurosis will soon avenge her upon the unloved husband and cause him just as much unpleasantness and sorrow as the real truth would cause him had he known it" (1931, p. 47).

36. David and Vera Mace, in their *Marriage, East and West* (1960), claim that Indian girls are "raised to love" their "arranged" husbands and that they actually do. See William Goode (1964).

37. As Kingsley Davis puts it: "Where exclusive possession of an individual's entire love is customary, jealousy will demand that exclusiveness. Where love is divided according to some scheme, jealousy will reinforce the division. . . . Whereas Westermarck (a historian of the family) would say that adultery arouses jealousy and that therefore jealousy causes monogamy, one could maintain that our institution of monogamy causes adultery to be resented, and therefore creates jealousy" (1936, pp. 400, 403). For Davis, jealousy involves another feeling, fear—fear of losing something one already has, has rights to, or wants to have (p. 395). This section of my chapter draws heavily on an unpublished paper by Frieda Armstrong, "Toward a Sociology of Jealousy" (1975).

38. Clanton and Smith (1977), p. 67. As ideological shifts filter down to the experts, the ranks of the emotional deviants who listen to the experts also change. For a social change to be deep, to strike bottom, to be permanent, it must have as one of its signs a change in who seems or feels "out of it." Some whose feelings used to be hidden in secrecy and guilt now come out to live comfortably under the umbrella of new emotional conventions whereas others who were once protected are now subjected to doubt and guilt. What has changed is the deep connection between situations and the interpretations and feelings with which people respond to them. Aside from this kind of deep change, there is only attitudinal fashion.

39. What holds true for rules in the private realm also holds true for the public realm. As citizens we look for guidance in how to interpret the news and also for guidance in what to feel—legitimately, appropriately, rationally—about it. The government is one opinion leader that helps us in this effort. The San Francisco *Chronicle* of January 25, 1978, had as a banner headline: "Soviet Nuclear Spy Satellite Disintegrates Over Canada." The report continued:

"There was serious concern, both in Washington and in other world capitals, that radioactive debris might have been strewn down a reentry path hundreds of miles long. The fact that [the] satellite was carrying a nuclear reactor and was mysteriously decaying was known to the United States as early as December 19 but was kept secret because, in the words of one White House security adviser, 'we were trying to head off a recreation of Mercury Theater.' The reference was to the fa-

mous radio broadcast of Orson Welles' Mercury Theater in 1938 in which Martians were reported to have landed at Glover's Mill, N.J. The net result was near hysteria among many Americans who had not realized that the Halloween broadcast was fiction."

The implicit feeling rule is that we should trust the U.S. government to tell us when an emergency is at hand. In this case, public fear of a potential nuclear disaster was discounted as resembling hysteria over a fictional event, a silly and after all funny trick on the folks back in 1938. A real near-disaster was compared to a make-believe one; the two were given equivalence. Thus the distinction between appropriate alarm and inappropriate alarm, between a rational and an irrational emotion, may rest in the end on what events opinion leaders choose to compare to fiction. The person who is "overexercised" in one era may have a fair crack at being a prophet in the next.

References

Armstrong, Frieda. 1975. "Toward a sociology of jealousy." Unpublished paper, Department of Sociology, University of California, Berkeley.

Beck, Aaron. 1971. "Cognition, affect, and psychopathology." *Archives of General Psychiatry* 24:495–500.

Brown, Barbara. 1974. *New Mind, New Body.* New York: Harper & Row.

Campbell, Sarah F. (ed.) 1976. *Piaget Sampler.* New York: Wiley.

Clanton, Gordon, and Lynn G. Smith. 1977. *Jealousy.* Englewood Cliffs, N.J.: Prentice-Hall.

Cohen, Albert. 1966. *Deviance and Control.* Englewood Cliffs, N.J.: Prentice-Hall.

Davis, Kingsley. 1936. "Jealousy and sexual property." *Social Forces* 14:395–410.

Douglas, Mary. 1973. *Natural Symbols.* New York: Vintage.

Durkheim, Émile. 1965. *The Elementary Forms of the Religious Life.* Tr. Joseph Ward Swain. New York: Free Press.

Freud, Sigmund. 1931. *Modern Sexual Morality and Modern Nervousness.* New York: Eugenics Publishing Co.

Friedman, Stanford B., Paul Chodoff, John Mason and David Hamburg. 1963. "Behavioral observations on parents anticipating the death of a child." *Pediatrics* 32:610–625.

Gellhorn, E. 1964. "Motion and emotion: the role of proprioception in the physiology and pathology of the emotions." *Psychological Review* 71:457–472.

Glick, Ira O., Roster Weiss, and C. Murray Parkes. 1974. *The First Year of Bereavement.* New York: Wiley-Interscience.

Goffman, Erving. 1959. *The Presentation of Self in Everyday Life.* New York: Doubleday Anchor.

Gold, Herbert. 1979. "The smallest part." Pp. 203–212. In William Abrahams (ed.), *Prize Stories, 1979. The O'Henry Award.* Garden City, N.Y.: Doubleday.

Goode, William. 1964. "The theoretical importance of love." Pp. 202–219. In Rose Coser (ed.), *The Family, Its Structure and Functions.* New York: St. Martin's Press.

Gorer, Geoffrey. 1977. *Death, Grief, and Mourning*. New York: Arno Press.

Horowitz, Mardi J. 1970. *Image Formation and Cognition*. New York: Appleton-Century-Crofts Educational Division, Meredith Corporation.

Koriat, A., R. Melkman, J.R. Averill, and Richard Lazarus. 1972. "The self-control of emotional reactions to a stressful film." *Journal of Personality* 40:601–619.

Latane, Bibb, and John Darby. 1970. *The Unresponsive Bystander*. New York: Appleton-Century-Crofts.

Lazarus, Richard. 1975. "The self-regulation of emotion." Pp. 47–67. In L. Levi (ed.), *Emotions: Their Parameters and Measurement*. New York: Raven Press.

Lewis, C. S. 1961. *Grief Observed*. New York: Seabury Press.

Lief, H. I., and R. C. Fox. 1963. "Training for a 'detached concern' in medical studies." Pp. 12–35. In H. I. Lief, V. F. Lief, and N. R. Lief (eds.), *The Psychological Basis of Medical Practice*. New York: Harper & Row.

Lindemann, Erich. 1944. "Symptomatology and management of acute grief." *American Journal of Psychiatry* 101:141–148.

Lofland, Lyn H. 1982. "Loss and human connection: an exploration into the nature of the social bond." Chap. 8. In William Ickes and Eric Knowles (eds.), *Personality, Roles, and Social Behavior*. New York: Springer-Verlag.

Lyman, Stanford, and Marvin Scott. 1970. *A Sociology of the Absurd*. New York: Appleton-Century-Crofts.

Mace, David, and Vera Mace. 1960. *Marriage East and West*. Garden City, N.Y.: Double-day.

Mandelbaum, David G. 1959. "Social uses of funeral rites." Pp. 189–219. In H. Feifel (ed.), *The Meaning of Death*. New York: McGraw Hill.

Mead, George Herbert. 1934. *Mind, Self, and Society*. Charles Morris (ed.). Chicago: University of Chicago Press.

Mills, C. Wright. 1956. *White Collar*. New York: Oxford University Press.

———. 1963. "The professional ideology of social pathologists." In Irving L. Horowitz (ed.), *Power, Politics and People: The Collected Essays of C. Wright Mills*. New York: Ballantine.

Parsons, Talcott. 1951. *The Social System*. Glencoe, Ill.: Free Press.

Parsons, Talcott, Robert Bales, and Edward Shils. 1953. *Working Papers in the Theory of Action*. Glencoe, Ill.: Free Press.

Pelletier, Kenneth. 1977. *Mind as Healer, Mind as Slayer? A Holistic Approach to Preventing Stress Disorders*. New York: Dell.

Peto, Andrew. 1968. "On affect control." *International Journal of Psychoanalysis* 49 (parts 2–3): 471–473.

Riesman, David. 1952. *Faces in the Crowd: Individual Studies in Character and Politics*. New Haven: Yale University Press.

———. 1953. *The Lonely Crowd: A Study of the Changing American Character*. New Haven: Yale University Press.

Schafer, Roy. 1976. *A New Language for Psychoanalysis*. New Haven: Yale University Press.

Sennett, Richard (ed.). 1977. *The Psychology of Society*. New York: Vintage.

Sennett, Richard, and Jonathan Cobb. 1973. *Hidden Injuries of Class*. New York: Vintage.

Stanislavski, Constantin. 1965. *An Actor Prepares*. Tr. Elizabeth Reynolds Hapgood. New York: Theatre Arts Books. First published 1948.

Weiss, Robert. 1976. "Transition states and other stressful situations: their nature and programs for their management." Pp. 213–232. In G. Caplan and M. Killilea (eds.), *Support Systems and Mutual Help: A Multidisciplinary Exploration*. New York: Grune and Stratton.

Wheelis, Allen. 1980. *The Scheme of Things*. New York and London: Harcourt Brace Jovanovich.

Wolff, Kurt H. 1950. *The Sociology of Georg Simmel*. New York: Free Press.

21 | THE DEVELOPMENT OF FEELING NORMS UNDERLYING ROMANTIC LOVE AMONG ADOLESCENT FEMALES

Robin W. Simon, Donna Eder, and Cathy Evans

In American society, love is an important emotion (Cancian 1985, 1987; Cancian and Gordon 1988; Hochschild 1983a; Swidler 1980). Like other feelings, romantic love is a *social* sentiment, for which a cultural label and a set of ideological beliefs exist (Gordon 1981). Embodied in ideological beliefs

From Simon, R., Eder, D., and Evans, C., *Social Psychology Quarterly* 55: 29–46, © 1992 by The American Sociological Association. Reprinted by permission.

about love are "feeling norms" which guide individuals' romantic feelings and behaviors (Hochschild 1979, 1983a).[1] Feeling norms that underlie romantic love not only influence whether we should or should not love (Hochschild 1983a), but also help us identify the appropriate object of romantic feelings. Yet in spite of the importance attached to love in American culture, we know little about the content of the feeling norms that govern romantic love and the ways in which cultural knowledge about love is acquired socially.

Sociological research on emotion at both macro and micro levels of analysis has emphasized the normative aspects of love in America. Swidler (1980) examined historical change in the ideology of love (i.e., beliefs about the experience and expression of love), which she argues is linked to changing conceptions of adulthood in Western culture. According to Swidler, current beliefs about love emphasize individualism, self-actualization, and independence, in contrast to earlier beliefs, which emphasized social commitment, self-sacrifice, and dependence.

Like Swidler, Cancian and Gordon (Cancian 1985, 1987; Cancian and Gordon 1988) examined historical change in the content of love ideology, which they claim is due to structural transformations in the family and economy. They argue further, however, that even though contemporary love ideology emphasizes self-development (as opposed to self-sacrifice), the polarization of gender roles since the nineteenth century continues to encourage females' preoccupation with love and interpersonal relationships and males' preoccupation with occupational achievement for self-fulfillment.

Other research focuses on the ways in which individuals express and experience love. This research emphasizes the normative nature of love at the social psychological level. Cancian (1985, 1987) found that husbands and wives prefer styles of expressing love that are consistent with gender stereotypes. Whereas wives tend to express love through emotional closeness and verbal expression, husbands tend to express love by giving instrumental aid and through sex. Yet because American culture recognizes only the feminine style of love, Cancian argues that females continue to be viewed both by themselves and by others as

more skilled at love than males, a situation that creates conflict between men and women in marriage.

Whereas Cancian focused on the expression of love, Hochschild examined romantic feelings. Like Cancian's study, Hochschild's research underscores gender differences in love and highlights the importance of romantic feelings to women. In her study of college students (1983a), she found that females were more likely than males to give a greater degree of attention to the love experience. Females also were more likely than males to engage in "emotion work" with respect to love. That is, when their actual feelings departed from feeling norms, women were more likely to report that they consciously manipulated their feelings by either evoking the emotion (e.g., trying to fall in love) or suppressing the emotion (e.g., trying to fall out of love), so that their feelings would coincide with social norms. According to Hochschild, women attend more to love and perform more feeling work on love because they lack control over the courtship process, even while they depend on marriage for structural mobility.

Overall, the research discussed above suggests that love, like other emotions, is shaped by cultural beliefs, which include feeling norms.

Individuals continually interpret, evaluate, and modify their feelings (and expressions) according to existing beliefs about the emotion (Gordon 1981; Hochschild 1979; Thoits 1989). Yet although these studies provide insight into the normative influences on love, they do not elaborate the content of feeling norms underlying romantic love in American culture.[2] Moreover, although an assumption underlying this research is that cultural knowledge about love is acquired socially, research to date has not directly examined affective socialization processes. The absence of research on emotional socialization is striking in view of the observed gender differences in love and the importance that females appear to attach to romance in American society.

This paper examines the development of feeling norms underlying romantic love among early adolescent females. Adolescence is relevant to the study of romantic socialization of females; previous research documents that romance and male-female relationships are important to white adolescent girls. During adolescence, many girls become interested in romance and begin to form romantic relationships (Eder 1988; Eder and Sanford 1986; Griffin 1985; Lees 1986; McRobbie 1978; L. Rubin 1977; Schofield 1982). Research also shows that in adolescence, girls' earlier concerns with academic and athletic achievement are replaced with concerns about being popular, well-liked, and attractive (Rosenberg and Simmons 1975; Youniss and Smollar 1985).

These studies point to the peer group as central for promoting the importance of romance to adolescent females, and suggest that relationships with boys are a means by which girls attain social status and popularity. Whereas some authors emphasize that simply having a boyfriend enhances girls' peer group status, others claim that being in a romantic relationship also validates girls' attractiveness, which in turn increases their popularity and self-image (Holland and Eisenhart 1990; Schofield 1982; Wulff 1988). Yet although adolescence is a period when females become interested in romance and male-female relationships, we argue that during this period, girls also are obtaining normative information about romantic feelings in the context of female friendships. To date, little attention has been given to *how* adolescent females acquire general cultural knowledge about romantic love and develop specific norms to guide romantic feelings.

In this paper we discuss the content of feeling and expression norms underlying romantic love as they emerge in adolescent girls' peer culture. We also discuss the various ways in which feeling norms are communicated to group members. Although adolescent girls may obtain normative information about romantic feelings in other social relationships and in other social contexts—as well as through media such as romance novels, music, television, and films—the focus of this paper is limited to affective socialization processes among peers in school contexts because we do not have data on those other socialization agents. Peer groups, however, are an important source of emotional socialization because of the primacy of these groups to youths. In interaction with peers, young people draw on norms and beliefs that are available in the broader culture and make them meaningful by applying them to their everyday concerns

and activities (Corsaro and Rizzo 1988; Mead 1934). By focusing on peer group socialization, we show that while adolescent girls are acquiring cultural knowledge about love, they also are creating and continuously negotiating feeling norms which pertain to the emergent concerns of their peer culture.

DATA AND METHODS

We collected the data for this paper as part of an ethnographic study of adolescent socialization and peer interaction in a middle school. The school that was selected for the study was located in a medium-sized mid-western community. The school enrolls sixth-, seventh-, and eighth-grade students from a range of socioeconomic backgrounds, including youths from upper middle-class and lower working-class families. Most of the students were white, but a small number of black youths were enrolled at the school. The school was large, with approximately 250 students in each grade.

Data on peer interaction and relations were collected over a three-year period and involved a variety of methods, including participant observation, audio and audiovisual recording, and in-depth group interviews. Three female researchers observed a total of 10 female peer groups during lunch periods twice a week, over periods ranging from five to nine months. Three of these groups were studied for two years. The groups were representative of groups at different status levels within the school as well as of different-sized cliques. Data were obtained on high- through low-status peer groups and on peer groups that ranged in size from dyads to groups of 12 members.[3]

In order to examine groups at each grade level, we observed two eighth-grade groups, three-seventh grade groups, and two sixth-grade groups during the first year of the study. In the second year, we followed two seventh-grade groups into the eighth grade. Because the sixth-grade groups had dissolved by the second year, however, we observed two new seventh-grade groups (consisting of some of the girls from the original sixth-grade groups) in addition to a group of eighth-grade special education students. In the third year, we followed a seventh-grade group into the eighth grade. Table 1 shows the grade level, status lev-

Table 1 Grade Level, Status Level, and Number of Members of Each Group Observed in Each Year of the Study

Grade Level	YEAR 1			YEAR 2			YEAR 3		
	8th	7th	6th	8th	7th	6th	8th	7th	6th
STATUS LEVEL									
High	12[a]								
Medium high	9	9	2	9[b]					
Medium low		7,5	12	7[b]	8,4		8[b]		
Low				6					

[a] In addition to 12 female group members, this group also contained nine male members.

[b] Groups that had been observed the previous year.

el, and size of each group that we observed during each year.

At the beginning of the study, we told the students that we were interested in their lunch-room activities and conversations. Because we spent time with each group and avoided assuming any authority over the students, a high degree of rapport was established. Several weeks into the study, many students felt free to swear in front of us and often assured other students that we were "okay."

After observing groups for a minimum of three months, we made and transcribed audio and/or video recordings of conversations with eight of the groups. In addition, we conducted in-depth interviews on romance with the girls in two groups that had a strong interest in this topic. Field notes and transcriptions of naturally occurring conversations among these girls show that their views about romance were similar to those of girls in other groups that also had romantic interests. We coded each type of data for content relevant to the topic of romance. We conducted computer searches on the codes in order to identify all references to romance and feeling norms.

Data from interviews, recorded conversations, and field notes are employed in this paper. It is important to combine these various types of data to study thoroughly the development of feeling norms underlying romance. Data from in-depth interviews reveal the girls' current beliefs and norms about romantic love but fail to show how their knowledge is acquired

through daily activities. For that purpose we turned to an examination of field notes and transcripts of naturally occurring conversations. These types of data are essential for identifying not only the content of feeling norms that underlie romantic love, but also the processes through which these norms are developed and conveyed in day-to-day interaction. Also, by examining daily speech activities we can examine how emotion norms and beliefs are reflected in actual discourse. Without this level of analysis, it is easy to assume greater conformity to emotion norms than actually exists. Finally, our analysis of field notes helps us identify certain feeling norms which are so taken for granted that they are no longer regarded as constraints.

Although data from all of the groups were analyzed for this paper, some groups of girls were more interested in romance and had more contact with boys than others. Among the girls who had romantic interests, relationships with boys varied considerably. In fact, at this school, the term "going together" was used widely by both girls and boys to refer to a variety of romantic relationships, ranging from those which lasted several months to those which lasted one or two days. In some cases, the girl and the boy spent their lunch period together; in others, the couple had minimal contact at school.[4] In most cases, the relationships were brief (less than two weeks) and were limited to some social contact at school, which sometimes included expressions of affection such as hand holding and kissing. Interestingly, even though many of the high-status girls were going with boys, they engaged in fewer conversations about romance than girls in the medium high- and medium low-status peer groups. Most conversations about romance took place when boys were absent, so these girls may have discussed romance less frequently because boys were regular members of their lunch group. The group that discussed romance the least was the low-status group of special education students, none of whom had a boyfriend. Thus, although the feeling norms *and* the affective socialization processes discussed in this paper are likely to be generalizable to other groups of white adolescent females who are interested in romance and in male-female relationships, they are not meant to reflect the experiences of all girls of this age.

FEELING NORMS UNDERLYING ROMANTIC LOVE IN ADOLESCENT FEMALE PEER CULTURE

We begin with the observation that romantic love was a frequent topic of conversation among the female students. By the seventh grade, most of the girls at the school had become concerned with romance and had begun to form relationships with boys. While the girls were obtaining normative information about romantic love, the feelings and behavior that group members considered appropriate were still in the process of negotiation. Some feeling norms were generally accepted; others were not shared by all group members. An examination of the girls' talk about romantic love revealed that they used a variety of discourse strategies to communicate normative information and clarify feeling norms.

Norm 1: Romantic Relationships Should Be Important, but Not Everything in Life.

Previous research shows that white adolescent females tend to embrace traditional feminine concerns of romance, marriage, and domesticity and to reject both academic and athletic values (Eder 1985; Griffin 1985; Kessler et al. 1985; Lever 1978; McRobbie 1978). Although romance was salient to most of the girls in this study, group members had mixed attitudes about the importance of relationships with boys

in relation to their other interests and activities. Some girls thought "they could not live without boys"; others believed that "learning about themselves and their schoolwork" was primary (interview, eighth-grade group, March 30, 1983). Concerns about the relative importance of romantic love required the development of a feeling norm among adolescent females.

One such norm that had begun to emerge in some peer groups was that romantic relationships should be important, but not everything in life. Many seventh- and eighth-grade girls agreed that relationships with boys were important. Group members, however, also were becoming critical of friends who were perceived as "boy-crazy," a term used by adolescents to describe girls who made boys their primary interest and activity. As the following two examples illustrate, this norm still was being negotiated when the girls were in the eighth grade.

In the first example, one group of girls debates the relative importance of romantic relationships. This exchange was part of an in-depth group interview about romance novels, which many eighth-grade girls liked to read. Ellen, Hanna, Natalie, Peg, and Tricia had been discussing why they liked reading romance novels when the researcher asked them how important romantic love was to them. Ellen began by expressing her view that boys are the most important thing in her life, a view that runs counter to the emerging feeling norm.[5]

1	Ellen:	Boys [are] the most important thing in my life. That's what I
2		marked it on my value chart today.
3	Hanna:	Yes. I know.
4	Researcher:	Why? Why are boys the most important // thing?
5	Hanna:	Boys, um (pleasure)
6	Ellen:	You can't live without 'em!
7	Natalie:	You can't live // with 'em and you can't live without 'em!
8	Peg:	You can't live with 'em.
9	Ellen:	You can too.
10	Tricia:	That's // a matter of opinion.
11	Ellen:	There is no way—there is no way a girl could live her
12		whole life without a boy.
13	Tricia:	I can.
14	Ellen:	You can live your whole life without a boy?
15	Tricia:	Yeah. // I'm not goin' to, though.

16 Peg: Uh uh!
17 Ellen: (be isolated) you never kissed one or nothin'.
18 Natalie: Lesbies can.
19 Researcher: That's true.
20 Tricia: You wouldn't know, Natalie. ((laughing)) (interview, eighth grade, March 30).

In this example it is clear that group members had conflicting views about the relative importance of romance, and expressed their opinions openly. Yet even though the girls engaged in a normative debate, they expressed conflict in a playful, nonserious way. Rather than responding defensively to Ellen's question in Line 14, Tricia said teasingly that even though she could live without boys, she was not going to do so. In Line 18, Natalie's substitution of the word "lesbies" for lesbians contributes to the playfulness of this exchange.

Whereas normative debates often were carried out in a playful and joking manner, conflict exchanges over normative issues were sometimes quite serious. This was especially true when lighter disputes were unsuccessful at producing normative consensus, as in the next example. The following exchange was part of the same group interview. At this point Ellen not only had stated repeatedly that boys were her central interest, but also had been flirting with some boys at a nearby table.

 1 Researcher: What about you, Tricia? How do you feel // about it all?
 2 Peg: Ellen, // I'm only teasin', gosh! ((singsong voice))
 3 Tricia: I feel the same way that Peg does. Especially now when
 4   we're just about to go into high school, our grades are more
 5   important than // boys.
 6 Natalie: See, we may be friends // with them, but we're not sluts.
 7 Researcher: Um hum. ((To Tricia))
 8 Hanna: Will you repeat that, please? ((angry voice))
 9 Tricia: No, /1/ you /2/ don't qualify.
10 Natalie: /1/ I know, but we're not sluts.
11 Ellen: /2/ (   ) fuck you (you guys))! ((Ellen stomps off, angry
12   and upset)) (interview, eighth grade, March 30).

In both examples, the girls openly expressed their conflicting views about the relative importance of romance and clarified this feeling norm to group members. In the second example, however, the conflict escalated and became more serious and more heated. Tricia and Peg became annoyed when the emerging norm was violated repeatedly, and engaged in confrontations when their friends' attitudes and behaviors did not match their expectations. In Lines 6 and 10, for example, Natalie accuses violators of this norm of being "sluts." Responses to norm violations are important ways in which group members develop and communicate knowledge about interpersonal and interactional norms (Eder and Sanford 1986; Mehan

1979). Although conflict was not resolved in either of these exchanges, the girls learned through these debates what their friends viewed as appropriate and inappropriate feeling and behavior with respect to this norm. Romantic love was a salient emotion for most of these girls, but several were concerned with setting some limits on its importance.

The Object of Romantic Feelings   According to Gordon (1981, p. 567), "sentiments," such as romantic love, are feelings that are "organized around a relationship to a social object, usually another person." While the girls were developing a norm about the relative importance of romance, they also were acquiring cultural knowledge about the object of romance. In fact, by the eighth grade, three norms concerning the object of romantic feelings had emerged.

Norm 2: One Should Have Romantic Feelings Only for Someone of the Opposite Sex

The most basic feeling norm concerning the object of romance was that one should have romantic feelings only for someone of the opposite sex. By the time they had become actively interested in romance, a norm of heterosexuality had developed in these groups of girls. In contrast to the previously discussed feeling norm, there was considerable consensus for this norm. In view of the general negative view of homosexuality at the school and the label attached to alleged norm violators, it is not surprising that this norm was widely accepted. We found that the girls used a variety of discourse strategies to clarify and reinforce the norm of heterosexuality to friends. The way in which this norm was communicated depended upon whether alleged norm violators were nongroup or group members.

One way in which the norm of heterosexuality was communicated was through gossip about nongroup members' deviant affect and behavior. Girls who did not express romantic interest in boys or who had gender-atypical interests often were the targets of gossip. For example, Sandy and Paula were discussing Sandy's sister in the sixth grade, who did not share their romantic interest in boys and who was interested in sports and in becoming a mechanic.

> Sandy said her sister is extremely different from her and has absolutely no interest in boys—she considers boys pests. Sandy referred to her sister as a tomboy. She said that since her sister is a tomboy, if she liked boys then she would be queer, but on the other hand, if she liked girls then she would really be queer. Then Paula added jokingly that if she didn't like anyone at all she would still be queer. I [researcher] said, "It sounds like she doesn't have a chance" (field notes, seventh grade, May 24).

This example shows that Sandy and Paula were reinforcing a feeling norm of which they had only limited understanding. Girls at this school were establishing violations of the norm of heterosexuality on the basis of gender-inappropriate behavior. Sandy's sister's outward disinterest in boys as well as her nontra-

ditional interests and behaviors were considered by these group members to be deviant with regard to the norm of heterosexuality. Yet, by establishing violations of this norm on the basis of nonstereo-typical gender-role behavior, the girls were reinforcing and reproducing existing gender norms that ultimately constrain their own behavior.[6]

In general, it was not uncommon for girls and boys who were not actively pursuing romantic relationships or who routinely engaged in gender-inappropriate behavior to be labeled homosexual. In fact, children at the school who were perceived to be deviant in other ways were the objects of these allegations as well (Evans and Eder 1989). Unpopular students who were viewed as unattractive and/or unintelligent also were singled out for group discussions in which they were accused indirectly of being homosexual.

> Annie said, "I'm gonna beat that girl up someday," referring to twins and a little chubby girl in a green sweater who were sitting at the middle of the table pretty far down. So we all turned to look at her and Marsha agreed that she was really disgusting, that "they're gay" (field notes, seventh grade, February 3).

Rather than relying on the display of romantic feelings toward someone of the same sex as an indication of affective deviance, Annie and Marsha accused these girls of being "gay" solely on the basis of physical appearance.

A second way in which the norm of heterosexuality was communicated was by teasing group members. Humor often was used when the girls confronted their friends about norm violations. Group members frequently teased one another about behaviors that could be interpreted as homosexual, such as close physical contact between friends. Although many girls still viewed close physical contact between friends as acceptable, others were beginning to redefine such expressions of affection as inappropriate.

> The little girl with glasses came over and actually sat on Andrea's lap. She's so tiny that she can do this easily, and Andrea laughed and said, "You're really not my type" (field notes, sixth grade, May 20).

Not only did the girls tease one another about overt expressions of affection; they also chided one another about their actual feelings. Statements concerning both positive and negative affect for females were a frequent source of group humor.

> ... they were talking about why would somebody like this particular girl. Debby said, "I wouldn't like her!" Melinda said, "Well, I should *hope* not" (field notes, eighth grade, April 20).

In addition to teasing one another about their feelings and behaviors, group members also chided each other about their best-friend relationships. In fact, adolescence is a period in which female friendships are faced with a dilemma. Even while intimate feelings between close friends usually deepen, girls routinely tease one another about the romantic implications of these relationships.

> Julie said something about how Bonnie and somebody were considered her best mates. Right away Mia said, "Ooooh ..." as this sort of implied that they were gay. Hillary picked up on that and went "Ooooh!" (field notes, eighth grade, April 9).

The final way in which the norm of heterosexuality was communicated was through self-denial. Self-denials often were used to clarify the nature of intimate female friendships. Although many girls at the school continued to have strong positive feelings for their female friends, verbal and behavioral expressions of affection frequently were followed by a disclaimer. In light of the pressures for heterosexuality from peers and the seriousness of norm violations, it is not surprising that many girls at the school became quite concerned that their own feelings and behaviors towards their close friends might be perceived by others as homosexual.

> Sally was really talkative today, and it was interesting to see her being so talkative. She was going on and on about how somebody would sign her letters "love you queerly." She said, "I always sign my letters 'love you dearly, but not queerly.'" But then she was joking, saying, "I didn't know what that meant," until Mary explained it to her. Then they were joking about how innocent she was and didn't even know what "queer" meant (field notes, seventh grade, March 3).

Whereas self-denials often were humorous, denials of affective deviance with respect to the norm of heterosexuality sometimes were quite serious. The girls were especially self-conscious about expressions of affection that were overt and therefore readily observable. They were concerned that nongroup members would misinterpret these visible signs of affection as romantic.

> Alice told me that she had taken a bunch of photographs recently. She said it was embarrassing because most of the pictures were taken when people happened to be hugging and kissing each other, and that she hoped she got hold of the pictures before her mother did when they got back from being developed. She said, for example, "Natalie and another girl were hugging each other in friendship" (which meant that she wanted me to know that that was differentiated from a romantic hug) (field notes, eighth grade, February 7).

Not only was Alice embarrassed by the hugging and kissing in the photographs, but she also was concerned that if her mother saw the pictures, she might interpret these actions as homosexual. By distinguishing between a "friendship" hug and a "romantic" hug, however, Alice clarified both to herself and to the researcher that this behavior was within the realm of acceptable conduct.

Overall the norm of heterosexuality was communicated among adolescent females through gossip, teasing, and self-denials. In these discussions, group members collectively explored what does and does not constitute homosexual feeling and behavior in order to develop an understanding of this feeling norm and of norm violations. Through these discussions, however, the girls not only expressed their own homophobic concerns but also supported and maintained the broader cultural norm of heterosexuality. Many girls at the school continued to value intimate relationships with females; nevertheless they upheld and reproduced what Rich (1980) called "the norm of compulsory heterosexuality."

Norm 3: One Should Not Have Romantic Feelings for a Boy Who Is Already Attached

Another feeling norm that had emerged in regard to the object of romance was that one should not have romantic feelings for a boy who is already attached. A corollary of this norm was that if one had such feelings, they should not be expressed. In most groups, the development of this norm was a direct response to changes in group members' romantic activities. The norm of exclusivity had only minimal relevance during an earlier phase, when the girls were first becoming interested in romance, but this norm had become highly salient by the time they began to form relationships with boys.

Early in the seventh grade, most of the girls talked about the boys they liked,[7] but often were shy about letting boys know their feelings. As long as romantic activities consisted of only talking about the objects of their affection, the norm of exclusivity had little significance. In fact, during this stage in the development of their romantic activities, it was not uncommon for many group members to like the same boy. Just as they might have other interests in common, sharing a romantic interest in a particular boy was considered to be acceptable, if not appropriate.

> Interestingly enough, Marsha and Josephine talked about how they both liked this guy Jack. They pointed him out to me and I [researcher] said, "Oh, oh, you both like the same guy?" They said, "Oh yeah, it's okay. We can do that. We always like the same people, but we don't get mad at each other" (field notes, seventh grade, March 30).

In an interview with another group of seventh-grade girls, it became clear that the distinction between *liking* and *going with* the same boy is important. The former is permissible; the latter is not.

1 Carrie:	They can like, like, like as much as they want, but they
2	don't // (go)
3 Marla:	They don't two-time!
4 Researcher	But what?
5 Carrie:	They can like a person as much as they want.
6 Researcher:	Can two friends *go* together // with the same boy?
7 (Alice):	Oh, they don't have any choice // (they)
8 Carrie:	No.
9 Bonnie:	No (interview, seventh grade, May 24).

Throughout this year, many girls began to pursue boys openly and to make their feelings more public, often through a friend who served as an intermediary. Once a group member had acted openly on her feelings and formed a relationship with a boy, it was no longer acceptable for other girls either to have or to express romantic feelings for him. At this point in the development of their romantic activities, the norm of exclusivity had become highly salient, and violations began to be perceived as a serious threat. Most of the girls became concerned about violations; they were resentful and jealous of those who did not abide by the norm of exclusivity.

Gossip was one way in which the girls clarified and reinforced this norm. In the following example from a seventh-grade interview, Natalie is accusing Rhoda, an attractive group member, of flirting with her and Tricia's boyfriends.

1 Natalie:	Rhoda, every time I get a boyfriend or Tricia gets a boyfriend
2	# or or we like somebody, she starts # y'know messing around
3	with him and everything and # y'know—and everything, she
4	shows her ass off and so, they start *likin'* her, right? And she
5	did that, she was trying to do that to Sammy Jones #
6	Tricia's boyfriend # ya know, the one that broke up with her
7	after four months (interview, seventh grade, May 24).

Although gossip episodes such as this do not inform norm violators about the deviant nature of their behavior, they communicate normative information to other group members (Eder and Enke 1988; Fine 1986; Goodwin 1980).

The girls considered it inappropriate to have or express romantic feelings not only for a boy who was involved with someone else, but also for a boy whom a group member was in the process of pursuing. Group members sometimes engaged in confrontations with alleged norm violators in order to communicate their inappropriate behavior and affect. In the next exchange, several members of a seventh-grade group directly accuse Carol of flirting with Ted, a boy Betty is pursuing but not currently going with. Although Carol argues initially that she has not done anything wrong, later she agrees to be an intermediary for Betty in order to resolve the dispute.

1	Mary:	Ted came up to Carol and said she—that he loved her.
2	Linda:	Who?
3	Betty:	*Carol!*
4	Carol:	What?
5	Betty:	I don't like you no more.
6	Carol:	What'd I do?
7	Linda:	Taking Betty's boyfriend.
8	Carol:	I didn't either! ((pounds table as she half laughs))
9	Mary:	It wasn't Carol's *fault,* though.
10	Betty:	*Yes it was!* She *flirts!*
11	Carol:	I was just walking there // ( ).
12	Betty:	You *flirt,* You *flirt.* Yes, you //
13	Carol:	I didn't even do nothing. ((laughter))
14	Betty:	You *flirt,* Carol! You're mean! I don't like you no more.
15	Carol:	You won't (mind me) after I get done talking # *if* you still
16		want me to.
17	Betty:	Huh?
18	Carol:	If you—do you want me to still talk to him? // ((Betty
19		nods)) Alright, shut up. God.
20	Nancy:	Hell, she called me up, she goes, "Nancy, call Ted and talk to
21		him."
22	Betty:	(I sank you) ((silly voice)) (taped conversation, seventh grade, May 5).

This example is interesting because it shows that these girls expect their friends to know not only with whom they are going, but also their *intentions* to become romantically involved with certain boys. Acceptable contact with these boys is limited to behavior that will promote their friends' romantic interests (e.g., serving as intermediaries), and excludes any friendly behavior that might encourage romantic feelings to develop. As shown in the previous example, such behavior makes a girl subject to the negative label "flirt."[8] It is also noteworthy that group members use confrontations such as this to sanction inappropriate behavior and affect. Because violations of the norm of exclusivity have serious consequences for group members, including the possibility of being in competition with friends over boys, it is not surprising that confrontations sometimes are used to clarify and reinforce this norm.

Although most group members increasingly saw the need for the norm of exclusivity to protect themselves from unpleasant feelings of jealousy, some girls were reluctant to give up the freedom to have or express romantic feelings whenever they desired. Because norm violations were viewed as serious, girls who continued to defy this norm occasionally engaged in playful modes of interaction whereby they could express their "deviant" feelings while acknowledging the norm of exclusivity.

For example, several seventh-grade girls were teasing Mary about "liking" Wally and dragged her over to the ball diamond, where Wally was playing softball. The teasing consisted of trying to get Mary to

talk with him and telling Wally that Mary wanted to "go in the stairwell" with him. Mary refused to talk to Wally. This reaction led to some joking exchanges among the other group members, several of whom also had romantic feelings for Wally.

1	Carol:	I'll take him if you don't.
2	Elaine:	Whoo! You hear that one, Wally?
3	Carol:	Well, I don't care.
4	Elaine:	Wally, Wally, Wally, Wally. She says she'll take
5		ya if Mary don't want ya. ((Unrelated talk for
6		five turns.))
7	Elaine:	She said she'd take ya if Mary don't want ya.
8	Mary:	What'd you tell him Elaine? Elaine // ( )
9	Linda:	Hey you! If Mary don't want ya and Carol don't
10		want ya, I'll take ya!
11	Carol:	Uh uh, I will. I'll take him if Mary don't and
12		then if I don't, you do (taped conversation, seventh grade, April 7).

Here the girls use playful teasing to inform Wally of their romantic feelings, while acknowledging at the same time that they will wait to act on these feelings until Mary no longer "wants" him. The joking nature of this exchange provides these girls with more freedom to express their feelings for Wally and thus to violate the norm of exclusivity.[9]

This finding suggests that feeling and expression norms do not determine adolescent girls' affect and behavior, but serve as an important cultural resource which is incorporated into their action. Through expressing their knowledge of this norm, in fact, these girls succeed in expressing their feelings for a boy who is being pursued by a friend. At the same time, their ability to transform cultural knowledge into a playful frame gives them an opportunity to violate the norm without negative sanctions.

In brief, when group members began to pursue boys and form romantic relationships, the girls developed the norm of exclusivity to deal with their new concerns. They communicated this norm through gossip and confrontations as well as in more playful modes of discourse. Yet even though norm violations were viewed negatively by most of the girls, several group members did not feel compelled to abide by this norm. Instead they responded with "resistance" by

continuing to hold and express romantic feelings for boys who were already "taken." In some cases their resistance was communicated through playful teasing, which allowed them to express their normatively inappropriate feelings while simultaneously showing their awareness of the norm of exclusivity.

Norm 4: One Should Have Romantic Feelings for Only One Boy at a Time

The third feeling norm pertaining to the object of romance was that one should have romantic feelings for only one boy at a time. A corollary was that if one had romantic feelings for more than one boy, these feelings should not be expressed. In some groups, the development of the norm of monogamy reflected the girls' awareness of the societal norm of monogamy. In other groups, however, this norm was developed to deal with the problems created by having multiple boyfriends.

For example, when we asked one group of seventh-grade girls about the possibility of going with more than one person at a time, the reason they gave for avoiding this behavior was the likelihood of creating jealousy among boyfriends. Because jealousy and other forms of conflict among males were expressed frequently in physical fights, the consequences of creating jealousy were considered to be quite serious.

I asked if you could only go with one person at a time and she said, "It depends on who you're talking about." She said that you should only go with one at a time but that some girls went with more than one. I asked why they shouldn't do that, and she said because "then you get a couple of jealous boyfriends on your hands" and they might end up getting into a fight, and that it was best to avoid that (field notes, seventh grade, April 27).

Some girls continued to have multiple boyfriends, but were careful to become involved only with boys who were separated geographically. As long as a boy was unaware of his girlfriend's other romantic involvements, jealousy and its negative consequences could be avoided. For some of these girls, in fact, having multiple boyfriends was a source of status—something they bragged about to their female friends.

Effie and Laura had a long conversation. Laura told Effie that she was going with two guys, one from Royalton and another from California. She said that they were both going to be coming down this summer and she didn't know what to do. She presented this as a dilemma, but she was laughing about it. She really wanted to show that she was popular with boys (field notes, eighth grade, April 6).

Although some groups developed the norm of monogamy to deal with the practical problems associated with having multiple boyfriends, in other groups the development of this norm reflected group members' knowledge of the cultural norm of monogamy. When we asked one group of seventh-grade girls whether two people could go with the same boy, their response turned to the inappropriateness of having multiple romantic partners.

1	Researcher:	How come two people can't go with the same boy at the same
2		time? It seems like you could logi-
3	Ellen:	Because you're only supposed to—when you go with a person
4		like if you
5	Natalie:	It's like a bigamist.
6	Ellen:	Oh . . .
7	Natalie:	You know, when you
8	Ellen:	Like a what?
9	Natalie:	A bigamist. Like when you go with somebody. Like it's, it's
10	Ellen:	Two-timing.
11	Natalie:	When you go with each other the same—when you go with each
12		other it's kinda like gettin' married or somethin', you
13		know, and like if you're goin' with two people at the same
14		time it's like a bigamist.
15	Ellen:	Like Natalie did!
16	Natalie:	Yeah, I did that once.
17	Ellen:	Yeah, with Steve and Robert.
18	Natalie:	I did it twice. ((Natalie and Ellen burst out laughing)) (interview, seventh grade, May 24).

This example illustrates that the girls are drawing on their knowledge of the societal norm of monogamy (which pertains to marriage) in order to develop a feeling norm regarding multiple partners which is relevant to their own romantic relationships. The exchange also shows that even though these girls agreed that it was inappropriate to have romantic feelings for

more than one boy at a time, violations of this norm were not perceived as serious.

By the time these girls were in eighth grade, however, having romantic feelings for more than one boy was no longer viewed as acceptable. Moreover, they used different strategies to clarify this norm and to sanction deviant affect and behavior. In the following exchange, Ellen and Hanna are telling the other girls about what happened at church the night before. Because Ellen is already going with Craig, she is first accused and later reprimanded for going to church solely to meet other boys.

1	Ellen:	We were sittin' there starin' at guys at church last night,
2		me and Hanna were, and—
3	Hanna:	And she saw one that looked just like Craig.
4	Natalie:	But # // I was—
5	Ellen:	I wasn't starin' at him.
6	Hanna:	That was groaty.
7	(Natalie:)	You're going with Craig.
8	Ellen:	I know. I stared at Steve. ((laughs))
9	Hanna:	I know, but he looks like him in the face,
10	Natalie:	But, um, he just—
11	Peg:	You // go to church for a different reason than that, Ellen!
12	Natalie:	I // get stuck on one guy.
13	Peg:	Then you shouldn't of been there (interview, eighth grade, March 30).

Although Peg and Natalie considered this violation to be serious, Ellen continued to view it as humorous, laughing as she acknowledged that she "stared" at another boy. Given Ellen's reluctance to consider the seriousness of her violation, Peg and Natalie used more confrontive strategies to inform her about the inappropriateness of her affect and behavior with respect to this norm.[10]

As girls begin to take this norm seriously, they need to become more aware of their romantic feelings. They may even begin to modify their emotions on certain occasions, changing romantic attractions to non-romantic feelings in order to avoid norm violations. Sometimes the girls explicitly discussed their feelings toward boys, thus showing their close monitoring of these feelings. Awareness of romantic feelings was especially important during times of transition from one boyfriend to another. Because "going together" arrangements typically lasted less than two weeks, these transitions were frequent.

> Gwen and Ellen went "cruising" with some boys over the weekend. The boy Gwen was with asked her to go with him but he broke up with her the next morning because another boy that Gwen went with last week threatened to beat him up. So then the other boy asked her back with him Monday morning and she's going with him again now. She said that "one thing I can say for certain is that I love (the boy she's going with), but I can also say for certain that I really like (the boy she went with on Saturday)" (field notes, eighth grade, March 30).

Through Gwen's claim that she "loves" the boy she is currently going with and "likes" the boy she went with on Saturday, her feelings appear to conform with the norm of monogamy. Although it is not clear whether her current feelings are the result of emotion (or expression) work, it is clear that she pays close attention to her feelings and can discuss them with "certainty."[11]

Other girls expressed more confusion about their emotions. In some cases, their confusion stemmed from the discrepancy between their *actual* feelings and the feelings they thought they *ought* to have. Even though they knew that they *should* have romantic feelings for only one boy at a time, girls sometimes found themselves feeling multiple attractions.

> I heard Karla being teased when a specific boy walked by. Her friends were saying that she had a crush on him and once they yelled it at the boy. Karla acted rather embarrassed and angry about this. When they yelled at the boy, they asked Karla if it was true that she liked him. Karla said that she did like him "for a friend." They said that they had seen her walking with him in the halls. After a long pause

Karla asked Laura rather indignantly, "How could I like him when I'm already going with somebody?" Effie said, "Two-timing." Karla was embarrassed and seemed rather mild in her denial (field notes, eighth grade, April 21).

Karla's feelings are creating some discomfort for her because they do not conform readily to this feeling norm. She claims that she likes the other boy only "for a friend," but she expresses embarrassment as well as anger toward her friends, who perceive it to be a stronger attraction. Although we do not know whether Karla subsequently modified her feelings and/or expressions toward this boy, emotion work might be necessary in situations such as this, if girls are to abide by the norm of monogamy.[12]

Norm 5: One Should Always Be in Love

The final feeling norm that emerged was that one should always be in love. This norm differed from those discussed previously in that it was not devised to deal with group concerns, but was developed largely to deal with the concerns of individuals. Whereas violations of most feeling norms had consequences for other group members and peers (e.g., the norms of heterosexuality, exclusivity, and monogamy), violations of this final norm had consequences only for individual girls. Because such violations did not affect others, this norm was held even less widely than those discussed previously. For many girls at the school, however, this emotion norm was a basic part of their knowledge and understanding of romantic love.

For some girls, the onset of their first romantic attraction was the beginning of a continuous state of being in love, often with frequent changes in the object of their feelings. In fact, simply having romantic feelings may have been more important than the actual boys to whom these feelings were directed. For example, a researcher noticed that a girl had "I love" written on her hand and asked her about it. Although this girl's romantic feelings had no particular target, she explained that she was ready to add the name of a boy as soon as a suitable target was found.

The importance of always being in love became particularly evident when relationships with boys end-

ed. For instance, when girls realized that a boy they had been going with now liked someone else, they often redirected their romantic feelings toward someone new.

> She said that she was just going to go up and ask him if he had any intention of going with her again, and if he didn't, she was just "going to have to find someone else." I don't think she has the concept in her mind that she could possibly not be involved with anyone (field notes, eighth grade, March 23).

The salience of this norm was related to the duration of adolescent romantic relationships. Although it might seem that "long-term" relationships would be preferred because girls would not continually have to seek out new boyfriends, some girls reported that being in a long-term relationship was a disadvantage because it took them out of circulation.

> Apparently Alice's boyfriend broke up with her today and she was unhappy. She saw him walk by the media center and called to him several times, but he ignored her purposely. She said that the worst of it was that she had gone with him several months, and during that time had progressively cut herself off from contact with other boys so that she didn't even have any male friends left (field notes, eighth grade, March 4).

Within four days Alice had a new boyfriend, but her comments show that replacing her old boyfriend was an important concern.

During the early stage in the development of their romantic activities, when the girls were beginning to have romantic feelings but did not act on them, all group members could adhere easily to this norm. Once they started to form romantic relationships, however, only the girls who were popular with boys could continually attract new boyfriends. In fact, the status associated with being popular with boys contributed to the salience of this norm among the girls at this school. At the same time, group members also had a hand in reinforcing this feeling norm.

> When Nancy came up she asked "Who do you like now, Carol?", a question which Nancy often asks Carol. Carol said, "Pete." Nancy said, "Oh yeah." Shortly after that Linda said, "Guess who Pete likes?" Betty said, "Carol." Nancy said, "God, you guys get

everything you want" (field notes, seventh grade, April 14).

Even though less popular girls could not attract new boyfriends so easily, nevertheless they were able to abide by this norm. One strategy commonly used by these as well as by the more popular girls was to "recycle" the boys with whom they had had a previous relationship.

```
1 Ellen:    And then she went with George and then she went to likin' Tom
2           again.
3 Natalie:  Yeah. ((pause)) But sometimes it kinda switches on and off, like
4           s—like you'll like one boy and then you'll get tired of 'im and
5           you go with somebody else and then you'll like him again. Like
6           with Bryan and Dale. I used to do that a lot (interview, seventh grade, May 24).
```

Natalie's comments suggest that her and her friends' feelings for former boyfriends sometimes are recreated for the purpose of conforming to this norm. Natalie's comments also imply that conformity is likely to result in emotion work on the part of these girls, who sometimes evoke romantic feelings for boys they were previously "tired of."[13]

The advantages of conforming to this norm include appearing to be popular with boys as well as providing ongoing evidence of a heterosexual orientation; both are important concerns to girls at this age. At the same time, however, conformity carries several possible costs. One such cost is that emotion work may be necessary in order to always be in love. Although we can only speculate at this point, adolescent girls sometimes may create romantic feelings for boys to whom they are not attracted so they can conform to this norm. Hochschild (1983b) argued that when insincere feelings are created routinely, people lose touch with their actual feelings. Insofar as girls have insincere feelings, it is possible that eventually they will have difficulty in distinguishing between their "real" romantic feelings and their less authentic feelings, which they created in order to satisfy the requirements of this norm.

A second potential cost stems from the dilemma faced by adolescent females as a result of their adherence to this norm. On the one hand, girls consider being continuously in love as socially desirable because it is a way to reaffirm their popularity with boys and thus to increase their own status in relation to other females. On the other hand, group members who both attract too much attention from males and appear to be indiscriminate in their choice of romantic partners are often criticized by their friends for being "sluts," and ultimately are viewed in a negative manner.

DISCUSSION

In this paper we argue that adolescence is a period during which females acquire cultural knowledge about romantic love, including the social norms that guide romantic feelings. In addition to obtaining normative information about romance, we found that the girls in this study had developed several feeling and expression norms to deal with their own concerns about romantic love. By the seventh and eighth grade, norms concerning the relative importance of romantic relationships as well as the appropriate object of romantic feelings had emerged in these groups of friends. Whereas some of these norms were highly developed and generally accepted (e.g., the norms of heterosexuality, exclusivity, and monogamy), others were not held by all group members and still were being negotiated (e.g., the norm concerning the relative importance of romantic relationships).

We also found that adolescent girls used a variety of discourse strategies to communicate normative information and to reinforce emotion norms to friends. In general, group members informed one another about feeling and expression norms through light and playful language activities, as well as through serious and confrontive modes of discourse. Language that involved humor was one of the more common discourse strategies used by these girls. Through joking and teasing remarks, group members could point out their friends' norm violations in an indirect, nonthreatening manner. Moreover, teasing and joking were ways in which the girls could show their awareness of feeling norms while simultaneously expressing their own normatively inappropriate emotions.

The girls also commonly used gossip and confrontations to clarify and reinforce feeling norms. Although gossip did not directly inform norm violators of their inappropriate affect and behavior, it provided normative information to other group members. Finally, confrontations sometimes were used when indirect strategies were ineffective at producing normative consensus and when norm violations had negative consequences for group members. In these exchanges, girls expressed social disapproval of affective deviance through accusations, insults, and reprimands. Not surprisingly, such exchanges often involved considerable conflict and tension. Overall, through these various language activities and modes of discourse, the girls conveyed what they viewed as appropriate and inappropriate in regard to the group's feeling and expression norms.

Even though girls obtain normative information about romantic love from friends, they do not always abide by emotion norms. Rather, our analysis of discourse revealed that group members sometimes responded with "resistance" and intentionally defied their group's feeling and expression norms. Therefore, feeling and expression norms underlying romantic love constrain but do not determine adolescent females' affect and behavior. Further research is necessary to determine the degree to which girls resist other emotion norms, as well as to identify the full range of emotion management processes used by adolescent females.

Romance is highly salient, however, because having a boyfriend enhances girls' popularity with peers at an age when being popular is important for their self-image. In fact, two norms that emerged in these peer groups reveal the salience of romance to girls during this period: the norms concerning the relative importance of romantic relationships and the importance of being in love continually. It is possible that even after romantic relationships become tied less closely to peer group status, females continue to feel that they always should be in a romantic relationship with a male in order to validate their attractiveness and worth to self and to others.

Although it was not our purpose to examine the actual emotional experiences of adolescent girls, our findings support the view that emotions are in part socially constructed and that feeling and expression are subject to normative influences. By focusing on romantic socialization in adolescent peer groups, we have shown how, in everyday interaction with friends, females obtain normative information about romantic feelings as well as maintaining, reproducing, and recreating one aspect of their society's emotion culture.

The focus on emotional socialization among adolescent peers also is important for understanding emotion processes more generally. Affective socialization, as a fluid, negotiated process that nonetheless leads to conformity to social norms, often is overlooked when attention is restricted to adult-child interaction and relations among adults. Our findings illustrate that older children not only acquire cultural knowledge about emotion but also challenge, refine, and alter this knowledge.

Although the results of our study should be generalizable to other adolescent white females, there is some evidence suggesting that black and other nonwhite females are less concerned with romance (Griffin 1985). This difference may occur because historically, nonwhite females have been less dependent than white females on marriage for economic sustenance or mobility. Additional research is necessary to assess whether the affective socialization processes described in this paper are specific to white girls, or whether they apply to girls from a variety of social and cultural backgrounds.

It also is important to learn more about affective socialization processes among females in adulthood. For example, it is conceivable that women make a greater distinction between feelings and expressions than girls, accepting a wider range of feelings but monitoring their expressions more closely. Women also may use different strategies when resisting the feeling and expression norms underlying romantic love. Interactional data on married and single women would be helpful in beginning to address these issues.

In this paper we begin to identify feeling norms that underlie romantic love among early adolescent females as well as outlining the social processes by which normative information about romantic feelings is obtained. This research, however, raises questions about affective socialization processes that we did not address here. We limited our analysis to peer group socialization in school, but it is likely that children also acquire cultural knowledge about romantic feelings through other social relationships and in other social contexts. For example, to what extent do children acquire normative information about romantic feelings from family members such as parents, siblings, and cousins?

Moreover, we focused on the ways in which adolescent females obtain normative information about romantic feelings in everyday interaction. Yet, girls also may acquire cultural knowledge about love through romance novels, television, and films. Do these media present explicit normative information about romantic feelings? If they do so, how is this information interpreted and used by adolescent females?

Furthermore, does romantic socialization differ for adolescent males? We know little about the ways in which boys gain normative information about romantic feelings. Are the affective socialization processes described here specific to females, or are they found also in adolescent male peer groups?

Finally, can we attribute gender differences in the experience, expression, and importance of love in adulthood, reported by Cancian (1985, 1987) and Hochschild (1983a), to these earlier affective socialization processes? Insofar as romantic love is more salient to adolescent females than to adolescent males, what are the implications of these differences not only for male-female romantic relationships, but also for gay and lesbian relationships, in adult life? Our understanding of romantic love in American culture will be broadened only when these questions are addressed.

NOTES

Address all correspondence to Robin W. Simon, Department of Sociology, Ballantine Hall 744, Indiana University, Bloomington, IN 47405. An earlier version of this paper by the senior author was presented at the annual meeting of the Midwest Sociological Society in St. Louis, April 1989. We gratefully acknowledge Brian Powell, Sheldon Stryker, and Peggy Thoits for their helpful suggestions on this paper. We also would like to thank Stephanie Sanford for her assistance in data collection and Daniella Simon for her help in data interpretation. This research was supported by NIMH Grant 36684.

1. Feeling norms are social norms that prescribe the appropriate intensity, duration, and target of emotions in social situations and relationships (Gordon 1981; Hochschild 1979). For a detailed description and analysis of sympathy norms, see Clark (1987). Stearns and Stearns (1986) and Cancian and Gordon (1988) provide insightful discussions of historical changes in emotion norms, regarding anger. For an examination of historical change in social norms concerning grief, see Lofland (1985).

2. Although Cancian's (1987) and Cancian and Gordon's (1988) research provides insight into the content of feeling norms governing love, they focus on norms that guide marital love and do not examine the content of norms underlying nonmarital romantic love.

3. We determined the status levels of the groups through participant observation. Students described those who sat on one side of the cafeteria as "popular" and those who sat on the other side as "grits." We studied four groups that sat on the "popular" side of the cafeteria: one high-status group that consisted of cheerleaders and their closest friends and three medium high-status groups. We also studied six groups on the "grit" side: five medium low-status groups and one low-status group, which consisted of special education students. Group size was determined by the numbers of students who sat with the group for at least one month of the period during which the group was observed. Not all members were present during the entire period, however, and many groups had visitors who sat with the group only occasionally.

4. Often the best friend of the girl and of the boy arranged these relationships by contacting the interested parties over the telephone, so that the couple might not have had much direct contact either before or after they started "going together."

5. All names are pseudonyms. The following notations are used in the examples from transcripts:

   ( ) refers to an uncertain or unclear utterance or speaker;
   (( )) refers to nonverbal behavior;
   // refers to the point at which the next speaker begins talking during someone else's turn;
   /1/ first interruption; /2/ second interruption;
   # refers to a brief pause.

6. See Berger and Luckman (1967) for a theoretical discussion of both the functions of language in the social construction of reality and the objectification of norms through socialization.

7. Although Zick Rubin's (1970, 1973) research shows that "liking" and "loving" are distinct emotional states, the girls in this study used these emotion words interchangeably, especially when referring to their romantic feelings for boys.

8. The label "flirt" has a double meaning among adolescent females. Whereas the term sometimes is used to describe girls who express romantic feelings toward a group member's boyfriend, it is also used to describe girls who express romantic

feelings for more than one boy. In the previous example, the girls used it in the former sense. Like the labels "gay" and "slut," the girls also use the label "flirt" to refer to an emotional social type. Emotional social types are persons who routinely violate emotion norms and who serve as examples in correcting young people's feeling and/or expression. See Gordon (1989) for a discussion of the functions of the emotional social type in childhood emotional socialization.

9. Although an alternative interpretation of this exchange is that the girls actually are supporting Mary's romantic interest rather than violating the norm of exclusivity, ethnographic data on these girls show that several of them in fact had romantic feelings for Wally. Because Mary was somewhat overweight, the girls did not take her interest in him seriously.

10. As among the college students in Waller's (1937) classic study of the "rating and dating complex," our data show that same-sex peers are more important than romantic partners in regulating adolescent girls' romantic feelings and behaviors.

11. Although our data do not permit us to assess whether these girls altered their emotions and/or expressions in order to conform to feeling norms, research by developmental psychologists shows that by age 11, children know that internally experienced affect need not be expressed (Saarni 1979) and that certain affective states can be manipulated intentionally (Harris and Olthof 1982).

12. One possible interpretation of these data is that these feeling norms concern how adolescent girls should conduct discourse about romantic love, rather than how they should feel and behave. The girls' normative statements in the interviews about affect and behavior, however, suggest that these norms are merely "rhetorical devices." Another possibility is that these norms pertain not to emotion per se but rather to romantic relationships. Indeed, it is difficult to disentangle the two, especially because the girls' conversations are not laden with emotion words. On the basis of the combination of ethnography, in-depth interviews, and naturally occurring discourse, however, we are convinced that these are norms about feelings corresponding to romantic relationships.

13. Although the scope of this paper does not include an examination of the role of the media in disseminating normative information about romantic feelings to adolescent females, studies of media messages indicate that teenage girls typically are portrayed in popular magazines, romance novels, and television programs as either having a boyfriend or actively seeking one (Cantor 1987). These messages may contribute to the development and maintenance of the feeling norm regarding the importance of being in love continually.

REFERENCES

Berger, Peter L. and Thomas Luckman. 1967. *The Social Construction of Reality: A Treatise in the Sociology of Knowledge.* New York: Anchor.

Cancian, Francesca M. 1985. "Gender Politics: Love and Power in the Private and Public Spheres." Pp. 253–64 in *Gender and the Life Course,* edited by Alice S. Rossi. New York: Aldine.

———. 1987. *Love in America: Gender and Self Development.* Boston: Cambridge University Press.

Cancian, Francesca M. and Steven L. Gordon. 1988. "Changing Emotion Norms in Marriage: Love and Anger in U.S. Women's Magazines since 1900." *Gender and Society* 2(3):308–42.

Cantor, Muriel. 1987. "Popular Culture and the Portrayal of Women: Content and Control." Pp. 190–214 in *Analyzing Gender,* edited by Beth Hess and Myra Marx Ferree. New York: Sage.

Clark, Candace. 1987. "Sympathy Biography and Sympathy Margin." *American Journal of Sociology* 93:290–321.

Corsaro, William A. and Thomas A. Rizzo. 1988. "Discussione and Friendship: Socialization Processes in the Peer Culture of Italian Nursery School Children." *American Sociological Review* 53:879–94.

Eder, Donna. 1985. "The Cycle of Popularity: Interpersonal Relations Among Female Adolescents." *Sociology of Education* 58:154–165.

———. 1988. "Teasing Activities Among Adolescent Females." Paper presented at conference "Gender Roles through the Life Span," Ball State University, Muncie, IN.

Eder, Donna and Janet Enke. 1988. "Gossip as a Means of Strengthening Social Bonds." Paper presented at the annual meeting of the American Sociological Association, Atlanta.

Eder, Donna and Stephanie Sanford. 1986. "The Development and Maintenance of Interactional Norms Among Early Adolescents." *Sociological Studies of Child Development* 1:283–300.

Evans, Cathy and Donna Eder. 1989. "'No Exit': Processes of Social Isolation in the Middle School." Paper presented at the annual meeting of the American Sociological Association, San Francisco.

Fine, Gary Alan. 1986. "The Social Organization of Adolescent Gossip: The Rhetoric of Moral Evaluation." Pp. 405–23 in *Children's Worlds and Children's Language,* edited by Jenny Cook-Gumperz, William Corsaro, and Jurgen Streeck. Berlin: Moulin.

Goodwin, Marjorie H. 1980. "He-Said-She-Said: Formal Cultural Procedures for the Construction of a Gossip Dispute Activity." *American Ethnologist* 7:674–95.

Gordon, Steven L. 1981. "The Sociology of Sentiments and Emotion." Pp. 562–92 in *Social Psychology: Sociological Perspectives,* edited by Morris Rosenberg and Ralph H. Turner. New York: Basic Books.

———. 1989. "The Socialization of Children's Emotions: Emotional Culture, Competence, and Exposure." Pp. 319–49 in *Children's Understanding of Emotion,* edited by Carolyn Saarni and Paul Harris. New York: Cambridge University Press.

Griffin, Christine. 1985. *Typical Girls?: Young Women from School to Job Market.* London: Routledge and Kegan Paul.

Harris, Paul and Tjeert Olthof. 1982. "The Child's Concept of

Emotion." Pp. 188–209 in *Social Cognition: Studies of the Development of Understanding,* edited by George Butterworth and Paul Light. Chicago: University of Chicago Press.

Hochschild, Arlie R. 1979. "Emotion Work, Feeling Rules, and Social Structure." *American Journal of Sociology* 85(3):551–75.

———. 1983a. "Attending to, Codifying and Managing Feelings: Sex Differences in Love." Pp. 250–62 in *Feminist Frontiers: Rethinking Sex, Gender, and Society,* edited by Laurel Richardson and Verta Taylor. New York: Addison-Wesley.

———. 1983b. *The Managed Heart: Commercialization of Human Feeling.* Berkeley: University of California Press.

Holland, Dorothy and Margaret Eisenhart. 1990. *Educated in Romance: Women, Achievement, and College Culture.* Chicago: University of Chicago Press.

Kessler, S., D. Ashenden, R. Connell, and G. Dowsett. 1985. "Gender Relations in Secondary Schooling." *Sociology of Education* 58:34–47.

Lees, Sue. 1986. *Sexuality and Adolescent Girls.* London: Hutchinson.

Lever, Janet. 1978. "Sex Differences in the Complexity of Children's Play and Games" *American Sociological Review* 43:471–483.

Lofland, Lyn H. 1985. "The Social Shaping of Emotion: Grief in Historical Perspective." *Symbolic Interaction* 8:171–90.

McRobbie, Angela. 1978. "Working Class Girls and the Culture of Femininity." Pp. 96–108 in *Women Take Issue,* edited by The Women's Study Group, Centre for Contemporary Cultural Studies. London: Hutchinson.

Mead, George Herbert. 1934. *Mind, Self, and Society.* Chicago: University of Chicago Press.

Mehan, Hugh. 1979. *Learning Lessons: Social Organization in the Classroom.* Cambridge: Harvard University Press.

Rich, Adrienne. 1980. "Compulsory Heterosexuality and Lesbian Existence." *Signs: Journal of Women in Culture and Society* 5:631–60.

Rosenberg, Florence and Roberta Simmons. 1975. "Sex Differences in the Self-Concept in Adolescence." *Sex Roles* 1:147–59.

Rubin, Lillian B. 1977. *Worlds of Pain: Life in the Working-Class Family.* New York: Basic books.

Rubin, Zick. 1970. "Measurement of Romantic Love." *Journal of Personality and Social Psychology* 16:265–73.

———. 1973. *Liking and Loving: An Invitation to Social Psychology.* New York: Holt, Rinehart and Winston.

Saarni, Carolyn. 1979. "Children's Understanding of Display Rules for Expressive Behavior." *Developmental Psychology* 15(4):424–29.

Schofield, Janet. 1982. *Black and White in School.* New York: Praeger.

Stearns, Carol Z. and Peter N. Stearns. 1986. *Anger: the Struggle for Emotional Control in America's History.* Chicago: University of Chicago Press.

Swidler, Ann. 1980. "Love and Adulthood in American Culture." Pp. 120–47 in *Themes of Work and Love in Adulthood,* edited by Neil J. Smelser and Erik H. Erickson. Cambridge: Harvard University Press.

Thoits, Peggy A. 1989. "The Sociology of Emotions." *Annual Review of Sociology* 15:317–42.

Waller, Willard. 1937. "The Rating and Dating Complex." *American Sociological Review* 2:727–34.

Wulff, Helena. 1988. *Twenty Girls: Growing Up, Ethnicity and Excitement in a South London Microculture.* Stockholm: University of Stockholm Press.

Youniss, James and Jacqueline Smollar. 1985. *Parents and Peers in Social Development: A Sullivan-Piaget Perspective.* Chicago University of Chicago Press.

FURTHER READING

Cahill, Spencer and Rebin Eggleston. 1994. "Managing Emotions in Public: The Case of Wheelchair Users." *Social Psychology Quarterly* 57: 300–312.

- The emotional challenges that wheelchair users face in public and the consequent management of their own and others' feelings.

Clark, Candace. 1987. "Sympathy Biography and Sympathy Margin." *American Journal of Sociology* 93: 290–321.

- Discusses the social feeling rules involved in sustaining sympathy.

Lofland, Lyn. 1985. "The Social Shaping of Emotion: The Case of Grief." *Symbolic Interaction* 8: 171–190.

- How grief is experienced in different historical periods.

Schachter, Stanley and Jerome E. Singer. 1962. "Cognitive, Social, and Physiological Determinants of Emotional State." *Psychological Bulletin* 69: 379–399.

- A classic study of the social and cognitive factors involved in interpreting emotional arousal.

Smith Allen C. and Sherryl Kleinman. 1989. "Managing Emotions in Medical School: Students' Contacts with the Living and the Dead." *Social Psychology Quarterly* 52: 56–69.

- How medical students manage their feelings interacting with dead bodies.

MOTIVES

We commonly treat motives as the reasons for what we do. Psychologists are especially interested in establishing motives as causes of conduct. In this view, the actions people take result from impulses that prompt them to behave in one way or another. These impulses or motives come from inside and take many forms. At one end of the spectrum, we trace what we do to our so-called primary or biological needs. These may be needs like thirst or hunger, which ostensibly causes us to eat or drink. Psychologists also identify motives they call "stimuli," such as frustration or rejection. These motives, they say, can lead to aggression or withdrawal. At the other end of the spectrum, we encounter more socially based causes for behavior. Peer group pressure, we hear, prompts the need to conform. This need, in turn, leads teenagers to act, dress, and talk just like their friends.

Psychologists aren't the only ones to think about motives in this way. We all do it. It's even the basis for people's jobs. Consider medical examiners or coroners, for instance. Let's say that Pete Smith has just fallen to his death from the 12th floor of a building. The coroner needs to assign a cause of death. Since no one saw the incident, the coroner will need to ascertain what went on that led Pete to plunge to his death. Perhaps it was a homicide. Someone pushed Pete out the window. Perhaps it was an accident. Pete was a window washer who slipped off precarious scaffolding. Perhaps it was suicide. But in this case, the coroner would have to determine what went on inside Pete's proverbial head. This is a search for motives. Was Pete depressed about his failure to get a promotion at work? Was he in despair because he'd been caught in an affair with a younger woman and was about to be exposed to his wife and family? Was Pete scared to face the prospect of dealing with a recently diagnosed disease like cancer?

Day in and day out, all of us assign motives to each other's actions. We refer to internal causes of conduct that range from bodily states to social conditioning. Indeed, part of our ability to understand others' actions rests on knowing their motives. Even the simplest social encounters hinge on knowing one another's motivations. Say, for example, Sue walks in the door, straight from a hard day at the office. Tom, her husband, calls out from the kitchen, "How was your day, honey?" But he doesn't get a response. Tom could make sense of this silence in a number of ways, all of them requiring the assignment of motives. "Oh, that's just Sue being absentminded," he might think. Her motive for not responding is a personality trait. That explains everything. "Maybe she's worried about work," Tom might think. A tough day at the office could lead her to ignore everyone—another reasonable motive. Or maybe, thinks Tom, she's just an inconsiderate jerk. Assigning this motive, of course, is probably a step in the direction of a marital spat.

In each instance, the motive that's assigned makes a big difference in how the evening is going to proceed. The same behavior may lead to strikingly different understandings and reactions, depending on how the motive behind it is defined. This is also true when we assign motives to our own actions. Sue might tell Tom that she was distracted. She'd just picked up the mail and was trying to figure out how the credit card bill could be so high. Or Sue might tell Tom she was ignoring him because she was angry, recalling some cross words they exchanged over breakfast. Whatever motives we choose to convey, they are crucial to how others respond to us. In the first instance, Tom might attend to Sue's concern over the bill and then ask about her day once more. In the second case, it may become "round two" of the breakfast table fight. Sue's silence remains the same, but the motives she and Tom assign to it make all the difference in the world.

As important as they are, we never actually observe motives. They're inner states that we can't ever see. Yet, in practice, these features of inner lives are crucial for understanding the actions that they seemingly motivate. Oddly enough, in everyday life, motives are designated *after* the actions they ostensibly cause. We can hardly assign motives to events that haven't happened yet. Still, we share the belief that motives cause behavior. We act as if they precede the actions that they cause. An interactional approach to inner lives doesn't blindly accept this belief. Instead, it treats motives as claims about, or explanations for, conduct. As features of talk and interaction, motives are working *accounts* for what people say and do. They are social building blocks of this aspect of our inner lives.

ABOUT THE READINGS

Years ago, philosopher **John Dewey** suggested that motives are socially constructed. In **"On Motive,"** he frames motives as a type of explanation we use to account for particular behaviors. Dewey defies conventional wisdom, writing that motives are "in truth extra-psychological." That locates them *outside* the individual. Reading on, we learn that Dewey thinks that motives are verbal attributions, explanations we offer, *after the fact,* for behavior. We may attribute Johnny's ravenous grab for a cookie to the child's hunger, for example. "Johnny must be starving," we may sympathetically exclaim as Johnny rips through a package of Oreos. In this scenario, Johnny's behavior is innocent because it's attributed to natural causes. But if, for some reason, we find Johnny's behavior displeasing, we may attribute to it the motive of greed or selfishness. Then, Johnny's not so innocent. Indeed, he may be in for big trouble. From this perspective, a motive isn't an inner psychological state. It's a communicative act that shapes the interpretation of persons and their behaviors.

In **"Situated Actions and Vocabularies of Motive,"** C. Wright Mills puts this counterintuitive view into historical and situational perspective. Like Dewey, Mills thinks of motives as explanations, not internal causes. He calls them "vocabularies" that communicate the causes for what people say and do. But, Mills adds, we don't attribute motives to ourselves and to others arbitrarily. Situations and history partly determine which attributions make sense and are convincing. For example, we may say we wear red hats everyday to ward off evil spells and spirits. Of course, that motive wouldn't make much sense today. It wouldn't be very convincing. We might have gotten away with the hat wearing and its motive, however, in a historical era when people believed in ghosts, spirits, and incantations. We're likely to be more convincing today by saying we are big St. Louis Cardinals fans. Mills points out, "Acts often will be abandoned if no reason can be found that others will accept." This places motives squarely within social situations. They are integral parts of our social worlds. We use them to reasonably account for what we do.

Joseph Hopper's chapter **"The Rhetoric of Motives in Divorce"** considers the motives used in divorce proceedings. Like Mills, Hopper sees motives as rhetorical accounts—in this case accounts for decisions to divorce. He's also careful to tie motive attribution to particular social situations, insisting that usage isn't arbitrary. Hopper discusses two vocabularies of motive used by divorcing partners. The person initiating the divorce emphasizes the importance of individual needs over marital commitment. The other partner typically invokes marriage vows, emphasizing interpersonal and familial responsibilities. Hopper also notes that motives emerge as accounts *after the fact,* only as partners gain a clear sense of their respective roles in the divorce proceedings. The rhetoric of motives is something divorcing partners learn as they move through the process, not something inside them that causes them to act as they do.

22 | ON MOTIVE
John Dewey

Any one who observes children knows that while periods of rest are natural, laziness is an acquired vice—or virtue. While a man is awake he will do something, if only to build castles in the air. If we like the form of words we may say that a man eats only because he is "moved" by hunger. The statement is nevertheless mere tautology. For what does hunger mean except that one of the things which man does naturally, instinctively, is to search for food—that his activity naturally turns that way? Hunger primarily names an act or active process not a motive to an act. It is an act if we take it grossly, like a babe's blind hunt for the mother's breast; it is an activity if we take it minutely as a chemico-physiological occurrence.

The whole concept of motives is in truth extra-psychological. It is an outcome of the attempt of men to influence human action, first that of others, then of a man to influence his own behavior. No sensible person thinks of attributing the acts of an animal or an idiot to a motive. We call a biting dog ugly, but we don't look for his motive in biting. If however we were able to direct the dog's action by inducing him to reflect upon his acts, we should at once become interested in the dog's motives for acting as he does, and should endeavor to get him interested in the same subject. It is absurd to ask what induces a man to activity generally speaking. He is an active being and that is all there is to be said on that score. But when we want to get him to act in this specific way rather than in that, when we want to direct his activity that is to say in a specified channel, then the question of motive is pertinent. A motive is then that element in the total complex of a man's activity which, if it can be sufficiently stimulated, will result in an act having specified consequences. And part of the process of intensifying (or reducing) certain elements in the total activity and thus regulating actual consequence is to impute these elements to a person as his actuating motives.

A child naturally grabs food. But he does it in our presence. His manner is socially displeasing and we attribute to his act, up to this time wholly innocent, the motive of greed or selfishness. Greediness simply means the quality of his act as socially observed and disapproved. But by attributing it to him as his motive for acting in the disapproved way, we induce him to refrain. We analyze his total act and call his attention to an obnoxious element in its outcome. A child with equal spontaneity, or thoughtlessness, gives way to others. We point out to him with approval that he acted considerately, generously. And this quality of action when noted and encouraged becomes a reinforcing stimulus of that factor which will induce similar

The Collected Works of John Dewey, Middle Works: Volume 14, Human Nature and Conduct © 1983 by the Board of Trustees, Southern Illinois University, reprinted by permission.

acts in the future. An element in an act viewed as a tendency to produce such and such consequences is a motive. A motive does not exist prior to an act and produce it. It is an act *plus* a judgment upon some element of it, the judgment being made in the light of the consequences of the act.

23 | SITUATED ACTIONS AND VOCABULARIES OF MOTIVE
C. Wright Mills

The major reorientation of recent theory and observation in sociology of language emerged with the overthrow of the Wundtian notion that language has as its function the "expression" of prior elements within the individual. The postulate underlying modern study of language is the simple one that we must approach linguistic behavior, not by referring it to private states in individuals, but by observing its social function of coordinating diverse action. Rather than expressing something which is prior and in the person, language is taken by other persons as an indicator of future actions.[1]

Within this perspective there are suggestions concerning problems of motivation. It is the purpose of this paper to outline an analytic model for the explanation of motives which is based on a sociological theory of language and a sociological psychology.[2]

As over against the inferential conception of motives as subjective "springs" of action, motives may be considered as typical vocabularies having ascertainable functions in delimited societal situations. Human actors do vocalize and impute motives to themselves and to others. To explain behavior by referring it to an inferred and abstract "motive" is one thing. To analyze the observable lingual mechanisms of motive imputation and avowal as they function in conduct is quite another. Rather than fixed elements "in" an individual, motives are the terms with which interpretation of conduct *by social actors* proceeds. This imputation and avowal of motives by actors are social phenomena to be explained. The differing reasons men give for their actions are not themselves without reasons.

First, we must demarcate the general conditions under which such motive imputation and avowal seem to occur.[3] Next, we must give a characterization of motive in denotable terms and an explanatory paradigm of why certain motives are verbalized rather than others. Then, we must indicate mechanisms of the linkage of vocabularies of motive to systems of action. What we want is an analysis of the integrating, controlling, and specifying function a certain type of speech fulfils in socially situated actions.

The generic situation in which imputation and avowal of motives arise involves, first, the *social* conduct or the (stated) programs of languaged creatures, i.e., programs and actions oriented with reference to the actions and talk of others; second, the avowal and imputation of motives is concomitant with the speech form known as the "question." Situations back of questions typically involve *alternative* or *unexpected* programs or actions which phases analytically denote "crises."[4] The question is distinguished in that it usually elicits another *verbal* action, not a motor response. The question is an element in *conversation*. Conversation may be concerned with the factual features of a situation as they are seen or believed to be or it may seek to integrate and promote a set of diverse social actions with reference to the situation and its normative pattern of expectations. It is in this latter as-

From *American Sociological Review*. 1940, v. 5: 904–13.

sent and dissent phase of conversation that persuasive and dissuasive speech and vocabulary arise. For men live in immediate acts of experience and their attentions are directed outside themselves until acts are in some way frustrated. It is then that awareness of self and of motive occur. The "question" is a lingual index of such conditions. The avowal and imputation of motives are features of such conversations as arise in "question" situations.

Motives are imputed or avowed as answers to questions interrupting acts or programs. Motives are words. Generically, to what do they refer? They do not denote any elements "in" individuals. They stand for anticipated situational consequences of questioned conduct. Intention or purpose (stated as a "program") *is* awareness of anticipated consequence; motives are names for consequential situations, and surrogates for actions leading to them. Behind questions are possible alternative actions with their terminal consequences. "Our introspective words for motives are rough, shorthand descriptions for certain typical patterns of discrepant and conflicting stimuli."[5]

The model of purposive conduct associated with Dewey's name may briefly be stated. Individuals confronted with "alternative acts" perform one or the other of them on the basis of the differential consequences which they anticipate. This nakedly utilitarian schema is inadequate because: (a) the "alternative acts" of *social* conduct "appear" most often in lingual form, as a question, stated by one's self or by another; (b) it is more adequate to say that individuals act in terms of anticipation of *named* consequences.

Among such names and in some technologically oriented lines of action there may appear such terms as "useful," "practical," "serviceable," etc., terms so "ultimate" to the pragmatists, and also to certain sectors of the American population in these delimited situations. However, there are other areas of population with different vocabularies of motives. The choice of lines of action is accompanied by representations, and selection among them, of their situational termini. Men discern situations with particular vocabularies, and it is in terms of some delimited vocabulary that they anticipate consequences of conduct.[6] Stable vocabularies of motives link anticipated consequences and specific actions. There is no need to invoke "psychological" terms like "desire" or "wish" as explanatory, since they themselves must be explained socially.[7] Anticipation is a subvocal or overt naming of terminal phases and/or social consequences of conduct. When an individual names consequences, he elicits the behaviors for which the name is a redintegrative cue. In a *societal* situation, implicit in the names of consequences is the social dimension of motives. Through such vocabularies, types of societal controls operate. Also, the terms in which the question is asked often will contain both alternatives: "Love or Duty?", "Business or Pleasure?" Institutionally different situations have different *vocabularies of motive* appropriate to their respective behaviors.

This sociological conception of motives as relatively stable lingual phases of delimited situations is quite consistent with Mead's program to approach conduct socially and from the outside. It keeps clearly in mind that "both motives and actions very often originate not from within but from the situation in which individuals find themselves. . . ."[8] It translates the question of "why"[9] into a "how" that is answerable in terms of a situation and its typal vocabulary of motives, i.e., those which conventionally accompany that type situation and function as cues and justifications for normative actions in it.

It has been indicated that the question is usually an index to the avowal and imputation of motives. Max Weber defines motive as a complex of meaning, which appears to the actor himself or to the observer to be an adequate ground for his conduct.[10] The aspect of motive which this conception grasps is its intrinsically social character. A satisfactory or adequate motive is one that satisfies the questioners of an act or program whether it be the other's or the actor's. As a word, *a motive tends to be one which is to the actor and to the other members of a situation an unquestioned answer to questions concerning social and lingual conduct.* A stable motive is an ultimate in justificatory conversation. The words which in a type situation will fulfil this function are circumscribed by the vocabulary of motives acceptable for such situations. Motives are accepted justifications for present, future, or past programs or acts.

To term them justification is *not* to deny their efficacy. Often anticipations of acceptable justifications will control conduct. ("If I did this, what could I say? What would they say?") Decisions may be, wholly or in part, delimited by answers to such queries.

A man may begin an act for one motive. In the course of it, he may adopt an ancillary motive. This does not mean that the second apologetic motive is inefficacious. The vocalized expectation of an act, its "reason," is not only a mediating condition of the act but it is a proximate and controlling condition for which the term "cause" is not inappropriate. It may strengthen the act of the actor. It may win new allies for his act.

When they appeal to others involved in one's act, motives are strategies of action. In many social actions, others must agree, tacitly or explicitly. Thus, acts often will be abandoned if no reason can be found that others will accept. Diplomacy in choice of motive often controls the diplomat. Diplomatic choice of motive is part of the attempt to motivate acts for other members in a situation. Such pronounced motives undo snarls and integrate social actions. Such diplomacy does not necessarily imply intentional lies. It merely indicates that an appropriate vocabulary of motives will be utilized—that they are conditions for certain lines of conduct.[11]

When an agent vocalizes or imputes motives, he is not trying to *describe* his experienced social action. He is not merely stating "reasons." He is influencing others—and himself. Often he is finding new "reasons" which will mediate action. Thus, we need not treat an action as discrepant from "its" verbalization, for in many cases, the verbalization is a new act. In such cases, there is not a discrepancy between an act and "its" verbalization, but a difference between two disparate actions, motor-social and verbal.[12] This additional (or "*ex post facto*") lingualization may involve appeal to a vocabulary of motives associated with a norm with which both members of the situation are in agreement. As such, it is an integrative factor in *future* phases of the original social action or in other acts. By resolving conflicts, motives are efficacious. Often, if "reasons" were not given, an act would not occur, nor would diverse actions be integrated. Motives are common grounds for mediated behaviors.

Perry summarily states the Freudian view of motives "as the view that the real motives of conduct are those which we are ashamed to admit either to ourselves or to others."[13] One can cover the facts by merely saying that scruples (i.e., *moral* vocabularies of motive) are often efficacious and that men will alter and deter their acts in terms of such motives. One of the components of a "generalized other," as a mechanism of societal control, is vocabularies of acceptable motives. For example, a businessman joins the Rotary Club and proclaims its public-spirited vocabulary.[14] If this man cannot act out business conduct without so doing, it follows that this vocabulary of motives is an important factor in his behavior.[15] The long acting out of a role, with its appropriate motives, will often induce a man to become what at first he merely sought to appear. Shifts in the vocabularies of motive that are utilized later by an individual disclose an important aspect of various integrations of his actions with concomitantly various groups.

The motives actually used in justifying or criticizing an act definitely link it to situations, integrate one man's action with another's, and line up conduct with norms. The societally sustained motive-surrogates of situations are both constraints and inducements. It is a hypothesis worthy and capable of test that typal vocabularies of motives for different situations are significant determinants of conduct. As lingual segments of social action, motives orient actions by enabling discrimination between their objects. Adjectives such as "good," "pleasant," and "bad" promote action or deter it. When they constitute components of a vocabulary of motives, i.e., are typical and relatively unquestioned accompaniments of typal situations, such words often function as directives and incentives by virtue of their being the judgments of others as anticipated by the actor. In this sense motives are "social instruments, i.e., data by modifying which the agent will be able to influence [himself or others]."[16] The "control" of others is not usually direct but rather through manipulation of a field of objects. We influence a man by naming his acts or imputing motives to them—or to "him." The motives accompanying institutions of war, e.g., are not "the causes" of war, but they do promote continued integrated participation, and they vary from one war to the next. Working vocabularies of motive have careers that are woven through changing institutional fabrics.

Genetically, motives are imputed by others before they are avowed by self. The mother controls the child: "Do not do that, it is greedy." Not only does the child learn what to do, what not to do, but he is given standardized motives which promote prescribed actions and dissuade those proscribed. Along with rules and norms of action for various situations, we learn vocabularies of motives appropriate to them. These are the motives we shall use, since they are a part of our language and components of our behavior.

The quest for "real motives" supposititiously set over against "mere rationalization" is often informed by a metaphysical view that the "real" motives are in some way biological. Accompanying such quests for something more real and back of rationalization is the view held by many sociologists that language is an external manifestation or concomitant of something prior, more genuine, and "deep" in the individual. "Real attitudes" versus "mere verbalization" or "opinion" implies that at best we only infer from his language what "really" is the individual's attitude or motive.

Now what *could we possibly* so infer? Of precisely *what* is verbalization symptomatic? We cannot *infer* physiological processes from lingual phenomena. All we can infer and empirically check[17] is another verbalization of the agent's which we believe was orienting and controlling behavior at the time the act was performed. The only social items that can "lie deeper" are other lingual forms.[18] The "Real Attitude or Motive" is not something different in kind from the verbalization or the "opinion." They turn out to be only relatively and temporally different.

The phrase "unconscious motive" is also unfortunate. All it can mean is that a motive is not explicitly vocalized, but there is no need to infer unconscious motives from such situations and then posit them in individuals as elements. The phrase is informed by persistence of the unnecessary and unsubstantiated notion that "all action has a motive," and it is promoted by the observation of gaps in the relatively frequent verbalization in everyday situations. The facts to which this phrase is supposedly addressed are covered by the statements that men do not always explicitly articulate motives, and that *all* actions do not pivot around language. I have already indicated the conditions under which motives are typically avowed and imputed.

Within the perspective under consideration, the verbalized motive is not used as an index of something in the individual but *as a basis of inference for a typical vocabulary of motives of a situated action.* When we ask for the "real attitude" rather than the "opinion," for the "real motive" rather than the "rationalization," all we can meaningfully be asking for is the controlling speech form which was incipiently or overtly presented in the performed act or series of acts. There is no way to plumb behind verbalization into an individual and directly check our motive-mongering, but there is an empirical way in which we can guide and limit, in given historical situations, investigations of motives. That is by the construction of typal vocabularies of motives that are extant in types of situations and actions. Imputation of motives may be controlled by reference to the typical constellation of motives which are observed to be societally linked with classes of situated actions. Some of the "real" motives that have been imputed to actors were not even known to them. As I see it, motives are circumscribed by the vocabulary of the actor. The only source for a terminology of motives is the vocabularies of motives actually and usually verbalized by actors in specific situations.

Individualistic, sexual, hedonistic, and pecuniary vocabularies of motives are apparently now dominant in many sectors of twentieth-century urban America. Under such an ethos, verbalization of alternative conduct in these terms is least likely to be challenged among dominant groups. In this milieu, individuals are skeptical of Rockefeller's avowed religious motives for his business conduct because such motives are not *now* terms of the vocabulary conventionally and prominently accompanying situations of business enterprise. A medieval monk writes that he gave food to a poor but pretty woman because it was "for the glory of God and the eternal salvation of his soul." Why do we tend to question him and impute sexual motives? Because sex is an influential and widespread motive in our society and time. Religious vocabularies of explanation and of motives are now on the wane. In a society in which religious motives have been debunked on a rather wide scale, certain thinkers are skeptical of those who ubiquitously proclaim them. Religious motives have lapsed from selected portions of modern populations and other motives have become "ultimate" and operative. But from the monasteries of medieval Europe we have no evidence that religious vocabularies were not operative in many situations.

A labor leader says he performs a certain act because he wants to get higher standards of living for the workers. A businessman says that this is rationalization, or a lie; that it is really because he wants more money for himself from the workers. A radical says a college professor will not engage in radical movements because he is afraid for his job, and besides, is a "reactionary." The college professor says it is because he just likes to find out how things work. What is reason for one man is rationalization for another. The variable is the accepted vocabulary of motives, the ultimates of discourse, of each man's dominant group about whose opinion he cares. *Determination of such groups, their location and character, would enable delimitation and methodological control of assignment of motives for specific acts.*

Stress on this idea will lead us to investigations of the compartmentalization of operative motives in personalities according to situation and the general types and conditions of vocabularies of motives in various types of societies. The motivational structures of individuals and the patterns of their purposes are relative to societal frames. We might, e.g., study motives along stratified or occupational lines. Max Weber has observed:[19]

> . . . that in a free society the motives which induce people to work vary with . . . different social classes. . . . There is normally a graduated scale of motives by which men from different social classes are driven to work. When a man changes ranks, he switches from one set of motives to another.

The lingual ties which hold them together react on persons to constitute frameworks of disposition and motive. Recently, Talcott Parsons has indicated, by reference to differences in actions in the professions and in business, that one cannot leap from "economic analysis to ultimate motivations; the institutional patterns

always constitute one crucial element of the problem."[20] It is my suggestion that we may analyze, index, and gauge this element by focusing upon those specific verbal appendages of variant institutionalized actions which have been referred to as vocabularies of motive.

In folk societies, the constellations of motives connected with various sectors of behavior would tend to be typically stable and remain associated only with their sector. In typically primary, sacred, and rural societies, the motives of persons would be regularly compartmentalized. Vocabularies of motives ordered to different situations stabilize and guide behavior and expectation of the reactions of others. In their appropriate situations, verbalized motives are not typically questioned.[21] In secondary, secular, and urban structures, varying and competing vocabularies of motives operate coterminously and the situations to which they are appropriate are not clearly demarcated. Motives once unquestioned for defined situations are now questioned. Various motives can release similar acts in a given situation. Hence, variously situated persons are confused and guess which motive "activated" the person. Such questioning has resulted intellectually in such movements as psychoanalysis with its dogma of rationalization and its systematic motive-mongering. Such intellectual phenomena are underlaid by split and conflicting sections of an individuated society which is characterized by the existence of competing vocabularies of motive. Intricate constellations of motives, for example, are components of business enterprise in America. Such patterns have encroached on the old style vocabulary of the virtuous relation of men and women: duty, love, kindness. Among certain classes, the romantic, virtuous, and pecuniary motives are confused. The asking of the question: "Marriage for love or money?" is significant, for the pecuniary is now a constant and almost ubiquitous motive, a common denominator of many others.[22]

Back of "mixed motives" and "motivational conflicts" are competing or discrepant situational patterns and their respective vocabularies of motive. With shifting and interstitial situations, each of several alternatives may belong to disparate systems of action which have differing vocabularies of motives appropriate to them. Such conflicts manifest vocabulary patterns that have overlapped in a marginal individual and are not easily compartmentalized in clear-cut situations.

Besides giving promise of explaining an area of lingual and societal fact, a further advantage of this view of motives is that with it we should be able to give sociological accounts of other theories (terminologies) of motivation. This is a task for sociology of knowledge. Here I can refer only to a few theories. I have already referred to the Freudian terminology of motives. It is apparent that these motives are those of an upper bourgeois patriarchal group with strong sexual and individualistic orientation. When introspecting on the couches of Freud, patients used the only vocabulary of motives they knew; Freud got his hunch and guided further talk. Mittenzwey has dealt with similar points at length.[23] Widely diffused in a postwar epoch, psychoanalysis was never popular in France where control of sexual behavior is not puritanical.[24] To converted individuals who have become accustomed to the psychoanalytic terminology of motives, all others seem self-deceptive.[25]

In like manner, to many believers in Marxism's terminology of power, struggle, and economic motives, all others, including Freud's, are due to hypocrisy or ignorance. An individual who has assimilated thoroughly only business congeries of motives will attempt to apply these motives to all situations, home and wife included. It should be noted that the business terminology of motives has its intellectual articulation, even as psychoanalysis and Marxism have.

It is significant that since the Socratic period many "theories of motivation" have been linked with ethical and religious terminologies. Motive is that in man which leads him to do good or evil. Under the aegis of religious institutions, men use vocabularies of moral motives: they call acts and programs "good" and "bad," and impute these qualities to the soul. Such lingual behavior is part of the process of social control. Institutional practices and their vocabularies of motive exercise control over delimited ranges of possible situations. One could make a typal catalog of religious motives from widely read religious texts, and test its explanatory power in various denominations and sects.[26]

In many situations of contemporary America, conduct is controlled and integrated by *hedonistic* language. For large population sectors in certain situations, pleasure and pain are now unquestioned motives. For given periods and societies, these situations should be empirically determined. Pleasure and pain should not be reified and imputed to human nature as underlying principles of all action. Note that hedonism as a psychological and an ethical doctrine gained impetus in the modern world at about the time when older moral-religious motives were being debunked and simply discarded by "middle class" thinkers. Back of the hedonistic terminology lay an emergent social pattern and a new vocabulary of motives. The shift of unchallenged motives which gripped the communities of Europe was climaxed when, in reconciliation, the older religious and the hedonistic terminologies were identified: the "good" is the "pleasant." The conditioning situation was similar in the Hellenistic world with the hedonism of the Cyrenaics and Epicureans.

What is needed is to take all these *terminologies* of motive and locate them as *vocabularies* of motive in historic epochs and specified situations. Motives are of no value apart from the delimited societal situations for which they are the appropriate vocabularies. They must be situated. At best, socially unlocated *terminologies* of motives represent unfinished attempts to block out social areas of motive imputation and avowal. Motives vary in content and character with historical epochs and societal structures.

Rather than interpreting actions and language as external manifestations of subjective and deeper lying elements in individuals, the research task is the locating of particular types of action within typal frames of normative actions and socially situated clusters of motive. There is no explanatory value in subsuming various vocabularies of motives under some terminology or list. Such procedure merely confuses the task of explaining specific cases. The languages of situations as given must be considered a valuable portion of the data to be interpreted and related to their conditions. To simplify these vocabularies of motive into a socially abstracted terminology is to destroy the legitimate use of motive in the explanation of social actions.

NOTES

1. See C. Wright Mills, "Bibliographical Appendices," Section I, 4: "Sociology of Language" in *Contemporary Social Theory,* ed. by Barnes, Becker & Becker, New York, 1940.

2. See G. H. Mead, "Social Psychology as Counterpart of Physiological Psychology," *Psychol. Bul.,* VI: 401–408, 1909; Karl Mannheim, *Man and Society in an Age of Reconstruction,* New York, 1940; L. V. Wiese-Howard Becker, *Systematic Sociology,* part I, New York, 1932; J. Dewey, "All psychology is either biological or social psychology," *Psychol. Rev.,* vol. 24:276.

3. The importance of this initial task for research is clear. Most researches on the verbal level merely ask abstract questions of individuals, but if we can tentatively delimit the situations in which certain motives *may* be verbalized, we can use that delimitation in the construction of *situational* questions, and we shall be *testing* deductions from our theory.

4. On the "question" and "conversation," see G. A. DeLaguna, *Speech: Its Function and Development,* 37 (and index), New Haven, 1927. For motives in crises, see J. M. Williams, *The Foundations of Social Science,* 435 ff., New York, 1920.

5. K. Burke, *Permanence and Change,* 45, New York, 1936. I am indebted to this book for several leads which are systematized into the present statement.

6. See such experiments as C. N. Rexroad's "Verbalization in Multiple Choice Reactions," *Psychol. Rev.,* Vol. 33:458, 1926.

7. Cf. J. Dewey, "Theory of Valuation," *Int. Ency. of Unified Science,* New York, 1939.

8. K. Mannheim, *Man and Society,* 249, London, 1940.

9. Conventionally answerable by reference to "subjective factors" within individuals. R. M. MacIver, "The Modes of the Question Why," *J. of Soc. Phil.,* April, 1940. Cf. also his "The Imputation of Motives," *Amer. J. Sociol.,* July 1940.

10. *Wirtschaft und Gesellschaft,* 5, Tubingen, 1922, "'Motiv' heisst ein Sinnzusammenhang, Welcher dem Handelnden selbst oder dem Beobachtenden als sinnhafter 'Grund' eines Verhaltens in dem Grade heissen, als die Beziehung seiner Bestandteile von uns nach den durchschnittlichen Denk- und Gefühlsgewohnheiten als typischer (wir pflegen in sagen: 'richtiger') Sinzusammenhang bejaht Wird."

11. Of course, since motives are communicated, they may be lies; but, this must be proved. Verbalizations are not lies merely because they are socially efficacious. I am here concerned more with the social function of pronounced motives, than with the sincerity of those pronouncing them.

12. See F. Znaniecki, *Social Actions,* 30, New York, 1936.

13. *General Theory of Value,* 292–93, New York, 1936.

14. Ibid., 392.

15. The "profits motive" of classical economics may be treated as an ideal-typical vocabulary of motives for delimited economic situations and behaviors. For late phases of monopolistic and regulated capitalism, this type requires modification; the profit and commercial vocabularies have acquired other ingredients. See N. R. Danielian's *AT & T,* New York, 1940, for a suggestive account of the *noneconomic* behavior and motives of business bureaucrats.

16. *Social Actions,* 73.

17. Of course, we could infer or interpret constructs posited in the individual, but these are not easily checked and they are not explanatory.

18. Which is not to say that, physiologically, there may not be cramps in the stomach wall or adrenalin in the blood, etc., but the character of the "relation" of such items to social action is quite moot.

19. Paraphrased by K. Mannheim, op. cit., 316–17.

20. "The Motivation of Economic Activities," 67, in C. W. M. Hart, *Essays in Sociology,* Toronto, 1940.

21. Among the ethnologists, Ruth Benedict has come up to the edge of a genuinely sociological view of motivation. Her view remains vague because she has not seen clearly the identity of differing "motivations" in differing cultures with the varied extant and approved vocabularies of motive. "The intelligent understanding of the relation of the individual to his society . . . involves always the understanding of the types of human motivations and capacities capitalized in his society . . ." "Configurations of Culture in North America," *Amer. Anthrop.,* 25, Jan.–Mar. 1932; see also: *Patterns of Culture,* 242–43, Boston, 1935. She turns this observation into a quest for the unique "genius" of each culture and stops her research by words like "Apollonian." If she would attempt constructively to observe the vocabularies of motives which precipitate acts to perform, implement programs, and furnish approved motives for them in circumscribed situations, she would be better able to state precise problems and to answer them by further observation.

22. Also motives acceptably imputed and avowed for one system of action may be diffused into other domains and gradually come to be accepted by some as a comprehensive portrait of *the* motive of men. This happened in the case of the economic man and his motives.

23. Kuno Mittenzwey, "Zur Sociologie der psychoanalystischer Erkenntnis," in Max Scheler, ed. *Versuche zu einer Sociologie des Wissens,* 365–375, Munich, 1924.

24. This fact is interpreted by some as supporting Freudian theories. Nevertheless, it can be just as adequately grasped in the scheme here outlined.

25. See K. Burke's acute discussion of Freud, op. cit., Part I.

26. Moral vocabularies deserve a special statement. Within the viewpoint herein outlined many snarls concerning "value-judgments," etc., can be cleared up.

24 | THE RHETORIC OF MOTIVES IN DIVORCE
Joseph Hopper

Sociologists have long argued that we need to reconceptualize our common sense notion of motives. Beginning with the insights of Kenneth Burke (1935/1954), and then with the influential statement on motives by C. Wright Mills (1940), we have been urged to see motives not as inner dispositions that cause action, but rather as rhetorical constructs that define action with respect to particular social contexts. While these insights have led to fruitful lines of analysis and empirical inquiry, many researchers working in the area of motives tend to assume that Burke and Mills were right. In this article, I offer evidence that they were right by showing two vocabularies of motive that emerged after the events that the vocabularies purportedly explained. I examine ethnographic data on divorce and show that the motives people used to explain their divorces can only be understood as rhetorical devices that imposed a sense of order onto situations that were otherwise fraught with ambiguous and contradictory events, emotions, and inclinations toward behavior. With this evidence on motives, I also argue that efforts to characterize divorce as an orderly, sequential process in which one stage of dissolution leads to the next may be mistaken.

RESEARCH ON VOCABULARIES OF MOTIVE

Burke (1935/1954) set the task for an interpretive sociology of motives when he noted: "A motive is not some fixed thing, like a table, which one can go and look at. It is a term of interpretation, and being such it will naturally take its place within the framework of our *Weltanschauung* as a whole. . . . The few attributions of motive by which a man explain[s] his conduct . . . [are] but a fragmentary part of this larger orientation" (p. 25). Motives, he argued, are not mental or biological states that somehow impel action; rather, motives are social constructs through which actors impose meaning onto situations. Saying "I married him because I wanted his money," for example, makes certain behaviors intelligible in particular social and historical contexts (Mills, 1940), and the pecuniary motive reflects more upon those varied contexts where it makes sense and less upon any presumed mental disposition of the actor. Social theorists have since pushed these insights even further. Foote (1951), for example, links the rhetorics of motive with the problematic nature of self and identity, saying that motives are "symbolic constructs which not only organize . . . acts in particular situations but make them recognizably recurrent in the life-history of any person" (p. 15) (see also Campbell, 1991). Blum and McHugh (1971) discuss the grammatical "deep structures" in social life to explain how and why motives are proffered in the first place. Additionally, Scott and Lyman's (1968) influential article on accounts has generated several lines of theoretical refinement and speculation (Blumstein, 1974; Hewitt & Stokes, 1975; Nichols, 1990; Stokes & Hewitt, 1976), as has Garfinkel's (1967) work in ethnomethodology.

The problem is that, while many sociologists use this new rhetorical conception of motives in their empirical work, many do not test whether the conception is warranted in the first place. They do not show, for example, that the motives actors give do not "match up" with the situations that the motives are intended to explain. Too many researchers take it for granted that motives are rhetorical constructs that function in social interaction, and so they proceed to describe the structures, categories, and interactional techniques of account making used by their research subjects. Consider a few examples. Ray and Simons (1987) classify the range of vocabularies used by convicted murderers, but they fail to show that the motives given have less to do with "inner dispositions" impelling action and more to do with persuading an audience. Blum-stein (1974) describes conditions under which ac-counts are honored, but in doing so he abandons the question of whether accounts are rhetorics in the first place. Other empirical studies offer typologies and de-scriptions of accounts (Croghan & Miell, 1992; Kalab, 1987; Sarat & Felstiner, 1988; Scully & Marolla, 1984; Weinstein, 1980), but unless these studies show some disparity between the accounts given and the sit-uations they purportedly explain, why should we sup-pose the motives proffered to be anything but indica-tors of the causes of behavior? Ethnomethodologists and discourse analysts, for their part, do the same. They purposefully eschew any concern with "mo-tives" and take up instead the analytical problem of "motive attributions" (Potter & Wetherell, 1987; Shar-rock & Watson, 1984).

Such analyses are usually insightful enough, and they at least demonstrate the heuristic value of Burke's and Mills' conception of motives. But as sev-eral sociologists have argued recently (Bruce & Wal-lis, 1983, 1985; Campbell, 1991; Wallis & Bruce, 1983), contemporary research too often shifts the problem away from motives to motive-talk, without ever proving that they are one and the same thing, or without ever proving that there is no necessary con-nection between the two. Thus, as Yearly (1988) notes, the question remains: Are "accounts of interest as putative explanations of action or only as part of an interpretative repertoire?" (p. 582). The common sense notion of motives is problematic, he argues, but most research has simply failed to prove it wrong. Most research describes the local interactional proce-dures through which social action is made account-able, giving up entirely the "tireless search for reasons and intentions" (p. 581). To be sure, this is an impor-tant analytical move that yields "empirical dividends" (p. 587), but it fails to prove that motives are rhetori-cal constructs. If motives are rhetoric, then data about motives can be subject to rhetorical analysis; but too many studies fail to establish that motives are indeed rhetorical constructs.

Here I offer an empirical demonstration that mo-tives do not necessarily correspond with the complex situations that motives are intended to explain. In ex-amining the vocabularies of motive that divorcing peo-ple offer, my purpose is not to motive-monger or seek the "real" causes of divorce, either psychological or so-cial. Nor is my purpose to argue, along with the eth-nomethodologists, that we should abandon the search for motives and focus only on the structures of ac-counting and motive imputation. Rather, my purpose is to offer empirical evidence that vocabularies of motive are indeed rhetorical constructs, and that they function to impose order upon sets of behaviors, circumstances, and events that would otherwise seem chaotic.

IMPLICATIONS FOR DIVORCE RESEARCH

The motives-as-rhetoric thesis has not been sufficient-ly proven, nor has it had much influence in the area of family studies (McLain & Weigert, 1979). But if proven, it would give further evidence that social or-der in family life is something accomplished largely through interpretive activities (Eheart & Power, 1988; Gubrium, 1988; Gubrium & Buckholdt, 1982; Gubri-um & Holstein, 1990; Gubrium & Lynott, 1985; Han-del, 1985; LaRossa, 1988; Lynott, 1983; Miller, 1990; Weigert & Hastings, 1977). Burke and Mills argued that the orderliness of social life comes about because we endow it with order, and that one way in which we do this is by assigning motives to ourselves and to oth-ers. This would throw into doubt any processual, de-velopmental models of social phenomena that ignore the essentially interpretive nature of social life.

Over the past twenty years, scholars have tried to go beyond correlating social and psychological vari-ables with divorce in order to delineate the orderly process through which divorce happens. Most of this research conceptualizes divorce as a series of defin-able stages in what might be called a sequential or de-velopmental view of divorce. Vaughan's (1986) find-ings best exemplify this view. She outlined a detailed step-by-step process by which two people slowly un-couple: One partner harbors a secret discontent, slow-ly shifts activities, then drifts even further from her spouse and so confirms the discontent; she begins talking with others, making the secret public, and fi-nally confronts the partner. Then the process shifts into a series of back-and-forth maneuvering between partners, and so on. In the end, both "initiator" and "partner" successfully split as they have slowly become autonomous and separate from each other. Other family researchers have delineated a similar process of divorce, one that begins with secrets, revelations, and then moves on to the dynamics of separation (Duck, 1982; McCall, 1982; Ponzetti & Cate, 1986). Or they have offered some other variation of a multistage, linear model of the course of dissolution (Ahrons & Rogers, 1987; Crosby, Gage, & Raymond, 1983; Crosby, Lybarger, & Mason, 1986; Federico, 1979; Kersten, 1990; Kessler, 1975; Price-Bonham & Balswick, 1980; Salts, 1979). Exchange theorists, too, typically conceptualize the process as a sequential one in which rational considerations of costs and benefits begin shifting, moving one or both partners away from commitment and towards divorce (Levinger, 1979; Lewis & Spanier, 1979; Palisi, 1984; Scanzoni, 1979; Sprecher, 1992; Yoder & Nichols, 1980).

But as divorcing people think about, articulate, and explain what happened in their marriages (and even as they fill out formal questionnaires), it may be a rhetorical accomplishment that they organize the whole series of events. If Burke and Mills are right, then key elements of these stories—motives, intentions, and causes—are constructs that generate meaning for both teller and audience . . . and if motives are rhetorics, what else might be? The motives-as-rhetoric thesis begins to suggest that the course-of-relations stories divorcing people tell are also defining rhetorics; as such, developmental views of divorce may be artifacts of the ways in which divorcing people make sense out of chaos and ambiguity.

A second purpose in examining the vocabularies of motive, then, is to suggest that divorce may be an essentially disorganized process rather than a patterned series of stages. The divorcing situations I learned about were immensely complex—so complex and indeterminate, in fact, that any number of outcomes could have resulted. Yet divorcing people almost always explained their situations by invoking one of two distinct vocabularies of motive.

RESEARCHING VOCABULARIES OF MOTIVE AMONG DIVORCING PEOPLE

In the spring of 1991, I began a broadly defined ethnographic research project on divorce. I attended divorce information workshops, met with directors and counselors of social service agencies, and attended a single father's support group through one of the agencies. I also began working with a divorce resource and training center based in Colorado, and through this center I began attending a 10-week divorce seminar along with thirty women and men who were recently divorced or soon to be divorced. In all of these settings, I gathered information about divorce through participant observation, and I began finding people who agreed to discuss their relationships and subsequent divorces with me. I interviewed people from every setting and supplemented these with interviews obtained through personal contacts and telephone responses from fliers.

I asked 32 people for interviews, 30 of whom agreed. Most interviews were conducted in the participant's home or in my home, several were done over the telephone, and a few were conducted in a restaurant or at my university office. Most interviews lasted about 2 hours; a few went as long as 5 hours. All of the interviews were taperecorded and subsequently transcribed. Additionally, I kept detailed notes from conversations with many people whom I met and talked with but did not interview formally, and I updated these notes regularly with new facts and impressions from ongoing conversations. Elsewhere I have detailed the methods, the settings, the procedures, and the sample of this study (Hopper, 1993), so here I will focus on key methodological issues associated with the problem of motives.

After 10 interviews and 3 months of work on the project, I began to focus explicitly on the phenomenon of nonmutual divorce. From the start, I noticed that nearly all divorcing people could identify themselves as either the "initiator" of the divorce or as the "partner" who was left, and I was struck by the fact that no one described divorce as a mutual decision even though in most cases noninitiating partners, as well as initiators, had been considering divorce. Thus I began directing my discussions and interviews around this topic. Among other things, I began asking questions about motives: I asked initiators why they decided to leave the marriage and to speculate on why their partners had not; I asked noninitiating partners why they opposed their divorces (which they almost always did) and why they had not initiated their divorces.

As the research progressed, I discovered a pattern: Nearly all divorcing people invoked one of two themes when describing their motives, and which of the two they invoked depended upon whether they were initiators or noninitiating partners. At the same time, however, I could find no such pattern among the events, intentions, and feelings that had happened during the relationship and immediately prior to one person deciding to initiate a divorce. In other words, I could find little correspondence between the motives that divorcing people articulated and the earlier experiences that they drew upon to explain those motives. Hence I began to document two incongruous aspects of the divorcing experience: First, I documented the two dominant vocabularies of motive that divorcing people used to talk about their divorces in interviews and in other formal and informal group contexts; second, I documented the chronology of "what happened" in each case, recording in detail the bewildering complexity of events, actions, and intentions that each divorcing person described as having occurred throughout marriage and divorce.

Documenting these two incongruous aspects of the divorcing experience raised two important methodological issues that deserve brief mention here. First, certain limitations were imposed by not having truly longitudinal data. Thus, in order to compare motives furnished after divorce with the happenings before divorce, I attempted to extrapolate a longitudinal perspective by piecing together information gathered through informal conversations, participant observation, and in-depth interviews. I did this in a number of ways. In each interview, for example, I attempted to get an accurate historical account of the marriage by soliciting retrospective narratives, probing for facts and documentation of facts, and returning to important events several times during the course of an interview. I often cross-checked interview data with in-field notes from conversations in order to verify the reliability of reported events. Another way in which I pieced together longitudinal information was by gaining a broad sample through which to infer and substantiate general temporal phases in the divorcing process—for example, by comparing the account of

one person who was six months into a divorce with the account of another person who was just beginning a divorce. This was possible because interviewees were in several different phases of the divorcing process: Many were in the very midst of their divorces, others were 3 to 4 years out of their divorces, and one woman was 17 years out. Finally, in one man's case I was able to document the entire dissolution process that began with generalized confusion about his relationship, that moved toward his partner's decision to leave, and then ended with the traumatic aftermath of divorce. I kept notes on our informal conversations throughout the process, and conducted a formal taped interview after the divorce. The longitudinal data that I gathered in this case, even though it constitutes a small portion of the whole, helped to confirm many of the impressions and conclusions that I had generated from other sources.

The second methodological issue had to do with problems inherent in comparing the events before divorce with the seemingly constructed, rhetorical nature of motives. Admittedly, I was unable to know about events before divorce except via the words and accounts of those getting divorced. But I was able to discern that these accounts of predivorce experiences revealed ambiguities and contradictions that were almost never present once divorcing people moved into a discussion of motives. Again, I probed for facts and accurate historical accounts, and I cross-checked interview data with in-field notes. People did not seem to change their stories about their experiences substantially over time, nor did they seem to selectively reveal or conceal information during lengthy interviews. They described failings on both sides, along with a fundamental uncertainty and indeterminacy in their marriages. In contrast, when they described their motives, they seemed to communicate a remarkably unidimensional stance toward those multifaceted experiences.

EMERGENT VOCABULARIES OF MOTIVE IN DIVORCE

In this section I describe the two main vocabularies of motive that divorcing people used to explain their divorces: Whatever the specifics of their situations, initiators generally articulated a vocabulary of individual needs and noninitiating partners invoked a vocabulary of familial commitment. Before describing these vocabularies of motive, however, I document the ambivalence, the discontent, and the back-and-forth complexity of marital relationships before divorce. Ostensibly, these divorcing people used the two vocabularies to explain why they had either initiated or opposed their divorces; but here I demonstrate the incongruity between what was happening before the divorce and the explanatory motives that were invoked afterwards. The two vocabularies *emerged only after a decision to divorce had been made,* and only as partners gained a clear sense of their respective roles in divorce as either initiators or noninitiating partners.

Before Divorce: Indeterminacy and Ambivalence

Once divorce begins, people usually identify themselves as either the one who wants the divorce or as the partner who does not want the divorce. Indeed, other studies have noted that most divorcing people describe their divorces as nonmutual and that they have no difficulty specifying who decided on a divorce and who did not (Buehler, 1987; Buehler, Hogan, Robinson, & Levy, 1986; Goode, 1956; Hill, Rubin, & Peplau, 1979; Nevaldine, 1978; Pettit & Bloom, 1984; Spanier & Thompson, 1984).

In this study, the motives that divorcing people attributed to their actions cohered around their identities as either initiators or noninitiating partners: They described what led them to seek a divorce or, conversely, they described why they opposed a divorce. However, nothing prior to a divorce seemed to predict who would become the initiator and who the partner. Thus, I found little to substantiate the subsequent claims that divorcing people made about their motives for either initiating or opposing. I found no antecedent pattern of behaviors, feelings, or social processes that matched up with the two vocabularies that later emerged. Instead, I found consistent evidence that predivorce experiences were not different and that most relationships were characterized by three things: a long period of discontent, multiple complaints, and ambivalence. Furthermore, the feelings and intentions that initiators described were precisely the same feelings and intentions

that noninitiators described. Hence, as I document the discontent, the multiple complaints, and the ambivalence in the following paragraphs, I provide paired quotes: One quote exemplifies how initiators described their marriages, and the other quote exemplifies how noninitiators described their marriages.

First, all divorcing people described themselves as having been keenly aware of their marital problems for a long time, and many had seriously contemplated divorce at other points in the marriage. Even among those who first described themselves as surprised by divorce, the road to divorce was a long one: They admitted that the dissolution had been happening for at least a few years, sometimes for 10 to 20 years. Moreover, it seemed clear in my interviews that the problems divorcing people described were not being identified merely in retrospect because most were able to recall specific events, thoughts, or comments that demonstrated such awareness. Several detailed past conversations with friends; a few mentioned early proposals that their spouse live in a separate house; some told about discussing separation with marriage counselors on and off throughout the relationship. One initiator recalled, for example:

> I can remember talking to friends quite a while before we split up, and wondering out loud whether it could ever work, whether it really ever should work. And we talked about it. We had fights and threatened to break up before. Probably for the last 2 years before we broke up, we'd had fights. At least on a couple of occasions, we'd all but broken up, and at the last minute decided not to.

And as a noninitiating partner in the midst of her divorce after 25 years of marriage said:

> Eleven years back I was ready to take steps. Yeah, I was ready to leave. And he was the one that convinced me, "No, I'm worth fighting for, and the relationship is worth fighting for, and let's work on it." I was ready to leave then, and he knew it, and I was real serious.

Second, as they looked back and described the long history of marital trouble, all of these divorcing people described multiple complaints that they had about their marriages, which they factored into explanations as to why their marriages fell apart. They were quick to describe their frustrations, their pain, and the widening distance that developed between them and their spouses. They listed basic differences in sociability, with one person wanting a wide circle of friends and the other not. Women often described gender roles that became more unequal over time, fueling a slow, building resentment. Both women and men talked about infidelity, physical and emotional abuse, isolation, trouble with in-laws, alcoholism, codependency, disagreements about children, intellectual and political differences, violence, differences in hobbies, conflicts over television, and sexual tensions. And as Riessman (1990) found, nearly all divorcing people traced their problems to "a lack of communication." The list of complaints that any one person furnished was extensive: Most enumerated at least four or five complaints, and most insisted that the many problems had made their marriages irrevocably unworkable. Again, this was true for both initiators and noninitiators.

At the same time that they listed complaints, however, divorcing people easily reported good things about their marriages. They liked having someone at home, someone to talk with about their day. They described camping trips, holidays and birthdays, the dream of having one's own family and home. They loved their children. They described feelings of security, safety, and comfort. Even the marital roles themselves—being a wife, husband, father, or mother—were sources of contentment and stability for them (Hagestad & Smyer, 1982; Levinger, 1979). As one woman summed it up, "Even with all the tough times that we've had, there have been some real positive times, too."

The third thing that all divorcing people described, then, was intense indecisiveness and ambivalence about their marriages. They had numerous complaints that they believed condemned their marriages to failure, while at the same time they treasured the good things. For example, one man who later opposed his divorce pulled out his journal for me and read from two lists that he had composed several months before his wife left him. The two lists outlined five things that he liked about his wife and five things that he disliked—all of which documented his own ambivalence and the fact that he had been weighing his alternatives and considering divorce even before his wife left. An-

other man who described himself as an initiator recalled this episode:

> I went to Alaska for a while about 4 months before [my son] was born. And I remember thinking all the time that I was there, "Well, when I get back we're going to work out some way of being together. Because we really need to live together to have a child." And then I remember thinking one day, I don't know how it came to me, that it was just ludicrous. It was just ridiculous for me to think that.

Likewise, a noninitiating partner told me about her ambivalent feelings during the 6 months that preceded her husband asking for a divorce, and during which she traveled around the country deciding what to do:

> It was a very sad time. When I was away from him I missed him terribly and wanted to be back together. And couldn't wait to see him, call him, and write him letters. When I got back with him, I could be back less than 24 hours and I needed to go. I needed to absolutely get away from him again. And then the same thing would happen. I would go away, I'd miss him, I'd just feel terrible, I'd want to be near him. It was just on and on.

Prior to nearly every divorce, then, there was a long period of assessment, with both initiators and noninitiating partners describing similar experiences and feelings of indecision and ambivalence. They described pain, dissatisfaction, and feelings of being trapped; at the same time, they described good things that they did not want to forgo. This is what made divorce such an agonizing decision and process, no matter what side of divorce they were on. Additional evidence that predivorce experiences are similar for both initiators and partners comes from two quantitative survey studies: Pettit and Bloom (1984) have demonstrated that initiators and partners tend to report similar patterns of marital dissatisfaction and stress prior to their divorces; similarly, Black, Eastwood, Sprenkle, and Smith (1991) have reported that both groups of people see the same attractions to marriage and the same barriers to leaving prior to their divorces.

The point here is that whatever the "real" motives behind the subsequent actions in divorce, I found no antecedent patterns by which to discern motives for one partner initiating and the other opposing. Given the uncertainty and ambivalence that both partners felt, and given the circumstances in which divorcing people described both fatal flaws and good things about their relationships, it seemed that many outcomes were possible in nearly every marriage that I learned about. The partners might have stayed together, for example. Or the noninitiating partner might have been the one to call the marriage off. The reality was that both partners felt confusion and ambivalence, and this complex mixture of events and intentions seemed to make the outcome of any particular marriage largely uncertain.

The Initiator's Vocabulary of Motives

Despite the uncertainty before divorce, divorcing people knew immediately who had initiated their divorces. An initiator, they said, was simply the one who made the final decision to end a marriage. And once the initiator's identity had been established, a discernible vocabulary of motives emerged that helped make the initiator's decision seem reasonable and "motivated." This vocabulary cut through the complexity of what was happening before and made sense out of the initiator's transition from ambivalence.

Before describing the initiator's vocabulary of motives, it is worth contrasting once again the complexity of the predivorce situations with the easy and unambiguous designation of the initiator. Despite other events prior to the divorce, during the divorce, or afterward, and despite the back-and-forth bickering about who did what to spoil the marriage, the initiator was decisively identified as the person who finally declared, "I want out." One or both partners might have had an affair; one partner might have started feeling depressed and sought counseling where marital problems were discussed; one partner might have gotten a lawyer to assess the legal and financial possibilities of a divorce. But despite my efforts to trace the initiator's position back to these critical events happening prior to divorce, and hence despite my efforts to discern the motives for one person rather than another making the decision, I found nothing that necessarily determined who initiated the split. Additionally, I found that once the dissolution began, the initiator was not necessarily the one who filed the papers in court nor the one who moved out of the home. The initiator was simply the partner who made the decision to leave.

Whatever the factors that led to divorce, though, initiators began articulating a common vocabulary of motives. They began seeing their situations in a new way, selecting out certain information and interpreting that information in order to make their decisions seem legitimate and inevitable, and they did this by articulating a vocabulary that emphasized individualism. They began negating the good things and emphasizing the bad. In doing so, they began to emphasize the importance of individual needs over commitment. They described marriage as a functional arrangement, and they explained their divorces in terms of emotional and practical needs being unfulfilled. The needs varied among the people I talked with: Some people wanted more emotional closeness, some wanted less; some wanted a more extensive social life outside the marriage, others wanted less; several people wanted more room for personal growth, autonomy, and individual career goals. Whatever their needs, the many complaints described earlier took on new shades of meaning, now being articulated around a rhetoric of self-need. Complaints about alcoholism making a marriage unworkable turned into: "I just couldn't stand the alcohol anymore. It was ruining my life." Complaints about lack of communication turned into: "I never got any support and intimacy from her, which is what I needed." A lesbian woman, for example, first described all sorts of personality and lifestyle conflicts with her lover that she believed doomed her relationship to failure. When I asked about why she finally decided to leave, she answered:

> I'm just thinking now of the official reason that I broke up. It was like we were doing more what she wanted than what I wanted. And that didn't feel good. She was doing a PhD. And I wanted to be doing a PhD. And I was feeling frustrated, like I was giving up some of my stuff. It was kind of like I wasn't sure: When she's through with it, is it then going to be my turn? Some of that . . . I guess I was being a bit selfish, to an extent.

Other initiators talked in more general terms about self-fulfillment:

> I was just feeling kind of discontented like there was something wrong. That my needs weren't being met, I guess.

> I wanted to take care of me. And I knew as long as

I stayed in the relationship that I would always take care of somebody else because that's just the way I was. It's probably stupid, but I felt that I couldn't grow and I couldn't be independent as long as I was in that position.

I was feeling bad about myself, and what did I really want to do with my life. Because there was some real dissatisfaction that I wasn't feeling fulfilled myself.

Every person described multiple frustrations and discontent in the years leading up to divorce; but when initiators began describing the divorce itself and the patterns of interaction that ensued, they talked with a one-sided and forceful emphasis on personal needs. Perhaps what most highlighted this before-and-after contrast was the decisiveness that they felt about having initiated divorce as opposed to the uncertainty they had expressed earlier. In the following excerpt, for example, an initiator describes her husband moving out and how she coped in the days immediately following. Her story captures the sense in which disorganization and uncertainty were transformed into surety:

I walked into the bedroom and it was a total mess in there, and I just stood there and tears rolled down my face. It was really hard. He came over and we just held each other for a while. Then he got all the rest of his stuff that he could take in the truck, and left. I was really depressed. I guess I was depressed for about a day and a half. Particularly the very next day . . . walking around . . . and my house was a total disaster area. Nothing was in its place. And I felt very disorganized. And I didn't have a bed. It was just a mess. Then Wednesday morning I woke up and I was ironing and I was thinking, "Cynthia, you've got to get your stuff together here. You've got to get your act together. Why are you feeling this way?" What I had to do was think about the reasons why I was wanting this. And about that time George called and there was some problem with something. As I hung up I thought, "This is exactly why I want it. What just happened, this is exactly why." Then I just had to think about all the different reasons why, and get mad again, and think, "Yes, you have done the right thing."

And another initiator said:

I feel a great sense of relief that I know it's over, that

I don't have any hesitations at all about ending it. There isn't a question in my mind as to whether I would go back with him ever. I know that I would never do that. I don't have any hesitations left— where I did for some time.

Even initiators were sometimes perplexed by their previous doubts; when asked about why they decided to get a divorce, they would turn my question around and say, "The real question is why I stayed in the marriage as long as I did." As they established their motives for initiating divorce by highlighting their discontent, the happy moments shifted to the background and became fragments that were recalled piecemeal over the course of a lengthy interview.

In sum, initiators began emphasizing the negative aspects of marriage and they framed that emphasis within a discernable vocabulary of motives that allowed them (and their partners) to interpret their status as initiator. Despite the myriad events characterizing and leading up to each individual divorce, most initiators articulated this common vocabulary of motives by which they subsequently understood and talked about their divorces. And because this vocabulary derived more generally from a "socially valid" discourse (Garfinkel, 1956) about personal needs and self-gratification, the motives that initiators furnished made their decisions seem reasonable and justifiable. Furthermore, it seemed clear that these descriptions emphasizing personal fulfillment were formulated after the decision to initiate.

The Noninitiating Partner's Vocabulary of Motives

In most cases, partners who did not initiate their divorces maintained forceful and bitter opposition to the efforts of their spouses who did. This section describes the vocabulary of motives that emerged among most noninitiators. Again, a striking fact about noninitiators' opposition and their emergent vocabulary was that neither the opposition nor the proffered motives derived in any simple way from longstanding antecedent marital dynamics. It is important to reiterate, then, that noninitiating partners were not characterized by a peculiar set of actions and feelings prior to the breakup; as other research (Jones, 1986) has shown as well, noninitiating partners typically acknowledged their marital problems and described themselves as unhappy. Most non-initiating partners even told me that they had been contemplating a divorce themselves.

When initiators seized control of the process by declaring the marriage over, however, partners responded by articulating an opposition that made the divorce painful and contentious. Sometimes they pleaded with the initiators, asking for another chance at making the marriage work. Several arranged for joint counseling, though the counseling usually manifested opposing efforts with the initiator attempting to smooth the divorce transition and the partner hoping to save the marriage. Sometimes the partner harassed the initiator with frequent phone calls and uninvited visits. A few became violent, destroying property or attempting to kill or hurt the initiator. The level of hostility and hatred astonished even divorcing people; almost in disbelief, they would relate sensational and lurid stories about violence, sabotage, and vandalism. Not every partner was aggressively hostile towards the initiator, but in most cases the partner played a decisive role in transforming the relationship from one of mutual ambivalence and unhappiness into one of deep antagonism.

Partners thus found themselves in a paradoxical situation: While having felt ambivalent and uncertain about the relationship prior to the divorce, now they found themselves resolutely opposing any effort to dissolve it. One partner, for example, recalled an incident in which she had been nearly ready to leave the marriage herself:

> I walked into the room where he was and he wouldn't even look at me. And I said, "I can't live like this. This is killing me." And he said, "I don't care, whatever you want you can have, you can have the house, you can have all the money, I just want out." And I fell apart. I literally fell apart. I thought I was just going to die. I begged him not to go, and can't we please work on it, and we'll go to a counselor and we'll do all this stuff.

Yet noninitiating partners managed to smooth over the disjuncture between confused frustration during marriage and resolute opposition during and after the divorce. Here the data consistently reveal one way in which they did this: They invoked a common vocabulary of motives that helped make sense of having been

left, and that helped explain and justify their subsequent opposition to divorce. Just as initiating was most characterized by a particular stance toward marriage and divorce, so too was opposing, and this stance was clearly manifested in a vocabulary of motives that emphasized family and commitment.

Whereas initiators worked to resolve ambivalent feelings with a one-sided emphasis on negative aspects of the relationship, partners responded by laying claim to the other side of ambivalence and began emphasizing the good. They began comparing their relationships with those of friends and relatives, emphasizing the ways in which their own were superior. They began seeing their marriages in a new light, selecting out certain information and interpreting that information in order to make their opposition seem legitimate and inevitable. To be sure, they still acknowledged the complaints that they had about their marriages, and most even admitted that some of these complaints were grounds for believing that their marriages were irreconcilable. But they began articulating their complaints within a larger rhetorical context in which commitment and family were primary. They invoked the vows they had made and talked about the sanctity of promises. They talked about persistence, about sacrifice, about working through tough times, and about responsibility. In sum, they invoked a moralistic vocabulary about commitment and about not giving up.

As an example, consider the following verbatim dialogue from an interview that I conducted with a man who had been separated from his wife for 6 years. He detailed the many problems in his marriage, and he described an agreement that he had with his wife about finalizing a divorce "when the time was right." To his surprise, however, she decided to initiate the divorce on her own. The dialogue begins with a question from me:

JH: When she said she was ready to split up, that was OK with you?

INFORMANT: No. No. I had been working my butt off trying to keep our relationship together. Trying everything I could. I say, "Boy, you fight this thing. You do something to keep your relationship together, especially if you have kids. You do something to keep this relationship going." Our grandparents—

they didn't get along all the time. There's just no way in the world that they got along together all the time. But it's a struggle, they were able to work something out between themselves to maintain a relationship.

JH: You would have stuck it out?

INFORMANT: Oh yeah, I'd still be right there.

Another woman detailed a litany of complaints with such angry forcefulness that I was surprised when she said that her spouse, rather than she, initiated divorce. She described and explained her subsequent opposition:

In a lot of ways I think a lot of it's from my dad. My mom treated my dad like shit. But my dad believes in honor and a sense of duty. I think I somehow got those values. You tell someone you're going to be there forever, then you're going to work on it. You're going to be there. And you may have really shitty times, but you're going to be there. You work on these things. We fucking got married, you know? I mean we did the rings and everything. And said forever. And that to me meant, OK, that's what you're going to do. Work on that.

And another noninitiating partner explained her opposition to divorce despite not even liking her spouse anymore:

Did you always like your mother? Did you always like your dad? So to me commitment was about that. That you could say to someone, "I don't really like you very much, but I'm going to stay here a while and hang out, and see how it's going." There are times that you need to commit to something that you don't like.

In several interviews I pointed out the obvious disparity between noninitiators' ambivalent intentions and feelings before divorce and their resolute opposition during divorce. I pressed them to explain these contradictions, and they gave fascinating answers—answers suggesting that even they could see the after-the-fact, constructed, and rhetorical nature of their motives. One woman, for example, told me a long story about the emotional turmoil she felt in her marriage, recognizing clearly that divorce seemed like a good idea given a realistic assessment of the marriage. Nevertheless, she ended up opposing her divorce, and she talked at length about commitment. When I pointed out the incongruity, she puzzled over it:

Yeah, I know. It's another contradiction. But I do think you should try and try and try and work through these things. But maybe it's the only way I can think about these things. You do a lot of thinking and rewording to make the pain go away or to make it make some kind of sense, somehow.

On one level, then, even noninitiating partners acknowledged that their motives were retrospectively assigned, and interview data like these provide further confirmation of the hypothesis that motives are rhetorical constructs that assign meaning to events after they happen.

CONCLUSION

Beneath the intelligibility of social life lies a messy reality full of what Burke calls "discrepant and conflicting stimuli" (p. 30). Nevertheless, social actors manage to coordinate their activities by ascribing meaning to the events and objects and people around them, and by mutually negotiating patterns of social life through which the world becomes intelligible. Burke's and Mills' critical insight was that motives are social constructs that serve to ascribe meaning to the goings on of social life, and that one way in which humans create order out of chaos is by imputing motives. Whatever the true causes of action (if we can even conceive of such a thing), and whatever the "inner springs" that impel individuals to behave as they do, when we talk about motives we are talking about an order of symbolic reality through which social life is negotiated. As Blum and McHugh (1971) assert, "To give a motive is not to locate a cause of the action, but is for some observer to assert how a behavior is socially intelligible. . . . [A motive] is to be understood grammatically (as part of the meaning of an action) rather than as a factual report on some contingent, antecedent event" (pp. 100–101).

The data presented here give evidence that the motives humans routinely ascribe to their own behaviors and others' behaviors have no essential and necessary connection to antecedent events. When the people I talked with reflected upon the events leading up to divorce, most acknowledged the almost accidental nature of who became the initiator and who became the noninitiator. But once those positions emerged, they became the basis on which divorcing partners invoked one of two typal vocabularies of motive. The implication, of course, is that the motives by which divorcing people interpret their behaviors have less to do with actual events leading up to divorce and more to do with an emergent symbolic order structured around the initiator and noninitiator identities.

As startling as this conclusion may seem, it should not be misinterpreted as arguing that motives are merely fabrications used cynically by social manipulators, or that motives are merely rationalizations used unwittingly by social dupes. I want to propose, along with another recent interpreter of Mills and Burke (Marshall, 1981), that motives are in some sense "true." They are not true in the sense of being causes of behavior, but rather in the sense that social actors derive them from actual prior events even though they rhetorically constitute and use them afterwards. It helps to keep in mind Burke's notion that motives are "shorthand words for situations" (p. 31)—situations that are characterized by "discrepant and conflicting stimuli." In divorce, even though motives come into play only after the two positions in divorce are designated and identified, nearly everyone describes an agonizing ambivalence beforehand: They want to leave their marriages and at the same time they want to stay. They feel unhappy, frustrated, and personally unfulfilled in their relationships, but they desperately want to be married and to have a supportive and satisfying home life. Whatever would make for a subsequent vocabulary of unfulfilled needs is already there for either partner to seize upon; and whatever would make for a subsequent vocabulary of commitment is already there for either partner to seize upon. Once partners reach the almost arbitrary designation of who is the initiator and who is not, it is a simple matter for the initiator to see and to believe that personal frustration was the motive for initiating; likewise, it is a simple matter for the noninitiator to see and to believe that commitment was the motive for opposing divorce.

Thus our strong sense that motives are not merely "made up" *ex post facto* is a good one. They aren't, at least not entirely. In divorce, the events, feelings, facts, and "motives" that would explain one line of action over another were present antecedent to the divorce. But just as many events, feelings, facts, and

motives that would explain numerous other possible outcomes were there as well. The motives were there to be discovered, whether a person initiated divorce or opposed it. Thus noninitiators really were committed all along (as were initiators) and initiators really were personally frustrated all along (as were their partners). As sense-making, symbol-using creatures, one way that we sort through these complex situations is by ascribing motives, and by identifying the elements "all along" that led to certain patterns of behavior.

NOTE

Many thanks to Alan Booth. An earlier version of this paper was presented at the 1993 meeting of the American Sociological Association.

REFERENCES

Ahrons, C. R., & Rogers, R. H. (1987). *Divorced families: A multidisciplinary developmental view.* New York: Norton.

Black, L. E., Eastwood, M. M., Sprenkle, D. H., & Smith, E. (1991). An exploratory analysis of the construct of leavers versus left as it relates to Levinger's social exchange theory of attractions, barriers, and alternative attractions. *Journal of Divorce and Remarriage, 15,* 127–139.

Blum, A. F., & McHugh, P. (1971). The social ascription of motives. *American Sociological Review, 36,* 98–109.

Blumstein, P. W. (1974). The honoring of accounts. *American Sociological Review, 39,* 551–566.

Bruce, S., & Wallis, R. (1983). Rescuing motives. *The British Journal of Sociology, 34,* 61–70.

Bruce, S., & Wallis, R. (1985). 'Rescuing motives' rescued: A reply to Sharrock and Watson. *The British Journal of Sociology, 36,* 467–470.

Buehler, C. (1987). Initiator status and the divorce transition. *Family Relations, 36,* 82–86.

Buehler, C. A., Hogan, M. J., Robinson, B. E., & Levy, R. J. (1986). The parental divorce transition: Divorce-related stressors and well-being. *Journal of Divorce, 9,* 61–81.

Burke, K. (1950). *A rhetoric of motives.* Englewood Cliffs, NJ: Prentice Hall.

Burke, K. (1954). *Permanence and change* (3rd ed.). Berkeley: University of California Press. (Original work published 1935.)

Campbell, C. (1991). Reexamining Mills on motive: A character vocabulary approach. *Sociological Analysis, 52,* 89–97.

Croghan, R., & Miell, D. (1992). Accounts of intimate support relationships in the early months of mothering. In J. H. Harvey, T. L. Orbuch, & A. L. Weber (Eds.), *Attributions, accounts, and close relationships* (pp. 221–243). New York: Springer-Verlag.

Crosby, J. H., Gage, B. A., & Raymond, M. C. (1983). The grief resolution process in divorce. *Journal of Divorce, 7,* 3–18.

Crosby, J. H., Lybarger, S. K., & Mason, R. L. (1986). The grief resolution process in divorce: Phase II. *Journal of Divorce, 10,* 17–40.

Duck, S. (1982). A topography of relationship disengagement and dissolution. In S. Duck (Ed.), *Personal relationships: Vol. 4. Dissolving personal relationships* (pp. 1–30). London: Academic Press.

Eheart, B. K., & Power, M. B. (1988). An interpretive study of adoption: The interplay of history, power, knowledge, and emotions. *Journal of Contemporary Ethnography, 17,* 326–348.

Federico, J. (1979). The marital termination period of the divorce adjustment process. *Journal of Divorce, 3,* 93–106.

Foote, N. N. (1951). Identification as the basis for a theory of motivation. *American Sociological Review, 16,* 14–21.

Garfinkel, H. (1956). Conditions of successful degradation ceremonies. *American Journal of Sociology, 61,* 420–424.

Garfinkel, H. (1967). *Studies in ethnomethodology.* Englewood Cliffs, NJ: Prentice-Hall.

Goode, W. J. (1956). *After divorce.* Glencoe, IL: Free Press.

Gubrium, J. F. (1988). Family responsibility and caregiving in the qualitative analysis of the alzheimer's disease experience. *Journal of Marriage and the Family, 50,* 197–207.

Gubrium, J. F., & Buckholdt, D. R. (1982). Fictive family: Everyday usage, analytic, and human service considerations. *American Anthropologist, 84,* 878–885.

Gubrium, J. F., & Holstein, J. A. (1990). *What is family?* Mountain View, CA: Mayfield.

Gubrium, J. F., & Lynott, R. J. (1985). Family rhetoric as social order. *Journal of Family Issues, 6,* 129–152.

Hagestad, G. O., & Smyer, M. A. (1982). Dissolving long-term relationships: Patterns of divorcing in middle age. In S. Duck (Ed.), *Personal relationships: Vol. 4. Dissolving personal relationships* (pp. 155–188). London: Academic Press.

Handel, G. (Ed.). (1985). *The psychosocial interior of the family* (3rd ed.). New York: Aldine.

Hewitt, J. P., & Stokes, R. (1975). Disclaimers. *American Sociological Review, 40,* 1–11.

Hill, C. T., Rubin, Z., & Peplau, L. A. (1979). Breakups before marriage: The end of 103 affairs. In G. Levinger & O. C. Moles (Eds.), *Divorce and separation* (pp. 64–82). New York: Basic Books.

Hopper, J. (1993). Oppositional identities and rhetoric in divorce. *Qualitative Sociology, 16,* 133–156.

Jones, B. W. (1986). The ambivalent spouse syndrome. *Journal of Divorce, 10,* 57–67.

Kalab, K. A. (1987). Student vocabularies of motive: Accounts for absence. *Symbolic Interaction, 10,* 71–83.

Kersten, K. K. (1990). The process of marital disaffection: Intervention at various stages. *Family Relations, 39,* 257–265.

Kessler, S. (1975). *The American way of divorce.* Chicago: Nelson-Hall.

LaRossa, R. (1988). Renewing our faith in qualitative family research. *Journal of Contemporary Ethnography, 17,* 243–260.

Levinger, G. (1979). A social psychological perspective on marital dissolution. In G. Levinger & O. C. Moles (Eds.), *Divorce and separation* (pp. 37–60). New York: Basic Books.

Lewis, R. A., & Spanier, G. B. (1979). Theorizing about the quality and stability of marriage. In W. R. Burr, R. Hill, F. I. Nye, & I. L. Reiss (Eds.), *Contemporary theories about the family* (Vol. 1, pp. 268–294). New York: Free Press.

Lynott, R. J. (1983). Alzheimer's disease and institutionalization: The ongoing construction of a decision. *Journal of Family Issues, 4,* 559–574.

Marshall, G. (1981). Accounting for deviance. *The International Journal of Sociology and Social Policy, 1,* 17–45.

McCall, G. J. (1982). Becoming unrelated: The management of bond dissolution. In S. Duck (Ed.), *Personal relationships: Vol. 4. Dissolving personal relationships* (pp. 211–231). London: Academic Press.

McLain, R., & Weigert, A. (1979). Toward a phenomenological sociology of family: A programmatic essay. In W. R. Burr, R. Hill, F. I. Nye, & I. L. Reiss (Eds.), *Contemporary theories about the family* (Vol. 2, pp. 160–205). New York: Free Press.

Miller, L. J. (1990). Violent families and the rhetoric of harmony. *British Journal of Sociology, 41,* 263–288.

Mills, C. W. (1940). Situated actions and vocabularies of motive. *American Sociological Review, 5,* 904–913.

Nevaldine, A. (1978). *Divorce: The leaver and the left.* Unpublished doctoral dissertation, University of Minnesota.

Nichols, L. (1990). Reconceptualizing social accounts: An agenda for theory building and empirical research. *Current Perspectives in Social Theory, 10,* 113–144.

Palisi, B. J. (1984). Symptoms of readiness for divorce. *Journal of Family Issues, 5,* 70–89.

Pettit, E. J., & Bloom, B. L. (1984). Whose decision was it? The effects of initiator status on adjustment to marital disruption. *Journal of Marriage and the Family, 46,* 587–595.

Ponzetti, J. J., Jr., & Cate, R. M. (1986). The developmental course of conflict in the marital dissolution process. *Journal of Divorce, 10,* 1–15.

Potter, J., & Wetherell, M. (1987). *Discourse and social psychology.* London: Sage.

Price-Bonham, S., & Balswick, J. O. (1980). The noninstitutions: Divorce, desertion, and remarriage. *Journal of Marriage and the Family, 42,* 959–972.

Ray, M. C., & Simons, R. L. (1987). Convicted murderers' accounts of their crimes: A study of homicide in small communities. *Symbolic Interaction, 10,* 57–70.

Riessman, C. K. (1990). *Divorce talk: Women and men make sense of personal relationships.* New Brunswick, NJ: Rutgers University Press.

Salts, C. J. (1979). Divorce process: Integration of theory. *Journal of Divorce, 2,* 233–240.

Sarat, A., & Felstiner, W. L. F. (1988). Law and social relations:

Vocabularies of motive in lawyer/client interaction. *Law and Society Review, 22,* 737–769.

Scanzoni, J. (1979). A historical perspective on husband-wife bargaining power and marital dissolution. In G. Levinger & O. C. Moles (Eds.), *Divorce and separation* (pp. 20–36). New York: Basic Books.

Scott, M. B., & Lyman, S. M. (1968). Accounts. *American Sociological Review, 33,* 46–62.

Scully, D., & Marolla, J. (1984). Convicted rapists' vocabulary of motive: Excuses and justifications. *Social Problems, 31,* 530–544.

Sharrock, W. W., & Watson, D. R. (1984). What's the point of 'rescuing motives'? *The British Journal of Sociology, 35,* 435–451.

Spanier, G. B., & Thompson, L. (1984). *Parting: The aftermath of separation and divorce.* Beverly Hills: Sage Publications.

Sprecher, S. (1992). Social exchange perspectives on the dissolution of close relationships. In T. L. Orbuch (Ed.), *Close relationship loss: Theoretical approaches* (pp. 47–66). New York: Springer-Verlag.

Stokes, R., & Hewitt, J. P. (1976). Aligning actions. *American Sociological Review, 41,* 838–849.

Vaughan, D. (1986). *Uncoupling.* New York: Oxford University Press.

Wallis, R., & Bruce, S. (1983). Accounting for action: Defending the common sense heresy. *Sociology, 17,* 97–111.

Weigert, A. J., & Hastings, R. (1977). Identity loss, family, and social change. *American Journal of Sociology, 82,* 1171–1185.

Weinstein, R. M. (1980). Vocabularies of motive for illicit drug use: An application of the accounts framework. *The Sociological Quarterly, 21,* 577–593.

Yearly, S. (1988). Settling accounts: Action, accounts and sociological explanation. *The British Journal of Sociology, 39,* 578–599.

Yoder, J. D., & Nichols, R. C. (1980). A life perspective comparison of married and divorced persons. *Journal of Marriage and the Family, 42,* 413–419.

FURTHER READING

Dowd, James J. 2000. "Hard Jobs and Good Ambition: U.S. Army Generals and the Rhetoric of Modesty." *Symbolic Interaction* 23: 183–205.

- Discusses the accounts given by U.S. Army general officers to explain their success in an environment that discourages careerism and self-aggrandizement.

Hewitt, John P. and Randall Stokes. 1975. "Disclaimers." *American Sociological Review* 40: 1–11.

- Treats "disclaimers" as a particular kind of account, taking a future, rather than a past, orientation to motive talk.

Kalab, Kathleen A. 1987. "Student Vocabularies of Motive: Accounts for Absence." *Symbolic Interaction* 10: 71–83.

- Examines the accounts given by students that construct their motives for being absent from class.

Scott, Marvin B. and Stanford M. Lyman. 1968. "Accounts." *American Sociological Review* 33: 46–62.

- Classic article that sets forth the idea that accounts are the vocabulary of motives.

Scully, Diana and Joseph Marolla. 1984. "Convicted Rapists' Vocabulary of Motives: Excuses and Justifications." *Social Problems* 31: 530–544.

- Examines the constructed motives of convicted rapists.

—— SECTION 5 ——

COMPETENCE

People typically think of competence as a personal characteristic. Intelligence, aptitudes, and creativity are just a few of the types of competences we distinguish. But like minds and motives, we can also view competence as a social construction. Doing so leads us to examine the interactional process by which competence is assigned to particular individuals.

Sociologist Nikolas Rose (1998) (see Further Reading) has called the 20th century the "psy" era. By this he means that the "psy" professions—psychology, psychiatry, psychoanalysis, psychotherapy—came into their own as disciplines, becoming significant influences in everyday life. Today, there's an increasing prevalence of psychological assessment. Virtually every personal trait can be measured. IQ scores. Job performance evaluations. Proficiency ratings. Nearly every aspect of personal behavior is appraised and assessed. The "psy" professions are at the forefront of the construction of inner life, especially personal competence.

Schools, businesses, governments, and myriad other institutions routinely assess individual skills and competence. Intellectual ability probably gets the most attention. Virtually everyone has taken intelligence and achievement tests. From third-grade reading tests to the familiar test battery of acronyms, we take ACTs, SATs, GREs, and LSATs. The tests probe and prod our psyches for competence in one graded skill after another. If you don't score well, you aren't making the grade. You aren't measuring up. You aren't getting ahead. We also measure progress back to normalcy for those who may have drifted off track. We assess those who have fallen by the wayside because they are disabled, developmentally challenged, ill, or incorrigible to gauge the help they need and the progress they make.

These evaluations focus on the individual and his or her abilities. Unfortunately, evaluators haven't attended closely to how the assessment process itself constructs its own outcomes. The central issue here is how the evaluation process defines what competence means in the first place. Traditionally, evaluators take for granted that properly conducted assessments produce information that is exclusively about the competence of the person being tested or evaluated. Needless to say, this practice pinpoints the inner life of that person.

There's increasing interest, however, in turning this perspective on its head. Researchers are investigating how formal test-taking and evaluation processes themselves produce the competence and incompetence they otherwise only seek to document. More and more, it's clear that assessment practices actually create the competencies they seemingly only measure. By the same token, competence is constructed in walks of everyday life in which evaluation isn't explicitly at stake. In practice, competence isn't a personal feature of an individual. It's something that's attributed to persons through everyday interpretive and evaluative procedures.

This perspective raises all sorts of questions. Some researchers, for example, look at how the interactions between test takers and evaluators work to produce evidence of competence or incompetence as the case may be. Others consider how family members create and sustain the impression that their domestic affairs are normal, not dysfunctional. We are increasingly finding that competence, like other aspects of inner life, is a feature of how people interact with one another to accomplish their everyday goals.

ABOUT THE READINGS

In practice, the formal definition or evaluation of competence centers on social relationships. The individual being assessed is on one side of the relationship. He or she may be a child taking a reading test or an adult taking a vocational aptitude assessment. Evaluators are on the other side of the relationship. Teachers, psychologists, and human resource specialists often fill this role. Most of what we know about competence comes from information taken from the first side of the relationship, from the people being evaluated. The readings in this section point us to the other side. They consider the part that those who administer tests or conduct evaluations play in the construction of competence.

In **"Constructing Competence," James A. Holstein** and **Jaber F. Gubrium** review a variety of studies that show how competence is interactionally constructed. These studies display how the evaluation of different aspects of individual competence—intelligence, aptitudes, and achievement, among others—doesn't simply reveal traits of the individual being evaluated. The evaluation also reflects the evaluators' contribution to the resulting measures and scores. We should emphasize that the "part evaluators play" is not just a matter of how well the evaluators do their job. It also refers to the role they play in actually producing the scores in collaboration with their subjects.

For example, Holstein and Gubrium discuss how verbal exchanges between a child and a clinician produce answers to a language skills test. It's not simply the child who produces the answers. The answers that emerge are a *joint* production. Children are often tentative in proceeding through the test, anticipating clues for the "right" answers. Sometimes a clinician senses that a child gets the point of a question and knows a correct response. But the child may start to give a technically incorrect answer. The clinician may then steer the child to a more correct way of responding that better reflects "what we know the child knows." As in other assessment procedures, providing a correct or positive response is not just a matter of getting the right answer. It also involves communicating an answer that is counted as correct in the scoring process. Any score that emerges from interactional testing therefore represents contributions by both the test taker and the test administrator. Still, test scores are viewed as if they were markers of only the test taker's competence.

Laypersons also collaborate to construct personal competence. In **"The Social Construction of Unreality: A Case Study of a Family's Attribution of Competence to a Severely Retarded Child," Melvin Pollner** and **Lynn McDonald-Wikler** take us into a bizarre family situation. Mary, the 5-year-old daughter, is clinically diagnosed as severely retarded. Family members, however, say that Mary is "really a fast child." She "puts on an act of being retarded" in public. That is, "she fakes it." The selection examines how family members maintain the sense that Mary is competent even though others see her differently. The emphasis is on family members' interpretive work, not on Mary herself.

The selection describes how family members construct Mary as normal in the face of massive contradictory evidence. Pollner and McDonald-Wikler identify six interactional strategies or "family practices" used by family members: framing, postscripting, puppeteering, semantic crediting, putting words in the child's mouth, and explaining in the "bright" direction. These are all collaborative procedures through which family members sustain Mary's competence. Mary's seemingly personal traits become virtually everybody's business.

25 | Constructing Competence
James A. Holstein and Jaber F. Gubrium

"Maturity" and "competence" are popular terms for describing standards of human growth and development. Many life course theorists—Freud, Erikson, Piaget, and Kohlberg, among others—have used physical growth as a model for the development of psychosexual, cognitive, affective, and moral aspects of the person. In these approaches, the individual grows from relative simplicity to greater complexity of structure and differentiation of function. The physical and social environments may stimulate or retard development, but the sequence or hierarchy of stages follows biogenetic characteristics. Maturity and competence reflect the gradual emergence of innate capacities.

Of course, some individuals seem to mature more quickly or develop greater competencies than others. While acknowledging the developmental course of human growth, some psychologists have been more interested in the correlates of variation, leading them to investigate both the personality characteristics of the mature or competent individual (e.g., Heath 1965; Elkind 1967; Rogers 1964; Carlson 1965; McKinney 1968) and the environmental conditions that stimulate maturation (e.g., Havinghurst 1951; Hunt 1961). Their findings lead to the conclusion that development is not an inevitable unfolding process, but depends on the proper combination of human potential and environmental contingencies.

Sociologists have also been interested in maturity and competence, but have generally worked with the concept of socialization rather than human development. The concept references both what is to be learned and its functions. The former includes a wide variety of norms, values, skills, and expectations required for the social integration of the person and the stability of society. Socialization is considered to be functional for both the person and the social order if it provides for individual and social integration. Infants are considered incomplete, incompetent, and asocial;

they are not yet human inasmuch as they have not been socialized. They cannot yet participate in the integrative work of society, that is, perform in its network of interdependent roles and positions. Through experience gained within a variety of formal and informal settings and institutions, they gradually acquire the cultural resources and interpersonal understandings by which they both recognize themselves and are recognized by others as competent members of the social order.

Maturity and competence, then, are typically construed as individual qualities that people acquire or develop with age and experience. Despite their many differences, psychological theories of human development and sociological ideas about socialization share a strikingly similar view in this regard. The fully socialized or mature adult provides the standard by which we judge competence. Change is developmental—moving in the direction of more complete socialization—if it results in greater maturity, rationality, or responsibility. Lack of change or movement "off course" is seen as faulty socialization, inadequate development, personality defect, immaturity, and the like. The child is naturally deficient vis-a-vis the adult. Although children may have their own sets of interpretive skills, the skills are valuable only if they contribute to further development. If there is perceived continuity between a child's current behavior and desirable future states, we say that growth is evident. Perceived discontinuity between the present and the desired future signals problems. The warning is signaled by labels such as "immature," "irrational," "incompetent," and "unenculturated," depending on whether the interpreter is, say, an ordinary citizen, teacher, psychologist, sociologist, or anthropologist (MacKay 1973).

Conventional theories of aging share the common-sense perspective that development or socialization brings about real changes in individual capability. Change is considered an objective feature of human behavior. It can be differentially evaluated for whether it appears to be moving in the proper direction, toward greater maturity, personal and social integration, and cognitive differentiation and elaboration. Competence is something real, an objective thing that can be studied with scientific precision to reveal process and effect.

Following the theme that life change is socially constituted, this chapter suggests a different perspective. Instead of being a set of traits, we analyze maturity, competence, and related terms as labels people use to assign evaluative meaning to individual capability. In this context, traits are interpretively and interactionally assigned. Orienting primarily to present-time matters, we examine how maturity and competence are circumstantially accomplished.

SITUATED ASSIGNMENT

Developmental psychologists traditionally focus their attention on the particular skills, general abilities, and personality characteristics that individuals acquire at sequential life stages, while sociologists usually consider the structures and processes by which persons internalize the norms, values, and attitudes of their society. Both approaches tend to cast the person as a passive participant in these processes. More significantly, from our standpoint, they fail to examine how various competencies are actually recognized and displayed, how people interpret behavioral displays as indices of competence.

Conventional theories are not sufficient for understanding how personal and social structures are produced and maintained in daily interaction. Developing biogenetic capabilities have no inherent or self-evident meaning. They are assigned meaning by those who witness behavior and interpret it in specific situations, based on tacit and shared understandings of human growth and development. The interpretive practices through which persons identify, label, and judge relative competence show that maturity, wisdom, ability, realism, competence, and related terms are a constitutive vocabulary for assigning developmental meaning to the individual's present capability. Equally important, the vocabulary takes its specific content and relevance from concrete settings and situations.

Competence is a concern in all walks of life. Leiter (1974), for example, describes how typifications of capability are used by teachers to differentiate students. It is evident that the teachers, as others do in different circumstances, invoke their practical agendas and use relevant aspects of their background knowledge of everyday classroom relations to formulate their constructions. One familiar type of student they recognize is the "immature child." This child is easily distracted, cannot sit still during a lesson, and has a short attention span. Boys are less capable than girls in this regard, as are children who are physically smaller than others their own age. A second type is the "bright child." This child learns quickly, without demanding much time or effort from the teacher. His or her social skills may be poor but if he or she learns quickly and his or her verbal skills are good, the child is considered to be bright. A third type of child is the "behavior problem." This child is usually a boy, often of large build, who fights with other children for "no reason at all." A fourth type is the "independent child." He or she can work with very little supervision and finishes assigned tasks before beginning other activities. In other settings, these same children might be typified somewhat differently, such as a child being "basically a good boy" at home or "irreverent" at church, again reflecting the practical issues and local cultures of the context (Gubrium 1989).

The teachers described by Leiter were able to assign children to a "mature" and an "immature" class in one case and to specific teacher types (mamma types, strongly academically oriented, weak academically) in another. They accomplished their classifications without apparent embarrassment or sensitivity to the ad hoc, situated nature of the process. It was routine business for them, undertaken as part of their educational activities. Teachers did not question one another's actions, in principle, nor did they argue about the appropriateness of the categories. The apparent ease with which the teachers applied the typology shows that a system of normative usage was referenced, allowing teachers to sense they were "talking the same language" and pursuing the same objectives in an orderly and rational way.

The teachers possessed the interpretive skills to see and describe behavioral displays as examples of general types, as well as the accounting skills to explain their classifications to an interviewer. Life course imagery filtered in throughout their discussions. Consider the following exchange between a teacher (T) and an interviewer (I) (Leiter 1974:44–45):

T: Now this is Pa, . . . a very interesting child because he's one of the ones who's extremely bright but he is a behavior problem in school. And umm one of the reasons he's a behavior problem is because he—well, I guess I really shouldn't say he's a behavior problem but he's immature. Because he's young and we probably expect too much of him. He's an October birthday which would make him one of the youngest in the class. . . .

I: What are some of the things that give you the impression that he was bright?

T: Oh, he has a fantastic memory. In the group I can read a story and he can be looking out the window or talking to his neighbor and I can ask him the question and he knows the answer like that, you know. At first I would, he would be talking so after I read something or if we'd been discussing something I would say "Pa, what have we been talking about?" And I was doing it because I figured he wouldn't know—and he did.

I: Um humm.

T: And so it was in the total group that he's catching a lot of what they're hearing and if he's a child who can talk to his neighbor and still know the answer you know you've got a bright child on your hands. . . .

Specific behaviors may likewise be assessed for competence. Turning to later life, consider how a so-called activity of daily living—the ability to control one's bowels—was interpretively constituted at Murray Manor, a nursing home for the aged (Gubrium and Buckholdt 1979). A highly touted bowel-training program had been instituted to help residents become more self-sufficient. The program required staff nurses to monitor effectiveness in terms of participants' ability to control their bowel movements. While this would seem to be rather straightforward, in practice it was mediated by locally contingent understanding. On one occasion, for example, an aide entered a resident's room to find that the resident had fully soiled her bed and clothing with feces. One of the nurses on the floor noticed the aide cleaning up and remarked, "I guess Helen's at it again, huh? The program is not helping her too much, is it?" (p. 121). The aide, who was none too pleased at having to tend to the mess, blurted:

Oh, she knows damn well what she's doing. She just shit everywhere because I was busy helping Stella [another resident] down the hall and you know how she hates Stella. Well, . . . she [Helen] just had to wait a little longer until I could finish. She didn't like that, of course. So she got mad and just BMed all over the place. (p. 121)

Later, when it was time to record Helen's progress in the training program, the aide did *not* count the episode as an instance of incontinence, explaining, "That was different. Helen knew what she was doing and was just trying to get back at me" (p. 122).

The next day, the same aide entered Helen's room to find Helen "red-faced and squirming." She quickly took her to the bathroom where Helen promptly moved her bowels. Helping Helen off the toilet, the aide complimented her on her control. Later, the aide informed a nurse that Helen was "clean" all day, adding, "I think she's really coming around, you know what I mean? I think she's gonna come out one of the best on the floor" (p. 122). While Helen's attributed intentions had been used earlier to discount a soiling episode as incontinence, here intention is glossed over to produce the day's "fact" of total control.

IMPUTING READINESS

For developmental psychologists, the idea of readiness refers to the successful mastery of the characteristic skills of a stage of growth as a prelude to moving on the next. Recall that Piaget, for example, argued that the child cannot begin to perform concrete operations until he or she can extract concepts from experience and make intuitive use of them. Although such skills are not strictly defined by age, they are thought to conform generally to certain age periods.

Notions of developmental readiness are not the exclusive concern of human scientists, however. They are given serious attention and used by laypersons in the commonsense management of their everyday affairs. Assumptions about relationships between age, training, experience, and background and a person's competence to perform adequately in real-life settings guide much of our everyday thinking. Some schoolteachers, for example, believe that children are not "ready to read" until they are six and a half years old (see Hamblin et al. 1971). The teachers locate the reason for this in the children's developmental readiness and not in the historical development or organizational structure of the school. There also is the commonsense theory concerning the relationship between age and the ability to be an "informed" voter. For decades, a person had to be twenty-one years old to vote. Now, apparently because our younger citizens are developing more quickly and have more education, we, as a society, have decided that eighteen-year-olds are capable of participating rationally in the election process. And take the example of a friend of the authors who once applied for the position of chair of the sociology department at a major university. His teaching and publication record were apparently fine enough to place him among the finalists for the job. When he visited the campus, however, department members became quietly concerned about how "young" he was (thirty-one at the time) and how young he looked. Presumably a desirable chairman was more mature, or at least looked more mature. The candidate was not offered the job. Off the record, several department members implicitly linked age and experience with competence as they informally accounted for the decision.

Individual characteristics such as physical size and chronological age are used for imputing readiness in schools in much the same way as educational credentials are used in employment decisions. Take the following rationales teachers provided for placement decisions (Leiter 1974). In this case, teachers were deciding who would go on to first grade and what kind of first grade class would be best for each child.

. . . Then we have had one other little boy who is very, very immature and he was a November birthday. Just a little, little boy. (p. 43)

. . . Maybe I ought to put her five plus because she does have a May birthday. (p. 33)

. . . Because he's young and we probably expect too much of him. He's an October birthday which would make him one of the youngest in the class. (p. 44)

. . . She's a large child. Now, here's a case where even though she would not be ready for first grade—she's ready for a low first grade—but even if she were not ready in other ways, I still would pass her on to a first grade because that girl . . . another year in kindergarten? Look how big she'd be before she went into the first grade. (p. 63)

Shared understandings linking age and size to behavior help teachers "make sense" of both their observations of children and their assessments of the children's competence and readiness. Age and size criteria were invoked both to make the decision and to justify and explain it.

Age, of course, is only one criterion by which to assess competence. Training or, more important, the certification of training, is also relevant. Persons are not presumed to be ready or qualified for most important work unless they have the proper credentials, such as a college or graduate degree, professional license, or certificate of apprenticeship. The process of training itself represents a life course preparation that is understood and invoked to signal readiness. Commonsense reasoning tells us that education, for example, has a strong positive, and desirable, relationship with both personal well-being and economic productivity. The idea is supported by the so-called human-capital economists who inform us that improvements in the quality of human resources are a major source of economic growth (Schultz 1962).

Ivar Berg (1971) questions the validity of arguments that imply a simple, direct relationship between education and job performance. He reports that interviews with personnel directors, managers, and foremen reveal adamant claims that better-educated workers are better employees. They presumably are more promotable and possess more "stick-to-it-tiveness." Yet respondents also indicate that the actual content of the training is not as important as the fact that employees have completed a program and thus supposedly demonstrate desirable personal qualities. Berg thus reinterprets the meaning of education and training, contending that training is a putative indicator of an ability to adapt and persevere as much as it represents acquired competence.

Few of the firms Berg studied had ever tested their assumptions, so Berg attempted to do a systematic study of the relation between education and job performance. His conclusion was that there was little, if any, evidence for believing that more highly educated persons performed better on the job. To produce these findings, however, Berg had to create measures of job performance, such as absenteeism, turnover, and job satisfaction. Concern over the relative worth of training hinged on interpretive matters relating to just what it was that education was supposed to affect.

Berg also argues that the sorts of decisions involved in many jobs that require advanced educational credentials do not need the kinds of skills that education and training are supposed to provide. He illustrates his point by quoting a report produced by three Brookings Institution economists in which they describe pricing decisions in "a representative sample of large enterprises," decisions that officially require a good deal of training and technical skill. Berg notes (1971:73) that complex decisions were indeed made, but he characterizes them as being of the "it seemed like a good idea" variety, rather than decisions based on the application of general rules or formulas. He then goes on to argue that the kinds of skills that are ostensibly acquired from education or training are not really the ones needed on the job.

Our interest in Berg's analysis is not to join in the debate about the relevance of educational credentials. Instead, we wish to show how the relevance of education and training is interpretively assembled and *used* to typify persons, to elaborate the notion of readiness, and to make accountable, organizationally relevant decisions. A wide spectrum of opinions coexist and compete. Human-capital theorists hold that training is a necessary investment; they believe competence is a prerequisite for productivity. Some administrators say educational attainment is used to assess a person's "readiness" to be a competent, trustworthy employee. Educated persons are said to be better gambles for the company. Other managers and personnel directors say that important skills are learned on the job; from this point of view, competence is an outgrowth of performance. And while the reasoned and reasonable explanations compete, nearly half of the "well-trained" college recruits leave their companies within the first five years on the job. The point is not that one explanation is better than another but that a variety of accounts centering on competence and training—professional, scientific, and commonsense—are available and are used to make sense of organizational behavior and outcomes.

The various typifications are self-sustaining. For example, when "well trained" recruits fail to work out, the belief in the positive relation between training and job performance is not abandoned. Instead, descriptions of existing capabilities are reformulated. Organizational personnel argue that those who leave "think they are better than they are." They are called "kids who want too much" or "who haven't yet learned the facts of life, that you have to bide your time." In other words, despite their education, they "really" are not yet competent or mature.

COLLABORATIVE ACCOMPLISHMENT

Clearly, the interpretive activity that constitutes life change and human development is concretely social. Indeed, interaction is so deeply implicated in the production of traits and behaviors that our commonsense belief that these are features of particular individuals must be questioned. The competence, maturity, or developmental readiness established by tallying correct and incorrect answers is typically attributed to the testtaker. A child, for example, takes an IQ test on which he or she responds to questions correctly or incorrectly. The test results are then treated as an indicator of the child's intelligence. But if test answers—putative documents of competence, intelligence, readiness, and so on—are joint productions, attributing test scores to the testtaker alone obscures the interactional process involved, the complex interactional skills of both tester and testtaker. Let us now consider in greater detail how intellectual competence is interactionally produced.

Educational or developmental testing are prototypic instances of the construction and documentation of individual characteristics. Standardized procedures are employed to elicit responses to predetermined questions. The test-taker's responses to the questions are believed to represent the test-taker's competence or development on the dimension being evaluated.

Close examination of the testing process reveals cooperative interactional practices that are central to the production of test results. Yet these practices are invisible in reports of performance.

Courtney Marlaire and Douglas Maynard (1990) have studied testing procedures in a developmental disabilities clinic. The clinic attempts to diagnose and correct children's problems that might be the result of mental retardation, learning disability, attention deficit disorder, autism, or other developmental disorders. Clinicians use a variety of tests to assess intelligence, aptitudes, achievement, and general development.

Marlaire and Maynard note that these tests rely upon vast unacknowledged interactional processes and skills to produce test scores for the children. While the scores are treated as documents of the children's competence, Marlaire and Maynard argue that they are better understood as the "collaborative productions" of the children and their testers.

Consider, for example, a test that requires the child to provide a synonym for the stimulus word. The testing takes place within verbal exchanges between a child (*CH*) and a clinician (*CL*) like the following sequence:[1]

1. CL: Tell me another word that means angry.
2. CH: S—[.5-second silence while child gazes at the clinician,
3.   who is looking at the test instrument.] Angry, mad.
4. CL: Good. Tell me another word that means the same as lawn.
5. CH: Onk.
6. CL [*points with pencil*]: Lawn.
7. CH: Long—longer?
8. CL: Okay. Tell me another word that means small.
9. CH: Smaller?
10. CL: Another word that means the same.
11. CH: Kay. Small.
12. CL: Yeah, what's another word that means small?
13. CH: Little.
14. CL: Good. You're thinking good now. (Marlaire and Maynard 1990:94)

Superficially, the procedure seems to be a straightforward pattern of stimulus and response, but Marlaire and Maynard point out a necessary interactional component to the child's replies. The child is tentative in proceeding through this test. At line 2 she starts a reply, then hesitates. At line 5 she offers a sound mimicking the clinician's prompt (*onk*) that is not clearly a response to the question. In response to the first hesitation, the clinician strongly and positively responds to the child's eventual answer, confirming its correctness, then moves to another question. The child is credited with a correct response (line 4). In the second instance, however, the clinician repeats the prompt (line 6). This signals the unacceptability of *onk* and provides the child with another opportunity to answer correctly. The exchange thus elaborates the stimulus and provides the child with an additional chance to give the "right" answer. When the correct answer fails to emerge in the child's next utterance, the clinician accepts the answer as given ("okay,"—line 8) and moves on to another prompt. This effectively completes the test item sequence and results in an incorrect response for that item.

Later in the test (lines 8–14), a similar exchange takes place. The clinician asks for another word meaning "small," and the child replies with a version of the prompt ("Smaller?"). This utterance is ambiguous; it is not clear if it is the child's answer or an attempt to clarify or repair the clinician's question. The clinician takes it as the latter and offers an alternate version of the the prompt, soliciting "another word that means the same" but omitting the original stimulus item—"small" (line 10). The child responds by repeating the omitted word (line 11), leading the clinician to repeat the entire prompt (line 12). Thus, instead of responding to the child's utterances as candidate (and incorrect) replies, the clinician treats them as bids for further information or clarification. The clinician's *elaborations* lead to the child's correct answer at line 13.

From this, and similar exchanges, it is clear that the emergence of right and wrong answers depends on the tester as well as the test taker; producing test scores is a collaborative venture. Note, in the next example, how an answer requires both a reply from the test taker and the clinician's acceptance of the child's reply as an answer. Until the answer is mutually established, the testing sequence remains open-ended, with the child's competence unresolved. In the test sequence, the child is asked to specify the appropriate behavior for the situation that the clinician describes. The child has responded to several such prompts before this excerpt begins.

1. CL: What do you do if you cut your finger?
2.   [1 second silence]
3.   What would you do if you cut your finger?
4. CH: Put a Band-aid on it.
5. CL: That's right. What do you do when you're sick?
6. CH: Go to the doctuw.
7. CL: That's right.
8.   [1 second silence]
9.   What do you do when you see your hands are dirty?
10. CH: Go wash em.
11. CL: That's right. [.75 second silence] What do you do if you
12.   go into a room and it's all dark in the room?
13.   [1 second silence]
14. CH: Sweep.
15. CL: Okay. C—is there anything else you can do?
16. CH: Yeah.
17. CL: Let's say you wanna play in the room and you walk in the
18.   room.
19. CH: You wanna pway in the room, you walk in the woom, you
20.   know I have a wight switch on mine, to tuwn the lights
21.   on and off.
22. CL: Yah, so you can turn the lights on and off, can't you.
23. CH: Y.
24. CL: So if it's dark and you wanna play, you turn the lights on.
25. CH: Yup.
26. CL: Yup. Good fer you. (Marlaire 1990:255–56)

As Marlaire (1990) shows, the sequence from line 11 through line 26 clearly results in a co-produced answer. The clinician refuses the child's first answer ("Sweep,"—by which the child may mean "sleep") and asks for another one (line 15). The ensuing exchange finds the clinician elaborating the scenario (line 17) and the child further developing the clinician's input (lines 19–21). At line 22, the clinician elaborates on the child's description, suggesting the behavioral possibility that follows from the presence of a light switch that can be turned on and off. By line 24, the clinician has essentially provided the correct answer for the test prompt, with which the child agrees.

While the score that resulted from this test was treated as a document of the child's competence and maturity, it was the interactional exchange that allowed for its production. Shorn of its interactional particulars, it became an accountable test score, that is, one that will be taken as a reliable, valid, and objective indicator of the child's developmental stage or level. As Marlaire and Maynard (1990) suggest, the practices and skills of both participants in the test are overlooked when assessments are made. Yet they are the invisible interactional scaffolding upon which such tests depend. The more general point relates to where we typically locate competence. While we commonsensically understand it to be an individual characteristic—a matter of an individual capability— we can see that competence is occasioned and interactionally constructed.

Competence is an issue for persons of all ages. Negotiating the routine transactions of everyday life without incident or disruption generates a tacit sense of competence, yet interactional breakdowns may occasion doubt, if not outright questions. But, as Michael Lynch (1983:161) suggests, passing for competent or normal in everyday life does not simply reveal mastery of social conventions; it is a constant project involving others.

Lynch presents a number of common ways by which persons manage others' ostensibly problematic behaviors so as to sustain routine interaction and the others' appearance of competence or normalcy. He notes, for example, how we frequently *humor* others, maintaining a veneer of agreement and geniality even as potential interactional troubles simmer. Instances are commonplace. One manages interactions with an "eccentric" aunt by not discussing specific topics and

persons that "set her off." An aging grandmother is mollified—"kept on an even keel"—by agreeing with everything she says and otherwise keeping quiet. She *is screened* off from anything that might "agitate" her. A circle of friends and relations manage the household and do all the driving for a "distracted" acquaintance, *taking over* his responsibilities so he cannot display his inability to discharge them. Or when things go wrong, others provide *accounts* and *excuses,* or *cover up,* for the offending person. The upshot of such practices is to insulate the person being interactionally managed from circumstances that might evoke untoward behavior. Failing this, such behavior can be interpretively monitored and recast. In the process, normalcy is sustained and competence is preserved.

Competence can be managed even when it is the explicit object of attention. Consider, for example, some exchanges from involuntary mental hospitalization hearings where one of the practical issues being considered is the candidate patient's interactional competence or the candidate patient's ability to manage consequential situations without "talking crazy," a colloquial sign of incompetence (Holstein 1988, 1993). In defending the candidate patient, counsel attempts to prevent "crazy talk." The following extract is from the direct examination of a candidate patient, Katie Maxwell (KM), by the Public Defender (PD) who was handling her case.[2]

1. PD: If they let you go today, Katie, do you have a place to live?
2. KM: Uh huh my mother's (place).
3. PD: Where is your mother's place?
4. KM: In Bellwood.
5. PD: What's the address?
6. KM: One twenty Acton street. I can come // and go as I please.
7. PD [breaking in]: That's fine Katie.
8.   Does your mother say you can live with her?
9. KM: Yeah it's okay with her.
10. PD: Can you eat your meals there?
11. KM: Yeah there's no one there // always watching me.
12. PD [breaking in]: You can just answer yes or no. Okay?
13. KM: Okay.
14. PD: Do you have clothes at your mother's house?
15. KM: Yes.
16. PD: Can you dress yourself?

17. KM: Of course I can.
18. PD: Do you get an (SSI) check in the mail?
19. KM: Yes.
20. PD: Will you give it to your mother?
21. KM: Yes.
22. PD: And will you let her give you your medication?
23. KM: Yeah, whenever I // need it.
24. PD [*breaking in*]: That's good Katie. (Holstein 1988:462–63)

This exchange reveals a set of conversational practices that promote forms of talk that help display a sense of the candidate patient's interactional competence. Note, for example, how the PD's questions were formulated to elicit brief, direct answers. All but one question (line 5) were answerable in a single word. The PD established the adequacy of such answers both explicitly, by instructing the witness simply to answer yes or no (line 12) and tacitly, by accepting brief answers as complete and moving directly to the next question without hesitation. Speaker transition was immediate as the PD claimed her preallocated turn. When Maxwell attempted to elaborate on her answers, however, the PD broke into her response. In three instances (lines 6, 11, and 23), Maxwell tried to embellish or qualify her minimal answer to the PD's question and, each time the embellishments met with intrusions of simultaneous speech. The content of each overlapping utterance indicated that the patient's answer was adequately completed (e.g., line 7:

"That's fine Katie."), and, just as significantly, the intrusions into the patient's turns discouraged continuation. The PD thus managed the patient's talk to accomplish the appearance of concise, direct testimony. The PD organized her questions to constrain Maxwell's answers at the first possible turn-completion point (see Sacks et al. 1974), trying to keep testimony directly responsive to the questions asked.

A continuing worry in these hearings, from the PD's point of view, is that candidate patients may begin to "talk crazy." For example, when Maxwell began to elaborate answers at lines 6, 11, and 23, the PD immediately broke in, competing for speakership perhaps as a precaution against Maxwell's iteration of inappropriate answers. On other occasions when talk that might be heard as "crazy" or inappropriate begins to emerge, PDs move quickly to terminate it, as in the following instance involving candidate patient Fred Smitz (FS).

1. PD: Where would you live?
2. FS: I think I'd go to a new board and care home not populated
3.   by rapists//and Iranian agents
4. PD [*breaking in*]: Fine, Mr. Smitz now would you take your
5.   medication?
6. FS: I would if it didn't pass//through the hands of too many
7.   Russians.
8. PD [*breaking in*]: Do you get an SSI check, Mr. Smitz? (Holstein 1988:463–64)

Here, the candidate patient initially offered an apparently appropriate answer in line 2, but then began to introduce referents that could be heard as delusional. The PD broke in, using the patient's name to refocus his attention, then moved immediately to a new question about medication. In line 6, the patient answered and again began a qualification that culminat-

ed in a hearably delusional reference. The PD simultaneously produced another new question. The effect of these intrusions was to override, if not obliterate, the seemingly inappropriate talk that was emerging. Development of topics introduced by "crazy" utterances was aggressively curtailed for the sake of the clients' competence. While the management of witnesses' responses is a feature of all courtroom proceedings, PDs have a special substantive interest in candidate patients' responses in commitment hearings.

While PDs question candidate patients in ways that manage their competence, soliciting brief answers and discouraging elaborations, District Attorneys (DAs), who argue for commitment, encourage more expansive testimony, hoping to elicit instances of incompetence or "crazy" talk. The practice is illustrated in the following excerpt. After asking candidate patient Lisa Sellers (LS) fourteen consecutive questions in a relatively straightforward manner, the DA began a new approach.

1. DA: How do you like summer out here, Lisa?
2. LS: It's okay.
3. DA: How long have you lived here?
4. LS: Since I moved from Houston
5. [Silence 1 second]
6. LS: About three years ago.
7. DA: Tell me about why you came here.
8. LS: I just came.
9. [Silence 1 second]
10. LS: You know, I wanted to see the stars, Hollywood.
11. [Silence 1 second]
12. DA: Uh huh
13. LS: I didn't have no money.
14. [Silence 1 second]
15. LS: I'd like to get a good place to live.
16. [Silence 5 seconds]
17. DA: Go on. [spoken simultaneously with next utterance]
18. LS: There was some nice things I brought.
19. [Silence 1 second]
20. DA: Uh huh
21. LS: Brought them from the rocketship.
22. DA: Oh really?
23. LS: They was just some things I had.
24. DA: From the rocketship?
25. LS: Right.
26. DA: Were you on it?
27. LS: Yeah.
28. DA: Tell me about this rocketship, Lisa. (Holstein 1988:467)

While the sequence culminates in Ms. Sellers's hearably delusional references to a rocketship, the DA was instrumental in cultivating its display. Throughout the exchange, he encouraged Sellers to take extended and unfocused turns at talk by removing interactional constraints on her speaking turns. He asked very general questions or open-ended requests for information (lines 1, 3, 7, and 17) so that it was never clear precisely when Sellers might have finished her answer. He repeatedly refused to take up his turn at the possible completion of her turns, allowing silence to develop and thus inviting her to fill it. In the face of these repeated silences, Sellers continued to speak and eventually made reference to the rocketship. At this point, the DA responded immediately with "Oh really? (line 22), encouraging confirmation.

Now, this type of response marks a significant noticing that might have accomplished several things.

First, it could focus attention on the prior utterance so as to invite further talk on the subject. Such noticings might also call attention to a "faulted" quality of an utterance, suggesting the need for repair. Here, the DA highlighted Ms. Sellers's statement about the "rocketship." His use of "Oh really?" could be heard as an expression of surprise or disbelief, a call for elaboration that invited Ms. Sellers to dispel implied doubts by altering, repairing, retracting, or reframing the problematic utterance. That she declined to retract or explain the claim might be interpreted as further evidence that she was incapable of recognizing and correcting conversational "gaffes" that any competent interactant would probably not make, and certainly would repair, if given the opportunity.

Clearly, this "incompetent" talk is an interactional achievement. The DA requested testimony from the candidate patient, but repeatedly withheld acknowledgment of the testimony's adequacy, promoting more unfocused talk in the process. He further encouraged Sellers to speak, using "Uh huh" to indicate an understanding that an extended unit of talk was in progress and was not yet complete (Schegloff 1982), and by declining possible turns at talk altogether. He resumed an active role in the dialogue only after hearably "crazy talk" emerged, at which point he attempted to focus the discussion on the "crazy" topic and encourage Sellers to elaborate. For her part, Sellers sustained the ongoing conversation by terminating silences that had begun to emerge at failed speaker-transition points. She repeatedly elaborated responses and eventually produced the "crazy" talk cited as evidence of her interactional incompetence. But, ironically, it was her ability to cooperate with the DA in extending the conversation—her *conversational* competence—that allowed for the emergence of that very talk.

While involuntary commitment proceedings are not typical everyday interactions, we find similar displays in more commonplace settings. Since interactants' practical interest in everyday encounters is generally to conduct the exchange so that everything goes smoothly (Garfinkel 1967), we are much more likely to collaborate in the production of competence than to promote the sorts of interactional disruptions that make incompetence visible and interaction difficult. In either case, however, it is clear that much of what

we commonsensically attribute to individuals as internal or individual traits and abilities can be construed as social constructions.

Interactional monitoring and management may lead one to actually speak and act for others in the interest of sustaining the public impression of competence, a form of interlocutorship. Consider the following encounter that took place in a neighborhood market. An elderly couple, Henry and Millie, met a female acquaintance named Marge. After exchanging greetings with Millie, Marge turned to Henry and initiated the following "conversation":

MARGE: So how have you been feeling Henry?

MILLIE: Oh, he's been perkin' right along.

MARGE: Think winter's about through huh Hank?

MILLIE: He sure does. He's really happy to be able to get out.

Without a word from Henry, Henry's thoughts and feelings are conveyed by his wife. This "conversation" takes place in the sequential environment of questions and answers that, in most important respects, resembles normal conversation (see Sacks et al. 1974). Typically, speakers transfer speakership by explicitly or tacitly designating the next speaker. While Millie has apparently violated what might be seen as Marge's right to select the next person to talk, Marge does not treat it as such. Instead she asks another question, indicating that, for all practical purposes, the original question has been adequately understood and answered, thus confirming the trajectory of the conversation. Marge and Millie do the talking in this sequence, while Henry's silence makes him an accomplice in sustaining the impression of "his" participation as competent.

Nowhere is this sort of practice more poignant, perhaps, than in the case of victims of Alzheimer's disease (Gubrium 1986a, 1986b). Alzheimer's disease, or senile dementia, is widely assumed to "rob" persons of their minds. Victims experience confusion, forgetfulness, depression, disorientation, and agitation. Severe dementia virtually disables the victim so that one no longer recognizes once-familiar persons or objects and is unable to manage routine activities such as eating, voiding, and grooming. Yet, while the victim's outward appearance and gestures may provide little or no indication of an underlying competence, dedicated caregivers may persist in sustaining the last glimmers of a once-vital, competent person.

Caregivers, for example, often express the sentiment that "it is up to us" to look and listen carefully for what the Alzheimer's victim is trying to communicate. A familiar claim is that those who truly love the person can make the difference between the continued realization of the victim's personhood as opposed to his or her becoming the "mere shell" of a former self. In the words of a member of an Alzheimer's disease caregiver support group:

> We all have gone through it. I know the feeling . . . , like you just know in your heart of hearts that he's [the Alzheimer's victim] in there and that if you let go, that's it. So you keep on trying and trying and trying. You've got to keep the faith, that it's him and just work at him, 'cause if you don't . . . well, I'm afraid we've lost them. (Gubrium 1986b:41)

Caregivers may persist in "articulating" the victim's mind long after he or she has lost any capacity for self-expression. Contrary to Mead's (1934) view that the individual expresses him or herself to others, the Alzheimer's experience finds others literally speaking and "doing" the mind of the victim as a way of preserving it. Mind thus becomes a social entity, something interactionally assigned and sustained, both by and for whomever assumes it to exist.

Whether it is dealing with victims of senile dementia, developing children, an "embarrassing" husband, or an "eccentric" aunt, characteristics like mind, maturity, and competence are pervasively dialogic—interactionally constructed, sustained, and preserved (Coulter 1979, 1989; Pollner 1975; Gergen and Davis 1985). The sheer ubiquity of competence-sustaining practices thus requires an analytic reassessment of just what competence is in everyday life. As we notice the extent to which the meaning of traits and behaviors is socially constructed, we must reconsider the entire issue of the human agency involved, as well as its attendant structures—mind, self, personality, intelligence, and the like. Persons across the life span are constitutively assisted in displaying their competence. Examples are commonplace in everyday interaction. The competence of children (Marlaire 1990; Marlaire and Maynard 1990; Mehan 1973, 1974; Pollner and Mc-

Donald-Wikler 1985), college students (Holstein 1983; Lynch 1983), young and midlife adults (Holstein 1988; Sampson et al. 1962; Yarrow et al. 1955), and old people (Gubrium 1986a, 1986b) have all been documented as social accomplishments.

ACCOUNTING FOR INCOMPETENCE

Whereas competence-producing practices may be practically invisible, ascriptions of incompetence are often accompanied by behavioral explanations. Everyday reasoning can invoke accounts (Scott and Lyman 1968) for deviance or incompetence that sound remarkably sociological or criminological, or even gerontological, as Gubrium and Wallace (1990) and Holstein (1990) show for everyday reasoning about the causes and consequences of age-related experiences.

Consider the practice of accounting for delinquency in this regard. Juvenile delinquents are believed to be incompetent in terms of various criteria that are especially tuned into age or life course location. Psychologists locate problems of youth in emotional conflicts of one sort or another. Sociologists investigate factors such as the family, adult community, peer influences, and/or the structural inconsistencies that lead to delinquency. The fact that delinquency exists—as indicated by police, court, school, and other records—is more or less taken for granted. Yet the social process of recognizing delinquents and reaching some decision about their official classification is by no means a straightforward application of legal statutes to behavioral displays.

Irving Piliavin and Scott Briar (1964) report, for example, that police exercise considerable discretion in encounters with juveniles. Five alternative dispositions are available: outright release, release and submission on an interrogation report, official reprimand and release to parent, citation to juvenile court, and arrest and confinement. Police discretion is supported by an unofficial belief among police officers that correctional or rehabilitation alternatives do not help most young people, as well as by the official training manual, which states that "age, attitude, and prior criminal record" should be considered in all but the most serious offenses. The character of the juvenile, in most cases, rather than the specific offense, is officially used to determine disposition. The process closely resembles the decision-making process that Robert Emerson (1969) describes in juvenile courts.

Piliavin and Briar note that in the field, officers have little or no information on the past offenses, school performance, personal adjustment, or family situation of individual juveniles. Decisions are based on cues that emerge from the immediate encounter and that are used to assess character. These cues include age, race, grooming, dress, and especially demeanor. Those who act their age—appearing neither overly immature nor worldly beyond their years—are generally not seen as serious problems. Juveniles who are contrite, show fear of sanctions, and are respectful are judged to be "salvageable" and are released with only a reprimand. Those who display nonchalance, rebelliousness, or impenitence are seen as "would-be tough guys" or "punks." Black males are judged to be particularly problematic and are most likely to be stopped and interrogated, and they receive more serious sanctions.

Police discretion, then, is considerable, even in very serious cases. Take the following two situations involving alleged sex offenses observed and recorded by Piliavin and Briar (1964) in this regard.

Case 1

The interrogation of "A" (an eighteen-year-old lower-class white male accused of statutory rape) was assigned to a police sergeant with long experience on the force. As I sat in his office while we waited for the youth to arrive for questioning, the sergeant expressed his uncertainty as to what he should do with this young man. On the one hand, he could not ignore the fact that an offense had been committed; he had been informed, in fact, that the youth was prepared to confess to the offense. Nor could he overlook the continued pressure from the girl's father (an important political figure) for the police to take severe action against the youth. On the other hand, the sergeant had formed a low opinion of the girl's moral character, and he considered it unfair to charge "A" with statutory rape when the girl was a willing partner to the offense and might even have been the instigator of it. However, his sense of injustice concerning "A" was tempered by his image of the youth as a

"punk," based, he explained, on information he had received that the youth belonged to a certain gang, the members of which were well known to, and disliked by, the police. Nevertheless, as we prepared to leave his office to interview "A," the sergeant was still in doubt as to what he should do with him.

As we walked down the corridor to the interrogation room, the sergeant was stopped by a reporter from the local newspaper. In an excited tone of voice, the reporter explained that his editor was pressing him to get further information about this case. The newspaper had printed some of the facts about the girl's disappearance, and as a consequence the girl's father was threatening suit against the paper for defamation of the girl's character. It would strengthen the newspaper's position, the reporter explained, if the police had information indicating that the girl's associates, particularly the youth the sergeant was about to interrogate, were persons of disreputable character. This stimulus seemed to resolve the sergeant's uncertainty. He told the reporter, "unofficially," that the youth was known to be an undesirable person, citing as evidence his membership in the delinquent gang. Furthermore, the sergeant added that he had evidence that this youth had been intimate with the girl over a period of many months. When the reporter asked if the police were planning to do anything to the youth, the sergeant answered that he intended to charge the youth with statutory rape.

In the interrogation, however, three points quickly emerged which profoundly affected the sergeant's judgment of the youth. First, the youth was polite and cooperative; he consistently addressed the officer as "sir," answered all questions quietly, and signed a statement implicating himself in numerous counts of statutory rape. Second, the youth's intentions toward the girl appeared to have been honorable; for example, he said that he wanted to marry her eventually. Third, the youth was not in fact a member of the gang in question. The sergeant's attitude became increasingly sympathetic, and after we left the interrogation room he announced his intention to "get 'A' off the hook," meaning that he wanted to have the charges against "A" reduced or, if possible, dropped.

Case 2

Officers "X" and "Y" brought into the police station a seventeen-year-old white boy who, along with two older companions, had been found in a home having sex relations with a fifteen-year-old girl. The boy responded to police officers' queries slowly and with obvious disregard. It was apparent that his lack of deference toward the officers and his failure to evidence concern about his situation were irritating his questioners. Finally, one of the officers turned to me and, obviously angry, commented that in his view the boy was simply a "stud" interested only in sex, eating, and sleeping. The policemen conjectured that the boy "probably already had knocked up half a dozen girls." The boy ignored these remarks, except for an occasional stare at the patrolmen. Turning to the boy, the officer remarked, "What the hell am I going to do with you?" And again the boy simply returned the officer's gaze. The latter then said, "Well, I guess we'll just have to put you away for a while." An arrest report was then made out and the boy was taken to Juvenile Hall. (Piliavin and Briar 1964:211)

The presumed character of the person is not the only consideration that influences police discretion in particular cases. Researchers have reported, for example, that situational factors such as the presence of an audience or a complaining witness, or a satisfactory place other than jail to deposit the person, may influence the decision to arrest or release (Sudnow 1965; Bittner 1967a, 1967b). From the constructionist perspective, it is important to note how mundane theories of criminality are used to interpret "what really happened" and what sort of person was involved. One cannot predict the disposition of cases merely from a knowledge of the law. Theory-like accounts of people's actions, including hypotheses about why different kinds of people behave as they do and what they can be trusted to do in the future, articulate behavioral displays with the penal code. In an important sense, the law is used to justify whatever practical decisions or character imputations criminal justice personnel have made.[3] If the person is judged to be a "good risk," a way can be found to avoid formal booking and detention. Likewise, the law can be used to legitimize more punitive treatment for "bad risk" cases. The work of law-enforcement personnel in interpreting the meaning of behavioral displays and in articulating behavior with the law is an important instance of what Robert Emerson and Sheldon Messinger (1977) call the "micropolitics" of trouble, interactional negotiations through which persons are judged to be incom-

petent, immature, and such, and through which practical decisions are made.

Aaron Cicourel's *The Social Organizational of Juvenile Justice* (1968) provides further illustration of the accounting process among probation officers who decide the meaning of the particular actions of young persons on probation. Cicourel argues that the probation officer and youthful offender implicitly develop a sense of trust between themselves that includes expressed feelings of regret about previous behavior, admission that it was wrong, and promises to try to do better. Future behavior is interpreted in light of this implicit trust. The probation officer, for example, may reevaluate past behavior and conclude that there actually was no basis for the trust or that the present incident really does not require any basic reinterpretation of the trusting relationship but only a reminder of its existence.

Consider the following dialogue between a female probation officer (PO) and Audrey (A), a fifteen-year-old female juvenile who had been reported to the police by school officials for fighting. Audrey was already on probation at the time of the incident. The following segment of the conversation comes after Audrey has admitted that it is wrong to fight and has promised that in the future she will simply "walk away" from situations where a fight may be brewing.

PO: Well, Audrey, you've overcome a lot of your problems, you really have. But now that we see maybe another problem is going to start getting you in trouble, this is the time to start handling that problem. [*Pause.*] Right? Not wait until it becomes so serious that it is difficult to tell other people that you're going to stop doing it. Now they'll still believe you, like Mr. James. If you're not going to fight any more or not get mixed up in this stuff any more, he'll believe you. But if you went on doing it for a couple of months, you know, he'll find it difficult to believe you, wouldn't he?

A: Yes.

PO: So you stick by what you've told him [*pause*], that you're not going to get in any more trouble, all right? [cut off as "all right" is uttered]

A: You know, I could have went to juvie again, but Mr. James say uh . . . [cut off by probation officer].

PO: I know it. He helped you.

A: I know, 'cause he said I hadn't been in no trouble since I had been in.

PO: See [*pause*], so that good time helped you. If you had gotten in trouble right away he wouldn't have known if you could behave yourself. And he probably would have, you know, let you go to Juvenile Hall, but since you had all this—how many months?—six or seven months?

A: I figured eleven months.

PO: Eleven months.

A: At the home.

PO: Eleven months with no real difficulties either at home or at school, right?

A: Yeah.

PO: So that's why he knew if you said you won't get in more trouble he knows you can if you stick by that.

A: You see I gotta . . . [cut off by probation officer].

PO: He trusts you, Audrey, so it is up to you to keep his trust. . . . [The conversation continues.] I, I would have to figure out what would be best for you, Audrey. I don't know what would be best, but if you don't stop having these problems that you just started having, I'd have to think up something.

A: Oh, I can stop having problems.

PO: Well, then you'd better. You show me that you can and then I won't have to make any decisions. Right? I'm coming out here today mainly just to warn you about what can happen if you do any more of this. Do you understand that?

A: Uh, hmm.

PO: You have anything you want to talk about? If you want to stay there, well, this is fine with me. I go along with that. I think it's a real good idea. I'm not saying forever. I can't promise you forever either. Right?

A: Yeah. (Cicourel 1968:153–57)

Cicourel notes that the probation officer has not chosen to see this incident as a violation of probation. Yet the officer makes it clear that further troubles may force her to a different conclusion. The juvenile apparently displayed a "cooperative" or "right" attitude on this occasion, but there is a warning that future problems may cause the officer to reevaluate her interpretation of "what is best" for the juvenile.

The probation officer must now articulate her interpretation of the meaning of Audrey's recent behavior and her decision about what should be done about it with general policies or rules of the criminal justice system. The articulation is accomplished by producing a report (a portion of which is presented here) which manages the impression or interpretation that the probation officer wishes to give:

> A couple of minor incidents since—yesterday she and some other girls jumped on a laundry truck at school and Audrey didn't obey bus driver on bus. However, Mr. J. reports that Audrey's attitude was good—admitted everything and promised she wouldn't any more. (Cicourel 1968:163)

The description of the situation as "minor" and of Audrey's attitude as "good—admitted everything and promised she wouldn't any more" justified the decision to treat this incident as insignificant and not to reevaluate the current disposition. Audrey had earlier been placed in a foster home after she had been accused of several thefts. The probation officer discovered what she called "a lack of adult and parental supervision and control. Both parents are employed and either unable or uninterested in having Audrey properly supervised." To the probation officer it was "obvious that Audrey has quite a problem with thievery and should have some type of professional help."

Hospital authorities agreed: "She has an . . . extremely low self-esteem which she compensates by stealing" (Cicourel 1968:131). Audrey was thus typified as a clinical type, a girl with "deep underlying problems" that caused her to break the law. The probation officer interpreted her current behavior as one more unfortunate example of Audrey's difficult, but potentially winnable battle with emotional problems, rather than an additional episode in a developing career of a hopeless "criminal" type. Thus, Audrey's troubled life course was given a psychological, rather than criminal, cast.

The production of a delinquent career does not simply grow out of the juvenile's experience. Probation officers, police, school authorities, and parents participate in the work of deciding what has really happened to a troubled youngster, what the behavior means in terms of the kind of person this is, and what can be expected from him or her in the future. The youth may behave in ways that can be taken as signs of good character, cooperation, rebelliousness, defiance, being in or out of line with age, and myriad similar typifications. The talk of the parents, their personal appearance and the condition of their home, and their expressed (or lack of) concern for their child is used by police and probation officers to reveal positive resources for change or continuing contributions to delinquency (see Gubrium and Holstein 1990, chap. 5).

The police apply commonsense theories of criminality to view some juveniles as "kids with normal problems" and others as "future criminals" who need to be dealt with now. The probation officers, armed with vernacular psychological explanations of juvenile problems and rehabilitation, see deep, emotional problems rooted primarily in the family and cultural environment and secondarily in schools and peer relationships. Juvenile courts routinely respond in similar ways to what they consider typical troubled lives (Emerson 1969). All told, the full range of ordinary reasoning has many conceptually affinities with the spectrum of conventional approaches to life change presented in chapter 1, showing native facsimiles of scientific usage.

Cicourel (1968) describes the production of delinquent careers in detailed case studies. We draw on his study for the following illustration of the ways that police and probation officers use practical theories to decide what to do with a troublesome youth—a boy named Smithfield. Smithfield, an African American, was accused of burglary, petty theft, and defiance of school authority on at least eight occasions over a period of three years. The following reports on the boy's behavior were prepared by school personnel:

Smithfield is mentally retarded, or at least appears that way. He would profit from placement in a special class. Smithfield responds well to praise and recognition, and these methods should probably be used in teaching self-control and acceptable social behavior [sixth grade]. (Cicourel 1968:204)

During the time that Smithfield has been in the room, his adjustment has been very ineffective. His social values seem to be functioning at a different level than the rest of the class. He appears to have no personal goals and does not appear to recognize significant problems which face him. The antagonistic

attitude with which he meets both students and teachers aggravates all of his social situations [seventh grade]. (p. 207)

Would rather tell a lie than tell the truth. A typical sentence: "I didn't do it. Besides you did not catch me." Has a hard time keeping his hands off other people's property. I have changed his seat in class several times, hoping he would improve, to no avail. . . . What suggestions can one make for a boy who is dishonest, a chronic liar, a very poor student, and constant trouble-maker [eighth grade]. (p. 217)

The accounts provided by the school give a graphic picture of Smithfield and his troubles. His academic progress is poor and he is considered disruptive, a chronic troublemaker, and a liar.

There also were reports from juvenile authorities. According to one report:

Smithfield appears to be an emotionally disturbed boy who has considerable difficulty relating to peers. He is loud and aggressive, and has a tendency to pick fights with the smaller and less physically adept group members. He refuses to accept authority of any nature. When counselled, concerning his negative conduct and attitude, he becomes emotionally upset using crying tactics as a means of getting sympathy instead of admonishment. (pp. 218–19)

Apparently the police and school officials agree that something is wrong with Smithfield. They describe him as a poor student, mentally retarded, emotionally disturbed, aggressive, and disrespectful of authority. The "underlying problems," however, are not consistently revealed. They are left to the diagnostic skill or interpretive ability of the probation officer who determines not only what is wrong but what should be done, implicating the family in the process (see Gubrium 1992). The probation officer reports the following:

Mrs. Elston [Smithfield's mother] is handicapped in coping with her son's problems, primarily because of her inability to be firm. She does realize, after firm counselling, that it is her responsibility as a parent to work with agencies that are attempting to assist her. It is encouraging to note the mother figure has taken a firmer attitude in the matter of her delinquent son and will attempt to be more realistic in the future. (Cicourel 1968:211)

Cicourel notes that there is little the probation officer can add to the above remarks. At this point it appears to the officer that a change of environment as well as schools possibly will assist those concerned in rehabilitating this child. Cicourel continues his description of the case:

> It appeared to this writer that Mrs. Elston was able to control Smithfield's activities and companions for a long period of time but that during the current year Smithfield acquired undesirable companions without the knowledge of his mother. Consequently, his general attitude regressed. The school personnel have acknowledged that they are willing to continue working with Smithfield and the minor's mother has acknowledged a desire to continue working with him and further acknowledges that she will contact the Probation Officer if the minor does not conform. Therefore, the Probation Officer is recommending that Smithfield be continued on probation and allowed to remain in the custody of his mother, but it is further recommended that the court instruct the minor and his mother regarding their responsibilities and inform them that if they are not able to meet them, the Court will find it necessary to remove the minor from his home and place him elsewhere. (p. 221)

These official reports do not reveal the complete range of practical information used by the police, school officials, and probation officers to interpret Smithfield's behavior as exemplary of a type of person. For example, while it was not evident in the foregoing extracts, Smithfield's racial and social-class background was cited by the police to account for their claim that he would be a source of trouble and a likely suspect whenever there is a crime. The police assumed that he would lie about his involvement and would attempt to conceal evidence. An unhappy marriage that ended in the separation of the boy's parents and the supervision of "trouble-prone" children by an overburdened mother was also useful information for the probation officer. Such knowledge apparently allowed the officer to "understand" how such behavior and attitudes could develop and to suggest remedial intervention.

The reports do not provide sufficient detail to allow us to know what Smithfield actually did or said on particular occasions. But even if we had more descriptive information, the reports would still require interpretation. Individuals do not simply possess imma-

ture, incompetent, delinquent, or similar characteristics that are self-evident in their behavior, even while they may be recounted as such. Smithfield's case was made understandable through the application of commonsense theories about "boys like Smithfield." Race, family problems, cultural deprivation, bad peer influences, and other undesirable effects were believed to be evident or easily "read" from his behavior. Police, school, and probation personnel took this for granted.

In order for a person to be salvageable, the origin of his problem must be found in some set of correctable conditions. Home, school, or peer groups can figure in a process of intervention, both as putative causes and as justifications for proposed solutions (Darrough 1990). In Smithfield's case, the typification of a juvenile as an "emotional problem" provided the probation officer with a ready-made account for a variety of problematic behaviors as well as a general strategy for change. The probation officer was reluctant to recommend severe punishment because he believed he had identified the reasons for the problems and felt sure that remedial action could be helpful. Knowing that the police believed that probation officers were too "soft" on delinquents and that punishment was called for in more cases, the probation officer's official reports to the court downplayed the significance of the delinquent activity as such. He argued instead for a clinical interpretation of "deep problems," which might be corrected with the appropriate treatment. For the probation officer, Smithfield was salvageable, while for the police he was on the course of an inevitable delinquent career, reflecting the respective officers' organizational standpoints.

INTERPRETIVE VARIABILITY

Patterns revealing competence are actively assembled, reflecting practical circumstances and orientations. The job is never finally completed, as persons' characteristics and competence, and the meaningful course of their development, are not interpretively fixed. As concrete as they may seem to us in everyday life, traits, identities, and competencies are reformulated in light of changing information, orientations, and the practical demands of circumstance.

Consider, for example, Houston Wood's analysis

of the fluid character of traits, problems, and incapacities attributed to patients on an inpatient psychiatric ward (reported in Mehan and Wood 1975). The ward staff used a variety of categories to characterize the patients in their charge. They saw the ward as populated by "babies," "good patients," "niggers," "sociopaths," "depressives," and "lost souls," among others. While some terms were borrowed from professional vocabularies, they all were used as vernacular categorizations that reflected the attendants' practical concerns about, and appraisals of, those being labeled.

One patient, Jimmy Lee Jackson, was originally typified as a "nigger" by the ward attendants. For them, Jackson was "lazy, and . . . without morals or scruples." The attendants said that Jackson was "cunning" and would attempt to ingratiate himself with staff in order to get attention and special treatment (Mehan and Wood 1975:21). To the extent Jackson's past or future was noted, it referenced the purported life course of the typical "nigger."

One evening, Jackson suffered from a toothache. Unable to get the staff to do anything about it, he rammed his arm through a window pane in one of the ward's locked doors, inflicting severe lacerations that required many stitches. Out of the bloody scene emerged an account of the incident as a suicide attempt. A new typification of Jackson accompanied the account. Virtually overnight, Jackson was interpretively transformed from being a "nigger" into being a "depressive." His past behavior on the ward—behavior that had made it "clear" that he was a "nigger"— was reinterpreted in light of his suicide attempt and what it now implied about the kind of patient Jackson actually was. Particulars were reconstructed to fit with the new categorization. Prior "laziness" was now a manifestation of depression. Behaviors previously seen as disingenuous were regarded as sincere. Ward personnel now listened to Jackson with sympathy. They gave him whatever he requested and no longer pressured him to do more work on the ward. The attendants came to believe that Jackson had *always* been a depressive and that they had always seen him as such.

The staff treated Jackson as a depressive for quite some time. Wood reports, however, that new events and circumstances later led staff members to alter the characterization. They reinterpreted the window-breaking incident, reformulating the "suicide" attempt as a "fake," an attempt to "con" the staff. Jackson became known as a "sociopath" and behavior toward him aligned with the new view.

As Jimmy Lee Jackson's problems and characteristics were transformed, the ongoing process of interpretation reorganized the course of his problematic behaviors on the ward. His history of troubles did not build progressively and incrementally from incident to event toward a final outcome in a cumulative fashion. Instead, his problem and its history were reformulated through interpretive leaps, from one understanding of what had happened to another— a process Foucault (1965) might have described as a practical archaeology of madness at the level of social interaction. The process of interpretation made visible concrete life patterns, which could evaporate in an instant with the application of a new framework.

Organizational Embeddedness

As fluid as the interpretation process is, it is not without substantive organization. Particular, local categories combine with more general vocabularies to give a situated cast to competence. In a manner of speaking, one interpretive domain's assigned sense of competence for a person is not necessarily the same as another's. Local interpretive cultures and practical goals and orientations influence the assignment of meaning; context delimits the diversity of interpretation. Despite the variability of interpretations of Jimmy Lee Jackson, for example, the categories applied all reflected the psychological orientation and custodial concerns of the psychiatric ward, with its staff's decided bent toward psychological vocabularies. In general terms, the process that yields patterns of competence, development, and change is situationally sensitive, indeed organizationally embedded (Gubrium 1988).

The situated character of interpretive practice is vividly illustrated in a case one of the authors (Holstein) observed at a child guidance clinic. The clinic had several departments and programs providing a variety of outpatient therapies and services for children reporting emotional and related troubles. One client, twelve-year-old Charles Grady, was originally referred to the clinic by the police department as a "diversionary alternative" to the juvenile justice system. He had a history of disruptive behavior in school and a growing record of informal encounters with the police. After being apprehended for loitering at a fast-food restaurant with a "rowdy" group of boys and refusing to leave, a police juvenile officer told Charles and his parents that Charles would either have to enroll in the clinic's Delinquency Prevention Program or face charges in juvenile court.

One of the central principles that guided the program was the belief that juveniles engaged in deviant and disruptive activities in response to peer-group pressure, a vernacular version of conventional theorizing about the identification of selves in relation to others. One of the clinic's goals was to provide positive alternatives to so-called gang pressures. Charles was assigned to a peer group led by a counselor named Mr. Burke. Under Burke's guidance, Charles was integrated into adult-supervised, peer-oriented activities that took him away from his normal after-school routines. Burke explained that the problem with boys like Charles was they were extremely susceptible to the bad influences of friends and others of their own age group whom they looked up to or admired. Charles, and others like him, would gravitate toward gang membership because "preadolescence is a time when kids are looking for acceptance, approval, anything to prove that they belong." According to Burke, Charles's misbehavior in school, his brushes with the law, and his tendency to get into fights and skirmishes was proof that Charles was trying to impress a crowd of "undesirables," to become one of them. Charles's inability to integrate into normal activities and settings was considered to be a manifestation of his need to belong to another group.

Three weeks into the program, Charles was again apprehended by the police, this time for minor vandalism on school property. Returned to the clinic, Charles's case was evaluated by the Youth Programs supervisor and one of the staff therapists, a Mr. Miller. In the course of the discussion, Miller commented on the results of the cognitive and emotional development tests Charles had been administered at intake.

Miller suggested that perhaps he should "take a look at Charles," and, following a two hour interview, he offered an alternate perspective on Charles' problem. Writing in Charles's case file, Miller indicated that Charles's "antisocial outbursts" were due to "misdirected frustration and energy." Shifting the characterizing discourse from the social to the psychosexual, Miller noted that Charles was "going through a difficult adolescence. He has difficulty adjusting to newly developed sexuality and physical maturity. He vents his feeling and frustrations in aggressive outbursts and senseless acts of hostility and destruction." Miller recommended that Charles begin weekly therapy sessions, explaining to the supervisor that "Charles' psychosocial development and social skills haven't caught up with his hormones," which was now understandable in the context of Charles's referral to the clinic's youth program, which was psychologically oriented.

Charles' participation in clinic activities continued, apparently without major incident, for another month. Reports from the school and file entries by both Burke and Miller, however, indicated that Charles was still prone to disruptions and fighting. By sheer coincidence, Charles's parents arranged for Charles to have a general physical examination by a physician, Dr. Cook, in anticipation of enrolling Charles in a summer camp. During the examination, Charles's mother apparently mentioned some of Charles's recent troubles. She later told the supervisor at the clinic that Dr. Cook had suggested the possibility that her son was hyperactive. Cook apparently had done some tests and written a prescription for Ritalin, the local pharmacological treatment of choice at the time. Mrs. Grady reported that the doctor said, "Charles acts so immature because he probably has some sort of medical disorder."

As the case moved from one setting to another, its interpretive jurisdiction changed. Charles's traits and behaviors fell into three contrasting organizational contexts, each with its own behavioral understandings. Burke brought a distinctly social outlook to the interpretive enterprise, while Miller's focus was oriented to Charles's psychosexual makeup. As might be expected, the MD's interpretation was physiological. Their views were not idiosyncratic, however, as each oriented to professional and organizational ways of dealing with the problem under consideration. Burke worked within a "socialization" program, Miller within a psychotherapeutic setting, and Cook in a medical office with its arsenal of psychopharmaceutic resources at his disposal.

The emergent interpretations of Charles and his problem reflect practical objectives and local interpretive groundings. Charles's life course is embedded in related organizational and professional outlooks and concerns. Burke, for example, characterized Charles as a "preadolescent" in the throes of a battle with peer pressure. For Miller, the psychotherapist, the problem was Charles's adolescence with its untamed hormonal advances outstripping Charles's ability to cope with, and properly channel, them. Dr. Cook portrayed Charles's disruptive behavior as "immature," the product of hyperkinetic disorder. The life course was prominent in each of these descriptions, but each located the boy differently. While organizational embeddedness does not determine how its participants categorize things and occurrences, it does provide locally "customary and usual" means of doing so. And, in the process, the locally-grounded discourses "deprivatize" persons' characteristics and problems, making ostensibly private, personal traits into matters of public interpretation.

NOTES

1. These transcripts have been slightly simplified from the original published versions.

2. In the following excerpts, double slashes (//) indicate the onset of simultaneous speech.

3. Ironically, criminals reference their own rules or code to make sense of "deviant" behavior. See, for example, Wieder's (1988) account of telling the "convict code."

REFERENCES

Berg, I. 1971. *Education and Jobs.* Boston: Beacon Press.

Bittner, E. 1967a. "Police Discretion in Emergency Apprehension of Mentally Ill Persons." *Social Problems* 14:278–92.

———. 1967b. "The Police on Skid Row: A Study of Peace-Keeping." *American Sociological Review* 32:699–715.

Carlson, R. 1965. "Stability and Change in the Adolescent Self-Image." *Child Development* 36:659–66.

Cicourel, A. V. 1968. *The Social Organization of Juvenile Justice.* New York: Wiley.

Coulter, J. 1979. *The Social Construction of Mind.* London: Macmillan.

———. 1989. *Mind in Action.* Atlantic Highlands, NJ: Humanities Press.

Darrough, W. 1990. "Neutralizing Resistance: Probation Work as Rhetoric." Pp. 163–88 in *Perspectives on Social Problems,* v. 2 ed. G. Miller and J. Holstein. Greenwich, CT: JAI Press.

Elkind, D. 1967. "Egocentrism in Adolescence." *Child Development* 38:1025–34.

Emerson, R. M. 1969. *Judging Delinquents.* Chicago: Aldine.

Emerson, R. M., and S. Messinger. 1977. "The Micro-Politics of Trouble." *Social Problems* 25:121–34.

Foucault, M. 1965. *Madness and Civilization.* New York: Random House.

Garfinkel, H. 1967. *Studies in Ethnomethodology.* Englewood Cliffs, N.J.: Prentice-Hall.

Gergen, K., and K. Davis, eds. 1985. *The Social Construction of the Person.* New York: Springer-Verlag.

Gubrium, J. F. 1986a. *Oldtimers and Alzheimer's.* Greenwich, Conn.: JAI Press.

———. 1986b. "The Social Preservation of Mind: The Alzheimer's Disease Experience." *Symbolic Interaction* 9:37–51.

———. 1988. *Analyzing Field Reality.* Beverly Hills: Sage.

———. 1989. "Local Culture and Service Policy." Pp. 94–112 in *The Politics of Field Research,* ed. J. Gubrium and D. Silverman. London: Sage.

———. 1992. *Out of Control: Family Therapy and Domestic Disorder.* Newbury Park, Calif.: Sage.

Gubrium, J. F. and D. R. Buckholdt. 1979. "Production of Hard Data in Human Service Organizations." *Pacific Sociological Review* 22:115–36.

Gubrium, J. F., and J. A. Holstein. 1990. *What Is Family?* Mt. View, Calif.: Mayfield.

Gubrium, J. F., and B. Wallace. 1990. "Who Theorizes Age?" *Aging and Society* 10:131–49.

Hamblin, R., D. Buckholdt, D. Ferritor, and M. Kozloff. 1971. The *Humanization Process.* New York: Wiley.

Havighurst, R. J. 1951. *Developmental Tasks and Education.* London: Longman.

Heath, D. H. 1965. *Explorations of Maturity.* New York: Appleton-Century-Crofts.

Holstein, J. A. 1983. "Grading Practices: The Construction and Use of Background Knowledge in Evaluative Decision-making." *Human Studies* 6:277–92.

———. 1988. "Court Ordered Incompetence: Conversational Organization in Involuntary Commitment Hearings." *Social Problems* 35:442–57.

———. 1990. "The Discourse of Age in Involuntary Commitment Proceedings." *Journal of Aging Studies* 4:111–30.

———. 1993. *Court Ordered Insanity: Interpretive Practice and Involuntary Commitment.* Hawthorne, N.Y.: Aldine de Gruyter.

Hunt, J. 1961. *Intelligence and Experience.* New York: Ronald Press.

Leiter, K. 1974. "Ad Hocing in the Schools: A Study of Placement Practices in the Kindergartens of Two Schools." Pp. 17–75 in *Language Use and School Performance,* ed. A.V. Cicourel et al. New York: Academic Press.

Lynch, M. 1983. "Accommodation Practices: Vernacular Treatments of Madness." *Social Problems* 31:152–63.

MacKay, R. 1973. "Conceptions of Children and Models of Socialization." In *Childhood and Socialization,* ed. H. P. Dreitzel. New York: Macmillan.

McKinney, J. P. 1968. "The Development of Choice Stability in Children and Adolescents." *Journal of Genetic Psychology* 113:79–83.

Marlaire, C. L. 1990. "On Questions, Communication, and Bias: Educational Testing as 'Invisible' Collaboration." Pp. 233–60 in *Perspectives on Social Problems,* ed. G. Miller and J. Holstein. Greenwich, Conn.: JAI Press.

Marlaire, C. L., and D. W. Maynard. 1990. "Standardized Testing as an Interactional Phenomenon." *Sociology of Education* 63:83–101.

Maynard, D. W. 1984. *Inside Plea Bargaining.* New York: Plenum.

Mead, G. H. 1934. *Mind, Self, and Society.* Chicago: University of Chicago Press.

Mehan, H. 1973. "Assessing Children's School Performane." In *Childhood and Socialization,* ed. H. P. Dreitzel. New York: Macmillan.

——. 1974. "Accomplishing Classroom Lessons." Pp. 76–142 in *Language Use and School Performance,* ed. A. V. Cicourel et al. New York: Academic Press.

Mehan, H., and H. Wood. 1975. *The Reality of Ethnomethodology.* New York: Wiley.

Piliavin, I., and S. Briar. 1964. "Police Encounters With Juveniles." *American Journal of Sociology* 70:206–14.

Pollner, M. 1975. "'The Very Coinage of Your Brain': The Anatomy of Reality Disjunctures." *Philosophy of Social Sciences* 5:411–30.

Pollner, M., and L. McDonald-Wikler. 1985. "The Social Construction of Unreality: A Case Study of a Family's Attribution of Competence to a Severely Retarded Child." *Family Process* 24:241–54.

Rogers, C. 1964. "Toward a Modern Approach to Values: The Valuing Process in the Mature Person." *Journal of Abnormal and Social Psychology* 68:160–67.

Sacks, H., E. Schegloff, and G. Jefferson. 1974. "A Simplest Systematics for the Organization of Turn-Taking in Conversation." *Language* 50:696–735.

Sampson, E., S. Messinger, and R. Towne. 1962. "Family Processes and Becoming a Mental Patient." *American Journal of Sociology* 68:88–96.

Schegloff, E. A. 1982. "Discourse as an Interactional Achievement." Pp. 73–91 in *Georgetown University Roundtable on Languages and Linguistics,* ed. D. Tannen. Washington, D.C.: Georgetown University Press.

Schultz, T. W. 1962. "Reflections on Investment in Man." *Journal of Political Economy* 70:1–8.

Scott, M. B., and S. M. Lyman. 1968. "Accounts." *American Sociological Review* 33:46–62.

Sudnow, D. 1965. "Normal Crimes: Sociological Features of the Penal Code in a Public Defender Office." *Social Problems* 12:255–76.

Wieder, D. L. 1988. *Language and Social Reality.* Lanham, Md.: University Press of America.

Yarrow, M. R., C. G. Schwartz, H. S. Murphy, and L. C. Deasy. 1955. "The Psychological Meaning of Mental Illness in the Family." *Journal of Social Issues* 11:12–24.

THE SOCIAL CONSTRUCTION OF UNREALITY

A Case Study of a Family's Attribution of Competence to a Severely Retarded Child

26

Melvin Pollner and Lynn McDonald-Wikler

In recent years attention has been drawn to the ways in which what group members take to be given, natural, or real is a subtly organized achievement (Berger, 1969; Cicourel, 1973; Garfinkel, 1967). The social world of the group is not a simple reflection of what is "out there" but a continuously developed and sustained construction. The maintenance of a collective construct requires work—information must be selected, edited, and interpreted; anomalies must be explained; heretics from within and critics from without must be discounted, dissuaded, managed, or avoided. As Berger (1969) suggests:

> Worlds are socially constructed, socially maintained. Their continuing reality, both objective (as common, taken-for-granted facticity) and subjective (as facticity imposing itself on individual consciousness), depends upon *specific* social processes, namely those processes that ongoingly reconstruct and maintain the particular world in question. (p. 45)

The family is no different. Indeed, in many respects it is an especially intense locus of these constructive processes (Berger & Kellner, 1970). In *The Family's Construction of Reality,* Reiss (1981), for example, proposes that "family paradigms"—the fundamental assumptions a family holds about itself and the world—are realized and conserved through interactional patterns. These patterns create the family's everyday reality and enable members "to experience their own values and assumptions as if they were unquestionable components of outer reality" (p. 228).

The conception of family reality as an interactionally achieved construction may prove especially valuable in exploring the dynamics by which families maintain seemingly extreme, bizarre, or aberrant versions of reality. Although the psychological dynamics and functions of such constructions have received attention (Pulver & Brunt, 1961; Wikler, 1980) and despite numerous case histories in the literature (Gralnick, 1942), relatively little is known about the concrete, detailed activities in which family members use, manage, and "realize" these versions of reality in their day-to-day activities. The constructionist standpoint corrects this imbalance by inviting close examination of the artful, minute, and continuous work through which what might be characterized as "myth," "distortion," or "delusion" from outside the family is rendered a reality for those on the inside.[1]

We have applied this general perspective to a family diagnosed as *folie à famille* and attempted to discern the "reality work"—practices of reasoning, speaking, and acting—through which members documented and maintained their particular world. The family in question was initially encountered at a large psychiatric institute to which the parents had turned in their search for a remedy for 5 1/2-year-old Mary's unusual behavior. Family members stated that Mary was a verbal and intelligent child who malingered and refused to speak in public in order to embarrass the family. Extensive clinical observation and examination revealed Mary to be severely retarded and unable to perform at anywhere near the level of competence claimed by her parents and two older sibs. Clinical materials collected included videotaped recordings of each family member interacting with the child in the institute. Initial viewings of the tapes suggested that family members' transactions were permeated by subtle, almost artful, practices that could function to create the image of Mary as an intelligent child. Intensive examination of these and other materials yielded a repertoire of such practices, and they constitute a central focus of this report. Although our analysis was driven by the assumption that family members were constructing their reality, our subsequent reflections suggested more complicated possibilities whose dimensions we shall explore in our concluding discussion.

CASE DESCRIPTION

Mary's parents came to a psychiatric institute for an inpatient psychiatric evaluation of their 5 1/2-year-old daughter.[2] Their presenting complaint was that, although at home their child acted normally, she refused to do so in public. They wanted the reason for this peculiar and difficult-to-manage behavior to be identified and then treated. In public, they claimed, she acted retarded. Each of the four family members who lived with Mary agreed with this description:

FATHER (aged 42):   She's really a fast child, if anything. Once she even read a note aloud that I had passed over to my wife not intending for Mary to see it.

MOTHER (aged 39):   She puts on an act of being retarded in public while acting normally at home.

HALF-SISTER (aged 18):   I've had 10-minute long normal conversations with her, but she won't talk in front of most people.

BROTHER (aged 12):   I don't know why she fakes it; she's like any other 5-year-old.

Prior to coming for the inpatient evaluation, the

child had been taken to several reputable outpatient clinics in the general geographical area for work-ups. These had been, according to the parents, frustrating experiences, and they had not received the help they sought. In each case they were essentially told (father's report) that Mary was severely retarded. This was rejected by the parents and instead was regarded by them as an indicator of Mary's capabilities—she had fooled the clinicians. Therefore, they had continued their search for a thorough, long-term evaluation.

Mary was admitted to the children's ward in the Neuropsychiatric Institute, which specialized in evaluation and treatment of retarded children. The admission was made with the clearly stated contingency that the family remain intensively involved with the professional staff throughout her stay. Mary was observed 24 hours a day for eight weeks (except on weekends when she routinely returned home) by a professional nursing staff. The pediatrician and social worker for the ward had their offices on the ward and so had frequent occasions to observe Mary's behavior informally in addition to their formal evaluations. Mary was evaluated by specialists in developmental disabilities from the following disciplines (each using several standardized measures as well as narrative summaries of impressions to reach their conclusions): neurology, psychiatry, pediatrics, psychology, special education, psychiatric nursing, vocational rehabilitation, physical therapy, audiometry, speech pathology, dentistry, social work.

While recognizing the similarity with cases of elective mutism (Rosenberg & Lindblad, 1978), there was no deviation in any of the findings, and there was unanimous agreement on the diagnosis: Mary was severely retarded. She was mildly cerebral palsied; she had petit mal seizures; she was more than three standard deviations below average in height and weight; her language development was below that of a 9-month-old; her receptive language abilities seemed nonexistent, except for intonation; she was not sufficiently maturationally developed to be toilet trained; etc. There was no time at which anyone felt or mentioned in the discussion of their findings that emotional disturbance or resistance or noncooperation was interfering with the validity of their test results. The

evaluation was conclusive in every way; her IQ was set at approximately 20 to 25.

Although by standardized MMPI testing, no psychosis was evident and all members of the family were normal or above in intelligence, the family was diagnosed as delusional. A highly refined testing procedure indicated the mother was disposed to delusions under stress. She was seen as the locus of the family delusion, and the entire family was diagnosed as a case of *folie à famille, imposée.*

In contrast to the professional diagnosis, the family claimed that:

1. Mary is like other children her age; she is normal; she can talk.
2. Mary is often crabby and obstinate; when she's in such moods, she won't cooperate.
3. Mary puts on an act of "being retarded" in public, which the family cannot understand.
4. The professional staff had been fooled by Mary.

Our analysis of the available materials has been instigated by the following questions: How does the family do it? What sorts of skills, practices, and strategies are utilized to create and then "discover" Mary's competence? A number of images and anecdotes had heuristic value for discerning the nature of the family accomplishment. We occasionally thought of a Zen tale, for example, which goes something like this: A Zen master is asked by a novice to draw a perfect circle. The master draws a wretchedly ragged figure. The novice quickly notes that the figure is hardly a "perfect circle." "That is correct," responds the master, "but it is a perfect whatever-it-is." The tale captured for us what we felt was a dominant thrust of the family's practices—they had ways of transforming what others regarded as incompetent performance into exhibits of intelligence and responsiveness. The yield of our analysis has been a set of practices by which family members created Mary's "perfection."

FAMILY PRACTICES
Framing

There were several ways in which family members verbally or physically prestructured the environment to maximize the likelihood that *whatever* Mary did could be seen as meaningful, intentional activity. In "framing," Mary's family would establish a definition of the immediate situation and use it as a frame of reference for interpreting and describing any and all of Mary's subsequent behavior. Playing a game with Mary was perhaps the prototype of such framing activity. For example, once the game of "catch" was inaugurated as a definition of "what we are now doing," a variety of game-relevant dimensions for understanding and describing Mary's behavior came into effect. She could be seen as either "catching the ball," "not catching the ball," "dropping the ball," "throwing well," and so forth. The game provided a vocabulary for describing activities that occurred while the frame was in effect. Even activities that seemed to fall outside the frame were describable: Mary's nonresponsiveness might be formulated as "not playing" or "playing very poorly." Framed within the structure of an activity and described with the activity-specific terminology, Mary's behaviors were endowed with an aura of significance and responsiveness. In the exchange in Table 1, for example, Mary's passivity was reformulated into game-relevant terms; the ball tumbling out of Mary's hands was described by Mary's sister as an error; i.e., Mary "dropped" it.

To a certain extent the very structures of discourse provided frames that constituted the possibility of interpreting Mary's behavior as intelligent and responsive. For example, once a question was posed or an in-

vitation proffered, Mary's subsequent behavior might be reviewed for the ways in which whatever she was doing could serve as a response (Schegloff, 1968). Mary, of course, was impervious to the content of such overtures and often to the sheer fact of the overture itself; she never responded to a question or complied with a command behaviorally or verbally. Yet family members often formulated Mary's behaviors following these overtures as deliberately chosen and meaningful courses of activity even if Mary's behavior consisted of the completely unperturbed continuation of what she had been doing prior to the immediate transaction. In one sequence, for example, the mother twice requested "Give Mommy the ball"; when Mary simply continued to stand while holding the ball, the mother said "You don't want to give me the ball," thereby narratively transforming obliviousness into a willful reluctance to give the ball.

In the transaction in Table 2, Mary's involvement with a piling toy was framed by the mother's invitation to build a block house. Mary's continued fingering of the piling toy was then formulated as a deliber-

Table 1 Framing (Game)

Verbal Exchange	Movements
Do you want it?	
You gonna catch it for me? Huh?	
Come on.	
Come on.	
Put your hand out.	
Come on.	
Come on.	Sister puts ball in Mary's hand and Mary doesn't hold onto it.
Uh, uh (*laughs*).	
Almost dropped it.	Ball falls.
Come on.	Sister throws it to Mary who can't catch it, it drops again.
Come on (*laughs*).	

Table 2 Framing (Question)

Verbal Exchange	Movements
MO: Let's see, what have we got in here?	Mo pulls out piling toy, sets it on table away; M stands watching.
MO: How about building a block house?	Mo looks up at M, M looks at box.
M: Um mmmm.	Mo takes ball out; Mary puts a leg on the table and reaches in box touching the blocks.
MO: O.K.? M: Ahhhuy aiieo gege. MO: Shall we build a house? MO: Or are you gonna do that? M: Uh. MO: Let's build a house. Whup!	Mo takes blocks out and puts them on the table; Mary climbs onto table and reaches for piling toy, begins to pull off a section. After placing box on floor, Mo places hands on toy ball and removes them from the table top and looks at her. M has piece of toy, which Mo removes from her hand. M sits back on her heels, and M drops a toy. Mo reaches for her waist and lifts her down from table onto her lap.

ately chosen alternative. The formulation of Mary's activity was itself stated as a question—"Or are you gonna do that?"—with the subsequent result that Mary had been asked a sequence of questions that almost totally exhausted alternative possibilities for activity. In the face of options that covered the range of immediate possibilities—blocks or continued involvement with the piling toy—almost anything Mary did, even if she continued to do what she had been doing all along, could serve as material for inferring an intelligent choice.

Postscripting

If framing served prospectively to generate a "space" within which Mary's behaviors might assume meaning, postscripting attempted to generate or discern significance after the fact. In postscripting, family members would in effect track or follow Mary's ongoing behaviors and develop physical or verbal contexts that could render the behaviors intelligent and interactionally responsive.

Perhaps the clearest form of postscripting was expressed in what might be called "commanding the already done," in which family members requested Mary to engage in an activity she had already initiated. That is, family members observed the beginnings of possible actions and then ordered their completion. When done quickly with finesse, the inversion of the temporal sequence was hardly noticeable and the aura of competence enhanced; to the casual eye Mary seems to be following orders.

1. As Mary lay down on the floor, father said, "Mary, you just lie there." She does.
2. As Mary reached up to father with part of a toy in her hand, he said, "Give me that one, too." She gave it to him.
3. As Mary looked at her sister and climbed onto the chair, her sister said, "And you sit down." Mary sat down.

A somewhat more sophisticated form of postscripting entails the interposition of actions into the stream of Mary's behaviors. By discerning a pattern or developmental possibility in Mary's behaviors, the successful postscripter could integrate his or her actions with Mary's so as to achieve the appearance of

coordinated interactional activity. Thus, for example, at one point the sister dropped a block while Mary was intently banging a block on the table. As Mary sat down on the floor, the sister bent down from her chair, saying, "Let's find that block."

Puppeteering

In framing and postscripting, Mary's behaviors were endowed with significance through the artfulness of prebehavior and postbehavior interpretations. In effect, Mary's behaviors were treated as "givens" around which an edifice of meaning was constructed. On some occasions, however, instead of working with whatever Mary happened to do, family members would "create" Mary's behavior. Specifically, Mary would be physically maneuvered through various tasks. Moreover, the maneuvering was accompanied or followed by commentary implying that Mary was performing as an autonomous and responsive agent. We refer to this practice as "puppeteering," and when executed in a masterful way it could succeed in creating the illusion of independence. Indeed, initial viewings of videotaped sequences in Table 3 suggested that Mary could respond to requests and follow instructions. An instruction would be given, the observer would shift visually to view Mary, and Mary could be observed to approximate the behavior that had been requested of her. It was not until later in the analysis, however, that the sequencing of family talk and family touching was seen to be related to the active production of her behavioral response. Mary's movements were often artifacts of the family's physical engineering of her body.

Semantic Crediting

Mary was responsive to a range of different stimuli, all of which were nonverbal. These were fairly predictable, and they were appropriate for a child with her mental age. [Table 4 contains] a partial list of stimuli Mary responded to, with the corresponding behaviors (from hours of observation on ward and on tape).

These are events that elicited predictable behavioral reactions from Mary, even when embedded in a context that included other stimuli such as talk. Indeed the fact that these triggering items almost invariably occurred in a semantically meaningful configuration created ambiguity as to precisely which features of the

Table 3 Puppeteering

Verbal Exchange	Movements
MOTHER AND MARY	
MO: Okay, now.	Mo sitting on floor next to the table, setting up a circle of blocks on table. Mary just slipped to floor. Mo picks M up under her arms to a standing position. With one hand Mother points to the middle of the circle of blocks, *other arm is around and behind M with hand on M's arm; she pushes* M's arm, which has block in it, toward the middle while looking at the table—then looks at M. M's arm moves forward, then stops, and M slips to the floor again.
Put your block in the middle.	
M: Ah hayee.	
MO: Put your block in—	
SISTER AND MARY	
SI: Give me this; give me that. All right; take these, put them in the truck; take the blocks and put them in the truck; *Come on take the block.*	S grabs the stick and block out of M's hand one at a time, puts her hand briefly on M's hand, then touches the blocks, then touches the truck in pointing gesture.
	S puts her hand on M's arm and lifts it over to the block and onto the block; M holds onto a block briefly.
FATHER AND MARY	
FA: I'm not gonna talk to you unless you get the ball. Now you go over there and get the ball. Come on Mary.	Fa sitting on chair, M standing by his knee. Fa moves slightly away from M and puts one hand under his chin. Fa puts hand on M's shoulder and pushes her toward the table; lets go of her.

Table 4 Stimuli and Responses

Stimuli	Responses
A sudden loud noise: a shout, a knock on the door, a clapping of hands, etc.	Often causes Mary to turn toward the source of the noise, stop what she is doing, look and walk toward the source
A sudden movement within her peripheral vision	Often causes Mary to look in that direction, pause
A person reaching out to Mary, hand out, palm open, or arms outstretched	Often causes Mary to move toward that person or reach out with her hand
A person slapping her or shaking her suddenly	Often causes Mary to pause, orient herself, look at the person, make a face
Having an object placed close to her while she's watching	Often causes Mary to look at it, touch it, explore it, pick it up, or put it to her mouth
A person walking away	Often Mary will follow
Being near a door knob	Often Mary will touch and fiddle with it

environment Mary was reacting to. Insofar as attention was displaced to the utterance accompanying a triggering event or gesture, such as an outstretched arm, it appeared that Mary was able to understand the verbal message, when in fact she was simply responding to a behavioral cue. Table 5 furnishes examples of how these cues might be embedded in or accompanied by a verbal message thereby permitting the inference that Mary's subsequent activity was in response to the meaning of the utterance.

The inference that one would make about Mary's mental acuity would vary dramatically according to which stimulus one considered to be the crucial one: the verbal request or the accompanying cues. The familial claim, of course, was that she understood the words spoken to her and that her competence far exceeded the level of responsiveness involved in merely reaching for an outstretched hand or turning to a loud noise.

Putting Words in Mary's Mouth

Perhaps the most dramatic, and the most difficult to understand, set of practices were those by which the family created the semblance of Mary's linguistic competence. From the point of hearing of an outside observer-listener, Mary's utterances were interactionally capricious and unintelligible and without promise of any sort of cryptointelligibility. Family members, on the other hand, were insistent that Mary spoke and spoke well, albeit not always and not everywhere. Although it is difficult to specify precisely what family members heard and how they came to hear it, we have located certain interactional styles that seemed to contribute to the image that Mary responded at a timely and appropriate place in a conversational sequence, that she responded intelligently and intelligibly, and

Table 5 Semantic Crediting

Verbal Exchange	Movements
MOTHER AND MARY	
MO: Come on. (*knock on door*)	
	M looks around and Mo stands up. M reaches for Mo's hand. Mo pulls away and points to the door.
I think somebody wants to get in. Do you wanna open the door?	
Open the door.	M goes to the doorknob and puts both hands on it and twists it.
MO: Come on.	Mo opens the door. Mo seated by the table, M lying on the floor fiddling with the blocks in her hand. *Mo taps M's foot, then holds out hand close to M.* M lolls on floor, *slowly gets up.*
Get up (*whisper*).	
Get up (*fierce*).	
Get up (*enunciated*)	
FATHER AND MARY	
FA: You sit in my lap. Come on.	Fa sitting on chair, his hands on his knees, M walking toward him; holds his hands out toward her; she backs off and leans back against a chair. *Fa reaches out with hand, almost touching M,* she raises a leg, then *touches his hand briefly with her own.* He takes hold and picks her up onto lap.
M: Euuuhhn.	
FA: I don't care *whether you* want to; *come on.*	
SISTER AND MARY	
SI: Mary—	Si sitting on chair, M next to her. M drops block out of truck, Si reaches over and picks it up, puts it back in the truck, *slaps M's hand* while looking at her face; *M looks up at her for a moment.*
Hey.	
Now listen!	

that what she said was inter-subjectively available. We shall comment on but one aspect of the interactional patterns by which the family sustained the myth of Mary's interactional skill.

Often, when Mary made an utterance, a family member would repeat what Mary said. But, of course, they did not repeat it at all, for they would babble were they to do so. More precisely, then, when family members "repeated," they were actually creating a novel, intelligent utterance and stating it as though they were repeating what they had heard Mary say or imply.

While putting words in Mary's mouth, they implicitly claimed that she was putting her words in theirs. Table 6 presents several examples of such "statement by re-statement." They were excerpted from a tape Mary's family made at home and offered as somewhat unsat-isfactory (to them) evidence of Mary's competence.

Although we are unable to specify how family members were prompted to "repeat" precisely what they chose to "repeat," we can appreciate one of the possible functions of these procedures for the collec-tive, sense-making enterprise. Specifically, such prac-tices introduced a degree of determinacy and integrity to Mary's talk and allowed family consensus on what Mary has said. In "repeating," or heavily implying the meaning of Mary's utterance by their response, family members were in fact creating and broadcasting the meaning. If we are not mistaken, such work allowed

Table 6 Putting Words in Mary's Mouth

1. Mary is wearing a newly bought robe.
FA: Want to see it in the mirror?
M: [Gurgling.]
FA: She doesn't like it.
MO: You don't like the robe? It fits you.
M: [Gurgling].
MO: What did you say about Daddy?
M: Mmmmmm, [gurgle].
FA: She thinks it's too cheap!

2. Encouraging her to talk into the recorder:
FA: OK, you tell me your name and age into that thing, and I'll give you $5 to go out and buy a present that you want to buy yourself.
M: [Gurgling.]
FA: Your name and age—
M: Goo ga [gurgle].
FA: She's bargaining with me for more money!

3. Later:
MO: Time for your pills, Mary.
M: Mmmmm.
MO: Time for your pills.
M: [Gurgling.]
MO: You don't think you need them.
M: Mmmmm, ga.
MO: I think you need them.

the family to avoid embarrassing disagreements, to perpetuate the fiction that Mary was speaking intelligibly, and to develop a shared version of precisely what Mary said.

Explaining in the "Bright" Direction

Although the previously described practices often succeeded in imparting an aura of intelligence and responsiveness to Mary's behaviors, they also provided opportunities for behaviors to be specifically and recognizably inadequate. A parentally inaugurated game of catch, for example, generated the possibility of "missing" or "dropping" the ball over and over and over again. Thus, the practices were not a guarantee of the semblance of competence; they could become methods for displaying incompetence. Indeed, there were a number of occasions on which family members found Mary's behavior remiss, in error, or unresponsive. But such occasions did not result in attributions of incompetence. On the contrary, members could transform these episodes into evidence of Mary's sophistication.

Almost any system of belief is capable of furnishing secondary elaborations that will preserve the sense of the system's validity in the face of seemingly discrediting or subversive evidence. The belief in Mary's competence was protected by a network of such "epicyclical" explanations (Polanyi, 1964; Pollner & Wikler, 1979). Mary's ostensible failures were continuously reinterpreted as successes of sorts or else explained away as the product of normal transient mood shifts or lapses of attention. Thus, for example, instances in which Mary's behavior seemed to defy interpretation as a directly responsive action were treated as the product of Mary's postulated proclivity toward "teasing" and "pretending." Indeed, the fact that psychiatric staff had one version of Mary and her family another was attributed to Mary's faking or malingering. Other failures were explained away by the family as products of orneriness, lack of cooperation, or momentary inattentiveness, as in the interaction between Mary and her father presented in Table 7.

In effect, the belief "Mary is competent" functioned as an "incorrigible assumption" (Gasking, 1965), that is, as an assumption that would not be withdrawn or reevaluated in light of empirical events.

Table 7 Explaining in the Bright Direction

FA:	Go get the ball, Mary.
M:	Eigaga.
FA:	Come on, Mary, go get the ball. Come on, come on, go get the ball. You're not being the least bit cooperative, Mary, you just lie there; okay, you going to sleep? Come on, get me the ball. The ball, Mary.
M:	Ummm.
FA:	Hey, I don't care whether you want to or not; do you want to get belted? Go get the ball! Come on. Come on, Mary.
M:	Uhnn.
FA:	Huh?
M:	Ewaiuhh.
FA:	Mary, you're making it harder on yourself. Come on. Come on with me, and I'll go over and get the ball with you. Give me your hand.
M:	Guheaa.
FA:	You're being a bad girl, Mary.
M:	Agaa.

Instead, empirical events were interpreted so as to render them compatible with the fundamental claim "Mary is competent." The net effect of such explanatory and descriptive practices was to inhibit the growth of what could have been an enormous catalogue of incompetence. Each instance was explained away in a fashion congenial to the basic belief. Indeed, insofar as "faking" or "cheating" are higher-level activities requiring sophisticated reflections and interpersonal manipulations, there is a sense in which ostensible failures ultimately served to enhance Mary's image among family members.

DISCUSSION

In a more literal sense than is usually intended, a *folie à famille* makes and lives in its own little world. We have attempted to examine some of the practices through which that world or *nomos* is reproduced and maintained. Although we have succeeded in identifying several practices, questions and issues abound both with respect to the case at hand and *folie à famille* generally.

The first issue is the extent to which the practices discerned were characteristic of the family's routine transactions with Mary. The videotapes were made in a clinic waiting room with several staff members behind a one-way mirror making consequential decisions on the basis of what they observed. It is a difficult task in general and an impossible one in this case, given the absence of materials on routine family relations, to assess the correspondence between performance in clinical and nonclinical settings. It is quite easy on the other hand to imagine ways in which the relation might be problematic, that is, the ways in which family performance in the clinic might have been different from interaction in the home. The very request to interact with Mary under the gaze of others, for example, might have induced a level of self-consciousness and an intensity of effort uncharacteristic of interaction in the home. It is also possible that Mary herself was different in the home. This, of course, was the claim of the family. Although every piece of clinical information weighed against the competence attributed to Mary by the family, the familiarity of household objects and routines may have contributed to higher levels of displayed competence than observed in the clinic. These are possibilities that defy closure owing to the limits of our materials.

A related issue is the extent to which family members believed or experienced their version of Mary. It is possible if not plausible that family members varied in the depth and nature of their acceptance of the delusional content (Evans & Marskey, 1972). Although again our materials preclude closure, it is of interest to note that family members varied in the adroitness with which they were able to create the aura of Mary's competence for observers—and perhaps for themselves. Mary's mother, for example, by virtue of her active involvement with Mary could achieve a more convincing display of Mary's competence than any other family member. The possibility of various depths and types of commitments to the family delusion means that, although some may have been true believers, others may have had to be continually though implicitly urged to voice the family line and to partake of the appropriate practices. Thus a comprehensive analysis of the "how" of the maintenance of

shared delusion would explicate the interactional dynamics by which members are rewarded for honoring the family *doxa* and castigated for heretical tendencies.[3]

A final issue of consequence focuses on the origin of these practices. And although once again we plead limitations of materials, our reflections have taken us to a point suggesting that reformulation of the nature of the practice of delusion may be in order. Initially focused on the "how" of delusion, we did not have well-articulated notions regarding the origin of these practices save for the assumption that they were mobilized or developed in the interest of sustaining a belief that was important in the interpersonal and intrapersonal dynamics of family members. In effect, we regarded the practices and, for that matter, the belief itself as more or less *de novo* creations. As we completed the bulk of our analysis, we noted that the practices we discerned were similar to those many parents seem to employ with their preverbal children. Parent-infant interaction is replete with episodes in which adults playfully treat the child's babbling as an intelligent and complex utterance or manipulate the child through complex sequences of activity while praising the child for the excellence of her performance or describe whatever the child is doing at a particular moment as though it were an intentional project of the child (Bruner, 1983; Lock, 1981; Wertsch, 1978). In the language of our report, interaction between adults and preverbal children is replete with "putting words in the child's mouth," "puppeteering," and "framing."[4]

The similarity between observed family practices and those characteristic of adult/young-child interaction suggests the origins of the former. It may be that family practices are not novel creations but a perseveration of once appropriate practices. Mary's family may have initially interacted with Mary in the fashion that all families interact with infants in the preverbal stage. Somehow those practices persisted despite the fact that Mary was now over five years old and had not acquired the skills and competencies appropriate for her age. Given this possibility, it is not that the family constructs a new world so much as they refuse to relinquish an old one. Accordingly, the question of interest may not be how did the practices originate, but rather how do they endure.

A detailed explication of the processes that might promote the perseveration of "outmoded" practices is beyond the scope of this paper, though some features may be portrayed in a few broad strokes. Consider that families will often have good reason for disattending or otherwise not confronting an actual loss, such as the decline of the position, prestige, or competence of one of its members or the loss of some anticipated state of affairs such as a successful career, happy family life, or healthy child. The psychological and interpersonal costs of addressing such losses may be great. The loss may touch on the foundations of a person's sense of self, other family members' sense of him, family members' relation to one another, and even their relations to others outside the nuclear family. Accordingly, there may be attempts to evade or forestall directly confronting the nature and significance of the loss. There are, of course, a variety of ways to accomplish this. Family members may tacitly agree not to talk about the matter. In other instances, perhaps especially when the loss is not (yet) definitive or clear-cut, the family may persevere in the practices and outlook characteristic of the preloss period—the husband is on the verge of success; we are a happy family; our daughter is a healthy, normal child. Permeated by the sense of catastrophe on the one hand and of hope on the other, these "little tribes in distress" (First, 1975) may continue to do what they have always done.

Depending upon the nature of the threatened loss, old practices may be retained for indefinite lengths of time without confronting directly contradictory or disconfirming information. As the hoped-for reality recedes into the horizon and the dreaded loss becomes actual, however, the retention of old practices means that the family enters a sham world or, more to the point, is left with a sham world (Henry, 1973). Initial participation in sham may have an accelerating effect: A little sham leads to a lot of sham as family members become reluctant and perhaps unable to cease the fiction for fear not only of calling attention to the lost object but also for fear of acknowledging that for the past few minutes, weeks, years, they have been living a fiction. Shamming after all is shameful, particularly

with loved ones, and thus participants may find that having taken one step into this world they must take another—and cover their tracks.

CONCLUSION

Folie à deux (or "shared delusion") is often catalogued among the more exotic pathologies, involving as it does several individuals—the classical number, of course, is two—who share and participate in the same delusional system (Wikler, 1980). Though there may be many differences between these little tribes and other collectivities, the commitment to beliefs whose foundation in reality is problematic is not in itself a distinguishing criterion. As Berger (1969) has noted, all collectivities construct a meaningful order or *nomos,* and every *nomos* is erected in the face of chaos and "irreality." Although it would be naïve and misleading to treat *folie à deux* as nothing but a variant of the *nomos*-building processes characteristic of other groups, there is heuristic value in underscoring the fact that these groups develop meaningful worlds that, like all such symbolic constructs, must be nourished and protected through specific practices of reasoning, speaking, and acting.

In an earlier work, Wikler (1980) explored some of the clinically relevant features of this particular case for family therapists, as an example of the syndrome of *folie à famille.* In this paper, we have examined the practices through which a family, diagnosed as *folie à famille,* sustained its world. Our analysis led us to suggest that some forms of "delusion" may involve not the construction of novel symbolic realms but the buttressing of old ones. Although it is highly unlikely that all forms of *folie à deux* originate through retention of outmoded practice, it is plausible and in keeping with the ubiquitousness of the phenomena (Ferreira, 1963; Gralnick, 1942; Greenberg, 1954; Wikler, 1980) to consider the possibility that, in some instances, shared "delusions" arise not as the consequence of an elected or induced set of practices and beliefs that fly in the face of reality but as a result of reality flying away from an established set of practices and anticipations.[5] Whether this interpretation extends beyond the current case awaits detailed descriptions of the processes by which families create their worlds and respond to the inevitable tremors.

NOTES

1. The social constructionist attitude does not provide privileged exemptions for "expert" or "scientific" constructions of reality. The tacit practices by which clinicians develop, coordinate, use, and defend their versions of reality are as amenable to analysis as those of the families they study. For certain clinical purposes, however, it is necessary to avoid what can turn into an infinitely regressing form of analysis (as when, say, an analysis of the social construction of reality is itself viewed as a construction). Nevertheless, the ceaseless relativism inherent in the constructionist perspective is useful in that it heightens appreciation of the tacit commitments and practices implicated in the development of one's own "authoritative" version of "what really happened."

2. Extensive background and biographical information as well as transcripts of the audiotapes and videotapes used in this report are available in Wikler (1976).

3. The work of Henry (1973) and Goode (1980) provides examples of the kind of "clinical ethnography" necessary to get at family dynamics as they occur in the home setting.

4. In an unpublished paper, David Helm suggests these practices may be characteristic of interaction with any person whose verbal capacity or intelligence is perceived as limited, impaired, or otherwise problematic. A number of colleagues have suggested that similar practices are found in interaction with pets. An unusual development in this regard is a recent critical review of the research on the linguistic ability of primates. Umiker-Sebeok and Sebeok (1980) argue that ostensibly positive evidence may be more an artifact of researchers' procedures and interpretations than a reflection of genuine linguistic competence. Several of the practices identified by the Sebeoks as the source of artifactual evidence are remarkably similar to the practices described in this report. The Sebeoks note, for example, some of the "no-forfeit" practices through which a primate's signing behaviors, no matter how unusual, are treated as evidence of linguistic ability—anomalous signs are interpreted as jokes, insults, or metaphors. In characterizing the immediate social context of talking primate projects, the Sebeoks all but state the possibility of a *folie à famille*. A team constitutes "a tightly knit social community with a solid core of shared beliefs and goals in opposition to outside visitors, as well as against groups elsewhere which are competing for scarce research resources" (pp. 7–8). The research teams, they indicate, are often led by investigators married to one another (e.g., the Gardners, Premacks, and Rumbaughs), with graduate students and younger colleagues serving as "uncles and aunts" of the subjects.

5. One implication of this portrayal of the path to *folie à famille* is that it is continuous and does not require reference to any qualitatively distinct psychological traits that dispose or propel individuals on their way. This is a problematic assumption, and it may be that there is a crevice between preservation of old practices and "delusion," across which one can leap only if propelled by, say, dependency needs of extreme intensity. It may, however, be worth considering that the point at which the leap occurs is much further away from home base than previously thought and that many families take the path a goodly distance before encountering the schism.

REFERENCES

Berger, P. (1969). *The sacred canopy.* Garden City, NY: Doubleday.

Berger, P., & Kellner, H. (1970). Marriage and the construction of reality. In H. P. Dreitzel (Ed.), *Recent sociology* (No. 2). New York: Macmillan.

Bruner, J. (1983). *Child's talk. Learning to use language.* New York and London: Norton.

Cicourel, A. V. (1973). *Cognitive sociology: Language and meaning in social interaction.* Harmonds-worth, UK: Penguin.

Evans, P., & Marskey, H. (1972). Shared beliefs of dermal parasitosis: Folie partagée. *Brit. J. Med. Psychol., 45,* 19–26.

Ferreira, J. (1963). Family myth and homeostasis. *Arch. Gen. Psychiat., 9,* 457–463.

First, E. (1975). The new wave in psychiatry. *New York Review of Books, 22,* 8–15.

Garfinkel, H. (1967). *Studies in ethnomethodology.* Englewood Cliffs, NJ: Prentice-Hall.

Gasking, D. (1965). Mathematics and the world. In A. Flew (Ed.), *Logic and language.* Garden City, NY: Doubleday.

Goode, D. (1980). Behavioral sculpting: Parent-child interaction in families with retarded children. In J. Jacobs (Ed.), *Phenomenological approaches to mental retardation.* Springfield, IL: Charles C Thomas.

Gralnick, A. (1942). Folie à deux—The psychosis of association. A review of 103 cases and the entire English literature: With case presentations. *Psychiat. Quart., 16,* 230–263, 491–520.

Greenberg, P. H. (1954). Folie à deux. *Guy's Hospital Reports, 4,* 381–392.

Henry, J. (1973). *Pathways to madness.* New York: Vintage.

Lock, A. J. (Ed.). (1981). *Action, gesture and symbol: The emergence of language.* London: Academic Press.

Polanyi, M. (1964). *Personal knowledge.* New York: Harper & Row.

Pollner, M., & Wikler, L. (1979). "Cognitive enterprise" in einem Fall von Folie à Famille. In H. G. Soeffner (Ed.), *Interpretative Verfahren in den Sozial—und Textwissenschaften.* Stuttgart: J. B. Metzler.

Pulver, S. E., & Brunt, M. Y. (1961). Deflection of hostility in folie à deux. *Arch. Gen. Psychiat., 5,* 257–265.

Reiss, D. (1981). *The family's construction of reality.* Cambridge, MA: Harvard University Press.

Rosenberg, J. B., & Lindblad, M. B. (1978). Behavior therapy in a family context. *Fam. Proc., 17,* 77–82.

Schegloff, E. A. (1968). Sequencing in conversational openings. *Am. Anthrop., 70,* 1075–1095.

Umiker-Sebeok, J., & Sebeok, T. A. (1980). Introduction: Questioning apes. In J. Umiker-Sebeok & T. A. Sebeok (Eds.), *Speaking of apes.* New York: Plenum.

Wertsch, J. V. (1978). Adult-child interaction and the roots of metacognition. *Quarterly News-letter of the Institute for Comparative Human Development, 2,* 15–18.

Wikler, L. (1976). *Delusions of competence: A socio-behavioral study of the maintenance of a deviant belief system in a family with a retarded child.* Unpublished doctoral dissertation, University of California, Irvine.

Wikler, L. (1980). Folie à famille: A family therapist's perspective. *Fam. Proc., 19,* 257–268.

FURTHER READING

Anderson, Elijah. 1990. "Street Etiquette and Street Wisdom." Pp. 207–236. in *Streetwise* Chicago: University of Chicago Press.

- Discusses the social organization of wisdom in an African American urban community.

Anderson, Milton L. 1994. "The Many and Varied Social Constructions of Intelligence." Pp. 119–138 in *Constructing the Social,* edited by Theodore R. Sarbin and John I. Kitsuse, London: Sage.

- A history of the construction of the concept and the measurement of intelligence.

Holstein, James A. 1993. *Court-Ordered Insanity: Interpretive Practice and Involuntary Commitment.* New York: Aldine de Gruyter.

- A comprehensive study of the construction of the varied contours of mental incompetence in court proceedings.

Lynch, Michael. 1983. "Accommodation Practices: Vernacular Treatments of Madness." *Social Problems* 31:152–163.

- Discusses how family members and close associates accommodate troublesome persons who have not been, and may never be, defined as mentally ill.

Rose, Nikolas. 1998. *Inventing Our Selves: Psychology, Power, and Personhood.* Cambridge, England: Cambridge University Press.

- Provides a historically based constructionist view of the "psy" professions.

SECTION 6

THE BODY AND THE PHYSICAL SELF

The self seems to be the most public side of our inner lives. It's the inner part of us that we present to others in talk and interaction. It's also the part to which others respond as they communicate with us. Yet, as seemingly public as it appears, the self remains physically invisible. We take it, for example, that a particular facial expression "re-presents"—but doesn't actually show—the self. The face stands for the self, but it isn't the self itself. We recognize this distinction when we wonder whether, say, a smile doesn't really hide sorrow or whether an angry look isn't masking fear.

As a practical matter, we constantly look to the body for signs of what lies within. Facial expressions, eye contact, and posture, among myriad aspects of our physical bearing, can speak volumes about our inner selves. Consequently, we are deeply concerned with appearances. "Looks" can immediately convey our identities. Our culture and its advertisers bombard us with endless messages that the way we look influences the way others appreciate us. Appearance affects the way we feel about ourselves, too. Indeed, "good looks" are among the most widely publicized commodities in contemporary life. *Our Bodies, Ourselves* (Boston Women's Health Book Collective 1973) is not only the title of a popular book on women and identity, but also is today's rallying cry of the physical self.

Of course, features of the body don't automatically signal the self that's inside. It's what bodily signs *mean* that's important. Like dimensions of self, the various meanings of the body are constructed in social interaction. Male and female bodies, for example, signify particular qualities that we expect to find in men's and women's inner regions. Certainly there's variation among those sharing the same body types, but there are many common expectations. The same goes for expectations associated with skin color, height, weight, and posture. Sometimes we call this stereotyping, which has both positive and negative connotations. But all of us construct meanings about the inner selves of others based only on what we see on the outside. It's an unavoidable part of everyday interaction.

Bodily deformity and disfigurement send especially strong signals. Their meanings often translate into social *stigmas*—socially devalued bodily markings. These markings can be as highly visible as a missing limb or as inconspicuous as a small birthmark. They may be as rare as albino skin pigmentation or as common as male pattern baldness. Bodily stigmas transmit negative meanings, despite the fact that there is nothing inherent in the physical condition to support the social meanings.

Even the slightest body stigma can have life-changing social consequences. Consider, for example, the ridicule aimed at an overweight second grader, solely because of the shape of his body. In response, the child may withdraw or lash out. In either case, social meanings prompt his reaction. Or think of the lengths to which some adults go to conceal aging selves by rejuvenating their bodies through cosmetic surgery. Tummy tucks, nose jobs, and wrinkle removal ostensibly transform outer bodies. But plastic surgery is as much about inner selves as it is about surface restoration. A toupee, for better or worse, is as much for a man's self as it is for his scalp.

ABOUT THE READINGS

Mary M. Gergen and **Kenneth J. Gergen's** chapter **"Narratives of the Gendered Body in Popular Autobiography"** explores how the body figures into accounts of success and failure. Looking at popular autobiographies of celebrities, the Gergens are interested in how gender relates to the meaning of the body. Although these are celebrities' stories, they nevertheless resonate with the way the rest of us describe our bodies in relation to our own successes and failures.

Male celebrities generally talk about their bodies in instrumental terms. They view them as tools for accomplishing things. When their bodies are in good working order, they don't pay much attention to them. Indeed, for the men, being fixated on one's body verges on unmanliness. This view changes somewhat as the men get older. When their bodies break down, the men are disappointed. But, again, this view is instrumental. The men are unhappy, for example, that they can't accomplish the things they used to.

Female celebrities' accounts are different. They're more ego involved with their bodies. The women present life stories in which the body and the self are intertwined. Across the life course, their bodies continually signify who they are as persons. Their self-worth is intimately tied to their bodies and their appearances. Putting the men's and women's stories together, the Gergens show how gender is closely tied to embodiment.

Karen March's chapter considers a different kind of intertwining. **"Who Do I Look Like? Gaining a Sense of Self-Authenticity Through the Physical Reflection of Others"** deals with the relation between physical resemblances and inner selves. According to March, family resemblances—such as having the same shape of nose or body build as one's mother—affect one's feelings about being a part of the family. "Table talk"—casual comments made about each other around the dinner table—can be serious business when physical resemblance comes up. A seemingly trivial comment, such as "when you smile like that, you look like your mother," constructs identity in familial terms. It ties the inner self of the daughter to the physical selves of both the mother and the daughter.

What happens when individuals have little or no basis for making such connections? March interviewed a number of persons who had been adopted, but who had not found their biological parents. She describes how these adoptees convey an incomplete sense of self because they can't see physical connections between themselves and their relatives. Table talk in adoptive families can inadvertently marginalize adoptees simply because a lack of references to family resemblances momentarily leaves them out. For many adoptees, meeting their birth relatives and comparing physical characteristics provides a kind of self-authenticity that is otherwise missing from their lives. March's article shows how important the body can be for constructing self and identity.

Finally, **Carolyn Ellis** explores the implications of minor bodily imperfections. In **"'I Hate My Voice': Coming to Terms with Minor Bodily Stigmas,"** Ellis explains that small stigmas—such as lisps—sometimes have a greater impact than major ones because those who have them know that they are always there, but others may hardly notice. Ignoring small stigmas leaves their presence and meaning unresolved, putting those who have them in a double bind. Should minor imperfections be pointed out, they can become the object of unwanted attention. If, on the other hand, one never mentions the imperfections, one has no way of knowing what others think about them. Ellis shows us some of these difficulties in poignant detail as she recounts challenges she has personally encountered.

27 | NARRATIVES OF THE GENDERED BODY IN POPULAR AUTOBIOGRAPHY

Mary M. Gergen and Kenneth J. Gergen

One of the commonplace truths of contemporary culture is that people are born either male or female, and that these two groups of people exhibit differing characteristics related to their sexes across the life span. Except for rare instances, people identify themselves in the most profound ways as either male or female, and become acutely aware of qualitative changes in what it is to be a man or a woman as they age. Yet, how we understand these matters is subject to broad debate. Let us contrast two positions, the one stressing *essence* and the other *meaning*. It is frequently presumed that facts about gender differences, along with views about human development more generally, are (or should be) derived from systematic observation of behavior. What we believe about gender development is, ideally, a reflection of the actual essence of gender differences across the life span (cf. reviews of sex difference research in Maccoby and Jacklin, 1974; Money and Ehrhardt, 1972). Scientific knowledge on this account represents a distinct advancement over folk psychology because scientific observation of essential differences is more systematic and rigorous.

Yet, though the essentialist view is commonplace, it is also delimited. A growing body of scholarship now places central emphasis on the formative effects of understanding itself. That is, what we take to be knowledge of gender and development over the life span are not reflections of the essences; rather, our presumptions of knowledge enter, reflexively, into daily affairs to shape the contours of human activity (cf. Steier, 1991). On this latter account, the possession of full breasts or a bald head is of no necessary consequence in itself—no more, let's say than other observable facts, such as having brown eyes or large toes. However, if full breasts and a bald head come to

demark discrete stages of development, and the members of such classes are thereby defined as more or less emotional, rational, passive, sexy, or moral, then having full breasts or a bald head may importantly shape one's life chances, activities, and satisfactions.

Further, as people live out their lives, engaging in various courses of action, they often support the matrix of preexisting meanings attached to various physical characteristics. In this way the current cultural meanings, whatever they are, exert their effects on others, even into future generations. In a broad sense, one is thus born into a culture composed of interlocking patterns of meaning and action (Bruner, 1986). These meanings give specific significance to various biological characteristics, rendering them socially visible or insignificant, deeming them valuable or debilitating, using them to designate differences or similarities. The result of this process of cultural construction is a deep sense of the *natural* differences between men and women as they develop and age over the life span.

From the social constructionist perspective, meanings are not private and subjective events, but public and shared.[1] Meanings are generated through the discursive practices of the culture, transmitted from adults to children within various cultural contexts. Because such practices are inherently fragile and subject to continuous alteration, various significations can be foregrounded in one cultural enclave but overlooked in another. Cultural patterns of speaking and acting at any time may be viewed as a patchwork of discourses, each with its different history and context of usage.[2] In order to carry out relationships, it is thus necessary to borrow from various repositories of discourse to achieve mutual coordination of action.[3] At the same time, most recognizable cultures also contain a body of more or less interdependent, enduring, and broadly sustaining discourses. Thus, for example, in the United States a common discourse on justice may enter into relationships in the courtroom, the classroom, or the living room. In this case, each localized usage may support a more or less pervasive array of cultural meanings.

In the present offering we explore a small repository of discourse within the culture; although relatively insignificant in the literary landscape, this body of writing provides significant bearings for negotiating the life course. Our particular interest is in narrative construction, and most focally, the stories people tell about their lives. In our view, the narrative is the central means by which people endow their lives with meaning across time.[4] Thus, as people are exposed to the popular narratives within the culture, they learn how to regard themselves, how to make themselves intelligible to each other, and how to fashion their conduct. In Paul de Man's (1979) words, "We assume that life produces the autobiography . . . , but can we not suggest, with equal justice, that the autobiographical project itself may produce and determine life?" (p. 920).

To the extent that narratives are gendered, furnishing different structures of meaning for men as opposed to women, so do they contribute to cultural patterns that differentiate between the genders and prescribe both what is likely and unlikely during a lifetime. Thus, as men and women tell the stories of their bodies—what they mean and how they should be considered—so do these stories affect the course of their relationships with others, their career potentials, and their life satisfactions. If the stories of embodiment differ importantly between men and women, they may also generate estrangements. To live in a different story of the body from another can render an impasse of understanding. Male and female actions toward each other may be misunderstood, and relationships dwindle into lonely alienation.

AUTOBIOGRAPHY AND THE FASHIONING OF THE LIFE COURSE

One of the most accessible forms of narrative available to contemporary North American readers is the autobiography. Highly marketable in the United States, the bestseller list each week usually includes at least two autobiographies in the top ten nonfiction books (cf. *New York Times,* 1990–92 booklists). These autobiographies vary in their instantiations, but bestsellers are frequently based on formula formats prescribed by publishing houses. These forms allow celebrities, often abetted by professional writers who specialize in this form, to tell their life stories in a revealing and engrossing way. Despite their mass appeal, we believe the popular autobiography is far more than a mode of public entertainment. Rather, such works operate much like secularized primers for the "good life" (Stone, 1982). They provide an idealized model of the life course—furnishing direction, sanctioning deviation, and providing benchmarks against which the common person can measure and judge their development. Autobiographies such as these are not, of course, the only such sources for rendering the life course meaningful. However, because they bear an intertextual relationship with other popular sources of narrative—television documentaries, Hollywood films, and magazine stories, as well as other fictional fare—their significance is noteworthy.

The function of the autobiography as a life course model is revealed in the narrator's positioning of self vis-à-vis the reader. As Eakin (1985) points out, the autobiographer typically takes "the stance of the wise and fatherly elder addressing the reader as son or niece" (p. 29). The principal form of the autobiographical relationship is expert to novice, elder to younger, master to apprentice, or powerful to powerless. The edifying principle behind autobiographies is also revealed in their central themes and the personages selected to write about themselves. The central emphasis of the autobiography is on success and failure, and particularly how to achieve the former and avoid the latter. The authors are typically figures widely recognized for their cultural achievements (Olney, 1980). Classical autobiographies almost exclusively delineate the life of cultural heroes—those who have achieved greatness through their accomplishments (Jelinek, 1980). Readers benefit by being able to fantasize about the pleasures of escaping their humdrum circumstances and learning the ways and means to a notable life.

The Emergence of the Female Voice

What kind of image of the life span does the popular autobiography present? There has been no systematic study of this question, but the answers can be ascertained, in part, by reference to the historical development of the autobiographical form itself. Although the history of autobiography is in its infancy, scholars suggest that its particular form took shape with the rise of the bourgeoisie, and the accompanying concept of the self-made man (Lejeune, 1975, Pascal, 1960). Similarly, Weintraub (1978) argues that the development of autobiography is closely linked in Western culture with the emerging value of the unique and independent individual. "The fascination with individual specificity leads to deep intrigue with life stories" (Eakin, 1985, p. 204). In this view, autobiographical figures represent a culturally and historically situated model of an ideal self.

With the emphasis on individual achievement, autobiographies tend to follow the classical lines of the "monomyth," a form that Joseph Campbell (1949/1956) has designated as the most fundamental in Western civilization. In its clearest form, the monomyth is the saga of a hero who triumphs over myriad impediments. When applied to the life span, the monomyth is a heroic trajectory. It thus tends to recognize youth as a preparatory period, early and middle adulthood as induction and struggle to attain one's goals, and mature adulthood and old age as full achievement and later consolidation and appreciation of one's successes. The form of the heroic life span is indeed like a skewed arc, with the apex at the climactic moment of highest attainment. The particular time in the life span is dependent upon the goals, but in the popular autobiography it is usually formed so that this point is approximately three quarters of the way through the text. In the autobiography, the form of the story is singular, linear, and progressive to the climax, and usually stable thereafter.

Yet, it is also clear that this account of the autobiography is most relevant to—if not the unique provenance of—prominent public figures; in almost all cases, the high status man. The chief features of the monomythic tale speak most directly to the life span of a man, not a woman (Gergen, 1992). As Mary Ma-

son (1980) has described, "The self presented as the stage for a battle of opposing forces and where a climactic victory for one force—spirit defeating flesh—. . . simply does not accord with the deepest realities of women's experience and so is inappropriate as a model for women's life-writing" (p. 210). Included in the monomythic story are several women's roles, none of which is considered heroic. Women are cast in roles that are defined as stable, passive, or service oriented. Women are thematized as fair maidens to be wooed and won, mothers and wives, witches and sorcerers.[5] Women tend to be objects of quest, or forces that impede the hero in pursuit of his quest.

Earlier work on gendered forms of autobiography (M. Gergen, 1992; in press) indicates that in contrast to men's accounts, women's story lines are multiple, intermingled, ambivalent as to valence, and recursive. Whereas men's stories concentrate on the pursuit of single goals, most often career oriented, women's are more complex. Women's stories usually weave together themes of achievement, along with themes of family obligations, personal development, love lives, children's welfare, and friendship. Whereas men's stories are rarely revealing about emotional experiences, traumas, self-deprecation, self-doubt, and self-destructiveness, women's stories often express these aspects. Because of these multiple themes and self-expressions, the tone or movement of women's stories are never unidirectional, focused, or contained. Thus the content and the form of men's and women's autobiographies are distinct. The men's stories, however, exhibit the cardinal characteristics of the idealized form of autobiography. Women's forms are deviant.

Gendered Narratives of the Embodied Self

Although there are substantial differences in the narrative forms located in male as opposed to female autobiographies, our special interest is in a specific form of content, namely embodiment. As reasoned above, the body doesn't "speak for itself." Rather, as a culture, we invest it with meaning—giving it importance (or not), treating its changes as significant (or not), and elaborating these meanings in such a way that life satisfactions blossom or are obliterated. The question, then, is how these culturally acclaimed authors embody themselves over the life span. How do they define, elaborate, and give significance to their physical being? How do males and females differ in the model they provide for the experience and treatment of one's body through the life course?

To explore these issues we shall consider how famous men and women account for their bodies from their youth through adulthood and old age. A sample of autobiographies of 16 men and women published in the United States in the past 7 years will serve as the basis for this discussion. These books were chosen to reflect the range of autobiographies available in the popular market. This selection includes people who have accomplished noteworthy activities, and are not merely associated with or related to famous people. The authors of this sample do vary in age, primarily because many of them—in particular the athletes and performers—became famous in their youth. The male autobiographies include those of: Ansel Adams, John Paul Getty, Lee Iacocca, T. Boone Pickens, Ahmad Rashad, Donald Trump, Jr., Thomas Watson, Jr., and Chuck Yeager. The female autobiographers are Joan Baez, Sydney Biddle Barrows, Nien Cheng,[6] Linda Ellerbee, Gelsey Kirkland, Martina Navratilova, Joan Rivers, and Beverly Sills. Although the full complexity of these accounts cannot be conveyed in this chapter, illustrative quotations will allow dominant themes to become apparent.

BODILY INSCRIPTION FROM CHILDHOOD TO PUBERTY

Remarkable differences between men's and women's accounts of their bodies begin to emerge from their earliest reminiscences of childhood. Two facets of this difference deserve notice. First, men have very little to say about their physical beings, except to note how effective their bodies were in attaining their goals. Second, men display little affect when making these descriptions. Perhaps the time lag between event and reportage has stifled any sense of connectedness that once may have existed for the author, and/or the inclusion of any emotional reactions might seem inappropriate. In any case, the body is virtually an absent figure in their reminiscences. Women's stories tend to be far more embodied. Beginning with the early years, women include greater detail in the descriptions of the body, and they are often emotional in describing their embodied lives.

A typical example of the "indifferent" male author is Thomas J. Watson, Jr. (1990), powerful long-term boss of IBM. After looking at a homemade film of his first grade class in 1921, Watson (1990) reports only, "I'm the tallest, long boned and ungainly" (p. 4). More poignant to the reader, but apparently not to the owner, is photographer Ansel Adams's (1985) account of how he acquired his misshapen nose:

> On the day of the San Francisco earthquake [April 17, 1906] . . . I was exploring in the garden when my mother called me to breakfast and I came trotting. At that moment a severe aftershock hit and threw me off balance. I tumbled against a low brick garden wall, my nose making violent contact with quite a bloody effect. The nosebleed stopped after an hour, but my beauty was marred forever—the septum was thoroughly broken. When the family doctor could be reached, he advised that my nose be left alone until I matured; it could then be repaired with greater aesthetic quality. Apparently I never matured, as I have yet to see a surgeon about it. (pp. 7–8)

For Adams, the contorted nose that punctuated his face simply became irrelevant to his life.

For women, the physical tribulations of childhood are often felt strongly and deeply, sometimes for many years. Feelings of present day self-worth seem strongly conditioned by the physical nature of the person they were. For example, comedienne Joan Rivers (1986), now a Barbie-doll look-alike, has made a career out of comic references to her misbegotten self. As she describes a family photograph:

> When I make jokes . . . about being fat, people often think it is just my neurotic imagination. Well, on the right, with her mother and sister during a vacation trip to Williamsburg, Virginia, is the thirteen year-old fat pig, wishing she could teach her arms and hips to inhale and hold their breath. (p. 183)

Fat also plagued the prima ballerina, Gelsey Kirkland (1986). She describes her dancing debut at camp as a form of self-defense for her misshapen body: "The other children taunted me about the disproportions of my body. I never let them know how much I was stung by their disparagements . . . I turned my abdominal bulge to advantage by performing a belly dance to amuse those in my cabin" (p. 10). Tennis star Martina Navratilova (Navratilova and Vecsey 1985) had the reverse problem: being too small. "I was tiny, not an ounce of fat on me—nothing but muscle and bone— just sheer energy. In school I was kind of embarrassed about being so small, but on the tennis court it didn't really matter that much" (p. 24).

In terms of development over the life span, the impact of physiognomy for both boys and girls often turns on the extent to which its effects are intensified or altered in puberty. For men in contemporary Western culture, the adolescent challenge largely takes place within the arena of athletics. The body's abilities to measure up to the competition is all-important in athletics particularly. For these males, it is in this period that body and identity are more closely linked than at any other time in the life span. Chuck Yeager (Yeager and James 1985), the man with the "right stuff," looks back with pleasure: "By the time I reached high school, I excelled at anything that demanded dexterity . . . In sports, I was terrific at pool and pingpong, good in basketball and football" (p. 11). Having an athletic body also helped ease a racially tense social scene for footballer Ahmad Rashad (1988), as well as contributing to his self-esteem. "If you lived in my neighborhood, . . . you tended not to go to Eastside—they would kick your ass over there. Because of my brother and my athletic ability, the law of the street didn't apply to me" (p. 47). T. Boone Pickens, Jr. (1987), the billionaire "take-over" tycoon describes himself: "Fortunately, I was well coordinated . . . Only five feet nine inches tall, . . . but a basketball player" (p. 17). In effect, being short was a threat to adolescent identity; being coordinated was a fortunate compensation. Donald Trump (Trump and Schwark 1987), New York's bad-boy builder, avoids any physical description of himself as a youth, except to relate that he was physically aggressive, to the point of giving a music teacher a black eye when he was in second grade "because he didn't know anything" (p. 71).

Lee Iacocca (Iacocca and Novak 1984) turned the story of his youthful illness into gains in the realms of gambling and sex. "I came down with rheumatic fever. The first time I had a palpitation of the heart, I almost passed out—from fear. I thought my heart was popping out of my chest . . . But I was lucky. Although I lost about forty pounds and stayed in bed for six months, I eventually made a full recovery" (p. 16). While convalescing, he started playing poker and reading books. "All I could remember about the book [*Appointment in Samarra*] was that it got me interested in sex" (pp. 16–17).

An exception to the bravado and self-assuredness of the vast majority of autobiographers, Watson (1990) portrays himself as unathletic. "While I was skinny and taller than most other kids, I was no athlete. My eye-hand coordination was terrible, so I hated baseball." Late in his life he proves himself by going sailing in dangerous waters away from medical supports, in part to overcome his fears of dying following a heart attack. A theme of overcoming his bodily and psychological defects is a stronger undercurrent in his book than in others. His success in mastering himself is illustrated, however.

For the adolescent girl, character is not made so much on the playing fields as in private chambers. Because girls seem more fully identified with their bodies, bodily changes at puberty become an enormous issue for identity formation. It is as if the body, which seemed a reasonably stable and controllable aspect of the girlhood self, begins to undo one's identity in adolescence. Spontaneously, it can make one hideous or desirable, both of which are problematic shifts in identity. Unlike men, it is a rare woman whose personal narrative is not concentrated on the unsettlement of adolescent transformation. As Navratilova (Navratilova and Vecsey 1985) comments, "The girls started to fill out in the sixth or seventh grade, but I didn't wear a brassiere until I was fourteen—and God knows I didn't need one then. I was more than a little upset about developing so late" (p. 24). Later she gains in stature: "My new weight gave me some curves I never thought I'd have, and they gave me the idea that I was a full-grown woman at seventeen" (p. 122). Joan Baez (1987) described her entry into junior high school as marked by rejection, which stemmed from her physical appearance. Without much pathos she recounted her image: "Joanie Boney, an awkward stringbean, fifteen pounds underweight, my hair a bunch of black straw whacked off just below my ears, the hated cowlick on my hairline forcing a lock of bangs straight up over my right eye" (p. 30). In high school her self-evaluation echoed a degree of self-confidence, mixed with doubt: "On the one hand I thought I was pretty hot stuff, but on the other, I was still terribly self-conscious about my extremely flat chest and dark skin" (p. 43). Beverly Sills (Sills and Linderman 1987), the great opera singer and director of the New York City Opera, describes her anguish:

> I developed breasts earlier than any of my classmates, and that was a great source of anguish for me. I was already feeling tall and gawky, and when it became obvious in gym class that I was the only girl who needed a bra, I didn't just become miserable, I became *hysterical.* I was so unhappy with the sheer size of me that my mother bought me a garter belt, which was about seven inches wide, and I wore it around my chest. (p. 17)

As a more general surmise, through the period of childhood and adolescence, boys and girls develop dramatically different interpretations of their body. Boys describe their bodies as separated from self, and as more or less useful instruments to attain their will. Whereas the male's identity is alienated from physical form, females tend to define themselves in terms of their body. This tendency is congenial to the views of many object relations theorists who hold that daughters are much more strongly linked to their mothers' identities through the similarities of their bodies, but sons are taught that they are distinct and separate from their mothers. Boys must suppress their identification with their mothers and cleave to the unknown world of men outside the home (cf. Chodorow, 1978; Dinnerstein, 1977). To elaborate in the context of autobiography, it is possible that the distinctiveness that men acquire of self from mother becomes fulfilled in their alienation from their own bodies. That is, they echo their mother's actions in regarding their bodies as "other." In support of this complex relationship, theorist Jane Flax (1990) speculates that men desire the unity with the mothering figure that characterizes girl-mother relationships, and their rejection of the "female" in themselves and others [including their embodied natures] is a constant discipline required "to avoid memories of, longing for, suppressed identification with, or terror of the powerful mother of infancy."

She cites "a long line of philosophic strategies motivated by a need to evade, deny, or repress the importance of . . . mother-child relationships" (1990, p. 232).

THE ADULT YEARS: LIVING WITHIN AND BEYOND THE BODY

The tendency in narrative for men to distance themselves from their bodies intensifies in adulthood. The major plot in adult male autobiographies is focused on career development; these careers are typically defined independently from the body. The discourse of career tends toward the transcendent—emphasizing ideals, goals, values, and aspirations as opposed to organicity. The body, if mentioned at all, tends to be characterized as servant to the master's plans and purposes, whether for career or pleasure. For most of one's activities the body is simply taken for granted; it seems not to be a matter of particular interest or concern. Metaphorically, the body is considered a machine possession, and like one's automobile, its normal operation should enable one to get on with the real business of life. Only on occasion does the body enter the register of meaning, and that is when it serves as an asset or a liability to ends that lie beyond. Thus, as Yeager (Yeager and James 1985) describes, "Being in our early twenties, we were in good physical shape and at the height of our recuperative powers—which we had to be to survive those nights. That was our Golden Age of flying and fun. By the time we reached thirty, our bodies forced moderation on us" (p. 180). In effect, one simply goes on until the machine begins to break down. Watson (Watson and Petre 1990) describes an attempt to turn a disenabling threat into a career gain: "I developed a pain in my right side that turned out to be appendicitis. Getting operated on gave me a chance to postpone taking the exams by six weeks, so I was able to study and pass" (p. 47).

At times the male autobiographer is surprised to find the body makes a difference. Donald Trump (Trump and Schwark 1987), commenting on his early efforts to join a prestigious Manhattan club (with a lack of modesty about his body that is not found in women's autobiographics), is shocked to find his body is a consideration: "Because I was young and good-looking, and because some of the older members of the club were married to beautiful young women, [the officer of the club] was worried that I might be tempted to try to steal their wives" (p. 96). Having a good body can thus be a career impediment. It can also cause other troubles, especially for the man who takes too much pride in his athletic abilities. Consider J. P. Getty's (1986) attempt to pass himself off as a boxer. Enticing his friend Jack Dempsey to spar with him, he finds himself in difficulty in order to impress some young ladies:

> A few moments after we began to spar, I realized that Jack was pulling his punches. My *macho* was taking all the punishment, for there were two or three very attractive young women friends watching at ringside. I wanted not only to test my ability as a boxer but also to prove myself . . . "Damn it, Jack, treat me just as you would any professional sparring partner." . . . I swung my lefts and rights as hard as I could. Jack . . . moved back a pace or two.
>
> "Okay, Paul," he said, "If you insist . . ."
>
> The first punch was hard. Jack swung again—and connected. That was that . . . I picked myself up off the canvas, fully and finally convinced that I would thenceforth stick to the oil business. (pp. 276–7)

One might also note from this little tale that Getty was willing to subject his body to abuse in order to satisfy his "macho" needs.

Because the body as an asset is taken for granted—much like the beating of a heart—it is only its potential for failure that must be confronted. The male reaction is expressed in two major ways: *anxiety* and *denial*. Among autobiographers, overtly expressed fear of dysfunction is largely reserved to men whose career success is closely linked to physical condition. Thus Rashad (Rashad and Bodo 1988) comments:

> injuries are the ultimate reality for a pro athlete—they throw a shadow over your days . . . Football is like the army in that you know that a third of your men will become casualties. You just hope it isn't you that gets hit. Football is not just a job, it's an adventure—until it comes time to get killed. (pp. 118–19)

However, by far the more common reaction to the threat of dysfunction is denial. Again consider Rashad:

> On a pass play early in the game, Ferguson threw to me . . . As I caught the ball, cornerback Jimmy Marsalis undercut me, rolling with his full body weight on my left knee.
>
> The pain was excruciating, but the invulnerable Keed did the natural thing: I bounced up off the turf, pretending nothing was wrong. I didn't want to be hurt, and I insisted on walking it off. That provided the next real sign that something was wrong: I couldn't put my foot down . . . As the trainers came out, I insisted to them, "Nah, it ain't too bad. It'll be all right. There's nothing wrong with this baby." (p. 179)

A more dramatic illustration of defensiveness at work comes from Chuck Yeager's (Yeager and James 1985) account of his emergency exit from a crashing plane. Yeager's parachute caught on fire as he ejected himself from the cockpit. Upon hitting the ground, he wanders toward a passerby who has seen him land:

> My face was charred meat. I asked him if he had a knife. He took out a small penknife . . . and handed it to me. I said to him, "I've gotta do something about my hand. I can't stand it anymore." I used his knife to cut the rubber lined glove, and part of two burned fingers came out with it. The guy got sick. (p. 360)

Yeager himself registers no reaction.

Women's accounts of embodiment in the adult years stand in marked contrast to men's. The woman's sense of identity remains closely tied to her physical condition. It is not so much that the body is used instrumentally—as a means to some other end outside the body. Rather, to be in a certain bodily condition is to "be oneself." Consider the detail in which Joan Baez (1987) describes her bodily being as she readies herself for a major performance:

> I am in my room by two o'clock, tired, wired, and thinking about what to wear. I turn my suitcase upside down, littering the floor from wall to wall to get a good look at my entire out-of-date collection of rags and feathers. By three o'clock I have finally ironed a yellow parachute skirt and cobalt blue blouse, dug out the belt with the big silver circles and the necklace made of spoon ladies linked together,

and the nineteen-dollar black sandals bedecked with rhinestones. I spend an extra twenty minutes hunting down my half slip . . . They escort me to the green room. All the saliva in my mouth evaporates on the way. I have to go to the bathroom desperately, but it's too far and won't do any good anyway, so I sit tight, sip water, and ask Mary not to let anyone talk to me. (pp. 355–7)

This is not to say that women do not speak of using their bodies as instruments of achievement. For women, appearance constitutes an integral part of every story they tell and they are often keenly aware of shaping their bodies for ulterior ends. In the dramatic tale of survival in a Chinese detention prison during the era of the Cultural Revolution, Nien Cheng (1986) described the day her long ordeal with the Red Guard began. Two men from her company arrive unannounced at her home to take her to her "trial." She delayed going downstairs to have more time to think what she should do to preserve herself in this tense situation. She strives to create an impression of herself through her appearance. "I put on a white cotton shirt, a pair of gray slacks, and black sandals, the clothes Chinese women wore in public places to avoid being conspicuous . . . I walked slowly, deliberately creating the impression of composure" (p. 8). Effects of appearance on career goals continues to be especially relevant to women in the public eye. Comments by Linda Ellerbee (1986), a television journalist, are telling:

I was told to lose weight if I wished ever to anchor again at NBC News. I wonder if anyone's ever said that to Charles Kuralt . . . Regarding my hair—I have lots of hair—I've paid attention to commands to tie it back, bring it forward, put it up, take it down, cut it, let it grow, curl it, straighten it, tame it—and I stopped doing so before someone asked me to shave it off . . . Maybe I'd just gotten older, not mellower, or maybe I'd had it up to here with men telling me to do something about my hair. (p. 119)

Because women describe themselves as deeply embodied, they are more often candid than men about the discomforts and threats to their bodies. A typical example is furnished by Beverly Sills (Sills and Linderman 1987), as she describes her bout with ovarian

cancer at the age of 45: "I was lucky. I had a tumor the size of a grapefruit, but the doctor removed it entirely." Then she adds a gratuitous aside from a medical standpoint: "After my operation, I probably weighed about 125 pounds. I don't think I'd weighed 125 pounds since I was four years old" (p. 264). Returning to the stage very quickly, she mentions the pain she suffered. "To be blunt about it, I was in agony . . . the pain was almost unbelievable," but she did it anyway. "The plain truth is that if I had canceled, I would have worried that I was dying" (p. 267).

After her arrest and imprisonment, Nien Cheng (1986) minutely describes her experiences in prison as embodied ones of privation. Her description is rich with details of her bodily states, her illnesses, and her deteriorating condition: "After some time, hunger became a permanent state, no longer a sensation but an ever present hollowness. The flesh on my body slowly melted away, my eyesight deteriorated, and simple activities such as washing clothes exhausted my strength" (p. 185).

Given women's close identification with their bodies, it is also possible to appreciate why violations of the body are so unsettling for the woman: They represent invasive negations of one's identity. Consider Sydney Biddle Barrows's (Barrow and Novak 1986) account of how nude photos were taken of her and published in national newspapers. With a boyfriend in Amsterdam:

We went to the houseboat and sampled our new friend's excellent hashish. After a while, [the friend] tactfully disappeared, leaving us together in the shimmering afternoon sun . . . I was delighted to have him snap some shots of me in my skimpy summer clothes. Pretty soon, he started flattering me: I looked so terrific, the light was just right, so why didn't I take off my clothes and let him shoot some nude photographs? (p. 22)

Later when Barrows was arrested for running a high-class escort service, her former boyfriend sold the photos to the *New York Post*:

I was devastated. I could live with being called the Mayflower Madam, and I could even tolerate having my real name known. But now nude photographs of me were being splashed across two of the largest newspapers in the country! I couldn't believe that Rozansky had so shamelessly betrayed me, and I was disgusted that I had ever given him the time of day. (p. 290)

Other intimacies of the body were shared by Ellerbee (1986), who describes her illegal abortion:

> I'd been one of those women . . . who'd gotten pregnant, then gotten the name of someone through a friend of a friend, paid six hundred dollars cash, and waited, terrified, at my apartment until midnight when a pimply-faced man showed up, exchanged code words with me, and came in, bringing cutting tools, bandages and Sodium Pentothol—but no medical license I could see. I was lucky. I did not bleed uncontrollably. I did not die. I recovered. I was no longer pregnant. But I wasn't the same, either. No woman is. (p. 96)

From the standpoint of the unity of mind and body, it is also possible to understand why women's stories—and seldom men's—often contain instances of bodily alteration, mutilation, or destruction. When a woman is unhappy with her identity—feeling like a failure, wishing for a change in identity—the frequent result is some form of bodily obliteration. Ballerina Gelsey Kirkland (Kirkland and Lawrence 1986) described a period of despair: "I wanted to lose my identity . . . [at night, sleeping] I was able to dream my way into somebody else's body. I was no longer Gelsey" (p. 205). At another point, when she has lost her boyfriend, "I went through another round of cosmetic surgery. I had my earlobes snipped off. I had silicone injected into my ankles and lips" (p. 126). Joan Rivers (Rivers and Meryman 1986) turned such events into comedy:

> That winter, in fact, suicide become one of my options; a way to strike back at all the people who did not appreciate me, a way to make them pay attention and be sorry . . . I wanted to do something terrible to myself, expend my powerless rage on my body, so I went into the bathroom and with a pair of scissors crudely chopped off my hair. (p. 249)

Summing up the narratives of embodiment for the adult years, we find that the man's bodily self fades even more into the background as career interests expand. The career is typically tied to ideas and ideals, power and prestige, and not to corporality. In contrast, women typically remain wedded to their bodies regardless of their career interests and abilities. In their identification with their bodies, self and bodily activities are one.

EMBODIMENT IN THE LATTER YEARS

Because popular autobiographies tend to embrace the traditional criteria of the well-formed narrative,[7] their endings are extensions of that which proceeds. Especially for the male, the story line is a coherent one, with the writer describing early events in such a way that later outcomes are almost necessitated. Thus, in accounting for the body in the later years, much of the groundwork has already been laid. For the younger male autobiographer, the life account will be notable for its absence of body talk. Discursively, career success serves almost as an epiphany, enabling the male to achieve a state of the pure ideal. For males who do write from a more elderly position, however, matters are more complex. For here there are pervasive signs of what the culture defines as bodily deterioration. Issues of embodiment, then, begin to break through the seamless narrative of career advancement.

Three primary reactions tend to dominate the male autobiography. First, there is a *self-congratulatory* theme. If one's body has remained in reasonably good health, one may offer it (as separated from "I, myself") some form of adulation. Like a motorcar that has outlasted those of one's friends, one may feel proud to be the owner of the machine. This orientation flavors Getty's (1986) commentary on aging: "I am eighty-three. Cold, damp winters do bring on attacks of bronchitis . . . I can't lift weights or swim for hours or walk five miles at the brisk pace I did ten years ago . . . Luckily, I can afford the best medical care available" (p. 275). With a "touch" of the "chronic," Getty appears to revert to the earlier defensive posture.

Among those writers who are not so fortunate as Getty, two other orientations are taken toward the body. One is *begrudging admission* that one has a body, and that it must be given its due. This approach is taken by Chuck Yeager (Yeager and James 1985):

> My concession to aging is to take better care of myself than I did when I was younger . . . Nowadays, I hunt as much for the exercise . . . as for the sport . . .

I'm definitely not a rocking-chair type. I can't just sit around, watch television, drink beer, get fat, and fade out. (pp. 422–3)

This begrudging interruption of the heroic narrative is more dramatically illustrated in Ansel Adams's (1985) revelations of his chronic and increasingly disabling problems: "As I cleared the decks for future projects, I found an ever-present complicating factor: Health. My mind is as active as ever, but my body was falling farther and farther behind" (p. 365). (The reader may note that the "real" Adams is the mental form, and the body is a recalcitrant fellow-traveller who is lagging behind.) Adams (1985) describes his heart surgery (a triple bypass and valve replacement). "Without surgery I was fast reaching an embarrassing state of inactivity; I could not walk a hundred feet without the crippling symptoms of chest pains and shortness of breath" (p. 366). Yet, the sense of bodily infringement on the idealized masculine narrative is revealed in Adam's (Adams and Alinder 1985) description of recovery: "My only complaint was a pestiferous vertigo . . . In two months the vertigo vanished and I was able to drive the late Congressman Philip Burton to Big Sur for his first view of that marvelous region; he soon became one of the leaders in the fight for its preservation" (p. 366). Back to business as usual.

A third orientation to the aging body is often encountered in the male autobiography, essentially a *trauma of broken defenses*. Because of the ravages to the body in the later years, the picture of the self during the middle years—detached from natural anchors—can no longer be maintained. With the disruptive sense of being the victim of "a dirty trick," the male at last confronts the possibility of finitude. Watson's (Watson and Petre 1990) description of his heart attack is illustrative:

In mid-November, I was in my office and Jane Cahill, my executive assistant, started to come in the door. Then she stopped cold, because I had my head down on the desk, "Are you all right?" she asked.

"I'm fine. I'm tired."

That night I woke up with a pain in my chest. It wasn't very intense but it wouldn't go away. Olive was in the Caribbean with friends, so I drove myself to the emergency room at Greenwich Hospital . . . having a heart attack. (p. 392)

Employing the metaphor of the body as the serviceable machine, Watson also reveals his sense of vulnerability; "When you have a heart attack, you realize how fragile your body is. I felt that mine had let me down, damn near entirely, and for several months I had very volatile reactions to insignificant things" (p. 394).

It would be useful to make broad comparisons between older male autobiographies and those written by older women. Unfortunately, however, few women write popular autobiographies when they are past 60. For this genre of literature, women's reputations tend to result from achievements of the early years. Lifetimes that culminate in professional heroics are rarer for women than for men. For those older women who do contribute to the genre, the body continues to figure importantly in two ways. First, although one might anticipate a drawing away from bodily identification as it become more problematic, this does not seem to be the case with women. Instead, the writers continue to "live their bodies," in spite of the body's transformation. Beverly Sills's (Sills and Linderman 1987) account of her body's reaction to her chores in the management of the opera company after her retirement as a diva is illustrative: "I was working like a horse, my blood pressure was way up, and I was eating six meals a day . . . I came into my job as general director weighing 150 pounds; on June 16, 1984 when I visited the endocrinologist, I weighed 220 pounds" (p. 345)

There is a second theme located in the accounts of women, including those in later years, that is far more subtle in its manifestation, but pervasive and profound. Because the woman's body is so closely identified with the self, one's bodily relations with others essentially extend the self. In the same way that violations of the body are defacements of identity, so are investments of the body in others' modes of unifying self and other. Thus, in pondering the preceding years and the meaning of one's life, women are more given to thinking about their children, lovers, and parents—those with whom the body has been intimately shared—and others, such as friends, who are now part of oneself. Nien Cheng's (1986) autobiography is a continuous knitting of her life to her daughter's especially. After the memorial service for her daughter, killed by the Red Guard, she describes a night without sleep:

> Lying in the darkened room, I remembered the years that had gone by, and I saw my daughter in various stages of her growth from a chubby-cheeked baby ... to a beautiful young woman in Shanghai ... I blamed myself for her death because I had brought her back to Shanghai in 1949. (p. 495)

This recounting of significant connection is not wholly reserved for the old age, however. Even when the younger women think back on their lives, their ruminations tend to center on those related through extensions of the body. When Navratilova (Navratilova and Vecsey 1985) won the Wimbledon Championship, she expressed her first thoughts on winning as: "For the first time I was a Wimbledon champion, fulfilling the dream of my father many years before. . . . I felt I was on top of the world" (p. 190). Joan Baez (1987) writes an epilogue in which she describes her family and friends, those who have been important in her life. In the final pages she talks of going to a party in Paris with her son. When she returns home:

> Mom will have a fire going in the kitchen and perhaps a Brahms trio on the stereo. Gabe will fall into bed, and I will sit in front of the fire, dressed like a Spanish princess, telling Mom how the sun rose, piercing through the mist over the lake ... and how there was peace all around as the castle finally slept. (pp. 377–8)

For men, rumination about the significance of intimates plays but a minor role in their stories. When one is on the grand highway of monomyth, it is important to travel light. Thus Yeager and Getty, for example, speak only in passing of deaths and illnesses within the family; Trump describes himself, his family members, and his then wife, Ivana, as "rocks." The major exception to this general disregard is the father's death, which often receives considerable attention. The importance of the father's death can be traced to the threat it symbolizes to the male portrayal of invulnerability. Because one can see within the father's death the possibility of one's own finitude, added attention is needed to keeping the defenses strong. There is no male autobiographer who could write as Nien Cheng (1986), who is an old woman when she is

finally allowed to leave China. Leaving Shanghai harbor she continues to speak of bodily sensations, the feeling of the heavy rain, her lack of umbrella or raincoat, her "staggering up the slippery gangway," the "wind whipping my hair while I watched the coastline of China receding." She ponders her daughter's fate. "I felt guilty for being the one who was alive. I wished it were Meiping standing on the deck of this ship, going away to make a new life for herself" (pp. 534–5).

EMBODIED SELVES OVER THE LIFE SPAN

The popular autobiography is both a repository of cultural meanings and a model for future lives. As the present analysis indicates, autobiographical stories differ dramatically in the meanings they impart to the male as opposed to the female body over the life span. The male autobiographer suggests that the man should be "above bodily concerns," more invested in culture than nature, in rationalities and values as opposed to the corporal.[8] To be fixed on one's body would be unmanly, narcissistic, and perhaps effeminate. To put matters of corporality aside is also highly functional for the male in terms of career. More hours can be devoted to achievement, and with fewer complaints. It is only in the later years that the male autobiographer admits an important relationship between self and body, and it is often an admission of shock, fear, and sorrow. The grand story is being brought to a close by a secret villain, and that villain dwells within.

Female autobiographers present a life story in which body and self are more unified. To be a woman is to be embodied; to fail in attending to one's corporality would be to ignore the cultural codes of being. Bodies serve a more central role in women's lives and consciousness than they seem to in men's. As Adrienne Rich (1977) has put it: "I know no woman—virgin, mother, lesbian, married, celibate—whether she earns her keep as a housewife, a cocktail waitress, or a scanner of brain waves—for whom her body is not a fundamental problem" (p. 14). This embodiment lends itself to a far greater sense of unity with others—particularly with those who have shared the flesh. To be embodied in this way is thus to be in significant relationship with others. At the same time, the discourse of embodiment sets the stage for deep unsettlement during puberty, for self-mutilation during periods of disappointment, and for a more profound sense of aging in the later years.

Inevitably an analysis such as this raises questions of the cultural good. For if one lives the life course within frameworks of meaning, and these meanings invite and constrain, celebrate and suppress, then one may ask whether it might be otherwise. If we could alter the forms of meaning—whether in autobiography or elsewhere—should we do so? From the female standpoint, there is much to reject in the male version of life and the practices that they favor. The male life course seems a strange "out of body" experience, one that devalues potentially significant aspects of human life. For the male, the female's mode of indexing life seems often irrelevant to the tasks at hand, and lends itself to emotional instability. However, rather than conceptualizing themselves as participants in "the longest war," perhaps both genders might benefit from new syntheses that would expand life story options for all. At the same time, however, further attention is needed to the cultural patterns in which these discourses are embedded. So long as the power relationships between men and women appear to favor the male version of reality and value, so long as the workplace makes little allowance for embodied selves, and so long as relationships are treated in a utilitarian manner, new stories might not be able to survive. Yet, one might hope that within dialogues, through reciprocal and reflexive endeavors, and via political and social changes, new stories might encourage new practices and prospects—and we might hope that embodied stories would be available to all (see K. Gergen, in press).

NOTES

1. For further discussion of meaning as discursive rather than psychological, see Gergen (1991).

2. See Bakhtin's (1981) concept of *heteroglossia.*

3. For more extended accounts of the mutual management of meaning, see Pearce and Cronen, 1980.

4. See also Bruss (1980), Rabuzzi (1988), Russ (1972), Sprinker (1980), and White (1978).

5. See Frye (1957) and Rich (1977).

6. Nien Cheng's (1986) autobiography, *Life and Death in Shanghai,* is exceptional within this group because she was not well known before her book was published, and she did not write with the help of a professional writer. Her volume was selected for inclusion in this sample because it was a best-seller and, in addition, she was a businesswoman and an older woman author. These characteristics are difficult to find in best-selling autobiographies by women.

7. See Gergen and Gergen (1983, 1988) for further discussion of these criteria.

8. It should be emphasized that the subject of concern here is how embodiment is described in autobiographies. It is possible that in private spheres men express their embodiment much as women do in print. This possibility remains to be explored.

REFERENCES
Autobiographical

Adams, Ansel, with Mary Street Alinder. (1985). *Ansel Adams. An autobiography.* Boston: Little, Brown.

Baez, Joan. (1987). *And a voice to sing with: A memoir.* New York: New American Library.

Barrows, Sydney Biddle, with William Novak. (1986). *Mayflower madam.* New York: Arbor House; London: MacDonald.

Cheng, Nien. (1986). *Life and death in Shanghai.* New York: Penguin.

Ellerbee, Linda. (1986). *And so it goes: Adventures in television.* New York: Berkley Books.

Getty, J. Paul. (1986). *As I see it: An autobiography of J. Paul Getty.* New York: Berkley. (Original work published 1976).

Iacocca, Lee, with William Novak. (1984). *Iacocca. An autobiography.* New York: Bantam Books.

Kirkland, Gelsey, with Greg Lawrence. (1986). *Dancing on my grave.* Garden City, NY: Doubleday.

Navratilova, Martina, with George Vecsey. (1985). *Martina.* New York: Fawcett Crest.

Pickens, T. Boone, Jr. (1987). *Boone.* Boston: Houghton Mifflin.

Rashad, Ahmad, with Peter Bodo. (1988). *Rashad.* New York: Penguin.

Rivers, Joan, with Richard Meryman. (1986). *Enter talking.* New York: Delacorte.

Sills, Beverly, and Lawrence Linderman. (1987). *Beverly.* New York: Bantam Books.

Trump, Donald, with Tony Schwark. (1987). *Trump: The art of the deal.* New York: Warner Books.

Watson, Thomas J., Jr., and Petre, Peter. (1990). *Father son & co. My life at IBM and beyond.* New York: Bantam Books.

Yeager, Chuck, and Leo James. (1985). *Yeager, an autobiography.* New York: Bantam Books.

General

Bakhtin, Mikhail. (1981). *The dialogical imagination: Four essays* (Michael Holquist, ed.). Austin: University of Texas Press.

Bruner, Jerome. (1986). *Actual minds, possible worlds.* Cambridge: Harvard University Press.

Bruss, Elizabeth W. (1980). Eye for I: Making and unmaking autobiography in film. In J. Olney (ed.), *Autobiography: Essays, theoretical and critical.* Princeton, NJ: Princeton University Press.

Campbell, Joseph. (1956). *Hero with a thousand faces.* New York: Bollingen. (original work published 1949).

Chodorow, Nancy. (1978). *The reproduction of mothering: Psychoanalysis and the sociology of gender.* Berkeley: University of California Press.

de Man, Paul. (1979). Autobiography as de-facement. *Modern Language Notes, 94,* 920.

Dinnerstein, Dorothy. (1977). *The mermaid and the minotaur: Sexual arrangements and the human malaise.* New York: Harper & Row.

Eakin, Paul John. (1985). *Fictions in autobiography: Studies in the art of self-invention.* Princeton, NJ: Princeton University Press.

Flax, Jane. (1990). *Thinking fragments.* Berkeley: University of California Press.

Frye, Northrup. (1957). *Anatomy of criticism: Four essays.* Princeton, NJ: Princeton University Press.

Gergen, Kenneth J. (1991). *The saturated self.* New York: Basic Books.

Gergen, Kenneth J. (in press). *Social construction: Critique and re-creation in the postmodern community.* Chicago: University of Chicago Press.

Gergen, Kenneth J., and Gergen, Mary M. (1983). Narrative of the self. In T. Sarbin and K. Schiebe (eds.), *Studies in social identity.* New York: Praeger.

Gergen, Kenneth J., and Gergen, Mary M. (1988). Narrative and the self as relationship. In L. Berkowitz (ed.), *Advances in experimental social psychology* (Vol. 21). San Diego, CA: Academic Press.

Gergen, Mary M. (1992). Life stories: Pieces of a dream. In G. Rosenwald and R. Ochberg (eds.), *Telling lives.* New Haven, CT: Yale University Press.

Gergen, Mary M. (in press). The social construction of personal histories: Gendered lives in popular autobiographies. In T.

Sarbin and J. Kitsuke (eds.), *Constructing the social.* London: Sage.

Jelinek, Estelle C. (1980). *Women's autobiography. Essays in criticism.* Bloomington: Indiana University Press.

Lejeune, Philippe. (1975). *Le pacte autobiographique.* Paris: Seull.

Maccoby, Eleanor, and Jacklin, Carol. (1974). *The psychology of sex differences.* Stanford, CA: Stanford University Press.

Mason, Mary G. (1980). Autobiographies of women writers. In J. Olney (ed.), *Autobiography. Essays theoretical and critical.* Princeton, NJ: Princeton University Press.

Money, John, and Ehrhardt, A. A. (1972). *Man & woman. Boy & girl.* Baltimore, MD: Johns Hopkins University Press.

Olney, James. (1980). *Autobiography. Essays theoretical and critical.* Princeton, NJ: Princeton University Press.

Pascal, Roy. (1960). *Design and truth in autobiography.* Cambridge, MA: Harvard University Press.

Pearce, W. Barnett, and Cronen, Vern. (1980). *Communication, action, and meaning.* New York: Praeger.

Rabuzzi, Kathryn Allen. (1988). *Motherself. A mythic analysis of motherhood.* Bloomington: Indiana University Press.

Rich, Adrienne. (1977). *Of woman born: Motherhood as experience and institution.* New York: Norton.

Russ, Joanna. (1972). What can a heroine do? Or why women can't write. In S. Koppelman Cornillon (ed.), *Images of women in fiction.* Bowling Green, OH: Bowling Green University Popular Press.

Sprinker, Michael. (1980). Fictions of the self: The end of autobiography. In J. Olney (ed.), *Autobiography: Essays theoretical and critical.* Princeton, NJ: Princeton University Press.

Steier, Frederick. (ed.). (1991). *Method and reflexivity: Knowing as systemic social construction.* London: Sage.

Stone, Albert E. (1982). *Autobiographical occasions and original acts. Versions of American identity from Henry Adams to Nate Shaw.* Philadelphia: University of Pennsylvania Press.

Weintraub, Karl J. (1978). *The value of the individual: Self and circumstance in autobiography.* New York: Random House.

White, Hayden. (1978). *The tropics of discourse.* Baltimore, MD: Johns Hopkins University Press.

WHO DO I LOOK LIKE?

28

Gaining a Sense of Self-Authenticity Through the Physical Reflections of Others

Karen March

Until recently, the majority of adoptions in North America involved a legal contract that sealed all adoption records, severed all biological family ties, and limited the amount of biological background information released to adoptees and their families (Garber 1985; Sachdev 1989). Increasingly, these adult adoptees are seeking contact with birth relatives (Wegar 1997). Search behavior emerges from adoptees' sense of personal fragmentation at being unable to integrate their biological backgrounds as a part of self (March 1995; Pacheco and Eme 1993; Sachdev 1992). Many adoptees have expressed this sense of disunity in the question, Who do I look like? (Anderson 1989). For searching adoptees, answering this question requires face-to-face contact with biological relatives who physically resemble them.

In this article I examine the association between search and contact outcome and physical self. For the purpose of this analysis, I define physical self as the image one has of self as a single entity with distinguishable physical traits. Drawing on a symbolic interactionist analytic framework, I define self as a social process formed in interaction with others. Secrecy in adoption highlights the significance of biological background for self because it denies adoptees access to personal information that others in their society readily possess. The question, Who do I look like? illustrates the importance of this knowledge for physical self because it draws attention to the body and the need to account for the source of one's physical traits.

Lack of biological background information means not being able to place self in the social context expected by others. It also means not being able to envision self as a single entity with distinguishable physical traits. Searching adoptees express a sense of incompleteness from not knowing the source of their physical characteristics. This sense of incompleteness creates personal doubt about their bodily perceptions. Part of adoptees' desire for contact derives from the need to remove these doubts by meeting biological relatives who match them physically. In this way, their search represents an attempt to access the biological template used by others in developing a sense of physical self.

By removing the biological source of their bodily self-reference, secrecy also removes the adoptees' ability to place self within the genealogical talk used to establish family membership and intergenerational continuity. Consequently, adoptees cannot locate their position in a unique group of physical beings endowed with a distinct genetic heritage and culture. Because the body carries the characteristics representing this position, it becomes a symbol of the "unknown." Thus, searching adoptees express a sense of alienation from their physical bodies and the genetic heritage that they represent. They experience a sense of disunity of self because they cannot integrate their biological background information as a part of self.

Contact with biological relatives removes the barriers of secrecy and verifies the adoptees' source of self as a physical being belonging to a distinct group of other physical beings. Of particular interest in this article is adoptees' view that their bodily perceptions are validated by face-to-face contact with biological relatives who physically resemble them. This contact eliminates the sense of alienation produced by their own bodies and their sense of uncertainty over physical self. However, adoptees do not passively accept the attributes assigned to them. Rather, as social actors, they assess and interpret the significance of each physical characteristic before ascribing it to their own bodies. Change in physical self therefore depends on the symbolic meaning attached to these physical characteristics and the adoptees' previous image of self as a single entity with distinguishable physical traits.

Despite the variation in contact outcome, adoptees experience a sense of self-completion from contact. This unity of self emerges from their sense of having merged their biological background as a part of self. Furthermore, by establishing their genetic heritage and intergenerational position, contact places adoptees in the biological family context valued by their society. This genealogical placement produces a sense of self-authenticity, that is, a feeling that their image of self is genuine and can no longer be held in question. Face-to-face contact with biological relatives who physically resemble them provides additional validation of their genetic heritage.

Thus, physical matching sustains self-image and reinforces the sense of self-authenticity created by integrating biological background as a part of self. This physical matching locates adoptees in a biological family and anchors their position within generations. From this perspective, the search and contact accounts presented in this article provide a useful set of conditions for examining the relationships existing among the physical body, the self, and the reflected appraisals of others.

METHODOLOGY

Much of the data for this article stem from a larger study conducted on adoptee searching behavior and birth mother contact (March 1995). That study consisted of fifteen months of participant observation with two self-help search groups in Ontario, Canada, and in-depth interviews with sixty adoptees, seven birth parents, and four adoptive mothers. To enhance my understanding of the contact process, I also attended public meetings on proposed changes to adoption legislation, examined the search and contact literature, followed two adoptees through their search, and read autobiographies of searching adoptees (Fisher 1973; Lifton 1979; Redmond and Sleightholm 1982). Since that time I have gathered data on a postcontact support group of adoptees, birth parents, and adoptive parents.

I still read the most current search and contact literature, follow media coverage of legislative changes in the release of adoption information, and sporadically attend meetings with a self-help search group in my community. Close friendships with three reunited adoptees, one adoptive mother, and two birth mothers keep me aware of the issues involved in long-term contact outcome.

FRAMEWORKS OF ENVISIONING SELF

The adoptees in this study perceived themselves as occupying a secondary position in a society and culture that defines them as Other (March 1995). This sense of being Other was based on their status as nonbiological family members in a society and culture where biological kinship is paramount (Miall 1996; Wegar 1997). Also, secrecy in adoption had denied them access to the information used by others in society to designate biological heritage. Envisioning their bodies from this dominant perspective, their sense of physical self was socially constructed around a "lack." To quote one searcher:

> You feel kind of empty. There's part of you missing. Like, every time you look in the mirror, you think, there's someone out there. Someone I'm related to. Who I must resemble. My eyes, my nose, my shape. Whose are they really? I couldn't picture myself. I felt blank. (Female, age 29)

This quote demonstrates the difficulty that adoptees encountered in forming an image of self as a separate being with identifiable physical traits. Because their body had a material base, they could contrast its morphology with other objects in their environment and create a partial sense of physical self. Thus, when looking in the mirror, the woman quoted above perceived "my eyes, my nose, my shape." At the same time, she knows that her physical characteristics have an unknown biological source. Judging self from the perspective of the majority raised in a biological family structure, she questioned the origin of her physical traits.

In this way, the missing information produced by adoption became internalized as missing parts of physical self. Consequently, when visualizing self as a single entity, these adoptees experienced gaps in their identification and recognition of particular aspects of their bodies, that is, a sense of incompleteness in physical self. They described this sense of incompleteness as a feeling of being "blank," "empty," "with parts missing."

Constrained by this sense of incompleteness, the adoptees in this study developed personal doubt about the appropriateness of their physical characteristics. Using the gaze of others as the basis of their bodily self-reference, they engaged their adoptive status in the self-body dialogue involved in objectifying their own bodies. Thus, in contemplating her face in the mirror, the woman quoted above did not merely see a pair of eyes; she saw a pair of eyes belonging to an unknown biological relative. Since she could not evaluate the appearance of this unknown other, she believed she could not adequately assess her own physical traits. Similarly, the adoptees in this study reported a lack of trust in their bodily evaluations. That distrust undermined their confidence in their bodily perceptions. For this reason, they reported experiencing uncertainty over physical self, that is, a sense of not possessing an acceptable image of self as a single entity with distinguishable physical traits. As discussed in the following section, that sense of uncertainty was reinforced by their inability to identify themselves as complete members of their adoptive families.

FAMILY IDENTIFICATION AS A FRAMEWORK OF LOOKING

The importance of blood kinship is learned as an adopted child comes to understand the social implications of being adopted (Wegar 1997). For the adoptees in this study, such understanding emerged through "table talk." According to Peters (1993), table talk involves social interactions in which children are designated as possessing family traits matching those of other family members. Over time, after hearing such messages consistently repeated, children internalize the biological inheritances assigned to them. They come to perceive themselves as strong or weak, short or tall, handsome or pretty, that is, as being similar to the family member with whom they have been matched. Through table talk, children acquire family identification and develop a sense of self as represen-

tatives of both past and future generations (Mykhalovskiy 1997; Peters 1993).

The adoptees in this study experienced a comparable process of table talk in which others were identified as possessing inherited family traits. Typically, they were excluded from those interactions because they lacked the required biological kinship ties. As much of the content of table talk focuses on the physical similarity between biological family members, this exclusion reaffirmed their sense of having no bodily self-reference. They could not internalize their adoptive family's traits as a part of self and had been denied the opportunity to internalize those attributed to their biological family. Thus, one woman (age 35) said her search was motivated by wanting to know who she looked like.

> You come into a room, or you're sitting there, and they talk about how so and so looks like Uncle Jim. They ignore you. Or they notice you and stop talking. Or they change the subject. It makes you want something that is biologically yours. I never grew up feeling insecure or anything. But it was just a piece that was missing. Like, you hear all the kids talking at school about their cousins and you talk about yours but you also know that those people aren't your cousins. Not really! You feel a bit on the outside. I felt phony.

Another woman (age 28) remarked:

> I remember when I was little and people would come in and say, "He looks like X and she looks like Y and who do you look like?" My mother told me to say that I look like myself. I would say it. But it was hard. You want to look like someone because everyone else does.

In the context of table talk, the question Who do I look like? signifies much more than curiosity over the unknown source of one's physical traits. This question is deeply interwoven with other questions concerning family membership, intergenerational continuity, social acceptability, and personal identity. The adoptees in this study perceived table talk as reaffirming their perception of self as Other and reinforcing their adoptive status as a person possessing an unknown biological background. Of particular note, they perceived table talk as identifying them as belonging elsewhere—to a different family, separate from the adoptive family in which they were raised. For this reason, adoptees who had been "physically matched" (Feigleman and Silverman 1984) with their adoptive families also claimed:

> People would say, "You look like your mother, or you look like your father." It bothers me because I know that it's not right. I can't look like them. Because I'm not part of them. I love them and everything. I just don't belong to them. I guess that the biological means a lot to me. My parents have done nothing wrong. But my mom told me that I started asking questions when I was five. Like about my background and where I really came from. (Female, age 21)

The heavy concentration in table talk on biological inheritance and biological matching intensified the sense of incompleteness and uncertainty over physical self that the adoptees in this study reported. More important, it exposed the most obvious factor distinguishing them as Other. Through table talk these adoptees learned the significance of biological family membership as a way of placing and evaluating self as a physical being. From this perspective their body acquired additional symbolic meaning. It did not belong entirely to them. Rather, it stemmed from an unknown biological source possessing a separate genetic heritage than their adoptive family. Furthermore, this biological source represented their connection to past, present, and future generations of unique physical beings. Adoption had severed their position within this intergenerational family structure. Thus, when explaining their need to search, these adoptees noted a disunity of self, that is, a sense of being disconnected from the source of self as a physical being. They described this sense of disunity as a feeling of "being ungrounded," "lacking roots" or "being unreal." To quote one man (age 30):

> My search represented a need for a biological connection. I felt a vacuum there because I was unrelated to people. I didn't have any ties or connections to anyone. My adoptive parents. Even my wife and children. It's different somehow. I wanted an anchor. To connect me. Make me real. I'm much more peaceful now. In the sense that before there were a lot of unknowns. I tended to fill those unknowns with a lot of negatives. Finding them removed that. It gave me roots.

Because their bodies carried the physical characteristics representing that source, this sense of disunity confounded physical self. These adoptees could not effectively imagine self as a single entity with distinguishable physical traits because they could not visualize the source of those physical traits.

GAINING A NEW FRAMEWORK OF LOOKING

Like other searchers, the adoptees in this study experienced a sense of completion from a "filling in the gaps" created by secrecy in adoption (Pacheco and Eme 1993; Sachdev 1992; Wegar 1997). Significantly, they associated this sense of completion with being able to see their physical characteristics reflected in biological relatives. For example, in describing her first face-to-face contact experience with her birth mother, one woman (age 42) said:

> When I saw her, I knew that I belonged to her. Like, when the social worker was talking to me on the telephone, she asked me to describe myself and I said, "Small, thin, dark-haired, a big nose." One of the first things my birth mother said to me was, "What do you mean a big nose?" I looked at her. My nose was exactly the same as hers. I immediately said, "It doesn't seem big now." And I felt it! I really felt beautiful inside. And her hand movements are just like mine. It's incredible! She looks so much like me. For instance, I have these bushy eyebrows. Before I went to meet her, I plucked them so they wouldn't look so bad. But when I saw her, she had the same eyebrows. I started to laugh and I told her, "You have the same eyebrows. But they look okay on you." It was like I didn't have to worry anymore. She looked okay. Everything looks fine on her. So now I know it looks fine on me. I really feel beautiful now. Complete. (Female, age 42)

This woman gained a stronger perception and acceptance of her own body in seeing similar physical traits in the form of a biological relative. The other adoptees in this study described similar effects from face-to-face contact. It was therefore common to hear such phrases as, "I feel more comfortable with my body now," or "I know I look okay now" in their accounts of contact outcome.

A small number of adoptees reported emotional

distress at what they perceived as "unattractive" features. For example, one woman (age 24) observed:

> I've always had to fight my weight. Now I know why. I never want to look like her. She's so heavy. I was really upset for a while. But, seeing her, it just made me more determined in my fight against my own weight.

In contrast, a woman (age 39) who encountered a comparable reflection remarked:

> When she came through the door, she had to squeeze by me. I laughed. Because I have been dieting all of my life. I realize now that it isn't my fault. I come from a background of people who are built like that. It's no longer a personal failing. I mean I still try to keep my weight down, but I don't get so upset about it as I used to.

These examples reveal a continuum of satisfaction with contact based on the types of physical reflections perceived, how the adoptee viewed self being portrayed in those reflections, and the meaning attached to those bodily characteristics. Although contact gave these adoptees a stronger sense of certainty over physical self, it did not produce a radical change in their bodily perceptions. They had developed a sense of physical self through a comparison of their own body morphology with other objects in their environment and through previous self-body dialogues. Drawing on those experiences, their biography became a resource in helping them to internalize the reflected images of biological relatives in a way that fit with this previous sense of physical self. Thus, one woman expressed relief over her birth mother's weight while the other became upset.

Secrecy in adoption had created the adoptees' sense of incompleteness and uncertainty over physical self. By eliminating the secrecy, the adoptees were able to gain access to their genetic heritage and their source of self as a physical being. Contact also removed the restrictions placed on the self-body dialogue by not knowing this information. For these reasons, the adoptees reported a change in self from contact. They had replaced their sense of disunity of self with a sense of self-completion or a unity of self. This unity of self stemmed from their sense of having merged their biological background information with their image of self as a single entity with distinguishable physical traits. The adoptees described it as a feeling of "being whole now," "being complete," or "having finally put all of the puzzle pieces together."

Adoptees who received biological background information from a third party or through pictures and film clips experienced a more limited sense of self-completion. In addition, those who noted little physical similarity between themselves and their birth mother, or members of her family, expressed less certainty over physical self. Often, these adoptees sought contact with the birth father and his family as a way of fulfilling this need. To quote one woman (age 44) who found her birth mother deceased:

> She didn't have any other children, so I couldn't meet them. And the rest of her family didn't know about me, so I never contacted them. Her husband sent pictures and told me as much about her as he could. So it filled in some of the gaps. Her physical appearance surprised me because I couldn't see that she looked a lot like me. But they are only pictures. Maybe if I had met her I would be able to see more. Like, her shape isn't like mine. It's more like my daughter's. But her mannerisms. They are a lot alike in families too. I'm trying to find my birth father now. Maybe he can give me some of that.

The process of biological matching carries symbolic meaning. It validates the source of self as a physical being. Furthermore, biological matching substantiates one's unrivaled position within an intergenerational group of physical beings possessing unique characteristics. Adoptees who saw physical similarities between birth relatives and self could place themselves more effectively in the biological context valued by their society. Adoptees who perceived little physical similarity had more difficulty recognizing their genetic heritage and acknowledging their position in the biological family structure. Consequently, when describing the effects of contact outcome, adoptees who experienced biological matching reported, "I knew immediately I belonged there," "I felt real for the first time," or "It made me feel connected." In contrast, adoptees such as the woman who had found out that her birth mother was deceased noted a less dramatic effect and sought other biological counterparts who might provide a stronger intergenerational connection.

Despite contact outcome, the adoptees in this study claimed a sense of authenticity of self by removing the secrecy surrounding their biological background. This sense of authenticity was characterized by a belief that their image of self was genuine and could no longer be held in question. These adoptees had identified the source of self as a physical being and established their place in the biological family context demanded by their society. They had changed their status as a person with an unknown biological background into a person who could claim access to that part of self. This change validated their image of self as a single entity possessing distinguishable physical traits. This change gave adoptees the sense of authenticity of self denied to them by secrecy in adoption.

CONCLUSION

The accounts of search and contact presented in this study support the interest raised in the symbolic interactionist literature about the relationship between the body and the self (Charmaz 1999; Denzin 1984; Gagne and Tewksbury 1999; McCarthy 1989; Olesen 1992). Accepting the cultural standard of biological kinship as paramount, these searching adoptees experienced distrust in their images of self because they lacked the biological template used by their society to support those images. The social meanings attached to their bodily traits made contact imperative for them because it provided access to these hidden parts of self. In this sense, their need to see their physical characteristics reflected in the form of biological relatives highlights the significance of physical appearance for self and the symbolic value assigned to the body and its physical characteristics.

ACKNOWLEDGMENTS

I would like to acknowledge Kathy Charmaz and Virginia Olesen for comments made on earlier drafts of this article. Their dedication to sound scholarship has enhanced both my present analysis and my future intellectual growth. I cannot thank them enough.

Direct all correspondence to Karen March, Department of Sociology and Anthropology, Carleton University, Loeb B744, Ottawa, Ontario, Canada K1S 5B6; *e-mail:* kmarch@ccs.carleton.ca.

REFERENCES

Anderson, Robert A. 1989. "The Nature of Adoptee Search: Adventure, Cure or Growth?" *Child Welfare* 68:623–32.

Charmaz, Kathy. 1999. "The Body, Identity and Self: Adapting to Impairment." Pp. 95–112 in *Health, Illness and Healing: Society, Social Context and Self,* edited by K. Charmaz and D.A. Paterniti. Los Angeles: Roxbury.

Denzin, Norman K. 1984. "On Understanding Emotion: The Interpretive-Cultural Agenda." Pp. 85–116 in *Research Agendas in the Study of Emotions,* edited by T.D. Kemper. New York: State University of New York Press.

Feigleman, William and Arnold R. Silverman. 1984. *Chosen Children: New Patterns of Adoption Relationships.* New York: Praeger.

Fisher, Florence. 1973. *The Search for Anna Fisher.* New York: Arthur Fields.

Gagne, Patricia and Richard Tewksbury. 1999. "Knowledge and Power, Body and Self: An Analysis of Knowledge Systems and the Transgendered Self." *Sociological Quarterly* 40:59–83.

Garber, Ralph. 1985. *Disclosure of Adoption Information.* Report to the Honourable John Sweeney, Minister of Community and Social Services, Government of Ontario.

Lifton, Betty Jean. 1979. *Lost and Found: The Adoption Experience.* New York: Dial Press.

March, Karen. 1995. *The Stranger Who Bore Me: Adoptee-Birth Mother Interactions.* Toronto: University of Toronto Press.

McCarthy, E. Doyle. 1989. "Emotions Are Social Things: An Essay in the Sociology of Emotions." Pp. 51–72 in *The Sociology of Emotions: Original Essays and Research Papers,* edited by D.D. Franks and E.D. McCarthy. Greenwich, Connecticut: JAI.

Miall, Charlene. 1996. "The Social Construction of Adoption: Clinical and Community Perspectives." *Family Relations* 45:309–17.

Mykhalovskiy, Eric. 1997. "Reconsidering 'Table Talk': Critical Thoughts on the Relationship between Sociology, Autobiography, and Self-Indulgence." Pp. 229–51 in *Reflexivity and Voice,* edited by R. Hertz. Thousand Oaks, CA: Sage.

Olesen, Virginia. 1992. "Extraordinary Events and Mundane Ailments: The Contextual Dialectics of the Embodied Self." Pp. 205–20 in *Investigating Subjectivity: Research on Lived Experience,* edited by C. Ellis and M.G. Flaherty. Newbury Park, CA: Sage.

Pacheco, Frances and Robert Eme. 1993. "An Outcome Study of the Reunion between Adoptees and Biological Parents." *Child Welfare* 72:53–64.

Peters, Eric. 1993. "Table Talk." Pp. 77–90 in *Men and Masculinities: A Critical Anthology,* edited by T. Haddad. Toronto: Canadian Scholar's Press.

Redmond, Wendy and Sherry Sleightholm. 1982. *Once Removed: Voices from Inside the Adoption Triangle.* Toronto: McGraw-Hill Ryerson.

Sachdev, Paul. 1989. *Unlocking the Adoption Files.* Lexington, MA: Lexington Books.

———. 1992. "Adoption Reunion and After: A Study of the Search Process and Experience of Adoptees." *Child Welfare* 71:53–68.

Wegar, Katarina. 1997. *Adoption, Identity and Kinship: The Debate over Sealed Birth Records.* New Haven: Yale University Press.

"I HATE MY VOICE"

29 | Coming to Terms with Minor Bodily Stigmas

Carolyn Ellis

"I hate my voice," the clerk says, spitting out the word "hate." As I leave the store, his words reverberate inside my body, enter my consciousness, and only now, many months later, find their way out onto these pages. I hate my voice too, but I never have said so to anyone.

The words uttered by this clerk have moved me to write about hating my voice as an example of "minor bodily stigmas," those small physical imperfections that make us fear we stand out and might be rejected. While often evident to others, minor bodily stigmas rarely are severe enough to become the focus of attention or to interrupt social interaction. Nonetheless, minor body stigmas often are "interiorized" to such a degree that they produce distress and anxiety regarding how others perceive and attribute meanings to them and how these characteristics influence self-presentation, social location, and subsequent action. I begin with the story of the shopping excursion that initially raised these issues to my consciousness.

My partner Art abruptly makes a ninety-degree turn into a small Greenwich Village store. I follow him into a kaleidoscope of colored handbags propped in layers on every shelf, hanging side by side on walls, and dangling like mobiles from the ceiling. My hand affectionately pats the functional bag I have carried on my shoulder for more than a decade.

A small board of earrings off to the side immediately catches my eye. You see, I have a harmless earring fetish, aptly demonstrated by the numerous pairs occupying every inch of spare space in my bathroom—on cork boards, pegs, wicker shelves, even decorating the top of the toilet tank. For me, earrings signify frivolity and lightness in a life that often threatens to become overly serious. Earrings decorate and let me play with my surface identity, yet ironically do not violate my feminist consciousness that eschews other decorations such as makeup and high-heeled shoes.

Since a petite woman stands in front of the earring display, I reluctantly turn back to the pocketbooks. "These are nice," I say with mild enthusiasm to my partner Art, who closely examines the various styles.

"These are all hand-made, tanned, and designed. Real leather," the handsome, middle-aged, African American clerk says quietly in a melodic voice as he passes by and disappears into a back room. His graceful, flowing stride matches his soft, rhythmic voice.

Although the clerk's words remind me of the environmental incorrectness of leather, I place a bag on my shoulder. It contours snugly against the upper part of my hip, allowing my left hand to fall comfortably on top. As I fantasize owning this attractive purse, I search discreetly for the price tag unobtrusively attached to the bottom. When I see the price, I put the bag on the shelf and start for the door, almost colliding with Art who is heading down the narrow aisle toward me. "How much?" he asks quietly, his hands placed momentarily on my shoulders to steady our near collision.

"Too much," I say without looking up, as I move around him and continue walking slowly toward the door.

"Everything is half price," the clerk says soothingly, as he reenters the store from the back room. He speaks as though he just remembered the sale and not because he saw my response to the price tag.

"Everything?" I ask.

"Yes, everything." My eyes open wide in delight, although I quickly narrow them to conceal that my earlier disinterest was connected to price.

Now I'm especially interested in examining the earrings. Since the same woman continues to monopolize the earring board, I think of approaching her from the side, excusing myself, and reaching in front of her to take an earring from the display. But, no, the awkward movement would violate shopping etiquette regarding space and turn taking. Besides, she holds in her hands earrings from the two pairs that, from a distance, seem the best. I watch her as she holds the earrings in front of her lobes, tilting her head, first to the right, then the left, and back again, many times. Still grasping both earrings, she pushes her lush black hair behind her ears with the three available fingers on each hand, then brushes it quickly forward, showing no signs of making up her mind.

I drift slowly to the pocketbooks along the back wall, and Art follows. Picking up the bag I had admired, I hold the price tag so that it is visible to both of us. We calculate silently: $490 divided in half is $245. Art's raised eyebrows ask what I think. "Still too much," I convey by narrowing and moving my eyes quickly to the right and left, puckering my eyebrows and mouth slightly. Nevertheless, to occupy time until I can get to the earrings, I put the bag on my left shoulder for Art to see.

"It sure looks better than what you're carrying," Art responds, nodding toward my old pocketbook, suddenly transformed into a dirty, misshapen bag that too comfortably sags against my right side. Slightly embarrassed because the clerk is listening, I chuckle, "Yes, there is quite a difference, isn't there? Guess I do need a new one."

When Art offers, "I'll buy it, for your birthday," I understand his sudden interest in pocketbooks.

"No, I won't let you," I reply, unwilling to forgo one of his patented birthday surprises and anyway not wanting such an expensive gift.

"The bags are lovely," I say to the clerk, who stands just close enough to be invited into the conversation yet not intrude. The clerk describes the materials in the pocketbooks and their artistic construction. "They're all made by the owner. . . . He combines the colors. . . ." I hear only part of his well-practiced speech, though I am lulled by his voice.

Just then Art reaches up for a bag high on a shelf, a bag I haven't yet noticed, our different vistas no doubt affected by his extra seven inches of height. Slightly larger than what I am used to, the purse he pulls down is a beautiful tweed of light brown, dark brown, and almost black leather, overlaid with half circles that give it the texture of alligator skin. A vertical, leather braid and long double shoulder straps communicate a casual yet elegant look.

"Wow," I say, taking the bag from Art's hands, obviously searching for the price tag this time. I laugh at the absurdity of the marked price; at the same time I do quick calculations: "$290," I whisper to Art.

"This one is the best," I say. Art looks pleased that I like his discovery. "Beautiful, could go with black or brown, the right size, the snap is easy, but . . ." I inspect the inside, "it has only one side pocket. I like lots of pockets so I can organize my things and find them easily."

"It's your call," Art announces, looking disappointed.

I continue examining the bag, stroking the leather, placing it on, then off my shoulder, turning around to see how it swings. "Do you have one with more pockets?" I ask the clerk, my enthusiasm apparent. I anticipate he will answer no and I will feel relieved to have a way out of this overly expensive purchase.

"No, but some women put in plastic pouches to keep things together." This quick inadequate answer lets me know he's heard this comment before even though he has no solution. I consider and reject the plastic pouch idea as I move to place the bag back on the shelf.

"The one you're holding converts into a backpack," the clerk says, again piquing my interest. He shows me how to loop the straps through the snap on the bottom. I put the straps over my back, look into the mirror, then back at Art. I like my stylish, sophisticated, yet playful image, just the right suggestion of "hippie," yet not enough to indicate that I am stuck in the sixties or trying to look younger than I am. "I think I have to have this," I say, my usual preface to buying something expensive.

"Do it," Art says. "If you won't let me buy it for you, buy it as a gift for yourself."

Now on a buying spree, I finally approach the woman still trying on earrings. To make my intrusion more appropriate, I say, "Those are nice on you. Both pairs." I speak to her neck and the side of her hair. The partial image of her face with different earrings held up to each ear reflects back at me from the mirror she looks into. She stands so that I see the earring closest to me, but her face is turned away to such a degree that I must awkwardly walk around her to see the other earring. When I do, she turns that side of her face away.

"They're a gift for a friend, not for me," she says, sounding apologetic.

Since her voice is friendly, I continue, "Still they're lovely on you. Let me see the other one again?" I ask. When she turns to face me, she quickly raises her elbow so that her hand and wrist turn in front of her face, all the while holding the two earrings to her ears. I admire the earring before she hurriedly buries her face back into the mirror.

I scan the small display of earrings. Just as I thought, she has the two pair I like most. Feeling disingenuous now, I hope she doesn't buy both of them. From my partial view, I try to decide which pair I want, although choosing is difficult without seeing the earrings against my face and fine, light brown hair. The beige bone tubes linking a red ball at the top to an opaque white glass circle at the bottom are elegant but would demand I wear red, not one of my favorite colors. I am pulled to the pair with darker bone cylinders connecting a white ball to a pink glass circle, translucent enough to reflect the color of my clothing. Although not as dramatic, they have that funky yet sophisticated look with which I identify—not so extreme that they will attract undue attention, yet they

are sure to engender mild celebration, a second glance perhaps, or a few words of approval and admiration.

The woman continues to hold the earrings to her ears. I can tell from her intense, yet microscopic movements that she tries hard to imagine how they'd look on her friend. Perhaps she pretends to be her friend. "They're the two best," I say, to make her feel confident of her choices and to hurry her along.

"Oh, yes," she says still facing away from me and providing only a partial reflection in the mirror. Does she think that the face in the mirror is different from the face I would see if she turned around? "But they're not for me," she repeats.

"I don't know what your friend looks like, but they look wonderful on you," I say. She turns around for a moment, eyes open wide, looking straight at me for the first time, now not hiding, as if to ask, "Do you mean it?" I admire the Asian face in front of me, though I am surprised to see scars extending into her chin, around her mouth, and up both sides of her face. I nod, then smile at her. She turns back quickly, and I move away so as not to appear to rush her.

When the woman finally moves from the display, I'm happy to see she has left behind my favorite pair. I quickly take the bone earrings from the display and glance at the back. Half price, only $40; what a steal. As I carry my purchases to the counter, the bargain makes me feel better about the cost of the purse.

While the clerk wraps the earrings the woman chose, I show her the pair I am about to buy. When she smiles at me, I see her face is more scarred than I thought, the surgically repaired sides unmatched in size and shape. I wonder if she had enjoyed pretending her friend's face was her own as she looked in the mirror. Is that why the purchase took so long? I wonder if she ever buys a gift to decorate her face. Might she see her face differently after this experience? Maybe she'll keep the earrings for herself, be unwilling to let something go that looks so good on her.

"This is buffalo bone," the clerk says, turning now to my purchase and pointing toward the cylinders. "This white bead is over four hundred years old. It's from China. The bottom disk is clear quartz." His description reminds me that neither of my purchases is environmentally correct.

I begin to pull items out of my old pocketbook,

packing them into my new one. Empty, my old bag tiredly sags into itself, readied for retirement. The clerk laughs out loud when I say, "I guess my husband was right. I did need a new purse." I think again that the clerk is attractive. In addition to his harmonious voice, he has a pleasant face, soft demeanor, and an open and inviting interactive style.

"Have you lived in the city long?" I ask, intrigued to know more about him.

"Oh, yes," he says and smiles, "for twenty-five years."

"I lived on Long Island for eight years," I reply, to draw a connection.

"Where?"

"Stony Brook."

"I grew up in Riverhead," he says.

"That's a long way from Manhattan," I respond, chuckling and emphasizing "long," as I think of the potato and cauliflower farmland of Riverhead, an area stuck between Stony Brook's radical intellectuals and East Hampton's rich and famous.

"Only about ninety miles," he says, not getting my double meaning.

"But culturally it's much farther than that," I explain.

"Oh, yes," he says, and smiles again. "My family still lives there."

I wonder what a black family did in Riverhead twenty-five years ago. Maybe they were farmers or migrant workers. I think that this man is similar to me—grew up in a small town, probably with parents who had little education, then moved away.

"Would you like a shopping bag for this one?" he asks, pointing to my old purse.

"Thanks, that would make it easier to carry."

I put the earrings I purchased into my new pocketbook and hand the old one to the clerk. Treating my old pocketbook with the same gentle reverence he would a new one, he smooths out the wrinkles, wraps it gently with purple tissue paper, and inserts it carefully into a shopping bag.

I pick up the package and start toward the door. "Did you get the earrings?" he asks, at the same time I look back and say, "By the way, I love your voice."

"What?" he asks, frowning and somewhat befuddled.

"Yes," I respond, our conversation now out of sync. "Your voice. I love your voice."

"Oh, I *hate* my voice!" he says, blushing through his dark brown skin, his speech taking on a coarse edge.

"I'm sure others must tell you this all the time," I say. "Your voice, I mean. How nice it sounds."

He leans over the counter, rolls his eyes, and waves his hands in dismissal, as if my compliment is the most absurd thing he has ever heard. "I've always hated my voice," he continues loudly. "I won't even let it be taped. I can't stand hearing it. Oh, I'll speak into an answering machine, if I have to, but I don't even like to do that." The words fly fiercely from his mouth.

As he talks, the roughness of his words more and more camouflages the melodic qualities of the voice that attracted me so strongly. Concentrating on his face as he talks, I note that his front teeth are crooked. Suddenly I hear the sound, more apparent in the passionate voice he uses now than when he spoke calmly before. Later, when I recreate this scene in my mind, I will realize that the imperfection was always there, lingering in all his quiet talk. For now, though subconscious, a sense of identification starts to form.

"The earrings?"

"What?"

"Did you get them?"

"Oh . . . yes," I say, patting my new backpack, as a distinct image of putting them carefully inside comes into focus. Taking his repeated question as the end of the conversation, I follow Art through the doorway. "Well, now maybe you'll change your attitude about your voice," I say, unwilling to drop the conversation.

"No, maybe you'll change *your* attitude about my voice," he says in a surprisingly aggressive tone, as the door swings shut. I sense that his anger is not at me, but at himself, his voice, a lifetime of self-consciousness about how he talks, and how others hear his sounds. I am amazed at the vehemence and passion with which he uttered the last words to me, a stranger.

Out on the street, my emotions and desires collide as I hurry to catch up with Art who has walked a few steps ahead. I want to rush back into the store and continue to talk to the tall, good-looking, African American man with the crooked teeth and melodic voice, to the one who has a slight lateral lisp on the "s" sound that he tries to cover by speaking softly, to the one who hates his voice.

I understand how he feels. I want him to know that I hate my voice too, hate it every time I have to listen to it, every time I have to say a word that has an "s" sound. I'd tell him how much I hate repeating my office phone number—974-3626—even my last name. We'd laugh at how often I practiced before recording the message on my home answering machine and then how many times I recorded it before I was satisfied. "Hello. You have reached 989-0544 [better to say "o," not zero]. Please [the "l" and "s" combination are a disaster] leave a message [double "s" in that one] at the sound [remember to place tongue in the "t" position] of the tone."

I'd tell him that I make my living with my voice and how, as a professor in a speech communication department, I fear I'm judged by my voice. I want to tell him how hard it is to speak in public without being aware of my voice; how I sometimes hear the slurred "s" sound as I talk, my self-consciousness at the moment making the slurring worse; how I rarely make short comments in a public forum because I know I am most nervous then about my lisp; how I refuse to watch myself on videotape because I don't want to be confronted with my voice. I can't stand to hear my voice either, I'd tell him with passion, perhaps a touch of anger and frustration, and not worry that, in that self-conscious, emotional state, my lisp would be more apparent, and I more aware of it.

At that moment, I realize that I have never admitted these feelings to anyone. I am ashamed of the strength of these feelings. I regret, yet am relieved, that the opportunity to have talked with the African American man about our mutual experience has passed.

As my emotions recede to a familiar and protected place, I say to Art, "I think I gave that man a very important gift. What I said to him, I mean. I know why he hates his voice."

We both say, "Because he has a lisp." I am surprised, and then I am not, that Art understands exactly what has happened in our interaction. So he heard the lisp, too. Just like he hears mine. Just like other people hear mine.

"I understand because of my own lisp," I continue, feeling self-conscious even with Art and realizing, as I speak, that the word "lisp," cruelly enough, is probably the most difficult word in the English language for someone with a lisp to say. Perhaps I should call it a slur. No, slur is the second hardest word to say. Problems with "s"? No wonder I never talk about it.

"Go back and talk with him about your lisp," Art suggests.

I don't admit how uncomfortable that would make me. Instead I say, "I'd like to, but that would take away the gift, to admit I heard his speech problem, I mean." I know how happy I would feel if someone admired my voice, seemingly without noticing my lisp. I smile as I remember once receiving a misdialed call and continuing to talk to the man who said I had a beautiful, sensuous voice; I was too delighted to wonder at the time if he was an obscene caller.

"What I don't understand is why you think you gave him a gift. He certainly didn't react as though he were receiving one."

"Did he think I was insincere, or making fun of him?" I wonder aloud. Then, "I don't believe how much I just paid for a pocketbook," I say, suddenly changing the subject. "If it had been marked $290 to start with, I doubt I would have bought it. Probably the man's melodic voice lulled me to buy," I laugh. "Or my unconscious identification with him. Or the magic of watching the woman try on her friend's face," I add.

When Art looks questioningly at me, I tell him about the woman buying the earrings. I am not surprised when he remembers her but says he never noticed her scarred face. She did a good job of hiding herself. I think about how the woman reacted as though I *had* given her a gift when I complimented her face. I wonder about the differences between her reactions and the clerk's. Do they relate to gender? Ethnicity? Severity of the stigma? To the constant visibility of her scar? Or are the reactions simply a reflection of individual differences? I wonder whether the clerk and customer recognized my speech problem. Do they identify with me as I now do with them?

"Don't tell anyone," Art says, interrupting my thoughts.

"What?"

"How much you paid, for the bag, I mean. You deserve it."

"Don't worry. I'd feel weird if my friends knew I'd spent that much for a handbag."

"Look. There's another handbag store," Art points out, "on the next block."

"And another," I say soon afterward. "I've never noticed so many interesting pocket-book stores."

"And this one has handbags made into backpacks, similar to yours," Art says. "But, of course, not as nice," he hurries to add.

"Of course not," I say loudly, to reduce any dissonance I still feel over the cost of my purchase. "This morning I had no eye for attractive handbags, now I see them everywhere!"

"Like being exposed to a new word or concept," Art responds. "Suddenly you notice it's always been there and you become more aware of its existence. The phenomenon is much more salient."

"Sure is," I respond. Silently, I wonder whether lisps also work that way.

CATEGORIZING OUR COMMONALITIES

"I Hate My Voice" is a "true" autoethnographic story (Ellis 1997). The narrative displays concrete interactional details of an episode in which minor bodily stigmas played a significant role and evolved into a topic of conversation in a public setting. Thus, it follows the tradition of research on stigmas in which investigators observe brief interactional sequences in public spaces (e.g., Cahill and Eggleston 1995; Gardner 1991; Goffman 1963; Gussow and Tracy 1968). This story deviates from traditional stigma research in a number of ways: most obviously, it *shows* through *narrative* rather than *argues* from *data* (Bochner 1994); it deals with a kind of stigma—minor bodily stigmas—that has been ignored by sociologists; it contextualizes stigmas within non-stigmatized mundane interactions; it describes complex interactions among stigmatized people (Gussow and Tracy 1968), instead of concentrating solely on encounters between "normals" and stigmatized; and, most importantly, it begins to examine how living with a stigma feels over time, how subjective responses are managed, and the thoughts and

feelings associated with one's self-construction as a stigmatized person (e.g., Perry 1996).

The remainder of this article moves back and forth among theory, narrative, and personal experience to try to understand and convey the process of living with a stigma. I try to show that the personal and the categorical go hand in hand in understanding the interactional experience of minor bodily stigmas (cf. Daly 1997). In this section, I examine minor bodily stigmas as both a category of stigma and as felt experience in order to ameliorate some of the criticisms of Erving Goffman's (1963) broader concept of stigma. I discuss how minor bodily stigmas are experienced as an interactional double bind (Bateson, Jackson, Haley, and Weakland 1956)—to notice or not to notice—and an emotional double bind—of moral character as well as physical appearance.

Rather than a strict category of specific attributes, minor bodily stigmas might better be presented as a point on a continuum of relational activity (Laurel Richardson, personal communication). Since a relational language to describe such experience is lacking (Goffman 1963, p. 3; Bochner 1984; Haley 1963), I employ the language of attributes and categories as heuristic devices. Minor bodily stigmas may include "blemishes" potentially perceptible by sight (that is, impaired appearance such as buck teeth, hair lips, moles, scars, acne, psoriasis, scales, baldness, red hair, curly hair, big breasts, flat breasts, tall or short stature, heavy or skinny bodies; missing or damaged body parts, such as chipped or crooked front teeth, missing or malformed digits on fingers or toes, scoliosis, or one leg shorter than another; or impeded bodily movement such as tics, shaking, limping, squinting, unbalanced eye tracking or crossing); by hearing (that is, minor speech problems, such as lisping and mild stuttering, or speech impaired by lack of hearing); by smell (that is, chronic halitosis, body odor, or putrid cysts); or by the presence of an aid or sign of impairment (that is, a toupee, hearing aid, thick glasses, brace, or cane). Whether a particular characteristic is treated as a minor bodily stigma depends on the context in which it occurs, its degree of perceived distance from some imagined or accepted norm, the bearer's self-perception, and others' reactions.

To be included as minor bodily stigmas, these characteristics should be involuntary and perceived by self and/or some others as undesirable. Sometimes people are born with minor bodily stigmas, such as birthmarks; other times these attributes, such as scars or baldness, are acquired through aging or accidents. The characteristics may be present always, as in the case of disfigurement, or their performance may vary according to interactional context, as in the case of stuttering. Although not necessarily detectable at all times, minor bodily stigmas are difficult to hide. Still, they rarely if ever serve as master statuses or stand in the way of everyday life. Since only on rare occasions (such as in plastic surgery) are holders able to rid themselves of stigmatized characteristics, *they must figure out ways to live with minor bodily stigmas.* Many develop concealing or coping mechanisms (e.g., Rochford 1983), while some, paradoxically, turn a potential stigma into something valued, such as a tall woman becoming a basketball player or model. In either case, except in severe forms of a stigma (e.g., extreme stuttering [Carlisle 1985] or hearing impairment [Perry 1996]), the solution usually is an informal interactive effort rather than a formal collective one (such as the formation of support groups).

The category of minor bodily stigmas refers to a small and similarly situated subset of characteristics normally included under the general label of stigma. Goffman's *Stigma* (1963), out of which most of the work on this topic grows, dealt with such disparate attributes as serious physical deformities, unemployment, criminal behavior, addiction, homosexuality, radical political orientations, and particular racial characteristics, without distinguishing between voluntary and involuntary activities. In his discussion of physical deformities, Goffman (1963) briefly mentioned a few minor bodily stigmatized characteristics (e.g., stuttering, scars, hair lips, misshapen noses, and hearing impairment) but these were not his primary interest.

A number of researchers have argued that Goffman's concept of stigma is "so inclusive as to be uninformative" (Cahill and Eggleston 1995, p. 682; see also Murphy, Scheer, Murphy, and Mack 1988; Susman 1994). Since *Stigma* (Goffman 1963), researchers

usually have isolated one segment of the stigmatized population at a time; for example, J. Ablon (1984) studied dwarfs, G. Becker (1980) focused on older deaf people, and M. Angrosino (1997) examined adults with mental retardation. Or they have concentrated on a segment categorized by a particular symbol of stigma, such as S. Cahill and R. Eggleston's (1995) work on wheelchair users, or by location, such as R. B. Edgerton's (1967) study of former state hospital inmates. A few researchers have focused on one type of stigma that fits under minor bodily stigmas, for example, speech problems such as stuttering (Carlisle 1985; Petrunik and Shearing 1983; Rochford 1983) or physical blemishes such as burns, birth defects, dermatological disorders, height, weight, and eye problems (Beuf 1990; Herman, Zanna, and Higgins 1986; Millman 1980). Those who have examined more inclusive categories of stigmatized behavior have concentrated on Goffman's (1963, p. 4) three major categories of stigma, consisting of "physical deformities" (e.g., Susman 1994; Davis 1961; Frank 1988), "blemishes of individual character" inferred from actions regarded as deviant, such as homosexuality or alcoholism (e.g., Kowalewski 1988), and the "tribal stigma of race, nation, and religion" (e.g., Broaded 1991), or they have continued to study stigmas in general (e.g., Jones, Farina, Hastorf, Markus, Miller, and Scott 1984).

Neither Goffman nor those following him have defined or examined the interactional particularities that differentiate minor bodily stigmas from severe and obvious physical disabilities or other stigmas. Perhaps minor bodily stigmas have been neglected by social scientists because of their perceived unimportance; a lack of publicly displayed talk and feelings about them in daily discourse; the mild, often subtle, reactions they generate from others; or the lack of clearly defined boundaries to define the category as well as the situated variability of attributes included therein. After all, what may be a minor stigma for one person may be major for another but nonexistent for a third, varying with age, gender, ethnicity, and across interactional situations.

The category of minor bodily stigmas shares many characteristics with Goffman's broader concept of stigma. As Goffman noted, there is nothing crediting or discrediting in the attributes themselves. Rather stigmas occur in the context of relationships with others (Goffman 1963, p. 3); to some extent, we all take on both normal and stigmatized roles (p. 138); and ambivalence is built into the way both the holder and beholder view the characteristic (p. 38). Goffman argued that the same features are involved whether a "major" or "picayune" differentness is at question (p. 130).

In light of their interactional particularities, however, minor bodily stigmas deserve more attention than the phrase "picayune differentness" indicates. For example, the more minor the stigmatized characteristic, the more ambiguous the interaction may be: others' reactions and the holder's self-definition regarding the attribute can be hidden easily. Normally, a minor bodily stigma does not interrupt communication—thus, few situations require the stigma to be either acknowledged or actively concealed to maintain interaction. The holder of a stigma may wonder whether others have noticed the blemish and, if they have, whether they consider it stigmatizing. Interactants may wonder if the holder is aware of its presence and, if so, how it is defined and coped with. The very "smallness" of the stigma may make interactants less, rather than more, willing to call attention to the characteristic. The ambiguity in whether, when, under what circumstances, and by whom these attributes are noticed and defined is integral to the complex interactional character of minor bodily stigmas, more so even than in situations involving more critical stigmas.

Minor bodily stigmas appear to have become more important markers of difference today than Goffman may have anticipated when he published *Stigma* in 1963. Americans seem preoccupied with minor physical blemishes (Valdez 1997), as demonstrated by the consumer-driven development of plastic surgery (liposuction, aesthetic reconstruction, spider-vein removal, tummy tucks, and face-lifts), cosmetics, exercise clubs, weight reduction plans, psychotherapy, and the emphasis given to overcoming natural signs of aging and avoiding the negative consequences of being overweight or out of shape.

This ideal image is largely a creation of mass media. The perfectly airbrushed and computerized models in magazines and the heavily made-up and rehearsed characters on TV ads show few signs of the stress and physical blemishes that they and we suffer in everyday life. At the same time, we (women especially) are reminded of our own blemishes and the need to do something about them by advertising that plays into anxieties about imperfections, holding out remedies for overcoming the tendency to smell, look, or feel bad. Perhaps we are reminded of them as well as we laugh heartily at sitcoms, such as *Seinfeld,* where the main characters plot secretly to deal with or avoid someone with a minor bodily stigma, such as oversized hands and nose or a bald head (David Payne, personal communication). Are we laughing at the person with the stigmatized characteristic, the stigmatized characteristic itself, the *Seinfeld* characters who react inappropriately to minor bodily stigmas, our own hangups about our blemishes, or to relieve our anxieties about them? Whichever, minor bodily stigmas have become a salient part of everyday life, yet we have little guidance about how to act, talk, or think regarding them. That we have some guidance from support groups, lawmakers, media, and social scientists for responding to other stigmatized characteristics (such as disability, sexual orientation, or race) may make us even more apprehensive about our actions toward those with minor bodily stigmas—we think we *should* know how to regard them but we don't.

This leaves interactants in a Batesonian double bind (Bateson 1972; Bateson et al. 1956) in two ways. First, without rules for how to deal with the minor bodily stigmas of others, social interactants often are confused about how to respond appropriately. If I mention my stigma, will it be easier or more difficult to interact around it? If you mention my stigma, is that evidence that my "spoiled identity" is salient for you or that the blemish is so trivial that it can be spoken of offhandedly? If you don't mention it, is that evidence of its triviality or its unmentionability (Robert Drew, personal communication)? If you do mention it, will I see you as an insensitive and uncaring person? Is our silence meant to protect each other's identities and, as Goffman (1956) says about embarrassment, the interactional encounter as well?

Second, the holder of a minor bodily stigma must cope with a subjective double bind of feeling not only shame for having the stigma but metashame as well—feeling ashamed for feeling ashamed about a seemingly trivial blemish, a point that Goffman (1963, p. 130) mentions in passing. The blemish is so small that we shouldn't care; at the same time, it is so big that it prevents us from measuring up to the images of perfection we are encouraged to seek by mass media. Thus, bearers suffer a blemish in moral character that might impact their experiences as much, if not more than, the blemish in physical appearance.

Stories of stigma, most told in response to my request on a list serve, demonstrate some of the complex relationships between responses to stigma and the bearer's feelings. For example, a woman wrote about her sister's birthmark on her neck. "For years, I don't think she was ever affected by it and then in the vulnerable adolescent years, someone made a comment and it was turtlenecks for years, followed by two types of treatment to rid herself of this." Another related that when someone mentions her eye-tracking problem, her composure dissolves almost instantaneously. A third wrote that it does not bother her when people inquire about her hearing aids, yet she is "very conscious and embarrassed" about the birthmark on her cheek "even though no one ever mentioned it." The type and frequency of comments also play a part in how people feel about the minor bodily stigmas they bear. For example, a tall woman suggested that the frequency and variety of people's comments about her height, some positive and some negative, probably desensitized her to the idea that being tall was a stigma.

These stories also display the deep emotional pain, shame, and metashame connected to minor bodily stigmas. For example, a woman with an amputated finger tip said, "I feel almost embarrassed to call it a minor stigma. . . . It is such a tiny stigma, but wow, it rules my life." The woman who has the eye that doesn't track properly wrote, "If you ever want to see me lose my shit during an interaction, arrange to be present when someone asks why my eyes don't move like they should. . . . My heart seems to suddenly freeze rather painfully, before resuming its normal beat. My goodness, someone notices! I'm a freak, a fucking freak." In addition, Susan Krieger (1996, pp. 74–75) wrote, "If only my hair would be straight, I used to feel, I would be like everyone else. I would be happy."

Such stories indicate that these stigmatized characteristics, though minor, often are so problematic that bearers go to great lengths to pass as "normals." For example, the woman with an eye-tracking problem wrote: "The way I have usually dealt with my eye problem is to turn my head a little to the right, so that I am looking at people more out of my left eye." Another wrote about the missing tip of her finger: "I do everything I can to hide it (put my right hand in a fist so the finger is less noticeable, etc.)." And, Krieger (1996, p. 75) described sleepless nights on large, hard curlers.

With the exception of Krieger's contribution, the severity and complexity of the felt experience of stigma has not been developed in social science literature and is more likely to be found in novels, popular literature, and short stories (e.g., Jezer 1997; Updike 1989). This lack of attention by social scientists may stem from the interactionist emphasis on the "beholder" rather than the "holder" of an experience such as a stigma. Research is almost always conducted from the perspective of distanced observers with privileged insight, such as in Goffman's *Stigma* (1963). As Ann Branaman (1997, p. lii) points out, "In *Stigma* (1963), Goffman defines personal identity in terms which require no corresponding subjective experience of the individual at all. What matters is not how the individual identifies him or herself but rather how he or she is identified by others." Likewise, the emphasis in C. H. Cooley's (1902) looking-glass self is on how we tend to see ourselves as we imagine others see and judge us. What about the individual looking into the looking glass who often takes an active role in presenting a particular characterization of self to others (Branaman 1997; Goffman 1959)? Except for the case of a one-way mirror, the looking glass reflects two ways—others also tend to see us as they imagine we see and judge ourselves, and the self feeling that results from the looking-glass process in turn affects how others see and judge us.

With these conceptual ideas in mind, I next continue my exploration, begun in the opening narrative, of my own minor speech problem. In contrast to most interactionist work on stigmas, I concentrate on telling my story from the perspective of the involved, emotional, interacting subject who feels a moral as well as a physical stigma. In place of a static, categorical portrayal of stigma emphasizing strategies or patterns in brief encounters and others' rejection of the holder of a stigma, my goals are to intersect categorical understanding with concrete experiences of stigmas in day-to-day life (Scott 1970) and to connect the complexity and variability of interaction around stigma (Anspach 1979; Hahn 1985; Thomas 1982) in a public setting (Cahill and Eggleston 1995, p. 682) with the intimate experience of dealing with stigma over time (Frank 1988; Wright 1983) in sustained relationships (Bogdan and Taylor 1989). In contrast to work on speech disorders, research designed with the goal of *correcting* stigmas (but see Carlisle 1985; Petrunik and Shearing 1983; Rochford 1983), my narrative concentrates on *living and coping with* stigmas and recognizing the commonality of vulnerability that our differences may mask (Perry 1996, p. 259).

BREAKING MY SILENCE

To display or not to display; to tell or not to tell; to let on or not to let on; to lie or not to lie; and in each case, to whom, how, when, and where.

Erving Goffman, Stigma

And, of course, I am afraid—you can hear it in my voice—because the transformation of silence into language and action is an act of self-revelation and that always seems fraught with danger. . . . I speak now these words . . . to break that silence and bridge some of those differences between us, for it is not difference which immobilizes us, but silence. And there are so many silences to be broken.

Audre Lorde, The Cancer Journals

I have been silent about my lisp, rarely volunteering feelings or thoughts. Unlike stigmas where distinct physical markers, such as wheelchairs, are evident (Cahill and Eggleston 1995), few people have ever admitted noticing my lisp or initiated a conversation about it. In the few incidents I remember, the details stand out and remain vivid (cf. Richardson 1996).

The most painful memory I recall regarding my speech involves the first time someone acknowledged my lisp. As a child, I never suspected I had a problem with speaking, and the public recognition shattered my self-image. The event occurred in third grade when my teacher refused to let me read aloud to the class, a favorite activity for which I always volunteered whenever the opportunity arose. In front of the class in response to my outstretched waving hand, the teacher said, "Carolyn, I'd rather you didn't read because your voice is so hard to understand." That day I hid behind the girl sitting in front of me and cried. I thought I read so beautifully, with so much expression, and I always knew all the words. Hard to understand? Wasn't I the best reader in the class? Embarrassed beyond words, I never again volunteered to read in class, nor did the teacher ask me.

Many years later, in Spanish class, a high school teacher said, "You have a natural Castilian Spanish." Smiling and nodding, she demonstrated the slurred "s" sound, holding it long with lots of slur and loose spit sounds for emphasis. Although she was trying to "normalize" my speech, I turned red, feeling put on the spot and uncomfortable that my speech needed normalizing. After that, I hated Spanish with its frequent "s" sounds and spoke it aloud only when the teacher demanded.

My next memory is of a drama teacher who refused to give me a part in the high school senior play, even a minor one, while all my friends had major roles. "Because of your voice," was all she would say. Frankly, I didn't want her to elaborate. I attended the play, all the while feeling left out and disconfirmed, an experience that stood out all the more because of the rarity of these feelings during high school. By then, it was hard to deny that others perceived my speech as a problem.

I have no memory of similar incidents during college and graduate school, although I remember being quiet in classes. But I believe I was more concerned then with learning to "speak clearly" in other ways that, at that point, seemed more important than my lisp and over which I could exert some control (cf. Richardson 1996). With my dictionary, and sometimes with close friends, I practiced saying unfamiliar words. In front of the mirror, I rehearsed speaking without the heavy southern accent I had carried from small-town Virginia to New York—the accent that always reappeared when I talked to my relatives over the phone. In interaction, I practiced interrupting aggressively yet politely and speaking assertively, similar to others I admired in the northeastern university setting. I worked hard to develop a voice that clearly articulated ideas, if not sounds. I wanted the voice of a professor—even if it had a lisp attached.

Early in my first teaching job, a student from an undergraduate class I had taught told me that at first my voice "drove her crazy" but that after a while she liked the class so much she "didn't notice it." Soon after that, a colleague said that it was a shame my parents never did anything about my speech. These comments motivated me to go to speech therapy.

At first I dreaded hearing my voice so accurately represented on the high-tech recording machines—no denying my lisp then—but I loved listening to myself toward the end of therapy, when I had "improved." Years later, I ran into my speech therapist at a party. When I reminded him I had been his client, he said (in front of others), "So let me hear you talk." My face turned red and I was speechless, knowing that if I spoke I would "let him down." This situation felt quite different from the lack of stress I experienced during therapy.

The problem is that speech therapy "works" only when I remember to place my tongue for "s" sounds in the same way I place my tongue behind by front teeth to make "t" sounds. When I read aloud, I get into the rhythm of proper placement. But when I have to think on my feet—well, it's just too much to consider at one time, and the practice (though I drilled myself for hours a day for months) never became routine. Besides, focusing on the "t" sound and making it so often and unnaturally makes my jaw muscles ache.

I told my mother I was in speech therapy, to see what she would say, since no one in my family had ever mentioned my speech to me. "There's nothing wrong with the way you talk," she said. "Did you ever notice I spoke differently from others when I was a kid?" I asked, wanting to know when this problem started, longing to get to the "cause." "You didn't talk no different than anybody else," she said and changed the subject.

But not everyone agrees with my mother. Once a colleague mentioned my speech problem in a scholarly article. He described meeting me: "I was surprised by her accent. She had a slight lisp and a southern trailer park drawl" (Shelton 1995, p. 83). Actually, I celebrated the chutzpah it took for this author to mention my lisp in a public forum. I thought he had thrown in "southern trailer park drawl" for literary effect—there wasn't much of the southern speech left; I wondered how much "lisp" was for effect as well. How stigmatizing could it be if a friend would say it in print?

I fantasized about people reading this passage. Would they wonder how it made me feel? Would they imagine how they'd feel if they were me? I didn't mind being noticed for difference as long as the difference wasn't too extreme—sort of similar to the effect I looked for in choosing my earrings. At the same time, I feared this passage might make people more aware of my lisp, similar to the effect of examining pocketbooks in the story that began this article.

The few times I've opened up conversation about my lisp with my partner Art, he has maintained, "I hardly ever notice it. Your speech—the slight lisp, if you want to call it that—is part of your total presentation, not a characteristic that stands out." While his response pleases me, sometimes I'd like more concrete details. I think of asking, "How does my lisp compare to the lisp of the clerk in the store?" But I don't. After reading an early draft of this article, Art asked if I wanted to talk about my lisp. Actually I didn't. That's the strange thing. Sometimes I think I really don't have a problem, and that my focusing on it, such as in writing this article, makes a big deal out of what is, or at least should be, a minor inconvenience. After all, I often go long periods—at least weeks—without thinking about my speech. I am proud of my ability to teach and give speeches, and I think of myself as an effective speaker. As far as I know, my lisp has never stood in the way of friendships or romantic attachments.

Other times, I know I suffer from my speech difficulty, and I define it is an impediment, not merely an inconvenience. Yet Art has trouble pronouncing his "l's" so that "roll" becomes "row," "cool" becomes "cole," and neither of us thinks of his speech as impaired. So why do I think of my own as impeded? Is there something specific about the "s" sound that makes it more likely to be stigmatized? Certainly we have a commonly known label of "lisp" for this problem, while there is no such label for difficulties with other letters of the alphabet. I wonder if our evaluations would be the same if we spoke a language that had fewer "s" sounds (Rhonda Rubin, personal communication). Even so, what is there to say about my lisp that will help? I know too well that the most successful strategy is to forget about it, because the more self-conscious and anxious I am about doing well, the worse the lisp seems to be (cf. Carlisle 1985). There doesn't seem to be much I can do one way or the other about the way I talk.

How I do and should feel about, experience, and cope with my minor stigma are not simple issues. Since I'm ambivalent regarding how to think about and whether to talk about my lisp and how others' responses will affect me, most of the time I have found Art's rather neutral reaction and the silence surrounding my stigma comforting. Given my hesitations and concerns then, how did I decide to write about something so uncomfortable to acknowledge and reveal?

My decision was influenced by the scene I describe in the opening narrative. Fortuitously, telling this story allowed me to confront my stigma first through other characters, thus giving me the distance (and courage) I needed to begin this exploration. Having such intense emotions and reflections after interacting in the store made me think more deeply and analytically about the meaning of stigma in my life. Seeing the similarity between the clerk and me revealed my lisp as a social problem, where before I had considered it solely as a personal idiosyncrasy. Encountering the woman with facial disfigurement presented the commonalities of lisps and scars and spurred me to seek other stories about how people deal with minor bodily stigmas in our culture.

The more I wrote about and theorized from my personal experience, the less inhibited I felt writing openly about this issue—there's no lisp in my writing. The writing process itself and imagining readers provided companionship and a chance to "try on" my stigma. Yet I still gave vague answers—"a shopping trip"—to those who asked what I was writing about, since I did not want to talk face to face with others, who could observe the lisp as we discussed it. I feared that level of reflexivity and awareness and the resulting self-consciousness (and increased lisping) would make me feel out of control. Given that I have written

and spoken rather easily about many personal topics in my life—for example, death, intimate relationships, and bodies (Ellis 1993; 1995; 1996)—my difficulties in revealing myself seemed extreme. The rough journey made me realize how much I experienced my lisp as a stigma and how horribly difficult it was to speak out.

In February 1997, six months after writing the introductory story to this article, I broke the secrecy surrounding this work by agreeing to be on a panel on stigmas, organized by Janet Yerby, for the National Communication Association conference. That task left me encouraged yet a bit unsettled—I was taking a big risk to talk openly about my voice problem to academics who often judge each other according to verbal performances. How, I wondered, would I be able to present this work at a conference? Should I try to control my lisping when I presented? I recalled Janet Yerby saying, "I never noticed your lisp as a problem. It's in the background. The lisp makes your presentations more down to earth, like you're a little vulnerable, and that's good. But that kind of thing adds only when you give a competent performance, as you do." Yet, Art had told me that the only time he noticed my voice was when I read papers at conventions. "I can tell you are working to control your voice then. I wish you'd just forget about it and read more naturally." I felt the remnants of my third grade teacher saying she didn't like the way I read. Reading without a lisp was the only time I felt proud of my voice. How ironic! To Art, my attempts at speaking "correctly" sounded odder than when I spoke "incorrectly."

I had solicited the feedback, and I appreciated how hard it was to give. I wondered how this feedback would affect me. What if it had been more negative? How will others react to me after reading this article? When I present it, might it be the only public performance I've ever given in which I don't worry about my voice? Or might I worry even more now that I've made my lisp into an object to be noted, talked about, dissected, and commented on?

The last set of questions brings me finally to another awareness. People interacting with me will more likely be concerned with how I, an ethnographer of stigmas, perceive *their* blemishes than how I sound. I have to wonder then whether this article will help those who anxiously experience their minor stigmas. Have I bought into a category (stigma), and created a version (minor bodily stigmas), that might be better left ignored? Might my work serve to remind people of their "flaws" when they would be better left unacknowledged? As a result of this work, might others redefine a personal characteristic as a stigma? Will the awareness brought to life then tighten the double bind that we all are made to feel regarding how we negotiate our stigmas? What seems to be called for is a way to reframe stigmatized experience, to unravel the knot that entangles us.

SPEAKING THE UNSPEAKABLE/ CONNECTING TO OTHERS

"What are you up to these days?" my colleague Rob asks, as he stands in the open door-way of my office.

"Oh, just getting through the semester and writing a paper on stigma." I feel a twinge of nervousness since, with this lead-in, I have invited Rob, an expert on Goffman, to probe for details.

"A paper about stigma? What on?" he asks.

"Minor bodily stigmas," I respond. "It's a category that not much has been written about. Most attention has been paid to the other kinds of stigmas Goffman discusses. Like disability and deviance." The mini-lecture I give lets me postpone answering Rob's real question.

"What are you examining exactly?"

"It's an autoethnographic study," I respond quickly, stepping into risky territory but still evading Rob's question. It's April 1997 and I've done several rewrites by now. Still, I have not shown this paper to anyone. Am I ready to talk about what I'm doing? Perhaps Rob might be satisfied with what I've already told him, or, sensing my hesitation, he might steer away from the original question, as most people do. A part of me hopes he won't; still I continue to buy time. "You know, we all have little physical characteristics that bother us. It's amazing, almost everybody I talk to admits to something. Like . . . ," I hesitate as I search for examples.

At the same time, I focus on Rob's thick glasses. The right side seems much thicker than the left, almost hiding his eye from my view. He seems to turn his head away as though he is keeping that eye out of my sight line. I have noticed before that it's hard to tell when Rob is looking at me, but I'd never recognized it to this degree.

I carefully leave out any mention of stigma concerning vision. ". . . oh, like having the tip of your finger cut off . . . or a birthmark or speech difficulties." I have moved another step toward inviting attention to myself. Perhaps I am fishing to see if Rob has noticed my speech, and if he'll say anything about it.

"You mean Loyd?"

"What?" His question seems to come out of left field and I wonder for a moment whether he has been following what I said.

"Loyd, our colleague. You know . . . the end of his finger is missing."

Hesitating, I search for an image of Loyd's shortened finger.

"When I first met Loyd and he shook my hand," Rob continues, "he mentioned immediately that he was missing the end of his finger."

I ask, "On his right hand?" to which Rob shakes his head yes. "Wow," I continue, "that counters my argument that we usually don't point out minor bodily stigmas to others."

"Well, Loyd did, and it surprised me. I wondered how often he had to do that and how awful it must be."

"Yeah, me too," I respond and think that having to acknowledge the problem to others upon shaking hands is probably as problematic as having a fingertip missing. "You know, now I think I do remember about Loyd's finger, but if someone had asked me if I had a colleague with a missing finger tip, I think I would have said no."

"It's not something you'd readily notice."

"No, it isn't."

"You said your study was autoethnographic. . . . So what are you studying?"

Although I feel my face flush a bit, I like Rob's direct question. I ease into my answer. "Well, it's a story about an interaction in a store with someone who has problems speaking, ah . . . , with the 's' sound." My tongue was in position to say "lisp" instead of "s," but I moved quickly away from the slurred "sp" sound. It is difficult to place my tongue correctly behind my upper teeth for the "t" sound as I slide into the "s" and then move immediately into the "p" sound, which demands my tongue be behind my lower teeth. No doubt I also still resist using lisp as a label. I continue, "Talking with the clerk makes me confront my own speech problem so then I introspect about my own experiences. I want to show how a narrative description of a scene can be connected to introspection about one's life and then to theory. I try to theorize from my own experience and use my experience to clarify and expand theory, extending my observations to other people."

I have given Rob many points to respond to now, so that he can, if he desires, ignore the revelation of my speech problem. Rob goes straight for the jugular. "You know, your lisp has always been ground for me," Rob replies thoughtfully.

"What?" I ask, not understanding, probably because I am too focused on his use of the word "lisp" and the direction of the conversation.

"You know, ground not figure. Except right now, as we're talking about it. Now it's figure. And I just noticed that you just said an 's' sound without lisping."

"Probably because I was self-conscious about focusing on it in our conversation so I tried to say it right, which I can do if I concentrate," I respond proudly.

"I guess my stigma is that I'm a few pounds overweight," Rob reveals, patting his tummy. We've never spoken in this way before, and I note that my revelation has permitted his. "My friends are always kidding me about my weight, saying I need to lose a few pounds."

I note Rob's size; the "extra" pounds look good on him. Maybe it's that vulnerability-competence dialectic at play: Rob is articulate and competent, yet being a few pounds overweight makes him seem a little vulnerable and approachable. It's an attractive combination. He appears to enjoy life and not be taken up with body image, weight control, and exercise. Perhaps the image is false, I think, since I also am a few pounds overweight, and I think about weight and exercise. Yet I don't consider my size a stigmatized characteristic.

"It's interesting that your friends kid you about your weight. That challenges another thing I thought about minor bodily stigmas—that people don't say anything to you about it. Maybe it's because weight is

such a commonplace topic in our society." I realize as we continue talking that I didn't invalidate his "few extra pounds," and I wonder if he will conclude from my omission that I too think he is overweight. Maybe I should have said something.

"Well, I think people feel okay teasing you if it's only a few pounds, but if you're a lot overweight, they don't say anything," Rob offers.

"Maybe because they think you can do something about the problem. People must assume I can't do anything about my speech, or that a severely overweight person can't do anything about their weight." I wonder, at what point does "a few pounds" become "a lot overweight"?

Rob nods, seemingly in agreement. "Don't get me wrong," I add before he can say anything. "I don't have all this figured out. It's just amazing that we all have these stigmas and often they affect us so intensely, yet we don't talk about them."

"Yeah, also I have my glasses. I started wearing them in second grade," Rob says, grabbing onto his glasses, "so I was called four-eyes all the time." He says nothing else about his vision, and I don't either. But from Rob's serious expression, I sense that his vision, not his weight, is his most bothersome minor bodily stigma.

"Geez, I have to go to class," I say, looking at my watch and hurriedly gathering my books. "What's interesting is bodily difference that is not considered a stigma. Like with Art," I continue, as we walk down the hall. "He has double-jointed fingers, but he doesn't consider them a stigma. He likes them and sometimes shows them to people. He says he used to hold them up to scare kids." I demonstrate and Rob laughs at the image.

"Let's talk again," I say as we reluctantly part.

"Yes, let's," Rob replies enthusiastically.

"You'll probably be a character in my story now." (I laugh as I recall Janet Yerby telling me she'd rather be a character than a citation in my paper.)

"That's fine. Use our conversation any way you want."

On my way to class, I duck into the bathroom to collect my thoughts for a moment. I think about how confirming Rob's comments were. Yes, Rob acknowledged he had noticed my stigma, but he basically validated what Art and Janet had said—that my problem was not something that dominated my presentation of self. Having a sense of how others saw me made me feel better, more confident of myself really; this felt much better than keeping silent and wondering.

Maybe someday I'll be able to say "lisp" without flinching, I think, looking into the bathroom mirror. Maybe someday I'll view my speech as simply a variation, more similar to a southern accent or Castilian Spanish, instead of a stigma. Maybe someday I'll be able to read my paper in a public presentation without correcting for my "ss." Who said all our voices have to sound the same? I glance again at how well the turquoise, purple, and silver earrings I have on match the colors in my shirt. I brush my hair back so my ears are in full view and flip my handbag over my shoulder, smiling as I walk out the door.

BREAKING THROUGH OUR CATEGORIES

This article offers autoethnographic storytelling as an alternative to the common practices of concealing, underplaying, manipulating, or denying stigmatized differences, practices that allow the "world of normals" to go unchallenged (Branaman 1997, p. lix). In telling my own story, I seek to understand minor bodily stigmas and to decenter the normal in terms of these differences in the same way others before me have decentered the normal relative to race and disability. I problematize these categories by consciously moving back and forth, in and out of them.

Since my conversation with Rob, I have engaged in a number of discussions about minor bodily stigmas with people who have read this article or heard me present it. Similar to Rob, these readers have helped me understand that my lisp is minor, though this validation was not primarily what I sought. After all, I realized from the beginning that my stigma was minor, but that knowledge had not helped me cope. Instead, the minor quality of my lisp generated a larger moral problem of feeling ashamed of feeling ashamed of something so small.

The alliance with people who share these feelings has lessened the burden of undesired difference. Readers have drawn comparisons from their own lives, telling vivid stories and expressing strong feelings about their interiorized anxiety, shame, and dread. Many have said that reading about my lisp encouraged them to speak about their stigmas, often for the first time. Focused on our common experiences, our talk defused some of the feelings of shame and stigmatization that we shared.

Although the physical manifestation of my lisp has not changed in any appreciable way, I rarely feel shame or metashame about it now. Without shame, the physical part of my lisp just does not seem like a big deal, and perhaps it *is* less physically prominent without the accompanying emotional stress of feeling shame. Sometimes I am able to laugh with others now about the ways we have twisted ourselves into pretzels to conceal and cope with our stigmas. I seem to have stopped fantasizing about how much better my life would be without a lisp. I noticed my lisp the other day in class; what stood out for me was how long it had been since I last paid attention to it. After this exploration, I doubt my lisp will ever have the same hold over me again.

I do not claim, however, that I am now completely comfortable about my lisp. Two nights before I submitted this article for publication, I dreamed I was giving a speech and my lisp was so severe that no one in the audience could understand what I said. Then, before I actually presented a paper from this work at the National Communication Association meetings in November 1997, I practiced it aloud daily for three weeks, making sure that I could say "lisp" without stumbling. Immediately before the presentation, I worried that I had practiced so much that I wouldn't lisp at all. Would the audience then wonder why I had written about such a trivial topic? If I did lisp, after all this practice, would I feel shame? These events help me hesitate whenever I move toward romanticizing stigma or claiming "recovery."

Nevertheless, I have been able to reframe my lisp as part of my total identity. Now I even think of what I like about my voice—its expressiveness in tone and the face work that goes with it—and consider the ways in which my lisp may have contributed positively to who I have become (cf. Updike 1989). Perhaps my lisp reminds me to think before I speak and to try to have something worthwhile to say before I do. Perhaps my lisp makes it difficult to talk like a professor, preventing me from lecturing at the drop of a question and rushing to fill every hole in conversation. Perhaps my lisp enhances my desire to speak clearly in other ways, such as in my writing. Perhaps my lisp makes me a better listener, reminding me to be more empathic and sensitive to others' differences, insecurities, and frailties. Perhaps my lisp allows others to approach me more easily because they see me as vulnerable. Perhaps my lisp helps me serve as a role model—if she can do it, so can I. And perhaps my lisp has given me the gifts that accompany hardheaded determination, making me work harder to succeed and overcome my limitations.

I doubt that I would have been able to move outside the category of minor bodily stigmas without first immersing myself in it. Categories too often limit us without our being aware of their influence; once we are aware, too often we assume there is no use in trying to break through them. Telling and analyzing my personal story not only helped generate and make visible the category of minor bodily stigma, it also provided a way through. The categorical story offered a name to my experiences where before there was only dread; the personal story connected real people with feelings to the labels, where before there were only tactics of concealment and denial. This research helped me understand the inextricable connections between categorical and personal knowledge.

The fear I had initially that concentrating on lisps or minor bodily stigmas in general might make me and others see them everywhere—as concentrating on pocketbooks in the first story made us see pocketbooks everywhere—held true. But in seeing stigma everywhere, I came to see it nowhere. Now I expect to encounter minor bodily stigmas, but in the way that I expect to see beards or brown hair or hear accents and dialects. Minor bodily stigmas have become part of the landscape of human variability and commonality.

In surrendering attachment to myself as minor bodily stigmatized, I am able now to take attention off my mouth and how I speak myself out there. I end then where I began, with my ears, eager to hear others' stories of minor bodily stigmas, so that we all might continue "coming to terms with" and, in the process, learning to cope better with our differences, however minor they may be.

ACKNOWLEDGMENTS

Thanks to Arthur Bochner, Spencer Cahill, Robert Drew, and Laurel Richardson for critical readings of this manuscript. Also, thanks to Leigh Berger, Norman Denzin, Karen Fox, Joan George, John Harvey, Krista Hirschmann, Carol Jablonski, Tanya Keenan, Judith Perry, Loyd Pettegrew, Lisa Tillmann-Healy, Sheree Wood, Janet Yerby, participants on the QUALS-L Listserve, and reviewers of *The Sociological Quarterly* for assistance.

Direct all correspondence to Carolyn Ellis, Professor of Communication and Sociology, Department of Communication, University of South Florida, CIS 1040, 4202 E Fowler Ave., Tampa, FL 33620-7800; e-mail: cellis@chumal.cas.usf.edu

REFERENCES

Ablon, J. 1984. *Little People in America: The Social Dimensions of Dwarfism.* New York: Praeger.

Angrosino, Michael. 1997. *Opportunity House: Ethnographic Stories of Mental Retardation.* Walnut Creek, CA: AltaMira Press.

Anspach, R. R. 1979. "From Stigma to Identity Politics: Political Activism among the Physically Disabled and Former Mental Patients." *Social Science and Medicine* 13A:765–772.

Bateson, Gregory. 1972. *Steps to an Ecology of Mind.* New York: Ballantine Books.

Bateson, Gregory, Don Jackson, Jay Haley, and John Weakland. 1956. "Toward a Theory of Schizophrenia." *Behavioral Science* 1:251–264.

Becker, G. 1980. *Growing Old in Silence: Deaf People in Old Age.* Berkeley: University of California Press.

Beuf, Ann Hill. 1990. *Beauty Is the Beast: Appearance-Impaired Children in America.* Philadelphia: University of Pennsylvania Press.

Bochner, Arthur. 1984. "The Functions of Human Communication in Interpersonal Bonding." Pp. 544–621 in *Handbook of Rhetorical and Communication Theory,* edited by Carroll Arnold and John Waite Bowers. Boston: Allyn and Bacon.

———. 1994. "Perspectives on Inquiry II: Theories and Stories." Pp. 21–41 in *Handbook of Interpersonal Communication,* edited by M. L. Knapp and G. R. Miller. Thousand Oaks, CA: Sage.

Bogdan, Robert, and Steven Taylor. 1989. "Relationships with Severely Disabled People: The Social Construction of Humanness." *Social Problems* 36:135–148.

Branaman, Ann. 1997. "Goffman's Social Theory." Pp. xiv–lxxxii in *The Goffman Reader,* edited by Charles Lemert and Ann Branaman. Cambridge, MA: Blackwell.

Broaded, C. Montgomery. 1991. "China's Lost Generation: The Status Degradation of an Educational Cohort." *Journal of Contemporary Ethnography* 20:352–379.

Cahill, Spencer, and Robin Eggleston. 1995. "Reconsidering

the Stigma of Physical Disability: Wheelchair Use and Public Kindness." *The Sociological Quarterly* 36:681–698.

Carlisle, Jock. 1985. *Tangled Tongue: Living with a Stutter.* Toronto: University of Toronto Press.

Cooley, C. H. 1902. *Human Nature and Social Order.* New York: Scribner's.

Daly, Kerry. 1997. "Re-Placing Theory in Ethnography: A Postmodern View." *Qualitative Inquiry* 3:343–365.

Davis, Fred. 1961. "Deviance Disavowal: The Management of Strained Interaction by the Visibly Handicapped." *Social Problems* 9:121–132.

Edgerton, R. B. 1967. *The Cloak of Competence: Stigma in the Lives of the Mentally Retarded.* Berkeley: University of California Press.

Ellis, Carolyn. 1993. "'There Are Survivors': Telling a Story of Sudden Death." *The Sociological Quarterly* 34:711–730.

———. 1995. *Final Negotiations: A Story of Love, Loss, and Chronic Illness.* Philadelphia: Temple University Press.

———. 1996. "Maternal Connections." Pp. 240–243 in *Composing Ethnography,* edited by Ellis and Bochner. Walnut Creek, Calif.: AltaMira.

———. 1997. "Evocative Autoethnography: Writing Emotionally about Our Lives. Pp. 115–139 in *Representation and the Text: Re-framing the Narrative Voice,* edited by W. Tierney and Y. Lincoln. New York: State University of New York Press.

Ellis, Carolyn, and Arthur P. Bochner, eds. 1996. *Composing Ethnography: Alternative Forms of Qualitative Writing.* Walnut Creek, CA: AltaMira Press.

Frank, Gelya. 1988. "Beyond Stigma: Visibility and Self-Empowerment of Persons with Congenital Limb Deficiencies." *Journal of Social Issues* 44:95–115.

Gardner, Carol Brooks. 1991. "Stigma and the Public Self: Notes on Communication, Self, and Others." *Journal of Contemporary Ethnography* 20:251–262.

Goffman, Erving. 1956. "Embarrassment and Social Organization." *American Journal of Sociology* 62:264–271.

———. 1959. *The Presentation of Self in Everyday Life.* Garden City, NY: Doubleday/Anchor Books.

———. 1963. *Stigma: Notes on the Management of Spoiled Identity.* Englewood Cliffs, NJ: Prentice-Hall.

Gussow, Zachary, and George S. Tracy. 1968. "Status, Ideology, and Adaptation to Stigmatized Illness: A Study of Leprosy." *Human Organization* 27:316–325.

Hahn, H. 1985. "Towards a Politics of Disability: Definitions, Disciplines, and Policies." *Social Science Journal* 22:87–105.

Haley, Jay. 1963. *Strategies of Psychotherapy.* New York: Grune and Stratton.

Herman, C. Peter, Mark Zanna, and E. Tory Higgins. 1986. *Physical Appearance, Stigma, and Social Behavior.* Hillsdale, NJ.: Lawrence Erlbaum.

Jezer, Marty. 1997. *Stuttering: A Life Bound Up in Words.* New York: Basic Books.

Jones, Edward, Amerigo Farina, Albert Hastorf, Hazel Markus, Dale Miller, and Robert Scott. 1984. *Social Stigma: The Psychology of Marked Relationships.* New York: W. H. Freeman.

Kowalewski, M. R. 1988. "Double Stigma and Boundary Maintenance: How Gay Men Deal with AIDS." *Journal of Contemporary Ethnography* 17:211–228.

Krieger, Susan. 1996. *The Family Silver: Essays on Relationships Among Women.* Berkeley: University of California Press.

Lorde, Audre. 1980. *The Cancer Journals.* San Francisco: Aunt Lute Books.

Millman, M. 1980. *Such a Pretty Face: Being Fat in America.* New York: Berkeley Press.

Murphy, Robert, Jessica Scheer, Yoland Murphy, and Robert Mack. 1988. "Physical Disability and Social Liminality: A Study in the Rituals of Adversity." *Social Science and Medicine* 26:235–242.

Perry, Judith. 1996. "Writing the Self: Exploring the Stigma of Hearing Impairment." *Sociological Spectrum* 16:239–261.

Petrunik, Michael, and Clifford Shearing. 1983. "Fragile Facades: Stuttering and the Strategic Manipulation of Awareness." *Social Problems* 31:125–138.

Richardson, Laurel. 1996. "Speech Lessons." Pp. 231–239 in *Composing Ethnography,* edited by Ellis and Bochner.

Rochford, E. Burke. 1983. "Stutterers' Practices: Folk Remedies and Therapeutic Intervention." *Journal of Communication Disorders* 16:373–384.

Scott, Robert. 1970. "The Construction of Conceptions of Stigma by Professional Experts." Pp. 255–290 in *Deviance and Respectability: The Social Construction of Moral Meanings,* edited by J. D. Douglas. New York: Basic Books.

Shelton, Allen. 1995. "Foucault's Madonna: The Secret Life of Carolyn Ellis." *Symbolic Interaction* 18:83–87.

Susman, Joan. 1994. "Disability, Stigma and Deviance." *Social Science and Medicine* 38:15–22.

Thomas, D. J. 1982. "Interactions." Pp. 54–70 in *The Experience of Handicap,* edited by D. J. Thomas. New York: Methuen.

Updike, John. 1989. *Self-Conscious Memoirs.* New York: Fawcett Crest.

Valdez, Linda. 1997. "Baby-Boomer Moms Send Mixed Messages to Their Daughters." *Tampa Tribune,* May 20, p. 7.

Wright, B. A. 1983. *Physical Disabilities: A Psychosocial Approach.* New York: Harper and Row.

FURTHER READING

Becker, Howard S. 1953. "Becoming a Marijuana User." *American Journal of Sociology* 59: 235–242.

- A Classic article about how group life mediates the interpretation of bodily sensations for marijuana users.

Furman, Frida K. 1997. *Facing the Mirror: Older Women and Beauty Shop Culture.* New York: Routledge.

- An ethnographic study of a beauty salon and the experience of bodily self-presentation.

Goffman, Erving. 1963. *Stigma: Notes on the Management of Spoiled Identity.* Englewood Cliffs, NJ: Prentice-Hall.

- A Classic statement about the social organization of bodily and other stigmas.

Hesse-Biber, Sharlene. 1996. *Am I Thin Enough Yet? The Cult of Thinness and the Commercialization of Identity.* New York: Oxford University Press.

- A richly detailed study of the attractions of thinness among adolescents and young women.

Sanders, Clinton R. 1989. *Customizing the Body.* Philadelphia: Temple University Press.

- The body and the physical self in the world of tattooing.

PART 4 ---

SOCIAL
WORLDS

"Social worlds" is a familiar term. We may say, for example, that a group of teenagers lives in its own social world. This suggests that the teenagers have their own unique interests and concerns that are distinct from those of both younger and older persons. Their social world organizes their daily affairs, their inner lives, and their relations with other people. The group may even have a distinct territory, too, where they live out their social world—perhaps the high school cafeteria or a popular local hangout. Of course, social worlds may also be geographically diffuse. There may be no particular place that's identified as the site of a social world, as in the world of stamp collectors, which includes people scattered all over the globe.

Social world is also a familiar sociological concept. It's a convenient way of describing a distinctive social sphere. It's a realm of experience with specific, identifiable characteristics. For example, we may speak of the social world of the New York City taxi cab driver and contrast it with the social world of the Manhattan executive. Although the two may inhabit the same geographic space, their social worlds would feature specific professional, personal, and economic circumstances. There are myriad social worlds in contemporary life. They're as diverse as the social worlds of "Star Trekkies," soccer moms, and computer games, for instance. As important or trivial as they may seem, they are real and consequential to their participants.

341

They reflect a common culture that results when people share particular outlooks, orientations, and experiences (see Strauss 1978; Unruh 1983). Considered in this way, social worlds are discrete domains of identity and interaction. They are social realms where people share perspectives, systems of ideas, and common ways of acting and reacting.

In this book, we build upon this notion of social world, but we use it somewhat differently. For us, a social world is a working experiential reality. It comprises the *entire* panorama of experience for its participants—at least for the time being and the purposes at hand. It's more than a discrete, but circumscribed, realm of experience. The term "world" implies that it's more comprehensive than that. As we encounter a world of lived experience, we apprehend it as a comprehensive constellation of meaningful things and actions. It has distinctive parameters, signposts, and frontiers. This constellation of meanings takes shape and gains substance through social interaction. In practice, a social world is more than a mere part of experience. When it's engaged, it's an encompassing outlook or orientation to oneself and others that is constructed, conferred, and activated as the sum total of working experience, for all practical purposes. A social world includes the inner lives and interpersonal relations of those who engage it.

Imagine the social world of a 10 year old. We've all passed through that time of life, so we have some sense of what the world is from that perspective. For one thing, it's a world populated by particular roles—little kids, big kids, and adults. The distinctions between grade levels at school make all the difference in the world. A fourth grader, for example, simply doesn't play with second graders. On the other hand, "old" people are all pretty much the same—30, 50, or 70 years old—there's hardly a difference to the 10 year old. Work and play have distinct meanings and places in that world. The former is located at school, or at home when chores need to be done. The latter involves "fun." It's all but inconceivable that the two may intersect to the 10 year old.

The social world appears quite differently to a 50 year old. It's a world of responsibilities, commitments, and obligations. With luck, one's work may be fun. In terms of family life, it's hard to distinguish where parental duties end and enjoying "quality time" begins. Everyone under 30 years old is a "kid." Fifty can be "the prime of life" or "over the hill." It all depends upon the individual's orientation to career, family, finances, physical and mental health, and myriad other features of everyday life. The parameters and meanings of this social world emerge from the complex interactions and encounters that make up lived experience for the 50 year old. This is true for all social worlds. They are interactionally constructed experiential realities.

VARIABLE SOCIAL WORLDS

Notice that we've illustrated more than a single social world. Indeed, we often refer to social worlds in the plural. It's important to remember that what we experience as the social world at one time and place may change into a different social world at any moment. We are always participating in some social world—a working reality that takes its particular meaning, characteristics, and self-organizing impulses from talk and interaction. But this world and its meaningful features can change by virtue of how interaction shapes our orientation to the experience at hand. This means that we inhabit multiple social worlds—a number as vast as the alternating social contingencies that make up everyday life.

We may think of social worlds as experiential universes. We encounter these worlds by way of particular categories of meaning. That is, we see them through specific interpretive lenses.

We understand them in terms of distinct vocabularies and familiar metaphors. Because these worlds can be continuously transformed, we inhabit "multiple realities," as social phenomenologist Alfred Schutz (1970) put it. As our working realities shift, the picture and meaning of our experience changes. This change, in turn, alters the operating relevancies of our inner lives.

Social worlds change all the time. Some social worlds, however, are more fleeting than others. The social world of Little League baseball, for example, may encompass only a few hours a week—on game days—for example. For those brief times, the camaraderie, the game, and the popsicles afterward fully make up the Little League social world. But when the day is done, back at home, the world of video games or teenage romance novels may take over. In contrast, other social worlds may have greater duration or durability. The social world of a budding young artist, for example, may command virtually all his or her waking moments.

Because they are products of talk and interaction, social worlds are not set in stone. They are always potentially in flux—fluid, dynamic, temporary, transient, and changing. Of course, they don't seem that way while we are engaging them. Then, they are very real, very solid, and seemingly quite permanent. But as circumstances change, so do social worlds. Some of these changes can take place in relation to history or culture. Others are more situational.

Cultural or Historical Variation

First, let's consider how social worlds vary culturally or historically. One way to think of a social world is as a set of "conditions of possibility" for what reality may amount to (see Foucault 1979). At different points in time or in different cultural locations, our societies and cultures provide us with distinct possibilities for the realities of our social worlds. Imagine how different the world must appear to members of a culture such as our own who believe in the insights of science versus how it may appear to members of a culture who believe that wisdom emanates from, say, oracles or inspired visions. Turn back to the reading selection by Hugh Mehan and Houston Wood in Section 1 of Part 2 for vivid illustrations of alternative social worlds.

But changes occur within cultures as well as between them. And as they do, the social realities they construct change with them. When a scientific outlook, for instance, replaces a cultural belief in oracles, an entirely new set of possibilities for what could be "real" is likely to emerge. The social world of gender in the United States has undergone just this kind of change as the meaning of "female" has shifted over the years.

The women's suffrage movement of the 19th and early 20th centuries was virtually mind-boggling. American culture moved from categorizing women as mere chattel to viewing them as full participants in social, political, and economic affairs. Whereas women were once confined to the household, they now have access to the wider worlds of education, business, and employment. Whereas women were denied the right to vote, they now occupy seats in Congress, the president's cabinet, and the Supreme Court. As the world changed, so did the meaning of being female. The possibilities for what women could be inside—their minds, intellects, and ambitions, for example—expanded simultaneously. The social categories of "male" and "female" were redefined in relation to one another, as well as in terms of social relations more generally. The landscape of today's gendered social world is vastly different from that of the early 20th century because of the strikingly different meanings associated with gender in those worlds.

More recent examples of cultural change abound. Before the mid-1980s, for instance, the term "homelessness" didn't exist as a category for constructing experience; homelessness wasn't viewed as a distinct social world (Spencer 1996). It's not that there weren't people without homes. Plenty of people found themselves indigent and living "on the streets." But they weren't called "homeless." Without the category and its associated working reality, a social world of "homelessness" didn't exist. Nor did the inner lives of the homeless. Until the category and reality of *the* homeless emerged, no one cared to understand what these people were like as a group or as individuals. No one asked what motivated them, what they thought of themselves, or how they felt about their experiences. Being on the streets was a residual category, whose social psychological dimensions were yet to be constructed.

Many other social worlds have emerged in recent years. A world marked by random violence (Best 1999) is a striking recent example. New visions of inner lives accompany these new social worlds. We now have "hate crimes," with their perpetrators and victims (Jenness, 1996), "stalking" and "stalkers" (Lowney and Best 1996), and the "crack epidemic" and "the crack addict" (Reinerman and Levine 1996). These are now landmark identities on the social landscape. Yet they were nowhere to be found until the end of the 20th century. This is not to say that phenomena or actions resembling them didn't exist. But we didn't construct them into shared kinds of experience and identity with characteristics of their own.

Social movements are typically responsible for the creation and widespread use of new experiential categories. Interest groups, along with their stakeholders and claims makers, promote and publicize new constructions of everyday life. For example, the women's suffrage movement of the 19th century and the women's liberation and feminist movements of the 20th century were social forces that redefined what it meant to be female, which, in turn, altered what the gendered social world could possibly look like. These movements virtually reinvented the conditions of possibility for how women (and men) constructed their experiential realities.

In a sense, social movements are in the business of developing possibilities for new social worlds. Or they may aim to get rid of old ones. Either way, they transform inner lives. In the process of respecifying what it meant to be a woman, for example, the women's movement also engaged in the "politics of self." The movement specified and legitimated new opportunities for the kinds of selves that women could rightfully claim in American society.

This may be hard to imagine in the 21st century. There was a time, however, when women in the United States couldn't vote. They had no right to resist their husbands' wishes and desires. They held no standing in the realms of law, commerce, and industry. The identities that were available to them—and, by the same token, their own inner lives—were so drastically constrained and curtailed as to be virtually unrecognizable today. Today's female selves would have been equally unrecognizable 100 years ago. Given the social categories available at the time, "today's woman" would likely have been viewed as masculine, if not morally reprehensible. Women's vocabularies of motive, areas of competence, and even emotions—essentially their entire inner lives—have changed in parallel to changes in the gendered social world.

Situational Variation

While cultural and historical changes transform social worlds and inner lives, the interactional dynamics of social situations also have their impact. Everyday interaction further shapes the conditions of possibility for our working realities. Social worlds aren't imposed upon us from the outside. They have to be "worked up," so to speak. Culture and history aren't distant, all-powerful interpretive templates. Rather, we encounter alternate social worlds through the lived interactions of our everyday lives.

Consider, for example, how the social worlds of leisure and work can alternate from moment to moment even in the most casual everyday situations. On Saturday morning, Matthew

Yoshi, a partner in an up-and-coming software development firm, heads out to the golf course. It's time to unwind from a long week on the job. The sun is shining, and his game is "on." Every drive's in the fairway, and he's always around the green. He hasn't three-putted yet. For the time being, Matt hasn't a care in the world, except perhaps for lowering his handicap. It's a beautiful day. The grass and the trees couldn't be greener. The sky couldn't be bluer. Matt's swapping good-natured insults with his two playing partners, longtime friends. They're rehashing last night's ball game and the Yankees' prospects for the pennant. A $2 bet here and there keeps the golf "interesting." Everybody's loose and relaxed. And Matt has picked up a few bucks along the way.

Just as Matt's group prepares to tee off on the back nine, another golfer approaches them from the clubhouse. "Mind if I make it a foursome?" he inquires politely. "No problem." As the golfers introduce themselves to each other, however, Matt's day—his very world, his working social reality—changes abruptly.

"I'm Ty, Tyler DeGuere," offers the new guy. "I haven't been out here much. Just getting set up here in town."

"Holy crap!" says Matt to himself. "This is Tyler DeGuere, head of that new 'e-business' that's marketing herbal aphrodisiacs over the Internet. They're gonna be huge. We've been trying to get these guys interested in some of our software applications for weeks, but they're too busy making money to give us a meeting."

Suddenly, what was once a genial, carefree recreational outing has turned into a business opportunity. Matt's social world—previously revolving around relaxation and leisure—has suddenly been transformed into a world of commerce. Matt didn't have to go into the office or put on a tie. He didn't need his laptop or cell phone, his Palm Pilot or his pager. The physical setting hadn't changed, but the social world sure had. And so did the inner lives of the persons on the scene.

A simple exchange of introductions set off the transformation. In an interactional moment, Matt's whole world shifted. Once Matt realized who his new golfing "buddy" was, he was up to his ears in a whole new reality. But this new social world didn't emerge automatically. In many respects, it was already ready for action, a social world waiting to happen, so to speak. It just wasn't the working social world at that particular time and place.

The culture of business success, especially in the rapidly expanding and deadly competitive realm of e-commerce, had taught Matt that he had to be ready to jump at every opportunity, no matter how unexpected or serendipitous. Matt's business experience over the past weeks, even years, set the stage for him now to play out a recognizable and pervasive business world. Tyler DeGuere was a crucial part of this schema. As a golfing partner on an ordinary Saturday morning, he was nothing special—just another "good Joe." But as a piece of a larger business puzzle, Ty's mere presence transformed the operating social and experiential landscape. The social world of business opportunity was always there. Perhaps it was imperceptible, deep in the background. Ty's appearance literally "activated" it—brought it into view and soon put it into practice. This made it Matt's paramount reality, at least for the time being. With Ty on the scene, Matt's world wasn't the same.

So what's different? How did the social world change? For Matt, this was no longer a recreational outing. It wasn't exclusively a world of leisure and relaxation. The relevant features of the scene were no longer the sun, the grass, the trees, and the humorous banter. To be sure, they provided a pleasant backdrop, but now business took center stage in a world revolving around software applications and worldwide product distribution. An hour ago, Matt was intent on a perfectly struck drive, 250 yards, dead center of the fairway. In the context of recreational golf, that was his goal, even his obsession. In a world of business, however, Matt was intentionally pushing his drives way out to the right, so he could follow Ty into the rough and commiserate about their incurable slices and bad lies. The "perfect shot" now had little to do with golfing prowess and everything to do with sales opportunities.

Should Matt knock his approach stiff to the pin? Think again. Best lay up a few feet farther away than Ty's ball. Make sure not to show him up. How about those Yankees? The Yankees' prospects be damned; Ty's from Chicago and a long-time Cubs fan. "How about that 12-game winning streak? It's a crime that the Cubbies haven't played in 'the Series' since 1945. You just gotta love that Sammy Sosa. By the way, what business did you say you were in? . . . What sort of tracking and distribution software are you using out at your place?"

Seen through the lenses of business opportunity, the golf course became every bit as much a part of the world of work and commerce as any office or boardroom. Matt's working social world occupied the same physical space, comprising the same physical parameters, as his world of leisure. Many of the situation's social features even remained the same. Yet, virtually every object and action took new shape as the business world supplanted the world of leisure. As Matt's interactions took a "commercial" turn, they conferred new meaning and significance on nearly every aspect of the situation. Matt entered a new experiential reality, populated by new personas.

SOCIAL WORLDS IN PRACTICE

Social worlds aren't abstractions. Matt's day at the golf course vividly demonstrates how real and consequential they are. The transformation of his world of leisure into a business world wasn't simply imaginary. It wasn't philosophical or theoretical. Social worlds aren't just mental fabrications. Rather, they come to us through the actual *practice* of everyday life. The meaningful contours of lived experience are shaped by purposeful social encounters.

Activating Social Worlds

Social worlds may exist as potential schemes of experience, but they remain mere conditions of possibility until they are pressed into service by the demands of real-life interaction. Possible social worlds are not the same as the social worlds that emerge in talk and interaction. Even the seemingly most consequential features of social worlds aren't constant, objectively given features of experience. Rather, working social realities must be "activated" to be part of everyday life.

Consider, for example, how nationality and ethnicity as social worlds become salient and consequential *in practice*. In the late 1980s and early 1990s, the Yugoslavian men's national basketball team was among the world's finest. It came to be known as the "Yugoslav Dream Team." The team dominated international competition, producing stars who made their ultimate mark playing alongside Michael Jordan in the American NBA. Team members hailed from all over the country—Croatia, Serbia, Bosnia, and Slovenia.

By all accounts, this was an extraordinary squad. Individually, its players were men of character and goodwill. They came together with an unrivaled singleness of purpose, solidarity, and fellowship. They lived together, trained together, traveled together, played together. Truly embodying an overused sports cliché, this group of young men from widely different backgrounds became a single "family." They were "close as brothers" (Cornell and Hartman 1998).

The tragedy of civil war that erupted in 1991 tore apart the Yugoslav Federation. In the process, it also established social worlds of ethnicity as the paramount realities of all Yu-goslavs, including the "brothers" on the national team. Although they had "always" been Serbs, Croats, and Bosnians—at least in the sense that ancestries could be traced to different geo-graphic locales in the region—the players' ethnic differences were submerged. They were al-ways conditions of possibility, of course. But, on a day-to-day basis, they were experientially irrelevant to the teammates' "hoop dreams."

As the war's genocidal mayhem spread, the social world of these extraordinary players was inescapably altered. The players' homeland crumbled around them. Atrocities of "ethnic cleansing" were everyday fare. Players increasingly saw differences where they once saw only teammates. Violent ethnic rivalries pervaded everyone's lives as the players directly confront-ed political and military conflicts. This was real life, not simply headlines in the newspaper or film clips on the TV news. No one was immune. Hometowns were bombed into oblivion. Friends and relatives were left homeless. Loved ones died.

All this inevitably penetrated the fellowship of the Dream Team. When asked about rela-tions among teammates, future NBA star Toni Kukoc admitted that his social world had changed: "It always gets down to asking how's your family, how's mine . . . and when you touch on families, you have to touch on the war, and when you touch on the war, you're on op-posite sides" (Wolff 1996:88). The issue was unavoidable.

In a country torn by civil war, the simplest aspects of everyday life made ethnic ties con-spicuous. It happened even where ethnicity had previously been "no big deal." Once simply a Dream Teamer, Kukoc was now *Croatian.* Kukoc's teammate, Teo Alibegovic, had become a *Bosnian Muslim* in a social world constructed out of ethnic division and destruction. "You know, I never knew what nationality anyone was when we were playing with each other," re-called Alibegovic wistfully. "And I bet you they never knew what I was. . . . Well, now we know" (Wolff 1996:90). *In practice,* the social worlds of Kukoc, Alibegovic, Vlade Divac, and the rest now revolved around ethnic difference as much as basketball prowess.

If social worlds are conceptually "always already there," they are not socially consequential until they are activated or realized. Activation may come in the form of dramatic events, such as the cataclysmic destruction of the World Trade Center, which activated worlds of terrorism, militarism, and patriotic fervor, among others. But it also takes place in the mundane give-and-take of everyday interaction. A gendered world, for example, is not simply a uniform code of gendered meanings to be considered and automatically applied. Rather, the parameters of a gendered world—what gender actually means in relation to lived experience—are constantly under construction. Cultural meanings provide recipes for organizing experience, but situation-al contingencies always have their say, too.

Let's look at the interactive detail of how this process works in relation to a particular social world, where gender and severe personal troubles intersect. Whereas our illustration may por-tray somewhat unusual circumstances, it depicts phenomena that are common in more ordinary settings as well. Nowadays, when persons are psychologically troubled or become troublesome to those around them, psychiatric hospitalization provides a remedy for the intra- and interper-sonal havoc at hand. Persons are admitted to mental hospitals so they can be evaluated and treated, but sometimes "patients" resist. They don't want to sacrifice their freedom while un-dergoing treatment. In some cases, *involuntary* commitment procedures are invoked. Of course, not all troublesome behavior or psychological troubles lead to involuntary hospitaliza-tion. But even if such cases are extreme, they can nonetheless illustrate the interactional work that goes into producing a gendered social world.

Involuntary commitments are formal legal proceedings. Judges decide if persons who are deemed to be mentally ill should be hospitalized because they pose a danger to themselves or others or if they are so gravely disabled that they can't adequately care for themselves (see Holstein 1993). Potential patients are typically represented by private attorneys or public defenders (PDs). Attorneys for the state (district attorneys, or DAs) argue for commitment. A mental health professional is usually asked to render an opinion about the candidate patient's mental health. Eventually, the candidate patient gets to speak for himself or herself. During these hearings, we often see a gendered world emerge, but the meaning and significance of gender is far from constant. This world is shaped and specified in social interaction.

Take the case involving Gerald Simms, where gender was used to provide standards for how a "normal" man should behave. The testifying psychiatrist initially characterized Simms as a "severely troubled man" and gave the following reason for his diagnosis of schizophrenia:

> Mr. Simms suffers from drastic mood swings. His affect is extremely labile. One minute he'll be in tears, the next he's just fine. He fluctuates. His affect may be flattened, then elevated. One moment he'll be telling you about his cleaning business, then he'll flip out of character and cry like a brokenhearted schoolgirl over the most insignificant thing. Something that should never upset a grown man like Mr. Simms. During his periods of flattened affect, he seems to lose all interest. . . . His passivity—he's almost docile in a very sweet sort of way. He just smiles and lets everything pass. It's completely inappropriate for an adult male. (Holstein 1993: 155)

Initially, the relevance of Simms's gender to the psychiatrist's diagnosis was hardly apparent. Subsequently, however, the psychiatrist explained his diagnosis by articulating Simms's behavior with standard gender expectations. He portrayed Simms's emotions as inappropriate—crying like "a brokenhearted schoolgirl" over matters that should "never upset a grown man." He framed being pleasant and passive as a "problem" for a man living in a gendered world. Note how it was not just Simms's gender that was highlighted. The psychiatrist invoked a wide variety of expectations connected with gender more generally. He juxtaposed and contrasted them with one another to make the point that Simms wasn't normal. The psychiatrist *used* features of a gendered world to establish Simms's "abnormality," putting that gendered world into place in the process.

In a gendered social world, the meaning of being male or female isn't simply dictated by personal traits or individual characteristics. The experiential contours of that world are continually asserted and negotiated. In the actual practice of involuntary commitment hearings, gender is continuously made salient and significant, but not necessarily in the same ways. Let's look at this process in relation to another case, involving Arlene Bluman, a 33-year-old white woman. In this instance, the DA based her case for commitment on Bluman's inability to function and her recurrent social impairment. She concluded that Bluman wasn't fit to live in the community because she was vulnerable to a variety of perils.

> She [Bluman] has a repeated history of failure in non-institutional settings. There is abundant evidence that she has trouble keeping herself together when she's released. She has trouble managing her money. She has trouble with almost everything—interacting with others, getting along with people, taking her medications. She simply isn't ready to resume a normal life at this point. . . .

The PD in the case countered by suggesting that Ms. Bluman's home environment was adequately suited for a person of her type. As the following extract shows, the PD argued that the home was fine *for a woman* with special needs.

My client has a place to live. It's everything a woman needs. The landlord, a Mr. Dietrich, has agreed to rent her a room with a kitchen . . . he lives in the building and says he'll look in on her from time to time. . . . She'll sign over her SSI check to him the day it arrives. . . . Arlene has some problems, but she's aware of them now. She just needs a little help. This woman will not be much trouble. How much trouble can a woman like her be? She won't cause anyone any harm. Looking after a woman in that situation won't require very much. The landlord—Mr. Dietrich—says he's willing and I believe that Miss Bluman can manage very well with him helping take care of her.

Explicitly invoking gender as a relevant consideration, the PD argued that, as a woman, Bluman was easily managed. She was basically harmless. Her gender, in this case, was constructed as synonymous with manageability. Mr. Dietrich's gender was implicitly invoked as well, to support the claim that he would surely be able to manage this harmless woman.

The judge, however, had other ideas. Once again, gender was at the heart of the discussion. As the exchange veered in a new direction, gender took on different meanings.

JUDGE: It seems that Arlene might be taken care of all right But that's what worries me. Would we be doing the right thing by placing this woman in the care of some strange man? Now, hopefully his intentions are honorable, but can we know that for sure? . . . I don't feel good about a woman living alone in this kind of arrangement. And what about the other tenants? . . . What do we know about them? This makes me very uneasy. A woman is very vulnerable. I'm concerned about her safety. I'm concerned that this may not be the most proper thing to do.

PD: We have no reason to believe that anything improper at all would happen. Just because she's a woman doesn't mean she has to be protected from every male that's out there. . . . What this woman needs is just a little help to get by. Should we distrust anyone who offers to help? . . .

JUDGE: No. . . . We're talking about a woman's best interest here. A woman's. And I've got to make that the basis for my decision. Ms. Bluman's not well yet, and even if she were, I don't know as I'd recommend her living in a place like this. It's important that there would be someone there that could take care of her. I'm sure he would, but that's my worry. That he would take care of her, if you know what I mean.

The practical contours of a gendered social world were at stake in this exchange. What it means to be male or female is far from definite. Rather, working definitions emerge strategically in the flow of talk and interaction. The judge argued that men are predatory, openly suggesting that they are likely to take improper advantage of women. He also portrayed women as vulnerable. This particular woman—Ms. Bluman—was especially vulnerable because of her mental problems. The PD, of course, disagreed. He minimized the vulnerability associated with femininity and refused to categorize all men as predators. Clearly, the essential parameters of this social world were not set in stone, but were realized in the course of the discussion. The interacting parties activated gender as a consequential feature of the practical reality at hand.

Institutionalizing Social Worlds

When patterns of activity become routine and highly anticipatable, we refer to them as social institutions. Everett Hughes (1984) called these customary ways of acting and interacting the "going concerns" that organize everyday life. Their concerted activities give our everyday lives structure and predictability. Social institutions provide the enduring categories of meaning that we use to map out how we act, who we are, and with whom we interact. They are prominent landmarks of our social environments.

In the involuntary commitment hearings just described, the "going concern" was dealing with potential havoc that mentally ill persons may cause. The proceedings focused on both psychiatric troubles and the more-or-less tenable situations that mentally ill persons may inhabit. These persons were typically viewed in terms of their manageability and vulnerability. In the proceedings, gender often intersected with the troubles under consideration. The ensuing discussions produced "institutionalized" versions of both gender and psychiatric troubles.

Institutions, however, can never dictate the parameters of social worlds. Instead, they provide normative expectations—prevalent conditions of possibility for what social worlds may be. As we saw in the involuntary commitment hearings, what the social world ended up looking like, in practice, was always up for grabs to some extent, even if its appearance was fairly predictable in light of existing institutional groundings. For instance, within the institutional purview of an alcohol abuse treatment center, a "drinking problem" may be framed as a "disease." It may be an "addiction" that rules a "victim's" life. In this world, the "alcoholic" is powerless to resist on his or her own. He or she needs outside intervention and support of one kind or another to hold the disease at bay "one day at a time." It's a distinctive and increasingly familiar social world.

The "same" drinking problem, however, may be constructed entirely differently in another institutional setting. In a fundamentalist Christian church, for example, alcoholism may be more of a spiritual or moral transgression than a sickness. The social world of the church may be every bit as encompassing as that of the treatment center. But it would present vastly different moral contours for alcoholism. The point is not that one way of viewing drinking problems is better than the other. Rather, different institutions give their participants different recipes for how to construct their inner lives and inhabit their social worlds.

Readers may recall a vivid example of this from the discussion of Charles Grady in the Part 3, Section 5, selection titled "Constructing Competence." Charles's identity changed dramatically as he traveled from one institutional setting to another. He was nothing but a small-time street punk to the police, who picked him up for loitering and vandalism. The social world of police officers revolves around law and order, detecting transgressions and exacting compliance. The category "punk" has specific connotations that help officers know just what kind of person they are dealing with. But when Charles was sent to a "Delinquency Prevention Program," he found himself immersed in a social world made up of strikingly different categories (also see Emerson 1969). The world of reform and rehabilitation introduced notions of "reference groups," "peer pressure," and "viable alternatives." Here, Charles became a "vulnerable" kid, looking for social approval, hoping to belong. His inner life was now a feature of a different working reality. After this, Charles became a "psychosexually maladjusted adolescent" in a psychiatric treatment program. Finally, he was an "immature" and "hyperactive" boy in a medical setting, where he was diagnosed as suffering from "attention deficit disorder." Each institutional setting had its own working social world, complete with psychological blueprints for inner life. In each situation, the participants constructed Charles's persona in terms of the categories, terminology, concerns, remedies, and sense of Charles's thoughts and desires that were locally pertinent. The "same" person hardly looked the same from one institution to the next.

But, again, it's important to emphasize that institutions only provide conditions of possibility for who and what we are. They don't dictate or unilaterally assert inner lives or social worlds. Treatment personnel within an organization, for example, may disagree on how they see a boy like Charles and his problems. Institutionalized social worlds may be so multifaceted that they are never completely normative or predictable in practice. Moreover, it's never fully clear where the borders of various social realities lie.

For example, at Cedarview, a residential treatment program for emotionally disturbed children (see Buckholdt and Gubrium 1985), inner lives and social worlds were typically seen in terms of behavioral psychology. It was a social world of visible conduct, stimuli and responses, rewards, punishments, and reinforcement schedules. The treatment program was designed to shape *behaviors,* not personalities or dispositions. The program's social world revolved around these concerns. Interest in children's inner lives was officially limited to what could be gleaned from their visible actions. The deep recesses of the children's thoughts and feelings were institutionally ignored.

Such was daily life at Cedarview. That is, until midafternoon on Fridays, when the weekend was close at hand. At this time, many of the children and most of the staff members went home. For the few remaining children and adult staffers, it seemed like the social world of behavioral treatment suddenly went "on vacation." From Friday to Monday, talk of rules and regulations virtually ceased. "Aw, come on. It's the weekend," was the rallying cry of a different reality. Nonclinical identities displaced the psychological labels that identified the children who inhabited Cedarview during regular business hours. Over the weekend, the typical ways of viewing residents and their activities were suspended. Weekday realities were put on hold, as it were. Routines were relaxed, judgments withheld, reinforcements ignored. The institution—as a possible clinical reality—was still very much in place. *In practice,* however, it was set aside for the weekend. A more conventional social world of children and their adult caretakers took over. Taken together, we may say that multiple social realities were housed under one institutional roof. To get along on the premises, one had to learn when and where different social worlds might predominate.

FINAL REMINDERS

Our discussion of inner lives and social worlds brings us to a fascinating conclusion. As different as they may sometimes seem, "inner" and "outer" realms of experience are made from the same interactional cloth in practice. Superficially, they appear to occupy separate domains of our lives, but they are both social constructions. They are things of our own making. Often, they appear to be distant from us, either outside, beyond our control, or deeply embedded inside us. Nevertheless, they are products of what we do together through social interaction.

Not only are inner lives and social worlds both social constructions, but they help to construct each other. Who we are and the social worlds that we inhabit affect what we think, feel, and do. In fundamental ways, our inner lives and social worlds shape the way we act and interact. And since they both contribute to interaction, each helps to construct the other.

This process of mutual construction gives rise to a working paradox. Interaction creates both our inner lives and social worlds. At the same time, those inner lives and social worlds provide the substance and direction for interaction. We emphasized this unceasing linkage between inner lives and social worlds in the introductory essays for Parts I and II. Readers should recall an important point we made at the time. *Social life is reflexive,* some aspects of social encounters produce other aspects of those encounters. These encounters, in turn, affect the production of the social actions and objects that seemingly kicked off the process in the first place. It's a complex, circular process. Explaining it in a linear fashion is as futile as trying to explain which came first, the chicken or the egg.

Our aim hasn't been to straighten out this process. Instead, we've tried to expand the reader's appreciation for the complex self-producing and self-sustaining quality of social life.

That's what a *sociological* social psychology is all about. It highlights how social interaction produces inner lives and the social worlds that are the working realities of experience. It shows us how we create the circumstances of our lives at the same time that we are shaped by these very same circumstances. It reminds us how deeply interconnected the various aspects of lived experience can be.

Our final reminder is a point that bears repeating. We construct our inner lives and social world through everyday interaction. Having created, them, in their varied guises, we continue to live by them.

REFERENCES

Best, Joel. 1999. *Random Violence.* Berkeley: University of California Press.

Buckholdt, David R. and Jaber F. Gubrium. 1985. *Caretakers.* Lanham, MD: University Press of America.

Cornell, Stephen and Douglas Hartman. 1998. *Ethnicity and Race.* Thousand Oaks, CA: Pine Forge Press.

Emerson, Robert M. 1969. *Judging Delinquents.* Chicago: Aldine.

Foucault, Michel. 1979. *Discipline and Punish.* New York: Vintage Books.

Holstein, James A. 1993. *Court-Ordered Insanity.* Hawthorne, NY: Aldine de Gruyter.

Hughes, Everett. 1984. *The Sociological Eye.* New Brunswick, NJ: Transaction Books.

Jenness, Valerie. 1996. "Hate Crimes in the United States: The Transformation of Injured Persons into Victims and the Extension of Victim Status to Multiple Constituencies." Pp. 213–238 in *Images of Issues,* (2d ed., edited by Joel Best). Hawthorne, NY: Aldine de Gruyter.

Lowney, Kathleen S. and Joel Best. 1996. "Stalking Strangers and Lovers: Changing Media Typifications of a New Crime Problem." Pp. 33–58 in *Images of Issues,* (2d ed., edited by Joel Best). Hawthorne, NY: Aldine de Gruyter.

Reinerman, Craig and Harry G. Levine. 1996. "The Crack Attack: America's Latest Drug Scare, 1986–1992." Pp. 147–186 in *Images of Issues,* (2d ed., edited by Joel Best). Hawthorne, NY: Aldine de Gruyter.

Schutz, Alfred. 1970. *On Phenomenology and Social Relations.* Chicago: University of Chicago Press.

Spencer, J. William. 1996. "From Bums to the Homeless: Media Constructions of Persons Without Homes from 1980–1984." Pp. 39–58 in *Perspectives on Social Problems,* Vol. 8, edited by James A. Holstein and Gale Miller. Greenwich, CT: JAI Press.

Strauss, Anselm. 1978. "A Social World Perspective." Pp. 119–128 in *Studies in Symbolic Interaction,* edited by Norman K. Denzin. Greenwich, CT: JAI Press.

Unruh, David R. 1983. *Invisible Lives.* Beverly Hills CA: Sage.

Wolff, Alexander. 1996. "Prisoners of War." *Sports Illustrated.* June 3, pp. 80–90.

WORLDS OF RACE AND ETHNICITY

Today, it's often difficult to discuss how race figures in our day-to-day lives. For all the talk about diversity, we sometimes find ourselves uncomfortable in admitting to racial differences, even while there are some who see race at every turn. There are times when some of us treat race as *the* crucial factor in how we define who we are or how we will act. There are other times when race recedes so far into the background as to virtually disappear. Race seems to matter, but then it doesn't. Race is everywhere and nowhere, all at once.

Race may provide the quintessential illustration of how social worlds can change from one moment to the next. For example, many white Americans will tell you that "race doesn't matter" in how they conduct their lives. This isn't simply denial or ignorance. It's the legacy of decades of trying to forge a society in which rights, resources, and status aren't determined by racial considerations. For some, it's a matter of political correctness, for better or worse. But it's also the upshot of living in circumstances in which, for all practical purposes, "white" is not a race. For many people, being white in America means an absence of conscious racial identity. It means that everyday life doesn't deliberately revolve around matters of race or ethnicity. "Whiteness" has been the standard for being "normal" or absolutely ordinary. It's the social *norm,* to use a more sociological term. All this implies that race isn't an especially important parameter of the social world—at least not for whites. It's part of others' worlds, but not theirs. "Others" are Asians or Hispanics or African Americans. For a white person, "I'm just me."

But this can be the case for white people only in situations that are predominantly and constantly "white." What happens, however, when a white person finds himself playing basketball on a playground, and all the other players are African American? Or when a teenager notices that she seems to be the only person at the shopping mall who isn't speaking Spanish or Chinese? These are situations that heighten racial consciousness. The self of which we become aware now has definite racial and ethnic contours.

Try to visualize a social world in which such racial self-consciousness exists. Imagine, for instance, an English literature class with mostly nonwhite students and a black professor. What is the social world like for the white student who finds him or herself in the minority in this class? Or, for that matter, what would it be like for students of color to find themselves in the majority? Would their outlooks—what they say, feel, and do—be different? How might being in the minority affect the way the social world—especially its racial aspects—appears to a white person?

It's likely that this hypothetical classroom would become a social world revolving around race and ethnicity. Certainly, not everything would become a racial matter. But it would certainly be a new challenge for many white students, who typically take their own race for granted. It's a different social world when "being white" seems to matter. The world's not the same when being white makes *you* different. This world would suddenly resemble the world that many—if not most—persons of color in America confront every day, especially when they move beyond their immediate homes and communities.

When we're aware of the racial and ethnic dimensions of social worlds, they take new shape and texture. When a person walking through a particular neighborhood knows that the color of his skin can be sufficient cause for residents to be wary and suspicious or for the police to stop and question him, it affects his outlook on that world. When a police officer's experience patrolling a community tells her that certain "types" of people are especially likely to be part of the so-called criminal element, it influences the way she views her beat. When jurors' personal experiences with the criminal justice system tell them that authorities do, in fact, tip the scales of justice in favor of, or against, members of particular racial or ethnic groups, it's understandable for those jurors to have "reasonable doubts" about how the police and prosecutors develop and present "evidence" in a murder trial. Race and ethnicity are key components of such social worlds. They can significantly shape how we view ourselves and others.

ABOUT THE READINGS

Social worlds of race and ethnicity are *constructed*—both culturally and situationally. At times, race remains in the background. At other times, racial aspects of social experience can move front and center with remarkable force and presence. **Langston Hughes's** classic observation, **"That Powerful Drop,"** is as poignant as it is succinct. It shows us how race can become the very essence of a social world.

As fundamental as they are, racialized selves and identities are also socially constructed: We aren't simply black or white. We have to work at being who we are. We literally *do* "being black" or "being white." **Robin D. G. Kelley** provides a fascinating account of how an African American male works to construct particular aspects of being black. **"Confessions of a Nice Negro, or Why I Shaved My Head"** describes how the author *managed* his appearance in order to be both suitably black, yet nonthreatening to whites. Kelley shows us how he *does* "being a Nice Negro." Parts of Kelley's narrative clearly resonate with what Goffman told us about the presentation of self earlier in this book.

At the same time, however, Kelley shows us that we don't control every aspect of how we are perceived. Sometimes he found himself "doing being black" when he least expected it. The appearance of the body itself—over which we have only limited control—is capable of speaking volumes about who we are, even when we remain verbally silent. Of course, awareness that this happens can also be used as a tactic for self-presentation. Kelley, for instance, explains how much he accomplished through the simple, fortuitous act of shaving his head.

The selections by Hughes and Kelley stand in stark contrast to **Pamela Perry's** insights in **"White Means Never Having to Say You're Ethnic: White Youth and the Construction of 'Cultureless' Identities."** Perry begins her study of two high schools by showing readers how "normal" it is to be white in a world where race is seldom a conscious consideration. In a nearly all-white high school, being white is taken for granted. Nevertheless, the construction of whiteness, Perry argues, is ubiquitous. It happens everywhere. Students just don't seem to notice. For white students, race is something others may have. But being white is nothing special or distinctive for them. It's simply natural.

In comparison, Perry shows how a multiethnic setting makes race much more problematic for whites. In a high school where whites are in the minority, students constantly confront what it means to be white—or any other race or ethnicity. The diverse cultural mix brings race and ethnicity to a high level of consciousness. It's ironic, however, that white students construct racial identities that are similar to those of the students at the all-white school. In both schools, being white comes to mean being "cultureless," especially in comparison to members of other ethnic or racial groups. These groups, of course, are defined principally in terms of their cultures.

Finally, **Beverly Daniel Tatum** describes how language is central to the construction of ethnicity. Asking **"Who Are You if You Don't Speak Spanish?"** in the article subtitled **Language and Identity Among Latinos,** Tatum explores the interrelations among language, self, and identity. For Latino teenagers, using, or avoiding the use of, Spanish is often a key to establishing the parameters of their social worlds and the selves that populate them.

30 | THAT POWERFUL DROP
Langston Hughes

Leaning on the lamp post in front of the barber shop, Simple was holding up a copy of the *Chicago Defender* and reading about how a man who looks white had just been declared officially colored by an Alabama court.

"It's powerful," he said.

"What?"

"That one drop of Negro blood—because just *one* drop of black blood makes a man colored. *One* drop—you are a Negro! Now, why is that? Why is Negro blood so much more powerful than any other kind of blood in the world? If a man has Irish blood in him, people will say, 'He's *part* Irish.' If he has a little Jewish blood, they'll say, 'He's *half Jewish*.' But if he has just a small bit of colored blood in him, BAM!—'*He's a Negro!*' Not, 'He's *part* Negro.' No, be it ever so little, if that blood is black, '*He's a Negro!*' Now, this is what I do not understand—why our *one* drop is so powerful. Take paint—white will not make black *white*. But black will make white *black*. One drop of black in white paint—and the white ain't white no more! Black is powerful. You can have ninety-nine drops of white blood in your veins down South—but if that other *one* drop is black, shame on you! Even if you look white, you're black. That drop is really powerful. Explain it to me. You're colleged."

"It has no basis in science," I said, "so there's no logical explanation." . . .

31 | CONFESSIONS OF A NICE NEGRO, OR WHY I SHAVED MY HEAD

Robin D. G. Kelley

It happened just the other day—two days into the new year, to be exact. I had dashed into the deserted lobby of an Ann Arbor movie theater, pulling the door behind me to escape the freezing winter winds Michigan residents have come to know so well. Behind the counter knelt a young white teenager filling the popcorn bin with bags of that awful pre-popped stuff. Hardly the enthusiastic employee; from a distance it looked like she was lost in deep thought. The generous display of body piercing suggested an X-generation flowerchild—perhaps an anthropology major into acid jazz and environmentalism, I thought. Sporting a black New York Yankees baseball cap and a black-and-beige scarf over my nose and mouth, I must have looked like I had stepped out of a John Singleton film. And because I was already late, I rushed madly toward the ticket counter.

The flower child was startled: "I don't have anything in the cash register," she blurted as she pulled the bag of popcorn in front of her for protection.

"Huh? I just want one ticket for *Little Women,* please—the two-fifteen show. My wife and daughter should already be in there." I slowly gestured to the theater door and gave her one of those innocent childlike glances I used to give my mom when I wanted to sit on her lap.

"Oh god . . . I'm so sorry. A reflex. Just one ticket? You only missed the first twenty minutes. Enjoy the show."

Enjoy the show? Barely 1995 and here we go again. Another bout with racism in a so-called liberal college town; another racial drama in which I play the prime suspect. And yet I have to confess the situation was pretty funny. Just two hours earlier I couldn't persuade Elleza, my four-year-old daughter, to put her toys away; time-out did nothing, yelling had no effect, and the evil stare made no impact whatsoever. Thor-

oughly frustrated, I had only one option left: "Okay, I'm gonna tell Mommy!" Of course it worked.

So those five seconds as a media-made black man felt kind of good. I know it's a product of racism. I know that the myth of black male violence has resulted in the deaths of many innocent boys and men of darker hue. I know that the power to scare is not real power. I know all that—after all, I study this stuff for a living! For the moment, though, it felt good. (Besides, the ability to scare with your body can come in handy, especially when you're trying to get a good seat in a theater or avoid long lines.)

I shouldn't admit this, but I take particular pleasure in putting fear into people on the lookout for black male criminality mainly because those moments are so rare for me. Indeed, my *inability* to employ black-maleness as a weapon is the story of my life. Why I don't possess it, or rather possess so little of it, escapes me. I grew up poor in Harlem and Afrodena (the Negro West Side of Pasadena/Altadena, California). My mom was single during my formative preadolescent years, and for a brief moment she even received a welfare check. A hard life makes a hard nigga, so I've been told.

Never an egghead or a dork, as a teenager I was pretty cool. I did the house-party circuit on Friday and Saturday nights and used to stroll down the block toting the serious Radio Raheem boombox. Why, I even invaded movie theaters in the company of ten or fifteen hooded and high-topped black bodies, colonizing the balconies and occupying two seats per person. Armed with popcorn and Raisinettes as our missiles of choice, we dared any usher to ask us to leave. Those of us who had cars (we called them hoopties or rides back in that day) spent our lunch hours and precious class time hanging out in the school parking lot, running down our Die Hards to pump up Cameo,

---

Funkadelic, Grandmaster Flash from our car stereos. I sported dickies and Levis, picked up that gangsta stroll, and when the shag came in style I was with it—always armed with a silk scarf to ensure that my hair was laid. Granted, I vomited after drinking malt liquor for the first time and my only hit of a joint ended abruptly in an asthma attack. But I was cool.

Sure, I was cool, but nobody feared me. That I'm relatively short with dimples and curly hair, speak softly in a rather medium to high-pitched voice, and have a "girl's name" doesn't help matters. And everyone knows that light skin is less threatening to white people than blue-black or midnight brown. Besides, growing up with a soft-spoken, uncharacteristically passive West Indian mother deep into East Indian religions, a mother who sometimes walked barefoot in the streets of Harlem, a mother who insisted on proper diction and never, ever, ever used a swear word, screwed me up royally. I could never curse right. My mouth had trouble forming the words—"fuck" always came out as "fock" and "goddamn" always sounded like it's spelled, not "gotdayum," the way my Pasadena homies pronounced it in their Calabama twang. I don't even recall saying the word "bitch" unless I was quoting somebody or some authorless vernacular rhyme. For some unknown reason, that word scared me.

Moms dressed me up in the coolest mod outfits—short pant suits with matching hats, Nehru jackets, those sixties British-looking turtlenecks. Sure, she got some of that stuff from John's Bargain Store or Goodwill, but I always looked "cute." More stylish than roguish. Kinda like W. E. B. Du Bois as a toddler, or those turn-of-the-century photos of middle-class West Indian boys who grow up to become prime ministers or poets. Ghetto ethnographers back in the late sixties and early seventies would not have found me or my family very "authentic," especially if they had discovered that one of my middle names is Gibran, after the Lebanese poet Kahlil Gibran.

Everybody seemed to like me. Teachers liked me, kids liked me; I even fell in with some notorious teenage criminals at Pasadena High School because *they* liked me. I remember one memorable night in the ninth grade when I went down to the Pasadena Boys' Club to take photos of some of my partners on the basketball team. On my way home some big kids, eleventh-graders to be exact, tried to take my camera. The ring-leader pulled out a knife and gently poked it against my chest. I told them it was my stepfather's camera and if I came home without it he'd kick my ass for a week. Miraculously, this launched a whole conversation about stepfathers and how messed up they are, which must have made them feel sorry for me. Within minutes we were cool; they let me go unmolested and I had made another friend.

In affairs of the heart, however, "being liked" had the opposite effect. I can only recall having had four fights in my entire life, all of which were with girls who supposedly liked me but thoroughly beat my behind. Sadly, my record in the boxing ring of puppy love is still 0–4. By the time I graduated to serious dating, being a nice guy seemed like the root of all my romantic problems. I resisted jealously, tried to be understanding, brought flowers and balloons, opened doors, wrote poems and songs, and seemed to always be on my knees for one reason or another. If you've ever watched "Love Connection" or read *Cosmopolitan,* you know the rest of the story: I practically never had sex and most of the women I dated left me in the cold for roughnecks. My last girlfriend in high school, the woman I took to my prom, the woman I once thought I'd die for, tried to show me the light: "Why do you always ask me what I want? Why don't you just *tell* me what you want me to do? Why don't you take charge and *be a man?* If you want to be a real man you can't be nice all the time!"

I always thought she was wrong; being nice has nothing to do with being a man. While I still think she's wrong, it's an established fact that our culture links manhood to terror and power, and that black men are frequently imaged as the ultimate in hypermasculinity. But the black man as the prototype of violent hypermasculinity is as much a fiction as the happy Sambo. No matter what critics and stand-up comics might say, I know from experience that not all black men—and here I'm only speaking of well-lighted or daytime situations—generate fear. Who scares and who doesn't has a lot to do with the body in question; it is dependent on factors such as age, skin color, size, clothes, hairstyle, and even the sound of one's voice. The cops who beat Rodney King and the jury who acquitted King's assailants openly admitted that the size, shape, and color of his body automatically made him a threat to the officers' safety.

On the other hand, the threatening black male body can take the most incongruous forms. Some of the hardest brothas on my block in West Pasadena kept their perms in pink rollers and hairnets. It was not unusual to see young black men in public with curlers, tank-top undershirts, sweatpants, black mid-calf dress socks, and Stacey Adams shoes, hanging out on the corner or on the basketball court. And we all knew that these brothas were not to be messed with. (The rest of the world probably knows it by now, too, since black males in curlers are occasionally featured on "Cops" and "America's Most Wanted" as notorious drug dealers or heartless pimps.)

Whatever the source of this ineffable terror, my body simply lacked it. Indeed, the older I got and the more ensconced I became in the world of academia, the less threatening I seemed. Marrying and having a child also reduced the threat factor. By the time I hit my late twenties, my wife, Diedra, and I found ourselves in the awkward position of being everyone's favorite Negroes. I don't know how many times we've attended dinner parties where we were the only African Americans in the room. Occasionally there were others, but we seemed to have a monopoly on the dinner party invitations. This not only happened in Ann Arbor, where there is a small but substantial black population to choose from, but in the Negro mecca of Atlanta, Georgia. Our hosts always felt comfortable asking us "sensitive" questions about race that they would not dare ask other black colleagues and friends: What do African Americans think about Farrakahn? Ben Chavis? Nelson Mandela? Most of my black students are very conservative and career-oriented—why is that? How can we mend the relations between blacks and Jews? Do you celebrate Kwanzaa? Do you put anything in your hair to make it that way? What are the starting salaries for young black faculty nowadays?

Of course, these sorts of exchanges appear regularly in most black autobiographies. As soon as they're comfortable, it is not uncommon for white people to take the opportunity to find out everything they've always wanted to know about "us" (which

also applies to other people of color, I'm sure) but were afraid to ask. That they feel perfectly at ease asking dumb or unanswerable questions is not simply a case of (mis)perceived racelessness. Being a "nice Negro" has a lot to do with gender, and my peculiar form of "left-feminist-funny-guy" masculinity—a little Kevin Hooks, some Bobby McFerrin, a dash of Woody Allen—is regarded as less threatening than that of most other black men.

Not that I mind the soft-sensitive masculine persona—after all, it is the genuine me, a product of my mother's heroic and revolutionary child-rearing style. But there are moments when I wish I could invoke the intimidation factor of blackmaleness on demand. If I only had that look—that Malcolm X/Mike Tyson/Ice Cube/Larry Fishburne/Bigger Thomas/Fruit of Islam look—I could keep the stupid questions at bay, make college administrators tremble, and scare editors into submission. Subconsciously, I decided that I had to do something about my image. Then, as if by magic, my wish was fulfilled.

Actually, it began as an accident involving a pair of electric clippers and sleep deprivation—a bad autocut gone awry. With my lowtop fade on the verge of a Sly Stone afro, I was in desperate need of a trim. Diedra didn't have the time to do it, and as it was February (Black History Month), I was on the chitlin' lecture circuit and couldn't spare forty-five minutes at a barber shop, so I elected to do it myself. Standing in a well-lighted bathroom, armed with two mirrors, I started trimming. Despite a steady hand and what I've always believed was a good eye, my hair turned out lopsided. I kept trimming and trimming to correct my error, but as my flattop sank lower, a yellow patch of scalp began to rise above the surrounding hair, like one of those big granite mounds dotting the grassy knolls of Central Park. A nice yarmulke could have covered it, but that would have been more difficult to explain than a bald spot. So, bearing in mind role models like Michael Jordan, Charles Barkley, Stanley Crouch, and Onyx (then the hip-hop group of the hour), I decided to take it all off.

I didn't think much of it at first, but the new style accomplished what years of evil stares and carefully crafted sartorial statements could not: I began to scare people. The effect was immediate and dramatic. Passing strangers avoided me and smiled less frequently. Those who did smile or make eye contact seemed to be deliberately trying to disarm me—a common strategy taught in campus rape-prevention centers. Scaring people was fun for a while, but I especially enjoyed standing in line at the supermarket with my bald head, baggy pants, high-top Reeboks, and long black hooded down coat, humming old standards like "Darn That Dream," "A Foggy Day," and "I Could Write a Book." Now *that* brought some stares. I must have been convincing, since I adore those songs and have been humming them ever since I can remember. No simple case of cultural hybridity here, just your average menace to society with a deep appreciation for Gershwin, Rodgers and Hart, Van Heusen, Cole Porter, and Jerome Kern.

Among my colleagues, my bald head became the lead subject of every conversation. "You look older, more mature." "With that new cut you come across as much more serious than usual." "You really look quite rugged and masculine with a bald head." My close friends dispensed with the euphemisms and went straight to the point: "Damn. You look scary!" The most painful comment was that I looked like a "B-Boy wannabe" and was "too old for that shit." I had to remind my friend that I'm an OBB (Original B-Boy), that I was in the eleventh grade in 1979 when the Sugar Hill Gang dropped "Rapper's Delight," and that *his* tired behind was in graduate school at the time. Besides, B-Boy was not the intent.

In the end, however, I got more questions than comments. Was I in crisis? Did I want to talk? What was I trying to say by shaving my head? What was the political point of my actions? Once the novelty passed, I began getting those "speak for the race" questions that irritated the hell out of me when I had hair. Why have *black men* begun to shave their heads in greater numbers? Why have so many black athletes decided to shave their heads? Does this new trend have some kind of phallic meaning? Against my better judgment, I found myself coming up with answers to these questions—call it an academician's reflex. I don't remember exactly what I said, but it usually began with black prizefighter Jack Johnson, America's real life "baaad nigger" of the early twentieth century, whose head was always shaved and greased, and end-

ed with the hip-hop community's embrace of an outlaw status. Whatever it was, it made sense at the time.

The publicity photo for my recent book, *Race Rebels,* clearly generated the most controversy among my colleagues. It diverged dramatically from the photo on my first book, where I look particularly innocent, almost angelic. In that first photo I smiled just enough to make my dimples visible; my eyes gazed away from the camera in sort of a dreamy, contemplative pose; my haircut was nondescript and the natural sunlight had a kind of halo effect. The Izod shirt was the icing on the cake. By contrast, the photograph for *Race Rebels* (which Diedra set up and shot, by the way) has me looking directly into the camera, arms folded, bald head glistening from baby oil and rear window light, with a grimace that could give Snoop Doggy Dogg a run for his money. The lens made my arms appear much larger than they really are, creating a kind of Popeye effect. Soon after the book came out, I received several e-mail messages about the photo. A particularly memorable one came from a friend and fellow historian in Australia. In the course of explaining to me how he had corrected one of his students who had read an essay of mine and presumed I was a woman, he wrote: "Mind you, the photo in your book should make things clear—the angle and foreshortening of the arms, and the hairstyle make it one of the more masculine author photos I've seen recently????!!!!!"

My publisher really milked this photo, which actually fit well with the book's title. For the American Studies Association meeting in Nashville, Tennessee, which took place the week the book came out, my publisher bought a full-page ad on the back cover of an ASA handout, with my mug staring dead at you. Everywhere I turned—in hotel elevators, hallways, lobbies, meeting rooms—I saw myself, and it was not exactly a pretty sight. The quality of the reproduction (essentially a high-contrast xerox) made me appear harder, meaner, and crazier than the original photograph.

The situation became even stranger since I had decided to abandon the skinhead look and grow my hair back. In fact, by the time of the ASA meeting I was on the road (since abandoned) toward a big Black Power Afro—a retro style that at the time seemed to be making a comeback. Worse still, I had come to participate in a round-table discussion on black hair! My paper, titled "Nap Time: Historicizing the Afro," explored the political implications of competing narratives of the Afro's origins and meaning. Overall, it was a terrific session; the room was packed and the discussion was stimulating. But inevitably the question came up: "Although this isn't directly related to his paper, I'd like to find out from Professor Kelley why he shaved his head. Professor Kelley, given the panel's topic and in light of the current ads floating about with your picture on them, can you shed some light on what is attractive to black men about baldness?" The question was posed by a very distinguished and widely read African-American literary scholar. Hardly the naif, he knew the answers as well as I did, but wanted to generate a public discussion. And he succeeded. For ten minutes the audience ran the gamut of issues revolving around race, gender, sexuality, and the politics of style. Even the issue of bald heads as phallic symbols came up. "It's probably true," I said, "but when I was cutting my hair at three-o'clock in the morning I wasn't thinking 'penis.'" Eventually the discussion drifted from black masculinity to the tremendous workloads of minority scholars, which, in all honesty, was the source of my baldness in the first place. Unlike the golden old days, when doing hair was highly ritualized and completely integrated into daily life, we're so busy mentoring and publishing and speaking and fighting that we have very little time to attend to our heads.

Beyond the session itself, that ad continued to haunt me during the entire conference. Every ten minutes, or so it seemed, someone came up to me and offered unsolicited commentary on the photo. One person slyly suggested that in order to make the picture complete I should have posed with an Uzi. When I approached a very good friend of mine, a historian who is partly my Jewish mother and partly my confidante and *always* looking out for my best interests, the first words out of her mouth were, "Robin, I hate that picture! It's the worst picture of you I've ever seen. It doesn't do you justice. Why did you let them use it?"

"It's not that bad," I replied. "Diedra likes it—she took the picture. You just don't like my bald head."

"No, that's not it. I like the bald look on some men, and you have a very nice head. The problem is the photo and the fact that I know what kind of person you are. None of your gentleness and lovability comes out in that picture. Now, don't get a swelled head when I say this, but you have a delightful face and expression that makes people feel good, even when you're talking about serious stuff. The way you smile, there's something unbelievably safe about you."

It was a painful compliment. And yet I knew deep down that she was telling the truth. I've always been unbelievably safe, not just because of my look but because of my actions. Not that I consciously try to put people at ease, to erase conflict and difference, to remain silent on sensitive issues. I can't quite put my finger on it. Perhaps it's my mother's politeness drills? Perhaps it's a manifestation of my continuing bout with shyness? Maybe it has something to do with the sense of joy I get from stimulating conversations? Or maybe it's linked to the fact that my mom refused to raise me in a manner boys are accustomed to? Most likely it is a product of cultural capital—the fact that I *can* speak the language, (re)cite the texts, exhibit the manners and mannerisms that are inherent to bourgeois academic culture. My colleagues identify with me because I can talk intelligently about their scholarship on their terms, which invariably has the effect of creating an illusion of brilliance. As Frantz Fanon said in *Black Skin, White Masks,* the mere fact that he was an articulate *black* man who read a lot rendered him a stunning specimen of erudition in the eyes of his fellow intellectuals in Paris.

Whatever the source of my ineffable lovability, I've learned that it's not entirely a bad thing. In fact, if the rest of the world could look a little deeper, beyond the hardcore exterior—the wide bodies, the carefully constructed grimaces, the performance of terror—they would find many, many brothas much nicer and smarter than myself. The problem lies in a racist culture, a highly gendered racist culture, that is so deeply enmeshed in the fabric of daily life that it's practically invisible. The very existence of the "nice Negro," like the model-minority myth pinned on Asian Americans, renders the war on those "other," hardcore niggas justifiable and even palatable. In a little-known essay on the public image of world champion boxer Joe Louis, the radical Trinidadian writer C. L. R. James put it best: "This attempt to hold up Louis as a model Negro has strong overtones of condescension and race prejudice. It implies: 'See! When a Negro knows how to conduct himself, he gets on very well and we all love him.' From there the next step is: 'If only all Negroes behaved like Joe, the race problem would be solved.'"[1]

Of course we all know this is a bunch of fiction. Behaving "like Joe" was merely a code for deference and patience, which is all the more remarkable given his vocation. Unlike his predecessor Jack Johnson—the bald-headed prize fighter who transgressed racial boundaries by sleeping with and even marrying white women, who refused to apologize for his "outrageous" behavior, who boasted of his prowess in every facet of life (he even wrapped gauze around his penis to make it appear bigger under his boxing shorts)—Joe Louis was America's hero. As James put it, he was a credit to his race, "I mean the human race."[2] (Re)presented as a humble Alabama boy, God-fearing and devoid of hatred, Louis was constructed in the press as a raceless man whose masculinity was put to good, patriotic use. To many of his white fans, he was a man in the ring and a boy—a good boy—outside of it. To many black folks, he was a hero because he had the license to kick white men's butts and yet maintain the admiration and respect of a nation. Thus, despite similarities in race, class, and vocation, and their common iconization, Louis and Johnson exhibited public behavior that reflected radically different masculinities.

Here, then, is a lesson we cannot ignore. There is some truth in the implication that race (or gender) conflict is partly linked to behavior and how certain behavior is perceived. If our society, for example, could dispense with rigid, archaic notions of appropriate masculine and feminine behavior, perhaps we might create a world that nurtures, encourages, and even rewards nice guys. If violence were not so central to American culture—to the way manhood is defined, to the way in which the state keeps African-American men in check, to the way men interact with women, to the way oppressed peoples interact with one another—perhaps we might see the withering away of white fears of black men. Perhaps young black men wouldn't feel the need to adopt hardened, threatening postures merely to survive in a Doggy-Dogg world. Not that black men ought to become colored equivalents of Alan Alda. Rather, black men ought to be whomever or whatever they want to be, without unwarranted criticism or societal pressures to conform to a particular definition of manhood. They could finally dress down without suspicion, talk loudly without surveillance, and love each other without sanction. Fortunately, such a transformation would also mean the long-awaited death of the "nice Negro."

Not in my lifetime. Any fool can look around and see that the situation for race and gender relations in general, and for black males in particular, has taken a turn for the worse—and relief is nowhere in sight. In the meantime, I will make the most of my "nice Negro" status." When it's all said and done, there is nothing romantic or interesting about playing Bigger Thomas. Maybe I can't persuade a well-dressed white couple to give up their box seats, but at least they'll listen to me. For now. . . .

NOTES

1. C. L. R. James, "Joe Louis and Jack Johnson," *Labor Action,* 1 July 1946.

2. Ibid.

32 | WHITE MEANS NEVER HAVING TO SAY YOU'RE ETHNIC
White Youth and the Construction of "Cultureless" Identities
Pamela Perry

"How would you describe white American culture?" I ask Laurie, a white, middle-class senior at Valley Groves High,[1] a predominantly white, suburban public school near the Pacific Coast of northern California. She pauses, her face looking visibly perplexed as if she did not understand the question or her mind was drawing a blank. Wondering if she heard me over the roar of the cappuccino machine in the background, I awkwardly reiterate, "Like, you know, what would you say white American culture is like?"

"I wouldn't be able to tell you. I don't know." She pauses again and laughs nervously. "When you think about it, it's like—[a longer pause]—*I don't know!*"

About twenty miles away from Valley Groves is the postindustrial city of Clavey. Clavey High School is composed of a brilliant mosaic of students from different ethnic and racial groups, about 12 percent of whom are white. In an interview with Murray, a white, Jewish, middle-class senior, he and I talked a great deal about the consequences of race in the United States and what privileges come with being a white person here. When I probed into his identification with being white or Jewish, he said,

> [Cultural pride] doesn't make sense to me. To me it doesn't. I mean, what difference does it make what my great, great grandfather was or his whole generation. That's not affecting my life. . . . I'm still here now. I've got to make what's best for me in the future. I can't harp on what the past has brought.

Laurie and Murray express what the racial category "white" means to each of them. Although their responses differ markedly, they share something fundamental; they perceive white raciality as cultureless. For Laurie, whiteness is not culturally defined. She lives within it but cannot name it. It is taken for granted. For Murray, to be cultural means having emotion-al attachment to tradition and history. He eschews culture, in this regard, and lives in the present, looking forward.

I chose these two excerpts from qualitative research I carried out in 1994–97 at Valley Groves, a predominantly white, suburban high school, and Clavey, a multiracial, urban high school. The focus of this research was on what differences, if any, the two demographically distinct contexts made on the ways white youth reflected on and constructed white identities. I found that it made a large difference: white students at Valley Groves did not reflect on or define white identity as a culture and social location to the extent that the white youth at Clavey did. Moreover, white identities at Clavey tended to be altogether more variable and contradictory than at Valley Groves. Elsewhere, I argue that these differences in white identities were conditioned by different experiences and structures of interracial association (Perry 1998).

I make a similar argument in this article but with a focus on the only similarity between the ways whites at both schools defined white identity. They defined white as cultureless. By that, I mean that white identity was understood to have no ties or allegiances to European ancestry and culture, no "traditions." To the white youth, only "ethnic" people had such ties to the past. The students would agree with George DeVos (1975) that a "feeling of continuity with the past" distinguishes an "ethnic" group from peoples with more "present-oriented" or "future-oriented" identities (p. 17)—such as whites.

However, although white students at Valley Groves and Clavey shared this perception of white identity, they did not arrive at it by the same processes. In what follows, I present and interpret ethnographic and interview data to argue that at Valley

Pamela Perry, *Journal of Contemporary Ethnography* 30: 56–91, copyright © 2001 by Pamela Perry. Reprinted by permission of Sage Publications, Inc.

Groves, the tendency for youth to explicitly define themselves and other whites as people without culture came about through processes of *naturalization*—the embedding of historically constituted cultural practices in that which is taken for granted and seems "normal" and natural. At Clavey, culturelessness was achieved through processes of *rationalization*—the embedding of whiteness within a Western rational epistemology and value paradigm that marginalizes or subordinates all things "cultural."

Although there is some scholarly debate over whether there is such a thing as "white culture" (Ignatiev and Garvey 1996; Roediger 1994), my argument here is not so much about whether there is or is not a white culture but about the power whites exercise when *claiming* they have no culture. Culturelessness can serve, even if unintentionally, as a measure of white racial superiority. It suggests that one is either "normal" and "simply human" (therefore, the standard to which others should strive) or beyond culture or "postcultural" (therefore, developmentally advanced).

This work seeks to advance on theories and research in critical white studies, the sociology of education, and racial-ethnic identity formation by vividly illustrating the social construction of white identities and culture in schooling and the ways that different social-structural contexts differently influence constructions of whiteness, including the construction of white as cultureless or the norm.

PREVIOUS SCHOLARSHIP ON WHITE CULTURE

While I was conducting my research, the field of "critical white studies" was birthing with a dizzying amount of literature on whiteness. Widely interdisciplinary, whiteness scholarship cannot be reduced to any small set of theoretical currents, but it may be safe to say that it has been preeminently concerned with exposing the ways white domination is sustained and reproduced in invisible ways. Scholars within critical white studies have revealed the perniciousness of whiteness as it hides in literature, art, and popular culture (Dyer 1997; Giroux 1997; Hill 1997; hooks 1992; Morrison 1993; Pfeil 1995); work and educational institutional structures (Essed 1996; Fine et al. 1997);

pedagogy (Giroux 1997; McCarthy and Crichlow 1993); the law and property rights (Haney Lopez 1996; Harris 1993; Lipsitz 1995); the values and identities of whites in the historical past (Allen 1994; Almaguer 1994; Goldberg 1993; Ignatiev 1995; Jacobson 1998; Lott 1993; Roediger 1991, 1994; Saxton 1990; Ware 1992); and the historical present (Frankenberg 1993, 1997; Gallagher 1995, 1997; Hartigan 1997, 1999; Kenny 2000b; Segrest 1994; Wellman 1977; Wray and Newitz 1997).

Among whiteness scholars, *whiteness* and *white culture* are frequently conflated, especially when whiteness is understood as a whole symbolic system and way of life through which whites make sense of themselves and their social relations. Possibly because of this, few have directly addressed the invisibility of white culture as a set of "bounded"—that is, clearly named and defined—practices and values with historical antecedents. Among those who have, Ruth Frankenberg (1993) has best articulated a widespread understanding that white culture is "invisible" because it is constructed as "normal." The white women she interviewed felt that they were culturally empty. Frankenberg argues that the women's discourses suggest that their felt sense of cultural emptiness stems from a dualistic sense of unbounded white versus bounded (nonwhite) others. As the norm and standard, white culture has no definition, only those who *deviate* from the norm have "culture." And therein lies the toxicity of the construction of white as the (cultureless) norm: it serves as a basis on which to measure the humanity and social standing of others.

Historian David Roediger (1994) has a slightly different critique of white culture. Like Frankenberg (1993), he observes that white culture is devoid of a kind of bounded quality. He asserts that whites lack any community or direct continuity with some past, unlike African Americans or even white ethnics like Italian Americans. However, Roediger does not believe that culturelessness is merely a false consciousness but the truth about whiteness. For Roediger, there is no white culture, and white domination is exercised not from a racial norm-other dualism but through "an identity based on what one isn't and on whom one can hold back" (p. 13). I understand Roediger to be arguing that white culture is not merely absent, it is, in a sense, anticulture—predicated on subjugating those "with" culture.

I do not agree with Roediger (1994) that white culture is altogether nonexistent. It may be invisible and taken for granted for many whites, but it is "real," often oppressively so.[2] One objective of this and my wider work is precisely to make white culture visible and thus disarm its cloaked perniciousness. However, Roediger's implication that white culture is by definition anticulture is more descriptive of the power of whiteness than, merely, white as "norm," which can imply that it is "neutral" or passive in its effects. Two other scholars, anthropologist Renato Rosaldo (1989) and philosopher David Theo Goldberg (1993), have produced elaborated arguments on the theme of white anticulture. Rosaldo points out that everyone has culture; it fundamentally shapes all people's understanding of themselves and the world. But the *visibility* of one's culture differs according to social status. Drawing on observations in the Philippines, Mexico, and the United States, Rosaldo argues that cultural invisibility is a characteristic of all those who hold full citizenship and institutional power in the nation state. Cultural invisibility is a privileged status marking the most "rational" (and, hence, deserving of power and privilege) peoples against those who are not rational, those who are "cultural" (pp. 198–99). He introduces the concept "postcultural" to define cultural invisibility and to codify how the *denial* of culture marks one's place on the high end of the social hierarchy. Rosaldo's argument suggests that, if at one time Western Europeans had to define themselves as cultural to set themselves apart and superior to "savages," today, with much of the world "civilized" under Western domination, whites must claim a new and higher rung—the postcultural—to maintain their privileged status.

Evident in the above arguments is the understanding that white culture has historically been molded by the values and sociodiscursive constructs of the European Enlightenment and, specifically, the rule of reason. Goldberg (1993) lays this out thoroughly in his book *Racist Culture*. He asserts that racial exclusions and inclusions have historically been made and authorized by Western rational authority. The grounds for exclusion of non-Westerners has been reason or, rather, the claimed absence of reason. However, the standards of "Reason in modernity arose against the backdrop of European domination and subjugation of nature, especially human nature" (p. 119). Hence, Goldberg argues, irrationality does not refer to the inability to meet expectations of "logical noncontradiction or consistency" but rather the inability to "exhibit the values, metaphysical attitudes, epistemological principles, or cognitive styles of 'whitemales'" (ibid.). Those values, attitudes, principles, and styles include individual responsibility and self-determination, a self-concept that is wedded to freedom from the past, and the primacies of the mind over the body, the intellect over emotion, and order over chaos.[3]

These scholars, to varying degrees and in divergent ways, point out that white culture *is* Western European rational culture and that whites (white, propertied males, especially) are the unconditional beneficiaries of rationalism in that they are constructed as the most rational and, therefore, the most superior of all peoples.[4] Being rational, whiteness must deny culture to the extent that culture is understood as sets of practices that carry affective and valued continuities with the past. Rational whiteness is postcultural. It is anticulture.

This explains, in my view, the persistence of cultureless whiteness in the two different schools in this study; cultureless whiteness is a form of hegemonic power and, therefore, widespread. However, my work suggests that different contexts may require different strategies to maintain the illusion of cultureless whiteness. I propose that the naturalization of whiteness most easily occurs where white cultural practices are ubiquitous and self-confirming, such as at Valley Groves High. In contexts in which naturalization processes are weak, such as Clavey High, where whites are a numerical and cultural minority, then rationalization processes come into the foreground.

METHOD AND REFLECTIONS

The vast wealth of excellent scholarship on the social construction of identities in schooling fundamentally shaped my research focus and methodology (Bourdieu and Passeron 1977; Davidson 1996; Eckert 1989; Fordham 1996; Fordham and Ogbu 1986; Kinney 1993; MacLeod 1987; Thorne 1993; Valenzuela 1999). The main focus of my work was what role, if any, close interracial association in school had on the racial consciousness and identities of white youth. Therefore, in choosing my research sites, I looked for two schools: one predominantly white and located in a predominantly white town or city; the other multiracial, minority white and located in a minority white town or city. It also concerned me that the schools be in the same geographical region, of similar size and academic standing, and with student bodies of similar socioeconomic backgrounds to keep those factors as "constant" as possible. I studied census data and school statistics for different towns and cities across the United States before I decided on Valley Groves, which was 83 percent white, and Clavey, which was 12 percent white. Although Clavey was located in a city and Valley Groves a suburb, Clavey was very similar to Valley Groves in all respects besides racial composition, largely due to the fact that Clavey's catchment area encircled a largely middle- to upper-middle-class population. Particularly important for my research was that white students at Clavey were primarily middle class, which allowed me to focus on middle-class whites in both schools.

I spent two and a half years in the schools doing participant observation and in-depth interviewing. Daily practices included sitting in on classrooms with students, hanging out with them during breaks and lunch, attending school club meetings, and participating in student-administrator advisory committees, especially those concerned with race and cultural awareness on campus. I also observed or helped out with after-school programs and events, such as school plays, major rallies, games, and the junior and senior balls of each school. To familiarize myself with the music and leisure activities the students were involved in, after hours I listened to the local rap, R & B, punk, alternative, and classic rock radio stations; bought CDs of the most popular musical artists; went to live underground punk and alternative concerts; read fanzines and other youth magazines; watched MTV; studied music that students dubbed for me;

and attended a large rave produced by some Clavey students.

Although I looked somewhat younger than my age (thirty-eight when the research began), I made concerted efforts to minimize the effects of age difference on how students related to me. I did not associate with other adults on campus. I dressed casually in attire that I was comfortable in, which happened to be similar to the attire students were comfortable in: blue jeans, sandals or athletic shoes, T-shirt or sweat-shirt, no jewelry except four tiny hoop earrings—one in one ear, three in the other. I had students call me by my first name, and I did not talk down to them, judge them, or otherwise present myself as an authority figure. To the contrary, I saw the students as the authorities, and they seemed to appreciate that regard. Those efforts, on top of having developed some popular-cultural frames of reference with the students, contributed to my developing some very close relationships with several of the students and fairly wide access to different peer groups and cliques on campus. Having stood in the middle of secret hideouts, food fights, fist fights, tongue lashings, and over-the-top fits of goofiness, I can say that in most cases, I seemed to have little impact on students' behaviors.

My other most apparent traits—race, gender, and middle-class/intellectual appearance—had both positive and negative effects. I connected most readily and easily with girls. The results were that I have more narrative data and in-depth material from girls than boys. At Clavey, however, I did make a few close relationships with boys that I believe helped balance my findings at that school. Similarly, my class background made crossing class differences awkward at times for me and for some participants, particularly working-class males. However, since I was focusing on middle-class white students, my own middle-class whiteness seemed to work mostly on my behalf. With respect to students of color, of which I interviewed quite a few, my race limited my ability to hang out with them in groups at school. Because my focus was on white students, I do not feel this limitation seriously compromises my argument, but deeper perspectives from students of color would certainly have improved it.

I formally interviewed more than sixty students at Valley Groves and Clavey. They included, at Valley Groves, fourteen white youth, one Filipino female, and a group of ten African-American students. At Clavey, I interviewed twenty-two white youth, ten African American youth, two Chinese American, one Filipino, and two Latino youth. A little more than half of my interviewees were female and the rest male. Most were middle class, but six were working class.[5]

I did not randomly sample interview participants because I had very specific desires regarding to whom I wanted to speak: liberals and conservatives; whites, blacks, Asians, and Latinos; punks, hippies, homies, alternatives, rappers, and such; high achievers and low achievers; girls and boys; middle class and working class. So I sought out interviewees through multiple methods. Mostly, I directly approached students I observed in classrooms or in their cliques, but I also went to club meetings and asked for volunteers and, for the hard to find students, sought recommendations or introductions from youth.

Interviews took place on campus, in coffee shops, and in students' homes and generally lasted two hours. Students and their parents signed consent forms that explained that I was examining racial identities and race relations in the two demographically distinct contexts. In the interviews, I explored youth's experiences at school, their experiences of racial difference, how they thought of themselves racially, how they thought of racial-ethnic others, their cultural interests and other significant identities, and what types of meanings they gave to their interests and identities. Interviews and informal discussions were also a time for me to discuss with youth my interpretations of school practices, youth cultures, and other events around campus. Students spoke candidly and openly; they seemed eager to talk to an adult who would listen to and treat them respectfully.

The interviews were tape-recorded and transcribed. They and my field notes were manually coded and analyzed along the way to illuminate processes, practices, terms, and conceptions calling for deeper investigation or changes in focus. Along the way, also, I read widely, looking for existing studies and theories that might shed analytical light on my observations. My final coding and analysis were carried out without

the aid of software—only colored markers, a Xerox machine, and lots of post-its.

IDENTITY NATURALIZATION AT VALLEY GROVES HIGH: PASSIVE CONSTRUCTION OF WHITE AS CULTURELESS

Valley Groves is a suburban city of roughly 115,000 people. Its residents are solidly white and middle to upper-middle class. In 1990, 83 percent of the population of Valley Groves was white, and the median household income was $42,095. Inside Valley Groves High School's catchment area is Mapleton, a small suburb of about 7,500 people. Ninety percent of Mapleton residents are white, and their median household income in 1989 was $70,000.

The racial and class demographics of Valley Groves and Mapleton cities were reflected in the composition of the Valley Groves High student body and staff. In the 1995–96 school year, white youth made up 83 percent of the school population, followed by Hispanics (7 percent), Asians (5 percent), Filipinos (2 percent), and African Americans (2 percent). The fifty-three teachers, five administrators, three campus supervisors, and fifty-odd service and administrative staff were 85 percent non-Hispanic white. There was only one African American among them.

Raymond Williams (1976) wrote,

Hegemony supposes the existence of something that is truly total . . . which is lived at such a depth, which saturates the society to such an extent, and which, as Gramsci put it, even constitutes the limit of common-sense for most people under its sway. (Pp. 204–5)

At Valley Groves, whiteness "saturated" youth's lived experience. White youth and adults overwhelmed the demographic landscape. When I asked white students at Valley Groves how they would rate their experiences of people of color, most said "very little" or "none at all." In the school yard during lunch or break, students sauntered into the "quad," a large patio area in the center of the campus, to meet with friends and grab a bite to eat. At these times, the most open and public spaces were a sea of blonde- and brown-haired white girls and boys in blue jeans and T-shirts sporting logos of their favorite rock band or skateboard company. The popular and nondescript kids (usually called "normal") occupied the main quad, and the counterculture white students—druggies, skaters, hicks—claimed territory in outside areas adjoining the quad.

Some African American, Asian, or Latino students joined with white friends, and, when they did, they assumed the styles and demeanors of the crowd they were in, be it "popular," "skater," or merely "normal." Then, there were the students of color who clustered in groups of like-kind, racial ethnically. They wore their own styles; spoke in Tagalog, Spanish, or black English; and usually hung out in the cafeteria, classrooms, or distant corners of the campus, locations that kept them virtually invisible to the majority of students in and around the quad.

Similar spatial demographics, in which racial-ethnic difference was placed where it did not challenge the white norm, existed in the classroom structure (Fine 1989). The mainstream students—the popular kids, athletes, and college-bound youth—were in the honors and other high-tracked classes. The "regular" classes were made up of a hodge-podge of different types of youth—middle-class mainstream, working class, countercultural. With the exception of some of the high-tracked math classes, in which Asian American students were overrepresented, high and regular-tracked courses were disproportionately white, with small numbers of minority youth distributed equally among them. Just where the students of color were I am sorry to say I never learned the answer to, except that one day I saw a large (disproportionate) number of them in a remedial class.

Whiteness saturated Valley Groves school life not only demographically but culturally as well. The dominant culture at Valley Groves—that which oriented the social organization of students, common styles and practices, and expected behaviors—was homologous with the dominant culture outside of the campus, namely, a white European American culture. By "white European American culture," I refer to two features of American culture, broadly. First, although the dominant culture in the United States is syncretic, that is, composed of the different cultures of the peoples that populate the United States, several of its core characteristics are of European origin. These include, as I have already suggested, the values and practices derived from the European Enlightenment, Anglican Protestantism, and Western colonialism, such as rationalism, individualism, personal responsibility, a strong work ethnic, self-effacement, and mastery over nature. I include, also, carryover or "melted" material cultures of Western, Eastern, and Southern European peoples, such as hamburgers, spaghetti, cupcakes, parades, and line dancing. Second, by virtue of being numerically and politically dominant, whites tend to share certain dispositions, worldviews, and identities constituted by that, especially in predominantly white communities. Currently, a race-neutral or "color-blind" worldview and sense of oneself as normal are examples of that.

At Valley Groves, student cliques and social categories revolved around a norm-other dichotomy in which normal meant that one conformed to the dominant culture and expectations placed on them, and other meant one did not. For example, when I asked Billy how he would describe his group of friends he said,

"Normal. We don't smoke or drink or anything and [we] wear clothes we would call normal."

"And what is that?" I asked.

"Not oversized, baggy clothes like the skaters wear, or, obviously, we don't wear cowboy hats or boots."

The normal clothes Billy referred to were the styles one might find at mainstream department stores like The Gap: loose, not overly baggy blue jeans; cotton T-shirts and blouses; sundresses; khaki shorts. The kids who did not dress or act normal served to define the boundaries of what was and was not normal. For instance, skaters wore excessively baggy pants and overall filthy clothes; "hicks" wore ten-gallon cowboy hats, tooled-leather boots, and tight jeans with big brassy pants buckles; and druggies flagrantly carried and consumed illicit drugs. (*Flagrant* is the key word here since, as a popular girl told me, "Popular kids do drugs. They just don't want anyone to know it.") Carli, a white girl who considered herself "hippie," referred to the nonmainstream kids as "rebels." She said, "I call them rebels 'cause they know the system sucks."

This norm-other dichotomy was race neutral. Maria, a popular senior of Mexican-American descent on her mother's side, told me that the "first cut of students starts with who is popular" and who fits in with the other cliques on campus. Anyone, regardless of racial-ethnic ascription, could be popular, a skater, a druggie—even a "homie," which, as groups went at Valley Groves, was the most nonwhite. Price of admission was conformity to the styles and demeanor of the group. Hence, black kids who were skaters were not "black skaters," nor were white kids who were homies "white homies"; they were simply "skaters" and "homies," respectively. A white skater I spoke to pointed to an African American boy in his crowd and said, "That doesn't matter. We all love to skate together, hang out together." And when I asked black students if the white kids who were homies were considered "wanna-be black," they looked flatly at me and said, "No." Ron, who was a homie himself, said, "One of the guys who hangs out with us is white. He's not a racist and we've known each other for years."

Students' measuring sticks for gauging normal styles, behaviors, and expectations were the common, everyday practices and the system of rewards at school. On any given day at Valley Groves High, students attended classes and romped into the Quad at break and lunch to purchase anything from fresh cinnamon rolls, cupcakes, rice crispy bars, and fudge for snacks to pizza, hamburgers, meat loaf, and spaghetti for something more substantial. On occasion, leadership students played rock music over the loudspeakers while students talked among themselves in their friendship groups. Circulating through the youth were members of the administrative staff, who would greet students by their first names and engage them in casual conversation, and the team of grounds supervisors, all of whom were greying, middle-aged women. One was affectionately referred to as "Grandma."

"These are all good kids," is what administrators, teachers, and ground supervisors would say to me nearly every time I spoke with them. As Bourdieu (1977) argues, the embodiment of practices and ideas into that which feels normal, natural, and "common sense" requires collective reinforcement and approval. Adult approval rating of the students was high, and they let students know that with their smiles and friendly banter. It was demonstrated also, I believe, through the grounds supervisors, who, by virtue of

their title (as opposed to "security") and appearance, demonstrated an implicit trust the adults had that students would, for the most part, comply with expected behaviors. (At least, adults trusted that the white students would comply. Students of color, especially black boys who wore hip-hop styles, told me that they experienced considerable racial profiling by school administrators and the grounds supervisors. This explicitly racial treatment of students of color was either not witnessed by whites or rubbed out of their minds, which I believe played a role in maintaining the pretense of race neutrality on campus.)

At schoolwide rallies and events, collective consensus, reinforcement, and approval of white American norms came from an even wider span of individuals: school adults, other students, and the outside community. Such events seemed to secure a broad consensus of what is true, right, and white but always through nondiscursive practice, never by saying and, thus, never sayable. For example, homecoming—a high school tradition that celebrates the school football team—was a time to raise school spirit and, thus, excite the interest and imagination of the most students possible. It was, for me, an excellent time to observe shared assumptions and normative expectations of students and observe the rewards and sanctions applied to different types of behaviors.

One day during homecoming week, students held rallies in the gym for the entire student body. To the thunder of heavy-metal music, rivers of white students flowed into the gym and took seats in different quadrants of the auditorium reserved for different grade levels. Just before the official ceremony began, two big, husky white males (appearing to be seniors) dragged into the center of the auditorium a small boy (appearing to be a freshman) whose feet and legs were bound with silver duct tape. The crowd laughed and applauded. The two husky guys pumped their fists in the air to encourage the crowd then dragged the boy off center stage. After a brief greeting, members of the student leadership committee introduced the junior varsity and varsity football players. The players came out in succession and formed a line across the middle of the gym floor. The boys were all white except for three black players on the junior varsity team and, on the varsity team, two boys with Hispanic surnames.

As his name was called, each player stepped forward to acknowledge the applause. Most did so with an air of shyness or humility, their heads bowed, cheeks blushing, shoulders pulled up to their ears. Two boldly strutted out, trying to play up the roar of the crowd, but their efforts fell flat.

Then, the varsity cheerleaders bolted to center stage, leaping energetically before getting into formation for their choreographed performance. The girls were all thin, some overly so, and wore uniforms with close-fitted bodices that made them look all the smaller. But their body size betrayed their strength. Their routine, driven by the firm beat of a heavy-metal tune, was rigorously gymnastic, with lots of cartwheels, flips, and pyramid constructions that were punctuated by the top girls falling trustingly into the arms of their comrades. Long, silky blonde hair parachuted out with each acrobatic stunt. Through the performance, the audience remained silent and attentive, with an occasional collective gasp at the girls' athleticism, until the show was over. At that time, the cheerleaders received roaring, vocal applause.

On the day after the rally was the homecoming parade. The parade took off from the basketball field and wound its way onto a residential side street. Four adult males, two of whom appeared to be Mexican American, led the parade mounted on prancing horses and wearing Mexican serapes and sombreros. The front two carried large replicas of the California and American flags. Following the horsemen were two convertibles, one of which was a white Corvette carrying the (white) city mayor, who waved ceremoniously to the onlookers on the sidewalks.

The music of the marching band, which followed closely behind the mayor, announced the arrival of the parade along its path. A group of eight white and one African American female dancers led the band, tossing and spinning colored flags in sync with the beat of the band's percussion section. The fifty musicians in the band, most of whom appeared white with five or six exceptions, marched militarily in tight formation and played their instruments with competence and finesse. Following the band was a procession of American-built pickup trucks carrying, first, the varsity and junior varsity football players, then the "royalty"—the senior "king" and "queen" and underclass "princes"

and "princesses"—and finally, an open-bed truck loaded with seniors, hooting and cheering as if their graduation day had already arrived.

The parade made its way through several blocks of residences before returning to the main street and slowly making its way back to the school. Proud parents were perched on the sidewalks with their thirty-five-millimeter and video cameras in hand. Community residents stepped onto their front landings to wave and cheer as the parade passed their homes. Others peered out through large pane windows with cats in arms and dogs at heel.

The homecoming rally and parade were, in my view,[6] packed with assumptions, values, behaviors, and origin stories that privileged white European American perspectives as well as gender, sexuality, and class-based norms (all of which tend to coproduce one another). At the rally, for example, the display of the hog-tied freshman reinforced that white (male) dominance is sustained not only through the subordination of nonwhite others but of "other" whites as well (Hartigan 1997, 1999; Thandeka 1999; Wray and Newitz 1997). Second, the virtues of personal mastery and self-effacement were exemplified by the humble postures of the football players and reinforced by the slights the audience gave to those who presented themselves with more bravado. And, finally, the cheerleaders' thin, bounded physiques and gravity-defying athletic feats demonstrated that the girls had successfully learned to subjugate their bodies and overcome nature.

The homecoming parade, with its display of the national and state flags, American cars, marching band, and school royalty, was a stunning way to observe the coproduction of whiteness, Americanness, citizenship, and gendered codes of conduct. Included was even an origin story of white American colonial victory over Mexico. And, by virtue of who was there and who was not, the knitting together of the themes of mastery, domination, nationhood, and industry with whiteness was seamless. Other cultures in the school and community were not represented in the parade. There were no Filipino dancers, Asian martial artists, or African-American rappers. The event was performed by whites and for whites and, thus, little contradicted the cultural and political assumptions at play.

In sum, at Valley Groves High, white people and white European American culture saturated school life. White youth had little to no association with people or cultures that would place whiteness in relief in such a way that students might reflect on it and consciously define it.

NO TIES

Given this sociocultural milieu, white youth could say nothing when I asked them to describe white culture; they had no words to describe that which comes naturally. Laurie, whom I quoted at the beginning of this article, struggled to describe white culture and finally succumbed to "I don't know!" Billy, a popular white senior, had a similar response. I asked him what he thought was culturally specific about white American culture. After a long pause in which he said only, "hmmm," he asked, "Like, what's American culture?"

"Uh-huh," I replied.

"Hmmm. [Another long pause]—I don't really know, 'cause it's like [pause]—just [pause]—I'm not sure! I don't know!"

However, Valley Groves white students were not always speechless about white identity. When my questions probed into the youth's social experiences and identities as whites and not their cultures, they could find something to say. Not too surprisingly, most told me that being white meant you had no cultural ties. Students I spoke to would explain that they had mixed European roots that held no significance to them; therefore they were "just white." For example, I asked Mara, a Valley Groves senior, what she would say if a census taker asked her, straight out without any prompting, "What are you?"

MARA: Like a race?

PGP: Could be a racial category.

MARA: I'd have to answer "Very white." I am, yeah. I am 100 percent white.

PGP: I noticed on your [consent form] you said you had a mix of European backgrounds, and you wrote, "Pretty much WHITE." Is that what "white" means to you, a European mix?

MARA: I just think that there's not much—I don't really think of myself as European. I think of myself as a white American girl. . . . I don't really go back to my roots, though I know I have family and where they come from but they're all white races.

PGP: You don't have any heartfelt devotion to your European past?

MARA: Not really. My family has lived here for generations, so I don't really draw on that.

Laurie had a similar response:

We're a bunch of everything. My great, great Grandmother is Cherokee. Whenever I fill out [questionnaires] about what's my ethnic background I write "white" because everything is so random. We have German, some family from Wales—but that means nothing to me. . . . I don't have ties to anything. I haven't heard about anything my parents have been through except for my grandparents in wars. It's all been about people, not culture.

Answers like Mara's and Laurie's, of which there were many, reflect that, although white youth at Valley Groves may not have thought about whiteness as a culture, they did think about it as a social category (Phoenix 1997), as a "group position" (Blumer 1958) with respect to other racial-ethnic groups. To Valley Groves students, whites were a group because they did not have culture, and "minorities" did. Through mixed-European and other cultural amalgamation, whites were a new breed, a hybrid, removed from a past that was meaningless to them and for the loss of which they held no remorse.

Valley Groves whites were speaking from the "postcultural" perspective that Rosaldo (1989) asserts is the perspective of all who are members of the dominant group of Western-style nation states. Naturalized whiteness complements and helps constitute this kind of postcultural identity because of the stability garnered from the fit between societal norms and the constructed identity of whites (powell 1997). The us-them construction revolves around "majority" (those who all look and act normal to one another) and the "minority" (those who do not look or act like the majority). Naturalized whiteness is securely grounded in and validated by the normal way of things in the present and therefore does not seek meaning in a cultural or past orientation.

CLAVEY HIGH SCHOOL: WHEN WHITE IS NOT THE NORM

Once a port of entry for African American, Mexican, and Asian immigration into northern California, Clavey City today has one of the most racially/ethnically diverse populations for its size in the United States. Of its 372,000 residents, 33 percent are white, 44 percent are black, 19 percent are of Hispanic origin, and 15 percent are of Asian origin. Median household income in 1989 was $27,095. More than 16 percent of families in Clavey City live below poverty.

Clavey High School stands like a fortress overlooking a dense urban landscape. The schools magnet academies draw in youth from all over the city, bringing in a mosaic of students from different racial and ethnic groups. At the time of my research, whites comprised 12 percent of the two thousand students at Clavey. African Americans were the majority, making up 54 percent of the school. They were followed in numbers by Asian Americans (23 percent), then Hispanics (8 percent), Filipinos (2 percent), and a few Pacific Islanders and Native Americans. At any given moment during lunch break, one could tour the campus and hear students speaking in standard English, black English ("ebonics"), Eritrean, Cantonese, Mandarin, Korean, Spanish, Spanglish, Tagalog, Samoan, Russian, and Vietnamese, among others.

The racial composition of the administrative and teaching staff at Clavey was also quite diverse. The principal of Clavey was a white male, but the other top administrators, two assistant principals and the dean, were African American. Of all the administrators and their staff, 50 percent were African American, 25 percent were Asian, and 25 percent were white. Clavey teachers were 53 percent white, 30 percent African American, 8 percent Asian American, 6 percent Hispanic, and 3 percent Pacific Islander.

Life at Clavey High was very different from that at Valley Groves. White youth at Clavey were in daily, up-close association with marked racial and cultural difference to whiteness, and race was the primary means of sorting out who was who and where one belonged in the social organization of the school. Clavey's tracking structure, which I say more about

later, was racially segregated, with whites and Asians disproportionally represented in the high-tracked classes and African Americans and Latinos overrepresented in the low-tracked classes. As well, certain areas on the campus were "where the white kids hang out"; others were "where the black (or Asian American or Latino) kids hang out." And student cliques and subcultures were racially marked such that "straights" (who were like "normal" kids at Valley Groves), alternatives, hippies, and punks were all "white people's groups"; rappers, athletes, gangsters, and "fashion hounds" were "black people's groups"; housers, natives, newly arrived, and martial artists were "Asian people's groups"; and so forth. This meant that the styles, slangs, vernaculars, and demeanors that marked identification with a certain clique or subculture simultaneously inferred racial identification. In a word, peer group activities *racialized* youth.

Speaking to this fact and the sanctions that came with crossing racialized boundaries in styles or leisure activities, Gloria, an immigrant from El Salvador, said to me,

> For my race, if you start wearing a lot of gold, you're trying to be black. If you're trying to braid your hair, you'll be accused of trying to be black. I'm scared to do things 'cause they might say, "that's black!" Or if you're Latino and you listen to that, you know, Green Day—that [alternative rock] kinda thing. If you listen to that, then you wanna be white. . . . "Oh my god, why you listening to that music?" they'd say, . . . Aren't you proud of who you are?

Also different from Valley Groves was the dominant school culture. Overall at Clavey, African American youth claimed the majority of open, public spaces, and black popular cultural forms and practices shaped the normative culture of the school. By "black popular culture," I refer to the music, styles, and other meaningful practices that have risen out of black communities; are linked, if remotely, to diasporic traditions; and, most significantly, mark black identity and peoplehood (Gilroy 1991, 1993; Rose 1994; Wallace 1992). Hall (1992) defines three things that are distinctive of black diasporic culture: (1) *style* as the "subject of what is going on," (2) *music* as the "deep structure of [black] cultural life," and (3) the *body* as "canvases of representation" (p. 27). Gilroy (1991) adds that the body in black culture carries "potent meanings" (p. 226) because it rests at the core of historical efforts of blacks to assert their humanity.

Unlike at Valley Groves, where the dress code did not diverge much from white adult mainstream style, at Clavey, basic elements of black hip-hop style were generalized into the normative styles for all youth. One informant called it the "leveler" style because it made all who wore it "the same." This basic style included clean, oversized, and sagging denim pants or sweatpants; large and long untucked T-shirts or hooded sweatshirts; large, bulky parkas; and sparkling-clean athletic shoes. The look was particularly common for boys, but girls' styles were also influenced by it. Only if and when students wanted to mark a distinctive style and/or racial identification did they embellish on this basic, baggy theme. Duncan, a middle-class, white male skater and "raver" (someone who frequents rave parties) told me,

> We all wear baggy pants, right? So parents think! But you find that ravers have cut-off bottoms to their [sagging] jeans, they wear bigger t-shirts they have hanging out of their pants, they carry packs that's full of crap that they take everywhere.

What Duncan specified as "raver" style, other students specified as "white," particularly the cut-off bottoms to large pants. Other markers of white kids' styles were Van shoes, instead of Nike or Fila brands (which marked black style), and macramé or silver-chain neck chokers.

Informal and formal activities on campus were also shaped by black popular culture. During breaks or at lunchtime, the ambient din of casual conversation was composed of the sounds, words, and inflections of black English and the most recent innovation in "street" slang. Lunchtime events, school rallies, and dances were enlivened with rap and R & B music, predominantly, with an occasional reggae tune or specially requested techno or alternative song. Often, students performed raps on the steps in front of the cafeteria or graced an audience with a spontaneous hip-hop dance performance.

Homecoming week at Clavey, like at Valley Groves, was a time to unite the school and raise the collective spirit. So, leadership students made attempts to appeal to the breadth of diverse interests and cultures of the school with "fashion shows" of traditional or native garments and a variety of games designed to mix students up. At lunch, they played a range of music, from R & B to techno and alternative rock, but songs by African-American and Afro-Carribean artists were predominant. The main events—the rally and game—were attended by and played predominantly to a majority-black audience.

The rally took place during lunch on the day of the "big game." Students, of which all but a few were black, crammed into the auditorium to the heartbeat pulse of a rap song. The rally opened with a greeting from the student body president and a soulful a cappella song performed by three African-American students. Then the cheerleaders, composed of one white and ten black girls, sprung out onto the gym floor. Their choreographed routine was fluid, rhythmic, and dancelike, with movements drawn from traditional and contemporary African and African-American dance forms. To the infectious beat of an upbeat R & B song, the girls playfully flirted with their appreciative audience with beckoning hand and eye gestures. Several boys succumbed to the urge to dance in dialogue with the girls and leapt down to the floor to join them, but they were met by the arresting hands of campus security. Others, boys and girls alike, stood up and swayed or danced in place until the performance was over. Then, the varsity football players were called to line up in the center of the auditorium. The players were African American with the exception of two white boys and one Latino. When each name was announced, the football player leapt forward a few steps and embraced the cheers from the crowd. Each took his moment in the limelight proudly, with his fist in the air or maybe a little dance to augment the roar of his audience.

At Clavey, there was no homecoming parade that extended into the community, like at Valley Groves. At the game, a small procession of vehicles featuring the elected school "emperor" and "empress" circled the football field during half time. There was no marching band, either, but the award-winning school gospel choir sang several lively songs at halftime.

In short, school life at Clavey was heavily infused with styles, music, and activities that marked the identities and cultures of the majority black students. This had a few important implications for the experiences and identities of the white students. First, white was not the norm, either numerically or culturally. Barry, a middle-class, "straight" white male, told me, "School is like a foreign country to me. I come here to this foreign place, then go home where things are normal again." When I asked white students why they did not attend the rallies and dances, they said things like, "I don't enjoy the people," "They don't play my kind of music," and "I can't dance to that music." All in all, the message was that they could not relate to the dominant school culture.

Furthermore, whiteness was not entirely taken for granted. The racial organization of Clavey's social life, curricular structure, and schoolwide activities meant that white students were forced to grapple with their identities as whites and participate in active contestation over the meanings of white identity and culture. No white student I spoke to at Clavey was completely unable to describe something about white culture. All had reflected on it to some extent, even if only to ruminate on how difficult it was to define. And some youth could say a lot about white culture. One white, middle-class senior girl, Jessie, elaborated extensively on differences in attitudes toward food consumption that she noticed between her white, Filipino, and Chinese American friends, and she commented on how much more visible white culture is to her in places outside of California. She said, "Minnesota, Denver and . . . places like that. It seems like . . . you know, you've got the whole thing going on—beer bread, polka, parades, apple pie and things like that."

Most stunning to me about the white students at Clavey was not what they said explicitly about white culture but what they said implicitly. In our discussions about the types of music they liked and why, white students would tell me that they liked rock or punk or alternative music and not rap or R & B because "their" music spoke more to their "interests" or experiences as whites. For example, Kirsten and Cindi were good friends. They both were from middle-class homes, were juniors at the time, and liked alternative rock. Kirsten was white, European American, and Cindi was part white and part Chinese, although she

admittedly "looked white" and hung out solely with other white youth. I asked them why they thought students tended to self-segregate on campus:

CINDI: I think there is . . . the factor that some people feel like they may not have very much in common with someone from a different race, which in some ways is true. Because you have, like, different music tastes, different styles of clothes. Also, like what your friends think.

KIRSTEN: Or like different things you do on weekends.

CINDI: Yeah, so I think that's something that separates the races.

KIRSTEN: It's kind of interesting because my musical interests have changed. . . . It seems like [in junior high school] everyone, regardless of if they were black or white or Asian, . . . listened to the [local rap and R & B station.] But then I think when you are little you don't really . . . have too much of an identity of yourself. As you get older and mature more you, like, discover what your "true being" is. So then people's musical tastes change. [Later in the conversation.] I think punk is more of a "I don't get along with my parents" kind of music and rap is more of "lets go kill someone" music.

CINDI: Punk . . . expresses a simpler anger. It's just kind of like "Oh, I broke up with my girlfriend" . . . something like that. Usually rap has more to do with killing and gangs—stuff that doesn't really relate to me.

In this discussion, Kirsten and Cindi defined white identity and culture in terms of interests and tastes in leisure culture. This "discourse of taste" (Dolby 2000) was the language of choice among all groups of students for articulating racial-ethnic differences. Behind it was the belief that different life experiences accounted for different tastes. Sometimes, white youth named fairly explicit experiences they believed were most common to or defining of whites. Class experience, expressed by Kirsten and Cindi in terms of the type of neighborhood one lived in, was often evoked by youth. Other times, white youth spoke in terms of intangible but presumably race-based, emotional, aesthetic, and ethical sensibilities they felt when they listened to, say, punk or alternative music but not when they listened to rap.

ACTIVE CONSTRUCTION OF WHITE AS POSTCULTURAL

Ironically, even as Clavey whites demarcated white culture and identity boundaries through their popular-cultural tastes and leisure activities, they also imagined whiteness as cultureless, as postcultural. This was not as explicit as it was at Valley Groves. It would show its face when white students referred to people of color as people with "race" or "ethnicity," as though whites had neither. Tina, a working-class junior who had always been a racial minority in school and had many close black and Latino friends, told me that she "had a lot of ethnicity in [her] family . . . His-panic, Korean. We all get along." By this she meant that white relatives had married "out" of whiteness and into culture, ethnicity.

Common also was the explicit and implicit definition of white as empty, meaningless, bland, and without tradition. This comment by Eric touches on all of those:

> I think it's more difficult [to define white culture] for Americans because the culture of America is more just consumption. In America, we buy stuff, and that's the basis of our culture. If you talk to people who want to come to America?—They want things. TV is a very American thing. We don't have lengthy traditions. . . . A lot has been lost because of the good ol' melting pot. I heard a cool one about a salad bowl—that's what America is, and along comes the dressing and turns everything into dressing flavor. Vegetables all got that white American spin on it.

Note, too, that Eric equates "white" with "American" until his last line, when he specifies "white American." That is a faux pas that whites often fall into because of the dominant construction of white as the "unhyphenated" American standard.

Finally, several Clavey white students told me that they did not like to think about themselves as "white" but as "human." These students also expressed a more explicitly rationalist construction of whiteness that denied the significance of a past orientation and exalted a more individualistic and present- or future-oriented construction of the self. White, middle-class boys expressed this most boldly, which might be expected

given that they are triply constructed as the most rational by race, class, and gender.

Murray, whom I quoted at the beginning of this article, best exemplifies this latter perspective. In Murray's comments, we can read several tenets of Western rational thought and a postcultural identity: the irrationality of past-oriented values, the future orientation of the self, and individual responsibility. Daniel was a white, middle-class, "straight" male with some Portuguese ancestry. He made comments similar to Murray's:

> People have suggested I am a person of color or mixed. Then I decided, no, I'm European American. Ancestry doesn't matter. . . . People look back in the past and judge you for it, and I don't think that's right. Sure, people enslaved people. At one time every race had slaves. I think you need to move on and see what's going on now. History is important but you have to work on getting together now and don't use that as a divide.

A few scholars have observed a propensity among whites to deny the significance of the past, slavery particularly, in affecting the life chances of African Americans today. Some argue that this denial is a kind of defensive mechanism whites adopt to exonerate themselves from taking responsibility for the legacies of slavery and past discrimination against African Americans and other minorities (Gallagher 1995). I take a slightly different position and suggest that white identity and culture is constructed in such a way that the values of individuality, personal responsibility, and a future-oriented self create a cognitive inability to see things any other way (see also Alba 1990; Blauner 1989). A past orientation simply does not make sense to many whites from their cultural perspective.

In sum, at Clavey, white culture was not entirely naturalized and taken for granted; it was reflected on and even defined somewhat, particularly through the language of tastes and popular culture. To an extent, however, white students also considered themselves unmarked American, nonethnic, unmarked human, and/or present oriented. In a word, they saw themselves as cultureless. I might add that several students of color I spoke to also were quick to define white culture in terms of styles and tastes but not in terms of tradition. Johnetta, an African American senior, said, "It's hard to generalize [about white culture] because there's no ready answer to what is white culture."

Whereas I have proposed that the naturalization of whiteness greatly facilitated the passive construction of postcultural whiteness at Valley Groves, I suggest that at Clavey, different and more active social processes were in play. Namely, Western rational ways of knowing and making sense of social relations permeated Clavey school and social practices. As I have argued, Western rationalism exiles tradition and culture from the realms of truth and relevance and replaces them with reason. That which is reasonable or rational is separated from and raised above that which is not, like the elevation of mind over body, intellectual over emotional, and order above chaos. Whiteness benefits from those hierarchical dualities by being linked with the higher value of each—with orderliness, self-control, individualism, and rationality, which, not coincidentally, are recognized as standard or normal behaviors. Otherness is defined in terms of that which is passionate, chaotic, violent, lazy, irrational, and—since marginal to the norm—cultural.

Two school practices in particular stood out for me in terms of the ways they seemed to structure the meanings all youth gave to their experience through a Western rational value paradigm. The first and most obvious of those was the tracking structure. Scholars have long argued that racial segregation in tracking reproduces racial inequalities in the wider society, largely by preparing high-tracked students, who tend to be middle-class white and Asian, better than low-tracked students, who tend to be black, Latino, and poor white and Asian (Gamoran et al. 1995; Oakes 1985, 1994; Oakes and Guiton 1995). Tracking also reproduces racial inequalities by reinforcing, if not constituting, racial stereotypes. Jeannie Oakes (1994) has argued that "all but the most extraordinary schools have their stereotypes and prejudices reinforced by racially-identifiable high- and low-tracked classes" (pp. 86–87). She asserts that tracking "institutionalizes racist conceptions of intellectual capacity" (ibid.). I would add to her argument that tracking also institutionalizes the values of mind over body and self-

control over lack of restraint and racializes those who are superior and inferior in those respects.

At Clavey, the high-tracked classes, those designed to prepare students for high-ranking colleges and universities, were 80 percent white and Asian, according to a school survey. Conversely, "preparatory" classes, which filled graduation requirements, were overwhelmingly black and Latino. Remedial classes were 100 percent black and Latino. Although, officially, youth were tracked according to their intellectual or achievement levels, the discourses that surrounded tracking at Clavey suggested that *behavior* (including expected behavior) was just as relevant.

Students in the high-tracked classes were generally understood to be "well-behaved," "good" students. In those classrooms, students acted in the utmost orderly fashion: always listening attentively and taking notes, speaking only when called on. They considered themselves hard working and sophisticated in their abilities to defer gratification, such as to study during lunch instead of hang out and have fun with their friends. They justified their privilege to be in the accelerated classes on these grounds and blamed underachievement on the behaviors of the underachieved. Linda, a white Jewish girl in accelerated classes, represented this viewpoint in the following comment:

> It's so sad because these kids could be pushed so far beyond what they are [doing]. Like, it's unbelievable. When I see a twelfth grader holding a geometry book, I cringe inside me. Because, *you can learn, you can do it!* People are so lazy, they don't care. They have no goals, no ambitions. It's frustrating! I don't get it!

The "lazy" and unambitious kids Linda referred to were black and Latino students in the preparatory classes. Other commonly used terms to describe those classes and the students in them were "bonehead," "rowdy," and "out of control." And, indeed, some of those classes had students who were inattentive or disruptive and who could, on occasion, set the whole class off into a blaze of rowdiness. But those students were aware that they had been assigned to the least valued and negatively stereotyped classes in the school. If they did not hear it through common discourse, they deduced it from the classes themselves.

They were overcrowded and short of chairs, books, and other course materials. Sometimes, they did not even have full-time teachers. It is not a stretch to suggest that preparatory students behaved in "bonehead" ways that they thought were expected of them (Eder 1981; Baron, Tom, and Cooper 1985; Lightfoot 1978; Ferguson 1998; Steele and Aronson 1998).

In sum, tracking at Clavey asserted more than, simply, intellectual superiority but also the values of mind over body and self-control over lack of restraint. Furthermore, it marked standard, acceptable forms of behavior—standards within which middle-class whites and Asians were squarely located practically and symbolically.

"Multicultural" programs and discourses were other school practices that positioned whites as the school's most rational and postcultural. At Clavey, there were two main, formal multicultural events: the "cultural assemblies" and "multicultural week." Once every other month or so, an ethnic club—the African-American Student Union, the Asian Student Union, Latino Student Union, or the Inter-Tribal Student Union—would put on a schoolwide assembly. A common assembly featured traditional ceremonial dances and rituals, music and song, poetry readings, historically informative slide shows, and clothing displays, all arranged and performed by the students.

Lunchtime activities during multicultural week were another opportunity for students to publicly display elements of their cultural heritage. Each day of the week was designed to feature a particular aspect of a culture—the music, dance, clothing, written texts, or narratives. For example, on a day featuring traditional or national clothing styles, youth held a fashion show in which African-American youth in dashikis, Chinese-American girls in brocade gowns, and Mexican-American youth in ceremonial dance costumes paraded before youth gathered outside the cafeteria.

These events had their merits. They gave voice and visibility to the cultures and perspectives of people historically silenced by white colonialism. African-American and Asian youth told me that they enjoyed having the opportunity to present their culture as well as learn about others. I propose, however, that multicultural events at Clavey coterminously reproduced white su-

premacist, rationalist tenets of white colonialism by making whiteness culturally invisible.

Rosaldo (1989) argues that, "as the Other becomes more culturally visible, the self becomes correspondingly less so" (p. 202). I believe this was true for many Clavey whites. When white students spoke about the assemblies, they usually expressed enthusiastic appreciation for "the chance to learn about so many cultures." But learning about other cultures merely gave them more references by which to define what they were not. As well, when they spoke in this way, it was as if "cultures" were like books—objective things that existed outside of the self but could be consumed to pleasure the self (Farley 1997). In a conversation with four middle-class white girls at Clavey, I asked them how they thought their experience at Clavey would influence their adulthood.

ANN: I think it's going to be a very positive thing. [Melissa interjects: Yeah.] Because it teaches us how to deal with different kinds of people.

SERA: Yeah, you learn more about others. . . . It's a positive experience.

MELISSA: Yeah, you gain street smarts. You gain stuff.

Greater knowledge of other cultures was something Ann, Sera, and Melissa appreciated because it gave them tools to enhance their sociability, but it did not make them reflect on their sociocultural location as whites. When other white students at Clavey spoke to me about the value of the multicultural events, they made very similar kinds of statements and inferences. Overall, multicultural events, as "add-on" school practices in which white students could pleasurably gaze on racial-ethnic others without putting themselves on the line, reinforced a sense of whiteness as center and standard (cultureless) and racial-ethnic others (by virtue of having culture to display) as different and marginal to that.

Furthermore, no white students I spoke to questioned why there was not a white-American cultural assembly. Granted, to most this was untenable, largely because it might be taken as a white-supremacist act. I talked to students about school clubs for whites only, and they categorically dismissed the idea. One said, "There'd be a riot!" Another said, "It wouldn't be right. It would be taken all wrong." But it was also untenable because, as another student put it, "White is all around. It doesn't need special attention." The idea that white culture does not need special attention (read: white is the norm and standard) seemed to be another message multicultural events gave to white students. As if for the eyes of whites only, multiculturalism at Clavey gave white students new references to add to their mental cache of exotic others while further obscuring the invisible power of white culture.

CONCLUSION

For a while now, scholars of race and whiteness have understood that the construction of white culture as the invisible norm is one of the most, if not *the* most pernicious, constructions of whiteness in the post–civil rights era. However, very few have examined the everyday social processes by which white people come to think of themselves as normal and culturally empty (Frankenberg 1993; Kenny 2000a, 2000b; Twine 1997), and among those, no one has done a comparative study illuminating the ways that different social-structural institutional contexts influence different constructions of white identity as cultureless. My research suggests that, at Valley Groves, a predominantly white high school, white identity seemed cultureless because white cultural practices were taken for granted, naturalized, and, thus, not reflected on and defined. At Clavey, a multiracial school, white culture was not taken for granted—white youth thought about and defined it to an extent, particularly through their interests and tastes in popular culture. However, in part, whites also reflected on their sociocultural location through the lens of European American rational authority, which school structures and practices helped construct and reinforce. That lens refracted whiteness into all that was good, controlled, rational, and cultureless and otherness into all that was bad, out of control, irrational, and cultural. It may be that when naturalization processes are not possible because of close interracial association, then rationalization processes must come into play to preserve white hegemony.

This argument has theoretical and practical implications for critical white studies, the sociology of education, and general theories and research in racial-

ethnic identity formation. Within critical white studies, there are two prevalent sets of assumptions about white culture that this research advances. The first is that white people experience themselves as culturally empty because whiteness is hegemonic and, therefore, undefined. To disrupt the insidious power of white culture, then, we must expose and define it. My study suggests that this is true but not everywhere the truth. The multiracial experiences of white youth at Clavey suggest that making white culture visible is not sufficient for challenging the construction of white as norm. What is also necessary are efforts to expose, challenge, and transform the rule of reason that frames white culture as rational and, therefore, *beyond* culture, postcultural or even anticultural.

Another assumption among some scholars of critical white studies, particularly "New Abolitionists," is that white culture is experienced as empty because, simply, there is no white culture. I am less concerned with the question of whether there really is a white culture than with what is reproduced through *denying* there is a white culture. The argument I have presented here proposes that the concept of culture denotes more than, simply, a way of life organized around sets of symbolic practices. It connotes a relationship of power between those who "have" culture (and are, thus, irrational and inferior) and those who claim not to (and are, thus, rational and superior). More research and thought needs to go into examining the ways postcultural whiteness is inculcated in daily practice and into the profits whites gain by denying that they have a culture.

This research also contributes to the growing scholarship on social and cultural reproduction in education. Although considerable research has examined the reproduction and subversion of societal norms in schools, including racial norms (for example, Carter 1999; Conchas 2000; Davidson 1996; Fordham 1996; Fine et al. 1997; Kenny 2000a; McCarthy and Critchlow 1993; Valenzuela 1999), more is still needed that closely examines the symbolic impact of certain school practices on how white students make sense of their own identities and the identities of people of color. This research only touched the surface of that and came on some disturbing and unexpected findings, namely, the active construction of postcultural whiteness. Research and evaluations of multicultural and other programs designed to redress racial inequalities have focused primarily on students of color. Important insights might be gained from more attention to white students and the meanings they assign to their experiences of those same programs.

Finally, this research embellishes on theories of racial-ethnic identity formation by vividly illuminating the socially constructed and contingent nature of race. Racial identities are made, not born, and they are made through the interaction of the specific social, structural, political, and cultural composition of a given context (Blumer 1958; Pinderhughes 1997). This means that racial identities are not fixed or uniform but variable and multiple. They may even be contradictory. These observances are often lost among scholars of whiteness and white racism who tend to represent whites and white identities as everywhere and always the same and contradictions as a form of "contemporary race prejudice" (Williams et al. 1999). My research affirms that the hegemonic construction of white as cultureless is stubbornly persistent but that even *it* is not the same across all contexts. To more effectively dismantle white domination, we need to be aware of and ready to work with its different manifestations and internal contradictions. Future research and antiracist scholarship may benefit from deeper exploration of the variability of white racial identities and the processes by which white racial domination is reproduced and subverted in distinct contexts.

NOTES

AUTHOR'S NOTE: This study was supported in part by grants from the sociology department of the University of California at Berkeley and the Doreen B. Townsend Center for the Humanities. A grant from the Spencer Foundation supported the writing of this piece. I am solely responsible for all views and statements made. My deepest admiration and thanks go to all of the youth who participated in this project. I also thank Rob Benson, Robert Bulman, Katherine Rosier, Michael Wilson, Matt Wray, Ana Yolanda Ramos Zayas, and the anonymous readers for JCE for their helpful comments on this article.

1. All names of cities, schools, and individuals in this article are pseudonyms.

2. Please do not interpret my assertion that culture is "real" to mean that I see it as a fixed and immutable "thing" that is consistent with all members of a culturally defined group. Cultures are constituted by social, geographical, historical, and political processes, which make them variable and always changing (see Rosaldo 1989). However, in a given time and place, a culture may appear fixed and stable, especially in conditions of domination and oppression (Hall 1996). The same argument applies to my use of the concept "race." However, I have yet to find a way to satisfactorily resolve the tension between, on one hand, analyzing and deconstructing racial categories and stereotypes to dismantle them and, on the other, reifying and reproducing those same categories and stereotypes in the process. I acknowledge that my assertions in this piece about white and black culture uncomfortably balance on that tension.

3. See also Ferguson (1997).

4. Ferguson (1997) argues that the property qualification in the U.S. Constitution for the right to American citizenry was used to justify the exclusion of nonwhites, women, and unpropertied men on the grounds that land ownership "epitomizes a *rational,* virtuous, masculine, and politically necessary control of the world" (my emphasis, p. 157). Only the most rational had the right to be citizens.

5. I judged socioeconomic class by considering both parent occupation and quality-of-life issues.

6. Although I tried throughout this research to reflect on and take into consideration the race, class, gender, and other biases I bring to my representations and interpretations of the students' practices and assumptions at both Valley Groves and Clavey, I cannot claim to have succeeded in that 100 percent.

REFERENCES

Alba, Richard. 1990. *Ethnic identity: The transformation of white America.* New Haven, CT: Yale University Press.

Allen, Theodore. 1994. *The invention of the white race, vol. 1: Racial oppression and social control.* London: Verso.

Almaguer, Tomas. 1994. *Racial fault lines: The historical origins of white supremacy in California.* Berkeley: University of California Press.

Apple, Michael W. 1995. *Education and power.* New York: Routledge.

Baron, Reuben, David Y. H. Tom, and Harris M. Cooper. 1985. Social class, race and teacher expectations. In *Teacher expectancies,* edited by Jerome B. Dusek. Hillsdale, NJ: Lawrence Erlbaum.

Blauner, Bob. 1989. *Black lives, white lives: Three decades of race relations in America.* Berkeley: University of California Press.

Blumer, Herbert. 1958. Race prejudice as a sense of group position. *Pacific Sociological Review* 1 (1): 3–7.

Bourdieu, Pierre. 1977. *Outline of a theory of practice.* Cambridge, UK: Cambridge University Press.

Bourdieu, Pierre, and J. C. Passeron. 1977. *Reproduction in education, society and culture.* Beverly Hills, CA: Sage.

Carter, Prudence L. 1999. Balancing acts: Issues of identity and cultural resistance in the social and educational behaviors of minority youth. Ph.D. diss., Columbia University, New York.

Conchas, Gilberto Q. 2000. Structuring failure and success: Understanding the variability in Latino school engagement. Working paper, Harvard Graduate School of Education.

Davidson, Ann Locke. 1996. *Making and molding identity in schools: Student narratives on race, gender, and academic engagement.* Albany: State University of New York Press.

De Vos, George. 1975. Ethnic pluralism: Conflict and accommodation. In *Ethnic identity: Cultural continuities and change,* edited by George De Vos and Lola Romanucci-Ross. Chicago: University of Chicago Press.

Dolby, Nadine. 2000. The shifting ground of race: The role of taste in youth's production of identities. *Race, Ethnicity, and Education* 3 (1):7–23.

Dyer, Richard. 1997. *White.* New York: Routledge.

Eckert, Penelope. 1989. *Jocks and burnouts: Social categories and identity in high school.* New York: Teachers College Press.

Eder, Donna. 1981. Ability grouping as a self-fulfilling prophecy: A micro-analysis of teacher-student interaction. *Sociology of Education* 54 (3): 151–62.

Essed, Philomena. 1996. *Diversity: Gender, color and culture.* Amherst: University of Massachusetts Press.

Farley, Anthony Paul. 1997. The black body as fetish object. *Oregon Law Review* 76 (3): 457–535.

Ferguson, Robert A. 1997. *The American Enlightenment, 1750–1820.* Cambridge, MA: Harvard University Press.

Ferguson, Ronald F. 1998. Teachers' perceptions and expectations and the black-white test score gap. In *The black-white test score gap,* edited by Christopher Jencks and Meredith Phillips, 318–74. Washington, DC: Brookings Institution.

Fine, Michelle. 1989. Silencing and nurturing voice in an improbable context: Urban adolescents in public school. In *Critical pedagogy, the state, and cultural struggle,* edited by Henry Giroux and Peter McLaren, 152–73. Albany: State University of New York Press.

Fine, Michelle, Lois Weis, Linda C. Powell, and L. Mun Wong, eds. 1997. *Off white: Readings on race, power and society.* New York: Routledge.

Fordham, Signithia. 1996. *Blacked out: Dilemmas of race, identity, and success at Capital High.* Chicago: University of Chicago Press.

Fordham, Signithia, and John Ogbu. 1986. Black students' school success: Coping with the "burden of 'acting white.'" *Urban Review* 18 (3): 176–206.

Frankenberg, Ruth. 1993. *White women, race matters: The social construction of whiteness.* Minneapolis: University of Minnesota Press.

———. 1997. *Displacing whiteness: Essays in social and cultural criticism.* Durham, NC: Duke University Press.

Gallagher, Charles A. 1995. White reconstruction in the university. *Socialist Review* 24 (1&2): 165–87.

———. 1997. White racial formation: Into the twenty-first cen-
tury. In *Critical white studies: Looking behind the mirror,* edited by Richard Delgado and Jean Stefancic, 6–11. Philadelphia: Temple University Press.

Gamoran, Adam, Martin Nystrand, Mark Berends, and Paul C. LePore. 1995. An organizational analysis of the effects of ability grouping. *American Educational Research Journal* 32 (4): 687–715.

Gilroy, Paul. 1991. *"There ain't no black in the Union Jack": The cultural politics of race and nation.* Chicago: University of Chicago Press.

———. 1993. *The black Atlantic: Modernity and double consciousness.* Cambridge, MA: Harvard University Press.

Giroux, Henry. 1996. *Fugitive cultures: Race, violence, and youth.* New York: Routledge.

———. 1997. Rewriting the discourse of racial identity: Towards a pedagogy and politics of whiteness. *Harvard Educational Review* 67 (2): 285–320.

Goldberg, David Theo. 1993. *Racist culture: Philosophy and the politics of meaning.* Cambridge, UK: Blackwell.

Hall, Stuart. 1992. What is the "black" in black popular culture? In *Black popular culture,* edited by Gina Dent, 21–33. Seattle, WA: Bay.

———. 1996. Introduction: Who needs identity? In *Questions of cultural identity,* edited by Stuart Hall and Paul du Gay, 1–17. London: Sage.

Haney Lopez, Ian F. 1996. *White by law: The legal construction of race.* New York: New York University Press.

Harris, Cheryl. 1993. Whiteness as property. *Harvard Law Review* 106:1707–91.

Hartigan, John, Jr. 1997. Locating white Detroit. In *Displacing whiteness: Essays in social and cultural criticism,* edited by Ruth Frankenberg, 180–213. Durham, NC: Duke University Press.

———. 1999. *Racial situations: Class predicaments of whiteness in Detroit.* Princeton, NJ: Princeton University Press.

Hill, Mike, ed. 1997. *Whiteness: A critical reader.* New York: New York University Press.

hooks, bell. 1992. *Black looks: Race and representation.* Boston: South End.

Ignatiev, Noel. 1995. *How the Irish became white.* New York: Routledge.

Ignatiev, Noel, and John Garvey, eds. 1996. *Race traitor.* New York: Routledge.

Jacobson, Matthew Frye. 1998. *Whiteness of a different color: European immigrants and the alchemy of race.* Cambridge, MA: Harvard University Press.

Kenny, Lorraine Delia. 2000a. Doing my homework: The autoethnography of a white teenage girl. In *Racing research, researching race: Methodological dilemmas in critical race studies,* edited by France Winddance Twine and Jonathan Warren. New York: New York University Press.

———. 2000b. *Daughters of suburbia: Growing up white, middle class, and female.* New Brunswick, NJ: Rutgers University Press.

Kinney, David A. 1993. From nerds to normals: The recovery of identity among adolescents from middle school to high school. *Sociology of Education* 66 (1): 21–40.

Lightfoot, Sara Lawrence. 1978. *Worlds apart: Relationships between families and schools.* New York: Basic Books.

Lipsitz, George. 1995. The possessive investment in whiteness: Racialized social democracy and the "white" problem in American studies. *American Quarterly* 47 (3): 369–87.

Lott, Eric. 1993. *Love and theft: Blackface minstrelsy and the American working class.* New York: Oxford University Press.

MacLeod, Jay. 1987. *Ain't no makin' it.* Boulder, CO: Westview.

McCarthy, Cameron, and Warren Crichlow, eds. 1993. *Race, identity and representation in education.* New York: Routledge.

Morrison, Toni. 1993. *Playing in the dark: Whiteness in the literary imagination.* New York: Random House.

Oakes, Jeannie. 1985. *Keeping track: How schools structure inequality.* New Haven, CT: Yale University Press.

———. 1994. More than a misapplied technology: A normative and political response to Hallinan on tracking. *Sociology of Education* 76 (2): 84–89.

Oakes, Jeannie, and Gretchen Guiton. 1995. Matchmaking: The dynamics of high school tracking decisions. *American Educational Research Journal* 32:3–33.

Perry, Pamela. 1998. Beginning to see the white: A comparative ethnography in two high schools of the racial consciousness and identities of white youth. Ph.D. diss., University of California, Berkeley. Forthcoming publication by Duke University Press.

Pfeil, Fred. 1995. *White guys: Studies in postmodern domination and difference.* New York: Verso.

Phoenix, Ann. 1997. "I'm white! So what?" The construction of whiteness for young Londoners. In *Off white: Readings on race and power in society,* edited by Michelle Fine, Linda C. Powell, Lois Weis, and L. Mun Wong, 187–97. New York: Routledge.

Pinderhughes, Howard. 1997. *Race in the hood: Conflict and violence among urban youth.* Minneapolis: Minnesota University Press.

powell, john a. 1997. Reflections on the self: Exploring between and beyond modernity and postmodernity, *Minnesota Law Review* 81 (6): 1481–1520.

Roediger, David. 1991. *The wages of whiteness: Race and the making of the American working class.* New York: Verso.

———. 1994. *Towards the abolition of whiteness.* New York: Verso.

Rosaldo, Renato. 1989. *Culture and truth: The remaking of social analysis.* Boston: Beacon.

Rose, Tricia. 1994. *Black noise: Rap music and black culture in contemporary America.* Hanover, NH: Wesleyan University Press.

Saxton, Alexander. 1990. *The rise and fall of the white republic.* New York: Verso.

Segrest, Mab. 1994. *Memoirs of a race traitor.* Boston: South End.

Steele, Claude M., and Joshua Aronson. 1998. Stereotype threat and the test performance of academically successful African Americans. In *The black-white test score gap,* edited by Christopher Jencks and Meredith Phillips, 401–27. Washington, DC: Brookings Institution.

Thandeka. 1999. The cost of whiteness. *Tikkun* 14 (3):33–38.

Thorne, Barrie. 1993. *Gender play: Girls and boys in school.* New Brunswick, NJ: Rutgers University Press.

Twine, France Winddance. 1997. Brown-skinned white girls: Class, culture, and the construction of white identity in suburban communities. In *Displacing whiteness: Essays in social and cultural criticism,* edited by Ruth Frankenberg, 214–43. Durham, NC: Duke University Press.

Valenzuela, Angela. 1999. *Subtractive schooling: U.S.-Mexican youth and the politics of caring.* Albany: State University of New York Press.

Wallace, Michelle (a project of). 1992. *Black popular culture.* Edited by Gina Dent. Seattle, WA: Bay.

Ware, Vron. 1992. *Beyond the pale: White women, racism and history.* New York: Verso.

Wellman, David. 1977. *Portraits of white racism.* Cambridge, UK: Cambridge University Press.

Williams, David R., James S. Jackson, Tony N. Brown, Myriam Torres, Tyrone A. Forman, and Kendrick Brown. 1999. Traditional and contemporary prejudice and urban whites' support for affirmative action and government help. *Social Problems* 46 (4):503–27.

Williams, Raymond. 1976. Base and superstructure in Marxist cultural theory. In *Schooling and capitalism: A sociological reader,* edited by R. Dale, 202–10. London: Routledge and Kegan Paul.

Wray, Matt, and Annalee Newitz, eds. 1997. *White trash: Race and class in America.* New York: Routledge.

33 "WHO ARE YOU IF YOU DON'T SPEAK SPANISH?"
Language and Identity Among Latinos
Beverly Daniel Tatum

Language is inextricably bound to identity. Language is not only an instrumental tool for communication, but also the carrier of cultural values and attitudes. It is through language that the affect of *mi familia,* the emotions of family life, are expressed. Richard Rodriguez, author of *Hunger of Memory* and critic of bilingual education, describes what happened in his family when the nuns at his parochial school told his Mexican parents to stop using Spanish at home, so their children might learn English more quickly. Gradually, he and his parents stopped speaking to each other. His family was "no longer so close; no longer bound tight by the pleasing and troubling knowledge of our public separateness. . . . The family's quiet was partly due to the fact that as we children learned more and more English, we shared fewer and fewer words."[1] What did it mean to his understanding of familism, and other aspects of ethnic identity when he relinquished his Spanish?

For Jose, a young Puerto Rican man, the answer to this question is clear.

> I think that the only thing that Puerto Ricans preserve in this country that is Puerto Rican is the language. If we lose that, *we* are lost. I think that we need to preserve it because it is the primordial basis of our culture. It is the only thing we have to identify ourselves as Puerto Rican. If you don't know your language, who are you? . . . I believe that being Puerto Rican and speaking Spanish go hand in hand.[2]

This sentiment was echoed repeatedly by other young Puerto Rican adults who were interviewed by Maria Zavala as part of a study of language and ethnic identity among Puerto Ricans.[3]

However, these young people had also learned that their language was devalued by the dominant culture.

Those who had spent their childhoods in the United States in particular recalled feeling ashamed to be bilingual. Said Margarita,

> In school there were stereotypes about the bilingual students, big time. [Since] they don't speak "the" language, they don't belong here. That's number one. Number two, they were dumb, no matter what. . . . Everyone said "that bilingual person," but they didn't realize that bilingual means they speak *two* languages. To them bilingual was not a good thing. There was a horrible stigma attached to them and I think I fell in the trap sometimes of saying "those bilingual people" just because that was what I was hearing all around me.[4]

A common coping strategy in childhood was to avoid the use of Spanish in public, a strategy akin to the "racelessness" adopted by some African American students. Said Cristina, a young woman raised in the United States, "I remember pretending I didn't know how to speak Spanish. You know, if you pretended that you were that American then maybe you would get accepted by the White kids. I remember trying not to speak Spanish or speaking it with an [English] accent."[5]

However, avoiding the use of Spanish does not guarantee acceptance by the dominant society. A growing awareness of this reality and the unfolding process of adolescent identity development led these students to reclaim their Spanish, a process integral to their exploration of Puerto Rican identity. Cristina, now a college student, explains:

> I'm a lot more fluent with English. I struggle with Spanish and it's something that I've been trying to reclaim. I've been reading a lot of literature written by Latinos lately, . . . some Puerto Rican history. Before [college] I didn't even know it existed. Now I'm reading and writing more and more in Spanish and

I'm using it more in conversations with other Puerto Ricans. Now I have confidence. I don't feel inferior any more. I used to in high school, I did. People don't want you to speak Spanish and before I was one of those that's very guilty of not speaking it because I didn't want to draw attention to me, but now you can't tell me not to speak Spanish because for me that's the biggest form of oppression. My kids are going to speak Spanish and they're going to speak it loud. They're not going to go with the whispering stuff. As a matter of fact, if a White person comes by, we're going to speak it even louder. I am going to ingrain that in them, that you need to be proud of that.[6]

Zavala effectively demonstrates that while these young people are still in the process of exploring identity, the resolution of their feelings about the Spanish language is a central dimension of the identity development process. The linguicism—discrimination based on language use—to which they all had been subjected had been internalized by some, and had to be rejected in order for them to assert a positive sense of identity.

While Zavala's study focused only on Puerto Ricans, sociologist Samuel Betances argues that for Latinos the Spanish language is a unifying theme. He writes, "in essence, the core which links Hispanics/Latinos is language, i.e., the theme of Spanish and English as vital to a healthy membership in both the larger society and in the ever growing emerging ethnic interest group."[7]

Given the strong connection between language and identity, it seems very important for educators to think carefully about how they respond to Latino children's use of Spanish at school. As Nieto points out, schools often work hard to strip away the child's native language, asking parents to speak English to their children at home, punishing children with detention for using their native language at school, or even withholding education until children have mastered English.[8] While of course fluency in English is a necessary educational goal, the child's fluency in Spanish need not be undermined in order to achieve it.

There is increasing evidence that the level of proficiency in one's native language has a direct influence on the development of proficiency in the second language. Contrary to common belief, it makes sense to use students' native language to reinforce their acqui-

sition of English. While it is not possible here to review the varieties of bilingual education and the political controversies surrounding them, the positive effects of bilingual education, from lower dropout rates to increased literacy development, have been demonstrated again and again.[9] Bilingual education, in which children are receiving education in content areas in their native language, as well as receiving structured instruction in English, is more effective than English as a second language (ESL) instruction alone, because the children can build on their previous literacy. Research suggests that it takes five to seven years on average to develop the level of English proficiency needed to succeed academically in school. For this reason, late-exit bilingual education programs—in which students remain until they have developed adequate English proficiency for high-level academic work—are particularly effective. Such programs have not only cognitive benefits, but social and emotional ones as well. Students who are encouraged to maintain their Spanish are able to maintain close family ties through their shared use of the language and their parents feel more comfortable with the school environment, increasing the likelihood of parental involvement at school.[10] Nieto and others are quick to point out that bilingual education alone cannot completely reverse the history of school failure that Latino students have experienced. But it does challenge the alienating and emotionally disruptive idea that native language and culture need to be forgotten in order to be successful.

The attempted destruction of an oppressed people's native language has been an issue not only for Latinos, but also for American Indians. In fact, Indian education as carried out by the U.S. government in the nineteenth and early twentieth centuries served as the model for the early Americanization efforts in Puerto Rico.[11] The physical and cultural dislocations visited upon Native Americans still have major implications for the identity development of Indian youth today.

NOTES

1. R. Rodriguez, *Hunger of memory: The education of Richard Rodriguez* (New York: Bantam, 1982), p. 23.
2. M. Zavala, "Who are you if you don't speak Spanish? The Puerto Rican dilemma" (presented at the American Educa-

tional Research Association Annual Meeting, New York, April 1996).

3. M. Zavala, "A bridge over divided worlds: An exploration into the nature of bilingual Puerto Rican youths' ethnic identity development" (master's thesis, Mount Holyoke College, South Hadley, MA, 1995).

4. Zavala, "Who are you if you don't speak Spanish?" p. 9.

5. Ibid.

6. Ibid., p. 11.

7. S. Betances, "African-Americans and Hispanic/Latinos: Eliminating barriers to coalition building" (presented at the Ethnic Diversity Roundtable, Chicago Urban Policy Institute and the Joint Center for Political and Economic Studies, April 15, 1994).

8. Nieto, *Affirming diversity, The sociopolitical context of multicultural education,* 2d ed. (White Plains, NY: Longman, 1996), ch. 6.

9. For a review of this literature, see C. E. Moran and K. Hakuta, "Bilingual education: Broadening research perspectives," pp. 445–62 in J. Banks and C. M. Banks (Eds.), *Handbook of research on multicultural education* (New York: Simon & Schuster, 1995).

10. Nieto, *Affirming diversity,* p. 200.

11. See J. Spring, *Deculturalization and the struggle for equality: A brief history of the education of dominated cultures in the United States* (New York: McGraw-Hill, 1997).

REFERENCES

Betances, S. "African-Americans and Hispanic/Latinos: Eliminating barriers to coalition building." Paper presented at the Ethnic Diversity Roundtable, Chicago Urban Policy Institute and the Joint Center for Political and Economic Studies, April 15, 1994.

Moran, C. E., and K. Hakuta. "Bilingual education: Broadening research perspectives." Pp. 445–62 in J. Banks and C. M. Banks (Eds.), *Handbook of research on multicultural education.* New York: Simon & Schuster, 1995.

Nieto, S. *Affirming diversity: The sociopolitical context of multicultural educationm,* 2d ed. White Plains, NY: Longman, 1996.

Rodriguez, R. *Hunger of memory: The education of Richard Rodriguez.* New York: Bantam, 1982.

Spring, J. *Deculturalization and the struggle for equality: A brief history of the education of dominated cultures in the United States,* 2d ed. New York: McGraw-Hill, 1997.

Zavala, M. "A bridge over divided worlds: An exploration into the nature of bilingual Puerto Rican youths' ethnic identity development." Master's thesis, Mount Holyoke College, South Hadley, MA, 1995.

Zavala, M. "Who are you if you don't speak Spanish? The Puerto Rican dilemma." Presented at the annual meeting of the American Educational Research Association, New York, April 1996.

FURTHER READING

Anderson, Elijah. 1978. *A Place on the Corner.* Chicago: University of Chicago Press.

- A study of social life among African American men in an urban neighborhood.

Anderson, Elijah. 1992. *Streetwise: Race Class and Change in an Urban Community.* Chicago: University of Chicago Press.

- Blacks and whites from a variety of backgrounds speak candidly about their lives, their differences, and their struggles for identity.

Blee, Kathleen M. 1996. "Becoming a Racist: Women in Contemporary Ku Klux Klan and Neo-Nazi Groups." *Gender & Society* 10: 680–702.

- Using life-history narratives and in-depth interviews, the author examines how women racial activists relate self-understandings to racist movement goals.

Liebow, Elliot. 1967. *Tally's Corner.* Boston: Little, Brown.

- A classic study of the jobs, family life, and social networks of black street-corner men.

Rawls, Anne Warfield. 2000. "Race as an Interaction Order Phenomenon." *Sociological Theory* 18: 241–275.

- A study of interaction between Americans who self-identity as black and white. The study reveals underlying expectations regarding conversation that differ between the two groups.

Stack, Carol B. 1974. *All Our Kin.* New York: Harper & Row.

- An ethnographic study of kinship and strategies for survival in a black community.

THE GENDERED WORLD

We commonly identify ourselves as men and women, girls and boys. We classify others in the same terms. Indeed, we regularly operate with the moral certainty that there are two—and only two—sexes into which the human population is divided. Thanks to the influence of the social sciences, it's now commonplace to distinguish between sex and gender. Sex is an ascribed, biological status. Gender is a culturally, socially, and psychologically achieved or learned status or role. But we still divide the world into two groups—two genders, two sexes. We assume that everyone who is normal fits one category or the other.

We thus live in a gendered social world. Many features of social life alternately step forward and recede in our consciousness. They assert, retract, and revamp our social worlds. But gender tends to be in the foreground most of the time. Even when gender isn't prominently in the picture, our actions and interactions take into account the sex categories to which we assign one another. Our interest in gender may appear incidental; it sometimes seems like "no big deal." But gender is almost always a significant feature of the social landscape we occupy.

We constantly rely upon displays of, and assumptions about, gender to supply basic understandings of who we are and what we're doing. It's hard to imagine a social world where gender doesn't matter. It's rare for us to encounter circumstances where gender isn't relevant to what we say, do, or feel. It's equally difficult to cope with situations when there's even the slightest uncertainty about a person's gender. How, for instance, would you go about interacting with a stranger you just met if you didn't know it was a man or a woman? How would this affect what you say and do? What could you reliably expect from this person?

For years, the television show *Saturday Night Live* ran a sketch about a character named Pat. Pat was thoroughly androgynous. That is, Pat wasn't clearly male or female, in dress, appearance, or behavior. Even the name "Pat" could "go either way." Pat's indistinct gender humorously vexed the other characters in the sketches. Part of the humor came from the many tricks and schemes contrived by other characters to get Pat to reveal his or her identity. But the sketch was especially telling because it showed how uncomfortable others were in simply not knowing. Normal interaction ceased as everyone joined in the search for Pat's gender and sexuality.

Such searches are usually unnecessary in everyday life. If our normative expectations aren't obviously betrayed, we presume we know the gender of those with whom we interact. Nearly everyone works full time at "doing gender" in order to display an appropriate sexual identity, even though they're not aware of doing so. The gendered social world, in other words, is a social space where people are constantly *accomplishing* gender as they interact with one another.

Still, some social scientists have tended to picture this gender work in overly simple terms. They tell us that we *learn* to be female or male. If everything works out as it should, we eventually *acquire* gendered identities. Having achieved these identities, we then get on with our lives. In due time, we are *socialized* to gender roles, or so these social scientists say. But this is a rather formulaic view of the territory. It suggests that there are social scripts or prescriptions that we internalize and follow in order to be proper men and women.

Everyday life, however, tells us that there are no strict gender formulas. It's more complicated than that. "Doing gender" must be interactionally tuned to the situation at hand. Gender displays must fit the demands of particular occasions. Astute improvisation is the key. Cultural norms and expectations may provide general recipes for crafting gendered selves and worlds, but these recipes must constantly be put into place.

ABOUT THE READINGS

A gendered social world isn't simply there. It has to be worked up through social interaction. In fact, **Barrie Thorne** argues that some of the most important work of "doing gender" is actually accomplished by children *at play*. In **"Gender Play: Creating a Sense of 'Opposite Sides,'"** Thorne takes readers inside the construction and reproduction of the gendered world of elementary school children. This social world arises on the playground as children divide themselves along gender lines.

Thorne uses the term "borderwork" to describe how children construct and sustain gender differences. She argues that kids develop identities as "boys" and "girls" through games and informal rituals. Playing "chase the girls," for instance, requires separate and distinct "teams" that necessarily oppose one another. In such games, children establish gender by displaying team membership. Being a boy or being a girl thus depends less on what children *are* and more on what they *do* in the context of playground activities. Their social worlds are forged in play and crystallized around the boundaries that establish the "opposite sides" in games of teasing, spying, and the like. Such games cultivate and accentuate differences and dualities that come to be associated with gender.

As vast as the differences between boys and girls seem to be at school, however, the world of strict gender distinctions can be easily transformed. Away from school—playing together in the backyard, for instance—children can play out entirely different social worlds. In these circumstances, doing "being a boy" and "being a girl" doesn't always seem to matter so much.

Doing gender isn't all play, however. It can be an extremely earnest enterprise. There may be no more serious venue for gender displays than prom night. In her book of the same title, **Amy L. Best** gives readers keen insights into how **"Fashioning the Feminine"** is done by girls in preparation for "a night to remember." Femininity in its highest form is constructed in the elaborate costumes, coiffures, and other adornments that girls concoct to be at their feminine best. Cultural standards of feminine beauty combine with ubiquitous messages about the need to shine on this most special occasion. Prom night thus presents young women with a gender project par excellence.

The essence of the project is the "body work" that girls do to enter into this highly stylized, gendered world. Best shows readers how even the physical self is fashioned in response to social demands. Teenage girls use prom-night rituals to define their most intimate, personal selves. But it's also clear that those selves and the bodies that ostensibly secure them are part of a highly gendered, decidedly public, social world.

Constructing gender is serious "business" when it becomes a commercial venture. In **"Beer Commercials: A Manual on Masculinity,"** **Lance Strate** examines how the advertising industry creates a gendered world into which men are expected to fit. This chapter isn't so much about how masculinity is *done* in practice, as it is about the range of masculine identities that are available for application. It describes contemporary masculinity ideals, so to speak. These are goals that men should shoot for if they are to establish themselves as "real men" in a gendered world.

GENDER PLAY
34
Creating a Sense of "Opposite Sides"
Barrie Thorne

> It's like girls and boys are on different sides.
> —*Heather, age eleven, discussing*
> *her experiences at school*

When I first began to wander the Oceanside School playground, with gender on my mind, I came upon a noisy group at the edge of a grassy playing field. A tall, brown-haired girl leaned toward two shorter boys and yelled, "You creeps! You creeps!" Then she laughingly pretended to hide behind a much shorter girl at her side. As one of the boys moved toward them, he asked, "What did you call me?" "Creep!" the tall girl, Lenore, repeated emphatically as she turned and slowly began to run. The boy, Ronnie, loped after her for about fifteen feet and grabbed her ponytail, while she shrieked. Lenore then spun around, shook loose, and reversed the direction of the chase, setting out after Ronnie. In the meantime, Sherry chased after Brad with her arms extended. As they ran, Brad called, "Help, a girl's chasin' me!" When Sherry approached him, she swung her right leg into the air and made an exaggerated karate kick. Then they reversed directions, and Brad started running after Sherry.

I could tell from the laughter and stylized motions that this was a form of play, and I immediately recognized the genre from my own childhood schoolyard days: boys-chase-the-girls/girls-chase-the-boys. This kind of encounter, when "the girls" and "the boys" become defined as separate and opposing groups, drew

me like a magnet; it seemed like the core of their gender relations. I gradually came to see that the occasions when boys and girls interact in relaxed and non-gender-marked ways are *also* significant, although, and this bears thought, it is more difficult to analyze and write about the relaxed situations within the rubric of "gender." Gender is often equated solely with dichotomous difference, but gender waxes and wanes in the organization and symbolism of group life, and that flux needs close attention.

This chapter, which attends closely to *meaning,* examines boys' and girls' experiences of varied situations of "together" and "apart." It explores the ways in which boys and girls interact to create, and at other points to dismantle, group gender boundaries, or a sense of "the boys" and "the girls" as separate and opposing sides. It also probes the magnetism of gender-marked events for observers, for participants, and in the realms of memory.

BORDERWORK

Walking across a school playground from the paved areas where kids play jump rope and hopscotch to the grassy playing field and games of soccer and baseball, one moves from groups of girls to groups of boys. The spatial separation of boys and girls constitutes a kind of boundary, perhaps felt most strongly by individuals who want to join an activity controlled by the other gender. When girls and boys are together in a relaxed and integrated way, playing a game of handball or eating and talking together at a table in the lunchroom, the sense of gender as boundary often dissolves. But sometimes girls and boys come together in ways that emphasize their opposition; boundaries may be created through contact as well as avoidance.

The term "borderwork" helps conceptualize interaction across—yet interaction based on and even strengthening—gender boundaries. This notion comes from Fredrik Barth's analysis of social relations that are maintained across ethnic boundaries (e.g., between the Saami, or Lapps, and Norwegians) without diminishing the participants' sense of cultural difference and of dichotomized ethnic status.[1] Barth focuses on more macro, ecological arrangements, whereas I emphasize face-to-face behavior. But the insight is similar: *although contact sometimes undermines and reduces an active sense of difference, groups may also interact with one another in ways that strengthen their borders.* One can gain insight into the maintenance of ethnic (and gender) groups by examining the boundary that defines them rather than by looking at what Barth calls "the cultural stuff that it encloses."[2]

When gender boundaries are activated, the loose aggregation "boys and girls" consolidates into "the boys" and "the girls" as separate and reified groups. In the process, categories of identity that on other occasions have minimal relevance for interaction become the basis of separate collectivities. Other social definitions get squeezed out by heightened awareness of gender as a dichotomy and of "the girls" and "the boys" as opposite and even antagonistic sides. Several times I watched this process of transformation, which felt like a heating up of the encounter because of the heightened sense of opposition and conflict.

On a paved area of the Oceanside playground a game of team handball took shape (team handball resembles doubles tennis, with clenched fists used to serve and return a rubber ball). Kevin arrived with the ball, and, seeing potential action, Tony walked over with interest on his face. Rita and Neera already stood on the other side of the yellow painted line that designated the center of a playing court. Neera called out, "Okay, me and Rita against you two," as Kevin and Tony moved into position. The game began in earnest with serves and returns punctuated by game-related talk—challenges between the opposing teams ("You're out!" "No, exactly on the line") and supportive comments between team members ("Sorry, Kevin," Tony said, when he missed a shot; "That's okay," Kevin replied). The game proceeded for about five minutes, and then the ball went out of bounds. Neera ran after it, and Tony ran after her, as if to begin a chase. As he ran, Rita shouted with annoyance, "C'mon, let's play." Tony and Neera returned to their positions, and the game continued.

Then Tony slammed the ball, hard, at Rita's feet. She became angry at the shift from the ongoing, more cooperative mode of play, and she flashed her middle finger at the other team, calling to Sheila to join their side. The game continued in a serious vein until John ran over and joined Kevin and Tony, who cheered; then Bill arrived, and there was more cheering. Kevin called out, "C'mon, Ben," to draw in another passing boy; then Kevin added up the numbers on each side, looked across the yellow line, and triumphantly announced, "We got five and you got three." The game continued, more noisy than before, with the boys yelling "wee haw" each time they made a shot. The girls—and that's how they now seemed, since the sides were increasingly defined in terms of gender—called out "Bratty boys! Sissy boys!" When the ball flew out of bounds, the game dissolved, as Tony and Kevin began to chase after Sheila. Annoyed by all these changes, Rita had already stomped off.

In this sequence, an earnest game, with no commentary on the fact that boys and girls happened to be on different sides, gradually transformed into a charged sense of girls-against-the-boys/boys-against-the-girls. Initially, one definition of the situation prevailed: a game of team handball, with each side trying to best the other. Rita, who wanted to play a serious game, objected to the first hint of other possibilities, which emerged when Tony chased Neera. The frame of a team handball game continued but was altered and eventually overwhelmed when the kids began to evoke gender boundaries. These boundaries brought in other possibilities—piling on players to outnumber the other gender, yelling gender-based insults, shifting from handball to cross-gender chasing—which finally broke up the game.

Gender boundaries have a shifting presence, but when evoked, they are accompanied by stylized forms of action, a sense of performance, mixed and ambiguous meanings (the situations often teeter between play and aggression, and heterosexual meanings lurk within other definitions), and by an array of intense emotions—excitement, playful elation, anger, desire, shame, and fear. I will elaborate these themes in the context of several different kinds of borderwork: contests; cross-gender rituals of chasing and pollution; and invasions. These stylized moments evoke recurring themes that are deeply rooted in our cultural conceptions of gender, and they suppress awareness of patterns that contradict and qualify them.

Contests

Girls and boys are sometimes pitted against each other in classroom competitions and playground games. Since gender is a relatively unambiguous and visible category of individual identity that divides the population roughly in half, it is a convenient basis for sorting out two teams. When girls and boys are on separate teams, gender may go unremarked as a grounds of opposition, as in the beginning of the team handball game; but more often gender, marked by talk and other actions, becomes central to the symbolism of the encounter. In the Oceanside fourth-fifth—grade classroom, where regular seating was almost totally divided by gender, the students talked about a boys' side and a girls' side. Drawing on and reinforcing the kids' self-separation, Miss Bailey sometimes organized the girls and the boys into opposing teams for spelling and math competitions.

Early in October, Miss Bailey introduced a math game. She would write addition and subtraction problems on the board, and a member of each team would race to be the first to write the correct answer. She designated the teams with two score-keeping columns on the blackboard: "Beastly Boys" . . . "Gossipy Girls." Several boys yelled, "Noisy girls! Gruesome girls!" and some of the girls laughed in response. Shaping themselves into a team, the girls sat in a row on top of their desks; sometimes they moved their hips and shoulders from side to side in a shared rhythm and whispered "pass it on." The boys stood along the wall, with several reclining against their desks. When mem-

bers of either group came back victorious from the front of the room, they passed by their team members and did a "giving five" handslap ritual with each in turn.

By organizing boys and girls into separate teams and by giving them names with (humorously) derogatory gender meanings, Miss Bailey set up a situation that invited gender antagonism. Disparaging the other team/gender and elevating one's own became a running joke. A few weeks later, when the teacher once again initiated the math game, Tracy ran to the board, grabbed the chalk, and wrote two column heads: "Boys" . . . "Great Girls." Then Bill ran up, erased the "Great," and substituted "Horrible."

When teachers organize gender-divided classroom contests, students pick up on and elaborate the oppositional and antagonistic meanings. When free to set up their own activities, kids also sometimes organize girls-against-the-boys games, especially of kickball. Compared with games where each side has a mix of girls and boys, these gender-divided games are highly unstable, which may, of course, be the intention and much of the fun. As in the team handball example, the participants usually end up tugging the thread of gender and sexual meanings and thereby unraveling the ongoing game.

For example, on the fifth-sixth—grade side of the Ashton playground, I came upon a kickball game with all boys in the field and all girls up to kick; about a fourth of the players on each side were Black and the rest were white, but the emphasis on gender seemed to submerge potential racial themes. As the game proceeded, it was punctuated by episodes of cross-gender chasing. When one of these episodes involved a boy chasing a girl who had the rubber ball, the game changed into an extended version of "keepaway," with girls and boys on opposite sides, and a lot of chasing, pushing, screaming, and grabbing.

Chasing

Cross-gender chasing dramatically affirms boundaries between boys and girls. The basic elements of chase and elude, capture and rescue are found in various kinds of tag with formal rules, as well as in more casual episodes of chasing that punctuate life on playgrounds.[3] These episodes begin with a provocation, such as taunts ("You creep!"; "You can't get me!"), bodily pokes, or the grabbing of a hat or other possession. A provocation may be ignored, protested ("Leave me alone!"), or responded to by chasing. Chaser and chased may then alternate roles. Christine Finnan, who also observed schoolyard chasing sequences, notes that chases vary in the ratio of chasers to chased (e.g., one chasing one, or five chasing two), the form of provocation (a taunt or a poke); the outcome (an episode may end when the chased outdistances the chaser, with a brief touch, wrestling to the ground, or the recapturing of a hat or a ball); and in use of space (there may or may not be safety zones).[4] Kids sometimes weave chasing with elaborate shared fantasies, as when a group of Ashton first- and second-grade boys played "jail," with "cops" chasing after "robbers," or when several third-grade girls designated a "kissing dungeon" beneath the playground slide and chased after boys to try to throw them in. When they captured a boy and put him in the dungeon under the slide, two girls would guard him while other boys pushed through the guards to help the captured boy escape.

Chasing has a gendered structure. Boys frequently chase one another, an activity that often ends in wrestling and mock fights. When girls chase girls, they are usually less physically aggressive; for example, they less often wrestle one another to the ground or try to bodily overpower the person being chased. Unless organized as a formal game like "freeze tag," same-gender chasing goes unnamed and usually undiscussed. But children set apart cross-gender chasing with special names. Students at both Oceanside and Ashton most often talked about "girls-chase-the-boys" and "boys-chase-the-girls"; the names are largely interchangeable, although boys tend to use the former and girls the latter, each claiming a kind of innocence. At Oceanside I also heard both boys and girls refer to "catch-and-kiss," and at Ashton, older boys talked about "kiss-or-kill," younger girls invited one another to "catch boys," and younger girls and boys described the game of "kissin'." In addition to these terms, I have heard reports from other U.S. schools of "the chase," "chasers," "chase-and-kiss," "kiss-chase," and "kissers-and-chasers." The names vary by region and school but always contain both gender and sexual meanings.[5]

Most informal within-gender chasing does not live on in talk unless something unusual happens, like an injury. But cross-gender chasing, especially when it takes the form of extended sequences with more than a few participants, is often surrounded by lively discussion. Several parents have told me about their kindergarten or first-grade children coming home from school to excitedly, or sometimes disgustedly, describe "girls-chase-the-boys" (my children also did this when they entered elementary school). Verbal retellings and assessments take place not only at home but also on the playground. For example, three Ashton fourth-grade girls, who claimed time-out from boys-chase-the-girls by running to a declared safety zone, excitedly talked about the ongoing game: "That guy is mean, he hits everybody"; "I kicked him in the butt."

In girls-chase-the-boys, girls and boys become, by definition, separate teams. Gender terms blatantly override individual identities, especially in references to the other team ("Help, a girl's chasin' me!"; "C'mon Sarah, let's get that boy"; "Tony, help save me from the girls"). Individuals may call for help from, or offer help to, others of their gender. And in acts of treason, they may grab someone from their team and turn them over to the other side. For example, in an elaborate chasing scene among a group of Ashton third-graders, Ryan grabbed Billy from behind, wrestling him to the ground. "Hey girls, get 'im," Ryan called.

Boys more often mix episodes of cross-gender with same-gender chasing, a pattern strikingly evident in the large chasing scenes or melees that recurred on the segment of the Ashton playground designated for third- and fourth-graders. Of the three age-divided playground areas, this was the most bereft of fixed equipment; it had only a handball court and, as a boy angrily observed to me, "two stinkin' monkey bars." Movable play equipment was also in scarce supply; the balls were often lodged on the school roof, and for a time the playground aides refused to hand out jump ropes because they said the kids just wanted to use them to "strangle and give ropeburns." With little to do, many of the students spent recesses and the lunch hour milling and chasing around on the grassy field. Boys ran after, tackled, and wrestled one another on the ground, sometimes so fiercely that injuries occurred. Girls also chased girls, although less frequently and with far less bodily engagement than among boys. Cross-gender chases, in every sort of numeric combination, were also less physically rough than chasing among boys; girls were quick to complain, and the adult aides intervened more quickly when a boy and a girl wrestled on the ground. Cross-gender chasing was full of verbal hostility, from both sides, and it was marked by stalking postures and girls' screams and retreats to spots of safety and talk.

In cross-gender and same-gender chasing, girls often create safety zones, a designated space that they can enter to become exempt from the fray. After a period of respite, often spent discussing what has just happened, they return to the game. The safety zone is sometimes a moving area around an adult; more than once, as I stood watching, my bubble of personal space housed several girls. Or the zone may be more fixed, like the pretend steel house that the first- and second-grade Ashton girls designated next to the school building. In the Oceanside layout the door to the girls' restroom faced one end of the playground, and girls often ran into it for safety. I could hear squeals from within as boys tried to open the door and peek in. During one of these scenarios eight girls emerged from the restroom with dripping clumps of wet paper towels, which they threw at the three boys who had been peeking in, and then another burst of chasing ensued.

Variations by Age   Although the basic patterns of cross-gender chasing are remarkably persistent across all age levels, I noticed some variations by age. Several times I saw younger children go through a process of induction, as in the early fall at Ashton when a second-grade boy taught a kindergarten girl how to chase. He slowly ran backward, beckoning her to pursue him, as he called, "Help, a girl's after me." She picked up the loping movement and paced herself behind him, as he looked back to make sure she was following. Then he slowly veered around and said, "Now I'll chase you."

Chasing often mixes with fantasy scenarios in the play of younger kids. An Ashton first-grade boy who said he was a "sea monster" made growling noises and curled his fingers like claws at the end of his out-stretched arms as he stalked groups of girls. "There's a sea monster, c'mon, we gotta save our other friend, you know, Denise," Bonnie said to the three other girls beside her on the sidewalk. They ran from "the sea monster" to grab Denise's hand and then move into the safety of their "steel house." By the fourth and fifth grades, chasers have perfected the exaggerated movements and sounds—stalking, screams, karate kicks—that accompany scenes of chasing among older girls and boys, and that help frame them as play.

Sexual meanings, highlighted by names like "chase-and-kiss" and "kissers-and-chasers," infuse cross-gender chasing at every age. The threat of kissing, most often girls threatening to kiss boys, is a ritualized form of provocation, especially among younger kids. When Shana, a third-grader, brought a tube of lipstick from home, she and her friends embellished games of kissin' by painting their lips dark red and threatening to smear the boys with kisses. This caused an uproar on the playground, and both boys and girls animatedly talked about it afterward. "The kiss gives you cooties," a boy explained to me.

I only once saw kisses used as a weapon in within-gender relations, when Justin, a second-grade boy, puckered his lips and told another boy that he would kiss him if he didn't leave him alone; the threat worked, and the other boy left. I never saw a girl use a kiss to threaten another girl, although young girls sometimes kissed one another with affection.

At both schools overt threats of kissing were more prevalent among younger kids, but they sometimes appeared in the play of fourth-, fifth-, and sixth-graders. At Oceanside I watched Lisa and Jill pull along Jonathan, a fourth-grade boy, by his hands, while a group of girls sitting on the jungle gym called out, "Kiss him, kiss him." Grabbing at his hair, Lisa said to Jill, "Wanna kiss Jonathan?" Jonathan wrenched himself away, and the girls chased after him. "Jill's gonna kiss your hair," Lisa yelled.

Sexual meanings may extend beyond kisses to other parts of the body. Margaret Blume, who observed on the Oceanside playground several years after I did, recorded a variant of chasing that the third- and fourth-graders called "scoring high with the girls."[6] When Margaret talked with a group who had been playing the game, a girl named Becky exclaimed, "They're trying to pinch our butts!" "Do you pinch them back?" Margaret asked. "No, I scratch; I hit them." A boy bragged, "I got fifty [pinches] now." "I guess we're popular," Becky said to Lois, as they both giggled.

Among fifth- and sixth-graders, cross-gender chasing involves more elaborate patterns of touch and touch avoidance than among younger kids. As I watched the stylized motions of grabbing at girls in ways that avoided their fronts, it seemed to me that older chasers often took account of girls' "developing" (or soon-to-be-developing) bodies, especially the growing visibility of their breasts. Principals, teachers, and aides generally ignored cross-gender chasing among younger kids, unless it got physically rough. Sometimes adults found it amusing, as when a first-grade teacher came up to me on the playground and, teasing the little girls who were standing next to her, told me, "Write down that first-grade girls kiss the boys." But if a fourth-, fifth-, or sixth-grade girl and boy ended a chase by wrestling on the ground (an infrequent occurrence; that sort of physical pummeling between boys and girls diminished with age), playground aides were quick to intervene, even when it was clear the tussle was being enacted in a mode of play. The Ashton principal told the sixth graders that they were not to play "pom-pom tackle," a complicated chasing game, because it entailed "inappropriate touch" between boys and girls.

Troupes At every age some kids gravitate to boys-chase-the-girls, while others, both girls and boys, avoid it. Individuals may gain a reputation for their interest in cross-gender chasing, like a second-grade girl who was teased for being a "kisser." But younger boys and girls mix bursts of chasing with other activities, rather than making it the focus of all their playground time. This continues to be true for older boys; for example, Bill, a fifth-grader whom an Oceanside aide said was "crush-prone," often played chasing games with girls, but he engaged in other playground activities as well. In both schools, however, a handful of fifth- and sixth-grade girls organized themselves into troupes who roamed the playground in search of "action"—primarily chasing—with boys. (Once the word "troupe" occurred to me, it stuck because it so aptly grasps the imagery of the wandering and performing female groups.)

At the center of a troupe are usually one or more "well-developed" (in both schools, the favored adult word for big-breasted and tall) girls, such as Lenore, who led the Oceanside chase scene described at the beginning of this chapter. The other girls (troupe numbers range from two to six), who may or may not be "developed," follow the lead of those at the center. Other groups of girls who stick together on the playground, like the ones I came to think of as "the jump rope girls," engage mostly with one another and the activity at hand. In contrast, the members of a wandering troupe spend their time in an open-ended search for ritual contact with boys. Troupes cover a lot of territory; they stride across the playground, looking around, wearing their breasts like badges, and drawing boys into bouts of chasing.

In both schools there were interracial troupes of girls. For example, two white girls and three Black girls, all of them fifth- and sixth-graders, constituted the largest and most visible troupe on the Ashton playground. One of the white girls and two of the Black girls were tall and had breasts and full hips. The other two girls were shorter and flat-chested. They walked along together, sometimes five in a row, sometimes snapping their fingers in shared rhythms or doing dance steps. Their stylized motions evoked the culture of African-American dance and movement, which, of course, is a major influence on U.S. teen culture.

One day, when this troupe came near three white boys, one of the Black girls leaned over and said tauntingly, "It's not nice to talk about Mother Nature." The boys ran, and she chased them for a short distance and then returned to the striding troupe. Then one of the white girls stuck out her foot, threatening to trip two white boys who stood at the fringes. She broke into a run, as one of the boys chased after her. Another white girl said, "I won't let him touch you," and ran after him. He grabbed at her hands; she kicked her leg out, got him down, and sat on him. He pushed her off and walked away, while the rest of the girls stood watching and laughing. The girls reconstituted their row and walked along until they came to the grassy field where a small group of fifth- and sixth-grade boys were playing football. One of the girls ran over, caught the football, and tossed it to another member of the troupe. The boys, who were much shorter than the three tallest girls, rushed to get the ball, but the girls kept it away from them. In a gesture unusual for boys this age, they went to complain to an aide, "Us boys can't play football without the girls gettin' in"; "The girls are gettin' in the way." The aide told the girls to leave the boys alone.

These girls were highly visible because of their size and mobility, their coordinated movements and display, and their unusual actions. Only twice did I see a group of girls—both times this troupe—deliberately disrupt the ongoing play of boys; it is usually boys who invade the activities of girls. This group claimed space and asserted themselves with a style that mixed sexuality with claims to power. Some other playground participants seemed to regard this group with ambivalence. A sixth-grade girl pointed to the group and said to me, with an edge of resentment, "They're so proud, they think they're so smart; they go marching around."

"Cooties" and Other Pollution Rituals

Episodes of chasing sometimes entwine with rituals of pollution, as in "cooties" or "cootie tag" where specific individuals or groups are treated as contaminating or carrying "germs." Cooties, of course, are invisible; they make their initial appearance through announcements like "Rochelle has cooties!"[7] Kids have rituals for transferring cooties (usually touching someone else, often after a chase, and shouting "You've got cooties!"), for immunization (writing "CV"—for "cootie vaccination"—on their arms, or shaping their fingers to push out a pretend immunizing "cootie spray"), and for eliminating cooties (saying "no gives" or using "cootie catchers" made of folded paper).[8] While girls and boys may transfer cooties to one another, and girls may give cooties to girls, boys do not generally give cooties to other boys.[9] Girls, in short, are central to the game.

Either girls or boys may be defined as having cooties, but girls give cooties to boys more often than vice versa. In Michigan, one version of cooties was called "girl stain"; the fourth-graders in a school on the East Coast used the phrase "girl touch."[10] And in a further shift from acts to imputing the moral character

of actors, individuals may be designated as "cootie queens" or "cootie girls."[11] Cootie queens or cootie girls (I have never heard or read about "cootie kings" or "cootie boys") are female pariahs, the ultimate school untouchables, seen as contaminating not only by virtue of gender, but also through some added stigma such as being overweight or poor.[12] And according to one report, in a racially mixed playground in Fresno, California, "Mexican" (Chicano/Latino) but not Anglo children gave cooties; thus inequalities of race, as well as of gender and social class, may be expressed through pollution games.[13] In situations like this, different sources of oppression may compound one another.

I did not learn of any cootie queens at Ashton or Oceanside, but in the daily life of schools *individual* boys and girls may be stigmatized and treated as contaminating. For example, a third-grade Ashton girl refused to sit by a particular boy, whom other boys routinely pushed away from the thick of all-male seating, because he was "stinky" and "peed in his bed." A teacher in another school told me that her fifth-grade students said to newcomers, "Don't touch Phillip's desk; he picks his nose and makes booger balls." Phillip had problems with motor coordination, which, the teacher thought, contributed to his marginalization.

But there is also a notable gender asymmetry, evident in the skewed patterning of cooties; *girls as a group are treated as an ultimate source of contamination,* while boys *as* boys—although maybe not, as Chicanos or individuals with a physical disability— are exempt. Boys sometimes mark hierarchies among themselves by using "girl" as a label for low-status boys and by pushing subordinated boys next to the contaminating space of girls. In Miss Bailey's fourth-fifth–grade class other boys routinely forced or maneuvered the lowest-status boys (Miguel and Alejandro, the recent immigrants from Mexico, and Joel, who was overweight and afraid of sports) into sitting "by the girls," a space treated as contaminating. In this context, boys drew on gender meanings to convey racial subordination. In contrast, when there was gender-divided seating in the classroom, lunchroom, music room, or auditorium, which girls sat at the boundary between groups of girls and groups of boys had no apparent relationship to social status.

Boys sometimes treat objects associated with girls as polluting; once again, the reverse does not occur. Bradley, a college student, told me about a classroom incident he remembered from third grade. Some girls gave Valentine's Day cards with pictures of Strawberry Shortcake, a feminine-stereotyped image, to everyone in the class, including boys. Erik dumped all his Strawberry Shortcake valentines into Bradley's box; Bradley one-upped the insult by adding his own Strawberry Shortcake valentines to the pile and sneaking them back into Erik's box.

Recoiling from physical proximity with another person and their belongings because they are perceived as contaminating is a powerful statement of social distance and claimed superiority. Pollution beliefs and practices draw on the emotion-laden feeling of repugnance that accompanies unwanted touch or smell. Kids often act out pollution beliefs in a spirit of playful teasing, but the whimsical frame of "play" slides in and out of the serious, and some games of cooties clearly cause emotional pain. When pollution rituals appear, even in play, they frequently express and enact larger patterns of inequality, by gender, by social class and race, and by bodily characteristics like weight and motor coordination. When several of these characteristics are found in the same person, the result may be extreme rituals of shaming, as in the case of cootie queens. Aware of the cruelty and pain bound up in games of pollution, teachers and aides often try to intervene, especially when a given individual becomes the repeated target.

What is the significance of "girl stain," of the fact that girls, but not boys, become cast as an ultimate polluting group? Beliefs in female pollution, usually related to menstruation and reproductive sexuality, can be found in many cultures but not, at least from the reports I've been able to find, among prepubertal children. Cooties, which is primarily played by first-, second-, and third-graders (or kids ages six to nine), is therefore unusual. These pollution rituals suggest that in contemporary U.S. culture even young girls are treated as symbolically contaminating in a way that boys, as a group, are not. This may be because in our culture even at a young age, girls are sexualized more than boys, and female sexuality, especially when "out of place" or actively associated with children, con-

notes danger and endangerment. Furthermore, even before birth girls are, on the whole, less valued than boys; it is still the case, for example, that prospective parents more often wish for a son than a daughter. Pollution rituals connect with themes of separation and power, to which I will return later in the chapter.

Invasions

In contests and in chasing, groups of girls and groups of boys confront one another as separate "sides," which makes for a kind of symmetry as does the alternation of chasing and being chased. But rituals of pollution tip the symmetry, defining girls as more contaminating. Invasions, a final type of borderwork, also take asymmetric form; boys invade girls' groups and activities much more often than the reverse. When asked about what they do on the playground, boys list "teasing the girls" as a named activity, but girls do not talk so routinely about "teasing boys."[14] As in other kinds of borderwork, gendered language ("Let's spy on the girls"; "Those boys are messing up our jump rope game") accompanies invasions, as do stylized interactions that highlight a sense of gender as an antagonistic social division.

On the playgrounds of both schools I repeatedly saw boys, individually or in groups, deliberately disrupt the activities of groups of girls. Boys ruin ongoing games of jump rope by dashing under the twirling rope and disrupting the flow of the jumpers or by sticking a foot into the rope and stopping its momentum. On the Ashton playground seven fourth-grade girls engaged in an intense game of four-square; it was a warm October day, and the girls had piled their coats on the cement next to the painted court. Two boys, mischief enlivening their faces, came to the edge of the court. One swung his arm into the game's bouncing space; in annoyed response, one of the female players pushed back at him. He ran off for a few feet, while the other boy circled in to take a swipe, trying to knock the ball out of play. Meanwhile, the first boy kneeled behind the pile of coats and leaned around to watch the girls. One of the girls yelled angrily, "Get out. My glasses are in one of those, and I don't want 'em busted." A playground aide called the boys over and told them to "leave the girls alone," and the boys ran off.

Some boys more or less specialize in invading girls, coming back again and again to disrupt; the majority of boys are not drawn to the activity.[15] Even if only a few boys do most of the invading, disruptions are so frequent that girls develop ritualized responses. Girls verbally protest ("Leave us alone!"; "Stop it, Keith!"), and they chase boys away. The disruption of a girls' game may provoke a cross-gender chasing sequence, but if girls are annoyed, they chase in order to drive the boy out of their space, a purpose far removed from playful shifting between the roles of chaser and chased. Girls may guard their play with informal lookouts who try to head off trouble; they are often wary about letting boys into their activities. And they sometimes complain to playground aides.

Complaining to Adults

There is an empirical as well as stereotypical association of younger kids, and of girls of all ages, with complaining to adults about the behavior of other kids.[16] The word "tattling" is often used for this behavior, which conveys the telling of tales, of secrets, and thus the betrayal of one's kind. The negative connotation builds in a judgment I want to query. Sometimes the less powerful, or those not trained to be physically aggressive, have little recourse except to complain to adults.[17]

As Mrs. Smith's kindergarten students entered the culture of schooling, they continually assessed the reach of adult authority, including whether and when to "tell" on one another. Boys and girls peppered their daily talk with threats like "I'm gonna' tell the teacher" and "I'm tellin'." Mrs. Smith tried to set limits by simply ignoring the requests for intervention and by repeatedly telling the students that she wanted "none of that tattling stuff." The amount diminished over time, but "tattling" continued even when the teacher refused to intervene.

Students develop codes about when it is appropriate to complain to an adult about the misconduct of peers, with boys placing and accepting firmer limitations than girls.[18] The boys' code is illustrated by a brewing conflict on the Ashton playground. A third-grade boy wearing a dark-green shirt angrily leaned toward a girl who was holding the arm of a boy in a blue jacket and said, "He hit me in the gut; he's dead."

The girl let go of the second boy's arm and said, "He's yours." The boy in the green shirt continued, "I already beat his butt," as he and the other boy, both with hostile facial expressions, squared off to fight. As they pushed toward each other, a much taller boy came up behind and said calmly, "Break it up." The two pushed some more as the tall boy inserted himself between them. The boy in the blue jacket stomped away, calling over his shoulder, "I'm tellin'." "Only tattletales tell," the boy in the green shirt taunted after him. The boy who had threatened to tattle continued to walk off the playing field but didn't approach an adult.

Girls also chastise one another for being tattletales, but they do so far less often than boys. And when boys invade their play, girls are quick to complain to the playground aides, who sometimes intervene, especially when physical harm (like breaking a pair of glasses) or active sexuality (such as an older girl and boy wrestling on the ground) seem to be at stake. Sometimes, however, the aides ignore or challenge girls' complaints. A third-grade girl came up to a playground aide and complained, "Robert's hurtin' me." The aide dismissed the charge, saying, "You've been chasing him; go on."

Aides recognize that boys invade girls' ongoing play much more than the reverse, and they frequently witness these scenes since most of the girls' games (jump rope, foursquare) take place in the cement area by the building, where the aides usually stand. (This vantage point, as well as the fact that they are all women, may lead aides to see the playground world more from the vantage point of girls than of boys.) Anticipating trouble, Ashton aides often shooed away boys from areas where girls were playing, even when the boys hadn't done anything to provoke. This strategy may have warded off immediate conflicts, but it enhanced gender separation on the playground.

Aides do not anticipate trouble from girls who seek to join groups of boys, with the exception of girls intent on provoking a chase sequence. Indeed, if they seek access to a boys' game, girls usually play with boys in earnest rather than breaking up the game. The scenario of girls complaining and of aides then intervening may limit boys' aggression, but it also supports boys' views of girls as weaker and as tattletales.[19] Girls have less access than boys to physical aggression, which gives some of them little recourse except to turn to adults. But power derived from adults does not transfer to settings where those adults are not present or will not intervene.

IS BORDERWORK "ALL IN PLAY"?

I once asked Jeremy, one of the Oceanside fifth-graders, why girls and boys in Miss Bailey's class formed separate lines. "So they won't fight so much," he promptly replied. A variety of terms—"fighting," "teasing," "hassling," "bothering"—have been used to suggest the heightened emotions and the playful and real conflict that characterize borderwork.[20] Are the various incidents I have described really "fighting?" Or are they mostly "play?" When a girl repeatedly yells "You creep!" at a boy, is she insulting him or just fooling around? When a boy and a girl chase each other and wrestle on the ground, are they fighting, or expressing real sexual desire, or is it "all in fun?" Of course it all depends on context, and meanings are often mixed. Ambiguity is a feature of all types of borderwork and contributes to their volatility.

The anthropologist Gregory Bateson once observed that "play" does not name actions but the "frame" for actions.[21] An incident may at first glance look like a fight, but if the participants smile, restrain their physical force, use certain tones of voice, and engage in exaggerated movements, they can cue that it is a "play fight" and therefore not to be taken seriously. The cues, or metacommunication (that is, the communication *about* communication), signal the message "this is play." The "play" frame, like the related frame of "humor," brackets an encounter, setting it apart from ongoing, more "serious" life. Situations of play and humor have a loosened relationship to consequences; if pressed to take responsibility for their actions, participants can say, "we're only playing" or "this is just a joke."[22] The frames of play and humor "lighten up" a situation, moving it toward the more voluntary and spontaneous, and emphasizing process rather than product.[23]

All forms of borderwork partake, to varying degrees, in the frame or mode of "play." Some types of borderwork, like boys against the girls in kickball or in classroom math competitions, are organized as games, a rule-governed type of play. Episodes of chasing and cooties are more informal; participants signal the play frame by using scripted talk ("Help! A girl's chasin' me!"), laughter, stylized movements, and exaggerated kicks in the air. And when they disrupt a game of jump rope, boys often wear playful expressions and bend over with laughter when the jumper gets tangled in the rope.

"Play" is a fragile definition; participants have to continually signal the boundary that distinguishes play from not-play, and play and humor easily slide in and out of other, more "serious" meanings. This ambiguity creates tension, since one is never sure in what direction it will swing; a tease may move from playful to irritating to malicious and back again. Multiple layers of meaning also provide maneuvering room to try out one message with the option of falling back on another, safer meaning; the ambiguity lessens potential risks and leaves room for denial. Aggression and sex are the dangerous desires in school, as elsewhere in the world, and these are the messages that often lurk within the lightened frames of play and humor that surround episodes of borderwork.

The Theme of Aggression

I have already touched on varied kinds of aggression, ranging from verbal insults to outright physical coercion, that thread through incidents of borderwork. When girls and boys confront one another as rival groups, their boundaries defined by gender, the situation invites verbal insults, like those that accompanied the math game in Miss Bailey's class. Sometimes kids voice insults in anger, as when Rita, Neera, and Sheila yelled, "Bratty boys! Sissy boys!" in the heated-up game of team handball. At other times, the rivalry may be more playful and almost ritualized, as when three girls, sitting in one of the waiting lines that crisscrossed the Ashton lunchroom floor, chanted in cheery unison, "Girls are smart, boys are bogue" ("bogue" means "stupid and uncool"). The boys across from them smiled and, quickly fishing for a retort, came up with "Boys are better, girls are dumb."

Kids often carry out episodes of playground chasing in a whimsically scripted way, providing many cues that "this is play." But in both same-gender and cross-gender chasing, provocations that violate bodies, possessions, and selves may not be intended or perceived as very playful, and they may spur an angry pursuit. In the course of my fieldwork one of the few times I heard overtly racist insults was during episodes of cross-gender chasing; "Na, na, colored boy," a white third-grade girl at Ashton School yelled at an African-American boy, who then chased her. At Oceanside Lenore, a fifth-grade white girl, repeatedly yelled "Mexican monkey" as she chased with a Chicano boy. Chasing sequences may contain physical as well as verbal aggression, with the chased being pummeled to the ground, tripped, and sat upon. This kind of "play fighting" sometimes shades into "real fighting," especially among boys, whose chasing tends to be quite physical. In cross-gender chasing, when girls complain to aides that the boys are getting too rough, or on the rarer occasions when boys complain, the frame of play breaks down and the issue of aggression comes to the fore.

In the charges and countercharges that attend some episodes of tattling, one party may define the situation as a serious violation, while the other party insists that they were "just playing." This pattern recurs in the wake of playground invasions; boys, far more often the invaders, often claim a play frame, but girls, more often the targets of invasion, refuse to accept that definition. The asymmetry increases with age; many fourth- and fifth-grade girls see male invasions as a playground nuisance that simply makes them angry. This pattern resembles the structuring of sexual harassment. The harasser, nearly always male, often claims that verbal and physical intrusions into the target's personal space are "all in fun," while the target, usually female, sees it as unwanted and even coercive attention. Hierarchies help determine whose version of reality will prevail.[24]

Kids and adults often use the word "teasing" to describe episodes of chasing and invasion; "teasing" suggests targeted humor, with an angry or aggressive edge. This mix again provides multiple possibilities for action and interpretation. Teasing may express affection and solidarity, but, as Freud persuasively demonstrated, humor may also be a guise for hostility. The ambiguity titillates, and the possibly serious import of humor may be raised for negotiation.[25]

Sexual and Romantic Themes

The ambiguities of borderwork allow the signaling of sexual or romantic, as well as aggressive, meanings, and the two often mix together. If a girl repeatedly chases a particular boy, or vice versa, it may be taken as a sign of "liking." Participants are fully aware of this potential interpretation, as shown during one vivid incident when a participant suddenly, teasingly named that tune. On the Ashton playground, Ken, a third-grader, growled and stalked after two of his classmates, Sharon and Jenny, who ran to the proclaimed safety of "the cage," as they called the area by the bars. Lisa came over and taunted, "Ken can't get me," and Ken chased her while she screamed. Then Ken circled back to the area of the bars and, his arms outflung, ran after Sharon and Jenny. The pursuit ended when Ken grabbed Jenny, and they ended up face-to-face with his arms around her. Jenny suddenly, teasingly said, "What you huggin' me for?" "I'm not," he replied in a slightly stunned voice, while she flashed a triumphant smile. Ken quickly let go.

Running after someone, pinning their arms from the front or behind, or verbally insulting them may all be intended and/or interpreted as positive signs of attention. A woman college student remembered "antagonizing guys" in fifth grade; "you chased them, yelled at them, and called them shocking names, but you really liked the guy." Invasions may also, ambiguously, convey positive interest, as noted by Susan Allen Toth in her memoirs of growing up in Ames, Iowa, in the 1950s. She describes summers in the community swimming pool when she was on the cusp of puberty:

> Tommy or Bob or Lon glided under water toward us, often in twos or threes, as though they needed support. We girls pretended not to notice them coming until they spouted to the top, with loud shouts, and pounced on us to dunk us. . . . Being shoved under water was recognized as a sign that a boy had noticed you. He had at least taken the trouble to push you down. We certainly never complained, though I sometimes swallowed water and came up coughing. At other times the boys would ignore us and engage in their own elaborate games, diving for pennies or playing tag. We girls clung to the side, hanging onto the gutters, and watched.[26]

Other researchers have pondered the mix of aggression and liking that infuses boundaries between boys and girls. In her research in a desegregated junior high, Janet Schofield observed a lot of physical "bothering" and "pushing" not only between girls and boys, but also between Blacks and whites. But she argues that these forms of hassling differ in fundamental ways: "Whereas relations with gender outgroups are fundamentally influenced by the knowledge of future positive ties, relations between blacks and whites are fundamentally shaped by the history and present existence of racial separation, hostility and discrimination in our society."[27]

Schofield's argument about the history and structure of race relations, and racism, in the United States is well taken. But this interpretation tends to naturalize gender relations instead of observing that they are *also* shaped by history and by patterns of separation, hostility, and discrimination. Adult cross-gender relations cannot be chalked up simply as "future positive ties"; not everyone is heterosexual, and the "liking" relations of adults, as well as of fifth-graders and junior high students, mix caring and antagonism, pleasure and hostility. These patterns should not be taken for granted; gender relations, like race relations, are always changing, and, they can be deliberately altered.

Issues of Power

Power is another consequential structure that moves in and out of the leavening frame of "play." Much borderwork is symmetrical—girls and boys both avoid one another, exchange insults, square off as separate sides in games of math or kickball, or alternate roles in games of chasing. But telling asymmetries skew the marking of gender difference toward patterns of male dominance among children as well as, although generally less than, among adults.

Space, an especially valuable resource in the crowded environment of schools, is the locus of one basic asymmetry between girls and boys. On school playgrounds boys control as much as ten times more space than girls, when one adds up the area of large playing fields (plus basketball courts and, at Oceanside, skateball courts) and compares it with the much smaller areas (for jump rope, hopscotch, foursquare, and doing tricks on the bars) where girls predominate.[28] In addition to taking up more space, boys more often see girls and their activities as interruptible; boys invade and disrupt all-female games and scenes of play much more often than vice versa. This pattern, coupled with the much larger turf under boys' control, led Zella Luria, another playground observer, to comment that playgrounds are basically male turf; even girls' smaller enclaves are subject to invasion.[29]

Boys' control of space can be seen as a pattern of claimed entitlement, perhaps linked to patterns well documented among adults in the same culture. For example, there is ample evidence, reviewed and analyzed by Nancy Henley, that adult men take up more personal and public space than adult women. Furthermore, men more often interrupt or violate the space, as well as talk, of women.[30]

Beliefs about female pollution also express and help maintain separation between the genders, and female subordination, in the social relations of U.S. elementary school children as well as in cultures of the Mediterranean and of highland New Guinea.[31] But, as anthropologists have recently argued, pollution beliefs have multiple and even contradictory dimensions.[32] In some contexts women, and girls, may use belief in female contamination to further their own ends and even as a source of power. Male susceptibility to female pollution can be experienced as a source of vulnerability; if a girl is designated as having cooties or threatens to plant a dangerous kiss, it is the boy who has to run.[33] In complex dialectics of power, boys treat girls' spaces, activities, and sheer physical presence as contaminating, but girls sometimes craft their perceived dangerous qualities into a kind of weapon. Several of the third-grade boys who talked about the "lipstick girls who gave cooties" seemed not only excited but also a little fearful. Furthermore, on some occasions girls and boys who *share* other features in the crisscross mix of social identities—who, for example, are Anglos (rather than Chicanos) or who are not cootie queens—unite in treating some "Other" as polluting. In these contexts, "sides" shift, and being a girl or boy becomes less important than *not* being the school pariah or a member of a racially marginalized group. Gender dominance is only one strand of an intricate mesh of power relationships.

The dynamics of power in children's social relationships are extremely complex, and in many ways, in the words of a playground aide, "girls give as well as get." Girls sometimes turn pollution into a weapon; they challenge and derogate boys; they guard their own play and respond angrily to invasions; they stave off provocations by ignoring them; they complain to adults. But in several notable ways, girls act from a one-down position, a pattern both enacted and dramatized in the processes of borderwork.

WHY IS BORDERWORK SO MEMORABLE?

The imagery of "border" may wrongly suggest an unyielding fence that divides social relations into two parts. The image should rather be one of many short fences that are quickly built and as quickly dismantled. Gender boundaries are episodic and ambiguous, and *the notion of "borderwork" should be coupled with a parallel term—such as "neutralization"—for processes through which girls and boys (and adults who enter into their social relations) neutralize or undermine a sense of gender as division and opposition.*[34] The situations (e.g., less crowded in space, with fewer potential witnesses and participants) and practices (e.g., teachers or children organizing encounters along lines other than gender) that draw girls and boys together are a first step. But these "with" situations can go in varied directions: when girls and boys are together, gender may be marked and boundaries evoked, the theme of this chapter, or gender may become muted in salience.

At the beginning of the chapter I described a team handball game in which gender meanings heated up. Heated events also cool down. After the team handball game transmuted into a brief scene of chasing, the recess bell rang and the participants went back to their shared classroom. Ten minutes later the same girls and boys interacted in reading groups where gender was of minimal significance. Gender boundaries may also be dismantled on the playground, as when boys and girls left their mostly gender-divided activities while defending Don against mistreatment by a teacher who

was on "yard duty." In that incident, girls and boys found another source of solidarity—being in the same class and chafing under the authority of the adult "yard duty"—and gender divisions receded in importance.

Here I must stress *levels of analysis.* As *individuals,* we are (with a few ambiguous exceptions, such as transsexuals) each assigned to a fixed gender category, and by age three we develop relatively firm individual identities as either girls or boys. Over the course of our lives we continually enact and construct individual gender (being a male, being a female, with multiple styles of masculinity and femininity) through talk, dress, movement, activities.[35] But when the level of analysis shifts from the individual to *groups and situations,* gender becomes more fluid. A boy may always be a "boy," and that fact will enter into all of his experiences. But in some interactions he may be much more aware of that strand of his identity than in others, just as his ethnicity or age may be more relevant in some situations than in others. Multiple identities may also compound one another; sometimes it is highly salient that one is an African-American boy.

The salience of gender may vary from one situation to another, and gender and other social divisions (age, ethnicity, social class) may, depending on the context, "abrade, inflame, amplify, twist, dampen, and complicate each other" (in the phrasing of R. W. Connell and his colleagues).[36] Given these complexities, why are the occasions of gender borderwork so compelling? Why do episodes of girls-chase-the-boys and boys-against-the girls *seem* like the heart of what "gender" is all about? Why do kids regard those situations as especially newsworthy and turn them into stories that they tell afterward and bring home from school? And why do adults, when invited to muse back upon gender relations in their elementary school years, so often spontaneously recall "girls-chase-the-boys," "teasing girls," and "cooties," but less often mention occasions when boys and girls were together in less gender-marked ways? (The latter kinds of occasions may be recalled under other rubrics, like "when we did classroom projects.")

The occasions of borderwork may carry extra perceptual weight because they are marked by conflict, intense emotions, and the expression of forbidden desires. These group activities may also rivet attention because they are created by kids themselves, and because they are ritualized, not as high ceremony, but by virtue of being stylized, repeated, and enacted with a sense of performance.[37] I have described the scripted quality of contests, chasing, invasions, and tattling. This ritual dimension, as Mary Douglas has written, "aides us in selecting experiences for concentrated attention" and "enlivens the memory."[38] Cross-gender chasing has a name ("chase-and-kiss"), a scripted format (the repertoire of provocations and forms of response), and takes shape through stylized motions and talk. The ritual form focuses attention and evokes dominant beliefs about the "nature" of boys and girls and relationships between them.

Erving Goffman coined the term "genderism" to refer to moments in social life, such as borderwork situations, that evoke stereotypic beliefs. During these ritually foregrounded encounters, men and women "play out the differential human nature claimed for them."[39] Many social environments don't lend themselves to this bifurcated and stylized display, and they may even undermine the stereotypes. But when men engage in horseplay (pushing, shoving) and mock contests like Indian wrestling, they dramatize themes of physical strength and violence that are central to hegemonic constructions of masculinity.[40] And in various kinds of cross-gender play, as when a man chases after and pins down a woman, pretends to throw her off a cliff, or threatens her with a snake, the man again claims physical dominance and encourages the woman to "provide a full-voiced rendition [shrinking back, hiding her eyes, screaming] of the plight to which her sex is presumably prone."[41] In short, men and women—and girls and boys—sometimes become caricatures of themselves, enacting and perpetuating stereotypes.

Games of girls-against-the-boys, scenes of cross-gender chasing and invasion, and episodes of heterosexual teasing evoke stereotyped images of gender relations. Deeply rooted in the dominant culture and ideology of our society, these images infuse the ways adults talk about girls and boys and relations between them; the content of movies, television, advertising, and children's books; and even the wisdom of experts, including social scientists. This hegemonic view of gender—acted out, reinforced, and evoked through the various forms of borderwork—has two key components:

1. *Emphasis on gender as an oppositional dualism.* Terms like "the opposite sex" and "the war between the sexes" come readily to mind when one watches a group of boys invade a jump rope game and the girls angrily respond, or a group of girls and a group of boys hurling insults at one another across a lunchroom. In all forms of borderwork boys and girls are defined as rival teams with a socially distant, wary, and even hostile relationship; heterosexual meanings add to the sense of polarization. Hierarchy tilts the theme of opposition, with boys asserting spatial, physical, and evaluative dominance over girls.

2. *Exaggeration of gender difference and disregard for the presence of crosscutting variation and sources of commonality.* Social psychologists have identified a continuum that ranges from what Henri Tajfel calls the "interpersonal extreme," when interaction is largely determined by *individual* characteristics, to the "intergroup extreme," when interaction is largely determined by the *group membership* or social categories of participants.[42] Borderwork lies at the intergroup extreme. When girls and boys are defined as opposite sides caught up in rivalry and competition, group stereotyping and antagonism flourish. Members of "the other side" become "that boy" or "that girl." Individual identities get submerged, and participants hurl gender insults ("sissy boys," "dumb girls"), talk about the other gender as "yuck," and make stereotyped assertions ("girls are crybabies"; "boys are frogs; I don't like boys").

Extensive gender separation and organizing mixed-gender encounters as girls-against-the-boys set off contrastive thinking and feed an assumption of gender as dichotomous and antagonistic difference. These social practices seem to express core truths: that boys and girls are separate and fundamentally different, as individuals and as groups. Other social practices that challenge this portrayal—drawing boys and girls together in relaxed and extended ways, emphasizing individual identities or social categories that cut across gender, acknowledging variation in the activities and interests of girls and boys—carry less percep-

tual weight. As do efforts by kids and adults to challenge existing gender arrangements. *But the occasions
where gender is less relevant, or contested, are also
part of the construction of gender relations.*

I want to conclude by raising another interpretive
possibility. The frames of "play" and "ritual" set the
various forms of borderwork a bit apart from ongoing
"ordinary" life. As previously argued, this may enhance the perceptual weight of borderwork situations
in the eyes of both participants and observers, highlighting a gender-as-antagonistic-dualism portrayal of
social relations. But the framing of ritualized play
may also give leeway for participants to gain perspective on dominant cultural images. Play and ritual can
comment on and challenge, as well as sustain, a given
ordering of reality.[43]

The anthropologist Clifford Geertz interprets the
Balinese cockfight, a central ritual and form of gam-
ing in that culture, not as a direct expression of the hierarchy of Balinese social structure but rather as a
"metasocial commentary upon the whole matter of as-
sorting human beings into fixed hierarchical ranks and
then organizing the major part of collective existence
around that assortment." The cockfight has an intepre-
tive function; it is a "Balinese reading of Balinese experience, a story they tell themselves about themselves."[44]

Geertz's interpretation came to my mind when I
watched and later heard an aide describe a game the
Oceanside students played on the school lunchroom
floor. The floor was made up of large alternating
squares of white and green linoleum, rather like a
checkerboard. One day during the chaotic transition
from lunch to noontime recess, Don (the same boy
whose protest against unjust punishment was actively
supported by a united group of girls and boys later in
the year) jumped, with much gestural and verbal fan-
fare, from one green square to another. Pointing to a
white square, Don loudly announced, "That's girls'
territory. Stay on the green square or you'll change
into a girl. Yuck!"

It occurred to me that Don was playing with gender dualisms, with a basic structure of two oppositely
arranged parts, whose boundaries are charged with
risk. From one vantage point the square-jumping
game, as a kind of magical playing with borderwork,

may express and dramatically reaffirm structures basic
to, although far from exhaustive of, the gender relations of the school. In the dichotomous world of either
green or white, boy or girl, one misstep could spell
transformative disaster. But from another vantage
point, Don called up that structure to detached view,
playing with, commenting on, and even, perhaps,
mocking its assumptions.

NOTES

1. Fredrik Barth, "Introduction" to *Ethnic Groups and
Boundaries.* I am grateful to Fred Erickson for suggesting the
relevance of Barth's analysis. Sandra Wallman's writing (e.g.,
"The Boundaries of Race") on the process of marking race and
ethnic boundaries is also suggestive. Several years after I had
worked out the significance of Barth's insight for understanding
children's gender relations, I discovered a similar project in
Berentzen's ethnography of a preschool in Norway, *Children
Constructing Their Social World.*

2. Barth, "Introduction," p. 15.

3. For a taxonomy of children's games that distinguishes
chasing from other forms, see Brian Sutton-Smith, "A Syntax
for Play and Games."

4. Christine R. Finnan, "The Ethnography of Children's
Spontaneous Play."

5. For brief descriptions of cross-gender chasing on school
playgrounds, see ibid. (observations in Texas); Raphaela Best,
*We've All Got Scars: What Boys and Girls Learn in Elementary
School* (the Central Atlantic region); Kathryn M. Borman,
"Children's Interactions in Playgrounds" (the Midwest); Corsaro, *Friendship and Peer Culture* ("cross-gender approach-
avoidance" play, including chasing, in a nursery school on the
West Coast); Sue Parrott, "Games Children Play: Ethnography
of a Second-Grade Recess" (second-grade boys in Minnesota
tell about playing "girls-catch-the-boys"); Andy Sluckin, *Growing Up in the Playground* ("kiss-chase" in a British school); and
Stephen Richert, *Boys and Girls Apart: Children's Play in
Canada and Poland* ("kissing girls," a children's chasing game
in Ottawa, Canada, and "kisser catchers," in the Bahamas).

6. I would like to thank Margaret Blume for sharing her
fieldnotes and giving me permission to cite this example.

7. The word "cooties" may have its origins among soldiers
in foxholes in World War I, who used the term for head lice
(Robert L. Chapman, *New Dictionary of American Slang*).
When the soldiers returned home, some playfully called their
wives and other women "cooties," and "The Cooties" was the
name of at least one Veterans of Foreign Wars women's auxiliary club. Since the late 1940s a toy company has marketed a
children's game called Cooties, which involves rolling a dice to
draw body pieces and constructing an antlike plastic creature.
Iona Opie and Peter Opie (*Children's Games in Street and Play-*

ground) have recorded versions of cootie tag from England, Spain, Madagascar, and New England. With new times come new forms of contamination; I recently heard reports of children saying to one another, "Don't touch me; I don't want your AIDS."

8. Cootie catchers are a variant of the fortune-telling devices made of folded paper that are described and illustrated in Mary Knapp and Herbert Knapp, *One Potato, Two Potato: The Secret Education of American Children,* pp. 257–259 and in Iona Opie and Peter Opie, *The Lore and Language of School-children,* pp. 341–342.

9. This pattern was also found by Sue Samuelson, a folklorist, who gathered reports about how the game has been played ("The Cooties Complex").

10. Kevin Karkau, "Sexism in Fourth Grade." Richert (*Boys and Girls Apart*) reports Canadian children talking about "girl germs" but not "boy germs."

11. Thanks to Bob Emerson for this insight.

12. College students have told me about cootie queens in the elementary schools they attended; one reported that she had been a cootie queen when she was in fourth grade, a memory fraught with shame and suffering. She speculated that the stigma was related to her being overweight, as well as new to the school.

13. Samuelson, "The Cooties Complex." A friend of mine relayed a student's description of interactions in a school in a Canadian community divided between whites and more impoverished Native Americans. If a white girl accidentally touched a "native" girl, the white girl would quickly say "superstuff" and run to touch another white girl or boy to pass on, and thereby undo, the pollution.

14. I observed this in casual conversations at Ashton and Oceanside; the pattern also emerged in the memories of college students: both men and women recalled "chasing," but men talked more generally about "teasing girls." In extensive observations of elementary school children in West Germany, Oswald and his colleagues ("Gaps and Bridges") found a lot of mutual "bothering" between first-grade boys and girls. By fourth grade, boys bothered girls much more than the reverse; girls coped by complaining to adults and by ignoring or rebuking the botherers.

In a study of U.S. first-graders, Linda Grant ("Black Females' 'Place' in Desegregated Classrooms") found that where an initiator could be discerned, boys were responsible for 59 to 90 percent of physically aggressive encounters between boys and girls. Ruth G. Goodenough ("Small Group Culture and the Emergence of Sexist Behavior: A Comparative Study of Four Children's Groups") computed the ratio of negative to positive behavior in relations between the genders in four different kindergartens. She found a wide range, from one classroom with a relatively even balance of negative and positive behaviors to one where boys' negative behaviors to girls outweighed their positive behaviors by a ratio of thirty-one to one. In that classroom, boys repeatedly disrupted girls' play, while girls rarely disrupted the activities of boys. The girls in that classroom were generally more timid and less spontaneous than girls in the more egalitarian kindergarten

Patricia S. Griffin ("'Gymnastics Is a Girls' Thing': Student Participation and Interaction Patterns in a Middle School Gymnastics Unit"), who observed in a coed gymnastics class at a U.S. middle school, also found a dramatic gender asymmetry. Boys, as individuals and in groups, hassled girls (by getting in their way, butting into line, giving orders, teasing, mimicking, yelling and laughing at them) much more than the reverse. The girls responded by physically moving away, acquiescing (e.g., letting boys butt into line), ignoring, and asking the boys to stop. Boys generally interacted with girls only to hassle them; girls generally interacted with boys only when they responded to being hassled.

15. In quantified observations among elementary school children in West Germany, Oswald and his colleagues ("Gaps and Bridges") also found that a few boys—four out of fourteen in a group of fifth-graders—were responsible for most of the "bothering"; they made "plaguing girls" into a kind of sport. This pattern may relate to the emergence of school "bullies," although that topic has been studied more in the context of boy-boy than of boy-girl (or girl-girl) relationships.

Dan Olweus (*Aggression in the Schools*) found that of one thousand Swedish boys, ages twelve to sixteen, 4 to 6 percent were, in the perceptions of teachers and other students, extreme bullies; another 4 to 6 percent were "whipping boys," or frequent targets of bullying. In research in Norway Olweus found that boys engaged in three times as much bullying as girls; girls' bullying tended to be more subtle, like spreading rumors. In 1983 the Norwegian government, with Olweus's help, launched a national campaign to end bullying in elementary and junior high schools. Educational materials about the bully problem were given to school staff and families, and teachers were urged to give a clear message that bullying is not acceptable, to initiate talks with victims and bullies, and to give generous praise when rules were followed. When rules were violated, teachers and parents were advised to consistently use nonhostile, noncorporal punishment. According to Olweus, this national campaign reduced bullying by as much as half (Peter Freiberg, "Bullying Gets Banned in Norway's Schools").

16. Boys succinctly express this stereotype in their equation of "tattletales, crybabies, and girls," although a girl will sometimes insult a boy by using these female-typed names.

17. Conversations with Nancy Henley illuminated this point. "Tattling" resonates with "nagging"; both belittling terms are used more to refer to females than to males, and as labels and as actual forms of verbal recourse, they may be associated with having less power.

18. Linda Grant ("Gender Roles and Statuses in School Children's Peer Interactions") found that in four of six first-grade classrooms girls tattled on boys more than the reverse. Teachers also varied widely in their rules about and responses to tattling; for example, one teacher more often reprimanded the

tattler than the target, while another more often punished the target.

19. Kids recognize the scripted quality of these encounters. A third-grade girl told Jean Doyle, who interviewed students about their daily life, that boys "bother" girls and "the girls tell the teacher and she will punish them" ("Helpers, Officers, and Lunchers: Ethnography of a Third-Grade Class," p. 155). An Oceanside fifth-grade boy provided a different perspective on the same scenario: "Girls are always getting boys into trouble. They tease us and when we react, they tell on us and it's us who get into trouble."

20. Perhaps because most of the students at both Oceanside and Ashton were white and working-class, I witnessed little systematic hassling along lines of race and/or social class. Researchers in schools with larger proportions of students from different races and social classes have found those boundaries marked by teasing and bothering, with gender cutting across. Judith Lynne Hanna (*Disruptive School Behavior: Class, Race, and Culture*) observed in a recently desegregated "magnet" elementary school composed mostly of Black working-class and white middle-class students. She found recurring patterns of verbal and physical aggression that the children called "meddlin," including insults and taunts, menacing body postures, pushing, hitting, poking, and fighting. Working-class Black boys most often engaged in meddlin, and Black girls did more meddlin, especially in response to provocation, than white girls. The targets of meddlin were sometimes social equals of the aggressor but were most often the vulnerable: newcomers, children with physical handicaps or unusual dress, poor athletes, or those afraid to stand up to provocation. Some white and more Black children responded to meddlin by reciprocating; middle-class children, Black and white, were more likely to comply with demands or to disengage by using humor, negotiation, withdrawal, or the mediation of a teacher or another child. Hanna connects this use of verbal and physical aggression to patterns of bodily self-assertion in African-American culture; she also suggests that when children lack material or academic resources, they may resort to physical means to gain power. Meddlin took place mostly among Blacks and was not specifically targeted against whites as a group, but whites were put off by it and more often saw it as aggression rather than play, a perception that contributed to racial separation.

In observations in a desegregated junior high school, Schofield (*Black and White in Conflict*) also found an association between being Black, working-class, and male, and engaging in physical hassling. Targets who were white were quicker than those who were Black to interpret the hassling as intimidation.

21. Bateson, *Steps to an Ecology of Mind,* pp. 177–193. Just as a picture frame tells a viewer to interpret what lies inside differently than the wallpaper that surrounds it, so an interactional frame sets apart a different space of meaning. In *Frame Analysis: An Essay on the Organization of Experience,* Erving Goffman extended Bateson's insight.

22. Joan P. Emerson ("Negotiating the Serious Import of Humor") analyzes tricky everyday negotiations about whether a joking comment will be taken in a humorous or serious vein.

23. For a thorough review of the vast literature on play, especially in reference to children's activities, see Schwartzman, *Transformations.* The definition of play has been extensively debated; for every list of characteristics (such as spontaneous, voluntary, unproductive), counter-examples can be found, perhaps in part, as this discussion emphasizes, because the line between "play" and "real" is inherently problematic.

24. See Nancy Henley and Cheris Kramarae, "Miscommunication, Gender, and Power."

25. Sigmund Freud, *Jokes and Their Relation to the Unconscious,* and Emerson, "Negotiating the Serious Import of Humor."

26. Susan Allen Toth, *Blooming: A Small-Town Girlhood,* pp. 29–39. The reframing of insults as a sign of liking persists in patterns of male dominance among adults; battered women sometimes try to interpret male violence as a sign of caring. See Henley and Kramarae, "Miscommunication, Gender, and Power."

27. Janet Schofield, "Complementary and Conflicting Identities: Images of Interaction in an Interracial School," p. 85.

28. A pattern of boys having access to more space than girls of the same age can also be found in research on the daily lives of kids outside school. Roger Hart (*Children's Experiences of Place*) gathered information on the space traversed by forty-seven boys and forty girls, ages five through twelve, in a town in New England. At all ages, boys traveled almost twice as far as girls; for example, among fifth- and sixth-graders, boys averaged a distance of almost half a mile, and girls around one fourth of a mile. Parents gave boys permission to roam more freely than girls and were more likely to turn an eye when a son rather than a daughter broke the rules.

In a study of 764 sixth-graders in California, Medrich and his colleagues (*The Serious Business of Growing Up*) found boys were more physically mobile than girls, with some striking individual variations; for example, girls who played team sports were more physically mobile than other girls. They also found African-Americans were more physically mobile than whites or Asian-Americans; African-American boys roamed the farthest of any gender/ethnic group. Lever ("Sex Differences in the Games Children Play") found, as have other researchers, that when they are not in school, fifth-grade boys more often play in out-of-door activities, and girls are more likely to play in and around their houses. In a comparative study of six cultures, Whiting and Edwards (*Children of Different Worlds*) found that boys more often traveled beyond the immediate neighborhood except in one culture, the Taira in Okinawa, where, at an early age, girls, as well as boys, were allowed to roam freely throughout the community.

29. Personal communication from Zella Luria.

30. Nancy Henley, *Body Politics: Power, Sex, and Nonver-*

bal Communication; also see Thorne et al., eds., *Language, Gender, and Society.*

31. In a classic statement, Mary Douglas argued that "pollution is a type of danger which is not likely to occur except where the lines of structure, cosmic or social, are clearly defined" (*Purity and Danger,* p. 113). Thus, depending on the context, pollution rituals may help sustain social divisions along lines of gender, race, ethnicity, social class, or age. For writings on female pollution beliefs and rituals in varied cultures, see Thomas Buckley and Alma Gottlieb, eds., *Blood Magic: The Anthropology of Menstruation.*

32. Buckley and Gottlieb, *Blood Magic.*

33. Feminist psychoanalytic theories may help explain why males may feel threatened by females and "things feminine" and thus may treat girls as polluting. Chodorow's theory (*The Reproduction of Mothering*) may also help account for a related asymmetry: to say that a boy is "like a girl" is more insulting and personally threatening than to say that a girl is "like a boy." In the repertoire of children's teases I sometimes heard the taunting charge that a given boy "is" a girl ("Ben is a girl 'cause he's sitting at the girls' table"), but I never saw kids tease a girl for "being" a boy.

34. The process I am calling "neutralization" is called "decategorization" in Marilyn B. Brewer and Norman Miller, "Beyond the Contact Hypothesis: Theoretical Perspectives on Desegregation." In the process of decategorization, social categories like Black and white are made less salient than in "category-based contact."

35. See West and Zimmerman, "Doing Gender."

36. See Connell et al., *Making the Difference,* p. 182.

37. For a review of debates about use of the term "ritual," see Sally F. Moore and Barbara Myerhoff, eds., *Secular Ritual.*

38. Douglas, *Purity and Danger,* pp. 63–64.

39. Goffman, "The Arrangement between the Sexes," p. 321.

40. See Connell, *Gender and Power,* on the notion of "masculinities," some dominant or hegemonic, and others, like gay masculinity, more submerged.

41. Goffman, "The Arrangement between the Sexes," p. 323. Henley (*Body Politics*) earlier identified this type of cross-gender play as a reinforcement of male dominance.

When I was in the third grade in 1949–50, our teacher had us keep journals about events at school. When I recently read my entries, which are carefully printed in pencil on wide notebook lines and illustrated with crayon drawings, I was startled to discover my matter-of-fact recording of two gender scenarios in which I was part of the objectified category of "the girls." In one entry about a class picnic, I wrote: "Some boys found watersnakes and scared the girls. After that we went home." The other is in a short report on a playground clean-up day: "Gerald teased the girls by putting earthworms down our necks, and as soon as all the weeds were out we went home."

42. Henri Tajfel, "Social Psychology of Intergroup Relations."

43. See Schwartzman, *Transformations.*

44. Clifford Geertz, "Deep Play: Notes on the Balinese Cockfight," p. 26.

REFERENCES

Barth, Fredrik. "Introduction." In *Ethnic Groups and Boundaries,* ed. Fredrik Barth, 9–38. Boston: Little, Brown, 1969.

Bateson, Gregory. *Steps to an Ecology of Mind.* New York: Ballantine, 1972.

Berentzen, Sigurd. *Children Constructing Their Social World: An Analysis of Gender Contrasts in Children's Interactions in a Nursery School.* Bergen, Norway: Department of Social Anthropology, University of Bergen, 1984.

Best, Raphaela. *We've All Got Scars: What Boys and Girls Learn in Elementary School.* Bloomington: Indiana University Press, 1983.

Borman, Kathryn M. "Children's Interactions in Playgrounds." *Theory Into Practice* 18 (1979): 251–257.

Brewer, Marilynn B., and Norman Miller. "Beyond the Contact Hypothesis: Theoretical Perspectives on Desegregation." In *Groups in Contact,* ed. Norman Miller and Marilynn B. Brewer, 281–302. New York: Academic Press, 1984.

Buckley, Thomas, and Alma Gottlieb, eds. *Blood Magic: The Anthropology of Menstruation.* Berkeley: University of California Press, 1988.

Chapman, Robert L. *New Dictionary of American Slang.* New York: Harper and Row, 1986.

Chodorow, Nancy. *The Reproduction of Mothering.* Berkeley: University of California Press, 1978.

Connell, R. W., Dean J. Ashenden, Sandra Kessler, and Gary W. Dowsett. *Making the Difference: Schools, Families, and Social Division.* Boston: Allen and Unwin, 1982.

Corsaro, William A. *Friendship and Peer Culture in the Early Years.* Norwood, N.J.: Ablex Publishing, 1985.

Douglas, Mary. *Purity and Danger.* New York: Praeger, 1966.

Doyle, Jean. "Helpers, Officers, and Lunchers: Ethnography of a Third-Grade Class." In *The Cultural Experience,* ed. James P. Spradley and David W. McCurdy, 147–156. Chicago: Science Research Associates, 1972.

Emerson, Joan P. "Negotiating the Serious Import of Humor." *Sociometry* 32 (1969): 169–181.

Finnan, Christine R. "The Ethnography of Children's Spontaneous Play." In *Doing the Ethnography of Schooling,* ed. George Spindler, 358–380. New York: Holt, Rinehart and Winston, 1982.

Freiberg, Peter. "Bullying Gets Banned in Norway's Schools." *APA (American Psychological Association) Monitor,* October 1990, p. 30.

Freud, Sigmund. *Jokes and Their Relation to the Unconscious.* [1905]. New York: Norton, 1963.

Geertz, Clifford. "Deep Play: Notes on the Balinese Cockfight." *Daedalus* 101 (1972): 1–37.

Goffman, Erving. "The Arrangement between the Sexes." *Theory and Society* 4 (1977): 301–336.

———. *Frame Analysis: An Essay on the Organization of Experience.* New York: Harper and Row, 1974.

Goodenough, Ruth G. "Small Group Culture and the Emergence of Sexist Behavior: A Comparative Study of Four Children's Groups." In *Interpretive Ethnography of Communication,* ed. George Spindler and Louise Spindler, 409–445. Hillsdale, N.J.: Lawrence Erlbaum, 1987.

Grant, Linda. "Black Females' 'Place' in Desegregated Classrooms." *Sociology of Education* 57 (1984): 98–110.

———. "Gender Roles and Statuses in School Children's Peer Interactions." *Western Sociological Review* 14 (1984): 58–76.

Griffin, Patricia S. "'Gymnastics Is a Girls' Thing': Student Participation and Interaction Patterns in a Middle School Gymnastics Unit." In *Teaching in Physical Education,* ed. T. J. Templin and J. Olson, 71–85. Champaign, Ill.: Human Kinetics Publishers, 1983.

Hanna, Judith Lynne. *Disruptive School Behavior: Class, Race, and Culture.* New York: Holmes and Meier, 1988.

Hart, Roger. *Children's Experience of Place.* New York: Irvington, 1979.

Henley, Nancy, and Cheris Kramarae. "Gender, Power, and Miscommunication." In *"Miscommunication" and Problematic Talk,* ed. Nikolas Coupland, Howard Giles, and John M. Wiemann, 18–43. Newbury Park, Calif.: Sage Publications, 1991.

Karkau, Kevin. "Sexism in the Fourth Grade." Pittsburgh: KNOW, 1973. (Reprinted in *Undoing Sex Stereotypes.* See Guttentag, Marcia, and Helen Bray.)

Knapp, Mary, and Herbert Knapp. *One Potato, Two Potato: The Secret Education of American Children.* New York: Norton, 1976.

Lever, Janet. "Sex Differences in the Games Children Play." *Social Problems* 23 (1976): 478–487.

Medrich, Elliott A., Judith Roizen, Victor Rubin, and Stuart Buckley. *The Serious Business of Growing Up: A Study of Children's Lives Outside School.* Berkeley: University of California Press, 1982.

Moore, Sally F. and Barbara Myerhoff, eds. *Secular Ritual.* Amsterdam: Van Gorcum, Assen, 1977.

Olweus, Dan. *Aggression in the Schools.* New York: Wiley, 1978.

Opie, Iona, and Peter Opie. *Children's Games in Street and Playground.* Oxford: Clarendon Press, 1969.

Oswald, Hans, Lothar Krappman, Irene Chowdhuri, and Maria von Salisch. "Gaps and Bridges: Interactions between Girls and Boys in Elementary School." In *Sociological Studies of Child Development,* vol. 2, ed. Peter Adler and Patricia Adler, 205–223. Greenwich, Conn.: JAI Press, 1987.

Parrott, Sue. "Games Children Play: Ethnography of a Second-Grade Recess." In *The Cultural Experience,* ed. James P. Spradley and David W. McCurdy, 206–219. Chicago: Science Research Associates, 1979.

Richert, Stephen. *Boys and Girls Apart: Children's Play in Canada and Poland.* Ottawa, Canada: Carleton University Press, 1990.

Samuelson, Sue. "The Cooties Complex." *Western Folklore* 39 (1980): 198–210.

Schofield, Janet W. *Black and White in School.* New York: Praeger, 1982.

———. "Complementary and Conflicting Identities: Images of Interaction in an Interracial School." In *The Development of Children's Friendships,* ed. Steven R. Asher and John M. Gottman, 53–90. New York: Cambridge University Press, 1981.

Schwartzman, Helen B. *Transformations: The Anthropology of Children's Play.* New York: Plenum, 1978.

Sluckin, Andy. *Growing Up in the Playground.* London: Routledge and Kegan Paul, 1981.

———. "A Syntax for Play and Games." In *Child's Play,* ed. R. E. Herron and Brian Sutton Smith, 298–307. New York: Wiley, 1971.

Tajfel, Henri. "Social Psychology of Intergroup Relations." *Annual Review of Psychology* 33 (1982): 1–39.

Thorne, Barrie, Cheris Kramarae, and Nancy Henley, eds. *Language, Gender, and Society.* New York: Newbury House, 1983.

Toth, Susan Allen. *Blooming: A Small-Town Girlhood.* Boston: Little, Brown, 1978.

Wallman, Sandra. "The Boundaries of 'Race': Processes of Ethnicity in England." *Man* 13 (1978): 200–217.

West, Candace, and Zimmerman, Don H. "Doing Gender." *Gender & Society* 1 (1987): 125–151.

Whiting, Beatrice B., and Carolyn P. Edwards. *Children of Different Worlds.* Cambridge, Mass.: Harvard University Press, 1988.

35 | FASHIONING THE FEMININE
Amy L. Best

Before the twentieth century, girls simply did not organize their thinking about themselves around their bodies. Today, many young girls worry about the contours of their bodies—especially shape, size, and muscle tone—because they believe the body is the ultimate expression of the self. The body is a consuming project for contemporary girls because it provides an important means of self-definition, a way to visibly announce who you are to the world. From a historical perspective, this particular form of adolescent expression is a relatively recent phenomenon.

—*Joan Jacobs Brumberg,* The Body Project

The popular 1999 teen prom films *She's All That* and *Never Been Kissed* are Cinderella-inspired tales of transformation. As the narratives unfold, the central female characters, both wallflowers, submit to a series of changes culminating in their emergence as beauty queens at the prom. Each wins the adulation of her peers, and best of all, each gets the man of her dreams. In these Hollywood productions, the process of getting ready for the prom is a privileged space in which bodies are magically reworked and identities completely refashioned.

Predictably, the popular construction of the prom as a moment in which to reinvent the self is a gendered one; this narrative is almost always told through the voice of a girl and the transformation that occurs is mapped fundamentally through her body. This is because the prom belongs to "the feminine." The prom is a feminine space, conventionally thought to be the domain of girls. Constructed as such, it is a site where girls are expected to be heavily invested because they can use this space to solidify and display their feminine identities. Such expectations are inscribed in both popular culture forms and everyday talk. Girls are repeatedly told that going to the prom is a fundamentally important part to their being and becoming femi-

nine. In prom magazines, "making a statement" is the very promise of the prom: "the prom is your night to shine." "Dare To Stand Out" and "Be The Babe of the Ball" these magazines tell their readers. One magazine article asks, "On your special night will you steal the social scene?" The message is that a carefully fashioned feminine self is the key to an unforgettable prom. The packaging of the prom in this way virtually ensures girls' participation in the consumption of goods and in feminine body work. And why wouldn't girls want to make a dramatic statement about themselves at the prom? There is tremendous pleasure in the project of self-change.

Yet while girls are expected to take up the work of becoming feminine at the prom, they are also confronted with the inherent contradiction in doing this kind of work. The very practices that girls are expected to invest in and to find pleasurable are also dismissed as trivial. "When I was a freshman I couldn't wait to go. I worked at the postprom party at my school but by the time senior year came around it all seemed so irrelevant and unimportant to the future," one young woman wrote. The basic paradox lies in the following: the project of becoming feminine is defined as frivolous, and that which is frivolous is also feminine.[1]

So profound is this contradiction for girls that many young women I talked to expressed an initial ambivalence about going to the prom.[2] One white young woman wrote,

> I wasn't originally going to attend my prom simply because I was broke and didn't want to get dressed up for one night. But somehow my best friend convinced me to go. So then I went home and told my mom that I was going and she didn't believe me until two weeks later when I shelled out $50 for two tickets.

Elise, a biracial, bisexual student at Woodrow, originally rejected the prom because she felt it reflects a space ordered by a set of gendered practices that privilege consumption and heterosexuality. "At first I was like, screw the prom, you know. It's kind of cheesy. Everyone's going parading around, this is my dress, and who's he bringing?" But she also said later in the interview, "You know, I'm kinda getting into it." Elise did end up going, as did many young women who originally thought they might not. Most girls found themselves—for some reason or another—mysteriously "caught up" in the preparations for the prom despite their initial resistance. Only a few girls in this study decided they were not going to attend their proms. One young white woman discussed her decision to not go:

> I choose not to attend my junior or senior prom because it was not important to me. I had opportunities my sophomore, junior, and senior years to attend and I worked on the prom committee to organize the event. I think that the prom is blown completely out of proportion. I came from a small town and there were some people who became obsessed with the prom. This was the case with one of my friends. She got mad at me because I didn't want to go. I think my mom was a little hurt by this too because we didn't go dress shopping, etc.

Even the marketers of the prom magazines realize the weight of this contradiction. Consider one article from a 1997 special prom edition of *YM,* which began, "In your opinion, the prom is so, well, not hip. So though you're majorly excited for the big night, you're saying 'See ya!' to flowing ball gowns and stretch limos—you've got to make a statement girl!"[2]

The contradictions among delighting in the work of getting ready for the prom, of wanting to be seen, and of feeling that the prom is an event having little true social value point to an ongoing tension (significantly beyond that of the prom) that many girls experience when taking up a position of femininity in a culture organized around consumption in which men and the practices authorized by masculine ideologies are privileged. Leslie Roman and Linda Christian-Smith, in their book *Becoming Feminine,* elaborate the connections between the contradictory nature of popular cultural forms and the struggles girls face in becoming feminine. As they explain, "At stake in the

struggles and contestations over these meanings are not only textual representations of femininity and gender relations in particular cultural commodities, but also their place and significance in the lives of actual women and men who consume, use and make sense of them in the context of their daily practices and social relations. The struggle for girls and women, then (whether they are feminist or not), over gendered meanings, representations and ideologies in popular cultural forms is nothing less than a struggle to understand and hopefully transform the historical contradictions of becoming feminine within the context of conflicting sets of power relations."[3] This chapter explores how this struggle, a struggle fundamentally formed in relation to the self, was narrated by girls as they prepared for and then attended their proms. While the prom highlights more general dilemmas about the continuing influence of dominant gender meanings on girls' lives and their bodies, it also emerges as a distinct site where context-specific forms of femininity—that surprisingly cut across race and class lines—arise. From hairstyles to dresses, these girls' narratives tell the story of the work and the lessons offered by the prom.

SEEING AND BEING SEEN: THE MAKING OF FEMININE BODIES

> I want something that makes my dad a little nervous . . . something pretty . . . maybe make him lose a little sleep. I want something that will make me the center of attention . . . I want something the other girls wish they could wear . . . something that makes everyone stop and stare.
> —*Advertisement for Flirtations,* Your Prom, 1996

Despite the tensions some girls initially felt about investing in an event that had been framed as silly and superficial, many young women looked forward to the prom as a place to be seen. As John Berger explains in his important book, *Ways of Seeing,* "A woman must continually watch herself. She is almost continually accompanied by her own image of herself. Whilst she is walking across a room or whilst she is weeping at the death of her father, she can scarcely avoid envisaging herself walking or weeping. From earliest childhood she has been taught and persuaded to survey herself continually."[4]

Proms are moments in which girls in particular are on display. The structuring of physical space at the four proms I attended ensured that the prom would be designated in this way: the entrances to the prom sites were situated so that girls could be looked at by others. "Even at the prom, people said it was the best looking dress, I remember," one young white woman offered. Many purposely delay their arrival to the prom so that they can make a grand entrance. As one African-American young woman wrote,

> When I stepped out of the limo I remember thinking that I was just the princess of the night. All lights were on me and this was my night. No one and nothing was going to spoil it for me. So we walked in about an hour late. When I made my entrance everyone's eyes were on me. I even remember one of my enemies sitting on the table that was right next to the door. And when she turned around and took a look at me her whole face fell. By the way she looked, it seems like she had just decided at the last minute she was going to the prom.

Though especially pronounced at the prom, being looked at is a normalized and naturalized dimension of life as a girl; as a result, its embeddedness within a gender and heterosexual order usually goes unnoticed.[5] One girl related,

> I'm looking forward to seeing everyone in a different dress. Everybody keeps telling everybody else what their dress looks like and you can get an idea but you can't *really* get an idea until you actually see it. You can get rolls and rolls of film and take lots of pictures.

As this young woman suggests, seeing carries as much significance as being seen in this cultural scene. While suggestive of the agency girls can claim in the space of the prom (being able to look rather than just being looked upon), this agency continues to be lodged in an organization of gender; the practice of seeing chiefly centers on girls' bodies, and in this way offers little room for girls to reject fully their participation in the project of becoming feminine.

Getting Ready

Your 30-Day Beauty countdown. Don't let prom put you in a panic! With one month to go, you've

still got tons of time to get perfect skin, beautiful hair and a hot bod. Just follow our head-to-toe guide to getting gorgeous.
> —*"Your 30-Day Beauty Countdown," article in*
> YM, 1997

Because of the importance of being seen in this context, preparations of the body are extensive. Many girls spent considerable time during interviews and in their written narratives providing detailed descriptions of their dresses and hair, how they came to select their dresses, and their efforts to coordinate what they wore with what their date wore. Sally, a white student from Woodrow, had originally bought two dresses, the first of which she returned once her friend found her a new dress.

AB: So what made you choose this dress over the first dress?

SB: The first dress was like, I would have to buy jewelry too. Like, dress it up and get, like, different shoes. It was very plain. It was, like, something you would wear out to a nice restaurant.

AB: How did you find your first dress?

SB: I was so lazy. I was like, I went to the prom last year. I don't feel like shopping again so I was like, I'll just look through catalogues. And I looked through a *Victoria's Secret* catalogue and I just picked out the first dress that I saw.

SB: That was the short dress?

AB: Yeah, so that's my big mistake. I didn't go looking around at stores or anything.

Sally, while initially ambivalent about the work required to experience the prom in a feminine way, ultimately acquiesces. Her self-critique for not initially engaging in the work that is in many ways for girls the very foundation of the prom points to the ongoing pressure many girls experience in fashioning themselves to be seen.

For a number of girls, how they worked and "disciplined" their bodies directly related to their having a successful prom. "When the day started off I thought it would be the best day. I had the perfect dress (no one had anything else like it) and my hair was done beautifully," one African-American young woman wrote. Success for her not only centers on but is bound to the body.

The process of preparing for the prom for many of these girls was as important as the end product, if not more so. Many girls declared that getting ready for the prom was an entire day's commitment (though preparations began months in advance). Hair, nails, and face were thoroughly worked over; many girls attended tanning salons, while others reported that they dieted to lose weight before the prom:

> All I can remember was that the prom wore me out. From half a day at school, to a morning appointment to get my hair done to an afternoon appointment for my friend to do her hair I was literally exhausted. I also remember fasting so that I could fit into my prom dress.

Another girl wrote,

> We all went shopping for dresses. This didn't take just one trip to the mall. We looked at dresses at every mall in the area and even traveled to malls where there is more selection. Some of my friends even had their dresses made by professional seamstresses. We all had our "dream dress" in mind and it was all a matter of finding it. Then, of course, we had to look perfect in those dresses, so a bunch of my friends and I joined the gym. We exercised three months before.

Social class emerges to organize these feminine practices in a range of ways. One girl, discovering on the day of the prom that her dress was too small, went out and bought another. Sally was able to buy two dresses, though she planned to return one. Clearly the availability of disposable income made this possible. For these girls, class status often means whether or not their parents are able to "support" their prom by covering the significant expense.

The availability of unlimited money enabled some girls to organize the activities in ways that directly hooked them into the spheres of consumption. Several young women enlisted the help of beauty professionals. One girl reported that she and her friends had rented a limousine to take them from the hair salon to lunch at a local café, while another girl and her friends hired a cosmetics representative to come to her home and do their makeup. One white middle-class girl wrote,

> I remember the preparation for my senior prom being really formal. I remember going to NYC to pick the dress, which took two days, starting to get ready at 10:30 in the morning. That day a group of six friends including myself made a day out of it: hair, nails, pedicures, facials, lunch—the works. Even though we all rode in the limo during the day while getting ready and going from place to place, we all took separate limos to the prom.

Most girls, constrained by limited money but also wanting to participate in this beauty work, compromised by getting just their hair, nails, or face done. Tracey, a young African-American woman, explains,

> I know it's like I have to get my hair done and then I have to get my nails done and that costs a lot of money. My dress was expensive, you know, my dress was $275. So it's like I'm broke. I have no money, you know, so if like somebody loans you jewelry or something, you know, that's a lot cheaper than going out and buying it.

Several girls, deciding that this beauty work should be done by professionals, sought jobs to pay for these added expenses; some even started separate bank accounts to save for the cost of the prom.

As many of these young women suggest, these preparations for the prom, while fundamentally being about setting oneself apart, were often a collective process. For many of these girls, talk started about how they intended to prepare for the prom months before the actual event. Some girls reported that these conversations transformed their initial ambivalence about the prom into excitement about the prospects of working on their bodies for the upcoming event.

The process of getting ready came to represent for many a space of shared experience. It was not uncommon for female family members, friends, and more experienced promgoers to assemble at one girl's house to get ready together. Consider my fieldnotes from observing as one young white woman, helped by two others, got ready for the prom:

> Susie came in from having taken a shower in a panic, wrapped in robe and towel. Her day, she said, had been a succession of preparations: getting the campsite ready for after the prom, having her nails done. She had had a French manicure. Susie left to put some clothes on after calling a friend to remind her to bring the boutonnieres. We, the three helpers, sat on the floor in the middle of the room, talking casually

about last year's prom, which one of the girls, Lori, had attended. Lori told us a story about sticking her head out the sunroof of the limo they had rented and messing up the big curls she had so carefully put in her hair. Lori was supposed to put those same big curls in Susie's hair. Before they began working on Susie's hair, Lori and her friend Donna decided to go have a smoke, on the roof, while Susie began drying her short bobbed hair. After a few minutes Lori came through the window "refreshed" and began working on Susie's hair. As Lori styled Susie's hair around the curling iron, the three girls chatted about the prom, how Susie had found her dress, their skipping school to lay out in the sun that day and the boys outside playing basketball in the driveway across the street. The conversation jumped from one topic to another quickly. From the pace of their talk it was easy to tell these three girls were good friends and that their lives were bound up with one another. What I realized after being there for just an hour was that while these girls came together ostensibly to help Susie prepare for her prom, the social significance of this space was more meaningful. More than just getting ready, this was a space to "rehash" aspects of their daily lives with other girls who shared in it. (May 1996)

The pleasure many of these girls expressed as they spoke about this collective process was difficult to miss. Consider the following three narratives written by young African-American women:

> The house is going to be filled with people coming to help me. My mom and her friends they're gonna come help me get ready and stuff and do my make-up. I'll already have my hair and nails done and then my friends are gonna come help me get dressed. They're gonna be taking pictures and videotaping. One of my friends, she's a year younger and then her sister's a year older. She graduated last year and I went last year and helped her get ready and get her stuff together. Her and her mom are gonna come help me. My grandmother will probably come over. My brother, his girlfriend and my niece, they're gonna come over and take pictures and watch when I leave.
>
> I woke up out of bed about 9:00 a.m. that morning because I had a million things to do. I called my cousin and we went shopping. We picked up my dress, accessories and shoes. After doing that I spent another 10 hours getting my hair and nails done. I didn't get home until about 6:15 and the limo was scheduled to pick me up at 6:30. So thanks to my

mother and cousin I was able to get ready in about 25–30 minutes.

> I have to go get my nails done. I don't want my hair to fall. How do I do this? How do I do that? I have to make sure I do the make-up, this that. Well, I don't wear make-up, but this is just what we were all talking about, just the girl-type of stuff. Like, "Oh make sure you bring an extra pair of pantyhose, make sure your shoes are this, that everything matches, you don't put on too much make-up because the light looks this way on your face." All that type of stuff.

Pictures were often taken to record the elaborate work that goes into getting ready.

The Burdens of Beauty

> Beauty Make Me Over: From Toned-down to Terrific; From Low-key to Luminous; From Sweet to Sophisticated.
>
> —*Beauty article in* Your Prom, 1996

Some girls, while enjoying the process of getting ready for the prom, were also aware of the extent to which these preparations are distinctly feminine. One white middle-class girl wrote:

> This elaborate process of preparation was done by most of the people attending the prom (well, girls). It was ridiculous when you think of all the time and money that went into one night. But it was fun.

Another young white woman wrote,

> This whole procedure for preparing for the prom was pretty hectic. That's because, I mean, I don't mean to create more stereotypes for my gender but, girls who do go to the prom have the tendency to over-exaggerate things. Speaking for most of my friends, we worried too much. There were many questions that ran through my mind as the prom night got closer and closer: what type of dress should I wear? Should I wear long or short? What color dress should I wear? How should I get my hair done? Who should do my hair? Should I do my nails? What type of jewelry should I wear with my dress? What type of shoes? While on the other hand guys have one major question: Should I rent or buy?

Like these two girls above, most took it for granted that boys and girls engaged in a different set of practices as they prepared for the prom. These young women are drawing from a set of social assumptions

about what it means to be a "man" or a "woman."
Treating gender as simply a matter of social difference
and not social power not only works to naturalize a
gendered division of labor, it also obscures how this
very talk produces and maintains a social organization
of gender. Mary and Sarah, two white students from
Woodrow, related,

MD: I don't think they [boys] really care quite as much
      as the girls do. I mean, like, what they care about is
      what they're doing before and what they're doing af-
      ter and with who.

SJ: They don't really have a lot to get ready.

MD: "My tux is a double-breasted gray." [she laughs]

SJ: The girls are—the girls have to do a lot more plan-
      ning with their dress and their . . .

MD: Yeah, go through their hair and their nails, their
      dress.

While many girls were willing to acknowledge
that the work required of them was entirely different
from the work required of boys to get ready for the
prom, few referred to these preparations as burdensome. Exceptions to the rule, two white young women
described their experiences as follows:

I'm all through with dress shopping. I'm done. It's
tiring. You go from store to store trying on dresses,
taking off clothes and putting it on, oh no. It's very
tiring shopping for a dress. I'm glad that part is over
with.
    Shopping for all the prom stuff was a hassle. I
went through four dresses and two pair of shoes until
I was set on the perfect outfit. The night before the
prom I ended up puking my brains out all night and
was running a high fever. My mother dragged me to
the beauty parlor drugged up, while I had my nails,
hair, and makeup done. They had to put extra makeup on me because I was so pale from being sick.

As this last young woman suggests, mothers are
central players in the prom, often as invested as these
girls in the project of becoming feminine. One young
woman laughingly reported to her friends in the bathroom at the prom that her mother had "attacked" her
with mascara. In these last two scenes, it is mothers
who enlist their daughters to do the work of looking
feminine for the prom. One girl is "dragged" by her
mother, while the second had been "attacked."

Though clearly expressed in jest, both provide compelling imagery of the ways the practices of femininity are passed from mother to daughter.

While at the prom, a lot of girls talked openly
among themselves about the labor-intensive work they
do on their bodies to achieve an idealized feminine image. Most common were girls' tales of struggles to find
the right dress and their efforts toward having the "perfect" hairstyle. Stories of this kind were exchanged and
compared at the prom in the girl's bathroom, a space at
the prom reserved exclusively for girls. After observing four proms, I realized that these bathroom discussions about their bodies, dresses, and preparations
were not only a source of pleasure, but were also an integral part of the actual prom. In my fieldnotes from
Hudson's prom this is most evident:

I watched girls come and go and check themselves
out in the mirror as they passed. Three girls came in
the bathroom and I started to talk with them as they
primped. One girl was wearing a green dress, with a
green sheer shawl and full tulle skirt and I told her
how pretty it was. She twirled around for me. I asked
her if she'd had it made and she said she had. She
told me she wanted it to be fuller on the bottom so
that she would get more attention. She also told me
that her jewelry came from the makeup artist who did
her makeup. She was heavily made up in green eye
shadow with her hair pulled up into large ringlets.
Her friend, who had also had her dress made to look
like a traditional ball gown, with a purse to match,
said her sister had done her makeup. The girl in the
green dress told me she had only had hers done by a
professional because she didn't know how to do it
herself. I asked her if she normally wore makeup and
she said no. The three of them talked among themselves about their lipstick, comparing prices, mostly.
One girl had bought hers for $2.00, while the other
had gone and gotten her lipstick from Lancome for
close to $15.00. Another girl walked by showing off
her gold shoes and said, "These are toe crackers."
Soon after another girl came by whose dress was
bursting at the sides. She and her friends were in
search of a pin of some sort. They had done a
botched job to repair the dress by the bathroom stalls.
This led to the three girls' discussion of the mistakes
about their own dresses. The girl in the green dress
pointed to some gapping around the neckline, while
the other pointed to her uneven hemline. (June 1997)

While in many ways this kind of "body talk" represents an articulation of feminine identity and mastery, it also undermines the idealization of feminine display because it exposes it as work that requires money, time, and body alteration. Contrary to the idea that femininity is something girls simply possess, their talk helps to define femininity as something one actively undertakes.[6] I overheard one girl as she rushed up to greet her friend in the beginning of Rudolph's prom, pointing to the top of her head, exclaiming, "Three hours, it took three hours to get my hair to look like this!"

More than just a set of frivolous practices of primping, these are fertile sites of identity negotiation and construction, where girls are making sense of what it means to be women in a culture that treats the surface of the body as the consummate canvas on which to express the feminine self. There is also a clear sense that many of these girls enjoyed the attention they received after such significant transformations—their labors were not in vain. Indeed, this is the very promise of the prom, highlighted in girls' talk, and telegraphed in prom films and magazines. The pleasure in being seen in "a new light" helps to gain girls' consent to consume, to ensure their participation in beauty culture and the ongoing creation of gender.

THE POLITICS OF PLEASURE

The achievement of femininity for the prom depends on an endless consumption of products; makeup, clothing, hair accessories, shoes, lingerie, handbags, and jewelry are all products readily available in a commodity market and heavily marketed as tools for feminine display and self-reinvention at the prom. These are tools that require time, patience, and skill to master. Susan Bordo elaborates on the more lasting effects this kind of exacting and intensive work has on women and how they experience life in their bodies, explaining, "Through the pursuit of an ever-changing, homogenizing, elusive ideal of femininity—a pursuit without a terminus, requiring that women constantly attend to minute and often whimsical changes in fashion—female bodies become docile bodies—bodies whose forces and energies are habituated to external regulation, subjection, transformation, 'improve-

ment'."[7] But this kind of body work is not just about producing disciplined bodies for consumption; there is more here. The meanings girls themselves attach to this work is significant for understanding why they engage in such practices in the first place.[8]

Engaging in the work of becoming "beautiful" for the prom represents a struggle to stake a claim to one's identity. For many of these girls, participating in beauty work enables them to occupy a position within a public space, a significant fact when considering women's historical relegation to the private sphere. As consumers of beauty culture, these young women are able to possess a sense of power and visibility by claiming public space that often is not experienced in their everyday lives in school, with family, or in their relationships with young men. They occupy hair salons, nail salons, and dress shops in a way similar to that of middle-class women in the 1920s who, just after winning the right to vote, proudly (and paradoxically) announced their new freedom by wearing shorter skirts, bobbing their hair, and smoking cigarettes in public.

Not only are these girls able to demonstrate a public commitment to feminine practices, they are also able to express their competence as beauty practitioners. The desire to do so is so significant that girls who were either unable (or sometimes unwilling) to indulge in the extravagances of the beauty/hair salon performed this work in private spaces, most often their homes. These girls created a situation resembling, in remarkable ways, the experience of going to a salon. Friends and female family members were enlisted to perform the beauty work provided to other girls by service workers. Though done in the private setting of home, getting ready signified a public act.

While young women arguably do beauty work for the prom to express their heterosexual desirability, they also do this work to experience a self-pleasure by making themselves feel special.[9] For many of these girls, the prom presents itself as an opportunity to indulge themselves in ways that many of them are simply unable to in their day-to-day school lives. Part of what makes this body work around the prom worth undertaking stems directly from how they experience everyday life as young women.

Teenage girls are often denied control over their

bodies, their desire, and their self-definition. Engaging in this elaborate consumption-oriented body work enables them to craft a space of self-control, self-definition, and self-pleasure that is experienced immediately. Many girls perceive adult women as possessing greater control over their lives than they as girls can. Transforming themselves to look more like adult women through these beauty practices allows many of them to feel more like adult women, to possibly experience adult freedoms and liberties, even if momentarily, and to negotiate those everyday constraints they experience because of their age and consequent position in society. Of course, the result is that the pleasure of excess conceals the ideological workings of the prom; proms structure girls' investments in both gender and heterosexuality, exacerbate their anxieties about the body, and focus their attention toward the all-consuming project of the body.

Fashioning the Feminine Self

The Dress

> I had been looking for prom dresses for months and I hadn't found anything I really liked and I just happened to walk back to where they keep the more expensive dresses in my store and I saw this dress and went, "This is the dress." Before I even put it on I was like, "This is my dress." I tried it on and all the ladies in the store were like, "Oh my god, that's so beautiful." I did my hair up a little bit, you know and it looked really nice. So I decided to get the dress.

Like this African-American woman, most of the young women in this study made some mention of the prom dress, detailing their efforts in finding it, as well as how it felt to wear it on the night of the prom. There was anxiety for some girls as they figured out what to wear; others enjoyed looking for a dress as a part of the process of doing beauty/body work. One white girl wrote,

> I don't remember anything eventful about the prom itself. I remember the major preparation that went into it, namely—FINDING THE DRESS. Everyone discussed first what style they wanted: long, short, strapless, black, sequined, etc. When we walked into the prom everyone (girls) greeted the other girls immediately with compliments on dress and hair.

Consider an African-American girl's comments:

> You can have the same hair style as anyone else. It doesn't matter, but that dress. I know me, the dress I picked out two years from now I don't want to look back on my prom pictures and be like, "What am I wearing?" So, I won't be like other girls. I won't regret having this dress.

Her statement is suggestive of the complex thinking girls engage in when selecting a prom dress. A range of factors must be considered: not only must she set herself apart through what she wears at the prom, the dress must also be remembered in a particular way. It must be able to endure changing styles and outlast current trends. She is conscious not to make the same mistakes as other girls. Her good taste, keen sense of style, and feminine judgment will be admired not only at the prom, but in years to come. How she remembers the prom is contingent on how she remembers the dress. One girl reported feeling like "a million dollars in my beautiful red dress" and that she had the time of her life, while another girl commented that she felt like "a princess for a day" because of what she wore—an unforgettable dress secured an unforgettable night. Significantly, one young woman ended up not going to her prom because her dress was not ready:

> Oh gosh, it's so sad. She's, um, my best friend and she basically didn't make it to the prom because her dress wasn't ready. She started, her sister goes to the Rhode Island School of Design, so she was designing her dress and everything. Doing it by hand, no pattern and they basically waited till the last minute to go to New York and get the fabric and they started her dress on Tuesday. The prom is Friday so she was all prepared except for the dress. She had her nails done, her hair done. She had the shoes, the pocketbook, everything, but her dress wasn't ready until 12:30 that night. Like, we were calling because she was supposed to sit at our table and she's just like, "It's not done. I can't come. It's not done," and I'm like, "You can't just slip on any dress? You spent all of this money on preparations. Just because your dress isn't made, just come anyway. You bought the bid." Like, she spent all of this money getting ready. She probably spent more money than I did because she didn't go last year, either, so I'm like, "Just come." But she wound up not coming.

Many girls spoke about their dresses not only with

an uncanny attention to detail, but with a striking familiarity and understanding of the meanings that underlie the style codes defined by the fashion industry:

> My dress, I believe, it's called watercress satin. It's the satin that has the sort of wood grain texture. It's not a shiny satin, it's a duller satin and its got a scoop neck and it has puffy sleeves. Mary and I used to call it a princess dress and this is the actual thing. My dress is more flared than hers is going to be. It's not way out. It stands a bit above the floor. So it's gonna be cream satin and then it's going to have some flowers on the collar.

Another white girl said,

> It's long, but unlike most long dresses it's not tight. It's not really squared off. It's just kind of like not fitted. It's like A-line and backless but, it's not like high cut in the neck and its got crisscrossing straps in the back and it's shimmery black . . . when it ripples, it ripples sparkles. Not just silver sparkles but multicolored sparkles. It's really, really faint glitter and you wouldn't see it normally. It has a silver image but, it's really blotted. Everybody else is going black.

Elise referred to her dress as "a great dress" because it showed off the new tattoo on her arm, a significant departure from how other girls spoke. Displaying her tattoo counters the cultural expectation that girls will relate to their bodies as spaces to demonstrate their commitment to feminine practices. Yet this can also be read as a dramatic statement she makes about herself through her body. As Joan Jacobs Brumberg has argued in her book *The Body Project,* tattooing and body piercing, though often considered outside the realm of the feminine, is still work on the body. Whether dramatic or subtle, work on the body is a feminine form of work.[10]

Hair

Just as the dress signifies an expression of the feminine self, enabling girls to make a statement about who they are, so does hair. For the prom, many girls treat their hair with the utmost care. Great attention is paid to how it looks, and whether or not its style compliments the style of dress worn. In many girls' narratives, hair was critically important to the overall construction of a "prom look." As mentioned earlier, many girls had their hair professionally styled. Several girls reported that hair salons were so overbooked on the day of the prom that they were forced to take hair appointments early in the morning and pray their hair would hold its shape until the fateful moment arrived. Hairstyles varied: one white girl discussing her hair offered, "I have a feeling I'm going to have braids and pearls. I have long red hair and I'm wearing a princess dress, so the hairdresser immediately said pearls and braids." Another girl, who wanted to create what she considered a more sophisticated look through her hairstyle, explained, "Since, I'm going to be wearing rhinestone jewelry, I'm gonna slick it back or something. I could do curls, but I look silly in curls. I'm going to be Miss Elegant for the night." For many girls the "up do," a symbol of sophistication and elegance, was most popular.

Hair seemed to be a particularly important site for some African-American girls in the articulation of a sense of self, perhaps even more so than the dress. Many African-American girls at the prom creatively displayed their hair through hair extensions, braids, and wraps. Glitter and rhinestones were artfully placed to draw attention to hair, often overshadowing the prom dress.

While few white girls would have been able to connect how they styled their hair to their being white, to see their hairstyles as an expression of their race identities, predictably, for African-American girls, hair seemed to have everything to do with race. Historically, hair has been an important symbol through which both style and identity politics have been expressed within the African-American community. Lisa Jones writes on the meaningfulness of these hairstyles, "These are elaborate constructions, with hair piled high, woven with ornaments and shaped like fans, wedding cakes, hourglasses and halos. Maybe they're crowns, maybe they're altars. What links African American/Africa–diaspora cultural practice with African traditional cultures is not the naturalness of the braids, it's the idea of construction. Hair in both traditions suggests spectacle and pageantry. It's always handled and adorned; hair is never left 'as is.' Hair exists to be worked."[11]

Challenging the idea that black women work on their hair to conform to white ideals of femininity, Kobena Mercer has argued that hair stylization within the black community signifies a creative play of identity rooted specifically in African-American beauty culture.[12] Similarly, I would argue that these creative expressions represent an attempt to resist hegemonic images of femininity and beauty rooted in white middle-class culture by articulating pride in racial self. This act may be especially meaningful at the prom because it is a highly visible and public spectacle formally tied to white institutions of schooling.

What He Wears Matters, Too

> Night of Nights. The best looks for this year's ball. "Suitable style" for him is just a page away, too.
> —*"Night of Nights," article in* Your Prom, 1996

Some girls express their feminine skills through the outfits they selected for their dates. Several of the girls I interviewed stated that what their date wore was more an expression of their own ability, not his, to assemble and organize appearance and style. I, too, can remember negotiating with my date what he was going to wear when I went to my own prom. I had insisted he wear a red plaid cummerbund and bow tie with his tails and went with him to the tuxedo rental shop to make sure he picked the right suit. "The guy matches to the best he can," one girl offered. Mark, an African-American student, discusses how he came to select his prom outfit and the role his girlfriend played in the decision:

AB: So how did you pick out your tuxedo?

ML: Well, I really didn't pick it out. Me and her went to get it and she was like, she got her dress way before the prom. But I had to match what she had so I didn't want to get a regular black tuxedo.

AB: How come?

ML: Because I figure everybody would have a regular tuxedo. I wanted to be different. I wanted to stand out. So I went there and she was like, This is what I want you to get. Like, not a regular one. She picked out everything. This is what I want you to get. Like, so, I got the white jacket. Like I said, she picked it out.

While his desire to be different may have been independent of her, Mark's girlfriend exerted considerable influence over how he was able to express his individuality. How a boyfriend dresses is often perceived as an expression of the girlfriend's good taste and style. Consider one white girl's comments about what her boyfriend wore to the prom:

> He had a little baby-blue handkerchief so it would match my dress. We didn't want to be tacky with a baby-blue vest or anything. I remember he got the cummerbund and I was like, "You need to get the vest." Everybody was getting vests and I was just like, "Why didn't you get a vest?"

This suggests an extension of the spaces where femininity can be demonstrated. Boys' bodies, in addition to girls' bodies, signify meaningful sites for the display and management of femininity at the prom. What matters is how it all comes together: how the dress looks beside the tux, and how well the corsage compliments the dress. Of course, this very coordinated presentation relies on an organized, even rigidly regulated, heterosexuality.

It Has to Be an Original

The importance of setting oneself apart is such a significant aspect of feminine consumption that one small dress shop from which many girls from Woodrow High School bought their dresses kept a record of who bought which dress and which school the girl attended to prevent girls at the same school from wearing identical dresses to their prom. Mary, a white student at Woodrow, elaborates on the importance of having an original look:

> The two other girls I'm going with, one girl is going to be wearing a silver dress with stockings, heels. She's dying her hair, well it's black now and she's gonna put silver hairspray in it and she's gonna, everything is gonna be silver. She got the idea from me, which is why I'm not doing it. I was going to go silver until two of my friends said, "Oh, we're going to go silver," and bought the dresses before mine was made. Okay, forget that.

Some girls went to great lengths to ensure that their dresses were originals. One young woman traveled out of state to find her dress, while another bought her dress from a small dress shop where she knew few girls from her school would shop. Terry, an African-American student at Woodrow, discussed how she would feel if someone had the same dress as she:

I would die if someone had my dress. I would die! Because I just love that dress and I really don't, I would be really surprised if someone had that dress. I really would. And my friend saw it and she's like, "Oh, my god! That dress is so pretty." And she's like, "I want to get that dress, after I saw it." I was like, "Too bad, you ain't gonna get it. That's my dress." I would die. This is like my prom and I own it. No, I don't want anyone to have the same dress as me. I would say, "Well I look better than anyone," to try to make myself feel better, but I would still be upset. I would still be mad. I know they [the store] have three of my dress.

Girls' talk about prom dresses in the weeks before the prom can also be a deliberate way of ensuring that other girls do not wear the same dress, as is suggested by Erin:

> The worst thing that could happen is to run into somebody with your dress. That's why you have to be kind of sneaky about it. Like, lots of girls will go around and ask, "What color are you wearing?" to make sure that we have a different color and always ask what does your dress look like. And you make sure someone doesn't have it and it's nothing close to yours. You know some people will draw their own dresses on papers and like, my friend she drew a dress, designed her own thing and she was going to have somebody make it for her because she wanted to make sure she had something like nobody else. She showed it to me, not to other people, because she didn't want other people stealing her idea.

SCHOOL, DRESSES, AND THE BODY

Getting ready for the prom enables many girls to cultivate and demonstrate their skills at coordinating and assembling a range of signs and symbols upon their bodies in a way that transforms who they are in school. As one African-American girl wrote,

> I wanted to wear something that would totally surprise people. In school I was known to constantly wear all black, if not mostly black outfits. So as my huge surprise to everyone, I ended up wearing a long white dress. It was white stain and chiffon with black lace on the side with white pearls on the lace.

The prom is a space in which young women can play with a range of identities, many of which are closed off to them within what Nancy Lesko refers to as the "body curriculum" of schools, a curriculum that operates to regulate and discipline girls' sexuality and desire.[19]

Most girls construct their appearances in ways that suggest their willingness to be seen; as one girl noted, "I remember everyone being surprised I had on make-up and all that." Without romanticizing the practices of dressing up, I do want to suggest that the prom represents a safe and playful space in which many girls may negotiate, in some ways challenging how adolescent girls are culturally represented. For many girls the style of dress worn is tied to sexuality and to sexual identities. Consider a Latina middle-class girl's comments,

> I'm such a tomboy. I never let my hair down and I rarely wear dresses. The prom was an experience. Everyone kept commenting on how beautiful I looked, "Why don't you let your hair down more often?" "You have a great figure; you shouldn't hide behind jeans and a T-shirt." My friends barely recognized me. People who've known me all my life stared at me.

The prom dress is critically important to this invention of a sexual self; as such, many girls buy dresses that are significantly beyond what they can normally afford to spend on everyday school clothes. Many girls at the proms I attended wore long, fitted dresses, many of them black, often with exposed backs and deep slits running up one leg. As one white girl described her dress,

> It's got rhinestones and spaghetti straps. It's got a scoop neck with rhinestones going all the way around. It's long, it's got a slit up the mid-thigh and then rhinestones going in the back criss-cross and then the back is completely open and then it kind of comes in at the sides so your sides are showing.

These young women are able to display their bodies in ways that they usually can't at school: arms and legs are bared, necklines revealed. "It was cut in here and here [gesturing to her sides] and came up around my neck and all this was beaded and it was like an open back with just the crosses and it was real tight and it just went out to like here. I loved it." As another described hers, "It's blue chiffon and it comes down to like the heel of my shoe, and it doesn't have a split in it which surprises me cause I wanted a split." I also overheard many girls proudly exchanging stories of their fathers' utter discomfort in seeing their daughters in such sexy dresses, testimonies that the girls had succeeded in transforming themselves.

When understood within an organization of schooling that emphasizes modesty and reserve in dress for girls, a sexy prom dress signifies a way to negotiate the sexual terrain of school.[20] Girls have so few spaces in which they can claim sexual agency.[21] Those who attempt to articulate their own sexual desire must negotiate their sexuality within a discursive organization of adolescent female sexuality most often ordered around images of sexual victimization, teen pregnancy, and sexual promiscuity.[22]

Through what they wear many girls seem to claim a visible (hetero)sexual identity that counters a (racially coded) bourgeois image of the adolescent girl as the bearer of sexual innocence.[23] While the activity of dressing up binds girls to an unequal order of gender, their actions and the meanings they attach to them reflect attempts to generate alternate meanings that enable them to exert some control over those sexual and social struggles that shape and pattern their everyday lives.

CAN GIRLS CONTEST THE PROM?

At stake here are familiar concerns. What leads girls to invest in feminine practices, particularly those that require the dramatic altering of their bodies? The transformation of self many of these girls desire reflects the ideologies organizing not only beauty culture within consumer capitalism but its entrenchment in an organization of class, gender, and (hetero) sexuality. For most girls choosing to attend the prom involves a series of negotiations that express a struggle to understand these social forms in relation to their lives. Their narratives illustrate the tensions girls experience as they make sense of the cultural codes of femininity.

There is a clear sense that many girls in this study are not normally as invested in femininity as they seem to be for the occasion of the prom. Many indicated to me that they usually do not wear makeup and only visit the hair salon to have their hair cut. In this way proms are much like weddings: women who

might normally reject the conventions of femininity suddenly find themselves strangely seduced by their appeal. Just as many women do for their weddings, girls pulled out all the stops for the prom: nails were manicured, eyebrows plucked, and hair professionally styled. In fact, for some young women, the prom is seen as a dress rehearsal for weddings. If young women invest in the body work for the prom or for their weddings, but not necessarily elsewhere, what, then, are the connections between gender and these settings?

Proms, as cultural sites, work to secure girls' consent to prevailing feminine forms. The gender and heterosexual controls within this cultural scene are so rigidly organized and so profoundly connected to bodily pleasure and self-pleasure that acts of resistance seem to be possible for only a few. The limits of resistance to these gender precepts seem to be determined by the very social organization of this space—proms are the domain of the feminine, where girls' pleasure in doing feminine appearance work and their desire to make a statement about themselves are especially pronounced.

On the day of my junior prom a close girlfriend, who had decided to wear pajamas and no makeup to school, approached me to ask why I had worn makeup and chosen to wear a skirt and nice sweater on the day of the prom, of all days. I didn't understand what she meant; since I wore skirts almost everyday to school, why would this day be different from any other? She told me pointedly that girls are supposed to look awful on the day of the prom so that when we arrive at the event the statement we make is more dramatic. In short, her plan ensured that on the night of the prom she would really wow them! This memory of my prom was recalled as I struggled to make sense of why girls, many of whom reject these aspects of femininity more generally, used these feminine codes as they defined, experienced, and talked about their proms.

What girls wear to their prom and the activities they participate in tie them in many ways to gender structures that concentrate their energies on body work. Yet at the same time, their actions provide an opportunity for them to respond to how their schools defined adolescent femininity, and defined the girls themselves. Understanding what girls respond to—

specifically, how schools restrict their sexual identities and expressions—is essential to understanding why girls invest in these activities, the pleasure they derive from them, and the meanings they attach to them.[24] Likewise, understanding how girls engage in negotiations over definitions of these activities is central to understanding how gender continues to operate as a pervasive force in our society.

Notes

1. Griggers, 1997.

2. "Discover Your Perfect Prom Look," *YM* special prom edition, 1997:37.

3. Roman and Christian-Smith, 1988:4.

4. Berger, 1977:46.

5. McRobbie, 1991; Montgomery, 1998; Willis, 1996.

6. See West and Zimmerman, 1987, for a discussion on how gender is actively constructed and reconstructed through day-to-day relations.

7. Bordo, 1993:166.

8. Carrington, 1989; Craik, 1989; Clark, 1987; Fiske, 1989a; McRobbie and Garber, 1981; Radner, 1995, 1989; Radway, 1984; Roman and Christian-Smith, 1988.

9. Hillary Radner (1989) suggests in her work on femininity and consumption that women find pleasure in the consumption of beauty culture because it provides a space in which women can be the agents of their own desire. Radner develops a compelling analysis of how feminine pleasure in the production of appearance is tied to beauty and culture industries. In the 1980s, she argues, these industries recognized the influence of women's struggle to articulate an autonomous self-identity on women's patterns of consumption. In so doing, the market repositioned beauty work within a discourse of self-pleasure; the focus shifted from making oneself over for others to doing it simply for oneself. Beauty work at this particular historical moment not only is rooted in the discourses of heterosexual desirability, but in a discourse of feminine desire (e.g., "I'm beautiful and I'm worth it").

10. Brumberg, 1997.

11. Jones, 1994:297.

12. Mercer, 1990.

13. See Bourdieu, 1984, for more on this notion.

14. "Big hair," often associated with shopping mall culture, is a signifier for a class-specific femininity that is very much a part of our cultural imagination. "Big hair" is tied to a series of other class/ethnic (Italian-American, Latina) signifiers: Camaros, tight acid-washed jeans, high-heeled boots, and heavy eyeliner. For examples, see movies such as *Working Girl, Jungle Fever, My Cousin Vinny,* and *The Wedding Singer.* These films, with the exception of *My Cousin Vinny,* depict women with "big hair" as either deferential, sexually loose, dependent on their boyfriends, consumed with beauty culture, and/or as especially loud.

15. "Don't Break the Bank," *HJ* prom special, 1996:16.

16. Bourdieu, 1984.

17. Blackman, 1998; Dwyer, 1998; Inness, 1998a, 1998b; Leadbeater and Way, 1996; Leonard, 1998; Sato, 1999.

18. See Fiske, 1989a, for a more extensive discussion of how consumers use the market in ways that disrupt its power.

19. Lesko, 1988a. See also Inness, 1998a, 1998b; McRobbie, 1991; Tolman, 1994; Walkerdine, 1990.

20. This may be especially pronounced for middle-class girls because the prom may represent for them a momentary chance to abandon their concerns with sexual respectability (Tolman, 1994).

21. Carrington, 1989; Fine, 1993; Krisman, 1987; Leahy, 1994.

22. Fine, 1993; Tolman, 1994.

23. See Clark, 1987; Haug, 1987; Lesko, 1988a, for more on this notion.

24. Angela McRobbie and Jennifer Garber (1981) argue along a similar line that working-class girls often embrace conventional feminine practices like wearing makeup and talking about boys in the classroom as a way to contest schools as middle-class organizations.

References

Berger, John. 1977. *Ways of Seeing.* London: Penguin.

Blackman, Shane J. 1998. "The School: 'Poxy Cupid!' An Ethnographic and Feminist Account of Resistant Female Youth Culture: The New Wave Girls." *Cool Places: Geographies of Youth Cultures,* ed. Tracey Skelton and Gill Valentine. London: Routledge.

Bordo, Susan. 1993. *Unbearable Weight: Feminism, Western Culture and the Body.* Berkeley and Los Angeles: University of California Press.

Bourdieu, Pierre. 1984. *Distinction: A Social Critique of the Judgment of Taste.* Cambridge, MA: Harvard University Press.

Brumberg, Joan Jacobs. 1997. *The Body Project: An Intimate History of American Girls.* New York: Random House.

Carrington, Kerry. 1989. "Girls and Graffiti." *Cultural Studies* 3 (89–100).

Clark, Ann K. 1987. "The Girl: A Rhetoric of Desire." *Cultural Studies* 1 (195–203).

Craik, Jennifer. 1989. "'I Must Put My Face On': Making Up the Body and Marking Out the Feminine." *Cultural Studies* 3 (1–24).

Dwyer, Clarie. 1998. "Contested Identities: Challenging Dominant Representations of Young British Muslim Women."

Cool Places: Geographies of Youth Cultures, ed. Tracey Skelton and Gill Valentine. London: Routledge.

———. 1993. "Sexuality, Schooling and Adolescent Females: The Missing Discourse of Desire." *Beyond Silenced Voices: Class, Race and Gender in United States Schools,* ed. Michelle Fine and Lois Weis. Albany: State University of New York Press.

Fiske, John. 1989a. *Understanding Popular Culture.* Boston: Unwin Hyman.

Griggers, Camilla. 1997. *Becoming Woman.* Minneapolis: University of Minnesota Press.

Haug, Frigga et al. 1987. *Feminine Sexualisation: A Collective Work of Memory.* London: Verso.

Innes, Sherrie A., ed. 1998a. *Delinquents and Debutantes: Twentieth Century American Girls' Cultures.* New York: New York University Press.

———, ed. 1998b. *Millennium Girls.* New York: Rowan & Littlefield.

Jones, Lisa. 1994. *Bulletproof Diva: Tales of Race, Sex and Hair.* New York: Anchor Books.

Kett, Joseph F. 1977. *Rites of Passage: Adolescence in America, 1790 to the Present.* New York: Basic Books.

Krisman, Anne. 1987. "Radiator Girls: The Opinions and Experiences of Working Class Girls In An East London Comprehensive." *Cultural Studies* 1 (219–30).

Leadbeater, Bonnie J. Ross and Niobe Way, eds. 1996. *Urban Girls: Resisting Stereotypes, Creating Identities.* New York: New York University Press.

Leahy, Terry. 1994. "Taking Up A Position: Discourse of Femininity and Adolescence in the Context of Man/Girl Relationships." *Gender and Society* 8:1 (48–72).

Leonard, Marion. 1998. "Paper Planes: Traveling and the New Grrrl Geographies." *Cool Places: Geographies of Youth Cultures,* ed. Tracey Skelton and Gill Valentine. London: Routledge.

———. 1988a. The Curriculum of the Body: Lessons from a Catholic High School." In *Becoming Feminine: The Politics of Popular Culture,* ed. Leslie G. Roman and Linda Christian-Smith. London: The Falmer Press.

———, ed. 1991. *Feminism and Youth Culture: From Jackie to Just Seventeen.* Boston: Unwin Hyman.

McRobbie, Angela and Jennifer Garber. 1981. "Girls and Subcultures." *Feminism and Youth Culture: From Jackie to Just Seventeen,* ed. Angela McRobbie. Boston: Unwin Hyman.

Mercer, Kobena. 1990. "Hair and Politics." *Out There: Marginalization in Contemporary Culture,* ed. Russell Ferguson, Martha Gerver, Trinh T. Minh-ha, and Cornel West. Cambridge, MA: MIT Press.

Montgomery, Maureen E. 1998. *Displaying Women: Spectacles of Leisure in Edith Wharton's New York.* New York: Routledge.

———. 1987. "Consumerism and Its Contradictions." *Cultural Studies* 1 (204–10).

Radner, Hillary. 1995. *Shopping Around: Feminine Culture and The Pursuit of Pleasure.* New York: Routledge.

———. 1989. "'This Time's For Me': Making Up and Feminine Practice." *Cultural Studies* 3 (301–21).

Radway, Janice. 1984. *Reading the Romance: Women, Patriarchy and Popular Literature.* Chapel Hill: University of North Carolina Press.

Roman, Leslie G. and Linda Christian-Smith, eds. 1988. *Becoming Feminine: The Politics of Popular Culture.* London: The Falmer Press.

Sato, Rika Sakuma. 1998. "What Are Girls Made of? Exploring the Symbolic Boundaries of Femininity in Two Cultures." *Millennium Girls,* ed. Sherrie Inness. New York: Rowan & Littlefield.

Tolman, Deborah L. 1994. "Doing Desire: Adolescent Girls' Struggle for/with Sexuality." *Gender and Society* 8:3 (324–42).

Walkerdine, Valerie. 1990. *Schoolgirl Fictions.* London: Verso.

West, Candice and Don Zimmerman. 1987. "Doing Gender." *Gender and Society* 1 (125–51).

West, Cornel. 1993. "The New Cultural Politics of Difference." *Race Identity and Representation in Education,* ed. Cameron McCarthy and Warren Crichlow. New York: Routledge.

Whiteley, Sheila, ed. 1997. *Sexing the Groove: Popular Music and Gender.* London: Routledge.

Willis, Susan. 1996. "Play For Profit." *Feminisms and Pedagogies of Everyday Life,* ed. Carmen Luke. Albany: State University of New York Press.

36 | BEER COMMERCIALS
A Manual on Masculinity
Lance Strate

Jocks, rock stars, and pick-up artists; cowboys, construction workers, and comedians; these are some of the major "social types" (Klapp, 1962) found in contemporary American beer commercials. The characters may vary in occupation, race, and age, but they all exemplify traditional conceptions of the masculine role. Clearly, the beer industry relies on stereotypes of the man's man to appeal to a mainstream, predominantly male target audience. That is why alternate social types, such as sensitive men, gay men, and househusbands, scholars, poets, and political activists, are noticeably absent from beer advertising. The manifest function of beer advertising is to promote a particular brand, but collectively the commercials provide a clear and consistent image of the masculine role; in a sense, they constitute a guide for becoming a man, a rulebook for appropriate male behavior, in short, a manual on masculinity. Of course, they are not the only source of knowledge on this subject, but nowhere is so much information presented in so concentrated a form as in television's 30-second spots, and no other industry's commercials focus so exclusively and so exhaustively on images of the man's man. Most analyses of alcohol advertising acknowledge the use of masculine characters and themes, but only focus on their persuasive function (see, for example, Atkin, 1987; Finn & Strickland, 1982, 1983; Hacker, Collins, & Jacobson, 1987; Jacobson, Atkins, & Hacker, 1983). In my own research on beer commercials (Postman, Nystrom, Strate, & Weingartner, 1987; Strate, 1989, 1990), the ads are analyzed as a form of cultural communication and a carrier of social myths, in particular, the myth of masculinity. A similar approach is taken by Craig (1987) in his analysis of Super Bowl advertising, and by Wenner (1991) in his analysis of beer commercials and television sports. A major concern in my research has been the relationship between alcohol advertising and drinking and driving, a problem especially among young, unmarried men. Drawing on that research, I will discuss here the ways in which the myth of masculinity is expressed in beer commercials.

Myths, according to semioticians such as Roland Barthes (1972), are not falsehoods or fairy tales, but uncontested and generally unconscious assumptions that are so widely shared within a culture that they are considered natural, instead of recognized as products of unique historical circumstances. Biology determines whether we are male or female; culture determines what it *means* to be male or female, and what sorts of behaviors and personality attributes are appropriate for each gender role. In other words, masculinity is a social construction (Fejes, 1989; Kimmel, 1987). The foundation may be biological, but the structure is manmade; it is also flexible, subject to change over time and differing significantly from culture to culture. Myth, as a form of cultural communication, is the material out of which such structures are built, and through myth, the role of human beings in inventing and reinventing masculinity is disguised and therefore naturalized (and "biologicized"). The myth of masculinity is manifested in myriad forms of mediated and nonmediated communication; beer commercials are only one such form, and to a large extent, the ads merely reflect preexisting cultural conceptions of the man's man. But in reflecting the myth, the commercials also reinforce it. Moreover, since each individual expression of a myth varies, beer ads also reshape the myth of masculinity, and in this sense, take part in its continuing construction.

Myths provide ready-made answers to universal human questions about ourselves, our relationships with others and with our environment. Thus, the myth of masculinity answers the question: What does it

---

mean to be a man? This can be broken down into five separate questions: What kinds of things do men do? What kinds of settings do men prefer? How do boys become men? How do men relate to each other? How do men relate to women? Let us now consider the ways in which beer commercials answer these questions.

What kinds of things do men do? Although advertisers are prevented from actually showing an individual drinking beer in a television commercial, there is no question that drinking is presented as a central masculine activity, and beer as the beverage of choice. Drinking, however, is rarely presented as an isolated activity, but rather is associated with a variety of occupational and leisure pursuits, all of which, in one way or another, involve overcoming challenges. In the world of beer commercials, men work hard and they play hard.

Physical labor is often emphasized in these ads, both on and off the job. Busch beer features cowboys riding horses, driving cattle, and performing in rodeos. Budweiser presents a variety of blue-collar types, including construction workers, lumberjacks, and soldiers (as well as skilled laborers and a few white-collar workers). Miller Genuine Draft shows men working as farm hands and piano movers. But the key to work is the challenge it poses, whether to physical strength and endurance, to skill, patience, and craftsmanship, or to wit and competitive drive in the business world. The ads do associate hard work with the American dream of economic success (this theme is particularly strong in Budweiser's campaign), but it is also presented as its own end, reflecting the Puritan work ethic. Men do not labor primarily out of economic necessity nor for financial gain, but rather for the pride of accomplishment provided by a difficult job well done; for the respect and camaraderie of other men (few women are visible in the beer commercial workplace); for the benefit of family, community, and nation; and for the opportunity to demonstrate masculinity by triumphing over the challenges work provides. In short, work is an integral part of a man's identity.

Beer is integrated with the work world in three ways. *First,* it is represented in some commercials as the product of patient, skillful craftsmanship, thus par-

taking of the virtues associated with the labor that produced it; this is particularly apparent in the Miller beer commercials in which former football player Ed Marinaro takes us on a tour of the Miller brewery. In effect, an identity relationship between beer and labor is established, although this is overshadowed by the identification between beer and nature discussed below. *Second,* beer serves as a reward for a job well done, and receiving a beer from one's peers acts as a symbol of other men's respect for the worker's accomplishment—"For all you do, this Bud's for you." Beer is seen as an appropriate reward not just because drinking is pleasurable, but because it is identified with labor, and therefore can act as a substitute for labor. Thus, drinking beer at the end of the day is a symbolic reenactment of the successful completion of a day's work. And *third,* beer acts as a marker of the end of the work day, the signal of quitting time ("Miller time"), the means for making the transition from work to leisure ("If you've got the time, we've got the beer"). In the commercials, the celebration of work completed takes on a ritualistic quality, much like saying grace and breaking bread signal the beginning of meal time; opening the can represents the opening of leisure time.

The men of beer commercials fill their leisure time in two ways; in active pursuits usually conducted in outdoor settings (e.g., car and boat racing, fishing, camping, and sports; often symbolized by the presence of sports stars, especially in Miller Lite ads) and in "hanging out," usually in bars. As it is in work, the key to men's active play is the challenge it provides to physical and emotional strength, endurance, and daring. Some element of danger is usually present in the challenge, for danger magnifies the risks of failure and the significance of success. Movement and speed are often a part of the challenge, not only for the increased risk they pose, but also because they require immediate and decisive action and fine control over one's own responses. Thus, Budweiser spots feature automobile racing; Michelob's music video-like ads show cars moving in fast-motion and include lyrics like "I'm overheating, I'm ready to burn, got dirt on my wheels, they're ready to turn"; Old Milwaukee and Budweiser commercials include images of powerboat, sailboat, and canoe racing; Busch beer features cowboys on galloping horses; and Coors uses the slogan, "The Silver Bullet won't slow you down." Activities that include movement and speed, along with displays of coordination, are particularly troubling when associated with beer, in light of social problems such as drinking and driving. Moreover, beer commercials portray men as unmindful of risks, laughing off danger. For example, in two Miller Genuine Draft commercials, a group of young men are drinking and reminiscing; in one they recall the time when they worked as farm hands, loading bales of hay onto a truck, and the large stack fell over. In the other, the memory is of moving a piano, raising it up by rope on the outside of a building to get it into a third-story apartment; the rope breaks and the piano crashes to the ground. The falling bales and falling piano both appear dangerous, but in the ads the men merely joke about the incidents; this attitude is reinforced visually as, in both cases, there is a cut from the past scene to the present one just before the crash actually occurs.

When they are not engaged in physical activity, the men of beer commercials frequently seek out symbolic challenges and dangers by playing games such as poker and pool, and by watching professional sports. The games pose particular challenges to self-control, while spectator sports allow for vicarious participation in the drama of challenge, risk, and triumph. Even when they are merely hanging out together, men engage in verbal jousts that contain a strong element of challenge, either in the form of good-natured arguments (such as Miller Lite's ongoing "tastes great—less filling" conflict) or in ribbing one another, which tests self-control and the ability to "take it." A sense of proportion and humor is required to overcome such challenges, which is why jokers and comedians are a valued social type in the myth of masculinity. Women may also pose a challenge to the man's ability to attract the opposite sex and, more important, to his self-control.

The central theme of masculine leisure activity in beer commercials, then, is challenge, risk, and mastery—mastery over nature, over technology, over others in good-natured "combat," and over oneself. And beer is integrated into this theme in two ways: one obvious, the other far more subtle. At the overt level, beer functions in leisure activities as it does in work:

as a reward for challenges successfully overcome (the race completed, the big fish landed, the ribbing returned). But it also serves another function, never explicitly alluded to in commercials. In several ways drinking, in itself, is a test of mastery. Because alcohol affects judgment and slows reaction time, it intensifies the risks inherent in movement and speed, and thereby increases the challenge they represent. And because it threatens self-control, drinking poses heightened opportunities for demonstrating self-mastery. Thus beer is not merely a reward for the successful meeting of a challenge in masculine work and leisure, but is itself an occasion for demonstrating mastery, and thus, masculinity. Beer is an appropriate award for overcoming challenge because it is a challenge itself, and thereby allows a man to symbolically reenact his feat. It would be all but suicidal for advertisers to present drinking as a challenge by which the masculine role can be acted out; instead, they associate beer with other forms of challenge related to the myth of masculinity.

What kinds of settings do men prefer? In beer commercials, the settings most closely associated with masculinity are the outdoors, generally the natural environment, and the self-contained world of the bar. The outdoors is featured prominently as both a workplace and a setting for leisure activity in ads for Busch beer, Old Milwaukee, Miller Genuine Draft, and Budweiser. As a workplace, the natural environment provides suitable challenge and danger for demonstrating masculinity, and the separation from civilization forces men to rely only on themselves. The height of masculinity can be attained when the natural environment and the work environment coincide, that is, when men have to overcome nature in order to survive. That is why the cowboy or frontiersman is the archetypical man's man in our culture. Other work environments, such as the farm, factory, and office, offer their own form of challenge, but physical danger is usually downplayed and the major risk is economic. Challenge and danger are also reduced, but still present, when nature is presented as a leisure environment; male bonding receives greater emphasis, and freedom from civilization becomes freedom for men to behave in a boyish manner.

In the ads, nature is closely associated with both masculinity and beer, as beer is presented as equivalent to nature. Often, beer is shown to be a product that is natural and pure, implying that its consumption is not harmful, and perhaps even healthy. Moreover, a number of beers, including Rolling Rock, Heileman's Old Style, and Molson's Golden, are identified with natural sources of water. This identification is taken even further in one Busch beer commercial: We see a cowboy on horseback, herding cattle across a river. A small calf is overcome by the current, but the cowboy is able to withstand the force of the river and come to the rescue. The voice-over says, "Sometimes a simple river crossing isn't so simple. And when you've got him back, it's your turn. Head for the beer brewed natural as a mountain stream." We then see a six-pack pulled out of clear running water, as if by magic. The raging water represents the power and danger of nature, while the mountain stream stands for nature's gentler aspect. Through the voice-over and the image of the hand pulling the six-pack from the water, beer is presented as identical with the stream, as bottled nature. Drinking beer, then, is a relatively safe way of facing the challenge of raging rivers, of symbolically reenacting the taming of the frontier.

Beer is identified with nature in a more general way in the ads for Old Milwaukee, which are usually set in wilderness environments that feature water, such as the Florida Everglades, and Snake River, Wyoming. In each ad, a group of men is engaged in recreational activities such as high-speed air-boating, flat-bottom boat racing, or fishing. Each commercial begins with a voice-over saying something like, "The Florida Everglades and Old Milwaukee both mean something great to these guys." Each ad includes a jingle, which says, "There's nothing like the flavor of a special place and Old Milwaukee beer." In other words, Old Milwaukee is equivalent to the special place. The place is special because it is untouched by civilization, allowing men to engage in forms of recreation not available elsewhere. It therefore must be fairly inaccessible, but since beer is presented as identical to the place, drinking may act as a substitute for actually going there.

Beer is also identified with nature through animals. For example, the symbol of Busch beer, found on its label and in its commercials, is a horse rearing on its hind legs, a phallic symbol that also evokes the idea of the untamed. And in another Busch ad, a young rodeo rider is quickly thrown from his mount; trying to cheer him up, an older cowboy hands him a beer and says, "Here. This one don't buck to so hard." Thus, the identification of beer and nature is made via the horse. Drinking beer is like rodeo-riding, only less strenuous. It is a challenge that the rider can easily overcome, allowing him to save face and reaffirm masculinity. Budweiser beer also uses horses as a symbol: the Budweiser Clydesdales, a breed of "draft" horse. Whereas the Busch Stallion represents the frontier wilderness, the Clydesdales stand for the pastoral. Also, Colt 45 malt liquor, by its very name, invokes images of the Old West, horses, and of course guns, another phallic symbol. Another way in which beer is identified with nature and animals is through Budweiser's "Spuds McKenzie" and Stroh's "Alex," both dogs that behave like humans; both are in turn identified with masculinity as they are male characters, and canines are the animals most closely associated with masculinity.

As a setting for masculine activity, the bar runs a close second to nature, and many commercials seem to advertise bar patronage as much as they do a particular brand of beer. Of course, the drinking hall has a venerable history in Western culture as a center for male socializing and tests of skill, strength, and drinking ability. It is a setting featured prominently in the myths and legends of ancient Greece, and in Norse and Old English sagas. The pub is a popular setting in British literature, as is the saloon in the American Western genre. Like its predecessors, the bar of the beer commercial is presented as a male-dominated environment, although it sometimes serves as a setting for male-female interaction. And it is generally portrayed as a relaxed and comfortable context for male socializing, as well as a place where a man can find entertainment and excitement. The bars are immaculate and smokeless, and the waitresses and bartenders are always friendly; thus, along with nature, bars are the ideal male leisure environment. The only exception is the Bud Light bar, where men who are so uninformed as to ask for "a light" rather than a specific brand are subjected to pranks by the bartenders; still, even in this case the practical jokes are taken in stride, reaffirming the customer's masculinity.

It is worth noting that in the romanticized barroom of beer commercials, no one ever pays for his drinks, either literally or in terms of alcohol's effects. In other words, there are no consequences to the men's actions, which is consistent with the myth of masculinity's tendency to ignore or downplay risk and danger. The bar is shown as a self-contained environment, one that, like the outdoors, frees men from the constraints of civilization, allowing them to behave irresponsibly. Moreover, most settings featured as drinking-places in beer commercials are probably places that people would drive to—and drive home from. Because the action is confined to these settings, however, the question of how people arrived and how they will get home never comes up.

How do boys become men? In the world of beer commercials, boys become men by earning acceptance from those who are already full-fledged members of the community of men. Adult men are identified by their age, their size, their celebrity, and their positions of authority in the work world and/or status in a bar. To earn acceptance, the younger man must demonstrate that he can do the things that men do: take risks, meet challenges, face danger courageously, and dominate his environment. In the workplace, he demonstrates this by seizing opportunities to work, taking pride in his labor, proving his ability, persisting in the face of uncertainty, and learning to accept failure with equanimity. Having proven that he can act out the masculine role, the initiate is rewarded with beer. As a reward, beer symbolizes the overcoming of a challenge, the fulfilling of the requirements for group membership. The gift of beer also allows the adult male to show his acceptance of the initiate without becoming emotional. Beer then functions as a symbol of initiation and group membership.

For example, one of Budweiser's most frequently aired commercials during the 1980s features a young Polish immigrant and an older foreman and dispatcher. In the first scene, the dispatcher is reading names from a clipboard, giving workers their assignments. Arriving late, which earns him a look of displeasure from the foreman, the nervous young man takes a seat in the back. When he is finally called, the dispatcher stumbles over the immigrant's foreign name. The young man walks up to the front of the room, corrects the dispatcher's mispronunciation—a risky move, given his neophyte status, but one that demonstrates his pride and self-confidence. He receives his assignment, and the scene then shifts to a montage of the day's work. At the beginning, he drops a toolbox, spilling its contents, a mishap noted by the foreman; by the end of the day, however, he has demonstrated his ability and has earned the respect of his co-workers. The final scene is in a crowded tavern; the young man walks through the door, making his way to the bar, looking around nervously. He hears his name called, turns around, and the foreman, sitting at the bar, hands him a beer. In both the first and final scene, the immigrant begins at the back of the room, highlighting his outsider status, and moves to the front as he is given a chance to prove himself. The commercial's parallelism is not just an aesthetic device, but a mythic one as well. Having mastered the challenge of work, the neophyte receives the reward of a beer, which is both a symbol of that mastery and an invitation to symbolically reenact his feat. By working hard and well, he gains acceptance in the work world; by drinking the beer, he can also gain acceptance into the social world of the bar. The foreman, by virtue of his age, his position of authority, and his position sitting at the bar in the center of the tavern, holds the power of confirmation in both worlds.

The theme of initiation is also present in a subtle way in the Bud Light ads in which someone orders "a light," is given a substitute such as lamp or torch, and then corrects himself, asking for a "Bud Light." As one of the commercials revealed, the bartenders play these pranks because they are fed up with uninformed customers. The bizarre substitutions are a form of hazing, an initiation into proper barroom etiquette. The mature male is familiar with brands of beer, knows what he wants, and shows decisiveness in ordering it. Clearly, the individuals who ask for "a light" are inexperienced drinkers, and it is important to keep in mind that, to the barroom novice (and especially to the underage drinker), bars and bartenders can seem very threatening. While the substitute "lights" come as a surprise to the patrons, and thus threaten their composure, they are a relatively mild threat. The customers are able to overcome this challenge to their self-control, correct their order, and thereby gain entry into barroom society.

The biological transition from childhood to adulthood is a gradual one, but in traditional cultures, it is symbolized by formal rituals of initiation, rites of passage which mark the boundary between childhood and adulthood, clearly separating these two social positions. In our own culture, there are no initiation rites, and therefore the adolescent's social position is an ambiguous one. A number of events and activities do serve as symbols of adulthood, however. The commercials emphasize entry into the work world as one such step; financial independence brings the freedom of adulthood, while work is an integral part of the adult male's identity. As a symbol of initiation into the work world, beer also functions as a symbol of adulthood. And although this is never dealt with in the commercials, drinking in and of itself is a symbol of adulthood in our culture, as is driving, particularly in the eyes of underage males. Bars are seen as exclusively adult environments, and so acceptance in bars is a further sign of manhood. In the commercials, bars and workplaces complement each other as environments in which initiation into adulthood can be consummated.

How do men relate to each other? In beer commercials, men are rarely found in solitary pursuits (and never drink alone), and only occasionally in one-to-one relationships, usually involving father-son or mentor-protégé transactions. The dominant social context for male interaction is the group, and teamwork and group loyalty rank high in the list of masculine values. Individualism and competition, by contrast, are downplayed, and are acceptable only as long as they foster the cohesiveness of the group as a whole. Although differences in status may exist between members of the group and outsiders, within the group equality is the rule, and elitism and intellectualism are disdained. This reflects the American value of egalitarianism and solidifies the importance of the group over individual members. The concept of group loyalty is extended to community and to country, so that patriotism is also presented as an important value for men.

The emotional tenor of relationships among men in beer commercials is characterized by self-restraint. Generally, strong emotions are eschewed, especially overt displays of affection. In the workplace, mutual respect is exhibited, but respect must be earned through ability and attitude. In leisure situations, humor is a major element in male interactions. Conversations among men emphasize joking, bragging, story-telling, and good-natured insults. The insults are a form of symbolic challenge; taking a ribbing in good spirit is a demonstration of emotional strength and self-mastery. By providing a controlled social context for the exchange of challenges and demonstrations of ego strength and self-control, the group provides continuous reinforcement of the members' masculinity. Moreover, gathering in groups provides men with the freedom to act irresponsibly; that is, it allows men to act like boys. This is particularly the case in the Miller Lite ads that feature retired sports stars, comedians, and other celebrities.

In beer commercials, drinking serves several important functions in promoting group solidarity. Beer is frequently the shared activity that brings the group together, and in the ads for Miller Genuine Draft, sharing beer acts as a reminder of the group's identity and history. Thus, beer becomes a symbol of group membership. It also serves as a means for demonstrating the group's egalitarian values. When one man gives a beer to another, it is a sign of acceptance, friendship, or gratitude. In this role, beer is also a substitute for overt display of affection. Although the commercials never deal with why beer takes on this role, the answer lies in the effects of alcohol. Certainly, its function as mood enhancer can have a positive influence on group interaction. And, as previously discussed, alcohol itself constitutes a challenge, so that drinking allows each member of the group to publicly demonstrate his masculinity. Alcohol also lowers inhibitions, making it easier for men to show their affection for one another. The well-known saying that you cannot trust a man who does not drink reflects the popular conception that under the influence of alcohol, men become more open and honest. Moreover, the effects of drinking on physical coordination make a man less of an immediate threat. All these properties contribute to beer's role as a medium of male bonding and a facilitator of group solidarity.

In general, men are not portrayed as loners in beer commercials, and in this respect the ads differ markedly from other expressions of the myth of masculinity. There are no isolated Marlboro men in the Busch frontier, for example. When he saves the calf from being swept away by the river, the Busch cowboy appears to be on his own, but by the time he is ready for his reward, another cowboy has appeared out of nowhere to share his beer. In another Busch ad, a jingle with the following lyrics is heard: "There's no place on earth that I'd rather be, than out in the open where it's all plain to see, if it's going to get done it's up to you and me." In this way, the ideal of individual self-reliance that is so central to the American myth of the frontier is transformed into group self-reliance. In the world of beer commercials, demonstrating one's masculinity requires an audience to judge one's performance and confirm one's status. Moreover, the emphasis the ads place on beer drinking as a group activity undermines the idea that it is in any way problematic. One of the most widespread stereotypes of problem drinkers is that they are solitary and secretive loners. The emphasis on the group in beer commercials plays on the common misconception that drinking, when it is done socially and publicly, cannot be harmful.

How do men relate to women? Although the world of beer commercials is often monopolized by men, some of the ads do feature male-female interaction in the form of courtship, as well as in more established relationships. When courtship is the focus, the image of the man's man gives way to that of the ladies' man, for whom seduction is the highest form of challenge. And while the obvious risk in courtship is rejection by the opposite sex, the more significant danger in beer ads is loss of emotional self-control. The ladies' man must remain cool, confidant, and detached when faced with the object of his desires. This social type is exemplified by Billy Dee Williams, who plays on his romantic image in Colt 45 commercials. Strangely enough, Spuds McKenzie, Budweiser's "party animal," also fits into this category, insofar as he, like Alex, is treated like a human being. In his ads, Spuds is surrounded by the Spudettes, three beautiful young women who dance with him, serve him, even bathe him. The women are attractive enough to make most males salivate like Pavlov's dogs, but Spuds receives their attentions with casual indifference (and never betrays the insecurities that haunt his cousin Snoopy

when the *Peanuts* dog assumes his "Joe Cool" persona). While the commercials do not go so far as to suggest bestiality, there is no question that Spuds is a stud.

Emotional control is also demonstrated by the male's ability to divide his attention. For example, in one Michelob commercial, a young woman is shown leaning over a jukebox and selecting a song; her expression is one of pure pleasure, and she seems lost in thought. Other scenes, presumably her memories, show her dancing in the arms of a handsome young man. His arms are around her neck, and he is holding in one hand, behind her back, a bottle of beer. This image emphasizes the difference between the myths of masculinity and femininity; her attention is focused entirely on him, while his interests extend to the beer as well as the woman. According to the myth of masculinity, the man who loses control of his emotions in a relationship is a man who loses his independence, and ultimately, his masculinity; dividing attention is one way to demonstrate self-control. Michelob also presents images of ladies' men in the form of popular musicians, such as the rock group Genesis, rock star Eric Clapton, and popular vocalist Frank Sinatra. Many male pop stars have reputations as sexual athletes surrounded by groupies; in the ads, however, they function as modern troubadours, providing a romantic backdrop for lovers and facilitating social interaction. Acting, like Spuds McKenzie, as mascots for the beer companies, they imply that the beer they are identified with serves the same functions.

By far the most sexist of beer commercials, almost to the point of farce, are the Colt 45 ads featuring Billy Dee Williams. One of these, which is divided into three segments, begins with Williams saying: "There are two rules to remember if you want to have a good time: Rule number one, never run out of Colt 45. Rule number two, never forget rule number one." In the next segment, Williams continues: "You want to know why you should keep plenty of Colt 45 on hand? You never know when friends might show up." As he says this, he opens a can and a woman's hand reaches out and takes it. In the third segment, he concludes, "I don't claim you can have a better time with Colt 45 than without it, but why take chances?" As he says this, the camera pulls back to reveal Williams standing, and an attractive woman sitting next to him. The ad ends with a picture of a Colt 45 can and the slogan, "The power of Colt 45: It works every time." There are a number of ways to interpret this pitch. First, malt liquor has a higher alcohol content than beer or ale, and therefore is a more *powerful* beverage. Second, the ad alludes to alcohol's image as an aphrodisiac, despite the fact that it actually reduces male potency. As noted, the Colt 45 pistol is a phallic symbol, while the slogan can be read as a guarantee against impotency—"it works every time." Third, it can be seen as referring to alcohol's ability to make men feel more confident about themselves and more interested in the opposite sex. And fourth, it plays on the popular notion that getting a woman drunk increases her desire for and willingness to engage in sex. Williams keeps Colt 45 on hand not just for himself, but for "friends," meaning "women." His secret of seduction is getting women to drink. In the ad, the woman is eager to drink Colt 45, implying that she will be just as eager to make love. The idea that a woman who drinks is "looking for it" is even clearer in a second ad.

This commercial begins with the title "Billy Dee Williams on Body Language." Moving through an outdoor party, Williams says, "You know, body language tells you a lot about what a person is thinking. For instance, that means she has an interest in the finer things in life." As he says this, the camera pans to show an attractive women sitting at a bar alone, holding her necklace. She shifts her position and strokes her hair, and Williams says, "That means she also wants a little fun in her life, but only with the right man." At this point, the woman fills her glass with Colt 45, as Williams says, "And now she's pouring Colt 45 and we all know what that means." He then goes over to her and asks if she would mind if he joined her, and she replies, "You must have read my mind." Williams responds, "Something like that," and the ad ends with the same slogan as the first. What is implied in this commercial is that any woman who would sit by herself and drink must be looking to get picked up; she is sending out signals and preparing herself to be seduced. And although she is making herself approachable, she must wait for Williams to make the first move. At the same time, the woman appears to be vain, fondling her jewelry and hair. And in both ads, the women are seated while Williams stands. This portrayal of the woman's woman, based on the myth of femininity, is the perfect counterpart to Williams' image as a ladies' man.

When the commercials depict more established relationships, the emphasis shifts from romance and seduction to male activities in which women are reduced largely to the role of admiring onlookers. Men appear to value their group of friends over their female partners, and the women accept this. Women tend to be passive, not participating but merely watching as men perform physical tasks. In other words, they become the audience for whom men perform. For the most part, women know their place and do not interfere with male bonding. They may, however, act as emotional catalysts for male interaction, bringing men together. Occasionally, a woman may be found together with a group of men, presumably as the girlfriend or wife of one of the group members. Here, the presence of women, and their noninterference, indicates their approval of masculine activity and male bonding, and their approval of the role of beer in these situations. Even when a group of men acts irresponsibly and/or boyishly, the presence of a woman shows that this behavior is socially sanctioned.

Alternate images of femininity can be found in beer commercials, but they are generally relegated to the background; for the most part, the traditional roles of masculinity and femininity are upheld. One exception is a Michelob Light ad that features Madeline Kahn. Introduced by a male voice-over, "Madeline Kahn on having it all," she is lying on her side on a couch, wearing an expensive-looking gown and necklace, and holding a bottle of beer. Kahn does a short humorous monologue in which she acknowledges her wealth and glamour, and the scene shifts to a shot of the beer, as the male voice-over says, "Michelob Light. You *can* have it all." While this represents something of a concession to changing conceptions of femininity, the advertisers hedge their bets. The male voice-over frames, and in a sense controls, Kahn's monologue, while Kahn position, lying on her side, is a passive and seductive one. To male viewers, the commercial can easily imply that "having it all" includes having a woman like her.

CONCLUSION

In the world of beer commercials, masculinity revolves around the theme of challenge, an association that is particularly alarming, given the social problems stemming from alcohol abuse. For the most part beer commercials present traditional, stereotypical images of men, and uphold the myths of masculinity and femininity. Thus, in promoting beer, advertisers also promote and perpetuate these images and myths. Although targeted at an adult audience, beer commercials are highly accessible to children; between the ages of 2 and 18, American children may see as many as 100,000 of these ads (Postman et al., 1987). They are also extremely attractive to children: humorous, exciting, and offering answers to questions about gender and adulthood. And they do have an impact, playing a role in social learning and attitude formation (Wallack, Cassady, & Grube, 1990). As Postman (1979) argues, television constitutes a curriculum, one that children spend more time with than in schoolrooms. Beer commercials are a prominent subject in television's curriculum, a subject that is ultimately hazardous to the intellectual as well as the physical health of the young. The myth of masculinity *does* have a number of redeeming features (facing challenges and taking risks are valuable activities in many contexts), but the unrelenting one-dimensionality of masculinity as presented by beer commercials is clearly anachronistic, possibly laughable, but without a doubt sobering.

REFERENCES

Atkin, C. K. (1987). Alcoholic-beverage advertising: Its content and impact. *Advances in Substances Abuse (Suppl.) 1,* 267–287.

Barthes, R. (1972). *Mythologies* (A. Lavers, Ed. and Trans.). New York: Hill & Wang. (Original work published 1957).

Craig, S. (1987, March). *Marketing American masculinity: Mythology and flow in the Super Bowl telecasts.* Paper presented at the annual meeting of the Popular Culture Association, Montreal.

Fejes, F. (1989). Images of men in media research. *Critical Studies in Mass Communication, 6*(2), 215–221.

Finn, T. A., & Strickland, D. (1982). A content analysis of beverage alcohol advertising, #2: Television advertising. *Journal of Studies on Alcohol, 43,* 964–989.

Finn, T. A., & Strickland, D. (1983). The advertising and alcohol abuse issue: A cross media comparison of alcohol beverage advertising content. In M. Burgeon (Ed.), *Communication yearbook* (pp. 850–872). Beverly Hills, CA: Sage.

Hacker, G. A., Collins R., & Jacobson, M. (1987). *Marketing booze to blacks.* Washington, DC: Center for Science in the Public Interest.

Jacobson, M., Atkins, R., & Hacker, G. (1983). *The booze merchants: The inebriating of America.* Washington, DC: Center for Science in the Public Interest.

Kimmel, M. (Ed.). (1987). *Changing men: New directions in research on men and masculinity.* Newbury Park, CA: Sage.

Klapp, O. E. (1962). *Heroes, villains, and fools: The changing American character.* Englewood Cliffs, NJ: Prentice-Hall.

Postman, N. (1979). *Teaching as a conserving activity.* New York: Delacorte.

Postman, N., Nystrom, C., Strate, L., & Weingartner, C. (1987). *Myths, men and beer: An analysis of beer commercials on broadcast television.* Falls Church, VA: AAA Foundation for Traffic Safety. (ERIC Document Reproduction Service No. ED 290 074).

Strate, L. (1989). The mediation of nature and culture in beer commercials. *New Dimensions in Communications, Proceedings of the 47th Annual New York State Speech Communication Association Conference 3,* 92–95.

Strate, L. (1990, October). *The cultural meaning of beer commercials.* Paper presented at the Advances in Consumer Research Conference, New York.

Wallack, L., Cassady, D., & Grube, J. (1990). *TV beer commercials and children: Exposure, attention, beliefs, and expectations about drinking as an adult.* Washington, DC: AAA Foundation for Traffic Safety.

Wenner, L. (1991). One part alcohol, one part sport, one part dirt, stir gently: Beer commercials and television sports. In L. R. Vande Berg & L. A. Wenner (Eds.), *Television criticism: Approaches and applications.* New York: Longman.

FURTHER READING

Cahill, Spencer. 1989. "Fashioning Males and Females: Appearance Management and the Social Reproduction of Gender." *Symbolic Interaction* 12: 281–298.

- Explores appearance management in young children's gender constructions.

Kessler, Suzanne J. and Wendy McKenna. 1978. *Gender: An Ethnomethodological Approach.* Chicago: University of Chicago Press.

- A thorough discussion of gender as a social construction.

Kimmel, Michael S. and Michael Kaufman. 1994. "Weekend Warriors: The New Men's Movement." Pp. 259–288 in *Theorizing Masculinities,* edited by Harry Brod and Michael Kaufman. Thousand Oaks, CA: Sage.

- The social organization of men's groups and their implication for masculinity.

Mason-Schrock, Douglas. 1996. "Transsexuals' Narrative Constructions of the 'true self'." *Social Psychology Quarterly* 59: 176–192.

- Shows how transsexuals collaborate to fashion their biographies.

Ornstein, Peggy. 1994. "Fear of Falling: Sluts." Pp. 51–66 in *School Girls.* New York: Doubleday.

- Discusses the use of the category "slut" in constructing school social status.

Sandstrom, Kent L. 1996. "Redefining Sex and Intimacy: The Sexual Self-Images, Outlooks, and Relationships of Gay Men Living with HIV/AIDS." *Symbolic Interaction* 19: 241–262.

- Examines how gay men living with HIV/AIDS come to terms with the intimate implications of their illness.

SECTION 3

SOCIAL WORLDS OF AGE AND THE LIFE COURSE

The life course and one's location in it are typically viewed as matters of chronological age. These are undeniable features of personal experience through time. It's as if you are a young adult when you're in college and when you hit 40, you're middle aged, and that's that. We tend to treat life as an unfolding sequence of ages and stages that individuals experience as they get older. Life's segments appear to be patterned, predictable, and obvious.

When we think of our social worlds as interactionally constructed, however, we need to re-consider the meanings of age and the life course in our everyday lives. From this point of view, the life course isn't a predetermined march through time. Instead, chronological time and progression through stages are ways of conceptualizing the passage through life. They are concepts that people *use* interactionally to make sense of their ongoing experiences. When we say that the life course is socially constructed and used, we mean that people actively assemble, articulate, and organize meanings that they attach to age and life change. They collaborate in creating what it means to be old, young, or in between, as part of the practical work of understanding experience through time. Age and time don't simply "march on." Instead, they are actively assembled in those terms.

For example, people often use chronological age to define selves and situations, but its meaning is far from predetermined or obvious. Some may call a 30-year-old man a "boy wonder" in the corporate board room, for instance. But we'd say the same man was "over the hill"—an "ancient mariner," as it were—in Olympic swimming competition. The meaning of his age comes from the context of its use. Such descriptions convey a sense for where a 30-year-old stands in a developmental sequence, but their meanings are tied to the situations at hand. They depend on comparisons with other people in similar situations. Clearly, mere chronological age isn't the key to understanding the man's current stations in the life course.

It's also clear from this example that the life course isn't a singular patterned progression. People depict different courses to accommodate the interpretive demands of diverse social worlds. For example, we can formulate the life course as a positive *developmental* sequence to depict the "maturation" of a young person. Or we can portray a *spiral of decline* to describe a person suffering from Alzheimer's disease or from failing physical health. The metaphors we use for aging vary dramatically. Sometimes we use the image of sand running out in an hourglass. Other times, we compare the passage of time to the perpetual cycling of a wheel that always returns to its point of origin. The lesson is not that one metaphor is more accurate than the other in describing the patterned progression of experience. Rather, it's that we *use* various metaphors to convey diverse meanings for experience through time. In this way, the meaning of age and its place in our social worlds is continually under construction.

Still, it's becoming more and more common to picture experience in terms of age-related phases and stages. We're all familiar with stagewise depictions of child development. Later in life, we see and hear our lives laid out in terms of mid- and later-life "crises." The important point to remember is that these phases and stages are interpretive devices, not intrinsic features of lives in progress. They emerge at particular points in history and are applied in different situations and circumstances. The *meaning* of age in everyday life is the critical issue.

ABOUT THE READINGS

In **"Preadolescent Clique Stratification and the Hierarchy of Identity,"** Patricia A. Adler and **Peter Adler** describe how elementary school children go about the business of being successful "kids." Typically, we take it for granted that people simply pass through various stages of life. They navigate each stage more or less successfully to move on or grow up. The Adlers show that "being a kid" is more complicated than this.

Preadolescence presents both the extraordinary challenge of being popular and the fear of being excluded. Some kids will do just about anything to be one of the "populars." Being "cool" is everything. Being a "nerd" or a "loser" is tantamount to the end of the world, even if these are just the judgments of 12 year olds. The Adlers outline some of the ways that the experience of childhood is constructed by the children who are actually living through and "doing" preadolescent life. They show how the various meanings of age-status markers are actively created and sustained. Kids don't passively internalize a preteen social world and automatically identify themselves in those terms. They *do* it in the ways they act and interact.

Carol Rambo Ronai offers a different take on the life course as she examines the aging experience of women in their late teens and 20. It seems unusual that aging would be a concern for such "young" women. But for the subjects of Ronai's study, "getting old" is especially foreboding because these women are strip-tease artists known as "table dancers." In **"Managing Aging in Young Adulthood: The 'Aging' Table Dancer,"** Ronai explores the identity implications of advancing age for women who make their living by putting their bodies on public display. The meaning of age comes to the fore as dancers confront questions such as "When are you *too old* to dance?" or "When do you begin to *show your age?*" Ronai vividly describes how the women's identities are tied to the meaning of their age in relation to their physical bodies in these circumstances.

Katherine Newman provides a glimpse of another age-related social world in her chapter

"Place and Race: Midlife Experience in Harlem." Newman presents the world of middle age among African American residents of poor Harlem neighborhoods in New York City. These people in their 40s and 50s experience the life course differently than do their white counterparts. Newman describes a generation whose lives are distinctively shaped by where and when they grew into adulthood. The unique challenges they confront are revealed in the interpretive benchmarks they use to account for their lives through time. Place, race, and family also bear heavily on what it means to be middle aged in Harlem.

Returning to more traditional concerns, **Sarah H. Matthews** describes how the aging experience is managed in **"The Social World of Old Women."** Surprisingly, Matthews tells us that being old is sometimes not very important to how the women define themselves. Age isn't always crucial to how older persons relate to others. Instead, it emerges in relation to particular social relationships. Still, age is almost always on the social horizon because others can make age relevant to interaction. Matthews shows how older women work to control how others apply the label "old" to them. She demonstrates how women manage their social worlds and their self-images by staving off definitions that would consign them to the scrap heap of old age.

37 | PREADOLESCENT CLIQUE STRATIFICATION AND THE HIERARCHY OF IDENTITY
Patricia A. Adler and Peter Adler

Preadolescents' peer friendship groups constitute one of the most profound and meaningful elements of their lives. Having a circle of close and loyal friends can signify the difference between an active, exciting, and secure social life, and one that is filled with uncertainty, insecurity, and degradation. While research on adolescents has shown that their friendship groups form the most salient element of their school experience (Cusik 1973; Everhart 1983; Willis 1981) and provide the basis for their peer culture (Everhart 1983; Fine 1987; Willis 1981; Wulff 1988), this topic remains underaddressed with respect to the lives of elementary school children. Yet elementary school friendship groups are not only organized, but highly differentiated and stratified.

Studies of adolescent friendship groups, from middle and junior high school to high school, have found that teenagers categorize clusters of people according to their social type. For example, Coleman (1961) described four groups in the stratification system of the adolescents he studied; the leading crowd, the exemplars, the local leaders, and a group he referred to as being unpopular. Canaan (1987), Eckert (1989), and Eder (1995) have discussed the formation of groups in junior highs or middle schools based on styles and interests, where people such as jocks, preppies, greasers, skaters, druggies, or eggheads, can come together and find like-minded people. Researchers have also shown that adolescents stratify these clusters hierarchically in terms of popularity and prestige (Brown and Lohr 1987; Cohen 1979; Coleman 1961; Cusik 1973; Eckert 1989; Eder 1995; Hollingshead 1949; Ianni 1989; Kinney 1993; Larkin 1979; Lesko 1988; Lightfoot 1983; Schwartz 1987; Schwartz and Merten 1967; Schwendinger and Schwendinger 1985; Snyder 1972; Weis 1974). This type of differentiation, however, has not been noted at the elementary level. Scholars have pointed to very little variety in terms of the types of groups available within or between different ranks that surface in older and larger school populations (Canaan 1987; Eder 1995). Research on the friendship groupings of elementary-school-age children have focused either on gender clusterings (Thorne 1993), on divisions within the group (Best 1983), or only tangentially on social stratification (Kless 1992). These treatments overlook the sophistication with which preadolescent children typologize each other both within and between groups according to their recognition and respect—the elements of which status is composed.

Social psychologists have identified people's self-concept or identity as the location of their feelings about themselves, the image they hold as experiencing beings interacting with the world (Epstein 1973; Rosenberg 1979; Turner 1968, 1976). A central theme in the literature on the self-concept is that the content and organization of identities reflect the content and organization of society (Gecas 1982). Symbolic interactionists have focused on the way identities are socially constructed in interaction, based on people's shared understandings of social roles, rules, symbols, and categories (Cooley 1902; Foote 1951; James 1890; Mead 1934; Stryker 1968; Thomas 1923). Identities are then expressed, maintained, negotiated, and modified in the enactment and presentation of these categories, through people's perceptions of the reactions and evaluations of others (Goffman 1959; McCall and Simmons 1966; Stone 1962; Weinstein 1969). Identities symbolize self-meanings, and are acquired in particular situations based on people's comparison of their roles to others and others' counter-roles (Lindesmith and Strauss 1956; Turner 1956). At the same time identities form the core of our self-esteem, the emotional dimension of our selves. Identities thus specify the content and evaluation of our

selves, and guide and regulate our subsequent thoughts, feelings, and behavior, operating cybernetically to reciprocally relate the individual and the social structure (Stryker 1980).

Scholars have explored numerous sources that contribute to the foundation of identity, among them appearance (Stone 1962), occupation (Hughes 1971; Snow and Anderson 1987), linguistic structures (Goodwin 1990), and interaction partners (Robinson and Smith-Lovin 1992). Our research highlights the role of friendship groups in affecting the formation of children's conceptions of self. Children learn, in interacting both within and between friendship groups, what kind of social competence, currency, and charisma they possess. Their efforts locate them in clearly identifiable positions along the peer status hierarchy. This analysis posits a *structural-relational* base to identity, a model that simultaneously draws on and integrates the processual (Blumer 1969) and structural (Stryker 1980) perspectives on symbolic interactionism. It conceives people's friendship group affiliation as forged and maintained through situational, negotiated interaction, yet crystallized into symbolic clusters of stratified roles that influence the character and interpretation of their subsequent interaction. The processual, micro perspective meets the structural, macro perspective at the Simmelian level of analysis (Simmel 1950), in the crystallized interactions that are recurrent between members of these groups.

In this article we directly address the status and relational dimension as basis for inter- and intragroup stratification, showing the powerful hierarchies among preadolescent children. Drawing on seven years of participant–observation research, we outline the typologies of social groups commonly found among preadolescents. In contrast to teenagers' diverse and loosely arranged groups, preadolescent social groups tend to be smaller, less eclectic, and more socially restricted by their encapsulation in homerooms. As a result, their status stratification tends to be more unidimensional, a single popular crowd dominating over the grade and other groups lining up beneath it. We look at variations in the character, composition, and social experience associated with membership in groups at different positions, and at the consequences of friendship group membership for a so-cial-relational hierarchy of identity. We conclude by addressing the foundations of this identity hierarchy in relation to theories of identity and levels of analysis.

METHODS

This research draws on data gathered through longitu-dinal participant observation and interviews with stu-dents in the upper grades (third through sixth) of ele-mentary schools. Over the course of seven years (1987–1994) we observed and interacted with chil-dren both inside and outside of their schools. The chil-dren we studied came from seven large public and five small private schools that drew from middle- and up-per-middle-class neighborhoods (with a smattering of children from lower-socioeconomic areas) in a large, predominantly white university community with a population of around 85,000. As is consistent with the demographics of the community, the majority of chil-dren we observed attended public schools. The data we present describe and analyze the concerns and ide-ologies of this overwhelmingly middle- and upper-middle-class population. While doing our research, we occupied several roles: parent, friend, counselor, coach, volunteer, and carpooler (see Fine and Sand-strom 1988). We undertook these diverse roles as they naturally presented themselves and as deliberate re-search strategies, sometimes combining the two as op-portunities for interacting with children became avail-able through familial obligations or work/school requirements. As a research team, we were diverse in gender, which enabled us to interact well with both boys and girls and to employ a range of roles and perspectives.

In interacting with children we tried to develop and expand on the "parental" research role by observ-ing, casually conversing and interacting with, and in-terviewing children, children's friends, other parents, and teachers. This built upon our natural parenting ac-tivities, contacts, interests, and style, taking us into lo-cations and events populated by children. We did much of our research outside of school settings. We followed our daughter and son, their friends and ene-mies, the children of our neighbors and friends, and other children we met through our involvement in youth leisure activities through their school and out-of-school experiences. Studying circles in which our children were members usually provided a boost to the research: We had a "membership role" (Adler and Adler 1987) in the setting and came into contact with children and their parents naturally; we knew and in-teracted with many of them over a period of years; and we could triangulate (Denzin 1989) by observing them, talking with them, and hearing about them from others. Our children inadvertently obliged us by occu-pying or passing through different strata of the clique hierarchy: One was consistently in the popular group, but the other moved between the popular, the wan-nabe, the isolate, and the middle levels.[1] We also gath-ered data inside of school settings, conducting indi-vidual and group interviews with children outside of and in their classrooms.

Though most studies of children focus on institu-tionalized educational settings, we gathered data in both school and out-of-school recreational settings, becoming actively involved in a variety of "after-school" arenas such as organized youth sports, ex-tracurricular academic activities, and neighborhood play. While our main understanding of the setting and the behavior of the participants was derived from our years of participant-observation with nearly a hundred children of each gender,[2] we augmented these data with more focused conversations with children. We conducted in-depth, unstructured interviews with ap-proximately forty boys and girls from a variety of ages and social groups, culling individuals from the popu-lar inner clique, the wannabes, the nonpopular middle circles, and the social isolates. We selected interview subjects by soliciting volunteers from children (and recommendations from teachers to round out under-represented groups) in public school settings as well as by approaching children (both directly and through their parents) in recreational and afterschool settings. As a result, most of our interviews were conducted with children who attended public schools, although some of the children we recruited from afterschool settings attended private schools (five). We selected individuals to interview over whom we had no author-ity, either through academic, recreational, or familial relations. Of these forty children, approximately thir-ty-five were involved in some sort of extracurricular, afterschool activities (although most of the activities were not connected with us). We interviewed children wherever it was most convenient for them, in either their homes or their schools. Parents, teachers, and children we had already talked to helped us with our research by referring new subjects to us, helping us to sample in accordance with theoretical standards (Glaser and Strauss 1967) for others in different situations. We continued this snowball referral method (Biernacki and Waldorf 1981) until we felt that we had adequately covered the range of existing social roles and experiences and had reached theoretical saturation. We then conducted selected interviews with seven teachers at three different public elementary schools to get a broader overview of social cliques and their dynamics from individuals whose experiences were more comparatively rooted in working with many different groups of children over the years. Throughout the data-gathering process we engaged in continual inductive analysis (Becker and Geer 1960), developing categories and typologies of behavior that fit within these different status strata and forging them into the identity hierarchy we present in the conclusion.

THE STATUS HIERARCHY

Children from all the schools we studied described the arrangement of members of their grade into a hierarchy based on peer status. Variations in the nature and composition of these strata might be influenced by the size of the school, the demographics of its population, the grade level, and the organization of classrooms (open versus closed) (Hallinan 1979). For every age level, within each gender group, and in every school with a population of more than eighty students per grade, the social system was composed of four main strata: the high, wannabe, middle, and low ranks.[3] At the high end was the popular clique, comprising the exclusive crowd. Below them were the wannabes, the group of people who hung around the popular clique hoping for inclusion. Next was the middle group, composed of smaller, independent friendship circles. At the bottom were the social isolates who found playmates only occasionally, spending most of their time by themselves.[4]

The Popular Clique

At the top of every grade was the popular clique. Members of this group were often referred to by themselves and others as "the cool kids."

Composition and Character   Several features distinguished the makeup of this group.

Size—The popular clique formed the largest friendship circle in the grade. In some grades it was an integrated whole, in others it was composed of interrelated and overlapping subgroups. The size of this clique grew as children advanced through the elementary grades, starting out small and incorporating new members each year. By the fourth and fifth grades it usually encompassed around one-third of the entire population. Taylor, a fifth-grade boy, outlined the relative size of the four social groups he saw in his grade:

> The cool group is at the top, say 35 percent of the kids. Then you've got the cool followers [wannabes], the ones that follow the cool kids around, they're around 10 percent. The medium group is the biggest, around 45 percent. They're all divided up into little groups, but there's a lot of them. Then the rest are in the outcast group, maybe 10 percent there, too.

Visibility—Members of the popular clique had the most active social lives, both during school and outside of it, had the largest number of friends, appeared to have the most fun, and as Eder (1995) has noted, commanded the most attention in the grade. They spent their time talking and whispering, running from one activity to the other, busying themselves with friends, and having dates and parties after school and on weekends. The greatest amount of crossgender interaction occurred within this group, as boys and girls talked on the phone after school, socialized at parties and movies, and "went" (steady) with each other, as Best (1983) also described. Their activities, social liaisons, and breakups were known about not only within their own circle, but by the rest of the grade as well.

Dominance—This group of people set the tone for, and in many ways influenced, the behavior of the entire grade. Miss Moran, a fourth-grade teacher, offered her observations of the popular clique's dominance:

> I see the popular clique as controlling the rest of the

class, so the middle group, although they're not part of it, depending on the agenda of the powerful clique, they will respond in a certain way or they will act in a certain way. They're not totally separate. The popular clique controls everything, classroom climate, as far as who feels comfortable blurting out an answer to a question. They just have a lot of power. So that even the people who are not popular but relatively comfortable will always keep an eye on the popular clique.

Although nonmembers did not directly engage with the popular people in their activities, jokes, or games, they were aware of them and set their attitudes and behavior in relation to them.

Exclusivity—Another feature that differentiated the popular crowd from the others in the grade was its exclusivity. Cliques are closed friendship groups, guarding their borders from undesirable interlopers. Located at the top of the status hierarchy, popular clique members accepted as friends only those judged worthy. They might dangle membership in front of others, as the members of Best's (1983) exclusive "Tent Club" did, but this did not mean that they would let them into the clique. Joe, a sixth-grade nonpopular boy, offered his view on the exclusionary behavior of clique leaders:

JOE: I've noticed a lot of things called clubs, and they usually have enrollment tests, and I've seen these be very demanding, and I've seen these be kind of trivial and stupid, but always it's something for the leader to laugh at the other one, and, for instance, give the leader control of the other person. But I still think that by doing that, and the other people doing that, they're kind of telling the leader, okay, I'll do whatever you want. And so then that goes into a cycle, so the leaders ask for more, they do it, they ask for more, they do it, and on and on and on.

The more individuals could be manipulated into self-debasing actions, the slimmer their chances of being accepted into the group, and the more they were taunted with futile opportunities for membership just to amuse the leaders and reinforce their influence. Most cliques admitted new members only when an existing member sponsored them and the leader approved, when people moved into the school system or neighborhood who looked highly desirable, or when power

plays or fights broke out, motivating conflicting members to include and elevate newcomers who would support them (for a further discussion of this process, see Adler and Adler 1995).

Role Stratification   As fundamental to cliques as their exclusivity was the internal hierarchy of their role structure. Although the movement of people within a clique might be fluid and shifting, people moved among a cluster of positions that were characterized by certain regular features. Differences in popularity, power, and control separated members in positions more central to the group from those at the periphery.

Leaders—The most powerful and pivotal role in the clique was the leader's. Cliques usually took the single-leader mode, with one person serving as the most forceful of the group, dominating over all the others. The leader had the power to set the clique boundaries, include or exclude potential members, raise or lower people in favor, and set the collective trends and opinions. Single-leader cliques coalesced around this central person and had an undisputed pyramid structure with different layers of subordinate strata arranged below.

A second form that cliques less commonly took involved two leaders. Two leaders could operate in tandem, as friends, or more independently, often with an element of competition. When two friends ran a clique together, they tended to be best friends, to operate in a unified manner on issues, and to use their combined power to dominate over others. In other cases, two powerful leaders might belong to a clique and not align themselves so completely. Ben, a fourth-grade boy, explained how his broader clique was divided into two subgroups independently led by Todd and Steven:

Todd had people who liked him more than Steven, but still liked Steven. Steven had others who liked him more than Todd, but still liked Todd. They formed together into one group and played together. But Steven had more followers than Todd, and so he was the most powerful. But he couldn't always get Todd and his friends to follow him all the time.

Second Tier—Just below the leaders were the second-tier clique members. This notch was usually occupied by one or two people at a time. Individuals in this position were close to the top, the next tier falling a significant step below them. Melanie, a fifth-grade girl who occupied the second tier with a friend, described the structure of her fourth-grade clique:

> We had three levels, kind of. There was Denise in the center, and then me and Kristy kind of just close to the center, and then there was another level beyond us, way beyond us. But we were pretty much scared of Denise.

Individuals could attain second-tier status in one of two ways. Some came to this highly placed position because they were best friends with the leader. This type of relational status was dependent, however, on the favor of the clique leader. If friendships and alliances shifted, as they were apt to do, the person(s) in the second-tier position could be replaced with a new status occupant. Melanie discussed how she was ejected from the role she had occupied in her fourth-grade clique when her best friend, the leader, abandoned her:

> Yeah. Denise liked me best for awhile, and she and I were real close. So, even though she was the leader, I was up there too. But then the boys started liking Kristy because she was a blonde. And my boyfriend dumped me and went off with Kristy. And then Denise was best friends with Kristy and was just a bitch to me. I went way down, way.

The other way people attained a position close to the top was through their own power. They might have followers who liked and supported them, they might have had high ranking before the current leader assumed prominence, or they may have contributed to unseating a previous leader.

Followers—The third clique role was occupied by the followers, who formed the bulk of the people in the group. Although less visible than the leaders, followers formed an indispensable part of the clique, as their unhesitant acceptance of leaders' actions and authority legitimated the leaders' role. They were connected to the group by their relation to one or more central members, and occupied positions that varied in status. Blake, a fifth-grade boy, described the hierarchy of members in his clique, carefully noting the gap between the two higher tiers and the followers:

> Bob was at the top, number one, and Max was number two. They were pretty much the most popular people. Then there was a jump between them and the rest of the group. Nobody was at three, but Marcus was a three and a half, and so were three other guys. A few people were at three and three-quarters, then Josh was a four and John was a four. Everyone else moved between three and a half and four including me. It could shift a lot.

The composition of the followers, while marked by subtle shadings, was fluid and mobile, with members moving up and down as they were targeted for ridicule or favor by more leading members. Some people were secure followers, while others held a more precarious position. Yet while different followers had their own clump of immediate friends, the leaders were sought by all of the clumps.

Relationships Relationships within the popular group were significantly affected by its exclusivity, prestige, and power.

Status Striving—Popular clique members were sensitive to their social position, both within the grade and within the clique. Maintaining their membership in the popular crowd and at the highest rank within it took concerted effort. Friendships were strongly influenced by underlying status concerns. Less-popular people tried to curry favor with more-popular people in order to improve their standing in the group. They imitated leaders' behavior and supported leaders' opinions to enhance their acceptance and approval. In turn, leaders acted to maintain their own popularity and control by seeking the continuing endorsement of other group members. Actions and friendships, then, were always subtly influenced by the consequences they might have on power and position, making them more self-consciously manipulative.

Loyalty—Several factors undercut the strength of the loyalty bonds that might have developed among members of the popular clique, giving their relationships a fragile quality. First, as Best (1983) noted in the Tent Club, the underlying preoccupation with rank and status created an atmosphere of competition, setting members against each other in their quest to remain accepted and well-regarded. Second, the dynamics through which leaders carved out and maintained their power undercut loyalty. One of the primary ways leaders held dominance was by alternately gracing followers with their favor and then swinging the other clique members against them. Over time, everyone had the opportunity to experience the vicissitudes of this treatment, with its thrill of popularity and its pain of derogation. This shifting treatment prevented potential rival leaders from gaining a toehold of influence at the same time as it reinforced leaders' control over clique followers. Clique members liked and admired, but also feared, their leaders and these people's power to make their lives miserable. Few had the courage to defy the leaders and stand up against them when they or their friends became the butt of teasing and exclusion.[5] They knew that alliance with stigmatized clique members would cast them into the painful position these others occupied. As a result, they learned that the price of loyalty was severe, and that it was safer not to stick up for their friends but to look out for themselves instead. They thus joined with leaders in ridiculing other group members. A third factor weakening the loyalty bond within popular clique relations lay in the means by which clique members were chosen. Inclusion in the clique was determined by group leaders rather than by the general membership, and followers often embraced new members because they were popular with leaders rather than because they, themselves, liked them. As a result, when these individuals were cast into disfavor, as Eder (1995) also noted, other clique members did not jump to their defense. Tracy, a fourth grade girl from the middle level, offered her view of the fickleness of the relationships that characterized the popular people:

> Some of the popular group, they just hang out with those people to be popular and they are not their friends; and if someone is being teased, they will just say in some instances, like, "I don't really care," since she was only in there to be popular, not really to be my friend. And for the popular group, some of the people who are really mean, they don't have that many people to help them out when other people are doing the same thing to them, since they have been so mean to others.

Members of the popular clique might thus find themselves in a group with people that they liked only slightly or not at all.

Stability and Flux—Some members of the popular clique held long-lasting relationships. Constancy among best-friend pairs existed, and connections within smaller subgroups often endured. Like status and position, however, individuals' relationships and membership within the popular clique integrated flux and insecurity with this stability. Popular people changed their friends from time to time, getting sick of hanging out with some people and moving on to others within the group.[6] As one popular fifth grader noted in reflecting on the fluidity of people's friendship patterns, "They move around a lot. Some of them are friends with most of the same people, but most of them are friends with different people." In addition, people moved into and out of the group. Of those exiting, some left to join with new friends, while others were expelled. Any clique member could be thrown out of the group, and this awareness was widespread, although some were more vulnerable than others. Followers were the most easily dislodged, as they had the weakest base of support and least power. They could be cast out if the leaders turned against them and turned everybody else against them, as Best (1983) noted in describing Billy's fall from leadership in the Tent Club. But leaders, too, could be dumped if they acted bad enough. Mark, a popular fifth grader, recalled the expulsion of one clique leader:

MARK: Preston used to be the most popular kid in school but he got too lazy and he took advantage of kids. So kids dumped him.

Q: *That's not so easy, to dump the most popular kid, is it?*

MARK: Yeah. When everybody doesn't like him, it's like, See ya.

Q: *And what makes everyone turn against someone?*

MARK: If they take advantage of you. Like, say, Preston used to always say, like, "Go get me that piece of paper," and if you didn't get that piece of paper you were *uncool* (inflects with over-dramatic flair). People didn't like being *uncool* for not serving somebody. So he got kicked out.

Preston's expulsion was consequential and enduring. By six months later, none of his former friends had taken him back. He had fallen hard, tumbling down past the followers and wannabes into a threesome in the middle ranks. More common than these permanent actions, however, were temporary expulsions. Individuals could be kicked out by their friends and readmitted shortly thereafter. Ryan, a fourth-grade boy, talked about the vicissitudes of people's exits from and reentries into relationships with the popular clique:

> It's happened to me before. I've been kicked out, and some other people. You have to watch what you wear, what you say. It's hard, but you get over it. Like just some days people are in bad moods. Other days, they let you in. So it kind of depends on mood.

Membership in the popular clique, because of its exclusive character, was thus fragile and uncertain.

The Wannabes

The cool people and their accepted followers constituted the ranks of the popular clique. Surrounding them and striving, less successfully, for acceptance were the wannabes to the popular clique.

Composition and Character Wannabes were the people referred to by Taylor, earlier, when he fairly accurately noted that the "cool followers" comprised around 10 percent of the grade. Clique members occasionally included individuals outside of their strict borders into their games or activities. In so doing, they usually invited participation from individuals with a peripheral, or borderline, status. These were people who were not explicitly members of the clique but who hung around the group hoping to be incorporated into activities. They fell below the clique followers, even those who had some friends outside the group, on the stratification hierarchy because the followers were fully accepted group members. Wannabes usually had most of their friends outside of the group, but were partly accepted by some people on the inside. Mr. Clark, a fifth-grade teacher, described their configuration:

> I think a lot of those kids want to be liked by the popular kids, so therefore they are willing to hang out until they are accepted. And then when the group accepts them and lets them in, even if it's for just a while, then they feel good because all of a sudden these popular kids are now their friends. They feel

good because they are getting acknowledged by somebody from that top group. If they are going to widen the group, these are the people they will turn to. They're not really in, but they're not altogether out.

In short, wannabes held the lowest status of any near-clique members.

Attempts at Inclusion In most instances when clique members deigned to play with outsiders, these marginals were readily available. Stacy, a fourth-grade popular girl, described why the pool of borderline people waited to be included:

> The wannabes try to hang around, and try to be in, and try to do stuff that is cool, but they aren't really cool. But they think they are, and if we play with them, they think they'll get cooler, so they're always ready if we want them.

In making efforts to be included, wannabes copied the behavior of the popular people. They imitated their clothing and hair styles, bought the same kind of music, and tried to use the same vocabulary.[7] According to fifth graders, they'd use remarks like, "Hey, man, what's up?" instead of "Hello," or they'd say they were "hanging out" instead of "playing." The thrust of these linguistic efforts was to assert their coolness through a pseudomaturity, to act like teenagers. Several middle-rank third-grade girls secretly mocked the cool wannabe girls because they all adopted a particular mannerism of the leader, that of running her fingers through her hair and shaking her head in a distinctive manner. Every time one of them did this, these other girls would look at each other and try not to laugh, often unsuccessfully. Wannabes also tried to lure popular people into friendship with what Rizzo (1989) has called "friendship bids": overnight or party invitations, material possessions such as sport cards to trade or clothes to borrow, and trips with their family to movies or other entertainment events. For these offerings they received some attention, but it was often short-lived.

Their efforts to be included also resulted in their exhibiting some extreme behavior. They would run and fetch things for popular people, carry their messages to others, and threaten to beat up people who were out of favor with the crowd. Even when they were not being belittled, they acted out and made fools of themselves. In the children's peer culture, such vulnerability was quickly noticed and regarded as a sign of insecurity and weakness.[8] Rather than helping them become accepted, it was taken as a sign of desperation, thrusting them further outside of the group (for a further discussion of these exclusion mechanisms, see Adler and Adler 1995).

Temporary Inclusion   People around the periphery might be called upon by popular people to join their clique activities for a variety of reasons. Boys' play, which usually involved sports, commonly occurred within moderately large groups (Adler, Kless, and Adler 1992; Lever 1976; Thorne 1993). If their clique was too small to accommodate a particular sport, boys often invited outsiders to participate. Ryan, the fourth-grade boy quoted earlier, explained who participated in his clique's activities:

> The more people that you have playing football or basketball or something the better, because then you have more people to pass to, and more people to block, or whatever, so they like to include, if we are playing sports, they like to include more people. But if we're just kind of hanging out, just kind of sitting around and talking, it's just the main people and no borderline ones.

In addition to simply having larger and more differentiated teams, boys often invited marginals to play with them because it was easier to play aggressively against people who were less close friends. In fact, poor treatment of the people who occupied the borderline status seemed fairly common. This involved a complex combination of acceptance and rejection: On the one hand they were more accepted than the total rejects, yet they experienced the bulk of the rejection behavior, as they were the ones who tried to be included, and were alternately welcomed and shunned. Laura, a sixth-grade girl looking back at fifth grade, tried to explain the relation of the borderline tier and their treatment by the rest of the clique:

LAURA: We would pretty much treat them like shit, but they were our friends. We would treat them like shit, but we would be nice to them, and they would always just come back.

Q: They were in the crowd but they were on the margins?

LAURA: Yeah. It kind of just depended on what we wanted. We kind of used them in a way. But we were friends with them, but sometimes we were just like "Pffft" (gestures condescendingly, like she is blowing them off). . . . Just to have somebody to be mean to; that's who we'd be mean to.

Individuals who stood outside the main circle of the group's membership thus filled the important function of defining clique boundaries, as shifting as they were, and of making all fully accepted clique members, no matter what their ranking, appreciate the benefits of their insider status. Clique members usually recognized the positive role these people filled, and although they derided wannabes, they worked to retain their attention.

Buffering the Popular Clique   When they were not playing with the cool kids, the wannabes formed smaller friendship groups of their own. They hung out alone or congregated with each other in circles of two, three, or four people. These were not strong friendship groups, however, as each person thought he or she was better than the rest and belonged with the popular clique. Wannabes also served as a buffer zone, accepting rejects from the top group. Individuals who were discarded by their popular friends could find inclusion there. Miss Moran, the fourth-grade teacher mentioned earlier, offered her observations of the status differentials between the popular clique and the wannabes, and the way the wannabes buffered the popular clique:

Q: When kids fall out of the popular group, what usually happens to them, do the lower groups embrace them?

MISS MORAN: It depends why they fall out. If they fall out because they're popular and having a tiff with somebody else in the popular group, then, boy, they're a hot product in the wannabe and middle groups, like wow. But if they fell out because they're a wannabe, one of the ones trying to fit in, then sometimes they'll fall all the way down and no one will grab them except at the very bottom.

Wannabes accepted the popular rejects to improve

their own status. Most popular rejects maintained at least a few ties to people who were still popular, and connecting themselves to semipopular people might result in their gaining more popularity. Popular people saw right through this transparent strategy. In scoffing at the wannabes, Lauren, a popular third grader, noted, "People that we dump go into the middle, and the wannabes down there all think they are cool because they used to be cool and they are talking to them, but what really happened is they got booted." Accepting rejects diminished wannabes' status further with the people whose acceptance they sought. Yet even though the popular people scoffed at the wannabes from their high perch, when they became the object of exclusion, they valued wannabes' intermediate status. Holding some ties into the popular clique, wannabes were not as far removed from the upper echelons as were members of the middle circles. Mark, the popular fifth-grade boy, discussed the role of the wannabes in his fall from the reentry into popularity:

Q: *When you got kicked out of the cool group, who did you hang out with?*

MARK: I hung out with, like, the wannabes of the cool kids. For, like, a couple of weeks. And then my old friends said, This guy's okay, and they let me back in. And then I was back in the cool group.

Q: *So you didn't go down to the medium kids?*

MARK: No. I knew that if I hung out with the medium kids for too long I was never going to get back into the cool group.

Q: *So the wannabes of the cool kids are higher up than the medium kids?*

MARK: Yeah. Because they're like risking it, they're just enough trying to be cool that they are noticed. And sometimes the cool kids let them in. So they're kind of on the map, the edges.

Middle-Level Friendship Circles

After the popular group and its hangers-on, the main body of each grade fell into the middle rank.

Composition and Character   These were the people who were considered nonpopular, who didn't try to be cool or to be accepted by the cool people.

Size—Constituting approximately half of each grade, this group was large and fairly amorphous, made up of many different subgroups and subtypes. Mrs. Perkins, a fifth-grade teacher, offered her observations of the composition of the middle group:

They're not all one group; they're very diverse. On the strong end, they're very well-adjusted kids, who may be above the popular games, who may not want to get into the teasing; they may not want to get into the power struggles, and sometimes are very stable kids. Then I've got some kids who are just not as socially astute, who don't wear the right clothes, but still [are] well-rounded kids, healthy. And then I'd say you have some computer nerd types who seem to be very socially inept, but not in a bad sense. Just in a kind of dorky sense.

People in the middle rank clustered into small groups of friendship circles. This could range anywhere from pairs of best friends or threesomes, to slightly larger groups. Middle friendship circles rarely got too large, or they tended to develop cliquish tendencies. Nicole, a fourth-grade girl from the middle stratum, described the social clumpings surrounding her:

They're the people that mind their own business, sort of people that get in a group, maybe three to five people. They just stick to that group, don't even attempt to make other friends, and nobody attempts to penetrate into the group, except for just a few exceptions.

Others corroborated this assessment, referring to the middle friendship circles as "just a slop of two- or three-person groups," or as "a couple of people in a parking lot, just all standing together, talking in little groups of three, couple of them are friends."

Internal Stratification—In contrast to the popular clique's strongly tiered ranking, middle friendship circles had only a weak hierarchical system, operating between the different friendship circles rather than within them. The higher-status aggregations might accept and be considered acceptable by the popular group's rejects, such as by Preston, the formerly popular clique leader who tumbled down into the middle range. The intermediate circles minded their own business and played among themselves. The lower middle circles might be just one step above the social isolates. Mark, the popular fifth grader, characterized these latter groups by saying, "These are the kids who have the guts not to just hang out in the sandbox, but are still pretty far down."

Most nonpopular people recognized their middle-level status and accepted it. They shared the realization that they were not the type to be included in the elite circles, offering various accounts to explain this. Some described themselves as too quiet or too shy to be the "popular type," while others described themselves as "the type that other people don't like." If they were ever unsure about this, the popular people made sure to reinforce these perceptions by picking on them and deriding them, both individually and in groups.

Openness—One of the strongest features that differentiated middle friendship circles from the cliques found at the upper end of the status hierarchy, apart from their size, was their willingness to accept people. Whereas popular groups were exclusive, maintaining tight control over their boundaries and keeping important members in and undesirables out, middle friendship groups more readily welcomed people who wanted to join in or play with them. Timmy, a third-grade boy from a middle circle, described how his group accepted outsiders to play:

> Sometimes, a lot of people who really aren't in will get together and form a big game of basketball and they will let anyone come in because they are a lot nicer, so if someone gets ejected from a group, they usually come over. We've had a lot of people from the popular group come over to the unpopular people because they want to play a game and the popular people usually cheat or don't treat them fairly.

Leadership   Another characteristic that differentiated middle friendship circles from cliques was their democratic leadership structure. While cliques had clearly defined leaders and a strongly articulated hierarchy of internal stratification, friendship circles were much more egalitarian. They were not identified by a single core person, no one person led the decisions about what they should do or think, and no leader dominated the delineations of the borders. Mary, a fifth-grade nonpopular girl, talked about the demo-

cratic nature of the leadership structure in the middle circles:

> Usually, someone would just suggest something, and usually we either like it or we, if we don't like it, then somebody else would suggest something else. We don't usually have a person that chooses what we're gonna do. We just all of a sudden choose something and we see if everybody else likes that idea.

Relationships   The friendship bonds in the middle circles were also distinctive from those of the popular clique.

Intimacy—Relationships in these circles were often more intimate and intense than those in the popular or wannabe groups. This was partly due to the small size of these friendship circles and the frequency of members' interactions. Popular people had many more people with whom they regularly socialized, and they tended to regard all members of the clique as their friends. Wannabes had a weak and diffused group that never coalesced, being focused instead around the popular clique. In contrast, members of middle circles had many fewer individuals with whom they interacted. Marty, a fifth-grade nonpopular boy, offered his observations about the difference in friendship relationships between the middle and popular levels:

> I would probably say that if you were a member of the smaller groups that you would have more one-on-one experience, and you would probably get even closer and closer. And if you're in the more popular groups, you probably wouldn't stay with one person for very long, and you'd keep on moving from subgroup to subgroup, because the whole group is larger. They're like groups of twenty or thirty kids.

Loyalty and Trust—The lack of competition for status stratification within the nonpopular circles also affected the character of their relationships. People did not have to be as conscious about who was in better favor, about losing favor, or about getting picked on by their own friends as they did in the popular clique. Consequently, they had a greater degree of loyalty and trust among their friends and felt freer to discuss sensitive issues. Ariana, a nonpopular fourth-grader, talked about the nature of the relationships in her circle:

> I have lots of friends that are not in the popular

group, that are in the middle, so I always knew that there was someone to turn to. With my friends you can always express your feelings and say that this person is really hurting my feelings, and then maybe we will all talk it over. There's no one who is mean in our group, who thinks she's better than the rest of us or who lords it over all of us. So we know we can really count on each other, like if anyone makes fun of us, we know that our friends will always stick up for us.[9]

Stability and Flux—Like the popular cliques, middle friendship circles exhibited both turnover and constancy in their relationships and membership. Some people remained in their groups or friendships over long periods. They bonded tightly with friends, spent considerable time at school, home, and recreational activities together, and developed close relational ties. Others developed an orbit surrounding a certain group that they moved into and out of over a period of time. Adam, a fifth-grade boy, described the ebb and flow of his relationship with his core middle friendship group:

Q: *So would you say that these groups are fairly stable, or that this kind of breaking off and re-forming is more common?*

ADAM: I would say it's in between. I have gone from together for two years, broken up for a week, together for two days, broken up for three weeks, over and over.

Q: *And when you get back together, do you go back to the same people or do you go into another group?*

ADAM: Same people.

Miss Moran, the fourth-grade teacher, summed up the pattern of stability and flux among the people in the middle circles she observed with this remark:

> There's a lot of going back and forth among the group, like for instance one week two people do something and the next week another two people will do something out of the same group. But it doesn't seem to be a big deal, like who's with who this week. People shift around more comfortably in the middle range, but also you've got your lasting friendships too. You've got some friends who are just good friends. They spend the weekend together, hang out together.

Individuals had a greater degree of social security, however, because there were not the kind of capri-

cious, demanding leaders ready to expel them from the group. People left middle circles because they got into fights with other people in the group, or because they did not want to do what others wanted to do. Sometimes two people would gang up on one, leaving that person isolated. Other times a larger group would get fed up with someone. Nick, a fifth-grade boy from a middle circle, described the collective group dynamics associated with people's exit from such groups:

Q: *So one could get kicked out of a group like that?*

NICK: Right, but only if most of the people got agreement from each other. They could use persuasion, they could use insults, they could use reasons why the other people would want that person kicked out. They could make up stories, which I've seen a lot, about the other person, they could spread rumors, and so forth. But what they can't do, which the popular people do, is to have one person decide that you're uncool and just kick you out on his own.

Social Isolates

Past the ranks of the middle circles, the small groups of people who had two or three friends, were those individuals who had no real friends. These loners, drifters, "dweebs," and "nerds" occupied the bottom stratum of the grade, and stuck out in everyone's view. Kless (1992) labeled these people pariahs while Eder (1995) referred to them as isolates and Best (1983) called them losers.

Composition and Character Other kids noticed the social isolates and clearly differentiated them from the middle people at the low end of the acceptable realm. These were the people who wandered around the playground at recess, making up a game by themselves, talking to an adult playground aide, or just hanging around the sidelines. At lunch they ate by themselves, as nobody wanted to sit with them. When it came time to form into groups they were chronically left out. When asked to reflect on the reasons for people's isolation, Tracy, a middle-rank fourth-grade girl, and Adam, a middle-rank fifth-grade boy, offered these independent observations:

TRACY: There are some kids who just go outside and try to hang around people, but they don't really fit in with them, so they just stay there but not talk.

ADAM: They're different. It's a lot like segregation. If you're different, you go off and sit alone.

Tracy's and Adam's remarks indicate that people perceived these individuals as apart from the rest of the grade, mostly because of something inherent in their own nature.[10] They were different; they did not fit in with the others. Something about the way they looked or the way they acted deviated from the norm.

While the composition of the social isolates might vary, the number of people in this category held relatively constant. Mr. Goodwin, a fourth-grade teacher, reflected on the size of this group:

Q: In thinking of the group of people at the bottom, how many would there be of these?

MR. GOODWIN: Thinking in terms of every year, I would say, total, in the last five years, there's probably twelve or thirteen of those kids. So out of the 125 or so students I have had, that's about 10 percent. I don't know. There's regular nerds and then there's kids who are real behavioral problems, who frighten the other kids. They're the ones who're really way out there, just socially not fitting in.[11]

The Spiral of Rejection   Although they spent considerable time alone, social isolates longed to be included in the interaction and play of their classmates. From time to time they would make attempts to join in various conversations and games.

Limited Acceptance—These efforts occasionally yielded some success, they being taken into activities, tolerated or somewhat included in the lunchroom, or made part of a collective action strategy. Ryan, the popular fourth-grade boy discussed earlier, explained the way people without friends could get included in the activities of the popular group:

> There are some people who have no friends, or maybe sometimes one or two, and sometimes they just sit down and read in the classroom or sit outside and kind of don't do much. But sometimes even if we don't like the person, sometimes the really unpopular kids get included just because they're needed in a game, and say six people are needed and maybe we have five people. They want one more people to make teams even, then they can ask someone who is just sitting around if they want to do something.

In a case like this, the added people would feel included for the duration of the game. Timmy, the middle-rank third grader, talked about a friend of his who was very isolated. He discussed his friend's attempts to be included in interaction with others:

Q: Does he try to be included in groups?

TIMMY: Yeah, he does that a lot, and he usually gets included, except he's not really part of it, like if someone's having a conversation with someone, he tries to be a part of it, but he doesn't really know anything about it, so he's not part of the whole thing. I think that's what makes him feel lonely because he's not part of [being] with anyone, he's not part of, like, the group of kids, really.

Rejection and Degradation—More often, however, isolates' attempts at inclusion were unsuccessful. When they summoned the nerve to ask other people if they could join them in play, they would be laughed at and treated poorly. People made sport out of teasing them and picking on them. While popular leaders degraded their followers, followers degraded the wannabes, and wannabes degraded the middle people, everyone could safely offset their own humiliation by passing it on to individuals at the lowest stratum. No one came to these individuals' defense, and everyone could unite in feeling superior to them. People called them names, started fights with them, made fun of their clothing and appearance, and talked about them as having "cooties" (Thorne 1993). People rebuffed those labeled as losers from play with hardly a care for their feelings. Terry, the fourth-grade middle-level boy, discussed the way loners were rejected cruelly by groups of people, particularly those at the popular rank:

> At recess they [isolates] maybe just go out and talk or something to other people, but they don't really play games or anything. They try to, but some people don't let 'em. Sometimes people say, just to be mean, that the game is full, when there's only five people or ten people, but then they let other people in after.

Withdrawal and Isolation—After a series of such encounters, the potential benefit of social interaction tended to no longer seem worth the risk of degradation and humiliation. Mary, the middle-level fifth-grade girl discussed earlier, offered her observation of what frequently happened when social isolates made repeated unsuccessful attempts to be included with others:

Q: And do people at the bottom ever try to get in with other friendship groups?

MARY: Once or twice, and then the people shatter their self-confidence so they don't try again.

Such encounters often led loners to retire further into seclusion and cease interacting with people. They ate lunch by themselves every day, often stayed inside at recess, and went home right after school. People who experienced prolonged or severe isolation sometimes invoked the ultimate recourse: They transferred to another school.

Relationships While isolates spent much of their time alone, they drifted in and out of some relationships and sought out people in lesser positions they could more safely befriend.

Mutual Rejection—Most of the people in the bottom stratum were aware of the presence of other social isolates. These individuals could be found drifting by themselves in the playground or being taunted and teased by more socially successful people. When people clumped together into groups for play, the loners were left hanging around the edges. In many cases, however, rather than forming their own groups, isolates' reaction to others in similar situations was mutual rejection. They were no more eager to befriend these outcasts than were others in the class. Meredith, a third-grade social isolate, expressed her lack of interest in her social peers:

Q: So what might you do then at recess?

MEREDITH: Well, sometimes I look at how people are playing, it makes me feel good. Sometimes I just play a simple game by myself. Just games by myself that I make up.

Q: Are there other kids that are also playing by themselves?

MEREDITH: Well, I have to say there're sure to be, but very little. A very little group of them.

Q: So, do you ever play with any of them?

MEREDITH: No, not really.

Q: How come? You don't like them?

MEREDITH: Sort of that. There's different reasons.

Miss Moran, the fourth-grade teacher, explained why she thought social outcasts shunned each other:

Q: Is it a stigma to be friends with another person down there?

MISS MORAN: Yeah. Well, for instance, if I were to say, "Okay, make groups," and there's two or three of them standing around, and they have to be in a group with each other, it's obvious to everyone that those are the leftovers. And some of them are knowledgeable enough to not want to be in that situation, although a few seem so out of it that they are oblivious.

Desperation Friendships—Despite the potential stigma, there came a time when social isolates got desperate and made friends. They could no longer stand the loneliness and boredom, and they overcame their feelings of distaste for other pariahs. They managed to put up with annoying behavior and overlook the teasing of high-status people, even if it increased when they joined with other isolates. Tracy, the fourth-grade middle-level girl, described how some loners joined together:

TRACY: Eventually some of them will meet someone else that they kind of like, and then they will start hanging out with them, and then after about half the year it will become a little group of two or three people.

Q: So people don't always stay by themselves forever?

TRACY: Right, eventually some of them find someone, or they just get so lonely they force themselves to be with someone.

Mrs. Perkins, the fifth-grade teacher, gave her view of how social isolates overcame their aversion to being friendly and came to form relationships:

> Their friendships are based on availability, not on any commonality. I mean the commonality, I guess, is that they're social outcasts. Some kids don't want to accept that. They eventually do accept it and I think they're happier when they finally do accept that and say, Okay, I've got a friend here, even though I know what everyone thinks of this friend.

Descended Friendships—Despite their stigmatized status in the peer social hierarchy, most individuals were able to turn somewhere, even if it was not in their school or in their grade, to find companionship.

Having some friend, even if that person was of lower status, was critical. Otherwise isolates spent all their time after school and on weekends watching television, playing video games, reading books, participating in organized afterschool activities, and hanging around with their parents. Forming friendships with younger people was easier for social isolates, because they were often able to leave the stigma of their outcast status behind and adopt a high status in a new school or neighborhood crowd on the basis of their advanced age and grade. Roger, a severely isolated third grader, described his most steady companion:

> Mostly I play with my next door neighbor, Eric; he's two years old. I really help out with him, cause his dad's usually at work, and his mom has arthritis. So when I come over it's a big help for them. They go run errands. Mostly Eric wants me to come along. They say it's okay because they could get more done when they're doing errands when I'm around. Like, I take care of Eric, tell him not to take the things off the shelf, it helps them a lot. 'Cause if he sees something when they're not looking, then they have to go there and put it back, and then they have to find the area again, and he does it again, a lot of junk. So I help out a lot.

Roger was able to find a regular playmate by going outside of both his school's status system and his age system. When pariahs made inroads into new crowds, their acceptance was sometimes short-lived, however, as news travelled, and their outside friends discovered their pariah status. This often resulted in their being dropped.

THE IDENTITY HIERARCHY

People's location at the various levels of the social stratification hierarchy led them to vastly dissimilar interactional experiences. The size of their group, the type and intensity of its activities, the nature of the relationships within it, and its relative super/subordination to other groups were all colored by this ranking system. These features led people to develop feelings about themselves, or self-concepts, that were anchored in their social-relational placement. This resulted in a second form of stratification: the identity hierarchy.

The Popular Clique

Individuals in the elite, leader stratum of the popular clique sat atop the identity hierarchy. They compared other people unfavorably with themselves, regarded their own activities as the most exciting and fun, and believed that everybody was envious of them. They basked in the attention they received from the rest of the grade, and were proud to think that they could convince anyone they wanted to follow them or to join their group. They considered their interest a prize bestowed on those lower than them, to be received with eagerness. Some people believed that cool leaders had the most positive self-identity merely by virtue of their position, although Eder (1995) has noted that those in her study were also frequently disliked. Mary, the fifth-grade middle-level girl, expressed this relational viewpoint:

> Well, I think that with the leaders of the big group, they usually have the most self-esteem because there's no one else to make fun of them; there's no one else for them to be competing with unless there's another person that's a leader, and they can really do anything that they want, so I think they have the most self-esteem.

Yet other members of the group did not share this positive identity. Followers suffered through their subordination to the leaders, by being bossed around, derided, and stigmatized, and by frequently worrying about losing their position in the group. Despite how they presented themselves to outsiders, Blake, the popular fifth-grade boy, noted that "the people in the top group are insecure also, especially the followers, because you get made fun of, then your self-esteem goes." Mr. Clark, the fifth-grade teacher, explained why this came back to affect the self-concepts of all members of the popular group:

> Your self-esteem, the day-to-day worries about self-esteem, are going to be much more pronounced with the popular group, even if you're on the top. You're going to have setbacks, and your popularity's such a big issue that you're always feeling either attacked or you're feeling on top of things.

Middle Friendship Circles

After those in the popular clique, members of the middle friendship circles had the most positive self-identities, lacking both the social pretensions and the status insecurities plaguing the popular clique members. Individuals in the middle group generally felt good about themselves. While they had to endure status derogation from popular clique members, they derived significant security from the loyalty of their friends. They did not have to worry about coming in to school and finding that all their friends had been on the phone the night before and had decided that they were out of favor. They could trust their friends to stick up for them and not betray them. They knew that fights might occur, but that they would be over, and that their friends would still be faithful to them. Mary, the fifth-grade middle-level girl, talked about the feelings of confidence she derived from the relationships within her group:

> I would rather be in my own circle of friends and be, everyone's nice and everything, instead of having to deal with what the leader says and being bossed around, having to do what they say and do to be in that group. It makes me feel like I am worth something, instead of always having to sell myself to be popular.

People in the middle level held many shared views about members of the other strata. There was some degree of envy towards the popular clique, both for the abundance of their friends and the excitement of their activities, yet their feelings towards them were predominantly negative. They often noted the way the cool people acted as though they were superior, and referred to them as having "swelled heads" and "big egos," and as being "full of themselves." As Eder (1995) also observed, they rejected the popular people's attitude of superiority toward them. Terry, a fourth-grade middle-rank boy, offered his views of the popular crowd:

Q: What do you think of the kids that think they're cool?

TERRY: Mostly they're just jerks.

Q: Why is that?

TERRY: 'Cause they treat other kids a lot more mean, they pick on kids, pick on little kids, they screw up loads. They spray paint on the walls and stuff. They like to get in trouble.

Middle people reserved their harsher criticism for the wannabes, however. As did the popular people,

they regarded the wannabes as weak and insecure. They watched as the wannabes unsuccessfully imitated the popular people. Ariana, the fourth-grade girl noted earlier, offered a commonly held negative view of the wannabes:

Q: What do the middle people tend to think about the wannabes?

ARIANA: Well, from my experience, we'd just laugh. We'd laugh at how they are being dragged around by other people.

Q: They are making fools of themselves for people?

ARIANA: Right. How they will go to any extent to be with those people. What makes them happy? All they want is to be with those people. But they never get the job, 'cause they always get shoved out. There's no sense of, there's nobody being themselves.

Thus, while members of middle friendship circles suffered from being ridiculed by the popular people, they enjoyed an autonomy that the status-seeking wannabes lacked. Individuals at the middle rank derived a great deal of security and self-esteem from the loyalty of their friends. They might not have had the status and excitement of the large popular group membership and the most privileged activities, but their relationships flourished because they were internally focused and supportive, and their identities were strong.

Wannabes

Although the wannabes ranked higher on the status hierarchy than the people from the middle rank, they paid a high price for it in self-esteem. The wannabes' position in the social status system was unique. They were defined not by their own social group, but by their relation to a group to which they only marginally belonged. They were not members of the popular clique, yet neither were they independent of it. They forged their behavior, attitudes, and relationships by fervently looking up to the clique above them, hoping for a trickle-down of attention that would draw them into greater favor. They desperately aspired to be accepted by people who toyed with them, using them for their own benefit. They suffered by always desiring something that they never really attained, enduring the frustration of experiencing it temporarily only to lose it again. They knew that the people they wanted as friends did not want them, and mocked, teased, and derided them. Scott, a fourth-grade wannabe, explained the contradictory treatment he experienced from the popular people:

> With the popular group you get to do more stuff, you get to have more play, you get to have more fun at recess, you get to play with all the people that are kind of up on theirselves, have big egos, and really think they're great. You play with them but they don't—in football they never pass to you, and in basketball they never really pass to you, so there're advantages to being in the popular group but there's a lot of disadvantages to being in the popular group.

But the wannabes did not have secure membership in their own friendship circles to use as a safety net. If they were to let go of their clutch onto the popular crowd, they knew that they might tumble into the isolate rank. They therefore clung to the liminality of the in-between, striving for acceptance but never fitting in. Mr. Goodwin, the fourth-grade teacher, analyzed the way this made them feel:

> The ones who are really feeling the pain are the ones who're hanging onto this popular group, but I think they're the ones who are really low in self-esteem. They don't seem to enjoy anything for the sake of it, they're just kind of analyzing things from the outside. And therefore, if they're not part of the group, they're trying to figure out what's wrong with them. . . . I guess the point I'm really trying to make is that there's that small group of kids who don't fit in either group; they're not happy. They're not happy with themselves, they're not happy with where they are, and they try so hard. . . . I would say they have some social problems, identification problems. They don't know who they are really yet, or where they want to be.

Wannabes' intense status aspirations thus yielded them intense status insecurity. They suffered the continual anguish of domination and exclusion at the hands of the popular clique. They lacked the loyalty and trust of the true friendships found in the middle circles. Their identities were stronger than that of an isolate only by virtue of the companionship and social activities in which they were able to engage, which gave them some feeling of self-worth.

Social Isolates

At the bottom of the status hierarchy, isolates were also at the bottom of the identity hierarchy. Most isolates recognized the effects of their low social status on their ability to form relationships and be included in social activities. Although they tried not to think that there was something wrong with them, their wonder about themselves sometimes surfaced. Mr. Clark, the fifth-grade teacher, expressed his concerns about the feelings and identities of the social isolates:

> I think some who are down there, who are kind of nice kids, are feeling quite a bit of pain. They probably sit there now and then and say, What's wrong with me? Why does no one . . . I know where I am, I'm way down here with these weird kids. And I think there's some pain there. I've asked myself this question, Why are these kids down there, and I'm sure that they probably do too.

Unlike people in the other three strata, who all had some group that they disdained, whether higher or lower, the pariahs held contempt for no group. Their feelings about the people in the other groups fell into one of two categories: envy and dislike. Many isolates envied the social standing and relationships accompanying location in the higher strata. They looked longingly at the activities of the popular crowd and wished they were a part of it. Rudy, the third-grade isolate, expressed his feelings about the cool kids:

RUDY: They do a lot of cool things at recess. They dig in the sandbox, they always get in a long group of, like a lot of bunch of kids, like in different grade classes, but then they break up to another group of kids.

Q: *So you think that would be better to be in a bigger group of kids?*

RUDY: Well, it would be more comfortable, for me anyways.

Social isolates' exclusion from nearly all social activities, coupled with the extreme degradation they suffered at the hands of the popular and wannabe crowds, left them with the lowest sense of self-worth. Social isolates' exclusion, rejection, ostracism, and limited scope of activities carried a heavy toll on their feelings about themselves. They tried to deceive themselves into thinking they had friends or that they were accepted, but they could only sustain this image for so long. They occasionally tried to manage their stigma by ignoring it, but they ultimately had a hard time disguising their pariah status, and had to accept their disvalued identity.

CONCLUSION

Elementary school children's social experiences are strongly affected by the location of their friendship group along the continuum of status and popularity. Those who attain membership in the elite popular clique enjoy the benefits of a more expansive social life and a superior position relative to other crowds, but they pay for this with a greater anxiety about their place within the group. Wannabes, forming the periphery around the popular crowd, have the opportunity to participate in some popular-group activities and thus derive a measure of reflected status, but they never attain membership in the group that they fervently seek. Most people fall into the largest category, composed of smaller, mid-level friendship circles that garner low prestige and suffer degradation from the popular people, but whose members care less about their social ranking and enjoy secure relationships with friends. At the bottom of the grade are the social isolates, combining pariah social status with a virtual lack of viable peer friendships. The identity stratification of the groups is thus somewhat different from the hierarchical arrangement based on status; the top and bottom strata remain constant but the positions of the middle rank and wannabes are reversed. Members of middle circles, by virtue of the loyalty and support they derive from their strong friendship relations with their peers, hold more positive self-concepts than the higher-status wannabes, despite the latters' circulation within the broader confines of the popular clique.

While many differences have been noted between the culture and experiences of preadolescent girls and boys (Best 1983; Eder 1995; Fine 1987; Goodwin 1990; Lever 1976; Thorne 1993), the stratification of their peer societies into typological groups and the interactional dynamics both within and among these groups appear to be fairly consistent for members of both genders. Preadolescent boys' and girls' social worlds are thus different in some ways similar in

others. While we have noted that boys and girls stratify themselves in popularity according to different factors (Adler, Kless, and Adler 1992), there is more similarity to the friendship structures and interactions across gender than up and down the status hierarchy. Boys and girls are thus both competitive and cooperative, hierarchical and leveling, and they compose their peer societies into stratified groups that are fundamentally comparable.

This research asserts the importance of social position to identity. A question raised, however, concerns the precise nature of the relationship between social position and identity. Our data suggest that the hierarchical ordering based on popularity and status is not strictly replicated in the identity arena. This varies from the direct stratification of status ranking and self-esteem found by sociologists who have studied the prestige hierarchy of occupations (Hodge, Siegel, and Rossi 1964) and the prestige hierarchy of ethnic and racial groups (Bogardus 1959). In addition, most social psychologists, as Rosenberg (1981, p. 603) has noted, have "tended to take it for granted that those ranking lower in the various status hierarchies would have lower self-esteem than the more favored members of society."

The structural-relational hierarchy of identity inferred by our data is more complex than this, as it is grounded in two complementary elements, *status* and *relationship.* Status, the first dimension, is composed of four features: a pure *rank-orientation,* based on prestige, recognition, and visibility; an *attractiveness* component tied to popularity and desirability; a *power and dominance* feature embodying the ability to ridicule or pick on others while remaining safe from such degradation; and *leadership,* the ability to influence and have one's opinions accepted by others. The second dimension, relationship, is also defined by four component features: *camaraderie,* the freedom from loneliness that comes with having friends; *loyalty,* the degree of trust and allegiance in those friendships; *security,* or the stability and certainty of one's membership in the group; and *role in group,* involving one's core centrality versus marginality or peripherality in intragroup relations. Together, these two elements combine to stratify groups and their members along the identity hierarchy, as Table 1 illustrates.

Table 1 A Hierarchy of Group Identity

	Status	Relationship
Popular	+	−+
Middle	−	+
Wannabe	−+	−
Isolate	− −	− −

The necessity of relational criteria in addition to those of pure status for understanding the identity hierarchy illustrates the need for integrating the perspectives of the processual and structural branches of symbolic interactionism. The processual approach focuses on the social situation as the context in which identities are interactionally negotiated, conceiving identity as situated, emergent, and reciprocal (Becker 1964; Blumer 1969; Glaser and Strauss 1965; Stone 1962; Strauss 1978). The structural interactionists emphasize identities as internalized roles, behavioral expectations associated with a position or status and thereby more directly tied to the social structure (Burke and Tully 1977; McCall and Simmons 1966; Stryker 1980). The importance of status elements to identity reifies the structuralists' concern with individuals' self-conceptions as based on social position and connected to social structure. The relational elements of identity are rooted in the emergence and negotiation of individuals' reciprocal friendship relations, thus evoking an interactional base in the social situation. Yet children's definitions and evaluations of self do not arise out of a combined patchwork of structural and processual influences, but are firmly grounded in a more integrated *structural-relational* foundation. This foundation is rooted in what Simmel (1950) considered the key element, or level, of analysis necessary to understanding society: "sociation," the crystallized interactions that bind groups of people together and at the same time distinguish them from each other. The crystallized interactions that repeatedly characterize children's interactions both within and between groups are what mark the groups' character, distinguish them in relation to one another, and set the members' identities. This includes such patterned interactions as the repeated exclusion of wannabes by the popular clique members, the failures by the social isolates to find acceptance with any group, and the

nonhierarchical, leaderless character of the middle friendship circles. This structural-relational identity rooting shows us that both processual and structural interactionists may have drifted too far from the critical center in their focus on negotiated interaction and social structure. These theoretical tensions may best be resolved by searching for the confluence of the two approaches at the Simmelian level of sociation rather than by focusing on their distinctiveness.

While the research on adolescent social typologization and stratification primarily depicts junior high and high school peer culture as divided into a plethora of groups focused around diverse substantive interests (Canaan 1987; Eckert 1989; Eder 1995), this research supports the more limited, unidimensional group differentiation suggested by Best (1983), Kless (1992), and Thorne (1993) for the elementary, preadolescent peer society. Future research could benefit from addressing the change in group typologization as children move from preadolescent to adolescent society and the factors primarily responsible for that transformation. Specific factors to consider include such possibilities as the increased size of junior high and high schools over elementary schools, the transition from the elementary school homeroom structure to the departmentalization of junior high and high school classes, and the role of the age and maturity of the populations.

This research was limited by its white, middle-class subject base. It may well be that race and class variables significantly affect the character of group typologization and stratification, injecting elements from the larger, adult society into the childhood model, or that the different ages of maturity characteristic of different population groups might affect the timing of the shift from the simpler to the more intricate model. Future research examining the stratification of children's social groups in populations with a broader or more comparative range of these demographic characteristics might help to answer some of these questions.

NOTES

We would like to thank the editors and reviewers of this article for helpful comments on earlier drafts.

1. For a further discussion of methodological, epistemological, and ethical issues associated with researching in the parental role, see Adler and Adler (1996).

2. On the basis of our participant-observation, we selected the theme of the article, developed our understandings of children's behavior, constructed a preliminary outline of the article, and forged a rough, unstructured interview guide.

3. Kless (1992) noted only three clear groups: the leading crowd, the middlers, and the pariahs, failing to distinguish a wannabe cluster. This may be due to the larger size, greater diversity, and more variable classroom structure of the schools our subjects attended. For schools with a population of under eighty students per grade (such as Kless studied), that stratum tended to disappear, being replaced with only scattered individuals or not replaced at all.

4. Complicating and augmenting this typology of stratification were overlaps and movement between the ranks. Some people straddled ranks, occupying a gray zone between the popular, wannabe, or middle levels with friends in each, or drifting between isolation and a friend or two. Others aspired to and saw themselves in ranks where they were not fully accepted, commonly hanging out on the borders of the popular crowd, wanting to be accepted but achieving only sporadic success. Still others were in flux between ranks, having been kicked out of their group and searching to reestablish themselves, or temporarily drifting on their own, hoping to be taken back by their former friends.

5. Eder (1995) specifically points out that this dynamic is common to both boys' and girls' subcultures.

6. As Rizzo (1989) noted, however, people were more likely to be closer friends with people in their class.

7. Eder (1995) also observed that nonathletes who tried to imitate the dress of popular athletes were often viewed negatively.

8. Eder (1995) has remarked upon the prevalence of insecurity-based behavior in this age group generally.

9. Youniss and Smollar (1985) have noted that friendship choices based on intimacy and openness, rather than popularity, do not become more widespread until adolescence.

10. As Eder (1995) also noted, people from lower socioeconomic strata and minority groups were disproportionately represented in this position.

11. This number is consistent with the relative number of isolates Hallinan (1979) observed in the elementary schools she studied.

REFERENCES

Adler, Patricia A., and Peter Adler. 1996. "Parent-as-Researcher: The Politics of Researching in the Personal Life." *Qualitative Sociology* 19(1):35–58.

———. 1995. "Dynamics of Inclusion and Exclusion in Preadolescent Cliques." *Social Psychology Quarterly* 58(3):145–162.

———. 1987. *Membership Roles in Field Research.* Newbury Park, CA: Sage.

Adler, Patricia A., Steven J. Kless, and Peter Adler. 1992. "Socialization to Gender Roles: Popularity Among Elementary School Boys and Girls." *Sociology of Education* 65:169–187.

Becker, Howard S. 1964. "Personal Change in Adult Life." *Sociometry* 27:40–53.

Becker, Howard, and Blanche Geer. 1960. "The Analysis of Qualitative Field Data." Pp. 652–660 in *Human Organization Research,* edited by Richard Adams and Jack Preiss. Homewood, IL: Dorsey.

Best, Raphaela. 1983. *We've All Got Scars.* Bloomington, IN: Indiana University Press.

Biernacki, Patrick, and Dan Waldorf. 1981. "Snowball Sampling." *Sociological Research and Methods* 10:141–163.

Blumer, Herbert. 1969. *Symbolic Interactionism: Perspective and Method.* Englewood Cliffs, NJ: Prentice-Hall.

Bogardus, E. S. 1959. "Race Reactions by Sexes." *Sociology and Social Research* 43:439–441.

Brown, B. Bradford, and Mary Jane Lohr. 1987. "Peer-Group Affiliation and Adolescent Self-Esteem: An Integration of Ego-Identity and Symbolic-Interaction Theories." *Journal of Personality and Social Psychology* 52:47–55.

Burke, Peter J., and J. Tully. 1977. "The Measurement of Role-Identities." *Social Forces* 55:881–897.

Canaan, Joyce. 1987. "A Comparative Analysis of American Suburban Middle Class, Middle School and High School Teenage Cliques." Pp. 385–406 in *Interpretive Ethnography of Education,* edited by George Spindler and Louise Spindler, Hillsdale, NJ: Lawrence Erlbaum.

Cohen, Jere. 1979. "High School Subcultures and the Adult World." *Adolescence* 14:491–502.

Coleman, James S. 1961. *The Adolescent Society.* New York: Free Press.

Cooley, Charles H. 1902. *Human Nature and Social Order.* New York: Scribner's.

Cusik, Phillip A. 1973. *Inside High School.* New York: Holt, Rinehart, and Winston.

Denzin, Norman K. 1989. *The Research Act.* 3rd. ed. Englewood Cliffs, NJ: Prentice-Hall.

Eckert, Penelope. 1989. *Jocks and Burnouts.* New York: Teachers College Press.

Eder, Donna. 1995. *School Talk: Gender and Adolescent Culture.* New Brunswick, NJ: Rutgers University Press.

Epstein, S. 1973. "The Self Concept Revisited or a Theory of a Theory." *American Psychologist* 28:404–416.

Everhart, Robert B. 1983. *Reading, Writing, and Resistance.* Boston: Routledge Kegan Paul.

Fine, Gary Alan. 1987. *With the Boys.* Chicago: University of Chicago Press.

Fine, Gary Alan, and Kent L. Sandstrom. 1988. *Knowing Children.* Newbury Park, CA: Sage.

Foote, Nelson N. 1951. "Identification as the Basis for a Theory of Motivation." *American Sociological Review* 26:14–21.

Gecas, Victor. 1982. "The Self-Concept." *Annual Review of Sociology* 8:1–33.

Glaser, Barney G., and Anselm L. Strauss. 1967. *The Discovery of Grounded Theory.* Chicago: Aldine.

———. 1965. *Awareness of Dying.* Chicago: Aldine.

Goffman, Erving. 1959. *The Presentation of Self in Everyday Life.* Garden City, NY: Doubleday.

Goodwin, Marjorie H. 1990. *He-Said-She-Said.* Bloomington, IN: Indiana University Press.

Hallinan, Maureen. 1979. "Structural Effects on Children's Friendships and Cliques." *Social Psychology Quarterly* 42:43–54.

Hodge, R. W., P. M. Siegel, and P. H. Rossi. 1964. "Occupational Prestige in the U.S." *American Journal of Sociology* 70:286–302.

Hollingshead, August B. 1949. *Elmtown's Youth.* New York: Wiley.

Hughes, Everett. 1971. *The Sociological Eye.* Boston: Little, Brown.

Ianni, Francis A. J. 1989. *The Search for Structure: A Report on American Youth Today.* New York: Free Press.

James, William. 1890. *Principles of Psychology,* 2 Vols. New York: Henry Holt.

Kinney, David A. 1993. "From Nerds to Normals: The Recovery of Identity Among Adolescents from Middle School to High School." *Sociology of Education* 66:21–40.

Kless, Steven J. 1992. "The Attainment of Peer Status: Gender and Power Relationships in the Elementary School." Pp. 115–148 in *Sociological Studies of Child Development,* Vol. 5, edited by Patricia A. Adler and Peter Adler. Greenwich, CT: JAI.

Larkin, Ralph W. 1979. *Suburban Youth in Cultural Crisis.* New York: Oxford University Press.

Lesko, Nancy. 1988. *Symbolizing Society: Stories, Rites, and Structure in a Catholic High School.* Philadelphia: Falmer.

Lever, Janet. 1976. "Sex Differences in the Games Children Play." *Social Problems* 23:478–87.

Lightfoot, Sara Lawrence. 1983. *The Good High School: Portraits of Character and Culture.* New York: Basic.

Lindesmith, Alfred R., and Anselm L. Strauss. 1956. *Social Psychology.* New York: Holt, Rinehart and Winston.

McCall, George J., and Jerry L. Simmons. 1966. *Identities and Interactions.* New York: Free Press.

Mead, George H. 1934. *Mind, Self and Society.* Chicago: University of Chicago Press.

Rizzo, Thomas A. 1989. *Friendship Development Among Children in School.* Norwood, NJ: Ablex.

Robinson, Dawn T., and Lynn Smith-Lovin. 1992. "Selective Interaction as a Strategy for Identity Maintenance: An Affect Control Model." *Social Psychology Quarterly* 55:12–28.

Rosenberg, Morris. 1981. "The Self-Concept: Social Product and Social Force." Pp. 591–624 in *Social Psychology,* edited by Morris Rosenberg and Ralph H. Turner. New York: Basic.

———. 1979. *Conceiving the Self.* New York: Basic.

Schwartz, Gary. 1987. *Beyond Conformity or Rebellion: Youth and Authority in America.* Chicago: University of Chicago Press.

Schwartz, Gary, and Don Merten. 1967. "The Language of Adolescence: An Anthropological Approach to the Youth Culture." *American Journal of Sociology* 72:453–468.

Schwendinger, Herman, and Julia Schwendinger. 1985. *Adolescent Subcultures and Delinquency.* New York: Praeger.

Simmel, Georg. 1950. *The Sociology of Georg Simmel,* translated and edited by Kurt H. Wolff. New York: Free Press.

Snow, David, and Leon Anderson. 1987. "Identity Work Among the Homeless: The Verbal Construction and Avowal of Personal Identities." *American Journal of Sociology* 92:1336–1371.

Snyder, Eldon E. 1972. "High School Students' Perceptions of Prestige Criteria." *Adolescence* 6:129–136.

Stone, Gregory P. 1962. "Appearance and the Self." Pp. 86–118 in *Human Behavior and Social Processes,* edited by Arnold Rose. Boston: Houghton Mifflin.

Strauss, Anselm L. 1978. *Negotiations: Varieties, Contexts, Processes, and Social Order.* San Francisco: Jossey-Bass.

Stryker, Sheldon. 1980. *Symbolic Interaction: A Social Structural Version.* Menlo Park, CA: Cummings.

———. 1968. "Identity Salience and Role Performance." *Journal of Marriage and the Family* 4:558–564.

Thomas, W. I. 1923. *The Unadjusted Girl.* Boston: Little, Brown.

Thorne, Barrie. 1993. *Gender Play.* New Brunswick, NJ: Rutgers University Press.

Turner, Ralph H. 1976. "The Real Self: From Institution to Impulse." *American Journal of Sociology* 81:989–1016.

———. 1968. "The Self-Conception in Social Interaction." Pp. 93–106 in *The Self in Social Action,* edited by C. Gordon and K. Gergen. New York: Wiley.

———. 1956. "Role Taking, Role Standpoint, and Reference Group Behavior." *American Journal of Sociology* 61:316–328.

Weinstein, Eugene. 1969. "The Development of Interpersonal Competence." Pp. 753–775 in *Handbook of Socialization Theory and Research,* edited by D. Goslin. Chicago: Rand McNally.

Weis, Joseph G. 1974. "Styles of Middle-Class Adolescent Drug Use." *Pacific Sociological Review* 17:251–286.

Willis, Paul. 1981. *Learning to Labour.* New York: Columbia University Press.

Wulff, Helena. 1988. *Twenty Girls: Growing Up, Ethnicity, and Excitement in a South London Microculture.* Stockholm Studies in Social Anthropology, No. 21. Stockholm: University of Stockholm.

Youniss, J., and J. Smollar. 1985. *Adolescent Relations with Mothers, Fathers and Friends.* Chicago: University of Chicago Press.

38 | MANAGING AGING IN YOUNG ADULTHOOD
The "Aging" Table Dancer
Carol Rambo Ronai

According to several strip bar owners and other bar personnel in a large metropolitan area in the Southwest where this study was conducted, strip-tease dancers are getting old at a younger age. Studies conducted well over a decade ago (Boles and Garbin 1974a, 1974b, 1974c; Carey, Petersen, and Sharpe 1974; Gonos 1976; McCaghy and Skipper 1969, 1972; Salutin 1971; Skipper and McCaghy 1970, 1971, 1978) report a median age of 23. Those interviewed for this study consider the average age to be 19 or 20. An explanation is succinctly offered by Santino;[1] a respondent and bar owner:

> It used to be that dancers catered to older customers, but now, younger and younger customers are coming into the bar all the time. When customers are forty to fifty years old, it's okay for a dancer to be thirty years old, but when the customers are in their twenties, they are interested in younger dancers, not older ones.

Asked why he thinks younger customers are going to strip bars, Santino explains:

> These guys come here instead of going to a singles bar. Girls in singles bars are too much trouble for them; they're difficult to start talking to, stuck-up, and you don't get to see them undressed. Here, it's their [the dancers] job to talk to you. Plus, these guys think there is a better chance of taking out one of these women, than a woman you meet in a regular bar.

This article considers the social and personal consequences of an aging process experienced in the late teens and early twenties by strip-teasers known as "table dancers." While occupational identity is tied to biological aging, it is also a social construction. If one traces the career routes and occupational transitions of the table dancer, one can readily see that she has the ability to manage the definitions of age and usefulness

assigned to her. Based on the table dancer's experience in exotic dance bars, I contend that since most of the aging literature and its theoretical formulations are limited to the latter end of the life course, namely, old age, the experience of aging as a descriptive category of earlier years is ignored, in particular as this applies to the meanings assigned to age at various times and in various contexts of life. In relation to gerontology, this perspective is a way of arguing that aging is neither a clear matter of final disengagement nor a particular activity level, but something used, situated, and managed (Holstein 1990).

The concept "managed utility" is introduced to convey how dancers manipulate the definitions assigned them regarding age-appropriateness for their occupation (Neugarten and Hagestad 1976). For dancers the definition of old is both bodily and socially contingent, the dancer herself being active and reactive in her ability to control the contexts and conditions contributing to definitions of her age. It is my hope that separation of aging from old age, a distinction often conflated in gerontology, will add an important dimension to formulating a general processual approach to aging as an experience across the life course.

TABLE DANCING AND AGING

In exotic dance bars, "dance" refers to a staged stripping routine as well as a one-on-one individualized "turn-on." Appearing in full costume on stage, the stripper gradually removes her clothing while dancing. Depending on local ordinances, the stripper disrobes until she is clothed in a full bikini top and bottom, pasties and t-back panties, or nothing. Between acts, strippers stroll the floor and fraternize with customers. In some bars, strippers make money when

Reprinted from *Journal of Aging Studies,* Vol. 6, Carol Rambo Ronai: "Managing Aging in Young Adulthood: The Aging Table Dancer," 1992, with permission of Elsevier Science.

customers buy them drinks, but the main source of income is table dancing.

Table dances are "sold" in a complicated negotiation process, the aim of which is to convince the individual customer that he is "turned on" to her and/or that she is "turned on" to him, that is, being sexually attracted. The table dancer controls the situation so that she is not caught disobeying "house" or bar rules, many of which spill over the edge of what local authorities would consider illegal. For example, at two of the bars studied, "charging" for a table dance is considered soliciting. Like the "word games" used by the masseuse to bypass direct solicitation (Rasmussen and Kuhn 1976), dancers regularly "suggest" a donation, called a "contribution," usually an amount ranging from five to twenty dollars a dance, depending on what is locally customary.

Persuaded to buy a dance, the customer is led to a dark secluded area of the bar designated for table dancing. Depending on the dancer's interpretation of local ordinances, she leans over her seated patron, her legs inside his, and sways suggestively to the rhythm of the music playing in the bar. Customers are allowed to touch the hips, waist, back, and outsides of a dancer's legs. Many men try and some succeed in gaining greater advantage. Customers attempt to touch dancers' bodies by inserting fingers into briefs or fondling breasts. In practice, the range of sexual activity in the bar includes infrequent "hand jobs" (the dancer masturbating the customer), oral sex, and, less frequently, sexual intercourse. Commonly, the dancer and customer engage in body-to-penis friction, a form of which is humorously called "talented knees" by participants in the stripbars.

Staged stripping routines and individual table dances put considerable emphasis on physical attraction, but more importantly, sexual appeal. First impressions are derived from the dancer's appearance, in particular, the appearance of her body. Loss of physical attractiveness risks loss of credibility and influence. Unlike the aging athlete, where physical performance is declining, aging for the dancer means that she is no longer persuasive sexually (Salutin 1971). While she still may be an adept dancer, her body loses appeal as a sexual object. Sustaining the resources she

formerly possessed—youth and beauty—becomes strained and in the eyes of customers has diminished sexual utility, that is, a form of aging.

How does a dancer know she is too old to dance and what does a dancer do when she is showing her age? Popular theories of aging such as the disengagement (Cumming et al. 1960) or activity theory (Cavan et al. 1949) lack in explanation. They take aging and retirement to be marked events that happen towards the latter part of the life course. Aging is presumed to happen in old age. Even symbolic interactionists, who commonly treat life events as contextual and definitional matters, presume the existence of an inevitable "life course" with regular age-related markers (Marshall 1979). Accordingly, the aim is to predict or understand the factors that produce or enter into aging in old age.

The gerontological conception of aging seems to have ignored the variety of situations and structures—besides chronological age—that engage participants in the *experience* of aging. A dancer's activities, for one, are informed by her own and others' underlying conceptions about aging in particular contexts. What is more, aging research has been too focused on conventional contexts (Stephens 1976). The strip tease literature, on its own, has not subjected its data to the analysis of "normal" experience, thus eclipsing questions of aging, role transformations, and the like. The literature portrays stripping as a *deviant* activity, focusing on contingencies of a deviant career (Skipper and McCaghy 1970), deviant patterns in early life (McCaghy and Skipper 1972), and structural factors facilitating lesbian and other deviant behavior (McCaghy and Skipper 1969; Salutin 1971).

PROCEDURE

Consideration of the aging table dancer's experience as "normal" evolved from reflections on data gathered in a field study of interaction strategies among strip tease artists (Rambo 1987; Rambo Ronai and Ellis 1989; Rambo Ronai 1992). For eight years, I have had insider access to the table dancing scene in the region where the study was conducted. Access began as part of dancing for employment. Opportunistically using an available social setting (Riemer 1977), I became a "complete-member-researcher" (Adler and Adler 1987) and undertook a field study of the dancers' everyday world. I subsequently left the occupation, but over the years maintained contacts in the field by occasionally re-entering it as a participant.

A growing interest in body image and self-conception led to consideration of the place of an aging process in the table dancers' self-acceptance and acceptance by others. "Aging" table dancers were interviewed and asked about the process of getting old in the occupation. The first three dancers approached were offended by the question, and, in turn, asked me questions like "Why are you asking *me* this?" and "What are you *really* saying?" The third dancer was so offended that she terminated the interview with "I haven't got time for this bullshit." In time, however, by talking casually with younger and older dancers, informing each of other dancers I had spoken with, and by asking what kinds of options they generally thought older dancers in the bar setting had, I was able to avoid what could have been an insurmountable barrier to data collection.

With a few exceptions, most of the dancers were unwilling to discuss their thoughts and feelings about their own aging. They were willing, though, to tell stories about other dancers whom they felt had "gotten old." Together with field observations, these and other stories form the data base of this study. The stories suggest how serious the consequences of aging are for the dancer's acceptance, and how active the dancer can be in managing the process. Stories, other accounts, and observations were recorded in the form of field notes, as close as possible to their actual expression. Altogether, over thirty dancers, fifteen customers, three bartenders, four managers, and four bar owners were interviewed and their stories obtained.

AGING AS MANAGED UTILITY

A dancer manages the definitions assigned the physical consequences of aging by shifting her resources to either leave the occupation or continue working in the bar setting. Leaving the occupation or "getting out" is a clear exit. It is rare and usually needs planning. Re-

maining in the setting requires a dancer to carve out a niche that either does not rely on attractiveness or depends on a rearrangement of attractiveness as the priority of a new role.

At no point can it be confidently said the dancer has quit, or retired, even though there are gradual transitions or situated "disengagements." A dancer's career path is dynamic in character, highly responsive to definitions of utility negotiated or managed in the context of her particular experience. "Retirement" is more a matter of what roles evolve from her situation than a matter of leaving, departure, or final exit.

Getting Out

A popular way out of the dance world is to find a so-called "sugar daddy," which is an older, wealthy man willing to take care of a woman in exchange for companionship and/or sexual favors. As one dancer observed of two friends:

> It was like one minute they weren't interested in settling down and the next, boom! They started dating lots of older guys instead of the young ones they used to. It was really gross. But maybe it'll be different when I get older. Anyway, they both got married to these guys like 20 years older than them. One is divorced now and she is out at Mammy Larry's [a strip bar] datin' round for another one.

According to Santino, a bar owner, "shopping" for a sugar daddy can start for some as young as twenty-one years of age, adding:

> They look for someone old enough to always consider them young so they won't be abandoned later for a younger woman. Also, the guy has to have money and he has to treat her "well."

Santino relayed a story of a woman who found a sugar daddy at twenty-three and quit stripping. After ten years, she divorced and started dancing again at thirty-three, in search of another man. According to Santino, she was open about her mission and often joked with him, "I'm going to blow this joint as soon as I find myself a man." She subsequently left the bar a second time after moving in with another man.

Some dancers attempt to save money to buy a business or support themselves while attending school. Few are successful. According to most stories, even if a dancer manages to get out, she usually returns to the stripping business. One dancer who returned worked a hot dog cart that she and her boyfriend bought together. She was only earning $50.00 a day. As she commented:

> I worked my ass off out there in that hot sun. I spent more time with that fuckin' cart than I would spend dancing in a cool air-conditioned bar where I could earn a couple hundred dollars. I can even drink—it's part of the job—if I want.

She left her boyfriend, a bar manager trying to get her out of the business and stuck him with the hot dog cart. Referring to another dancer who tried to leave the trade, a young woman who had recently received her state board cosmetology license, Mae, an older dancer, explained to the young woman while changing in a dressing room:

> Don't worry, you'll be back. Mark my words. They all come back some time. You won't make enough money, especially when you're used to this. You're spoiled on that money. You'll see.

No One Just Quits

Many contextual factors keep dancers dancing. Aging in the stripper's world is more a matter of leaving and returning than retirement per se. When asked if he knew anyone who quit the business, Santino remarked:

> This business spoils you—male, female alike. No one just quits dancing or any other job around it. There is too much money to be made. I know of a bar manager right now trying to buy this bar. I've hired lots of guys as bouncers that have gone on to manage at other clubs. I started out with a B.A. in business, managed this bar for a while and a religious bookstore I inherited. I sold the bookstore and used the proceeds to buy this bar. There is just too much money here to get out of it. I'm trying to get out now, before I get in too deep. Talk to me in a year. We'll see.

"No one just quits" is a common phrase among dancers, customers and bar workers. Money is said to be the primary inducement to strip, in addition to easy hours, easy work (no responsibility), and gifts (Skipper and McCaghy 1970). Many dancers are supporting a husband, a boyfriend, children, or a combination

of the three. One woman danced to support a bisexual girlfriend who acted as a housekeeper and nanny for her child, and a boyfriend who was a part-time bouncer at the bar where she worked as well as being the cook at home. The need for easy money to support such lifestyles keeps them "in the life" (Salutin 1971). Other than attractive bodies and performance routines, most dancers have limited skills. Few have sufficient training or education to make as much money in other occupations as they do now (Carey, et al. 1974; Skipper and McCaghy 1971).

Dancers are typically aware of the public's negative conception of the trade (Salutin 1971). The stigma of a deviant identity drives them closer together in defense against outsiders negative conceptions. The longer a dancer stays in the trade, the more likely she will be entangled by its associations, activities, and relationships. Relatedly, in a discussion of prostitutes, Prus and Vassilakopoulous (1979) state:

> With each overlapping set of interests—namely, financial, friendship, and intimacy—the involved persons are not only likely to find that contact with "straight society" becomes less important, but that disengagement "from the life" even when so desired, becomes more difficult and costly.

Carving Out a Niche

One response to bodily aging or uselessness is to seek a promotion to a role not as dependent on physical attractiveness. Take Marge in this regard. Coy about her age, Marge was a night manager estimated to be in her late forties. An ex-dancer who was fond of such items of the trade as whips, paddles, blonde wigs, and evening gowns, she went on stage once a night and danced, much to the delight of other dancers and the customers. She sat and drank with customers and occasionally did table dances. Regarding her situation, she once noted:

> I've been in this business in one shape or form for a long time. I was a dancer when this bar was located at the corner of Fifth and Main. I started waitressing after a while, you know, a couple days a week, and dance a couple days. I've tended bar, waited tables, even been on the door [as a bouncer]. Finally, it seemed like all the girls would listen to me any way. So they just went ahead and made me night manager.

It's easy for me now. I can dance if I want to, but I don't gotta do anything if I don't feel like it. One thing about this business—if you prove yourself, they take care of their own.

At first blush, this might suggest that Marge and the bar's owner mutually contributed to an inevitable disengagement from dancing. Marge gradually withdrew from her role as a dancer, but it was not an automatic, nor inevitable process. She carved out a niche for herself in the bar setting. She was free to dance if she chose, while being able to literally shape her environment to do as she pleased. She disengaged from dancing by trading the role of sex object for a managerial role. The reconstructed role with its related age identity did not produce a genuine or final disengagement from the bar scene or her dancer role, but, locally redesigned her circumstance and the consequent meaning of usefulness.

Some dancers are recognized alcoholics. They carve out their niche by drinking with customers. At several bars, dancers were required to "sell," that is, have a customer pay for a certain number of drinks. If dancers fell below their quota, they were required to pay for the drinks themselves. If they sold over the requirement, they earned a dollar for every drink sold. In this scheme of things, it was relatively easy to become habituated to alcohol. Besides, as some women put it, "You can handle the bullshit better with a buzz on."

As this type of dancer gets older, she usually gets heavier and becomes less active on stage because of her fear of falling while drunk. She gradually cuts back on table dances. But she can carve out a niche at the bar, waiting for customers to offer her a drink as a way of having someone in turn, sit and talk. Eddie, a heavy drinker, said of Nancy, an aging dancer:

> I like her. I take care of her; she takes care of me. She ain't nothing to look at but she's good people, good company. We have a good time. She's got moxie. She likes to bet with me on stuff. She'll say like, "I'll bet you ten bucks that broad will stand on her head on stage." She's great!

It was said that Nancy drank so much that the management put her on a limit of five half-shots of liquor per hour, thus curtailing her particular form of adaptation.

Some dancers have impressive social skills, used to cultivate regular customers. Women who carve out their niche in this way tend to be in their thirties and forties. The dancer interacts with the customer in a manner to make him feel as if some type of involved, long-term relationship were taking place. This is called "getting them going." Mae was well known for her ability in this regard. One evening Mae was given a mink coat by a customer, but she returned it to him. Asked why she returned the coat, Mae answered, "I couldn't hock it for very much, and I won't use it here in Florida. I'd rather get money." Asked how, then, she would earn money, she explained, "I'll get more money from him by being the type of person who gives this stuff back than if I keep it. I have lots of customers who give me stuff nicer than that mink." As a bouncer/drinker who knew Mae explained further, "It's true, Mae can really get them going." Referring to one of Mae's more impressive gifts, he remarked, "That necklace was a grand, easy."

As the dancer grows older and her appearance becomes less desirable, attractiveness as a component in self-management takes on a lower priority. She may make up for declining visual sex appeal with wholesale sexual activity. There are many stories about the older dancer who "does tricks" to get by, something most younger dancers need only leave to customers' imaginations. Younger and more attractive strippers are not as compelled to perform sexual favors to make money. Trina was exemplary in this regard. She was considered pretty but "rough around the edges," being about ten pounds over what was considered desirable and having a few extra lines on her face. Regarding aging and sexual favors, she noted:

> The longer you dance, the more bullshit you'll have to put up with. You'll gradually start to let them get away with stuff. You know, for the money. When you get older you have to work on getting them [the customer] into it.

That older dancers typically recast their situation into a compromise of necessity, was tacitly understood by regular customers. As one customer cryptically put it, "Guys sometimes prefer older dancers because they work hard for you." I once spoke with a dancer named Maxine about this. She was "near 50" and only sat with "certain customers."

CR: I noticed that you don't sit with too many customers. Is that intentional?

MAXINE: You bet. You can't be too careful with some
of the jokers that come in here. I don't put up with
any shit, you know what I'm saying here. No shit.
You never know who could be a cop. I only sit with
guys I know, guys I've known for years.

CR: I don't want you to get offended . . .

MAXINE: Then don't say nothing you might regret.

CR: How can you make any money if you don't meet
new people?

MAXINE: [Laughing] Oh that. Well, you see, I got my
regulars. I got their phone numbers. When I go to a
new bar, they follow me. I give 'em a call. When you
start out, well, you're young, you know what I mean.
You can handle their crap. Out of all those guys you
meet you find a few you treat "special" and they stay
with you. You saw me with that one guy yesterday? [I
nod agreement] Well he gave me five hundred dollars.
Now later today I'm expecting Sam in. He's usually
good for a hundred or two between his Friday and Saturday visits. Even if I don't see another customer all
week, I'm set for a while. You follow this? [I nod].

I later observed some of Maxine's "special" treatment. During a table dance, she allowed Sam to make
oral contact with her breasts while his hands roamed
her body. By catering only to regulars, Maxine protected herself from potential arrest from undercover
agents while making a great deal of money from the
few men who visited her in the bar, even though she
was "elderly."

The constant onslaught of propositions, paired
with an increased performance of sexual favors,
tempts some older dancers into prostitution. Salutin
(1971) implies that the general population regard them
as prostitutes anyway; so there is nothing to lose in
terms of status. Yet those who turn occasional "tricks"
insist they are not like full time "whores" or "street
walkers." They claim to engage in sexual activity only
when they need the money. Still, older dancers can
make a satisfactory, relatively safe living by using the
bar as a place of contact for prostitution (Prus and Irini 1980). A schedule of "regulars," whom the older
dancer "tricks for" outside the bar, provides security
and predictability. She need not worry about where
her money is coming from or being arrested.

When a stripper ages, she may find herself fired
from a bar where she has worked for a long time, or
forced to quit because she no longer makes money at
the location. Aging dancers who cannot create a niche
for themselves in bars where they are currently employed wind up in lower status clubs (Salutin 1971).
Bars have reputations in this regard. A bar may be
known for its "celluloid queens," where every
physique in the house is perfect because all the
dancers have had plastic surgery to enhance bodily attractiveness such as liposuction or breast and buttocks
implants. Some bars are known to have beautiful
"stuck up" girls, others for their friendly average-
looking girls, and still others for "sleazy" women with
whom anything is said to go.

Accordingly, the "demotion" of aging dancers who
can't carve a niche goes from beautiful to friendly to,
finally, sleazy. Related stories form a kind of social
control in their own right. Santino, for one, often took
misbehaving dancers on "the circuit," visiting other
bars in descending order of status for an "attitude adjustment." He stated that dancers usually were sobered
by the experience and "straightened up their act."

The status of a bar and physical attractiveness
work in tandem to define aging. A dancer may be too
young, or too attractive to work a particular bar. A
"elderly" twenty-five-year-old dancer in the company
of nineteen-year-olds may find herself broke. But if
she moves to a lower status bar, she may regain her
youth and rejuvenate her earning potential, until she
has aged there as well. Managers also work the age
angle. A manager or owner of a "dive" will hire on
older, attractive dancer who is younger than his other
dancers in hopes of luring clientele and other attractive dancers. Other dancers may become angry because the younger, more attractive dancer monopo-
lizes the business in the bar. Management may
become wary if many dancers in their bars become
"rough around the edges." Too many unattractive women working a higher status bar will bring down that
bar's public standing. Bar owners have been known to
ask young attractive dancers if they have young attractive friends who would like to dance. They solicit help
with stories typically beginning "If this bar gets a bad
reputation for old ugly dancers, you stop making money because the customers will stop coming." What

managers fail to mention is that young attractive dancers can move on to better bars.

SEPARATING AGE FROM AGING

Aging is a process both physical and social. Experientially, there is not set definition for what or who is old, even while there seems to be general agreement among gerontologists that old age occurs in the later years. The aging experience is socially constructed by individuals and through contexts that assign meaning to the physical body.

Meanings change over time because contexts change, something eminently social. The bar's physical setting may be the same, the people employed in the bar and those who patronize it may be the same, but the dancer starts to exhibit external signs of unattractiveness. As chronologically young as she may be, she can be old. Her body is not as supple and her dance not as animated as it once was. Her gestures towards customers are construed to be abrupt, demanding, nagging, less patient than before. A dancer's sexual utility and the sincerity of her presentation come into question. Appearing and acting like an old dancer breaks the tacit rule that women who sell their bodies in one form or another should be selling young, attractive, and cooperative commodities.

Popular theories of aging fail to account for the processes examined here. Dancers' and others' stories and accounts suggest that aging is an experience not necessarily just of later life, nor socially automatic or inevitable. In separating age from aging, and making visible the management of an aging experience, we learn the life course contingencies of being old.

ACKNOWLEDGMENTS

An earlier version of this article was presented at the Gregory Stone Symposium on Emotions and Subjectivity held in St. Petersburg Beach, Florida, January 1990. I thank Carolyn Ellis, Michael G. Flaherty, Jaber Gubrium, Danny Jorgensen, Hernan Vera, and two anonymous reviewers for their comments and suggestions.

NOTE

1. The names of persons and places have been fictionalized.

REFERENCES

Adler, P. A. and P. Adler. 1987. "The Past and the Future of Ethnography." *Journal of Contemporary Ethnography* 16:4–24.

Boles, J. and A. P. Garbin. 1974a. "The Strip Club and Customer-Stripper Patterns of Interaction." *Sociology and Social Research* 58:136–44.

Boles, J. and A. P. Garbin. 1974b. "The Choice of Stripping for a Living." *Sociology of Work and Occupations* 1:110–23.

Boles, J. and A. P. Garbin. 1974c. "Stripping for a Living: An Occupational Study of the Night Club Stripper," Pp. 312–35 in *Deviant Behavior: Occupational and Organizational Bases,* edited by Clifton Bryant. Chicago: Rand McNally.

Carey, S. H., R. A. Peterson, and L. K. Sharpe. 1974. "A Study of Recruitment and Socialization in Two Deviant Female Occupations." *Sociological Symposium* 11:11–24.

Cavan, R. S., E. W. Burgess, R. J. Havighurst, and H. Goldhammer. 1949. *Personal Adjustment in Old Age.* Chicago: Science Research Associates.

Cumming, E., L. R. Dean, D. S. Newell, and I. McCaffrey. 1960. "Disengagement: A Tentative Theory of Aging." *Sociometry* 23:23–35.

Gonos, G. 1976. "Go-Go Dancing: A Comparative Frame Analysis," *Urban Life* 9:189–19.

Holstein, J. A. 1990. "The Discourse of Age in Involuntary Commitment Proceedings." *Journal of Aging Studies* 4:111–30.

Marshall, V. W. 1979. "No Exit: A Symbolic Interactionist Perspective on Aging." *International Journal of Aging and Human Development* Pp. 345–58.

McCaghy, C. H. and J. K. Skipper. 1969. "Lesbian Behavior as an Adaptation to the Occupation of Stripping." *Social Problems* 17:262–70.

McCaghy, C. H. and J. K. Skipper. 1972. "Stripping: Anatomy of a Deviant Life Style," Pp. 362–73 in *Life Styles: Diversity in American Society,* edited by S. D. Feldman and G. W. Thielbar. Boston: Little, Brown.

Neugarten, B. L. and G. U. Hagestad. 1976. "Age and the Lifecourse," in *Handbook of Aging and the Social Sciences,* edited by H. B. Binstock and E. Shanas. New York: Van Nostrand Reinhold.

Prus, R. C. and S. Irini. 1980. *Hookers, Rounders and Desk Clerks: The Social Organization of the Hotel Community.* Salem, Wisconsin: Sheffield.

Prus, R. C. and S. Vassilakopoulos. 1979. "Desk Clerks and Hookers: Hustling in a 'Shady' Hotel." *Urban Life* 8:52–71.

Rambo, C. 1987. "Negotiation Strategies and Emotion Work of the Stripper." Unpublished Masters Thesis, Department of Sociology, University of South Florida.

Rambo Ronai, C. and C. Ellis. 1989. "Turn-on's for Money: Interactional Strategies of the Tabledancer." *Journal of Contemporary Ethnography* 18:271–98.

Rambo Ronai, C. 1992. "A Night in the Life of an Erotic Dancer/Researcher: the Emergent Construction of a Self," in

Subjectivity in Social Research: Windows on Lived Experience, edited by Carolyn Ellis and Michael Flaherty. Newbury Park, CA: Sage.

Rasmussen, P. and L. Kuhn. 1976. "The New Measure: Play for Pay." *Urban Life* 5:271–92.

Riemer, J. W. 1977. "Varieties of Opportunistic Research." *Urban Life* 15:467–77.

Salutin, M. 1971. "Stripper Morality." *Transaction* 8:12–22.

Skipper, J. K. and C. H. McCaghy. 1970. "Stripteasers: The Anatomy and Career Contingencies of a Deviant Occupation." *Social Problems* 17:391–405.

Skipper, J. K. and C. H. McCaghy. 1971. "Stripteasing: A Sex Oriented Occupation," Pp. 275–96 in *The Sociology of Sex,* edited by James Henslin. New York: Appelton-Century Crofts.

Skipper, J. K. and C. H. McCaghy. 1978. "Teasing, Flashing and Visual Sex: Stripping for a Living," Pp. 171–93 in *The Sociology of Sex,* edited by James Henslin and E. Sagarin. New York: Schocken.

Stephens, J. 1976. *Loners, Losers and Lovers: Elderly Tenants in a Slum Hotel.* Seattle: University of Washington Press.

39 | PLACE AND RACE
Midlife Experience in Harlem

Katherine Newman

Developmentalists interested in the subjective experience of midlife in the United States are often drawn to the study of middle-class Americans who have, on the whole, experienced "canonical" careers and now contemplate the pleasures and strains of retirement. How do they maintain their identities when the defining features of corporate employment slip through their fingers? Under what conditions do they remain psychologically resilient in the face of declining physical strength? What adaptations do they undergo as their children leave home and their roles as parents begin to recede, perhaps just in time to contend with the need to care for elderly parents who are now dependent upon them? These are the questions that confront many researchers hoping to understand what midlife means in American society.

Yet just as earlier researchers sought to broaden our understanding of childhood and adolescence by moving beyond the white middle class to the experience of minorities passing through the life course, it is important to expand the study of midlife in America to incorporate the expectations and experiences of African-Americans and other ethnic groups who may differ in the problems they face at midlife. A mosaic approach, represented through its examination of midlife in different national cultures, needs to be applied internally, to the study of midlife in America. Only when the study of midlife is expanded to include minority communities will we have a full appreciation for the complexity of this life stage.

As an initial step along this path, this essay explores the experiences of men and women in their forties and fifties who live in poor neighborhoods of Harlem in New York City. They came to participate in this study because children in their households—their own or those of other close family members—were already part of my on-going study of youths in low-wage service-sector jobs in the inner city.[1] These parents, aunts, and uncles are all long-time residents of Harlem and for the most part are among the working poor themselves. They work as building superintendents in slum neighborhoods, home attendants for the elderly, housekeepers for wealthy families, and transit workers who clean the subways at night.

Most have experienced bouts of unemployment; some have been through precipitous slides in their standard of living, moving, for example, from the well-paid military to the low-wage service sector.

Their economic lives are punctuated by insecurity, but they remain doggedly attached to the labor force, believing that working for a living is a necessary aspect of human dignity. They have tried to transmit the same values, both by word and by example, to their own children, with varying degrees of success. Indeed, as I explain below, they have had to contend with the fact that their upstanding morality must compete for their children's attention with the mean streets that surround them. Much of their midlife experience, then, consists of intervening between their children or grandchildren and the forces of destruction loose in the ghetto.

The meaning of these experiences, the ways in which they "add up" to a sense of satisfaction or disappointment, cannot be fully understood in a presentist mode. Middle age, unlike previous life stages, builds up against a backdrop of earlier experiences.[2] It is an important consolidation of a trajectory whose curves may have been hard to discern earlier in life. It is part of a long process of arrival that culminates in old age, but begins, I would argue, in the middle of life, when youth is clearly in the past and old age is visible on the distant horizon. Given this, it is particularly important to recognize the influence of place, period, and in this case, race, in organizing prior life experience. For the social, political, and economic context within which this generation of midlife Harlem dwellers reached their mature years differs quite dramatically from the context of their childhood years. Indeed, there is relatively little continuity between their communities of origin and their communities of midlife "destination," and the differences cast a long shadow over the meaning of middle age.

Some of the discontinuity is quite positive in its impact. Men and women who grew up in the South before the Civil Rights movement have aged into a climate of race relations that, whatever its faults may be, they see as a distinct improvement over the police state they experienced in their youth. But other forms of social change have been negative to the point of near debilitation. Northern urban neighborhoods that were, in the 1950s and 1960s, home to a stable, employed, and basically safe black community have become devastated wastelands that are dangerous places to live.[3] Ghetto dwellers confront middle age in places

where going outside after dusk is risky, where advancing age renders them physically vulnerable. African-Americans in Harlem reach this life stage with both forms of discontinuity—the encouraging and the terrifying—in the background. If we are to understand how this social history colors their assessment of their mature years, we must understand the trajectory of their lives as they moved through distinctive historical periods and geographical locales.

THE JIM CROW SOUTH

The great migration of African-Americans out of the rural South began in the period between the two world wars, but gathered steam in the 1940s and 50s, the era when the oldest of my informants were children (see Lehmann 1993). Nearly 5 million Americans left the agricultural areas of the South for the greater opportunities of the industrial north during this period—the largest internal migration in U.S. history. There is a tendency in much of the historical literature on this movement to focus upon what the migrants found when they arrived in the north. Contemporary history begins, it would seem, with life in New York or Chicago.

But if we are to understand what this migration experience means today, in particular, the ways in which it shapes perceptions of an urban midlife in the 1990s, we must back up and understand life as it was lived in small towns in the South. For this migrant generation, some small town in a rural area was "home," the place to which they returned every summer, the place where their grandparents, aunts, and uncles remained.[4] Life was a seasonal affair in these agricultural communities. Sharecroppers who worked the land and settled up with the landlord every year supplemented their income with jobs in the local mills processing peanuts, tobacco, or some other crop. Women took in washing and did other kinds of domestic work to add to the family coffers. Older children took their place in this wage labor and sharecropping economy, working in the fields when they were not in school. Younger children took care of the littlest ones in the house, often for many hours while the able-bodied adults were out working.

Alvia Ford—an African-American woman now in

her early fifties—grew up outside a small town in Alabama, one of ten children in a sharecropper household. Her grandparents, aunts, uncles, and cousins all lived in the same community and had done so for generations. She rode a bus many miles to school every day, something she enjoyed as much for the company as for the education. But poverty put a stop to her schooling: "We were dirt poor. There wasn't enough money to buy clothes. So, in the seventh grade, I got left back for a year. I didn't have shoes and clothes to wear to school, so I just missed the seventh grade."

Men and women who come from communities like Alvia's remember living without running water and running low on food; they always recall the sense most sharecroppers had that it was impossible to get ahead. Factory work was the only local alternative for making ends meet. Poorly paid and deadly dull, agricultural mills were nonetheless essential elements of the rural economy. Barbara James, a fifty-year-old black woman from a small town in Georgia, remembered how limited the opportunities were for her family:

> There wasn't any factories, and like I said, in the two towns where my grandparents growed up in and where I growed up in, there wasn't nothing else left for you to do. I mean, you had maybe one or two supermarkets. So . . . that was it. And there wasn't any kind of [manufacturers] there, just peanuts and cotton and stuff like that. That was all the kind of work you had to do, so that's mostly what everybody did in those days. They [were sharecroppers]. If they wasn't farming for they self, they were farming for the white man. And it's still the same [in my town]. . . . With my father, he worked at the peanut mill for so long, I don't even know what year he left there. He decided to go twenty-four miles away and he ended up getting a job at the Marine base and worked there until he retired. My brothers, they worked in the peanut mill.

As far as Alvia and Barbara recall, the best a family could hope for was to just get by. Nothing better than that, nothing approaching prosperity, was ever likely to happen in small-town Alabama or Georgia.

Being black and poor in a southern community was hardly remarkable. Everyone around Barbara had the same standard of living. What stands out in her mind about growing up in her hometown was the fact that there was absolutely nothing to do there—no entertainment, no excitement, endless sameness. Like Alvia, Barbara had all her kin in town where they had lived for as long as anyone knew. But that was half the problem: she already knew everyone there and realized that she was not likely to see anything new as she got older.

> [There's] nothing really they do there, except visit, you know? You can go from house to house and meet peoples and things like that, but that's about it. There's nothing there to do. There's no movies. You would have fun on Friday and Saturday night because they would have a "juke joint," a cafe and a DJ where they play music. You can go there and dance a half hour and you can do the same on Saturday night, but the place have to close at twelve o'clock, so that's it. After Saturday night there's no more fun, so you sit out in the yard and that's it.

Barbara's hometown was really two communities: one white and one black, with little contact between the families on either side of the dividing line. On the black side of town, the community was so small that she knew every house in the area:

> Nobody goes by the names of the streets. Where my mother lived at, they called it "the bottom." It's in town, but they called it "the bottom." Its not a big town, its just like a little neighborhood. All black on one side. You have houses over on the other side which is where the white live at, where they church is at and everything. But [my neighborhood] was a little block of black people, that's all.
>
> You don't have very many street lights . . . and there's like houses sitting on both sides of the street. It's like a Western town. You seen the Westerns, right? You seen the hitching posts where they tie horses. Well, that's the way my whole town was for so many years. They just tore the last hitching post down ten years ago. No kind of business . . . nobody wants to move there. So this town has been like this since I was a little kid and it's never going to change.

Small-town life was slow and familiar, qualities that came to have some meaning for Alvia and Barbara as they got older and moved north to the hustle and noise of the big city. But for young people who knew—through magazines, radio, and eventually television—that there was a big world beyond Alabama and Georgia, small towns began to feel like deadweights around their shoulders. For African-Americans, of course, living in a small, segregated community was a schizophrenic experience. Close knit ties among friends and kin were paralleled by open hostility and constant, belittling barbs from whites across the tracks. As Barbara tells it, racial hatred enveloped every aspect of daily life:

> The whites was real nasty. . . . They never referred to the black mens as "mens." It was always "boy." That's the way [whites] treated [blacks] and we were used to it. I would have loved to go to school with white kids, but I didn't. It wasn't allowed when I was going. The black had they own school, the white had they own school, they own bus. They still had their signs up—Whites Only. You couldn't sit in restaurants, you couldn't go in and eat. Certain bathrooms you couldn't go in. If you working in the white peoples' house you couldn't go in the front door, you had to go in the back door or the side door. If you rode in the car with them, you had to ride in the back seat. That's the way it was.

Jimmy Hardin—at fifty-six a little bit older than Alvia or Barbara—was actually born in New York. But like most people of their generation, the ties to the South were strong. He spent every summer of his youth in two communities in the South, one in Georgia and one in North Carolina, where his grandparents lived. For Jimmy, the experience of living down south was a running confrontation with racial hatred. Where Barbara and Alvia had been raised to live with the indignities of southern bigotry, Jimmy's northern upbringing led him to resist demands for deference:

> One time I was going to school, so I got on the . . . school bus, and basically when you get down south they have a sign up there, "Niggers to the rear." I'm telling you "Niggers to the rear!" You know? So this is a school bus, we're always clowning around, so I was talking to a guy, then accidentally got on the bus and turned my behind and sat down on the wrong spot. There was a white man sitting next to me. He [said] "Nigger are you crazy? Get back there, get back there!" There was a panic in there, you know? I said, "Oh shit, this may be lynch time," 'cause the way he just swelled up, you know, "Nigger!"
>
> I was not supposed to stand on corners, you know? But I started hanging out. Them cops come

down, they come down, they move [you] off the corner. It's not like it up here, you know. Cops will pass [young people] by five or six times [here in New York] but they just leave them standing. But down south, you can't be congregating on corners. Them crackers are mean. I never got in no serious trouble down in the South, maybe just said something with them crackers, you know, or refusing to buck when they want me to buck.

Ultimately, Jimmy's relatives had to "hustle [him] out of the South" because they were afraid he would get into serious trouble with the police or endanger their safety. The years of exposure to the open racism of the Deep South left an indelible impression on Jimmy, setting a benchmark from which he evaluated race relations in the north in his youth and in his mature years.

The combination of racism and extremely limited economic opportunity in the South prompted many African-American youths to enlist in the armed forces—then, as now, a major route of upward mobility and freedom from the suffocation of small-town life. Barbara and Alvia saw most of their brothers and other boys of their generation off to the army, becoming frontline soldiers in Vietnam or the part of the Cold War military in Europe.

> When I was growing up, [all there was] was the cotton fields and stuff like that for my brothers. The two oldest ones . . . never really got good jobs until they left home. My oldest brother, he left when he was about eighteen. The next oldest one, he joined the marines when he was fighting in Vietnam. So . . . all of them have been in the services except for two. I think that's what you mostly got their training . . . and they [now] doing the jobs that they doing because they all, you know, went into the army. That's all that was left for the boys down there, otherwise they stayed and worked on the farms. Most of them, they chose to go into the army.

When today's generation of midlife Harlem residents examine their lives in middle age, they do so against a background of profound change. They were liberated from a degree of racial oppression that is hard for many of today's youth to imagine. They were able to seek out opportunities that would have been unthinkable for their own parents in middle age. The men who joined the army were able to see the world—

a chance that no one in their families had ever had before—and learn trades that were utterly closed to them in the rural South. Most of all, Harlem's middle-aged migrants were able to escape to the city that fired the imagination of the nation's African-Americans.

HARLEM IN THE POSTWAR YEARS

Barbara and Alvia were among the first in their family to move to New York, joining cousins already living in Harlem. Domestic jobs were relatively easy to find, and although they did not pay well by urban standards, the wages were well beyond anything they had earned in agricultural factories or domestic work in the South. To hear them tell it, however, almost any wage would have made the move worth it. The excitement of living in a big city—with its twenty-four-hour street life, its music, its crowds—made Harlem a mecca for young blacks.

Harlem was a crowded, raucous community in the 1940s and 1950s when my older informants came to town. But it was not wholly unrecognizable to rural folk because so many southerners had come north in a chain migration pattern, settling in particular districts or on particular blocks that were dominated by friends and kin from their home-towns in South Carolina, Georgia, and the other southern states.[5] Social structures were dense in Harlem neighborhoods because the ties binding neighbors reached back into small towns where ascending relatives still lived and where young kids would be sent back in the summertime. Hence, when today's midlife adults were teenagers and young adults, they came to a big city that felt more life a cluster of close knit neighborhoods. Everyone looked out for one another; everyone knew their neighbors' children. Community was more than an abstract concept: it was a concrete experience of block parties, holiday rituals, churchgoing friends, and elders who kept a close watch on the streets.

Jane Easton, now fifty years old, is of the same generation as Barbara and Alvia. But like Jimmy Hardin, she was born in Harlem and grew up in the heart of the community. She remembers the tight-knit quality of her neighborhood, the neighborhood into which southerners like Barbara moved in the 1950s:

It was a nice neighborhood then, you know? You could leave the door open. Everybody knew everybody. . . . My grandmother used to go to work. She'd open the door to her friend's house and she'd say, "Go on Rosalie [Go on in]." You could run from one person's house to another and you didn't have to ring the bell 'cause the door would be open. We had fun when we were kids, running around. The neighborhood was safe. Everybody would come downstairs and you'd play, running in the fire hydrant and stuff like that. You could go to the store for your mother and stuff. You had the watermelon man coming [around] . . . and he yelled, "Watermelons!"

You knew everybody. You knew the lady that ran the grocery store. . . . My grandmother's family . . . owned the cleaners. You knew the man that owned the supermarket and the meat market. They knew you personally, you know . . . "Oh, you're Miss——'s granddaughter." It was a real family thing.

Jimmy Hardin remembers the same kind of atmosphere:

You could go outside your apartment and go down to the store and leave your door open. You'd have the next door neighbor living next to you, if you needed something from her icebox. At that time there wasn't all these frigidaires; you'd go in there and take something.

Jane and Jimmy agree that Harlem was not only a safe place to raise a family in those days, it was a community filled with disciplined adults who expected their children to adhere to strict standards of behavior. This is not to suggest that everyone in the community was an angel; but those who misbehaved were regarded as less than respectable, failing to hold to community standards that were widely embraced. "You had a home, and everybody's home looked nice and presentable. You ate dinner at a certain time. You had to be in the house at a certain time. You couldn't eat at nobody's house unless you called up and asked." Jimmy Hardin described how social order was maintained on his block through a network of adults who monitored the behavior of their own children and the children of their friends and kin closely.[6] Young people could not misbehave without their parents finding out about it:

When I was growing up, they had a lot of people [on the stoops], just stationed themselves waiting in front of the buildings and they'd talk about you. You know, "Oh, you ain't going to be no good when you grow up, you ain't doing nothing . . . ," you know? Other people encouraged you to go to school, try to do the right thing. "Don't mess with that boy, you're going to get in trouble with that boy." . . .

You had a strong environment. People couldn't come in the neighborhood and do [bad] things, 'cause these older people would get together, you know, and tell them, "You can't do that round here" or something like that.

The backbone of the community was a stable and employed adult population. Some people in Jane's family were small-business owners like her grandmother. But most had regular jobs working in factories or for middle-class and wealthy white families in the richer parts of the city. The truly fortunate among them had government jobs:

Some of the adults used to sew, some cleaned houses. My grandmother had people [who came to her shop] to iron. . . . A lot of people worked in the post office then. Some were teachers, and at that time we used to have a lot of people come from . . . City College to take the kids to different places, to see different things.

Typically mothers and fathers both worked, leaving older relatives and the oldest of the children at home to watch over the young ones after school. Kids were routinely shipped off to their relatives in the South—as Jimmy Hardin was every summer—when school was out. Family life was organized around the tasks of the breadwinners, the backbone of the whole enterprise. And kids learned early about the importance of contributing. As Jane continues,

When I was growing up, all the people that I knew was encouraged to do something else other than just sit around, you know. At least they got a job. Kids now . . . I was starting shining shoes when I was about nine, ten years old. Sell Sunday newspapers, you know, at the weekends.

THE END OF ORDER

From Jane Easton's perspective, this orderly, disciplined character has long since disappeared. Her neighborhood has become a dangerous place to live, with drug dealers and loose guns infesting the streets like a plague of locusts. Children can no longer run

free on the sidewalks and only a fool would leave his door open. She notes, "A young person will shoot you out of your shoes if you cough wrong. They killing they own selves now. See, we didn't have all that . . . drug dealing. It wasn't like this, the money, the drugs."

Jimmy confronts the same conditions in his Harlem neighborhood. Since he works as a building superintendent, he has to face the grim consequences of the local drug economy every day.

[In the old days] it was nice to get outside the house and go out in the street. Now it's almost like a threat to go outside. You don't know what direction any harm's coming from. You might think [everything is okay] then go outside and these guys shooting at each other across the street. I was walking down the street one time and I started smelling gunpowder, and they started shooting out there.

Violence has become so commonplace that middle-aged residents of Harlem and their children plan their movements around it. They know which buildings to avoid walking near, which streets are safe to cross, whom they can trust and to whom they must be give a wide berth. Intimate knowledge of the neighborhood, born of many years in residence, is also important as a survival strategy. The older adults have often known the drug dealers on the corner since childhood; they trade upon these long-standing acquaintances as a source of safety, figuring that they have much more to fear from strangers than locals. As James Langford, a forty-year-old African-American man who is raising seven children in Harlem, explained:

I know these people, you know, and I know what they do. They may sell this or that, but they don't look for trouble [with me]. They live down the block. . . . They know my family from when we were growing up. . . . They speak to my wife and my kids, but they basically don't bother us or make trouble. . . . But they may bring in other people that may cause trouble.

Navigation strategies and the capacity to trade on personal acquaintance do not always work. They are, however, the only "ecological" adaptations available to Harlem's poor if they are to survive the pathologies they face in public spaces.

African-Americans in the inner city confront the

fact that their economic circumstances condemn them to living in a place where these dangers are ever-present. Many, particularly those in midlife, long for the opportunity to leave the problems of the ghetto behind, to get on with their work lives and their family responsibilities safe from the relentless pressure of crime. But this requires resources that are out of their grasp and not likely to materialize in the future. Hence, law-abiding, hard-working, mature citizens of Harlem end up locked inside their own houses, unable to enjoy the freedoms that most working people in suburban communities take for granted.

If Harlem had always presented these obstacles, midlife adults who grew up there or moved to the community in their youth might have grown to equate life in the inner city with this kind of social disorganization. However, for today's generation of midlife adults, Harlem represents a place that has undergone a profound transformation—for the worse. It was not always a dangerous and difficult place to live. Indeed, it was regarded as exciting but safe, diverse but ordered. What has happened in the last twenty years, however, has been that Harlem has seen a near total loss of the job base that used to sustain it and a consequent rise in the myriad social problems that confront midlife adults in the form of street dangers. Midlife has become a life stage of vulnerability, a condition that did not obtain for previous generations, but one that most assuredly worries middle-aged men and women today.

This is not to suggest that everyone in the ghetto is involved in crime or in harassing their neighbors. On the contrary, the majority of people who live in high poverty areas of Harlem are the working poor, as are their teenage and young-adult children. In central Harlem, for example, where poverty rates are nearly 40% and official unemployment is now 18%, more than two-thirds of all households have at least one worker in them (City of New York 1993). Nonetheless, the working poor do not earn enough to live in problem-free neighborhoods. Inner-city minorities, in particular, are likely to reach middle age in the midst of communities where they feel under siege, even though most of the people they know personally are working and trying to manage their way around the bad apples.

The fact that living among conditions of crime and unemployment was not always necessary registers profoundly among midlife adults examining what they have accomplished in their lives. They speak with dignity of their participation in the working mainstream, even if this has meant a poorly paid job. But they cannot be proud of the kind of place where they have to live when that place is home to crack dealers who commit random acts of terror. Relegated to these circumstances, they feel the weight of the community's problems as inescapable and draining. Why they have to put up with this deterioration, why it happened in the first place, what is wrong with their people or their society that this should be their fate—all of these questions recur again and again, the refrains of midlife in a place where race and the changing economy has laid the groundwork for a ghetto experience of midlife vulnerability.

Along with danger comes the recognition that the inner city, or the segregated suburb, is a place that has been ignored and rejected by white society. Services and amenities commonplace in middle-class communities are utterly absent. Shattered windows are left broken. Graffiti fills the walls, street signs, bus stops, and schoolyards, and no one seems bothered enough to clean it. Streets are dirty and the pavement is broken. Police, often depicted in the popular press as unwelcome in poor, minority neighborhoods, are more often the target of complaint because they seem absent, unconcerned, or corrupt.[7]

While often tagged an urban problem, the morass of difficulties described above long ago engulfed the segregated suburbs outside of New York. Al Sampson, a forty-year-old African-American man, grew up on Long Island in the 1950s and 1960s, coming in and out of Harlem to visit his relatives and friends. As he reached high school, however, whites began to move farther out on the island, and African-Americans, anxious to leave inner-city apartments for private houses, started arriving in large numbers.

> When I was growing up here . . . in the beginning it was fifty/fifty [white and black]. By the time I graduated, it was probably 90 percent black and 5 percent . . . Latins and maybe 2 percent white and then whatever [left over]. They tried to mainline all the blacks into certain areas on Long Island, and they wouldn't want to give them social services.

Segregation deepened, adjacent white communities

drew their tax dollars inward, and the relentless degra-dation of Al's neighborhood began. Today, his com-munity is rundown and depressed:

> The main street is the worst thing. I've never been in a place where the main street doesn't even have one garbage can on the street, not one. My landlord owns a liquor store, has a garbage can outside the store, that's chained to the pole. This old plastic garbage can, and the guys still continue to throw their wine bottles [on the ground]. I live right next door to the building. They throw everything right outside on the ground. . . .

> The real problem [here] is the drugs. . . . There's a lot of crack houses. As far as robbery and all that, there's no one really to rob. There are very few stores, very few, and the homeowners don't really own anything. It's just the drugs, right out there, wide open, on the street. I'm talking about right across the street from the firehouse, where . . . police officers change shifts.

> [In other places] fire departments hold social functions and things like that, but here, nothing. . . . The police . . . can't stop the drug dealing that's go-ing on right across the street [from the fire station]. They're always at the train station . . . but right across the street, in front of my house . . . they can't stop [the drugs].

Depressed conditions breed trouble on the streets. Although Al knows how to take care of himself on the streets, he has found that a wise man steers clear of trouble and stays indoors:

> It's sort of a . . . a locked-in situation. Stay upstairs in my apartment and I don't bother anybody. I come out once in a while, but I don't get involved, you know? I mean, I know a lot of the people that are involved [in drugs], I speak to them. But I got more important things to do, like looking for work.

The best way for Al—a robust man, six feet tall—to protect himself is to stay close to the people that he knows, to confine himself to the bosom of his family and other close friends he can trust. While affluent Americans may greet midlife as a time of expansion, a time free of the confining obligations of child rearing and open for outward movement, the poor who live in ghettos experience midlife as a period of vulnerability, a time when one's best bet is to pull inward and seek the safety of the known.

This strategy may speak to Al's safety, but it does not do much for his self-esteem. For the neighborhood he lives in reflects back on his station in life and makes him feel that he is a person of minimal stand-ing. No one who has a choice visits his neighborhood; it is an undesirable place to live. Anyone who has to live there is, by this definition, an outcast, a failure. He feels helpless to change the situation, except to focus on extracting himself from it. But because that is much easier said than done, the character of the place in which he lives takes a toll on the character he be-lieves himself to be.

Of course, middle-aged minorities living in simi-lar circumstances do not always react this way. Bar-bara James, who works as a house-keeper for wealthy families on the East Side of Manhattan, comes home to her walk-up apartment in Harlem and confines her-self until she has to go back to work:

> I come in from work on Friday and that's it. I don't go back out again 'til maybe on Sunday. I go to church then, and that's right [around the block]. When service is over, I come back in my house and I don't go back out no more until Monday morning.

Yet, where Al sees his neighborhood reflected in his life, Barbara defines the threatening element as de-viant and distinguishes herself sharply from it. She de-scribes herself as decent, hard-working, churchgoing, and surrounded by an enemy element bound on ruin-ing her environment. She does not internalize the problems she experiences, she distances them. Their divergent reactions are easily understood as reflec-tions of the economic differences that separate Bar-bara from Al. Barbara works full-time and defines her-self as part of the mainstream world, albeit not a well-paid member. Dignity comes from the fact that she is dependent on no one and works to support her-self and her daughters. There are real cultural and class differences between her and the crack dealers she is so angry with.

Al, like many black men in midlife, has had a much rockier employment history.[8] After a long peri-od of time in the service, where he was able to live overseas, earn good money, and enjoy a respectable status, he was discharged in his mid-thirties, only to find that there were no decent jobs available to him. He returned to Long Island and reconnected with his friends from the old neighborhood, hoping to activate a network that would help in job hunting, but he discovered that his friends had never been able to find good jobs. In the time he had been in the service, they had taken entry-level jobs in local warehouses or factories. Some had prospered, but most had spent those ten years cycling in and out of low-wage jobs. The best they could do to help an old friend was to clear the way for a job that offered a fraction of his military wage.

> I got out of the Air Force . . . and [went] looking for a job. I took a job [in a warehouse] and a lot of guys who were there, I went to school with, or they went to school with somebody I knew or one of my brothers. . . . All the people who worked in the front office were white and all the people who did all the dirty work, maintenance, worked in the warehouses and things like that, were all black. Now all these guys that did all the physical labor, of course, they got paid less. It was really bad news. . . . One of the warehouse managers considered us as being "porch monkeys," words from his mouth.

It is hard for Al to accept this fate after having had a steady, respectable career for a decade. Returning home after so many years, only to find that his age-mates had "gone nowhere" during the ten years he had been gone, only added to the sense that there was no future. Since the end of the warehouse job, he has had only sporadic employment. Today, he is unemployed and depressed about his prospects.

It comes as little surprise that, given this history, he looks upon his physical surroundings and sees in the community's depression a mirror of his own troubles. His financial circumstances lock him in to a bad neighborhood, force him to be dependent upon the charity of family and friends, and make him feel like a failure. Unfortunately, circumstances like these are all too common among African-Americans, particularly among middle-aged men. For they have taken the brunt of the economic slowdown that has shuttered the factories where they once worked; they have seen their occupational prospects wither.

For men in midlife, this reality is particularly harsh. They cannot hide behind youth or fool themselves into thinking that something much better is around the corner. Like others in middle age, they as-

sess their accomplishments and, if they have suffered an occupational history of intermittent work or low-wage jobs, they come up short of the kind of biography they consider respectable. As Al put it,

> I'm forty years old, I'm unemployed, and even with all the experience and the different jobs I've had, for some reason I still find it difficult to move ahead in life. . . . All I can do really is menial tasks and then, if you have all this knowledge, they tell you that you're overqualified to do some of these menial tasks. So, like I say, it's really been rough for me.

When Al looks around his community, he sees the broken glass and the dead-end inhabitants of the streets and feels trapped by his inability to move out. The physical and social surroundings symbolize his economic impotence. Barbara, who must contend with similar social problems in her neighborhood, has a different vantage point. She has an identity that lifts her above her surroundings.

RACE AND FATE

The relationship between place and identity presses upon Barbara and Al not only because they have to contend with the consequences of living in an unsafe neighborhood, but because segregation and poverty have insured that African-Americans are—unlike other racial groups—faced with such a fate in such large numbers. As members of a stigmatized community, they feel compelled (both by themselves and by an abstract mainstream) to answer for this condition, to explain why "their people" are in such abiding trouble.[9] And when you live in a community with so much failure in evidence, it becomes a challenge to be answered, even by those who are solid and steady.

Midlife Americans who are white rarely face this query, even though millions of them are also poor or unemployed.[10] White Americans have no cultural identity as a group for which they have to answer. For minorities, however, reflection upon midlife achievements and failures is rarely an individual matter, at least not wholly so. As Ellis Cose (1993) and others have noted,[11] even those African-Americans who are successful in life are often "charged" with having abandoned their troubled counterparts in the ghetto or with the necessity to be a role model for unfortunate members of their racial group. They are implicitly asked to account for the plight of the urban underclass. African-Americans who live in inner-city communities are no less "responsible" (in an abstract sense) for explaining how these troubles came to be. The answers to these questions impinge upon their own experience of midlife because a subtext of racial failure lurks below the surface. Why did I do well in life (when so many of my people have not)? Why have I seen so much trouble in my life (just like the millions of other African-Americans who are similarly situated)? As Barbara put it:

> People can't get a good job, can't get a better place to live, nothing in life seem to go right. You got more people counting on failure than they do on anything, because it's like a every day thing to them. If they put it as a struggle, so they failing everyday at trying to do better, trying to get a better life. Me, I say I'm OK. Long as I'm alive . . . I ain't going to say I got good health, I don't know that, but I'm alive and my kids are OK and I'm OK.

My informants are steeped in the culture of inequality, a fractured experience of promise and betrayal, a constant test of personal dignity, a fundamentally hierarchical experience in which their "people" are almost always on the bottom. They are not, however, alone in this rat race for material and social prestige. Their fellow citizens are also entrenched in a struggle for well-being, one that has increasingly threatened the standard of living of millions of middle-class whites who have, in previous decades, had little to fear in terms of economic security. American society as a whole is preoccupied with an ongoing conversation over the moral dimensions of inequality.

On one side of this debate lie conservative believers in a natural order of stratification, modern-day social Darwinists who embrace the notion that those who are deserving will prosper (see Newman 1988). On the other side are liberals who believe that forces larger than any given individual can overwhelm even the deserving and that whole categories of people— especially African-Americans—start so far behind the starting line that no credence can be given to the idea of "fair competition." The former view places primacy of effort on the shoulders of the individual or the family; the latter gives greater emphasis in achieving

fairness to interventions either of government or of charity.

These cultural arguments are routine fare on broadcast talk shows such as those hosted by Rush Limbaugh and Sally Jessy Raphael. They figure prominently in tabloid stories of celebrity tragedy,[12] they are the deep structure of crime stories. The subtext is inescapable in virtually any discussion that attempts to answer the question: How did this group come to be where it is in the social pecking order? For my informants, explanations about the condition of their neighborhood or the behavior of their children can never be merely a matter of personal opinion. It is part and parcel of a larger debate over the link between race and fate.

But the answers given by any individual—in this case middle-aged African-Americans living in high poverty communities—are never so straightforward as the two polar opposites given above. Nor are individual views ever so internally consistent as my dichotomous account would suggest. Moreover, informants are aware that their views on the subject are part of a debate, and they attempt to refute other points of view as much as state their own in the course of explaining how race matters (or does not).

The dominant perspective among working poor African-Americans is that individuals are indeed responsible for their fate and that membership in a stigmatized racial group is no excuse for poor personal performance as a parent or a young adult. Indeed, those who damage their children through neglect or poor oversight are held fully accountable. Barbara James is certainly of this opinion. She believes that her community has seen a collapse in responsibility, with young people having children before they are ready and with drugs engulfing young men. And among this latter group, many of whom she knew as children, she holds parents responsible for poor supervision and guidance. The contrast between Barbara's strict upbringing and the troubled families in her midst could not be more stark:

> The kids that I watched grow up in this neighborhood, they are the young boys, they're the ones that's out there [dealing drugs] now. A lot of them out there, they don't have fathers and they mothers don't care, so long as they bring the money home. They

don't care. When I came up, things wasn't like that. My father, he wasn't anyone to play with. We had to go to church every Sunday morning, we had to go to Sunday school. . . . When Sunday morning come, you all think up a lie, you say "We can't go to church today, Dad, we don't have nothing to wear." So he'd tell us, "You ain't got nothing to wear, then you can't go out at night." So a bunch of kids go running through the house finding something to put on! . . . He was real strict; so was my mother. A whole lot different than what it is today.

Barbara James herself has raised her kids the old-fashioned way, and she believes that this is why they never succumbed to the temptations of the streets, as so many of their age-mates did. However, she lives in a community where many families have taken a different pathway. She "cuts them no slack" for these mistakes and attributes the connection between race and fate to the willful neglect of people in her own community.[13]

Al Sampson has a slightly different view. He shares Barbara's disgust for the failures of many parents he knows to raise their kids right:

> There's too much babying today. . . . [Parents] are pampering everybody. . . . Nowadays, parents are just giving in too much . . . there's no . . . it's a simple word that I'm trying to think of . . . more discipline, more discipline man. . . . I know a lot of parents out there and I know [them] from the age that I grew up in . . . and they're out there still getting high. . . . Nobody is really pushing the kids. . . . No respect, no respect for their elders.

However, Al also sees a larger system of racial stratification and bigotry that has placed African-Americans at a consistent disadvantage from the beginning:

> The color of your skin, your neighborhood and where you're from. That's how most people judge you. The way it should be is individually, but when they first look at, say an [employment] application, that's the first thing they're going to judge you by, the very first thing.
>
> [Race] matters a lot, it does. Because, you know, every time you look in the mirror you see the color of your skin and you see what black people have gone through. Really. There's no doubt in my mind [that race matters a lot].

Al's general observations are grounded in many particular experiences where he has been singled out for abusive treatment simply because he is African-American. He can recount endless examples such as these:

> A couple of weeks after [the 1993 mass murders on the Long Island Railroad], we were on the train. . . . Something must have happened on one of the lines further down. Now, you hardly ever see the cops on a train. But they're coming on there like the big gestapo. . . . They come on, they're going to stand me down. I said "You better keep on walking, 'cause I know you know I'm not the person you're looking for." The conductor's right there with them, but everybody black on the train is who they're stopping.
>
> I used to work for a family-run business and a lot of times I used to have to go to do personal work at their homes. You find a lot of times, especially if it's an all-white town and you're a black guy, you're driving through there, people lock their doors in their cars. I'm talking about in the middle of traffic, you'll see them locking their doors. The police will routinely run you . . . you know, stop you. One time . . . I was stopped for running a red light, which I know the light wasn't red. The cop . . . continued to give me a lecture about things with my car. . . . Then two or three other cars came by and one of the officers in one of the other cars says, I swear to God, "You having any problems here?" I mean, I'm one guy, in a car, by myself. But I'm in a white neighborhood. It always happens like that.

He is keenly aware that where jobs, housing, and the general standard of living are concerned, blacks are shoved to the bottom, their individual qualifications disregarded. Al would add, as do many of his middle-aged counterparts in the inner city, that African-Americans are further hampered by competition with new immigrant groups, principally with Latinos who have flocked to New York City from the Dominican Republic in recent years (and with Puerto Ricans in the past).

IMMIGRANT COMPETITORS

Native-born, inner-city blacks often point to the rising number of immigrants in New York City as a contributory cause of the economic inequality which their communities face. Whether the influx of immigrants depresses wages for Americans in the nation's ghetto is a matter of controversy among labor economists, but it is a closed case among the people I have studied.[14] Most

African-Americans believe that immigrants are willing to work for wages that no American—of any color—would accept, effectively undercutting African-Americans in a struggle for a piece of the pie (at the bottom of the social order). Others argue that the government was generous to immigrants, providing them with financial benefits (access to welfare, health clinics, and social services) that somehow they do not deserve. African-Americans I speak with sometimes suggest that the government, and the mainstream white world it represents, is more concerned about taking care of these newcomers than it is with improving the economic prospects of native-born blacks. Finally, because both groups suffer from poverty, they are often geographically contiguous, living in low-rent neighborhoods that border one another, throwing the competition between them into high relief. As Al put the matter:

> The only real work out there [on Long Island] . . . is the factories. Most of those factory jobs now are being held by, I hate to say it, but people of Hispanic or Latino [descent]. . . . When I first came back [from the Air Force], I went to a job interview and the foreman was a black guy, and he told me that they really don't like hiring people from where I'm from.
>
> [The government] let too many people in. You know that it is a law that when they let the Russian immigrants in or anybody, any immigrants . . . automatically, we have to take care of them. Automatically. They're set up, they're getting social services. That's how they get set up in these small businesses, while a black man, just let him try to get a small business loan. Drives you crazy. I'm serious. . . . You can't tell me that all these Colombians and Hondurans and all these people here are legals. I remember when you was going home you had to go way, way up town . . . to Spanish Harlem to find Puerto Ricans. Man, now the Dominicans are moving damn near all the way down to 125th Street [the heart of Harlem] . . .
>
> I get on the subway . . . [to come] up here when these kids are coming out of school. Listen and see what language they speak. I've got nothing against them, but if you let it get too far . . . then you can't control it.

Jane Easton, who is ten years older than Al but a longtime resident of Harlem, sees the same kind of competition for housing, for services, and for jobs, and she resents the attention given to immigrant Latinos. From her perspective, much of the recent slide of African-Americans in New York is attributable to their presence:

> Dominicans come here and they just take. They have good ones that work hard, but they have so many that just slide and pass. Doing nothing, taking up space, taking up jobs, and different things that somebody else might want, you know? That's why you have all this . . . we had homeless before, but not like this. Look at it!
>
> Old people that worked all they lives hard, and they don't even have enough money when they get . . . pension . . . to pay rent. . . . That's not right. And here [Dominicans] come in, "Give me a welfare check." "Here go you, have twenty or thirty kids." . . . An old person that's been here all their life and they can't even get a little room . . . that's safe. And here [the immigrants] come and just have babies.
>
> I heard this lady . . . talking to her granddaughter, she was so hurt, you know. She said, "I go now to the welfare . . . and they treat me like a piece of dirt." She said, "I worked all my life to get what I got, and then when times get hard . . . and they talk to me like I'm nothing. They [immigrants] come . . . having babies and they get anything." Your own kind, blacks [working in the welfare offices] are talking to blacks like they're nothing, you know? That's what makes [blacks] want to jump across that desk and beat the daylights out of one another, you know?

However, inside the stacked deck—consisting of one part white animosity toward blacks and one part competition from immigrants—Al and Jane believe that people must still take responsibility for their own actions. It is a "cop-out" in Al's judgment to lay the blame for one's fate at the door of racism, even though this is the unavoidable environment within which African-Americans must function.

> You have to realize, any situation that you're in today, it ain't because of [being] a black man. I mean, some of it, you know, it is, but if you want more out of life, you've got to work a lot more harder than what you did. Ain't nobody going to give you anything. You got to get out of here and get it.

For Al the two polar positions discussed earlier are blended into one. There is a "system" of structured inequality that does indeed make it much harder for

African-Americans to claim their fair share. Yet, even though these forces are arrayed against him, it is up to him—the acting subject—to make his way in the world, even to redouble his efforts. In this, he accepts the basic burden of the conservative position, that individuals must take responsibility for their own fate, even though he knows that such a burden differs dramatically for blacks than for others.

None of the people who participated in this study argued the more radical view that all the ills of the black community can be chalked up to racial injustice, with no provision for personal fault. Indeed, they characteristically frowned upon local political figures—like Al Sharpton or Louis Farrakan—who consider racism the most compelling diagnosis of the problems of the inner city. The variation lies along the continuum between Barbara and Al with some middle-aged ghetto dwellers seeing a larger hand for racial prejudice in the predicament of the community than others. But all of them accepted the mainstream cultural prescription that places individual agency and responsibility at the heart of explanations for the fate of individuals.

This confluence with mainstream culture, however, is little comfort for those upstanding middle-aged citizens of Harlem who nonetheless look around their neighborhood and see the boarded up buildings, the drug dealers menacing people on the street, and the many troubled families in their midst. For the emphasis on individual responsibility merely points back to the direction of the community and the metamorphosis that its older members have witnessed over time. They realize that many families, including most of their own, lead admirable, responsible, and stable lives, that they monitor the behavior of their children, instill a work ethic, and take care of their friends and relatives. But it falls to them to explain why so many people in their midst have dropped off the mainstream wagon, why there is so much trouble in their community.

Success as the Absence of Failure

Popular accounts of middle age recount the psychological experience of recognizing the finite character of human life and of "taking stock": measuring one's

accomplishments against some imagined plan for adult life. It is unclear how widespread this experience is, to what extent it happens absent the prodding of a researcher. In an openended elicitation of life stages, for example, the African-American informants in this project never mentioned "middle age" as a period in the life cycle, preferring instead a long period of undifferentiated adulthood, ending in a clearly defined segment called "old age," "going back to childhood," and a variety of other descriptors for the declining period at the end of life.

Older African-Americans clearly know that people age biologically, and they have definitive ideas about the normative behavior and responsibilities entailed in earlier stages of life. However, midlife is a missing category. They recognize that other social groups utilize the term, and therefore they have a distant recognition of its meaning for others. Bit it is not a cognitive category with any emic significance.

It is possible that this lacunae reflects the fact that midlife is part of a middle-class culture that these working poor men and women do not participate in. They are, for example, not free of responsibilities for dependent children even though they are in their fifties. Most have, at a minimum, adolescent children of their own still at home. Some are primary caregivers for grandchildren whom they are raising. None can foresee a time when they will have sufficient resources to retire on their own steam: Only those who have had a career as public-sector employees have pensions or retirement funds, and they are in the decided minority. Indeed, they often worry about how they will fare in old age since their comfort depends to a great extent on the resources (time and money) that their children will be able to make available to them. The question of just how widespread (or class or race bound) the concept of midlife is deserves much greater emphasis than this suggestive account.[15] Suffice it to say, for the moment, that it is not a prominent feature of the life cycle landscape for African-Americans in Harlem.

However, although my informants never offered the term (or any of its equivalents) in elicitation, their life histories are filled with lengthy discussions of the success stories and failures in their lives in these, their mature years. Their frame of reference, however, contrasts sharply with the cultural imagery of the suburban, white middle class where questions of success are concerned (see, esp., Newman 1993). For when the more privileged assess their lives, their referents involve occupational prestige and financial comfort: a successful person is one who has become a professional and whose children are following along a similar path. They are people who own nice homes and live in comfortable communities. African-Americans in the inner city are not unaware of this kind of benchmarking, but they do not engage in it very much. This is not to suggest, for a moment, that they do not think about financial stability or career mobility. In fact, most face degrees of instability that force them to pour a great deal of psychological energy into worries over finances and job security.

But they also face trials that are much graver, particularly where their children are concerned. Living in neighborhoods that are often dangerous, where drugs seem to be the only growth industry, where schools are often little more than warehouses, they look upon success as the absence of major failure. A middle-aged parent is to be congratulated if she or he has managed to raise a family where the children are not in trouble. Parents of sons worry constantly about the threatening nature of the streets, about the lure of the underground economy, about violent confrontations with police. From the age at which they are old enough to navigate the streets on their own, when parents can no longer expect to rein them in, sons are at risk. Daughters pose other kinds of problems. Parents are less worried about their physical safety and more worried that they will be vulnerable to exploitative relationships, and above all that they will get pregnant young and thus lose educational and employment opportunities. Great value is placed upon having children, but mature mothers realize as well that giving birth too young will cause their daughters a great deal of hardship.

In families where these problems have been bypassed, where parents have worked hard to keep their children free of influences they consider pernicious, seeing kids through to adulthood intact is a significant achievement. As Art Sands explained:

The thing over here is M-O-N-E-Y, you know what I mean? Prestige, money. . . . But my mother raised thirteen kids. . . . She died of a stroke, and there was many nights she'd be in the house crying and you'd know things would bother her. But she raised us. I mean, none of my brothers and sisters has spent any time in jail or ever been in any really serious trouble.

Barbara James makes the same kind of point in talking about her daughters, one of whom works in a fast food restaurant and the other of whom is in high school. She "knocks on wood" that they have escaped a fate that many of their friends and neighbors have succumbed to: "[I'm proud that] my girls haven't got pregnant yet. I never really had any trouble out of them, they really been great. . . . I always say, 'You can always come back home when you can't go nowhere else.'"

Alvia Ford, who works as a nursing home attendant, has not been so lucky. Her oldest son died young in the course of a conflict between competing drug kings. She buried him before he reached twenty-five. Her firstborn child, a twenty-eight-year-old daughter, is a crack addict who has cycled in and out of treatment programs to no avail. If Alvia buys her daughter clothes, she sells them for crack. Any money that Alvia keeps in the house is ripe for stealing. And now the daughter is sick:

I learned how to pray a lot, and I [kept my] Bible [near]. I told [my daughter] she'd be better off dead . . . and you're not supposed to say that to your child. But . . . that girl has hurt me so bad. And now she is an HIV carrier. They said to her, you could live forever as an HIV carrier, but if you don't keep yourself clean [free of drugs] it will turn into AIDS.

Alvia has had to confront these problems alone, with no help from the state agencies she has turned to for drug counseling and protection:

I asked this cop, I told him, please pick her up, take her to jail. He said, "I just can't pick her up for nothing." "Possession of drugs," I said. "Pick her up for possession of drugs. Once you take her downtown, then I can come and tell the judge she's a danger to herself, and he can put her away." But he can't never catch up with her.

After [my son] was dead for a while, I got happy again because I had my two daughters. But this daughter here is not far off [from dying] unless I can get help for her and soon. I don't know of any organizations, unless I took off from work and take her. But she got to be off the street.

For poor people in middle age, who know that life is finite and old age a period of vulnerability, troubled children can spell personal disaster. They add to a persistent anxiety that they face about their futures when they have no margin for error, no means to save for the time when they can no longer take care of themselves.

Alvia has been through a great deal of grief and hardship on account of her children. But she is also dependent upon them in the long run, for she will not have the resources to take care of herself as she moves from midlife to old age. She is going to have to rely on her kin when she can no longer work, and she must worry, in ways that few middle-class people do, about whether her children will be able and willing to take care of her:

> I'm telling people that I'm banking on my baby daughter . . . to be here for me in case, when I get old and I get sick, I have somebody to wait on me. I'm hoping and praying that [my oldest daughter] going to hear this voice and it's going to turn her around. But I don't think so.

Jimmy Hardin also feels anxiety about the future, for he knows that he operates close to the margins and that there is no one else who will look out for him if he ever finds that he cannot look out for himself:

> You got to get up every morning and try to go to work and do something. Once you lay down, that's it. If you're not able to work, you're totally destroyed if you don't have no one to rely on. . . . When everybody's trying to hold you down, you got to try to get up. . . . You . . . [can] rock back on your heels and . . . go down, like a person when they get hit. . . . That's how bad you can be doing sometimes. You don't have a dime in your pocket, and like the whole damn world is closing up on you, and you can be sick all inside with fear, hurt, scared of what's going to happen. Then some little spark comes in, and you say, "Man, get a hold of yourself." That's really fear, when you have nothing, and you can't look to any place to get anything.

The kind of problems Alvia's children have had with drugs and guns make them an extreme example of the difficulties poor parents face in their middle-age years. However, Alvia's friends and neighbors know that they too could wind up with problem children because they are so often exposed to people who might lead

them astray. Being a good parent, a vigilant parent, is no guarantee that one's children will turn out on the right side of life. Yet it is an imperative that Harlem's midlife parents feel keenly: their diligence, their monitoring, is crucial in increasing the odds that their children will turn out to be honorable people.

David and Lila Williams have been married twenty years and have seven children, the first of whom was born when Lila was seventeen. David works full-time for the New York Transit Authority on the night shift. Lila's job is to make sure her kids stay in school, go to work, and keep out of trouble. The parents agree that they must be vigilant in order to make sure their kids come through adolescence in Harlem in one piece. John explains:

> I don't want [my kids] to spend too much time out there on the street . . . you know, rubbing shoulders with certain people. Because some of them, they don't have really the best intentions. Sometimes the bad will rub off on the good instead of the good rubbing off on the bad. So I try to tell [my kids] if you want to go out, try not to be in front of the building where you've just got nothing to do. . . . It's better to go to the park, play some ball, run round the track, go ride a bike, do something, you know?
>
> Fellows that come to the house, I know their parents. The other guys that come [around], the other friends, I don't let them in my house. I just don't let anybody come in my house.
>
> [We] try to keep a record of what happens to them, how many times they're missing for a class. I call the school regularly. We were just at my daughter's school two weeks ago. I think that's a big concern, trying to make sure that they do what they're supposed to do at school.

Lila adds:

> [The biggest problems we faced when the kids were little] were watching their health, watching when they grew up. The area we lived in was . . . getting bad. So we couldn't let them go outside and play in the street. We had to, you know, take them where they needed to go. When they became teenagers, the biggest problem was just the people they were out with. The people that came to the house, the people they hung out with in school, they had a great influence on them. . . . When I found out that [my kids] were getting a negative influence [from certain

friends] you had to make sure they cut those out. And once we did that . . . there was a change in attitude of the children.

It would be comforting to these parents to believe that these strategies always pay off. Yet virtually everyone in the community can name families where the parents did everything possible to prevent their kids from "going bad," only to find they were fighting a loosing battle. Carol Estes talks about her neighbors, a hard-working couple with kids who are in deep trouble despite their best efforts:

[My friend] used to work at American Express. . . . Her husband works in the flea market on [the main thoroughfare in Harlem]. They pull together very hard to make things [work]. They don't bother people about things, and if you ever need a favor from her, you can just ask. . . . They have three children, and you can't blame them for what the children are doing. Their oldest son, I think he dropped out of eleventh grade. Their baby son, he got back in school because he got left back [a grade] last year. . . . Their middle son is messing with drugs, selling drugs, and he has got the baby son running behind him.

In a period of economic instability, even members of the solid middle class worry about the fate of their children. Opportunities appear to be closing down, the competition for a piece of the pie is fierce, and no one (save those with inherited wealth) can be absolutely sure that their efforts to foster their children's well-being will be successful. But they have many carrots to dangle in front of their kids. Families living in the poverty-stricken neighborhoods of central Harlem face more than the average rate of risk that their children will be dragged down by drugs and gangs. They can make few real promises about their children's futures. Given the pervasiveness of these problems, midlife parents can never be sure that their best efforts will be enough. Jane Eaton, who has a son in his early twenties and a nephew of the same age to raise, described this uncertainty well:

It's hard 'cause they have so much distractions out there, you know? 'Cause they see . . . it's this big temptation. They see, like, there's a lot of money to be made in selling drugs. But it's also very dangerous. If you got a "I don't care kid." well . . . I'm happy that my kids are sort of scared of the street. I'm

telling them, "Those guys will get you in jail." But you have a lot of . . . that fast money.

Harlem families in poor areas have no cocoon of protection that guarantees that such a tragic fate will never befall them. Hence, those who have managed, by good fortune and hard work, to see their families through the storms of adolescence and early adulthood without confronting these problems thank their blessings and define themselves as success stories.

CONCLUSION

It would be a mistake to try to understand the experience of middle age in a working poor African-American community like Harlem if one were to simply take the present on its own terms. Instead, I have tried to show that the particular problems that beset midlife men and women in this inner-city setting are "products" of a historical transformation that they have experienced in the course of their own lives. Harlem has gone from being a segregated working- and middle-class community in the 1940s and 1950s to a place where poverty is widespread and the social problems it engenders difficult to escape. This does not mean everyone in Harlem is poor or that an urban underclass has engulfed all of its residents. In fact, the "bad apples" are relatively few, but they cause major problems for the upstanding people who do not earn enough money to get away from them.

For people in midlife, this evolution has been a source of dismay. They remember rather vividly a different way of life, a disciplined existence of churchgoing neighbors, vigilant parents, and open doors. It is a transformation that has had an effect on many of them in the form of unemployment, deteriorating housing, and increasing danger on the streets. Now that most are parents, with children in their teenage years and early twenties, they confront the need to protect them from dangers that they did not have to contend with in their own youth. Moreover, they must come to grips with the fact that a sizable minority of their fellow Harlem dwellers have been unable to do the same. The children of these "failed" parents now menace the rest of the community.

Yet this generation of midlife adults also knows another kind of history, a history of place and race that is more positive. Having come up from the Jim Crow South, they have lived to see the Civil Rights era open doors that were tightly shut in their youth. They have moved from places where they could not walk the streets or board buses or attend schools of their choosing busted open with legal sledgehammers. Jane Easton is not sanguine about the current state of African-American ghettos, but she would never trade the present racial situation for that of the 1950s:

> You have a lot of different jobs available to you now, to minorities, that they didn't have before. You can practically be anything you want to be now. A long time ago, you couldn't. Who would have thought you would see a black mayor?"[16] You got a lot of black mayors, you got all kinds of jobs. I mean, who would have even thought, besides shining somebody's shoes or dealing up the office. Now you have the education. We haven't hit . . . president, but we're sure knocking on the door.

Jane is not suggesting that equality is a reality or that prosperity is a common condition in her community. On the contrary, she realizes that for most people life is very tough. She speaks of businesses moving across the border, of the impact of the North American Free Trade Agreement (NAFTA) on jobs, and the pressure on American wages that is driving so many working people below the poverty line. But she also knows many people her own age whose futures might have been nothing more than working in the peanut mills for lousy wages. Her vantage point of the present begins with this kind of past.

The generation of midlife Harlem dwellers represented in this chapter do not necessarily see eye-to-eye with their own children on these issues. Having never witnessed the Jim Crow South, their kids can only know this past as a history, not a lived reality. They have a different set of benchmarks, in which race appears to be hardening as a line of division. Nationalist movements in the ghettos, backlash movements in the white suburbs—these are the political realities that the younger generation has grown up with. And, one imagines, this divergent historical reality will shape the middle-age experience of new generations differently. This merely points back to the underlying thesis of this chapter: place (a combination of period and locale) and race matter a great deal in shaping images and experiences of middle age. I would argue that this is true, perhaps to an even greater degree, of midlife than of other points in the life cycle. To the extent that middle age involves a kind of assessment, a meditation upon where one has been and where one may be able to go in the last phase of life, midlife calls forth generational memories, cultural grids through which an individual's life trajectory, and the transformations of his or her community, are evaluated (see Newman 1996a).

NOTES

This paper is based upon a pilot study of African-Americans in middle age funded by a grant from the MacArthur Foundation Network on Successful Midlife Development to the Social Science Research Council. I wish to thank Bert Brim for his support of the Social Science Research Council seminar group and my colleagues in the seminar—Larry Aber, Jeanne Brooks-Gunn, David Featherman, Frank Furstenberg, Diane Hughes, Frank Kessel, Orlando Rodriguez, and Mary Waters—for the insights they have contributed that have found their way into this paper. I am particularly grateful to John Jackson, doctoral candidate in the Anthropology Department at Columbia University, for the work he contributed in the form of life history interviews with all of the informants discussed in this paper.

1. Participants in this project are the older relatives of young people working in fast food restaurants in central Harlem. Some two hundred of them—African-Americans, Dominicans, and Puerto Ricans—participated in my two-year study of low wage workers in 1993–95 (see Newman 1996b).

2. This is undoubtedly true of old age, too, but I would not argue it for other, earlier, stages.

3. Recent accounts suggest that the urban north is not alone in the trend toward increasing crime and drug traffic. In particular, the southern communities from whence my informants hail are also becoming more dangerous places to live. (See "In Selma, Everything and Nothing Changed" *New York Times*, 2 August 1994, p. 11.)

4. See Carol Stack (1996) for a description of persistent attachment to southern communities among blacks who were born in the north but have returned to the South in record numbers.

5. Black gay men in Harlem follow similar patterns of block settlement (Hawkeswood 1995).

6. Jimmy's memories parallel Elijah Anderson's (1990) research on the transformation of his inner-city neighborhood in Philadelphia. See also James Coleman (1988, 107) for a theoretical discussion of monitoring as an aspect of social capital.

7. The Mollen Commission, formed in 1993 to investigate police corruption in New York City, discovered that the Thirti-

eth Precinct (which covers much of the area where my informants live) has been mired in kickback schemes involving local drug dealers, harassment, and a variety of other forms of corruption. Many years of citizen complaints about the police had gone unheaded until this commission took an official look.

8. In general, black men have done poorly in the labor market compared to black women, in part because of educational differences, but also because women have been able to work in domains that were closed to men (e.g., domestic service), while the jobs that traditionally attract men have been evaporating with each wave of plant shutdowns.

9. One might be tempted to attribute this "burden to explain" to the research encounter. These interviews were all conducted by an African-American doctoral student with far more years of education than these informants. However, the same pressure to account for the fate of fellow members of one's racial group is documented in the literature on the African-American middle class. See Ellis Cose (1993) for more on this.

10. Charles Murray (1990), the conservative critic of the welfare system, has recently written popular articles warning that a white underclass is forming out of the increasing population of white women who are having out-of-wedlock births. It is conceivable that the old category of "white trash" may be resurrected here with many of the same consequences for nonpoor whites. At the moment, however, we are a long way from expecting whites in general to account for the deviant behavior of some member of their racial group.

11. See Feagin and Sikes (1994) in addition to Cose for further discussion of the psychological burdens of middle-class African-Americans charged with either abandoning their race brethren or explaining to others how the masses of blacks came to be poor.

12. The most prominent example in 1994 was the O. J. Simpson murder trial, a veritable litmus test of racial ideology that saw most whites believing he was guilty (giving no special dispensation for his upbringing in a poor black neighborhood) and a majority of blacks believing both in his innocence and the unfair nature of the judicial process (giving weight to Simpson's race in both aspects).

13. We shall see in the next section that many of my informants who still have young children at home do indeed spend a great deal of time and energy monitoring their behavior and their movements outside the home. Nonetheless, Barbara argues that there are far too few "old-fashioned" families of this kind.

14. Some economists have argued that there is no evidence for immigrant/native-born competition in the job market. Others have taken the opposite view-point and have said that in those areas where immigrants live, wage depression among the native born is widespread. See Borjas et al. (1992).

15. In a companion pilot study of middle-aged Latinos in New York City—conducted during the same 1993–95 time period—it became clear that there is no real Spanish equivalent for the term "middle age." The term had no meaning in Spanish, whether Puerto Rican, Mexican, or Dominican translators were used. Similarly, open-ended elicitation of life stages never yielded a single example of middle age as a "subdivision" of adulthood, much less a distinctive period in the life cycle.

16. She refers here to David Dinkins, then mayor of New York City.

REFERENCES

Anderson, E. 1990. *Streetwise.* Chicago: University of Chicago Press.

Borjas, George, Richard Freeman, and Lawrence Katz. 1992. "On the Labor Market Effects of Immigration and Trade." In *Immigration and the Workforce,* edited by G. Borjas and R. Freeman, 213–44. Chicago: University of Chicago Press.

City of New York, Department of Urban Planning. 1993. *Socio-Economic Profiles: A Portrait of New York City's Community Districts from the 1980 and 1990 Censuses of Population and Housing.* New York: Department of Urban Planning.

Coleman, James. 1988. "Social Capital in the Creation of Human Capital." *American Journal of Sociology,* suppl. 94:S95–S120.

Cose, Ellis. 1993. *Rage of the Privileged Class.* New York: HarperCollins.

Feagin, J., and M. Sikes. 1994. *Living with Racism: The Black Middle-Class Experience.* Boston: Beacon Press.

Hawkeswood, William. 1995. *One of the Children: Black Gay Men in Harlem.* Berkeley and Los Angeles: University of California Press.

Lehmann, Nicholas. 1993. *The Promised Land.* New York: Knopf.

Newman, Katherine. 1988. *Falling from Grace: The Experience of Downward Mobility in the American Middle Class.* New York: Free Press.

———. 1993. *Declining Fortunes: The Withering of the American Dream.* New York: Basic Books.

———. 1996a. "Ethnography, Biography and Cultural History: Generational Paradigms in Human Development." In *Ethnography and Human Development,* edited by Richard Jessor, Anne Colby, and Richard Shweder, 371–94. Chicago: University of Chicago Press.

———. 1996b. "Working Poor: Low Wage Employment in the Lives of Harlem Youth." In *Transitions through Adolescence,* edited by Julia Graber et al. Hillsdale, N.J.: Erlbaum Associates.

Stack, Carol. 1996. *Call to Home: African-Americans Reclaim the Rural South.* New York: Basic Books.

40 | THE SOCIAL WORLD OF OLD WOMEN
Sarah H. Matthews

This chapter will focus on how persons with weak stigmas, in this case old women, maintain their images of themselves. The ambiguity involved in applying the label "old" gives old women some latitude in defining themselves as "old" or "not old." Oldness is not a pivotal self-identity for most old people: old women in most situations reject the label old for themselves, even though they use it to describe others who are age peers. However, it is a pivotal social identity, one that others impute to the old woman, in those situations in which another of her status attributes is not more salient.

Numerous studies have focused on the "adjustment patterns" of those who accept and those who reject the label old for themselves (Brubaker and Powers, 1976; Kastenbaum and Durkee, 1964). Generally, findings indicate that under some conditions adopting the label is indicative of a "good adjustment" to old age (Phillips, 1957). Research has also been directed toward finding correlates of a self-definition of old, including widowhood, retirement, physical impairment, and others who think of the person as old, all of which have been shown to affect likelihood of describing oneself as old (Atchley, 1972; Blau, 1956; Preston, 1968). There is some question, however, about the everyday meaning of a response to this forced-choice question. The situation of being confronted by an interviewer and being asked to identify oneself as young, middle-aged, old, or elderly, is atypical, and responses in this situation may not spill over into daily round situations (Deutscher, 1973).

Others have focused on the political implications of the refusal of the aged to embrace the label "old," and within the field of social gerontology there is an ongoing debate concerning the validity of viewing the aged as an active or even a potential political interest group (Binstock, 1972; Rose, 1965). Maggie Kuhn, founder and leader of the Gray Panthers, attempts to "raise consciousness" and recruit politically oriented members by inviting listeners to follow her example and publicly proclaim that they are old and proud to be old. Although the membership of the Gray Panthers is growing, it is telling that a substantial portion of the members are not old themselves, but professionals concerned with the welfare of the aged.

The issues addressed here, however, are not related to adjustment or politics but to self-identity. Even though an old woman may not think of herself as old, she must deal with others in a variety of situations who do think of her as old. In addition, having internalized the stereotypes that author negative expectations of old behavior, she may find evidence in her own behavior that she is, after all, an old woman. The strategies for protecting her image of herself in these two situations, that is, those situations in which she interacts with others who assume she is an old woman and those in which she recognizes indications in her own thoughts and actions that she may be an old woman after all, will be addressed here.

Lofland (1976: 100) has pointed out that:

All encounters involve people in immediate interaction, but not all interactants need be in separate bodies. . . . To the degree that people engage in internal dialogues with themselves, we may speak of self-encounters, or in the context of situation and strategy analysis, self-management encounters.

The delineation of strategies here, then, are divided somewhat arbitrarily between encounters with others and encounters with self.

ENCOUNTERS WITH OTHERS

Even though the old woman does not think of herself as old, she must deal with situations in which other people think she is old. In conversations with others, especially younger others, the old woman is faced

---

with the assumption on the listener's part that she is an instance of the category "old woman." She must explain to people who assume she is an old woman that she is not. Thus, when an old woman is talking about old people in general she is careful to point out that she does not consider herself old. The observation that old women use one definition of old for themselves and another for age peers is closely paralleled in Rosow's (1967) research. He found that 50% of his sample described themselves as middle-aged, while at the same time 85% agreed that old people who felt middle-aged were simply deluding themselves.

One old woman who was a retired nurse and had worked with hospitalized old people said, "I just loved those old people. (pause) But see, I don't consider myself in that category." Another woman realizing that the person to whom she was speaking would need an explanation for why she excluded herself from the category "elderly," supplied one.

> I have seen so many elderly women (I don't know whether they were older than I, but some people age faster than others), and some of them could hardly walk, you know.

She does not think of herself as one of "the elderly," in this case, because she does not meet her situational criterion for being included, "unable to walk."

In managing encounters with others who may assume that they are "just old women," the informants used four strategies.

Suppress Evidence

One simple strategy an old woman may use is to avoid telling her age. As one informant said, "I never tell them how old I am. I just tell them I'm old enough." A woman aged eighty-plus recounted an experience at the Senior Citizens' Center that had occurred the previous day:

> They said, "Poor soul, she's in her eighties." I just laughed. They never count me. The lady yesterday was only seventy.

Another woman confided:

> I don't think they know my age. I don't ask them theirs. People don't think I'm as old as I am, so I don't go around blabbin' it.

Thus, she avoids confronting publicly the significance of her age. Of course, for some old women this strategy is not available. One informant stated, "I've always looked older than my age. I've sort of gotten used to it. You probably think I'm older than I am."

This strategy falls under the generic heading of "information management," a tactic available to persons with nonvisible discrediting attributes (Goffman, 1963). Chronological age is assumed to be visible and this strategy, logically, would not appear to be available to the old. However, most members of society have such strong beliefs that physical incapacity and old age are highly correlated that when an old person's age is mentioned many persons are completely surprised. For many old women, then, suppressing evidence is a successful strategy.

Different Definitions of Old

The old woman may have a definition of old that is based on criteria other than chronological age. The strategy follows logically since, as was noted above, old women have internalized societal definitions of old and at the same time view themselves personally as not belonging to the category. Slightly simplified, what occurs is that the old woman has one definition for other old people and one for herself. With this in mind, remarks such as the following take on meaning: "I don't think I ever got old. That's all there is to it. And I never will be. If I live to be one hundred, I'm not going to be old."

To make clear that she does not consider herself old, she may share her definitions that "It's what's inside that counts." As one old woman said:

> In the old vintage, eighty was the little black bonnet affair and that sort of thing. I don't think we should think of age chronologically at all. It's your outlook more than anything else.

Another old woman showed the interviewer a pamphlet entitled, "How to Stay Young Forever,"

> and I read this. Now if you practice this, you will be taking on the qualities associated with youth. People will never think about your age. They'll just think how young you are.

This is an overstatement of the point and very few of the old women would agree with so strong a proclamation, but many believe in the basic philosophy. Two other examples of old people's beliefs that they are young by virtue of what is inside are found in the following.

> I don't feel like I'm seventy-two. I'm surprised when I look in the mirror. I went down to get my hair cut the other day and I'm always surprised when I look down and see all that gray hair, because I don't feel gray-headed.
>
> Being old is like playing a character role. Inside you're just the same. But you have a lot of stuff clamped onto you. Various ailments. They won't kill me yet, but they're no joke. You can't walk twenty miles. You're just the same inside. You are doing a character part [J. B. Priestly, San Francisco Chronicle-Examiner, 1974].

Thus, each old person considers herself to be just an ordinary person and forgets whenever possible that she has the trappings of oldness. But when she must attend to the trappings, she explains that she is not what she seems. This strategy, more than the others, falls under both encounters with others and encounters with self.

Bring in Outside Sources

To increase the credibility of her belief in her "not oldness," she may bring in outside sources to say, in effect, "Other reputable people do not think of me as old."

> I think I'm pretty spry for my age. I'm only 83. I just had a birthday last Friday. People tell me I get along just fine.
>
> They don't treat me like I'm a helpless old lady. I thank God I'm as good as I am. Very few think of me as old as I am. They don't. People can't tell how old I am.

This strategy shows clearly the uncertainty with which the old woman views herself. She feels that her word alone is not sufficient proof and that, by citing others who think of her as not old or treat her as not old, she will somehow be more convincing to dubious listeners.

Avoid Threatening Situations

Avoiding situations in which her oldness may be the pivotal or general identity is one way to maintain a self-identity of "not old." She may do this by organiz-

ing her daily activities so that she is never in such a situation. As one woman stated,

> You know about young people, but I don't pay any attention to them. Go over here to K-Mart and they take up the whole sidewalk. And the way they look at you, they wouldn't get off that sidewalk. You have to go around them. . . . I don't like to go over there on Saturday or even late Friday afternoon because school's out.

This old woman can purposely avoid those potentially demeaning situations by doing her shopping during school hours. Another example which is less clear on the surface is: "I don't hear so I don't go to church. I listen to a service on TV." This seems like an adequate explanation if it is assumed that the only reason people attend church services is to hear a sermon, but the statement loses credence when the many social functions of the weekly gathering are considered. A more accurate statement might be: "I don't go to church because I can't participate in the stated reason for being there and that makes me very aware of my oldness."

Another form this strategy may take is to plan ahead to avoid doing things that others may think are a reflection of advanced age and thereby diminish credibility. On one occasion at a senior citizens center, a woman viewed the beginning of a downpour with some dismay. She had brought her raincoat, but had left it in the car. "I thought you'd laugh at me if I brought it in, old grandma with her raincoat and her boots." Thinking about her granddaughter's wedding that was to take place in the near future, one old woman described her nervousness:

> Of course I sort of get anxious and worried about whether I dress right or look right or not or whether I say the things I should say or shouldn't say, and, you know, sometimes you forget if you've got more information that you're supposed to.

Everyone may feel a tinge of anxiety before a formal occasion, but old people fear that a social faux pas will be viewed as an indication of senility. By taking special care to see that her props and conversations are correct, the old woman acts to protect her self-image.

The safest way to avoid potentially problematic situations is perhaps the most general, and that is simply to avoid verbal and nonverbal interaction, especially with young people, who are seen as the least sympathetic. As one woman put it:

> I mix with my own age. I don't feel at home with younger people. They're nice and I love them and I love to watch them enjoy themselves, but I don't mix with them. I'm a wet blanket at my age on their activities. So I don't want to spoil anyone's fun. I like my own age. I feel at home there.

Tales of what happens when encounters take place are fairly rare, perhaps because the old women manage their daily rounds so well that encounters themselves are rare. One such incident is reported to her peers by an old woman.

> I was walking home from shopping. I guess it was Thursday. And there was this young fella, see, and his friend. I was carrying my groceries. They were heavy. And I was walking, you know, kind of slow. And that young fella called, "Why aren't you in your grave?" He and his friend laughed [Hochschild, 1969: 165].

Another old woman recounted a similar incident. On her way to the grocery store, she had passed a group of small children,

> and I grinned at them because I like children, and one of them looked up and she said, "You're ugly, ugly, ugly." And I said, "Well, so are you." And one of them was going to hit me with a stick. I said, "If you do, I'll call the sheriff." . . . I was surprised to death. I must have had a long face because I didn't feel very good and it takes all of me to get there and all of me to get back. But I have to laugh about it now.

The highway is another public place where the old meet the young.

> There have been a few occasions with younger people. Well, when I say younger I don't mean in the middle twenties, I mean in the teens. I had the feeling they were saying, "The poor old soul," especially when I used to drive a car. They had the attitude, the look on their face, "What the devil are you doing out in a car? You belong home in a rocking chair." But I can truly say it wasn't very often. But I'm kind of stupid. It might be that I didn't even notice.

The most frequent examples are of interaction with grand-children.

> I would try to tell these kids what we used to do when

I was their age. "Oh, Grandma, they don't do that anymore. They don't do that anymore."

The safest adaptation to having what she says dismissed as irrelevant and outdated, a severe hardship to her self-identity, is simply to quit talking, not to put herself on the line. A conversation between two old women indicates that this is not uncommon.

> Goldie had helped her granddaughter find a job. The grand-daughter was surprised that Goldie's advice had been valid. Ellen said that she didn't like to give her children or grandchildren advice. They think she doesn't know what she's talking about because times have changed so much. She just doesn't bother any more to tell them what she thinks.

The risks involved in conversing with younger people, and even in encountering them in public settings, are often too great to warrant putting herself in such situations.

Disengagement theory is one explanation of this type of data. Cumming and Henry (1961: 14) write:

> the old person is less involved in the life around him than he was when he was younger. . . . Aging is an inevitable mutual withdrawal resulting in decreased interaction between the aging person and others in the social system he belongs to.

The data presented here indicate that lack of interaction is not mutually rewarding, but a response to a situation that is threatening to the old woman's self-identity.

ENCOUNTERS WITH SELF

In encounters with self, the old woman must deal with signs, both physical and social, which indicate that she is a "typical" old woman after all. Again, some of these strategies might also be considered encounters with others, but, for the most part, are strategies for coping with self-doubt rather than directly with the doubts of others.

What Seems Like Oldness Really Isn't

Occasionally the old woman recognizes things about herself that she associates with oldness, but she is quick to find other explanations.

> I used to be able to watch television. Now I fall

asleep in the middle of the darn show. . . . But my son-in-law, Bob, he's half my age, and he falls asleep.

They just can't realize that maybe it's swell for you, but if it's swell for you and cutting someone else's throat, what good is it? And I'm not just talking because it's almost over. I have always felt that way. I don't think I've changed in my philosophy or my ideals in life anymore than when I was fourteen years old and I still maintain that you can't have it all unless you're going to hurt someone else.

One old woman has noticed in the last year that she does not like to be with large groups of noisy people.

Now that may be my age. I think that perhaps being older, I can't tolerate it as well. That's being honest. And I think, too, the world is really noisier.

As these episodes indicate, doubt may rear its ugly head, but age is soon dismissed as the "real" cause of her behavior and her beliefs.

Attach New Meaning to Old Activities

One of the features noted above of growing old in American society is the attenuation that occurs in the number of bonds to other people. The social-structural facts of oldness include a reduction in the number of roles available to old people. Old people are retired and widowed and independent, which is a euphemistic way of saying they live alone. They are still parents and grandparents and siblings, but these roles have no particular content. They are weak ways of identifying oneself. The old widow, in losing important roles, has fewer ways of viewing herself. She can no longer identify herself as a nurse, for example, or the postman's wife, or even the retired postman's wife. Being retired or widowed are identities that are nonrelationships, and the roles that do relate to other people lack content (Rosow, 1974) and cannot be used to justify existence.

That justification for existence is important to old people can be seen in the extreme in this letter to Abby (San Francisco Chronicle-Examiner, 1973).

Dear Abby—You asked to hear from senior citizens: Would that some compassionate, benevolent God take this body and accept the soul of man on the day he voluntarily retires or is arbitrarily retired from his work and soon becomes . . . Useless Seventy

This occurs in less dramatic forms in old peoples' daily lives. For example, when I asked an old woman what she had been doing since I last saw her, she replied, "Nothing much," and after a slight pause, "But I've been active." This old woman is in all likelihood doing the same things she has always done—cooking, cleaning, marketing, watching television, visiting with friends—but she is no longer doing these things for anyone, and therefore has no estimable labels for what she is doing, no way to justify her existence to me or to herself. This is not totally situational. Even in "age dense" housing, this need to justify exists among age peers. Hochschild (1973) found that the women in the housing project she studied regarded their "downstairs activities" (making things for others or for money) as work and were suspicious of those who stayed upstairs and did not join them. Justification even between age peers would appear to be important, although acceptable justifications may be more easily negotiated among age peers.

The lack of justifying labels for herself, then, is a problem that is dealt with in two ways. One, illustrated above by "Useless Seventy," is to personally accept, sometimes bitterly, the stereotypical denotation of the old as worthless to society. This stance is not typical of the informants. Attaching new meaning to the old activities is a more common strategy. Crocheting, cleaning house, watching television become ways of "keeping busy," which is now the justification for living. One woman said that she missed her job when she retired, "Until I got myself interested in keeping busy." Another stated:

Main things I do are go to church and play bridge. Outside of that, when I'm home, in the evenings, I watch television and crochet. I keep busy all the time.

Again, one woman said:

But you'd be surprised about how busy I am all the time. It seems silly, retired, and nobody but yourself. You know, you haven't got time to do things. I don't get done what I think I ought to do.

Another woman plans her day to include something that will justify the day when it comes to an end.

If I'm active during the day, I feel better. I don't know. . . . When you feel like you've accomplished something, even if it's the washing or the ironing, you feel like you've accomplished something. But if you just sit around all day with no point in view, you don't feel as good. It's a funny thing. If you have some interest, something that holds your interest, whether it be sewing or writing letters, or doing wash or cleaning up your place, or cooking or something. But if you just lie around. . . .

By attaching new meaning to old activities, the old woman is able to justify her daily life and maintain her self-identity as not old. If she were old, she would be spending the day in a rocking chair, and, since she is active, she must not be old.

Accounts

In her relationships with her offspring, their spouses and, to a lesser degree, their children, a poor relationship is viewed by the old woman as damaging to her self-identity: stereo-typical old women are forgotten by their families. Only a few informants directly expressed dissatisfaction with such a relationship, blaming the offspring, or in most cases the offspring's spouses. However, most hinted at a less than satisfactory relationship by giving accounts, excuses, or justifications for their children and in-laws not spending more time with them. Lyman and Scott (1970: 112) write:

> An account is a linguistic device employed whenever an action is subjected to valuation inquiry. . . . An account is not called for when people engage in routine, common-sense behavior in a cultural environment that recognizes that behavior as such.

Lack of interaction with offspring, then, is not viewed as routine. Reasons must be given to explain why a son or daughter is not as attentive as the old woman would like, or others feel he or she should be, that do not tarnish her image of herself. One reason two people do not get together more often may be that one of the parties finds the time together unrewarding. This obviously is not an acceptable reason for the old woman if she is to maintain a favorable view of herself.

A common justification for lack of attention is that there is just not enough time in the day to get everything done one would like to do; other things come before Mother, and rightly so.

But as I said, if you keep a marriage together, keep a roof over their heads, keep them fed, and raise three girls, you have your hands full without worrying about your doting mother, don't you?

Or again:

> I have a daughter over on 61st Street, but she works so I don't see her as often.

Even less traditional activities can be used as excuses to avoid the possible conclusion that spending time with an old woman is unrewarding. One woman recounted her daughter-in-law's weekly schedule, which included volunteer work, painting classes, a trip to the hairdressers', cleaning house, doing the laundry, and even spending the weekend with the old woman's son. This busy schedule and her son's working precluded their spending time with her, and at the same time this explanation left her self-identity intact.

She may also explain inattention by saying, in essence, "My relatives do not spend a lot of time with me because I am not an old lady yet." The fact that she is leading an independent life, that their paths rarely cross, can be a source of pride, although, perhaps a wistful pride. One old woman said in a straightforward manner:

> I've always been self-sufficient and independent and my son knows that. Without even giving it a thought, he knows that he doesn't have to worry about me.

And another pointed with pride to her relationship with her son, comparing it to some of her age peers.

> I've been more concerned about his happiness than mine. He has a nice life now. That's very important for my well being. To know that your children are all right is important. I know that there's some around here who just wait for their children to call and they're calling them forty times a day. I never have been like that because I figure they have to live. They have to hold down jobs and they can't do it if Mamma is on the phone every once in a while, crying.

This excuse makes lack of attentiveness a virtue rather than a reflection on her advanced years.

A third form refers to the "natural order of things," what Lyman and Scott (1970: 116) designate as a biological drive or "fatalistic forces" excuse, that, of course, young relatives have many interests that do not include old people. The world is seen as including

some activities that are for the young only, young referring in some cases to sons and daughters only twenty years the old woman's junior. This excuse is potentially demeaning and is used not as an excuse for
inattentiveness when describing nonrelatives, but as a
slur. One woman described the plight of her sister-in-
law.

> You know the younger people. They have their ways
> of doing and the older people are just left to sit and
> do whatever they can do.

But for sons and daughters and grandchildren to be
out engaging in "young" activities is only right and
"natural."

> I can't be sitting here thinking, "Oh, gee whiz, here I
> am alone." Sometimes my boy calls me up, but
> sometimes he doesn't for a week or two. And why
> should he? He has his life. Why should he give up his
> happiness with young people just because I'm his
> mother and bore him?

One grandmother pointed out the "naturalness" of the
situation:

> They outgrow their grandmother like they do Santa
> Claus and other things. Used to be they'd run across
> the street to find you and now they'll run across the
> street to keep from meeting their grandma and hav-
> ing to explain her to their friends. You know when
> they are that age, they're so busy. I'm not being face-
> tious, but they do. They outgrow their grandparents
> like they do Santa Claus. It's a phase of life and it
> isn't that they don't have any need for me now be-
> cause they are busy with growing up.

If something occurs because it is "natural," because it
is just the way things are, it cannot be a reflection on
the old woman personally and her self-identity is left
unmarred.

This "natural order of things" includes a definition
of a good mother, mother-in-law, and grandmother relationship that excludes the old woman. A "good" relationship is defined by the old woman in such a way
that she is an observer, or, at best, a nonvoting participant, rather than an equal partner. For example, one
woman reported with pride that her daughter-in-law
had said of her:

> "Oh, I've got a good mother-in-law. She never both-
> ers. You never hear her complain." I don't know

about that so much. I try not to interfere in their life.
I had my life to live as I wanted to.

The old woman, then, must not make any demands on
the relationship lest she give the impression that she is
interfering. Another old woman reported succinctly,
"We have a very nice relationship. I try not to infringe
on their privacy." One woman explained that her son
had transferred his affection from her to his wife,

> which is a good thing. That's the way it should be. So
> they sit and chit and chat and chat away more than he
> and I do anymore. . . . Anything that I want to discuss
> with him I can, but as far as personal things, well, he
> discusses that with his wife.

The old woman is free, and often feels obligated, to
discuss her personal affairs with her son or daughter
but she does not expect her offspring to reciprocate,
and this is accepted as "right." The old woman, then,
maintains her self-identity in an inequalitarian relationship by righteously holding to a belief in the "natural order." That this definition of the relationship may
be accepted as natural, but not with great conviction,
is seen in bits of data such as this:

> I have a card here that I treasure from my little
> daughter-in-law that says, "To my very good friend."
> Now isn't that a nice thing to write to your mother-
> in-law?

When the relationship is defined as an equalitarian
one, a friendship one, even as peripherally as this, it is
joyfully noted. The old woman, then, calls on the "natural order" to justify also the quality of the attention
that does occur and, in so doing, maintains an image
of herself that is acceptable to her.

Reciprocity

The stereotypical old woman has little to offer in relationships with other people. Valuable relationships
among people are, ideally, mutually rewarding to all
parties, but old people, by virtue of their imputed stigma and lack of resources, have few rewards to offer
others. Maintaining a belief in reciprocity, that she is
giving as well as receiving, in relationships with others, is one way to escape an image of herself as a val-
ueless old person.

One way to maintain this belief in reciprocity is

for the old woman to feel that she is now getting a return on an investment she made in the past.

> If I ever need anything, they both will be very willing to help. When I worked I made pretty good money and I helped them a lot. I've helped them, so I think if I'm in need they would help me out, too.

This is an abstract sort of reciprocity and tends to be associated with inducing guilt feelings. It does little in the here-and-now to make the old woman feel deserving of affection. A here-and-now semblance of reciprocity can also be maintained. One woman had just spent the weekend at a lake with her son, daughter-in-law, and grandchildren, in a cabin she had purchased for them. When she purchased the cabin she explained to her son, "And I'll give it to you now. Then if I die overnight you won't have to go through court and get the $12,000." This old woman exchanged a cabin in the mountains for the right to be included in vacations.

Another old woman is quite blunt about the fact that she pays her relatives to come visit her. She may be dependent in that she needs them for transportation, household chores, outings, and company, but they get something in return. Speaking of her granddaughter's most recent visit, she said:

> When she was here the other day, I, now let me see what did I do for her? I gave her groceries, filled her car up with gas, and I must have given her some money.

This old woman in almost all descriptions of visits with relatives mentions the fact that she "pays her own way and then some." She is, of course, much more blatant than most of her age peers, but, therefore, serves as an excellent example. Another less overt example is found in the following response to a question about dependency. Speaking of her daughter this woman said:

> I have to depend on her for transportation, but she depends on me an awful lot. I still feel useful because if anybody is sick, or she gets behind on her ironing or something like that, she comes and gets me to help her. And then I do all her sewing, too. I feel I'm still needed. Once school is out, they will be going to Florida on vacation and they will be gone for three weeks and I'm going over to babysit the house, do the watering, and take care of the mail that comes in.

By making herself useful and seeing herself as needed, she is able to maintain this semblance of reciprocity and avoid feeling dependent and, therefore, old. This is also done with friends.

> I'm a doer for others and not a crier for myself and maybe that's why I have so many younger friends. Because I'll mind the kids. I'll make a dress. I'll do this and that. At the same time, I can call them and say, "My legs hurt me. Can you take me to the bank?"

This is an unusual case because of the age differences noted. Reciprocity between friends of the same age is "normal" and not particularly noteworthy. Hochschild (1973: 65–66) characterized the relationships between age peers in the public housing project she studied as "sibling bonds."

> Most residents of Merrill Court are social siblings. The custom of exchanging cups of coffee, lunches, potted plants, and curtain checking suggest reciprocity. . . . They trade, in even measure, slips from house plants, kitchen utensils, and food of all sorts. They watched one another's apartments when someone was away on a visit, and they called and took calls for one another.

Reciprocity becomes an issue when self-identity is threatened in nonegalitarian relationships.

Failure to maintain a relationship in which exchange takes place leads to ambivalence about the desirability of continuing the relationship.

> My granddaughter comes over so much. She has a car and she's a good driver and she comes over and says, "Now, if you have any errands, let's go." Well, sometimes I feel guilty. Well, gee, she comes over here and it's tear here and tear there. She likes to do it, but I feel guilty. I feel guilty.

Carp (1972: 68) found in a study of transportation needs of the elderly that a majority of the old people in her survey sample were nervous about the skill of drivers with whom they rode, and "nearly as many disliked becoming indebted to the person who provided the ride."

One strategy, then, for maintaining self-identity in relations with others is to point out the reciprocity that is part of the relationship. In doing so the old woman avoids viewing herself as dependent, a state associated with oldness.

DISCREPANT DEFINITIONS OF IDENTITY

Viewed generically the situation the old widows face in finding similarities between themselves and the stereotypical old woman is one all social actors confront when they hold different definitions of themselves than are held by others with whom they interact. Much research on persons defined as deviant, either because of their appearances (social identities) or their biographies (personal identities), has focused on the difficulties of maintaining an acceptable view of self when confronted by others who hold different assumptions and definitions. Davis (1961) focuses on the visibly handicapped and how they cope to maintain a "preferred definition of self." Jackman et al. (1963) considers the problems of the professional prostitute and the way she explains her behavior in order to think of herself as a moral person. Ray (1961) focuses on the problems the reformed drug addict faces in dealing with others who adopt the attitude "once a drug addict always a drug addict." These are only a few of the many examples in the literature.

Persons who are not considered deviant find themselves in similar situations, but, because they are not considered abnormal, their strategic management of self definition has not come under close scrutiny. Most people organize their lives, or have them organized automatically by structural constraints, so that they are not with people who question their images of themselves. Professors, for example, spend most of their time with other professors or admiring (or powerless) students, rather than with members of society who question the validity of higher education and the worth of devoting a lifetime to teaching and research. Physicians spend their time with other physicians, persons in medical fields, or patients, all of whom rarely question physicians' images of themselves as competent humanitarians. When a particular group threatens their self-images, legitimate methods for eliminating those others from doctors' life space are found, such as refusal to accept Medicaid patients, ostensibly because of the burdensome paper work or low fee schedules. Women who view themselves righteously and primarily as housewives and mothers are not found in "conciousness raising" groups, and, if they are, the topics for discussion do not resemble

those of groups composed of self-proclaimed feminists. Classical music buffs rarely find themselves in situations in which they must defend their taste in music (Benson, 1971), but, if they do, may credibly explain their position, for it is shared by others. For "normals," then, the social world is organized in such a way that self-identity is rarely questioned and, if it is, active or passive withdrawal from those situations is relatively easy and seen as legitimite.

This is not to say that professors, physicians, mothers, and feminists, do not have doubts about their respective self-identities. A physician, for example, must occasionally ask him or herself, "What if I really am motivated by economic self-interest?" Feminists must wonder if they really are simply "man haters." A favorable view of self, even under ideal circumstances, may be more difficult to maintain than is often assumed. "Defense mechanisms," which are usually relegated to the status of neurotic or psychotic symptoms, can more accurately be considered as positive, necessary, and ingenious methods for protecting self from the paralyzing effects of doubt (Lofland, 1976).

The old widows whose social worlds are under analysis here are more like the "deviants" than the "normals" in that their worlds are not neatly compartmentalized. Associating primarily with others who see them as they see themselves is difficult. The stereotypes about oldness are pervasive. Indeed, the old women share them. There are fewer others available to validate their self-images than there are for "normals."

All of the examples above are of actors who view themselves as better (more competent, wiser, more intelligent) than others with whom they may come into contact. Some actors may be pleasantly surprised to find that others are willing to accept them as they think of themselves. Research on attitudes toward the old shows that the old are not consistently viewed negatively (Brubaker and Powers, 1976), and the analysis here emphasizes the ambiguous nature of applying the label "old." There is, then, a very real possibility that those with whom the old widows interact have a higher opinion of them than is expected. The strategies the old women and others use to protect their self-images may prevent them from discovering that they are, in fact, admired by others, or at least, that others are willing to relegate their oldness or other attributes to the status of a basic identity. Evidence to support this is found in Kitsuse's (1962) analysis of attitudes of informants toward acquaintances whom they discovered were homosexuals. He found that the informants' opinions changed only slightly. By encapsulating themselves, the old widows, and others with weak stigmas, may be preventing themselves from discovering that situations are much less negative than they assume.

SUMMARY

It is certainly not news that members of stigmatized groups find ways to protect their images of themselves and old women are not exceptions. In encounters with others and encounters with self they are able to put forth points of view and explanations and to manage daily rounds so that their behavior and relationships are not seen as "typical" of old women generally, and, thus, are able to maintain acceptable self-images. Old women occupy a peculiar position because they have fewer ways than most "normal" members of society in which to redeem themselves and many of the strategies they use to maintain an acceptable self-identity separate them still further from the mainstream of social life.

REFERENCES

Atchley, Robert C., 1972, The Social Forces in Later Life. Belmont, Ca.: Wadsworth.

Benson, Joseph, 1971, "Classical Music and the Status Game." In Irving Louis Horowitz and Mary Symons Strong (eds.) Sociological Realities: A Guide to the Study of Society. New York: Harper & Row, pp. 240–245.

Binstock, Robert H., 1972, "Interest-Group Liberalism and the Politics of Aging." The Gerontologist 12:265–280.

Blau, Zena Smith, 1956, "Changes in Age and Status Identification." American Sociological Review 21:198–203.

Brubaker, Timothy H. and Edward A. Powers, 1976, "The Stereotype of 'Old': A Review and Alternative Approach." Journal of Gerontology 31(4):441–447.

Carp, Frances M., 1972, "Retired People as Automobile Passengers." The Gerontologist 12(1):66–72.

Cumming, Elaine and William E. Henry, 1961, Growing Old. New York: Basic Books.

Davis, Fred, 1961, "Deviance Disavowal: The Management of Strained Interaction by the Visibly Handicapped." Social Problems 9:120–132.

Deutscher, Irwin, 1973, What We Say/What We Do: Sentiments and Acts. Glenview, Ill.: Scott, Forseman.

Goffman, Erving, 1963, Stigma: Notes on the Management of Spoiled Identity. Englewood Cliffs, N.J.: Prentice-Hall.

Hochschild, Arlie Russell, 1969, "A Community of Grandmothers." Ph.D. dissertation, Department of Sociology, University of California, Berkeley.

———, 1973, The Unexpected Community. Englewood Cliffs, N.J.: Prentice-Hall.

Jackman, Norman R., Richard O'Toole, and Gilbert Geis, 1963, "The Self-Image of the Prostitute." Sociological Quarterly 4:150–160.

Kastenbaum, Robert and Nancy Durkee, 1964, "Elderly People View Old Age." In Robert Kastenbaum (ed.) New Thoughts on Old Age. New York: Springer Publishing, pp. 250–262.

Kitsuse, John I., 1962, "Societal Reaction to Deviant Behavior." Social Problems 9:247–256.

Lofland, John, 1976, Doing Social Life. New York: John Wiley.

Lyman, Stanford B. and Marvin B. Scott, 1970, "Accounts." In A Sociology of the Absurb. New York: Appleton-Century-Crofts, pp. 111–143.

Phillips, Bernard, 1957, "A Role Theory Approach to Adjustment in Old Age." American Sociological Review 22(2):212–217.

Preston, C.E., 1968, "Subjectively Perceived Agedness and Retirement." Journal of Gerontology 23:201–204.

Ray, Marsh B., 1961, "The Cycle of Abstinence and Relapse Among Heroin Addicts." Social Problems 9:132–140.

Rose, Arnold, 1965, "The Subculture of Aging." In Arnold Rose and Warren Peterson (eds.) Older People and Their Social World. Philadelphia, Penn.: F.A. Davis, pp. 3–16.

Rosow, Irving, 1967, Social Integration of the Aged. New York: Free Press.

———, 1974, Socialization to Old Age. Berkeley: University of California Press.

FURTHER READING

Copp, Martha. 1998. "Adult 'Adolescents': Social Control of Sexuality and Adulthood in People with Developmental Disabilities." *Sociological Analysis* 1: 113–135.

- An ethnographic study of the social construction of the life course and sexuality of disabled adults.

Fine, Gary Alan. 1986. "The Dirty Play of Little Boys." *Society* 24: 63–67.

- Aggressive pranks and sexual talk among boys in Little League baseball teams.

Gubrium, Jaber F. and Robert J. Lynott 1985. "Alzheimer's Disease as Biographical Work." Pp. 349–367 in *Social Bonds in Later Life,* edited by Warren A. Peterson and Jill Quadagno. Thousand Oaks, CA: Sage.
  • A study of how the disease figures into the interpretation of normacy and illness.
Holstein, James A. and Jaber F. Gubrium. 2000. *Constructing the Life Course.* Lanham, MD: Rowman & Littlefield.
  • A constructionist analysis of the life course.
Van den Hoonard, Deborah Kestin. 1997. "Identity Foreclosure: Women's Experiences of Widowhood as Expressed in Autobiographical Accounts." *Ageing and Society,* 17: 533–551.
  • Discusses how identity is mediated by a new world of widowhood.

—— SECTION 4 ——

FAMILY AS A SOCIAL WORLD

When people think of the family, they commonly conceive of it as a close-knit group of individuals related by blood, marriage, or adoption. It's a bounded universe of interactions and relationships with kin. The family is a world unto itself, located in and around the household, apart from other worlds.

An interactional perspective on social worlds is concerned with *how* such a world is constructed and sustained. From this standpoint, "family" is as much an *idea* as it is a social object. It's a collection of associated meanings, not just a group of people. To be sure, this is an unconventional view. It transforms family from being a concrete collectivity into also being a way of thinking and talking about people and their relations with one another. "Family" and related terms become a vocabulary for social relations, a set of interpretive resources for assigning meaning to people and relationships.

The language of domesticity constructs family *in practice.* We use phrases such as "He's like a father to me" to convey the depth, reverence, and permanence of a relationship. Labels, such as sorority "sisters" and fraternity "brothers," underscore affective ties and enduring commitments. Even street gangs and prison inmates use the terms "family," "brother," "sister," "mother," and "father" to describe relations with one another and to represent their solidarity in relation to outsiders.

By the same token, withholding family designations is a way of excluding persons or denigrating social relations. Consider what it means for a mother to cry to her children "You're no sons of mine!" This is a dramatic indictment of the sons' relationship with their mother. It speaks loudly about how the mother feels she is being treated, as well as how she feels about her erstwhile sons. Words do make a difference. What we call people is morally consequential and tells a great deal about how we relate to them. Using or withholding family designations is a way of conferring identity that has implications for both those who employ family discourse and those to whom it is applied.

Because the language of family life may be applied anywhere and at any time, the social world of family is not necessarily tied to households or any other specific location, for that matter. Nor is it an experiential realm shared by family members alone. Instead, a social world of family may be "activated" at any time and in any place that family meanings are used to make sense of relationships. Consider, for example, how often we hear the coach of a football or basketball team attribute the team's success to "being a family." It's a way of conveying the team's willingness and ability to work together, care for one another, and pursue collective goals. Being "family" in this case has little to do with households and everything to do with commitment and cooperation. Family doesn't reside in the kitchen or the living room. It identifies and accentuates acts of caring and sharing wherever they may happen. Perhaps more rarely, family discourse can also be used negatively to describe social relationships by drawing from the darker side of family life: domestic abuse, blind loyalty, and siblings' incessant squabbling, among other things. Family is as ubiquitous as the occasions of its descriptive application. It knows no geographic or kinship limits. Its imprints on a social world may be seen at any time and in any place where family discourse is employed.

ABOUT THE READINGS

"**What Is Family?**" seems like a simple inquiry. When it's posed in **Jaber F. Gubrium** and **James A. Holstein's** chapter, however, it ignites a discussion that leads to more questions than answers. The scenario is imaginary, of course, but the authors use it to highlight how easy it is to take things for granted when they seem extremely familiar to us. Family is one of those "things."

Gubrium and Holstein use an imaginary alien to make "family" seem anthropologically strange. They invite readers to set aside normal preconceptions to observe family as if it were the artifact of some exotic society. By making it appear strange, the authors are able to ask questions that we would otherwise think are obvious or trivial. In the case of family, Gubrium and Holstein ask readers to consider the question "What is family?" without jumping to the conclusion that everybody knows what it is. They ask readers to look and listen carefully to how family is constructed and used in social interaction. If one pays close attention, they argue, one can hear how family is literally "talked into being."

This theme runs through **Nancy Anne Naples's** poignant account of **"A Member of the Funeral."** The occasion of her father's death gives Naples pause to recount the interwoven stories of the biological and "fictive" families of which she has been a part. The situation is complicated by the fact that Naples is a lesbian, and many of her significant others don't fit into presumed patterns of family life. Nevertheless, they sometimes prove to be more of a family to Naples than her closest kin.

Notions of what family is, or is supposed to be, literally collide when Naples attempts to bridge the chasm between her biological family and the intimate friends that she calls her "real" family. The point that resonates throughout the account is that family is not simply a thing that is just "there." Instead, it is something that is "done". Biological kinship, for example, doesn't ensure the compassion and caring that the term "family" typically implies. Intimate ties can be fashioned between those who have neither biological nor legal connection. Naples describes a panoply of ways of "doing family" that remind us that the social construction process can involve profound emotion work.

Definitions of family are also at stake in **Catherine Kohler Riessman's** chapter **"Stigma**

and Everyday Resistance Practices." In this study of childless women in South India, Riessman examines how family is constructed in a cultural setting where a woman's status depends largely on motherhood. To be a respectable woman, one must bear and raise children. Childless women, Riessman tells us, are constantly questioned, devalued, and ridiculed about their family status. In South India, it's not ordinary and natural for women to be childless, and such women are considered highly deviant. In addition, they are ostracized, if not exiled, from the lives of conventional Indian extended families.

The women Riessman studied, however, do not necessarily succumb to the cultural definitions of their lives and selves. Some South Indian women actively resist discredited feminine identities, creating a space for alternatives that come in different terms. They find ways to successfully construct family and family membership, even while their culture marginalizes them. In listening to these women's words, we can literally hear how they transform stigmatized identities to construct alternative family worlds. From them, we learn that social worlds are not ironclad templates for identities. Instead, they provide ways of both being and resisting identity prescriptions.

41 | WHAT IS FAMILY?
Jaber F. Gubrium and James A. Holstein

"When *I* use a word," Humpty Dumpty said in rather a scornful tone, "it means just what I choose it to mean—neither more nor less."
"The question is," said Alice, "whether you *can* make words mean so many different things."
"The question is," said Humpty Dumpty, "which is to be master—that's all."
    —*Lewis Carroll,* Alice Through the Looking Glass

Professor Caswell, a renowned scholar of the family, quoted from Lewis Carroll whenever he had the opportunity to make a point about human nature. As he once concluded, "Alas, friends, big brass, and pedestrians, words are what we make of them." Nevertheless, Caswell expected more from the language of serious scholarship. Family studies was a science, and he believed that science harbored clear thinking and precise meanings.

Lately, though, Caswell had been bothered by a small figment of his imagination, a curmudgeon of

himself who talked back incessantly, especially when Caswell railed over the place of words and meanings in life and science. That little bit of himself seemed to emerge full-blown one day when Caswell turned to a favored classroom technique for prodding students out of their taken-for-granted view of things. "I shall assume the perspective of an extraterrestrial visitor," he told his students, "and you will see how your familiar world must look to a stranger." Caswell instructed them to imagine him as an androgynous cyborg—a cybernetically operated organism named "Borg."

Caswell had explained earlier that the family had taken many different forms throughout history and across cultures, producing diverse households. It ranged from what some call the extended family to its ever-popular nuclear counterpart of mother, father, and children. Caswell had been careful to point out that the varied configurations, in their particular historical and cultural contexts, were normal forms, not

From *What Is Family?* by Jaber F. Gubrium and James A. Holstein. 1990 Mayfield. Reprinted with permission of the authors.

to be judged more superior or less desirable just because they differed from each other or from what is commonplace today. He added that, in some social contexts, the family had such strong connections with other social forms, like the workplace, that it was much less distinguished as a special unit of life than it is now. Caswell suggested that the family might take on any number of shapes and functions and launched into a lengthy discussion of "alternate family forms" such as the commune. As most textbooks on the family purported, an exact definition of family was out of reach.

Attempting to show his class how to sort through the variety of ties that have been called family, Caswell asked the students to put themselves in Borg's place. "Pretend that you don't know what words mean at all, that you don't know to what or how words should be applied. Now let's try to figure out what the family really is." Caswell wanted to show the students how the word "family," while highly variable in its historical and cultural meanings, nonetheless could be used to designate a concrete form of life, one he had studied for the greater part of his scholarly career.

Caswell started by talking about tables rather than households or homes. Using the classroom table next to him, he noted that, like the table, the family had parts and at the same time was a whole. Running his hand over the top of the table and down one of the legs, he explained how the whole held together the parts and implied each part's functions. Each leg held the top above the floor. The top, in turn, not only made the legs' collective functions evident but also provided a surface upon which objects could be placed.

Again referring to a table's analogy with the family, Caswell indicated how tables come in as many sizes and shapes as the family. "Some are big, some small, some do certain things—just as some tables hold dishes and others hold saws, different families do altogether different things." He cautioned that, nonetheless, they are all families. Caswell described structure and function as something common to all, even while he carefully denoted family's human variations. "And so that alien who looks across history and from one culture to another notices many, many differences. As Borg might ask, 'How can you have so many words for so many different things?'" Caswell's point was that, despite the variety across history and culture, *the* family was a continuous part of human experience.

Now Borg—that curmudgeon in Caswell's mind—emerged to speak in her own voice. Like Humpty Dumpty, she asked in a scornful tone, "But, Professor Caswell, I see the table, the students see the table, but I don't recall having seen *the* family, any family. If you ask me to find other tables using this one as a guide, I can probably find them; but I don't think I could do the same if you showed me a family or even gave me pictures of families." Borg added that, in her casual wanderings on Earth, she hadn't actually seen a family, only people.

Caswell picked up the assigned family textbook. Like most such textbooks, it included colorful pictures of diverse families and households, showing a variety of cultural and historical origins. Caswell opened the book to the appropriate pages and told Borg that the pictures would be her guide to a mission: to locate family in its many forms.

Before Borg left, she repeated that all she could see in the pictures were people and houses, just as she could see people in the classroom and people out in the street. Borg wondered how she would be able to distinguish just any collection of people from the collection that constituted a family; in particular, she wondered whether housing could help distinguish what these humans called "family." She asked Caswell how she could differentiate a collection that looked just like the people in one of the textbook pictures from what, on an earlier trip around Earth, she had heard called a "gang." Caswell responded that she had found the key; namely, that Borg had to combine looking with listening. He explained that she needed to discover how collections of people referred to themselves before she could locate families.

As Borg set out, she understood that this mission was going to be more difficult than finding more tables after seeing a table. What if people disagreed? What if they claimed to be family in one place and disclaimed it in another? Tables didn't talk to, or about, themselves. It crossed Borg's mind that speech might be the source of much trouble in her quest. She mused, "If only people didn't talk about themselves to anyone, even themselves; if only they stayed silent and remained what they were."

Several weeks later Professor Caswell announced to the class that Borg had returned from her search. He asked her what she had found. To begin with, Borg had found many collections of people whom other people referred to as families, but whose alleged members did not. She found that when she revisited the members of the gang she had mentioned earlier and paid close attention to what they said about themselves, she heard the members not only refer to themselves as family, but also call each other brothers and claim filial responsibility for their actions. Yet this "family" wasn't a household. She added, "And what about Laura, a teenage girl who shrieked that she didn't have a sister when her twin spilled grape juice on Laura's brand new cashmere sweater?"

Considering her difficulties, Borg explained that originally she had drawn a hint from Professor Caswell's own research and taken the legal status of the collections of people she observed as a convenient shortcut to their family status. But many of those who had legal family ties stated flatly that they were not a family. Some even remarked that they weren't family in any sense of the term and never had been; others complained that they were family in name only. On the other hand, she discovered a wide variety of people who spoke with equal force and sentiment about how they were family and held each other accountable for the claim, yet were not legally bound. The legal status of these humans, Borg found, was a very poor guide to what they said, claimed, felt, or did about themselves.

Borg didn't want to insult Caswell, but she thought maybe she would get a more definitive picture of the family if she consulted some other family experts. Dictionaries were no help because they offered dozens of variations. She found that scholarly texts were not much better. A few of them said families were persons living together and related by blood, marriage, or adoption. Others stated that this excluded too many of today's "contemporary" families, where couples lived together without being married. Still others complained that this included too many groups; a few relatives living together—say, two unmarried brothers running a trucking business and sharing an apartment because one was always on the road—really shouldn't be thought of as a family. Some texts stated that it was best to keep it simple and think traditionally: a family was a married couple living together with their children. But others claimed that this wouldn't do; wouldn't this definition exclude single parents raising their children or married couples living apart or childless couples for that matter? Finally, other texts concluded that there was no single definition of the family, just families, stressing the diversity of the phenomenon plaguing Borg.

Borg wondered how these experts could possibly study the family if there was so little consensus about what it was. How did they create a scientific literature on the family if they didn't define it in a common way? Could these experts have been looking at the same thing? Who did know what the family was and what it was like? Law books and family textbooks were not going to be much help in answering these questions.

Borg took delight in the confusion that seemed to rule the experts' search for the family. She teased Caswell that they were no better at it than she was. She enjoyed recounting the ways humans connected words and things; in general, it seemed to have no universal rhyme or reason. Yet everyone seemed to understand one another. She'd been keeping track of what people said when she asked about families, and it was clear that she had actually heard much more about the thing she was searching for—family—than legal status or biological kinship implied. What seemed most evident, she noted, was that people seemed to *use* family in ways that legal or biological definitions could not capture. She wondered aloud, "Could it be that what family is to people is how family is *used* by them?" Borg was beginning to sound like Humpty Dumpty.

Caswell was both surprised and annoyed by the question. Was Borg implying that family was nothing more than a human construct and that people applied family imagery and familial categories like brother, sister, and cousin to all sorts of human relations, in and out of homes? To make matters worse, Borg was starting to sound like those family therapists—called "constructivists"—who were beginning to show how important language, meaning, and process were to definitions of family, if not social reality as a whole. Was Borg saying that family was not so much a thing, but a way of interpreting interpersonal ties?

Caswell calmed himself and asked hastily, "Well, then, my skeptical alien sidekick, if that's all the family is—just words—then it's not much of anything! What are we to do? Study words?" Borg knew immediately that she had hit a nerve. She didn't want to be unfaithful to what she had heard in her empirical wanderings, and she didn't want to back away from Caswell simply because Caswell was unnerved. She was as committed to her studies as Caswell was to his.

Borg explained that no one she had talked with, or whom she had heard talk with others, acted as if family were just a word. She added, in a curious turn of phrase, that all the words she heard about family were words about "it" or some form of "it," something concretely part of experience. The people she heard were making statements about something either real, not real enough, or too real to them, and were not just uttering words. "It" seemed to link words to concrete aspects of life.

When Caswell accused Borg of making an intellectual exercise out of her search for the family, she replied, "Okay, wise guy, you claim to be a serious student of human affairs. You give me an accurate guideline for finding what we're looking for." But Caswell's every guideline or rule for discerning family broke down as Borg mentioned the diverse and sundry ways that humans seemed to assign the term to their interpersonal relations. Some called friends family; some called pets family; some called multinational corporations family; and some refused to call wives, children, and parents family. Who was right? Some stated that they knew better than others whether they were real family because they lived in the home; others claimed that they knew more objectively because they weren't members of the household. Having access to the inner privacies of the household seemed to provide no better picture of what a family was like than did the many voices Borg heard in public. And what of the experts, the family scholars? Should we take their word over the word of those who actually live out the domestic affairs studied by the experts? Were these ordinary folk wrong?

Borg pointed out that because people talked and communicated with each other about what they were, both in and out of their homes, they weren't like tables, and one couldn't establish a table-like guideline for discerning what they were to each other. (At the back of her mind, Borg suspected that the problem she was having locating families also existed with tables—not because tables talked back, but because people used the object in different ways. She saved that question for another day.) In order to "see" what people were referring to, one had to listen to the way they used words and described their social relations, paying particular attention to the factors that affected their descriptions. Looking straight at Caswell, Borg blurted out, "You have to listen in order to see, Caswell!"

This time, Caswell knew that Borg was annoyed, just as he had been taken aback earlier. He hadn't intended the listening business to become so central to locating the familial; he had meant it only as a handy guide. Yet, now intrigued by Borg's reasoning, Caswell was bent on learning more about Borg's thoughts on seeing and hearing. He turned toward her and asked warmly, "Well, then, my friend, what is family?"

LANGUAGE USE AND THE CONSTRUCTION OF FAMILY

This book presents an answer to Caswell's question, which is telling in its own right. Caswell asked Borg not "What is *the* family?" but rather "What is family?" Was he on to Borg? What difference does the absence of the simple modifier "the" make?

In everyday life, we refer to many objects, both tangible and intangible. We speak of community, feelings, political allegiances, family, attitudes, households, and the nation, among other things. They are objects for us because we experience them as *things*. As parts of our experience, we take things to be somewhere outside the standpoint from which we refer to them, existing apart from our attention to them. We experience our community as a feature of some population that surrounds us. The nation is presumably an even more heterogeneous object in the more distant environment. Our references to them indicate that we experience even feelings and attitudes as things separate and distinct from us. For example, we sense that feelings exist inside the body, perhaps lying somewhere near the heart or in the gut.

To speak of things as lying outside the standpoint of reference to them is a statement about experience, not physical reality. The world of experience is not the same as the physical world or the world of nature. The experiential world is made up of meanings and language, not just physical objects and space. Location is a matter of reference, not only of place. In the world of experience, what lies inside and outside of us has more to do with the *relationship* of the thing under consideration to a point of reference than it does to the thing's location in space. In experience, things are things because we think of them, act toward them, and speak of them as such; we confirm our references by responding to them as if they were objects. Thus whether feelings ultimately lie inside or outside the body, we nonetheless experience them as object-like.

Standpoint and the referencing process are integral parts of language use. Every utterance is about something, some object of experience. As we speak and indicate to ourselves and others, we inexorably create and construct objects. To do anything less would require silence; to be strict about doing less would require turning off that "internal" voice we call mind.

The connection between language, speech, and objects of experience was at the center of Caswell's and Borg's perplexities. Because Borg was an alien and didn't know what family was, Caswell attempted to give her a picture-like guide to finding it. But whenever she seemed to find an instance of what Caswell called family, she heard a cacophony of voices. Some affirmed its existence; others denied it altogether. Some voices referred to family while others referred to "empty shells" or "houses without homes" to convey the absence of family among a collection of individuals. People seemed to connect family to place (if place was mentioned at all) with terms like "household," "home," and "home base." Some voices not only affirmed the absence of family but also redefined linkages that Borg had heard others call "family." For example, some called their homes "prisons," the occupants "inmates," and acted as if that were actually the case, not considering that there were legal or biologically related families housed there. And strangely

enough, she even heard prison inmates call the penitentiary home and their fellow inmates husband, wife, brother, sister—family.

Like "it," the simple modifier "the" flagged the problem facing Borg. When we speak of the character of *the* family, the structures and functions of *the* family, we imply a thing, a solid and evident, tangible or intangible object of experience, something with substance and boundaries. The implication applies whether our references are to the family as an entity or to particular families. For example, to speak of a specific family—say, *the* Martin family—is to describe a thing that is organized in a certain way, has an inside and an outside. Yet when we take the voices of those who speak for the Martin family into account, this thing loses its boundaries. As we listen to the father describe the Martin family, will he describe the same thing as the mother? Does the oldest child describe the Martin family similarly or differently? What of the youngest child? What of the maternal as opposed to paternal grandparents? What of the family physician, the social worker, or the oldest child's teacher, among a host of voices? Could it be that when we listen carefully and let those concerned define the Martin family, that "it" becomes many things, as potentially diverse as those who speak for it? And what of those ostensibly nonfamilial things that the Martins call "family" from time to time, like sorority "sisters" and lodge "brothers"? Even the family dog is considered to be and is treated like a true member of the family. Is this nothing but talk?

When Borg permitted herself to pay attention to what people said about family, she asked herself whether those she heard were speaking about *the* same thing. What disturbed Caswell was Borg's implication that neither she nor Caswell were in any position to state more truthfully than those concerned what was and wasn't family to them. As Caswell suggested at one point, could it be that what was said about family and the vehicle for saying it—words—were as much a part of the family as *the* family? Borg thought that was the case, but only partially so. She was concerned that Caswell might be implying that the family was a mere language game. Rather, she found people acting in good faith, using family language, and applying it to concrete social relations. People were not merely doing conversational contortions with the language. In their discourse, they were seriously sorting through observable signs of their relationships in order to figure what they were all about.

The article "the" seemed to prematurely objectify family—to impose boundaries on it before its potential breadth can be examined. Borg had been prepared to observe family in the same way one might observe physical objects like tables. She eventually discovered that before she could find *the* family, she needed to pay attention to how modifiers like "the" were indi-

rectly affecting her observations. Borg learned that she needed to pay very careful attention to how people used words to convey a concrete sense of family life in order to discern family. Thus she concluded that the simple modifier "the" was a sign of something much more important and that family discourse in general was quite telling of the status of the family in experience. Professor Caswell's reformulation of "What is the family?" into "What is family?" was indeed more profound than even Caswell realized.

42 | A MEMBER OF THE FUNERAL
An Introspective Ethnography
Nancy Anne Naples

Standing at my father's freshly dug grave holding the American flag the funeral director had just handed to me, I had the feeling I was in a bad made-for-TV movie. Since my mother was too sick with Alzheimer's to attend and I was the oldest of the six siblings, I was given the "honor." I thought it was especially odd since, given my left-leaning politics, I would be the least likely member of my family to fly the flag on the major military and other national holidays. As I watched my three sisters, two brothers, their spouses, and my fifteen nieces and nephews slowly make their way back to the cars with other members of my large "hetero-normal" extended family, I at once ached to be accepted as a part of their world and longed for my "real" family.

I flashed back to the last time I stood by this grave side. It was also a somewhat dreary fall day. My brother Donald, who was the nearest in age to me (born less than a year and a half after me) and who was closest to me in other ways as well, had died in a car crash. At this time, my father decided to buy a plot in the local cemetery in their suburban community just

north of New York City that would fit eight family members—less than needed if all of us wanted to be buried there, more if everyone else was buried with their own nuclear family. So now two of the plots are inhabited. I wondered who besides my mother would join them. I presumed that all the other siblings would be buried with their nuclear families. Maybe my father thought that since I was "single," namely had no "family" of my own, it would make sense for me to join them when the time came.

The significance of my singleness in the context of all the two parent male and female families who made up the funeral procession was not lost on my two aunts. Earlier at the funeral parlour I overheard one of my aunts say to another aunt, "You know, the one I feel the most sorry for is Nancy. She has nobody." Their hushed and worried exchange amused me somewhat, although I also felt a great deal of sadness since, as many gays and lesbians, I am rich with loving and intimate friends who I consider my "real" family. Yet in fact I was indeed alone at my father's funeral. Where was everybody?

When my brother Donald died in 1985, two of my most treasured "real" family were there for me. My lover Nina, who died in 1987 of breast cancer, and Peter, my brother-in-spirit who died of AIDS in 1996, were with me and were important witnesses over the years to the difficulties I had negotiating relationships with my family. Nina and Peter most assuredly would have been by my side had they been alive. Yet since neither Nina nor Peter were my legal or biological relations, their presence would have done little to shake the perception of my aloneness in the heteronormative world of my family.

Nina was my first female lover. We met in graduate school and I fell madly in love with her. When I "came out" to a lesbian friend about our relationship, she expressed great pleasure at my "coming to consciousness" or something to that effect. She made me feel that my more than fifteen years as a practicing heterosexual was something akin to false sexual consciousness. I resisted the revised grand narrative she attempted to impose on my sexual identity. I asserted that my relationships with men, as troubled as they were, were authentic expressions of my sexual desire. However, as I made this statement I remember feeling uncomfortable about laying claim to some authentic self.

Maybe my long heterosexual history has made it difficult for my siblings to accept my claim to a lesbian identity. Nina was incorporated into my family as my "best friend." No questions were asked about why I was no longer seeing my boyfriend Mark, nor did anyone ever ask why I never had another boyfriend after him. This seemed like an obvious question since I had dated boys since eighth grade, been married once, and lived with another man for several years. Nor did I take the initiative to explain. I just believed deep in my bones that coming out to my parents and siblings at the time would only strain my already conflict-ridden relationship with them. I did not feel that I had anything to gain from doing so and had much more to lose. I remember having drinks with Donald one Christmas eve. When he said he wanted to ask me something important about Nina, I held my breath for what I thought would be the inevitable question: Are you and Nina lovers? I remember how perversely relieved I was when he asked me a very different ques-

tion: Had I ever thought about her dying?—she was in the first of several rounds of chemotherapy treatment for breast cancer.

Not surprisingly, the unspoken but palpable homophobia I felt from my family was deeply woven into my own psyche. I colluded in the silence about it while Nina was alive. However, after she died I desperately wanted them to acknowledge who she was in my life and what her loss meant for me. I remember my mother commenting on what a good friend and social worker (my previous career) I was given my central role in Nina's care, which included taking her to doctors' appointments and chemo treatments, sleeping over at the hospital during the last months of her life, and acting as executor of her will. Not even the fact that she left me all her worldly possessions, the money from the successful lawsuit against the breast surgeon who misdiagnosed the cancer, and her precious dog, Lucy, could shake my family's construction of my "friendship" with Nina.

Given the diversity among my siblings, coming out to them was much easier as well as much harder than I anticipated. The reactions ranged from downright hostility and rejection to ambivalent acceptance (the subtle message was that as long as I did not speak too much about my life as a lesbian, they could accept it). My brother John, the most hostile one, was violently angry and said in an attacking tone that having a sister who was a lesbian was a great embarrassment for him and that he would surely lose friends because of it. My brother Paul refused to hear it at all. Lisa and Melissa, the youngest of the clan, were mildly accepting, although over the years it became clear that, as Lisa put it, they would rather "not think about it." Karen, the remaining sister, was the most profoundly disturbed by it. Karen became a born-again Christian in her early twenties and was very invested in the anti-homosexual position her church promulgated. Her comments about how homosexuality was a sin against God and that gays were sexually promiscuous, carriers of diseases, and a basic threat to the moral fabric of society greatly distressed me even though I was well versed in the religious right's view of what they disparagingly call the "homosexual lifestyle." Once, I tried to explain the epidemiology of the AIDS virus to her. I dispassionately noted that the majority of those infected throughout the world are practicing hetero-sexuals and that lesbians are not at especially high risk of HIV. Karen responded, "Well you have your opinion and I have mine." I realized in this brief attempt to present an other view that I was forced to sell out gay men who did have AIDS. I knew better. After all, I teach about homosexuality, compulsory heterosexuality, and the social construction of gender to large classes of undergraduates and have had to find that careful balance between encouraging a critical consciousness and directly challenging their world views.

Religion also served as a main wedge between my other siblings and me. We were brought up by a devotely Catholic mother, and all of us—with the exception of my sister Karen, who became a member of a conservative Christian church, and me—continued to attend mass regularly and participate in all the Catholic sacraments. They baptized each of their children in the Catholic Church. I attended most of the baptisms but became increasingly pained by the way this ritual further marginalized me in the family. My lack of religious affiliation and unmarried status made me unfit, in my siblings eyes, to be godparent to any of my fifteen nieces and nephews.

Regardless of their individual responses to my coming out as a lesbian, each sibling strongly warned me against telling my parents. I think they all firmly believed that, as my brother John said, "it would kill daddy"—a projection of their own fears and a threat that is frequently used to keep gays and lesbians in their closets. Of course I did not really believe that the simple statement about my sexual orientation would kill my father or mother. However, on one level I felt I had nothing to gain by taking the risk and, on another level, I figured my father already knew. After all, he was a firefighter in the West Village for 25 years, even helping to put out the fires of Stonewall. I rationalized that if he wanted to deal with my lesbian identity, he would bring it up himself. So we developed an unspoken contract. I would not name my relationships with women as lesbian and he would accept my girlfriends into his home, no questions asked. I thought that was fair for the most part. In retrospect, I realize that I somehow bought into the fear that my lesbian self was a shameful secret that might have the power if not to kill, at least to deeply harm others.

Over the more than ten years since I came out as a lesbian to my siblings, I tried to find a way to be a part of the family while also trying to protect myself from their rejection of my lesbian self. I maintained normalized relationships with all but my brother John and related to the other brother Paul through my sister-in-law, who seemed to be more open. I stopped celebrating Christmas and Thanksgiving with them. I would limit my visits to one or two days, staying over no more than one or two nights. Since my parents had moved from my childhood home on Staten Island to a small town just an hour and a half north of Manhattan, I could stay with my friends and drive up for the day. I did not discuss my relationships with my family and showed up unaccompanied, even when in a relationship, for most events such as Christenings, weddings, baby showers, and physical and mental health crises. I sent money or gifts for birthdays and Christmas, but generally kept my worlds separate. When I moved to California, just forty miles south of my sister Lisa, I expected some challenge in balancing the different worlds, but she happened to be one of the two supportive sisters so I was not too concerned about it.

Yet, in some ways, the geographic closeness did pose some additional dilemmas. I recall the Christmas of 1994 right after my nephew James was born. Wanting to be helpful, I offered to make Christmas dinner for Lisa and her husband, Michael. But Melinda, my lover at the time, did not want to do the holiday thing in this way. What she wanted was a quiet dinner with me at home. Caught between my different families, I decided to make dinner for us at home and later to bring dinner to Lisa and Michael. This seemed doable at the time. The first snag, however, occurred after I described the Sante-Fe-inspired meal I planned to make. Lisa explained that her husband would not eat what Melinda and I had decided on for the main course and that since she was breast-feeding James, she would have to pass on the jalapeno corn bread. Okay, I thought, I need another fall-back plan. I decided to make two dinners, one for Melinda and me, plus one for Lisa and Michael. I made two corn breads, one with and one without the jalapenos. After completing our main course, I put a chicken in the oven to roast. Naturally, all of this took extra time so Melinda and I sat down to eat later than I intended. With the fireplace burning brightly and the candles nicely lit on the table, Melinda was anticipating a very relaxed meal. I, on the other hand, was anxious that we were running late so I could not really enjoy the meal, which was also interrupted several times while I checked the chicken. Then the phone rang. It was my sister wondering where we were. She told me that Michael loved my cooking so that he skipped lunch and was starving. I explained that things were taking a bit longer but that I would be there soon. Melinda, however, did not want to join me on the trip up to my sister's and I struggled with her for a while until the phone rang.

It was Peter wishing me a Merry Christmas. I explained the dilemma to him and complained that Melinda would not come with me to my sister's. Having met many of my family members, he not-so-diplomatically said, "Why should she? Let her stay home if she wants." It did seem such an obvious solution but I now realized how much I wanted to merge my different worlds for that holiday. So out the door I went, telling Melinda I would be back as soon as I could to share desert with her. Arriving at my sister's, I went into a flurry of activity heating up and then serving the food. I felt like a volunteer for Meals-on-Wheels. And, of course, I could not relax with them much since I felt I needed to get back home or Melinda would start feeling abandoned. I can laugh at the scene now, but it more than symbolized the absurdity and frustration associated with my attempts to navigate between different family forms.

So, for the most part, my siblings did not have to see me in a relationship with a woman. My long history as a practicing heterosexual was enough to negate my claims to a lesbian identity. How could someone who was involved with men for so long really be a lesbian? I fit none of their stereotypes. My sister Karen rationalized my claim to a lesbian identity as follows: "Well, after all you had such bad relationships with men." The obvious implication was that if I met the right man, I would change my mind. Again I was faced with proving my authentic identity, this time foregrounding my lesbian self. Another cliché I recognized in my family's response was the one that links having a career with my not needing men. Here the traditional gender division of labor, which assigns women to the private sphere of the home and men to the public breadwinner, role was upset by the fact that I had a career and therefore did not need the male breadwinner. Of course, what logically follows that particular assumption is that women's full time employment is a basic threat to the heterosexual family form—an old but persistent concern.

My family is more traditional than many, I suppose. During the 1950s and 1960s, we even had a girl's side, and a boy's side of the dinner table. If you tried to cross over to the wrong side you suffered great insults. The boys were taught auto mechanics and electronics among other technical skills. The girls learned child care and cooking among other home-making skills. I always resisted. Fortunately my sister Karen, who was three years younger than me, took to these activities, and I put up such a stink about performing them that I was off the hook.

My siblings have all followed the traditional route. The women have taken their husbands' names and have, for the most part, placed their own careers on hold until all their children are in school. My life as an unmarried college professor of sociology and women's studies was so far from their own lives that they could hardly comprehend it except that they knew I attended a lot of conferences. Furthermore, they never wanted to learn more about it so I rarely discuss what I do with them. I do not think my experience here differs much from other academics who come from the working class. However, I fear that part of my family's reluctance to ask more about my life's work is that for them women's studies equals feminist equals lesbian—and therefore something about my lesbian world might come up. So it is best not to even start down that road.

I continued to keep my worlds relatively separate with a few moments of overlap until 1997 when my mother's Alzheimer's escalated and we had to put her in a nursing home. This precipitated more intense and regular contact with my family. This difficult event overlapped with the start of a new relationship with Sharon, a woman who said that she would not mind being integrated into my family. In fact, she said, "I'm good with lovers' families. They like me." I was so pleased to finally have the opportunity to merge my worlds. I neglected to warn her, however, that I had never successfully done so before. She did wonder why I became increasingly anxious as we drove closer to my father's house a week before Christmas. I even passed the turn off and drove her around the town and several of the surrounding towns before returning to complete the drive to the house. When we arrived at my father's home, my sister Melissa with her son and my hostile brother, John, were there.

My plan was to spend the night and go visit my other brother Paul's family before making the four-hour drive to Sharon's home the next afternoon. However, shortly upon our arrival, as I was wrapping presents in one of the bedrooms, John comes in and asks me in a very accusatory tone: "You're not going to make some big announcement that we should know about? Paul is afraid to come over because he thinks you are planning some big surprise." I was speechless with fury. I now wish I had thought of some clever rejoinder such as: "Oh, you must be watching too many episodes of *Ellen.* If so, you'd know I would only do it in an airport over a loud speaker." But instead, I was paralyzed with anger and fear. I emerged from the room, didn't say a word to Sharon, went to play with my nephew, and left her to interact with my father and brothers—the second of whom had shown up by this time. Paul proceeded to glare at her from the kitchen. He never spoke to her. It was as though Sharon had a neon sign on her chest that read in bold scarlet letters: BEWARE, LESBIAN IN THE HOUSE. Later she explained that she felt I had taken her to some anonymous suburban family and dropped her off where she had to introduce herself and be subjected to the critical gaze of the residents. I disappeared emotionally under the homophobic gaze of my brothers. Sharon was angry that I had left her with these "strangers." I tried to explain that I could not have anticipated my reaction since it was the first time I ever really allowed the two worlds to collide so directly. She said that I should have at least warned her that she was the first female lover that I had introduced into the family. I had mistakenly assumed that Nina was the first lover they had met. Since I came out to them after she died, I had wishfully thought that would count and so this introduction of Sharon should be no big deal.

The Christmas visit would send me on a very difficult soul searching journey to confront and effectively eject much of the self-hate I had internalized. This was indeed a very good thing for me in the long run. Unfortunately, in the short run, I was to face a series of painful internal and external crises before I felt purged of some of my own internalized homophobia.

So now fast forward to the week of my father's death, which was quite unexpected. He had problems with his lungs, emphysema, a series of bouts with pneumonia, but until this last week or so no one thought his illness was life-threatening. I won't go into the unfortunate series of medical events that contributed to his death, but state simply that I did not have much time to prepare for how I would balance my conflicting worlds while all this was going on.

As a consequence of the previous Christmas I had decided not to stay over with my family if I could avoid it. When I got the call from my youngest sister, Melissa, that I better get "home," I did not even think about what it would be like to stay with my siblings during the emotionally painful days leading up to my father's death. Since it involved coming to a collective decision about removing the breathing tube, I assumed it best to stay with them. I also thought I would be criticized harshly if I chose to stay in Manhattan with my friends Jen and Terry, whose apartment was in fact closer to the hospital. I rented a car at the airport and drove to Melissa's home in New Jersey.

The first couple of days were difficult but manageable. All six of us seemed to be getting along pretty well. I remember calling one of my aunts to give her an update and saying how good our communication was as we were debating the pros and cons of removing the ventilator. Each day I spoke to my soon-to-be ex-lover, Sharon (we were in the process of breaking up), who was trying to be supportive. She had initiated the break-up a few weeks earlier. I was resisting vehemently. I had some crazy idea in the back of my mind that this crisis might bring us closer together. Little did I know how wrong I was. Each day Sharon offered to come. I so wanted to take her up on her offer. After all, my siblings all had their spouses and children with them. I had neither lover nor friend. But I also knew, given the view of homosexuality held by my sister Karen, that it would be difficult to have my ex-lover with me, although I had no idea how messy it would become.

When Karen and her children began discussing the

possibility of moving up to my father's house so they could be closer to the other cousins, I finally saw an opportunity to invite Sharon to join me. When I mentioned that she was coming, Karen threw a fit. She ranted, "How could you I bring this into the family at such a time? What about the children? This is a time for the family to be together. It's not a time for us to have to deal with this." I tried to explain that Sharon was my family and that I needed the support. And, further, I was a lesbian whether my lover was with me or not. She refused to calm down and, in a huff, went up to pack hers and her children's bags.

Melissa, the youngest sibling, came to me pleading, "Nancy, do something!" So I took a deep breath, went to my sister Karen and said, "Fine, I'll tell my lover not to come." I thought that this was the only way we could get through the next couple of days. I felt defeated and so alone but I was, after all, the older sister, a role that I performed uncritically for much of my life. After this incident, I could no longer stay with them. I quietly packed my bags and said that I would go stay with my friends in Manhattan. I drove away thinking what a fool I was for forgetting where I really belonged. When I arrived at the airport, I should have gone directly to Jen and Terry's apartment for they were my part of my "real" family. How could I have gotten it so wrong?

To make matters worse, Sharon was profoundly offended by my decision to acquiesce to Karen's tantrum. She resented that I placed my need to keep peace in the family over our relationship and told me that if I had discussed my fear of merging the two worlds with her, she might have helped me come up with the solution that eventually I had to turn to anyway—staying with my friends in the city. Further, she painfully exclaimed, how did I think this made her feel as the one defined as a dreaded threat to the moral integrity of my family? I could not find the words to explain what it had been like for me the day before with my sisters.

This conversation took place over the phone. I had just left my father's bed in intensive care when I called her. When I asked her if she would be willing to come after my father died, she initially said, "Why should I? After all, one goes to a funeral to be supportive of the family and your family doesn't want me there." Well,

I was devastated to say the least. I called another dear friend and sobbed for an hour. When I returned to my father's bedside, he was dead. So you can see now why I increasingly felt as though the bad TV-movie kept getting worse. Here I was, the only family member left at the hospital, staying through the night to be with my father so that he wouldn't be alone when he died, only to get caught up in a competing drama down the hall. I hope the guilt I feel over this dreadful episode will diminish with time.

After my father died, the nurse contacted my other siblings and they all returned to the hospital. We each said goodbye in our own way and left. It was after 2 a.m. I drove back to Manhattan. Exhausted and traumatized by what just occurred, and I collapsed into bed.

The following day I spent a long time describing the events to Jen and Terry and called some of my other close friends. I also contacted Sharon and asked her once again if she would come to be with me. She finally agreed but we did not decide whether or not she would attend the wake and funeral. I felt a bit aimless that day and thought that, even though it would have been easier to avoid it, I should drive to my father's house and together with my siblings confront the reality of his death. I also resented letting Karen's fear of my lesbian existence keep me away. I did not want her to have that much power over my choices at this point. Anyway, very quickly after I arrived it became clear to me that my lesbianism and the fear that my lover would come to the wake and funeral was the central topic of conversation. I went into the living room and all but my brother Paul were sitting there. John turned to me and said, on behalf of my siblings, that they wanted to talk to me, that they wanted to know what it was going to be like. At first I did not understand what they wanted to know. I thought that maybe since I had experienced so much loss, they wanted me to explain what it would be like at the funeral or the wake. I asked what they meant.

My sister Lisa then turned to me and said, "We want to know what it is going to be like when your lover comes. Are you two going to be touching or whatever?" At this point, I chose not to let them know that Sharon was, in fact, my ex-lover. I thought if I said, "Oh, you don't have to worry. We broke up." It would only feed into their self-righteousness and belief that there was something dangerous about lesbian love. As John and my two youngest sisters tried to explain their concerns, I painfully noted the smug look on my sister Karen's face. Now she was not the sole voice, the religious fanatic with some extreme view, but rather, just another of my siblings, who all felt that it was an awful thing for me to be a lesbian. I wondered what they thought Sharon and I would do at the funeral parlour. Everyone but Karen had met her the previous Christmas, but paranoia had overtaken them and they clearly were not thinking rationally.

I, of course, felt attacked, horrified and desperately alone in my father's house. I knew that my siblings only felt free to express their hatred and fear of my lesbian self because he was dead. It made me miss him even more. I got up and started packing my things to leave. Lisa came in and tried to explain why she thought it was a good thing for us to have this discussion, that my lesbianism was no longer a taboo subject, that she loved me, and that my lover would always be welcome in her house. I was appalled at the thought that there should have to be any question about this. I replied that they should deal with their own irrational fears about my sexuality but to leave me out of their conversations in the future. How unloving and hateful could a group of people be—people who are supposed to love me and want the best for me! I understood then that I was tolerated as part of the family as long as they thought I was alone, had no one to love me, to hold me, to comfort me. As I drove back to Manhattan, I understood even more deeply that the precious intimate friendships I had constructed over the years were truer expressions of "real" family than my biological family ever had been.

I missed Nina and Peter more than ever. How different the energy that surrounded Nina's last weeks and her memorial service. Right after Nina died, Peter told me that he had asked her what he was supposed to do with me—since we weren't really "friends," not like he was with Nina. I inherited Peter from Nina. And, I guess, he inherited me as well. He replaced Donald as the brother I could talk to. There was so much I couldn't tell Donald. His own homophobia made him less than the best confident for me when

Nina was first diagnosed. I am so grateful to Nina for leaving Peter to me and me to him. We were "real" family for each other, Peter with no other kinfolk, me with lots of related kin but none I felt close to or who loved me as freely. Peter was there for me from the time Nina died until his own untimely death. I so much prefer the version of family I learned from Nina and Peter to the one my biological family embraces. For my biological family, the effort to "do family" takes the form of boundary maintenance—controlling who and what can enter for fear that the family constellation is so fragile any slight disruption will cause permanent damage. Ironically, in their efforts to patrol the borders, the illusive ties that kept me linked to my family have been irrevocably severed.

I don't expect to have any future contact with my two brothers or my sister Karen. For Karen, I would have to confess my "sin," repent, and renounce my "homosexual lifestyle." Equally unlikely, she would have to forsake the treasured religious beliefs that have provided an anchor for her since her early twenties. Recently her ten year old son sent a letter to all his aunts and uncles seeking money for a bike-athon to support a missionary for his church. I could no longer ignore my negative feelings about this church in order to fulfill my familial obligations as his aunt. And I do not expect to have any meaningful contact with Sharon. This also saddens me greatly for despite the fact that we could not negotiate my family nor build towards our own version of family, we did love each other.

Yet despite all the loses I have suffered over the years in both my families, I am an incurable romantic. I deeply long to create daily life with someone—to swap stories of the day, to perform mundane household tasks together, to share meals, and to regularly experience the pleasures of physical touch. Fortunately, I find myself in a new relationship; this time with someone who wants to "do" family in much the same way I envision. The process of negotiating my two families continues, however. My new lover is coming to visit soon. In order to miss the Los Angeles traffic the morning she returns home, it would be most convenient for us to stay with my sister Lisa, who lives ten minutes from the airport. Recall that she was the one who said that my lover would always be welcome in her home. Yet does this offer extend to an overnight stay? I fear calling her on it and bumping up once again against the razor sharp boundary of my biological family. I also want to protect my new lover from any hurt or rejection, to do a better job than I did for Sharon. I am torn. Should I just give up my desire to merge my worlds and book a room in a hotel by the airport or should I give my sister a chance to show up for me. It is a hard call.

Well, after my father's funeral everyone returned to his house for a luncheon. I returned with them, flag in hand, and spent my remaining hours in his house talking to my aunts and several of my favorite cousins. After they left, I wasn't sure what to do. I wandered from room to room, looked in closets, found the hard cover copy of my book that I had recently given my father, and took one of his flannel shirts off a hanger. I decided to call my ex-lover. But she was neither at her home nor her work phone. She and my friend Jen had, in fact, made it to the first night of the wake. Need I add that, not surprisingly, nothing dramatic happened. None of my siblings' fears about how our presence together might disrupt the dignified nature of the wake were realized. I did feel compelled to keep my physical distance from her. Sharon decided to leave the next morning. We both agreed that was best. But I was glad she came, even for the one night. The only surprising and touching moment occurred when my sister Melissa introduced herself to Jen and thanked her for taking care of me, her big sister.

When I decided I needed to leave my father's house after the funeral luncheon and return to my "real" family in Manhattan, I put on the flannel shirt and went looking for my brother John, who had been so outraged by my lesbian self. I gave him the flag and my book and told him I didn't expect him to read it but he could have it if he wanted. I drove away while he stood motionless in the driveway. I knew he would miss my father more than anyone since he lived the closest and had followed closely in his footsteps as a New York City firefighter. The house was recently sold and even though I never lived there, I felt the loss of the "family homestead." I also mourned the fantasy that one day I would be an accepted member of my biological family. Yet letting go of the need to keep my hetero-normal self alive, I have come to more fully

embrace and gain sustenance from my "real" family who have been there all along.

The process of writing the story of my father's funeral involved analyzing complex and changing relationships I have with members of both my so-called family of origin and my family of choice. Telling the story, writing the essay, and discussing the narrative I produced involved retelling and revising the story as well as re-experiencing many of the painful feelings I had while the story was unfolding for the first time. I was struck by the ways in which my relationship to the story and to the essay changed with each interaction with friends as readers and reviewers, with the story as text, and with myself as author. The purpose of this telling is simultaneously personal, political, and pedagogical. The questions I address in analyzing both the process of narrative construction and the narrative product include: How do we achieve visibility in our families? How do we resist reproducing patterns of exclusion in our families of choice? How do personal narratives function as tools for these interrelated goals?

The story I tell about my father's funeral emphasizes the emotional work involved in "doing family."[1] Family is not merely a natural constellation of individuals connected by biology and the state with some set of behaviors that everyone knows and willingly performs. Family must be achieved and constructed on a daily basis. Bisexuals, gays, lesbians, and all of us who do not fit into the normative heterosexual family model understand this well. But all of us, regardless of the family form we inherit or create, must work to sustain these relationships.

I draw on the symbolic constructionist perspective for my analysis of "doing family." Candice West and Don Zimmerman (1987) argue that "gender is fundamental, institutionalized, and enduring; yet, because members of social groups must constantly (whether they realize it or not) 'do' gender to maintain their proper status, the seeds of change are ever present" (Lorber 1987:124). As Barrie Thorne (1995:498) points out, "'Doing gender' is a compelling concept because it jolts the assumption of gender as an innate condition and replaces it with a sense of ongoing process and activity." Yet gender, and family, are more than performances. They are structured in ways that are not always visible to the performers. As Thorne (1995:499) argues, "gender extends beyond daily cultural performance, and it will take much more than doing drag and mocking naturalized conceptions to transform it. Gender—and race, class, and compulsory heterosexuality—extend deep into the unconscious and the shaping of emotions . . . and outward into social structure and material interests." In much the same way, I argue, how we perform "family" is shaped by material as well as cultural practices that are often invisible to us as we interact with family, friends, lovers, co-workers. However, the practice of ongoing self-reflection provides one strategy to make visible how daily interactions are shaped by dominant constructions and structures of family. Self-reflective practice is a collective activity that involves on-going dialogue, behaviors, and political activities that serve to challenge the more oppressive features of patriarchal families.

We first learn to do family and relationships more generally in the families in which we grow up, whether biological, adopted, or otherwise constituted. Since many of these families adhere to some version of compulsory heterosexuality (Rich 1980), our models for performing family are constrained by perscriptions of the "family ethic."[2] Consequently, developing alternative models of "doing family" forms a central task for gays and lesbians and others who do not fit into the normative heterosexual family form (see Lewin 1993; Weston 1991). We are also challenged by the complex negotiations and contradictions between the performance of family, gender, and sexuality expected by our families and the relationships we form as lesbians, gay men, bisexuals, or transgendered people. Unfortunately, we often find ourselves repeating behaviors and imposing expectations that were developed through our early family experiences, thus limiting relational expression to patriarchal patterns of interaction. The process of telling, retelling, writing, and rewriting this story provided me with the distance to see how my attempts to construct my own family form were circumscribed by the limited vision of family I brought into this activity.

The essay about my father's funeral can thus be read as an introspective ethnography (see Ellis 1991; Ronai 1995; Timmermans 1994). With this formula-tion, it is possible to view the process of its production through the lens of a family ethnography concerning the struggle of a white lesbian with a heterosexual history to become visible and accepted in her working class family. The self-reflective process I employ includes feedback from friends, some of whom appear in the story. This dialogic strategy provided me with an analytic distance from the experiences described. However, I also recognize the limitations of my angle of vision and how my positionality[3] in the story priviliges my version.

I utilize the biographical narrative approach in much of my scholarship on women's community activism and therefore value this methodology for exploring the development of and shifts in political consciousness and diverse political practices over time without artificially foregrounding any one dimension or influence (see Naples 1998). However, such narratives can not be taken up unproblematically. For, as the Personal Narratives Group (1989, 4) emphasize:

> The act of constructing a life narrative forces the author to move from accounts of discrete experiences to an account of why and how the life took the shape it did. The why and how—the interpretive acts that shape a life, and a life narrative—need to take as high a place on the feminist agenda as the recording of women's experiences.

Yet as both interpreter and subject of the interpretation, I find myself in a complicated relationship to the narrative I have produced. In fact, in attempting to present the story of how the events surrounding my father's funeral helped me reflect on the dilemmas of doing family, I was often amazed at how many different versions I could tell, depending on which aspects of the story I chose to emphasize or how I combined different facets of my self-presentation (also see Abu-Lughod 1993; Behar 1993; Wolf 1992; also see Naples 1998).

There are many who critique this form of storytelling, namely, the privileging of one particular account over the multiple stories that could be told about the same phenomenon or set of experiences (see, e.g., Patai 1994). Self-disclosure or "going public" (Naples with Clark 1996) with painful life events, emotional difficulties, and personal failures has been criticized within and outside of feminism, within and outside of the academy, and in multiple arenas from the arts to literature to academic research. Anthropologist Ruth Behar (1995: 12–13) notes that: "No one objects to autobiography, as such, as a genre in its own right. What bothers critics is the insertion of personal stories into what we have been taught to think of as the analysis of impersonal social facts."

Defined by some as "confessional modes of self-representation" (Bernstein 1992), taking the first person and centering one's own experiences as a basis for knowledge claims—once a privileged strategy for the production of feminist scholarship—is now viewed with suspicion by many (see, e.g., Armstrong 1990 cited in Alcoff and Gray 1993; Kaminer 1995). Those theorists critical of this move to discredit experiential theorizing argue that the decentering of women's experiences in feminist scholarship is a consequence of the growing acceptance of certain feminist projects within the academy and other institutions, thus diminishing the necessity of taking an oppositional stance with regard to knowledge production in the academy (see Naples 2001). Some fear that by valorizing women's experiences over other ways of knowing, women's studies classrooms do not measure up to academic standards of "excellence" (see Patai and Koertge 1994).

In contrast, I believe that experiential theorizing and the process of critical self-reflection it entails offers a way to uncover and render visible the complex dynamics of doing family. This process illustrates the theoretical insights of feminist standpoint epistemologies (see Collins 1990; Hartsock 1983; Lugones 1992; Naples 1999; Sandoval 1991; Smith 1987). Donna Haraway (1988:584), in her now classic article, "Situated Knowledges: The Science Question in Feminism and the Privilege of the Partial Perspective," argued that those subjugated by forces of oppression "are knowledgeable of modes of denial through repression, forgetting, and disappearing acts." In the midst of my family's exaggerated performance of heteronormativity, I often felt my lesbian self rendered invisible despite "coming out" to all my siblings. For much of my adult life I could not break through their denial. The events leading up to, and surrounding my father's death served to thrust my lesbian self into the center of their consciousness in such a way that it symbolized a threat to the integrity of the family unit. Of course, it was my father's death that fundamentally unraveled the tightly bound net that held us together. In many ways, I was unprepared for the rejection; in other ways, I had been preparing for it most of my conscious life. The crisis led to a re-evaluation of my relationship to my family as well as an opportunity to develop a new interpretive framework through which I might be able to construct a family that does not replicate the negative aspects of the earlier formation. However, I recognize the challenge posed by the legacy of doing family unreflectively for so many years.

The construction of this new interpretative framework involved a process of politicization whereby I began to attribute my discontent to structural, cultural, or systemic causes rather than to my personal failings or individual deviance (Taylor and Whittier 1992:114). For, despite my political and academic education and my own research on the development of "oppositional consciousness"[4] (Sandoval 1991), I had not achieved the angle of vision that permitted me to understand my own agency in reproducing the family dynamics I found so painful. Fortunately, as Nancy Hartsock (1996: 371) explains: "the development of situated knowledges can constitute alternatives: they open possibilities that may or may not be realized. To the extent that these knowledges become self-conscious about their assumptions, they make available new epistemologies and political options."

While I expect that I will gain more from this exercise than my readers, I hope that I have demonstrated the challenges we all face and the benefits that ensue when we do family self-reflectively, rather than treat family as a taken-for-granted institution outside of our own making. This lesson is one I have learned from my many lesbian, gay, bisexual, and heterosexual family and friends. The family form I recommend is one built on respect for differences and openness to the diversity of expressions of intimacy.

Since I start and end with my own perspective on doing family, I must acknowledge that others mentioned in my story, including former lovers and siblings, will have different stories to tell about the relational activities I describe. While we were all confronted with the emotional and structural dilemmas associated with my attempt to negotiate different approaches to family, the experiences and analyses of what this all means for "doing family" will necessarily differ. Furthermore, the narrative I have constructed is one that glosses over the complexities of the interpersonal negotiations between former lovers and family members. As Melinda emphasized, following her reading of an early draft of the essay, "through the selective reporting of one event [Christmas 1994], the reader is offered a universalized picture of my relationship to your family as distanced, unwilling to interface with their community and you in it . . . [T]he problem for me is that this nice vignette for the sake of argument doesn't match the reality for many, many times I interfaced with your siblings at holidays as well as with your parents so it just is not the "real story." Melinda and I were together for almost five years. Over that period of time there were many opportunities for her to visit with members of my family. One of my favorite pictures of her shows her holding my sister Lisa's newborn baby, Max, shortly after Christmas Day, 1994. Obviously, then, this story as I tell it takes on meaning not as an uncontestable sequence of events—namely, as what really happened or as true in some objective way—but in the emotional and interpretative framing that shaped my interactions with different families and individual family members.

While the story I tell is particular to my own coming to consciousness about the dilemmas of doing family, I believe it illustrates some of the conflicts between different constructions of family that many of us encounter. The features of my own story include the ways in which religion, class differences, as well as gender and sexuality increasingly widened the emotional and physical divide that ultimately severed me from my family as a complex unitary form. The struggle to negotiate my lived experiences as a lesbian within my family has helped me differentiate among the family members, distancing me from some siblings while drawing me closer to others. In this way, I can now integrate these particular members of my childhood family as chosen members of my family of choice, creating a much more affirming and flexible relational structure. For me, the challenge of doing family had always meant choosing between one form or the other, rather than finding a way to include different family members from my different families to-

gether. Given the very bounded way my family did familial relationships, however, it is not surprising that I encountered such difficulty. In her response to my essay, Melinda asked an obvious question about my family, one that I take up somewhat in the narrative, namely, "Do they/did they ever do much to include anyone?" She noted how they never asked about her or made an effort to get to know her when she did interact with them.

My introspective ethnography of doing family brought home to me how much I had privileged my childhood family's version, at times marginalizing my relationships with lovers and friends in order to show up for the family in a way they could handle and I would feel safe from their criticisms. This highlighted a point raised by my friend Jen who asked: "What are your responsibilities to past lovers and how has your participation in your family drama let them down?" And a question from another friend: "How do we create family without expecting our family of choice to fill in the emotional holes left from childhood?" Attempts to answer these poignant questions would require further self-reflection and dialogue and still would remain a work-in-progress. However, experiential theorizing and the self-reflective process it entails may offer a strategy to addess questions such as the ones these friends have posed.

The dilemmas of bisexuality also complicated my relationships with my family. Despite the postmodern critiques of essentialized identities and futile searches for some ultimate truth about a mythical unfractured self, I remember the satisfaction I felt when I read Ann Ferguson's (1991) conceptualization of her own "bisexual lesbian" identity. The category worked for me as a shortcut to describe my sexual history, although I have been lesbian-identified since 1980. Categories, as misguided as they may be to a postmodern sensibility, can be quite comforting and useful at times. Yet I also realize that while I adopt the term bisexual lesbian to make sense of my personal history it serves only as a fleeting comfort. It fails to capture the processes of negotiation and redefinition embedded in my ongoing identity construction. And, furthermore, had little meaning for my siblings, who really did not know how to make sense of my shift in sexual partners.

In reviewing this essay, Jen asked why my family had such significance for me. Others might have distanced themselves more quickly than I did in response to the homophobia I encountered from it. I believe in retrospect that part of the answer can be found in the intense emotional and practical hold that my large working class family had over me. As the oldest child in an Irish Catholic working class family, the pressures I felt to show up for the family in a variety of ways formed part of my earliest memories. As we grew older, I listened to my parents' great disappointment when one sibling, then a second, moved away. (I was the third to "leave.") We were expected to stay close, to be there for each other, in what was a fairly tightly bounded family constellation.

My long history as a practicing heterosexual provided a convenient backdrop for my family's denial of my lesbian existence. But today I can also see how internalized homphobia played a role in my willingness to remain silent and to continue to perform a version of my hetero-normative self into my forties. My need to maintain this role within my family had particular consequences for my women lovers, who were not as invested in performing such roles. Although it took me many years and the death of my father to fully acknowledge the shame that kept me silent, I also gained much strength from my lovers and others in my family of choice who taught me how to trust my heart, find my voice, and construct a new vision for doing family. I dedicate this essay to them.[5]

NOTES

1. The names of all but those who have died have been changed.

2. Mimi Abramovitz (1988:2) defines the "family ethic" as a "preoccupation with the nuclear family unit featuring a male breadwinner and an economically dependent female homemaker." The family ethic also privileges the white middle class family over working class and non-white racial ethnic families.

3. Linda Alcoff (1988, 433) uses the concept "positionality" to describe "the subject as nonessentialized and emergent from a historical experience."

4. Aldon Morris (1992:363) defines "oppositional consciousness" with "hegemonic consciousness" as: "that set of insurgent ideas and beliefs constructed and developed by an oppressed group for the purposes of guiding its struggle to undermine, reform, or overthrow a system of domination." The

power of "oppositional consciousness" lies in its ability "to strip away the garments of universality from hegemonic consciousness, revealing its essentialist characteristics" (p. 370).

5. My heartfelt thanks to Mary Bernstein, Peter Canavan, Lauren Cruz, Dawn Esposito, Val Jenness, Maya Hostettler, Kate Kinney, Theresa Montini, Nancy Rose, Bettina Soestwohner, Susan Stern, Paul Stern, Cynthia Truelove, and Gilda Zwerman for insightful comments on earlier drafts of this chapter.

REFERENCES

Abramovitz, Mimi. 1988. *Regulating the Lives of Women.* Boston: South End Press.

Abu-Lughod, L. 1993. *Writing Women's Worlds: Bedouin Stories.* Berkeley: University of California Press.

Alcoff, Linda. 1988. "Cultural Feminism Versus Post-Structuralism: The Identity Crisis in Feminist Theory." *Signs* 13(3):405–436.

Alcoff, Linda, and Laura Gray. 1993. "Survivor Discourse: Transgression or Recuperation?" *Signs* 18(2):260–290.

Armstrong, Louise. 1990. "The Personal Is Apolitical." *Women's Review of Books* (March), 1–44.

Behar, Ruth. 1993. *Translated Woman: Crossing the Border with Esperanza's Story.* Boston: Beacon Press.

———. 1995. *The Vulnerable Observer: Anthropology That Breaks Your Heart.* Boston: Beacon Press.

Bernstein, Susan David. 1992. "Confessing Feminist Theory: What's 'I' Got to Do with It?" *Hypatia* 7(2):120–147.

Collins, Patricia Hill. 1990. *Black Feminist Thought.* Boston: Unwin Hyman.

Ellis, Carolyn. 1991. "Sociological Introspection and Emotional Experience." *Symbolic Interaction* 14:23–50.

Ferguson, Ann. 1991. *Sexual Democracy: Women, Oppression, and Revolution.* Boulder: Westview.

Haraway, Donna. 1988. "Situated Knowledges: The Science Question in Feminism and the Privilege of the Partial Perspective." *Feminist Studies* 14(3):575–599.

Hartsock, Nancy. 1983. *Money, Sex and Power.* Boston: Northeastern University Press.

Hartsock, Nancy. 1996. Comment on Hekman's "Truth and Method: Feminist Standpoint Theory Revisited": Truth or Justice? *Signs: Journal of Women in Culture and Society.* 22(2):367–373.

Kaminer, Wendy. 1995. Review of *Voices from the Next Feminist Generation. New York Times Review of Books* June 4.

Lewin, Ellen. 1993. "Lesbian and Gay Kinship: Kath Weston's *Families We Choose* and Contemporary Anthropology. In "Theorizing Lesbian Experience, Special Issue." *Signs* 18(4):974–989.

Lugones, María. 1992. "On Borderlands/La Frontera: An Interpretive Essay." In "Lesbian Ethics: Special Issue," *Hypatia* 7(4):31–37.

Morris, Aldon D. 1992. "Political Consciousness and Collective Action." Pp. 351–373 in *Frontiers in Social Movement Theo-

ry, edited by Aldon D. Morris and Carol McClurg Mueller. New Haven: Yale.

Naples, Nancy A. 2001. "Negotiating the Politics of Experiential Learning in Women's Studies." *Locating Feminism* edited by Robyn Weigman. Durham, NC: Duke University Press.

———. 1999. "Towards a Comparative Analysis of Women's Political Praxis: Explicating Multiple Dimensions of Standpoint Epistemology for Feminist Ethnography." *Women & Politics* 20(1):29–57.

———. 1998. *Grassroots Warriors: Activist Mothers, Community Work, and the War on Poverty.* New York: Routledge.

Naples, Nancy A., with Emily Clark. 1996. "Feminist Participatory Research and Empowerment: Going Public as Survivors of Childhood Sexual Abuse." Pp. 160–183 in *Feminism and Social Change: Bridging Theory and Practice* edited by Heidi Gottfried. Champagne-Urbana: Illinois University Press.

Patai, Daphne, and Noretta Koertge. 1994. *Professing Feminism: Cautionary Tales from the Strange World of Women's Studies.* New York: Basic Books.

Personal Narratives Group, ed. 1989. *Interpreting Womens' Lives: Feminist Theory and Personal Narratives.* Philadelphia: Temple University Press.

Rich, Adrienne. 1980. "Compulsory Heterosexuality and Lesbian Existence," *Signs* 5:631–660.

Ronai, Carol Rambo. 1995. "Multiple Reflections of Child Sex Abuse: An Argument for a Layered Account." *Journal of Contemporary Ethnography* 23(4):395–426.

Sandoval, Chela. 1991. "U.S. Third World Feminism: The Theory and Method of Oppositional Consciousness in the Postmodern World." *Genders* 10:1–24.

Smith, D. E. 1987. *The Everyday World as Problematic: A Feminist Sociology.* Toronto: University of Toronto Press.

Taylor, Verta, and Nancy E. Whittier. 1992. "Collective Identity in Social Movement Communities: Lesbian Feminist Mobilization." Pp. 104–129 in *Frontiers of Social Movement Theory*, edited by Aldon D. Morris and Carol McClurg Mueller. New Haven: Yale University Press.

Thorne, Barrie. 1995. "Symposium: On West and Fenstermaker's 'Doing Difference.'" *Gender & Society* 9(4):497–499.

Timmermans, Stefan. 1994. "Dying of Awareness: The Theory of Awareness Contexts Revisited." *Journal of Health and Illness* 16(3):322–339.

West, Candice, and Don H. Zimmerman. 1987. "Doing Gender." *Gender & Society* 1:125–151.

Weston, Kath. 1991. *Families We Choose: Lesbians, Gays, Kinship.* New York: Columbia University Press.

Wolf, Margery. 1992. *A Thrice-Told Tale.* Stanford: Stanford University Press.

43 | STIGMA AND EVERYDAY RESISTANCE PRACTICES
Childless Women in South India
Catherine Kohler Riessman

How do married women experience and resist hegemonic definitions of family in everyday interaction? What strategies can legitimately be theorized as resistance, in the absence of a collective movement that challenges discrimination based on family form? To illuminate the answers to these questions, I examine the everyday practices of married women in South India who are childless. India is not exceptional in its emphasis on childbearing—making babies is the primary way women are expected to make families the world over, and in Western nations, women encounter stigma if they do not become mothers (Greil 1991; Miall 1986). But the Indian context puts gender ideology, parental power, and other structural issues into sharp relief. I examine how childless women attempt to construct families in a pronatalist society and how they experience and challenge stigma when they are not mothers because of either infertility or choice.

Married women who remain childless in India are invisible in social research, but they are highly visible in their families and communities. From the perspective of international development experts, involuntary childlessness is not a problem. From the standpoint of women leading lives in a country where status depends on motherhood, the meaning of childlessness is profound. One of the few studies in India of women

Catherine Kohler Riessman, *Gender and Society* 14: 111–35, copyright © 2000 by Catherine Kohler Riessman. Reprinted by permission of Sage Publications, Inc.

who visit an infertility clinic reveals considerable self-blame: "There is something wrong with me" was a common statement (Jindal and Gupta 1989). Voluntary childlessness is rare in India, and research about it is absent.

The institutional importance of motherhood in India cannot be overestimated, even as family life is undergoing change. The normative social biography for an Indian woman mandates childbearing after marriage. Motherhood is her sacred duty—a value enshrined in religious laws for Hindus, Muslims, Sikhs, and Christians alike. Bearing and rearing children are central to a woman's power and well-being, and reproduction brings in its stead concrete benefits over the life course: A child solidifies a wife's often fragile bond with a spouse in an arranged marriage and improves her status in the joint family[1] and larger community; and with a child, she can eventually become a mother-in-law—a position of considerable power and influence in Indian families. In old age, women depend on children (particularly sons) for economic security in a country like India with few governmental social welfare programs, and upon death, a son makes possible the essential rituals for Hindus. For families with significant property or wealth, sexual reproduction allows for social reproduction—the orderly transfer of privilege through inheritance to the next generation of kin. Motherhood, in a word, serves critical cultural functions in India's hierarchical society—stratified by gender, caste, and class—that are masked by psychological or sentimental discourses (e.g., it is "natural" for a woman to want to bear a child). Indian women are keenly aware that their reproductive capacities are an important source of power, especially when they lack it from other sources (Dube 1986; Jeffery, Jeffery, and Lyon 1989; Stone and James 1995; Uberoi 1993).

Western stereotypes and generalizations about Indian women are based on inadequate knowledge about class structure (India has a large middle class alongside a wealthy class and considerable poverty), regional context (women's status and opportunity for education vary markedly within India), and India's vibrant feminist organizations (working on health issues and violence against women, primarily). Although there continue to be severe constraints on women who remain unmarried or live in same-sex unions, power over women is certainly not absolute and hegemonic. Social

change in postcolonial India has reconfigured family form for married women, and patterns are continuing to evolve with economic liberalization. Contemporary pressures encourage couples (sometimes one spouse) to migrate to urban centers. Partly as a consequence, nuclear households are increasing (due to necessity, in some cases, and preferences of spouses, in others). Impoverished South Indian couples have various alternatives to the joint family, such as living with the wife's relatives or in other extended family arrangements—couples generally reside where circumstances are best. Changing household structures, in turn, are influencing (and are influenced by) ideas about marriage, including gender relations and continuing obligations to natal kin. Although arranged marriage remains dominant, and parental authority over young women is considerable, diversity is possible in the timing of marriage and childbearing and in the number of children—especially in India's burgeoning middle class. There are clear undercurrents of change in the motherhood mandate.[2] Although some delay may be tolerated, women are ultimately expected to marry and reproduce. Pronatalism remains the dominant ideology.

Given the mandate of motherhood, how do married women retain valued identities and sustain families when they are not mothers? Following Davis and Fisher (1993), I explore how women create some degree of freedom within the gendered margins of families and culturally prevalent definitions of womanhood. I examine intensive interviews with 31 married South Indian women—involuntarily and voluntarily childless—to explore their experiences of stigma and situated resistance practices. By *resistance,* I mean the transformative actions women initiate to press their own claims in relation to others who discriminate against them—a definition I expand below. This research contributes to comparative studies of gender and the family, and by inviting women's voices into fertility discourse, there are insights for area and social development studies as well. My analysis also raises questions about stigma theory as it has developed in the West.

RETHINKING STIGMA

Erving Goffman articulates how bodily signs that depart from the "ordinary and natural" are deeply discrediting: The person is reduced in the eyes of others "from a whole and usual person to a tainted, discounted one" (1963, 3). Goffman's insights have been extended to a variety of other, not always visible, conditions such as epilepsy (Schneider and Conrad 1980), HIV (Weitz 1991), divorce (Gerstel 1987), mental illness (Rosenfield 1997), and infertility in the United States (Miall 1986). Collectively, research suggests that when a condition is potentially stigmatizing, individuals strategically manage information about themselves in interactions. They control what others know about them by selective disclosure or concealment. An invisible and potentially stigmatizing attribute can remain hidden; an actor chooses whom to disclose to and when. The theory (a product of Western thought) assumes a self-determining, autonomous individual with choices and a mass society that allows for privacy—in Asian contexts, these are problematic assumptions that scholars are beginning to criticize (Kleinman et al. 1995; Riessman 2000).

Gussow and Tracy identify a second problematic assumption: The original theory does not offer the "possibility of any serious attempt by stigmatized individuals to destigmatize themselves," that is, for individuals to put forth their "stigma" as a difference rather than a failing (1968, 317). Goffman assumes that the stigmatized person holds the same beliefs about her or his condition as the rest of society; consequently, dealing with stigma becomes a focus of existence. The politics of Goffman's theory are displayed in his language: Individuals "manage" information about themselves; they "react" to (rather than resist or reject) the critical appraisals of others. But in the empirical world, there are countless instances in which individuals disavow dominant perspectives. Some scholars depict a self that is more active than the one in Goffman's original formulation (Frank 1988; Weitz 1991).

A third issue in stigma research is the role of social structure—specifically, the stigmatized person's social class, age, and gender. I will argue that women in different class contexts can mobilize different resistance strategies in the face of childlessness. Social class carries with it privilege that affects the experience of stigma, strategies, and resolution. Similarly, stigma can operate differently over the life course: The value of motherhood varies over a woman's life (e.g., it is critical in old age in countries that lack universal social security programs), and its meaning is contextual in other ways as well (e.g., in women's relations with kin compared with employers). The question of whether people are permanently stigmatized is a matter of lively debate in the theoretical literature (for a review, see Bell 1999a). Gender also matters: In cultural representations around the world, biological reproduction has been fused with women's bodies (Ginsburg and Rapp 1995), and consequently, fertility problems are seen as women's failings. In research in the United States on childlessness, gender occupies a prominent place (Greil 1991; Lasker and Borg 1994), but the intersection with social class and race does not (but see May 1995). Studies have almost exclusively reported on the experiences of middle-class white women of childbearing age. Yet, the import of an attribute that is potentially discrediting, such as childlessness, should vary depending on the position of the woman, the contexts in which she leads her life, and the material and interpretive resources she can bring to bear.

Feminist scholarship provides a useful corrective to some of the problems of stigma theory, especially studies of lives that focus on race/ethnicity and class and their relationship to gender. Contemporary theorizing emphasizes women's agency in situations where they face discrimination and abuse. Women with disabilities, for example, confront and resist dominant views (Fine and Asch 1988). Women modify their reproductive lives as the need arises (Greenhalgh 1995). Women grapple with their position as victims of a culturally constructed subordinate status at the same time as they search for creative ways to resist subordination (Bell 1999b; Davis and Fisher 1993; Franz and Stewart 1994; Langellier 1989; Mahoney and Yngvesson 1992).

DATA AND METHOD: A REFLEXIVE ACCOUNT

In studying women's agency, it is necessary to locate my own. A narrative account of methods suits the shifting nature of the project, the routes I took to travel in a changing field (Clifford 1997; Morawski 1994). [I traveled to South India in 1993 intending to study the meaning and management of infertility.] In the proposal, I wrote as a distant observer who would "collect data" and "produce findings." This positioning, in part, was for an imagined audience of grant reviewers, but it also reflected my distance from the topic and the field. As an outsider—a white Western woman with grown children, studying South Asian women who wanted to conceive—I hoped to give voice to their invisible concerns in a country dominated by a discourse of population control.

The subcontinent of India and its southern coast (Kerala),[3] where I lived and worked from 1993 to 1994, dissolved distance. Traveling on crowded trains, I even began to question my topic: "India has too many people," I wrote in field notes, "why am I studying infertility?" But fieldwork drew me into the topic, especially interviewing women (together with my Mayalayali research assistant, Liza) in a busy infertility clinic of a government hospital or in their homes in towns and villages. Potential research participants were identified by physicians at the clinic and by village sponsors in two geographic areas. [For a time, I lived in a fishing village and assisted in wedding preparations, working alongside childless women I had formally interviewed. Witnessing them in everyday life decentered my earlier notions of their subordination (Riessman 2000).]

I learned about dominant definitions of family from repeated questions about my own: "How many children do you have? Why aren't they married? Where is your husband?" (I was divorced at the time). From strangers on trains and others who asked about my personal life, I learned firsthand about compulsory motherhood, marriage, and stigma. Ironically, I lived in an apartment complex called "Choice Gardens," but I felt stigmatized by my Indian neighbors' responses to my family status. Like a divorced woman, a married woman who is childless in India exists at the margins, in a liminal space—socially betwixt and between. With these insights, the interviews focused with increasing intensity on how women construct lives when they are not mothers and the social support others do (or do not) provide.

As the focus of the project shifted, sampling was increasingly driven by theoretical questions (Glaser and Strauss 1967). Initially, my criterion was infertility, but early interviews revealed definitional complexities. Some women were involuntarily childless, but

the problem was not infertility. These women were rarely together with their husbands. Because of high unemployment in Kerala, men migrate to the Gulf States in search of jobs, returning on leave for several months a year (Gulati 1993). If conception did not immediately occur, the couple came to the clinic. Busy physicians were irritated by "Gulf wives" and instructed them to "stay with their husbands"—an impossible recommendation in the economic context. Social problems produced unwanted childlessness, and consequently, I abandoned a medicalized definition (infertility) and adopted a social one (childlessness). The decision, in turn, opened up another question: What about the voluntarily childless? A woman, identified as infertile by my village sponsor, told us she "didn't have the inclination" for children and was not actively seeking treatment. I became intrigued with stigma in such circumstances and decided to seek out women who were explicitly childless by choice (those who articulated the decision, as distinct from others who might be passing as infertile). The voluntarily childless proved very difficult to locate in rural Kerala,[4] but I did interview several.

The 31 women participants (all married, and ranging in age from 22 to 57) are diverse on a number of dimensions, including the reasons they are childless. More than two-thirds are Hindus, with many castes represented: Brahmins and Nairs (advantaged castes), Ezhavas, and Pulayas (a scheduled or "backward" caste that receives government benefits). Nearly a quarter of the women are Christian, and there are a few Muslims. About a quarter have family incomes below the Indian poverty line (less than Rs 1,000 per month), nearly 40 percent are in the low- to middle-income range, and a third are from the middle- to upper-income levels. More than half have not attended college, while 23 percent have some professional education. Twenty-three percent live in joint families, the same percentage live with other relatives in extended families, and 55 percent live in nuclear units (see Table 1). It is impossible to know to what extent my sample represents the population of voluntarily childless and infertile women in the region, but on several dimensions, the sample does reflect the population of the two districts in Kerala where I did fieldwork. The sample slightly overrepresents Hindu and

Table 1 Characteristics of Sample (in percentages)

Age	
20–29	52
30–39	26
40 and older	23
Years married	
1–4	32
5–9	32
10–14	13
15 or more	23
Religion	
Hindu	68
Christian	23
Muslim	6
None	3
Education	
Less than high school	19
High school equivalent	35
College	23
Professional school	23
Occupation	
Clerical/manual	13
Professional/business	29
Full-time homemaker	58
Household income	
Poverty (less than Rs 1,000/month)	29
Low to middle (Rs 1,000–3,999/month)	39
Middle to upper (Rs 4,000 or more/month)	32
Household type	
Nuclear	55
Joint	23
Extended	23

professionally educated women and nuclear families, when compared with district data Gulati, Rama-lingam, and Gulati 1996). Few Muslims entered the sample, compared to their presence in the region, reflecting perhaps religious differences in the management of infertility and the incidence of voluntary childlessness.

Interviews, conducted at a single point in either the women's homes or in a private room in the clinic, were taped and subsequently transcribed and translated when necessary. Liza and I conducted the interviews (seven were in English and the rest in Malayalam).[5] Liza interpreted for me when necessary, translated the majority of the interviews, checked the others, and worked closely with me to clarify linguistic terms as I coded the transcripts. During the inter-

views, we encouraged women to give extended accounts of their situations, including the reactions of others: husband, his family, her family, the neighbors. The conversational nature of the interviews yielded lengthy accounts of meaning and action, and several women said they felt relieved to be able to talk. Elsewhere (Riessman 1995, 2000), I have described the interview process—how the women saw Liza and, in turn, me; we were interpreted by women as we interpreted them. The metaphor of travel (Clifford 1997) conveys the efforts we made, and those our participants made, to converse across borders of class and culture.

Responsibility for the analysis is mine, accomplished over an extended period beginning in India, continuing (and changing) as I returned to the United States. I coded the interviews using a version of grounded theory procedures (Charmaz 1990), searching the texts for common thematic categories and then examining concepts in relation to one another as I constructed them from the categorical data. I examined reported instances of stigma—social interactions when women said they felt tainted or discredited because they did not have children. Many also hinted at efforts to disavow their imputed inferiority, and in an effort to get beyond my early thinking about women as victims of the ideology of compulsory motherhood, I focused increasingly on women's everyday resistance strategies (Collins 1990; Scott 1985)—how they confronted discrimination and brought about change. Returning from the field to a disciplinary space in the United States altered ideas of victimhood and also decentered my notions of autonomous selfhood. Indian women did not act alone, I realized; actions to resist stigma needed to be read in a social structural context that was related to the woman's position in the life course, educational and occupational privilege, and her network of family ties. Husbands entered my analytic field, particularly actions to support and protect wives from stigma (the shift was coterminous with my remarriage). Limitations of lived experience often constrain imaginative identification and alternative readings of a text.

Some might question whether one can legitimately study linguistically mediated modes of resistance with translated texts. Although not minimizing language (it is not an objective container of ideas), I hope the strength and consistency of my argument across participants justifies the examination of interview transcripts that are not in the native tongue. (See Riessman 2000 for an extended discussion of language, translation, and meaning.)

CONTEXTS OF STIGMA

Remaining childless after marriage challenges strong cultural beliefs about the "ordinary and natural" life course for Indian women, and virtually everyone Liza and I interviewed—those who are voluntarily and involuntarily childless alike—spontaneously recalled incidents when they felt reduced in the eyes of others because they were not mothers. Discrediting encounters between a woman and those around her range from annoying comments to incidents that deeply threatened her welfare. The environment where a woman leads her life influences exposure to stigma, which in turn reflects class position. For all women, however, selective disclosure of the "invisible" attribute was not an option, as stigma theory suggests. All women were repeatedly questioned about their family status in a variety of public and private contexts.

Encounters in Public Settings

Both poor and affluent women experience unwanted questioning while on trains, which are used by all groups in India to travel around the vast country and where interaction with other passengers is typical. A 34-year-old Hindu home-maker, married 10 years to a fisherman (doctors determined he has no sperm), describes a common experience: "When we go on a trip, everyone will ask 'How many children do you have?' . . . Once we get married everyone will ask only that, 'How many children do you have? Haven't you consulted anyone [a doctor]?'" An affluent, 32-year-old Hindu scientist married to a physician (they are voluntarily childless) told me an almost identical story: "You know how in India people ask questions. We just meet a stranger on a train and they ask, 'Are you married? How many children do you have? Oh, you don't have? When are you planning to have?'" For neither woman was the questioning welcome—it was "upsetting." As stigma theory predicts, the families

were marked as departing from the "ordinary and natural."

Poor women encounter harsh judgments from neighbors. The fertility of village women of childbearing age, and those who live in crowded urban settings, is visible to all. Houses are typically close together, and women have frequent contact with neighbors as they walk to the main road to shop or collect water at a central pump. Those with young children talk about others who do not have children. A 32-year-old Hindu who works with her fisherman husband encounters derisive comments when she walks with him: "Someone will say something, purposely for us to hear. Women make comments when we come through the lane." The content of these remarks is articulated by a 28-year-old Muslim woman who is married to a day laborer: "They [neighbors] will say 'Oh she has no child,' like that they'll say." A 26-year-old Christian, married to a fisherman, describes harsher encounters: "Neighbors they ridicule me. When I go out and all they ridicule me calling 'fool without a child,' like that . . . they ridicule and laugh." Another woman used the term *outcast* to describe how neighbors treat her because she cannot conceive. It was doubly difficult because she is from a "backward" (untouchable) caste.

Several young poor women identified the most hurtful name they are called, *machi,* a word in Malayalam that has no English equivalent: It refers to a farm animal that cannot breed. When asked about her neighbors, a 30-year-old Hindu quickly volunteered, "Do you know what they all say? When there is a quarrel over something, they'll say 'machi, machi.' Because of all these problems I came here [to infertility clinic]." Others scorn the kind of family she has created, because it is childless, despite the fact that the "failing" is his: He had a vasectomy before marriage (at age 14), not understanding its consequences. The cause of infertility in this case is India's coercive, state-sponsored population control policies.

Economically privileged women are protected from coercive state policies and from the harsh comments poor women encounter at the local level. Their educational and occupational status, and the environments in which affluent women live, generally shield them from curious neighbors. Nevertheless, questions are sometimes asked ("Why the delay?") and derogatory comments made: "Certain people [neighbors] like to insult us by saying we are issueless."

A 34-year-old Hindu teacher (I interviewed her in English) tried to explain to me: "Neighbors, every time they ask . . . In Malayalam they ask, you know, 'Vishesham' [any special news]? Every time." When I inquired, "Is it an insulting term?" she responded, "No, not that," and then explained it is "colloquial language," a way that others ask about pregnancy right after marriage. After 11 years of marriage, she finds persistent questioning "awkward," and then she agreed with my earlier formulation: "You feel insulted." However discrediting, the term *vishesham* alienates them from (potentially) childbearing women and stands in sharp contrast to *machi,* the term poor women repeated, which carries meanings of indelible disrepute and likens a woman's body (and worth) to a farm animal's.

Women of all class backgrounds spontaneously mentioned the intrusive questioning that occurs when they attend others' marriage celebrations, which figure importantly in Indian communities. Celebrations are typically large, elaborate, and expensive (poor families often go into debt), and relatives travel distances to attend them. Marriage is central to the production and reproduction of traditional families, and the event becomes a site for stigmatizing families without children.

No childless woman said she was excluded from a marriage celebration or other event, but many spoke of difficult encounters there. A 34-year-old Hindu in business with her fisherman husband said, "They have only that to talk about, our relatives, when we go to a house where there is a marriage. 'Didn't you try? Didn't you see a doctor?'" A 24-year-old Muslim homemaker, also from a poor community, responded to the interviewer's questions:

INTERVIEWER: When you go to such functions and all, how do you find people's reaction?

RESPONDENT: They will speak to each other. . . . They'll look at us and ridicule and talk and all.

INTERVIEWER: How do you feel then hearing all this?

RESPONDENT: I'll feel upset that—isn't it because I don't have children?

A Hindu professional from a middle-class community reported a similar incident, but with a very different outcome:

> Yes, I go for functions. My husband's friends and all after marriage—there were four friends . . . all four are married, one got married recently. All three don't have children so we sit and console each other. When we go for relations' marriages certain people will say something and all, but I don't take it seriously.

The contrast between the two incidents is striking. The first (poor) woman experiences shame and distress: Although others ridicule both husband and wife, she views the fertility problem as her fault ("Isn't it because I don't have children?"). Because she has not conceived, the problematic attribute belongs to her. Being a mother is a master status for village women who live in poverty; it overrides other identities. The second incident (told by a middle-class professional) also reports discrediting comments by others ("Certain people will say something"), but her response is not to stigmatize herself. She has an occupational identity and support from others who are childless ("We sit and console each other"). Consequently, the meaning of potentially stigmatizing comments can be transformed—not taken seriously. Social class, in a word, mediates self-stigma. Derogatory comments are encountered at public events by childless women in general, but self-derogation and the construction of an identity around the "shameful" condition can be avoided by women with educational and occupational leverage.

Encounters in Family Settings

Questioning and negative comments are difficult to ignore in intimate family exchanges. Kin ties are strong among all class groups in India, and obligations to parents intensify after marriage. Visiting relatives is the major form of socializing on weekends for couples living in nuclear families, and in joint families, the daughter-in-law is expected to provide parental and household care. As one young wife put it, "Only if there are children can you have a good position [in his family]." Several women (both poor and affluent) in love marriages (as opposed to arranged marriages) longed for children so that family conflict would subside: "If we have children, then there will be no more opposition to the marriage."

Although the wife's family does inquire and pressure her to get treatment,[6] women spoke most often about stigma in the context of the husband's family. Fertility significantly improves the wife's moral status there, and harm can fall on village women at the hands of in-laws when conception does not readily occur, especially if there are also problems with the dowry (for a case study, see Riessman 2000). Mothers-in-law, in particular, communicate the motherhood mandate. As keepers of family and clear beneficiaries of motherhood as they age, mothers-in-law embody the importance of reproduction. When conception does not occur, the wife is blamed by the mother-in-law: "Why is she like that [not conceiving]?" "Why are they sitting without children? It must be her idea." A 42-year-old woman living in poverty put it angrily: "It is my fault we don't have children, their son has no problem—that is her opinion." The wife carries the stigma; it is her body that does not reproduce.

The message affluent women receive is similar, but subtle and indirect. A scientist and voluntarily childless woman reported her mother-in-law's comment to her husband: "It's not possible for a woman not to want a child, no woman can ever want that." In this (exceptional) instance, the son was blamed ("You must be forcing her not to have a child") because of gender ideology: The desire for children is "ordinary and natural" for all women. Issues arise about inheritance of family property when there are no children. Consequently, there is strong pressure on affluent wives to reproduce, although they have some latitude in the timing of pregnancy in contemporary India as the professional education of women becomes more common. Childbearing can be delayed if there are compelling reasons, and some women gain support in the interim, even, occasionally, from mothers-in-law. A 31-year-old woman finishing her law degree said, "Whenever I get a doubt [about my fertility] my mother-in-law says, 'There is time.'"

What are the responses of husbands when wives do not conceive? For involuntarily childless women, husbands' reactions vary widely, but a few are extreme. Infertility, in Kerala, does not appear to be a sufficient condition to abandon a wife (at least I did not locate instances during fieldwork). But women fear abandonment. A 24-year-old Muslim, whose husband works as a laborer in the Gulf, said he does not reply to her letters. Two women said they had been battered (both are poor village women). One was a 29-year-old Hindu woman, married just three years to a coconut picker. She canes chairs to supplement his meager income. She said, "Chettan [honorific term] used to get angry. When I said my menses had come." During the first year of marriage, he would come home drunk and beat her.

More typically, wives describe husbands who, like themselves, are distressed about fertility problems. In these cases, husbands do not side with critical in-laws and neighbors but ally with wives against hostile others, and in those marriages where emotional bonds are strong, husbands provide considerable emotional support. Wives told how their husbands got angry at devaluing comments and urged their wives to answer back. Perhaps husbands also sense the problem may be theirs. The infertility clinic requires both spouses to be tested, and about a third of the time the problem lies in the husband's sperm.

Several women described tender conversations with spouses about infertility. A Hindu homemaker is philosophical after 10 years of marriage, aided by her fisherman husband's commitment to the family they have made together and his promise to provide for her in old age: "So many people without children are living happily. So Chettan with that in mind will say, 'It's OK even if we don't have any children. I will take care of you completely.'" There is a suggestion here that identity need not be permanently spoiled. Self-stigma can be transcended over the life course, particularly in the context of a loving marriage, even if devaluing comments by others cannot be avoided. The "problem" of infertility can be viewed as a difference rather than as a failing (Gussow and Tracy 1968).

WOMEN'S RESISTANCE TO STIGMA

South Indian women's responses to stigma are complex and contradictory. They collaborate in the reification of motherhood, and they also challenge the stigma accorded childless families. Women collaborate in the reproduction of gender hierarchy in marriage at the same time as they challenge parental hierarchy when they are blamed by in-laws for infertility. A feminist language of resistance represents the complexity of the process better than stigma theory's language of interpersonal management strategies. South Indian women cannot join militant groups of fellow sufferers (Goffman 1963) as Western women do—self-help groups have little meaning in the Indian context. Instead, women who are not mothers but who live in society with pervasive pronatalist ideologies (which they often share) find ways to construct families without biological children. They fight back when they are blamed. Some make serious efforts to destigmatize themselves. Efforts do not have to be public, organized, formal, or unambivalently intentional to qualify as resistance (Collins 1990; Ortner 1995; Scott 1985, 1990; Scott and Kerkvliet 1986). As Scott argues, "Everyday resistance is informal, often covert, and concerned largely with immediate, de facto gains" (1985, 33). Ortner further emphasizes transformative processes: "Things do get changed, regardless of the intentions of the actors or the presence of very mixed intentions" (1995, 175). Childless women engage in transformative actions that can be seen in even the smallest activities. As social class shapes their experience of stigma, so too do everyday resistance practices vary with class position.

There is considerable debate in the Western feminist literature about social class and resistance processes. To simplify, some claim that women at the bottom of the social hierarchy are silent because they often do not see domination, whereas others argue that working-class women not only see it but speak out about it and organize. Emily Martin presents these polar positions and argues for additional possibilities:

> Women may know their oppression but choose not to speak out about it, judging the risk to be too great. They may do nothing or, operating stealthily in the interstices of power, they may resist through devious ways of speaking or acting. (1987, 182)

Like Martin, I found South Indian women—poor and affluent alike—expressing consciousness of their victimization as possessors of an imputed flaw and expressing opposition in subtle ways at some points and in overt ways at others. Three general patterns of resistance can be identified. The first two practices in-

volve transformative thoughts and actions in everyday life. The third—overt rejection of the motherhood mandate by the decision to remain childless—is of a different order. Like other resistance practices, however, it is transformative; it intentionally undercuts the ideology of compulsory motherhood.

Resistant Thinking and Strategic Avoidance

Involuntarily childless women rethink stigmatizing interactions to give past incidents new meanings. Women also strategically avoid contexts where they expect to encounter difficulty. Looking first at resistant thinking, when women experience the sting of critical comments about their families from strangers, they attempt to reevaluate the incidents and deflect self-blame. "Not taking it seriously" is a typical response to intrusive questioning on a train, for example. Poor village women ridicule the causal imputations of other village women, as a 30-year-old Christian articulates: "Neighbors are saying that others have cast a spell so we can't have children. People talk like that. I don't believe any of it." Living in close proximity to neighbors, poor women cannot avoid contact. But they can reinterpret the comments they hear and locate the fault in the neighbors instead of in themselves. A 45-year-old Hindu woman who initially "used to feel very bad" when others ridiculed her, subsequently realized their ignorance—neighbors assumed the fertility problem was hers, but she knew better: Doctors had determined that her husband had no sperm. She was constructing a family with her husband and natal kin, including a niece and nephew. Resistant thinking for such women involves the "private, hidden space of . . . consciousness, the 'inside' ideas" that allow women to transcend the confines of oppression (Collins 1990, 92) based on restricted definitions of family.

Advantaged women, similarly, reinterpret meanings even when they choose not to confront intrusive questioning directly. A 32-year-old voluntarily childless scientist told the story of her first job interview, during which she was asked about her childbearing plans. She responded by "going into a great explanation" about their decision not to have children.

> Later, as I think about it, I think it was not necessary. I shouldn't have done that. . . . I shouldn't have been asked and I shouldn't have responded. I should have

said, "It's our personal decision. I don't wish to discuss it. It's a private matter. Is it relevant?"

Resistant thinking also occurs in family contexts, where it often substitutes for speaking out, because the costs of confronting parental power can be great. A 25-year-old Hindu woman, whose husband has been a day laborer in the Gulf States for the six years of their marriage, ridiculed his family's imputation that she is at fault: "He is not here, right? He is working abroad. He comes home only occasionally. Only if he is here continuously can we say what the problem is." She did not voice these thoughts to the in-laws with whom she lived, however; to do so would have challenged the parental hierarchy—one of India's major forms of inequality and asymmetry. In such situations, Ortner observes, "people often do accept the representations which underwrite their own domination. At the same time they also preserve alternative 'authentic' traditions of belief and value which allow them to see through those representations" (1995, 182). Resistant thinking allows women to see through the apparently benevolent actions of mothers-in-law that mask systematic patterns of exploitation.

Several recently married, socially advantaged women were quite aware of the precarious position they occupied in families with considerable property and no visible heirs. These involuntarily childless women reminded themselves of their educational and occupational advantage: They could survive outside of marriage and achieve economic self-sufficiency—assets no poor woman possessed. A 31-year-old Christian employed as an accountant said, "If my husband leaves me, I think I will be able to live because I have a job."

Affluent and poor women use purposeful strategies of avoidance in similar ways. Wherever possible, they chose not to enter settings where intrusive questions and critical comments are routinely encountered. To avoid becoming "upset," village women strategically maneuver: "When I see them [neighbors who ridicule her] from a distance, I'll avoid them. Mostly, I don't go to my mother-in-law's house. If I go there, friends and neighbors will ask [about fertility]." A "backward" caste woman is defiant: "I don't give anybody an opportunity to call me that [machi]." She avoids public functions and temple festivals and

chooses settings that allow for invisibility, such as film showings. In nuclear and extended families, wives decline visits to their husbands' families. As a 32-year-old Christian, married to a coconut picker, puts it: "Husband goes to visit the family. They don't like me so I don't go." With these actions, she resists hierarchical family relations, specifically the intrusions of the mother-in-law into the daughter-in-law's reproductive life. Educationally advantaged women talk of "keeping mum" and "keeping away from husbands' relatives" at large functions. Although avoidance strategies run the danger of self-imposed exile, the everyday resistance practices allow women a measure of control—safe spaces where they can resist objectification (Collins 1990) and criticism of their families' form.

Resistant thinking and avoidance strategies do not, of course, attack stigma and discrimination directly, but they may be tactically necessary. Open challenge of a dominant ideology is not always possible. In sequestered settings where meanings can be reformed, overt critiques of domination may develop (Scott 1990). Challenges to structural and ideological power develop from hidden spaces of consciousness (Collins, 1990, 1997), especially during periods of rapid social change. The gaps and fissures in contemporary South Indian society provide fertile spaces for contesting dominant definitions of family.

Speaking Out and Acting Up

Direct action against stigma involves talking back to challenge discriminatory behavior. Although verbal resistance stopped short of collective action (e.g., a social movement), I witnessed individual women directly confronting pronatalist attitudes and hostile circumstances. Extreme measures were required to confront the extreme discrimination poor women face. Some quarreled with mothers-in-law and left hostile joint families to return to their natal villages when conflict with in-laws became more than they could bear. When adopting this oppositional practice, impoverished women do not act alone: Husbands accompany them (Riessman 2000). Leaving the joint family is often (but not always) a response of those in love marriages rather than arranged ones. A 35-year-old Hindu homemaker married to a fisherman said, "We got out of there," referring to his family's household, where his mother made her do all the work and "used to gossip bad" about her. In the Indian context, quarreling and leaving the joint family challenge established age and gender hierarchies, particularly deference to mothers-in-law. But such actions were necessary in extreme situations to preserve marriage.

Poor women also talk back to husbands who blame them for fertility problems. Sometimes, they are gentle. A 24-year-old Muslim "Gulf wife" said: "He will say jokingly sometimes 'I'll marry another girl' . . . I'll tell him 'It's not only you who wants children, I also wish to have a child.'" Other times, women confront. The 29-year-old woman who had been beaten by her husband when she menstruated eventually refused to accept blame. She held him responsible for their infertility: "I will say, 'It must be your problem because you have taken so many medicines [for mental health problems]. Stop drinking and it will all become alright.'"

Viewed together, these statements point to some of the ways economically impoverished South Indian women who are involuntarily childless resist, stop, and survive victimization. They "sustained continuity [in families with husbands] under transformed circumstances," and they "transformed circumstances [left joint families] in order to maintain continuity [with husbands and kin]" (Mullings 1995). The transformative acts some women initiated—always with support—were not intended necessarily to challenge stigma against childless women as a group, nor were actions (such as leaving the joint family) always unambivalent. But women's actions brought about change in families and generated spaces for husbands and wives to make families on their own terms, accommodating fertility problems—often with sadness. They confronted subordination openly sometimes and behind the scenes at other times, in social spaces where dissent of the "official transcript" (Scott 1990) could be voiced. Besides speaking out and acting up, women also made do within a constraining social order—a strategy that is active and inventive and shows resilience against, rather than succumbing to, stigma (De Certeau 1984). Middle-aged women in particular came to resilience after years of denigrating interactions. They decided it was not worth confronting every "ignorant" comment.

The stigma affluent women face for their "deviant" families is not as harsh as what poor women encounter, and subtle resistance actions often suffice. Many affluent women use humor, like this 28-year-old Hindu psychiatrist who laughingly narrated an incident at work: "I was told 'How can you do family therapy? You don't have children.' I mean, this was done jokingly by a colleague of mine. . . . My argument is that I don't have to be a schizophrenic to treat a schizophrenic." Others become militant. A 34-year-old Hindu librarian, chafing against expectations, openly contests the terms of her subordination: "Everyone will start inquiring . . . only about having children. As if this is the aim of getting married. I say 'Is this the only aim in life? There are so many other things.'" Challenge of compulsory motherhood was cleverly accomplished by a 47-year-old Hindu professor, who told a story about a conversation:

> My brother's wife, for instance . . . she's a good 10 years younger than me . . . she tried to make me feel guilty . . . "there's a lacking." I said, "No, darling, there's no lacking in me, even pigs can . . . it's how you bring up the child that is important, not whether you can conceive or not."

For this woman (who, during the interview, spoke of stigma when she was young), age and subsequent higher education made a huge difference. With education and maturity, she acquired the tools to see through dominant ideologies and the confidence to confront them. Women who are stigmatized at one point in their lives can transform their situations later with new ideas and values that allow them "to define their current selves and lives as equal to or more valuable than their previous ones" (Weitz 1991, 146). Talking back challenges stigma by reallocating fault: The problem lies in the values of the accuser (and, implicitly, Indian pronatalism and gender ideology), not in the childless woman herself.

The everyday resistance practices of speaking out and acting up do not include two obvious strategies. First, wives did not attempt to deflect stigma by naming the husband as the reproductive "failure." Village women did not say in response to neighbors' insults, "My husband has a low sperm count" or "He had a vasectomy during Indira Gandhi's mass sterilization program." Disclosure of biomedical "fault" probably does happen in private family contexts, especially among the educationally privileged, but its apparent absence in public conduct requires exploration. (One might ask, of course, how often U.S. women who struggle with infertility publicly disclose precise causes.) The issues are further complicated in India by gender conventions, which constrain wives' behavior. Wives are expected to refer to husbands with deference in their interactions with others; impoverished women even use honorific terms (Chettan). Significant cultural boundaries prevent wives from publicly faulting husbands, even when they do so privately. Consequently, childless women become the targets of stigmatization. As Ortner (1995) cautions, however, we must resist the tendency to romanticize the dominated by sanitizing their internal politics. In this case, gender politics—specifically the refusal to challenge male privilege—render women (unintentional) collaborators in the stigmatization process. Their actions both sustain and defy the cultural forms that try to enclose them.

Second, there is no collective movement of women against compulsory motherhood. Although there are long-standing feminist interests and organizations in India (e.g., health activists are working to curtail coercive sterilization policies—an important cause of infertility), the difficulties of women who attempt to construct families without children remain private issues. As Patricia Collins (1997) cautions, individual women may benefit from local resistance practices, but there is no substitute for sustained improvement of women as a group, which is possible in collective moments that target structural power. I did witness mass demonstrations organized by feminist groups, including creative public theater designed to raise awareness about domestic violence (one street performance portrayed wife battering due to infertility and dowry issues). Behind the mask of a gendered behavioral conformity, I witnessed a dawning consciousness in the talk of several middle-aged educationally privileged women in my sample. They observed that the woman's body is presumed faulty when the couple is childless. As a lawyer articulated, "Women are the injured party." A teacher made a similar point: "People will think that the man is perfectly OK, the whole fault is with the lady. That has to be changed." An upper-class homemaker, nothing that without sons women

have financial difficulty in old age, said "The government should do something to care for them." Advocacy for childless women as a group is a necessary prerequisite for a social movement against compulsory motherhood.

Rejecting the Motherhood Mandate: Choosing to Remain Childless

Voluntarily childless women challenge pronatalism directly by the explicit decision to build families without children. Generalization is impossible because of small numbers in my sample (three women) and demographic similarity (all are economically advantaged and "Westernized").[7] However, the group illuminates theoretically the boundaries of resistance processes. As Scott says, "Those renegade members of the dominant elite who ignore the standard script . . . present a danger far greater than their minuscule numbers might imply. Their public . . . dissent breaks the naturalization of power made plausible by a united front" (1990, 67).

Dissent elicits opposition from a variety of sources. As a 29-year-old Hindu banking officer said, "You get a lot of pressure to have children. . . . It's the norm in India." She has put her career first and is criticized for it. A 32-year-old Hindu scientist expressed sadness about her distance from women, including colleagues, who cannot understand her decision. She articulates how it has affected relationships: "Women ask more. I think they find it very threatening. They put pressure on you, you know, 'You have to go through this experience' . . . it makes me wonder if they don't feel it [motherhood] is a choice." Young women who reject motherhood for themselves embrace the Western discourse of choice. But choice is a shaky defense in communities where few share the discourse. In the face of normative pressure and the lack of a critical mass, the voluntarily childless women I spoke to continue to feel that their families are different.

> The thing is when you keep answering a question 25 times [How many children?] you know, you get irritated, you begin to feel you are different. . . . It's the same thing with being single. They just can't accept it, something is wrong. How can you not want to get married?

The scientist observed that others "find it really difficult to understand" and she feels "out of place." The banking executive feels uncertain and deviant: "You begin to wonder whether you are right or wrong." With aging, social pressure lessens, but lingering doubts remain in the mind of a 57-year-old affluent homemaker: "Maybe I am an odd thing . . . crazy." Lacking support for voluntary childlessness, all the women I interviewed struggle with self-definition.

Yet, they innovate and develop strategies to deflect questions. The banking executive interprets the everyday treatment she encounters ("It just happens in India, you have people coming and asking the most personal questions"). She has a rehearsed response that suggests irreverence toward motherhood: "I'll say, 'Well, I haven't thought about it yet.'" The scientist's rehearsed response is strategically effective, learned after many annoying interactions on trains: "Treatment is going on," she says with a serious face, and the questioning stops. A kind of medical disclaimer (Miall 1986), ironically, the response blunts her otherwise militant stand against compulsory motherhood. She has grown tired of trying to explain to strangers a decision she and her husband have carefully made. India's population justifies the older homemaker's response: "When I go to parties people will ask me, as usual, 'How many children?' I say, 'We are controlling the population.'" Although humorous and strategic, the response is located in her deep political concerns about India's future: "When I see the schoolchildren coming out of school, the amount of children we are having in each section, I get nauseated . . . like, you know, ants coming out of the pit . . . too many children." Her childlessness is "doing good for the nation." What others view as a "flaw" she has transformed into an attribute.

Kin relations are particularly difficult, especially for young women because they must confront the naturalization of parental power in India, and they sometimes pay a high price. The mother-in-law of the banking executive "took her to task," saying she wanted a grandson. Her father-in-law's will left all the real property to the married daughter with children instead of dividing it between the siblings as is customary. Her husband also can be critical ("He feels I've made my career more important than my marriage"), and I

sensed he may not be as resolute as she about their decision. The scientist and her husband have planned a life together without children; nevertheless, they also have ongoing struggles with both sets of parents. Her parents pressure them by using a maturation argument ("You should go through the experience . . . you will not be able to grow up if you don't"), whereas his—a Brahmin family—use a class-based argument. She laughed as she narrated an incident to me involving her mother-in-law:

> Initially, she tried to sit and reason with us. She gave us a long explanation as to why the two of us, especially, should have children, you know. . . . She would tell us . . . "All these autorickshaw drivers, you know, the lower socioeconomic status who are not educated, not knowledgeable, they are producing so many children. You are so educated and you are so aware of things, you should have children. Because then there will be better people in the world if you have children." She tried to use that logic.

The eugenics argument fell on deaf ears, and the couple "joke about it." Logic about "continuing the family name" was rebutted and the sexism exposed: "I said, 'Your daughter has two children . . . you don't consider your daughter's blood the same as your son's?'" Nevertheless, despite sophisticated resistance strategies, the couple has grown weary of stigma in interactions with kin. They have chosen to live a considerable distance from both sets of parents, a kind of resistance by relocation (Veevers 1979). They are creating a space for their life together as a couple—enlarging and reconfiguring the meaning of family.

DISCUSSION

Married women in South India are defined and judged in relation to dominant family forms and associated gender ideologies, and these forms of power elicit patterns of resistance. There are many commonalties between South Indian and U.S. women and some clear differences. Social change is expanding possibilities for women in India in general, and in families in particular, but women continue to be constrained by pronatalism—the ideology of compulsory motherhood. They are stigmatized when they cannot (or choose not to) be mothers. In a context of social change, however, married women are finding ways to sustain marriages without biological children—constructing families they seek to position alongside the other family forms evident in India today. Despite diverse reactions and important differences among women (educational and occupational privilege strongly influence experiences of stigma, strategies, and resolution), childless women as a group are not passive when they confront marginalization and devaluation. Yet it is important to resist the tendency to romanticize. As Linda Gordon notes about battered women:

> We must be clear that concepts like agency and resistance do not mean victory; nor should they work to soften the ugly and painful history of victimization. Indeed, many forms of resistance [are] probably poor choices, although one might argue that the impulse to do something, however ineffective, [is] usually preferable to resignation. (1993, 142)

Although a difficult process, particularly for young women and those living in poverty and village contexts, childless women make efforts to strengthen themselves against stigma, even as they lack opportunities for solidarity with other women in a social movement.

Forms of nonorganized, everyday resistance practices (Collins 1990, 1997; Scott 1985, 1990; Scott and Kerkvliet 1986) do not overthrow systems or even lead to emancipation. Given the forms of power South Indian women are up against—parental authority, structures of deference, gender ideologies, and strict control of women's sexuality—forms of protest are necessarily veiled. We need theories of resistance that do not misattribute forms of consciousness that are not part of most Indian women's experience (e.g., a Western feminist discourse about choice) at the same time as we acknowledge everyday sites of struggle (Abu-Lughod 1990). Foucault, Davis and Fisher articulate the perspective I've adopted here:

> Modern power operates continuously, in a penetrating matter—a "capillary" circulating through the social body and exerting its authority through self-surveillance and everyday, disciplinary micropractices. . . . Power exercised in this way . . . depends for its very existence on the multiplicity of points of resistance.

Any study of resistance practices must be contextual, taking local conditions and possibilities for action into account, but resistance implies more than accommodation, coping, or adaptation in the face of difficult circumstances. Women's agency must be palpable, and consistent with such a definition, I identified empirical instances where women advocated for themselves and their marriages, noting the contexts where they thought and acted in ways that contend with ideologies of family and derogatory evaluations of their families. Following Ortner (1995), I assume subjective ambivalence and ambiguity in women's resistance processes; my definition does not require intention to bring about a change in family form (the majority of those interviewed, after all, wanted children). Rather, I looked to see whether a woman's act (or thought) had transformative effects—however small—on reconfigurations of family. South Indian women who are childless, "negotiating at the margins of power, sometimes constrained by but also resisting even undermining asymmetrical power structures" (Davis and Fisher 1993, 16), fight against stigma and, simultaneously, bring about change in families.

I identified several forms of resistance in women's accounts: taking a stand in an interaction (speaking out and acting up), holding one's ground by refusing to internalize a deviant label (resistant thinking), purposefully electing to sidestep a confrontation (strategic avoidance), and finally, rejecting motherhood altogether. Except for the last form, the resistance practices do not necessarily imply ideological emancipation from the sex/gender system of India or even from the motherhood mandate. The Bedouin women Abu-Lughod (1990) studied support existing systems of power (e.g., they observe practices of veiling) at the same time as they subvert power and are irreverent toward particular cultural practices in their families. Similarly, childless women in South India negotiate the boundaries of normalcy in families, but at the same time, some of their actions (e.g., protecting husbands from blame) strengthen other sites of power (e.g., male privilege). By extensively seeking medical help, in addition, involuntarily childless women aid the growing infertility industry in India (rather than adoption services) and set the stage for medical domination over their lives. Medical definitions individualize women's problems, making collective action unlikely (Riessman 1983). Power and resistance work in complex ways in everyday practice.

South Indian women are finding ways to construct families even when they cannot (or choose not to) perform hegemonic scripts. Although structures of gender domination remain, women are clearing spaces for various kinds of families and creating spheres of influence, authority, and power in marriage that do not depend on motherhood. I watched childless women enthusiastically mothering other children—those belonging to kin or servants in their households and those of colleagues and friends. In these and other ways, women are positioning themselves in larger extended family arrangements. Social class matters immeasurably: Village women living in or near poverty have more limited opportunities to avoid surveillance of fertility than advantaged women do, and judgments about infertility may be harsher in less-educated families and communities compared to affluent ones. Although my sample size did not permit comparisons based on religion and type of household, these and other contextual factors may also shape responses to childlessness.

Goffman's (1963) historically and culturally located theory, which emphasizes stigma management, neglects the transformative effects of everyday resistance practices. Childless women in India cannot "pass"; on a daily basis, they encounter beliefs about the "ordinary and natural" family. They resist normative definitions differently depending on the resources they can bring to bear, particularly their subjective and material positions in South Indian society—interpretive and socioeconomic realities alike. Although a Western feminist imagination might wish them to go further and confront gender politics directly, South Indian women are working in context. Constructing their own lives within determinant conditions (Davis and Fisher 1993), they are finding "devious ways of thinking, speaking, and acting . . . operating stealthily in the interstices of power" (Martin 1987, 182) of South Indian culture to create spaces for families.

Voluntarily childless women—rare in South India, I learned from fieldwork—are challenging stigma and hegemony directly. It is not an accident that the three women I located are upper-middle class, "Western-

ized" in thinking, and in two cases, professional. Working at the margins of the South Indian gender order, and possessing discursive and material resources unavailable to most Indian women, they are openly contesting the importance of motherhood. Opposition from kin can be significant and can jeopardize inheritance. Further study of women who are voluntarily childless is needed. (As noted, the distinction between voluntary and involuntary childlessness is not always clear.)

A series of questions remain for theorizing. First, is it productive to define conceptual boundaries between resistance to dominant family scripts and resilience when the script cannot be performed (e.g., with infertility)? Resistance, in my definition, includes transformative actions in which women press their own claims vis-à-vis others who stigmatize them; resilience suggests managing, enduring, and transcending stigma. Both resistance and resilience are necessary as childless women negotiate their everyday lives, and survival strategies undoubtedly slide into one another in everyday practice. Nevertheless, further conceptual "unpacking" would benefit theory. Second, to what extent does a liberatory discourse (e.g., feminism) shape Western readings of resistance in women's words? How might the same texts be read by native speakers and others sharing indigenous ideologies? Elsewhere (Riessman 2000), I open up these issues by examining a South Indian woman's narrative that was read differently by different participants (and the same participant over time). The "translating" nature of interpretation cannot be ignored in ethnographic research (Clifford 1997).

Third, what is the role of political context in legitimating women's everyday resistance practices? The history and politics of Kerala, for example, with the region's tradition of political mobilization, provide fertile ground for women to speak out, which may be lacking in other settings. Women's high levels of education and literacy facilitate thinking and acting against dominant views, and matrilineal traditions of the past have likely strengthened women's position and capacities in the present for self-authoring lives. Comparison of women's strategic action in families in contrasting geopolitical settings is needed. Finally, how do stigma and women's resistance practices vary across the life course? My research raises questions as to whether the identity of a childless woman is permanently spoiled. Because stigma is greatest during childbearing years, it is most difficult for young women to construct emergent and reconfigured families. It becomes easier in middle age, but structural barriers to lives without children return with aging (at least in the context of India). We need to further specify the facilitating conditions for resistance to power.

NOTES

AUTHOR'S NOTE: A version of this article was presented at the 1995 meetings of the American Anthropological Association, Washington, D.C. For research assistance, I thank Liza George, Celine Suny, Leela Gulati, and Drs. A. K. Chacko, Kaveri Gopalakrishnan, P. K. Shamala (my physician sponsors), and Chandran and James (my village sponsors). For critiques of earlier versions, I thank Elliot Mishler, Vicky Steinitz Susan E. Bell, Lora Bex Lempert, Marjorie DeVault, Vicky Steinitz, my philosophy study group, and two anonymous reviewers. Deepest thanks go to the women who taught me about childlessness during fieldwork. The Indo-U.S. Subcommission on Education and Culture, Council for the International Exchange of Scholars provided financial support for fieldwork.

1. In joint families, a married couple resides in the household of the husband's parents.

2. Russo (1976) coined the term *motherhood mandate* in relation to sex-typing in the United States and the expectation that women have at least two children.

3. Kerala, located along the extreme southwestern coast of India, is an exceptional state on a variety of indicators: a 75 percent literacy rate (vs. 39 for India) for women, a life expectancy at birth of 73 (vs. 57) for women, and a sex ratio of 1,036 females (vs. 929) per 1,000 males. The effective female literacy rate in Kerala approaches 86 percent (Gulati, Ramalingam, and Gulati 1996). There is debate about the precise causes of the state's advantaged position (Letters 1991). On the political economy, special ecology, and unique history of Kerala, see Jeffery (1993), Mencher (forthcoming), Nag (1988), and Ratcliffe (1978).

4. Affluent voluntarily childless couples may migrate to the large cities of India where there is greater anonymity and tolerance for various family forms.

5. Malayalam is a member of the Dravidian family of languages spoken in South India. My representation of the translated interviews has benefited from conversations with Liza while I was in India and with India specialists since my return to the United States.

6. Relatives have definite opinions about appropriate sites for treatment: temples, churches, and doctors are all recommended. Because of Kerala's extensive system of primary care, allopathic recommendations are most typical: "You shouldn't keep delaying, go see a doctor for a checkup."

7. *Westernized* is a term used by educated Indian professionals, some of whom have visited Europe and/or America or send their children for higher education there. It suggests the incorporation of Western values (e.g., choice for women, gender equality, individual rights). It also is used critically to refer to excesses of U.S. culture that Indians observe in the media. (U.S. soap operas, talk shows, and Hollywood movies have large audiences in India).

REFERENCES

Abu-Lughod, L. 1990. The romance of resistance: Tracing transformations of power through Bedouin women. *American Ethnologist* 17:41–55.

Bell, S. E. 1999a. Experiencing illness in/and narrative. In *Handbook of medical sociology.* 5th ed. Edited by C. Bird, P. Conrad, A. Fremont, and S. Levine. New York: Prentice Hall.

———. 1999b. Narratives and lives: Women's health politics and the diagnosis of cancer for DES daughters. *Narrative Inquiry* 9(2):1–43.

Charmaz, K. 1990. "Discovering" chronic illness: Using grounded theory. *Social Science and Medicine* 30:1161–72.

Clifford, J. 1997. *Routes: Travel and translation in the late twentieth century.* Cambridge, MA: Harvard University Press.

Collins, P. H. 1990. *Black feminist thought: Knowledge, consciousness and empowerment.* Boston: Unwin Hyman.

———. 1997. How much difference is too much? Black feminist thought and the politics of postmodern social theory. *Current Perspectives in Social Theory* 17:3–37.

Davis, K., and S. Fisher. 1993. Power and the female subject. In *Negotiating at the margins: The gendered discourses of power and resistance,* edited by S. Fisher and K. Davis. New Brunswick, NJ: Rutgers University Press.

De Certeau, M. 1984. *The practice of everyday life.* Translated by S. Rendall. Berkeley: University of California Press.

Dube, L. 1986. Seed and earth: The symbolism of biological reproduction and sexual relations of production. In *Visibility and power: Essays on women in society and development,* edited by L. Dube et al. New Delhi: Oxford University Press.

Fine, M., and A. Asch. 1988. Disability beyond stigma: Social interaction, discrimination, and activism. *Journal of Social Issues* 44:3–21.

Frank, G. 1988. Beyond stigma: Visibility and self-empowerment of persons with congenital limb deficiencies. *Journal of Social Issues* 44:95–115.

Franz, C. E., and A. J. Stewart, eds. 1994. *Women creating lives: Identities, resilience, and resistance.* Boulder, CO: Westview.

Gerstel, N. G. 1987. Divorce and stigma. *Social Problems* 34:172–86.

Ginsburg, F. D., and R. Rapp, eds. 1995. *Conceiving the new world order: The global politics of reproduction.* Berkeley: University of California Press.

Glaser, B. G., and A. L. Strauss. 1967. *The discovery of grounded theory.* Chicago: Aldine.

Goffman, E. 1963. *Stigma: Notes on the management of spoiled identity.* Englewood Cliffs, NJ: Prentice Hall.

Gordon, L. 1993. Women's agency, social control, and the construction of "rights" by battered women. In *Negotiating at the margins: The gendered discourses of power and resistance,* edited by S. Fisher and K. Davis. New Brunswick, NJ: Rutgers University Press.

Greenhalgh, S. 1995. *Situating fertility: Anthropology and demographic inquiry.* New York: Cambridge University Press.

Greil, A. L. 1991. *Not yet pregnant: Infertile couples in contemporary America.* New Brunswick, NJ: Rutgers University Press.

Gulati, L. 1993. *In the absence of their men: The impact of male migration on women.* New Delhi, India: Sage.

Gulati, L., Ramalingam, and I. S. Gulati. 1996. *Gender profile: Kerala.* New Delhi, India: Royal Netherlands Embassy.

Gussow, Z., and G. S. Tracy. 1968. Status, ideology, and adaptation to stigmatized illness: A study of leprosy. *Human Organization* 27:316–25.

Jeffery, P., R. Jeffery, and A. Lyon. 1989. *Labour pains and labour power: Women and childbearing in India.* London: Zed.

Jeffery, R. 1993. *Politics, women and well being: How Kerala became "a model."* New Delhi, India: Oxford University Press.

Jindal, U. N., and A. Gupta. 1989. Social problems of infertile women in India. *International Journal of Fertility* 34:30–33.

Kleinman, A., W.-Z. Wang, S.-C. Li, X.-M. Cheng, X.-Y. Dai, K.-T. Li, and J. Kleinman. 1995. The social course of epilepsy: Chronic illness as social experience in interior China. *Social Science and Medicine* 40:1319–30.

Langellier, K. 1989. Women's personal narratives: Strategies of resistance. Paper presented at Annual Meetings, Speech Communication Association, San Francisco.

Lasker, J. N., and S. Borg. 1994. *In search of parenthood: Coping with infertility and high-tech conception.* Rev. ed. Philadelphia: Temple University Press.

Letters: The Kerala difference. 1991. *New York Review of Books,* 24 October.

Mahoney, M. A., and B. Yngvesson. 1992. The construction of subjectivity and the paradox of resistance: Reintegrating feminist anthropology and psychology. *Signs: Journal of Women in Culture and Society* 18:44–73.

Martin, E. 1987. *The woman in the body: A cultural analysis of reproduction.* Boston: Beacon.

May, E. T. 1995. *Barren in the promised land: Childless Americans and the pursuit of happiness.* New York: Basic Books.

Mencher, J. The village over time: Kerala. Forthcoming. *Economic and Political Weekly.*

Miall, C. E. 1986. The stigma of involuntary childlessness. *Social Problems* 33:268–82.

Morawski, J. 1994. *Practicing feminisms, reconstructing psychology: Notes on a liminal science.* Ann Arbor: University of Michigan Press.

Mullings, L. 1995. Households headed by women: The politics of race, class, and gender. In *Conceiving the new world order: The global politics of reproduction,* edited by F. D. Ginsburg and R. Rapp. Berkeley: University of California Press.

Nag, M. 1988. The Kerala formula. *World Health Forum,* vol. 9, no. 2. Geneva: World Health Organization.

Ortner, S. B. 1995. Resistance and the problem of ethnographic refusal. *Comparative Studies in Society and History* 37:173–93.

Ratcliffe, J. 1978. Social justice and the demographic transition: Lessons from India's Kerala State. *International Journal of Health Services* 8:123–44.

Riessman, C. K. 1983. Women and medicalization: A new perspective. *Social Policy* 14:3–18.

———. 1995. Locating the outsider within: Studying childless women in India. *Reflections* 1(3):5–14.

———. 2000. "Even if we don't have children [we] can live": Stigma and infertility in South India. In *Narrative and cultural construction of illness and healing,* edited by C. Mattingly and L. C. Garro. Berkeley: University of California Press.

Rosenfield, S. 1997. Labeling mental illness: The effects of stigma vs. services. *American Sociological Review* 63:230–45.

Russo, N. F. 1976. The motherhood mandate. *Journal of Social Issues* 32:143–79.

Schneider, J. W., and P. Conrad. 1980. In the closet with illness: Epilepsy, stigma potential and information control. *Social Problems* 28:32–43.

Scott, J. C. 1985. *Weapons of the weak: Everyday forms of peasant resistance.* New Haven, CT: Yale University Press.

———. 1990. *Domination and the arts of resistance: Hidden transcripts.* New Haven, CT: Yale University Press.

Scott, J. C., and B. J. Tria Kerkvliet, eds. 1986. Special issue: Everyday forms of peasant resistance in South-East Asia. *Journal of Peasant Studies* 13(2).

Stone, L., and C. James. 1995. Dowry, bride-burning, and female power in India. *Women's Studies International Forum* 18:125–34.

Uberoi, P. 1993. *Family, kinship and marriage in India.* New Delhi, India: Oxford University Press.

Veevers, J. E. 1979. Voluntary childlessness: A review of issues and evidence. *Marriage and Family Review* 2:1–26.

Weitz, R. 1991. *Life with AIDS.* New Brunswick NJ: Rutgers University Press.

FURTHER READING

Berger, Peter and Hansfried Kellner. 1970. "Marriage and the Construction of Reality." Pp. 50–72 in *Recent Sociology No. 2,* edited by Hans Pieter Dreitzel. New York: Macmillan.

- A Classic article on the talk and interaction that constructs marriage.

DeVault, Marjorie L. 1991. *Feeding the Family.* Chicago: University of Chicago Press.

- A study of the social organization of caring and household labor as gendered work.

Gubrium, Jaber F. 1992. *Out of Control.* Thousand Oaks, CA: Sage.

- A comparative study of the institutional construction of domestic disorder.

Gubrium, Jaber F. and James A. Holstein. 1990. *What Is Family?* Mountain View, CA: Mayfield.

- An amply illustrated, constructionist framework for family studies.

Riessman, Catherine Kohler. 1990. *Divorce Talk.* New Brunswick, NJ: Rutgers University Press.

- A study of women's and men's accounts of family dissolution in the divorce experience.

Stack, Carol. 1974. *All Our Kin.* New York: Harper and Row.

- An intimate picture of family relations in a poor African American community.

——— SECTION 5 ———

WORLDS OF TROUBLE

Troubles seem to crop up everywhere. It's hard to imagine a social world without them. But as commonplace as they are, troubles are not all that easy to define. It's not that simple or straightforward to specify what is *really* a problem in everyday life. For example, everyone probably agrees that "homicide" is a profound trouble. But are all deaths at the hands of another "homicides?" Are all killings "bad?" Sometimes it's not clear just what passes for homicide and what may be considered a justified, or even righteous, killing. We would probably agree that it's "murder" when the perpetrator of a convenience store robbery fatally shoots the store clerk. But what about killings that are ostensibly done in self-defense or in wartime? And if this weren't difficult enough, we then have to contend with the definition of self-defense and war. Is the fleeing burglar who fires a fatal shot at a pursuing police officer acting in self-defense? Is the member of an antigovernment militia engaged in an act of war when she opens fire on a U.S. marshal who has come to check on her children's welfare? Is it homicide when the government exacts retribution through capital punishment?

An interactional approach to troubles focuses on the processes of interpretation that construct actions as problems. From this point of view, societal reaction defines trouble as much as does the original act in question. Rather than take troubles as given, we turn to how people make sense of "troublesome" acts that they encounter in the course of everyday life. We need to consider the definitional processes that designate acts as troublesome, dysfunctional, abnormal, and the like.

Cultural and historical circumstances provide us with categories for discerning and naming troubles. We define individuals and situations as troublesome in terms of the *available* trouble categories of the times, so to speak. For example, suicide and infanticide have not always been considered serious troubles, in different eras and cultures, despite how clear-cut their definition seems to be in the contemporary United States. And even here and now, these definitions can still stir considerable controversy. For instance, is it all right to take one's own life or to assist another in taking his or her life, when such "suicide" is designed to put an end to extreme suffering? Should we allow the destruction of human embryos in the name of life-saving scientific research? Are such acts really "suicide" and "infanticide?"

Troubles, such as social problems, crimes, and diseases, are constantly being defined and redefined. For example, social movements have been responsible for designating and transforming the interpretation of behaviors, such as marijuana use, homosexuality, and excessive drinking. Public campaigns have sometimes made distinct, identifiable troubles out of what, at other times and places, might be viewed as socially acceptable. Even conditions, such as attention deficit hyperactivity disorder (ADHD), have achieved their definitions as diseases with the help of social movements and the medical professions.

In practice, an actual instance of "trouble" needs to be successfully identified and labeled for it to achieve its experiential reality. The simple presence of a category or label isn't enough to produce actual instances of the trouble itself. For example, the mere existence of the diagnostic category "ADHD" doesn't guarantee that we will automatically encounter "hyperactive" children. Extensive definitional work is required to establish that a particular child is suffering from ADHD and is not simply "high strung," "disobedient," or "mischievous." Whereas in today's world, the formal definition of troubles often requires professional expertise, what is and isn't troublesome in the first place is often discerned in quite ordinary circumstances by people who have little or no professional interest or expertise. And, likely as not, situations that could conceivably be called troubles end up being called something else or even ignored.

ABOUT THE READINGS

Robert M. Emerson and **Sheldon L. Messinger** show readers just how political the troubles-defining process can be in their article **"The Micro-Politics of Trouble."** Turning their attention to social deviance—troubles that come to be called crime, mental illness, or drug use, for example—the authors ask readers to avoid jumping to conclusions. They urge us not to move directly to the "end point" in analyzing troubles. They insist that we not take the definition of troubles for granted and then try to explain them retrospectively. Emerson and Messinger encourage us, instead, to pay close attention to the interactional contingencies that affect how a trait or behavior comes to be viewed as a particular kind of trouble. The key is to look at *how* trouble takes shape in the interactions surrounding it.

While many circumstances may be troublesome, often no full-blown trouble develops. According to Emerson and Messinger, that's because nothing is made of them, interpretively speaking. If no one pays attention to an everyday transgression, it's likely to go unnoticed. As such, it stays off the definitional path to becoming a moral or legal offense. Emerson and Messinger look closely at the interpersonal factors that contribute to a potential trouble becoming either "nothing" or something more substantial and serious. They also point out how the selection of possible remedies for a potential trouble itself contributes to how an act or event is eventually defined.

Dorothy E. Smith applies this perspective in **"K Is Mentally Ill,"** a richly detailed examination of psychiatric troubles. She carefully explores an account of how a young woman ("K"—a pseudonym) came to be seen as mentally ill by others in her life. Smith is meticulous as she examines interactional details that are typically overlooked. The payoff is extraordinary because she is able to show us how people—in practice—establish that "K" is surely mentally ill. In a fascinating twist, Smith also reveals how we may draw a vastly different conclusion if we give a slightly different spin to the circumstances surrounding the case.

Finally, **"Ways of the Badass"** by **Jack Katz** focuses on how persons help construct definitions of themselves as real trouble. Whereas Smith analyzed how others defined "K" as mentally ill, Katz focuses on how people interactionally establish "bad" identities *for themselves.* The compelling question is "How does one go about being a badass?" It doesn't just happen; it must be accomplished. Badasses, Katz argues, are made, not born. In the process, one must, of course, establish a social world for the badass to comfortably occupy. Katz describes how this can become a full-time interactional project. He shows how one goes about "doing" trouble to establish both one's bad self and the social world surrounding the badass.

44 | THE MICRO-POLITICS OF TROUBLE
Robert M. Emerson and Sheldon L. Messinger

In his early evaluation and criticism, Gibbs (1966) argued that proponents of the labeling approach to deviance "might reasonably be expected to develop a theory of the reaction process." A number of recent statements from within the perspective have echoed this call (Kitsuse, 1972; Orcutt, 1973). Two issues demand particular attention. First, as Kitsuse has emphasized (1972:241), labeling proponents have provided few studies of *informal reaction.* Yet informal processes can establish deviant status independently of, but affecting "official labeling." Second, the labeling tradition has neglected relations between informal and official systems of reactions. Little existing research explores the conditions under which informal systems of control prove inadequate (but see Goffman, 1969), or the reciprocal effects of informal and formal control measures. In this paper we want to make a programmatic statement of a sociology of trouble, to pro-

vide a theoretical approach to these two types of societal reaction.

Our argument assumes that any social setting generates a number of evanescent, ambiguous difficulties that may ultimately be—but are not immediately—identified as "deviant." In many instances what is first recognized is a vague sense of "something wrong"—some "problem" or "trouble." Consideration of the natural history of such problems can provide a fruitful approach to processes of informal reaction and to their relation to the reactions of official agencies of social control. Specifically, this paper will explore the processes whereby troubles are identified, defined, responded to, and sometimes transformed into a recognized form of deviance.[1] Two points in this process hold particular significance for the movement toward deviance, and will receive major attention. The first arises when parties outside the trouble are mobilized around it, the second when those outsiders' involvement rests on formal authority rather than personal ties.

PRELIMINARY CONSIDERATIONS OF TROUBLES AND REMEDIES

Problems originate with the recognition that something is wrong and must be remedied. Trouble, in these terms, involves both definitional and remedial components. Some state of affairs is experienced as difficult, unpleasant, irritating, or unendurable. The perception of "something wrong" is often vague at the onset: a woman notices that she is gaining weight, or that she is frequently depressed; a husband realizes that his wife is drinking more than usual, or is beginning to stay out later after work; parents see their daughter getting overly interested in boys, or their son starting to hang out with a tough gang of friends. Clearly, a person may come to recognize the existence of these or other problems, and yet never do anything in response. It may be that after mulling the problem over the person decides it is really no problem after all (everybody feels down at times, a few pounds don't matter, or sexual mores have changed in today's world); or that while there is indeed something wrong, there is nothing that can be done or that the attempt to do something would be doomed from the start. A problem ignored may fester; or it may disappear. But often the recognition that something is wrong coincides with a weighing of remedies, perhaps resulting in an attempt to implement an appropriate one.

Sometimes an initial remedy will work; other times it will not. The latter case may lead to a search for other remedies, and as the search continues, troubles may assume a cyclical pattern (e.g., Goffman, 1969:361–69). A difficulty arises, a remedy is sought and applied; it works temporarily or not at all; then some new remedy is sought. The result tends to be a recurring cycle of trouble, remedy, failure, more trouble, and new remedy, until the trouble stops or the troubled person forsakes further efforts. As a consequence of these processes, the trouble is progressively elaborated, analyzed, and specified as to type and cause—"organized" to use the term Balint (1957) has applied to the early stages of illness.

Again, on first apprehension troubles often involve little more than a vague unease. This feeling may derive internally from the person affected, or externally, from the remark of an observant acquaintance. An understanding of the problem's dimensions may only begin to emerge as the troubled person thinks about them, discusses the matter with others, and begins to implement remedial strategies. The effort *to find and implement a remedy* is critical to the processes of organizing, identifying, and consolidating the trouble.

Consider the kind of remedial cycle that may evolve with certain physical ailments. As some bodily trouble comes to be recognized and some "tentative self-diagnosis" (Freidson, 1961) made, some remedial measures—perhaps absolutely minimal may be undertaken. In the case of a cold for example, this may involve taking it easy while waiting to see if the trouble disappears. If it does not, "more active measures like staying in bed for a day or so and taking aspirin" (Freidson, 1961:143) may be tried. Such remedies may end the trouble. If they do not, or if the "same trouble" recurs at some later time, the prior "cold" diagnosis may be questioned. An initially accepted interpretation of the trouble may then be recast, sometimes quite radically. For example:

> When the husband was in the Army he had a "cold" that lasted several weeks. After observing the symptoms for a few days, the man's wife insisted that the ailment could not be a cold—it must be an allergy and he should see a doctor. The husband felt that his wife was wrong and he refused to consult a doctor for treatment of a mere cold. The symptoms persisted for six or seven weeks and then vanished. The husband was discharged from the Army the following year and returned to civilian work. During that second year he again had a "cold" which lasted several weeks. His wife again insisted that he must have hay fever. She reminded him that in a conversation about it his uncle—a physician—also said he must be suffering from an allergy, and she finally persuaded him to consult a physician who was a friend of theirs. The physician-friend diagnosed the ailment as a cold and joked about the wife's diagnostic qualifications. Eventually the "cold" disappeared. During the third year the husband began sneezing again and his wife insisted that he consult another doctor. This time hay

fever was diagnosed and the symptoms were hence-forth controlled (Freidson, 1961:142–3).

This illustration suggests why "trouble" should not be conceptualized as simply the establishment of a particular definition of a problematic situation.[2] Such a view would imply that having defined or diagnosed a trouble in a certain way, the appropriate remedy is more or less specified: if overweight is the trouble, then dieting is the appropriate response; if illness, then visiting a doctor and getting the appropriate treatments seem required. In fact, the process of remedying troubles is much more open and emergent than this diagnose-then-respond formulation allows. As the foregoing incident dramatizes, any initial formulation of what the trouble "really is" is conditional upon the subsequent effects of the attempted remedy. The use of a remedy, while following from a particular definition of the trouble, simultaneously serves as a test of that definition. That the remedy works the first time is taken to confirm the initial diagnosis and the trouble's cause.[3] But this diagnosis only holds "until further notice" (Garfinkel, 1967), until, for example, a worsening of the trouble reopens the whole matter of just what is wrong and what can be done about it.

We do not deny that definition of what a trouble is affects what is done about it. But the effect is neither as linear nor as direct as is posited by the define-then-respond model. Naming something a problem has implications, prefiguring some solutions and removing others. To identify one's problem as "overweight," for example, is to preclude a formulation such as discrimination and social exclusion based arbitrarily on bodily appearance (the position advanced by advocates of Fat Power; see Allon, 1973), a formulation with very different remedial implications. But even the definition "overweight" tends more to delimit a range of possible remedies than to prescribe a particular one necessary response. A man, deciding he is too fat, may diet or he may decide to exercise. Or he can look to causes rather than consequences, and enter psychotherapy.

In sum, many troubles, particularly when first noted, appear vague to those concerned. But as steps are taken to remedy or manage that trouble, the trouble itself becomes progressively clarified and specified. In this sense the natural history of a trouble is intimately tied to—and produces—the effort to do something about it. Thus, remedial actions of varying sorts—living with, ignoring, isolating, controlling, correcting the trouble—are highly significant events not only in determining the fate of the trouble, but also in shaping how it is first perceived. Conceptually, the definition of a trouble can be seen as the emergent product, as well as the initial precipitant, of remedial actions.

RELATIONAL TROUBLES AND INTRINSIC REMEDIES

We have largely drawn upon situations in which troubles begin and are remedied *intrapersonally*. Of particular sociological interest, however, are troubles that are inextricably *interpersonal* matters. Important variations arise with such *relational troubles*—that is, those in which remedial efforts are addressed to another in a recognized relationship with the troubled person. For, unlike efforts to remedy personal troubles, trying to resolve relational troubles raises issues concerning the distribution of rights and responsibilities in that relationship.

The difference between individual and relational troubles, and their radically variant remedial implications, is readily apparent in the advice and trouble formulations offered a woman interviewed about how she came to begin psychotherapy:

She noticed her problems "when I found myself crying on my job, while I worked. Bursting into tears in the face of a friend, while talking. And finally sobbing so continuously I could not leave the house without sobbing into the face of the first person I'd meet who greeted me with the words, 'Hello, how are you?'" After several months of this a neighbor, who was a school teacher, "told me to go to a mental hygiene clinic for aid." This advice was judged helpful. Other unsolicited advice came from two physicians, one of whom "told me I had no heart trouble but mental aggravation that caused me pains in (my) chest," and another who "told me to get rid of my husband because he was no good," and this was not helpful.

She solicited advice from several friends and from her husband. "Friends all advised me to leave my husband. My husband will never listen to me when I talk without ridiculing me" (Kadushin, 1969:172).

This troubled person received advice both to seek help for her mental condition, a remedy assuming an intrapsychic core to her problem, and to leave her husband, a remedy positing an essentially relational character to her trouble.

This distinction should not be taken to imply that certain troubles are necessarily or mainly individual, others inherently relational. The difference derives less from the troubles themselves than from the perspective or framework from which they come to be viewed and treated. What begins as a personal trouble can be redefined and treated as a relational one, and vice versa. With bodily illness, for example, a psychosomatic diagnosis can transform any physical symptom, such as chest pains in the above case, into a product of some relational strain. Conversely, the relational dimensions of many forms of mental illness may disappear upon application of the medical model, or upon discovery of an organic cause for the troubled behavior.[4]

Moreover, movement of a trouble from an individual to a relational frame and vice versa is often propelled by the remedial cycle discussed previously. Thus, if a personal trouble persists despite intrapersonally directed remedies, the troubled person tends to become progressively uncertain as to just what the trouble is and what ought to be done about it. Here, as earlier, the troubled person may receive a variety of often conflicting interpretations about what is wrong, typically imparted in advice on managing the problem. As a result both intrapersonal and relational versions of the trouble may be entertained sequentially, or even simultaneously.

When troubles are addressed in relational terms, first remedial actions typically involve one party directly responding to and trying to influence the behavior of the other. Such corrective actions can be termed *intrinsic remedies*, since they can draw upon the interpersonal resources inherent in that relationship. Intrinsic remedies may first assume indirect and implicit forms. A wife disturbed by some behavior of her husband, may offer a variety of subtle cues that something is wrong: an awkward silence, a raised eyebrow, a grimace (e.g., see Goffman on "remedial interchanges," 1971:95—187). Then a process of interactional negotiation is possible between participants to resolve the trouble without explicit recognition that it has arisen; the subtle sanction the offended person offers may work, moderating the behavior of the offender accordingly, sometimes by "stopping," sometimes by "stopping and apologizing." Alternatively, the offender may ignore the attempted sanction, and the sanctioner may let it pass.

But the issue may continue, initially in fairly muted, even covert ways. Joking references may be made of it, humor here as elsewhere allowing involved parties to avoid explicit acknowledgement of the trouble between them, while communicating its underlying seriousness (J. P. Emerson, 1969). Or the trouble may become an open issue in the relationship. Management strategies may vary from "we need to have a talk about it" to accusations that the other's behavior is wrong and must change.

A direct complaint made to the other alters the basic dynamics of the trouble. This move publicizes, explicates, and radically changes a purely individual trouble. With a direct complaint, buried differences in perceptions of the nature or source of the trouble may be brought to light. Implicit expectations about relational rights and responsibilities may be explicitly asserted and perhaps contested. The trouble may become the direct focus of the relationship, generating a continuing dialogue in which what is wrong and what should be done about it are explored, possibilities elaborated, and options specified. In this way, a complaint not only organizes and consolidates the trouble, but also constitutes that trouble as a fully interpersonal matter.

Initial complaints may only mark the beginning of an extended remedial cycle. Early interpersonal remedies may have little or only temporary effect, and further strategies may be used to influence the other's behavior, with varying degrees of success. Jackson (1954:572) has described a typical series of remedies unsuccessfully invoked by wives in trying to control a husband's emerging drinking problem:

> Threats of leaving, hiding his liquor away, emptying the bottle down the drain, curtailing his money, are tried in rapid succession, but none is effective. Less punitive methods, as discussing the situation when he is sober, babying him during hangovers, and trying to drink with him to keep him in the home, are attempted and fail.

Such remedial attempts reveal and highlight the nature and severity of the problem.

Understanding these matters is complicated by the partial and retrospective character of troubles and accounts of their development. Particular versions of what the trouble is, how it arose, and what was done in response, are likely to be highly partisan and hotly contested. Those involved in the trouble need never come to an agreement about what the trouble is or even that it exists. A husband may complain to his wife about her staying out nights, for example, but the wife need neither see nor acknowledge her behavior as a problem. When confronted by her spouse's rebuke or threat, she may identify his behavior as the trouble—an unreasonable insistence that she stay home. Claims about the existence or nature of a trouble, are embedded in and products of the troubled situation itself.

Second, many troubles will only be formulated retrospectively, often in furtherance of such partisan interests. Earlier relational incidents may be interpreted in light of subsequent diagnoses of the trouble. Thus, an aggrieved party may come to the realization: now I see what it is that has been bothering me about the way you treat me; or, now I appreciate how I have always hated it when you did that. Moreover, it is often only later that parties to a trouble explicitly formulate the distinctive stages and components of the remedial process. The beginning of the trouble, for example, may only be discovered in retrospect; pin-pointing the cause stands as part of the ongoing interpersonal struggle to determine what the trouble is and what can be done. Similarly, that relational rights and responsibilities, or which ones, are at issue, may be articulated only later. Finally, the meaning of actions as complaints or attempted remedies can often be grasped only in retrospect: at some later, intolerable point, for example, the complainant may point to his or her past toleration of the trouble as evidence of persistent attempts to handle the problem fairly and justly.

As with incipient intrapersonal troubles, relational troubles may not become more difficult. The complaint and attendant remedy may work sufficiently to satisfy the troubled party. The trouble may simply continue as neither party accepts the other's version of what is wrong. The complaint may be made and then dropped and ignored, as the initially offended individual learns to live with the problem. Or, as Goffman (1969:364–5) notes, the troubled party may accede to the demands of the other, redefining what was trouble as legitimate behavior and reallocating relational rights and responsibilities accordingly. In these circumstances, willingness to accept (or at least to endure) the problem behavior of the other—and alternatively, the inclination to keep pressing the trouble by looking for further remedies or responses—provide critical contingencies in the development of a trouble. But there is a limiting condition: that neither party to the trouble ends the relationship that surrounds it. While in fleeting public contacts with others, denial or withdrawal are readily available responses (Goffman, 1963), this strategem is not as available or acceptable in troubles arising in enduring relations (Goffman, 1969:365). Where exit is precluded, troubles and remedial strategies greatly increase in complexity. Under such circumstances, pressures to seek outside remedies often accelerate.

COMPLAINTS AND THIRD-PARTY INTERVENTION

As intrinsic remedies fail and accommodation is not forthcoming, outside parties are apt to be brought into the trouble in active and central ways. Outsiders may have been involved in a relational trouble from its inception; the husband of the philandering wife, for example, may talk to his mother, sister, or best friend about his wife's behavior, why it occurs, and how to respond. And his understanding of what the trouble is and how to cope may be critically shaped by the views and analyses provided by such third parties. Yet as long as these outside parties function only in advice and support roles, the trouble remains essentially private. In particular, efforts to do something still come only from those originally party to the problem. However, when an outside party moves from giving advice to active intervention the structure of the trouble undergoes significant change.

In many instances the line between advising and more active intervention may be blurred. There are strong pressures for converting advisors into direct participants. Friends, counsellors, and therapists of one party may decide to become directly involved in the trouble, as, for example, by taking a husband aside and pointing out how upset his wife is with his drinking. Critical involvement emerges when the third party directly intervenes and establishes a relationship with the troubled parties, who thus no longer deal exclusively with one another. With this event the remedies considered are no longer intrinsic, but *extrinsic,* to the troubled relationship.

With the request for third party intervention, the following roles (see Goffman on "agent roles," 1961:136) become differentiated in the remedial process: First, there is a *complainant* announcing the presence of trouble by seeking remedial action. The complainant role may be distinct from the role of *victim,* the person held injured, harmed, or wronged. Next, there is the remedy agent or *troubleshooter* to whom the trouble is taken for remedy. Finally, one party to the trouble may come to be designated the *troublemaker* responsible.[5]

In general terms, the decision to seek outside intervention and the kind desired seem intricately linked with prior attempts to deal with the trouble—to avoid, isolate, or remedy it. Such factors as the kinds of controls and remedies available in the particular social situation, the availability of and limitations upon their use, the presence and strength of ties with outside parties and possible troubleshooters, and the degree of legitimacy accorded each outsiders' potential involvement in the troubled situation, all shape not only the nature of initial efforts to respond to the trouble within the relationship, but also the occasion and nature of outside intervention.

Efforts to obtain outside intervention tend to move through several stages. First, those initially invited to troubleshoot are typically close friends or relatives of at least one of the involved parties. The involvement of such intimate troubleshooters rests exactly on their personal relationship with one or all of the parties to the trouble. While such personal troubleshooters may be able to remedy the trouble, their intimacy may also prove a hindrance. For example, the legacy of their prior dealings with the parties may preclude a mutually acceptable solution from the start, as when the troubleshooter is already identified as an ally of one of the parties.

Second, troubles may evolve with the increasing movement toward official, licensed troubleshooters. In some cases, such involvement may proceed on a highly unplanned and episodic basis. As Jackson (1954) has noted of the drinking husband, outside agents may be drawn into the situation on an emergency basis (for example, a call for police protection), and then through more regular contacts with social agencies, doctors, and perhaps sanitaria and Alcoholics Anonymous. In other situations, specific official troubleshooters may be sought out by the troubled parties or their allies because of their expertise or neutrality, as when a couple decides to take their problems to a marriage counsellor.

Usually, the first such official agents to become involved in troubles are "generalists," including the police (Cumming, Cumming and Edel, 1965; Parnas, 1967), family doctors (Freidson, 1961, 1970), and ministers (Cumming and Harrington, 1963; Weiss, 1973). Initial preference for such troubleshooters reflects a variety of factors. Such agents are relatively available to lay complainants and their orientations are similar to what laypersons already know (Freidson, 1961): the generality and inclusiveness of their occupational mandates attract those-seeking remedies for relational troubles.

Even the initial choice of troubleshooter may prove highly consequential for the trouble. For the selection of a particular troubleshooter may preemptorially impose a definition on a trouble previously open or contested. Moreover, this selection may expose the differences between the troubled parties as irreconcilable. To suggest that one's spouse see a psychiatrist, for example, may bring previously latent discordances to a head. The proffered remedy thus exacerbates the prior trouble: "You want me to see a psychiatrist! You think I'm the crazy one?"

Furthermore, the effects of initial choice of troubleshooter may be consequential, if not necessarily irreversible, in determining whether, where, and how a trouble enters subsequent referral networks. When a trouble has resisted remedial efforts, or when it seems more appropriately handled elsewhere, initial troubleshooters tend to pass intractable problems on to new, often more specialized, troubleshooters. As in Goffman's notion of a "circuit of agents" (1961), troubles may be shifted from one agent to another, perhaps moving upward toward greater and greater specialization, perhaps toward increasingly coercive and punitive outcomes.

In moving through a circuit of troubleshooters, an initially ambiguous trouble tends to crystallize, as new ways and means of dealing with the problem are sought out and implemented and prior ways are determined to be ineffective and rejected. In this process, an individual may be definitely assigned the role of troublemaker and explicitly identified as deviant. As full-scale deviant remedies are tried and found to fail, the troublemaker may be referred to specialists in other areas of deviance, the nature of his or her trouble undergoing reinterpretation as new ways of eliminating, reducing, or confining the troublemaking are implemented.

It is important to understand how outside intervention radically transforms what were previously private troubles, for this transformation shows most clearly the negotiated (rather than intrinsic) nature of problems. Whereas disagreements about the nature of the trouble and how to remedy it were previously confined to (and under the control of) the initial parties, the involvement of a third party reconstitutes the trouble as a distinctly public phenomenon. As Gulliver (1969:14) has noted with regard to processes of dispute settlement, "the initial disagreement (is raised) from the level of dyadic argument into the public arena." With movement to a triadic situation, the original dyad can no longer orient exclusively to one another. Rather, each must attend to and seek to present his or her side to the third party. In the process, relational assumptions, claims, and expectations previously taken for granted will have to be openly proclaimed and justified. Moreover, to the extent that the troubleshooter holds standards for weighing relational claims divergent from those of the original parties, new grounds for asserted rights and responsibilities may have to be provided. Tacit claims and conduct treated as idiosyncracies of the relationship, for example, may now have to be explained and justified in more universal terms; indeed the parties may learn to their surprise and dismay that some behaviors on which they founded their claim of being troubled are seen by others as "normal" or even "desirable."

Taking a problem to an outside party may provide the first occasion for seeing the trouble as a coherent whole and formulating an explicit history of the trouble. As troubled individuals try to have their claims validated by the newly involved third party, earlier behaviors, problems, and situations may be reinterpreted and organized into progressing incidents of the trouble, while still others may be framed as attempted remedies. Thus, the need to account for past actions and to justify desired remedial responses to the third party may generate more closely documented histories of the origin, causes, and persistence of the trouble, along with the new and extended accusations of wrongdoing.

Finally, outside intervention directly affects the remedial circumstances as well as the definitional dimension of the trouble. In proposing remedial actions the concerns and reactions of the third party now have to be anticipated and attended to, as these factors assume crucial roles in how the trouble will be defined and treated. If official troubleshooters are involved, the trouble may be treated as a "case" and accumulate a distinctive official history as it moves through the system of referrals. Different sets of remedial concerns may become salient, and solutions may be imposed that neither of the original disputants wanted.

In summary, the attempt to obtain and shape the course of intervention may lead to the progressive clarification and specification of the nature and seriousness of the trouble. More concretely, what is done about outside complaints—in particular, when and how the troubleshooter intervenes, if that happens—defines and organizes the trouble. The intervention, then, may fundamentally shape what the trouble will become. To highlight the theoretical significance of these processes, we will now consider the issues troubles pose to a troubleshooter at the point of initial intervention.

DEALING WITH COMPLAINTS: CONTINGENCIES IN INTERVENING

To an outside troubleshooter, troubles pose issues of alignment: the troubleshooter must decide what stance to take toward the parties and issues. As Aubert (1965) has emphasized, troubleshooters may assume two general stances, responding to the trouble as conflict or as deviance.

In responding to trouble as conflict, the troubleshooter adopts a stance of nonalignment, either by refusing commitment to either side, or by equal commitment to both. In the former, the troubleshooter refuses to intervene. In the latter, the troubleshooter may try to become involved equally with the two parties by trying to mediate a settlement. For example, the police routinely respond to calls concerning family violence by mediating between husband and wife to provide an immediate if temporary resolution (Parnas, 1967:932–3). In adopting the role of mediator, the troubleshooter treats the trouble as a dispute or conflict, in that intervention is symmetrical (Aubert, 1965:18) with regard to the positions and claims of the two parties.

In contrast, in responding to troubles as deviance a troubleshooter confronts the problem of alignment head on, orienting to the complaint and trouble in terms of whose side to take. In special circumstances, police will foresake mediating domestic disputes and respond openly on the side of one of the troubled parties, for example, by arresting and removing from the home an assaultive husband (Parnas, 1967). With one-sided intervention of this sort, the trouble is established not as conflict but deviance, as the disputelike, relational core of the trouble is dissolved with the asymmetrical allocation of all wrongdoing to one party (now the deviant) and of all right to the other (now the victim).

A variety of factors determine the likelihood of symmetrical or asymmetrical intervention. In the first place, on the structural level, the assertion of certain types of rights and claims may be legally proscribed, as when the criminal law denies workers a legitimate right to strike, or a disputant a legitimate right to kill or rob an enemy. Such denial of legitimacy to the assertion of particular claims, of course prescribes one-sided intervention against the illegitimized claimant.

Second, troubleshooters often operate with a distinctive theory of trouble and interventional ideologies which require symmetrical or asymmetrical responses. The assumptions of the criminal law, for example, encourage absolute judgments in the allocation of blame, and its agents typically dispense one-sided sanctions against the wrongdoer. The medical-

ization of troubles, locating the source of the trouble in some physiological disfunctioning within the individual, similarly promotes asymmetrical solutions. Finally, those who handle instances of child abuse are precommitted to the ideology of wrongdoing and proceed by determining whether or not there is a perpetrator. In contrast, some troubleshooters operate with distinctive remedial theories that facilitate or even require not taking sides. Marriage counsellors frequently employ a therapeutic ideology to eschew judgments of right and wrong, adopting a uniformly neutral, "no fault" stance toward troubles. Any and every problem must be treated as a relational matter, even though the counsellor may privately conclude that one party is more to blame.

Third, the form of intervention is affected by the power of the troubleshooter relative to that of the original parties to the trouble. Intervention by third parties whose authority is dependent upon the support or agreement of those in the entered trouble tends to assume symmetrical forms.[6] Personal troubleshooters (friends, relatives) may take sides, but usually cannot impose their solution against the resistance of the other. Thus, personal troubleshooting tends to be an act of mediation: the third party has to negotiate a mutually acceptable settlement relying upon personal resources and sanctions. In contrast, many official troubleshooters possess the power to impose one-sided solutions through adjudicated decisions (Eckhoff, 1966) even in the face of opposition from one or both parties. When mediating efforts have proved unsatisfactory, official intervention may be sought by one or another side, to obtain exactly this sort of forced ending to an intractable situation.

The nature of outside intervention is also fundamentally shaped by contingent, situational factors. Troubles will move toward asymmetrical outcomes to the extent that one or both parties are resistant to compromise and have reserves of power and resources to support that position. In addition, the conditions under which third party intervention is sought may prefigure symmetrical and asymmetrical response. Troubleshooters may be sought as mediators, as when a couple agrees to take their marital difficulties to a marriage counsellor. On other occasions, one or another party to a trouble may seek intervention directly on his

or her side. The result is frequently sought by directing accusations of wrongdoing at the other, in this way
formulating the trouble as onesidedly as possible in
order to gain the desired intervention. When one party's accusation is made from a position of greater
power, the likelihood of one-sided intervention on that
persons's terms increases.

A complaint to a third party, whether in the form
of an accusation or a request for mediation, marks
only the starting point for ensuing intervention. Complaints are subject to scrutiny and to possible revision
by troubleshooters, who proceed with some awareness
that allegations may be distorted or false, that the proposed allocation of blame and responsibility may be
misleading or invalid, that the remedial action sought
may be exploitative, subversive, or illegitimate. In
light of such understandings, the troubleshooter may
implement remedial strategies unrelated to initial proposals. Thus, the troubleshooter may refuse to take
any side where one or both parties seek partisan intervention. A juvenile court probation officer may respond to allegations that a teenager is actively misbehaving and "beyond control" by cooling out the
parental accusers. A troubleshooter may come to take
one side in a trouble brought in for neutral mediation.
A troubleshooter may come to respond within the
framework initially proposed for the trouble, but either redefine the problem (for example, parent-child
differences reflect "a lack of communication"), or,
with accusatory complaints, reverse the proposed allocation of victim and wrongdoer roles. Goffman's mental patient who "thought he was taking his wife to see
the psychiatrist" (1961:138fn) provides a classic example of this last possibility.

These considerations highlight the importance of
how direction and terms of the troubleshooter's intervention may determine what the trouble becomes.
Even where the troubleshooter's intervention is
shaped by the actions of one or both of the troubled
parties, such that the remedy implemented merely rat-
ifies what has already been proposed, in analytic terms
it is the nature and direction of the outside intervention, particularly when authoritatively enforced, that
determines what the trouble is. This is not to say that
troubleshooters can intervene freely. Intervention may
be tightly constrained by the need to take into account

the prior history, positions, power, and concerns of the
troubled parties, by the dictates of the troubleshooter's
professional or institutional ideology, and by practical
institutional and situational factors. Any troubleshooter's intervention may be radically overturned and revised by a subsequent intervention (although the ease
with which this can be achieved declines as the trouble accumulates a documented history). Yet, it is the
nature and direction of outside intervention, particularly where carried out by officials, that produces the
forms of alignment distinctive of deviance and conflict, and which ultimately constitutes the trouble as
one or the other of these forms.

The processes of intervention that provide the key
to the consolidation of troubles do not involve simply
defining the situation as one meriting either a balanced
or a one-sided treatment and responding accordingly.
For third party aligning responses can proceed according to their own logic and dynamic, at times at odds
with a trouble's definitions as deviance or as conflict.
Professional ideologies may prescribe a pre-set response to all troubles without regard to the particulars
of a given case, as when marriage counsellors respond
relationally to any and all marital problems. But pragmatic, situational concerns may take intervention in a
direction which could not be predicted on the basis of
the troubleshooter's assessment of specific instances
of wrongdoing. Those committed to relational treatments may find themselves stymied in efforts to work
out a mutually acceptable solution, and may have to
resort to onesided responses as a practical expedient.
Thus, community mental health workers may encounter a situation where they clearly assess both parties as psychiatrically disturbed, yet may hospitalize
only one, deciding that the situation is too volatile to
remain unchanged (Emerson and Pollner, 1976). Conversely, troubleshooters may respond in an evenhanded fashion, while recognizing unequal distribution of rightness and wrongness among the parties (for
example, Bittner on police peacekeeping, 1967).
Troubleshooters may even intervene on behalf of the
party seen to be in the wrong, if such a response promises to provide a permanent end to the trouble (see, for
example, Bittner's analysis of police handling of the
case of "Big Jim," 1967:709–10). These instances
highlight the way particular forms of trouble, includ-

ing deviance and conflict, are produced *procedurally* by the responses of troubleshooters, and not simply by their definitions of the trouble.

TOWARD A SOCIOLOGY OF TROUBLE

In conclusion, we would like to explore some implications of the micro-politics of trouble proposed here for prevailing interactional approaches to deviance.

First, many such approaches cut into the production of deviants at late stages. Frequently, those who have suffered some major, perhaps irrevocable sanction, such as institutional placement, are identified as the subject population. Such sanctioning or placement provides an "end point" (which may later turn out to have been a "stage," of course), for treating an actor as a particular sort of deviant, and past activities and events are ordered as leading to this "end point." These sorts of deviant career notions, however, often organize events in ways foreign to perceptions prevailing earlier, when outcomes were in doubt and definitions ambiguous. In addition, these approaches focus on cases that have made it to an eventual deviant designation, neglecting those that have failed to do so. If not neglected outright, such cases are addressed in terms of this failure; why did they not make it? In this sense, deviant career models both presuppose and require deviant outcomes. In contrast, the concept of "trouble" directs attention not simply toward early phases of careers into deviance, but also toward non- and "pre-deviant" situations and settings generally. Moreover, the idea of trouble keeps open the possibility that many troubles with deviant potentiality can "come to nothing," or come to something devoid of imputations of deviance, or become one of several possible categories of deviance. In these ways, trouble comprehends and incorporates both the openness and indeterminacy of deviant outcomes, in part by abandoning the centrality of the notion of deviance itself.

Second, the micro-politics of trouble points toward a deepening of the basic imagery of deviant designation. It is axiomatic to the labeling approach that deviants are products of social definition; definition typically involving the imputation of immoral identity and defective status. Douglas, for example, views deviance as the product of a negotiation of "moral mean-

ings" (1971), and Katz (1972:192) conceptualizes deviance as the assignment of defective moral or ontological status. But an exclusive focus on "meanings" runs the risk of being one-sided. This paper has argued that definition can both shape and be shaped by response: specifically, that deviant designation is the product of remedial efforts[7] involving both interpretative and active components which can vary independently of each other. A deviant should be understood not only as one who is morally condemned, but also as one who is sided against. And while on some occasions moral condemnation seems to precede and cause the siding against, having been sided against generates the subsequent moral opprobrium for others.

Third, our approach emphasizes a point insufficiently explicit in many studies by proponents, and totally unseen by many critics of labeling: actions directed toward another (or oneself) as a "deviant" are heavily contingent on, although not totally determined by, the frames of reference and resources of complainants, victims, and official troubleshooters, when they are involved.[8] The "labeling approach," properly construed, does *not* hold that the activities of deviants are disregarded by complainants, victims, or officials, nor does it recommend that analysts disregard these activities. It does propose that analysts explicitly take into account *and attempt to account for* the role of complainants, victims, and officials in determining definitions and actions, and redefinitions and further actions. We both think the activities of those eventually treated as deviants (and those not so treated), and the activities of complainants, victims, and troubleshooters, are appropriately conceived as *variable* influences on both temporary and lasting outcomes. The conditions of such variation should be a major topic for inquiry and theorizing.

This consideration leads to one final implication of this approach. Although our paper has focused on the micro-political, interactional processes, we recognize and even insist that a fully developed sociology of trouble would also consider macro-politics. Such a macro-politics of trouble would inquire into the ways broader economic, political and social interests shape both the frames of reference and the institutionalized remedies available for identifying and dealing with trouble. Long-term social trends such as the formation of states and the centralization of state power, the shift from mercantilism to industrial capitalism and from laissez-faire to corporate capitalism, and the spread of bureaucratic forms of organization appear to have major implications for interpretations of and responses to troubles. It may be argued that the formation of states and the centralization of their power made some forms of punishment such as banishment and transportation impossible and helped motivate the establishment of prisons (see Langbein, 1976); that the rise of a market economy in labor helped motivate differentiation of specific categories of deviants, and that the welfare state is encouraging "decarceration" (see Scull, 1977); that legal developments are sometimes powerfully determined by economic ones, so that new forms of "crimes" are "recognized," legislated, and enforced (see Hall, 1952); or, finally, that remedial institutions in the form of bureaucracies work unceasingly to influence how certain activities, like the possession of marijuana, are treated and understood (see Dickson, 1973).

This is not the place, even had we the insight, to try to spell out these matters. We strongly urge that developing a "micro"-politics of trouble should not be taken to imply that developing a "macro"-politics of trouble is unimportant; we think both need to be developed and their relations examined. Our approach suggests that in addition to exploring how larger forces may affect individual and group activities which may come to be treated as deviant, such a macropolitics of deviance should explore in detail how actions toward and understandings of such activities are affected.

NOTES

1. Our approach parallels, on the interactional level, that recently proposed by Spector and Kitsuse (1973) for analyzing the definition and crystallization of *social* problems on a collective level. They propose a natural history model to examine the "claim-making and responding activities" (146) that lead to the identification of an emergent social problem.

2. Hewitt and Hall (1973), for example, adopt this perspective: In looking at how "quasi-theories" may further the imputation of deviance in problematic situations, they conceptualize the process as essentially one whereby disorderly events are explained (defined) and made meaningful.

3. Note that in Freidson's illustration, it is just because the

remedies based upon the hay fever diagnosis stopped the problem that all those involved—including the sociologist-analyst—accept the validity of that diagnosis to define the trouble.

4. In these situations, troubles are moved back and forth between "social" and "natural" frames (Goffman, 1974:21ff). One attraction of the medical model is that it "de-relationizes" troubles, thus, in the case of psychiatric disorders, relieving those close to the disturbed person of any responsibility for the disordered state of affairs.

5. Many remedial agents expect victim and complainant roles to be performed by the same person, and while this is not inevitably forthcoming, "disinterested" complainants may have to provide some sort of account for their involvement. The more general point is that victim and non-victim complainants may encounter different presentational problems in getting their complaints validated. Furthermore, complaints can be advanced, and interventions implemented, without definite allocation of victim and wrongdoer roles. Remedies involving mediation, to be considered below, either avoid these roles, or attribute part of each to both parties.

6. Symmetrical intervention of a mediative character tends to be characteristic of legal processes in tribal and traditional societies as legal agents usually lack any such authority. Anthropological studies of disputing and dispute settlement (e.g., Nader, 1965: Gulliver, 1969) provide a rich source of materials on these processes.

7. See also the specific proposal by Fletcher et. al. (1974:59) to shift the conceptual focus to "referral behavior rather than naming behavior" as the key process in the "labeling" of mental illness.

8. The difference made by the presence and preferences of complainants has been documented by the work of Donald J. Black and Albert J. Reiss, Jr. (1970), although theory about the matter remains undeveloped. Much work in "victimology" also implicitly raises some relevant questions, but so much attention has been given to the light victims can throw on "dark numbers," and the variable role of victims in "causing" deviance, that these questions have gone unanswered. A considerable amount of work in the labeling tradition has, of course, focused on the role of official troubleshooters.

REFERENCES

Allon, Natalie. 1973. "Group dieting rituals." *Society* 10 (January/February): 36–42.

Aubert, Vilhelm. 1965. *The Hidden Society.* Totowa, N.J.: Bedminster Press.

Balint, Michael. 1957. *The Doctor, His Patient, and the Illness.* New York: International Universities Press.

Becker, Howard. 1963. *Outsiders: Studies in the Sociology of Deviance.* New York: Free Press.

Bittner, Egon. 1967. "The police on skid-row: A study of peace keeping," *American Sociological Review* 32 (October): 699–715.

Black, Donald J. and Albert J. Reiss. 1970. "Police control of juveniles." *American Sociological Review* 35 (February): 733–747.

Cumming, Elaine, Ian M. Cumming and Laura Edell. 1965. "Policeman as philosopher, guide and friend." *Social Problems* 12 (Winter): 276–286.

Cumming, Elaine and Charles Harrington. 1963. "Clergyman as counselor." *American Journal of Sociology* 69 (November): 234–243.

Dickson, Donald T. 1970. "Marijuana and the law: Organizational factors in the legislative process." *Journal of Drug Issues* 3 (Spring): 115–122.

Douglas, Jack D. 1971. *American Social Order: Social Rules in a Pluralistic Society.* New York: Free Press.

Eckhoff, Torstein. 1966. "The mediator, the judge and the administrator in conflict-resolution." *Acta Sociologica* 10: 148–72.

Emerson, Joan P. 1969. "Negotiating the serious import of humor." *Sociometry* 32 (June): 169–81.

Emerson, Robert M. and Melvin Pollner. 1976. "Mental hospitalization and assessments of untenability." Presented at the Annual Meetings of the Society for the Study of Social Problems, New York.

Fletcher, C. Richard, Peter K. Manning, Larry T. Reynolds, and James O. Smith. 1974. "The labeling theory and mental illness." In Paul M. Roman and Harrison M. Trice (eds.), *Explorations in Psychiatric Sociology.* Philadelphia: F. A. Davis: 43–62.

Freidson, Eliot. 1961. *Patients' View of Medical Practice: A Study of Subscribers to a Prepaid Medical Plan in the Bronx.* New York: Russell Sage Foundation.

Garfinkel, Harold. 1967. *Studies in Ethnomethodology.* Englewood Cliffs, N.J.: Prentice-Hall.

Gibbs, Jack P. 1966. "Conceptions of deviant behavior: The old and the new." *Pacific Sociological Review* 9 (Spring): 9–14.

Goffman, Erving. 1961. *Asylums.* Garden City, New York: Doubleday.

——1963. *Behavior in Public Places.* New York: Free Press.

——1969. "The insanity of place." *Psychiatry* 32 (November): 352–388.

——1971. *Relations in Public.* New York: Basic Books.

——1974. *Frame Analysis: An Essay on the Organization of Experience.* Cambridge, Mass.: Harvard University Press.

Gulliver, P. H. 1969. "Introduction" to Case Studies of Law in Non-Western Societies. In Laura Nader (ed.), *Law in Culture and Society.* Chicago: Aldine; 11–23.

Hall, Jerome. 1952. *Theft, Law, and Society,* 2nd Ed. Indianapolis: Bobbs-Merrill.

Hewitt, John P., and Peter M. Hall. 1973. "Social problems, problematic situations, and quasi-theories." *American Sociological Review* 38 (June): 367–374.

Jackson, Joan K. 1954. "The adjustment of the family to the crisis of alcoholism." *Quarterly Journal of Studies on Alcohol* 15 (December): 562–586.

Kadushin, Charles. 1969. *Why People Go to Psychiatrists.* New York: Atherton Press.

Katz, Jack. 1972. "Deviance, charisma, and rule-defined behavior." *Social Problems* 30 (Fall): 186–202.

Kitsuse, John I. 1972. "Deviance, deviant behavior, and deviants: Some conceptual problems." In William J. Filstead (ed.), *An Introduction to Deviance.* Chicago: Markham: 233–243.

Langbein, John H. 1976. "The historical origins of the sanction of imprisonment for serious crime." *The Journal of Legal Studies* 5 (January): 35–60.

Nader, Laura. 1965. "The anthropological study of law." *American Anthropologist* 67 (December): 3–32.

Orcutt, James D. 1973. "Societal reaction and the response to deviation in small groups." *Social Forces* 52 (December): 259–267.

Parnas, Raymond I. 1967. "The police response to the domestic disturbance." *Wisconsin Law Review* 4 (Fall): 914–960.

Scull, Andrew T. 1977. *Decarceration: Community Treatment and the Deviant—A Radical View,* Englewood Cliffs. N.J.: Prentice-Hall.

Spector, Malcolm, and John I. Kitsuse. 1973. "Social problems: A reformulation." *Social Problems* 21 (Fall): 145–159.

Weiss, Robert S. 1973. "Helping relationships: Relationships of clients with physicians, social workers, priests, and others." *Social Problems* 20 (Winter): 319–328.

K IS MENTALLY ILL

45 | ## The Anatomy of a Factual Account[1]

Dorothy E. Smith

This paper analyzes an interview which tells how K comes to be defined by her friends as mentally ill. It is not just a record of events as they happened, but of events as they were seen as relevant to reaching a decision about the character of those events. This is a common feature of the kinds of records etc. with which the social scientist in the field of deviant behavior is concerned. The various agencies of social control have institutionalized procedures for assembling, processing, and testing information about the behavior of individuals so that it can be matched against the paradigms which provide the working criteria of class-membership whether as juvenile delinquent, mentally ill, or the like. These procedures, both formal and informal, are a regular part of the business of the police, the courts, psychiatrists, and other similar agencies (Cicourel 1969). A full description of the organizational practice of such agencies in these respects would be a description of one type of procedure by which a set of original and actual events is transformed into the currency of fact. A number of studies in the field of mental illness (Goffman 1961; Scheff 1964; Mechanic 1962; Smith 1975), show that descriptions of the activities of the official agencies are far from adequate in accounting for how people come to be defined as mentally ill. In this account it is K's friends who are doing the preliminary work. K does not get so far as the formal psychiatric agencies though this is foreshadowed. Accounts of "paths to the mental hospital" (Clausen and Yarrow 1955) suggest that a good deal of non-formal work has been done by the individual concerned, her family, and friends, before entry to the official process. These non-formal processes may also be described as a social organization which in this case precedes the production of an interview account of the kind I am concerned with here.

The term "social organization" is used here in a sense which leaves the question of planning or purpose open. Such a use of the concept can be compared with the economic concept of a market which makes possible the analysis of the activities of numbers of individuals buying and selling as a social organization which is unintended by its participants and which produces "market phenomena" as an unintended consequence. It is used here analogously to include as participants in the production of this account, not just the sociologist, the interviewer, and the respondent, but also those who brought about the original events and those who tried to reach a decision about what they were. It is thus a means of making explicit the various steps and activities that intervene between the reader of the account and the original events; and of showing how the acceptability of the interview as a factual account and as an account of someone who is, or is becoming, mentally ill is provided for. I have accordingly also stressed throughout the fact that we all recognize but normally bracket, namely that the sociologist is and must be an active participant in constructing the events she treats as data.

THE ORIGIN OF THE DATA

In an undergraduate course on deviance, I worked with a few students on a research project concerned with how the lay person comes to define someone as mentally ill. The research was modeled, though loosely, on Kitsuse's paper on "Societal reaction to deviant behavior" (Kitsuse 1962) which examines how people come to identify someone as homosexual. The interviewing approach used was less structured than Kitsue's. The interviewers were instructed to begin with the question "Have you ever known anyone you

---

thought might be mentally ill?" Respondents were to be told to define mental illness and to tell the story pretty much in their own way, but the interviewer was told to get information on four points:

(a) the incident or situation in which the respondent first came to think the person might be mentally ill;

(b) what the subject was doing then or in other previous situations that suggested this definition or which could later be seen as instances of that kind of behavior;

(c) what the relationship between the subject and respondent had been;

(d) and what others were involved in the process of definition, who the respondent had talked to, etc.

This interview may not be a model of what such interviews might be like. The interviewer's write-up did not include her own questions, nor was the interview tape recorded, which is the ideal, though at that time one not ordinarily available to undergraduates. But my interest in analyzing is in just the account it is. The interview was discussed in class. At that time I did not have the written account before me. The interviewer gave a verbal presentation. Hearing her account, I took it to be an account of a developing schizophrenic reaction of some type. I thought to myself, "The subject will get more and more disorganized and then one day things will go to pot at work and she'll be hospitalized." In other words, I heard the interviewer's account as an account of someone who was or was becoming mentally ill. The verbal account differed, and differed I believe in important ways, from the written account, in that it included some material that is not in the written account and omitted some that is. Later, however, I saw the typescript of the interview and it was just as clear to me that a rather different picture of the goings-on could be drawn and that I would have no trouble drawing it, at least as a tentative picture, on the basis of evidence internal to the interview. The alternative picture, very simply stated, was that what was going on was a kind of communal freezing-out process, very like that which Lemert describes in his paper on "Paranoia and the dynamics of exclusion" (Lemert 1962) and that if

there was anything odd in K's behavior (and reading the account suggested to me that there was doubt whether anything was psychiatrically very odd) it might reasonably be supposed that people do react in ways which seem odd to others when they are going through this kind of process.

The usual thing to do with this type of difficulty is to try to arrive at some kind of decision about which interpretation is correct. This would normally involve wanting more information, or examining with care what is already there. In this case most likely the decision would have to be that the interview was not adequate for this purpose. But what I had been struck with was the figure-ground effect, that first I saw the verbal account as mental illness and could still see distinctly the lineaments of that in the written interview, and that now I could see the alternative. So the interview can be read for the mental illness effect and then that is what you see (and clearly that had been what the interviewer had seen and had further communicated to me and the students in class); but having seen the alternative model it is then hard to see the one where the subject is mentally ill.

RECOGNIZING MENTAL ILLNESS

The criteria of class-membership in other types of deviant categories, such as homosexual, juvenile delinquent, etc., are fairly straightforward. A definite rule must have been broken or a norm deviated from. The process of showing that something an individual has done can be properly seen as an instance of breaking the rule is not by any means simple. Nevertheless the difficulty with the category "mental illness" is of another kind. The criteria of class-membership are not clear. It is not clear what norms are deviated from when someone is categorized as mentally ill. Yet it is clearly possible to describe behavior in such a way that people will make that definition with full confidence in its propriety. There must therefore be some set of rules or procedures for representing behavior as mentally ill types of behavior and those procedures must meet the normative conditions for recognizing individuals as members of the class of persons who are mentally ill. In the verbal account given by the interviewer in class, I, and I take it others present, recognized the behavior of the subject, K, as mentally ill behavior. The interview purports to be, and can be, recognized in the same way. Recognizing in events the "fact" that someone is mentally ill involves complex conceptual work. It involves assembling observations from actual moments and situations dispersed in time, organizing them, or finding that they can be organized, in accordance with the "instructions" which the concept provides. A simple, immediate, and convincing recognition of a fact at this conceptual level implies that much of the work of providing events with the appropriate conceptual order has already been done. All that the reader/hearer has to do is to discover in those events, or rather that account of events, the model which enables her to classify them as this or that kind of social fact. The conceptual schema which is the meaning of the term "mental illness" (as I know it) provides a set of criteria and rules for ordering events against which the ordering of events in the account may be matched, or tested. An account which is immediately convincing is one which forces that classification and makes any other difficult. And if it does, then the events of the account must already display the order giving them the shape of the fact for the reader/hearer. It is this which entitles me, I suggest, to analyze this account to discover (in a preliminary way) the lineaments of the concept of mental illness. The structure of this account with respect to how it may be seen as an account of someone being mentally ill is treated as isomorphic with the structure of the conceptual schema used to recognize it as such. In analyzing this account as an account of mental illness I am, I argue, *recovering the structure of the conceptual model which I make use of in recognizing that that is what it is.*

THE INTERVIEW ITSELF AS DATA

In this analysis the interview is not being viewed as an account from which we are trying to infer back to what actually happened. The effect of questions is not merely to generate information. The difference between questions in different forms is not merely that some yield more and others less information. The form of the question tells the respondent what sort of work she is being asked to do. It asks her to operate on

her knowledge, experience, etc., in a particular way. In this interview the opening question—"Have you ever known anyone you thought might be mentally ill?"— asks the respondent to do a matching operation, to find from her own experience an instance (presumably known only to her) which can be properly matched against criteria of class-membership assumed to be known at large. An interview of this kind is thus a process in which the respondent works up and tests the status of her experience, knowledge, and definitions of events against the knowledge etc. imputed to the interviewer as representative of the culture at large. This account therefore is a further step in establishing the propriety of the definitions made prior to the interview. Thus from the respondent's point of view the interview is a further though unanticipated step in the process of testing a categorization already made. She has her uses for the interview just as the interviewer and I have ours. What actually happened— whatever that was—was something that the respondent was, and still was in the interview (I believe), working up into an intelligible form, a form in which she could find the shape and direction of those events. The actual events can be looked upon as a set of resources upon which the respondent drew in creating for herself and the interviewer an account of what had happened. Of course the actual events were much richer, much less orderly, simply much more, than those arranged into an interview of an hour or so; and indeed, might have lent themselves to being worked up in different ways from that selected by the respondent. So radical processes of selection have gone on; a lot is left out and what is left in is ordered to provide a coherence for the reader which was not present in the events. Moreover some events are brought into the foreground as elements of the picture whereas others that are also there are treated as part of the background or of the machinery of the narrative. That may be conceived to be the work of the respondent.

There is, however, a second step before the interview arrives at the reader/hearer. This is the work of the interviewer. Since the interviewer was inexperienced and did not use a tape recorder, we may suppose that this was fairly substantial and do not know precisely what it had been. Thus the interview as we have it must be regarded as a cooperative working up of a now rather distant and wholly indeterminate set of events. In addition I have myself done some very minor editing to ensure further that the subject should be identifiable. In analyzing the account and the organization of its relationship to the actual events it claims to represent, we will not be concerned with the actual character of these events. Whether K was really mentally ill or not is irrelevant to the analysis. It is impor-

tant that I convey to the reader *that the data the paper is concerned with are wholly present to her—just as they are to me—in the typescript of the interview which she will find below.*

Here is the interview as I received it, plus minor alterations to conceal identities further. The punctuation is the interviewer's. The form and paragraphing are as the interviewer wrote it up.

1 Angela was interviewed about her impressions regarding a
2 friend, who will be called "K" for the purpose of this
3 study. Angela met K about 4 years ago, during her first
4 year at university. Angela had been to the same school
5 but in a grade below K and when introduced to K felt full
6 of admiration. Here was a girl, a year older, of such a
7 good family, a good student, so nice, so friendly, so
8 very athletic, who was willing to befriend her. K sug-
9 gested outings, and they went skiing, swimming, playing
10 tennis together. In the fall they shared in a carpool,
11 so that more people were immediately involved in the con-
12 tact. Nearly every morning K would cry in the car, being
13 upset about little things, and the girls would comfort
14 her. Sometimes she would burst into tears in the middle
15 of a conversation. She began to have trouble with her
16 courses, dropped some of them and switched some.
17 ANGELA: My recognition that there might be something
18 wrong was very gradual, and I was actually the last of
19 her close friends who was openly willing to admit that
20 she was becoming mentally ill. Angela found it easier to
21 explain things chronologically, and, in retrospect, it
22 appears that this would make the observations fall
23 more easily into place.
24 We would go to the beach or the pool on a hot day, and I
25 would sort of dip in and just lie in the sun, while K
26 insisted that she had to swim 30 lengths. It was very
27 difficult to carry on an intelligent conversation with
28 her, this became apparent when I wanted to discuss a
29 particularly good movie, and she would make childish
30 inane remarks, completely off the point.
31 Slowly my admiration changed to a feeling of bafflement.
32 I began to treat her more like a child who was perhaps
33 not too bright, and I became protective of her. I real-
34 ized that this change had taken place, when a mutual
35 friend, Trudi who was majoring in English, had looked
36 over one of her essays, and told me afterwards: She
37 writes like a 12 year old—I think there is something

38 wrong with her.
39 K is so intense about everything at times, she tries too
40 hard. Her sense of proportion is out of kilter. When
41 asked casually to help in a friend's garden, she went at
42 it for hours, never stopping, barely looking up. When
43 you meet her, you are struck, by a sweet girlish
44 appearance. She will sit quietly in company, smiling
45 sweetly at all times, and seems disarmingly appealing.
46 But when there were young men in the company, she would
47 find it harder than ever to carry on a conversation, and
48 would excuse herself and leave very soon. During all the
49 time that I have known her she has really never gone out
50 with a boy, although she did occasionally share with them
51 in athletic activities. It was obvious that she was ter-
52 rified of anyone getting too near to her, especially men.
53 And yet she used to pretend to us (and obviously to her-
54 self too) that she had this and that guy really keen on
55 her.
46 During this time Angela had become more friendly with
47 Trudi mainly because she felt she could discuss things
48 with her. Her friendship with K continued, but was con-
49 fined more to athletic activities.
50 At the beginning of the next academic year Trudi and
51 Angela had found an apartment which they wanted to share,
52 but it was too expensive for two. Since K's family had
53 moved away, she was sort of on her own. And Angela par-
54 ticularly felt sort of responsible, and it was agreed
55 that K would share the apartment. Trudi had her doubts
56 that it would work out, but Angela felt confident that
57 things would work out.
58 For a few days, before the apartment became available, K
59 went to stay with Angela in her home. Angela's mother had
60 always admired the girl, K, for her politeness and gen-
61 eral good manners, and made her most welcome. Angela
62 tried to prepare her mother for any odd behaviour, but
63 found she could not bring herself to this. On the first
64 morning, Angela's mother offered to make K's breakfast.
65 K very sweetly said: Oh I don't want to give you any
66 trouble, just anything, anything that you have got. So
67 Angela's mother enumerated the things available and K
68 after much coaxing, and shy smiles, asked for tea and a
69 hard boiled egg. At that time, Angela's mother's own
70 breakfast was ready on the table, coffee and a soft
71 boiled egg. Angela's mother turned to the stove to put
72 on an egg, and water for tea and when she came back to

73 the table, there was K smiling sweetly, eating the soft-
74 boiled egg and drinking coffee. At the time Angela's
75 mother thought, well she misunderstood me. But later she
76 noticed that K was unable to put on a teapot cover cor-
77 rectly, she would not reverse its position to make it
78 fit, but would simply keep slamming it down on the pot.
79 Angela's parents are very warm and quite vocal people.
80 Angela's relationships with them is particularly good and
81 rests on mutual respect and continued expressions of
82 affection since childhood. During K's stay, she had occa-
83 sion to observe Angela's father put his arm around his
84 daughter. K turned away in embarrassment, and later con-
85 fided to Angela's mother: You know my father never put
86 his arm around me.
87 A little while after the three girls began to share the
88 apartment, they had to face the fact that K was
89 definitely queer. She would take baths religiously every
90 night and pin up her hair, but she would leave the bath
91 dirty. She would wash dishes, but leave them dirty too.
92 They would try and live within a strict budget, and take
93 turns in cooking dinner and shopping for it, each for one
94 week. K invariably overshot the budget by several dol-
95 lars. She would buy the most impractical things, such as
96 a broom, although they already one, 6 lbs of ham-
97 burger at one go, which they would have to eat the whole
98 week. She would burn practically everything. When some-
99 thing had gone radically wrong, obviously by her doing,
100 she would blandly deny all knowledge, but got very upset
101 at little things, like a blown fuse. She did not seem to
102 absorb the simplest information regarding the working of
103 the stove or other household implements. She had definite
104 food-fads, and would take condiments such as ketchup,
105 pepper to excess. Also things like tinned fruit and
106 honey, she would eat them by the jar, at one go. We grad-
107 ually began to realize that she just could not cope and
108 we began to take over more and more of her
109 responsibilities. She had begun to work in an account-
110 ant's office and we told her that she probably had too
111 much to do in her first year of working at her new job,
112 and that she could cook at the weekends only, but that we
113 would do the shopping.
114 Trudi and I found ourselves discussing her foibles in her
115 absence. I still tried to find explanations and excuses—
116 I refused to acknowledge the fact that there was anything
117 definitely wrong with K. But she'd tiptoe through the

118 apartment, when there was no need to, she would always
119 speak in a whisper, and she was always smiling, it was
120 like a mask, even when we sensed that she was unhappy. As
121 if she was trying to put on a brave front: I am going to
122 be happy, even if it kills me. We began to notice that
123 she could never do two things at once, such as: watch TV
124 and knit, or knit and talk, or eat and talk, or eat and
125 talk and listen. If she talked her food would get quite
126 cold, she would start when everyone finished. Or she
127 would ask, when is dinner ready, and when told in about
128 10 minutes, she would go and prepare something quite dif-
129 ferent for herself.
130 At a third friend's, Betty's apartment, things came to
131 sort of a head. Betty is a Psychology major, and we had
132 gone there by chance, with K, had dinner and settled down
133 for a chat, when a boyfriend of Betty's walked in, an
134 easygoing friendly fellow whom K and I had not met
135 before. K wanted to go to the kitchen and wash dishes but
136 we dissuaded her. She sat down with us, and was her
137 usual retiring, sweet smiling self. Conversation was
138 lively, but she did not take part. A boy was dis-
139 cussed, but K had not him met him. However she suddenly cut
140 in: Yes, isn't he nice. Everything was quiet for a
141 moment, but I carried on talking sort of covering up for
142 her. A few minutes later she cut in again, with: Oh yes,
143 and the little black sheep and the lambs . . . This was
144 really completely out of touch. The young man thought K
145 was kidding him, but no doubt by our embarrassment could
146 tell something was wrong. K was upset and we suggested
147 that she went home, because she must be tired. Our apart-
148 ment was very near by.
149 At this point Betty suggested that something should be
150 done. It seems that all the girls involved were of a par-
151 ticular social stratum, the parents business people and
152 acquainted with each other. A woman friend of the family
153 was 'phoned and her advice was asked: Did you know that
154 K is not well, that she needs help, her behaviour is not
155 as it should be. The woman was willing to talk about
156 it, and admitted that this had been silently acknowledged
157 by the social circle for some time that K had seen a
158 psychiatrist some while back. This man had been recom-
159 mended by the family doctor, and although he had not
160 really been of much help, it was inconceivable that
161 anyone else could be approached, because of etiquette
162 etc. It was arranged that K should go back to the
163 psychiatrist.

DEFINITIONS

In talking about the interview material I make use of a set of terms which are defined below:

(a) *The reader/hearer* I or anyone else who reads or hears read the text of the interview.

(b) *The interviewer* The student who did the interview and who with the respondent constructed the text now available to the reader/hearer. The presence of the interviewer is identifiable in the text in the occasional use of the impersonal mode.

(c) *The respondent* The person who was interviewed by the interviewer and who co-operated with her in constructing the text. The respondent is represented in the text as the "teller of the tale," but is not methodologically equivalent since the teller of the tale is internal to the text and is therefore the joint product—as a personage—of the interviewer and the respondent.

(d) *The teller of the tale* has in part already been defined in the above definition of the respondent. The teller of the tale is the "I" of the account who is represented as telling the story of what happened.

(e) *Angela* et al. The sub-set personages who are represented as being actively involved in the process of categorization. This includes—Angela, Trudi, Angela's mother, Betty, and "a woman friend of the family." It excludes K, Angela's father, and Betty's boyfriend. This term is given further specification in the discussion of the construction of a factual account below.

(f) *The personages* Those persons internal to the account who are referred to as being in any way active in moving the events along, in however trivial a way. So that it includes all the main characters designated by the term Angela *et al.* It also includes K, Angela's father, and Betty's boyfriend. It does not, however, include persons who are reference personages only and not participants—i.e. K's family, and the psychiatrist.

The attentive reader will have noticed that this has a kind of Chinese box structure. The definitions identify different levels of responsibility for making the account and the contributions of various persons at each. In effect they yield a role structure for describing the social organization of the account. At the point where I am and where other readers of the interview are (the reader/hearers), there is the complete text. In the making of the text (apart from the slight intervention of the editor which I have neglected here since it is so minor) there is the concerted work of interviewer and respondent. The respondent is identified in the text as the "teller of the tale." The teller of the tale is telling a tale about a set of personages, one of whom is herself. Internal to the account as it is told is the personage "Angela" and the sub-set of personages who cooperate in working up the raw material of the events as they happened into a form which was then available to be transformed into the text we have before us. Then, at the level of personages at large, are those who were active in generating the original set of events, who were doing what happened and what constituted the raw material out of which Angela *et al.* constructed a view of K as mentally ill. Note, then, the one term which is common to all levels of the account, namely Angela. Within the conventions of the account, she is entered as one of those active in doing the events; she is entered as one of those conceptualizing the events (the Angela *et al.* level); she is entered as teller of the tale; and she is also, as one of the members of the text, entered as the respondent. The above set of definitions is thus not merely a convenience, it also lays bare the structure which related the text you and I have to the original events as they happened. You, as reader of what I now write, may also wish to add the penultimate if not the ultimate level, namely may analysis of the text.

PRELIMINARY INSTRUCTIONS

The first part of the interview, lines 1–16, is written as the interviewer's account of what Angela, the respondent, told her. At line 15, the mode changes to the tale as told by Angela with the interpolated explanation by the interviewer (lines 20–23) that Angela found it easier to tell the tale in chronological form. In lines 17–20 the reader/hearer is provided with a set of instructions about how the interview is to be read, what it is an account of, as follows:

My recognition that there might be something wrong was very gradual, and I was actually the last of her close friends who was openly willing to admit that she was becoming mentally ill.

(17–20)

I want to draw attention to two effects which are announced at this point and which in important ways provide a set of instructions for how the account is to be read. They are as follows:

1. That K is "becoming mentally ill" is asserted as a fact at the outset and is preserved as such throughout. The same construction is offered at various other points in the text: they had to face the fact that K was definitely queer;

(88–9)

We gradually began to realize that she just could not cope;

(106–7)

I refused to acknowledge the fact that there was anything definitely wrong with K.

(116–17)

Such constructions establish that K's state is to be treated as something which (a) is a fact and (b) is therefore already there prior to, and independently of, its being "admitted," "realized," "faced," or "acknowledged" by Angela or others.

2. We are also provided with a preliminary set of instructions for how to read further descriptions of K's behavior. These are to be read as the behavior of someone who is 'becoming mentally ill' (this has important effects for the authorization of the version which I shall elucidate below). The instructions to read the behavior as "odd," "wrong," etc., are repeated at intervals throughout the account. Indeed sub-collections are distinguished by markers consisting of some summary statement, the conclusion of a member of Angela *et al.* or the like, that K's behavior is definitely queer etc. These can be viewed both as summary conclusions of the previous sub-collection and as renewing or reminding the reader/hearer of the instructions for how to read what comes next (these may be found at lines 35–7, 61–3, 87–9, 115–17).

THE AUTHORIZATION OF THE VERSION

I take it as axiomatic that, for any set of actual events, there is always more than one version that can be treated as what has happened, even within a simple cultural community. This is because social events or facts at the level of those I am analyzing here involve a complex assembly of events occurring in different settings, at different times, sometimes before collections of persons. Further, the moment of actual observation is at that point where the consciousness of the individual is, and any process of assembly from the past can no longer draw on the total universe of resources which were at successive "moments" present to the observer. For these reasons, an endemic problem must always be how a given version is authorized as that version which can be treated by others as what has happened. Accordingly an important set of procedures concern who is allocated the privilege of definition and how other possible versions or sources of possible disjunctive information are ruled out.

Here I think these authorization procedures are at work:

1. Durkheim's (1960:102) rule that the definition of an act as deviant serves to sanction and legitimize a social order can be extended to authorize as representatives of that order those who make that judgement. Their rules or norms are to be recognized as rules and norms against which the behavior of the deviant is defined as deviant. Thus that we are told at the outset that K is mentally ill authorizes the version of those who realized or came to admit the fact of her illness. It authorizes or assigns to Angela the definitional privilege and—internal to the account—it authorizes also the version of Angela's friends at those points when Angela is still "unwilling to admit" the fact. The circularity of this process is a feature of the account. Its logical impropriety does not obstruct the effect. K's illness is present as a fact independently of the wishes of the "observers." Her deviance serves therefore to authorize the account of her deviance which is provided and the "rightness" of the judgement of those who defined her as such. In particular, the authorization of the judgement of the "teller of the tale" (Angela) and her associates requires the reader/hearer to treat as the proper collection of events, the collection we have before us. Their selection procedures are implicitly sanctioned even though it is not made clear what they are.

Possibly there is a further and more general process at work here not directly linked to Durkheim's rule (Durkheim 1960). Angela is presented as having been present as an observer of the events recounted. Recollected introspection of how I read the account suggests that something like a "willing suspension of disbelief" effect is operating—that is, I tended to suspend or bracket my own judgemental process in favor of that of the teller of the tale. The reader/hearer is always open to the challenge "How do you know? You weren't there."

2. Categorizations of deviance of the same family as mental illness serve to circumscribe the area of intelligible and warrantable behavior and belief. Since K is defined at the outset as becoming mentally ill and other members of the account are not, the boundaries in this instance are drawn so that K is excluded. This has the following consequences:

(a) Between K and Angela *et al.,* K's behavior may not be treated as a source of normative definition whereas Angela *et al.*'s may be so treated. Here is an instance where this stipulation clearly decides how the normative accent should be assigned:

> We would go to the beach or the pool on a hot day, and I would sort of dip in and just lie in the sun, while K insisted that she had to swim 30 lengths.
>
> (24–6)

Angela's beach behavior provides the norm in terms of which K's behavior is to be recognized as deviating.

(b) K is by this rule disqualified from participating in the construction of social facts. Hence any version that she might have presented is discounted from the outset. The definers are privileged to present their version without taking hers into account. This procedure cuts off a possible set of resources which might otherwise be available in making interpretations of what is happening—namely that set of resources available only to K. This legitimates the restriction of resources used in interpreting K's behavior to what is available to Angela *et al.* Here is an instance of this effect:

> Nearly every morning K would cry in the car, being upset about little things, and the girls would comfort her.
>
> (12–14)

In this instance, the reasons for K's crying are taken to be those immediate occasions which were directly observable to "the girls" and which were "little things," not sufficient to warrant her weeping. Angela does not raise the possibility that there might have been features of K's biography unknown to her and the others which would provide adequate reasons for K's disposition to cry so readily.

(c) Accordingly also it is not a problem or ought not to be a problem for the reader/hearer who properly follows the instructions for how the account is to be read, that no explanation, information, etc., from K is introduced at any point in the account. And it is not or ought not to be strange that at no point is there any mention of K being asked to explain, inform, etc. In sum then, the rules, norms, information, observations, etc., presented by the teller of the tale are to be treated by the reader/hearer as the only warranted set.

THE CONSTRUCTION OF THE ACCOUNT AS FACTUAL

The actual events are not facts. It is the use of proper procedure for categorizing events which transforms them into facts. A fact is something that is already categorized, already worked up to conform to the model of what that fact should be like. To describe something as a fact or to treat something as a fact implies that the events themselves—what happened—entitle or authorize the teller of the tale to treat that categorization as ineluctable. "Whether I wish it or not, it is a fact. Whether I will admit it or not, it is a fact."

If something is to be constructed as a fact, then it must be shown that proper procedures have been used to establish it as objectively known. It must be seen to appear in the same way to anyone. Here are some of the relevant procedures in this account:

1. The teller of the tale, Angela, is K's friend. Others involved are also described as her friends, or as having a definitely positive attitude towards her. This structural frame is continued throughout. Since the 'fact' to be realized or established is a negative one and the structural frame declares for only positive motives towards K, there are no grounds for suspecting

Angela's motives. The rhetoric of the fact is here that Angela is constrained to recognize it. It is a fact independently of her wish; she does not wish it and yet she is "forced to face" it. This provision tends only to remove a possible difficulty. There are others more fundamental to the construction of objectivity. The construction of a fact involves displaying that it is the same for anyone and that their recognition of it as a fact is based on direct observation, is constrained by the nature of the event itself and is not determined by a hearsay construction.

2. The following structure establishes a succession of independent witnesses. A series of steps can be identified, defined by the addition of one person to the circle of those who recognize or know that something is wrong:

(a) at lines 24–33, Angela alone;
(b) at lines 34–38, Angela and Trudi;
(c) at lines 58–78, Angela, Trudi, and Angela's mother;
(d) at lines 130–48, Angela, Trudi, Angela's mother, and Betty;
(e) at lines 152–8, Angela, Trudi, Angela's mother, Betty, and a woman friend of the family.

The last step in this account breaks out of the local circle of those personally known to Angela by disclosing that this same "fact" is known to others independently—it "had been silently acknowledged by the social circle for some time" (156–7); and also that it had the formal sanction of a psychiatrist. This simple additive formula is a familiar one from children's stories—e.g. that of Henny-penny who went to tell the king the sky was falling. A cumulative effect is established. At each step a new member is introduced. This construction is particularly striking because it overrules indications present in the interview that some of those personages had been around before. For example, there was a carpool—who was in it and saw K cry (10–12)? Angela was "the last of her close friends" who admitted etc. Did those friends include or exclude Trudi and Betty (18–19)? Trudi was a mutual friend of Angela and K (34–5); Betty's apartment is just "nearby" the apartment of Angela, Trudi, and K and the account of the encounter suggests a casual dropping in ("we had gone there by chance"—130–3) characteristic of a

continuing friendship. The phone call to a woman friend of the family (152–3) is apparently to someone hitherto unconnected, and apparently taps a social circle independent of those personally known to Angela. Yet it is also said that "all the girls involved were of a particular social stratum" and their parents were "business people and acquainted with each other" (151–2). The inference is possible that the two social circles were in fact not independent of one another. The additive structure establishing textually the independence of witnesses overrides other possible principles governing the recognition of new presences in a narrative. Introducing new characters as members of circles of friendship would generate quite a different order. The items I have referred to above are present merely as parts of the connecting machinery of the story; it is the order of witnessing that occupies the foreground.

3. This structure makes possible the treatment of each additional witness as independent of the others. The judgement of each is based on direct observation or by inference an opportunity for such observation:

(a) Angela: in the course of ordinary interpersonal encounters with K, her admiration changes to bafflement;

(31)

(b) Trudi looks over one of K's essays and comments afterwards, "She writes like a 12 year old. I think there is something wrong with her";

(36–8)

(c) Angela's mother observes two instances of K's odd behavior:

(63–78)

(d) Betty is present at a conversation during which K's contribution shows her to be "completely out of touch";

(130–44)

(e) "The woman friend of the family" may be taken to have opportunities of personal observation independently of those made by previous witnesses.

(152)

These features of the account establish the judgements as arrived at independently by each witness and on the basis of direct observation (or a reasonable basis for inferring the same) uncontaminated by previous prompting or definitional work which might be interpreted as a source of bias. Note in this connection that Angela specifically mentions that she did not prepare her mother for any "odd behavior" on K's part. The ordering of events in the narrative constructs the objectivity of the fact, the items which might serve to suggest the opposite are not only relegated to the background, they are also not constructed in the same way. They are merely, as it were, lying about. A careful search may identify them, but the work of bringing them into an order must all be done by the reader/ hearer.

THE CONSTRUCTION "MENTAL ILLNESS"

The account provides the reader/hearer with an itemized and specific account of K's character and behavior. The reader/hearer is thus apparently given an opportunity to judge for herself on the basis of a collection of samples of the behavior from which Angela *et al.* constructed the fact of K's mental illness. The instructions for reading the account contained in lines 18–20 of the interview ("I was actually the last of her close friends who was openly willing to admit that she was becoming mentally ill") are that the collection is to be read as the behavior of someone who is becoming mentally ill. Thus the items are to be tested against a concept of mentally ill behavior (which I shall abbreviate hereafter to m.i. type behavior). The reader/hearer thus knows at the outset how this collection of characterological and behavioral descriptions is to be interpreted. If the collection is viewed as a problem, then we have been told what the solution is. The problem presented by the account is not to find an answer to the question "what is wrong with K?," but to find that this collection of items is a proper puzzle to the solution "becoming mentally ill."

Earlier when I was discussing how the account is authorized, I pointed out that defining K at the outset as "becoming mentally ill" removes her from the circle of potential witnesses to the events. The collection of items must therefore establish or justify this exclusion. K must be construed as a person who does not recognize what anybody else would recognize, who

does not share the same cognitive ground as others. The description of her character and behavior must be worked up as a "cutting out" operation (the *OED* gives for "cutting out" "to detach (an animal) from the herd"), which serves to draw the boundaries of the circle to exclude her. The final moment when things "come to a head," i.e. when K is seen to be "completely out of touch" (lines 143–4), is the point at which the cutting out operation is completed. This is its conclusion.

A strategy usually identified with the "medical model" (see Scheff 1966: 19–22) of mental illness views m.i. type behavior as symptoms of a "disease" or "illness." Thus behavior is treated as arising from a state of the individual and not as motivated by features of her situation. Though the medical model is not explicit here, the same fundamental strategy is used. Constructing K's behavior as m.i. type behavior involves showing that it is not adequately motivated by K's situation of action. Her actions are shown as not fully provided for by the instructions which follow from a rule or from how a situation is defined.

We have established already that it is the teller of the tale's privilege both to define the rule or situation and to describe the behavior. A rule or a definition of the situation yields a set of instructions for selecting those categories of action which are appropriate as "responses." We (the reader/hearer) must take on trust that the coding procedures for going from the original and actual behavior to such descriptive categories have been properly done. This definitional privilege and the use which the teller of the tale makes of it are of considerable importance in the cutting out operation. Behavior which is properly responsive to a rule or situation shows that the actor recognizes that rule or situation in the same way as it is defined by the teller of the tale. If it is not properly responsive, the reader/hearer may find an alternative rule or situation to which it is; or she may decide to sanction the teller of the tale's definition. The authorization rules direct the reader/hearer to select the second of these alternatives. So when we find in this account instances of a lack of fit between behavior and a rule or situation, these work as part of the cutting out strategy.

By a lack of fit I do not mean, for example, what Austin (1962:14) means by infelicitous or "unhappy" behavior. I want to find something closer to what could be meant by "anomalous" behavior, i.e. behavior for which no rule or set of instructions can be found. I am suggesting that social rules and definitions of situations can be viewed as if they provide a set of instructions for categorizing responses. (I should emphasize that the notion of instructions here is a metaphor at this moment, but I find it helpful.) Any such set of instructions provides for categorizing responses in two main ways: (1) by selecting a set of categories for describing behavior complying with the instructions; and (2) by selecting a set of categories for describing behavior which does not comply. So any set of instructions which might be written in the form "do such and such" can also be written by a simple transformation rule in the form "do not do such and such," where the negation is not just logical exclusion but is antonymous—i.e. the contrary or opposite of the behavior required by the instructions. In this sense, then, non-compliance or infractions of a rule are fitting. The instructions do provide for them (there are, I think, some types of instructions where the deviant option is not available at all).

Behavior which does not fit is behavior which is not provided for by the instructions either way. It is then anomalous, and anomalies, I suggest, are what we have to find in the descriptions of K's behavior. The cutting out operation thus involves showing how K's behavior is not properly instructed by the definitions of the rules or situations which are provided. The instructions to read K's behavior as m.i. type required that the search go from the behavior described to find the relevant rule or definition of the situation under which that behavior can be seen not to fit, or rather to be anomalous. If it does not fit, then it can be taken that K does not recognize the rules or situations as anyone else would recognize them. The procedure is analogous to the lay identification of color blindness. Anyone (given that she knows the coding rules) can identify colours in the same way. If you find someone who cannot distinguish between red and green, you do not raise questions about whether red and green can be discriminated; you rather identify as a special state of that individual her being unable to make that discrimination. You say she is color blind. The attribution of mental illness behaves in the same way. It is the state of not being able to recognize the social reality which is there for anyone else and it is effectively defined in the process of that individual having been found not to do it. The process of finding that out is what I have designated the "cutting out operation."

The collection of items in this account is not grandly convincing. There are few if any items that stand up as immediately convincing. The teller of the tale has to do a good deal of working up in order to display K's behavior as m.i. type. This visibility of the work is one of the things that makes the account worth analyzing in such detail. There are descriptions of K's behavior which, deprived of the contextualizing work put in by the teller of the tale, would not look particularly out of the way. There are even some that might be viewed as positive characteristics if the perspective were shifted just a little—e.g. K's insisting "that she had to swim 30 lengths" (25–6) on a hot day at the pool is entirely appropriate for someone with a concern for fitness; or her working so devotedly in her friend's garden might be a particularly creditable interpretation of the obligations of friendship. So we can begin looking at this collection with the hunch that the teller of the tale has to do rather a lot of contextual work to show how the behavior can read as m.i. type.

The contextual work at the level of individual items is most apparent in a device which I will call a "contrast structure." A contrast structure would be one where a description of K's behavior is preceded by a statement which supplies the instructions for how to see that behavior as anomalous. Here are some examples:

> When asked casually to help in a friend's garden, she went at it for hours, never stopping, barely looking up
>
> (40–2)
>
> She would take baths religiously every night and pin up her hair, but she would leave the bath dirty
>
> (89–91)
>
> When something had gone radically wrong, obviously by her doing, she would blandly deny all knowledge,
>
> (98–100)

The first part of the contrast structure finds the instruction which selects the categories of fitting behavior, the second part shows the behavior which did not fit. The first part may define a social rule, or a definite occasion, or some feature of K's behavior. I have counted twenty-three discrete items of behavioral description. Of these, eleven are contrast structures. I have defined this category very loosely since I am using it only to identify what seems to be a typical procedure. Other items which are not constructed as contrast structures at the level of individual items, can be shown to be contrastive with reference to larger segments of the account. And of course there are other things going on, some of which I shall try to analyze later.

ANALYSIS OF SOME CONTRAST STRUCTURES

Contrast Structure Type One: Paradoxes of Pretending

The parts of the c-structure are separated and identified by the numerals i and ii:

(i) It was obvious that she was terrified of anyone getting too near to her, especially men.

(ii) And yet she used to pretend to us (and obviously to herself too) that she had this and that guy really keen on her.

(53–5)

Embedded in this structure are two statements about K's behavior. Both describe mildy deviant behavior. K is described as being terrified of anyone, especially men, getting close to her (i); and as pretending that some man is keen on her (ii). The first is a description of a presumably stable feature of K's personality and the second a description of a kind of behavior she used to engage in. The contrast structure packages them as a unit linked by "It was obvious . . . and yet. . . ." What is the effect?

In part ii of the c-structure, K is said to "pretend." To be pretending, the actor must be trying to make others believe, or to give them the impression, by means of a current personal performance in their presence, that the actor is *abc,* in order to disguise the fact that she is really *xyz.*[2] This, I think, is how this contrast structure works to represent K's behavior as m.i. type:

1. Part ii makes clear what information was available to the teller of the tale at the time the events referred to took place. The "It was obvious . . ." establishes that the teller of the tale and others knew at that time what it was that K was trying to dissemble. Lacking the modifier 'it was obvious', the reader/hearer could infer no more than that at some time or another the teller of the tale knew that K was pretending. But the effect of "it was obvious" goes beyond this.

2. What is obvious is what may be plainly seen or understood by anyone. It is available to anyone and *therefore available to K.* Part ii also has a retroactive effect on part i of the c-structure, so that the part i statement is both what is obvious and what K is concealing. But if it is obvious, then it is not only known to K but *she must also know that it is known.*

3. "Pretending" is intentional. The actor is trying to conceal *abc* by doing *xyz.* The term thus assigns to K a plan or at least a prefiguring of what the teller of the tale tells us she was doing. It also implies the following distribution of information so far as the actor is concerned:

> The actor knows that she is really *abc.* She believes that those she is trying to deceive do not know that she is really *abc.*

These are the "belief conditions" of pretending.

4. The inference from "It was obvious"—namely that others know and that K knows they know—removes one term of the required belief conditions, namely that the actor believes that those she is trying to deceive do not know what it is she is trying to conceal. So this c-structure yields a paradox as follows. Pretending gives the following "proper" alternatives under different belief conditions. Either:

> K believes that others know *abc.* Therefore she does not believe that she can conceal it from them.

Or:

> K believes that others do not know *abc.* Therefore she believes that she can conceal it from them.

But not what in fact we have:

> K believes that others know *abc.* Therefore she believes that she can conceal it from them.

The effect of "it was obvious" on "pretending" is to shift the two statements out of the normal deviance class into a paradox which cannot be internally resolved.

It is here that the instructions given at the beginning of the interview become important because they tell us which term to select in order to resolve the paradox. Changing the second term might raise questions about the accuracy of the teller of the tale's description of what K was doing. This is ruled out by the authorization rules (see above). Changing the first term implies that what is obvious to others is not obvious to K. Then K believes that others do not know *abc* even though it is obvious. So K is not on the same wavelength as others; she is not seeing what is obvious to anyone else. That is the cutting out operation.

The same device is at work in the following c-structure:

(i)   When something had gone radically wrong, obviously by her doing,

(ii) she would blandly deny all knowledge. . . .

(98–100)

Contrast Structure Type Two: Standard Pattern Rule Anomalies

Here is another kind of c-structure:

(i)   she would bath religiously every night and pin up her hair,

(ii) but she would leave the bath dirty.   (89–91)

This kind of c-structure works differently from the foregoing. Part i gives a rule which is derived from routine features of K's behavior; part ii shows that she also routinely violates that rule. The procedure is something like this—from the occurrence of *a* and *b* expect *c*. But you do not get *c*, you get *x*.

Note that the ordinary sociological notions of expectation do not work here, as they probably never really do. For the following reason: that to get the expectation of *c* from the occurrence of *a* and *b* involves reference to a model or pattern in which these items occur regularly in that sequence. Seeing them as a series implies having grasped a model or pattern which is known in advance and on other grounds. One kind of rule here is what might be called a "standard pattern rule," like the alphabet. For there is nothing that holds the alphabet together as an ordered series of letters ex-

cept customary usage. There would be no way in which you could infer which letter must follow from any other without knowing already how it occurs.

Another type of rule is a formation rule which generates the series. The typical exercise which illustrates this type of rule is one in which a "subject" is given a series of signs such as "1, 2, 3 . . ." or "2, 4, 6 . . ." and is asked to continue the series. She may be told what rule to follow in doing so, but it is a common intellectual game and one that IQ tests sometimes make use of, to ask the subject to derive the rule for continuing the series from the series as it has been presented to her. We have a procedure like that here. The reader/hearer is instructed, I think, in virtue of the contrast structure to find from the first part the rule for continuing the series. The rule which she will presumably find would be some kind of "be clean" rule which can be rewritten as [bathe religiously every night, pin up your hair, leave the bath clean]. Part ii of the contrast structure would, however, read back to the simple deviance transformation of that rule. The two procedures can be stated as follows (the arrow means "rewrite as"):

Be clean → [every night do the following: bathe, pin up your hair, leave the bath clean]

Do not be clean → [every night do not do the following: bathe, pin up your hair, or, if you bathe, do not leave the bath clean]

From the first part of the c-structure we get a formation rule which is antonymous to the formation rule derived from part ii. And vice versa. So we find that we cannot retrieve a rule that does for both. But this is weak as a construction of m.i. type behavior because it is fairly easy to find an alternative rule which provides for the coherence of the set. For although this assemblage does not work under formation rules derived from looking at the items as a series, it could work perfectly well under a standard pattern type of rule, e.g. I might say, "Well, some people who take a lot of trouble with their personal appearance etc. are otherwise slobs" (or inconsiderate, or what have you). "They just are that way," I might say. Which I take to be an appeal to a standard pattern rule which would permit this series.

A similar construction can be found later in the same paragraph as follows:

(i)   She would wash the dishes,

(ii) and leave them dirty too.   (91)

Here the contrast structure is not built syntactically but is derived from the contradiction between the two parts. It could be, I suppose, a normal incompetence to find someone who washes dishes but does not wash them very well, so that bits of noodle, egg, etc., can still be found on fork and plate after the washing up is done. Leaving them dirty after washing them is more than incompetent. Indeed it is almost Dada and an achievement in itself. To leave dishes dirty after washing them is not just normal incompetence. In fact it is almost "against nature" so that the straining to realize what K has made available as m.i. type behavior does here, I think, overstep the limits of credibility.

Another and somewhat more successful instance of this kind of c-structure is the following:

(i)   When you meet her, you are struck by a sweet girlish appearance. She will sit quietly in company smiling sweetly at all times, and seems disarmingly appealing.   (42–5)

(ii) But when there were young men in the company, she would find it harder than ever to carry on a conversation, and would excuse herself and leave very soon.   (46–8)

Contrast Structure Type Three: Normatively Generated Anomalies

Here is a contrast structure in three parts:

(i)   We would go to the beach or pool on a hot day,

(ii)   I would sort of dip in and just lie in the sun

(iii) while K insisted that she had to swim 30 lengths.   (24–6)

Part i identifies an occasion and part iii the behavior, but it is clear that parts i and iii alone are not sufficient to show how K's behavior is odd. The day is hot and K insists on swimming 30 lengths—so? The middle term (part ii), by giving an example of behavior which is properly instructed by that type of occasion, provides the norm that generates the behavioral anomaly. The first two parts combined set up a model of occasion and fitting behavior which is more restrictive than part i alone. I suspect that quite a lot of work is

done by the specification "hot day" since that sets the instructions for the "lazing" behavior which is confirmed as the rule by the description of Angela's behavior. Thus K's behavior is not instructed by the occasion as it is specified by both part i and part ii together. Part i by itself would permit the behavior described in part iii so that the model of the occasion must be elaborated to give the swimming thirty lengths as anomalous. More work is then done by giving K's behavior an obsessional cast. She "insisted that she had to swim 30 lengths." So it is displayed in an imperative form without being referred to a social structure which would warrant that imperative.

I think there is a definite imperfection in the account here because we are still close to the categorization of K as "so very athletic" (line 7), which plugs into a social structure which would warrant this imperative. True this term is not "active" at this point, i.e. it has not been brought forward by the teller of the tale to define the actors and their relationship. At this point the working category appears to be "friend," and since Angela appears to establish a "friends do the same things and have the same interests" model of friendship, that category probably also works to establish the relevance of what Angela does on a hot day at the pool as a model for what K should do.

More important is the operation of the authorization rules described above. These provide the instructions that have already established Angela's authoritative voice and, in this case, Angela's entitlement to treat her own behavior as a norm *vis-à-vis* which K's appears anomalous. The positioning of the reading subject has already been set up, and this c-structure relies on this in accomplishing K's actions as ill-fitting.

Other Types of Contrast Structures

Here is a c-structure that recalls the "obviously"/"blandly denied" contrast structure examined in type one. But there is something else involved here.

(i)   When something had gone radically wrong . . . she would blandly deny all knowledge

(ii) but got very upset at little things, like a blown fuse.   (98–101)

This c-structure can be expressed in the language of psychiatric symptomalogy as an instance of "inappropriate affect"—the degree of feeling should be proportionate to the "value" of the event. Correspondingly, the proper value of an event is displayed by exhibiting the proper degree of feeling in the response. If something has gone *radically* wrong, the upset should be proportionate. In the above instance, it is not K's *denial* that something has gone radically wrong that is operative (i.e. this is not an example of c-structure type one) but that it is *blandly* denied. K's indifference to a serious problem is contrasted with getting very upset at little things in part ii.

The matter may be formally stated as follows. The rule that the degree of feeling should be proportionate to the seriousness of the events may be written as instructions on how much to care when things go wrong, as follows:

> When something goes seriously wrong, be seriously upset.
> When something goes mildly wrong, be mildly upset.

So from the "something has gone radically wrong" given by part i of the c-structure, we get the instruction "be very upset." The negative transformation would read "do not be very upset." And that is what we have. I am not at this time sure whether that is properly provided for by the rule, because there are other instances which could be had by a straightforward transformation, for example:

> Nearly every morning K would cry in the car, being upset about little things.   (12–13)

It seems to me that this c-structure is one of those rules where the negative is not provided. Otherwise it would be hard to get the "inappropriate affect" effect, and we do get it. But in any case the c-structure above is reinforced by showing that a possibly negative transformation, "do not be upset" does not hold either since K does get very upset at little things. The c-structure here thus works rather like the ones in type two, because the rule you generate from either tail of the c-structure does not hold for the other. So K is shown not to discriminate properly between things that go radically wrong and little things that go wrong.

There is also a device which is not properly a contrast structure, except perhaps in reverse. I have suggested that the contrast structures are ways of supply-

ing the contexts with reference to which K's behavior can be seen as m.i. type, and the implication is that, if it were described without those contexts, then the description of the behavior alone would not do the trick. There are, however, some types of non-routine behavior which normally require contextualization, or rather require to be shown as specially situationally instructed, in order to establish them as properly motivated. Some examples from the interview are tiptoeing (117) and whispering (119). These kinds of behavior are, I think, usually provided with a "reason" since they are behaviors which do not occur routinely in our culture. Routine occurrences are those where either no explanation need be given because it is assumed that there is some routine explanation; or where the occurrence itself suggests its typical grounds for occurring. The strategy here is to exhibit these without supplying an adequate reason, as follows:

> She'd tiptoe through the apartment, when there was no need to.   (117–18)
> She'd always speak in a whisper. . . .   (118–19)

An analogous device is used in the instance discussed above ("She insisted that she had to swim 30 lengths.") where K's behavior is given an obsessional cast by depriving the imperative of proper warrant. I suspect that instances of this type will form a greater proportion in accounts of m.i. type behavior which are stranger than this.

Other Constructions of "Anomalies"

This section examines some items that do not display a contrast structure. It will address those few items where K is shown to have a peculiar relation to material objects. These are:

> She would buy the most impractical things, such as a broom, although they already had one.
>
>   (95–6)
>
> She did not seem to absorb the simplest information regarding the working of the stove or other household implements.
>
>   (101–3)
>
> She had definite food-fads, and would take condiments such as ketchup, pepper to excess. Also things like tinned fruit and honey, she would eat them by the jar, at one go.
>
>   (103–6)

K was unable to put on a teapot cover correctly, she would not reverse its position to make it fit, but would simply keep slamming it down on the pot.

(76–8)

G. H. Mead has described how ordinary material objects—tables, chairs, etc.—as well as more complex social forms, are constituted by socially organized responses which refine and elaborate their uses out of the possibilities given by their sheerly physical properties (Mead 1934: 75–82). The object itself, thus constituted in its social organization, may thus also be understood as yielding sets of instructions for how to act towards it, how it may be inserted into human programs of action. And as with occasions and situations, a failure to act within the terms provided by these instructions displays the actor as failing to recognize the object as it is for anyone else. In these examples we may notice a much stronger structure than that which arises when rules or definitions of situations are in question. The objects themselves are treated as sufficient. Their definition does not have to be further elaborated or worked up to show K's failure to enter into that intersubjective world which is "ours." Yet the constructions are implicitly more complex than they seem. I shall discuss the first of these in another and later context. Here I just want to draw the reader's attention to these instances of misusage—that, for example, tinned fruit and honey carry the "instruction" "use in bits at intervals"; that ketchup etc. carries the "instruction" "eat in small quantities"; that a teapot in relation to its lid is constructed so that the sticky-out bit on the top fits into a notch in the rim of the pot and hence the "instruction"—"if the top does not fit the first time around then rotate it until the sticky-out bit fits into the notch." And beyond these, not just that K does not recognize these objects as they are constituted for anyone else, but that she is also apparently unable to "absorb" the simplest information about such uses.

Similarly, departures from household budgeting rules are presented not as "extravagance" or normal incompetence, but as a failure to grasp the ordinary properties of things—a new broom when they already had one; six pounds of hamburger—and the social structures which define their uses. With respect to the broom, for example, it would have been odd on the part of the teller of the tale if she had said that K had "bought a spoon, although they already had one." The social structure of a household requires that its members eat simultaneously, but not that they sweep simultaneously; therefore a spoon for each is "needed," but only one broom. This follows from the form and typical inventory of occasioned activities characteristic of household organization in our culture. It is enough, however, in the account merely to refer to the inappropriate uses of the objects. The rules do not have to be further elaborated presumably because they may be taken to be known at large. Unlike other features, they are "obvious" without having to be declared as "obvious." The objects are treated as "carrying" or simply implying the rules for using them. The latter do not need further explication or identification. These analyses by no means exhaust the types of behavioral descriptions included in the account. But they are sufficient to show the kinds of analyses that can be done and to subtend the notion of the cutting out operation introduced earlier.

"Cutting out" is done by constructing relationships between rules or definitions of situations and descriptions of K's behavior such that the former do not properly provide for the latter. The behavior is then exhibited as anomalous. Reading back from the anomaly gives the effect that the rule or situation which obtains is not recognized by K as it is. The specification of what it is is entrusted to the teller of the tale, whose status as definer and witness has been sanctioned by the authorization rules. K is thereby excluded from the circle of those who know. The circle of those who know includes now—in virtue of the bridging function of the teller of the tale—both Angela et al. and ourselves as reader/hearers. The transition between the different logical levels is made possible by their common term, namely Angela who is both a personage in the story and the teller of the tale.

THE COLLECTION AS A WHOLE

Turning from the individual items, I want to see now how the collection works as a whole. Rather than trying to identify a set of rules that are breached when people are recognized as mentally ill, or when behavior is recognized as m.i. type behavior, I suggest that this indeterminacy be placed at the heart of the problem. The institution of mental illness, its conceptual organization, forms of social action, authorized actors and sites, and so forth, are concerned precisely with creating an order, a coherence, at those points where members of a community have been unable or unwilling to find it in the behavior of a particular individual. This suggests a rule for assembling this collection which says that "for this collection, find that there is no rule." There is a visual analogy to the effect I am trying to specify. Paintings such as Ben Cunningham's combine different perspectival instructions. The looker in imagination must be continually shifting her position in relation to the events in the painting. She is never permitted to adopt a decisive relation resolving them into a single perspectival direction. I am looking for an analogue of that here.

There are indications from other descriptions of how people come to be categorized as mentally ill that this indeterminacy may be an essential preliminary phase to arriving at that label. The process described by the teller of the tale, when "Trudi and I found ourselves discussing [K's] foibles in her absence. I still tried to find explanations and excuses . . ." (114–15) suggests that not being able to find them may be a regular feature of the process. Compare Yarrow, Schwartz, Murphy, and Deasy's account of wives' descriptions of the process by which they came to see their husbands as mentally ill:

> Initial interpretations, whatever their content, are seldom held with great confidence by the wives. Many recall their earlier reactions to their husbands' behavior as full of puzzling confusion and uncertainty. Something is wrong, they know, but, in general, they stop short of a firm explanation.
>
> (Yarrow et al. 1955:20)

Those wives who do not fairly early on arrive at the categorization "mentally ill,"

> cast around for situationally and momentarily adequate explanations. As the situation changes or as the husband's behavior changes, these wives find reasons and excuses but lack underlying or synthesizing theory. Successive interpretations tend to bear little relation to one another.
>
> (Yarrow et al. 1955:20)

This seems to be analogous to the process described above, whereby alternative rules are sought and discarded or extenuations and excuses are sought and discarded. While an explanation may hold for one instance, it does not hold up for the next. Treating the collection as a whole means that a rule or extenuation found for any item must also hold for other items. A microcosm of the process is exhibited in the passage describing K's behavior at Angela's mother's (63–78) home. The incident of the wrong breakfast is explained first of all by Angela's mother as a misunderstanding (75). That is an extenuation rule which removes any particular significance from the episode. But that principle cannot be extended to the following episode of the teapot lid. One cannot, so to speak, misunderstand a teapot. The previous extenuation is removed once it is held that the two episodes must be treated as "a collection" such that a rule that is found for one must also hold for the other.

There are probably many instances of items in this collection for which it would be easy to find extenuations or alternative rules. It is the stipulation "one rule for all" which inhibits this procedure and serves to fix the weaker anomalies. Take, for example, the household passage which runs from lines 87 through 109 of the interview. If the instructions to read the following behavior as "queer" are removed and if certain of the items are also removed, the passage reads as incompetence rather than mental illness, as follows:

> She would wash dishes, but leave them dirty too. They would try and live within a strict budget, and take turns in cooking dinner and shopping for it, each for one week. K (frequently) overshot the budget by several dollars. She would buy the most impractical things. . . . She would burn practically everything. . . . She did not seem to absorb the simplest information regarding the working of the stove or other household implements.
>
> (91–103)

This could add up to K just being a hopeless housekeeper. Adding the items which do not precisely fit that categorization, namely the bathing religiously item, the food-fads, the bland denial when things go radically wrong, makes it difficult to fix the explanation under the stipulation that any explanation you find must serve for all. Weaknesses in the construction at the level of individual items are worked up by setting them into multiple constructions, which just make it harder to find a simple rule which provides for the whole. For example, in the passage:

> They would try and live within a strict budget, and take turns in cooking dinner and shopping for it, each for one week. K invariably overshot the budget by several dollars. She would buy the most impractical things, such as a broom, although they already had one, 6lbs of hamburger at one go, which they would have to eat the whole week.
>
> (92–8)

This works, I think, by the cumulation of small things. Any one item could be discounted as accident (overshooting the weekly budget) or oversight (the surplus broom) or inexperience (six pounds of hamburger), but the sequence as a collection exhibits K's actions as instances of the underlying state. She "invariably" overshot the budget, so it could not be accident or oversight; buying an extra broom or six pounds of hamburger are expressed as instances or examples of what ails her. The grammar is conditional; not she did, but she *would* do this or that. The onus shifts from each particular as act or event to each particular as an expression or instance of K's state of being.

When we examine the workings of the collection as a whole, the active part the reader/hearer must play to find out how to read the narrative as an account of someone becoming mentally ill becomes more visible. The conceptual schema of mental illness operates, as I have suggested, like a set of instructions for how to go about dealing with doubtful instances or weaknesses in the story as a story of someone becoming mentally ill. Finding some items as anomalous depends on the reader/hearer bringing together one part of the account to interpret another. In an earlier example (of K's swimming thirty lengths of a pool on a hot day), I pointed out how generating the anomaly depended upon a privileging of Angela's standpoint already accomplished by the authorization rules; it depends also on inhibiting the bringing forward of an earlier reference to K as "very athletic." This is reader/hearer's work but it is work that is instructed by the mental illness schema.

The following example also depends on referencing an earlier segment of the interview to accomplish it as anomalous.

> It was very difficult to carry on an intelligent conversation with her, this became apparent when I wanted to discuss a particularly good movie, and she would make childish inane remarks, completely off the point.
>
> (26–30)

Here again we can see the operation of the authorization rules in establishing the normative standpoint from which the reader/hearer is to view K's behavior. But given this, the item still fails to meet the criteria for anomalous behavior. The deviant behavior is fully provided for by the rule; the inverse of intelligence is stupidity; vis-à-vis the norm of intelligent conversation, inane remarks are deviant. Reading this as anomalous calls for the reader/hearer to reference back to the characterization of K as a good student (7) that establishes the initial norm against which K's deterioration becomes apparent. The reader/hearer can then assemble a first-term—second-term problem like that described as type two, where each part of the c-structure yields a rule which does not provide for the behavior in the other. If K is intelligent, a good student, etc., then her conversation should be intelligent; if K's conversation is inane and off the point, then K is not able to participate intelligently in conversation, *ergo* she is not intelligent.

The local weaknesses that are presented in many items are obscured by the cumulation of items which give different sorts of renderings and by the way in which one part of the story can be brought to bear in interpreting another. The cumulation has a progressive effect. The reader/hearer looks for how each next item can be read as a further instance. Each further instance works retroactively on the previous one. It is this property of the collection as a whole, as well as the structure of particular items, which gives the effect I found in my first hearing of the interview material—namely of K becoming "more and more disorganized." The effect of disorganization attributed thus to K is produced by the reader being unable to come to rest on any principle of organization which would generate the whole collection.

CONCLUSION

This conclusion points to, although it does not fully design, a general procedure for the analysis of such accounts. It suggests to the reader/hearer that she might treat the foregoing analysis not just as saying something about mental illness but as having a more general sociological relevance.

The analysis of the account has dealt with two main aspects. First, its social organization. Under this term I include both the structure which relates the original events described in the text of the interview to the present of the reader/hearer and the authorization rules which instruct the reader/hearer on what criteria to use in determining the adequacy of the description and credibility of the account. Such a social organizational analysis could be made of any such text, including, of course, a clinical psychiatric history. Its specific features would be systematically different and would display typical features of the institutional structure which provide the general contexts of its production and uses. For example, clinical histories commonly include no authorization procedures and we may take it that these instructions are established externally to the text.

Second, the analysis of contrast structures and of the collection as a whole brings out a procedure for constructing an account of behavior so that it can be recognized by any member of the relevant cultural community as mentally ill type behavior. This procedure I have called the "cutting out" procedure. Cutting out is done by constructing relationships between rules and definitions of situations on the one hand and descriptions of K's behavior on the other such that the former do not provide for the latter. The aim of such an analysis would be to spell out this procedure as instructions for generating such descriptions. Their adequacy could then be proved (in the pudding sense) by using them to write descriptions and seeing whether others could recognize them as accounts of someone who is mentally ill.

I do not think I have succeeded in explicating the procedure to this degree, but I think I have gone far enough to justify that as a direction. I have suggested that an alternative account of what happened is possible. In fact, theoretically a number of alternative accounts are possible since the problem is only to show how in K's behavior can be found rules and contexts which provide for them adequately. There is certainly more than one way in which this might be done. One

important restriction on the reader/hearer's being able to work on the account in this way is stabilized by the authorization rules which give a "witness" a privileged status versus the reader/hearer. Any alternative account must be speculative. This consequence is to be understood as a product of the social organization of the account which places the reader/hearer at a disadvantage with respect to those who were involved, even though the outsider was not herself present but makes up her own account from the accounts of those who were.

The effect of the authorization rules here bears on another aspect of the account relevant to the making of alternative interpretations, namely the lack of sufficient information. It is a normal feature of such accounts that they do not contain irrelevant material. Irrelevant material is material which neither (a) establishes the adequacy of the authorization procedures used nor (b) is appropriate to and can hence be appropriated interpretively by the conceptual framework. The reader/hearer cannot go back to the personages of the original to recover material which might be relevant to an alternative construction. As a feature of the social organization, this may be contrasted with situations such as a court of law in which witnesses may be questioned to recover material making possible alternative accounts. Thus the construction of an alternative account in which K is not mentally ill is not possible on the basis of what is available.

I can, however, briefly show for some parts how it might be done. It would involve finding rules or contexts for K's behavior which would properly provide for the behavior described or, alternatively, being able to re-describe the behavior to the same effect. If the enterprise were successful *it would result in a description which would lack any systematic procedure for bringing these items together. The pieces of behavior would simply be fitted back into various contexts. The present account would disintegrate. The reader/hearer would be unable to recover from them a rule under which she could see what the account 'was all about'.*

Take, for example, K's insisting that she had to swim thirty lengths (25–6). Earlier I fitted that back to the description of her "as very athletic." This involves finding a context which motivates the act. It can be done in a rather more complex way with the following set of items. When it is done, as the reader/hearer will see, there is nothing that holds them together other than that both are about K.

Here then very sketchily: let us go back to the instance of the second broom (95–6). And add to it a later item as follows:

> Or she would ask, when is dinner ready, and when told in about 10 minutes, she would go and prepare something quite different for herself.
>
> (126–9)

This item, like the broom item, can be treated as showing that K does not share the ordinary practical knowledge of how a household is structured, i.e. that the rules are that members should eat simultaneously and that they should not or need not sweep simultaneously (it is not one of the inventory of concerted occasions that "doing" a household requires). These instances can be fitted to a context if we write a version of the relations among Angela, Trudi, and K which contradicts that given in the account. It is maintained throughout that Angela and Trudi and K are friends. This is the basis on which they share an apartment. Trudi has some reservations about K but it is not suggested that these are serious; K's performance in the household does not meet Angela's and Trudi's standards. Ordinary experiences of such household arrangements suggest that difficulties often do arise. Sociological experiences of three-person groups suggest that these are particularly difficult to manage without trouble (Caplow 1968). Yet nowhere is any irritation, annoyance, or dislike recorded. The two items of behavior that I have introduced here could be warranted by recovering a social organization contradicting the united household presented in the text. Or put in another way, K's behavior can be read as "recognizing" two households in one set of premises.

This preliminary reading can be tied into a more general reconstruction of what is reported from then on. There are indications of a ganging up process similar to that which Lemert (1962) has described in his paper on "Paranoia and the dynamics of exclusion." The last sequence when things came to a head can be interpreted in this frame: Angela et al. are together working up an account of K as mentally ill. K is excluded from this process, yet is the object of it. Angela et al. are involved with one another in the business of establishing that there is something wrong with K. Take K's reported utterance "Oh yes, and the little black sheep and the lambs . . ." (123) as recognizing this and it makes perfectly good sense. Angela et al. are the lambs and K is the little black sheep, the outsider, the no-good, the marginal member who is never fully a member.

The credibility of the account and the reader/hearer's obedience to the restrictions on search procedures, as well as her authorization of the teller of the tale, depend upon accepting Angela et al. as K's friends. The contradictory interpretation provides a context for much of what is reported of K after Angela and Trudi had decided that "she just could not cope" (107) and found themselves "discussing her foibles in her absence" (114). The friendship version of their relationship depends upon successfully defining K as "mentally ill." Conversely, defining K as "mentally ill" depends upon preserving that version. So I take it as crucial that it is K's statement about "the little black sheep and the lambs" which receives the gloss from the teller of the tale. "This was really completely out of touch" (143–4). The social organization of the account plays a crucial part in the construction of the fact that "K is mentally ill."

NOTES

1. This paper has been published previously as "K ist geisteskrank. Die Anatomie eines Tatsachenberichtes" in 1976 in E. Weingarten, F. Sack, and J.N. Schenkein (eds) *Ethnomethodologie. Beitrage zu einer Soziologie des Alltagslebens,* Frankfurt: Suhrkamp.

2. This sentence is lifted directly from Austin's paper on "Pretending" (Austin 1964: 113), but I have modified the wording and therefore supply it without quotes.

REFERENCES

Austin, J. L. (1962) *How to do Things with Words,* London: Oxford University Press.

Austin, J. L. (1964) "Pretending," in Donald F. Gustafson (ed.) *Essays in Philosophical Psychology,* Garden City, New York: Doubleday Anchor Books.

Caplow, Theodore (1968) *Two Against One: Coalitions in Triads,* Englewood Cliffs, NJ: Prentice-Hall.

Cicourel, Aaron V. (1969) *The Social Organization of Juvenile Justice,* New York: John Wiley.

Clausen, John A. and Yarrow, Madeleine (eds) (1955) "The impact of mental illness on the family," *Journal of Social Issues,* Special Issue, II (4).

Durkheim, Emile (1960) *The Division of Labor in Society,* Glencoe, Ill.: The Free Press.

Goffman, Erving (1961) *Asylums: Essays on the Social Situation of Mental Patients and Other Inmates,* Garden City, NY: Doubleday Anchor Books.

Kitsuse, John I. (1962) "Societal reaction to deviant behavior," *Social Problems* 9 (3) winter: 247–56.

Lemert, Edwin M. (1962) "Paranoia and the dynamics of exclusion," *Sociometry* 25: 2–20.

Mead, George Herbert (1934) *Mind, Self and Society: From the Standpoint of a Social Behaviorist,* Chicago, Ill.: University of Chicago Press.

Mechanic, David (1962) "Some factors in identifying mental illness," *Mental Hygiene* 46, January: 66–75.

Scheff, Thomas J. (1964) "The societal reaction to deviance: ascriptive elements in the psychiatric screening of mental patients in a midwestern state hospital," *Social Problems* 11 (4) spring: 401–13.

Scheff, Thomas J. (1966) *Being Mentally Ill: A Sociological Theory,* Chicago: Aldine Press.

Smith, Dorothy E. (1975) "The statistics on mental illness: what they will not tell us about women and why," in D. E. Smith and Sarah David (eds) *Women Look at Psychiatry,* Vancouver, BC: Press Gang.

Yarrow, M. R., Schwartz, C. A., Murphy, H. S., and Deasy, L. C. (1955) "The psychological meaning of mental illness in the family," in John A. Clausen and Madeleine R. Yarrow (eds) "The Impact of Mental Illness on the Family," *Journal of Social Issues,* Special Issue, II (4): 12–24.

46 | WAYS OF THE BADASS
Jack Katz

In many youthful circles, to be "bad," to be a "badass," or otherwise overtly to embrace symbols of deviance is regarded as a good thing. How does one go about being a badass? How can that become a compelling project?

One can develop a systematic understanding of the ways of the badass by distinguishing among three levels or degrees of intimating aggression. Someone who is "real bad" must be tough, not easily influenced, highly impressionable, or anxious about the opinions that others hold of him; in a phrase, he must not be morally malleable. He must take on an existential posture that in effect states, "You see me, but I am not here for you; I see you, and maybe you are here for me."

The second stage in becoming a badass is to construct alien aspects of the self. This construction may be achieved barbarically, by developing ways of living that appear hostile to any form of civilization, or by inventing a version of civilization that is not only foreign but incomprehensible to native sensibilities. If being *tough* is essentially a negative activity of convincing others that one is not subject to their influence, being *alien* is a more positive projection of the world in which one truly fits. The existential posture of the alien states in effect, "Not only am I not here for you, I come from a place that is inherently intractable by your world." The foreigner may often be charming; the alien is unnerving. Managing the difference between appearing to be interestingly foreign and disturbingly alien is a subtle business; much of the work of the adolescent badass plays on the fineness of the distinction.

Either alone or in combination with a posture of toughness, the perfection of an alien way is not sufficient to achieve the awesomely deviant presence of the badass. Toughs who set off sparks that call for attention but never explode risk being regarded as "punks." And many who elaborate alien ways achieve nothing more than the recognition of being "really weird." In addition to being tough and developing an alien style, the would-be badass must add a measure of meanness.[1]

To be "bad" is to be mean in a precise sense of the term. Badasses manifest the transcendent superiority of their being, specifically by insisting on the dominance of their will, that "I mean it," when the "it" itself is, in a way obvious to all, immaterial. They engage in violence not necessarily sadistically or "for its own sake" but to back up their meaning without the limiting influence of utilitarian considerations or a concern for self-preservation. At this level, the badass announces, in effect, "Not only do you not know where I'm at or where I'm coming from, but, at any moment, I may transcend the distance between us and destroy you. I'll jump you on the street, I'll 'come up side' your head, I'll 'fuck you up good'—I'll rush destructively to the center of your world, whenever I will! Where I'm coming from, you don't *want* to know!"

To make vivid sense of all the detailed ways of the badass, one must consider the essential project as transcending the modern moral injunction to adjust the public self sensitively to situationally contingent expectations. The frequent use of phallic metaphors is especially effective for making this process bristle with sensational moves. At the end of the chapter, I will clarify the distinctive relevance of masculine sexual symbols and suggest why being a badass is so disproportionately seductive to males.

BEING TOUGH

The ways of being tough may be summarized along two lines. First, a tough appearance may be accomplished by using symbols and practical devices that suggest an impenetrable self. Here we can place the attractions, to those who would effect a tough appearance, of leather clothing and metal adornments. Here, too, we can understand the connection of a publicly recognizable "toughness" with signs that unusual physical risks have been suffered and transcended; scars are an example. High boots frequently enhance a tough look, in some styles suggesting cowboys or motorcyclists, in other styles implying that the wearer has passed or expects to pass through some sort of disagreeable muck.[2]

Prominent among the devices of toughness are dark sunglasses. As the street name suggests, "shades," unlike sunglasses in general, pull down a one-way curtain in face-to-face interaction, accomplishing nicely the specific interactional strategy that is toughness. On the folk assumption that the eyes are windows to the soul, in face-to-face interaction we regularly read the eye movements of others for signs of the focus of their consciousness, to grasp their subjective location, and to track what is "here" to them. Simultaneously, we manage the direction of our gaze to shape the perception by others of what is "here" to us. Thus, we usually avert our gaze from passersby after an implicitly understood interval, so that our apparent continued attentions do not suggest an improperly intimate interest; conversely, if we want to suggest that the other is intimately "here" for us, we do not avert our gaze. Shades permit the wearer to detect what is "here" to passersby, while the wearer's focus of consciousness remains inaccessible to them. When this interactional reading does not hold, for example, when we know the wearer is blind, darkly tinted glasses will not work as a device for intimating toughness.

Because toughness manifests that one is not morally or emotionally accessible, one recognizable style of being tough is to maintain silence, sometimes referred to as a "stony" silence, in the face of extensive questions, pleadings, comic antics, and other efforts to evoke signs of sympathy. As an audible analog to the eyes' "shades," when "tough" guys have to say something to get things from others, they may mumble or speak in a voice muffled by gum, a tightly closed mouth, or a downcast face.

The symbols and devices of impenetrability are a simple ready-made way of being tough; many of them can literally be bought off the rack. What is culturally more complex and individually more challenging is the requirement to offset the moral malleability inevitably suggested when one enters communicative interaction. I may easily appear tough to you when I am not attempting to shape your understanding to any effect other than that I am tough. But if I want to do any other sort of business with you, my apparent rigidity will, sooner or later, become a problem. If I want to communicate substantive desires, I must attend to whether you have correctly interpreted my messages; if not, I am constrained to alter my expression to get the point across—all of which risks suggesting that, to shape your experience of me, I am willing to shape and reshape myself and, hence, that I am not so tough.[3]

It is common for young people to take on the first layer of toughness without being accomplished in the second. What appears to be a hard-and-fast toughness often dissolves in the first moments of substantive interaction. Thus, in the privacy of a bedroom, one may drape the body in leather and chains, practice a hard look in the mirror, apply apparently permanent but really erasable tattoos of skulls and crossbones, and so forth. When one enters a store to buy cigarettes, however, it may feel impossible not to wait one's turn with the clerk politely, and even to finish the transaction with a muttered "thanks."

The openings and closings of face-to-face interactions in public are routine occasions for indicating that one has the moral competence to be in society. With "How are you?" we often formally open and move into an interaction. The response, "And how are you?" without a pause is accepted and thus the interaction proceeds smoothly without either party explicitly responding to the question.[4]

The primary project of the questioner is usually to indicate that he is the sort of person who cares. Even though his failure to await a response might logically be taken to indicate just the opposite, the move makes sense to the participants because it indicates that the speaker is open to moral concerns. He has used convention to indicate that he is open to change based on the state of the other's being. Here is a little ceremony performed to ritualize the beginning of interaction, a ceremony in which each indicates to the other that he is capable of mediating his existence with others through social forms.

Compare a common ritual opening of interaction among adolescents who are attempting to be tough. When boys in American junior high schools pass each other in the halls while changing classes, they sometimes exchange punches aimed at each others' shoulders. They may then continue past each other or, even more oddly, they may abruptly abandon the dramatization of hostilities and pause for a short interchange

of affable comments that make no reference to the opening blows. Literally, the thrust of the message is the thrust of the message. Familiarity with this ritual breeds a competition to be first in detecting the other's presence and to land the first punch. In a little ceremony performed to mark the initial moments of interaction, each attempts to indicate to the other that he exists for the other in the first instance physically, independent of civility and social form.

Note that not only is the implicit statement the inverse of that made by the customary civil ritual, so is its irony. The tactful adult shows that he is the sort of person who cares by inquiring about the other's sensibilities and then proceeding without pausing for a response. But the playfully combative adolescent shows that he is present most fundamentally in his socially unrestrained physical being, by more or less artfully employing a well-established social form.

One of the most elemental ways of being tough is to mark the beginning and the ending of an interaction gutturally, with a sound that emanates from deep in the body and whose form indicates that the sound maker ("speaker" would not be quite accurate here) exists outside of civil conventions. Members of street gangs in Italian sections of Brooklyn in the 1950s would often signal their entrance into a street corner assemblage of their fellows with an "eh" (or "ay") that would trigger a cycle of responsive "ehs."[5] This utterance is guttural, both in significance and sensual practice; the physical exertion indicates to the others that he is present for them from his stomach—not from his mind or from any socialized sensibility.

Endings of interactions are again typical occasions for expressing a competently socialized moral character. The strength of the moral demands made during an interaction is revealed by the amount of culture and proficiency of skill required to end an interaction without retrospectively undermining its moral framework. Such verbal and written civil endings as "Take Care," "Yours Truly," and "Have a Nice Day" reaffirm the person's competent social sensibility. Despite a near-universal awareness of the banality of these forms, they remain difficult to avoid.

Such ritual endings are executed because people who have been interacting anticipate that a new threat will emerge at the end of the interaction. This threat is not to the future of their relationship (these conventions are used as much, perhaps more, among strangers who may well never see each other again as among friends), but to the reinterpretation of what has just transpired. Often formally prospective (*Have a nice day: I remain sincerely yours, take care, best wishes*), these devices are implicitly and more fundamentally retrospective. In effect, farewells assert that even though my care for you is so limited that I can now move on to other cares—even though by ending this interaction I may suggest that I have not been authentically here for you—I really have been deeply, sensitively involved with you all the while. The misleadingly prospective direction of the form is essential to suppress awareness of the implicit retrospective doubt, the existential doubt that either participant was (and perhaps ever can be) really "here" for the other. As phenomenal worlds begin objectively to separate, civil interactors rush to reaffirm that those worlds really were isomorphic and that each person really was morally sensitive to the other. I anticipate your sense that if I can break off abruptly from you, you may reflect, "He never really gave a shit about what I felt in the first place!"

To produce toughness is, in part, a matter of failing to perform these prophylactic rituals on the moral health of everyday life, but it is also a matter of inventing substitutes. Consider as a striking example of a guttural exiting ceremony, the *cholo's* "Shaa-haa!" In East Los Angeles, adolescent *vatos, cholos,* or "homeboys" frequently mill about in a casual mood that shows no particularly malevolent spirit until the assemblage is brought to a close when one of the participants utters a forceful or cool statement of bravado to which he appends a "Shaa" or "Shaa-haa," which the others join in.

The following instance was part of a homeboy's recollection of his first day in the tenth grade at Garfield High School in East Los Angeles. He was "holding up the wall" with fellow homeboys from his *barrio*—a traditional practice in which groups congregate at traditional spots, lean against the wall, and look out at groups clustered in other spots. The school bell rang to call students to class. The homeboys continued to mill about, aware that, with time, their passivity would take on an increasingly deviant signifi-

cance as a tacit rebellion against the school's attempt to control their interaction. A vice principal came over to urge the group to go to class, and one homeboy responded, "'Say, professor, don't you have something better to do? If you don't take my advise, go sit on the toilet and flush yourself down. Shaa-haa!'"[6]

Like "eh," "Shaa-haa" (which can be short or long and more syncopated or less, depending on the occasion) comes from deep in the body, from the very bottom of the throat, if not from the guts. It involves letting out a burst of air audibly, over a jutting jaw, with mouth open but without shaping lips to form letters, all to accomplish a broad, deep, serpentine hiss that is often succeeded by a machine-gun burst of belly laughing. Having publicly defined the interaction that preceded the termination as one in which all the boys were present in a gutturally direct, socially uninhibited way, the aggregation can disband and the participants can head toward class.[7] With this utterance, a group of young men can harmoniously articulate a common moral posture of being tough without fear that the medium will contradict the message.

In addition to opening and closing interactions, those who would be tough must routinely counter the moral vulnerabilities suggested in the very nature of human existence. For human beings eating, for example, is a figurative, as well as a literal, opening of the self. For tough guys, eating (and defecating, ejaculating, extracting mucus from the nose and throat, and so on) must be carefully cultivated to offset the breach of self inherent in the process. Sweating, however, should require no special ceremony for toughs: perspiring occurs simply in a transpiring; no act of opening the body is necessary to make visible these drops from inside.

In adolescent cultures, toughness is commonly displayed as a subtle negativity, barely glossed onto an otherwise morally sensitive interaction. Consider two everyday ironies from black street life, hand-slapping rituals and the use of "shit" to begin a turn at speaking in conversation. Handshaking is a conventional form for displaying a civil sensibility when face-to-face interactions begin or end. It expresses a gentle man's spirit by physically enacting a moral malleability and a moral vulnerability: I open my hand, my self, to feel the force of your presence, and vice versa; we are united by social form, such that each may be influenced by the other's will.

Young men in black ghettos have constructed from this convention a means of displaying a paradoxical form of social contract. With the hand slap, the moral malleability suggested by the handshake becomes a cooperative hitting—I hit you and I let you hit me. The moral vulnerability suggested by the offer and acceptance of physical contact is simultaneously countered by its opposite. The hitting or slapping, an action that in other contexts might be humiliating punishment, usually passes as an unremarkable gloss of toughness.

This dialectical principle is elaborated within ongoing group interactions as speakers and listeners seek and confer agreement. The more a listener agrees with a speaker, the harder he hits him, and conversely. As R. Lincoln Keiser noted:

> In general, when a hand-slapping episode occurs during social interaction it emphasizes agreement between the two parties. If an individual has said something someone thinks particularly noteworthy, he will put out his hand to be slapped. By slapping it, the alter in the relationship signals agreement. Varying the intensity of the slap response indicates varying degrees of agreement. A Vice Lord may say, "Five Lords can whup fifty Cobras!" and then put out his hand, palm up. Another club member responds by slapping the palm hard, thus indicating strong agreement. The first Vice Lord might then say, "I can whup ten Cobras myself!" and again put out his hand. This time, however, the second individual may respond with a much lighter slap.[8]

The more the listener indicates that he has been moved by the speaker, the more emphatically he simultaneously acknowledges and counters his malleability through enacting aggression.

"Shit," pronounced melodically over long vowel sounds ("Sheee-it"), has had an extraordinary run of popularity in black street life. It is a way for a speaker to begin a turn in conversation or to mark publicly the movement of his consciousness from one theme to another within a monologue. Compare, as the inverse in form and function, the British use of "Right" to begin a turn in conversation, for example, the Bobby's "Right, what's going on here?" the Mexican's use of "Bueno, es que" to begin a response to a question; and the use of "okay" by white middle-class adolescents in the U.S.

to begin a turn and repeatedly to reorient a narrative account in a conversation. Although with "shee-it" the speaker pulls himself out of a communal moral order even as he audibly begins to enter it, "Right," "Bueno," and "Okay" invoke a transcendent moral order to tie people together into a conversation at moments when the coordination of their sensibilities has become problematic. With "Right," the Bobby invokes a framework of moral approbation to begin the assertion of his authority. With "Bueno, es que," the Mexican begins to respond to a question by formally overcoming the dim, horrific possibility that the asking has inexorably alienated the speakers. With "okay, okay, okay," the young suburban American asserts his moral commitment to sustain order in conversation just as he anticipates that, because of problems in the evolving structuring of a narrative, it may soon fall into doubt.[9]

"Sheee-it" is elegantly negative, both in content and in form of delivery. When pronounced in a descending melody, the phrasing gives the word, even apart from its content, a cynical, negating tone. In content, shit is about as purely negative an image as any that could be thrown into a conversation. The existential fact that we are, each of us, literally (if also narrowly), walking, talking containers of excrement is remarkable for its typical absence from overt public attention. When used to start a speaker's turn in conversation, "shee-it" brilliantly executes a simultaneous expression of two dialectically related themes: (1) the fact that I speak to you coherently displays my ability to shape myself to fit into your understanding and (2) the fact that I begin by tying your impression of me to shit suggests that the social form I take on is but a thin veneer over a nature that is obdurately beyond social domination. The following example, which illustrates the point both in form and content, came from an interview with a member of a black street gang in San Francisco:

I feel my high school education is the most important thing in my life right now. That's how I feel.
[INTERVIEWER:] How long have you felt this way?
Shit. Maybe a year.[10]

These subculturally varied devices for producing a veneer of toughness are all counterveiling commentaries on the image of personal moral openness that is persistently implied in social interaction. To sustain interaction while remaining tough, one can repeatedly negate the continuously resurrected implication that one is sensitive to others by throwing shit onto the scene, with guttural outbursts, by physically hitting at the image of moral sensibility, and so forth. Attacks on the conventions and cliches of civil demeanor constitute one of the stock ways of being tough. An account of street gang violence in Glasgow, Scotland, provides a final illustration. According to one retelling by members of the "Young Team" of an attack on a solitary victim, the victim, a boy aged 14, rolled himself into a ball for self-protection and was then stabbed seventeen times in the back. Just before the attackers ran off, Big Sheila, a barmaid who was sympathetic to the Young Team, created a memorable closing line by dropping a handkerchief on the boy and offering: "That'll help ye tae mop yir brow."[11]

BEING ALIEN

Being tough is essentially a process of negation, achieved either with a visual block, a symbolic sartorial shield, an audible muffle, or a maneuver that inverts the suggestions of a morally open self that are inevitably born in such everyday activities as eating, meeting friends, and conversing. Of course, being tough is not sufficient to construct a deviant identity; we admire poker players, respect businessmen, and honor political leaders who appear to be "tough." In all cases, the quality being celebrated is a negative moral capacity—an ability not to give away, not to give up, and not to give in.

By developing ways of being alien, adolescents can move positively beyond the negativity of a tough posture without abandoning it and without embracing respectable conventions. In congruence with the statement made from the stance of toughness, "I am not here for you," adolescents have fashioned an ever-expanding set of subcultures in which they can style great swaths of their everyday lives with indications that they come from some morally alien place.

Street Styles

Across subcultures would-be badasses exploit the hermeneutic possibilities in walking. Young blacks who would strike up the admirable image of the "bad nigger" work on orchestrating their pace to a ghetto "bop." John Allen, a black from Washington, D.C., who became a "professional" stickup man, recalled that when he was first committed to a juvenile detention facility,

> I learned a lot of things. . . . it was a place where you fought almost every day because everybody trying to be tougher than the next person. As a kid you pay so much attention to how a dude's supposed to be a bad nigger, he really having his way around the joint with the counselors and with everybody. . . . So you wanna be like him, you wanna act like him and talk like him. I think down there I must of changed my voice about hundred times 'cause I had a high-pitched voice and was bothered being small. And I changed my walk from supercool to ultracool.[12]

In East Los Angeles, the night before his first day in high school, a barrio homeboy anxiously anticipated humiliating challenges. He debated whether to take a gun to school and practiced his "barrio stroll": "a slow, rhythmic walk with ample flamboyant arm movement, chesty posture, and head up towards the heavens."[13]

Each of these styles transforms walking from a utilitarian convention into a deviant esthetic statement made routinely in the practice of getting from here to there. Each suggests that the walker takes some special pleasure in the existential necessity of putting one foot in front of the other to get ahead. Each suggests that the walker will not take a simple "straight" path through the social structure. He will take up more attention and more space in his social mobility than is called for by civil routines, perhaps, with those flamboyantly swayed arms and his side-to-side gait or slightly jumping bop causing problems for pedestrians who are attempting to pass unnoticed in the other direction.

Most notably, each style of walking suggests not only that the walker is not here for the others around and "walks to a beat of a different drummer," but he is from a morally deviant place. The *ghetto* bop and the *barrio* stroll, identify the walker as a native of a place that is outside and antagonistically related to the morally respectable center of society. Similarly, the streetcorner male's habit of repeatedly making manual contact with his genitals and hoisting up his pants is a prominent way of pointing to the walker's animal life, a life carried on somewhere beyond the perception of respectable society. The currently popular "sag" look makes the same point by inverting these symbols. Pants are held by tight belts below the buttocks, where they permit the display of a "bad" ass covered by florid boxer shorts, which are often worn over a second, unseen pair of underpants.[14]

From Japan to Scotland to East Los Angeles, tattoos are appreciated as devices for embracing a deviant identity. Tattoos may be used minimally to suggest toughness by drawing attention to the skin as a barrier between the tattooed person and others. They also conjure up toughness by suggesting that the person has suffered and survived pain. Tattoos are not necessarily ominous, but often their content conveys an additionally "bad," alien theme by suggesting a totemic relationship with evil. In one circle of street fighting young men in Glasgow in the early 1970s, "Mick . . . sported on his forearm a red dagger entering the top of a skull and reappearing through its mouth. It was considered to be the finest tattoo in the neighbourhood."[15] Los Angeles cholos are partial to black widow spiders and death skulls. Hell's Angels sport swastikas, German crosses, and skulls-and-crossbones.

These symbols suggest that the wearer presumes himself fundamentally rooted in a world of deviance and so is unresponsive to conventional moral appeals. What is more interesting is that the same effect is often achieved with tattoos that are traditional, respectable symbols of moral content—of "Mom," "love," and American Eagles; in the Japanese criminal subculture of *yakuza*, the whole body may be tattooed with chrysanthemums.[16] Beyond suggesting toughness and almost regardless of content, tattoos emphasize personal intransigence and are symbols of permanent loyalty to a particular subgroup's interpretation of the Good. They seem to say, "Wherever I am, whatever is going on, without my even trying, this will be fundamental to who I am." Even when the moral commitment is to "Mom" or to the American flag, the tattoo will often have threatening, deviant overtones. (Contrast the morally innocuous wearing of pins bearing club or patriotic images: unlike tattoos and like college ties and tie-clips, these can be taken off.)

Like walking, the would-be badass may also fashion talking into a deviant esthetic. John Allen, the pro-

fessional "bad nigger" whose recollections of his street education in a juvenile detention facility were quoted earlier, noted: "There was a big thing there about talking. You had to express yourself, and you saying, 'Damn, jive, Listen man' and going through all the motions and changes."[17] In Glasgow, young street fighting men use a slang, reminiscent of Cockney forms, that hides its meaning through a multistep process of alteration from conventional expression. Thus, "It's jist yir Donald" means "It's just your luck": "Donald" calls up "duck," and "duck" rhymes with "luck." "Ya tea-leaf ye!" means "You thief!," which, if pronounced with their accent, would sound something like, tea-eef. "Ah fancy yir tin flute" means "I like your suit."[18]

The ethnographer who recorded these phrases grew up in Glasgow but was initially frustrated in attempting to understand the young toughs' everyday conversations. As Allen indicates with regard to the United States, "jive" talk is not a natural talent of ghetto blacks.[19] Within the local context of ghettoes, these argots are resources for taking the posture of an alien presence, a being who moves cooly above the mundane realities of others. As with being tough, being alien is not necessarily a posture taken toward conventional society. It is a way of being that may be taken up at any moment. As Allen's quote made clear, being ultra cool is most essential in the company of other tough young men. Being alien is a way of stating, "I am not here for you," when anyone—friend, family, or foe—may be the "you."

The ways of being alien begin to define an alternative deviant culture. As such, they call for the study of their distinctive esthetic unities. Here, I can only indicate a few lines of analysis that might be elaborated by investigations devoted solely to ethnographic documentation.

The Cholo

A coherent deviant esthetic unites various manifestations of the low-income youth culture of the barrio known as *la vida loca* and identified with the cholo, vato loco, or Mexican-American homeboy. Language, body posture, clothing fashions, car styles, and graffiti exhibit a distinctive, structurally similar, "bad" perspective. As individuals, young people in the barrio take on and shed this esthetic from situation to situation and to different degrees, but they continuously take for granted that affiliation with it will signify, to their peers and to adults alike, the transcendence of a line of respectability and the assumption of a high-risk posture of moral defiance.

In its essential thrust, the cholo esthetic assumes an inferior or outsider status and asserts an aggressive dominance. In body posture, this dialectic is achieved by dropping below or falling back and simultaneously looking down on others. Thus, when Mexican-American young men wish to take up a cholo or "bad" posture for a photograph, they often squat, placing their buttocks just off the ground, sometimes on their heels, while they throw their heads slightly back to a position from which they can glare down at the camera. This posture is not easily sustained; its accomplishment is at once an athletic test and an esthetic demonstration of "bad" toughness.[20]

This position might be characterized as an aristocratic squat. Reminiscent of a resource known to peasants throughout the world, the cholo's squat creates a place for him to sit when there are no chairs. But by throwing his head sharply back, the cholo takes on a paradoxically aristocratic air. Once in the lowered and reared-back position, a sense of superiority is attached to him, as it is to one who is born to privilege: naturally and necessarily, like a law of nature.

Faced by a squatting cholo, an observer sees himself observed by a down-the-nose glance, like the stereotype of a peasant under the regard of an aristocrat. For his part, the cholo accomplishes something magical: he simultaneously embraces and transcends an inferior status. Before your very eyes and dressed in an undershirt that has no sleeves to put anything up, the cholo drops down to the ground, becoming lower to you in physical position but putting you down morally. Miraculously, the cholo manages literally to look down on you from beneath you.

The dialectical structure and aggressive symbolic force of this body posture is also carried out in the classic *pachuco* stance and in the contemporary "barrio stroll." Unlike the cholo's aristocratic squat, the pachuco style is both historically dated and well-known outside Mexican-American barrios, in part because of the popularity of the play and then movie, *Zoot Suit.* Although the pachuco's Zoot Suit or "drapes" were fashions of the 1930s and 1940s, contemporary cholos proudly, and sometimes self-consciously, continue elements of the pachuco style, wearing overly large, multiply pleated, sharply pressed khaki pants and pointed, brightly shined black shoes. And if the narrator of *Zoot Suit* took an exaggerated back-leaning stance, the contemporary cholo is similarly inclined.[21]

When being photographed, a group of cholos will often divide up into some who squat, lean forward, throw their heads back, and cast their eyes down to meet the camera and some who stand, maintaining the wide angle between their side-pointed feet that the squatters also adopt, throwing the trunk slightly back, throwing their heads back even more, and casting their eyes down to meet the camera. This standing position is put into motion in the barrio stroll. In forward movement, the foot position adopted by squatting and stationary cholos is maintained, but now it becomes far more noticeable, causing a ducklike waddle. To balance out the waddle and the backward slant of the trunk, the barrio stroller bends his elbows sharply, drawing the hands up parallel to the ground.

In the stationary position and in the stroll, the "being low" of the squat is replaced by a "being outside." While the squatting cholo is in a remarkably low social position, the backward-inclined, standing and strolling cholo is remarkably beyond reach. The magical effect is that while being emphatically beyond conventional reach, the cholo appears to be unusually aggressive and assertive as he strides into your world.

The low position of the cholo's aristocratic squat is repeated in the automobile esthetic of the low rider. By altering stock shocks and springs, cholos make cars ride literally low. If the rear is lowered more than the front, the driver will naturally incline backwards. Even without mechanical alterations, they may achieve the same effect by driving with their arms fully extended, their trunk and head inclined back, and their eyes cast down at the world above.

The overall effect is less an approximation of the advertised modern man in an up-to-date car than a fantasy image of a prince in a horse-drawn chariot, sometimes racing with other chariots and sometimes promenading slowly through public boulevards. The cars themselves are restored and dressed up at a substantial expense. The challenge is to demonstrate a transcendent esthetic power by raising the dead and discarded to a vividly displayed superiority. The lowrider is a distinctively American construction of alien being; foreign cars are not used, but the style is pointedly different from anything Detroit has ever tried to get Americans to buy.

The form of graffiti that is popular among Mexican-American youths in Los Angeles also has an emphatically alien esthetic and a backward leaning slant. In New York City, graffiti, produced by blacks, Puerto Ricans, and others, is often colorful and graphic, sometimes extensively narrative, and cartoon figures are often mixed in with individual and gang names, threats, and ideological slogans. New York graffiti writers consider one of their highest achievements to be the creation of an integrated set of images running over up to ten subway cars. In East Los Angeles, graffiti is primarily monotonic calligraphy; as one writer put it, everything is in the line:

> Graffiti is all the same line, the same feeling, even though different people use it for a different purpose. . . . Anyway, I dig that line, I dug that line. That's how I got involved. It's my thing—that line.[22]

Experienced graffiti "writers" in New York denigrate "tags" (writing only a name or nickname) as amateurish and unsophisticated. But in Los Angeles, graffiti is called *plaqueasos*—from *placa,* which in various contexts means a car license plate, a policeman's badge, or a plaque announcing one's business to the world. The plaqueasos of Los Angeles are elaborated in line and adornment far beyond the "tags" derided by New York writers.

Mexican-American plaqueaso writers appear to be working from traditions that are so ancient and foreign as to make the content of their graffiti routinely indecipherable to outsiders, often even to residents of their own barrios. The emphasis in the content is on individual and gang names, phrases of bravado and threats, nightmarish (black widow spiders, laughing skulls) and deviant (the number 13 for the letter "M" for marijuana) iconography and a protective curse (*Con Savos* or *Con Safos,* often written simply as C/S) that is reminiscent of those inscribed on Egyptian

tombs. Individual letters in words, designed in a style that is unfamiliar to any written tradition known in the barrio, are often mixed with symbols (for instance, stars between letters), as in a hieroglyphics.

In a sensitive study of East Los Angeles graffiti, Jerry and Sally Romotsky argued that major styles of plaqueasos are based on Old English, Gothic, Dürer-like calligraphy.[23] Perhaps the style that is most difficult for outsiders to decipher is what plaqueaso writers call the "point" style. Romotsky and Romotsky showed that the point style is achieved essentially by tracing the outlines of blocky, Old English-style letters. In effect, plaqueaso writers achieve a strange, alien appearance by working out of Anglo-Saxon cultural traditions in a disguised way. They achieve a distinctive presence by the ingeniously simple device of negation, that is, leaving out the substance of letters.

A superior posture for plaqueaso is achieved by using the same dialectical technique that is used in body posture. When drawn in three dimensions, the letters sometimes march to one side or huddle together like colorful cartoon characters engaged in a light, comic spirit. But in their "bad" forms—when they announce the names of gangs or make ominous declarations, three-dimensional letters often rear back and come down heavily on the observer as they declare their author's existence.[24]

The same esthetic runs through clothing and language. Cholos favor armless undershirts, as if to embrace a sign of the working-class status that has been abjured by conventional fashion. Unlike garments that are manufactured to be worn as "tops," these tops are also bottoms: traditionally worn beneath shirts, their display is a negation that emphasizes what is not worn. And by studiously maintaining their undershirts in brilliant white, cholos proclaim their transcendence of dirty work. Plaid shirts, referred to in the barrios as "Pendletons," are part of the everyday uniform of many school-age cholos. Worn over a bright white undershirt, the Pendleton recalls the cotton plaid shirts common among impoverished Mexican immigrants as well as the expensive wool shirts associated with the Oregon manufacturer. As a practical matter, the style is alien to the reality of the cholos, whose first days of classes in the fall often have temperatures topping 100 degrees. With colorful bandanas wrapped around their foreheads, cholos look like they come from rural Indian areas rather than urban barrio neighborhoods.

Homeboys in East Los Angeles speak and write graffiti with elements from Calo, a unique amalgam of Spanish and English that continues a "pachuco" argot whose roots are in pre-World War II, Mexican-American gang life.[25] On the one hand, cholos often ridicule recently arrived Mexicans who are incompetent in English.[26] On the other hand, their version of Spanish is incomprehensible to native Mexicans as well as to many of their U.S.-born parents. Pachuco or Calo is not a foreign language; it is ubiquitously alien.

In sum, the cholo-pachuco style is a deviant posture of aggressive intrusiveness made from a position that is proudly outside the reaches of the various societies it addresses. Through the stationary and the walking body and in clothing, cars, everyday language, and stylized writing, the pachuco-cholo-homeboy-vato loco conjures up a deviance rooted in a world that is self-consciously and intrinsically alien. The special claim of this esthetic is not just that its bearers are tough, but that they are from a spiritually rich, morally coherent place that Anglo authorities, native Mexicans, parents, or conventionally styled peers may only grasp minimally and at a distance as existing somewhere over "there."

The Punk

Consider next the novel way in which the punk culture locates its bearers in an alien moral system. An observer of the original British working class-based punk culture offered this summary:

> The punks turned towards the world a dead white face which was there and yet not "there." These "murdered victims"—emptied and inert—also had an alibi, an elsewhere, literally "made up" out of vaseline and cosmetics, hair dye and mascara. But paradoxically, in the case of the punks, this "elsewhere" was a nowhere—a twilight zone—a zone constituted out of negativity.[27]

The alien character of punk culture has been achieved in several ways. One is to embrace as appearance enhancing the devices that, according to strong moral injunctions and contemporary fashion, ought to be kept hidden. Thus, safety pins and sanitary napkins are worn as adornments on shirts and skirts, lavatory chains are draped like a necklace on the chest, and makeup is applied in degrees and places that ensure that its application will be seen. And hair is not only dressed in unconventional ways but is dyed blue, green, intense red, yellows, and combinations of these colors that are not found naturally on any humans. The suggestion is of an alien culture whose standards are the opposite of conventional esthetic standards. The thrust of punk culture is not only foreign or "weird" but consistently antipathetic.

The alien theme in punk culture has not been limited to dress and appearance. Dancing "was turned into a dumbshow of blank robotics." The pogo—a dance style of jumping up and down, hands clenched to the sides, as if to head an imaginary ball, the jumps repeated without variation in time to the strict mechanical rhythms of the music—"was a caricature—a reductio ad absurdum of all the solo dance styles associated with rock music." Bands took names like the Unwanted, the Rejects, the Sex Pistols, the Clash, and the Worst and wrote songs with titles like "I Wanna be Sick on You" and "If You Don't Want to Fuck Me, Fuck Off." There was a "wilful desecration and the voluntary assumption of outcast status which characterized the whole punk movement."[28] A memorable example was a sort of pet hairdo constructed by carrying live rats perched on the head.[29]

Another alien theme, one that was given a particular reading in punk culture but that has had broad appeal to many "bad" youth cultures, might be called, being inured to violence. Clothes display holes and rips that suggest not wear but war; hair is shaped into daggers; makeup may suggest bruises, scars, and black eyes. In this theme, the suggestion of an alien origin for the punk is that he or she has just come to the instant social situation, to what is going on here, from a place that is, to all in civil society, somewhere inhospitably "there."

Despite radical differences in the substance of their symbols, the punk and cholo cultures dramatize a tough invulnerability and the status of a visitor in the conventional world. For the individual adolescent, the adoption of the cholo or punk style has often meant a weighty decision of moral citizenship. On the one hand, the bearer sets himself off as a member of an alien culture in the eyes of school and police authorities, parents, and conforming peers. On the other hand, the alien style enables even the loner to induct himself, through what sociologists call collective behavior, into a deviant community.

Punk culture was manifested during its classic stage in the mid-to-late 1970s by an informal social organization underlying a strong esthetic coherence. The punk style inevitably became commercialized, softened, and sold to "normal" adolescents and to middle-aged adults through beauty salons, high-priced boutiques, and mass-marketed music. But for several years, tens of thousands of adolescents were working out a personal style and helping to produce the emerging collective esthetic. By acquiring pieces of used clothing, costume jewelry, and miscellaneous "junk"; altering items already in their closets; and applying makeup and assembling outfits with a care for detail; adolescents, male and female, were literally fitting themselves into a controversial collective movement. That the culture as a whole achieved a persistent coherence even while the details of the punk "look" constantly changed could be taken by individual members as proof both of the autodidactical, idiosyncratic creativity of individual punks and of the existence of a common spiritual bond running through the age group, cutting across formal divisions of school classes, neighborhoods, sex, and ethnicity.

Many adolescents live alien subcultures with far more everyday meaning than simply that of a bizarre dressing ritual. Beyond exploring the reactions of conventional others, adolescents who are dressed in an alien style are recurrently challenged to behave in a distinctively cholo or punk (or "bad nigger," or Hell's Angel) style in routine interactions. How, for example, does one order food at a restaurant in punk style? How does one answer a teacher's question like a cholo?

If the alien adolescent is in exile from a society that does not and never has existed, we still must appreciate the transcendent loyalties that are being evoked. Alien adolescent subcultures are collective movements on the way toward class consciousness, but they rarely reach explicit self-awareness or survive efforts to organize them formally. The cholos' aristocratic squat and other elements of arch style suggest their inchoate collective efforts to weave themes from their unique historical reality: the Mexican peasant origins and U.S. agricultural exploitation of earlier generations combined with a revolutionary tradition in which battles between peasants and aristocrats were joined by bandit leaders. Just as the black ghetto pimp, dressed in a white suit and a planter's hat, defiantly embodies the stereotype of slave owners he has never known, so the cholo, looking down on his environment by taking up a stance beneath and outside, unwittingly but defiantly gives expression to his people's historical subjugation.

The punk movement in the United States emerged in the mid-1970s, coincident with the recession, rapid inflation, and the passage into political quiescence of the "sixties" generation. It emerged after the withdrawal from Vietnam, after the culmination of Watergate, and as the oil crisis was beginning to push up prices throughout the economy. Meanwhile the sixties generation, which originally gained collective self-consciousness, in part by taking over radio station formats and displacing the pop stars of the fifties, was now in its thirties, moving into higher income brackets, but still holding onto its cultural representation of youth. In rock music, the arena in which adolescents uniquely attempt to detect and define the waxing and waning of generations, scores of bands struggled for mass recognition in a youth market that was tenaciously dominated by stars and styles nearing middle age. Styled like a militant vanguard, the punk band represented, in the market of collective symbols, the distinctive historical struggle of the emerging generation. The punk movement was bitterly antihippie; rumors of attacks on sixties youth types were constant. And the punk music and performance style was not simply raucous but a move back to an historical era before the sixties. It was an effort to get back to the fertile, earliest, crudest days of rock and roll in the fifties, as if to begin the youth culture again but in a way in which the currently young could take their place.

To regard these as more than speculations is to miss the open-ended, protean quality of the subculture. What the movement is about in terms of collective material interest and historical position is necessarily unclear as long as it retains the openness to individual esthetic creativity that makes it a compellingly exciting process to its members. But not to speculate on underlying, implicitly sensed themes of collective class interest is to miss an essential element in the excitement of being in these movements. The alien subcultures of adolescence are vehicles for cooperative speculation, means of exploring, through the reactions of others to clothing and new speech forms, which devices "work" and which do not; which fit the alien soul and which are incomprehensible in it; and which compromise the alien order by evincing a subtle sympathy to mainstream conventions. To the extent that young people who do not know each other can create, through indirect interactions and informality, a rich coherence among such minor details as the shape of a line in graffiti, the colors painted on hair, a rag worn around the head, a stirring accent, or a memorable phrase uttered before a class, they can sense the reality of an alien spiritual home—a place as yet concretely present in no definable geography, but surely "there."

The Animal and the Cool

Cutting across the various alien adolescent subcultures is a dualism between the animalistic and the cool. One way to indicate that you are not just tough but essentially outside contemporary civilization is to manifest an animal incapacity for moral responsiveness. Hell's Angels embraced this folk anthropology with their studied affinity for dirt. Inverting the practice of teenagers who shrink "designer" jeans through multiple washings before wearing them skin tight in public, Hell's Angels would train new denim jackets through multiple baths in dirt and grease before wearing them on the road. To shock outsiders, they turned rituals of civil society into occasions for displaying their animal natures, as when one 250-pound Hell's Angel would greet another in a bar by taking a running jump into his arms and planting a wet kiss on his lips.[30] To be animal is to suggest chaotic possibilities—that, through you, at any moment, forces of nature may explode the immediate social situation.

Being cool is a way of being alien by suggesting that one is not metaphysically "here" in the situation that apparently obtains for others, but is really in tune with sensually transcendent forces in another, conven-

tionally inaccessible dimension. To be cool is to view the immediate social situation as ontologically inferior, nontranscendent, and too mundane to compel one's complete attentions. A common way of being cool is to realize or affect a moderate drug mood: the "cool cat" of black street life has its origins in the culture of the heroin world.[31] In Los Angeles barrios, an analogous, drug-related phenomenon is *tapaoism,* an air of being so into a deviant world *(la vida loca)* that one cannot "give a shit" about any situational restraints. In contexts of extreme poverty, a cool version of a "bad" look may be achieved by a self-consciously exaggerated display of luxury in the form of flashy styles worn casually. In their ghettoes, the pachuco who is "draped" in overflowing fabric and the black cat who is "dripping" in jewelry imply sources of wealth that must exist at a distance from conventional morality, in some underground realm, perhaps that of the pimp or the drug dealer.[32]

The two emphases of alien style have spawned different descriptions of fighting. On the animal side, in Puerto Rican street gangs in New York in the 1970s, to be beaten up was to be "dogged up." In many black ghettoes, group attacks on isolated individuals are described as "rat packing" or "wolf packing." In East Los Angeles, attempting to intimidate others with a fierce expression is known as doing a "maddog" look.

On the cool side, to Chicago's Vice Lords of the early 1960s, a fight was a "humbug," and some of the West Side branches became known as the "Conservative" Vice Lords. With "conservative" as with "humbug," they were assuming a pose of calm reserve toward what others find extremely upsetting. It also is cool to refer to risky deviant activities with a diminutive. John Allen, the "professional" stickup man, liked to talk about a period in his life in Washington, D.C., that was nicely organized—a time when he could do "my little sex thing," "my little drug thing," and "a little stickup."[33]

As used in black street culture, "shit," "jive," and "stone" have been used to express both the animal and the cool sides of an alien posture. To talk "jive" is to talk in a cool, poetically effective way, but it may also be to talk nonsense and to bullshit, as in the pejorative "don't give me that jive talk!" or "you jive motherfucker!" "Jive" and "shit" also refer to a gun. In this sense they suggest an overwhelming force that puts the individual beyond the restraints of civilized morality. To be "stoned" is, in one aspect, to be drugged beyond competence for morally responsive interaction. Stone is also a cool object; metaphysically, it emphasizes a hard, unmovable reality, as in the praiseworthy, "He's a stone motherfucker," or in The Black P. Stone Rangers, a famous gang name in Southside Chicago in the 1960s. The gang's name was supercool, since it exploited a double entendre ("stone" played off the name of a local street, Blackstone). Actually, the phrase was ultracool, in that it fortuitously created a triple or quadruple entendre; the club's name was celebrated by poetically inserting a "P" within the street name, which audibly set "stone" apart from "black" just long enough to register racial as well as metaphysical connotations.

Finally, a lack of expressiveness is used widely to construct alien adolescent subcultures in both animal and cool forms. "Animals" in fraternity houses and on sports teams represent a frequently admired way of being "bad" by showing themselves, in loud and wild forms, as being governed by inarticulate, uncivilized forces. On the cool side is the use of silence to affect the style of the professional killer or the Mafia chief. When asked by a sociologist, "What would you like to be when you grow up?" it is cool to answer, "an assassin."[34]

More elaborately, it is dramatically "bad" style to exercise power publicly through silent codes. Turtle, "the Chicano 'Fonz,'" first verbally dressed down homeboys from another barrio in a dangerous face-to-face confrontation and next gave a hand signal and walked away; then twenty or so of *his* homeboys "spontaneously" attacked in unison.[35] This move is "supercool" or extraordinarily "bad" owing to its doubly silent structure. It is a silent message that mobilizes a more profoundly silent dialectic. That is, the most minimal imaginable physical move causes a major physical attack, a momentary shift in posture produces a permanent change in being, a silent signal creates screaming pain, and a cool move turns on the heat and burns the victim.

No attack need follow such a silent message, however. A gesture by one, apparently undifferentiated, man that turns all the others in a place into his servants—for instance, in a bar, at the snap of a finger, an aisle is cleared and a central table is left vacant—also shows a bad "cool." Watching the silent signal and its results, both the participants and bystanders suddenly appreciate a powerful, alien presence. The indications are not only that a structure of authority clearly exists in the group, but that it is implicitly illicit: no formal indicia demarcate those who act as waiters, chauffeurs, and couriers from those who are served as customers, car owners, and chiefs. Exercised with an aura of mystery, "bad" because it cannot show its sources publicly, this power always exists at a distance from the situation that obtains here and now. For those under its spell, its sources are always in some unreachable location vaguely apprehended as over "there."

BEING MEAN

The person who would be tough must cultivate in others the perception that they cannot reach his sensibilities. Adolescents who would achieve a foreign and hostile presence in interaction must go further and participate in a collective project to produce an alien esthetic. But the shaping of a tough image and the practice of an alien sensibility are insufficient to ensure that one will be "bad." Those who would be bad are always pursued by powerful spiritual enemies who soften tough postures and upset the carefully balanced cultures of alienation, making them appear silly, puerile, and banal and thus undermining their potential for intimidation. To survive unwanted imitators, you must show that unlike the kids, you're not kidding; unlike the gays, you're not playing; unlike the fashionable middle class, you understand fully and embrace the evil of your style. You must show that you mean it.

By being mean, I refer to a distinctive sensuality worked into the experience of interaction. To complete the project of becoming a badass, it is necessary to impress on others the apprehension that, however carefully they may maintain a respectful comportment, you might suddenly thrust the forces of chaos into their world. If he is serious about being tough and alien, the would-be badass can inundate the routine social settings of his everyday life with this "awe-full," ominous character. But how can he show that he means it so clearly that he is never confused with childish, playful, or otherwise inauthentic imitators?

The key distinction is not between physical action and its symbolic representation. If the badass is to make everyday social situations routinely ominous, he cannot, as a practical matter, depend simply on violently harming others.[36] As has frequently been found in studies of street "gangs," those with the "baddest" reputations are not necessarily the best nor even the most frequent fighters. And in the qualitative materials which follow, the actual infliction of physical harm seems always imminent but is not.

Whether through physical attack or via dramatization at a distance, the badass conveys the specific message that he means it. If we ask, what is the "it" that he means? we miss the point. To construct and maintain an awesome, ominous presence, the badass must not allow others to grasp the goals or substantive meaning of his action. He must seem prepared to use violence, not only in a utilitarian, instrumental fashion but as a means to ensure the predominance of his meaning, as he alone understands it, whatever "it" may be.

To make clear that "he means it," the badass celebrates a commitment to violence beyond any reason comprehensible to others. For example, at a dance hall in Glasgow, Tim, a dominant personality in the Young Team, turned to Dave and pointed to a bystander, "'Ah don't fancy the look o' his puss. Go over an' stab him fur me.' Dave had duly carried out the request."[37] From London's East End, an ex-skinhead recalled, "We only 'it people for reasons, didn't we? . . . like if they looked at us."[38]

In conflicts between street gangs, there is little room for a reasoned exchange of grievances; "discussion" and "debate" risk suggesting a deferential bow to rational order that would undermine the project of the badass. Manny Torres, a member of the "Young Stars" in Spanish Harlem in the late 1950s, recalled that in his work as "warlord," debate was not a means of avoiding conflict but a signal that a fight was inevitable:

My job was to go around to the other gangs, meet with their chiefs, and decide whose territory was whose. And if we had any debate about it, it was my job to settle on when and where we would fight it out and what weapons we would use.[39]

Physically, badasses are always vulnerable; in U.S. ghettoes, someone can always "get to" them, since guns are widely available. But if they communicate that they will persevere without limitation until they dominate, then they force others to confront the same choice: are they willing to risk bodily injury, and even if they escape injury, are they willing to risk arrest? Is a momentary sensation of dominance worth it? The badass's logic of domination is to mean nothing more or less than meanness. He succeeds by *inducing others* to reason, to reflect on the extraneous meaning of violence, to weigh the value of experiencing dominance against the fear of physical destruction and legal punishment, when *he* will not make the calculation. Now and again, he must go at least a little bit mad.

Ethnographic details demonstrate the would-be badass's awareness of the necessity to dramatize his transcendence of rationality. Badasses are not irrational or antirational, and they certainly are not stupid. They understand precisely the nature of rationality and they position themselves carefully to manifest that their spirit, their meaning, is not limited by their need to make intelligible to others or even to themselves the purposive coherence or utilitarian sensibility of their action. Within this framework, we can understand the following comments by black Philadelphia street toughs to sociologist Barry Krisberg not as evidence of intellectual incompetence or moral insensitivity, but as the opposite. A group leader named William told Krisberg that he "wouldn't argue with someone—just stab them."[40] There was no need to argue or explain because: "'whatever comes to my mind, I know it got to be right because I'm thinking of it.'"[41] Another leader, Deacon, characterized his everyday posture with:

Doesn't have to be anything, it could be just the principle of a conversation. If I thought it was justifiable, like, they was trying to, like fuck over me, I would shoot them, whatever way that came into my mind at that moment.[42]

Where badasses congregate, showdowns are likely. In showdowns, we can sometimes see the eminently rational use of seemingly irrational violence to manifest a transcendence of rationality. In the following incident, drawn from R. Lincoln Keiser's ethnography of Chicago's Vice Lords, there is no suggestion of sadism or even of much anger; rather, there is a mutual recognition of the meanness required to be a badass. The background is a fight between two cliques within the Vice Lords, the Rat Pack and the Magnificent Seven. The speaker, a member of the Rat Pack, began a fist-fight with Fresh-up Freddie of the Magnificent Seven:

He couldn't touch me, so I said, "I quit," and I dropped my guard. That mother fucker, he hit me in the nose, hit me in the mouth, and my mouth started bleeding. Now Cool Fool had my jive [gun]. I said, "Fool, gimme my jive!" and Fool, he gave me my gun. I said to Fresh-up, "I ought to shoot you!" Now Fresh-up got the intention of snatching the gun. He done snatched three or four guns out of different fellows hands, and he started walking at me. He said, "Shoot me if you want to. I don't believe you going to shoot me." I knew what he's going to do when he got close, he going to grab the gun. I didn't want to kill him so I shot him in the arm. I had to shoot him. You see, if I hadn't done it, he would of took my gun away from me.[43]

Fresh-up was attempting to be the baddest, first by manifestly not limiting himself by principles of honor or conventional morality (he struck out at the speaker after the latter had "quit") and second, in moving to snatch the gun away, by demonstrating the other's moral weakness—the other's fear not of him but of the consequences of using the gun he possessed. The speaker shot, not necessarily out of fear that Fresh-up would take the gun and shoot him, but so Fresh-up would not transform the speaker's pretense of meanness into an evident bluff.

Being mean, then, is a pristinely rational social logic for manifesting that one has transcended rationality. Having grasped its paradoxical rationality, we can now more readily understand various ways in which badasses breathe awesomely mean airs into everyday life. To the would-be badass, being mean is not an abstract commitment but an exciting world of distinctive phenomena. Becoming a badass becomes seductive when one senses in interactional detail the transcendent significance of manifesting meanness. I will trace three segments of esthetically and sensually compelling ways of being mean under the categories:

"Soulful Chaos," "Paraphernalia of Purposiveness," and "Mind Fucking."

Soulful Chaos

The ominous presence of the badass is achieved in one respect by his ways of intimating chaos. The person who is most fearsomely beyond social control is the one who does not appear to be quite in control of himself because his soul is rooted in what, to us, is chaos.

The following is a poem written by an ex-skinhead.

Everywhere they are waiting, In silence.
In boredom. Staring into space.
Reflecting on nothing, or on violence. . . .
Then suddenly it happens. A motor-cycle
Explodes outside, a cup smashes.
They are on their feet, identified
At last as living creatures,
The universal silence is shattered,
The law is overthrown, chaos
Has come again. . . . [44]

In this poem, chaos is represented as the force that moves one from boredom to liveliness, awakening one's senses, providing essential energy, making the world a seductive place again. The suggestion is that chaos is at the very source of one's spiritual being.

If badasses are not often poets, they are most fundamentally creators of a special culture. Consider the explanation offered by Big L, a member of a Puerto Rican gang in Brooklyn in the 1970s, of why the Bikers have the reputation of being the baddest:

Rape old ladies. Rape young girls. Kick people out of their homes. Steal. Vandalize the whole neighborhood. Burn cars and all this. And they're bad. That's why they consider them bad. They're bad.[45]

Beyond the specific acts cited, the Bikers have, for Big L, a transcendent, ringing reality as bad, real bad, the baddest: his description quickly becomes a recitation in which the intonation of evil goes on and on, resonating in choruses of awe.

Rape and mayhem may sometimes be useful to construct a bad reputation, but as a routine matter, the badass will exploit a more cultured, symbolically economic means of sustaining an awful presence. He may dramatize a sadistic pleasure in violence to suggest that chaos is natural to him and, therefore, that it is always his potential. Skinheads described cutting someone with a razor as "striping," as if there was an esthetic appeal, a matter of artistic achievement, in the process of destruction. In Glasgow, another place where knives have been a favorite instrument of group violence, "team" fighters distinguish between being "slashed" and being "ripped" (the latter involving a special turning of the knife) and they further distinguish a method of kicking aimed at opening the wound.[46] When gangs have successfully established terrifying reputations, they are often accorded myths of bestial sadism. Ellison reported that in the 1950s in Brooklyn, members of the most feared gang, the Puerto Rican Flyers, were said to drink blood.[47]

By celebrating hedonism as the underlying motivation for their violence, badasses avoid the interpretation that their violence is contingent on the prospect of extrinsic rewards and, therefore, ultimately controllable by others. A Vice Lord explained to Keiser the essential attraction of "wolf packing":

> Wolf packing—like for instance me and some other fellows go out and knock you down 'cause we feel like it. That's what it is. I might take your money, but I really want to kick some ass anyway, so I decide to knock the first thing in my way down.[48]

Across various sociocultural settings, badasses sometimes seem to attack victims because they "need" a beating. A graffiti writer from the South Bronx recalled a time when a few Black Spades arrived at their clubhouse with guns, turned lights on, and discovered that some of those present were not of their group: "first they took and beat up a couple of guys because, though they weren't in a gang, they just needed a good ass-kicking at the time."[49] There is an ambiguity in this statement as to who "needed" the beating, the attackers or the victims. In some contexts, badasses posture virtually as altruistic servants of their victims' "need" for a beating. At other times, the "need to kick ass" is more clearly their own. In either case the suggestion is of soulful chaos: of a nature governed by overwhelming, destructive forces that demand release through the instrumentality of the badass or of irresistibly seductive weaknesses in victims that compel the badass to attack, like a priestly servant who is duty bound to preserve a certain harmony of evil in the world.

Being mean is achieved with a special economy by attacks directed at especially vulnerable victims and especially respectable places. Accompanying a Glasgow gang, Patrick described a rush into a public library. They began setting fire to newspapers in the Reading Room, knocked a magnifying glass out of the hand of an elderly man, and en route to the street, a male attendant in a green uniform was punched and kicked out of the way. "Some, behind me," he noted, "could hardly run for laughing."[50]

Ex-skinheads recalled an excursion to London's Hyde Park: "When we got to the Park we just went wild." Disturbing "Pakis," for example, by putting fingers in the way of a man taking pictures of his wife and children, was a focal activity. At the local park, they would throw stones at ducks; go to the cafe, order food, and not pay; and hide behind bushes waiting for a boat to come by, say to the child in it, "give me a lift, mate," and then collectively jump in, promptly sinking the boat.[51] Their targets were "nice" in a conventional moral sense. The attacks had no utilitarian purpose; many were treated exclusively as "fun." With these elements of context, meanness may be manifest with remarkably little physical effort.

In fights, meanness may be demonstrated by exceeding moral limitations and utilitarian justification. From the white ethnic gang scene of 1950s Brooklyn, Ellison recited

> the primer for gang kids. . . . When he's down, kick for the head and groin. . . . gang warfare is typified by a callous disregard for Marquis of Queensbury rules, or for that matter, rules of simple decency. When they fight, they are amoral . . . totally without mercy . . . almost inhuman. A cat that's down is a cat who can't bother you, man! Stomp him! Stomp him good! Put that lit cigarette in the bastard's eye! Wear Army barracks boots—kick him in the throat, in the face, kick him where he lives. Smash him from behind with a brick, cave in his effin' skull! Flat edge of the hand in the Adam's Apple! Use a lead pipe across the bridge of his nose—smash the nose and send bone splinters into the brain![52]

Paraphernalia of Purposiveness

All manner of weapons contribute to the badass's project of being mean. From a Philadelphia black gang leader, Krisberg recorded this spontaneous expression of affection:

> I love shotguns. . . . And if anybody ever bother me, that's what they better look out for. Cause I'm going to bring it. . . . Cause I know I ain't going to miss you.[53]

In adolescent "bad" society, weapons and their incidents are matters for sacred ritual. In the South Bronx in the early 1970s, the Savage Nomads were ordered by their leader to clean their guns meticulously twice, sometimes three times, in weekly, group sessions.[54] In Chicago, Ruth Horowitz observed Mexican-American gang members' fascination with the special instruments of violence.

> One afternoon I was sitting on a bench talking with the Lions. Suddenly all conversation stopped and attention was focused on Spoof and Fidel, two Senior Nobles in their mid-twenties. Spoof flipped his keys to the nearest Lion and told him to get his lounge chair from the trunk of the car. His orders were carried out silently. Spoof settled comfortably in his chair. He proudly produced three bullets: one had a cutoff head, one had a flattened head, and the third was unmodified. He carefully described just how each of the bullets reacted inside the body. Everyone listened quietly and a few asked technical questions. No one was allowed to hold the bullets. . . . Then we were treated to a show and history of their scars while the Lions nodded their approval and were properly awed. Even after the two departed, the Lions discussed nothing else for the rest of the evening.[55]

As Ellison observed in Italian gangs in 1950s Brooklyn, "the weapons of the gang kid have a charm all their own." In this setting, the charmed objects resembled a medieval knight's battery of arms: garrison belts with razor-sharp buckles to be wrapped around fists, raw potatoes studded with double-edged razor blades, zip guns, barracks boots with razor blades stuck between toe and sole, and Molotov cocktails.[56] One fellow drew special attention for possessing a flare-shooting Navy Very pistol. As Robert DeNiro effectively captured in the movie *Taxi Driver* (after he asks the mirror, "Are you looking at me?"), would-be badasses may spend hours practicing the rapid production of a knife or a gun with a special flourish.[57]

Among Chicago's Vice Lords, a three-foot sword was, for a time, a popular weapon for robbing passengers on the El. A gang member named Cupid recalled the time "my mother came up and busted me with six shotguns!" including a buffalo gun, and Cupid will

> never forget this. It was . . . crazy ass King Solomon, [in a fight with the Comanches] he had one of these little Hookvilles. It's a knife, a linoleum knife. Got a hook on the end. . . . [which he used when he caught "Ghengis Khan" and] Cut the stud's whole guts out![58]

Among the fighting teams in Glasgow, a member named Baggy kept a "sword" in his scooter and would often recount how, in a battle with the Milton Tongs at a bowling center, he had rushed to his scooter, taken up his sword, cut one boy, and watched the rest scatter. When stopped by bouncers at a dance hall, members of the Young Team were required to give up a concealed hatchet and bayonet, but one got by with a hidden, open razor. In a fight outside a dance hall, Tim charged into battle, brandishing his open razor, but only after grabbing a wine bottle that he broke on the wall, cutting his hand badly. Later, Tim embroidered his account of the fight, adding an air rifle. "The open razor and the broken wine bottle he had carried were apparently not sufficient to create the image he hankered after."[59] In the United States today, we might find the objects of awesome charm to be Uzi machine guns and Ninja stars.

Fascinated, charmed, seduced—the badass is completely taken by the paraphernalia of his purposiveness. Note that although some of these objects might fit presumptions about the power of phallic imagery, others (stars, garrison belts, and linoleum knives) surely do not. Note also that the fascination persists apart from any envisioned practical context of the use of these objects. Just to have these things, to hold them, inspect them, and observe them swiftly introduced into the focus of the moment is exciting. These objects suggest that others will have to take seriously the intentions of the badass who controls them, whatever those intentions may be—that he will mean it, whatever he may make of "it."

We might attribute the significance of these things to the power they represent, but "power" is an impoverished metaphor for this world of experience. "Being mean" picks up the evil undertones set off by the display of these objects. Many of these weapons are notable not just for their power but for their brutish, sadistic character; others, fitted for covert possession, are notably illicit in design. In contrast to "power," "being mean" captures the project at stake: to assume a tough, alien posture beyond all danger of mockery and metaphysical doubt that ensures that one will be taken seriously. These things excite by attesting to a purpose that transcends the material utility of power.

Mind Fucking

In various languages, badasses have a special affinity for the culture of "fuck you!" Chas, an East Los Angeles graffiti writer, recounted his transformation from "Chingaso."

> A friend gave me that nickname. Started calling me that about three years ago. . . . Now it's funny. I don't like "Chingaso" any more because it's too "bad," it's too heavy. "Chingaso" means the one who's a fucker. Not a stud, just one who fucks people up. I don't like that. I feel like I'm not saying the right thing out there. I like it, but I think I'm telling the right people the wrong thing. So I write "Chas" now.[60]

In Glasgow, both the police and the street toughs they attempt to control are deeply involved in the same culture. In the following account, Patrick, Tim, and Dave from the Young Team were at Saracen Cross, on their way to a dance hall:

> Tim was prevented from moving forward by the approach of two policemen, one of whom shouted across at him: "So fuckin' Malloy is oot again? Is yir fuckin' brothers still in fuckin' prison?" Tim's answers also made liberal use of Glasgow's favourite adjective. The second policeman turned to Dave and me, and, noticing the marks on Dave's face he began: "So ye goat fuckin' scratched, trying' tae get yir fuckin' hole."[61]

The confrontation ended when one of the policeman said, "Weil, get aff this fuckin' Cross, or Ah'll fuckin' book ye."

Used gramatically in myriad ways and conveyed through posture and conduct perhaps more generally than in explicit verbal form, the distinctive thrust of the "fuck" culture is captured nicely in the English form, "fuck you!" Although it may seem obvious, it is

worth a moment's pause to articulate just what makes this phrase so effectively "bad." To wish sex on another is not necessarily negative, but this is clearly not an alternative form for "Have a nice lay." Nor is the use of "fuck" for denoting sex necessarily negative; the phrase is universally "bad" while crude sex is not.[62]

At the essence of "fuck you!" is the silent but emphatic presence of the "I." "Fuck you!" implies the existence of the speaker as the key actor (compared to "get fucked!" and the appropriately feminine form, "fuck off!"). It is the assertion of an anonymous insertion—a claim to penetrate the other in his most vulnerable, sensitive center, in his moral and spiritual essence, without revealing oneself to the other. "Fuck you!" thus achieves its force through projecting an asymmetry of the most extreme sort between the fucker and the fucked; I will force myself to the center of your existence, while you will not grasp even the most superficial indication of my subjectivity.

In its essence, then, "fuck you!" is a way of being mean as a transcendent existential project. "Fuck you!" equals "I'll thrust my meaning into your world, and you won't know why, what for, what I mean; I'll hide the 'I' from you as I do it." Of course, in context "fuck you!" may connote anything from a dare to a muted message uttered on retreat. But with the existential significance of "fuck you!" in mind, we may more readily grasp, as devices for mind fucking, several widespread, practical strategies of would-be badasses that are otherwise deeply enigmatic.

The Bump

Consider the "accidental" bump, used either to begin a fight or to force a humiliating show of deference. Manny Torres recalled from his adolescent years in Spanish Harlem,

> walking around with your chest out, bumping into people and hoping they'll give you a bad time so you can pounce on them and beat 'em into the goddamn concrete.[63]

In the literature on adolescent street violence, there are innumerable analogous examples of fights beginning from what in one light appears to be accidental and minor physical contact. Sometimes the badass is the one arranging the accident, sometimes he is the one who is accidentally bumped. Thus, when some laborers accidentally nudged Pat at a Glasgow bar, he challenged them to a fight, immediately moving his hand into his jacket as if he had a weapon. Wee Midgie hit the laborers on their heads with a lemonade bottle, Pat and others kicked them in the face, and Tim cracked a bottle over their heads. The fighting team suddenly exited when someone shouted, "Run like fuck."[64]

To understand specifically what is happening in these scenes, it is insufficient to interpret the attackers as "looking for a fight." The enigmatic aspect is the dramatization of a "bump"—an accidental physical clash—as the necessary condition or catalyst of the violence. Pat and his friends seemed so intent on attacking these laborers that one wonders why they waited for the chance, unintentional nudge.

Nor will it do to project onto the attackers a felt necessity to neutralize moral prohibitions against unwarranted attacks, that is, that the attack would make no compelling sense to them until and unless they had the "excuse" of a bump. The same young men can be seen at other moments proudly attacking without the moral necessity of any excuse or justification, as when the party attacked is treated simply as one who "needs his ass kicked."[65] Attackers often arrange bumps that are publicly, self-consciously transparent. Why do they bother to feign accidents?

Because their focus is not on physical destruction or moral self-justification, but on the transcendent appeal of being mean. The feigned accident is not a moral necessity for attack; it is, however, a delightful resource for constructing from the attack the stature of the attacker as a badass. Manny and Pat did not "have to have an excuse" to attack. Nor were they compulsive sadists "getting off" on physical destruction. They were seduced by the bump. They rejoiced in the special reverberations that could be given the interaction by making the attack the product of a transparently "accidental" bump.

At its first, most superficial, level of appeal, the bump clarifies and enhances the meaning of a subsequent physical attack as the work of a badass. After a bump, an attack inevitably reflects the spatial metaphor, the existential dilemma of "here" and "there" with which all the ways of the badass are concerned.

The badass does not invent the revolutionary moral potential in the bump; he simply seizes on it. When you and I, two polite members of civil society, bump into each other, there is at once a literal and figurative invocation of the toughness of each of us. Wishing to avoid giving offense, with bated breath we race each other to the stage of apology. Through my apology, I drop any possible pretense of toughness, showing you that I am morally responsive to your well-being. In apologizing, I enact a shameful recognition that the bump occurred because, as far as I could tell, our phenomenal worlds had been independent; I had practiced an apparent indifference to your existence.

In the bump, what had been "here" to you, bounded off from me, penetrates my phenomenal isolation and becomes "here" to me, and vice versa. As quickly as polite members of civil society scurry to avoid the moral tensions that they sense have suddenly become potential, so can the badass flood the situation with awful possibilities. By treating the accidental bump as an obdurate, unforgettable fact of history, the badass opens up a glorious array of nasty courses of action.

No matter who was at "fault" for the bump, once the "bump" has occurred the badass can exploit a precious ambiguity to charge the situation with the tensions of a moral crisis. Any fool can see and only a coward would deny that the bump takes each into the other's phenomenal world. In the bump, you become "here" for me and I become "here" for you. The bump provides the grounds for each to wonder, Was it accidental? Or were you "fucking" with me, thrusting yourself into my world for purposes I could not possibly grasp?

At this stage, the least the would-be badass can do is obtain public testimony to his badass status. If the other tries to ignore the bump, the badass can easily make this attempt an obvious pretense for repeating the bump. He may stop at any point in this process, taking as his sole booty from the situation the victim's evidently artificial posture that "nothing unusual is happening."

More enigmatically, immediately after he has produced an intentional bump or received an obviously accidental bump, the badass may launch an attack without waiting for an apology, whether sincere or pretended. This, an even tougher, "badder" move, plays off the metaphor of mind fucking.

Once we have accidentally bumped for all to see, everyone knows that you must wonder whether I will let it go as an accident or charge you with an intentional attack. Everyone knows that you are wondering about my purpose and spirit and that merely by wondering, you are taking me into your world of moral judgment and putting me at risk of negative judgment. In other words, the bump suddenly raises the momentous possibility that "you are fucking with me." I can now, without more provocation, strike out physically to "fuck you up" as a transcendent response to your publicly visible "fucking with me."

Before examining elaborations on this interaction, we should take special note of the profound explosion of meaning that has already occurred. Through the most inarticulate, most minor physical contact between two individuals, without any apparent plan, intention, or reason, without any forewarning any man could detect, a small moral world has suddenly burst into full-blown existence. Once the bump has occurred, for whatever original cause or antecedent reason, everything has forever changed; the bump cannot be removed from moral history. A chain reaction can then sensibly follow in a spirit of coherent determinism. The badass, as it were, struts out as the Great Creator, capable of arranging the most transcendent cosmological experience from the chance encounters of everyday life; with a little bump, he has occasioned a moral Big Bang.

But this is only the first theme of significance that may be drawn by the badass from the "accidental" bump. That the accidental quality of the bump should be put in quotes is not only obvious to the would-be badass; he may arrange the bump so that it is obvious to all that the fictive accidental character of the bump is obvious to him, to the victim, to all. And with this move into universal moral transparency, the would-be badass moves the drama to the level of what might be called on the streets, "royal mind fucking."

"Whachulookinat?"

In perhaps all subcultures of the badass, there is a homegrown version of a mind-fucking strategy that is deeply rooted in the danger of eye contact. It is recognizable with the opening phrase, "Whachulookinat?"

A badass may at any moment treat another's glanc-

ing perception of him as an attempt to bring him symbolically into the other's world, for the other's private purposes, perhaps to "fuck with" him. This may be treated as a visual bump. As with the physical bump, the badass may allow the victim to cower his way out of danger by enacting a transparently artificial display of deference, for example, through offering profuse excuses and literally bowing out of the situation.

Of more interest are those situations in which the badass wishes further to exploit the potential to construct a transcendent theme of evil. Victims of "Whachulookinat?" frequently answer "Nothing"; with this response, they open up what sometimes seems to be an irresistible opportunity to fill the air with awesomely threatening meaning. "You callin me nothin?" is the well-known reply.

Just as he thought he had regained a measure of self-protective control over the situation through an effusive display of deference, the victim realizes that he has damned himself, for he has been caught in a lie. *He* is now the immoral party. Everyone knows that he had glanced at the badass. "Nothing" was intended as a ritual of deference, but the badass will not go along with the fiction. The badass suddenly adopts the posture of the only honest man in the transaction: he's being lied to, as all can see. But, he now has the right to ask, why? What malevolence moves the victim to lie and answer, "Nothing?" Has he been fucking with the image of the badass in the privacy of his mind? What is he covering up?

From this point, the badass can readily build tension by playing for a while with the victim, tossing him from one to the other horn of his dilemma. Now the badass treats the victim's "Nothing" as a lie, a fiction designed to cover up a shameful or hostile perspective. Next, the badass insists on a literal interpretation, that the victim's response should be taken as a claim that the existential value of the badass is really "nothing." Then, the badass mocks his own metaphysical stance; everyone knows that the badass knows that the "Nothing" was artificial and, therefore, that the badass's indignation is artificial. All know, as they have known all along, who is the victim and who is the badass—who is attempting to avoid any association with evil and who is embracing it.

In short, all recognize that by feigning victimization, the badass is really mind fucking the victim. The universal transparency of the badass's moral posturing makes it "royal mind-fucking"—a high art that may be practiced through a variety of analogous strategems. Thus, analogous to the simple mind fucking of attacking after a bump is the strategy described by Yablonsky of a New York boy who

> will approach a stranger with the taunt, "What did you say about my mother?" An assault is then delivered upon the victim before he can respond to the question.[66]

And analogous to the royal mind fucking constructed from the visual bumping of "Whachulookinat?" is the Vice Lords's practice of wolf packing. With several mates present, a Vice Lord begins an interaction with a stranger passing by with the formal request, but informal demand, "Hey, man, gimme a dime!" As Keiser noted, "If a dime were given, then a demand for more money would be made until finally the individual would have to refuse."[67]

Physical dominance is not the key concern, since it often seems a foregone conclusion. And, what is even more interesting is that, as some of the Glasgow incidents showed, it sometimes seems not to matter to the badasses that they might lose the battle. From the standpoint of physical power and outcome, these mind-fucking maneuvers are gratuitous. After all, one could physically destroy victims without entering into any interaction with them, for example, by shooting them without warning from a distance and without emerging from camouflage. The ambush of a stranger might maximize one's physical success, but it would not necessarily construct an identity as a badass.

Mind fucking, however, shows the badass in control of the meaning of the situation. Bumps are accidents or intentional provocations, depending on what the badass has in mind. The badass controls the moral ontology of the moment. On the one hand, he may allow life its little bumps, its give and take, recognizing that, owing to imperfections in the nature of social life for which no one is responsible, men must have at least small spaces free from responsibility. On the other hand, he may make life inexorably purposive, affording a man no rest from the moral implications of his conduct. The badass rules the moment as the mas-

ter of its metaphysics. Moral pretenses become real and unreal as if by magic, at the snap of his finger. At his discretion, words mean just what they say on the surface or are revealed to mask shamefully hidden intentions. "Nothing" will mean nothing at all or everything fateful, as he chooses. Apart from physical dominance, mind fucking allows the badass to demonstrate the transcendent character of his meaning.

FOREGROUND AND BACKGROUND: THE SEX OF THE BADASS

I have attempted to demonstrate that the details of the distinctive adolescent culture of the badass can be grasped as a series of tactics for struggling with what the adolescent experiences as a spatially framed dilemma—a challenge to relate the "here" of his personal world to the phenomenal worlds of others who he experiences as existing at a distance, somewhere over "there." Thus, being tough positions the self as not "here" for others. Being alien goes further, indicating that the self is not only not here for others but is native to some morally alien world; inevitably beyond the intimate grasp of others who are present here. And being mean produces its awful air by intimating that where the self is coming from is a place that represents chaos to outsiders and threatens constantly to rush destructively to the center of their world, attacking their most intimate sensibilities.

The ultimate source of the seductive fascination with being a badass is that of transcending rationality. What "rationality" means to the adolescent, as a challenge that stimulates his seduction to a world of deviance, is not primarily legal authority, institutional discipline, or social expectations of an ordered and integrated competence to reason. These phenomena may, at times, become the foils for badasses of all types, but more routinely, the provocative issue is a matter of demonstrating rationality as the modern moral competence to adjust the self to situationally specific expectations.

To understand the seductive quality of this project and why the data have been overwhelmingly though not exclusively from males, we might consider what, after all, makes the phallus so powerful a symbol for the badass. Phallic imagery is obviously prominent in the ways of the badass, from the "hardness" of the tough posture, to the "hot rodder" style, to the "cool" quality conferred on speech by random thrusts of "fuck," to the drama of "mind fucking." But the motivating, emotionally compelling concerns of the badass cannot simply be reduced to a sexual metaphor; the distinctive presence of the badass is not particularly erotic. Posed like a phallus, the badass threatens to dominate all experience, stimulating a focus of consciousness so intense as to obliterate experientially or to transcend any awareness of boundaries between the situation "here" and any other situation, "there." And in this appreciation, the phallus has the further, socially transcendent power to obliterate any awareness of boundaries between the ontologically independent, phenomenal situations of different people. The fascination here is with the paradoxical, distinctively masculine potential of the phallus: by threatening to penetrate others, the badass, this monstrous member of society, can absorb the whole world into himself.

NOTES

1. The differences between the three stages are not on a scale of symbolism versus real action. A physical fight can be nothing more than a show of toughness, while a stare-down can accomplish a consummate act of meanness.

2. As Werthman noted, "Not all black leather jackets communicate the same quality of 'toughness.' . . . One almost has to be committed to a fashion in order to read the nuances of self-image that can be expressed within it." See Carl Werthman, "Delinquency and Authority" (master's thesis, University of California at Berkeley, 1964), p. 118.

3. If these terms seem abstract for the realities of street life, consider the following dialogue between two Puerto Rican women who were members of a Brooklyn street gang and became uncomfortable with the tough image they embraced in their early adolescent years.

[WEEZA:]   We ain't really tough. We don't consider ourselves tough—not me.

[BOOBY:]   Because we try to communicate with people. But when they don't want to communicate with us, then that's their problem, not ours.

Anne Campbell, *The Girls in the Gang* (Oxford: Basil Blackwell, 1984), p. 155.

4. For a treatment of such interactions, see Erving Goffman, *Relations in Public* (New York: Harper & Row, 1971), pp.

75–77, 81. For an analysis of "How are you?" as a "greeting substitute," see Harvey Sacks, "Everyone Has to Lie," in *Sociocultural Dimensions of Language Use,* ed. Mary Sanches and Ben Blount (New York: Academic Press, 1975), pp. 57–79.

5. See Harlan Ellison, *Memos from Purgatory* (New York: Berkley, 1983).

6. Gus Frias, *Barrio Warriors: Homeboys of Peace* (n.p.: Diaz Publications, 1982), p. 21.

7. As ethnographic observers have emphasized, toughness, as opposed to socially sensitive, deferential civility, is hardly a constant feature of Mexican-American adolescent society. In the street gangs of Chicago, Horowitz noted, "Most [of these] young men have conventional social skills"; they take a woman's arm when crossing the street and walk on the curb side, skillfully order dinner in a restaurant, and shake hands and make polite conversation when introduced to a stranger. See Ruth Horowitz, *Honor and the American Dream* (New Brunswick, N.J.: Rutgers University Press, 1983), pp. 86–87. The point is that toughness is a contingent social production.

8. R. Lincoln Keiser, *The Vice Lords* (New York: Holt, Rinehart & Winston, 1979), pp. 43–44.

9. On the last point, comments by my colleague, Emanuel Schegloff, were helpful.

10. Werthman, "Delinquency and Authority," p. 88.

11. James Patrick, *A Glasgow Gang Observed* (London: Eyre Methuen, 1973), p. 69.

12. John Allen, *Assault with a Deadly Weapon,* ed. Dianne Hall Kelly and Philip Heymann (New York: McGraw-Hill, 1978), pp. 19, 22–23.

13. Frias, *Barrio Warriors,* p. 19.

14. My thanks here to Paul Price, a sociology graduate student and a staff member in a Los Angeles home for delinquent boys.

15. Patrick, *Glasgow Gang Observed,* p. 83.

16. Florence Rome, *The Tattooed Men* (New York: Delacorte Press, 1975).

17. Allen, *Assault with a Deadly Weapon,* p. 23.

18. Patrick, *Glasgow Gang Observed,* pp. 32, 33.

19. Allen, *Assault with a Deadly Weapon.*

20. See, for example, the photographs of the Maravillos of the 1940s and 1980s, in Frias, *Barrio Warriors,* p. 16.

21. Descriptions of dress and walk are available in Frias, *Barrio Warriors;* Alfredo Guerra Gonzalez, "Mexicano/Chicano Gangs in Los Angeles: A Sociohistorical Case Study" (Ph.D. diss., School of Social Welfare, University of California at Berkeley, 1981); Carlos Manuel Haro, "An Ethnographic Study of Truant and Low Achieving Chicano Barrio Youth in the High School Setting" (Ph.D. diss., School of Education, University of California at Los Angeles, 1976); and Hilary McGuire, *Hopie and the Los Homes Gang* (Canfield, Ohio: Alba House, 1979).

22. Gusmano Cesaretti, *Street Writers: A Guided Tour of Chicano Graffiti* (Los Angeles: Acrobat Books, 1975), p. 8.

23. Jerry Romotsky and Sally R. Romotsky, *Los Angeles Barrio Calligraphy* (Los Angeles: Dawson's Book Shop, 1976), pp. 23–24, 29, 32–33.

24. See, for example, the laughing skull in Cesaretti, *Street Writers,* and in Romotsky and Romotsky, *Los Angeles Barrio Calligraphy,* pp. 58–59.

25. George Carpenter Barker, *Pachuco* (Tucson: University of Arizona Social Science Bulletin, no. 18, 1958).

26. Frias, *Barrio Warriors,* p. 23; and Haro, "Truant and Low Achieving Chicano Barrio Youth," p. 363.

27. Dick Hebdige, *Subculture: The Meaning of Style* (London: Methuen, 1979), p. 65.

28. Ibid., p. 110.

29. Sandy Craig and Chris Schwarz, *Down and Out: Orwell's Paris and London Revisited* (London: Penguin Books, 1984), p. 107.

30. Hunter Thompson, *Hell's Angels* (New York: Ballantine Books, 1967), p. 253.

31. Harold Finestone, "Cats, Kicks, and Color," in *The Other Side,* ed. Howard S. Becker (New York: Free Press, 1964), pp. 281–97.

32. By the 1970s in New York ghettos, being "cool" had been around for decades and had apparently lost some of its force. It was replaced by "too cool" as a superlative in the adolescent lexicon. See Campbell, *Girls in the Gang,* p. 183. Now "chill out" is popular.

33. Allen, *Assault with a Deadly Weapon,* pp. 199–200.

34. Admiration for the "killer" is reported in David Dawley, *A Nation of Lords: The Autobiography of the Vice Lords* (Garden City, N.Y.: Doubleday Anchor Press, 1973), p. 32.

35. Frias, *Barrio Warriors,* p. 45.

36. Being a badass is not a status obtained in a fatefully violent moment and guaranteed for life. Like other charismatic figures, the badass is subject to the double challenge: (1) that he must always be open to challenge—there is no time off for the badass, no vacation from this occupation, which is indeed a vocation; and (2) that he must never fail any challenge. Cf. Max Weber, *Economy and Society* (New York: Bedminster Press, 1968), 3:1112–13.

37. Patrick, *Glasgow Gang Observed,* p. 49.

38. Pat Doyle et al., *The Paint House: Words from an East End Gang* (Harmondsworth, England: Penguin Books, 1972), p. 31.

39. Richard P. Rettig, Manual J. Torres, and Gerald R. Garrett, *Manny: A Criminal Addict's Story* (Boston: Houghton Mifflin, 1977), p. 19.

40. Barry Alan Krisberg, *The Gang and the Community* (San Francisco: R & E Research Associates, 1975), p. 15.

41. Ibid.

42. Ibid., p. 24.

43. Keiser, *Vice Lords,* p. 18.

44. Doyle et al., *Paint House,* p. 23.

45. Campbell, *Girls in the Gang,* p. 164.

46. Patrick, *Glasgow Gang Observed,* p. 43.

47. Ellison, *Memos from Purgatory,* p. 86.

48. Keiser, *Vice Lords,* p. 35.

49. Craig Castleman, *Getting Up: Subway Graffiti in New York* (Cambridge, Mass.: MIT Press, 1982), p. 93.

50. Patrick, *Glasgow Gang Observed,* p. 77.

51. Doyle et al., *Paint House,* pp. 28, 30.

52. Ellison, *Memos from Purgatory,* pp. 58, 61. Note that the evidence is of a "primer," not of a pattern of violence.

53. Krisberg, *Gang and Community,* p. 14.

54. William Gale, *The Compound* (New York: Rawson Associates, 1977).

55. Horowitz, *Honor and the American Dream,* p. 92.

56. Ellison, *Memos from Purgatory,* pp. 48, 60, 61.

57. Cf. Ellison's account of his practice before a mirror with a twelve-inch Italian stiletto in ibid.

58. Keiser, *Vice Lords,* p. 62.

59. Patrick, *Glasgow Gang Observed,* pp. 54, 56.

60. Cesaretti, *Street Writers,* p. 57.

61. Patrick, *Glasgow Gang Observed,* pp. 52–53.

62. No doubt in some erotic uses, the "bad" quality of "fuck you" is deemed delicious. As many a wag has noted, "fuck" is an especially versatile condiment in courses of conversations. An anonymous list, provided to me by an engineer who found it circulating in a local metal-coating plant, includes "positive" uses, as in "Mary is fucking beautiful"; inquisitive uses, as in "What the fuck?"; and ad hoc, sometimes ambiguous enhancements of emphasis, as in "It's fucking five-thirty." "Fuck" draws attentions beyond civility, and it is therefore widely attractive as a means by which a speaker suggests he has more passion or a more idiosyncratic feeling about a matter than convention will allow him to express. Our concern here is to grasp the specifically hostile and threatening forms, the "bad" power that the phrase can achieve.

63. Rettig, Torres, and Garrett, *Manny,* p. 18.

64. Patrick, *Glasgow Gang Observed,* p. 54.

65. See also ibid., p. 32. At a dance hall, Pat pushed his way onto the floor and bumped into three big guys who said, "Who the fuck are you pushin'?" Pat responded with "Ah'm pushin' you, thug face," whereupon fists began to fly, this time to Pat's great disadvantage.

66. Lewis Yablonsky, *The Violent Gang* (Baltimore: Penguin Books, 1966), pp. 202–3.

67. Keiser, *Vice Lords,* pp. 44, 45. See also Robert Lejeune, "The Management of a Mugging," *Urban Life* 6 (July 1977): 123–48.

FURTHER READING

Conrad, Peter and Joseph W. Schneider. 1985. *Deviance and Medicalization: From Badness to Sickness.* Columbus, OH: Merrill.

- A thorough discussion of how troubles come to be defined as sickness.

Gamson, Joshua. 1998. *Freaks Talk Back.* Chicago: University of Chicago Press.

- A study of tabloid talk shows, sexual noncomformity, and the staging of troubles.

Gubrium, Jaber F. and James A. Holstein (eds.). 2001. *Institutional Selves.* New York: Oxford University Press.

- Studies focused on how institutions construct troubled identities.

Holstein, James A. 1993. *Court-Ordered Insanity.* New York: Aldine de Gruyter.

- A study of the courtroom talk and interaction that mediates involuntary mental hospitalization proceedings.

Lemert, Edwin M. 1962. "Paranoia and the Dynamics of Exclusion." *Sociometry* 25: 2–20.

- A classic article on the social processes that lead to a categorization of paranoia.

Rosenhan, D. L. 1973. "On Being Sane in Insane Places." *Science* 179: 250–258.

- Another classic, on how the definition of the situation constructs participants as mentally ill.

Spector, Malcolm and John I. Kitsuse. [1977] 2001. *Constructing Social Problems.* New Brunswick, NJ: Transaction.

- The definitive statement regarding the process by which social problems categories are constructed.

AUTHOR INDEX

SUBJECT INDEX

Absolutism, 33
Abstract values, 32–33
Accounts, 277
  defined, 481
  of elderly women, 481–482
  of homelessness, 142–145
Acting units, 58–60
Action
  social, 55, 56–58, 60, 127, 250
  social construction of paths, 34–35
Actors
  minded, 193, 194–195
  social, 248
Adolescents. *See also* Girls
  badass, 524, 558–581
  white, 354–355, 362–380
Affective socialization, 228, 241, 242
African Americans, 363
  appearance and, 354, 356–361
  badass, 562, 563, 564, 566, 568, 569
  in Harlem. *See* Harlem
  in Jim Crow South, 459–462
  juvenile delinquency in, 282, 285
  middle age in, 430, 458–475
  "one drop" rule and, 354, 355
  play and, 391, 396, 402n
  proms and, 407, 408, 409, 412,
    413–414, 415
  white culture and, 366, 367, 368, 369,
    371–373, 374, 375
Age, 428–486. *See also* Life course
  African Americans and, 430, 458–475
  childless women and, 507
  table dancers and, 429, 451–458
  women and, 430, 476–485
Agency, 184–185
Agent roles, 529
Aggression themes, in play, 395–396
Agnes (transsexual), 69
AIDS and HIV, 494–495, 507
Akarams tribe, 46–47
Alcohol abuse, 350
  in homeless, 145–146, 157–158n
  in table dancers, 455

Alcoholics Anonymous (AA), 153
Alternative realities, 145, 146–148,
    152–153
Alzheimer's disease, 178, 180–190, 199,
    280–281, 429, 493, 496
  agency and, 184–185
  articulating mind in, 185–187
  demise of mind in, 187–189
  description of, 181–182
  description of study, 182
  hidden mind in, 182–184
Alzheimer's Disease and Related
    Association (ADRDA), 182, 186,
    188
Anomalies (behavioral), 548, 552
  normatively generated, 551
  standard pattern rule, 550–551
Asian Americans, 366, 367, 369, 371, 375,
    376
Attention deprivation, 140, 147, 148
Authorization rules, 544–545, 547, 550,
    555, 556
Autobiographies, celebrity, 302–303,
    304–316
Autoethnography
  on bodily stigmas, 335, 337
  on dogs, 192, 195

Battered women, 512, 515, 516, 518
Beauty, burdens of, 409–411
Behaviorism, 180
Bilingual education, 381, 382
Bisexuality, 405–406, 503
Black(s). *See* African Americans
Black popular culture, 371–372
Bodily stigmas, 302, 303, 323–340
Body, 109, 301–340
  in African-American culture, 371–372
  gendered, 302–303, 304–316
  looking-glass self and, 123
  making of feminine, 406–411
  schools, dresses, and, 415–416
  self distinguished from, 125, 126
  stigmas of, 302, 303, 323–340

Body language, 203, 204
Borderwork, 385, 386–400
  aggression themes in, 395–396
  memorable characteristics of, 398–400
  power issues in, 397–398
  sexual and romantic themes in, 396–397
Bullying, 401n
Busing, 32

Caste system, 508
Categorical distancing, 149–150, 151, 156
Categorical embracement, 151–152, 153,
    156
Categories, 52, 62–78
  biased, 65, 75, 76
  bodily stigmas and, 328–332, 337–338
  construction of discourse and, 75–76
  content, community, and, 73–75
  fixed structure assumption, 65, 75
  membership, 69–73
  particularization and, 66
  physical world and, 63
  as preformed and enduring, 65, 75
  problems with traditional research,
    65–66
  prototypes and. *See* Prototypes
  social psychology and, 63–65
  social world and, 63–64
Category puzzle, 72
Characters, 137, 138
Child abuse, 531
Childless women, 487–488, 505–522
Children
  behavior problem, 271
  bond with parents, 219–220
  bright, 271
  developmentally disabled, 275–277
  emotionally disturbed, 212, 351
  friendship groups in. *See* Friendship
    groups
  gender play in, 385, 386–404
  immature, 271
  imputing readiness to, 273
  independent, 271

591